Discovering COMPUTERS

Your Interactive Guide to the Digital World

COMPLETE

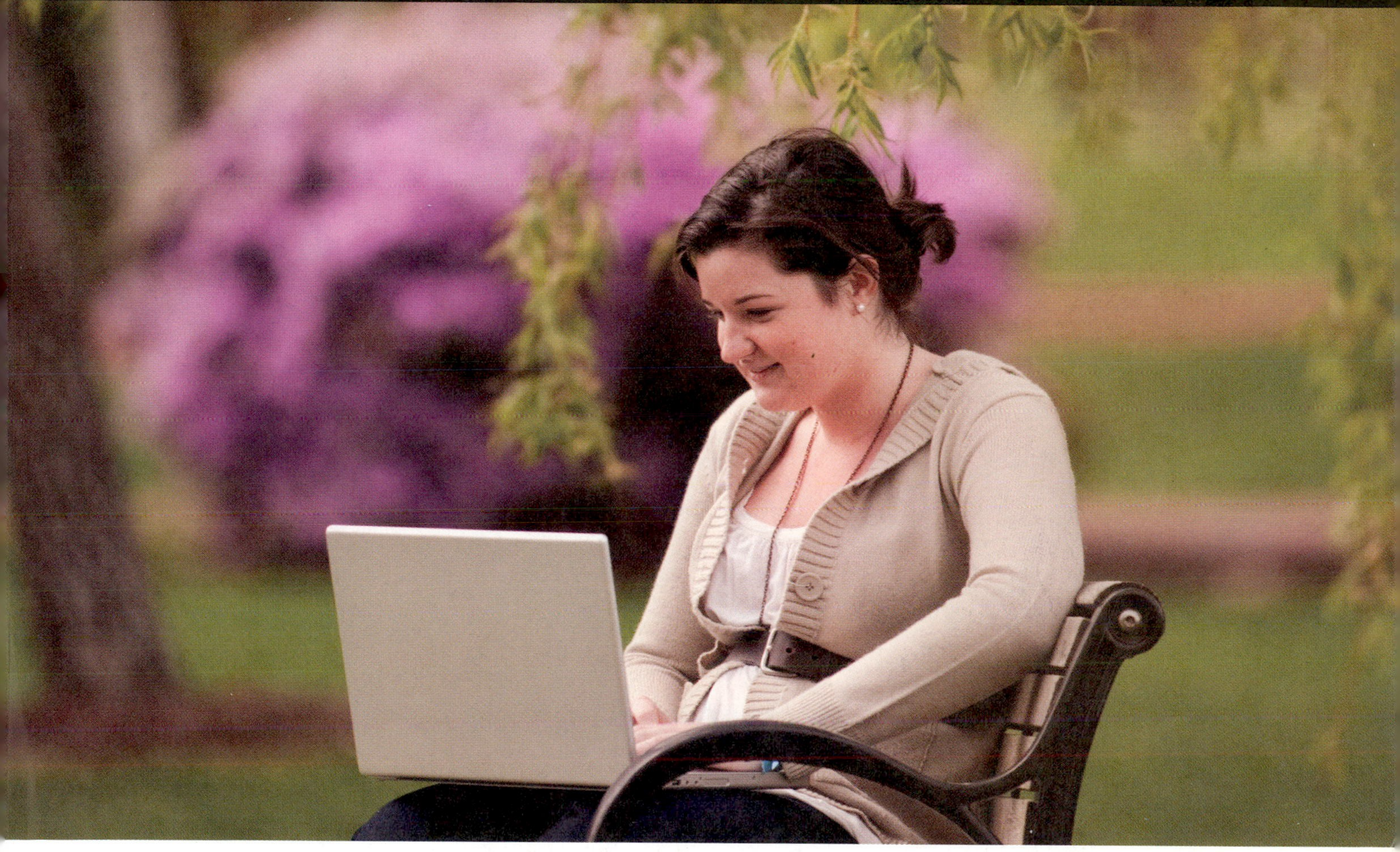

Gary B. Shelly
Misty E. Vermaat

Contributing Authors
Jeffrey J. Quasney
Susan L. Sebok
Steven M. Freund

Shelly Cashman Series®
A part of Course Technology, Cengage Learning

COURSE TECHNOLOGY
CENGAGE Learning™

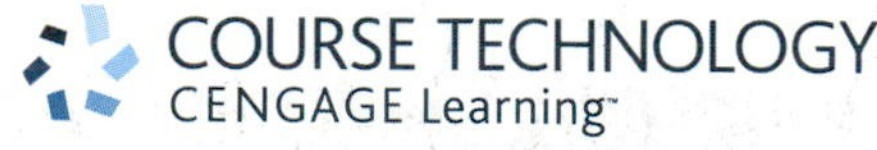

Australia • Brazil • Japan • Korea • Mexico • Singapore • Spain • United Kingdom • United States

Discovering Computers: Your Interactive Guide to the Digital World, Complete
Gary B. Shelly
Misty E. Vermaat

Vice President, Publisher: Nicole Pinard
Executive Editor: Kathleen McMahon
Associate Acquisitions Editor: Reed Curry
Associate Product Manager: Aimee Poirier
Editorial Assistant: Angela Giannopoulos
Director of Marketing: Elisa Roberts
Marketing Manager: Tristen Kendall
Marketing Coordinator: Adrienne Fung
Print Buyer: Julio Esperas
Content Project Manager: Matthew Hutchinson
Researcher: F. William Vermaat
Development Editor: Lyn Markowicz
Management Services: PreMedialGlobal
Interior Designer: Joel Sadagursky
Art Director: Marissa Falco
Text Design: Joel Sadagursky
Cover Design: Curio Press
Cover Photos: Tom Kates Photography
Illustrator: PreMedialGlobal
Compositor: PreMedialGlobal
Printer: RRD Menasha

Library of Congress Control Number: 2010943269

ISBN-13: 978-1-1115-3032-7

ISBN-10: 1-1115-3032-7

Course Technology
20 Channel Center Street
Boston, MA 02210
USA

Cengage Learning is a leading provider of customized learning solutions with office locations around the globe, including Singapore, the United Kingdom, Australia, Mexico, Brazil and Japan. Locate your local office at:
international.cengage.com/region

Cengage Learning products are represented in Canada by Nelson Education, Ltd.

Visit our Web site **www.cengage.com/ct/shellycashman** to share and gain ideas on our textbooks!

To learn more about Course Technology,
visit **www.cengage.com/coursetechnology**

Purchase any of our products at your local college bookstore or at our preferred online store at **www.cengagebrain.com**

Printed in the United States of America
2 3 4 5 6 17 16 15 14 13 12 11

Discovering Computers Complete

Your Interactive Guide to the Digital World

Table of Contents at a Glance

Discovering Computers Complete

Your Interactive Guide to the Digital World

Table of Contents

CHAPTER 5

Input 256

CHAPTER 6

Output 302

CHAPTER 7

Storage 350

CHAPTER 8

Operating Systems and Utility Programs 396

CHAPTER 13

Programming Languages and Program Development 662

Special Feature

CHAPTER 14

Enterprise Computing 718

CHAPTER **15**

Computer Careers and Certification 782

Table of Boxed Elements

ETHICS & ISSUES

FAQs

INNOVATIVE COMPUTING

LOOKING AHEAD

Preface

The Shelly Cashman Series® offers the finest textbooks in computer education. We are proud of the fact that the previous sixteen editions of this textbook have been the most widely used in computer education. With this edition of *Discovering Computers,* we have implemented significant improvements based on current computer trends and comments made by instructors and students, and are introducing an interactive, multi-media e-book and CourseMate Web site. *Discovering Computers: Your Interactive Guide to the Digital World* continues with the innovation, quality, and reliability you have come to expect from the Shelly Cashman Series.

In *Discovering Computers: Your Interactive Guide to the Digital World,* you will find an educationally sound, highly visual, interactive, and easy-to-follow pedagogy that, with the help of animated figures, relevant video, and interactive activities in the e-book, presents an in-depth treatment of introductory computer subjects. Students will finish the course with a solid understanding of computers, how to use computers, and how to access information on the Web.

Objectives of this Text, e-Book, and CourseMate Web Site

Discovering Computers: Your Interactive Guide to the Digital World, Complete is intended for use as a stand-alone solution or in combination with an applications, Internet, or programming textbook in a full-semester introductory computer course. No experience with computers is assumed. The objectives of this offering are to:

- Present the most-up-to-date technology in an ever-changing discipline
- Give students an in-depth understanding of why computers are essential components in business and society
- Teach the fundamentals of computers and computer nomenclature, particularly with respect to personal computer hardware and software, and the Web
- Present the material in a visually appealing, interactive, and exciting manner that motivates students to learn
- Assist students in planning a career
- Provide exercises, lab assignments, and interactive learning activities that allow students to learn by actually using the computer and the Web

Hallmarks of Discovering Computers

To date, more than six million students have learned about computers using *Discovering Computers*. With the Web integration and interactivity, streaming up-to-date audio and video, extraordinary step-by-step visual drawings and photographs, unparalleled currency, and the Shelly and Cashman touch, this book will make your computer concepts course exciting and dynamic. Hallmarks of Shelly Cashman Series *Discovering Computers* include:

A Proven Pedagogy

Careful explanations of complex concepts, educationally-sound elements, and reinforcement highlight this proven method of presentation.

A Visually Appealing Book that Maintains Student Interest

The latest technology, pictures, drawings, and text are combined artfully to produce a visually appealing and easy-to-understand book. Many of the figures include a step-by-step presentation (see page 145), which simplifies the more complex computer concepts. Pictures and drawings reflect the latest trends in computer technology. This combination of pictures, step-by-step drawings, and easy-to-read text layout sets the standard for computer textbook design.

- Present strategies for purchasing a desktop computer, a notebook computer, a Tablet PC, and personal mobile devices
- Provide alternative learning techniques and reinforcement via the Web
- Offer distance-education providers a textbook with a meaningful and exercise-rich digital learning experience

Distinguishing Features

Discovering Computers: Your Interactive Guide to the Digital World includes a variety of compelling features, certain to engage and challenge students, making learning with *Discovering Computers* an enriched experience. These compelling features include:

- Multi-media rich and interactive e-book and CourseMate Web site that engage students in learning about computer concepts.
- Animations, relevant and timely video, interactive in-chapter activities and Quiz Yourself reinforcement exercises embedded in the e-book, combined with the integration of interactive activities, videos, and end-of-chapter student assignments on the CourseMate Web site offer students an exceptional learning solution.
- Living Digitally and Web 2.0 features introduce and familiarize students with new and developing technology, making the technology accessible for introductory students.
- Innovative Computing, FAQ and Ethics & Issues boxes, Companies on the Cutting Edge, Technology Trailblazers, and High-Tech Talk articles enable relevant classroom discussion.

Latest Technologies and Terms

The technologies and terms your students see in *Discovering Computers* are those they will encounter when they start using computers. Only the latest application software is shown throughout the book.

Web Integrated

This book uses the Web as a major learning tool. The purpose of integrating the Web into the book is to (1) offer students additional information and currency on important topics; (2) use its interactive capabilities to offer creative reinforcement and online quizzes; (3) make available alternative learning techniques with Web-based learning games, practice tests, and interactive labs; (4) underscore the relevance of the Web as a basic information tool that can be used in all facets of society; (5) introduce students to doing research on the Web; and (6) offer instructors the opportunity to organize and administer their traditional campus-based or distance-education-based courses on the Web using various learning management systems.

Extensive End-of-Chapter Student Assignments

A notable strength of *Discovering Computers* is the extensive student assignments and activities at the end of each chapter. Well-structured student assignments can make the difference between students merely participating in a class and students retaining the information they learn. The student assignments in *Discovering Computers: Your Interactive Guide to the Digital World* include: Chapter Review, Key Terms, Checkpoint, Problem Solving @ Home, Problem Solving @ Work, Learn It Online, Learn How To, Web Research, and Critical Thinking. The Problem Solving and Critical Thinking student assignments also include Collaboration exercises, encouraging team work amongst students.

Instructor Resources

The Instructor Resources include both teaching and testing aids.

Instructor's Manual Includes lecture notes summarizing the chapter sections, figures and boxed elements found in every chapter, teacher tips, classroom activities, lab activities, and quick quizzes in Microsoft Word files.

Syllabus Easily customizable sample syllabi that cover policies, assignments, exams, and other course information.

Figure Files Illustrations for every figure in the textbook in electronic form. Figures are provided both with and without callouts.

Solutions to Exercises Includes solutions for all end-of-chapter student assignments. Also includes Tip Sheets, which are suggested starting points for the Problem Solving exercises.

PowerPoint Presentations — Course Presenter A one-click-per-slide presentation system that provides PowerPoint slides for every subject in each chapter. Several computer-related video clips are available for optional presentation. Course Presenter provides consistent coverage for multiple lecturers.

Test Bank & Test Engine Test Banks include 220 questions for every chapter, featuring objective-based and critical thinking question types, and including page number references and figure references, when appropriate. Also included is the test engine, ExamView, the ultimate tool for your objective-based testing needs.

Printed Test Bank A Rich Text Format (.rtf) version of the test bank that you can print.

Test Out/Final Exam Objective-based exam that can be used to test students out of your course, or as a final examination. Includes a master answer sheet.

Pretest/Posttest Carefully prepared tests that can be used at the beginning and the end of the semester to measure student progress. Includes master answer sheet.

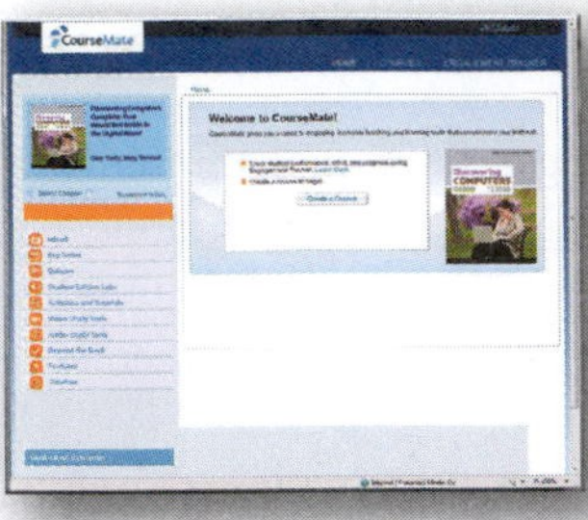

NEW! Computer Concepts CourseMate

The new Computer Concepts CourseMate for *Discovering Computers* is the most expansive digital site for any computer concepts text in the market today! The content in the CourseMate solution is integrated into each page of the text, giving students easy access to current information on important topics, reinforcements activities, and alternative learning techniques. Integrating the Computer Concepts CourseMate into the classroom keeps today's students engaged and involved in the learning experience.

The Computer Concepts CourseMate includes an integrated, multi-media rich and interactive digital book, and a variety of interactive Quizzes and Learning Games, Exercises, Web Links, Videos, and other features that specifically reinforce and build on the concepts presented in the chapter. These interactive activities are tracked within the CourseMate EngagementTracker, making it easy to assess students' retention of concepts. This digital solution encourages students to take learning into their own hands and explore related content on their own to learn even more about subjects in which they are especially interested.

All of these resources on the Computer Concepts CourseMate for *Discovering Computers* enable students to get more comfortable using technology and help prepare students to use the Internet as a tool to enrich their lives.

Contact Us

Colleges, Universities, Continuing Education Departments, Post-Secondary Vocational Schools, Career Colleges, Business, Industry, Government, Trade, Retailer, Wholesaler, Library, and Resellers
Call Cengage Learning at 800-354-9706

K-12 Schools, Secondary Vocational Schools, Adult Education, and School Districts
Call Cengage Learning at 800-354-9706

In Canada
Call Nelson Cengage Learning at 800-268-2222

Anywhere
www.cengage.com/coursetechnology

Visual Walkthrough of the Book

Current. Relevant. Innovative.
Teaching the Significance of Today's Digital World.

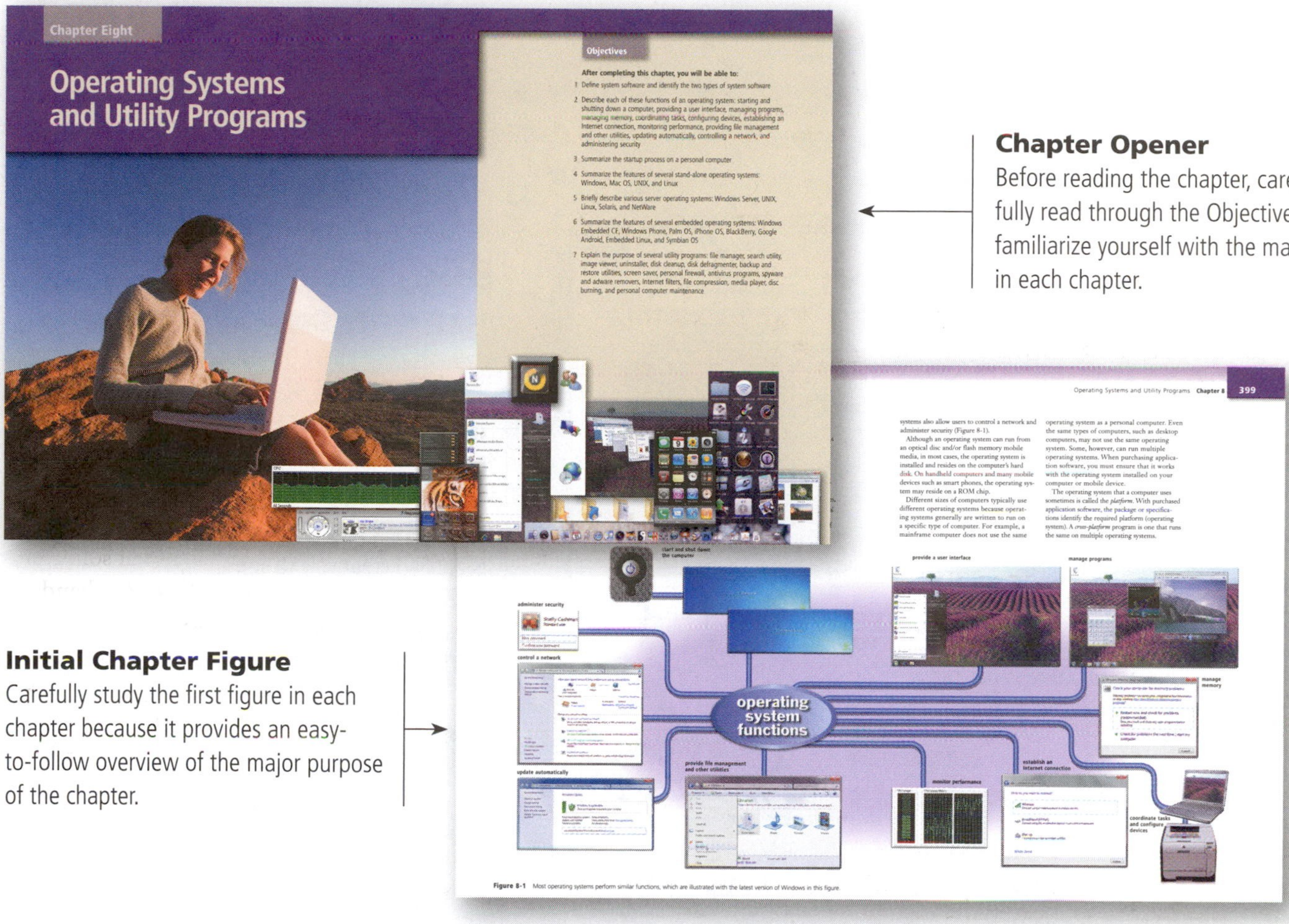

Chapter Opener
Before reading the chapter, carefully read through the Objectives to familiarize yourself with the material in each chapter.

Initial Chapter Figure
Carefully study the first figure in each chapter because it provides an easy-to-follow overview of the major purpose of the chapter.

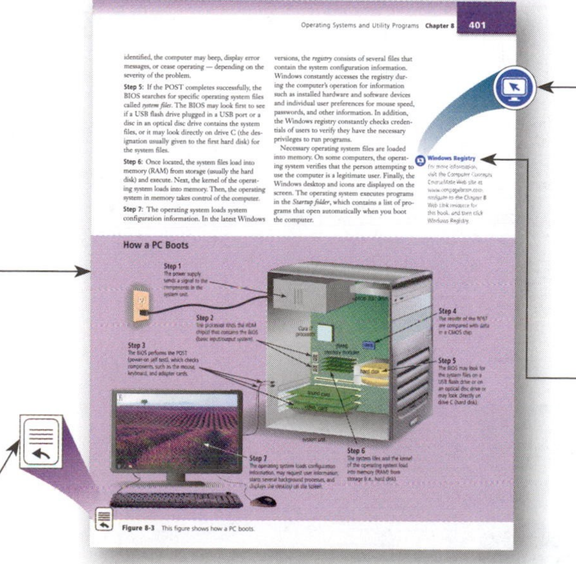

CourseMate Icon
Visit the Computer Concepts CourseMate Web site for access to many of the interactive chapter elements.

Step Figures
Each chapter includes numerous step figures that present the more complex computer concepts using a step-by-step pedagogy.

Web Links
Obtain current information and a different perspective about key terms and concepts by visiting the Web Links found in the margins throughout the book.

Interactive e-Book Activity Icon
Several elements in each chapter are interactive learning activities in the e-book and are identified by this icon.

FAQs

FAQ (frequently asked questions) boxes offer common questions and answers about subjects related to the topic at hand.

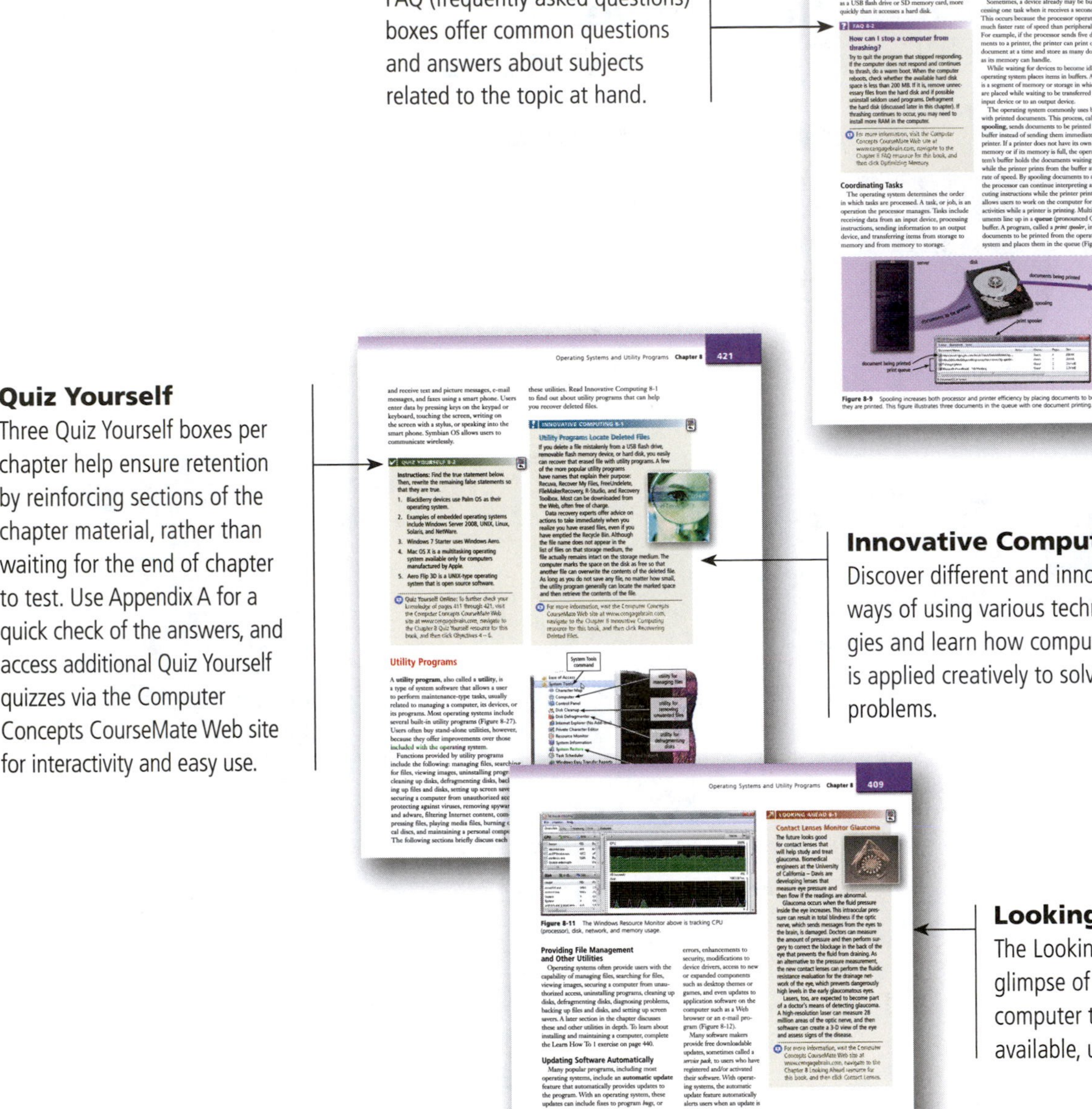

Quiz Yourself

Three Quiz Yourself boxes per chapter help ensure retention by reinforcing sections of the chapter material, rather than waiting for the end of chapter to test. Use Appendix A for a quick check of the answers, and access additional Quiz Yourself quizzes via the Computer Concepts CourseMate Web site for interactivity and easy use.

Innovative Computing

Discover different and innovative ways of using various technologies and learn how computing is applied creatively to solve problems.

Looking Ahead

The Looking Ahead boxes offer a glimpse of the latest advances in computer technology that will be available, usually within five years.

Ethics & Issues

Ethics & Issues boxes raise controversial, computer-related topics of the day, challenging readers to consider closely general concerns of computers in society.

Computer Usage @ Work

Learn about how computers are used in fifteen different professional industries, including transportation, hospitality, education, sports, and construction.

High-Tech Talk

The High-Tech Talk article at the end of each chapter expands on a topic covered in the chapter and presents a more technical discussion.

Companies on the Cutting Edge and Technology Trailblazers

Everyone who interacts with computers should be aware of the key computer-related companies and of the more famous leaders of the computer industry.

Operating Systems and Utility Programs **Chapter 8** 429

QUIZ YOURSELF 8-3

Instructions: Find the true statement below. Then, rewrite the remaining false statements so that they are true.

1. A pop-up blocker shrinks the size of a file(s).
2. An anti-spam program protects a computer against viruses by identifying and removing any computer viruses found in memory, on storage media, or on incoming files.
3. A personal firewall is a utility that detects and protects a personal computer from unauthorized intrusions.
4. You should uninstall files and disks regularly in the event your originals are lost, damaged, or destroyed.
5. Web filtering software writes text, graphics, audio, and video files to a recordable or rewritable disc.
6. Fragmenting a disk is the process of reorganizing it so that the files are stored in contiguous sectors.

Quiz Yourself Online: To further check your knowledge of pages 421 through 428, visit the Computer Concepts CourseMate Web site at www.cengagebrain.com, navigate to the Chapter 8 Quiz Yourself resource for this book, and then click Objective 7.

Chapter Summary

This chapter defined an operating system and then discussed the functions common to most operating systems. The chapter introduced a variety of stand-alone operating systems, server operating systems, and embedded operating systems. Finally, the chapter described several utility programs.

Computer Usage @ Work

Education

Teachers and students have been using computers in education for many years. Teachers have been taking advantage of advances in computer technology to help provide a better educational experience for their students.

Many grade schools throughout the United States, as well as other countries, enable parents to track their child's performance online. In the past, parents would rely solely on their child bringing home graded assignments and tests to know how he or she was doing. In some cases, parents would be surprised when they saw their child's grades on report cards every two to three

At the college level, many instructors today rely heavily on e-learning systems to provide students with Web-based access to course materials and assessments, discussion forums, chat rooms, and e-mail. Once used mainly in online classes, e-learning systems provide instructors with an easy way to allow students access to the class at any time of the day.

Most instructors go beyond e-learning systems and use additional technologies to enhance their classes. For example, digital media instructors might require students to upload their assignments to a photo sharing community, and an English instructor might save paper

430 **Chapter 8** Operating Systems and Utility Programs

High-Tech Talk

Touch Screen Technology: How the Screen Is So Smart

Touch screen technology is becoming a larger part of everyday life for many individuals. As presented in Chapter 5, a touch screen is a touch-sensitive display device that users can interact with by touching areas of the screen. People have been using touch screens for more than 30 years, and this technology now is being used in more places, such as in smart phones, point-of-sale terminals, automated teller machines, remote controls, GPS receivers, home security systems, and Tablet PCs.

Touch screen technology has evolved since its creation in the late 1960s. The first touch screens developed allowed users to press only one area at a time with the tip of their finger, and they were much less accurate than today's touch screens. As the technology is advancing, users are able to perform additional tasks, such as dragging their finger across the screen and touching more than one area of the screen at a time. For example, the iPhone and iPod touch allow you to zoom in pictures or other objects on the screen by placing two fingers close together on the screen, and then slowly moving them apart. Three types of touch screens most in use today are capacitive, resistive, and surface wave touch screens.

electrical charge, reducing the charge on the capacitive layer. Circuits located at each corner of the capacitive touch screen measure the change in electrical charge. The circuits then send this data to the touch screen controller, or software that is running on the computer. The controller then uses the data to calculate the location where the finger is touching the screen. Capacitive touch screens typically are high-quality and unaffected by items that do not conduct electrical charges. An example of the components of a capacitive touch screen is shown in Figure 8-41.

The second type of touch screen is a resistive touch screen. A metallic conductive and resistive layer held apart by spacers cover a *resistive touch screen*. When a user touches a resistive touch screen, the conductive and resistive layers connect in the location of the touch. An electronic current runs between the two layers, and the interruption in the current enables the touch screen controller to calculate the exact location of the touch. Although resistive touch screens usually are more affordable than capacitive touch screens, they are not as clear and can be damaged more easily.

The third type of touch screen uses surface wave technology. *Surface wave technology* passes ultrasonic waves over the touch screen. Touching the screen absorbs portions of the waves, which then allows the touch screen controller to calculate the position at which the object touched the screen. Because ultrasonic waves pass over the touch screen, it is easy for outside elements to damage the device. Touch screens using surface wave technology are the most advanced and often the most expensive of the three types.

Additional types of touch screen technologies exist, but they are not used as widely as the capacitive, resistive, and surface wave touch screens. *Optical touch screens* use cameras mounted at two corners of the screen to detect objects close to the surface. *Infrared touch screens* use light emitting diodes and light detectors at the edges of the touch screen to detect objects that break the beams of light traveling across the screen.

As touch screen prices continue to decrease, they most likely will be incorporated in an increasing number of computers and devices. Touch screens have increased productivity by allowing people to interact with devices more quickly than they can with a mouse or keyboard.

For more information, visit the Computer Concepts CourseMate Web site at www.cengagebrain.com, navigate to the Chapter 8 High-Tech Talk resource for this book, and then click Touch Screen Technology.

capacitive touch screen identifies where someone touches the screen by ...ces in electrical charges.

Operating Systems and Utility Programs **Chapter 8** 431

Companies on the Cutting Edge

VERISIGN Internet Infrastructure Services

Technology users desire immediate access to information and services. Their ability to communicate and conduct commerce securely is aided in large part by *VeriSign*. More than 30 billion times a day, people interact on the Internet, and their purchases, text messages, downloads, and other transactions are enabled and protected by VeriSign's infrastructure services.

Computer security company Semantic acquired VeriSign's Authentication division business in 2010 to strengthen encryption and identity services and help protect businesses and consumers by protecting information and detecting online fraud. Its domain name services department registers all .com, .net, .cc, and .tv domain names. The VeriSign Secured Seal, which has been issued to more than 100,000 domains in 145 countries, ensures companies and consumers that the Web site is secure.

The California-based company was founded in 1995 and has more than 2,200 employees worldwide.

RESEARCH IN MOTION (RIM) Wireless Mobile Communications Devices Manufacturer

By 2012, 800 million people worldwide are expected to access social networking Web sites on smart phones, up from 82 million in 2007. *Research in Motion (RIM)* helped fuel this networking frenzy by partnering with MySpace in 2008 to help connect networkers on the go. They can access MySpace Mobile on a BlackBerry smart phone, which is RIM's key product.

The Canadian company was founded in 1984 by Mike Lazaridis, who serves as its president and co-CEO. Lazaridis's vision for wireless technology developed in high school when he was a member of the local amateur radio and television club. He developed RIM's first major product, the Inter@active Pager, which was integrated in the first BlackBerry product in 1998. The BlackBerry gained attention for having the capability to combine a wireless mailbox with a corporate mailbox so that users could assess e-mail continuously.

Recently, Research in Motion launched BlackBerry App World, an application store that allows BlackBerry users to download personal and business programs.

For more information, visit the Computer Concepts CourseMate Web site at www.cengagebrain.com and then navigate to the Chapter 8 Companies on the Cutting Edge resource for this book.

Technology Trailblazers

STEVE WOZNIAK Apple Cofounder

Mixing fun with work comes naturally for *Steve Wozniak*. As Apple's cofounder, he says his computer designing career began and still continues to be a hobby filled with creativity, humor, games, and education. In his opinion, Apple's success evolved because he designed computers that had minimal parts and maximum performance.

Wozniak designed the original Apple computer in 1975 with Apple's current CEO, Steve Jobs, and wrote most of the software. Ten years later he cofounded Pixar, the award winning animation studio. He left Apple in 1985 to spend time with his family, work on community projects, and teach, but he still serves as an advisor to the corporation.

Wozinak was inducted into the Consumer Electronics Hall of Fame and the National Inventors Hall of Fame. One of his current passions is applying artificial intelligence to the area of robotics. He also is a member of the Silicon Valley Aftershocks, a polo team that plays using Segway electric transportation devices.

LINUS TORVALDS Linux Creator

Inductees to the Computer History Museum in Mountain View, CA, are noted for their contribution to computer technology. *Linus Torvalds* joined the Museum's Hall of Fellows in 2008 for his creation of the open source operating system, Linux.

When he developed an operating system in 1991, he announced his project in an Internet newsgroup. He made the source code available and asked readers for suggestions to enhance the product. Computer users responded by reviewing the system and offering enhancements. Three years later he released a greatly enhanced version he called Linux.

Torvalds developed this innovative operating system when he was a 21-year-old computer science student in Finland. Today, he leads the development of Linux as a fellow at OSDL (Open Source Development Labs), a not-for-profit consortium of companies dedicated to developing and promoting the operating system. Torvalds says his daily involvement with Linux involves coordinating and merging the lines of code submitted by users so that the software runs smoothly.

For more information, visit the Computer Concepts CourseMate Web site at www.cengagebrain.com and then navigate to the Chapter 8 Technology Trailblazers resource for this book.

STUDENT ASSIGNMENTS

End-of-Chapter Student Assignments

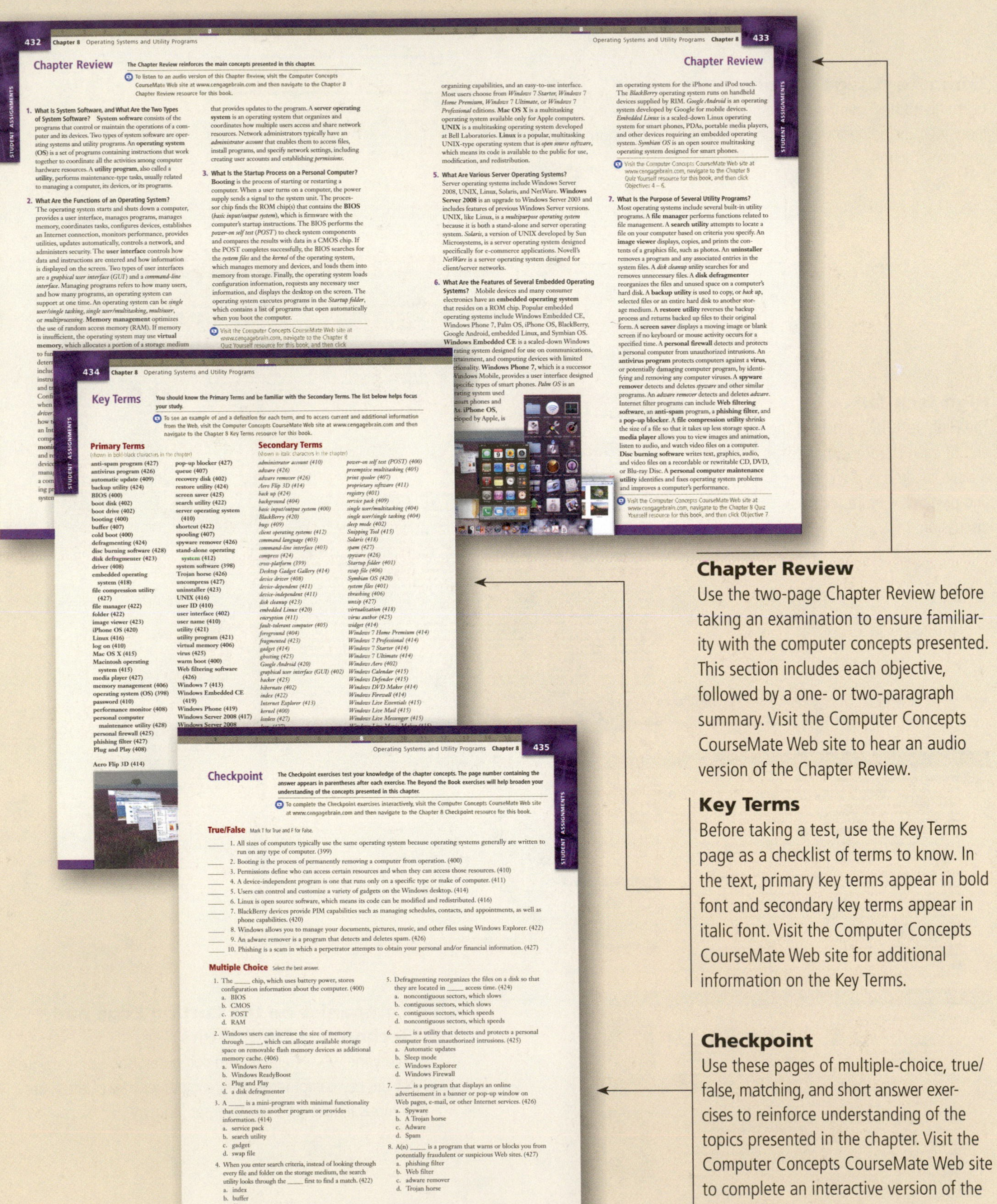

Chapter Review

Use the two-page Chapter Review before taking an examination to ensure familiarity with the computer concepts presented. This section includes each objective, followed by a one- or two-paragraph summary. Visit the Computer Concepts CourseMate Web site to hear an audio version of the Chapter Review.

Key Terms

Before taking a test, use the Key Terms page as a checklist of terms to know. In the text, primary key terms appear in bold font and secondary key terms appear in italic font. Visit the Computer Concepts CourseMate Web site for additional information on the Key Terms.

Checkpoint

Use these pages of multiple-choice, true/false, matching, and short answer exercises to reinforce understanding of the topics presented in the chapter. Visit the Computer Concepts CourseMate Web site to complete an interactive version of the Checkpoint exercises.

STUDENT ASSIGNMENTS

Learn It Online

The Learn It Online exercises, which include At the Movies online CNET videos, practice tests, interactive labs, learning games, and Web-based activities offer a wealth of online reinforcement.

Operating Systems and Utility Programs **Chapter 8** 437

Learn It Online

The Learn It Online exercises are interactive Web exercises designed to reinforce and expand your understanding of the chapter concepts. The descriptions below briefly summarize each exercise.

To complete the Learn It Online exercises, visit the Computer Concepts CourseMate Web site at www.cengagebrain.com, navigate to the Chapter 8 resources for this book, click the link for the exercise you want to complete, and then read the instructions.

1. **At the Movies — Free Online Antivirus** Watch a movie to learn why it is important to run antivirus software on your computer and how to scan your computer for malware online for no cost and then answer questions about the movie.
2. **Video and Audio: You Review It — Spyware** Search for, choose, and write a review of a video, podcast, or vodcast that discusses spyware.
3. **Student Edition Labs — Installing and Uninstalling Software and Keeping Your Computer Virus Free** Enhance your understanding and knowledge about installing and uninstalling software and keeping your computer virus free by completing the Installing and Uninstalling Software and Keeping Your Computer Virus Free Labs.
4. **Practice Test** Take a multiple choice test that checks your knowledge of the chapter concepts and review the resulting study guide.
5. **Who Wants To Be a Computer Genius²?** Play the Shelly Cashman Series version of this popular game by answering questions to find out if you are a computer genius. Panic buttons are available to provide assistance during game play.
6. **Wheel of Terms** Identify important key terms presented in this chapter by playing the Shelly Cashman Series version of this popular game.
7. **You're Hired!** Embark on the path to a career in computers by answering questions and solving puzzles related to concepts discussed in this chapter.
8. **Crossword Puzzle Challenge** Complete an interactive crossword puzzle to reinforce concepts presented in this chapter.
9. **Windows Exercises** Step through the Windows 7 exercises to learn about Windows, using a screen saver, changing desktop colors, customizing the desktop for multiple users, and backing up a computer.
10. **Exploring Computer Careers** Read about a career as a systems programmer, search for related employment advertisements, and then answer related questions.
11. **Web Apps — PhotoshopExpress** Learn how to use PhotoshopExpress to upload new photos as well as photos stored on other photo sharing communities, edit photos, create new pictures, and share them with others.

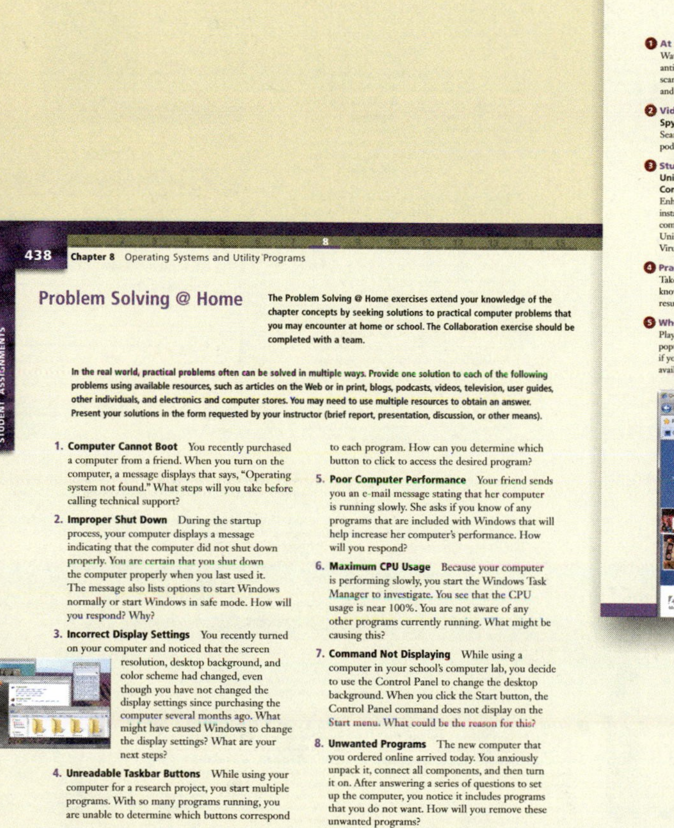

438 **Chapter 8** Operating Systems and Utility Programs

Problem Solving @ Home

The Problem Solving @ Home exercises extend your knowledge of the chapter concepts by seeking solutions to practical computer problems that you may encounter at home or school. The Collaboration exercise should be completed with a team.

In the real world, practical problems often can be solved in multiple ways. Provide one solution to each of the following problems using available resources, such as articles on the Web or in print, blogs, podcasts, videos, television, user guides, other individuals, and electronics and computer stores. You may need to use multiple resources to obtain an answer. Present your solutions in the form requested by your instructor (brief report, presentation, discussion, or other means).

1. **Computer Cannot Boot** You recently purchased a computer from a friend. When you turn on the computer, a message displays that says, "Operating system not found." What steps will you take before calling technical support?
2. **Improper Shut Down** During the startup process, your computer displays a message indicating that the computer did not shut down properly. You are certain that you shut down the computer properly when you last used it. The message also lists options to start Windows normally or start Windows in safe mode. How will you respond? Why?
3. **Incorrect Display Settings** You recently turned on your computer and noticed that the screen resolution, desktop background, and color scheme had changed, even though you have not changed the display settings since purchasing the computer several months ago. What might have caused Windows to change the display settings? What are your next steps?
4. **Unreadable Taskbar Buttons** While using your computer for a research project, you start multiple programs. With so many programs running, you are unable to determine which buttons correspond to each program. How can you determine which button to click to access the desired program?
5. **Poor Computer Performance** Your friend sends you an e-mail message stating that her computer is running slowly. She asks if you know of any programs that are included with Windows that will help increase her computer's performance. How will you respond?
6. **Maximum CPU Usage** Because your computer is performing slowly, you start the Windows Task Manager to investigate. You see that the CPU usage is near 100%. You are not aware of any other programs currently running. What might be causing this?
7. **Command Not Displaying** While using a computer in your school's computer lab, you decide to use the Control Panel to change the desktop background. When you click the Start button, the Control Panel command does not display on the Start menu. What could be the reason for this?
8. **Unwanted Programs** The new computer that you ordered online arrived today. You anxiously unpack it, connect all components, and then turn it on. After answering a series of questions to set up the computer, you notice it includes programs that you do not want. How will you remove these unwanted programs?

Collaboration

9. **Slow Computer** A fellow classmate has been complaining that his computer does not seem to be working properly. He complains that Windows takes too long to start and that it runs very slowly. You would like more practice troubleshooting computer problems, so you offer to look at his computer. When you start Windows, you notice that the hard disk has less than 100 MB of free space, many icons appear in the notification area, no antivirus software is installed, and more than 50 Windows updates are available for the computer. Form a team of three people and determine how to use the software that is included with Windows, in addition to any third-party software that may be needed, to resolve these computer problems. Compile your findings and submit them to your instructor.

Chapter 8 439

continue the boot process; however, you forgot the password. What are your next steps to allow the computer to continue the boot process, start Windows, and access the files on the hard disk?

3. **Frozen Manufacturer Logo** After turning on your computer, the computer manufacturer's logo displays on the monitor for several minutes. Suspecting that your computer might be frozen, you turn it off. Three minutes later, you turn the computer on and the same problem arises. What might be wrong?
4. **Automatic Updates** Two or three times per month, your coworker receives a notification on his computer that the computer recently has been updated. You ask your coworker about these messages, and he says that Microsoft periodically installs updates automatically to protect the computer from various threats, as well as to improve performance. You never have seen this for Windows Update. What could be causing this?
6. **Antivirus Schedule** You recently changed your work schedule so that you work until 6:00 p.m. instead of 5:00 p.m. At 5:00 p.m. each day, you notice that the antivirus program on your computer automatically begins scanning all files on your hard disk. This process slows your computer, and the program usually still is scanning when you leave the office. How can you change the configuration so that the antivirus program does not start until after you leave?
7. **Minimum Battery Power** When you use your notebook computer and it is not plugged in, the battery lasts for only one hour, but the documentation states that the computer can last for two hours on battery power. What are some ways that you can increase the battery life?

Collaboration

8. **Computers in Education** A private elementary school in your neighborhood has received a grant to create a computer lab with Internet access so that students can learn about computers and related technologies. Your neighbor, who also is a teacher at the school, asks for advice regarding how they should spend the grant money. Form a team of three people to determine the best configuration for the lab. One team member should research whether a PC or Mac is more beneficial. Another team member should research the application software that should be installed on these computers, and the other team member should determine what, if any, peripheral devices should be attached to the computers in the lab. Compile your findings and submit them to your instructor.

Problem Solving @ Home, Problem Solving @ Work, and Collaboration

Tackle everyday computer problems and put the information presented in each chapter to practical use with the Problem Solving @ Home and Problem Solving @ Work exercises. Work as a team to solve the Collaboration exercises.

STUDENT ASSIGNMENTS

Learn How To

Apply the concepts in the chapter to everyday life with these hands-on activities. Learn how the Learn How To activities fit into your life with relevant scenarios, visual demonstrations, and practice questions via the Computer Concepts CourseMate Web site.

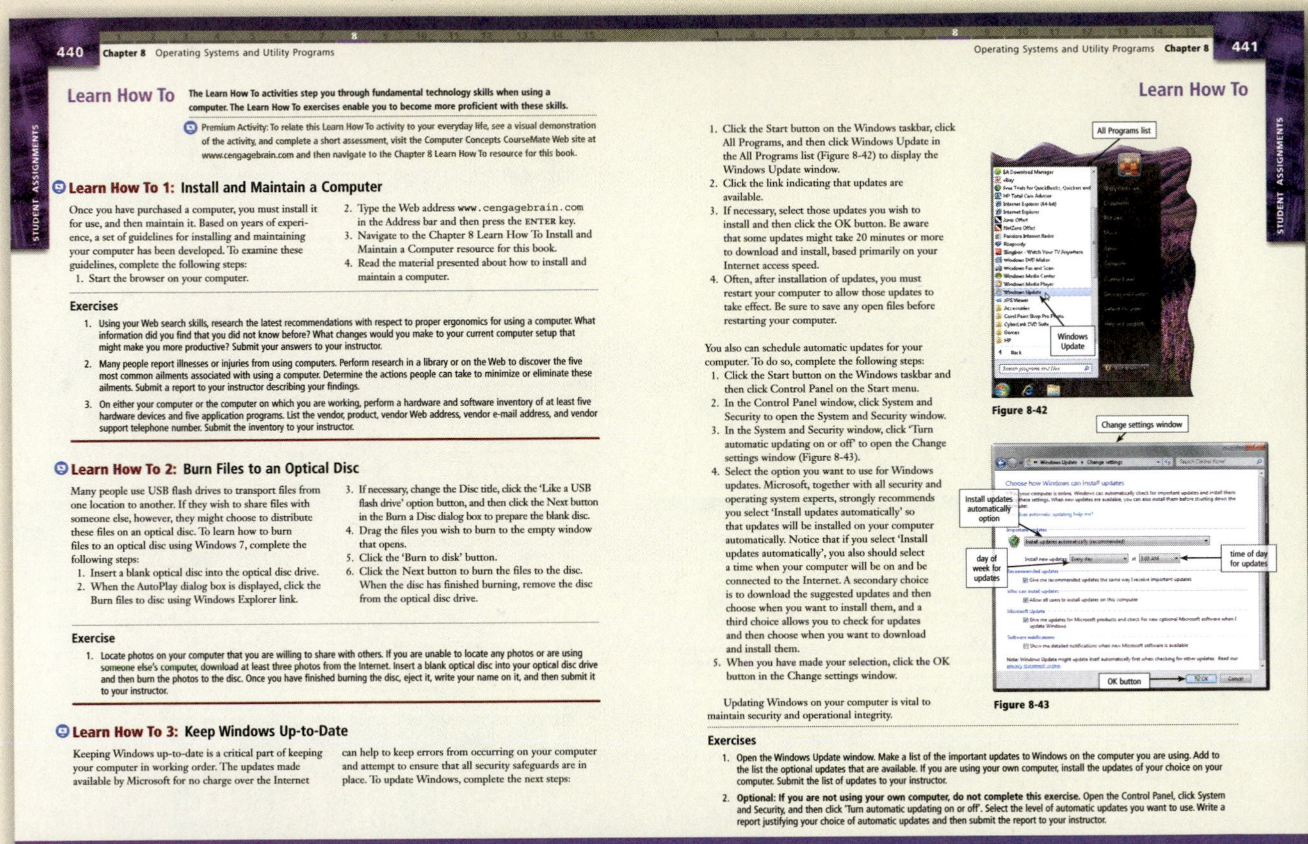

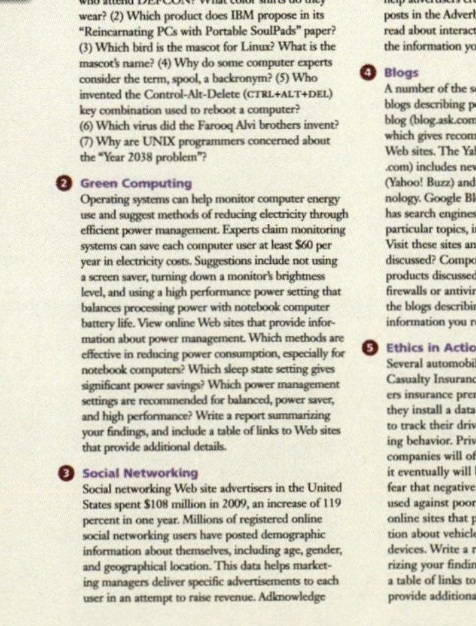

Web Research

Each Web Research exercise requires follow-up research on the Web and suggests writing a short article or presenting the findings of the research to the class.

STUDENT ASSIGNMENTS

Critical Thinking

Exercise your mind and construct creative solutions to these thought-provoking exercises presented in each chapter. The Critical Thinking exercises are constructed for class discussion, presentation, and independent research. The Collaboration exercise is designed for a team environment.

Operating Systems and Utility Programs **Chapter 8** 443

Critical Thinking

The Critical Thinking exercises challenge your assessment and decision-making skills by presenting real-world situations associated with the chapter concepts. The Collaboration exercise should be completed with a team.

To evaluate the situations below, use personal experiences and available resources such as articles on the Web or in print, blogs, podcasts, videos, television, user guides, other individuals, and electronics and computer stores. You may need to use multiple resources to form conclusions and make recommendations.

1. **Class Discussion — Downloading Music**
Many students at the local college have been using the college's computers to download music from the Internet. You have been asked to serve on a student committee to analyze and discuss this questionable use of the college's computers based on the following questions. Is it the college's responsibility to block music downloads? Why or why not? How would the college prevent students from downloading music? What is the difference between recording a song from the radio and downloading music from the Internet? Should violators be expelled, fined, required to attend a seminar on the ethical use of computers, or given a verbal warning? What recommendations would you give to the committee regarding the downloading of music?

2. **Class Presentation — Windows 7 Editions**
Your cousin is buying a new computer both for personal use and for operating his consulting business, which he runs out of his home. He is undecided about which edition of the Windows 7 operating system to purchase with his new computer. Windows 7 Professional is intended for business users. Windows 7 Home Premium is designed for home computing. Windows 7 Ultimate contains features both for home and business users. He has asked you to review the differences between each edition and help him decide which he should buy. Prepare a presentation comparing the similarities and contrasting the differences among the three editions. Be sure to include items such as features that are included with one edition that are not available in another and cost differences. At the end of your presentation, provide a recommendation and the reasons why the edition you chose would be best.

3. **Research — Complete Security Solutions**
Your neighbor started a new construction business and opened an office several blocks from your house. He is impressed by your computer knowledge and would like to hire you to set up his new computers. He mentions that because of the increasing security concerns on the Internet, he first would like you to install a program or programs designed to protect his computers from various security threats. What types of security threats exist on the Internet? Write a brief report describing two programs that provide a comprehensive security solution. What are the programs' functions? What computer requirements, if any, exist? Do the programs appear to be easy to install? What is their cost? Are subscription fees charged in order to receive automatic updates? In your opinion, are the programs worth the price? Why or why not?

Collaboration

4. **Operating Systems** Your team members are employed as analysts at Soap-n-Suds, an international manufacturer of laundry soaps. The company currently uses an early version of the Windows operating system on its 5,000 desktop computers. This year, the company plans to upgrade the operating system and, if necessary, its desktop computers. The vice president of information technology has asked your team to compare the latest desktop versions of the Windows operating system, Mac OS, and the Linux operating system. Assign each member of your team an operating system. Each member should use the Web and/or print media to develop a feature/benefit analysis along with the answers to the following questions. What is the initial cost of the operating system per computer? What are the memory and storage requirements? Will the operating system require the company to purchase new computers? Are training costs involved? Which operating system is best at avoiding viruses, spam, and spyware? Which operating system is easier to use? Why? Can the latest version of Microsoft Office run with the operating system? As a team, merge your findings into a team presentation and share your findings and recommendation with the class.

Special Features

Nine special features following Chapters 1, 2, 3, 6, 8, 11, 13, 14, and 15 encompass topics from the history of computers, to hot topics on the Web, including Web 2.0, to a buyer's guide, to the latest in new technology and digital communications.

Visual Walkthrough of the Computer Concepts CourseMate for Discovering Computers

Interactive. Current. Engaging. Your Interactive Guide to the Digital World!

Introduce the most current technology into the classroom with the Computer Concepts CourseMate for Discovering Computers. An integrated e-book and a wide range of online learning games, quizzes, practice tests, videos, and Web links expand on the topics covered in the text with hands-on reinforcement. The Pointer Icon integrated into each page of the text illustrates when to access the CourseMate Web site and quickly shows students the connection between the text and the digital solution.

Who Wants to Be a Computer Genius?²

The Who Wants to Be a Computer Genius?² learning game allows students to quiz themselves on chapter content within a dynamic and entertaining game scenario. Question results are provided instantly so that students quickly see which concepts they understand and which concepts they need to study. Page remediation is included with question results so students know exactly where in the text to find the information they need.

EngagementTracker

EngagementTracker makes assessing students easy by tracking student progress on the interactive activities. Clear and visual reports illustrate the class progress as a whole.

Wheel of Terms

Wheel of Terms is an interactive study tool for learning the Key Terms in each chapter. This learning game presents students with a short definition of one of the chapter's Key Terms and prompts them to type the correct term as the answer.

Online Content

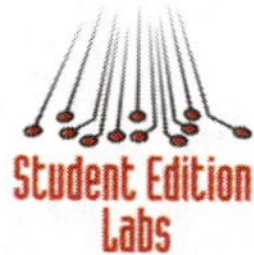

Student Edition Labs

Our Web-based interactive labs help students master hundreds of computer concepts, including input and output devices, file management and desktop applications, computer ethics, virus protection, and much more. Featuring up-to-the-minute content, eye-popping graphics, and rich animation, the highly interactive Student Edition Labs offer students an alternative way to learn through dynamic observation, step-by-step practice, and challenging review questions. Access the Student Edition Labs from the Discovering Computers: Your Interactive Guide to the Digital World Computer Concepts CourseMate Web site at www.cengagebrain.com or see the Student Edition Lab exercises on the Learn It Online pages at the end of each chapter. Also available on CD at an additional cost.

SAM 2010: Assessment & Training and Project Grading Solutions

SAM (Skills Assessment Manager) is a robust assessment, training and project-based system that enables students to be active participants in learning valuable Microsoft Office 2010 skills. A set of testbank questions ties directly to each chapter in this book. Let SAM be an integral part of your students' learning experience!

Content for Online Learning

Course Technology has partnered with the leading distance learning solution providers and class-management platforms today. To access this material, instructors will visit our password-protected instructor resources available at http://www.cengage.com/coursecare/cartridge/. Instructor resources include the following: additional case projects, sample syllabi, PowerPoint presentations per chapter, and more. For additional information or for an instructor username and password, please contact your sales representative. For students to access this material, they must have purchased a Course Cartridge PIN-code specific to this title and your campus platform. The resources for students may include (based on instructor preferences), but not limited to: topic review, review questions and practice tests.

CourseCasts Learning on the Go

Always available. . . always relevant.

Our fast-paced world is driven by technology. You know because you are an active participant — always on the go, always keeping up with technological trends, and always learning new ways to embrace technology to power your life. Let CourseCasts, hosted by Ken Baldauf of Florida State University, be your guide to weekly updates in this ever-changing space. These timely, relevant podcasts are produced weekly and are available for download at http://coursecasts.course.com or directly from iTunes (search by CourseCasts). CourseCasts are a perfect solution to getting students (and even instructors) to learn on the go!

CourseNotes — Technology in a Flash!

Course Technology's CourseNotes are six-panel quick reference cards that reinforce the most important and widely used features of a software application in a visual and user-friendly format. CourseNotes serve as a great reference tool during and after the student completes the course. CourseNotes are available for software applications, such as Microsoft Office 2010, Word 2010, PowerPoint 2010, Excel 2010, Access 2010, and Windows 7. Topic-based CourseNotes are available for Best Practices in Social Networking, Hot Topics in Technology, and Web 2.0. Visit www.cengage.com/ct/coursenotes to learn more!

About Our Covers

The Shelly Cashman Series is continually updating our approach and content to reflect the way today's students learn and experience new technology. This focus on student success is reflected on our covers, which feature real students from Bryant University using the Shelly Cashman Series in their courses, and reflect the varied ages and backgrounds of the students learning with our books. When you use the Shelly Cashman Series, you can be assured that you are learning computer skills using the most effective courseware available.

Chapter One

Introduction to Computers

Objectives

After completing this chapter, you will be able to:

1. Explain why computer literacy is vital to success in today's world
2. Define the term, computer, and describe the relationship between data and information
3. Describe the five components of a computer: input devices, output devices, system unit, storage devices, and communications devices
4. Discuss the advantages and disadvantages that users experience when working with computers
5. Define the term, network, and identify benefits of sharing resources on a network
6. Discuss the uses of the Internet and World Wide Web
7. Distinguish between system software and application software
8. Differentiate among types, sizes, and functions of computers in each of these categories: personal computers (desktop), mobile computers and mobile devices, game consoles, servers, mainframes, supercomputers, and embedded computers
9. Describe the role of each element in an information system
10. Explain how home users, small office/home office users, mobile users, power users, and enterprise users each interact with computers
11. Discuss how society uses computers in education, finance, government, health care, science, publishing, travel, and manufacturing

A World of Computers

Computers are everywhere: at work, at school, and at home. As shown in Figure 1-1, people use all types and sizes of computers for a variety of reasons and in a range of places. While some computers sit on top of a desk or on the floor, mobile computers and mobile devices are small enough to carry. Mobile devices, such as many cell phones, often are classified as computers.

Computers are a primary means of local and global communication for billions of people. Consumers use computers to correspond with businesses, employees with other employees and customers, students with classmates and teachers, and family members and military personnel with friends and other family members. In addition to sending simple notes, people use computers to share photos, drawings, documents, calendars, journals, music, and videos.

Through computers, society has instant access to information from around the globe. Local and national news, weather reports, sports scores, airline schedules, telephone directories, maps and directions, job listings, credit reports, and countless forms of educational material always are accessible. From the computer, you can make a telephone call, meet new friends, share opinions or life stories, book flights, shop, fill prescriptions, file taxes, take a course, receive alerts, and automate your home.

At home or while on the road, people use computers to manage schedules and contacts, listen to voice mail messages, balance checkbooks, pay bills, transfer funds, and buy or sell stocks. Banks place ATMs (automated teller machines) all over the world, so that customers can deposit

Figure 1-1 People use all types and sizes of computers in their daily activities.

and withdraw funds anywhere at anytime. At the grocery store, a computer tracks purchases, calculates the amount of money due, and often generates coupons customized to buying patterns. Vehicles include onboard navigation systems that provide directions, call for emergency services, and track the vehicle if it is stolen.

In the workplace, employees use computers to create correspondence such as e-mail messages, memos, and letters; manage calendars; calculate payroll; track inventory; and generate invoices. At school, teachers use computers to assist with classroom instruction. Students complete assignments and conduct research on computers in lab rooms, at home, or elsewhere. Instead of attending class on campus, some students take entire classes directly from their computer.

People also spend hours of leisure time using a computer. They play games, listen to music or radio broadcasts, watch or compose videos and movies, read books and magazines, share stories, research genealogy, retouch photos, and plan vacations.

As technology continues to advance, computers have become a part of everyday life. Thus, many people believe that computer literacy is vital to success in today's world. **Computer literacy**, also known as *digital literacy*, involves having a current knowledge and understanding of computers and their uses. Because the requirements that determine computer literacy change as technology changes, you must keep up with these changes to remain computer literate.

This book presents the knowledge you need to be computer literate today. As you read this first chapter, keep in mind it is an overview. Many of the terms and concepts introduced in this chapter will be discussed in more depth later in the book.

What Is a Computer?

A **computer** is an electronic device, operating under the control of instructions stored in its own memory, that can accept data, process the data according to specified rules, produce results, and store the results for future use.

Data and Information

Computers process data into information. **Data** is a collection of unprocessed items, which can include text, numbers, images, audio, and video. **Information** conveys meaning and is useful to people.

Many daily activities either involve the use of or depend on information from a computer. As shown in Figure 1-2, for example, computers process several data items to print information in the form of a cash register receipt.

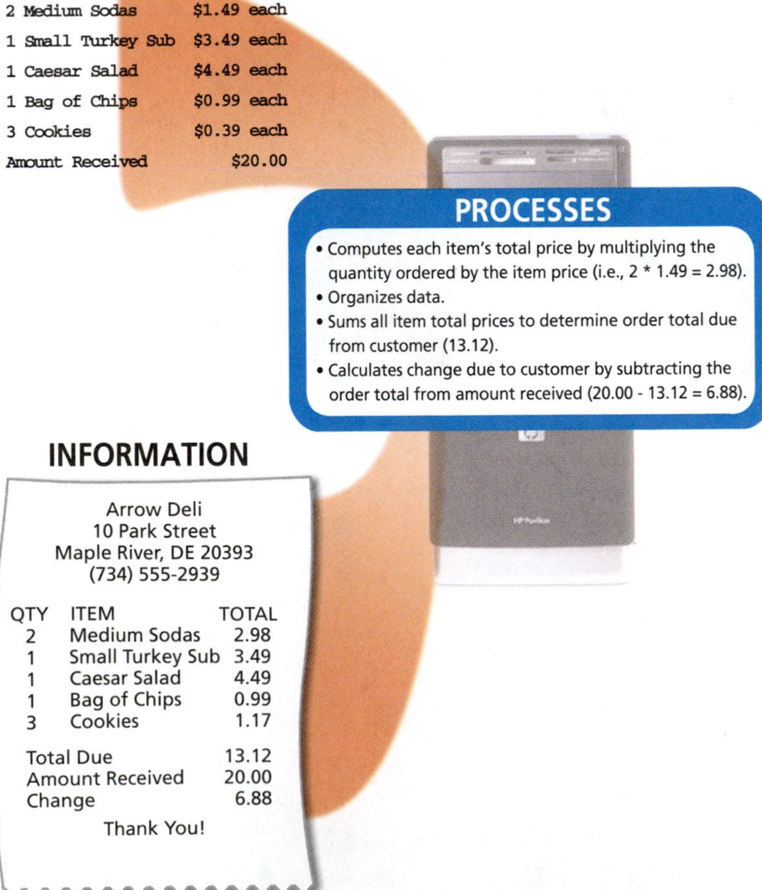

Figure 1-2 A computer processes data into information. In this simplified example, the item ordered, item price, quantity ordered, and amount received all represent data. The computer processes the data to produce the cash register receipt (information).

Information Processing Cycle

Computers process data (input) into information (output). Computers carry out processes using *instructions*, which are the steps that tell the computer how to perform a particular task. A collection of related instructions organized for a common purpose is referred to as software. A computer often holds data, information, and instructions in storage for future use. Some people refer to the series of input, process, output, and storage activities as the *information processing cycle*.

Most computers today communicate with other computers. As a result, communications also has become an essential element of the information processing cycle.

The Components of a Computer

A computer contains many electric, electronic, and mechanical components known as **hardware**. These components include input devices, output devices, a system unit, storage devices, and communications devices. Figure 1-3 shows some common computer hardware components.

Input Devices

An **input device** is any hardware component that allows you to enter data and instructions into a computer. Five widely used input devices are the keyboard, mouse, microphone, scanner, and Web cam (Figure 1-3).

A computer keyboard contains keys you press to enter data into the computer. For security purposes, some keyboards include a fingerprint reader, which allows you to work with the computer only if your fingerprint is recognized.

A mouse is a small handheld device. With the mouse, you control movement of a small symbol on the screen, called the pointer, and you make selections from the screen.

A microphone allows you to speak into the computer. A scanner converts printed material (such as text and pictures) into a form the computer can use.

A Web cam is a digital video camera that allows you to create movies or take pictures and store them on the computer instead of on tape or film.

Output Devices

An **output device** is any hardware component that conveys information to one or more people. Three commonly used output devices are a printer, a monitor, and speakers (Figure 1-3).

A printer produces text and graphics on a physical medium such as paper. A monitor displays text, graphics, and videos on a screen. Speakers allow you to hear music, voice, and other audio (sounds).

System Unit

The **system unit** is a case that contains the electronic components of the computer that are used to process data (Figure 1-3). The circuitry of the system unit usually is part of or is connected to a circuit board called the motherboard.

Two main components on the motherboard are the processor and memory. The *processor*, also called a *CPU* (*central processing unit*), is the electronic component that interprets and carries out the basic instructions that operate the computer. *Memory* consists of electronic components that store instructions waiting to be executed and data needed by those instructions. Although some forms of memory are permanent, most memory keeps data and instructions temporarily, which means its contents are erased when the computer is shut off.

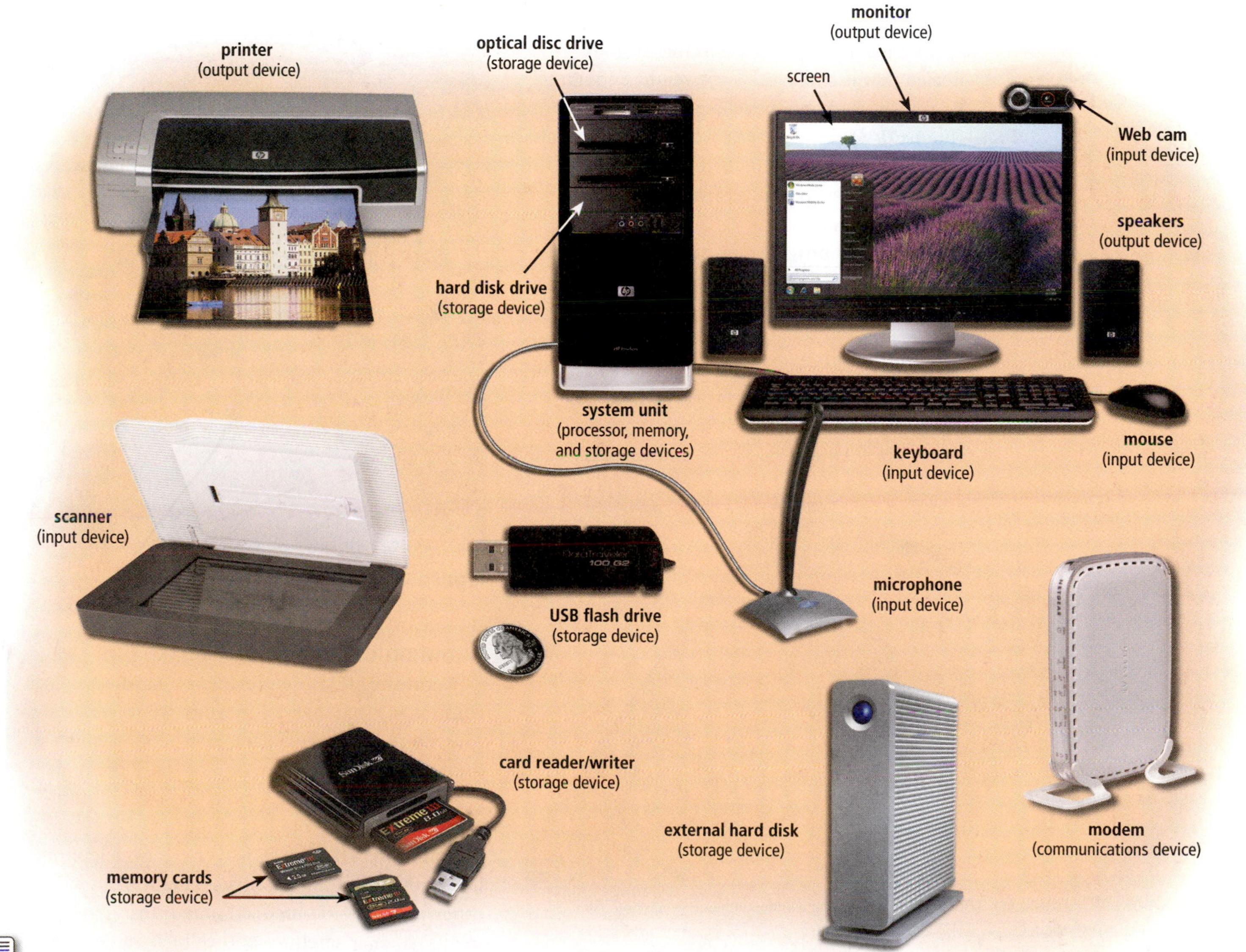

printer (output device)
optical disc drive (storage device)
monitor (output device)
screen
Web cam (input device)
speakers (output device)
hard disk drive (storage device)
system unit (processor, memory, and storage devices)
keyboard (input device)
mouse (input device)
scanner (input device)
microphone (input device)
USB flash drive (storage device)
card reader/writer (storage device)
external hard disk (storage device)
modem (communications device)
memory cards (storage device)

Figure 1-3 Common computer hardware components include a keyboard, mouse, microphone, scanner, Web cam, printer, monitor, speakers, system unit, hard disk drive, external hard disk, optical disc drive(s), USB flash drive, card reader/writer, memory cards, and modem.

Storage Devices

Storage holds data, instructions, and information for future use. For example, computers can store hundreds or millions of customer names and addresses. Storage holds these items permanently.

A computer keeps data, instructions, and information on **storage media**. Examples of storage media are USB flash drives, hard disks, optical discs, and memory cards. A **storage device** records (writes) and/or retrieves (reads) items to and from storage media. Drives and readers/writers, which are types of storage devices (Figure 1-3 on the previous page), accept a specific kind of storage media. For example, a DVD drive (storage device) accepts a DVD (storage media). Storage devices often function as a source of input because they transfer items from storage to memory.

A USB flash drive is a portable storage device that is small and lightweight enough to be transported on a keychain or in a pocket (Figure 1-3). The average USB flash drive can hold about 4 billion characters. You plug a USB flash drive in a special, easily accessible opening on the computer.

A hard disk provides much greater storage capacity than a USB flash drive. The average hard disk can hold more than 320 billion characters. Hard disks are enclosed in an airtight, sealed case. Although some are portable, most are housed inside the system unit (Figure 1-4). Portable hard disks are either external or removable. An external hard disk is a separate, freestanding unit, whereas you insert and remove a removable hard disk from the computer or a device connected to the computer.

Figure 1-4 Hard disks are self-contained devices. The hard disk shown here must be installed in the system unit before it can be used.

An optical disc is a flat, round, portable metal disc with a plastic coating. CDs, DVDs, and Blu-ray Discs are three types of optical discs. A CD can hold from 650 million to 1 billion characters. Some DVDs can store two full-length movies or 17 billion characters (Figure 1-5). Blu-ray Discs can store about 46 hours of standard video, or 100 billion characters.

Some mobile devices, such as digital cameras, use memory cards as the storage media. You can use a card reader/writer (Figure 1-3) to transfer the stored items, such as digital photos, from the memory card to a computer or printer.

Figure 1-5 A DVD in a DVD drive.

Communications Devices

A **communications device** is a hardware component that enables a computer to send (transmit) and receive data, instructions, and information to and from one or more computers or mobile devices. A widely used communications device is a modem (Figure 1-3).

Communications occur over cables, telephone lines, cellular radio networks, satellites, and other transmission media. Some transmission media, such as satellites and cellular radio networks, are wireless, which means they have no physical lines or wires.

Advantages and Disadvantages of Using Computers

Society has reaped many benefits from using computers. A **user** is anyone who communicates with a computer or utilizes the information it generates. Both business and home users can make well-informed decisions because they have instant access to information from anywhere in the world. Students, another type of user, have more tools to assist them in the learning process.

Advantages of Using Computers

Benefits from using computers are possible because computers have the advantages of speed, reliability, consistency, storage, and communications.

- **Speed:** When data, instructions, and information flow along electronic circuits in a computer, they travel at incredibly fast speeds. Many computers process billions or trillions of operations in a single second. Processing involves computing (e.g., adding, subtracting), sorting (e.g., alphabetizing), organizing, displaying images, recording audio, playing music, and showing a movie or video.
- **Reliability:** The electronic components in modern computers are dependable and reliable because they rarely break or fail.
- **Consistency:** Given the same input and processes, a computer will produce the same results — consistently. A computing phrase — known as *garbage in, garbage out* — points out that the accuracy of a computer's output depends on the accuracy of the input. For example, if you do not use the flash on a digital camera when indoors, the resulting pictures that are displayed on the computer screen may be unusable because they are too dark.
- **Storage:** A computer can transfer data quickly from storage to memory, process it, and then store it again for future use. Many computers store enormous amounts of data and make this data available for processing anytime it is needed.
- **Communications:** Most computers today can communicate with other computers, often wirelessly. Computers with this capability can share any of the four information processing cycle operations — input, process, output, and storage — with another computer or a user.

Disadvantages of Using Computers

Some disadvantages of computers relate to health risks, the violation of privacy, public safety, the impact on the labor force, and the impact on the environment.

- **Health Risks:** Prolonged or improper computer use can lead to injuries or disorders of the hands, wrists, elbows, eyes, neck, and back. Computer users can protect themselves from these health risks through proper workplace design, good posture while at the computer, and appropriately spaced work breaks. Two behavioral health risks are computer addiction and technology overload. Computer addiction occurs when someone becomes obsessed with using a computer. Individuals suffering from technology overload feel distressed when deprived of computers and mobile devices. Once recognized, both computer addiction and technology overload are treatable disorders. Read Ethics & Issues 1-1 for a related discussion.

ETHICS & ISSUES 1-1

How Can People Best Cope with Technology Overload?

Most people enjoy the benefits that technology brings to their lives, such as increased productivity. A growing problem, however, is observed among those suffering the effects of technology overload. People overloaded with technology often feel uncomfortable or nervous when they cannot use the Internet or a cell phone for even a short length of time. Some mental health experts believe that technology overload is a health problem that can be treated just as other compulsions are treated. While some disagreement exists over the specific definition, the general consensus is that a person has a problem with technology overload when the overuse of technology negatively impacts health, personal life, and professional life. For some, technology overload often leads to less time spent with family and has proven to be as potent a cause for divorce as gambling or substance abuse. Experts suggest balancing the use of technology in one's life and listening to others if they suggest that the overuse of technology is causing personal problems.

What steps can people or society take to cope with technology overload? How might one determine if he or she suffers from technology overload? How can technology companies help to alleviate the problem of technology overload? Should those identified as technology addicts be able to receive health insurance benefits for counseling services? Why or why not?

Ethics & Issues

For the complete text of the Ethics & Issues boxes found in this chapter, visit the Computer Concepts CourseMate Web site at www.cengagebrain.com and then navigate to the Chapter 1 Ethics & Issues resource for this book.

- **Violation of Privacy:** Nearly every life event is stored in a computer somewhere . . . in medical records, credit reports, tax records, etc. In many instances, where personal and confidential records were not protected properly, individuals have found their privacy violated and identities stolen.
- **Public Safety:** Adults, teens, and children around the world are using computers to share publicly their photos, videos, journals, music, and other personal information. Some of these unsuspecting, innocent computer users have fallen victim to crimes committed by dangerous strangers. Protect yourself and your dependents from these criminals by being cautious in e-mail messages and on Web sites. For example, do not share information that would allow others to identify or locate you and do not disclose identification numbers, passwords, or other personal security details.
- **Impact on Labor Force:** Although computers have improved productivity in many ways and created an entire industry with hundreds of thousands of new jobs, the skills of millions of employees have been replaced by computers. Thus, it is crucial that workers keep their education up-to-date. A separate impact on the labor force is that some companies are outsourcing jobs to foreign countries instead of keeping their homeland labor force employed.
- **Impact on Environment:** Computer manufacturing processes and computer waste are depleting natural resources and polluting the environment. When computers are discarded in landfills, they can release toxic materials and potentially dangerous levels of lead, mercury, and flame retardants.

Green computing involves reducing the electricity consumed and environmental waste generated when using a computer. Strategies that support green computing include recycling, regulating manufacturing processes, extending the life of computers, and immediately donating or properly disposing of replaced computers. When you purchase a new computer, some retailers offer to dispose of your old computer properly.

Green Computing

For more information, visit the Computer Concepts CourseMate Web site at www.cengagebrain.com, navigate to the Chapter 1 Web Link resource for this book, and then click Green Computing.

✓ QUIZ YOURSELF 1-1

Instructions: Find the true statement below. Then, rewrite the remaining false statements so that they are true.

1. A computer is a motorized device that processes output into input.
2. A storage device records (reads) and/or retrieves (writes) items to and from storage media.
3. An output device is any hardware component that allows you to enter data and instructions into a computer.
4. Computer literacy involves having a current knowledge and understanding of computers and their uses.
5. Computers have the disadvantages of fast speeds, high failure rates, producing consistent results, storing small amounts of data, and communicating with others.
6. Three commonly used input devices are a printer, a monitor, and speakers.

Quiz Yourself Online: To further check your knowledge of pages 4 through 10, visit the Computer Concepts CourseMate Web site at www.cengagebrain.com, navigate to the Chapter 1 Quiz Yourself resource for this book, and then click Objectives 1 – 4.

Networks and the Internet

A **network** is a collection of computers and devices connected together, often wirelessly, via communications devices and transmission media. When a computer connects to a network, it is **online**.

Networks allow computers to share *resources*, such as hardware, software, data, and information. Sharing resources saves time and money. In many networks, one or more computers act as a server. The *server* controls access to the resources on a network. The other computers on the network, each called a *client* or workstation, request resources from the server (Figure 1-6). The major differences between the server and client computers are that the server ordinarily has more power, more storage space, and expanded communications capabilities.

Many homes and most businesses and schools network their computers and devices. Most allow users to connect their computers wirelessly to the network. Home networks usually are small, existing within a single structure. Business and school networks can be small, such as in a room or building, or widespread, connecting computers and devices across a city, country, or the globe. The world's largest computer network is the Internet.

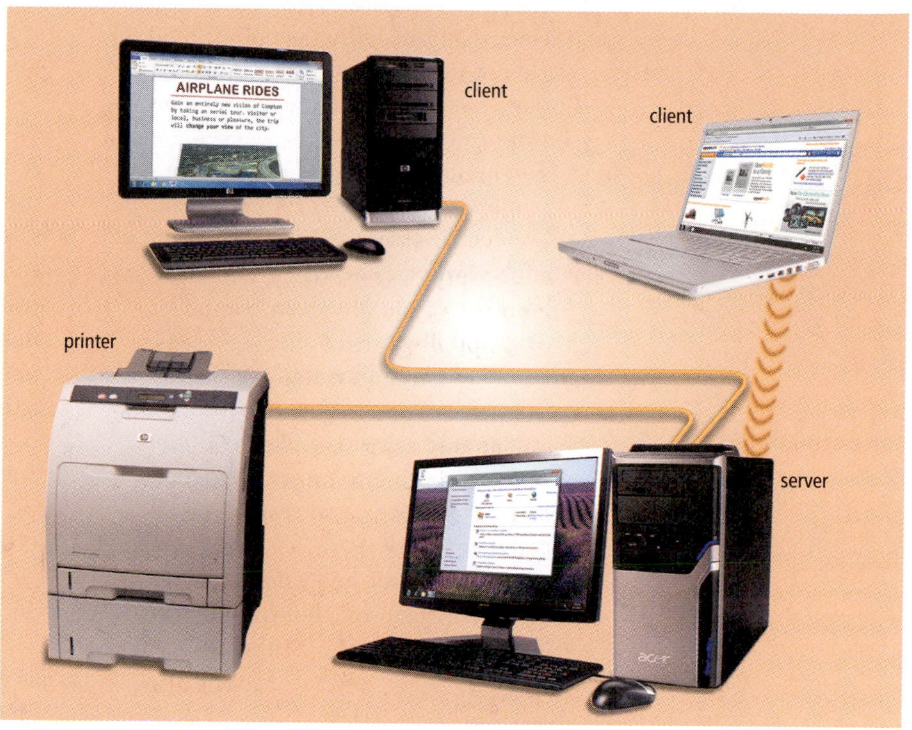

Figure 1-6 A server manages the resources on a network, and clients access the resources on the server. This network enables three separate computers to share the same printer, one wirelessly.

The Internet

The **Internet** is a worldwide collection of networks that connects millions of businesses, government agencies, educational institutions, and individuals (Figure 1-7).

Figure 1-7 The Internet is the largest computer network, connecting millions of computers and devices around the world.

More than one billion people around the world use the Internet daily for a variety of reasons, some of which are listed below and shown in Figure 1-8:

- Communicate with and meet other people
- Conduct research and access a wealth of information and news
- Shop for goods and services
- Bank and invest
- Participate in online training
- Engage in entertaining activities, such as planning vacations, playing online games, listening to music, watching or editing videos, and reading books and magazines
- Download music and videos
- Share information, photos, and videos
- Access and interact with Web applications

The Internet

For more information, visit the Computer Concepts CourseMate Web site at www.cengagebrain.com, navigate to the Chapter 1 Web Link resource for this book, and then click The Internet.

People connect to the Internet to share information with others around the world. E-mail allows you to send and receive messages to and from other users (read Ethics & Issues 1-2 for a related discussion). With instant messaging, you can have a live conversation with another connected user. In a chat room, you can communicate with multiple users at the same time — much like a group discussion. You also can use the Internet to make a telephone call.

Businesses, called access providers, offer users and organizations access to the Internet free or for a fee. By subscribing to an access provider, you can use your computer and a communications device, such as a modem, to connect to the many services of the Internet.

The Web, short for World Wide Web, is one of the more popular services on the Internet. Think of the Web as a global library of information available to anyone connected

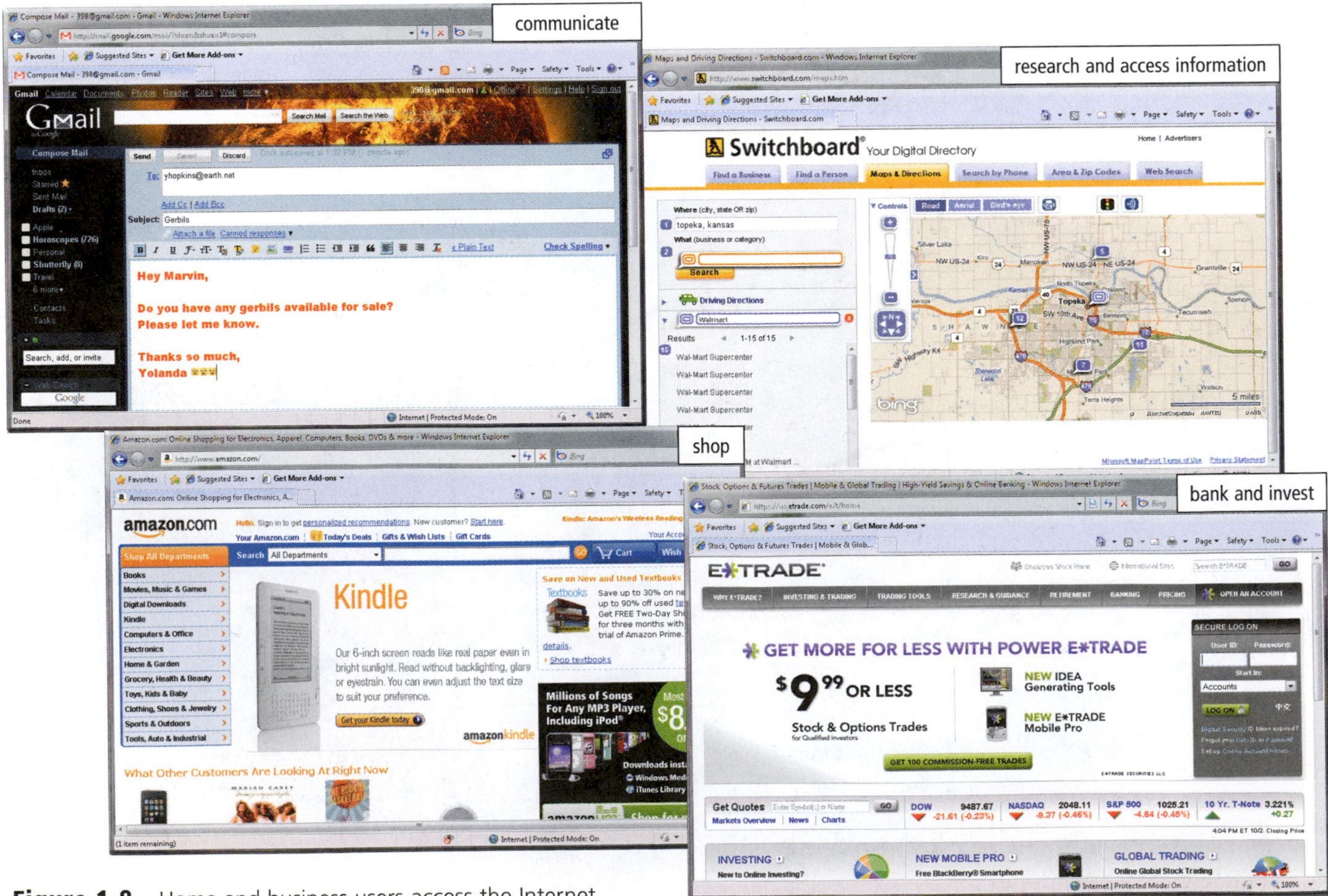

Figure 1-8 Home and business users access the Internet for a variety of reasons.

to the Internet. The **Web** contains billions of documents called Web pages. A **Web page** can contain text, graphics, animation, audio, and video. The nine screens shown in Figure 1-8 are examples of Web pages. Web pages often have built-in connections, or links, to other documents, graphics, other Web pages, or Web sites. A **Web site** is a collection of related Web pages. Some Web sites allow users to access music and videos that can be downloaded, or transferred to storage media in a computer or portable media player. Once downloaded, you can listen to the music through speakers, headphones, or earbuds, or view the videos on a display device.

Many people use the Web as a means to share personal information, photos, and videos with the world. For example, you can create a Web page and then make it available, or *publish* it, on the Internet for others to see.

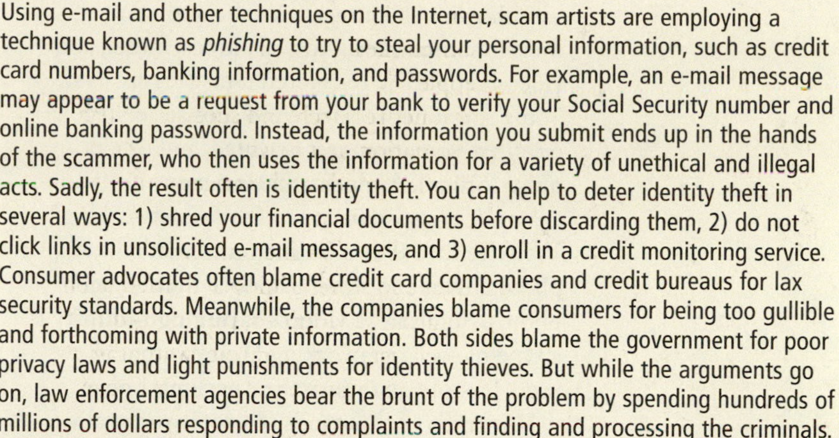

ETHICS & ISSUES 1-2

What Should Be Done about Identity Theft?

Using e-mail and other techniques on the Internet, scam artists are employing a technique known as *phishing* to try to steal your personal information, such as credit card numbers, banking information, and passwords. For example, an e-mail message may appear to be a request from your bank to verify your Social Security number and online banking password. Instead, the information you submit ends up in the hands of the scammer, who then uses the information for a variety of unethical and illegal acts. Sadly, the result often is identity theft. You can help to deter identity theft in several ways: 1) shred your financial documents before discarding them, 2) do not click links in unsolicited e-mail messages, and 3) enroll in a credit monitoring service. Consumer advocates often blame credit card companies and credit bureaus for lax security standards. Meanwhile, the companies blame consumers for being too gullible and forthcoming with private information. Both sides blame the government for poor privacy laws and light punishments for identity thieves. But while the arguments go on, law enforcement agencies bear the brunt of the problem by spending hundreds of millions of dollars responding to complaints and finding and processing the criminals.

Who should be responsible for protecting the public from online identity theft? Why? Should laws be changed to stop it, or should consumers change behavior? What is an appropriate punishment for identity thieves? Given the international nature of the Internet, how should foreign identity thieves be handled? Why?

online training

entertainment

download videos

share information

Web application

You also can join millions of people worldwide in an online community, called a **social networking Web site** or an *online social network*, that encourages members to share their interests, ideas, stories, photos, music, and videos with other registered users (Figure 1-9). Some social networking Web sites are college oriented, some business oriented, and others are more focused. A **photo sharing community,** for example, is a specific type of social networking Web site that allows users to create an online photo album and store and share their digital photos. Similarly, a **video sharing community** is a type of social networking Web site that allows users to store and share their personal videos.

Hundreds of thousands of people today also use blogs to publish their thoughts on the Web. A *blog* is an informal Web site consisting of time-stamped articles in a diary or journal format, usually listed in reverse chronological order. As others read the articles in a blog, they reply with their own thoughts. A blog that contains video clips is called a *video blog*. A *microblog*, such as Twitter, allows users to publish short messages, usually between 100 and 200 characters, for others to read. To learn more about creating and using blogs, complete the Learn How To 2 activity on pages 50 and 51.

Facebook

For more information, visit the Computer Concepts CourseMate Web site at www.cengagebrain.com, navigate to the Chapter 1 Web Link resource for this book, and then click Facebook.

Podcasts are a popular way people verbally share information on the Web. A *podcast* is recorded audio stored on a Web site that can be downloaded to a computer or a portable media player such as an iPod. A video podcast is a podcast that contains video and usually audio. At a convenient time and location, the user listens to or watches the downloaded podcast.

A **Web application** is a Web site that allows users to access and interact with software from any computer or device that is connected to the Internet. Examples of software available as Web applications include those that allow you to send and receive e-mail messages, prepare your taxes, organize digital photos, create documents, and play games.

Web sites such as social networking Web sites, blogs, and Web applications are categorized as Web 2.0 sites. The term **Web 2.0** refers to Web sites that provide a means for users to share personal information (such as social networking Web sites), allow users to modify the Web site contents (such as some blogs), and/or have software built into the site for users to access (such as Web applications).

Figure 1-9 Facebook is a popular social networking Web site.

? **FAQ 1-1**

What U.S. Web sites are visited most frequently?

A recent survey found that Google's Web site is visited most frequently, with Microsoft and Yahoo! not far behind. The chart below shows the five most frequently visited Web sites, as well as the approximate number of unique visitors per month.

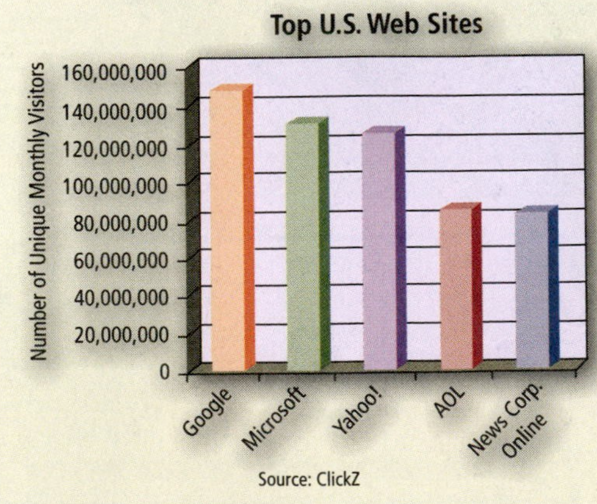

For more information, visit the Computer Concepts CourseMate Web site at www.cengagebrain.com, navigate to the Chapter 1 FAQ resource for this book, and then click Top Web Sites.

An *FAQ* (frequently asked question) helps you find answers to commonly asked questions. Web sites often post an FAQ section, and each chapter in this book includes FAQ boxes related to topics in the text.

Computer Software

Software, also called a **program**, consists of a series of related instructions, organized for a common purpose, that tells the computer what tasks to perform and how to perform them.

You interact with a program through its user interface. The user interface controls how you enter data and instructions and how information is displayed on the screen. Software today often has a graphical user interface. With a **graphical user interface** (**GUI** pronounced gooey), you interact with the software using text, graphics, and visual images such as icons. An *icon* is a miniature image that represents a program, an instruction, or some other object. You can use the mouse to select icons that perform operations such as starting a program.

The two categories of software are system software and application software. Figure 1-10 shows an example of each of these categories of software, which are explained in the following sections.

System Software

System software consists of the programs that control or maintain the operations of the computer and its devices. System software serves as the interface between the user, the application software, and the computer's hardware. Two types of system software are the operating system and utility programs.

Operating System An *operating system* is a set of programs that coordinates all the activities among computer hardware devices. It provides a means for users to communicate with the computer and other software. Many of today's computers use Microsoft's Windows, the latest version of which is shown in Figure 1-10, or Mac OS, Apple's operating system.

When a user starts a computer, portions of the operating system are copied into memory from the computer's hard disk. These parts of the operating system remain in memory while the computer is on.

Windows
For more information, visit the Computer Concepts CourseMate Web site at www.cengagebrain.com, navigate to the Chapter 1 Web Link resource for this book, and then click Windows.

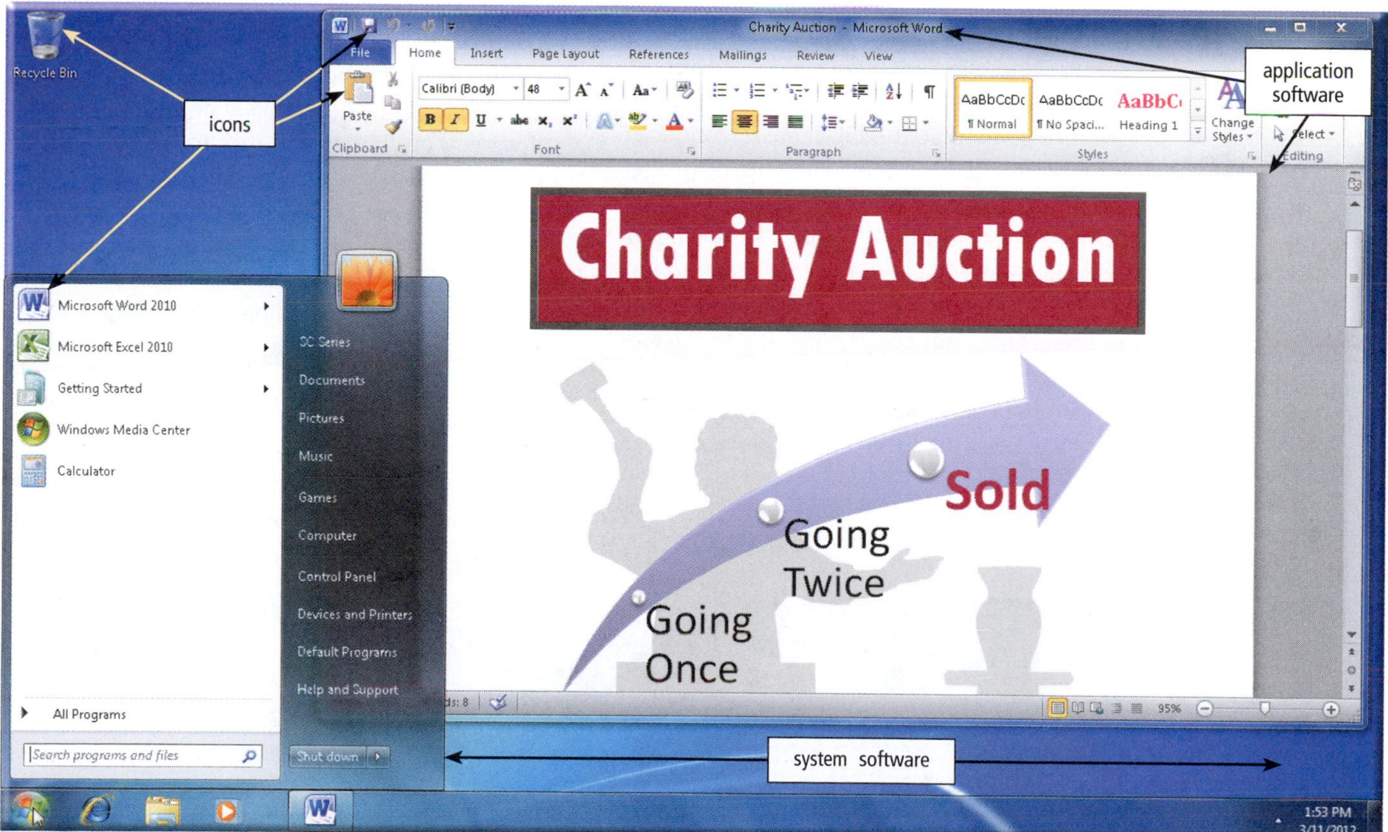

Figure 1-10 Today's system software and application software usually have a graphical user interface.

Utility Program A *utility program* allows a user to perform maintenance-type tasks usually related to managing a computer, its devices, or its programs. For example, you can use a utility program to transfer digital photos to an optical disc. Most operating systems include several utility programs for managing disk drives, printers, and other devices and media. You also can buy utility programs that allow you to perform additional computer management functions.

Application Software

Application software consists of programs designed to make users more productive and/or assist them with personal tasks. A widely used type of application software related to communications is a Web browser, which allows users with an Internet connection to access and view Web pages or access programs. Other popular application software includes word processing software, spreadsheet software, database software, and presentation software.

Many other types of application software exist that enable users to perform a variety of tasks. These include personal information management, note taking, project management, accounting, document management, computer-aided design, desktop publishing, paint/image editing, photo editing, audio and video editing, multimedia authoring, Web page authoring, personal finance, legal, tax preparation, home design/landscaping, travel and mapping, education, reference, and entertainment (e.g., games or simulations, etc.).

Software is available at stores that sell computer products (Figure 1-11) and also online at many Web sites.

FAQ 1-2

Who plays video games?

The introduction of computer and video games that cater to a broader audience has greatly increased the number of people who play them. According to the Entertainment Software Association, approximately 68 percent of the U.S. population plays video games. Of these, 40 percent are women. Further, 25 percent of Americans over 50 play video games, and the average game player is 35 years old.

For more information, visit the Computer Concepts CourseMate Web site at www.cengagebrain.com, navigate to the Chapter 1 FAQ resource for this book, and then click Game Demographics.

Installing and Running Programs

When purchasing software from a retailer, you typically receive a box that includes an optical disc(s) that contains the program. If you acquire software from a Web site on the Internet, you may be able to download the program; that is, the program transfers from the Web site to the hard disk in your computer.

The instructions in software are placed on storage media, either locally or online. To use software that is stored locally, such as on a hard disk or optical disc, you usually need to install the software. Web applications that are stored online, by contrast, usually do not need to be installed.

Installing is the process of setting up software to work with the computer, printer, and other hardware. When you buy a computer, it usually has some software preinstalled on its hard disk. This enables you to use the computer the first time you turn it on. To begin installing additional software from an optical disc, insert the program disc in an optical disc drive and follow the instructions to begin installation. To install downloaded software, the Web site typically provides instructions for how to install the program on your hard disk.

Figure 1-11 Stores that sell computer products have shelves stocked with software for sale.

Once installed, you can run the program. When you instruct the computer to **run** an installed program, the computer *loads* it, which means the program is copied from storage to memory. Once in memory, the computer can carry out, or *execute*, the instructions in the program so that you can use the program. Figure 1-12 illustrates the steps that occur when a user installs and runs a program. To learn more about starting and closing programs, complete the Learn How To 1 activity on page 50.

? FAQ 1-3

How do I know if computer software will run on my computer?

When you buy a computer, the box, the manufacturer's Web site, or the order summary will list the computer's specifications. Similarly, when you buy software, the software box or the product's Web site lists specifications. Your computer's specifications should be the same as or greater than the software specifications.

For more information, visit the Computer Concepts CourseMate Web site at www.cengagebrain.com, navigate to the Chapter 1 FAQ resource for this book, and then click Computer Software.

Installing and Running a Computer Program

Step 1: INSTALL

When you insert a program disc, such as a photo editing program, in the optical disc drive for the first time, the computer begins the procedure of installing the program on the hard disk.

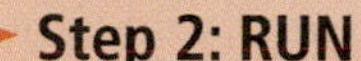

Step 2: RUN

Once installed, you can instruct the computer to run the program. The computer transfers instructions from the hard disk to memory.

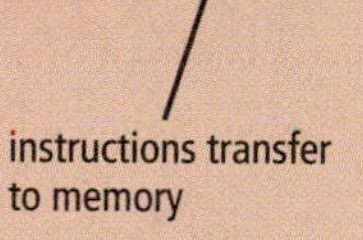

Step 3: USE

The program executes so that you can use it. This program enables you to edit photos.

Figure 1-12 This figure shows how to install and run a computer program.

Software Development

A *programmer*, sometimes called a computer programmer or *developer*, is someone who develops software or writes the instructions that direct the computer to process data into information. When writing instructions, a programmer must be sure the program works properly so that the computer generates the desired results. Complex programs can require thousands to millions of instructions.

Programmers use a programming language or program development tool to create computer programs. Popular programming languages include C++, Java, JavaScript, Visual C#, and Visual Basic. Figure 1-13 shows some of the Visual Basic instructions a programmer may write to create a simple payroll program.

Figure 1-13a (Visual Basic program instructions)

```
Public Class frmPayrollInformation

    Private Sub btnCalculatePay_Click(ByVal sender As System.Object, ByVal e As System.
    EventArgs) Handles btnCalculatePay.Click
        'This procedure executes when the user clicks the
        'Calculate Pay button. It calculates regular
        'and overtime pay and displays it in the window.

        ' Declare variables
        Dim strHoursWorked As String
        Dim strHourlyRate As String
        Dim decHoursWorked As Decimal
        Dim decHourlyRate As Decimal
        Dim decRegularPay As Decimal
        Dim decOvertimeHours As Decimal
        Dim decOvertimePay As Decimal
        Dim decTotalPay As Decimal

        ' Calculate and display payroll information
        strHoursWorked = Me.txtHoursWorked.Text
        strHourlyRate = Me.txtHourlyRate.Text
        decHoursWorked = Convert.ToDecimal(strHoursWorked)
        decHourlyRate = Convert.ToDecimal(strHourlyRate)

        If decHoursWorked > 40 Then
            decRegularPay = 40 * decHourlyRate
            Me.txtRegularPay.Text = decRegularPay.ToString("C")
            decOvertimeHours = decHoursWorked - 40
            decOvertimePay = (1.5 * decOvertimeHours) * decHourlyRate
            Me.txtOvertimePay.Text = decOvertimePay.ToString("C")
            decTotalPay = decRegularPay + decOvertimePay
            Me.txtTotalPay.Text = decTotalPay.ToString("C")
        Else
            decRegularPay = decHoursWorked * decHourlyRate
            Me.txtRegularPay.Text = decRegularPay.ToString("C")
            Me.txtOvertimePay.Text = "$0.00"
            Me.txtTotalPay.Text = decRegularPay.ToString("C")
        End If
    End Sub
End Class
```

Figure 1-13b (window appears when user runs program)

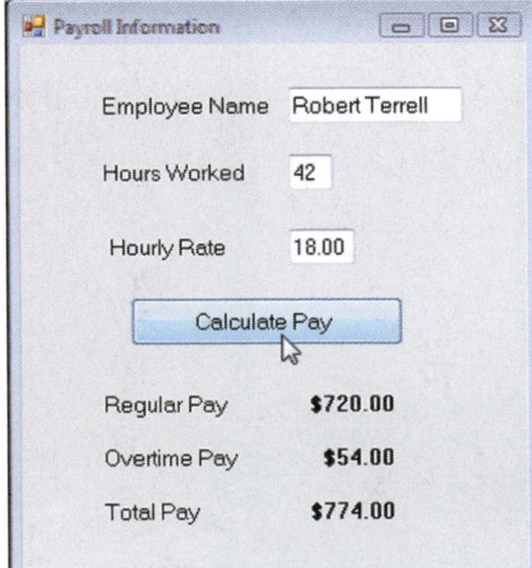

Figure 1-13 A programmer writes Visual Basic instructions to create the Payroll Information window.

QUIZ YOURSELF 1-2

Instructions: Find the true statement below. Then, rewrite the remaining false statements so that they are true.

1. A resource is a collection of computers and devices connected together via communications devices and transmission media.
2. Installing is the process of setting up software to work with the computer, printer, and other hardware.
3. Popular system software includes Web browsers, word processing software, spreadsheet software, database software, and presentation software.
4. The Internet is one of the more popular services on the Web.
5. Two types of application software are the operating system and utility programs.

Quiz Yourself Online: To further check your knowledge of pages 10 through 18, visit the Computer Concepts CourseMate Web site at www.cengagebrain.com, navigate to the Chapter 1 Quiz Yourself resource for this book, and then click Objectives 5 – 7.

Categories of Computers

Industry experts typically classify computers in seven categories: personal computers (desktop), mobile computers and mobile devices, game consoles, servers, mainframes, supercomputers, and embedded computers. A computer's size, speed, processing power, and price determine the category it best fits. Due to rapidly changing technology, however, the distinction among categories is not always clear-cut. This trend of computers and devices with technologies that overlap, called *convergence*, leads to computer manufacturers continually releasing newer models that include similar functionality and features. For example, newer cell phones often include media player, camera, and Web browsing capabilities. As devices converge, users need fewer devices for the functionality that they require. When consumers replace outdated computers and devices, they should dispose of them properly.

Figure 1-14 summarizes the seven categories of computers. The following pages discuss computers and devices that fall in each category.

Categories of Computers

Category	Physical Size	Number of Simultaneously Connected Users	General Price Range
Personal computers (desktop)	Fits on a desk	Usually one (can be more if networked)	Several hundred to several thousand dollars
Mobile computers and mobile devices	Fits on your lap or in your hand	Usually one	Less than a hundred dollars to several thousand dollars
Game consoles	Small box or handheld device	One to several	Several hundred dollars or less
Servers	Small cabinet	Two to thousands	Several hundred to a million dollars
Mainframes	Partial room to a full room of equipment	Hundreds to thousands	$300,000 to several million dollars
Supercomputers	Full room of equipment	Hundreds to thousands	$500,000 to several billion dollars
Embedded computers	Miniature	Usually one	Embedded in the price of the product

Figure 1-14 This table summarizes some of the differences among the categories of computers. These should be considered general guidelines only because of rapid changes in technology.

Personal Computers

A **personal computer** is a computer that can perform all of its input, processing, output, and storage activities by itself. A personal computer contains a processor, memory, and one or more input, output, and storage devices. Personal computers also often contain a communications device.

Two popular architectures of personal computers are the PC (Figure 1-15) and the Apple (Figure 1-16). The term, *PC-compatible*, refers to any personal computer based on the original IBM personal computer design. Companies such as Dell, HP, and Toshiba sell PC-compatible computers. PC and PC-compatible computers usually use a Windows operating system. Apple computers usually use a Macintosh operating system (Mac OS).

Two types of personal computers are desktop computers and notebook computers.

Figure 1-15 PC and PC-compatible computers usually use a Windows operating system.

Figure 1-16 Apple computers, such as the iMac, usually use a Macintosh operating system.

FAQ 1-4

Are PCs or Apple computers more popular?

While PCs still are more popular than Apple computers, Apple computer sales have been rising consistently during the past few years. In fact, Apple computer sales now account for more than 20 percent of all computer sales in the United States, with that number estimated to grow for the foreseeable future.

For more information, visit the Computer Concepts CourseMate Web site at www.cengagebrain.com, navigate to the Chapter 1 FAQ resource for this book, and then click Personal Computer Sales.

Desktop Computers

A **desktop computer** is designed so that the system unit, input devices, output devices, and any other devices fit entirely on or under a desk or table (Figures 1-15 and 1-16 on the previous page). In many models, the system unit is a tall and narrow *tower*, which can sit on the floor vertically — if desktop space is limited.

Some desktop computers function as a server on a network. Others, such as a gaming desktop computer and home theater PC, target a specific audience. The *gaming desktop computer* offers high-quality audio, video, and graphics with optimal performance for sophisticated single-user and networked or Internet multiplayer games. A *home theater PC (HTPC)* combines the features of a high-definition video/audio entertainment system with a desktop computer that is designed to be connected to a television and includes a Blu-ray Disc, digital video recorder, and digital cable television connectivity. These high-end computers cost more than the basic desktop computer.

Another expensive, powerful desktop computer is the workstation, which is geared for work that requires intense calculations and graphics capabilities. An architect uses a workstation to design buildings and homes. A graphic artist uses a workstation to create computer-animated special effects for full-length motion pictures and video games.

FAQ 1-5

Does the term, workstation, have multiple meanings?

Yes. In the computer industry, a *workstation* can be a high-powered computer or a client computer on a network. In an office environment, a workstation can refer to a work area assigned to an employee.

For more information, visit the Computer Concepts CourseMate Web site at www.cengagebrain.com, navigate to the Chapter 1 FAQ resource for this book, and then click Workstation.

Mobile Computers and Mobile Devices

A **mobile computer** is a personal computer you can carry from place to place. Similarly, a **mobile device** is a computing device small enough to hold in your hand.

The most popular type of mobile computer is the notebook computer. The following sections discuss the notebook computer and widely used mobile devices.

Notebook Computers

A **notebook computer**, also called a **laptop computer**, is a portable, personal computer often designed to fit on your lap. Notebook computers are thin and lightweight, yet they can be as powerful as the average desktop computer. A *netbook*, which is a type of notebook computer, is smaller, lighter, and often not as powerful as a traditional notebook computer. Most netbooks cost less than traditional notebook computers, usually only a few hundred dollars. An ultra-thin is another type of notebook computer that is lightweight and usually less than one-inch thick. Some notebook computers have touch screens, allowing you to interact with the device by touching the screen, usually with the tip of a finger.

On a typical notebook computer, the keyboard is on top of the system unit, and the monitor attaches to the system unit with hinges (Figure 1-17). These computers weigh on average from 2.5 to more than 10 pounds (depending on configuration), which allows users to transport the computers from place to place. Most notebook computers can operate on batteries or a power supply or both.

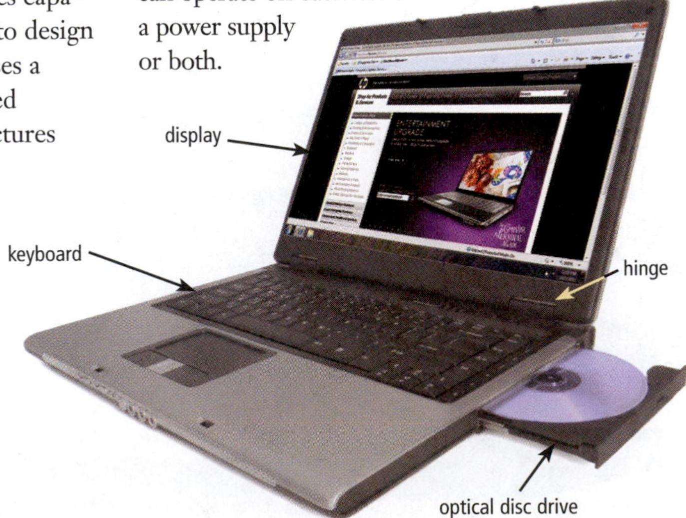

Figure 1-17 On a typical notebook computer, the keyboard is on top of the system unit, and the display attaches to the system unit with hinges.

Tablet PCs Resembling a letter-sized slate, the **Tablet PC**, or tablet computer, is a special type of notebook computer that you can interact with by touching the screen with your finger or a digital pen. A *digital pen* looks like a small ink pen but uses pressure instead of ink. Users write or draw on a Tablet PC by pressing a finger or digital pen on the screen, and issue instructions by tapping on the screen. One design of Tablet PC, called a *convertible tablet*, has an attached keyboard. Another design, which does not include a keyboard, is called a *slate tablet* (Figure 1-18) and provides other means for typing. Some Tablet PCs also support voice input so that users can speak into the computer.

Tablet PCs are useful especially for taking notes in lectures, at meetings, conferences, and other forums where the standard notebook computer is not practical.

Figure 1-18 The iPad is a widely used slate tablet.

Mobile Devices

Mobile devices, which are small enough to carry in a pocket, usually do not have disk drives. Instead, these devices store programs and data permanently on special memory inside the system unit or on small storage media such as memory cards. You often can connect a mobile device to a personal computer to exchange information between the computer and the mobile device.

Some mobile devices are **Internet-enabled**, meaning they can connect to the Internet wirelessly. With an Internet-enabled device, users can chat, send e-mail and instant messages, and access the Web. Because of their reduced size, the screens on mobile devices are small, but usually are in color.

Popular types of mobile devices are smart phones and PDAs, e-book readers, handheld computers, portable media players, and digital cameras.

Smart Phones and PDAs Offering the convenience of one-handed operation, a **smart phone** (Figure 1-19) is an Internet-enabled phone that usually also provides personal information management functions such as a calendar, an appointment book, an address book, a calculator, and a notepad. In addition to basic phone capabilities, a smart phone allows you to send and receive e-mail messages and access the Web — usually for an additional fee. Some smart phones communicate wirelessly with other devices or computers. Many also function as a portable media player and include built-in digital cameras so that you can share photos or videos with others as soon as you capture the image. Many smart phones also offer a variety of application software such as word processing, spreadsheet, and games, and the capability of conducting live video conferences.

Many smart phones have keypads that contain both numbers and letters so that you can use the same keypad to dial phone numbers

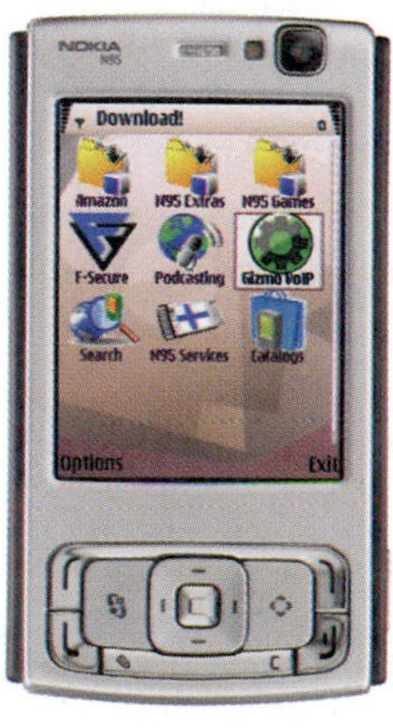

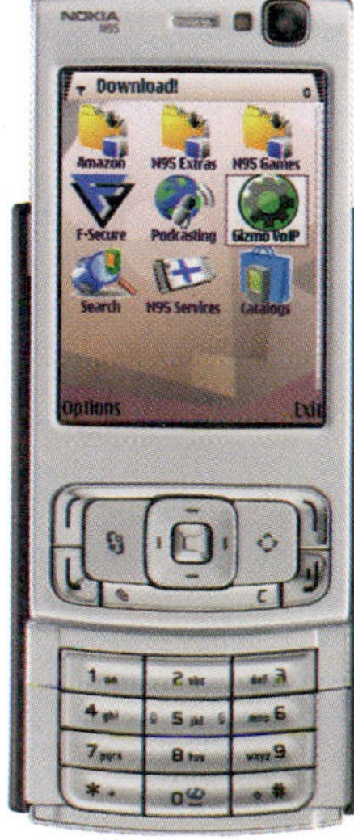

Figure 1-19 Some smart phones have touch screens; others have mini keyboards.

and enter messages. Others have a built-in mini keyboard on the front of the phone or a keyboard that slides in and out from behind the phone. Some have touch screens, where you press objects on the screen to make selections and enter text through an on-screen keyboard. Others include a stylus, which is similar to a digital pen but smaller and has less functionality.

Instead of calling someone's smart phone or cell phone, users often send messages to others by pressing buttons on their phone's keypad, keys on the mini keyboard, or images on an on-screen keyboard. Types of messages users send with smart phones include text messages, instant messages, picture messages, and video messages.

- A *text message* is a short note, typically fewer than 300 characters, sent to or from a smart phone or other mobile device.
- An *instant message* is a real-time Internet communication, where you exchange messages with other connected users.
- A *picture message* is a photo or other image, sometimes along with sound and text, sent to or from a smart phone or other mobile device. A phone that can send picture messages often is called a *camera phone*.
- A *video message* is a short video clip, usually about 30 seconds, sent to or from a smart phone or other mobile device. A phone that can send video messages often is called a *video phone*.

Camera Phone

For more information, visit the Computer Concepts CourseMate Web site at www.cengagebrain.com, navigate to the Chapter 1 Web Link resource for this book, and then click Camera Phone.

A **PDA** (*personal digital assistant*), which often looks like a smart phone, provides personal information management functions such as a calendar, an appointment book, an address book, a calculator, and a notepad. A PDA differs from a smart phone in that it usually does not provide phone capabilities and may not be Internet-enabled, support voice input, have a built-in camera, or function as a portable media player.

As smart phones and PDAs continue a trend of convergence, it is becoming increasingly difficult to differentiate between the two devices. This has led some manufacturers to refer to PDAs and smart phones simply as *handhelds*.

E-Book Readers An **e-book reader** (short for electronic book reader), or *e-reader*, is a handheld device that is used primarily for reading e-books (Figure 1-20). An *e-book*, or digital book, is an electronic version of a printed book, readable on computers and other digital devices. In addition to books, users typically can purchase and read other forms of digital media such as newspapers and magazines.

Most e-book readers have a touch screen and are Internet-enabled. These devices usually are smaller than tablet computers but larger than smart phones.

Figure 1-20 An e-book reader.

Handheld Computers A **handheld computer**, sometimes referred to as an *Ultra-Mobile PC* (*UMPC*), is a computer small enough to fit in one hand. Many handheld computers communicate wirelessly with other devices or computers and also include a digital pen or stylus for input.

Some handheld computers have miniature or specialized keyboards. Many handheld computers are industry-specific and serve the needs of mobile employees, such as meter readers and parcel delivery people (Figure 1-21), whose jobs require them to move from place to place.

FAQ 1-6

How popular is text messaging?

A recent study indicates that people are using their smart phones and cell phones for voice communications and text messaging more frequently than in previous years. Because of the increase in smart phone sales and the ease with which individuals can send text messages, approximately two billion text messages are sent each day.

For more information, visit the Computer Concepts CourseMate Web site at www.cengagebrain.com, navigate to the Chapter 1 FAQ resource for this book, and then click Text Messaging.

Figure 1-21 This handheld computer is a lightweight computer that enables delivery people to obtain and record information about their deliveries.

Portable Media Players A **portable media player** is a mobile device on which you can store, organize, and play digital media (Figure 1-22). For example, you can listen to music; watch videos, movies, and television shows; and view photos on the device's screen. With most, you download the digital media from a computer to the portable media player or to media that you insert in the device.

Figure 1-22 The iPod, shown here, is a popular portable media player.

Some portable media players are Internet-enabled so that you can access Web sites and send e-mail messages directly from the device. Many offer personal information management functions such as a calendar and address book, and include a variety of games and other application software.

Portable media players usually include a set of earbuds, which are small speakers that rest inside each ear canal. Some portable media players have a touch screen, while others have a touch-sensitive pad that you operate with a thumb or finger, to navigate through digital media, adjust volume, and customize settings.

Digital Cameras A **digital camera** is a device that allows users to take pictures and store the photographed images digitally, instead of on traditional film (Figure 1-23). While many digital cameras look like a traditional camera, some are built into smart phones and other mobile devices.

Although digital cameras usually have some amount of internal storage to hold images, most users store images on small storage media such as memory cards. Digital cameras typically allow users to review, and sometimes modify, images while they are in the camera. Some digital cameras connect to or communicate wirelessly with a computer or printer, allowing users to print or view images directly from the printer. Some memory cards can connect to a network wirelessly, so that you can transfer photos directly from the memory card in the camera to the Internet without requiring a computer.

Often users prefer to download images from the digital camera to the computer. Or, you can remove the storage media such as a memory card from the digital camera and insert it in a card reader in or attached to the computer.

Digital Cameras

For more information, visit the Computer Concepts CourseMate Web site at www.cengagebrain.com, navigate to the Chapter 1 Web Link resource for this book, and then click Digital Cameras.

Figure 1-23 With a digital camera, users can view photographed images immediately through a small screen on the camera to see if the picture is worth keeping.

Game Consoles

A **game console** is a mobile computing device designed for single-player or multi-player video games (Figure 1-24). Standard game consoles use a handheld controller(s) as an input device(s); a television screen as an output device; and hard disks, optical discs, and/or memory cards for storage. Weighing on average between two and nine pounds, the compact size of game consoles makes them easy to use at home, in the car, in a hotel, or any location that has an electrical outlet. Three popular models are Microsoft's Xbox 360, Nintendo's Wii (pronounced wee), and Sony's PlayStation 3. Read Innovative Computing 1-1 to find out how the medical field uses the Nintendo Wii.

A handheld game console is small enough to fit in one hand, making it more portable than the standard game console. With the handheld game console, the controls, screen, and speakers are built into the device. Because of their reduced size, the screens are small — three to four inches. Some models use cartridges to store games; others use a memory card or a miniature optical disc. Many handheld game consoles can communicate wirelessly with other similar consoles for multiplayer gaming. Two popular models are Nintendo DS Lite and Sony's PlayStation Portable (PSP).

In addition to gaming, many game console models allow users to listen to music, watch movies, keep fit, and connect to the Internet. Game consoles can cost from a couple hundred dollars to more than $500.

handheld game console

game console

Figure 1-24 Game consoles provide hours of video game entertainment.

! INNOVATIVE COMPUTING 1-1

Wii a Welcome Medical Skill Builder

A patient awaiting laparoscopic procedures may be less tense knowing that the surgeons have honed their dexterity and coordination using a Nintendo Wii. Preliminary studies have found that doctors can improve their fine motor control by playing video games that emphasize subtle hand movements used in minimally invasive surgeries. Researchers are developing Wii surgery simulators that will allow doctors to practice their skills at home or in break rooms at hospitals.

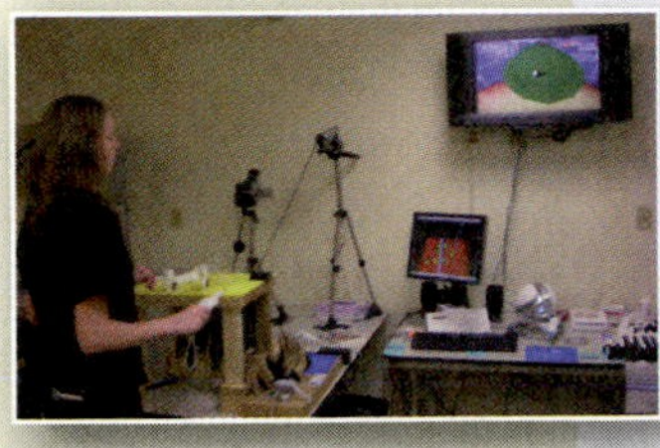

The Wii game system is finding a medical home in other nontraditional places. Physical therapists urge arthritic patients to use *Wiihabilitation* to build endurance and increase their range of motion. Therapeutic recreation with the Wii's sports games may help patients recovering from strokes, fractures, and combat injuries.

Researchers in a testing lab in California are experimenting with using the Wii's motion-activated controls in non-gaming applications, such as allowing doctors to explain X-ray images to patients.

For more information, visit the Computer Concepts CourseMate Web site at www.cengagebrain.com, navigate to the Chapter 1 Innovative Computing resource for this book, and then click Medical Wii.

Servers

A **server** controls access to the hardware, software, and other resources on a network and provides a centralized storage area for programs, data, and information (Figure 1-25). Servers can support from two to several thousand connected computers at the same time.

In many cases, one server accesses data, information, and programs on another server. In other cases, people use personal computers or terminals to access data, information, and programs on a server. A terminal is a device with a monitor, keyboard, and memory.

Figure 1-25 A server controls access to resources on a network.

Mainframes

A **mainframe** is a large, expensive, powerful computer that can handle hundreds or thousands of connected users simultaneously (Figure 1-26). Mainframes store tremendous amounts of data, instructions, and information. Most major corporations use mainframes for business activities. With mainframes, enterprises are able to bill millions of customers, prepare payroll for thousands of employees, and manage thousands of items in inventory. One study reported that mainframes process more than 83 percent of transactions around the world.

Mainframes also can act as servers in a network environment. Servers and other mainframes can access data and information from a mainframe. People also can access programs on the mainframe using terminals or personal computers.

Figure 1-26 Mainframe computers can handle thousands of connected computers and process millions of instructions per second.

Supercomputers

A **supercomputer** is the fastest, most powerful computer — and the most expensive (Figure 1-27). The fastest supercomputers are capable of processing more than one quadrillion instructions in a single second. With weights that exceed 100 tons, these computers can store more than 20,000 times the data and information of an average desktop computer.

Applications requiring complex, sophisticated mathematical calculations use supercomputers. Large-scale simulations and applications in medicine, aerospace, automotive design, online banking, weather forecasting, nuclear energy research, and petroleum exploration use a supercomputer.

Figure 1-27 This supercomputer, IBM's Roadrunner, can process more than one quadrillion instructions in a single second.

Embedded Computers

An **embedded computer** is a special-purpose computer that functions as a component in a larger product. Embedded computers are everywhere — at home, in your car, and at work. The following list identifies a variety of everyday products that contain embedded computers.

- Consumer Electronics: mobile and digital telephones, digital televisions, cameras, video recorders, DVD players and recorders, answering machines
- Home Automation Devices: thermostats, sprinkling systems, security monitoring systems, appliances, lights
- Automobiles: antilock brakes, engine control modules, airbag controller, cruise control
- Process Controllers and Robotics: remote monitoring systems, power monitors, machine controllers, medical devices
- Computer Devices and Office Machines: keyboards, printers, fax and copy machines

Because embedded computers are components in larger products, they usually are small and have limited hardware. These computers perform various functions, depending on the requirements of the product in which they reside. Embedded computers in printers, for example, monitor the amount of paper in the tray, check the ink or toner level, signal if a paper jam has occurred, and so on. Figure 1-28 shows some of the many embedded computers in cars.

Figure 1-28 Some of the embedded computers designed to improve your safety, security, and performance in today's automobiles.

Elements of an Information System

To be valuable, information must be accurate, organized, timely, accessible, useful, and cost-effective to produce. Generating information from a computer requires the following five elements:

- Hardware
- Software
- Data
- People
- Procedures

Together, these elements (hardware, software, data, people, and procedures) comprise an *information system*. Figure 1-29 shows how each of the elements of an information system in an enterprise might interact.

The hardware must be reliable and capable of handling the expected workload. The software must be developed carefully and tested thoroughly. The data entered into the computer must be accurate.

Most companies with mid-sized and large computers have an IT (information technology) department. Staff in the IT department should be skilled and up-to-date on the latest technology. IT staff also should train users so that they understand how to use the computer properly. Today's users also work closely with IT staff in the development of computer applications that relate to their areas of work.

Finally, all the IT applications should have readily available documented procedures that address operating the computer and using its programs.

Women in Technology
For more information, visit the Computer Concepts CourseMate Web site at www.cengagebrain.com, navigate to the Chapter 1 Web Link resource for this book, and then click Women in Technology.

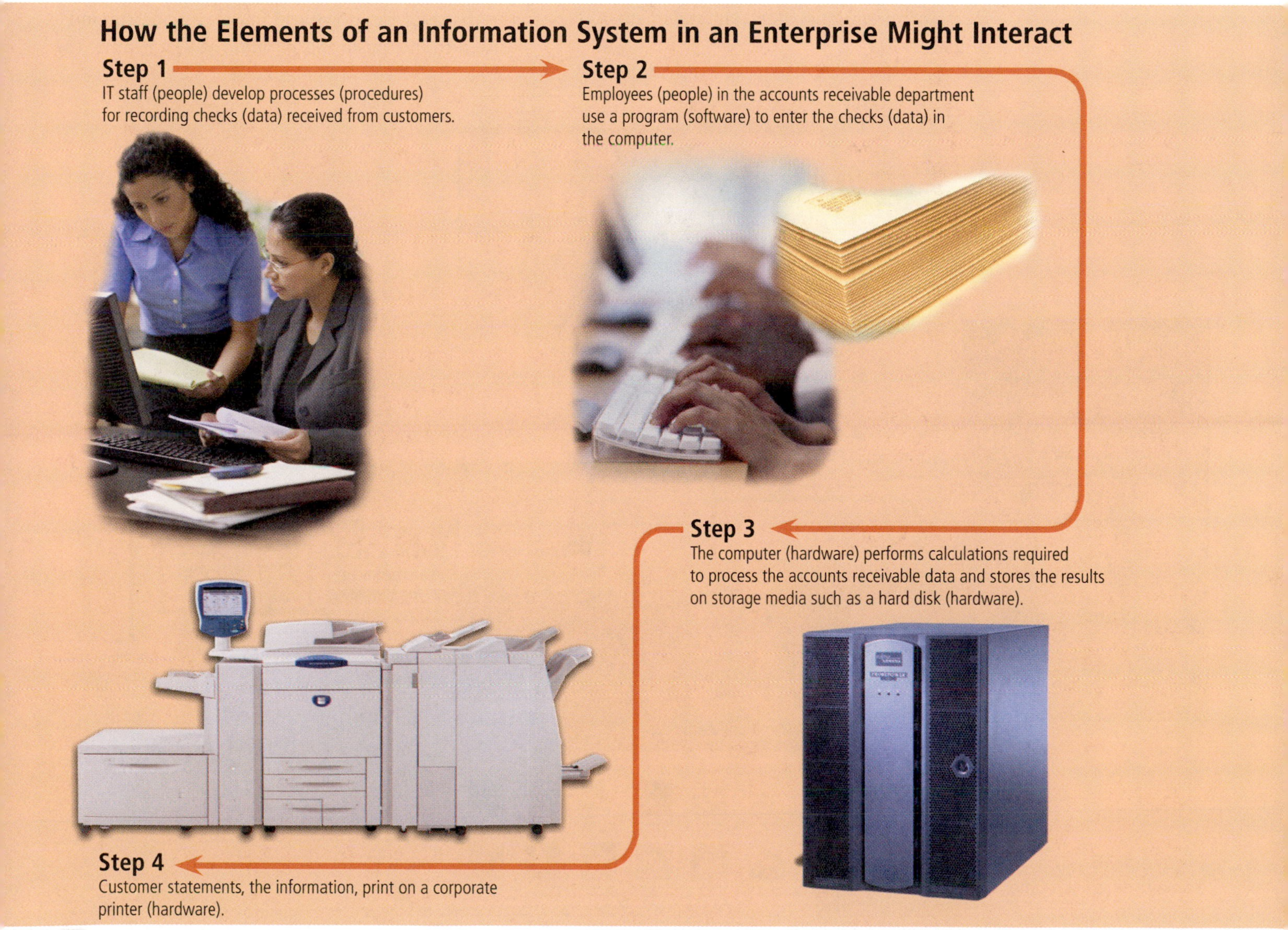

How the Elements of an Information System in an Enterprise Might Interact

Step 1
IT staff (people) develop processes (procedures) for recording checks (data) received from customers.

Step 2
Employees (people) in the accounts receivable department use a program (software) to enter the checks (data) in the computer.

Step 3
The computer (hardware) performs calculations required to process the accounts receivable data and stores the results on storage media such as a hard disk (hardware).

Step 4
Customer statements, the information, print on a corporate printer (hardware).

Figure 1-29 This figure shows how the elements of an information system in an enterprise might interact.

Examples of Computer Usage

Minorities in Technology

For more information, visit the Computer Concepts CourseMate Web site at www.cengagebrain.com, navigate to the Chapter 1 Web Link resource for this book, and then click Minorities in Technology.

Every day, people around the world rely on different types of computers for a variety of applications. To illustrate the range of uses for computers, this section takes you on a visual and narrative tour of five categories of users:

- Home user
- Small office/home office (SOHO) user
- Mobile user
- Power user
- Enterprise user

Home User

In an increasing number of homes, the computer no longer is a convenience. Instead, it is a basic necessity. Each family member, or **home user**, spends time on the computer for different reasons that include personal financial management, Web access, communications, and entertainment (Figure 1-30).

On the Internet, home users access a huge amount of information, conduct research, take college classes, pay bills, manage investments, shop, listen to the radio, watch movies, read books, file taxes, book airline reservations, make telephone calls, and play games (read Innovative Computing 1-2 to find out how some retailers use the Internet to help the environment). They also communicate with others around the world through e-mail, blogs, instant messages, and chat rooms using personal computers, smart phones, and other mobile devices. Home users share ideas, interests, photos, music, and videos on social networking Web sites (read Ethics & Issues 1-3 for a related discussion). With a digital camera, home users take photos and then send the electronic images to others. Using a Web cam, home users easily have live video calls with friends, family members, and others.

Many home users have a portable media player, so that they can download music or podcasts, and listen to the music and/or audio at a later time

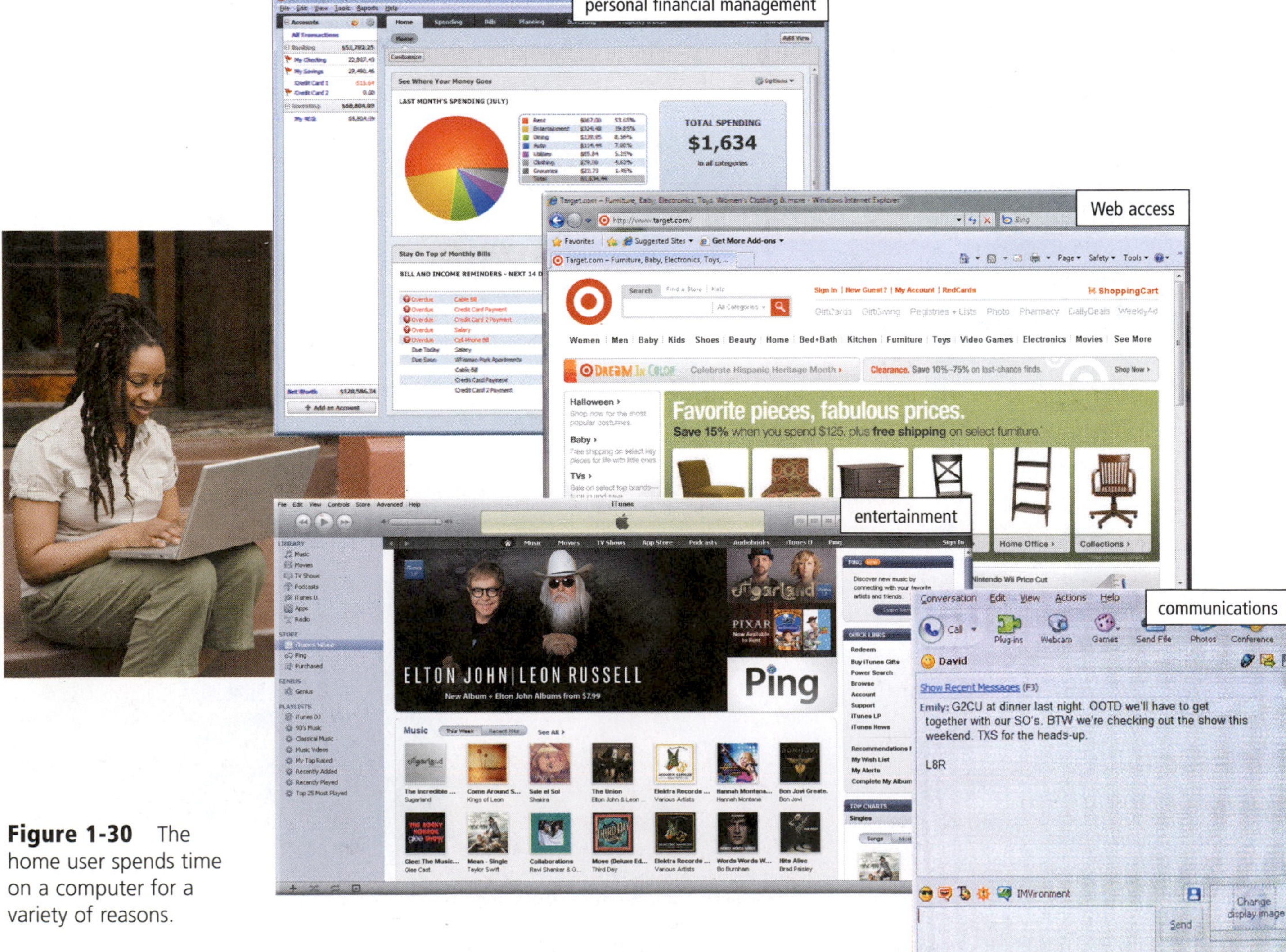

Figure 1-30 The home user spends time on a computer for a variety of reasons.

through earbuds attached to the player. They also usually have one or more game consoles to play video games individually or with friends and family members.

Today's homes also typically have one or more desktop computers. Many home users network multiple desktop computers throughout the house, often wirelessly. These small networks allow family members to share an Internet connection and a printer.

Home users have a variety of software. They type letters, homework assignments, and other documents with word processing software. Personal finance software helps the home user with personal finances, investments, and family budgets. Other software assists with preparing taxes, keeping a household inventory, setting up maintenance schedules, and protecting home computers against threats and unauthorized intrusions.

Reference software, such as encyclopedias, medical dictionaries, or a road atlas, provides valuable information for everyone in the family. With entertainment software, the home user can play games, compose music, research genealogy, or create greeting cards. Educational software helps adults learn to speak a foreign language and youngsters to read, write, count, and spell.

FAQ 1-7

How many households do not use the Internet or related technologies?

A recent survey estimates that 18 percent of U.S. households have no Internet access. Furthermore, about 20 percent of U.S. heads of households have never sent an e-mail message. The chart below illustrates the lack of experience with computer and Internet technology.

Lack of Experience with Technology

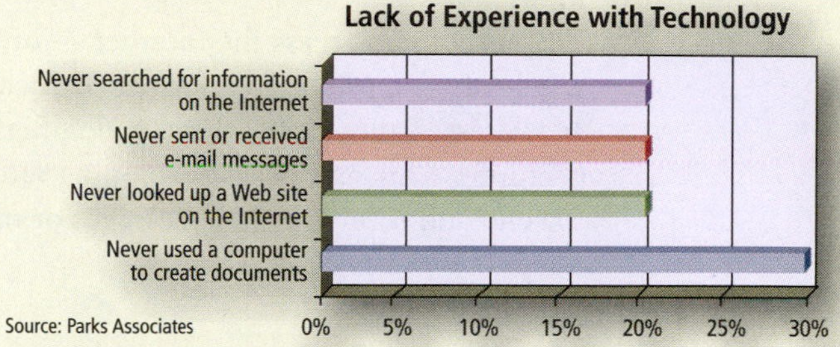

For more information, visit the Computer Concepts CourseMate Web site at www.cengagebrain.com, navigate to the Chapter 1 FAQ resource for this book, and then click Experience with Technology.

INNOVATIVE COMPUTING 1-2

E-Receipts Save Paper, Organize Life

You may need to find a new use for the old shoeboxes that are storing your receipts. Some environmentally conscious retailers are providing a service that issues receipts electronically so that consumers never will need to hunt for a little white slip of paper when returning an item or declaring an expense for income taxes.

Digital receipts, also called *e-receipts*, are sent automatically to an e-mail account or Web site where they can be sorted or deleted. One service links a consumer's credit cards to a receipt account on a specific Web site, so that every time the cards are swiped for a purchase, a receipt is sent to the consumer's account.

More than 70 percent of consumers say they would prefer having an e-receipt rather than a paper receipt. According to one estimate, nine million trees would be saved if no paper receipts were issued for one year.

For more information, visit the Computer Concepts CourseMate Web site at www.cengagebrain.com, navigate to the Chapter 1 Innovative Computing resource for this book, and then click Digital Receipts.

ETHICS & ISSUES 1-3

Who Should Look Out for the Safety of Social Networking Web Site Users?

In recent years, social networking Web site usage by children and adults exploded as a new means of communicating and socializing. Not surprisingly, the problems associated with this exciting way to interact with others mirror some problems in society in general. Problems include bullying, smear campaigns against individuals, and inappropriate contact between adults and minors. Recently, a high-school-aged girl secretly left the country with the intent of marrying an adult in a foreign country whom she met on a social networking Web site. Fortunately, authorities in the foreign country intercepted her at the airport and sent her home. Some parents claim that the government should intervene to ensure better monitoring of inappropriate behavior. While some social networking Web site companies have stepped up monitoring, they often claim that they are not responsible for the behavior of individuals, and parents and individuals should be responsible for inappropriate actions. Many individuals feel that the problems are simply a matter of personal responsibility and following some simple guidelines, such as the "golden rule."

Should social networking Web sites do a better job of telling their users what is safe or unsafe information to share? Why or why not? What role should parents play in overseeing their child's involvement in social networking Web sites? Why? Should police or other government authorities be responsible for maintaining order on social networking Web sites in the same way they are charged with maintaining order in society in general? Why or why not?

Small Office/Home Office User

Computers assist small business and home office users in managing their resources effectively. A **small office/home office** (*SOHO*) includes any company with fewer than 50 employees, as well as the self-employed who work from home. Small offices include local law practices, accounting firms, travel agencies, and florists. SOHO users typically have a desktop computer to perform some or all of their duties. Many also have smart phones or other mobile devices to manage appointments and contact information.

SOHO users access the Internet — often wirelessly — to look up information such as addresses, directions, postal codes, flights (Figure 1-31a), and package shipping rates or to send and receive e-mail messages or make telephone calls.

Many have entered the *e-commerce* arena and conduct business on the Web. Their Web sites advertise products and services and may provide a means for taking orders. Small business Web sites sometimes use a *Web cam* to show the world a live view of some aspect of their business.

To save money on hardware and software, small offices often network their computers. For example, the small office connects one printer to a network for all employees to share.

SOHO users often work with basic business software such as word processing and spreadsheet programs that assist with document preparation and finances (Figure 1-31b). They are likely to use other industry-specific types of software. An auto parts store, for example, will have software that allows for looking up parts, taking orders and payments, and updating inventory.

Figure 1-31a (Web access)

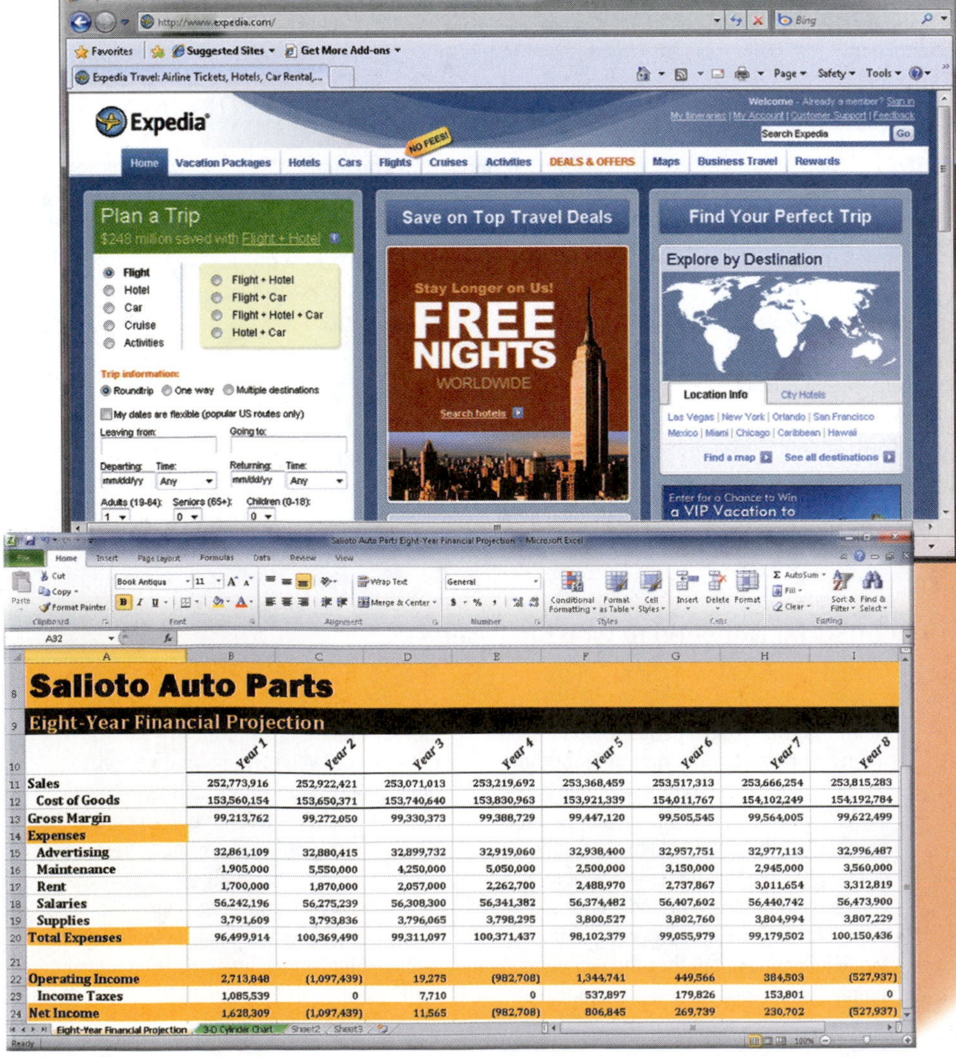

	Year 1	Year 2	Year 3	Year 4	Year 5	Year 6	Year 7	Year 8
Salioto Auto Parts								
Eight-Year Financial Projection								
Sales	252,773,916	252,922,421	253,071,013	253,219,692	253,368,459	253,517,313	253,666,254	253,815,283
Cost of Goods	153,560,154	153,650,371	153,740,640	153,830,963	153,921,339	154,011,767	154,102,249	154,192,784
Gross Margin	99,213,762	99,272,050	99,330,373	99,388,729	99,447,120	99,505,545	99,564,005	99,622,499
Expenses								
Advertising	32,861,109	32,880,415	32,899,732	32,919,060	32,938,400	32,957,751	32,977,113	32,996,487
Maintenance	1,905,000	5,550,000	4,250,000	5,050,000	2,500,000	3,150,000	2,945,000	3,560,000
Rent	1,700,000	1,870,000	2,057,000	2,262,700	2,488,970	2,737,867	3,011,654	3,312,819
Salaries	56,242,196	56,275,239	56,308,300	56,341,382	56,374,482	56,407,602	56,440,742	56,473,900
Supplies	3,791,609	3,793,836	3,796,065	3,798,295	3,800,527	3,802,760	3,804,994	3,807,229
Total Expenses	96,499,914	100,369,490	99,311,097	100,371,437	98,102,379	99,055,979	99,179,502	100,150,436
Operating Income	2,713,848	(1,097,439)	19,275	(982,708)	1,344,741	449,566	384,503	(527,937)
Income Taxes	1,085,539	0	7,710	0	537,897	179,826	153,801	0
Net Income	1,628,309	(1,097,439)	11,565	(982,708)	806,845	269,739	230,702	(527,937)

Figure 1-31b (spreadsheet program)

Figure 1-31 People with a home office and employees in small offices typically use a personal computer for some or all of their duties.

Mobile User

Today, businesses and schools are expanding to serve people across the country and around the world. Thus, increasingly more employees and students are **mobile users**, who work on a computer or mobile device while away from a main office, home office, or school (Figure 1-32). Examples of mobile users are sales representatives, real estate agents, insurance agents, meter readers, package delivery people, journalists, consultants, and students.

Mobile users often have mobile computers and/or mobile devices. With these computers and devices, the mobile user connects to other computers on a network or the Internet, often wirelessly accessing services such as e-mail and the Web. Mobile users can transfer information between their mobile device and another computer, such as one at the main office or school. For entertainment, the mobile user plays video games on a handheld game console and listens to music or watches movies on a portable media player.

The mobile user works with basic business software such as word processing. With presentation software, the mobile user can create and deliver presentations to a large audience by connecting a mobile computer or device to a video projector that displays the presentation on a full screen. Many scaled-down programs are available for mobile devices such as smart phones.

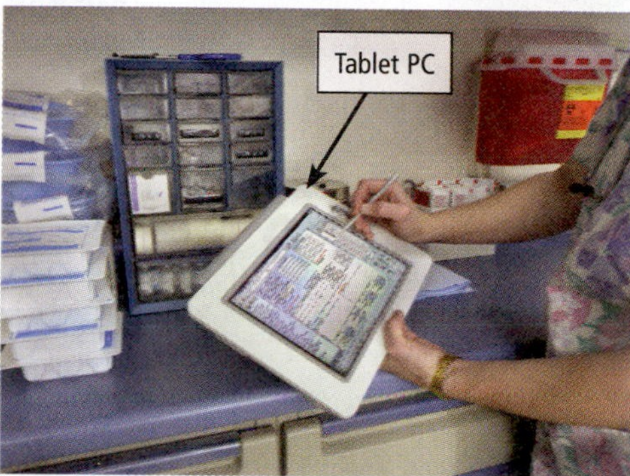

Figure 1-32 Mobile users have a variety of mobile computers and devices so that they can work, do homework, send messages, connect to the Internet, or play games while away from a wired connection.

Power User

Another category of user, called a **power user**, requires the capabilities of a workstation or other type of powerful computer. Examples of power users include engineers, scientists, architects, desktop publishers, and graphic artists (Figure 1-33). Power users often work with *multimedia*, combining text, graphics, audio, and video into one application. These users need computers with extremely fast processors because of the nature of their work.

The power user's workstation often contains industry-specific software. For example, engineers and architects use software to draft and design floor plans, mechanical assemblies, or vehicles. A desktop publisher uses software to prepare marketing literature. A graphic artist uses software to create sophisticated drawings. This software usually is expensive because of its specialized design.

Power users exist in all types of businesses. Some work at home. Their computers typically have network connections and Internet access.

Figure 1-33 This graphic artist uses a powerful computer to develop computer games.

Enterprise User

An enterprise has hundreds or thousands of employees or customers that work in or do business with offices across a region, the country, or the world. Each employee or customer who uses a computer in the enterprise is an **enterprise user** (Figure 1-34).

Many large companies use the words, *enterprise computing*, to refer to the huge network of computers that meets their diverse computing needs. The network facilitates communications among employees at all locations. Users access the network of servers or mainframes through desktop computers, mobile computers, and mobile devices.

Enterprises use computers and the computer network to process high volumes of transactions in a single day. Although they may differ in size and in the products or services offered, all generally use computers for basic business activities. For example, they bill millions of customers, prepare payroll for thousands of employees, and manage thousands of items in inventory. Some enterprises use blogs to open communications among employees, customers, and/or vendors.

Enterprise Computing
For more information, visit the Computer Concepts CourseMate Web site at www.cengagebrain.com, navigate to the Chapter 1 Web Link resource for this book, and then click Enterprise Computing.

Enterprises typically have e-commerce Web sites, allowing customers and vendors to conduct business online. The Web site also showcases products, services, and other company information.

The marketing department in an enterprise uses desktop publishing software to prepare marketing literature. The accounting department uses software for accounts receivable, accounts payable, billing, general ledger, and payroll activities.

The employees in the *information technology (IT) department* keep the computers and the network running. They determine when the company requires new hardware or software.

Enterprise users work with word processing, spreadsheet, database, and presentation software. They also may use calendar programs to post their schedules on the network. And, they might use smart phones or mobile devices to maintain contact information. E-mail programs and Web browsers enable communications among employees, vendors, and customers.

Many employees of enterprises telecommute. **Telecommuting** is a work arrangement in which employees work away from a company's standard workplace and often communicate with the office through the computer. Employees who telecommute have flexible work schedules so that they can combine work and personal responsibilities, such as child care.

Putting It All Together

The previous pages discussed the hardware and software requirements for the home user, small office/home office user, mobile user, power user, and enterprise user. The table in Figure 1-35 summarizes these requirements.

Figure 1-34 An enterprise can have hundreds or thousands of users in offices across a region, the country, or the world.

Categories of Users

User	Hardware	Software
Home 	• Desktop or notebook computer • Smart phone or other mobile device • Game consoles	• Business (e.g., word processing) • Personal information manager • Personal finance, online banking, tax preparation • Web browser • E-mail, blogging, instant messaging, chat rooms, and online social networking • Internet telephone calls • Photo and video editing • Reference (e.g., encyclopedias, medical dictionaries, road atlas) • Entertainment (e.g., games, music composition, greeting cards) • Education (e.g., tutorials, children's math and reading software)
Small Office/Home Office 	• Desktop or notebook computer • Smart phone or other mobile device • Shared network printer	• Business (e.g., word processing, spreadsheet, database) • Personal information manager • Company specific (e.g., accounting, legal reference) • Network management • Web browser • E-mail • Internet telephone calls
Mobile 	• Notebook computer equipped with a wireless modem, or a netbook or Tablet PC • Video projector • Smart phone or other mobile device • Handheld game consoles	• Business (e.g., word processing, note taking, presentation) • Personal information manager • Web browser • E-mail
Power 	• Workstation or other powerful computer with multimedia capabilities • Smart phone or other mobile device	• Desktop publishing • Multimedia authoring • Computer-aided design • Photo, audio, and video editing • Personal information manager • Web browser • E-mail
Enterprise 	• Server or mainframe • Desktop or notebook computer • Industry-specific handheld computer • Smart phone or other mobile device	• Business (e.g., word processing, spreadsheet, database) • Personal information manager • Accounting • Network management • Web browser • E-mail • Blogging

Figure 1-35 Today, computers are used by millions of people for work tasks, school assignments, and leisure activities. Different computer users require different kinds of hardware and software to meet their needs effectively.

Computer Applications in Society

The computer has changed society today as much as the industrial revolution changed society in the eighteenth and nineteenth centuries.

People interact directly with computers in fields such as education, finance, government, health care, science, publishing, travel, and manufacturing. In addition, they can reap the benefits from breakthroughs and advances in these fields. The following pages describe how computers have made a difference in people's interactions with these disciplines. Read Looking Ahead 1-1 for a look at how embedded computers may improve the quality of life.

LOOKING AHEAD 1-1

Embedded Computers May Improve Quality of Life

The weather forecast may be as close as your fingertips if plans to integrate embedded computers in everyday objects become a reality. Researchers are envisioning an umbrella with an embedded cell phone in the handle that will dial and then download the local forecast. The handle will glow green for good weather and flash red for imminent storms.

Dancers can pin a small flower with an embedded motion-detecting computer to their clothes. When they move, the embedded computer senses action and then synchronizes the tempo of music to this movement. Other embedded computers woven into clothing can monitor heart and breathing rates.

Wearing hidden embedded computers can help the elderly and people recovering from accidents and surgeries monitor their walking stride and pace. When their steps are uneven, the embedded computer can sound a warning and perhaps prevent a fall. Other embedded computers can give subtle feedback on the quality of physical activity.

For more information, visit the Computer Concepts CourseMate Web site at www.cengagebrain.com, navigate to the Chapter 1 Looking Ahead resource for this book, and then click Embedded Computers.

Education

Education is the process of acquiring knowledge. In the traditional model, people learn from other people such as parents, teachers, and employers. Many forms of printed material such as books and manuals are used as learning tools. Today, educators also are turning to computers to assist with education (Figure 1-36).

Many schools and companies equip labs and classrooms with computers. Some schools require students to have a mobile computer or mobile device to access the school's network or Internet wirelessly. To promote education by computer, many vendors offer substantial student discounts on software.

Sometimes, the delivery of education occurs at one place while the learning occurs at other locations. For example, students can take a class on the Web. Some classes are blended; that is, part of the learning occurs in a classroom and the other part occurs on the Web. More than 70 percent of colleges offer distance learning classes. A few even offer entire degrees online.

Figure 1-36 In some schools, students have mobile computers on their desks during classroom lectures.

Finance

Many people and companies use computers to help manage their finances. Some use finance software to balance checkbooks, pay bills, track personal income and expenses, manage investments, and evaluate financial plans. This software usually includes a variety of online services. For example, computer users can track investments and do online banking. With **online banking**, users access account balances, pay bills, and copy monthly transactions from the bank's computer right into their personal computers.

Many financial institutions' Web sites also offer online banking. When using a Web site instead of finance software on your computer, all your account information is stored on the bank's computer. The advantage is you can access your financial records from anywhere in the world (Figure 1-37).

Investors often use **online investing** to buy and sell stocks and bonds — without using a broker. With online investing, the transaction fee for each trade usually is much less than when trading through a broker.

Government

A government provides society with direction by making and administering policies. To provide citizens with up-to-date information, most government offices have Web sites. People in the United States access government Web sites to file taxes, apply for permits and licenses, pay parking tickets, buy stamps, report crimes, apply for financial aid, and renew vehicle registrations and driver's licenses. To provide these services, some Web sites require users provide personal information (read Ethics & Issues 1-4 for a related discussion).

Employees of government agencies use computers as part of their daily routine. North American 911 call centers use computers to dispatch calls for fire, police, and medical assistance. Military and other agency officials use the U.S. Department of Homeland Security's network of information about domestic security threats to help protect against terrorist attacks. Law enforcement officers have online access to the FBI's National Crime Information Center (NCIC) through in-vehicle notebook computers, fingerprint readers, and mobile devices (Figure 1-38). The NCIC contains more than 52 million missing persons and criminal records, including names, fingerprints, parole/probation records, mug shots, and other information.

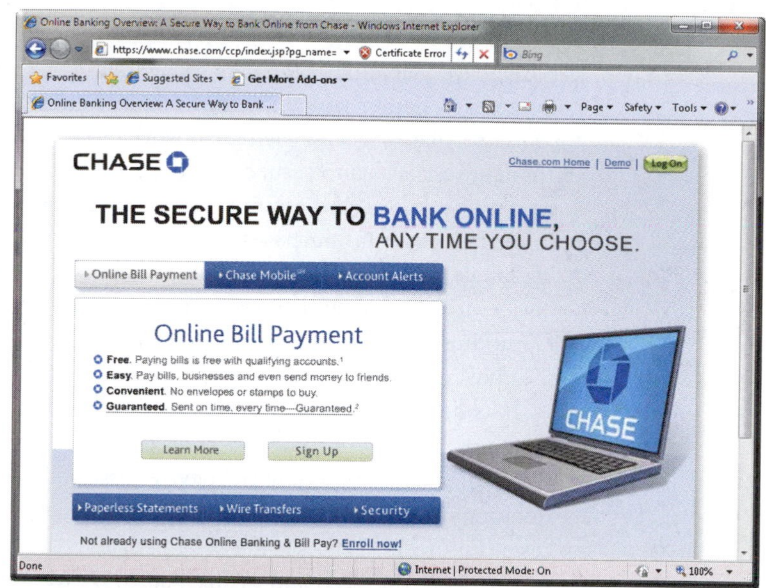

Figure 1-37 An online banking Web site.

Figure 1-38 Law enforcement officials have in-vehicle computers and mobile devices to access emergency, missing person, and criminal records in computer networks in local, state, and federal agencies.

ETHICS & ISSUES 1-4

Should You Surrender Privacy for Convenience, Security, Money, or Social Connections?

The chief executive officer of a large computer software company once declared, "Privacy is dead, deal with it." While a vast majority of people demand increased privacy, many of those same people do not hesitate to surrender personal information in exchange for some short-term benefit. In a recent study, one-third of Internet users admitted to making detailed personal information available on the Internet. Personal information has become similar to a currency that people give up in order to obtain a benefit. Benefits might be in the form of increased convenience, increased security, money savings, or social connections online. For example, increased convenience may be in the form of an automated toll collection device that also can track the user's location and speed, and allow the government to maintain a record of the user's whereabouts. Insistence on safety or security may mean tolerating video cameras in many public and private places. The use of a grocery store affinity card saves a few dollars but also allows the store to track an individual buyer's every purchase. Signing up for an online social network often requires the divulgence of personal information so that the service better can locate other members with similar interests. In each of these examples, some measure of privacy is sacrificed.

Should people limit the amount of personal information they exchange? Why or why not? What are the dangers and disadvantages of giving up some amount of privacy in exchange for a short-term benefit? What are some possible alternatives to exchanging privacy for a perceived benefit? Should companies or government organizations be required to purge your personal information if you request so? Why or why not?

Health Care

Nearly every area of health care today uses computers. Whether you are visiting a family doctor for a regular checkup, having lab work or an outpatient test, or being rushed in for emergency surgery, the medical staff around you will be using computers for various purposes:

- Hospitals and doctors use computers and mobile devices to maintain and access patient records.
- Computers monitor patients' vital signs in hospital rooms and at home.
- Robots deliver medication to nurse stations in hospitals.
- Computers and computerized devices assist doctors, nurses, and technicians with medical tests (Figure 1-39).
- Doctors use the Web and medical software to assist with researching and diagnosing health conditions.
- Doctors use e-mail to correspond with patients.
- Pharmacists use computers to file insurance claims.
- Surgeons implant computerized devices, such as pacemakers, that allow patients to live longer.
- Surgeons use computer-controlled devices to provide them with greater precision during operations, such as for laser eye surgery and robot-assisted heart surgery.

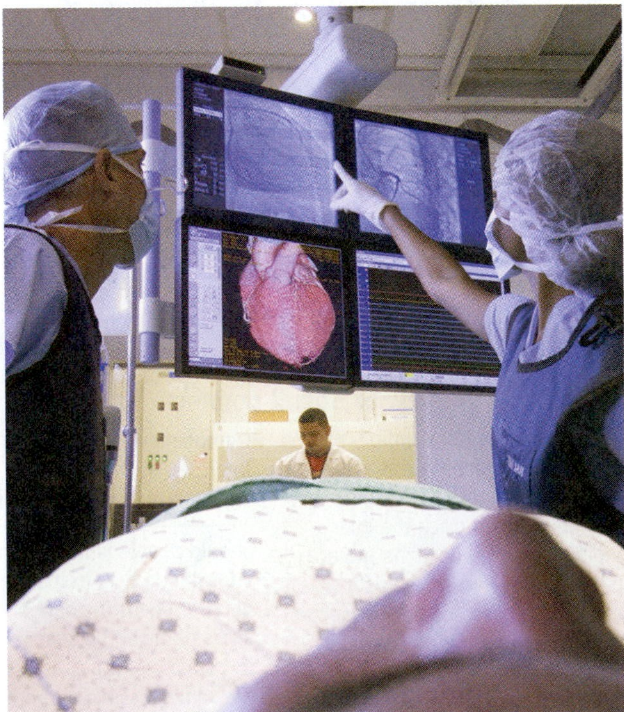

Figure 1-39 Doctors, nurses, technicians, and other medical staff use computers and computerized devices to assist with medical tests.

Many Web sites provide up-to-date medical, fitness, nutrition, or exercise information. These Web sites also maintain lists of doctors and dentists to help you find the one that suits your needs. They have chat rooms, so that you can talk to others diagnosed with similar conditions. Some Web sites even allow you to order prescriptions online.

Two forms of long-distance health care are telemedicine and telesurgery. Through *telemedicine*, health-care professionals in separate locations conduct live conferences on the computer. For example, a doctor at one location can have a conference with a doctor at another location to discuss a bone X-ray. Live images of each doctor, along with the X-ray, are displayed on each doctor's computer.

With *telesurgery*, also called *remote surgery*, a surgeon performs an operation on a patient who is not located in the same physical room as the surgeon. Telesurgery enables surgeons to direct robots to perform an operation via computers connected to a high-speed network.

Science

All branches of science, from biology to astronomy to meteorology, use computers to assist them with collecting, analyzing, and modeling data. Scientists also use the Internet to communicate with colleagues around the world.

Breakthroughs in surgery, medicine, and treatments often result from scientists' use of computers. Tiny computers now imitate functions of the central nervous system, retina of the eye, and cochlea of the ear. A cochlear implant allows a deaf person to listen. Electrodes implanted in the brain stop tremors associated with Parkinson's disease. Cameras small enough to swallow — sometimes called a camera pill — take pictures inside your body to detect polyps, cancer, and other abnormalities (Figure 1-40).

A *neural network* is a system that attempts to imitate the behavior of the human brain. Scientists create neural networks by connecting thousands of processors together much like the neurons in the brain are connected. The capability of a personal computer to recognize spoken words is a direct result of scientific experimentation with neural networks.

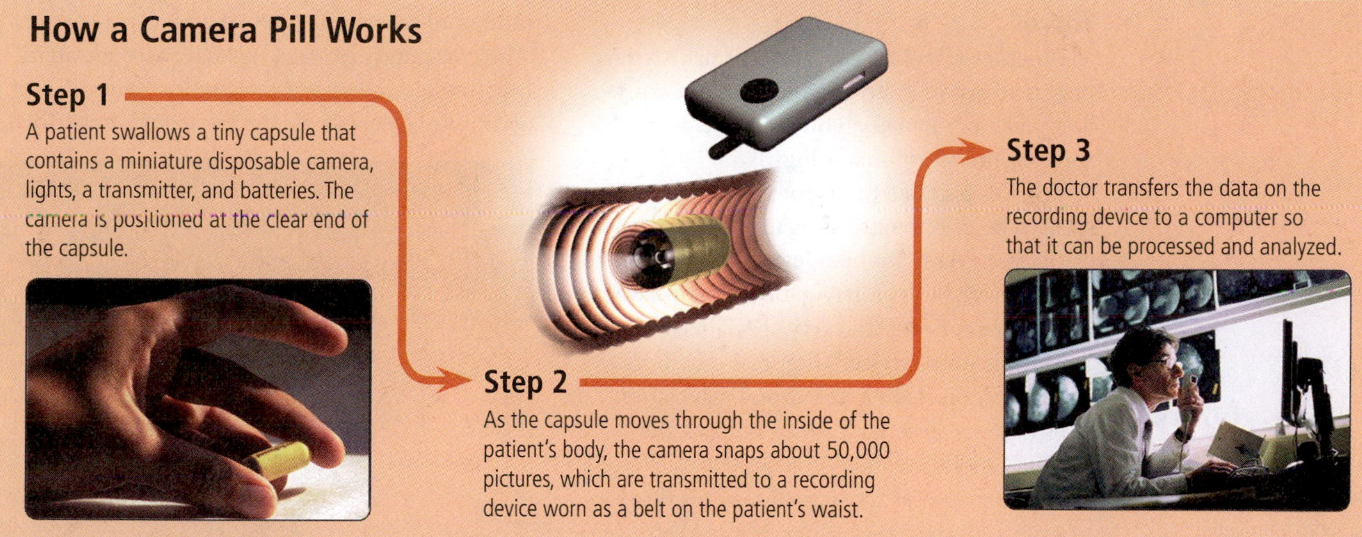

Figure 1-40 This figure shows how a camera pill works.

Publishing

Publishing is the process of making works available to the public. These works include books, magazines, newspapers, music, film, and video. Special software assists graphic designers in developing pages that include text, graphics, and photos; artists in composing and enhancing songs; filmmakers in creating and editing film; and journalists and mobile users in capturing and modifying video clips.

Many publishers make their works available online (Figure 1-41). Some Web sites allow you to copy the work, such as a book or music, to your desktop computer, mobile computer, smart phone, or other mobile device.

Figure 1-41 Many magazine and newspaper publishers make the content of their publications available online.

Travel

Whether traveling by car or airplane, your goal is to arrive safely at your destination. As you make the journey, you may interact with some of the latest technology.

Vehicles manufactured today often include some type of onboard navigation system, such as OnStar. Many mobile devices such as smart phones have built-in navigation systems. Some mobile users prefer to carry specialized handheld navigation devices (Figure 1-42). For a technical discussion about how navigation devices determine your location, read the High-Tech Talk article on page 40.

In preparing for a trip, you may need to reserve a car, hotel, or flight. Many Web sites offer these services to the public. For example, you can order airline tickets on the Web. If you plan to drive somewhere and are unsure of the road to take to your destination, you can print directions and a map from the Web.

OnStar

For more information, visit the Computer Concepts CourseMate Web site at www.cengagebrain.com, navigate to the Chapter 1 Web Link resource for this book, and then click OnStar.

Figure 1-42 This handheld navigation device gives users turn-by-turn voice-prompted directions to a destination.

Manufacturing

Computer-aided manufacturing (*CAM*) refers to the use of computers to assist with manufacturing processes such as fabrication and assembly. Industries use CAM to reduce product development costs, shorten a product's time to market, and stay ahead of the competition.

Often, robots carry out processes in a CAM environment. CAM is used by a variety of industries, including oil drilling, power generation, food production, and automobile manufacturing. Automobile plants, for example, have an entire line of industrial robots that assemble a car (Figure 1-43).

Special computers on the shop floor record actual labor, material, machine, and computer time used to manufacture a particular product. The computers process this data and automatically update inventory, production, payroll, and accounting records on the company's network.

Figure 1-43 Automotive factories use industrial robots to weld car bodies.

✓ QUIZ YOURSELF 1-3

Instructions: Find the true statement below. Then, rewrite the remaining false statements so that they are true.

1. A desktop computer is a portable, personal computer designed to fit on your lap.
2. A personal computer contains a processor, memory, and one or more input, output, and storage devices.
3. Each enterprise user spends time on the computer for different reasons that include personal financial management, Web access, communications, and entertainment.
4. A home user requires the capabilities of a workstation or other powerful computer.
5. Mainframes are the fastest, most powerful computers — and the most expensive.
6. The elements of an information system are hardware, e-mail, data, people, and the Internet.
7. With embedded computers, users access account balances, pay bills, and copy monthly transactions from the bank's computer right into their personal computers.

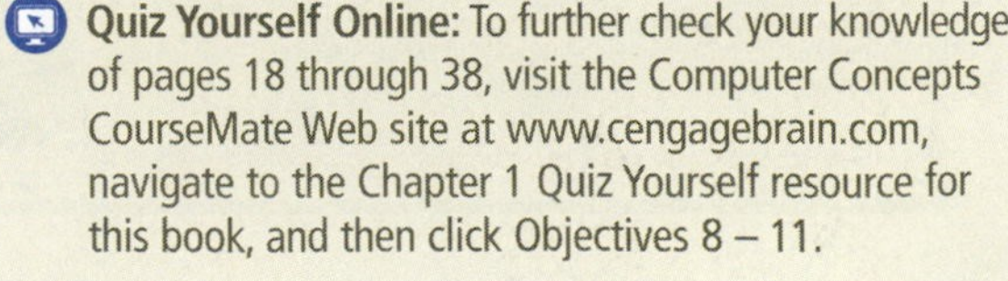

Quiz Yourself Online: To further check your knowledge of pages 18 through 38, visit the Computer Concepts CourseMate Web site at www.cengagebrain.com, navigate to the Chapter 1 Quiz Yourself resource for this book, and then click Objectives 8 – 11.

Chapter Summary

Chapter 1 introduced you to basic computer concepts such as what a computer is, how it works, and its advantages and disadvantages (read Ethics & Issues 1-5 for a related discussion). You learned about the components of a computer. Next, the chapter discussed networks, the Internet, and computer software. The many different categories of computers, computer users, and computer applications in society also were presented.

This chapter is an overview. Many of the terms and concepts introduced will be discussed further in later chapters. For a history of hardware and software developments, read the Timeline feature that follows this chapter.

ETHICS & ISSUES 1-5

Should Recycling of Electronics Be Made Easier?

Experts estimate that more than one billion computers have been discarded to date. The discarded items often are known as *e-waste*. As technology advances and prices fall, many people think of computers, cell phones, and portable media players as disposable items. These items often contain several toxic elements, including lead, mercury, and barium. Computers and mobile devices thrown into landfills or burned in incinerators can pollute the ground and the air. A vast amount of e-waste ends up polluting third world countries. One solution is to recycle old electronic equipment, but the recycling effort has made little progress especially when compared to recycling programs for paper, glass, and plastic.

Some lawmakers prefer an aggressive approach, such as setting up a recycling program that would be paid for by adding a small fee to the purchase price of computers and computer equipment, or forcing computer manufacturers to be responsible for collecting and recycling their products. California already requires a recycling fee for any products sold that include certain electronic equipment. Manufacturers have taken steps, such as offering to recycle old computers and using energy efficient and environmentally friendly manufacturing techniques, but some claim that consumers should bear the responsibility of disposing of their old computer parts. While some companies have set up recycling programs, many claim that forcing them to bear the cost of recycling programs puts the company at a competitive disadvantage when compared to foreign companies that may not be forced to maintain a recycling program.

Why is electronics recycling not as popular as other types of recycling? How can companies make it easier to recycle electronics while being compensated fairly for the cost of recycling? Should the government, manufacturers, or users be responsible for recycling of obsolete equipment? Why? Should the government mandate a recycling program for electronics? Why or why not?

Computer Usage @ Work

Transportation

What is transportation like without computers? Delivery drivers use clipboards to hold their records. Human navigators use paper maps to track routes for pilots. Ship captains rely solely on experience to navigate through shallow waters. Today, the transportation industry relies heavily on computer usage.

As presented in this chapter, many vehicles include onboard navigation systems to help you navigate from one location to another. These systems also usually provide other services such as dispatching roadside assistance, unlocking the driver's side door if you lock the keys in your vehicle, and tracking the vehicle if it is stolen.

The shipping and travel industries identify items during transport using bar codes, which are identification codes that consist of lines and spaces of different lengths. When you ship a package, the shipping company, such as UPS or FedEx, places a bar code on the package to indicate its destination to a computer. Because a package might travel to its destination by way of several trucks, trains, and airplanes, computers automatically route the package as efficiently as possible.

When you travel by airplane, baggage handling systems ensure that your luggage reaches its destination on time. When you check in your baggage at the airport, a bar code identifies the airplane on which the bags should be placed. If you change planes, automated baggage handling systems route your bags to connecting flights with very little, if any, human intervention. When the bags reach their destination, they are routed automatically to the baggage carousel in the airport's terminal building.

Pilots of high-technology commercial, military, and space aircraft today work in a glass cockpit, which features computerized instrumentation, navigation, communication, weather reports, and an autopilot. The electronic flight information shown on high-resolution displays is designed to reduce pilot workload, decrease fatigue, and enable pilots to concentrate on flying safely.

Boats and ships also are equipped with computers that include detailed electronic maps, help the captain navigate, as well as calculate the water depth and provide a layout of the underwater surface so that the captain can avoid obstructions.

As you travel the roadways, airways, and waterways, bear in mind that computers often are responsible for helping you to reach your destination as quickly and safely as possible.

For more information, visit the Computer Concepts CourseMate Web site at www.cengagebrain.com, navigate to the Chapter 1 Computer Usage @ Work resource for this book, and then click Transportation.

High-Tech Talk

Triangulation: Can You Find Me Now?

Have you wondered how a Nintendo Wii game console is able to determine the precise location of a Wii Remote while a player interacts with a game? How does the Wii console know where the player is pointing the Wii Remote, swinging it like a golf club, or motioning as if you are throwing a bowling ball? The answer is triangulation.

Triangulation is the process by which you can use trigonometry to determine the location of an object by measuring the angles from two or more fixed points. Surveyors often use triangulation to measure distance. Starting at a known location and elevation, surveyors measure a predetermined length to create a base line and then use an instrument called a theodolite to measure the angle to the unknown point from each side of the base line. The length of the base line along with the two known angles allows a computer or individual to determine the exact location of the third point (Figure 1-44). Electronic theodolites calculate angles automatically and then send the calculated angles to a computer for analysis.

In Figure 1-44, the distance between points A and B is known. The theodolite calculates angle CAB (α) and also calculates angle ABC (β). A human or computer can calculate the location of point C by determining the distance between points A and C and between points B and C. The formula used to determine the location of an object will vary depending upon the number of fixed points used in the measurement. With two fixed points, a relatively simple formula calculates the location of the third point. As the number of fixed points increases, the calculation becomes more complex.

Similarly, the Nintendo Wii game console uses triangulation to determine the location of a Wii Remote. When you set up a Wii game system, you place a sensor bar, which contains two infrared transmitters, near or on top of a television set. While you are using a Wii Remote, the Wii console determines the remote's location by calculating the distance and angles between the Wii Remote and the two transmitters on the sensor bar. Determining the location of a Wii Remote is relatively simple because the sensor bar only contains two fixed points: the transmitters.

A more complex application of triangulation occurs in global positioning systems. A *global positioning system* (*GPS*) is a navigation system that consists of one or more earth-based receivers that accept and analyze signals sent by satellites in order to determine the receiver's geographic location. GPS receivers are found in handheld navigation devices and many vehicles. GPS receivers use triangulation to determine their location relative to at least three geostationary satellites. Geostationary satellites, the fixed points in the triangulation formula, remain in the same location above the earth. Because 24 geostationary GPS satellites orbit the earth, a GPS receiver can increase its accuracy by using more than three satellites to determine its location by measuring the distance from each of the satellites, which always are a fixed distance apart, that are in range. In addition to determining position, GPS receivers also are able to calculate the speed of a moving object by recording its change in location from each satellite during a period of time. For instance, if a GPS receiver determines that you travel two-hundredths of a mile in one second, it automatically would be able to calculate that you are traveling at a rate of 72 miles per hour.

Another form of triangulation also can be used to determine the exact location of certain cell phones, usually after a caller dials for emergency assistance. Although some cell phones are not equipped with a GPS receiver, computers still can determine the phone's distance from other known locations, which might include cell towers. Because the location of two or more cell towers within range are known, computers easily can calculate the location of the cell phone. If you are unsure of whether the position of your cell phone can be determined automatically, always be prepared to give your location to an emergency dispatcher.

The next time you are passing a surveyor, playing a Nintendo Wii, following a prescribed route on a vehicle's navigation system, or observing emergency personnel respond to an accident, keep in mind that none of it might have been possible without the concept of triangulation.

Figure 1-44 Triangulation example.

For more information, visit the Computer Concepts CourseMate Web site at www.cengagebrain.com, navigate to the Chapter 1 High-Tech Talk resource for this book, and then click Triangulation.

Companies on the Cutting Edge

APPLE Innovative Industry Products

Apple recently sold a record 5.2 million of its latest iPhone models in one quarter, establishing the company's appeal to both consumer and corporate cell phone users. Apple is noted for introducing innovative products, starting with the Apple II, which was the first mass-marketed personal computer, in 1977 and the Macintosh, which featured a graphical user interface, in 1984.

Steve Jobs and Steve Wozniak founded Apple in 1976 when they marketed the Apple I, a circuit board they had developed in Jobs's garage. Under Jobs's direction as CEO, Apple developed the OS X operating system; iLife for working with photos, music, videos, and Web sites; and iWork, a collection of business programs. Apple also is leading the digital media revolution with its iPod portable media players, iPad tablet computer, and iTunes online store, which is the most popular Web site selling music. More than 10 million downloads occur each day from Apple's App Store, for a total download count exceeding 7 billion.

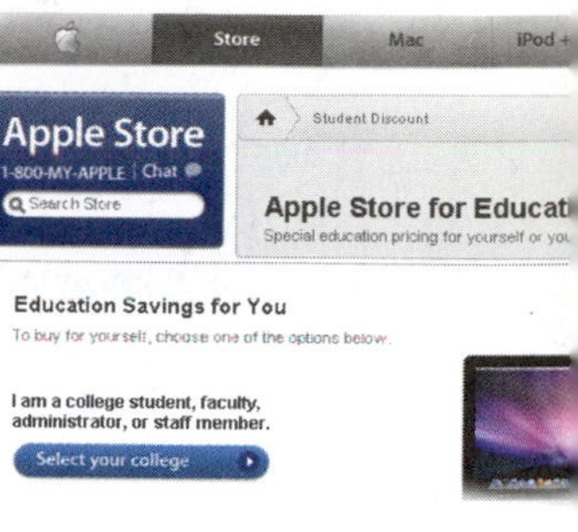

AMAZON Retailer Focused on Consumers

Online shoppers can find practically any product they desire on *Amazon*.com. Billing itself as the "Earth's most customer-centric company," it offers books, movies, electronics, clothing, toys, and many other items.

Jeff Bezos founded Amazon in 1995 knowing that book lovers would gravitate toward a Web site offering the convenience of browsing through millions of book titles in one sitting. He fulfilled orders for customers in every U.S. state and 45 additional countries during the first 30 days of business, all shipped from his Seattle-area garage.

The company has grown to permit third parties to sell products on its Web site. Its Kindle portable reader wirelessly downloads more than 450,000 books along with blogs, magazines, and newspapers to a high-resolution electronic paper display. Recently, it launched Kindle Singles, which are Kindle books with up to 30,000 words, the equivalent of two chapters of a typical book.

 For more information, visit the Computer Concepts CourseMate Web site at www.cengagebrain.com and then navigate to the Chapter 1 Companies on the Cutting Edge resource for this book.

Technology Trailblazers

BILL GATES Microsoft Founder

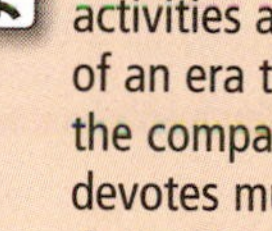

When *Bill Gates* stepped down from his day-to-day activities at Microsoft in 2008, his action marked the end of an era that shaped the computer world. He remains the company's chairman and advisor, but he now devotes much of his time directing the Bill & Melinda Gates Foundation, a philanthropic organization working to help people worldwide lead healthy, productive lives. His foundation currently is awarding $3 billion in grants to improve education and graduation rates via technology, with an emphasis on online learning.

Gates learned to program computers when he was 13 years old. Early in his career, he developed the BASIC programming language for the MITS Altair, one of the first microcomputers. He founded Microsoft in 1975 with Paul Allen, and five years later they licensed the first operating system, called PC-DOS, to IBM for $80,000. This decision to license, rather than sell, the software is considered one of the wisest business decisions Gates ever made. Today, Microsoft's Windows and Office products dominate the software market.

TOM ANDERSON MySpace Cofounder and President

Having more than 11 million friends is all in a day's work for *Tom Anderson*, the current president and one of the founders of MySpace, one of the world's largest online social networks. Every MySpace account includes Anderson as a default first friend who is invited to view each personal network.

When Anderson's own rock group failed, he needed a place to post his songs. He started MySpace in 2003 with his friend, Chris DeWolfe, as a free tool to help musicians promote their songs and allow music lovers to create their own Web pages devoted to sharing their favorite music with like-minded admirers. Two years later they sold the business to Rupert Murdoch's News Corporation for $580 million. Anderson graduated from the University of California – Los Angeles in 2001 with a master's degree in film and from the University of California – Berkeley in 1998 with a bachelor's degree in English and rhetoric.

For more information, visit the Computer Concepts CourseMate Web site at www.cengagebrain.com and then navigate to the Chapter 1 Technology Trailblazers resource for this book.

STUDENT ASSIGNMENTS

Chapter Review

The Chapter Review reinforces the main concepts presented in this chapter.

To listen to an audio version of this Chapter Review, visit the Computer Concepts CourseMate Web site at www.cengagebrain.com and then navigate to the Chapter 1 Chapter Review resource for this book.

1. Why Is Computer Literacy Vital in Today's World? **Computer literacy**, or *digital literacy*, involves having current knowledge and understanding of computers and their uses. The requirements that determine computer literacy change as technology changes. As computers become more a part of everyday life, many people believe that computer literacy is vital to success.

2. What Is a Computer, and What Is the Relationship between Data and Information? A **computer** is an electronic device, operating under the control of instructions stored in its own memory, that can accept data, process the data according to specified rules, produce results, and store the results for future use. **Data** is a collection of unprocessed items, which can include text, numbers, images, audio, and video. **Information** conveys meaning and is useful to people.

3. List and Describe the Five Components of a Computer. The electric, electronic, and mechanical components of a computer, or **hardware**, include input devices, output devices, a system unit, storage devices, and communications devices. An **input device** allows you to enter data or instructions into a computer. An **output device** conveys information to one or more people. The **system unit** is a case that contains the electronic components of a computer that are used to process data. A **storage device** records and/or retrieves items to and from **storage media**. A **communications device** enables a computer to send and receive data, instructions, and information to and from one or more computers.

4. What Are the Advantages and Disadvantages That Users Experience When Working with Computers? A **user** is anyone who communicates with a computer or utilizes the information it generates. Computers have the advantages of speed, reliability, consistency, storage, and communications. They perform operations at incredibly fast speeds, are dependable and reliable, consistently generate error-free results, can store enormous amounts of data, and can share processing with other computers. Disadvantages of computers relate to health risks, the violation of privacy, public safety, the impact on the labor force, and the impact on the environment.

Visit the Computer Concepts CourseMate Web site at www.cengagebrain.com, navigate to the Chapter 1 Quiz Yourself resource for this book, and then click Objectives 1 – 4.

5. What Is a Network, and What Are Its Benefits? A **network** is a collection of computers and devices connected together, often wirelessly, via communications devices and transmission media. Networks allow computers to share *resources*, such as hardware, software, data, and information. Sharing resources saves time and money. The world's largest computer network is the Internet.

6. How Are the Internet and World Wide Web Used? The Internet is a worldwide collection of networks that connects millions of businesses, government agencies, educational institutions, and individuals. People use the Internet to communicate with and meet other people; conduct research and access information and news; shop for goods and services; bank and invest; participate in online training; engage in entertaining activities; download music and videos; share information, photos, and videos; and access and interact with Web applications. The **Web**, short for World Wide Web, is a global library of documents containing information that is available to anyone connected to the Internet.

7. How Is System Software Different from Application Software? **Software**, also called a **program**, is a series of related instructions, organized for a common purpose, that tells the computer what actions to perform and how to perform them. **System software** consists of the programs that control or maintain the operations of a computer and its devices. Two types of system software are the *operating system*, which coordinates activities among computer hardware devices, and *utility programs*, which perform maintenance-type tasks usually related to managing a computer, its devices, or its programs. **Application software** consists of programs designed to make users more productive and/or assists them with personal tasks. Popular application software includes Web browsers, word processing software, spreadsheet software, database software, and presentation software.

Visit the Computer Concepts CourseMate Web site at www.cengagebrain.com, navigate to the Chapter 1 Quiz Yourself resource for this book, and then click Objectives 5 – 7.

Chapter Review

8. What Are the Differences among the Types, Sizes, and Functions in the Following Categories: Personal Computers (Desktop), Mobile Computers and Mobile Devices, Game Consoles, Servers, Mainframes, Supercomputers, and Embedded Computers? Industry experts typically classify computers in seven categories: personal computers (desktop), mobile computers and mobile devices, game consoles, servers, mainframes, supercomputers, and embedded computers. A **personal computer** is a computer that can perform all of its input, processing, output, and storage activities by itself. A **mobile computer** is a personal computer you can carry from place to place, and a **mobile device** is a computing device small enough to hold in your hand. A **game console** is a mobile computing device designed for single-player or multiplayer video games. A **server** controls access to the hardware, software, and other resources on a network and provides a centralized storage area for programs, data, and information. A **mainframe** is a large, expensive, powerful computer that can handle hundreds or thousands of connected users simultaneously and can store tremendous amounts of data, instructions, and information. A **supercomputer** is the fastest, most powerful, and most expensive computer and is used for applications requiring complex, sophisticated mathematical calculations. An **embedded computer** is a special-purpose computer that functions as a component in a larger product.

9. What Is the Role of Each Element in an Information System? An *information system* combines hardware, software, data, people, and procedures to produce timely and useful information. People in an information technology (IT) department develop procedures for processing data. Following these procedures, people use hardware and software to enter the data into a computer. Software processes the data and directs the computer hardware to store changes on storage media and produce information in a desired form.

10. How Do the Various Types of Computer Users Interact with Computers? Computer users can be separated into five categories: home user, small office/home office user, mobile user, power user, and enterprise user. A **home user** is a family member who uses a computer for a variety of reasons, such as budgeting and personal financial management, Web access, communications, and entertainment. A **small office/home office** (*SOHO*) includes any company with fewer than 50 employees, as well as the self-employed individual who works from home. SOHO users access the Internet to look up information and use basic business software and sometimes industry-specific software. **Mobile users** are employees and students who work on a computer while away from a main office, home office, or school. A **power user** uses a workstation or other powerful computer to work with industry-specific software. Power users exist in all types of businesses. An **enterprise user** works in or interacts with a company with many employees and uses a computer and computer network that processes high volumes of transactions in a single day.

11. How Does Society Use Computers in Education, Finance, Government, Health Care, Science, Publishing, Travel, and Manufacturing? In education, students use computers and software to assist with learning or take distance learning classes. In finance, people use computers for **online banking** and **online investing**. Government offices have Web sites to provide citizens with up-to-date information, and government employees use computers as part of their daily routines. In health care, computers are used to maintain patient records, monitor patients, deliver medication to nurse stations via robots, assist with medical tests and research, correspond with patients, file insurance claims, provide greater precision during operations, and as implants. All branches of science use computers to assist with collecting, analyzing, and modeling data and to communicate with colleagues around the world. Publishers use computers to assist in designing pages and make the content of their works available online. Many vehicles use some type of online navigation system to help people travel more quickly and safely. Manufacturers use **computer-aided manufacturing** (*CAM*) to assist with manufacturing processes.

Visit the Computer Concepts CourseMate Web site at www.cengagebrain.com, navigate to the Chapter 1 Quiz Yourself resource for this book, and then click Objectives 8 – 11.

STUDENT ASSIGNMENTS

Key Terms

You should know the Primary Terms and be familiar with the Secondary Terms. The list below helps focus your study.

To see an example of and a definition for each term, and to access current and additional information from the Web, visit the Computer Concepts CourseMate Web site at www.cengagebrain.com and then navigate to the Chapter 1 Key Terms resource for this book.

Primary Terms

(shown in bold-black characters in the chapter)

application software (16)
communications device (8)
computer (6)
computer literacy (5)
computer-aided manufacturing (38)
data (6)
desktop computer (20)
digital camera (23)
e-book reader (22)
embedded computer (26)
enterprise user (32)
game console (24)
graphical user interface (GUI) (15)
green computing (10)
handheld computer (22)
hardware (6)
home user (28)
information (6)
input device (6)
installing (16)
Internet (11)
Internet-enabled (21)
laptop computer (20)
mainframe (25)
mobile computer (20)
mobile device (20)
mobile users (31)
network (10)
notebook computer (20)
online (10)
online banking (34)
online investing (35)
output device (7)
PDA (22)
personal computer (19)
photo sharing community (14)
portable media player (23)
power user (31)
program (15)
run (17)
server (25)
small office/home office (30)
smart phone (21)
social networking Web site (14)
software (15)
storage device (8)
storage media (8)
supercomputer (25)
system software (15)
system unit (7)
Tablet PC (21)
telecommuting (32)
user (9)
video sharing community (14)
Web (13)
Web 2.0 (14)
Web application (14)
Web page (13)
Web site (13)

Secondary Terms

(shown in italic characters in the chapter)

blog (14)
CAM (38)
camera phone (22)
client (10)
convergence (18)
convertible tablet (21)
CPU (central processing unit) (7)
developer (18)
digital literacy (5)
digital pen (21)
e-book (22)
e-commerce (30)
e-reader (22)
enterprise computing (32)
execute (17)
FAQ (14)
gaming desktop computer (20)
garbage in, garbage out (9)
handhelds (22)
home theater PC (HTPC) (20)
icon (15)
information processing cycle (6)
information system (27)
information technology (IT) department (32)
instant message (22)
instructions (6)
loads (17)
memory (7)
microblog (14)
multimedia (31)
netbook (20)
neural network (36)
online social network (14)
operating system (15)
PC-compatible (19)
personal digital assistant (22)
picture message (22)
podcast (14)
processor (7)
programmer (18)
publish (13)
remote surgery (36)
resources (10)
server (10)
slate tablet (21)
SOHO (30)
telematics (26)
telemedicine (36)
telesurgery (36)
text message (22)
tower (20)
Ultra-Mobile PC (UMPC) (22)
utility program (16)
video blog (14)
video message (22)
video phone (22)
Web cam (30)

handheld computer (22)

Checkpoint

The Checkpoint exercises test your knowledge of the chapter concepts. The page number containing the answer appears in parentheses after each exercise. The Beyond the Book exercises will help broaden your understanding of the concepts presented in this chapter.

To complete the Checkpoint exercises interactively, visit the Computer Concepts CourseMate Web site at www.cengagebrain.com and then navigate to the Chapter 1 Checkpoint resource for this book.

True/False Mark T for True and F for False.

_____ 1. Many people believe that computer literacy is vital to success in today's world. (5)

_____ 2. Hardware consists of a series of instructions that tells the computer what actions to perform and how to perform them. (6)

_____ 3. The circuitry of the system unit usually is part of or is connected to a circuit board called the server. (7)

_____ 4. Green computing involves reducing the electricity consumed and environmental waste generated when using a computer. (10)

_____ 5. The client controls access to the resources on a network. (10)

_____ 6. Web pages rarely have built-in connections, or links, to other documents, graphics, other Web pages, or Web sites. (13)

_____ 7. A video sharing community is a type of social networking Web site that allows users to store and share their personal videos. (14)

_____ 8. A text message is a short note, typically fewer than 300 characters, sent to or from a smart phone or other mobile device. (22)

_____ 9. Because embedded computers are components in larger products, they usually are small and have limited hardware. (26)

_____ 10. Telecommuting is a work arrangement in which employees work away from a company's standard workplace and often communicate with the office through the computer. (32)

_____ 11. With online investing, the transaction fee for each trade usually is much more than when trading through a broker. (35)

Multiple Choice Select the best answer.

1. Computer literacy, also known as digital literacy, involves having a current knowledge and understanding of _____. (5)
   a. computer programming
   b. computers and their uses
   c. computer repair
   d. all of the above

2. _____ is/are a collection of unprocessed items, which can include text, numbers, images, audio, and video. (6)
   a. Data
   b. Instructions
   c. Programs
   d. Information

3. A _____ is a specific type of social networking Web site that allows users to create an online photo album and store and share their digital photos. (14)
   a. vodcast
   b. blog
   c. photo sharing community
   d. chat room

4. A _____ is recorded audio stored on a Web site that can be downloaded to a computer or portable media player. (14)
   a. podcast
   b. social networking Web site
   c. blog
   d. speaker

5. _____ consists of the programs that control or maintain the operations of the computer and its devices. (15)
   a. System software
   b. A communications device
   c. A graphical user interface (GUI)
   d. Application software

6. A(n) _____ message is a real-time Internet communication, where you exchange messages with other connected users. (22)
   a. text
   b. instant
   c. picture
   d. video

7. Many large companies use the word(s), _____, to refer to the huge network of computers that meets their diverse computing needs. (32)
   a. information technology
   b. enterprise computing
   c. telecommuting
   d. multimedia

8. _____ is a system that attempts to imitate the behavior of the human brain. (36)
   a. Telemedicine
   b. A kiosk
   c. E-commerce
   d. A neural network

Checkpoint

Matching

Match the terms with their definitions.

_____ 1. processor (7)
_____ 2. storage device (8)
_____ 3. online social network (14)
_____ 4. application software (16)
_____ 5. install (16)
_____ 6. execute (17)
_____ 7. portable media player (23)
_____ 8. digital camera (23)
_____ 9. multimedia (31)
_____ 10. neural network (36)

a. interprets and carries out basic instructions that operate a computer
b. carry out the instructions in a computer program
c. combines text, graphics, audio, and video into one application
d. programs designed to make users more productive and/or assist them with personal tasks
e. a system that attempts to imitate the behavior of the human brain
f. mobile device on which you can store, organize, and play digital media
g. online community that encourages members to share their interests, ideas, stories, photos, music, and videos with other registered users
h. set up software to work with a computer and other hardware components
i. device that allows users to take pictures and store the photographed images digitally, instead of on traditional film
j. records (writes) and/or retrieves (reads) items to and from storage media

Short Answer

Write a brief answer to each of the following questions.

1. What is a computer? ____________ What is the information processing cycle? ____________
2. Describe two health risks posed by computers. ____________ How might computers have a negative effect on the environment? ____________
3. What is a Web application? ____________ What are some features of a Web 2.0 site? ____________
4. What are seven categories of computers? ____________ What determines how a computer is categorized? ____________
5. How do Web sites benefit individuals' health care? ____________ How does telesurgery differ from telemedicine? ____________

Beyond the Book

Follow the book element instructions below; present your findings (brief report, presentation, discussion, or other means).

1. Ethics & Issues — Select an Ethics & Issues in this chapter (9, 13, 29, 35, 39), find a recent newspaper/magazine article that supports one point of view presented, and then evaluate the article.
2. Computer Usage @ Work — Use the Web or a recent newspaper/magazine to locate three additional unique usages of computer technology in the transportation industry (39). What makes the use of these technologies unique to the transportation industry?
3. Companies on the Cutting Edge and Technology Trailblazers — Use the Web or a recent business newspaper/magazine to locate an interesting fact about Apple, Amazon, Bill Gates, or Tom Anderson that was not presented in the chapter (41).
4. High-Tech Talk — Locate a recent newspaper/magazine article that discusses topics related to Triangulation (40). Would you recommend the article you found? Why or why not?
5. FAQs and Web Links — Use the Web or a recent newspaper/magazine to locate three additional facts about an FAQ (14, 16, 17, 20, 22, 29) and Web Link (10, 12, 14, 15, 22, 23, 27, 28, 32, 38) that were not presented in the chapter.
6. Looking Ahead — Use the Web or a recent newspaper/magazine to discover additional uses of the technology presented in Embedded Computers May Improve Quality of Life (34).
7. Innovative Computing — Use the Web or a recent newspaper/magazine to locate two additional interesting facts about Wii a Welcome Medical Skill Builder (24) and E-Receipts Save Paper, Organize Life (29).
8. Making Use of the Web — Visit three of the Fun and Entertainment Web Sites (125) and outline the information on each Web site and the possible uses for each Web site.
9. Timeline — Select an event from the Timeline (54) and then research the history surrounding the event using the Web or a magazine article.

Learn It Online

The Learn It Online exercises are interactive Web exercises designed to reinforce and expand your understanding of the chapter concepts. The descriptions below briefly summarize each exercise.

To complete the Learn It Online exercises, visit the Computer Concepts CourseMate Web site at www.cengagebrain.com, navigate to the Chapter 1 resources for this book, click the link for the exercise you want to complete, and then read the instructions.

1 At the Movies — Computer History in a Barn
Watch a movie to tour the Digibarn Computer Museum and then answer questions about the movie.

2 Video and Audio: You Review It — Social Networking
Search for, choose, and write a review of a video, podcast, or vodcast that discusses social networking.

3 Student Edition Labs — Using Input Devices and Using Windows
Enhance your understanding and knowledge about input devices and the Windows operating system by completing the Using Input Devices and Using Windows Labs.

4 Practice Test
Take a multiple choice test that checks your knowledge of the chapter concepts and review the resulting study guide.

5 Who Wants To Be a Computer Genius^2?
Play the Shelly Cashman Series version of this popular game by answering questions to find out if you are a computer genius. Panic buttons are available to provide assistance during game play.

6 Wheel of Terms
Identify important key terms presented in this chapter by playing the Shelly Cashman Series version of this popular game.

7 You're Hired!
Embark on the path to a career in computers by answering questions and solving puzzles related to concepts discussed in this chapter.

8 Crossword Puzzle Challenge
Complete an interactive crossword puzzle to reinforce concepts presented in this chapter.

9 Windows Exercises
Step through the Windows 7 exercises to learn how to use help, improve mouse skills, and identify computer information.

10 Exploring Computer Careers
Read about a career as a computer salesperson, search for relevant employment advertisements, and then answer related questions.

11 Web Apps — Google Maps
Learn how to locate businesses in your area, view a location's surroundings via satellite, and find directions from one location to another using Google Maps.

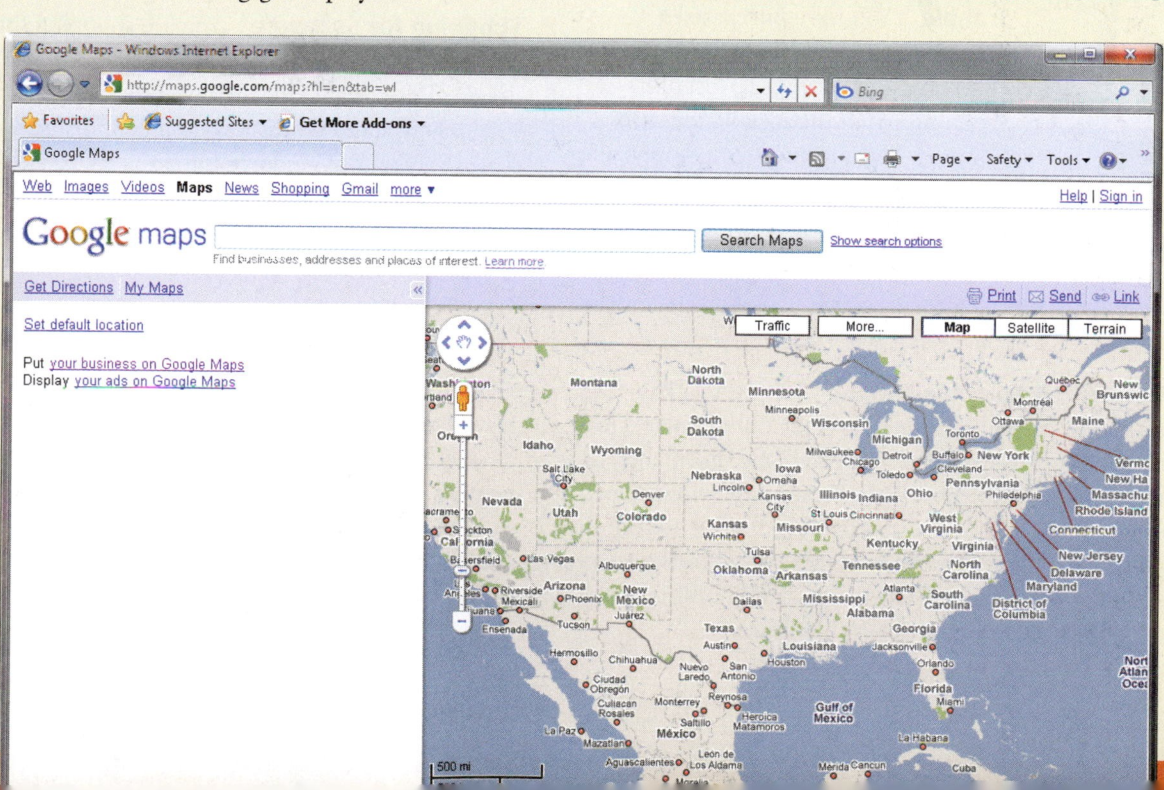

Problem Solving @ Home

The Problem Solving @ Home exercises extend your knowledge of the chapter concepts by seeking solutions to practical computer problems that you may encounter at home or school. The Collaboration exercise should be completed with a team.

In the real world, practical problems often can be solved in multiple ways. Provide one solution to each of the following problems using available resources, such as articles on the Web or in print, blogs, podcasts, videos, television, user guides, other individuals, and electronics and computer stores. You may need to use multiple resources to obtain an answer. Present your solutions in the form requested by your instructor (brief report, presentation, discussion, or other means).

1. **Incorrect Grade Report** Your grade report came in the mail today. On the grade report, your grade point average (GPA) is not what you expect. After computing it manually, you discover that the GPA on your grade report is incorrect. What might be causing the error?
2. **Suspicious Charges** Your credit card company called to inform you that your account has a suspicious charge. Upon further investigation, you realize that the charge does not belong to you. What will you do?
3. **Shared Printer Error** At the beginning of the semester, your roommate configured your computer so that it could print on the printer in his bedroom. He left for vacation three days ago, and you recently have noticed that you are unable to print to his printer from your computer. Each time you attempt to print, you receive an error message stating that the printer is unavailable. What might be wrong?

4. **Software Installation Trouble** You have purchased a new video game for your home computer and attempt to install it. Upon inserting the installation disc, however, nothing appears to happen on your computer. What is your next step?
5. **Problematic Player** After charging your portable media player overnight, you turn it on only to find that it is reporting a low battery. Seconds later, it shuts off automatically. What might be wrong?
6. **Inaccessible Media** You insert an optical disc with digital photos from your most recent family vacation, and discover that your computer will not read the optical disc. What might be wrong?
7. **Bank Account Postings** While reviewing your checking account balance online, you notice that debit card purchases have not posted to your account for the past several days. Because you use online banking to balance your account, you become concerned about your unknown account balance. What steps will you take to correct this situation?
8. **GPS Error** You are driving to your friend's house and are using your GPS receiver for directions. While approaching your destination, you realize that the GPS receiver instructed you to turn the wrong way on your friend's street. How could this have happened?
9. **Shopping for Software** You are shopping for software that will assist with your home landscape design. The package for the program you would like to purchase states that it was designed for the most recent version of Windows, but an older version is installed on your computer. How can you determine whether the program will run on your computer?

Collaboration

10. **Unsolicited Communications** Lately, you have been receiving many unsolicited e-mail messages, text messages, instant messages, and telephone calls. These messages not only are annoying, but they also are consuming large amounts of your time. Form a team of three people and decide what steps are necessary to minimize these unsolicited communications. One team member should research how to stop unsolicited e-mail messages, one team member should research how to stop unsolicited text messages and instant messages, and another team member should research how to stop unsolicited telephone calls. Finally, all team members should research where these unsolicited calls and messages might be originating and how to prevent being added to distribution lists in the future.

Problem Solving @ Work

The Problem Solving @ Work exercises extend your knowledge of the chapter concepts by seeking solutions to practical computer problems that you may encounter at work. The Collaboration exercise should be completed with a team.

In the real world, practical problems often can be solved in multiple ways. Provide one solution to each of the following problems using available resources, such as articles on the Web or in print, blogs, podcasts, videos, television, user guides, other individuals, and electronics and computer stores. You may need to use multiple resources to obtain an answer. Present your solutions in the form requested by your instructor (brief report, presentation, discussion, or other means).

1. **Insufficient Disk Space** Recently, you purchased a USB flash drive that you plan to use to store work-related files. When you attempt to store a file on the USB flash drive, the computer displays an error message indicating that the file will not fit. How could a brand new USB flash drive not have enough room to store the first file you attempted to store on it?
2. **Computer Replacement** The technical support department at your company has informed you that you will be receiving a new computer within the next week. Before they will replace your computer, they told you to back up anything that is important. What types of files do you feel are important to back up?
3. **Power Outage** The power in your office has been out for the last two hours and has just come back on. When you attempt to start your computer by pressing the power button, nothing happens. What is your next step before calling technical support?
4. **Incorrect Login Credentials** Upon returning to the office from a well-deserved two-week vacation, you turn on your computer. Upon entering your user name and password, an error message appears stating that your password is incorrect. What are your next steps?
5. **Software Installation** You are attempting to install a program on your office computer. After inserting the installation disc and specifying that you would like to begin the installation, your computer appears to begin installing the software. Halfway through the installation process, an error message appears stating that you must have administrative privileges to perform the installation. Why were you not informed immediately upon beginning the installation? What are your next steps?

6. **Dead Battery** While traveling for business, you realize that you forgot to bring the battery charger for your notebook computer. Knowing that you need to use the notebook computer to give a presentation tomorrow, what will you do to make sure that you have enough battery power?
7. **Discarding Old Computer Equipment** Your company has just given you a new computer to replace your current, outdated computer. Because of the negative environmental impact of throwing the computer away, your supervisor has asked you to suggest options for its disposal. How will you respond?

Collaboration

8. **Computers in Transportation** Your project team has been accepted to present a business proposal to a group of potential investors. Because the presentation will take place in San Francisco, CA, you will need to transport people and ship some materials to that location. Form a team of three people and determine how to use technology to ship materials and how to make travel arrangements. One team member should research the steps required to use a Web site to make flight reservations, one team member should determine the steps necessary to print a UPS shipping label from his or her computer and track the package while it is en route, and another team member should find directions from San Francisco International Airport to a nearby hotel.

Learn How To

The Learn How To activities step you through fundamental technology skills when using a computer. The Learn How To exercises enable you to become more proficient with these skills.

Premium Activity: To relate this Learn How To activity to your everyday life, see a visual demonstration of the activity, and complete a short assessment, visit the Computer Concepts CourseMate Web site at www.cengagebrain.com and then navigate to the Chapter 1 Learn How To resource for this book.

Learn How To 1: Start and Close a Program

You can start any program by using the Start button. Complete these steps to start the Web browser program called Internet Explorer:

1. Click the Start button ( ) at the left of the Windows taskbar on the bottom of the screen to display the Start menu.
2. Click All Programs on the Start menu to display the All Programs list (Figure 1-45).
3. Click the Internet Explorer in the All Programs list to start Internet Explorer (Figure 1-46).

An item in the All Programs list might have an open folder icon next to it. When this occurs, click the item and another list will appear. Click the program name in this list to start the program. Some program names might appear on the Start menu itself. If so, click any of these names to start the corresponding program.

The Start menu displays the names of the programs recently opened on the computer. You can start any of these programs by clicking the name of the program.

To close a program, click the Close button ( ) in the upper-right corner of the window. If you have created but not saved a document, Windows will ask if you want to save the document. If you do not want to save it, click the No button in the displayed dialog box. If you want to save it, refer to Learn How To 1 in Chapter 3 on page 188.

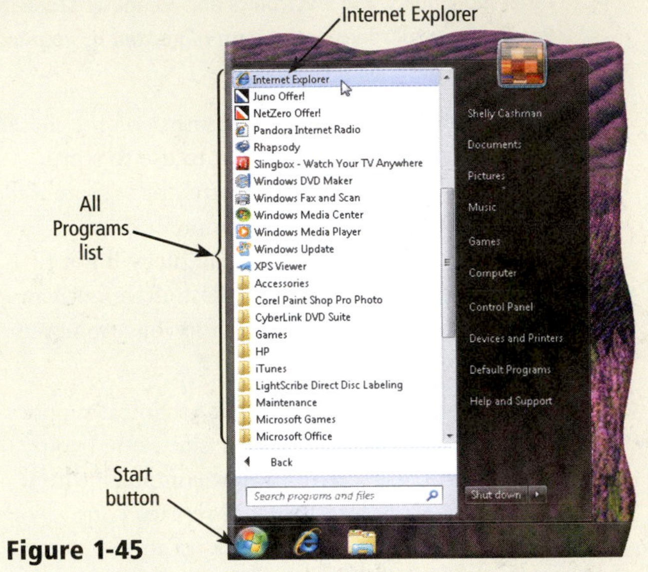

Figure 1-45

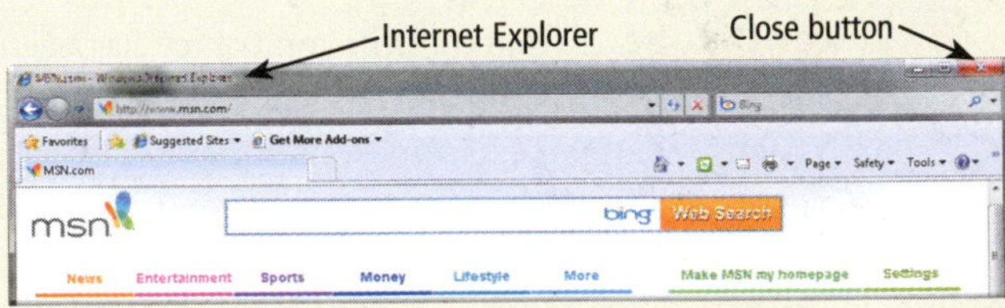

Figure 1-46

Exercises

1a. Using the Start button, start the program named WordPad found in the Accessories list in the All Programs list. WordPad is a word processing program. Type the following: `To start a program, click the program name in the All Programs list` and then type your name. Print the document, and then submit the printout to your instructor.

1b. Close the WordPad program. If you are asked if you want to save changes to the document, click the Don't Save button. Start the WordPad program again, type some new text, and then close the WordPad program. When the dialog box is displayed, click the Cancel button. What happened? Now, close the WordPad window without saving the document. Submit your answer to your instructor.

2. Using the Start menu, start the e-mail program on the computer. What is the name of the e-mail program? In the program window, what menu names are displayed on the menu bar at the top of the window? Close the e-mail program. Submit your answers to your instructor.

Learn How To 2: Create and Use Your Own Blog

A blog can contain any information you wish to place in it. For example, blogs contain addresses, thoughts, diaries, and anything else a person or group wants to share.

Once you have created a blog, you can update it. A variety of services available on the Web can help you create and maintain your blog. One widely used service is called Blogger. To create a blog using Blogger, complete the following steps:

1. Start your Web browser, type `blogger.com` in the Address bar, and then press the ENTER key to display the Blogger home page (Figure 1-47).
2. Click the CREATE A BLOG button.

Learn How To

3. Enter the data required on the 'Create Blogger Account' page. Your e-mail address and password will allow you to change and manage your blog. Your Display name is the name that will be shown on the blog as its author. Many people use their own names, but others use pseudonyms as their "pen names" so that they are not readily identifiable.
4. Click the Continue arrow and then enter your Blog title and Blog address. These are the names and addresses everyone will use to view your blog.
5. Click the Continue arrow to display the 'Choose a template' screen.
6. Choose a template for your blog and then click the Continue arrow to create your blog.
7. When the 'Your blog has been created!' screen appears, click the START BLOGGING arrow.
8. When the screen appears, you can post items for or view your blog, specify settings, and change the layout.
9. When you are finished, click the Sign out link at the top right of the screen to log out.
10. To edit your blog and add or change information on it, visit the Blogger home page, sign in by entering your user name and password, and then make changes.
11. Others can view your blog by entering its address in the browser's Address bar and then pressing the ENTER key.

Figure 1-47

Exercises

1. Start your Web browser and visit blogger.com. Click the 'Take a quick tour' link and go through all the screens that explain about a blog. What did you learn that you did not know? What type of blog do you find most compelling — a group or an individual blog? Why? Submit your answers to your instructor.
2. Optional: Create your own blog. Carefully name it and begin your posts at this time. What is your blog name and address? What is its primary purpose? Is it an individual or group blog? Write a paragraph containing the answers to these questions and any other information you feel is pertinent. Submit this paragraph to your instructor.

Learn How To 3: Use the Computer Concepts CourseMate Web Site for Discovering Computers

The Computer Concepts CourseMate Web site for Discovering Computers provides a variety of activities, exercises, and other resources. To use the site, you first must create a student account and then register this book, as described in the following steps:

1. Start the Web browser, type the Web address of `www.cengagebrain.com` in the browser Address bar, and then press the ENTER key to display the CengageBrain home page.
2. If you do not have an account, follow the on-screen instructions to sign up for a new account. If you have an account, log in with your user name and password.
3. Register this book by entering its Access Code in the appropriate text box and then clicking the corresponding button.
4. To open the resources for this book, click the button corresponding to Computer Concepts CourseMate Web site for Discovering Computers.

Exercise

1a. With a student account created and this book registered, type `www.cengagebrain.com` in the Address bar of your browser, press the ENTER key to display the CengageBrain home page, and then log in to your student account with your user name and password.

1b. Open the resources for this book by clicking the button corresponding to Computer Concepts CourseMate Web site for Discovering Computers.

1c. Select Chapter 1 and then click each resource listed below the chapter title to display the content associated with the selected resource.

1d. Write a report that describes the use of each of the Chapter 1 resources for this book. Which resource do you think will prove the most valuable to you when using the book and the Web site? Why? Which will be the least useful? Why? Submit your report to your instructor.

Web Research

The Web Research exercises broaden your understanding of the chapter concepts by presenting questions that require you to search the Web for answers.

1 Search Sleuth

Use one of the search engines listed in Figure 2-10 in Chapter 2 on page 85 or your own favorite search engine to find the answers to the following questions. Copy and paste the Web address from the Web page where you found the answer. Some questions may have more than one answer. If required, submit your answers to your instructor. (1) What company was the first to sell a USB flash drive? (2) What is the significance of the Universal symbol on Apple's Mac application programs? (3) Which retailers offer to dispose of old computers and other electronic products properly to help protect the environment? (4) What are three Illustrative Grant Commitments the Bill & Melinda Gates Foundation has made? (5) According to *Fortune*, at what company do MBA students most want to work when they graduate? (6) Who created the first set of icons for the Macintosh computer? What sound does her Clarus the Dogcow make? (7) What company manufactured the first notebook computer, the UltraLite, in 1989?

2 Green Computing

Computer usage requires electricity, whether to power the system unit and monitor, recharge batteries, or print. In addition, the computer manufacturing process depletes natural resources and often uses toxic chemicals. As you learned in this chapter, many environmentally conscious people practice green computing by attempting to reduce electricity and environmental waste. Examine your computing practices, and determine 10 ways that you can use less power on your computing equipment at home, work, and school. Consider how often you use the printer and the types of documents you print. Examine your monitor, system unit, and printer. Do you see any notation indicating they are environmentally sound? Do they hibernate or go into a power save mode when not being used? Write a 50-word summary of the green computing practices in your life.

3 Social Networking

One of the more popular social networking Web sites is Facebook. This quickly growing service differentiates itself from other online social networks by having widespread privacy controls. In addition, its development platform, called f8, allows developers to create programs (called applications) that users can add to a Web page. Hostels, for example, lets world travelers research and rate hostels and includes photos and descriptions. Visit the Facebook site (facebook.com), click the About link at the bottom of the page, and then read about Facebook's features. What are three of Facebook's top features? What information is given in the recent Facebook blog posts? Visit the AppRate Web site (apprate.com) and then summarize three Facebook application reviews and ratings.

4 Blogs

Blogs profiling the music industry discuss new technologies, legal issues, podcasts, and business news. Visit the CNET blog (news.cnet.com/tech-blogs) and then read and summarize at least three of the articles in the Most Recent Posts section. Locate the Crave, Gaming and Culture, and Green Tech features and then read and summarize at least one story from each blog. Then visit the iLounge (ilounge.com) Web site and read reviews of at least three new products for the iPhone. Would you purchase any of the products discussed? What books and buyer's guides are available to download from the Library? Which iPod cases and speakers received favorable reviews? Read and summarize at least three stories and associated comments in the News section.

5 Ethics in Action

The Internet has increased the ease with which students can plagiarize material for research paper assignments. Teachers are using online services, such as Turnitin and PlagiarismDetect.com, to help detect plagiarized papers and to help students understand how to cite sources correctly. Visit the Turnitin Web site (turnitin.com) and then write a summary of how this service is used. How does this service attempt to prevent plagiarism through the Turnitin Write Cycle? How prevalent is plagiarism on your campus? What is your school's official policy on disciplining students who submit plagiarized papers? Does your school have an honor code? If required, submit your summary to your instructor.

Critical Thinking

The Critical Thinking exercises challenge your assessment and decision-making skills by presenting real-world situations associated with the chapter concepts. The Collaboration exercise should be completed with a team.

To evaluate the situations below, use personal experiences and available resources such as articles on the Web or in print, blogs, podcasts, videos, television, user guides, other individuals, and electronics and computer stores. You may need to use multiple resources to form conclusions and make recommendations.

1. **Class Discussion — Reactions to Computer Problems** Virtually everyone who works with computers has experienced problems with computer software. Problems can range from not being able to install the software on your computer to installed software producing unanticipated results. Depending on the situation and time these problems occur, it can result in a great amount of user stress. Some people compare these types of problems to a craftsman's tools malfunctioning in the middle of a project. On the other hand, many people feel reactions to computer software problems tend to be more extreme than reactions to problems with other tools they use. Evaluate situations in which you have seen people react to computer software problems. Discuss how these users can reduce their frustration when dealing with such problems.

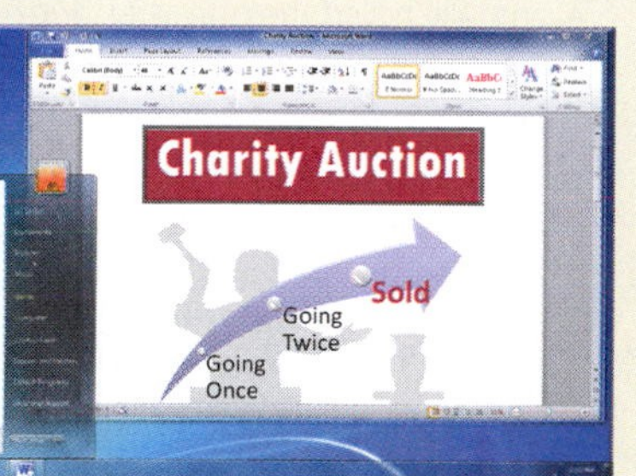

2. **Class Presentation — Technology in Education** You are a member of your local school district's board of education. During the past year, the number of computers purchased by the district increased by 85 percent, while the supply of library books declined by almost 10 percent. School officials claim that computers extend learning opportunities and develop the computer literacy needed in today's technological world. Yet, some parents complain that computer purchases represent frivolous, status-seeking spending. Notebook computers are purchased for teachers, while textbooks and library books are too old, too worn, and too scarce. Analyze how computers are being used in schools, and then present your recommendation of the percentage of the instructional materials budget that should be spent on computers versus the percentage that should be spent on library books and textbooks. Note the factors that influenced your decision.

3. **Research — Energy Efficiency** Increases in fuel prices result in increases in energy prices. When this occurs, many individuals and companies look at purchasing energy-efficient computers. These energy-efficient computers require less energy to operate and often look and perform similarly to equivalent computers that are not as energy efficient. Find two computers of identical configuration, where the only difference is energy consumption. How much energy does the energy-efficient computer save? Are energy-efficient computers more or less expensive? Will the difference in cost (if any) alter your preference to purchase an energy-efficient computer instead of one that is not energy efficient? What other ways might you be able to configure your computer to save energy? Compile your findings into a brief report and then submit it to your instructor.

Collaboration

4. **Recommending Technology Solutions** People use computers in a variety of fields, including education, finance, government, health care, science, publishing, travel, and manufacturing. Although the way people use computers varies, each use of a computer involves computer hardware, computer software, and normally some type of communications capability over networks, such as the Internet. Form a three-member team and choose a field in which you all are interested. Assign one member of your team to investigate hardware used in the field, another member to investigate software used in the field, and the third member to investigate communications capabilities used in the field. Each team member should develop a list of related items that may be used in the selected field. After the team's investigation, characterize a hypothetical business or organization in the field. Based on your investigation, recommend specific hardware, software, and networking capabilities that would be best for the business or organization. Each team member should provide an explanation for each selected item. Be sure to include comparisons of specific items. Prepare a report and/or presentation summarizing your investigations, describing the hypothetical business or organization, and outlining and supporting your recommendations.

Timeline

Milestones in Computer History

Visit the Computer Concepts CourseMate Web site at www.cengagebrain.com and then navigate to the Timeline Feature resource for this book.

1937 Dr. John V. Atanasoff and Clifford Berry design and build the first electronic digital computer. Their machine, the Atanasoff-Berry-Computer, or ABC, provides the foundation for advances in electronic digital computers.

1943 During World War II, British scientist Alan Turing designs the Colossus, an electronic computer created for the military to break German codes. The computer's existence is kept secret until the 1970s.

1945 John von Neumann poses in front of the electronic computer built at the Institute for Advanced Study. This computer and its von Neumann architecture served as the prototype for subsequent stored program computers worldwide.

1946 Dr. John W. Mauchly and J. Presper Eckert, Jr. complete work on the first large-scale electronic, general-purpose digital computer. The ENIAC (Electronic Numerical Integrator And Computer) weighs 30 tons, contains 18,000 vacuum tubes, occupies a 30 × 50 foot space, and consumes 160 kilowatts of power.

1947 William Shockley, John Bardeen, and Walter Brattain invent the transfer resistance device, eventually called the transistor. The transistor would revolutionize computers, proving much more reliable than vacuum tubes.

1951 The first commercially available electronic digital computer, the UNIVAC I (UNIVersal Automatic Computer), is introduced by Remington Rand. Public awareness of computers increases when the UNIVAC correctly predicts that Dwight D. Eisenhower will win the presidential election.

1952 Dr. Grace Hopper considers the concept of reusable software in her paper, "The Education of a Computer." The paper describes how to program a computer with symbolic notation instead of detailed machine language.

1957 The IBM 305 RAMAC computer is the first to use magnetic disk for external storage. The computer provides storage capacity similar to magnetic tape that previously was used but offers the advantage of semi-random access capability.

1959 More than 200 programming languages have been created.

1959 IBM introduces two smaller, desk-sized computers: the IBM 1401 for business and the IBM 1620 for scientists.

1957 FORTRAN (FORmula TRANslation), an efficient, easy-to-use programming language, is introduced by John Backus.

1952 1953  1957 1958  1959 1960

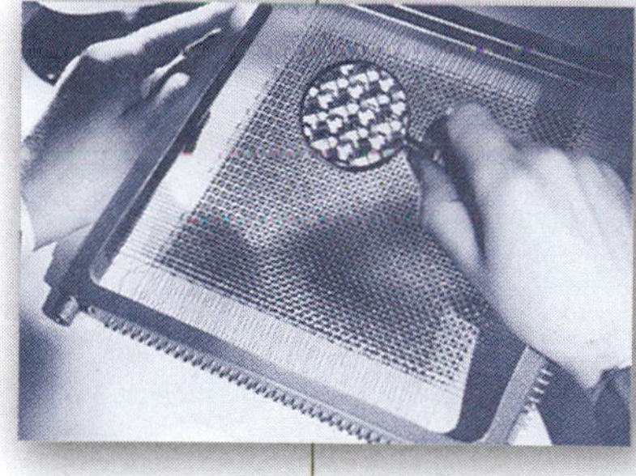

1953 Core memory, developed in the early 1950s, provides much larger storage capacity than vacuum tube memory.

1953 The IBM model 650 is one of the first widely used computers. The computer is so successful that IBM manufactures more than 1,000. IBM will dominate the mainframe market for the next decade.

1958 Jack Kilby of Texas Instruments invents the integrated circuit, which lays the foundation for high-speed computers and large-capacity memory. Computers built with transistors mark the beginning of the second generation of computer hardware.

1960 COBOL, a high-level business application language, is developed by a committee headed by Dr. Grace Hopper.

1965 Dr. John Kemeny of Dartmouth leads the development of the BASIC programming language.

1965 Digital Equipment Corporation (DEC) introduces the first minicomputer, the PDP-8. The machine is used extensively as an interface for time-sharing systems.

1968 In a letter to the editor titled, "GO TO Statements Considered Harmful," Dr. Edsger Dijkstra introduces the concept of structured programming, developing standards for constructing computer programs.

1968 Computer Science Corporation (CSC) becomes the first software company listed on the New York Stock Exchange.

1969 Under pressure from the industry, IBM announces that some of its software will be priced separately from the computer hardware, allowing software firms to emerge in the industry.

1969 The ARPANET network is established, which eventually grows to become the Internet.

ARPANET

1964 1965 1968 1969 1970

1964 The number of computers has grown to 18,000. Third-generation computers, with their controlling circuitry stored on chips, are introduced. The IBM System/360 computer is the first family of compatible machines, merging science and business lines.

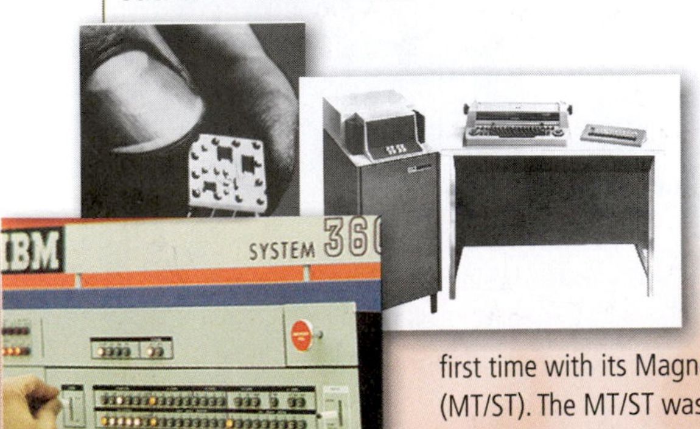

1964 IBM introduces the term word processing for the first time with its Magnetic Tape/Selectric Typewriter (MT/ST). The MT/ST was the first reusable storage medium that allowed typed material to be edited without having to retype the document.

1968 Alan Shugart at IBM demonstrates the first regular use of an 8-inch floppy disk.

1970 Fourth-generation computers, built with chips that use LSI (large-scale integration) arrive. While the chips used in 1965 contained up to 1,000 circuits, the LSI chip contains as many as 15,000.

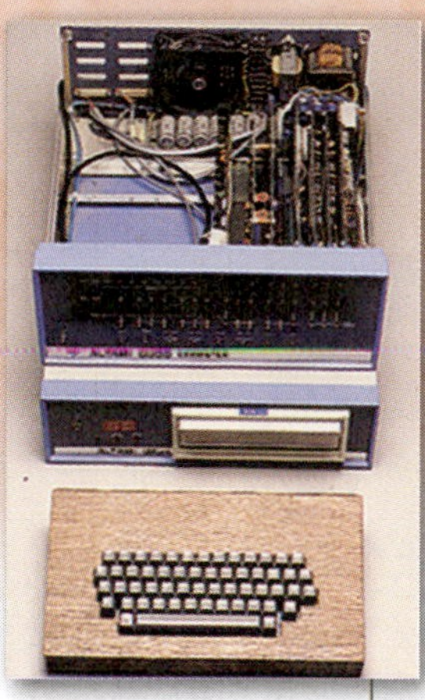

1975 MITS, Inc. advertises one of the first microcomputers, the Altair. The Altair is sold in kits for less than $400 and within the first three months 4,000 orders are taken.

1975 Ethernet, the first local area network (LAN), is developed at Xerox PARC (Palo Alto Research Center) by Robert Metcalfe.

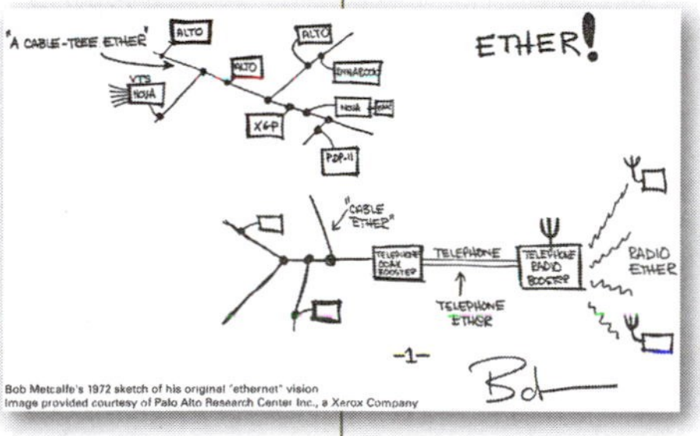

Bob Metcalfe's 1972 sketch of his original "ethernet" vision
Image provided courtesy of Palo Alto Research Center Inc., a Xerox Company

1979 The first public online information services, CompuServe and the Source, are founded.

1979 VisiCalc, a spreadsheet program written by Bob Frankston and Dan Bricklin, is introduced.

1981 The IBM PC is introduced, signaling IBM's entrance into the personal computer marketplace. The IBM PC quickly garners the largest share of the personal computer market and becomes the personal computer of choice in business.

1971 1975 1976 1979 1980 1981

1971 Dr. Ted Hoff of Intel Corporation develops a microprocessor, or microprogrammable computer chip, the Intel 4004.

1976 Steve Jobs and Steve Wozniak build the first Apple computer. A subsequent version, the Apple II, is an immediate success. Adopted by elementary schools, high schools, and colleges, for many students, the Apple II is their first contact with the world of computers.

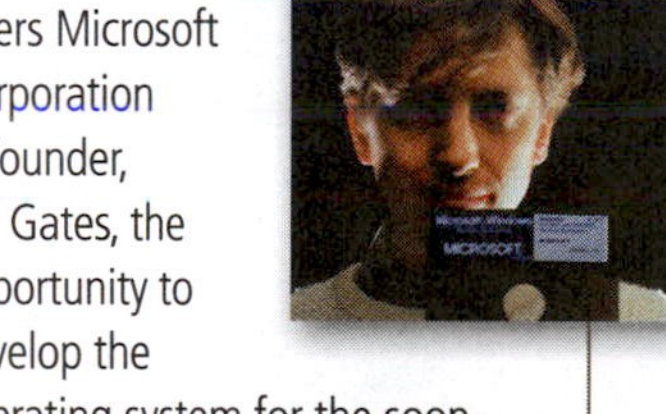

1980 IBM offers Microsoft Corporation cofounder, Bill Gates, the opportunity to develop the operating system for the soon-to-be announced IBM personal computer. With the development of MS-DOS, Microsoft achieves tremendous growth and success.

1980 Alan Shugart presents the Winchester hard disk, revolutionizing storage for personal computers.

1981 The first computer virus, Elk Cloner, is spread via Apple II floppy disks, which contained the operating system. A short rhyme would appear on the screen when the user pressed Reset after the 50th boot of an infected disk.

1982 3,275,000 personal computers are sold, almost 3,000,000 more than in 1981.

1982 Compaq, Inc. is founded to develop and market IBM-compatible PCs.

1982 Hayes introduces the 300 bps smart modem. The modem is an immediate success.

1984 Apple introduces the Macintosh computer, which incorporates a unique, easy-to-learn, graphical user interface.

1984 Hewlett-Packard announces the first LaserJet printer for personal computers.

1983 Instead of choosing a person for its annual award, *TIME* magazine names the computer Machine of the Year for 1982, acknowledging the impact of computers on society.

1983 Lotus Development Corporation is founded. Its spreadsheet software, Lotus 1-2-3, which combines spreadsheet, graphics, and database programs in one package, becomes the best-selling program for IBM personal computers.

1986 Microsoft has public stock offering and raises approximately $61 million.

1989 While working at CERN, Switzerland, Tim Berners-Lee invents the World Wide Web.

WWW

1991 Kodak announces the first digital SLR (single-lens reflex) camera. The Kodak DCS 100 is developed mostly for photojournalism purposes and stores the photos and batteries in a separate unit.

1989 Nintendo introduces the Game Boy, its first handheld game console.

1991 World Wide Web Consortium releases standards that describe a framework for linking documents on different computers.

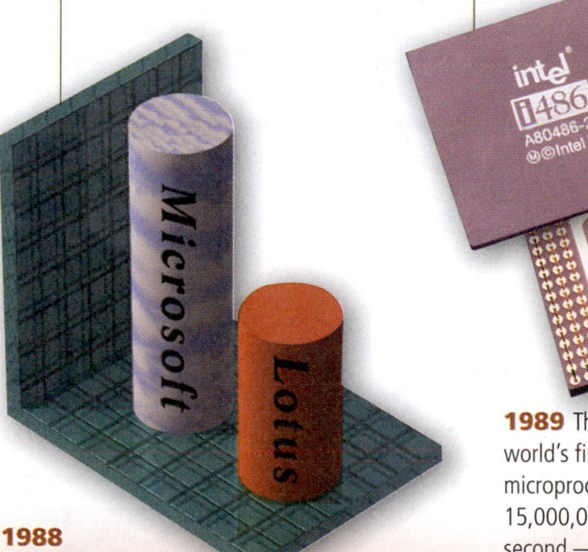

1988 Microsoft surpasses Lotus Development Corporation to become the world's top software vendor.

1989 The Intel 486 becomes the world's first 1,000,000 transistor microprocessor. It executes 15,000,000 instructions per second — four times as fast as its predecessor, the 80386 chip.

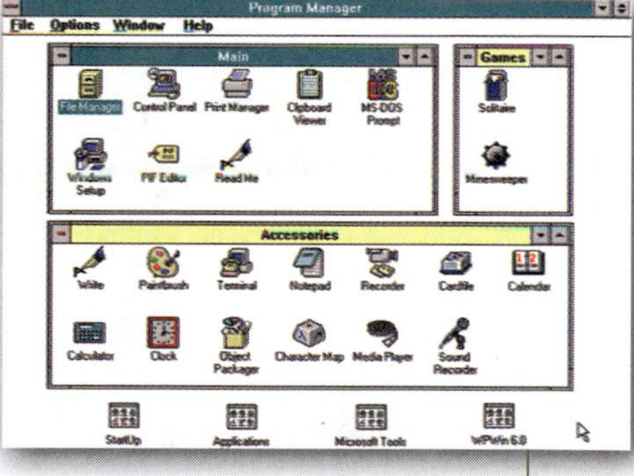

1992 Microsoft releases Windows 3.1, the latest version of its Windows operating system. Windows 3.1 offers improvements such as TrueType fonts, multimedia capability, and object linking and embedding (OLE). In two months, 3,000,000 copies of Windows 3.1 are sold.

1993 Several companies introduce computers using the Pentium processor from Intel. The Pentium chip contains 3.1 million transistors and is capable of performing 112,000,000 instructions per second.

1993 The U.S. Air Force completes the Global Positioning System by launching its 24th Navstar satellite into orbit. Today, GPS receivers can be found in cars, notebook computers, and smart phones.

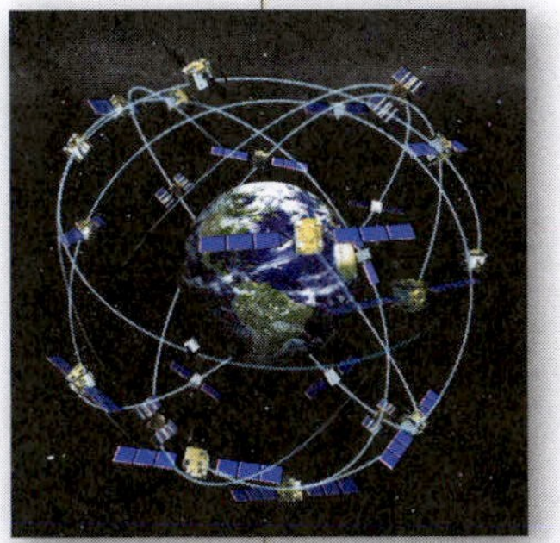

1994 Linus Torvalds creates the Linux kernel, a UNIX-like operating system that he releases free across the Internet for further enhancement by other programmers.

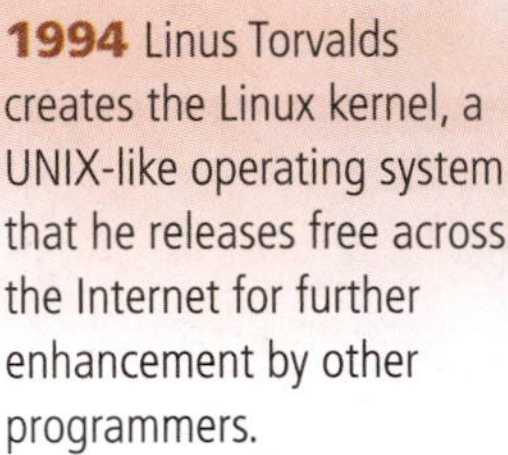

1994 Jim Clark and Marc Andreessen found Netscape and launch Netscape Navigator 1.0, a Web browser.

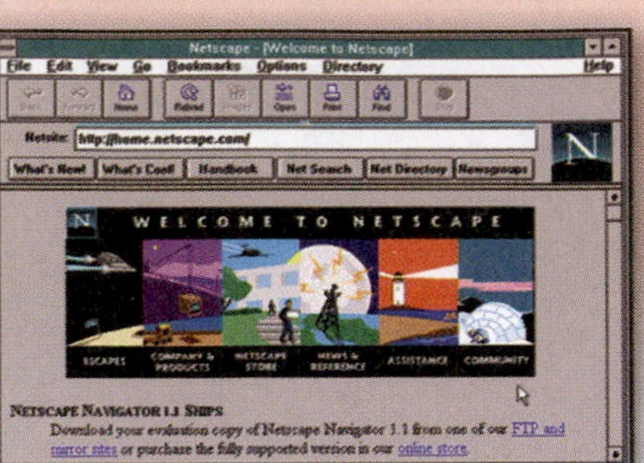

1994 Apple introduces the first digital camera intended for consumers. The Apple QuickTake 100 is connected to home computers using a serial cable.

1994

1993

1993 Microsoft releases Microsoft Office 3 Professional, the first version of Microsoft Office for the Windows operating system.

1993 The White House launches its Web site, which includes an interactive citizens' handbook and White House history and tours.

1994 Yahoo!, a popular search engine and portal, is founded by two Stanford Ph.D. students as a way to keep track of their personal interests on the Internet. Currently, Yahoo! has approximately 12,000 employees and more than 500 million unique visitors to its Web site.

1994 Amazon is founded and later begins business as an online bookstore. Amazon eventually expands to sell products of all types and facilitates the buying and selling of new and used goods. Today, Amazon has approximately 17,000 employees.

1995 Sun Microsystems launches Java, an object-oriented programming language that allows users to write one program for a variety of computer platforms.

1996 U.S. Robotics introduces the PalmPilot, an inexpensive user-friendly personal digital assistant (PDA).

1996 Microsoft releases Windows NT 4.0, an operating system for client-server networks.

1995 Microsoft releases Windows 95, a major upgrade to its Windows operating system. Windows 95 consists of more than 10,000,000 lines of computer instructions developed by 300 person-years of effort.

1997 Intel introduces the Pentium II processor with 7.5 million transistors. The new processor, which incorporates MMX technology, processes video, audio, and graphics data more efficiently and supports programs such as movie editing, gaming, and more.

1995 eBay, an online auction Web site, is founded. Providing an online venue for people to buy and sell goods, it quickly becomes the world's largest online marketplace as it approaches 100 million active users worldwide.

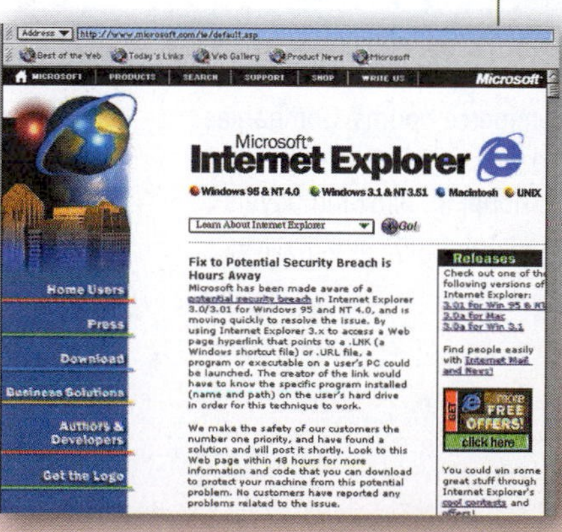

1997 Microsoft releases Internet Explorer 4.0 and seizes a key place in the Internet arena.

1998 Google files for incorporation and is now the most used search engine, capturing more than 60 percent of the market over other search engines.

1998 Apple Computer introduces the iMac, the next version of its popular Macintosh computer. The iMac wins customers with its futuristic design, see-through case, and easy setup.

1999 Microsoft introduces Office 2000, its premier productivity suite, offering new tools for users to create content and save it directly to a Web site without any file conversion or special steps.

1999 Open source software, such as the Linux operating system and the Apache Web server created by unpaid volunteers, begin to gain wide acceptance among computer users.

1999 Intel introduces the Pentium III processor. This processor succeeds the Pentium II and can process 3-D graphics more quickly. The Pentium III processor contains between 9.5 and 44 million transistors.

1998

1999

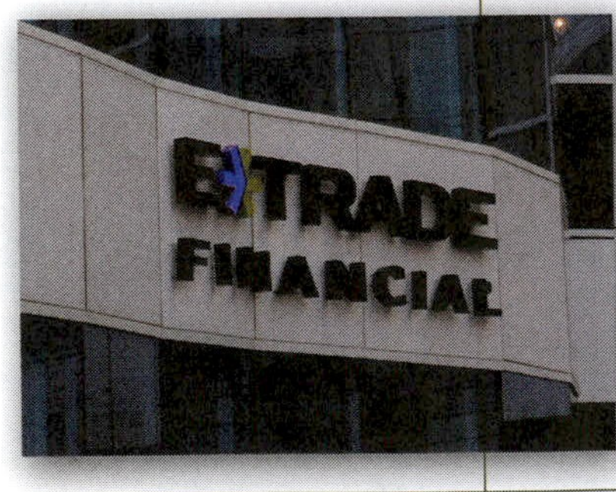

1998 E-commerce booms. Companies such as Amazon.com, Dell, and E*TRADE spur online shopping, allowing buyers to obtain a variety of goods and services.

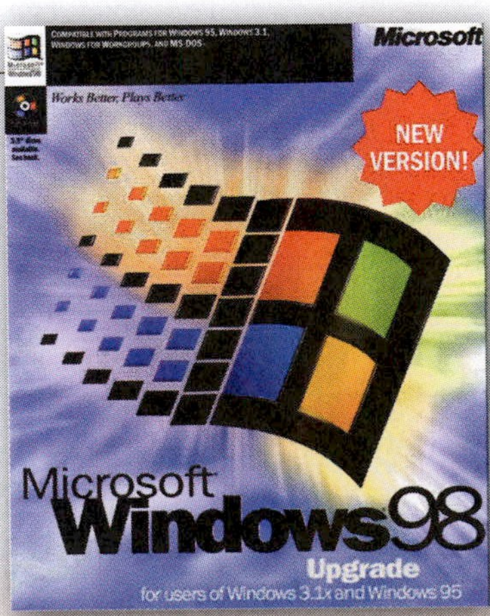

1998 Microsoft ships Windows 98, an upgrade to Windows 95. Windows 98 offers improved Internet access, better system performance, and support for a new generation of hardware and software.

1999 Governments and businesses frantically work to make their computers Y2K (Year 2000) compliant, spending more than $500 billion worldwide.

2000 Shawn Fanning, 19, and his company, Napster, turn the music industry upside down by developing software that allows computer users to swap music files with one another without going through a centralized file server.

2000 Microsoft ships Windows 2000 and Windows Me. Windows 2000 offers improved behind-the-scenes security and reliability.

2001 Microsoft releases major operating system updates with Windows XP for personal computers and servers. Windows XP is significantly more reliable than previous versions, features a 32-bit computing architecture, and offers a new look and feel.

2001 Intel unveils its Pentium 4 chip with clock speeds starting at 1.4 GHz. The Pentium 4 includes 42 million transistors.

2000

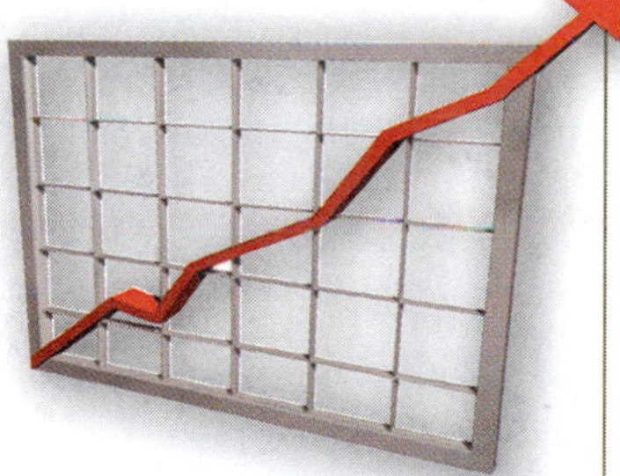

2000 E-commerce achieves mainstream acceptance. Annual e-commerce sales exceed $100 billion, and Internet advertising expenditures reach more than $5 billion.

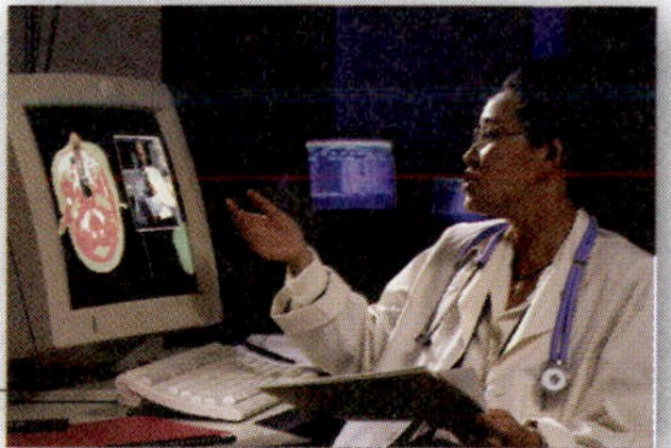

2000 Telemedicine uses satellite technology and video conferencing to broadcast consultations and to perform distant surgeries. Robots are used for complex and precise tasks.

2000 Dot-com companies (Internet based) go out of business at a record pace — nearly one per day — as financial investors withhold funding due to the companies' unprofitability.

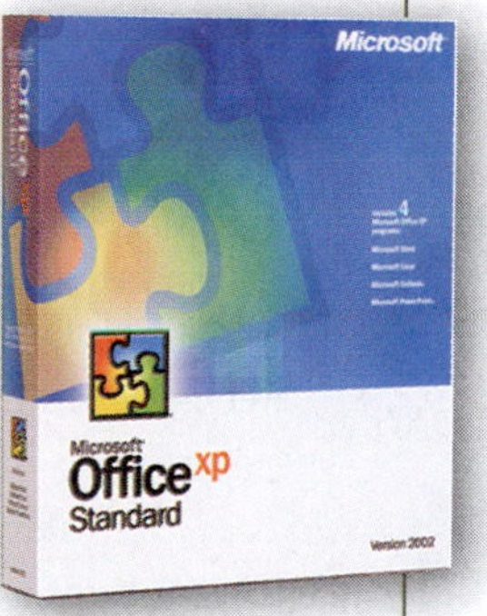

2001 Microsoft introduces Office XP, the next version of the world's leading suite of productivity software. Features include speech and handwriting recognition, smart tags, and task panes.

2001 Wikipedia, a free online encyclopedia, is introduced. Additional wikis begin to appear on the Internet, enabling people to share information in their areas of expertise. Although some might rely on wikis for research purposes, the content is not always verified for accuracy.

2002 After several years of negligible sales, the Tablet PC is reintroduced to meet the needs of a more targeted audience.

2003 Wireless computers and devices, such as keyboards, mouse devices, home networks, and wireless Internet access points become commonplace.

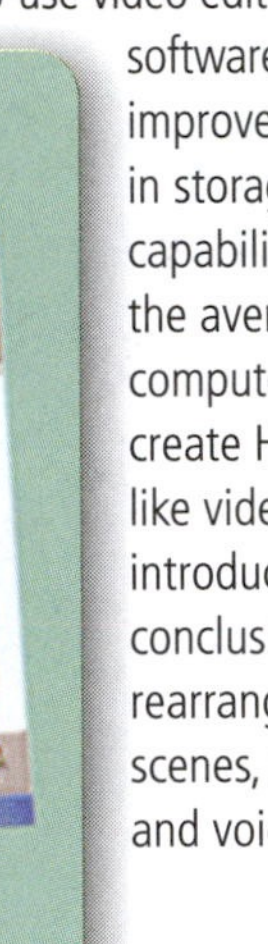

2002 Digital video cameras, DVD burners, easy-to-use video editing software, and improvements in storage capabilities allow the average computer user to create Hollywood-like videos with introductions, conclusions, rearranged scenes, music, and voice-over.

2003 Microsoft ships Office 2003, the latest version of its flagship Office suite. More than 400 million people in 175 nations and 70 languages are using a version of Office.

2002

2003

2002 Microsoft launches its .NET strategy, which is a new environment for developing and running software applications featuring ease of development of Web-based services.

2002 DVD burners begin to replace CD burners (CD-RW). DVDs can store up to eight times as much data as CDs. Uses include storing home movies, music, photos, and backups.

2002 Intel ships its revamped Pentium 4 chip with the 0.13 micron processor and Hyper-Threading (HT) Technology, operating at speeds of 3.06 GHz. This new development eventually will enable processors with a billion transistors to operate at 20 GHz.

2003 In an attempt to maintain their current business model of selling songs, the Recording Industry Association of America (RIAA) files more than 250 lawsuits against individual computer users who offer copyrighted music over peer-to-peer networks.

2003 MySpace, an online social network, is founded. MySpace allows users to share information, photos, and videos, as well as stay in touch with their friends and make new friends. MySpace eventually grows to nearly 200 million users, making it one of the more popular and successful online social networks.

2004 Companies such as RealNetworks, Microsoft, Sony, and Walmart stake out turf in the online music store business started by Apple Computer.

2004 USB flash drives become a cost-effective way to transport data and information from one computer to another.

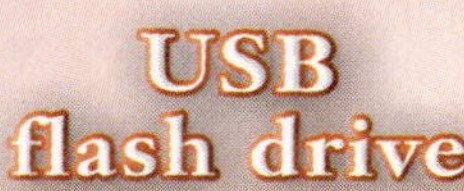

2004 Flat-panel LCD monitors overtake bulky CRT monitors as the popular choice of computer users.

2004 106 million, or 53 percent, of the 200 million online population in America accesses the Internet via broadband.

2004 Major retailers begin requiring suppliers to include radio frequency identification (RFID) tags or microchips with antennas, which can be as small as one-third of a millimeter across, in the goods they sell.

2004 The smart phone overtakes the PDA as the mobile device of choice.

2004 Facebook, an online social network originally available only to college students, is founded. Facebook eventually opens registration to all people and immediately grows to more than 110 million users with more than 10 billion photos, 30 million of which are uploaded daily.

facebook

2004

2004 Linux, the open source operating system, makes major inroads into the server market as a viable alternative to Microsoft Windows Server 2003, Sun's Solaris, and the UNIX operating systems.

2004 Sony unveils its PlayStation Portable (PSP). This handheld game console is the first to use optical discs.

2004 Mozilla releases its first version of the Firefox Web browser. Firefox provides innovative features that enhance the Web browsing experience for users, including tabbed browsing and a Search box. Firefox quickly gains popularity and takes market share away from Microsoft's Internet Explorer.

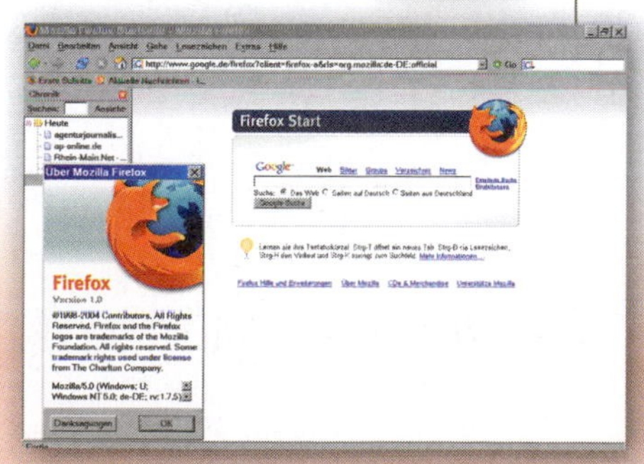

2004 Apple Computer introduces the sleek iMac G5. The new computer's display device contains the system unit.

2005 Apple releases the latest version of its popular pocket-sized iPod portable media player. First it played songs, then photos, then podcasts, and now, in addition, up to 150 hours of music videos and television shows on a 2.5" color display.

2005 YouTube, an online community for video sharing, is founded. YouTube includes content such as home videos, movie previews, and clips from television shows. In November 2006, Google acquires YouTube.

2005 Microsoft introduces Visual Studio 2005. The product includes Visual Basic, Visual C#, Visual J#, Visual C++, and SQL Server.

2005 Spam, spyware, phishing, pharming, spim, and spit take center stage, along with viruses, as major nuisances to the 801 million computer users worldwide.

2005

2005 Microsoft unveils Windows XP Media Center Edition 2005. This operating system focuses on delivering media content such as music, digital photos, movies, and television.

2005 Microsoft releases the Xbox 360, its latest game console. Features include the capability to play music, display photos, and network with computers and other Xbox gamers.

2005 Blogging and podcasting become mainstream methods for distributing information via the Web.

2006 Sony launches its PlayStation 3. New features include a Blu-ray Disc player, high-definition capabilities, and always-on online connectivity.

2006 Microsoft and Mozilla release new versions of their respective Web browsers. Microsoft's Internet Explorer 7 and Mozilla's Firefox 2 offer easier browsing through the use of tabs and allow search capabilities directly from the toolbar.

2006 Web 2.0, a term coined in 2004, becomes a household term with the increase in popularity of online social networks, wikis, and Web applications.

2006 Text, picture, and video messaging continue to increase as popular communications methods. In addition to people sending informal messages to each other, businesses and other institutions use messaging to allow people to vote in polls, receive targeted advertisements, and view news updates.

2006 Nintendo Wii is introduced and immediately becomes a leader in game consoles. The Wii is being used in revolutionary ways, such as training surgeons.

2006 Intel introduces its Core 2 Duo processor family. Boasting record-breaking performance while using less power, the family consists of five desktop computer processors and five mobile computer processors. The desktop processor includes 291 million transistors, yet uses 40 percent less power than the Pentium processor.

2006

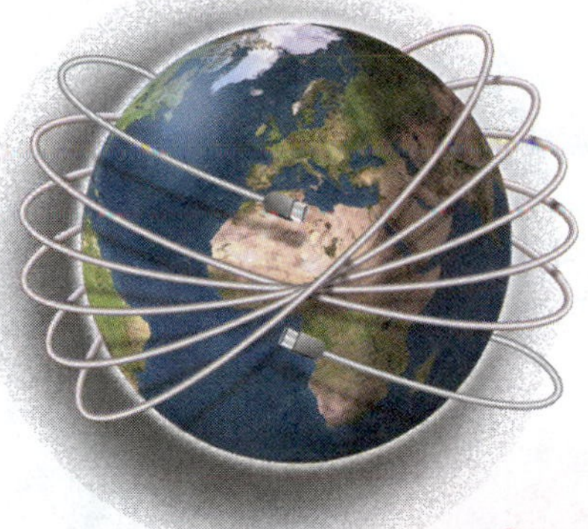

2006 IBM produces the fastest supercomputer, Blue Gene/L. It can perform approximately 28 trillion calculations in the time it takes you to blink your eye, or about one-tenth of a second.

2006 Nintendo releases the Nintendo DS Lite, a handheld game console with new features such as dual screens and improved graphics and sound.

2006 Apple begins selling Macintosh computers with Intel microprocessors.

2007 Intel introduces Core 2 Quad, a four-core processor made for dual-processor servers and desktop computers. The larger number of cores allows for more energy-efficient performance and optimizes battery performance in notebook computers.

2007 Video blogs, or vlogs, grow in popularity along with YouTube. Vlogs allow users to video their message instead of entering text via a regular blog. The growth in the popularity of vlogs is attributed to several factors, including the use of video portable media players. Podcasting also increases in popularity for the same reasons. A podcast is distinguished from other digital audio formats by its capability to be downloaded automatically.

2007 Apple introduces the iPhone and sells 270,000 phones in the first 2 days. iPhone uses iTouch technology that allows you to make a call simply by tapping a name or number in your address book. In addition, it stores and plays music like an iPod. Also, Apple sells its one billionth song on iTunes.

2007 VoIP (Voice over Internet Protocol) providers expand usage to include Wi-Fi phones. The phones enable high-quality service through a Wireless-G network and high-speed Internet connection.

2007 Apple releases its Mac OS X version 10.5 "Leopard" operating system, available in a desktop version and server version. The system includes a significantly revised desktop, with a semitransparent menu bar and an updated search tool that incorporates the same visual navigation interface as iTunes.

2007

2007 Blu-ray Discs increase in popularity, overcoming and replacing HD DVD in less than one year. A Blu-ray Disc can store approximately 9 hours of high-definition (HD) video on a 50 GB disc or approximately 23 hours of standard-definition (SD) video.

2007 Wi-Fi hotspots are popular in a variety of locations. People bring their computers to coffeehouses, fast food restaurants, or bookstores to access the Internet wirelessly, either free or for a small fee.

2007 Half of the world's population uses cell phones. More and more people are using a cell phone in lieu of a landline in their home.

2007 Microsoft releases Office 2007. New features include the most significant update to the user interface in more than a decade, including the introduction of the Ribbon, which replaces the toolbars in most of the programs, and the capability to save documents in XML and PDF formats.

2007 Microsoft ships the latest version of its widely used operating system, Windows Vista. Vista offers the Basic interface and the Aero interface, which offers several graphical features, including transparent windows. Internet Explorer 7 is included with Windows Vista.

2008 Microsoft introduces Windows Server 2008, the successor to Windows Server 2003.

2008 Bill Gates retires from Microsoft. He continues as chairman and advisor on key development projects.

2008 Dell offers a hybrid computer. Smaller than a desktop computer but larger than a notebook computer, these hybrid computers contain features comparable to their larger counterparts and can work more easily in a home entertainment environment.

2008 Netflix, an online movie rental company, and TiVo, a company manufacturing digital video recorders (DVRs), make Netflix movies and television episodes available on TiVo (DVRs).

2008

2008 WiMAX goes live! The advantage of this technology is the capability to access video, music, voice, and video calls wherever and whenever desired. Average download speeds are between 2 Mbps and 4 Mbps. By year's end, Sprint has approximately 100 million users on its network.

2008 Smart phones become smarter. Smart phones introduced this year include enhanced features such as touch screens with multi-touch technology, mobile TV, tactile feedback, improved graphics, GPS receivers, and better cameras.

2008 Computer manufacturers begin to offer solid state drives (SSDs) instead of hard disks, mostly in notebook computers. Although SSDs have a lower storage capacity, are more expensive, and slightly more susceptible to failure, they are significantly faster.

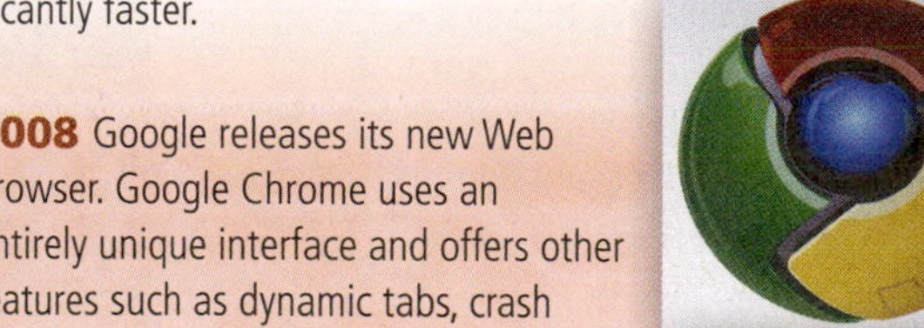

2008 Google releases its new Web browser. Google Chrome uses an entirely unique interface and offers other features such as dynamic tabs, crash control, and application shortcuts.

2008 Mozilla releases Firefox 3, the latest version of its Web browser. Firefox 3 offers greater security, a more user-friendly interface, and other improvements to enhance the Web browsing experience.

2009 In June 2009, federal law requires that all full-power television stations broadcast only in digital format. Analog television owners are required to purchase a converter box to view over-the-air digital programming.

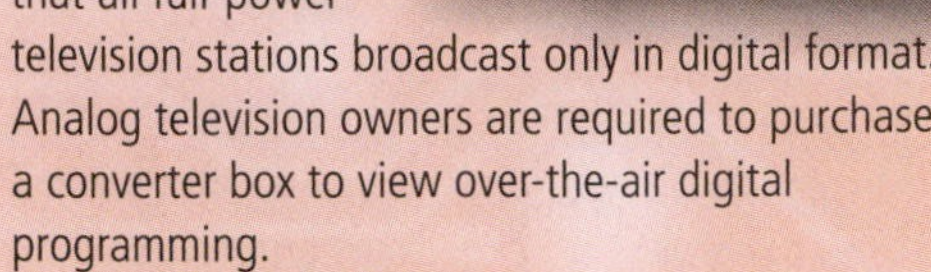

2009 Web applications continue to increase in popularity. Web applications make it easier to perform tasks such as word processing, photo editing, and tax preparation without installing software on your computer.

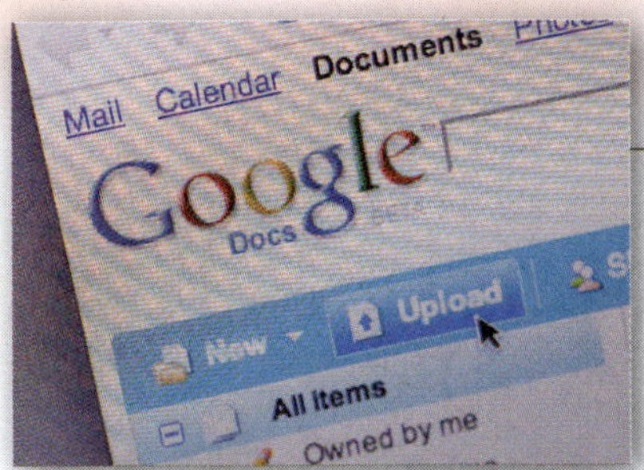

2010 Kinect for Xbox 360 changes the way people play video games. Game players now can interact with the game with a series of sensors, as well as a camera, tracking their movements in 3-D.

2009 Microsoft releases Internet Explorer 8, also known as IE8. IE8 offers new features such as InPrivate Browsing, Accelerators, and support for WebSlices.

2009 Microsoft releases the newest version of its Windows operating system, Windows 7. This version provides greater stability and security; a more flexible, user-friendly interface; and requires fewer computing resources to operate.

2009

2010

2009 Intel releases the Core i5 and Core i7 line of processors. These processors offer increased performance for some of the more demanding tasks. Intel also enhances its Core processor family by releasing multi-core processors, designed to increase the number of instructions that can be processed at a given time.

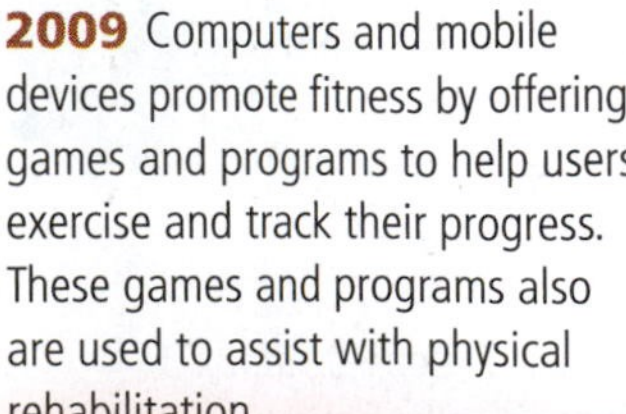

2010 AMD develops a 12-core processor, which contains two 6-core processors, each on an individual chip. Power consumption is similar to that of a 6-core processor but offers reduced clock speed.

2009 Computers and mobile devices promote fitness by offering games and programs to help users exercise and track their progress. These games and programs also are used to assist with physical rehabilitation.

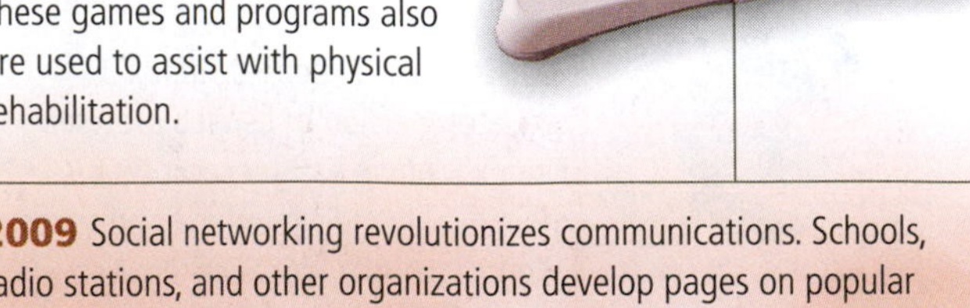

2009 Social networking revolutionizes communications. Schools, radio stations, and other organizations develop pages on popular online social networks, such as Facebook, creating closer connections with their stakeholders.

2010 Microsoft releases Office 2010, the latest version of its Office suite. This version is available in multiple editions and continues to help people work more efficiently. Office Web apps, available free to Windows Live users, offer online access to scaled-down versions of Word, PowerPoint, Excel, and OneNote.

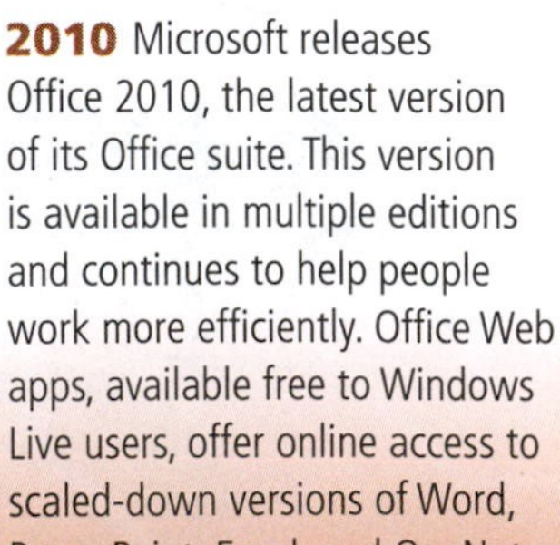

2010 Adobe releases the latest version of its design suite, Adobe CS5. This new suite has many performance and interface enhancements over previous versions and takes advantage of new technologies such as multi-touch.

2011 Individuals and enterprises increase their focus on green computing. Computer manufacturers not only sell more energy-efficient hardware, they also provide easy ways in which customers can recycle their old computers and devices.

2010 Hard disk capacity continues to increase at an exponential rate, with the largest hard disks storing more than 2.5 TB of data and information. Solid state storage also is becoming more popular, with storage capacities increasing and prices decreasing.

2010 Apple releases the iPad, a revolutionary mobile device with a 9.7-inch multi-touch screen. The iPad boasts up to 10 hours of battery life, connects wirelessly to the Internet, and is capable of running thousands of apps.

2011 Netbooks prove to be an attractive alternative to traditional notebook computers. Netbooks are smaller and lighter than traditional notebook computers, while providing nearly the same functionality.

2010

2011

2011 E-books and e-book readers explode in popularity. Many novels, textbooks, and other publications now are available digitally and can be read on an e-book reader, computer, or mobile device.

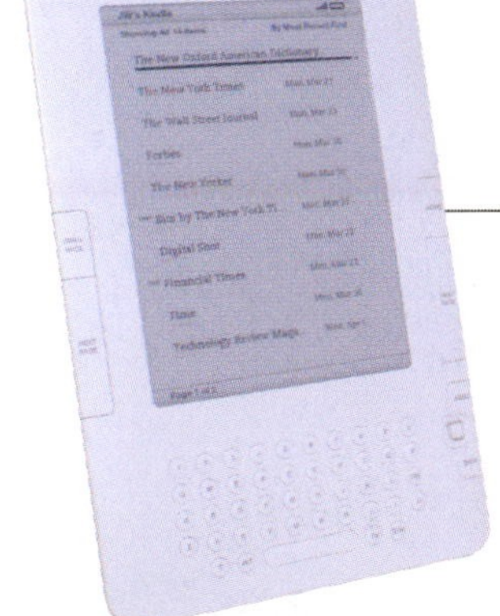

2011 Decreases in storage costs and increases in Internet connection speeds persuade more users to use cloud storage for their data. Cloud storage also provides users with the convenience of accessing their files from almost anywhere.

2011 A new generation of Web browsers is released to support HTML5, enabling Web pages to contain more vivid, dynamic content.

2011 More than 200 types of mobile devices are using Google Android, an operating system originally designed for mobile devices.

Chapter Two

The Internet and World Wide Web

Objectives

After completing this chapter, you will be able to:

1. Discuss the evolution of the Internet
2. Identify and briefly describe various broadband Internet connections and state differences between broadband Internet connections and dial-up connections
3. Describe the types of Internet access providers: Internet service providers, online service providers, wireless Internet service providers
4. Describe the purpose of an IP address and its relationship to a domain name
5. Explain the purpose of a Web browser and identify the components of a Web address
6. Describe how to use a search engine to search for information on the Web and differentiate between a search engine and a subject directory
7. Describe the types of Web sites: portal, news, informational, business/marketing, blog, wiki, online social network, educational, entertainment, advocacy, Web application, content aggregator, and personal
8. Explain how Web pages use graphics, animation, audio, video, virtual reality, and plug-ins
9. Identify and briefly describe the steps required for Web publishing
10. Describe the types of e-commerce: business-to-consumer, consumer-to-consumer, and business-to-business
11. Explain how e-mail, mailing lists, instant messaging, chat rooms, VoIP, newsgroups and message boards, and FTP work
12. Identify the rules of netiquette

The Internet

One of the major reasons business, home, and other users purchase computers is for Internet access. The Internet is a widely used research tool, providing society with access to global information and instant communications. Further, access to the Internet can occur anytime from a computer anywhere: at home, at work, at school, in a restaurant, on an airplane, and at a park.

The **Internet**, also called the *Net*, is a worldwide collection of networks that links millions of businesses, government agencies, educational institutions, and individuals. Each of the networks on the Internet provides resources that add to the abundance of goods, services, and information accessible via the Internet.

Today, more than one billion home and business users around the world access a variety of services on the Internet, some of which are shown in Figure 2-1. The World Wide Web, or simply the Web, and e-mail are two of the more widely used Internet services. Other services include chat rooms, instant messaging, and VoIP (Voice over Internet Protocol). To enhance your understanding of these Internet services, the chapter begins by discussing the history of the Internet and how the Internet works and then explains each of these services.

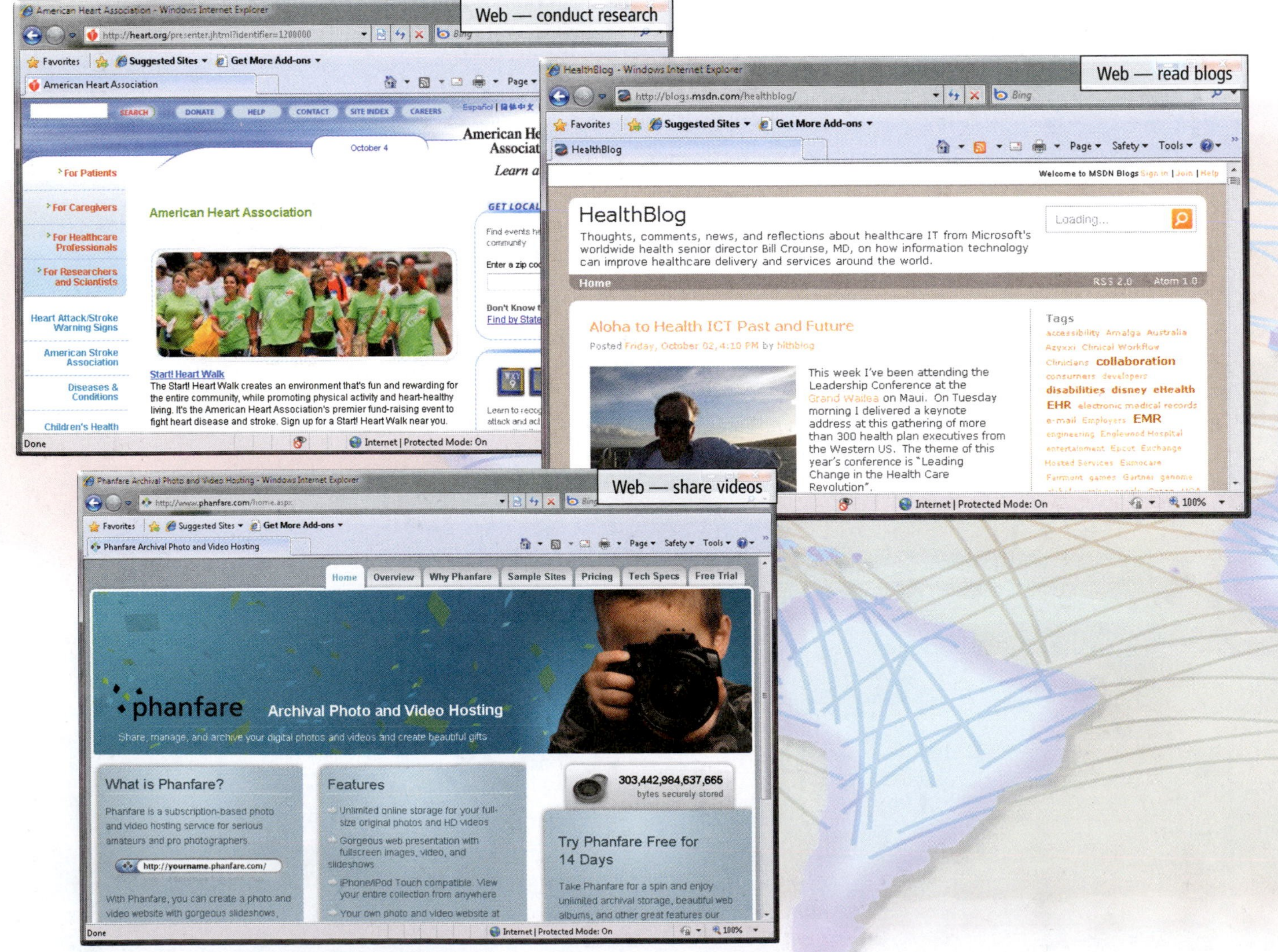

Figure 2-1 People around the world use a variety of Internet services in daily activities. Internet services allow home and business users to access the Web for activities such as conducting research, reading blogs, or sharing videos; to send e-mail messages; or to converse with others using chat rooms, instant messaging, or VoIP.

Evolution of the Internet

The Internet has its roots in a networking project started by the Pentagon's Advanced Research Projects Agency (*ARPA*), an agency of the U.S. Department of Defense. ARPA's goal was to build a network that (1) allowed scientists at different physical locations to share information and work together on military and scientific projects and (2) could function even if part of the network were disabled or destroyed by a disaster such as a nuclear attack. That network, called *ARPANET*, became functional in September 1969, linking scientific and academic researchers across the United States.

The original ARPANET consisted of four main computers, one each located at the University of California at Los Angeles, the University of California at Santa Barbara, the Stanford Research Institute, and the University of Utah. Each of these computers served as a host on the network. A *host*, more commonly known today as a server, is any computer that provides services and connections to other computers on a network. Hosts often use high-speed communications to transfer data and messages over a network.

As researchers and others realized the great benefit of using ARPANET to share data and information, ARPANET underwent phenomenal growth. By 1984, ARPANET had more than 1,000 individual computers linked as hosts. Today, more than 550 million hosts connect to the Internet.

Some organizations connected entire networks to ARPANET to take advantage of its high-speed communications. In 1986, the National Science Foundation (NSF) connected its huge network of five supercomputer centers, called *NSFnet*, to ARPANET. This configuration of complex networks and hosts became known as the Internet.

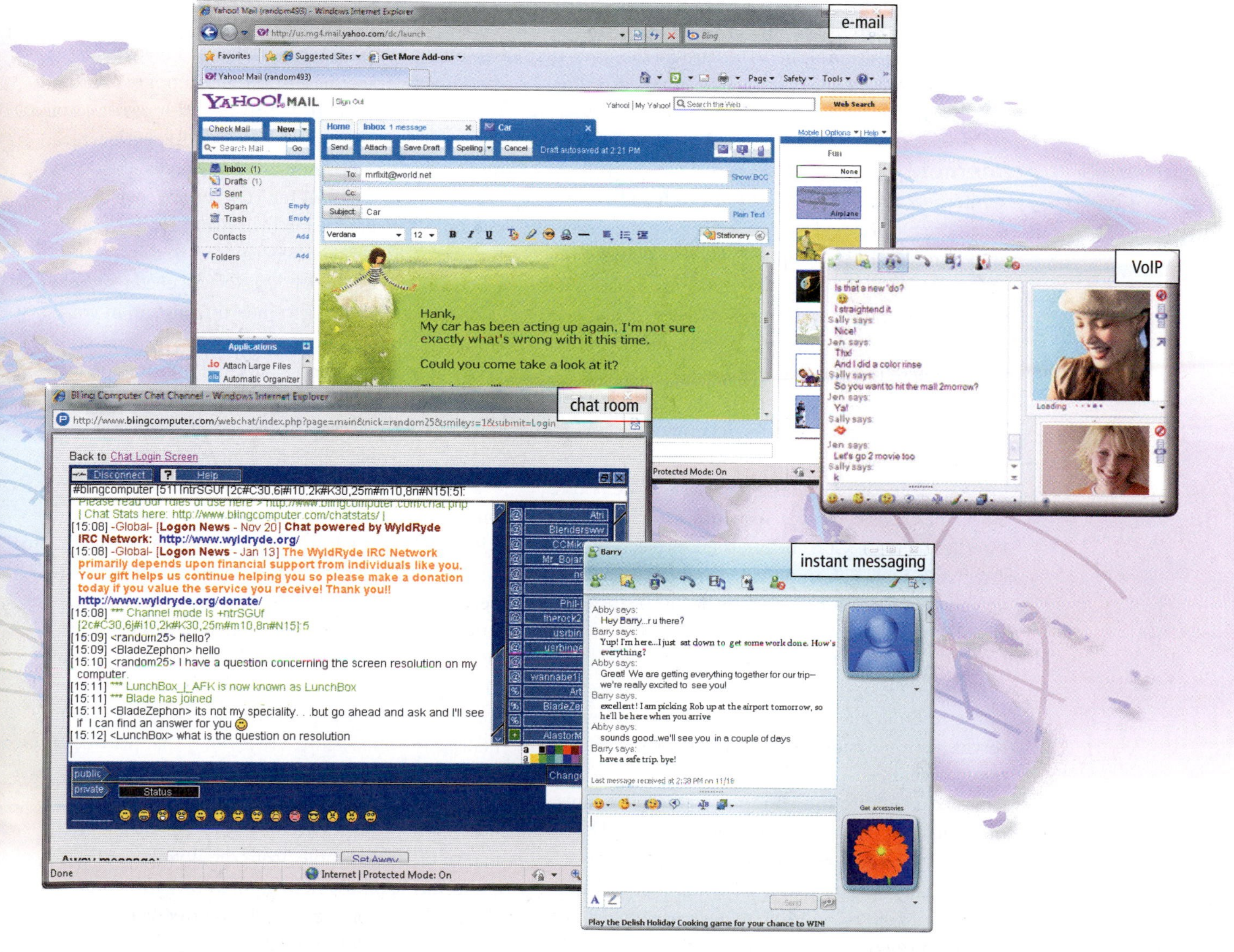

Until 1995, NSFnet handled the bulk of the communications activity, or **traffic**, on the Internet. In 1995, NSFnet terminated its network on the Internet and resumed its status as a research network.

Today, the Internet consists of many local, regional, national, and international networks. Numerous corporations, commercial firms, and other companies such as IBM provide networks to handle Internet traffic. Both public and private organizations own networks on the Internet. These networks, along with telephone companies such as Verizon and AT&T, cable and satellite companies, and the government, all contribute toward the internal structure of the Internet.

Each organization on the Internet is responsible only for maintaining its own network. No single person, company, institution, or government agency controls or owns the Internet. The World Wide Web Consortium (*W3C*), however, oversees research and sets standards and guidelines for many areas of the Internet. The mission of the W3C is to contribute to the growth of the Web. More than 350 organizations from around the world are members of the W3C, advising, defining standards, and addressing other issues.

W3C

For more information, visit the Computer Concepts CourseMate Web site at www.cengagebrain.com, navigate to the Chapter 2 Web Link resource for this book, and then click W3C.

Internet2

Internet2 is a not-for-profit research and development project that connects more than 200 universities and 115 companies via a high-speed private network. Founded in 1996, the goal of Internet2 is to develop and test advanced network technologies that will benefit Internet users in the short-term future. These technologies require an extremely high-speed network that exceeds the capabilities of today's Internet and networks. Examples of previous Internet2 projects that are now mainstream include telemedicine, digital libraries (online books, magazines, music, movies, speeches, etc.), and faster Internet services. Current Internet2 projects include interactive high-definition video and enhanced detection and resolution of network problems.

Connecting to the Internet

Many home and small business users connect to the Internet via high-speed *broadband* Internet service. With broadband Internet service, your computer or mobile device usually is connected to the Internet the entire time it is powered on. Examples of broadband Internet service include cable, DSL, fiber, radio signals, and satellite.

- *Cable Internet service* provides high-speed Internet access through the cable television network via a cable modem.
- *DSL* (digital subscriber line) provides high-speed Internet connections using regular copper telephone lines.
- *Fiber to the Premises* (*FTTP*) uses fiber-optic cable to provide high-speed Internet access to home and business users.
- *Fixed wireless* provides high-speed Internet connections using a dish-shaped antenna on your house or business to communicate with a tower location via radio signals.
- A *cellular radio network* offers high-speed Internet connections to devices with built-in compatible technology or computers with wireless modems.
- A **Wi-Fi** (wireless fidelity) network uses radio signals to provide high-speed Internet connections to compatible or properly equipped wireless computers and devices.
- *Satellite Internet service* provides high-speed Internet connections via satellite to a satellite dish that communicates with a satellite modem.

Employees and students typically connect their computers to the Internet through a business or school network. The business or school network connects to a high-speed broadband Internet service.

Many home users set up a Wi-Fi network, which sends signals to a communications device that is connected to a high-speed Internet service such as cable or DSL. Instead of using broadband Internet service, however, some home users connect to the Internet via dial-up access, which is a slower-speed technology. *Dial-up access* takes place when the modem in your computer connects to the Internet via a standard telephone line that transmits data and information using an analog (continuous wave pattern) signal. Users may opt for dial-up access because of its lower price or because broadband access is not available in their area.

Mobile users access the Internet using a variety of Internet services. Most hotels and airports provide wired or wireless Internet connections as a service to travelers. Wireless Internet services, such as Wi-Fi networks, allow mobile users to connect easily to the Internet with notebook computers, smart phones, and other mobile devices while away from a telephone, cable, or other wired connection. Many public locations, such as airports, hotels, schools, shopping malls, and coffee shops, are *hot spots* that provide Wi-Fi Internet connections to users with mobile computers or devices. At public locations, you may be required to agree to terms of service, obtain a password (for example, from the hotel's front desk), or perform some other action in order to connect to the Internet. Some cities provide free Wi-Fi Internet connections to all residents.

? FAQ 2-1

How popular is broadband?

According to a study performed by Pew Internet & American Life Project, 63 percent of American adults have broadband Internet connections at home. Adoption of broadband connections increases during good economic times, while some may hesitate to make the switch during an economic downturn. It is believed that once the price of a broadband connection decreases, and broadband is available in more rural areas, its popularity will increase further.

For more information, visit the Computer Concepts CourseMate Web site at www.cengagebrain.com, navigate to the Chapter 2 FAQ resource for this book, and then click Broadband.

Access Providers

An **access provider** is a business that provides individuals and organizations access to the Internet free or for a fee. For example, some Wi-Fi networks provide free access while others charge a per use fee. Other access providers often charge a fixed amount for an Internet connection, offering faster speeds or more services for higher rates. Typical monthly rates range from about $5 to $24 per month for dial-up, $13 to $70 for DSL, $20 to $75 for cable, $40 to $150 for FTTP, $30 to $80 for fixed wireless, $60 to $80 for cellular networks, and $50 to $120 for satellite. Many Internet access providers offer services such as news, weather, financial data, games, travel guides, e-mail, photo communities, and online storage to hold digital photos and other files. (A *file* is a named unit of storage.)

Access providers are categorized as regional or national ISPs, online service providers, and wireless Internet service providers (Figure 2-2).

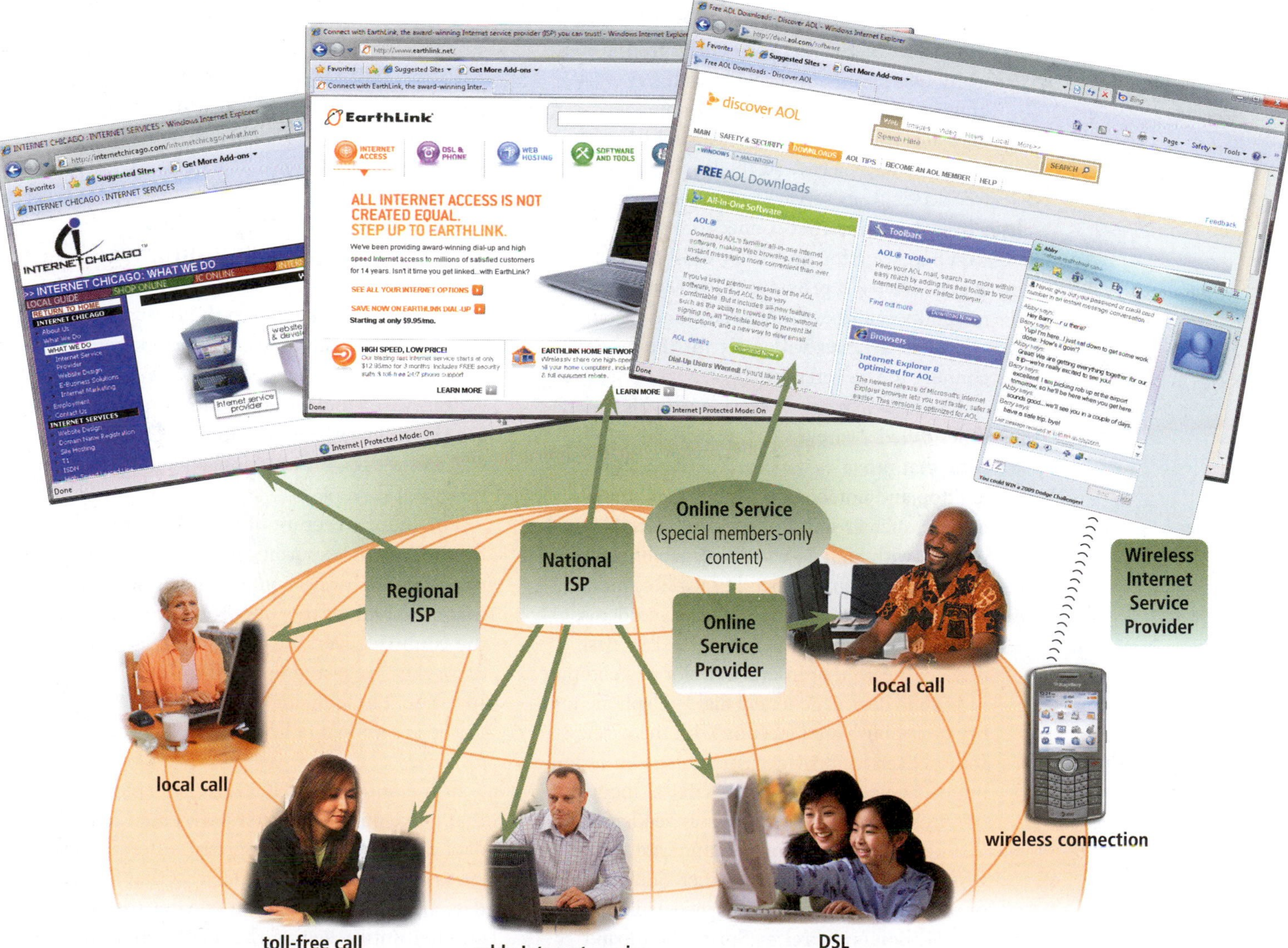

Figure 2-2 Common ways to access the Internet are through a regional or national Internet service provider, an online service provider, or a wireless Internet service provider.

An **ISP (Internet service provider)** is a regional or national access provider. A *regional ISP* usually provides Internet access to a specific geographic area. A *national ISP* is a business that provides Internet access in cities and towns nationwide. For dial-up access, some national ISPs provide both local and toll-free telephone numbers. Due to their larger size, national ISPs usually offer more services and have a larger technical support staff than regional ISPs. Examples of national ISPs are AT&T and EarthLink.

In addition to providing Internet access, an **online service provider (OSP)** also has many members-only features such as instant messaging or their own customized version of a Web browser. The two more popular OSPs are AOL (America Online) and MSN (Microsoft Network). AOL differs from many OSPs in that it provides gateway functionality to the Internet, meaning it regulates the Internet services to which members have access. AOL also provides free access to its services to any user with a broadband Internet connection.

When selecting an ISP or OSP for dial-up access, ensure it provides at least one local telephone number. Otherwise, long-distance telephone charges will apply for the time you connect to the Internet.

A **wireless Internet service provider**, sometimes called a wireless data provider, is a company that provides wireless Internet access to desktop and notebook computers and mobile devices, such as smart phones and portable media players, with built-in wireless capability (such as Wi-Fi) or to computers using wireless modems or wireless access devices. Wireless modems, which usually are in the form of a USB flash drive or a card that inserts in a slot in a computer or mobile device, generally dial a telephone number to establish a connection with the wireless Internet service provider. An antenna on or built into the computer or device, wireless modem, or wireless access device typically sends signals through the airwaves to communicate with a wireless Internet service provider. Some examples of wireless Internet service providers include AT&T, Boingo Wireless, Sprint Broadband Direct, T-Mobile, and Verizon Wireless.

Wireless Modems

For more information, visit the Computer Concepts CourseMate Web site at www.cengagebrain.com, navigate to the Chapter 2 Web Link resource for this book, and then click Wireless Modems.

? FAQ 2-2

What types of Web sites do mobile Internet users visit?

More than 87 million individuals subscribe to a wireless Internet service provider. Mobile Internet users most frequently visit weather, entertainment, and e-mail Web sites. The chart below illustrates various types of Web sites and their associated increase in traffic resulting from mobile Internet users.

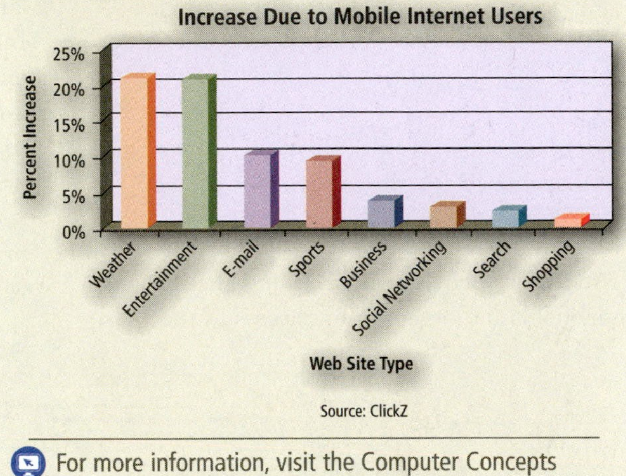

For more information, visit the Computer Concepts CourseMate Web site at www.cengagebrain.com, navigate to the Chapter 2 FAQ resource for this book, and then click Mobile Internet.

How Data and Information Travel the Internet

Computers connected to the Internet work together to transfer data and information around the world using servers and clients and various wired and wireless transmission media. On the Internet, your computer is a client that can access data, information, and services on a variety of servers.

The inner structure of the Internet works much like a transportation system. Just as interstate highways connect major cities and carry the bulk of the automotive traffic across the country, several main transmission media carry the heaviest amount of traffic on the Internet. These major carriers of network traffic are known collectively as the *Internet backbone*.

In the United States, the transmission media that make up the Internet backbone exchange data and information at several different major cities across the country. That is, they transfer data and information from one network to another until reaching the final destination (Figure 2-3).

How a Home User's Data and Information Might Travel the Internet Using a Cable Modem Connection

Step 1
You initiate an action to request data or information from the Internet. For example, you request to display a Web page on your computer screen.
Step 2
A cable modem transfers the computer's digital signals to the cable television line in your house.
Step 3
Your request (digital signals) travels through cable television lines to a central cable system, which is shared by up to 500 homes in a neighborhood.
Step 4
The central cable system sends your request over high-speed fiber-optic lines to the cable operator, who often also is the ISP.
Step 5
The ISP routes your request through the Internet backbone to the destination server (in this example, the server that contains the requested Web site).
Step 6
The server retrieves the requested Web page and sends it back through the Internet backbone to your computer.
Last Chance Buys
While supplies last!
Dell Mini 10
$299
SPECIALBUYS
e Values

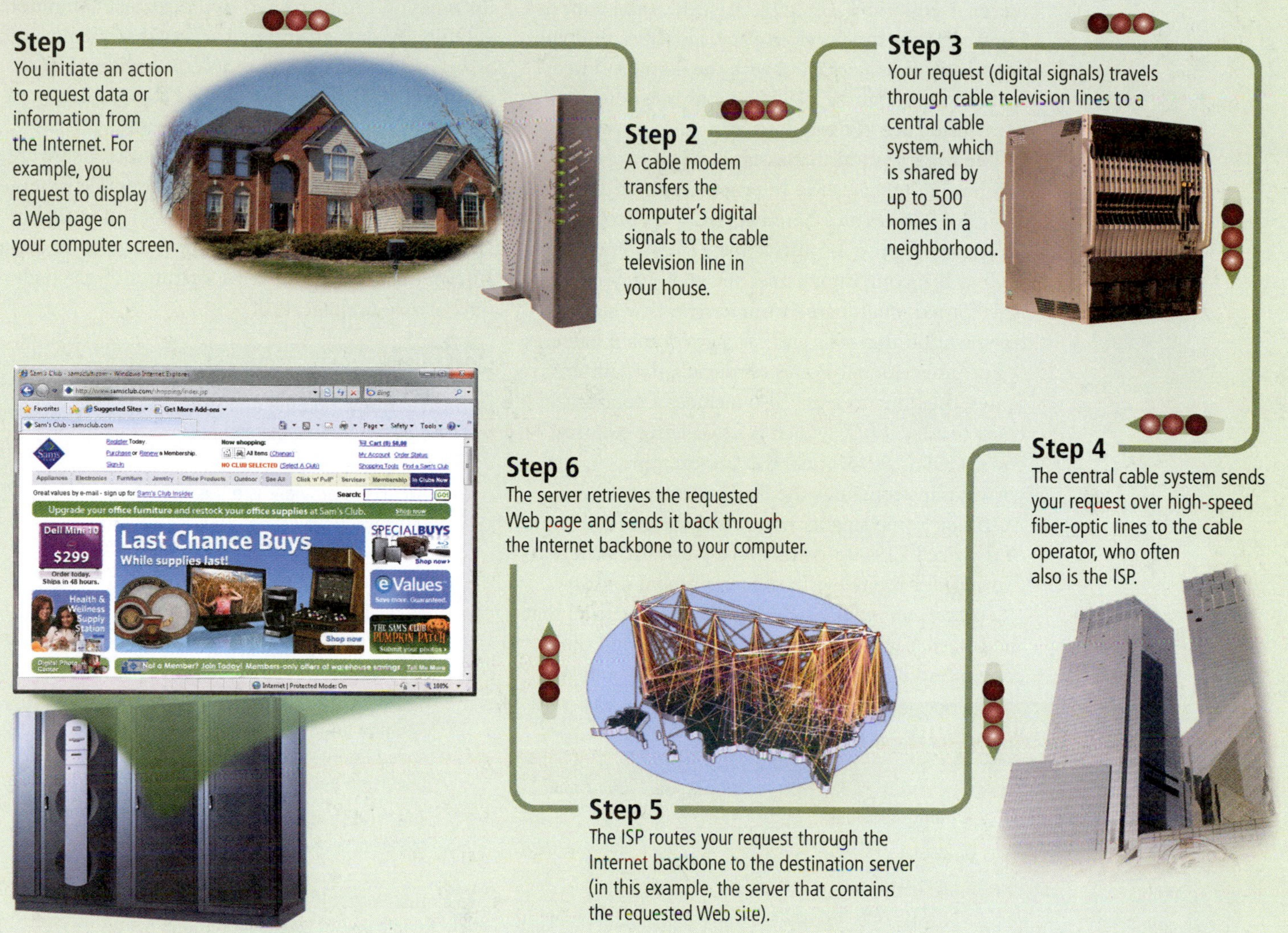

Figure 2-3 This figure shows how a home user's data and information might travel the Internet using a cable modem connection.

Internet Addresses

The Internet relies on an addressing system much like the postal service to send data and information to a computer at a specific destination. An **IP address**, short for Internet Protocol address, is a number that uniquely identifies each computer or device connected to the Internet. The IP address usually consists of four groups of numbers, each separated by a period. The number in each group is between 0 and 255. For example, the numbers 72.14.207.99 are an IP address. In general, the first portion of each IP address identifies the network and the last portion identifies the specific computer.

These all-numeric IP addresses are difficult to remember and use. Thus, the Internet supports the use of a text name that represents one or more IP addresses. A **domain name** is the text version of an IP address. Figure 2-4 shows an IP address and its associated domain name. As with an IP address, the components of a domain name are separated by periods.

The text in the domain name up to the first period identifies the type of Internet server. In Figure 2-4, for example, the www indicates a Web server.

IP address → 72.14.207.99
Domain name → www.google.com
top-level domain

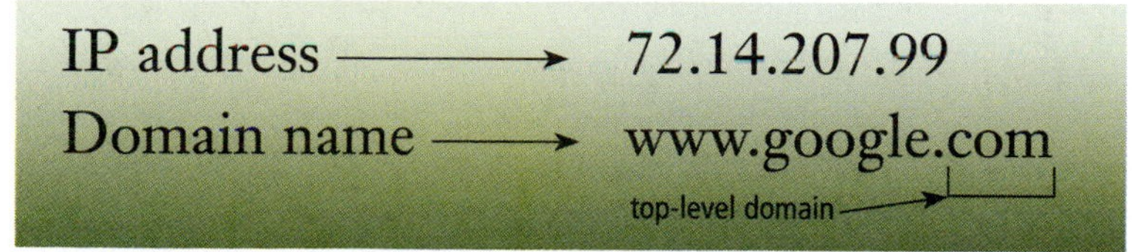

Figure 2-4 The IP address and domain name for the Google Web site.

Every domain name contains a *top-level domain* (*TLD*), which is the last section of the domain name. A generic TLD (*gTLD*), such as the com in Figure 2-4 on the previous page, identifies the type of organization associated with the domain. The Internet server and gTLD portions of a domain name often are not required.

The organization that assigns and controls top-level domains is the Internet Corporation for Assigned Names and Numbers (*ICANN* pronounced EYE-can). Figure 2-5 lists some gTLDs. For TLDs such as biz, com, info, name, net, and org, you register for a domain name from a *registrar*, which is an organization that sells and manages domain names.

For international Web sites outside the United States, the domain name also includes a country code TLD (*ccTLD*), which is a two-letter country code, such as au for Australia. For example, www.philips.com.au is the domain name for Philips Australia. Some smaller countries have granted use of their ccTLDs for commercial purposes, such as tv (Tuvalu) for the television/entertainment industry.

The *domain name system* (*DNS*) is the method that the Internet uses to store domain names and their corresponding IP addresses. When you specify a domain name, a **DNS server** translates the domain name to its associated IP address so that data and information can be routed to the correct computer. A DNS server is an Internet server that usually is associated with an Internet access provider. For a more technical discussion about DNS servers, read the High-Tech Talk article on page 382.

The growth of the Internet has led to a shortage of IP addresses. Thus, a new IP addressing scheme, called *IPv6*, may increase the number of available IP addresses. For a more technical discussion about Internet addresses and IPv6, read the High-Tech Talk article on page 110.

Examples of Generic Top-Level Domains

Generic TLD	Intended Purpose
aero	Aviation community members
biz	Businesses of all sizes
cat	Catalan cultural community
com	Commercial organizations, businesses, and companies
coop	Business cooperatives such as credit unions and rural electric co-ops
edu	Educational institutions
gov	Government agencies
info	Business organizations or individuals providing general information
jobs	Employment or human resource businesses
mil	Military organizations
mobi	Delivery and management of mobile Internet services
museum	Accredited museums
name	Individuals or families
net	Network providers or commercial companies
org	Nonprofit organizations
pro	Certified professionals such as doctors, lawyers, and accountants
tel	Internet communications
travel	Travel industry

Figure 2-5 In addition to the generic TLDs listed above, ICANN continually evaluates proposals for new TLDs.

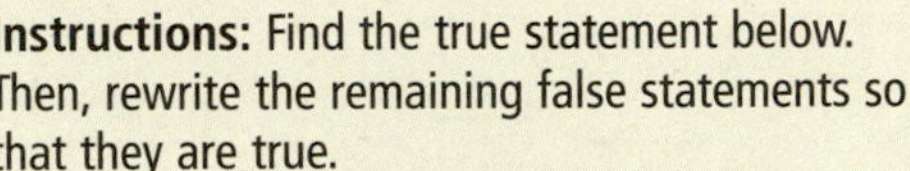

Instructions: Find the true statement below. Then, rewrite the remaining false statements so that they are true.

1. An access provider is a business that provides individuals and organizations access to the Internet free or for a fee.
2. A wireless Internet service provider is a number that uniquely identifies each computer or device connected to the Internet.
3. An IP address, such as www.google.com, is the text version of a domain name.
4. Satellite Internet service provides high-speed Internet access through the cable television network via a cable modem.
5. The World Wide Web Consortium (W3C) oversees research and owns the Internet.

Quiz Yourself Online: To further check your knowledge of pages 74 through 80, visit the Computer Concepts CourseMate Web site at www.cengagebrain.com, navigate to the Chapter 2 Quiz Yourself resource for this book, and then click Objectives 1 – 4.

The World Wide Web

Although many people use the terms World Wide Web and Internet interchangeably, the World Wide Web actually is a service of the Internet. While the Internet was developed in the late 1960s, the World Wide Web emerged in the early 1990s. Since then, it has grown phenomenally to become one of the more widely used Internet services.

The **World Wide Web** (*WWW*), or **Web**, consists of a worldwide collection of electronic documents. Each electronic document on the Web is called a **Web page**, which can contain text, graphics, animation, audio, and video. Additionally, Web pages usually have built-in connections to other documents.

Some Web pages are static (fixed); others are dynamic (changing). Visitors to a *static Web page* all see the same content. With a *dynamic Web page*, by contrast, visitors can customize some or all of the viewed content such as desired stock quotes, weather for a region, or ticket availability for flights.

A **Web site** is a collection of related Web pages and associated items, such as documents and pictures, stored on a Web server. A **Web server** is a computer that delivers requested Web pages to your computer. The same Web server can store multiple Web sites. Some industry experts use the term **Web 2.0** to refer to Web sites that provide a means for users to share personal information (such as social networking Web sites), allow users to modify Web site content (such as wikis, which are discussed later in this chapter), and have application software built into the site for visitors to use (such as e-mail and word processing programs). Read Looking Ahead 2-1 for a look at Web 3.0.

LOOKING AHEAD 2-1

Web 3.0 to Reinvent the Virtual World

The Web has evolved through versions 1.0 and 2.0, and work is underway to develop *Web 3.0*, also known as the *Semantic Web*. Some researchers predict that this next generation of the Web will perform practically any task imaginable. For example, your computer will be able to scan a Web page much as you do to look for specific useful information. If you need the location of the nearest eye doctor and the time when your brother's flight from Chicago actually will land, Web 3.0 first will provide those facts and then search your calendar, checking to see if your schedule allows time for the doctor's appointment before picking up your brother at the airport. In essence, the Web will become one huge searchable database, and automated agents of every type will retrieve the data we need to live productive lives.

W3C®

For more information, visit the Computer Concepts CourseMate Web site at www.cengagebrain.com, navigate to the Chapter 2 Looking Ahead resource for this book, and then click Web 3.0.

Browsing the Web

A **Web browser**, or **browser**, is application software that allows users to access and view Web pages or access Web 2.0 programs. To browse the Web, you need a computer or mobile device that is connected to the Internet and has a Web browser. The more widely used Web browsers for personal computers are Internet Explorer, Firefox, Opera, Safari, and Google Chrome.

With an Internet connection established, you start a Web browser. The browser retrieves and displays a starting Web page, sometimes called the browser's home page (Figure 2-6). The initial home

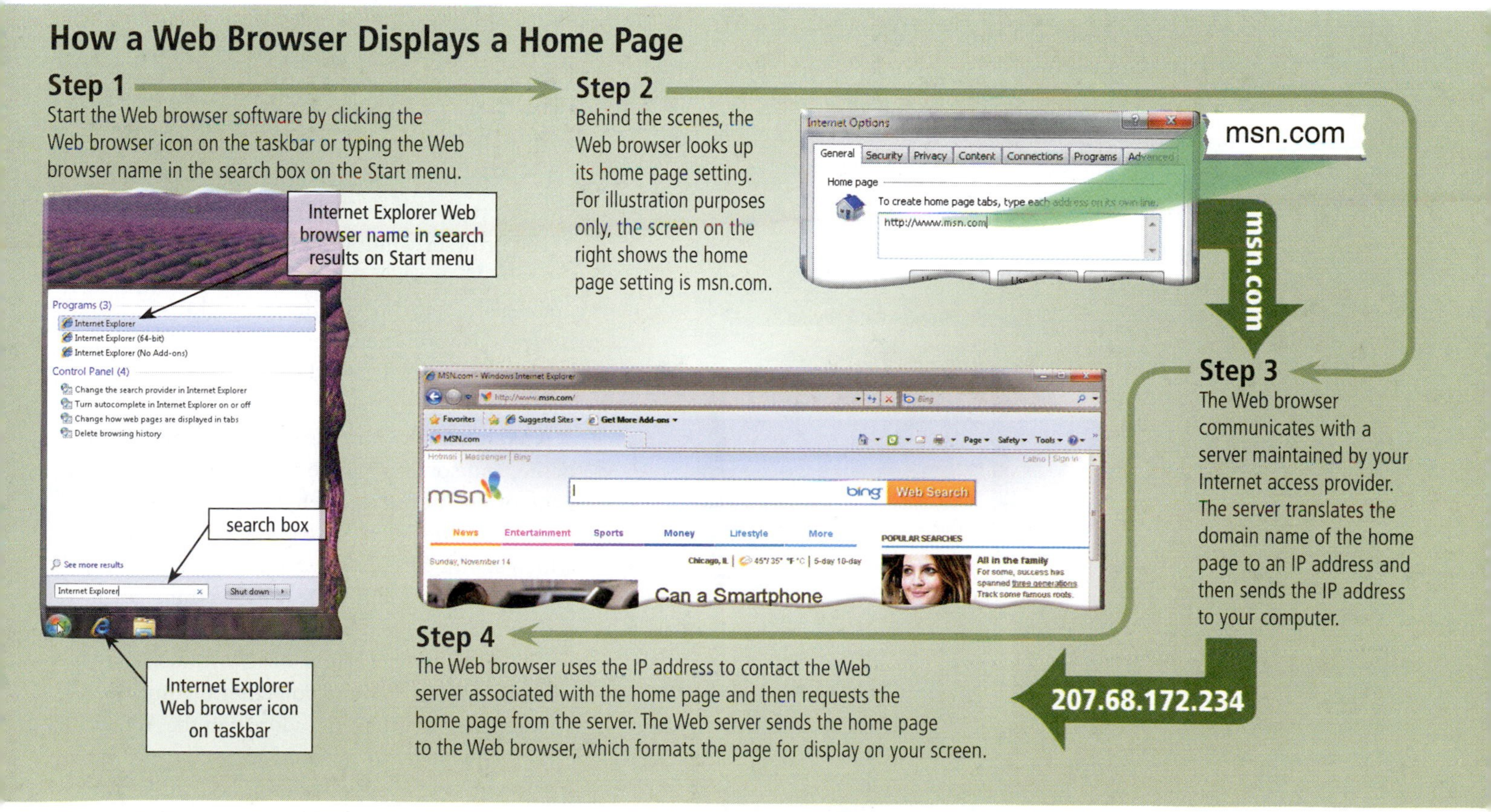

How a Web Browser Displays a Home Page

Step 1
Start the Web browser software by clicking the Web browser icon on the taskbar or typing the Web browser name in the search box on the Start menu.

Internet Explorer Web browser name in search results on Start menu

search box

Internet Explorer Web browser icon on taskbar

Step 2
Behind the scenes, the Web browser looks up its home page setting. For illustration purposes only, the screen on the right shows the home page setting is msn.com.

msn.com

Step 3
The Web browser communicates with a server maintained by your Internet access provider. The server translates the domain name of the home page to an IP address and then sends the IP address to your computer.

207.68.172.234

Step 4
The Web browser uses the IP address to contact the Web server associated with the home page and then requests the home page from the server. The Web server sends the home page to the Web browser, which formats the page for display on your screen.

Figure 2-6 This figure shows how a Web browser displays a home page.

page that is displayed is one selected by your Web browser. You can change your browser's home page at anytime.

Another use of the term, **home page**, refers to the first page that a Web site displays. Similar to a book cover or a table of contents for a Web site, the home page provides information about the Web site's purpose and content. Many Web sites, such as iGoogle, allow you to personalize the home page so that it contains areas of interest to you. The home page usually contains links to other documents, Web pages, or Web sites. A **link**, short for *hyperlink*, is a built-in connection to another related Web page or part of a Web page.

Internet-enabled mobile devices such as smart phones use a special type of browser, called a *microbrowser*, which is designed for their small screens and limited computing power. Many Web sites design Web pages specifically for display on a microbrowser (Figure 2-7).

For a computer or mobile device to display a Web page, the page must be downloaded. **Downloading** is the process of a computer or device receiving information, such as a Web page, from a server on the Internet. While a browser downloads a Web page, it typically displays an animated logo or icon in the browser window. The animation stops when the download is complete. The time required to download a Web page varies depending on the speed of your Internet connection and the amount of graphics involved.

iPhone

For more information, visit the Computer Concepts CourseMate Web site at www.cengagebrain.com, navigate to the Chapter 2 Web Link resource for this book, and then click iPhone.

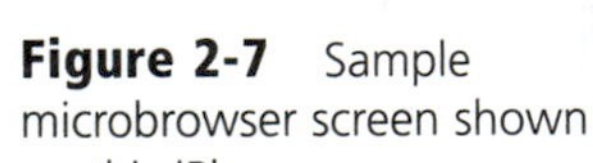

Figure 2-7 Sample microbrowser screen shown on this iPhone.

FAQ 2-3

Which Web browser currently has the highest market share?

Windows Internet Explorer (IE) currently is the most popular browser, with approximately 68 percent of the market share. The chart below illustrates the market share of the more popular Web browsers.

Market Share

4% 6% 22% 68%

Internet Explorer Firefox Safari Other

Source: Market Share by Net Applications

For more information, visit the Computer Concepts CourseMate Web site at www.cengagebrain.com, navigate to the Chapter 2 FAQ resource for this book, and then click Browser Market Share.

Web Addresses

A Web page has a unique address, called a **URL** (*Uniform Resource Locator*) or **Web address**. For example, the home page for the United States National Park Service Web site has http://www.nps.gov as its Web address. A Web browser retrieves a Web page using its Web address.

If you know the Web address of a Web page, you can type it in the Address bar at the top of the browser window. For example, if you type the Web address http://www.nps.gov/grsm/planyourvisit/wildlifeviewing.htm in the Address bar and then press the ENTER key, the browser downloads and displays the Web page shown in Figure 2-8.

A Web address consists of a protocol, domain name, and sometimes the path to a specific Web page or location on a Web page. Many Web page addresses begin with http://. The *http*, which stands for *Hypertext Transfer Protocol*, is a set of rules that defines how pages transfer on the Internet.

To help minimize errors, many browsers and Web sites do not require you enter the http:// and www portions of the Web address in the Address bar. If you enter an incorrect Web address, the browser may display a list of similar addresses or related Web sites from which you can select.

When you enter the Web address, http://www.nps.gov/grsm/planyourvisit/wildlifeviewing.htm in the Web browser, it sends a request to the Web server that contains the nps.gov Web site. The server then retrieves the Web page named wildlifeviewing.htm that is located in the grsm/planyourvisit path and delivers it to your browser, which then displays the Web page on the screen.

To save time, many users create bookmarks for their frequently visited Web pages. A *bookmark*, or *favorite*, is a saved Web address that you access by clicking its name in a list. That is, instead of entering a Web address to display a Web page, you can click a previously saved bookmark.

When you enter a Web address in a browser, you request, or *pull*, information from a Web server. Some Web servers also can *push* content to your computer at regular intervals or whenever updates are made to the site. For example, some Web servers provide the capability of displaying current sporting event scores or weather reports on your computer screen.

For information about useful Web sites and their associated Web addresses, read the Making Use of the Web feature that follows this chapter.

Navigating Web Pages

Most Web pages contain hypertext or hypermedia links. *Hypertext* refers to links in text-based documents, whereas *hypermedia* combines text-based links with graphic, audio, and video links. Links allow you to obtain information in a nonlinear way. That is, instead of accessing topics in a specified order, you move directly to a topic of interest. Branching from one related topic to another in a nonlinear fashion is what makes links so powerful. Some people use the phrase, **surfing the Web**, to refer to the activity of using links to explore the Web.

protocol
domain name
path
Web page name

http://www.nps.gov/grsm/planyourvisit/wildlifeviewing.htm

Address bar

Web page that is displayed after the Web address is entered

Figure 2-8 After entering http://www.nps.gov/grsm/planyourvisit/wildlifeviewing.htm as the Web address in the Address bar, this Web page at the United States National Park Service Web site is displayed.

A link can be text or an image. Text links may be underlined and/or displayed in a color different from other text on the Web page. Pointing to, or positioning the pointer on, a link on the screen typically changes the shape of the pointer to a small hand with a pointing index finger. Pointing to a link also sometimes causes the link to change in appearance or play a sound. For example, an underline may disappear, the text may change color, the image may change, etc. The Web page shown in Figure 2-9 contains a variety of link types, with the pointer on one of the links.

Each link on a Web page corresponds to a Web address or a document. To activate a link, you *click* it, that is, point to the link and then press the left mouse button. Clicking a link causes the Web page or document associated with the link to be displayed on the screen. The linked object might be on the same Web page, a different Web page at the same Web site, or a separate Web page at a different Web site in another city or country. To remind you visually that you have clicked a link, a text link often changes color after you click it.

Most current Web browsers support **tabbed browsing**, where the top of the browser displays a tab (similar to a file folder tab) for each Web page you open (shown in Figure 2-9). To move from one open Web page to another, you click the tab in the Web browser. Tabbed browsing allows users to have multiple home pages that automatically open when the browser starts. You also can organize tabs in a group, called a tab group, and save the group as a favorite, so that at any time you can display all tabs at once.

Because some Web sites attempt to track your browsing habits or gather personal information, some current Web browsers include a feature that allows you to disable and/or more tightly control the dissemination of your browsing habits and personal information. Read Ethics & Issues 2-1 for a related discussion.

Tabbed Browsing

For more information, visit the Computer Concepts CourseMate Web site at www.cengagebrain.com, navigate to the Chapter 2 Web Link resource for this book, and then click Tabbed Browsing.

Figure 2-9 This browser window has several open tabs. The current tab shows a Web page that has various types of links.

Ethics & Issues

For the complete text of the Ethics & Issues boxes found in this chapter, visit the Computer Concepts CourseMate Web site at www.cengagebrain.com and then navigate to the Chapter 2 Ethics & Issues resource for this book.

ETHICS & ISSUES 2-1

Should the Government Allow You to Sign Up for a Do-Not-Track List?

When you visit a Web site that includes an advertisement, someone probably is recording the fact that you visited that Web site and viewed the advertisement with your browser. Over time, companies that specialize in tracking who views which online advertisements can amass an enormous amount of information about your online Web surfing habits. Through tracking the Web sites a user visits, the products they buy, and the articles they read, a company may attempt to profile the visitor's beliefs, associations, and habits. Although a user may think he or she is anonymous while navigating the Web, the company can attempt through various means to link the user's true identity with the user's online profile. The company can sell online profiles, with or without the user's true identity, to other advertisers or organizations. Some privacy groups have called for the government to allow consumers to sign up for a do-not-track list modeled after the popular do-not-call list.

Should organizations be allowed to track your Web surfing habits? Why or why not? Should organizations be allowed to associate your real identity with your online identity and profit from the information? Should the government force companies to give you the option of not being tracked? Why or why not? What are the benefits and dangers of online tracking?

Searching the Web

The Web is a worldwide resource of information. A primary reason that people use the Web is to search for specific information, including text, pictures, music, and video.

The first step in successful searching is to identify the main idea or concept in the topic about which you are seeking information. Determine any synonyms, alternate spellings, or variant word forms for the topic. Then, use a search tool to locate the information.

Two types of search tools are search engines and subject directories. A **search engine** is a program that finds Web sites, Web pages, images, videos, news, maps, and other information related to a specific topic. A **subject directory** classifies Web pages in an organized set of categories, such as sports or shopping, and related subcategories.

Some Web sites offer the functionality of both a search engine and a subject directory. The table in Figure 2-10 lists the Web addresses of several popular general-purpose search engines and subject directories.

Widely Used Search Tools

Search Tool	Web Address	Search Engine	Subject Directory
A9	a9.com	X	
AlltheWeb	alltheweb.com	X	
AltaVista	altavista.com	X	
AOL Search	search.aol.com	X	
Ask	ask.com	X	
Bing	bing.com	X	
Cuil (pronounced cool)	cuil.com	X	
Dogpile	dogpile.com	X	
Excite	excite.com	X	X
Gigablast	gigablast.com	X	X
Google	google.com	X	X
Lycos	lycos.com	X	
MSN	msn.com	X	X
Open Directory Project	dmoz.org	X	X
WebCrawler	webcrawler.com	X	
Yahoo!	yahoo.com	X	X

Figure 2-10 Popular search engines and subject directories.

Search Engines A search engine is helpful in locating information for which you do not know an exact Web address or are not seeking a particular Web site. Thousands of search engines are available. Some search through Web pages for all types of information. Other search engines can restrict their searches to a specific type of information, such as the following items:

- Images — pictures, diagrams, and drawings.
- Videos — home videos, music videos, television programs, and movie clips.
- Audio — music, songs, recordings, and sounds.
- Publications — news articles, journals, and books.
- Maps — maps of a business or address, or driving directions to a destination.
- People or Businesses — addresses and telephone numbers.
- Blogs — specific opinions and ideas of others.

Search engines require that you enter a word or phrase, called **search text** or *search query*, that describes the item you want to find. Each word in the search text is known as a *keyword*. Your search text can be broad, such as spring break destinations, or more specific, such as Walt Disney World. Search engines often respond with thousands of results, whose content varies depending on the type of information you are seeking. Some results are links to Web pages or articles; other results are media, such as images or videos. You may find that many items that appear in the search results have little or no bearing on the item you are seeking. You can eliminate the superfluous items in your search results by carefully crafting search text that limits the search.

If you misspell search text, many search engines identify alternative search text. Some also provide suggested keywords, links, and/or images as you begin typing your search text.

Figure 2-11 shows one way to use the Google search engine to search for the text, Aspen Colorado ski resorts. The results of the search, called *hits*, shown in Step 3 include nearly 150,000 links to Web pages that reference Aspen Colorado ski resorts. Each hit in the list has a link that, when clicked, displays an associated Web site or Web page. Most search engines sequence the hits based on how close the words in the search text are to one another in the titles and descriptions of the hits. Thus, the first few links probably contain more relevant information. Read Ethics & Issues 2-2 for a related discussion.

How to Use a Search Engine

Step 1
Type the search engine's Web address (in this case, google.com) in the Address bar in the Web browser.

Step 2
Press the ENTER key. When the Google home page is displayed, type **Aspen Colorado ski resorts** as the search text and then point to the Google Search button.

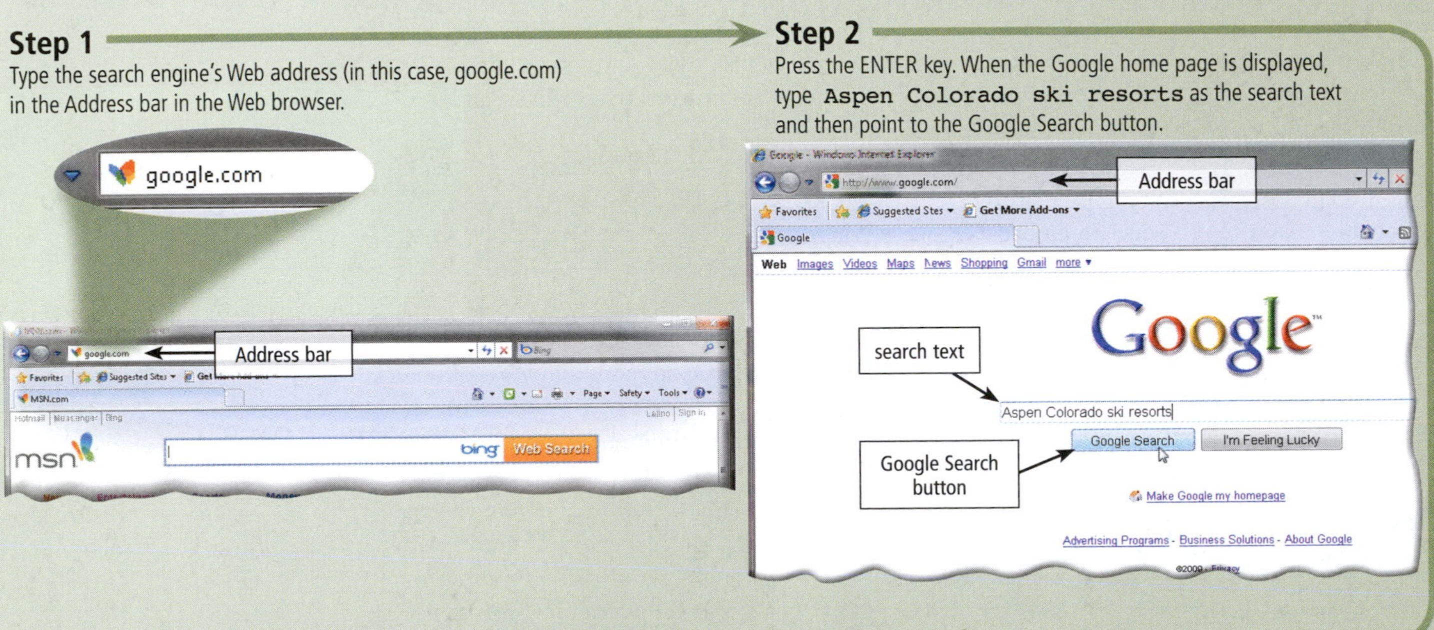

Step 3
Click the Google Search button. When the results of the search are displayed, scroll through the links and read the descriptions. Point to the Aspen Snowmass link.

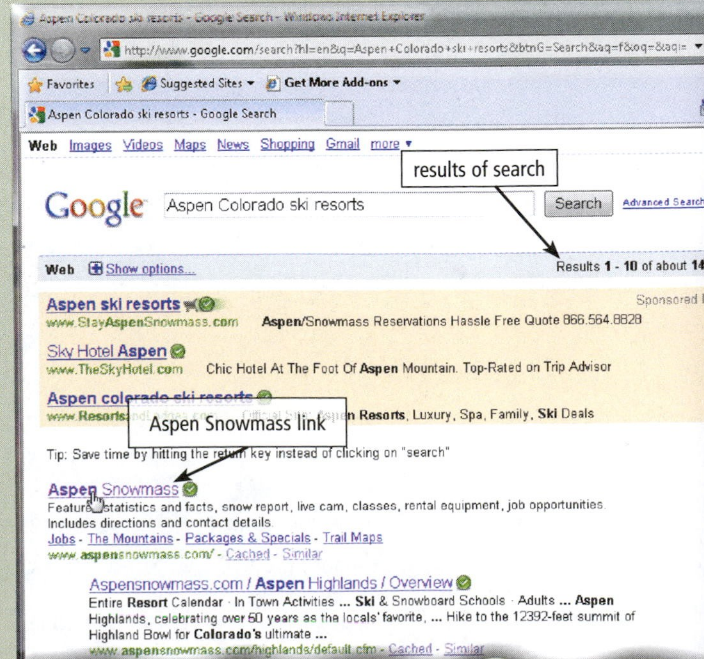

Step 4
Click the Aspen Snowmass link to display a Web page with a description and links to skiing in Aspen.

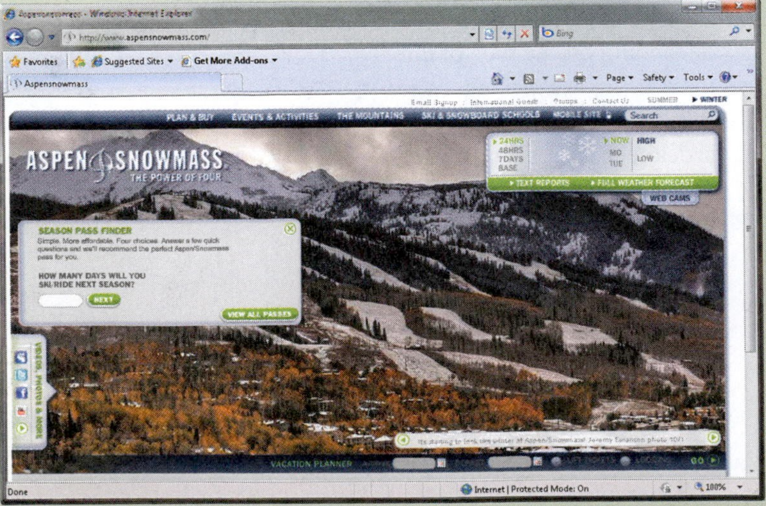

Figure 2-11 This figure shows how to use a search engine.

Some Web browsers contain an Instant Search box that, when filled in, uses a predefined or default search engine to perform searches (Figure 2-12). Using the Instant Search box eliminates the steps of displaying the search engine's Web page prior to entering the search text.

If you enter a phrase with spaces between the words in the search text, most search engines display results (hits) that include all of the words, except for common words (e.g., to, the, and). The table in Figure 2-13 lists some operators you can include in your search text to refine your search. Instead of using operators to refine your search text, many search engines have an Advanced Search feature that displays a form that assists with refining your search.

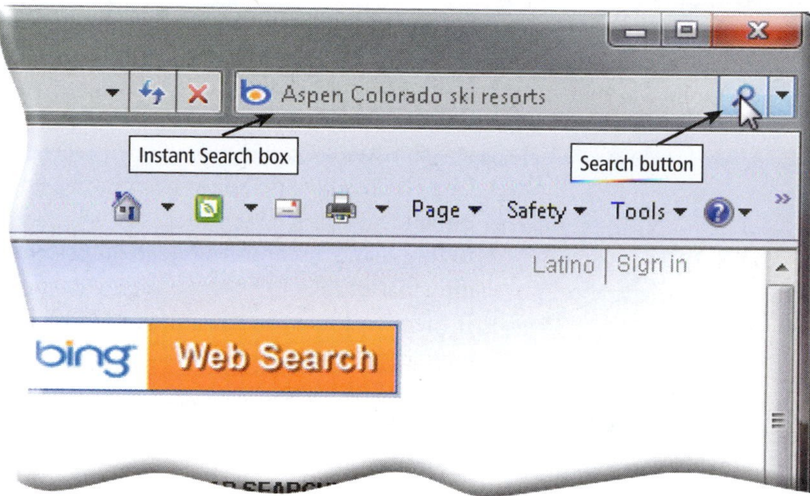

Figure 2-12 Using the Instant Search box combines Steps 1 and 2 in Figure 2-11.

ETHICS & ISSUES 2-2

Is It Ethical to Manipulate Search Engine Results?

Search engines attempt to present the most relevant and popular results to users when they perform searches. Search engines use special software to create indexes of topics from as many Web sites as possible. One key piece of information used by search engines to determine the relevance and popularity of a Web site is to examine how many other Web pages link to the Web site. Some individuals and groups take advantage of that fact and attempt to skew search results by creating hundreds or thousands of Web sites that link to a Web site that is the target of the effort. The practice of attempting to skew search engine results is known as *Google bombing*. One example of this is political activists Google bombing their opponents. When a person searches for a particular word or phrase with a negative connotation, the search results become skewed to return results about a political opponent of the Google bomber. A Google bomb can promote a product or service, or disparage a competing product or service. Google bombing often is used in a humorous manner. Comedians and television personalities sometimes request that their audience engage in some particular Google bomb. Opponents of Google bombing state that the practice lessens the public's trust in search engines and causes the search engines to be less accurate.

Is Google bombing ethical? Why or why not? How should Google bombers be handled? Why? Can Google bombing be stopped? Why or why not? Is there an ethical difference between Google bombs that attack a rival and those that are self-promoting? Why?

Search Engine Operators

Operator	Description	Examples	Explanation
Space or +	Display hits that include specific words.	art + music art music	Results have both words art and music — in any order.
OR	Display hits that include only one word from a list.	dog OR puppy dog OR puppy OR canine	Results have either the word dog or puppy. Results have the word dog or puppy or canine.
( )	Combine hits that include specific words with those that include only one word from a list.	Kalamazoo Michigan (pizza OR subs)	Results have both words Kalamazoo Michigan and either the word, pizza, or the word, subs.
-	Exclude a word from the search results.	automobile -convertible	Results include automobile but do not include convertible.
" "	Search for an exact phrase in a certain order.	"19th century literature"	Results have the exact phrase, 19th century literature.
*	Substitute characters in place of the asterisk.	writer*	Results include any word that begins with writer (e.g., writer, writers, writer's).

Figure 2-13 Use search engine operators to help refine a search.

Other techniques you can use to improve your searches include the following:

- Use specific nouns.
- Put the most important terms first in the search text.
- List all possible spellings, for example, email, e-mail.
- Before using a search engine, read its Help information.
- If the search is unsuccessful with one search engine, try another.

? FAQ 2-4

How many words do people typically use in search text?

According to research performed by OneStat, Internet users most often use only two words in their search text. The chart to the right illustrates the percentage of searches performed with search text of various lengths.

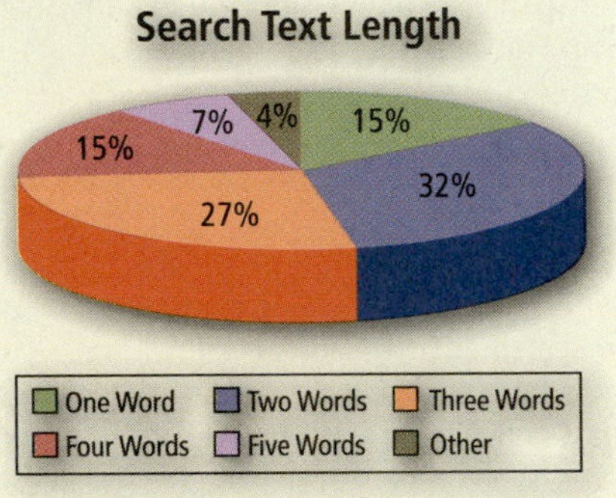

Search Text Length

One Word	15%
Two Words	32%
Three Words	27%
Four Words	15%
Five Words	7%
Other	4%

Source: OneStat

For more information, visit the Computer Concepts CourseMate Web site at www.cengagebrain.com, navigate to the Chapter 2 FAQ resource for this book, and then click Search Text.

Some search engines that work with navigation devices are location based, meaning they display results related to the device's current geographical position. For example, your mobile device can display all gas stations within a certain distance of your current location.

Many search engines use a program called a *spider* to build and maintain lists of words found on Web sites. When you enter search text, the search engine scans this prebuilt list for hits. The more sophisticated the search engine combined with precise search criteria, the more rapid the response and effective the search.

To learn more about searching for information, complete the Learn How To 2 activity on pages 120 and 121.

Subject Directories A subject directory provides categorized lists of links arranged by subject (Figure 2-14). Using this search tool, you locate a particular topic by clicking links through different levels, moving from the general to the specific. Each time you click a category link, the subject directory displays a list of subcategory links, from which you again choose. You continue in this fashion until the search tool displays a list of Web pages about the desired topic.

The major disadvantage with a subject directory is that users have difficulty deciding which categories to choose as they work through the menus of links presented.

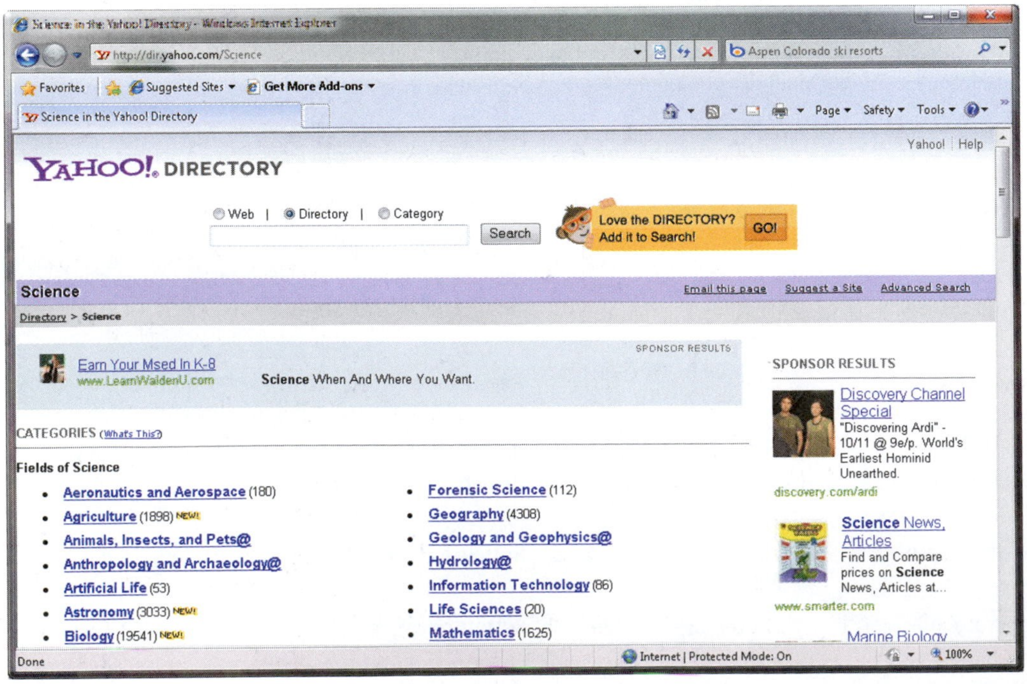

Types of Web Sites

Thirteen types of Web sites are portal, news, informational, business/marketing, blog, wiki, online social network, educational, entertainment, advocacy, Web application, content aggregator, and personal (Figure 2-15). Many Web sites fall in more than one of these categories.

Figure 2-14 A subject directory provides categorized lists of links.

Portal A **portal** is a Web site that offers a variety of Internet services from a single, convenient location (Figure 2-15a). Most portals offer these free services: search engine; news; sports and weather; Web publishing; reference tools such as yellow pages, stock quotes, and maps; shopping; and e-mail and other communications services.

Many portals have online communities. An **online community** is a Web site that joins a specific group of people with similar interests or relationships. These communities may offer online photo albums, chat rooms, and other services to facilitate communications among members.

Popular portals include AltaVista, AOL, Excite, GO.com, iGoogle, Lycos, MSN, and Yahoo!. A *wireless portal* is a portal designed for Internet-enabled mobile devices.

News A news Web site contains newsworthy material including stories and articles relating to current events, life, money, sports, and the weather (Figure 2-15b). Many magazines and newspapers sponsor Web sites that provide summaries of printed articles, as well as articles not included in the printed versions. Newspapers and television and radio stations are some of the media that maintain news Web sites.

Informational An informational Web site contains factual information (Figure 2-15c). Many United States government agencies have informational Web sites providing information such as census data, tax codes, and the congressional budget. Other organizations provide information such as public transportation schedules and published research findings.

Business/Marketing A business/marketing Web site contains content that promotes or sells products or services (Figure 2-15d). Nearly every enterprise has a business/marketing Web site. Allstate Insurance Company, Dell Inc., General Motors Corporation, Kraft Foods Inc., and Walt Disney Company all have business/marketing Web sites. Many of these enterprises also allow you to purchase their products or services online.

Figure 2-15a (portal)

Figure 2-15b (news)

Figure 2-15c (informational)

Figure 2-15d (business/marketing)

Figure 2-15 Types of Web sites. *(continued on next page)*

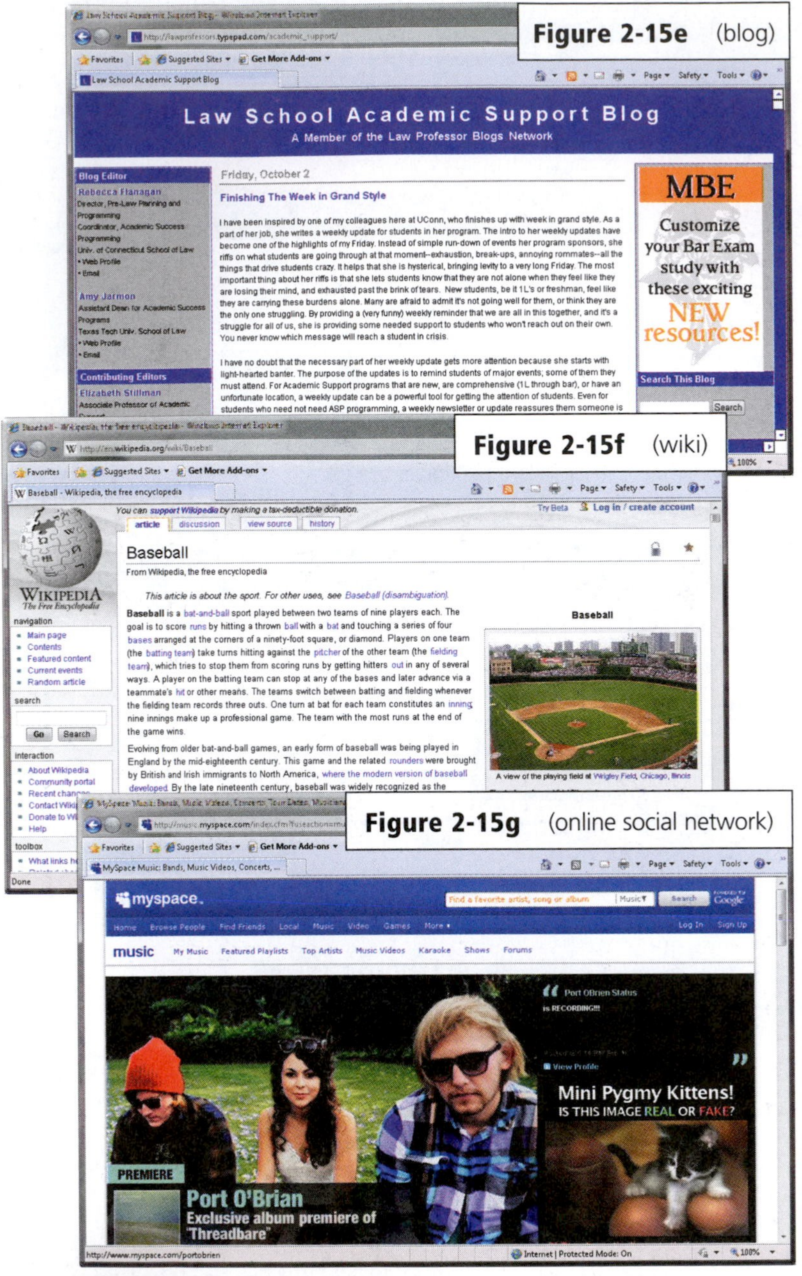

Figure 2-15 Types of Web sites. *(continued)*

Blog A **blog**, short for *Weblog*, is an informal Web site consisting of time-stamped articles, or posts, in a diary or journal format, usually listed in reverse chronological order (Figure 2-15e). A blog that contains video clips is called a **video blog**, or *vlog*. A **microblog** allows users to publish short messages, usually between 100 and 200 characters, for others to read. Twitter is a popular microblog. The term *blogosphere* refers to the worldwide collection of blogs, and the *vlogosphere* refers to all vlogs worldwide.

Blogs reflect the interests, opinions, and personalities of the author, called the *blogger* or *vlogger* (for vlog author), and sometimes site visitors.

Blogs have become an important means of worldwide communications. Businesses create blogs to communicate with employees, customers, and vendors. Teachers create blogs to collaborate with other teachers and students. Home users create blogs to share aspects of their personal life with family, friends, and others.

Wiki A **wiki** is a collaborative Web site that allows users to create, add to, modify, or delete the Web site content via their Web browser. Many wikis are open to modification by the general public. Wikis usually collect recent edits on a Web page so that someone can review them for accuracy. The difference between a wiki and a blog is that users cannot modify original posts made by the blogger. A popular wiki is Wikipedia, a free Web encyclopedia (Figure 2-15f). Read Ethics & Issues 2-3 for a related discussion.

Online Social Network An **online social network**, also called a **social networking Web site**, is a Web site that encourages members in its online community to share their interests, ideas, stories, photos, music, and videos with other registered users (Figure 2-15g). Most include chat rooms, newsgroups, and other communications services.

ETHICS & ISSUES 2-3

Should You Trust a Wiki for Academic Research?

As wikis have grown in number, size, and popularity, some educators and librarians have shunned the sites as valid sources of research. While many wikis are tightly controlled with a limited number of contributors and expert editors, these usually focus on narrowly-defined, specialized topics. Most large online wikis, such as Wikipedia, often involve thousands of editors, many of whom remain anonymous. Recently, television station reporters purposefully vandalized entries on Wikipedia for John Lennon and Elvis Presley in an attempt either to discredit Wikipedia or to test how quickly corrections are made. Editors quickly corrected the information. In other situations, rival political factions falsified or embellished wiki entries in an attempt to give their candidate an advantage. Some wiki supporters argue that most wikis provide adequate controls to correct false or misleading content quickly and to punish those who submit it. One popular wiki now requires an experienced editor to verify changes made to certain types of articles. Some propose that wikis should be used as a starting point for researching a fact, but that the fact should be verified using traditional sources.

Should wikis be allowed as valid sources for academic research? Why or why not? Would you submit a paper to your instructor that cites a wiki as a source? An encyclopedia? Why or why not? What policies could wikis enforce that could garner more confidence from the public? If a wiki provided verification of the credentials of the author, would you trust the wiki more? Why or why not?

Popular social networking Web sites include MySpace and Facebook, with Facebook alone boasting more than 300 million active users. In some social networking Web sites, such as Second Life, users assume an imaginary identity and interact with other users in a role-playing type of environment.

A **media sharing Web site** is a specific type of online social network that enables members to share media such as photos, music, and videos. Flickr, Fotki, and Webshots are popular photo sharing communities; PixelFish and YouTube are popular video sharing communities.

Educational An educational Web site offers exciting, challenging avenues for formal and informal teaching and learning (Figure 2-15h). On the Web, you can learn how airplanes fly or how to cook a meal. For a more structured learning experience, companies provide online training to employees; and colleges offer online classes and degrees. Instructors often use the Web to enhance classroom teaching by publishing course materials, grades, and other pertinent class information.

Entertainment An entertainment Web site offers an interactive and engaging environment (Figure 2-15i). Popular entertainment Web sites offer music, videos, sports, games, ongoing Web episodes, sweepstakes, chat rooms, and more. Sophisticated entertainment Web sites often partner with other technologies. For example, you can cast your vote about a topic on a television show.

Advocacy An advocacy Web site contains content that describes a cause, opinion, or idea (Figure 2-15j). These Web sites usually present views of a particular group or association. Sponsors of advocacy Web sites include the Democratic National Committee, the Republican National Committee, the Society for the Prevention of Cruelty to Animals, and the Society to Protect Human Rights.

Web Application A **Web application**, or *Web app*, is a Web site that allows users to access and interact with software through a Web browser on any computer or device that is connected to the Internet. Some Web applications provide free access to their software (Figure 2-15k). Others offer part of their software free and charge for access to more comprehensive features or when a particular action is requested. Examples of Web applications include Google Docs (word processing, spreadsheets, presentations), TurboTax Online (tax preparation), and Windows Live Hotmail (e-mail).

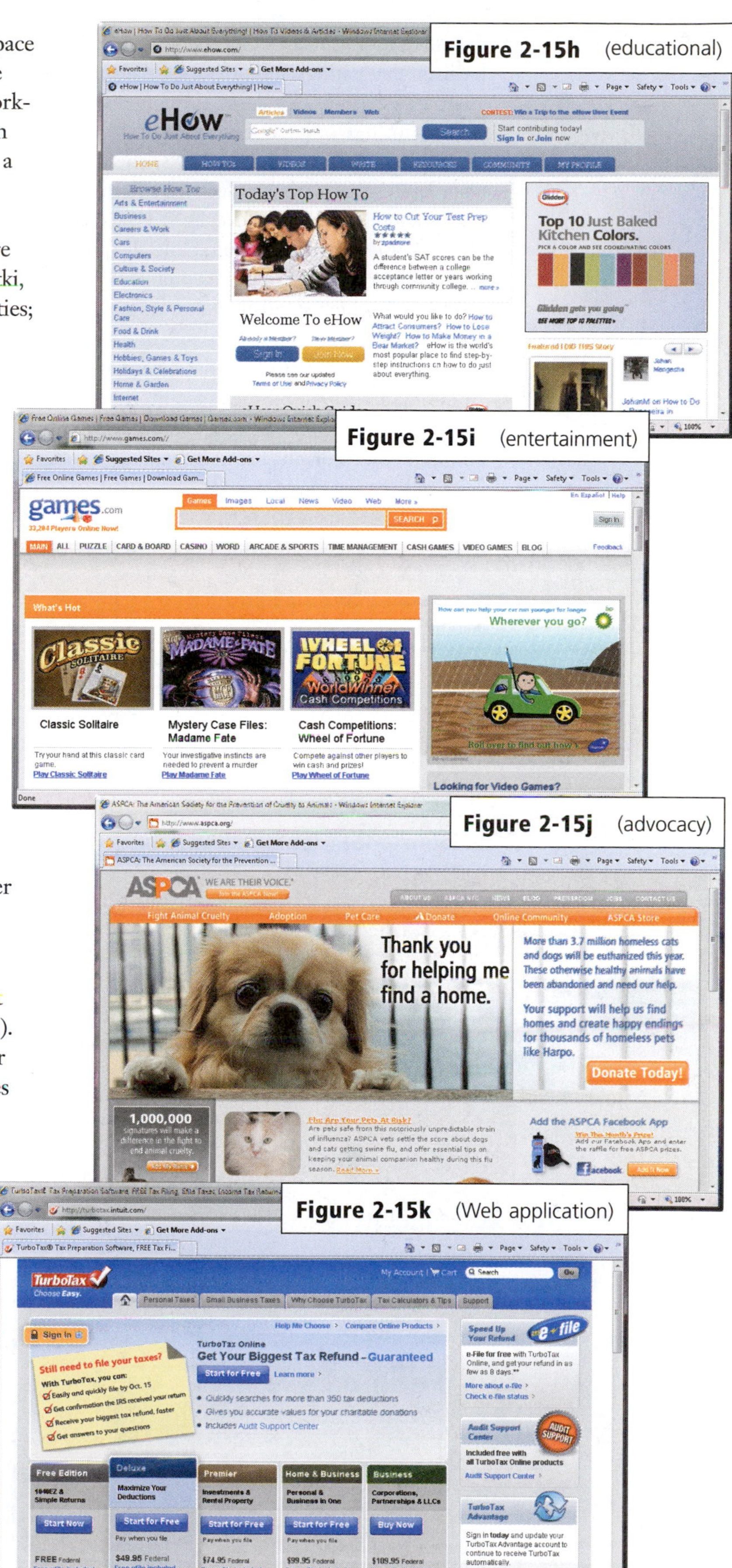

Figure 2-15 Types of Web sites. *(continued on next page)*

Content Aggregator A *content aggregator* is a business that gathers and organizes Web content and then distributes, or feeds, the content to subscribers for free or a fee (Figure 2-15l). Examples of distributed content include news, music, video, and pictures. Subscribers select content in which they are interested. Whenever the selected content changes, it is downloaded automatically (pushed) to the subscriber's computer or mobile device.

RSS 2.0, which stands for *Really Simple Syndication*, is a specification that some content aggregators use to distribute content to subscribers. *Atom* is another specification sometimes used by content aggregators to distribute content. Some current browsers include a feature, such as Internet Explorer's *WebSlices*, that enables content aggregators to mark sections of their Web pages as feeds to which users can subscribe.

Personal A private individual or family not usually associated with any organization may maintain a personal Web site or just a single Web page (Figure 2-15m). People publish personal Web pages for a variety of reasons. Some are job hunting. Others simply want to share life experiences with the world.

Figure 2-15l (content aggregator)

Figure 2-15m (personal)

Figure 2-15 Types of Web sites. *(continued)*

Evaluating a Web Site

Do not assume that information presented on the Web is correct or accurate. Any person, company, or organization can publish a Web page on the Internet. No one oversees the content of these Web pages. Figure 2-16 lists guidelines for assessing the value of a Web site or Web page before relying on its content.

Criteria for Evaluating a Web Site's Content

Evaluation Criteria	Reliable Web Sites
Affiliation	A reputable institution should support the Web site without bias in the information.
Audience	The Web site should be written at an appropriate level.
Authority	The Web site should list the author and the appropriate credentials.
Content	The Web site should be well organized and the links should work.
Currency	The information on the Web page should be current.
Design	The pages at the Web site should download quickly, be visually pleasing, and easy to navigate.
Objectivity	The Web site should contain little advertising and be free of preconceptions.

Figure 2-16 Criteria for evaluating a Web site's content.

Multimedia on the Web

Most Web pages include more than just formatted text and links. The more exciting Web pages use multimedia. **Multimedia** refers to any application that combines text with graphics, animation, audio, video, and/or virtual reality. Multimedia brings a Web page to life, increases the types of information available on the Web, expands the Web's potential uses, and makes the Internet a more entertaining place to explore. Multimedia Web pages often require specific hardware and software and take more time to download because they contain large graphics files and video or audio clips. Many Web sites have an option that allows visitors to disable multimedia, for example, if they have a slower-speed Internet connection.

The sections that follow discuss how the Web uses graphics, animation, audio, video, and virtual reality.

Graphics A **graphic**, or *graphical image*, is a digital representation of nontext information such as a drawing, chart, or photo. Today, many Web pages use colorful graphical designs and images to convey messages (Figure 2-17).

The Web contains countless images about a variety of subjects. You can download many of these images at no cost and use them for noncommercial purposes. Recall that downloading is the process of transferring an object from the Web to your computer. For example, you can insert images into greeting cards, announcements, and other documents. Read Innovative Computing 2-1 to find out how astronomers share graphics of the universe.

Of the graphics formats that exist on the Web (Figure 2-18), the two more common are JPEG and GIF formats. *JPEG* (pronounced JAY-peg) is a format that compresses graphics to reduce their file size, which means the file takes up less storage space. Smaller file sizes result in faster downloading of Web pages because small files transmit faster than large files. The more compressed the file, the smaller the image and the lower the quality. The goal with JPEG graphics is to reach a balance between image quality and file size. Digital photos often use the JPEG format.

GIF (pronounced jiff) graphics also use compression techniques to reduce file sizes. The GIF format works best for images that have only a few distinct colors, such as company logos. The newer *PNG* (pronounced ping) graphics format improves upon the GIF format, and thus may eventually replace the GIF format.

The BMP and TIFF formats listed in Figure 2-18 may require special viewer software, and they have larger file sizes. Thus, these formats are not used on the Web as frequently as JPEG, GIF, and PNG formats.

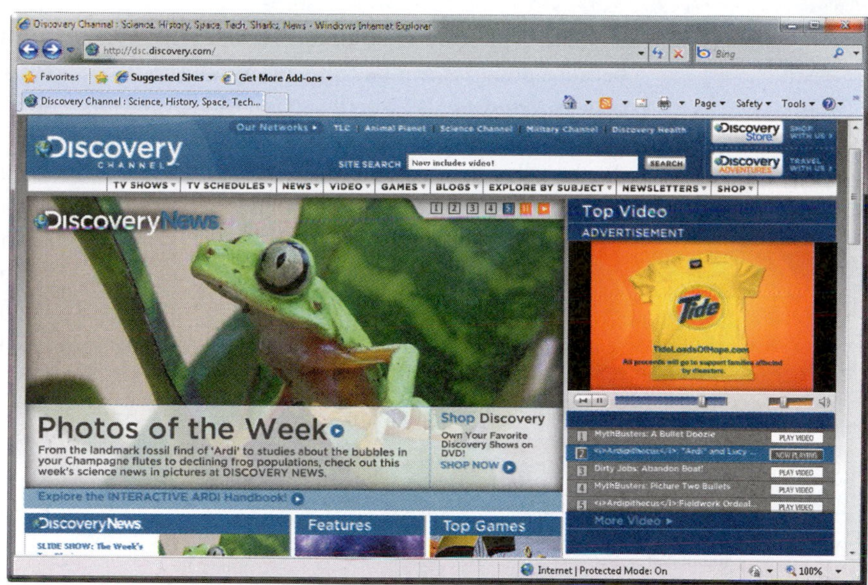

Figure 2-17 This Web page uses colorful graphical designs and images to convey its messages.

INNOVATIVE COMPUTING 2-1

View the Wonders of Space through the WorldWide Telescope

The phrase, reach for the stars, takes on a new meaning when using Microsoft's *WorldWide Telescope*. Users can access the Telescope from a Web browser or download free software. They then can view a variety of multimedia, including high-resolution graphics from telescopes located on Earth and in space, with Web 2.0 services to allow people to explore the final frontier from their computers.

Users can pan and zoom around the night sky by looking through a specific telescope, such as the Hubble Space Telescope, and view the universe in the past, present, or future. In addition, they can browse graphics of a specific planet, the Milky Way Galaxy, black holes, and other celestial bodies in our solar system, galaxy, and beyond. They also can select different wavelengths, such as X-ray or visible light, to search for objects. Astronomers and educators also have created narrated tours of the sky to help interpret the images.

For more information, visit the Computer Concepts CourseMate Web site at www.cengagebrain.com, navigate to the Chapter 2 Innovative Computing resource for this book, and then click WorldWide Telescope.

Graphics Formats Used on the Web

Abbreviation	Name	Uses
BMP	Bitmap	Desktop background, scanned images
GIF	Graphics Interchange Format	Simple diagrams, shapes, images with few colors
JPEG	Joint Photographic Experts Group	Digital camera photos
PNG	Portable Network Graphics	Web graphics
TIFF	Tagged Image File Format	Photos used by printing industry

Figure 2-18 The Web uses graphics file formats for images.

Some Web sites use thumbnails on their pages because graphics can be time-consuming to display. A *thumbnail* is a small version of a larger graphic. You usually can click a thumbnail to display a larger image (Figure 2-19).

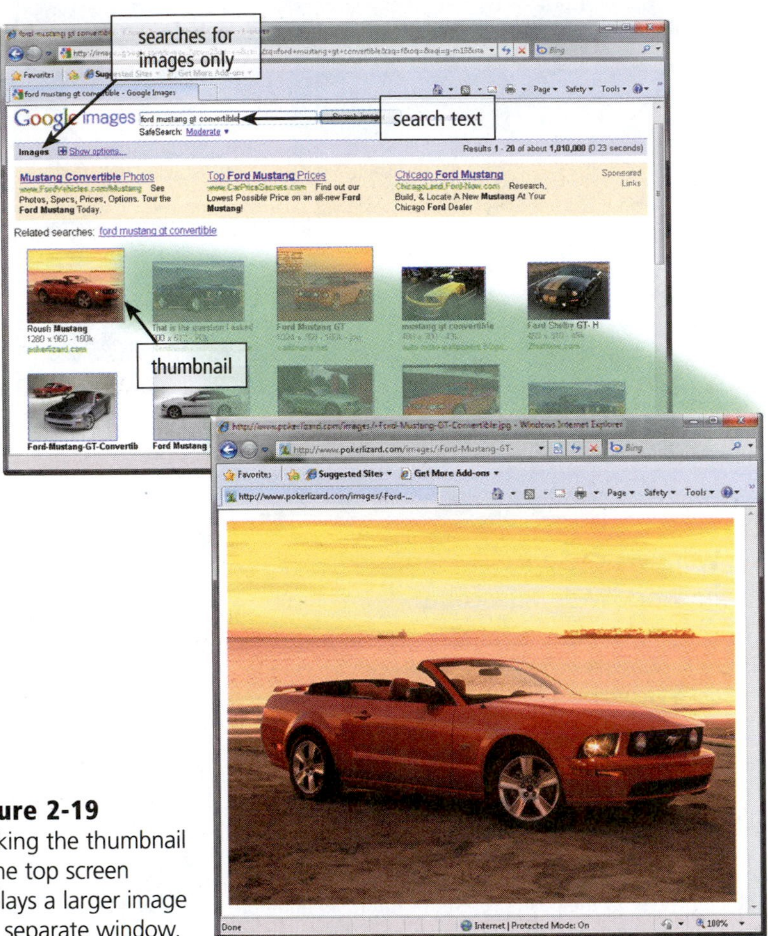

Figure 2-19
Clicking the thumbnail in the top screen displays a larger image in a separate window.

Animation Many Web pages use **animation**, which is the appearance of motion created by displaying a series of still images in sequence. Animation can make Web pages more visually interesting or draw attention to important information or links. For example, text that animates by scrolling across the screen can serve as a ticker to display stock updates, news, sports scores, weather, or other information. Web-based games often use animation.

Web page developers add animation to Web pages using a variety of techniques. Web page authoring programs, such as Adobe Flash and Microsoft Expression Web, enable Web site developers to combine animation and interactivity in Web pages. Developers unfamiliar with Web page authoring programs can create an *animated GIF*, which combines several GIF images in a single GIF file.

Audio On the Web, you can listen to audio clips and live audio. **Audio** includes music, speech, or any other sound. Simple applications consist of individual audio files available for download to a computer or device. Once downloaded, you can play (listen to) the contents of these files. Some common Web audio file formats are listed in Figure 2-20. Audio files are compressed to reduce their file sizes. For example, the **MP3** format reduces an audio file to about one-tenth its original size, while preserving much of the original quality of the sound.

Some music publishers have Web sites that allow users to download sample tracks free to persuade them to buy all the songs contained on the CD. Others allow a user to purchase and download an entire CD (Figure 2-21). It is legal to download copyrighted music only if the song's copyright holder has granted permission for users to download and play the song.

To listen to an audio file on your computer, you need special software called a **player**. Most current operating systems contain a player, for example, Windows Media Player. Some audio files, however, might require you to download a player. Players available for download include iTunes and RealPlayer. You can download the players free from the Web; some are plug-ins, which are discussed later in this chapter.

Some applications on the Web use streaming audio. **Streaming** is the process of transferring data in a continuous and even flow. Streaming allows users to access and use a file while it is transmitting. For example, *streaming audio* enables you to listen to music as it downloads to your computer. Many radio and television stations use streaming audio to broadcast music, interviews, talk shows, sporting events, music videos, news, live concerts, and other segments.

Podcasting is another popular method of distributing audio. A *podcast* is recorded audio, usually an MP3 file, stored on a Web site that can be downloaded to a computer or a portable media player such as an iPod. Examples of podcasts include music, radio shows, news stories, classroom lectures, political messages, and television commentaries. Podcasters register their podcasts with content aggregators. Subscribers select podcast feeds they want to be downloaded automatically whenever they connect. Most smart phone users who subscribe to a wireless Internet service provider can listen to streaming audio and podcasts.

Audio Web File Formats

Format	Description	Format	Description
AAC	Advanced Audio Coding	WAV	Windows waveform
AIFF	Audio Interchange File Format	WMA	Windows Media Audio (part of Windows Media framework)
ASF	Advanced Streaming (or Systems) Format (part of Windows Media framework)	RA	RealAudio sound file (supported by RealPlayer)
MP3	Moving Pictures Experts Group Audio Layer 3 (MPEG-3)	QT	QuickTime audio, video, or 3-D animation
Ogg	Free, unpatented audio and video format		

Figure 2-20 Popular Web audio file formats.

Figure 2-21 This figure shows how to purchase and download music using iTunes.

Video On the Web, you can view video clips or watch live video. **Video** consists of images displayed in motion. Most video also has accompanying audio. You can use the Internet to watch live and/or prerecorded coverage of your favorite television programs or enjoy a live performance of your favorite vocalist. You can upload, share, or view video clips at a video sharing Web site such as YouTube (Figure 2-22). Educators, politicians, and businesses are using video blogs and video podcasts to engage students, voters, and consumers.

Simple video applications on the Web consist of individual video files, such as movie or television clips, that you must download completely before you can play them on the computer. Video files often are compressed because they are quite large in size. These clips also are short in length, usually less than 10 minutes, because they can take a long time to download. The Moving Pictures Experts Group (*MPEG*) defines a popular video compression standard, a widely used one called *MPEG-4* or *MP4*. Another popular video format is Adobe Flash.

YouTube

For more information, visit the Computer Concepts CourseMate Web site at www.cengagebrain.com, navigate to the Chapter 2 Web Link resource for this book, and then click YouTube.

As with streaming audio, *streaming video* allows you to view longer or live video images as they download to your computer. Widely used standards supported by most Web browsers for transmitting streaming video data on the Internet are AVI (Audio Video Interleaved), QuickTime, Windows Media Format, and RealVideo. Like RealAudio, RealVideo is supported by RealPlayer.

FAQ 2-5

How are social networking Web sites and Internet video affecting Internet traffic?

A report from Cisco Systems states that Internet traffic will double every two years until 2012. The volume of Internet traffic is increasing mostly because of Internet videos and social networking. In addition, the increased use of video conferencing by business users also accounts for the increase in traffic.

For more information, visit the Computer Concepts CourseMate Web site at www.cengagebrain.com, navigate to the Chapter 2 FAQ resource for this book, and then click Internet Traffic.

Virtual Reality **Virtual reality (VR)** is the use of computers to simulate a real or imagined environment that appears as a three-dimensional (3-D) space. VR involves the display of 3-D images that users explore and manipulate interactively.

Using special VR software, a Web developer creates an entire 3-D environment that contains infinite space and depth, called a *VR world*. A VR world, for example, might show a house for sale. Potential buyers walk through rooms in the VR house by moving an input device forward, backward, or to the side.

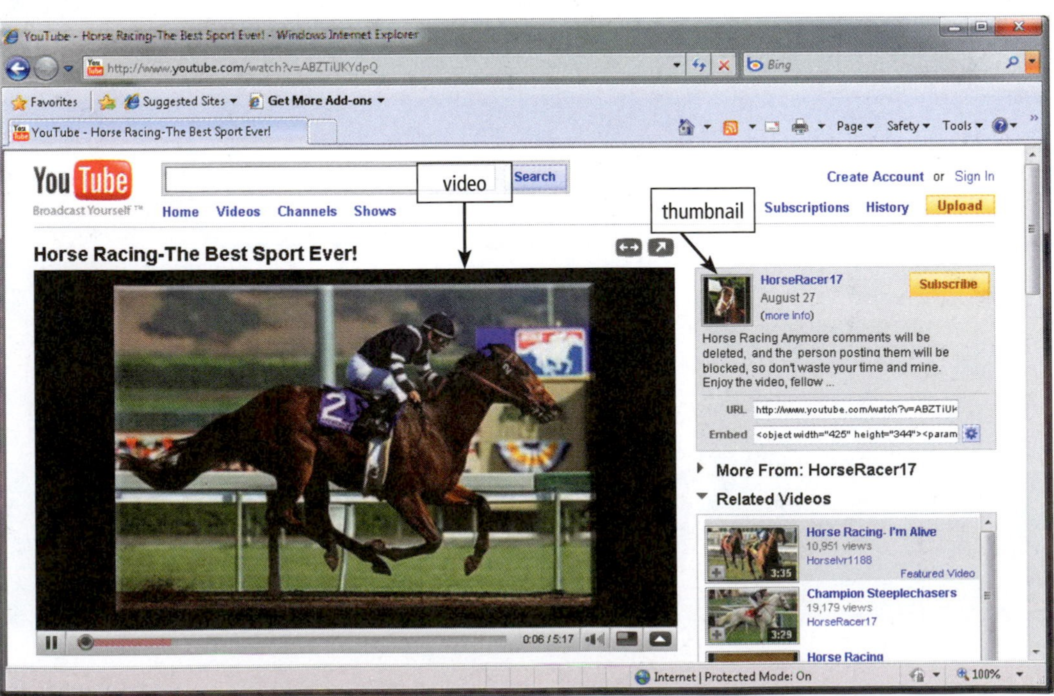

Figure 2-22 A video of a horse race.

Games and simulations on optical disc or on the Web often use VR (Figure 2-23). Many practical applications of VR also exist. Science educators create VR models of molecules, organisms, and other structures for students to examine. Companies use VR to showcase products or create advertisements. Architects create VR models of buildings and rooms so that clients can see how a completed construction project will look before it is built.

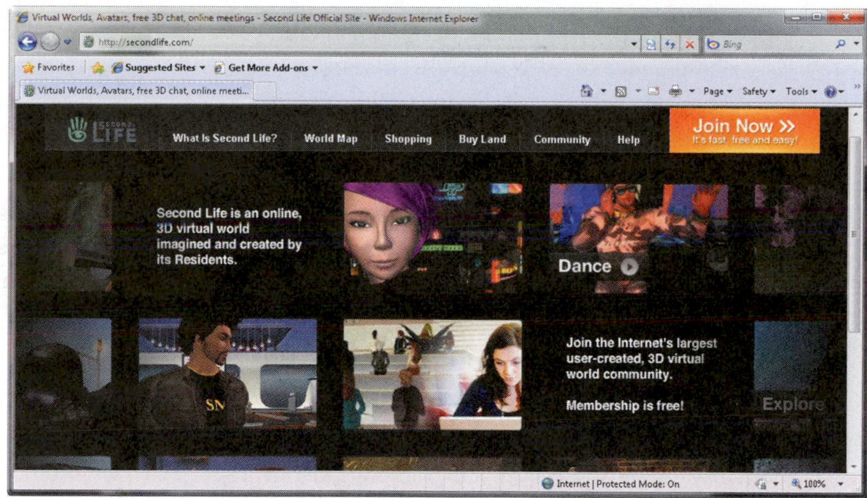

Figure 2-23 Residents (users) of the Second Life online social network interact with other online residents (users) in a VR world.

Plug-ins Most Web browsers have the capability of displaying basic multimedia elements on a Web page. Sometimes, a browser might need an additional program, called a plug-in. A **plug-in**, or *add-on*, is a program that extends the capability of a browser. You can download many plug-ins at no cost from various Web sites (Figure 2-24). Some plug-ins run on all sizes of personal computers and mobile devices. Others have special versions for mobile devices.

Web Publishing

Before the World Wide Web, the means to share opinions and ideas with others easily and inexpensively was limited to the media, classroom, work, or social environments. Generating an advertisement or publication that could reach a massive audience required much expense. Today, businesses and individuals convey information to millions of people by creating their own Web pages. The content of the Web pages ranges from news stories to product information to blogs.

Popular Plug-Ins

Plug-In Application	Description	Web Address
Acrobat Reader (Get ADOBE® READER®)	View, navigate, and print Portable Document Format (PDF) files — documents formatted to look just as they look in print	adobe.com
Flash Player (Get ADOBE® FLASH® PLAYER)	View dazzling graphics and animation, hear outstanding sound and music, display Web pages across an entire screen	adobe.com
Java (Java » Get it Now)	Enable Web browser to run programs written in Java, which add interactivity to Web pages	java.com
QuickTime (Get QuickTime Free Download)	View animation, music, audio, video, and VR panoramas and objects directly on a Web page	apple.com
RealPlayer (real RealPlayer DOWNLOAD)	Listen to live and on-demand near-CD-quality audio and newscast-quality video, stream audio and video content for faster viewing, play MP3 files, create music CDs	real.com
Shockwave Player (Get ADOBE® SHOCKWAVE® PLAYER)	Experience dynamic interactive multimedia, 3-D graphics, and streaming audio	adobe.com
Silverlight (Install Microsoft® Silverlight™)	Experience high-definition video, high-resolution interactive multimedia, and streaming audio and video	microsoft.com
Windows Media Player (Windows Media Player)	Listen to live and on-demand audio, play or edit WMA and MP3 files, burn CDs, and watch DVD movies	microsoft.com

Figure 2-24 Most plug-ins can be downloaded free from the Web.

Web publishing is the development and maintenance of Web pages. To develop a Web page, you do not have to be a computer programmer. For the small business or home user, Web publishing is fairly easy as long as you have the proper tools. To learn more about how to publish a document on the Web, complete the Learn How To 3 activity on page 121.

The five major steps in Web publishing are as follows:

1. **Plan a Web site.**
   Think about issues that could affect the design of the Web site. Identify the purpose of the Web site and the characteristics of the people whom you want to visit the Web site. Determine ways to differentiate your Web site from other similar ones.
2. **Analyze and design a Web site.**
   Design the layout of elements of the Web site such as links, text, graphics, animation, audio, video, and virtual reality. Required hardware may include a digital camera, Web cam, scanner, sound card, and microphone.
3. **Create a Web site.**
   Use a word processing program to create basic Web pages that contain text and graphics. Use Web page authoring software to create more sophisticated Web sites that include text, graphics, animation, audio, video, and special effects. For advanced features such as managing users, passwords, chat rooms, and e-mail, you may need to purchase specialized Web site management software.
4. **Deploy a Web site.**
   Transfer the Web pages from your computer to a Web server. Many Internet access providers offer their customers storage space on a Web server. Another option is a Web hosting service, which provides storage space on a Web server for a reasonable monthly fee. To help others locate your Web page, register your Web address with various search engines to ensure your site will appear in the hit lists for searches for certain keywords.
5. **Maintain a Web site.**
   Visit the Web site regularly to ensure the Web site contents are current and all links work properly.

Web Page Authoring Software

For more information, visit the Computer Concepts CourseMate Web site at www.cengagebrain.com, navigate to the Chapter 2 Web Link resource for this book, and then click Web Page Authoring Software.

✔ QUIZ YOURSELF 2-2

Instructions: Find the true statement below. Then, rewrite the remaining false statements so that they are true.

1. A blog is a Web site that uses a regularly updated journal format to reflect the interests, opinions, and personalities of the author and sometimes site visitors.
2. You can assume that information on the Web is correct and accurate.
3. Audio and video files are downloaded to reduce their file sizes.
4. Popular portals include iTunes, RealPlayer, and Windows Media Player.
5. The more widely used search engines for personal computers are Internet Explorer, Firefox, Opera, Safari, and Google Chrome.
6. To develop a Web page, you have to be a computer programmer.
7. To improve your Web searches, use general nouns and put the least important terms first in the search text.

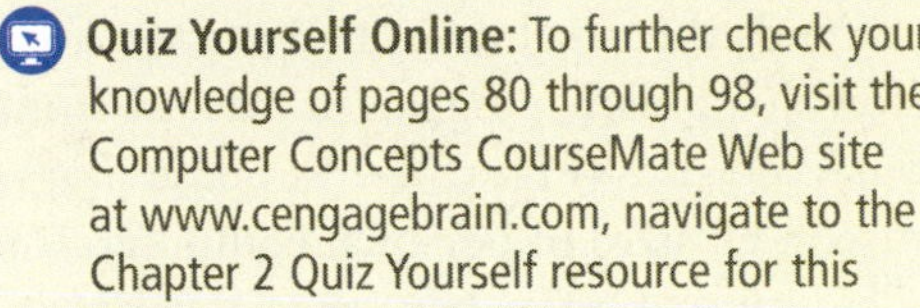

Quiz Yourself Online: To further check your knowledge of pages 80 through 98, visit the Computer Concepts CourseMate Web site at www.cengagebrain.com, navigate to the Chapter 2 Quiz Yourself resource for this book, and then click Objectives 5 – 9.

E-Commerce

E-commerce, short for *electronic commerce*, is a business transaction that occurs over an electronic network such as the Internet. Anyone with access to a computer or mobile device, an Internet connection, and a means to pay for purchased goods or services can participate in e-commerce. Some people use the term *m-commerce* (mobile commerce) to identify e-commerce that takes place using mobile devices.

Popular uses of e-commerce by consumers include retail, finance, travel, entertainment, and health. Users can purchase just about any product or service on the Web, including groceries, flowers, books, computers, music, movies, cars, airline tickets, and concert tickets. They also can pay bills, invest in stocks, make airline reservations, reserve a hotel or car, and fill prescriptions.

Three types of e-commerce are business-to-consumer, consumer-to-consumer, and business-to-business. *Business-to-consumer (B2C) e-commerce* consists of the sale of goods and services to the general public. For example,

Apple has a B2C Web site. Instead of visiting a retail store to purchase an iPod, customers can order one directly from Apple's Web site.

A customer (consumer) visits an online business through an **electronic storefront**, which contains product descriptions, images, and a shopping cart. The **shopping cart** allows the customer to collect purchases. When ready to complete the sale, the customer enters personal data and the method of payment, which should be through a secure Internet connection. *E-retail*, short for electronic retail, occurs when businesses use the Web to sell products (Figure 2-25).

FAQ 2-6

Is it safe to shop online?

Not always. Although 78 percent of shoppers find online shopping convenient, about 75 percent of surveyed individuals are hesitant to enter their personal or credit card information online. It always is best to conduct online transactions with well-established companies. If possible, research these companies and read about others' online shopping experiences before making a purchase. If you never have heard of a particular online business, do not entrust them with your credit card information.

For more information, visit the Computer Concepts CourseMate Web site at www.cengagebrain.com, navigate to the Chapter 2 FAQ resource for this book, and then click Online Shopping.

An Example of E-Retail

Step 1
The customer displays the e-retailer's electronic storefront.

Step 2
The customer collects purchases in an electronic shopping cart.

Step 3
The customer enters payment information on a secure Web site. The e-retailer sends financial information to a bank.

Step 4
The bank performs security checks and sends authorization back to the e-retailer.

Step 5
The e-retailer's Web server sends confirmation to the customer, processes the order, and then sends it to the fulfillment center.

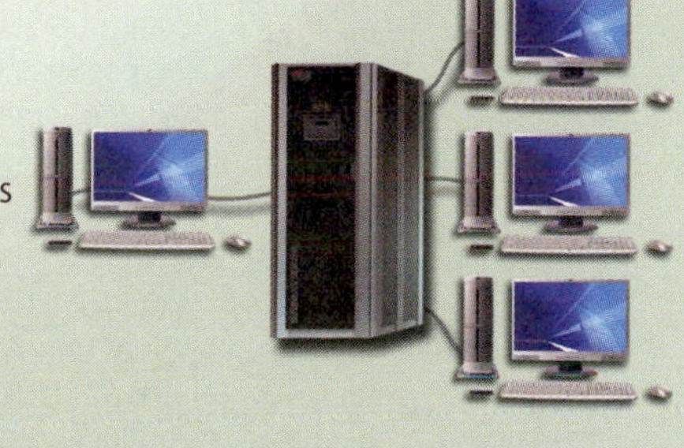

Step 6
The fulfillment center packages the order, prepares it for shipment, and then sends a report to the server where records are updated.

Step 7
While the order travels to the customer, shipping information is posted on the Web.

Step 8
The order is delivered to the customer, who may be required to sign a handheld computer or document to acknowledge receipt.

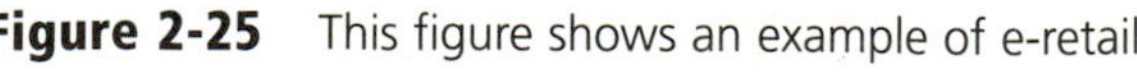

Figure 2-25 This figure shows an example of e-retail.

Consumer-to-consumer (C2C) e-commerce occurs when one consumer sells directly to another, such as in an online auction. With an **online auction**, users bid on an item being sold by someone else. The highest bidder at the end of the bidding period purchases the item. eBay is one of the more popular online auction Web sites.

As an alternative to entering credit card, bank account, or other financial information online, some shopping and auction Web sites allow consumers to use an online payment service such as PayPal or Google Checkout. To use an online payment service, you create an account that is linked to your credit card or funds at a financial institution. When you make a purchase, you use your online payment service account, which transfers money for you without revealing your financial information. Read Innovative Computing 2-2 to find out how shoppers can experience 3-D online stores.

Google Checkout

For more information, visit the Computer Concepts CourseMate Web site at www.cengagebrain.com, navigate to the Chapter 2 Web Link resource for this book, and then click Google Checkout.

Most e-commerce, though, actually takes place between businesses, which is called *business-to-business (B2B) e-commerce*. Businesses often provide goods and services to other businesses, such as online advertising, recruiting, credit, sales, market research, technical support, and training. For example, some MasterCard and Visa credit card companies provide corporations with Web-based purchasing, tracking, and transaction downloading capabilities.

INNOVATIVE COMPUTING 2-2

Shopping Becomes a Virtual Experience

Part of retail shopping at the mall or the grocery store is the ability to browse aisles, view labels, and compare products side by side. Online shoppers may be able to share these shopping experiences in three-dimensional environments complete with shelving, signs, overhead lighting, and outdoor plazas.

Software manufacturer Kinset, Inc. is leading the 3-D e-commerce development. Taking its cue from video games and the Second Life VR world Web site, Kinset has launched its product to big-name retailers, including Brookstone. Shoppers download and then install this software, connect to the Internet, and then begin their shopping experience.

When shoppers position their mouse pointer over an item, the information about the product is displayed. Pressing a specific key adds the item to a shopping cart, and another key brings the shopper to the checkout screen.

For more information, visit the Computer Concepts CourseMate Web site at www.cengagebrain.com, navigate to the Chapter 2 Innovative Computing resource for this book, and then click Online Shopping.

Other Internet Services

The Web is only one of the many services on the Internet. The Web and other Internet services have changed the way we communicate. We use computers and mobile devices to send e-mail messages to the president, have a discussion with experts about the stock market, chat with someone in another country about genealogy, and talk about homework assignments with classmates via instant messages. Many times, these communications take place completely in writing — without the parties ever meeting each other. Read Ethics & Issues 2-4 for a related discussion.

The following pages discuss these Internet services: e-mail, mailing lists, instant messaging, chat rooms, VoIP (Voice over IP), newsgroups and message boards, and FTP (File Transfer Protocol).

ETHICS & ISSUES 2-4

Should You Be Judged by Your Internet Communications?

Internet features, such as e-mail, instant messages, and chat, have become some of today's most popular methods of communications. Millions of people around the world send and receive various forms of Internet messages. The Internet links the geographically distanced, connects the economically separated, enables the physically challenged, and encourages the publicly timid. Almost all office workers are prolific users of Internet communications because their job depends on a great deal of collaboration with co-workers, management, vendors, and other departments.

Because of the ease of use of such forms of communications, people are writing more than ever before — but is it good writing? The carefully crafted letters of an era gone by, handwritten in beautiful penmanship, have been replaced by messages stylistically equivalent to notes on the refrigerator. The immediacy of the Internet often results in messages that are ill conceived, casually spelled, poorly worded, grammatically flawed, and tritely expressed. Despite experts suggesting that users always should proofread messages carefully before sending them, communications often are misinterpreted or come across as being rude.

Should employers require that employees adhere to e-mail authoring policies? In general, has e-mail's impact on communications been positive or negative? Why? Would you judge somebody by the quality of his or her e-mail message? Why or why not? Could someone's professional reputation be enhanced or hindered by the quality and effectiveness of his or her Internet communications?

E-Mail

E-mail (short for *electronic mail*) is the transmission of messages and files via a computer network. E-mail was one of the original services on the Internet, enabling scientists and researchers working on government-sponsored projects to communicate with colleagues at other locations. Today, e-mail is a primary communications method for both personal and business use.

You use an **e-mail program** to create, send, receive, forward, store, print, and delete e-mail messages. Outlook and Windows Live Mail are two popular desktop e-mail programs; Gmail and Windows Live Hotmail are two popular free e-mail Web applications. The steps in Figure 2-26 illustrate how to send an e-mail message using Outlook.

How to Send an E-Mail Message Using Outlook

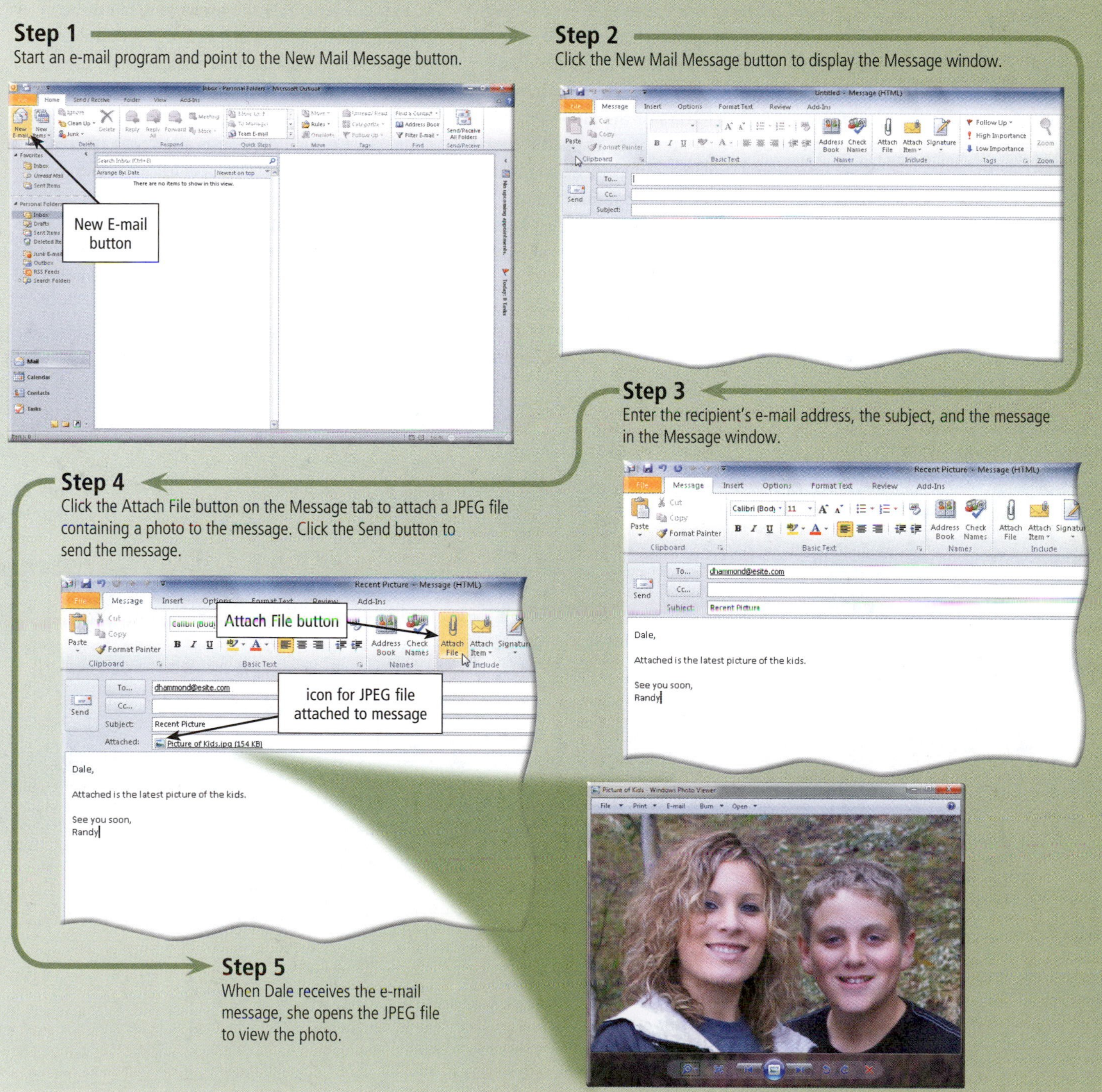

Figure 2-26 This figure shows how to send an e-mail message using Outlook.

The message can be simple text or can include an attachment such as a word processing document, a graphic, an audio clip, or a video clip. To learn more about how to attach a file to an e-mail message, complete the Learn How To 1 activity on page 120.

Just as you address a letter when using the postal system, you address an e-mail message with the e-mail address of your intended recipient. Likewise, when someone sends you a message, he or she must have your e-mail address. An **e-mail address** is a combination of a user name and a domain name that identifies a user so that he or she can receive Internet e-mail.

A **user name** is a unique combination of characters, such as letters of the alphabet and/or numbers, that identifies a specific user. Your user name must be different from the other user names in the same domain. For example, a user named Kiley Barnhill whose server has a domain name of esite.com might want to select kbarnhill as her user name. If esite.com already has a kbarnhill (for Ken Barnhill), Kiley will have to select a different user name, such as kileybarnhill or k_barnhill.

Sometimes, organizations decide user names for new users. In many cases, however, users select their own user names, often selecting a nickname or any other combination of characters for their user name. Many users select a combination of their first and last names so that others can remember it easily.

In an Internet e-mail address, an @ (pronounced at) symbol separates the user name from the domain name. Your service provider supplies the domain name. A possible e-mail address for Kiley Barnhill would be kbarnhill@esite.com, which would be read as follows: K Barnhill at e site dot com. Most e-mail programs allow you to create an **address book**, or contacts folder, which contains a list of names and e-mail addresses.

Figure 2-27 illustrates how an e-mail message may travel from a sender to a receiver using a desktop e-mail program. When you send an

Figure 2-27 This figure shows how an e-mail message may travel from a sender to a receiver.

e-mail message, an outgoing mail server that is operated by your Internet access provider determines how to route the message through the Internet and then sends the message. *SMTP* (simple mail transfer protocol) is a communications protocol used by some outgoing mail servers.

As you receive e-mail messages, an incoming mail server — also operated by your Internet access provider — holds the messages in your mailbox until you use your e-mail program to retrieve them. *POP3*, the latest version of POP (*Post Office Protocol*), is a communications protocol used by some incoming mail servers. Most e-mail programs have a mail notification alert that informs you via a message and/or sound when you receive new mail.

Mailing Lists

A **mailing list**, also called an e-mail list or distribution list, is a group of e-mail names and addresses given a single name. When a message is sent to a mailing list, every person on the list receives a copy of the message in his or her mailbox. For example, your credit card company may add you to its mailing list in order to send you special offers. To add your e-mail name and address to a mailing list, you **subscribe** to it (Figure 2-28). To remove your name, you **unsubscribe** from the mailing list.

Thousands of mailing lists exist about a variety of topics in areas of entertainment, business, computers, society, culture, health, recreation, and education. Many vendors use mailing lists to communicate with their customer base.

? FAQ 2-7

Can my computer get a virus through e-mail?

Yes. A *virus* is a computer program that can damage files and the operating system. One way that virus authors attempt to spread a virus is by sending virus-infected e-mail attachments. If you receive an e-mail attachment, you should use an antivirus program to verify that it is virus free.

For more information, read the High-Tech Talk article on page 178 and the section about viruses and antivirus programs in Chapter 8; and visit the Computer Concepts CourseMate Web site at www.cengagebrain.com, navigate to the Chapter 2 FAQ resource for this book, and then click Viruses.

E-Mail

For more information, visit the Computer Concepts CourseMate Web site at www.cengagebrain.com, navigate to the Chapter 2 Web Link resource for this book, and then click E-Mail.

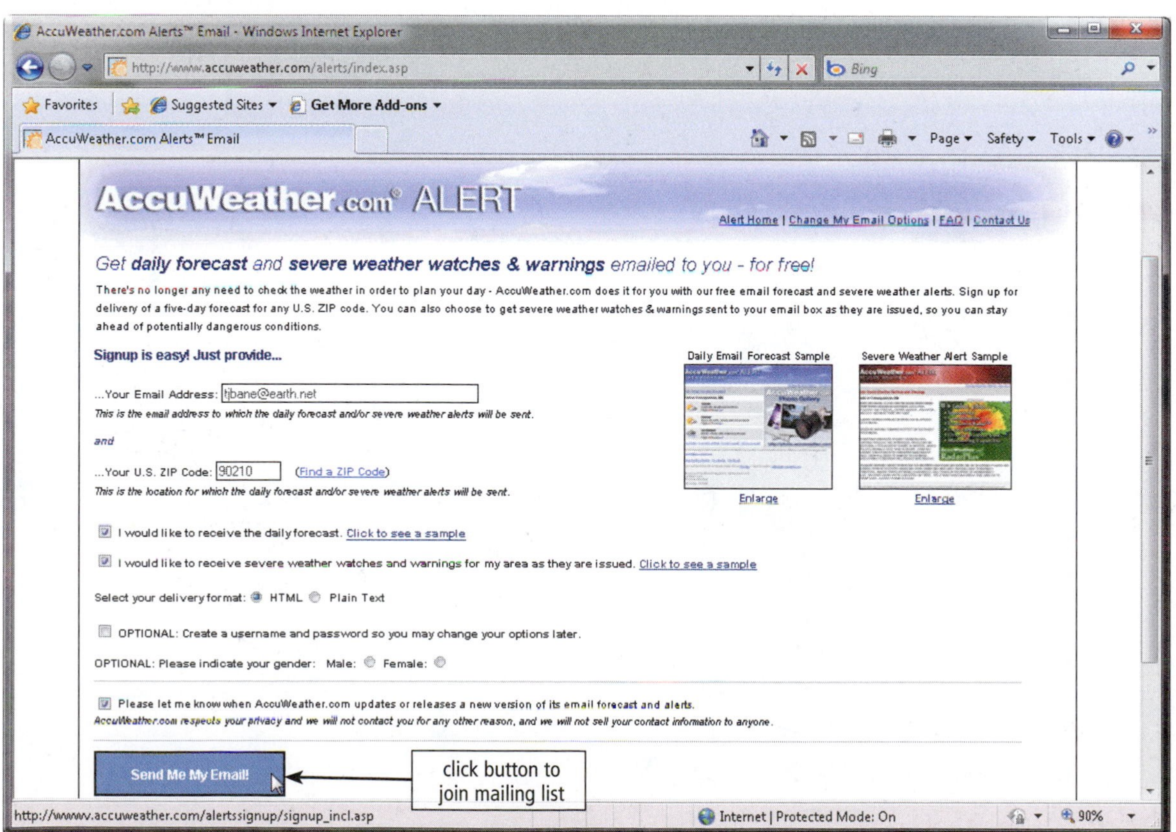

Figure 2-28 When you join a mailing list, you and all others on the mailing list receive e-mail messages from the Web site.

Instant Messaging

Instant messaging (**IM**) is a real-time Internet communications service that notifies you when one or more people are online and then allows you to exchange messages or files or join a private chat room with them. **Real time** means that you and the people with whom you are conversing are online at the same time. Some IM services support voice and video conversations (Figure 2-29). Many IM services also can alert you to information such as calendar appointments, stock quotes, weather, or sports scores. They also allow you to send photos

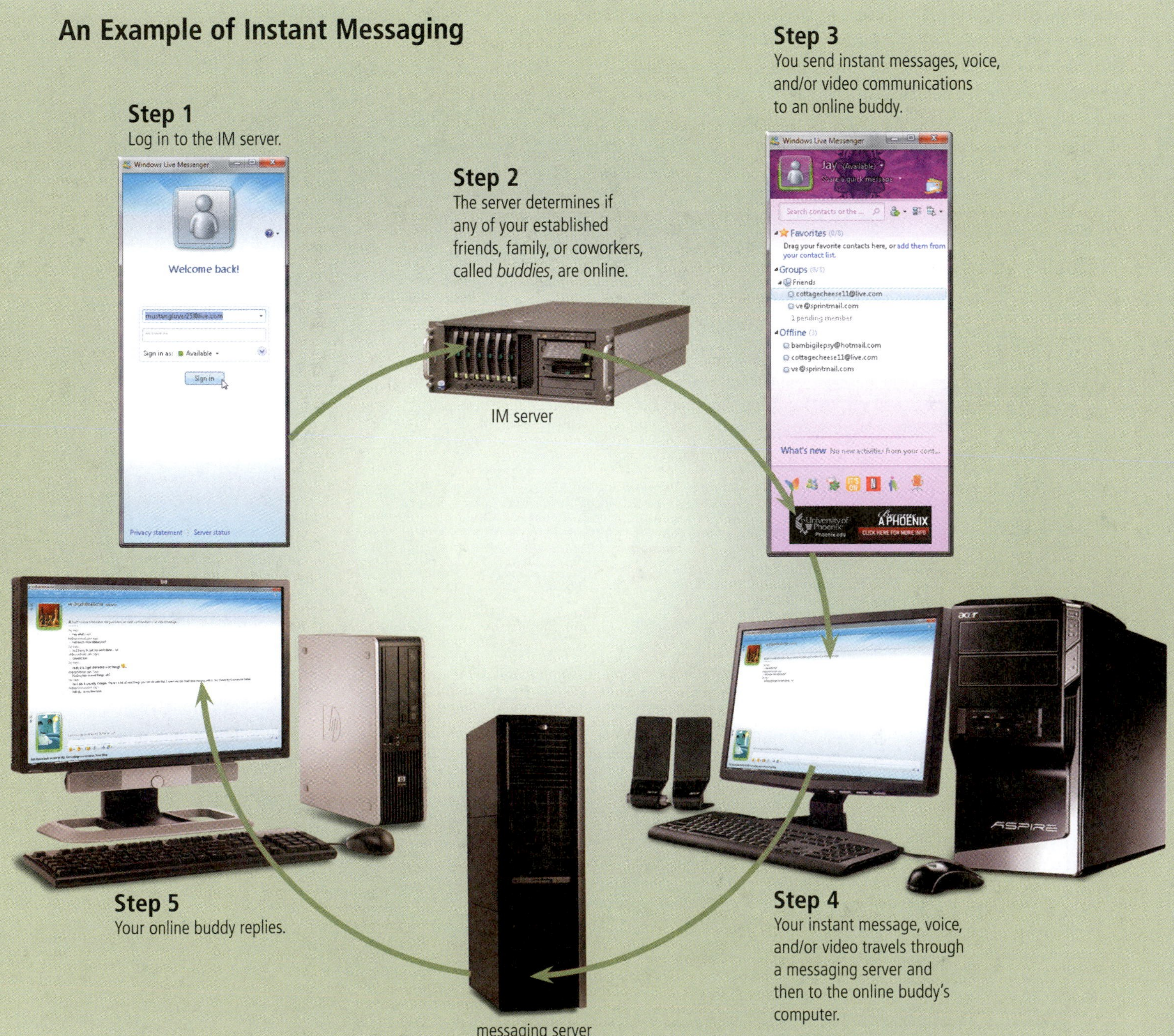

Figure 2-29 This figure shows an example of instant messaging.

or other documents to a recipient, listen to streaming music, and play games with another online party. For IM to work, both parties must be online at the same time. Also, the receiver of a message must be willing to accept messages.

To use IM, you may have to install *instant messenger* software on the computer or mobile device, such as a smart phone, you plan to use. Some operating systems, such as Windows, include an instant messenger. Popular IM software includes AIM (AOL Instant Messenger), Google Talk, MySpace IM, Windows Live Messenger, and Yahoo! Messenger.

Few IM programs follow IM standards. To ensure successful communications, all individuals on the contact list need to use the same or a compatible instant messenger.

FAQ 2-8

How popular are various online communications methods?

A research study conducted by Ipsos revealed that e-mail is expected to remain the preferred method of online communications during the next several years, at least. Methods of online communications expected to become more popular in the future include (listed from most popular to least popular) video conferencing, instant messaging, and text messaging.

For more information, visit the Computer Concepts CourseMate Web site at www.cengagebrain.com, navigate to the Chapter 2 FAQ resource for this book, and then click Online Communications.

Chat Rooms

A **chat** is a real-time typed conversation that takes place on a computer. A **chat room** is a location on an Internet server that permits users to chat with each other. Anyone in the chat room can participate in the conversation, which usually is specific to a particular topic.

As you type on your keyboard, a line of characters and symbols is displayed on the computer screen. Others connected to the same chat room server also see what you have typed (Figure 2-30). Some chat rooms support voice chats and video chats, in which people hear or see each other as they chat.

To start a chat session, you connect to a chat server through a program called a *chat client*. Today's browsers usually include a chat client. If yours does not, you can download a chat client from the Web. Some Web sites allow users to conduct chats without a chat client.

Once you have installed a chat client, you can create or join a conversation on the chat server to which you are connected. The chat room should indicate the discussion topic. The person who creates a chat room acts as the operator and has responsibility for monitoring the conversation and disconnecting anyone who becomes disruptive. Operator status can be shared or transferred to someone else.

Figure 2-30 As you type, the words and symbols you enter are displayed on the computer screens of other people in the same chat room. To save time many chat and IM users type abbreviations and acronyms for phrases, such as 'r u there?', which stands for 'Are you there?'.

Chat Rooms

For more information, visit the Computer Concepts CourseMate Web site at www.cengagebrain.com, navigate to the Chapter 2 Web Link resource for this book, and then click Chat Rooms.

VoIP

VoIP, (*Voice over IP*, or Internet Protocol) also called *Internet telephony*, enables users to speak to other users over the Internet. That is, VoIP uses the Internet (instead of the public switched telephone network) to connect a calling party to one or more local or long-distance called parties.

To place an Internet telephone call, you need a high-speed Internet connection (such as a DSL or cable modem); Internet telephone service; a microphone or telephone, depending on the Internet telephone service; and Internet telephone software or a VoIP router, or a telephone adapter, depending on the Internet telephone service. VoIP services also are available on some mobile devices that have wireless Internet service. Calls to other parties with the same Internet telephone service often are free, while calls that connect to the telephone network typically cost about $15 to $35 per month.

As you speak in a microphone connected to your computer or a telephone connected to the VoIP router or telephone adapter, the Internet telephone software and the computer's sound card or the VoIP router or telephone adapter convert your spoken words (analog signals) to digital signals and then transmit the digitized audio over the Internet to the called parties. Software and equipment at the receiving end reverse the process so that the receiving parties can hear what you have said. Figure 2-31 illustrates one possible configuration for VoIP.

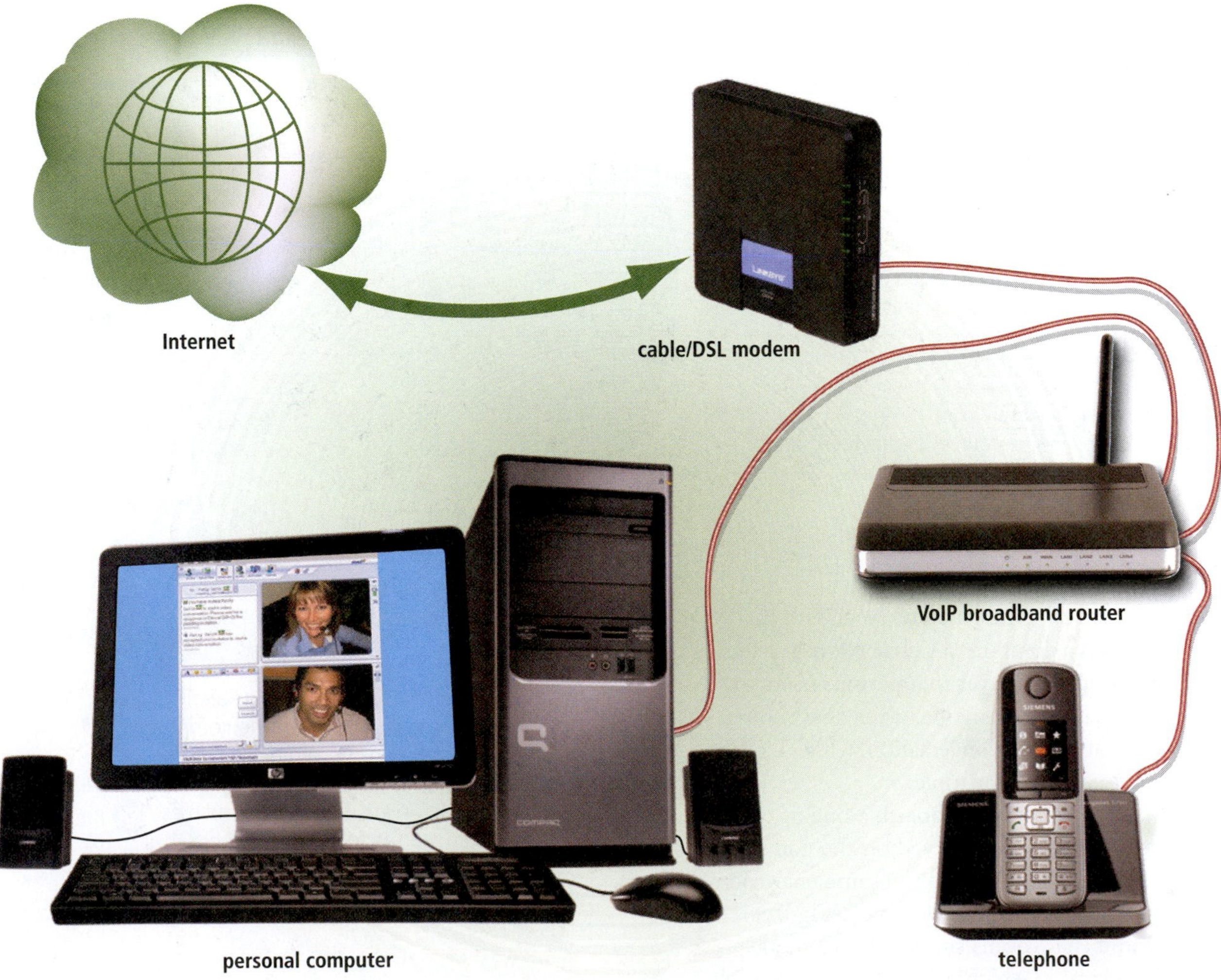

Figure 2-31 One type of equipment configuration for a user making a call via VoIP.

Newsgroups and Message Boards

A **newsgroup** is an online area in which users have written discussions about a particular subject (Figure 2-32). To participate in a discussion, a user posts a message, called an article, to the newsgroup, and other users in the newsgroup read and reply to the message. A *thread* or *threaded discussion* consists of the original article and all subsequent related replies.

A computer that stores and distributes newsgroup messages is called a news server. Some newsgroups require you to enter a user name and password to participate in the discussion. For example, a newsgroup for students taking a college course may require a user name and password to access the newsgroup. This ensures that only students in the course participate in the discussion.

To participate in a newsgroup, typically you use a program called a *newsreader*. Windows Live Mail includes a newsreader. Some Web sites, such as Google Groups, that sponsor newsgroups have a built-in newsreader.

A popular Web-based type of discussion group that does not require a newsreader is a **message board**. Many Web sites use message boards instead of newsgroups because they are easier to use.

FTP

FTP (File Transfer Protocol) is an Internet standard that permits file uploading and downloading with other computers on the Internet. Uploading is the opposite of downloading; that is, **uploading** is the process of transferring documents, graphics, and other objects from your computer to a server on the Internet. Web page authors, for example, often use FTP to upload their Web pages to a Web server.

Many operating systems include FTP capabilities. If yours does not, you can download FTP programs from the Web, usually for a small fee.

An *FTP server* is a computer that allows users to upload and/or download files using FTP. An FTP site is a collection of files including text, graphics, audio clips, video clips, and program files that reside on an FTP server. Many FTP sites have *anonymous FTP*, whereby anyone can transfer some, if not all, available files. Some FTP sites restrict file transfers to those who have authorized accounts (user names and passwords) on the FTP server.

Large files on FTP sites often are compressed to reduce storage space and download time. Before you can use a compressed (zipped) file, you must uncompress (unzip) it. Chapter 8 discusses utilities that zip and unzip files.

FTP

For more information, visit the Computer Concepts CourseMate Web site at www.cengagebrain.com, navigate to the Chapter 2 Web Link resource for this book, and then click FTP.

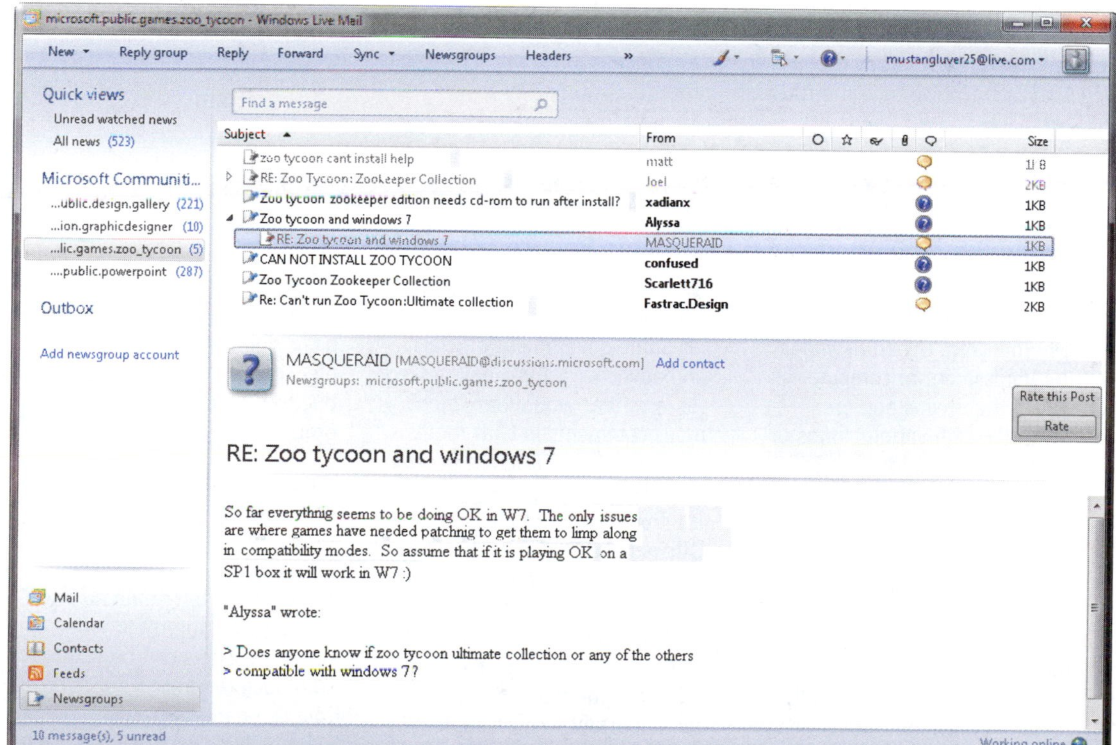

Figure 2-32 Users in a newsgroup read and reply to other users' messages.

Netiquette

Netiquette, which is short for Internet etiquette, is the code of acceptable behaviors users should follow while on the Internet; that is, it is the conduct expected of individuals while online. Netiquette includes rules for all aspects of the Internet, including the World Wide Web, e-mail, instant messaging, chat rooms, FTP, and newsgroups and message boards. Figure 2-33 outlines some of the rules of netiquette. Read Ethics & Issues 2-5 for a related discussion.

NETIQUETTE — Golden Rule: Treat others as you would like them to treat you.

1. In e-mail, chat rooms, and newsgroups:
   - Keep messages brief. Use proper grammar, spelling, and punctuation.
   - Be careful when using sarcasm and humor, as it might be misinterpreted.
   - Be polite. Avoid offensive language.
   - Read the message before you send it.
   - Use meaningful subject lines.
   - Avoid sending or posting *flames*, which are abusive or insulting messages. Do not participate in *flame wars*, which are exchanges of flames.
   - Avoid sending spam, which is the Internet's version of junk mail. *Spam* is an unsolicited e-mail message or newsgroup posting sent to many recipients or newsgroups at once.
   - Do not use all capital letters, which is the equivalent of SHOUTING!
   - Use **emoticons** to express emotion. Popular emoticons include

:)	Smile	:|	Indifference	:o	Surprised
:(	Frown	:\	Undecided		

   - Use abbreviations and acronyms for phrases:

btw	by the way
imho	in my humble opinion
fyi	for your information
ttfn	ta ta for now
fwiw	for what it's worth
tyvm	thank you very much

   - Clearly identify a *spoiler*, which is a message that reveals a solution to a game or ending to a movie or program.
2. Read the *FAQ* (frequently asked questions), if one exists. Many newsgroups and Web pages have an FAQ.
3. Do not assume material is accurate or up-to-date. Be forgiving of other's mistakes.
4. Never read someone's private e-mail.

Figure 2-33 Some of the rules of netiquette.

ETHICS & ISSUES 2-5

Would Banning Anonymous Comments Reduce Cyberbullying?

Recently, several high-profile cases highlighted the issue of cyberbullying. *Cyberbullying* is the harassment of computer users, often teens and preteens, through various forms of Internet communications. The behavior typically occurs via e-mail, instant messaging, and chat rooms, and can result in a traumatic experience for the recipient. The bullying may be in the form of threats, spreading of rumors, or humiliation. Usually, the perpetrators of cyberbullying remain anonymous. Many people believe that the anonymous nature of the Internet directly leads to this unscrupulous behavior. Some government officials and advocacy groups have asked for laws that would ban anonymous comments in chat rooms and require that Internet access providers verify and record the true identity of all users. Others have proposed that it be illegal to sign up for an e-mail account or instant messaging account with a fake screen name. Opponents of such plans claim that anonymity and privacy are too important to give up. They state, for example, that the right to be critical of the government in an anonymous forum is a basic right. The rights of everyone should not be infringed upon due to bad behavior of a small group of people.

Would banning anonymous comments reduce cyberbullying? Why or why not? What are the positive and negative aspects of the freedom to remain anonymous on the Internet? What other measures can be taken to reduce cyberbullying? What role can parents play in reducing cyberbullying?

Cyberbullying
For more information, visit the Computer Concepts CourseMate Web site at www.cengagebrain.com, navigate to the Chapter 2 Web Link resource for this book, and then click Cyberbullying.

QUIZ YOURSELF 2-3

Instructions: Find the true statement below. Then, rewrite the remaining false statements so that they are true.

1. A chat room is a location on an Internet server that permits users to chat with each other.
2. An e-mail address is a combination of a user name and an e-mail program that identifies a user so that he or she can receive Internet e-mail.
3. Business-to-consumer e-commerce occurs when one consumer sells directly to another, such as in an online auction.
4. FTP is an Internet standard that permits file reading and writing with other computers on the Internet.
5. Spam uses the Internet (instead of the public switched telephone network) to connect a calling party to one or more called parties.
6. Netiquette is the code of unacceptable behaviors while on the Internet.
7. VoIP enables users to subscribe to other users over the Internet.

Quiz Yourself Online: To further check your knowledge of pages 98 through 108, visit the Computer Concepts CourseMate Web site at www.cengagebrain.com, navigate to the Chapter 2 Quiz Yourself resource for this book, and then click Objectives 10 – 12.

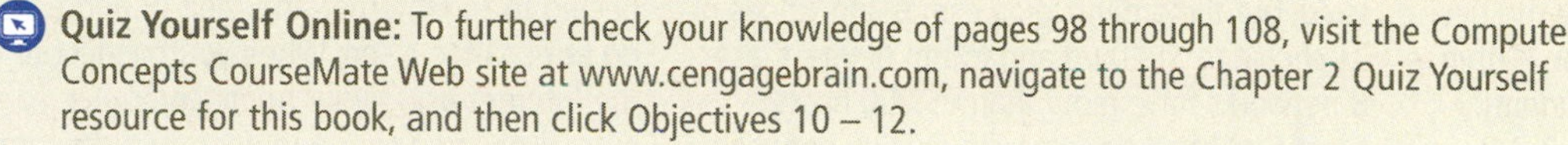

Chapter Summary

This chapter presented the history and structure of the Internet. It discussed the World Wide Web at length, including topics such as browsing, navigating, searching, Web publishing, and e-commerce. It also introduced other services available on the Internet, such as e-mail, mailing lists, instant messaging, chat rooms, VoIP, newsgroups and message boards, and FTP. Finally, the chapter listed rules of netiquette.

Computer Usage @ Work

Entertainment

Do you wonder how music on the radio sounds so perfectly in tune, how animated motion pictures are created, or how one controls lighting during a concert? Not only does the entertainment industry rely on computers to advertise and sell their services on the Internet, computers also assist in other aspects, including audio and video composition, lighting control, computerized animation, and computer gaming.

As mentioned in this chapter, entertainment Web sites provide music and movies you can purchase and download to your computer or mobile device; live news broadcasts, performances, and sporting events; games you can play with other online users; and much more.

As early as 1951, computers were used to record and play music. Today, computers play a much larger role in the music industry. For example, if you are listening to a song on the radio and notice that not one note is out of tune, it is possible that software was used to change individual notes without altering the rest of the song.

Many years ago, creating cartoons or animated motion pictures was an extremely time-consuming task because artists were responsible for sketching thousands of drawings by hand. Currently, artists use computers to create these drawings in a fraction of the time, which significantly can reduce the time and cost of development.

Computers also are used in the game industry. While some game developers create games from scratch, others might use game engines that simplify the development process. For example, LucasArts created the GrimE game engine, which is designed to create adventure games.

During a concert, lighting technicians use computer programs to turn lights off and on, change color, or change location at specified intervals. In fact, once a performance begins, the technicians often merely are standing by, monitoring the computer as it performs most of the work. A significant amount of time and effort, however, is required to program the computer to perform its required tasks during a live show.

The next time you listen to a song, watch a movie, play a game, or attend a concert, think about the role computers play in contributing to your entertainment.

For more information, visit the Computer Concepts CourseMate Web site at www.cengagebrain.com, navigate to the Chapter 2 Computer Usage @ Work resource for this book, and then click Entertainment.

High-Tech Talk

A Computer's Internet Protocol (IP) Address

Every computer on the Internet has a unique address, called an IP address, that distinguishes it from other computers on the Internet. Currently, two versions of IP addresses exist: IPv4 (Internet Protocol Version 4) and IPv6 (Internet Protocol Version 6). An IPv4 address has two parts that identify a specific computer: one part to identify the network where that computer resides and a second part to pinpoint the specific computer or host within that network. An IPv6 address has three parts: a global prefix to identify the network, a subnet to identify the location within the network, and the interface ID to identify the specific computer or host (Figure 2-34). Today, IPv4 addresses are more commonly used. For this reason, the terms IP address and IPv4 address are used interchangeably.

A typical IPv4 address — such as 72.14.207.99 — has four groups of numbers that range from 0 through 255. This form of the IP address sometimes is called a *dotted decimal number* or *dotted quad*. The four groups of numbers in the dotted quad are called octets, because they each have 8 bits when viewed in binary form for a total of 32 bits in the IP address. For instance, the binary form of 72.14.207.99 is 01001000.00001110.11001111.01100011. For more information about how the binary system works, see Appendix C.

Because each of the 8 bits can be 1 or 0, the total possible combinations per octet are 2^8, or 256. Combining the four octets of an IP address provides a possible 2^{32} or 4,294,967,296 unique values. The actual number of available addresses is about 3 billion, because some values are reserved for special use and are, therefore, off limits.

IP addresses, which are assigned by InterNIC (The Internet's Network Information Center), belong to one of three network classes: A, B, or C. In a Class A network, the first octet of the IPv4 address is assigned a number between 1 and 127. Large enterprises typically are assigned a Class A network, which can contain more than 16 million hosts; this allows network administrators to assign a value of their choice to the remaining three octets. Class B networks contain a number between 128 and 191 in the first octet. The second octet also is fixed, but the organization can assign values of its choice to the third and fourth octets. Class B networks have more than 65,000 hosts. Class C networks begin with a value between 192 and 223 and allow only the fourth octet to be customized. Class C networks can have only 254 hosts. Class D and E networks also exist, although they rarely are used.

To request data such as a Web page from a computer on the Internet, you need only an IP address. For instance, if you type the IPv4 address 72.14.207.99 in your Web browser's Address bar, the browser will display the home page on the machine hosting the Google Web site. Remembering an IP address is difficult at best — so you probably would just type the domain name, www.google.com, in the browser. The browser then contacts a domain name server (DNS) to resolve the human-readable domain name into a machine-readable IP address. Each domain name server houses a simple database that maps domain names to IP addresses. The DNS would resolve the human-readable domain name, www.google.com, into a machine-readable IP address, 72.14.207.99.

Domain names are helpful because they are easier for people to remember than IP addresses. You can learn more about a domain using the whois form at the Network Solutions Web site (www.netsol.com and then click the WHOIS link). If you type a domain name, such as google.com, the form displays the registration information for that domain, including its IP address.

Like all other computers, your computer must have an IP address to connect to the Internet or another computer that has an IP address. Servers generally have *static IP addresses*, because they usually are connected to the Internet and their IP addresses do not change often. When you connect to the Internet using your home computer, you most likely are using a temporary or *dynamic IP address*. Your access provider uses the *Dynamic Host Configuration Protocol (DHCP)* to assign your computer a temporary dynamic IP address from a pool of IP addresses. The dynamic IP address is unique only for that session. Once you disconnect, the DHCP server releases that IP address back in the IP address pool so that it can assign it to the next requesting computer. Even if you immediately reconnect, the DHCP server might not assign you the same IP address. Using DHCP and dynamic IP addresses means an Internet access provider needs only one IP address for each modem it supports, rather than one for each of its millions of customers.

Billions of IP addresses sounds like a lot. But, because so many computers and other devices connected to the Internet need unique IP addresses, a growing shortage of IP addresses exists. The newer IP addressing scheme is IPv6, also called IPng (IP Next Generation, which) will lengthen IP addresses from 32 bits to 128 bits and increase the number of available IP addresses to a whopping 3.4×10^{38}, or 340,000, 000,000,000,000,000,000,000,000,000,000, 000. Software is available that will install IPv6 on most current computers, although many networks and Internet service providers do not yet require its use. In fact, it could be many years before IPv6 completely replaces IPv4.

Do you want to know the IP address currently assigned to your computer? Click the Start button on the Windows taskbar and then click Control Panel. Click Network and Internet and then click View Network Status and Tasks. Finally, click View status and then click Details.

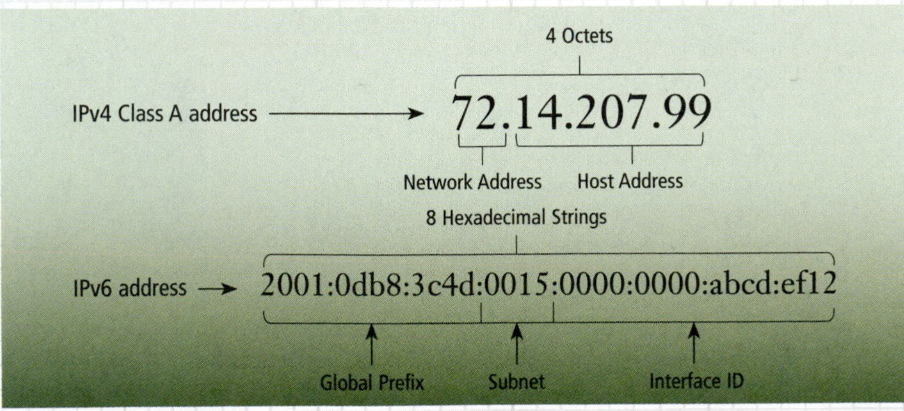

Figure 2-34 Components of IPv4 and IPv6 addresses.

For more information, visit the Computer Concepts CourseMate Web site at www.cengagebrain.com, navigate to the Chapter 2 High-Tech Talk resource for this book, and then click IP Addresses.

Companies on the Cutting Edge

GOOGLE **Popular Search Engine and Services**

Google founders Sergey Brin and Larry Page have done very little advertising, but their Web site has become a household word, largely on favorable word-of-mouth reviews. They launched the Web site in 1998 in a friend's garage with the goal of providing the best possible experience for their loyal users who are looking for information presented clearly and quickly.

Google regularly scans more than one trillion Web pages in search of unique phrases and terms. Its thousands of connected computers deliver organized search results for the hundreds of millions of queries users input daily. Recently, the company updated its Google Earth product to allow users to explore the Moon, and also updated its popular advertising product, AdWords. Among its other services are Google Docs and YouTube.

eBAY **World's Largest Online Marketplace**

Millions of products are traded daily on *eBay* auctions, whether it is across town or across the globe. The more than 88 million registered worldwide shoppers generate at least $1.8 billion in annual revenue through purchases on the main Web site, eBay, along with items on Shopping.com, tickets on StubHub, classifieds on Kijiji, and other e-commerce venues.

The shoppers likely pay for their merchandise using PayPal, another eBay service. This merchant service allows buyers to transfer money from savings accounts or use their credit card without having to expose the account number to the seller. Other eBay companies are Rent.com, which offers listings for apartments and houses, and Shopping.com, which allows consumers to find and compare products. Recently, eBay introduced a program to more easily identify its top-rated sellers. It also invited buyers and sellers to become members of the eBay Green Team, which encourages and promotes environmentally friendly business practices.

For more information, visit the Computer Concepts CourseMate Web site at www.cengagebrain.com and then navigate to the Chapter 2 Companies on the Cutting Edge resource for this book.

Technology Trailblazers

TIM BERNERS-LEE **Creator of the World Wide Web**

Being the creator of the World Wide Web is an impressive item on any resume, and it certainly helped *Tim Berners-Lee* become the 3Com Founders Professor of Engineering at the Massachusetts Institute of Technology in 2008. As a professor in the electrical engineering and computer science departments, he researches social and technical collaboration on the Internet.

Berners-Lee's interest in sharing information via Web servers, browsers, and Web addresses developed in 1989 while working at CERN, the European Organization for Nuclear Research, in Geneva, Switzerland. He continued to improve his design of a program that tracked random associations for several years and then became the director of the World Wide Web Consortium (W3C), a forum to develop Web standards, in 1994.

Recently, Queen Elizabeth bestowed the Order of Merit – the highest civilian honor – upon the British-born Berners-Lee.

MARK ZUCKERBERG **Facebook Founder and CEO**

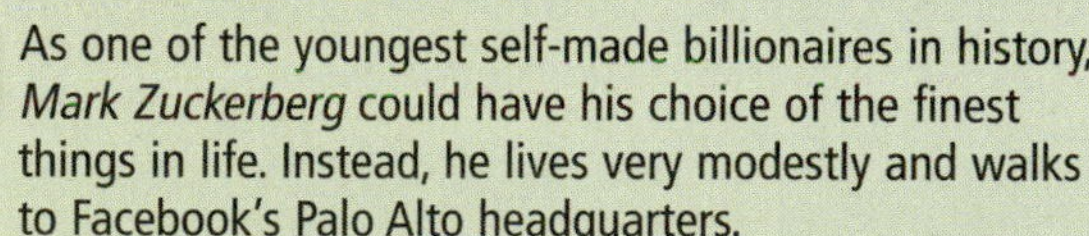

As one of the youngest self-made billionaires in history, *Mark Zuckerberg* could have his choice of the finest things in life. Instead, he lives very modestly and walks to Facebook's Palo Alto headquarters.

Both Microsoft and AOL had recruited Zuckerberg during his senior year in high school in New Hampshire. He declined their job offers and decided to attend Harvard. In college, he and some friends developed several projects, laying the foundation that led to Facebook's eventual start. Harvard administrators claimed these Web sites violated students' privacy. He, however, had instant success launching Facebook from his dorm room, and the Web site's popularity quickly spread to other Ivy League and Boston-area colleges and then worldwide. He left his studies at Harvard University in 2004 and moved to California.

Today, Zuckerberg says he spends the majority of his time running the $15 billion company on very little sleep.

For more information, visit the Computer Concepts CourseMate Web site at www.cengagebrain.com and then navigate to the Chapter 2 Technology Trailblazers resource for this book.

Chapter Review

The Chapter Review reinforces the main concepts presented in this chapter.

To listen to an audio version of this Chapter Review, visit the Computer Concepts CourseMate Web site at www.cengagebrain.com and then navigate to the Chapter 2 Chapter Review resource for this book.

1. **How Did the Internet Evolve?** The **Internet**, also called the *Net*, is a worldwide collection of networks that links millions of businesses, government agencies, educational institutions, and individuals. The Internet has its roots in *ARPANET*, a network started in 1969 to link scientific and academic researchers across the United States. In 1986, the National Science Foundation connected its huge network, called *NSFnet*, to ARPANET, creating a configuration of complex networks and hosts that became known as the Internet. Today, more than 550 million *host* computers connect to the Internet.

2. **What Are the Various Types of Internet Connections, and What Are the Differences between Broadband and Dial-Up Connections?** Many home and small business users opt to connect to the Internet via high-speed *broadband* Internet connections. *DSL* (digital subscriber line) provides Internet connections using regular copper telephone lines. *Cable Internet service* provides high-speed Internet access through the cable television network via a cable modem. *Fiber to the Premises* (*FTTP*) uses fiber-optic cable to provide high-speed Internet access. *Fixed wireless* provides high-speed Internet connections using a dish-shaped antenna to communicate via radio signals. A *cellular radio network* offers high-speed Internet connections to devices with built-in compatible technology or computers with wireless modems. A **Wi-Fi** network uses radio signals. *Satellite Internet service* provides high-speed Internet connections via satellite. Some homes and small businesses connect to the Internet with dial-up access. *Dial-up access*, which is slower-speed technology, takes place when the modem in your computer connects to the Internet via a standard telephone line that transmits data and information using an analog (continuous wave) pattern.

3. **What Are the Types of Internet Access Providers?** An **access provider** is a business that provides access to the Internet free or for a fee. An **ISP** (**Internet service provider**) is a regional or national access provider. An **online service provider** (**OSP**) provides Internet access in addition to members-only features. A **wireless Internet service provider** provides wireless Internet access to desktop and notebook computers and mobile devices with built-in wireless capabilities (such as Wi-Fi) or to computers using wireless modems or wireless access devices.

4. **What Is the Purpose of an IP Address, and What Is Its Relationship to a Domain Name?** An **IP address** (Internet Protocol address) is a number that uniquely identifies each computer or device connected to the Internet. The Internet relies on IP addresses to send data to computers at specific locations. The IP address usually consists of four groups of numbers, each separated by a period. A **domain name** is the text version of an IP address.

Visit the Computer Concepts CourseMate Web site at www.cengagebrain.com, navigate to the Chapter 2 Quiz Yourself resource for this book, and then click Objectives 1 – 4.

5. **What Is the Purpose of a Web Browser, and What Are the Components of a Web Address?** A **Web browser**, or **browser**, is application software that allows users to access and view Web pages or access Web 2.0 programs. With an Internet connection established, you start a Web browser, which then retrieves and displays a starting Web page, sometimes called a **home page**. The home page usually contains links to other Web pages. A **link**, short for *hyperlink*, is a built-in connection to another related Web page or part of a Web page. A **Web page** has a unique address called a **URL** (*Uniform Resource Locator*), or **Web address**. A Web address consists of a protocol, a domain name, and sometimes the path to a specific Web page or location on a Web page.

6. **How Do You Use a Search Engine to Search for Information on the Web, and What Is the Difference between a Search Engine and a Subject Directory?** A **search engine** is a program that finds Web sites, Web pages, images, videos, news, maps, and other information related to a specific topic. To use a search engine, you enter a word or phrase, called **search text** or a *search query*, that describes the item you want to find. Each word in the search text is known as a *keyword*. The search engine displays a list of *hits*. When clicked, each hit displays an associated Web site or Web page. A **subject directory** classifies Web pages in an organized set of categories and related subcategories. By clicking links, you move through levels to display a list of Web pages about a desired topic.

Chapter Review

7. What Are the Types of Web Sites? A **portal** is a Web site that offers a variety of Internet services from a single location. A news Web site contains newsworthy material. An informational Web site contains factual information. A business/marketing Web site promotes or sells products or services. A **blog**, short for *Weblog*, is an informal Web site consisting of time-stamped articles, or posts, in a diary or journal format, usually listed in reverse chronological order. A **wiki** is a collaborative Web site that allows users to create, add to, modify, or delete the Web site content via their Web browser. An **online social network**, or **social networking Web site**, encourages members to share their interests, ideas, stories, photos, music, and videos with other registered users. An educational Web site offers avenues for teaching and learning. An entertainment Web site provides an interactive and engaging environment. An advocacy Web site describes a cause, opinion, or idea. A **Web application**, or *Web app*, is a Web site that allows users to access and interact with software through a Web browser or any computer or device connected to the Internet. A *content aggregator* is a business that gathers and organizes Web content and then distributes, or feeds, the content to subscribers for free or a fee. A personal Web site is maintained by a private individual or family.

8. How Do Web Pages Use Graphics, Animation, Audio, Video, Virtual Reality, and Plug-Ins? Some Web pages use **multimedia**, which combines text with graphics, animation, audio, video, and/or virtual reality. A **graphic** is a digital representation of nontext information such as a drawing, chart, or photo. **Animation** is the appearance of motion created by displaying a series of still images in sequence. **Audio** includes music, speech, or any other sound. **Video** consists of full-motion images played back at various speeds. **Virtual reality (VR)** is the use of computers to simulate an environment that appears as three-dimensional space. A **plug-in**, or *add-on*, is a program that extends a browser's capability to display multimedia elements.

9. What Are the Steps Required for Web Publishing? **Web publishing** is the development and maintenance of Web pages. The five major steps to Web publishing are: (1) plan a Web site, (2) analyze and design a Web site, (3) create a Web site, (4) deploy a Web site, and (5) maintain a Web site.

Visit the Computer Concepts CourseMate Web site at www.cengagebrain.com, navigate to the Chapter 2 Quiz Yourself resource for this book, and then click Objectives 5 – 9.

10. What Are the Types of E-Commerce? **E-commerce**, short for *electronic commerce*, is a business transaction that occurs over an electronic network such as the Internet. *Business-to-consumer (B2C) e-commerce* consists of the sale of goods and services to the general public. *Consumer-to-consumer (C2C) e-commerce* occurs when one consumer sells directly to another, such as in an **online auction**. *Business-to-business (B2B) e-commerce* takes place between businesses that exchange goods and services.

11. How Do E-Mail, Mailing Lists, Instant Messaging, Chat Rooms, VoIP, Newsgroups and Message Boards, and FTP Work? **E-mail** (short for *electronic mail*) is the transmission of messages and files via a computer network. A **mailing list** is a group of e-mail names and addresses given a single name, so that everyone on the list receives a message sent to the list. **Instant messaging (IM)** is a **real-time** Internet communications service that notifies you when one or more people are online. A **chat room** is a location on an Internet server that permits users to conduct real-time typed conversations. **VoIP** (*Voice over IP*, or Internet Protocol), also called *Internet telephony*, enables users to speak to other users over the Internet, instead of the public switched telephone network. A **newsgroup** is an online area in which users have written discussions about a particular subject. A **message board** is a Web-based type of discussion group that is easier to use than a newsgroup. **FTP** (*File Transfer Protocol*) is an Internet standard that permits file **uploading** and **downloading** with other computers on the Internet.

12. What Are the Rules of Netiquette? **Netiquette**, which is short for Internet etiquette, is the code of acceptable behaviors users should follow while on the Internet. Netiquette rules include: keep messages short, be polite, avoid sending *flames* or *spam*, use **emoticons** and acronyms, clearly identify a *spoiler*, read the *FAQ*, do not assume material is accurate or up-to-date, and never read someone's private e-mail.

Visit the Computer Concepts CourseMate Web site at www.cengagebrain.com, navigate to the Chapter 2 Quiz Yourself resource for this book, and then click Objectives 10 – 12.

Key Terms

You should know the Primary Terms and be familiar with the Secondary Terms. The list below helps focus your study.

To see an example of and a definition for each term, and to access current and additional information from the Web, visit the Computer Concepts CourseMate Web site at www.cengagebrain.com and then navigate to the Chapter 2 Key Terms resource for this book.

Primary Terms

(shown in bold-black characters in the chapter)

access provider (77)
address book (102)
animation (94)
audio (94)
blog (90)
browser (81)
chat (105)
chat room (105)
DNS server (80)
domain name (79)
downloading (82)
e-commerce (98)
electronic storefront (99)
e-mail (101)
e-mail address (102)
e-mail program (101)
emoticons (108)
FTP (107)
graphic (93)
home page (82)
instant messaging (IM) (104)
Internet (74)
IP address (79)
ISP (Internet service provider) (78)
link (82)
mailing list (103)
media sharing Web site (91)
message board (107)
microblog (90)
MP3 (94)
multimedia (92)
netiquette (108)
newsgroup (107)
online auction (100)
online community (89)
online service provider (OSP) (78)
online social network (90)
player (94)
plug-in (97)
portal (89)
real time (104)
RSS 2.0 (92)
search engine (85)
search text (85)
shopping cart (99)
social networking Web site (90)
streaming (94)
subject directory (85)
subscribe (103)
surfing the Web (83)
tabbed browsing (84)
traffic (76)
unsubscribe (103)
uploading (107)
URL (82)
user name (102)
video (96)
video blog (90)
virtual reality (VR) (96)
VoIP (106)
Web (80)
Web 2.0 (81)
Web address (82)
Web application (91)
Web browser (81)
Web page (80)
Web publishing (98)
Web server (81)
Web site (81)
Wi-Fi (76)
wiki (90)
wireless Internet service provider (78)
World Wide Web (80)

blog (90)

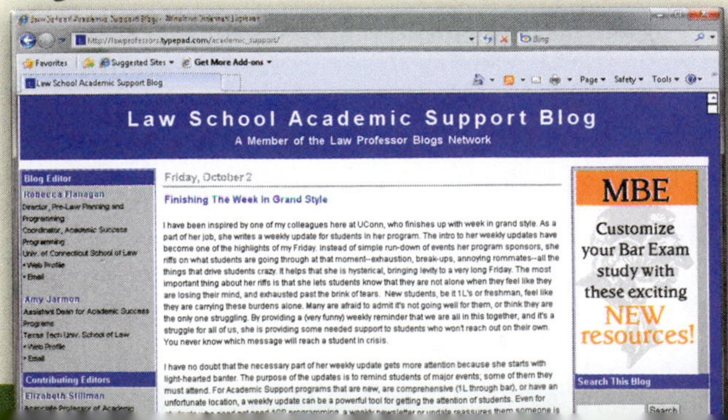

Secondary Terms

(shown in italic characters in the chapter)

add-on (97)
animated GIF (94)
anonymous FTP (107)
ARPA (75)
ARPANET (75)
Atom (92)
blogger (90)
blogosphere (90)
bookmark (83)
broadband (76)
buddies (104)
business-to-business (B2B) e-commerce (100)
business-to-consumer (B2C) e-commerce (98)
cable Internet service (76)
ccTLD (80)
cellular radio network (76)
chat client (105)
click (84)
consumer-to-consumer (C2C) e-commerce (100)
content aggregator (92)
dial-up access (76)
domain name system (DNS) (80)
DSL (76)
dynamic Web page (81)
electronic commerce (98)
electronic mail (101)
e-retail (99)
FAQ (108)
favorite (83)
Fiber to the Premises (FTTP) (76)
file (77)
fixed wireless (76)
flame wars (108)
flames (108)
FTP server (107)
GIF (93)
graphical image (93)
gTLD (80)
hits (86)
host (75)
hot spots (76)
http (82)
hyperlink (82)
hypermedia (83)
hypertext (83)
Hypertext Transfer Protocol (82)
ICANN (80)
instant messenger (105)
Internet backbone (78)
Internet telephony (106)
IPv6 (80)
JPEG (93)
keyword (85)
m-commerce (98)
microbrowser (82)
MP4 (96)
MPEG (96)
MPEG-4 (96)
national ISP (78)
Net (74)
newsreader (107)
NSFnet (75)
PNG (93)
podcast (94)
POP3 (103)
Post Office Protocol (103)
pull (83)
push (83)
Really Simple Syndication (92)
regional ISP (78)
registrar (80)
satellite Internet service (76)
search query (85)
SMTP (103)
spam (108)
spider (88)
spoiler (108)
static Web page (81)
streaming audio (94)
streaming video (96)
thread (107)
threaded discussion (107)
thumbnail (94)
top-level domain (TLD) (80)
Uniform Resource Locator (82)
vlog (90)
vlogger (90)
vlogosphere (90)
Voice over IP (106)
VR world (96)
W3C (76)
Web app (91)
Weblog (90)
WebSlices (92)
wireless portal (89)
WWW (80)

Checkpoint

The Checkpoint exercises test your knowledge of the chapter concepts. The page number containing the answer appears in parentheses after each exercise. The Beyond the Book exercises will help broaden your understanding of the concepts presented in this chapter.

To complete the Checkpoint exercises interactively, visit the Computer Concepts CourseMate Web site at www.cengagebrain.com and then navigate to the Chapter 2 Checkpoint resource for this book.

True/False

Mark T for True and F for False.

_____ 1. A single government agency owns and controls the Internet. (76)

_____ 2. DSL provides high-speed Internet connections through the cable television network. (76)

_____ 3. In general, the first portion of each IP address identifies the network and the last portion identifies the specific computer. (79)

_____ 4. A Web 2.0 Web site can never allow users to modify Web site content. (81)

_____ 5. A Web page has a unique address, called a URL or Web address. (82)

_____ 6. Hypertext combines text-based links with graphic, audio, and video links. (83)

_____ 7. The major disadvantage with a subject directory is that users have difficulty deciding which categories to choose as they work through the menus of links presented. (88)

_____ 8. Most social networking Web sites include chat rooms, newsgroups, and other communications services. (90)

_____ 9. Streaming disallows users from accessing and using a file while it is transmitting. (94)

_____ 10. A plug-in is a program that extends the capability of an add-on. (97)

_____ 11. Most e-commerce actually takes place between consumers, which is called consumer-to-consumer e-commerce. (100)

_____ 12. Flames are abusive or insulting messages. (108)

Multiple Choice

Select the best answer.

1. _____ offers high-speed Internet connections to devices with built-in compatible technology or computers with wireless modems. (76)
   a. Cable Internet service
   b. A digital subscriber line
   c. A cellular radio network
   d. Fiber to the Premises (FTTP)

2. As with an IP address, the components of a domain name are separated by _____. (79)
   a. commas
   b. periods
   c. colons
   d. semicolons

3. _____ combines text-based links with graphic, audio, and video links. (83)
   a. Hypertext
   b. Multi-linking
   c. Hypermedia
   d. Tabbed browsing

4. All of the following techniques can be used to improve Web searches except _____. (88)
   a. put the most important terms last
   b. read a search engine's Help information
   c. list all possible spellings
   d. if a search is unsuccessful, try another search engine

5. A _____ is a Web site that allows users to post short text updates, usually between 100 and 200 characters. (90)
   a. microblog
   b. wiki
   c. portal
   d. podcast

6. A(n) _____ is a small version of a larger graphic. (94)
   a. thumbnail
   b. MP3
   c. wiki
   d. portal

7. _____ is the process of transferring documents, graphics, and other objects from your computer to a server on the Internet. (107)
   a. Downloading
   b. Social networking
   c. Uploading
   d. Blogging

8. _____ is the code of acceptable behaviors users should follow while on the Internet. (108)
   a. Post Office Protocol
   b. The Golden Rule
   c. Netiquette
   d. An FAQ

STUDENT ASSIGNMENTS

Checkpoint

Matching

Match the terms with their definitions.

_____ 1. gTLD (80)
_____ 2. ccTLD (80)
_____ 3. DNS Server (80)
_____ 4. IPv6 (80)
_____ 5. link (82)
_____ 6. search engine (85)
_____ 7. MP3 (94)
_____ 8. player (94)
_____ 9. video (96)
_____ 10. VoIP (106)

a. built-in connection to another related Web page or part of a Web page
b. a two-letter country code for international Web sites outside the United States
c. enables users to speak to other users over the Internet
d. format that reduces an audio file to about one-tenth its original size
e. new IP addressing scheme that may increase the number of available IP addresses
f. translates the domain name to its associated IP address
g. software used to listen to an audio file on a computer
h. identifies the type of organization associated with a domain
i. program that finds Web sites, Web pages, images, videos, news, maps, and other information related to a specific topic
j. full-motion images that are played back at various speeds

Short Answer

Write a brief answer to each of the following questions.

1. Describe three different types of broadband Internet services. ____________ What is the difference between a regional ISP and a national ISP? ____________
2. How is a static Web page different from a dynamic Web page? ____________ What is a Web site? ____________
3. What is a Web application? ____________What are some features and examples of Web applications? ____________
4. What are three types of specifications used by content aggregators to distribute content? ____________ How might you evaluate the accuracy of a Web site? ____________
5. What is Web publishing? ____________ What are the five major steps in Web publishing? ____________

Beyond the Book

Follow the book element instructions below; then present your findings (brief report, presentation, discussion, or other means).

1. Ethics & Issues — Select an Ethics & Issues in this chapter (84, 87, 90, 100, 108), find a recent newspaper/magazine article that supports one point of view presented, and then evaluate the article.
2. Computer Usage @ Work — Use the Web or a recent newspaper/magazine to locate three additional unique usages of computer technology in the entertainment industry (109). What makes the use of these technologies unique to the entertainment industry?
3. Companies on the Cutting Edge and Technology Trailblazers — Use the Web or a recent business newspaper/magazine to locate an interesting fact about Google, eBay, Tim Berners-Lee, or Mark Zuckerberg that was not presented in the chapter (111).
4. High-Tech Talk — Locate a recent newspaper/magazine article that discusses topics related to A Computer's Internet Protocol (IP) Address (110). Would you recommend the article you found? Why or why not?
5. FAQs and Web Links — Use the Web or a recent newspaper/magazine to locate three additional facts about an FAQ (77, 78, 82, 88, 96, 99, 103, 105) and Web Link (76, 78, 82, 84, 96, 98, 100, 103, 105, 107, 108) that were not presented in the chapter.
6. Looking Ahead — Use the Web or a recent newspaper/magazine to discover additional uses of the technology presented in Web 3.0 to Reinvent the Virtual World (81).
7. Innovative Computing — Use the Web or a recent newspaper/magazine to locate two additional interesting facts about View the Wonders of Space through the WorldWide Telescope (93) and Shopping Becomes a Virtual Experience (100).
8. Making Use of the Web — Visit three of the Research Web Sites (126) and outline the information on each Web site and the possible uses for each Web site.

Learn It Online

The Learn It Online exercises are interactive Web exercises designed to reinforce and expand your understanding of the chapter concepts. The descriptions below briefly summarize each exercise.

To complete the Learn It Online exercises, visit the Computer Concepts CourseMate Web site at www.cengagebrain.com, navigate to the Chapter 2 resources for this book, click the link for the exercise you want to complete, and then read the instructions.

1 At the Movies — Tell Your Stories via Vlog
Watch a movie to learn about how to post your thoughts to a vlog and then answer questions about the movie.

2 Video and Audio: You Review It — VoIP
Search for, choose, and write a review of a video, podcast, or vodcast that discusses Voice over IP.

3 Student Edition Labs — Connecting to the Internet, Getting the Most out of the Internet, and E-mail
Enhance your understanding and knowledge about the Internet and e-mail by completing the Connecting to the Internet, Getting the Most out of the Internet, and E-mail Labs.

4 Practice Test
Take a multiple choice test that checks your knowledge of the chapter concepts and review the resulting study guide.

5 Who Wants To Be a Computer Genius²?
Play the Shelly Cashman Series version of this popular game by answering questions to find out if you are a computer genius. Panic buttons are available to provide assistance during game play.

6 Wheel of Terms
Identify important key terms presented in this chapter by playing the Shelly Cashman Series version of this popular game.

7 You're Hired!
Embark on the path to a career in computers by answering questions and solving puzzles related to concepts discussed in this chapter.

8 Crossword Puzzle Challenge
Complete an interactive crossword puzzle to reinforce concepts presented in this chapter.

9 Windows Exercises
Step through the Windows 7 exercises to learn about Internet properties, dial-up networking connections, and using Help to understand the Internet.

10 Exploring Computer Careers
Read about a career as a Web developer, search for related employment advertisements, and then answer related questions.

11 Web Apps — Windows Live Hotmail
Learn how to sign up for a free e-mail account, add a contact to your address book, and send an e-mail message.

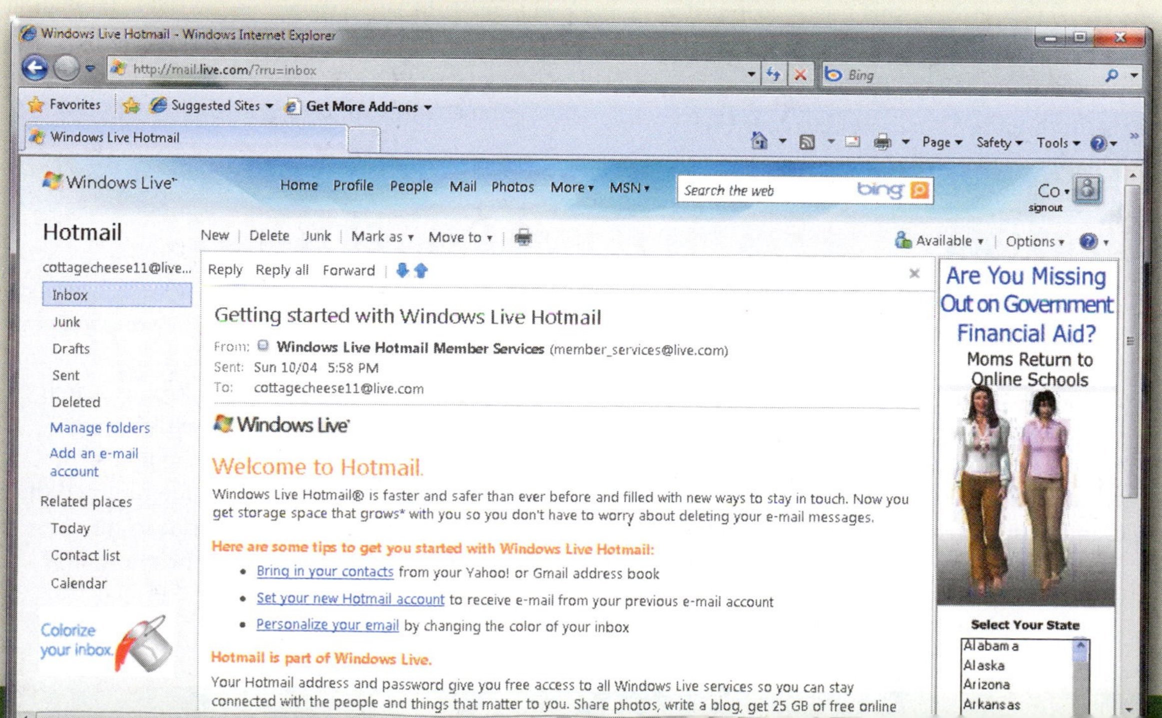

STUDENT ASSIGNMENTS

Problem Solving @ Home

The Problem Solving @ Home exercises extend your knowledge of the chapter concepts by seeking solutions to practical computer problems that you may encounter at home or school. The Collaboration exercise should be completed with a team.

In the real world, practical problems often can be solved in multiple ways. Provide one solution to each of the following problems using available resources, such as articles on the Web or in print, blogs, podcasts, videos, television, user guides, other individuals, and electronics and computer stores. You may need to use multiple resources to obtain an answer. Present your solutions in the form requested by your instructor (brief report, presentation, discussion, or other means).

1. **Page Not Displayed** When you type the Web address of your favorite news Web site in the Address bar of the Web browser, you immediately see an error message stating that the Web page cannot be displayed. You did not have problems accessing the Internet yesterday. Before calling technical support, how will you attempt to troubleshoot the problem?

2. **Slow Internet Connection** You just installed VoIP telephone service in your house. Each time you are on the telephone, however, you notice that your Internet connection slows down significantly. What could be causing this?

3. **No Wireless Connection** When you return home to visit your parents and turn on your new notebook computer, it does not connect automatically to their wireless network. What is your next step?

4. **Eliminating Pop-Ups** Each time you attempt to visit a Web site, many pop-up windows open on your computer. In fact, you sometimes close up to 10 windows that automatically appear. You used to browse the Web without this nuisance, but it is worsening by the day. What steps will you take to eliminate these pop-up windows?

5. **Incorrect Home Page** After starting your Web browser, you notice that your home page has changed. You display the Internet Options dialog box to change your home page back to its previous setting, close your browser, and then start the browser again. Surprisingly, your Web browser still navigates to a Web site other than the one you chose. What is your next step?

6. **Images Not Being Displayed** When you navigate to a Web page, you notice that no images are displaying. You successfully have viewed Web pages with images in the past and are not sure why images suddenly are not displayed. What steps will you take to view the images?

7. **Incorrect Search Engine** A class project requires that you conduct research on the Web. After typing the Web address for Google's home page and pressing the ENTER key, your Web browser redirects you to a different search engine. What could be wrong?

8. **Unsolicited Friend Requests** You recently signed up for an account on the MySpace social networking Web site. When you log in periodically, you find that people you do not know are requesting to be your friend. How should you respond?

9. **New Browser Windows** While browsing the Web, each time you click a link, the link's destination opens in a new browser window. You prefer to have each link open in a new tab so that your taskbar does not become cluttered. How will you resolve this?

Collaboration

10. **Finding Trustworthy Sources** Your history professor asked all of the students in her class to write a five-page paper about the Boston Tea Party. Instead of using books, you decide to find all of the relevant information you need on the Internet. After reading this chapter, you realize that not all Internet sources may be trustworthy, and that you must search the Internet for accurate Web sites. Form a team of three people and use various search engines to search for Web sites that discuss the Boston Tea Party. One team member should use the Google search engine, one team member should use the Yahoo! search engine, and one team member should use the Bing search engine. Which search engine displayed the most results overall? Which search engine returned the most relevant, trustworthy results? What search text did everyone use to narrow the search results to the most relevant Web sites? Did any of the search engines recommend alternate search text that might help to find relevant information?

Problem Solving @ Work

The Problem Solving @ Work exercises extend your knowledge of the chapter concepts by seeking solutions to practical computer problems that you may encounter at work. The Collaboration exercise should be completed with a team.

In the real world, practical problems often can be solved in multiple ways. Provide one solution to each of the following problems using available resources, such as articles on the Web or in print, blogs, podcasts, videos, television, user guides, other individuals, and electronics and computer stores. You may need to use multiple resources to obtain an answer. Present your solutions in the form requested by your instructor (brief report, presentation, discussion, or other means).

1. **Plug-In Required** Upon viewing a Web page, a message appears stating that you do not have the proper plug-in required to view the page's multimedia content. What is your next step?

2. **Blocked Instant Messenger** Today, you started a new job. After setting up your new computer, you download your favorite IM (instant messaging) program successfully and without issue. After attempting to enter your user name and password, however, the program does not connect to the IM service. You are certain that your user name and password are correct, so what else might be causing this?

3. **Access Denied** During your lunch hour, you decide to search the Web for possible vacation destinations. After visiting several airline and hotel Web sites, you attempt to visit the Web site for a Caribbean resort. Much to your surprise, the Web browser informs you that the Web site has been blocked. Why might this happen?

4. **Sporadic E-Mail Message Delivery** The e-mail program on your computer has been delivering new messages only every hour, on the hour. Historically, new e-mail messages would arrive and be displayed immediately upon being sent by the sender. Furthermore, your coworkers claim that they sometimes do not receive your e-mail messages until hours after they are sent. What might be the problem?

5. **E-Mail Message Formatting** A friend sent an e-mail message containing a photo to your e-mail account at work. Upon receiving the e-mail message, the photo does not display. You also notice that e-mail messages never display any formatting, such as different fonts, font sizes, and font colors. What might be causing this?

6. **Automatic Response** When you return from vacation, a colleague informs you that when she sent e-mail messages to your e-mail address, she would not always receive your automatic response stating that you were out of the office. Why might your e-mail program not respond automatically to every e-mail message received?

7. **Suspicious Web Site Visits** The director of your company's Information Technology department has sent you an e-mail message stating that you have been spending an excessive amount of time viewing Web sites not related to your job. You periodically visit Web sites not related to work, but only on breaks, which the company allows. How does he know your Web browsing habits? How will you respond to this claim?

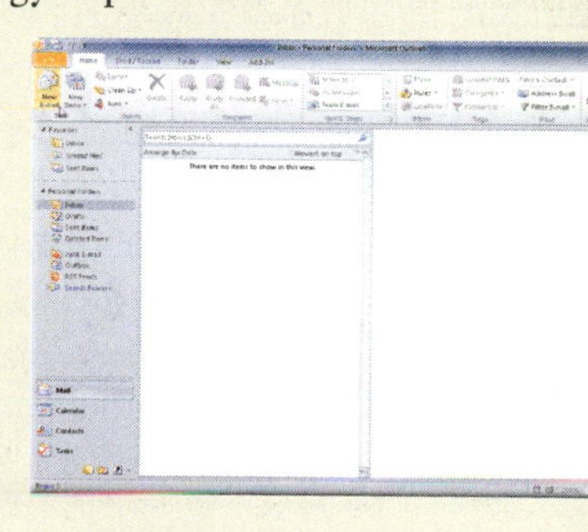

8. **Wrong Web Site** When attempting to visit your friend's Web site from your office computer, another Web site displays in its place. What might be wrong? What steps can you take so that you can visit his Web site?

Collaboration

9. **Computers in Entertainment** The drama department at a local high school is considering developing a movie and has asked for your help. The drama teacher would like to incorporate technology wherever possible, in hopes that it would decrease the costs of the movie's production. Form a team of three people to help determine what technology can be used to assist in the movie's production. One team member should research the type of technology that can be used during the filming process. Another team member should research the types of hardware and software available for editing footage, and the third team member should research the hardware and software requirements for creating the media to distribute the finished product.

Learn How To

The Learn How To activities step you through fundamental technology skills when using a computer. The Learn How To exercises enable you to become more proficient with these skills.

Premium Activity: To relate this Learn How To activity to your everyday life, see a visual demonstration of the activity, and complete a short assessment, visit the Computer Concepts CourseMate Web site at www.cengagebrain.com and then navigate to the Chapter 2 Learn How To resource for this book.

Learn How To 1: Attach a File to an E-Mail Message

When you send an e-mail message, it sometimes is necessary to attach a file to supplement the body of the e-mail message. Most e-mail programs allow you to attach a file to your e-mail messages easily, but many do not allow you to attach files exceeding a specified size limit (which varies by your e-mail service). You can attach a file to an e-mail message by completing the following steps:

1. Start your e-mail program and compose a new e-mail message to your recipient. Make sure that you have a descriptive subject and that you explain in the e-mail message that you are attaching a file.
2. To attach a file, locate and click the Attach File button or link. If you are unable to locate this button, you may find an icon with a picture of a paperclip or a menu command to attach a file. Some e-mail programs also may have a text box in the new message window with an adjacent Browse button. In this case, click the Browse button.
3. Locate and click the file you wish to attach and then click the Open (or Insert or Select) button (Figure 2-35).
4. Verify that your e-mail message contains the attachment and then click the Send button.

When the recipient opens the e-mail message, he or she also will be able to open the attachment.

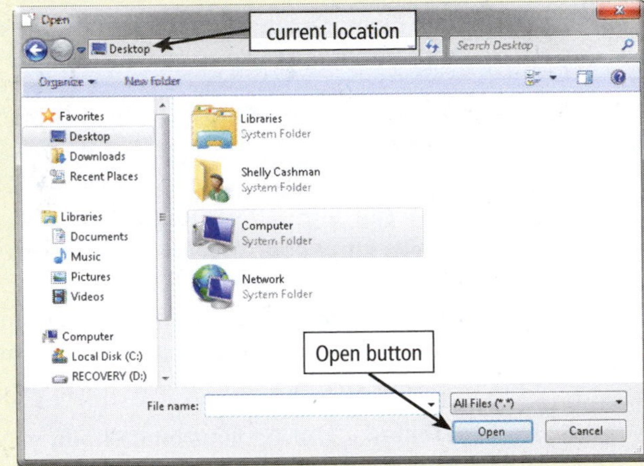

Figure 2-35

Exercises

1. Start your e-mail program. Compose a new e-mail message to your instructor, and attach a file containing your current course schedule. Verify that your message has been received and then close your e-mail program.
2. Locate three free e-mail Web applications. How many file attachments do these e-mail programs allow you to attach to one e-mail message? Is a maximum file size specified for an e-mail attachment? Can you pay to upgrade your e-mail account so that these restrictions are lifted? Submit these answers to your instructor.

Learn How To 2: Search the Web for Driving Directions, Addresses, and Telephone Numbers

In addition to searching the Web for information using search engines such as Google and Yahoo!, some Web sites are designed specifically to search for other information such as driving directions, addresses, and telephone numbers.

Search for Driving Directions

1. Start your Web browser, type `mapquest.com` in the Address bar, press the ENTER key to display the MapQuest home page, and then click the Directions tab.
2. Type the starting address (or intersection), city, state, and ZIP code (if you know it) in the appropriate text boxes in the Starting Location area of the Directions page.
3. Type the ending address (or intersection), city, state, and ZIP code (if you know it) in the appropriate text boxes in the Ending Location area of the Directions page.
4. Click the Get Directions button to display the driving directions.

Search for the Address and Telephone Number of a Business

1. If necessary, start your Web browser. Type `yellowpages.com` in the Address bar, and then press the ENTER key to display the Yellow Pages Local Directory home page.
2. Type the name of the business in the Find text box, and type the city, state, and ZIP (if you know it) in the Location text box.
3. Click the FIND button to display the search results.
4. Close your Web browser.

Learn How To

Exercises

1. If necessary, start Internet Explorer by clicking the Start button, and then click Internet Explorer on the Start menu. Type `mapquest.com` in the Address bar, and then press the ENTER key. Search for driving directions between your address and the address of a friend or family member. How many miles are between the two addresses? How long would it take you to drive from your address to the other address? Write a paragraph explaining whether you would or would not use MapQuest to retrieve driving directions. Submit this paragraph to your instructor.
2. Use the Web to search for another Web site that provides driving directions. Use the Web site to search for directions between the same two locations from Exercise 1. Are the driving directions the same as the ones that MapQuest provided? If not, why might they be different? Which Web site did you use? Do you prefer this Web site to MapQuest? Why or why not? Write a paragraph with your answers and submit it to your instructor.
3. Think about a company for which you would like to work. In your Web browser, display the Yellow Pages Web page (yellowpages.com) and then search for the address and telephone number of this company. If Yellow Pages does not display the desired information, what other Web sites might you be able to use to search for the address and telephone number for a company?

Learn How To 3: Publish Your Resume on the Web

Publishing your resume on the Web is a great way to distribute your resume to multiple people. To publish your resume on the Web, complete the following steps:

1. Using Microsoft Word, create a new resume or open an existing resume that you wish to publish on the Web. When you have finished creating the resume, click the Office Button and then click Save As on the menu.
2. Click the Desktop button in the Save As dialog box, type `resume` in the File name text box, click Web page in the 'Save as type' list, and then click the Save button.
3. Quit Microsoft Word.
4. Start your Web browser and then type `50Webs.com` in the Address bar. When the Web page is displayed, click one of the SIGN UP buttons (Figure 2-36).
5. Select the free Web hosting plan, click the 'Use a subdomain' option button, and then click the NEXT button.
6. Type the required information to sign up for the free plan. Make note of the subdomain you choose for your Web site. For example, if you type resume as your subdomain, your Web site address will be http://resume.50webs.com.
7. Click the check box to agree to the Terms and Conditions, and then click the Signup button. 50Webs will send your user name and password to the e-mail address you specified while signing up.
8. Click the Start button and then click Computer on the Start menu. In the Address bar, type `ftp://subdomain.50webs.com` (where subdomain should be replaced with the name of the subdomain you chose in Step 6). Type your user name and password in the Log On As dialog box, and then click the Log On button.
9. Double-click your Web site folder, and then drag your resume file from the desktop to the window containing your Web site files. If a resume_files folder exists on your desktop, you also should drag that folder to the window containing your Web site files.
10. In your Web browser, type `http://subdomain.50webs.com/resume.htm` (subdomain should be replaced with your chosen subdomain from Step 6).

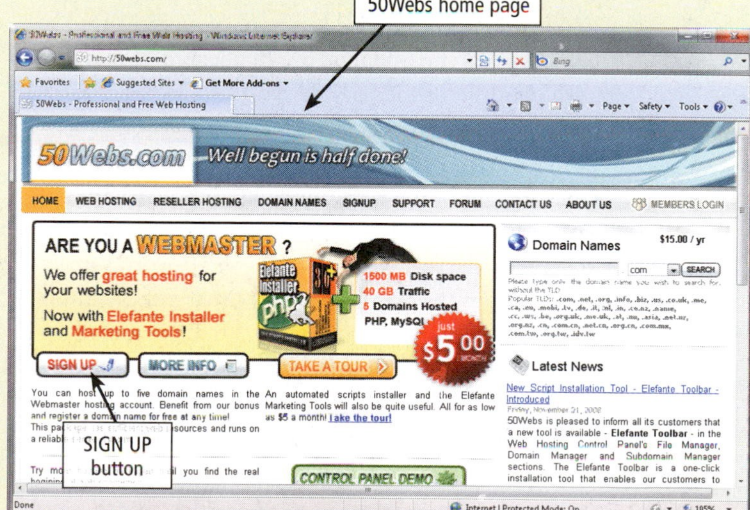

Figure 2-36

Exercise

1. Use Microsoft Word to create a Web page that you would like others to see when they visit your new Web site. Include your name, e-mail address, and any other information that you would not object to making public. Save the file as a Web page using the file name, index.htm. Upload the file to the 50Webs.com Web server and then send the Web page address to your instructor.

STUDENT ASSIGNMENTS

Web Research

The Web Research exercises broaden your understanding of the chapter concepts by presenting questions that require you to search the Web for answers.

1 Search Sleuth

Use one of the search engines listed in Figure 2-10 in Chapter 2 on page 85 or your own favorite search engine to find the answers to the following questions. Copy and paste the Web address from the Web page where you found the answer. Some questions may have more than one answer. If required, submit your answers to your instructor. (1) What were the title, date of publication, and purpose of the Internet Engineering Task Force's RFC 1 document? (2) What is the mission of the World Wide Web Consortium (W3C)? (3) What topic does the film *Adina's Deck* address? (4) What are the current figures on the Reporters Without Borders' Press Freedom Barometer? (5) What was eBay's original name, and what was the first item offered for auction? (6) Why did ConnectU sue Facebook in 2008 and 2004? (7) What is the cost to use Google's 411 service?

2 Green Computing

EcoSearch is a search engine dedicated to supporting the Earth's natural resources. Visit this Web site (ecosearch.org), use your word processing program to answer the following questions, and then, if required, submit your answers to your instructor. (1) From what company do the search results come? (2) Click the Learn More link on the page. What charities does EcoSearch support? (3) How can you get involved to help EcoSearch? (4) Click the EcoSearch Home link at the bottom of the page to return to the EcoSearch home page. In the text box, type `ecosearch donate profits` and then click the Search button. Click several of the resulting links and review the information. Write a 50-word summary of the information, including what percent of EcoSearch proceeds is donated to charities and how much money EcoSearch expects to donate each year.

3 Social Networking

MySpace is considered one of the pioneering Web sites that helped popularize the online social networking phenomenon. Calling itself "a place for friends," it allows the millions of registered members to create profiles for free and then invite friends to join their networks. The growth of this Web site has helped it emerge as one of the more popular search engines. Visit the MySpace site (myspace.com), type the name of your favorite musical artist or group in the search text box, and then click the Search button. How many search results were found? Visit some of these profiles. Which music videos, playlists, and ringtones are featured? How do you create and edit your own playlists and add a song to your profile? Then click the Safety Tips link at the bottom of the page and read the guidelines for posting information and reporting inappropriate content. Summarize the music profiles you viewed and the guidelines. If required, submit your summary to your instructor.

4 Blogs

Many of the best blogs in the blogosphere have received awards for their content and design. For example, loyal blogging fans nominate and vote for their favorite blogs by visiting the Blogger's Choice Awards Web site (bloggerschoiceawards.com). Visit this Web site, click the Best Blog Design, Best Blog About Blogging, and Best Education Blog links, and view some of the blogs receiving the largest number of votes. Then visit other award sites, including the Interactive Media Awards (interactivemediaawards .com), Bloggies (bloggies.com), and the Best of Blogs (thebestofblogs.com). Which blogs, if any, received multiple awards on the different Web sites? Who casts the votes? What criteria are used to judge these blogs?

5 Ethics in Action

Some Internet access providers have admitted they monitored their users' Web surfing activities without giving notice of this eavesdropping practice. Embarq and Charter Communications secretly tested advertising technology to gather data about specific Web searches and then display advertisements relating to these searches. Privacy experts claim these Internet access providers' practices violate federal privacy laws, including the wiretapping statute. Locate news articles discussing the Internet access providers' Web eavesdropping. Then locate Web sites that oppose this practice. Summarize the views of the advertisers and the privacy proponents. If required, submit your summary to your instructor.

Critical Thinking

The Critical Thinking exercises challenge your assessment and decision-making skills by presenting real-world situations associated with the chapter concepts. The Collaboration exercise should be completed with a team.

To evaluate the situations below, use personal experiences and available resources such as articles on the Web or in print, blogs, podcasts, videos, television, user guides, other individuals, and electronics and computer stores. You may need to use multiple resources to form conclusions and make recommendations.

1. **Class Discussion — Browser Comparison** Although Internet Explorer may be the most widely used Web browser, it is not the only Web browser in use. Evaluate and compare reviews of other Web browsers such as Google Chrome, Safari, or Firefox with Internet Explorer. Discuss the major differences between the browsers you researched and Internet Explorer. Examples of differences might include the number and types of features, how they display Web pages, and the speed at which they perform. Include in your discussion which browser you would recommend and the reasons for your recommendation.

2. **Class Presentation — Brick-and-Click Businesses** Many retailers, such as Best Buy, Barnes and Noble, and Toys R Us, are brick-and-click businesses. That is, they allow customers to conduct complete transactions at a physical location as well as online at a Web site. Choose a local brick-and-click business in which you have shopped at the physical location and then visit the Web site of the same business. Compare the type, availability, and cost (include tax and shipping) of products or services available. Analyze the advantages and disadvantages of dealing with the physical location versus the Web site of a brick-and-click business and then present your recommendation of whether you would rather shop at the physical location or at the Web site. Note the factors that influenced your decision. Next, locate a company that only conducts business online, but sells the same products as the brick-and-click business. How do the prices compare? Would you prefer to shop using this Web site instead?

3. **Research — Acceptable Use Policy** Most schools and businesses provide free Internet access to students and employees while they are at school or at work. While the school's or business's intention is for the Internet to be used for academic or work-related purposes, employees and students often find it easy to become involved with other activities on the Internet not related to their job or academics, which can degrade Internet access for others, or lead to poor job performance. For these reasons, many schools and businesses create an Acceptable Use Policy that outlines how students and employees should use the Internet. It also may outline consequences for unauthorized Internet use. Locate two Acceptable Use Policies that are published online. Compare these two policies, find two additional Acceptable Use Policies online, and then create a policy you believe would be fair to employees of a small business. Be sure to include guidelines for Internet use during breaks, use of IM programs, and the use of Web sites that are not related to their job.

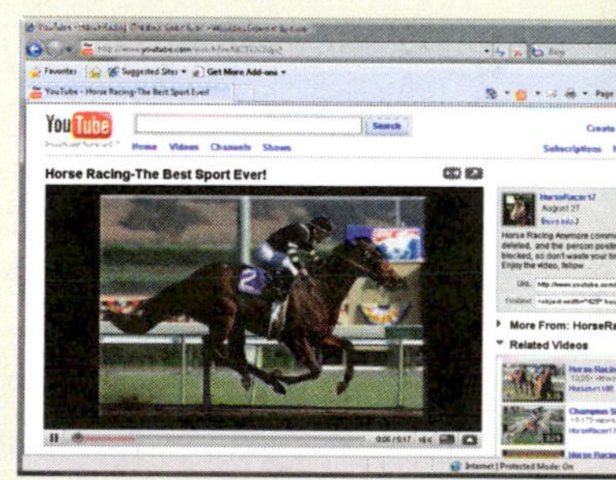

Collaboration

4. **Web Site Evaluation** You are vice president of operations for a major luxury hotel chain. You and three teammates want to start a new chain of discount hotels called Sleepy Hollow. You have made a plan that includes opening hotels initially in Seattle, Kansas City, Nashville, and Dallas. You plan to offer comfortable rooms, wireless Internet access, a business center, and a hot breakfast buffet. Besides offering reservations over the telephone, you want to develop a Web site that will allow customers to negotiate a nightly rate as their check-in time approaches. With your teammates, evaluate existing major hotel Web sites by listing the advantages and disadvantages of each. Assign each member the task of evaluating two of the following hotel chains: Marriot, Hilton, Holiday Inn, Ramada, Super 8, Motel 6, Days Inn, and Radisson. Team members should print the home page of the hotel chain to which they are assigned and evaluate their respective hotels' Web sites, paying particular attention to the following areas: (1) design of the Web site, (2) ease of use, (3) reservations, (4) awards programs, (5) special offers, (6) online Help, (7) information about the hotel, and (8) contact information for the hotel. Prepare a report and/or presentation summarizing your evaluations and ranking the sites in terms of their effectiveness. Be sure to include brief explanations supporting your rankings.

Making Use of the Web

INFORMATION LITERACY IS DEFINED as having the practical skills needed to evaluate information critically from print and electronic resources and to use this information accurately in daily life. Locating Web sites may be profitable for your educational and professional careers, as the resources may help you research class assignments and make your life more fulfilling and manageable.

Because the Web does not have an organizational structure to assist you in locating reliable material, you may need additional resources to guide you in searching. To help you find useful Web sites, this Special Feature describes specific information about a variety of Web pages, and it includes tables of Web addresses so that you can get started. The material is organized in several areas of interest.

Web Exercises at the end of each area will reinforce the material and help you discover Web sites that may add a treasure trove of knowledge to your life.

Areas of Interest	
Fun and Entertainment	Shopping and Auctions
Research	Weather, Sports, and News
Blogs	Learning
Online Social Networks and Media Sharing	Science
Travel	Health
Environment	Careers
Finance	Literature and Arts
Government	

Fun and Entertainment

That's Entertainment

Rock 'n' Roll on the Web

Consumers place great significance on buying entertainment products for fun and recreation. Nearly 10 percent of the United States's economy is spent on attending concerts and buying optical discs, reading materials, sporting goods, and toys.

Many Web sites supplement our cravings for fun and entertainment. For example, you can see and hear the musicians inducted into the Rock and Roll Hall of Fame and Museum. If you need an update on your favorite reality-based television program or a preview of an upcoming movie, E! Online and Entertainment Weekly provide the latest features about actors and actresses. The Internet Movie Database contains reviews of more than one million titles (Figure 1).

Watch the surfers riding the waves and romp with pandas at the San Diego Zoo. Web cams can display live video on Web pages, taking armchair travelers across the world for views of natural attractions, monuments, and cities. Many Web sites featuring Web cams are listed in the table in Figure 2.

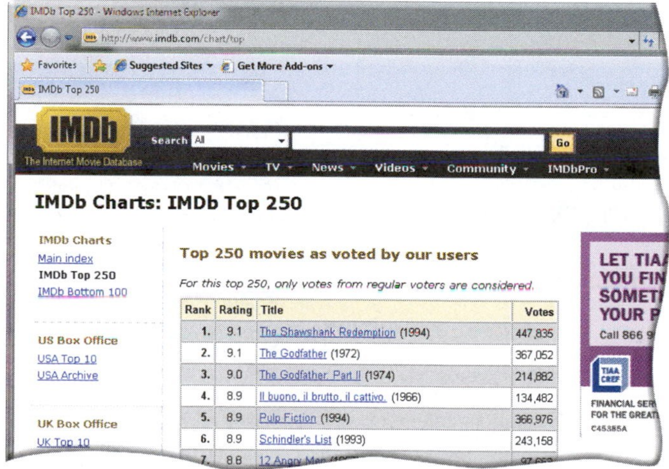

Figure 1 Visitors exploring the Internet Movie Database will find the latest news about their favorite television programs and movies.

Fun and Entertainment Web Sites	
Entertainment	**Web Address**
allmusic	allmusic.com
E! Online	eonline.com
Entertainment Weekly's EW	ew.com/ew
Games.com	games.com
Internet Movie Database	imdb.com
Old Time Radio (OTR) — Radio Days: A Radio History	otr.com
Rock and Roll Hall of Fame and Museum	rockhall.com
World Radio Network	wrn.org
Yahoo! Entertainment	entertainment.yahoo.com
Web Cams	**Web Address**
Camvista	camvista.com
Discovery Kids — Live Cams	kids.discovery.com/cams/cams.html
EarthCam — Webcam Network	earthcam.com
ESRL/GMD Mauna Loa Live Camera	esrl.noaa.gov/gmd/obop/mlo/livecam/index.html
Gatorland	gatorland.com/gatorcam.php
Geocaching — The Official Global GPS Cache Hunt Site	geocaching.com
Panda Cam San Diego Zoo	sandiegozoo.org/zoo/ex_panda_station.html
WebCam Central	camcentral.com
Wild Birds Unlimited Bird FeederCam	wbu.com/feedercam_home.html

For more information about fun and entertainment Web sites, visit the Computer Concepts CourseMate Web site at www.cengagebrain.com and then navigate to the Making Use of the Web Feature resource for this book.

Figure 2 When you visit Web sites offering fun and entertainment resources, you can be both amused and informed.

Fun and Entertainment Web Exercises

1. **Visit the Geocaching site listed in Figure 2.** Find the geocaches within five miles of your home or school and then print a map showing their locations. Then, visit the Discovery Kids — Live Cams Web site and view one of the animal cams in the Live Cams. What do you observe? Visit another Web site listed in Figure 2 and describe the view. What are the benefits of having Web cams at these locations throughout the world?

2. **What are your favorite movies?** Use the Internet Movie Database Web site listed in Figure 2 to search for information about two films, and write a brief description of the biographies of the major stars and director for each movie. Then, visit one of the entertainment Web sites and describe three of the featured stories. At the Rock and Roll Hall of Fame and Museum Web site, view the information about The Beatles and one of your favorite musicians. Write a paragraph describing the information available about these rock stars.

Research

Search and Ye Shall Find

Information on the Web

A recent Web Usability survey conducted by the Nielsen Norman Group found that 88 percent of people who connect to the Internet use a search engine as their first online action. Search engines require users to type words and phrases that characterize the information being sought. Bing (Figure 3), Google, and AltaVista are some of the more popular search engines. The key to effective searching on the Web is composing search queries that narrow the search results and place the more relevant Web sites at the top of the results list.

Keep up with the latest computer and related product developments by viewing online dictionaries and encyclopedias that add to their collections on a regular basis. Shopping for a new computer can be a daunting experience, but many online guides can help you select the components that best fit your needs and budget. If you are not confident in your ability to solve a problem alone, turn to online technical support. Web sites often provide streaming how-to video lessons, tutorials, and real-time chats with experienced technicians. Hardware and software reviews, price comparisons, shareware, technical questions and answers, and breaking technology news are found on comprehensive portals. Figure 4 lists popular research Web sites.

Figure 3 The Bing Web site provides a search engine for images, videos, shopping, news, maps, and travel.

Research Web Sites

Research	Web Address
A9.com	a9.com
AccessMyLibrary	accessmylibrary.com
AltaVista	altavista.com
Answers.com	answers.com
Ask	ask.com
Bing	bing.com
ChaCha	chacha.com
CNET	cnet.com
eHow	ehow.com
Google	google.com
HotBot	hotbot.com
Librarians' Internet Index	lii.org
PC911	pcnineoneone.com
Switchboard	switchboard.com
Webopedia	webopedia.com
ZDNet	zdnet.com

For more information about research Web sites, visit the Computer Concepts CourseMate Web site at www.cengagebrain.com and then navigate to the Making Use of the Web Feature resource for this book.

Figure 4 Web users can find information by using research Web sites.

Research Web Exercises

1. **Visit two of the research Web sites listed in Figure 4** to find three Web sites that review the latest digital cameras from Kodak and Canon. Make a table listing the research Web sites, the located Web site names, and the cameras' model numbers, suggested retail price, and features.

2. **Visit the Webopedia Web site.** Search this site for five terms of your choice. Create a table with two columns: one for the term and one for the Web definition. Then, create a second table listing five recently added or updated words and their definitions on this Web site. Next, visit the CNET Web site to choose the components you would buy if you were building a customized desktop computer and notebook computer. Create a table for both computers, listing the computer manufacturer, processor model name or number and manufacturer, clock speed, RAM, cache, number of expansion slots, and number of bays.

Blogs

Express Yourself

Blogosphere Growing Swiftly

Internet users are feeling the need to publish their views, and they are finding Weblogs, or blogs for short, the ideal vehicle. The blogosphere began as an easy way for individuals to express their opinions on the Web. Today, this communications vehicle has become a powerful tool, for individuals, groups, and corporations are using blogs to promote their ideas and advertise their products. It is not necessary to have a background in Web design to be able to post to a blog.

Bloggers generally update their Web sites frequently to reflect their views. Their posts range from a paragraph to an entire essay and often contain links to other Web sites. The more popular blogs discuss politics, lifestyles, and technology.

Individuals easily may set up a blog free or for a fee, using Web sites such as Blogger, Bloglines (Figure 5), and TypePad. In addition, online social networks may have a built-in blogging feature. Be cautious of the information you post on your blog, especially if it is accessible to everyone online.

Corporate blogs, such as The GM FastLane Blog, discuss all aspects of the company's products, whereas all-encompassing blogs, such as the MetaFilter Community Weblog and others in Figure 6, are designed to keep general readers entertained and informed.

Blogs are affecting the manner in which people communicate, and some experts predict they will one day become our primary method of sharing information.

Figure 5 Bloglines keeps readers abreast of the latest technology, entertainment, and political news in the blogosphere.

Blogs Web Sites

Blog	Web Address
A List Apart	alistapart.com
Blog.com	blog.com
Blog Flux	topsites.blogflux.com
Blogger	blogger.com
Bloglines	bloglines.com
Blogstream	blogstream.com
Davenetics*Remote Control Revolutionary	davenetics.com
Geek News Central	geeknewscentral.com
GM FastLane Blog	fastlane.gmblogs.com
kottke.org	kottke.org
MetaFilter Community Weblog	metafilter.com
Rocketboom	rocketboom.com
TreeHugger	treehuggertv.com
Twitter	twitter.com
TypePad	typepad.com

For more information about blogs Web sites, visit the Computer Concepts CourseMate Web site at www.cengagebrain.com and then navigate to the Making Use of the Web Feature resource for this book.

Figure 6 These blogs offer information about technology, news, politics, and entertainment.

Blogs Web Exercises

1. **Visit three of the blog Web sites listed in Figure 6.** Make a table listing the blog name, its purpose, the author, its audience, and advertisers, if any, who sponsor the blog. Then, write a paragraph that describes the information you found on each of these blogs.

2. **Many Internet users read the technology blogs to keep abreast of the latest developments.** Visit the Geek News Central and Bloglines blogs listed in Figure 6 and write a paragraph describing the top story in each blog. Read the posted comments, if any. Then, write another paragraph describing two other stories found on these blogs that cover material you have discussed in this course. Write a third paragraph discussing which one is more interesting to you. Would you add reading blogs to your list of Internet activities? Why or why not?

Online Social Networks and Media Sharing

Check Out My New Photos

Online Social Networks and Media Sharing Web Sites Gain Popularity

Do you ever wonder what your friends are doing? What about your friends' friends? The popularity of online social networks has increased dramatically in recent years. Online social networks, such as those listed in Figure 7, allow you to create a personalized profile that others are able to view online. These profiles may include information about you such as your hometown, your age, your hobbies, and pictures. You also may create links to your friends' pages, post messages for individual friends, or bulletins for all of your friends to see. Online social networks are great places to keep in touch with your friends and to network with professionals for business purposes.

If you would like to post pictures and videos and do not require the full functionality of an online social network, you might consider a media sharing Web site, which is a type of online social network. Media sharing Web sites such as YouTube and Phanfare (Figure 8) allow you to post media, including photos and videos, for others to view, print, and/or download. Media sharing Web sites, which may be free or charge a fee, provide a quick, efficient way to share photos of your last vacation or videos of your family reunion.

Online Social Networks and Media Sharing

Online Social Networks	Web Address
Club Penguin	clubpenguin.com
Facebook	facebook.com
LinkedIn	linkedin.com
MySpace — a place for friends	myspace.com
orkut	orkut.com
Windows Live Spaces	spaces.live.com
Media Sharing	**Web Address**
flickr	flickr.com
Phanfare	phanfare.com
Photobucket	photobucket.com
Picasa	picasa.com
Shutterfly	shutterfly.com
Yahoo! Video	video.yahoo.com
YouTube	youtube.com

For more information about online social networks and media sharing Web sites, visit the Computer Concepts CourseMate Web site at www.cengagebrain.com and then navigate to the Making Use of the Web Feature resource for this book.

Figure 7 Online social networks and media sharing Web sites are popular ways to keep in touch with friends, meet new people, and share media.

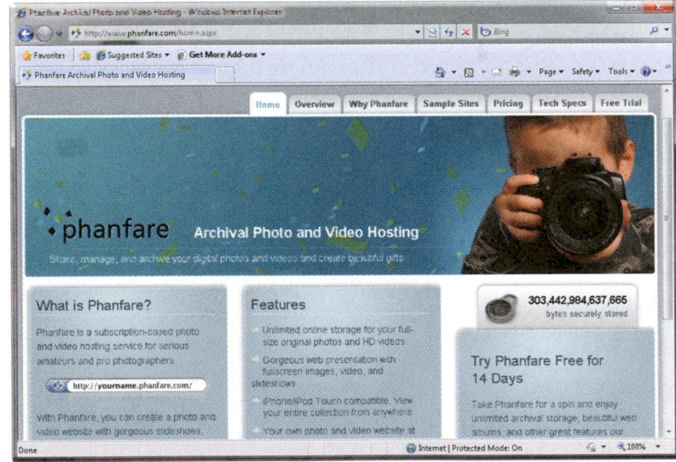

Figure 8 The Phanfare Web site allows users to share their photo and video files with people throughout the world.

Online Social Networks and Media Sharing Web Exercises

1. **Many individuals now use online social networks.** Visit two online social networks listed in Figure 7. (If you are attempting to access an online social network from your classroom and are unable to do so, your school may have restricted use of social networking Web sites.) Compare and contrast these two sites by performing the following actions and recording your findings. First, create a profile on each of these sites. If you find a Web site that charges a fee to sign up, choose another Web site. How easy is the sign-up process? Does either Web site ask for any personal information you are uncomfortable sharing? If so, what information? Once you sign up, make a list of five of your closest friends, and search for their profiles on each of these two sites. Which site contains more of your friends? Browse each site and make a list of its features. In your opinion, which site is better? Explain why.

2. **Media sharing Web sites make it extremely easy to share photos and videos with friends, family, and colleagues.** Before choosing a media sharing Web site to use, you should do some research. Visit two media sharing Web sites in Figure 7. Is there a fee to post media to these Web sites? If so, how much? Are these Web sites supported by advertisements? Locate the instructions for posting media to these Web sites. Are the instructions straightforward? Do these Web sites impose a limit on the number and/or size of media files you can post? Summarize your responses to these questions in two or three paragraphs.

Travel

Get Packing!

Explore the World without Leaving Home

When you are ready to arrange your next travel adventure or just want to explore destination possibilities, the Internet provides ample resources to set your plans in motion.

To discover exactly where your destination is on this planet, cartography Web sites, including MapQuest and Yahoo! Maps, allow you to pinpoint your destination. View your exact destination using satellite imagery with Google Maps and Bing Maps (Figure 9).

Some excellent starting places are general travel Web sites such as Expedia Travel, Cheap Tickets, Orbitz, and Travelocity. Many airline Web sites allow you to reserve hotel rooms, activities, and rental cars while booking a flight. These all-encompassing Web sites, including those in Figure 10, have tools to help you find the lowest prices and details about flights, car rentals, cruises, and hotels. Comprehensive online guidebooks can provide useful details about maximizing your vacation time while saving money.

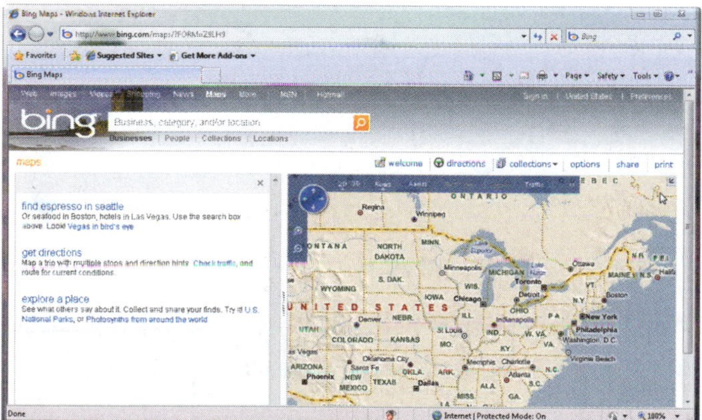

Figure 9 Bing Maps provides location information and satellite imagery for many regions on this planet.

Travel Web Sites

General Travel	Web Address
CheapTickets	cheaptickets.com
Expedia Travel	expedia.com
Kayak	kayak.com
Orbitz	orbitz.com
SideStep	sidestep.com
Travelocity	travelocity.com
Cartography	**Web Address**
Bing Maps	bing.com/maps
Google Maps	maps.google.com
MapQuest	mapquest.com
Maps.com	maps.com
Yahoo! Maps	maps.yahoo.com
Travel and City Guides	**Web Address**
Frommer's Travel Guides	frommers.com
GoPlanit	goplanit.com
U.S.-Parks US National Parks Travel Guide	www.us-parks.com
Virtual Tourist	virtualtourist.com

For more information about travel Web sites, visit the Computer Concepts CourseMate Web site at www.cengagebrain.com and then navigate to the Making Use of the Web Feature resource for this book.

Figure 10 These travel resources Web sites offer travel information to exciting destinations throughout the world.

Travel Web Exercises

1. **Visit one of the cartography Web sites listed in Figure 10** and obtain the directions from your campus to one of these destinations: the Washington Monument in Washington, D.C.; the Statue of Liberty on Ellis Island in New York; Disneyland in Anaheim, California; or the Grand Old Opry in Nashville, Tennessee. How many miles is it to your destination? What is the estimated driving time? Use the Google Maps Web site to obtain an overhead image of this destination. Then, visit one of the general travel Web sites listed in the table and plan a flight from the nearest major airport to one of the four destinations for the week after finals and a return trip one week later. Which airline, flight numbers, and departure and arrival times did you select?

2. **Visit one of the travel and city guides Web sites listed in Figure 10,** and choose a destination for a getaway this coming weekend. Write a one-page paper giving details about this location, such as popular hotels and lodging, expected weather, population, local colleges and universities, parks and recreation, ancient and modern history, and tours. Include a map or satellite photo of this place. Why did you select this destination? How would you travel there and back? What is the breakdown of expected costs for this weekend, including travel expenditures, meals, lodging, and tickets to events and activities? Which Web addresses did you use to complete this exercise?

Environment

The Future of the Planet

Making a Difference for Earth

From the rain forests of Africa to the marine life in the Pacific Ocean, the fragile ecosystem is under extreme stress. Many environmental groups have developed informative Web sites, including those listed in Figure 11, in attempts to educate worldwide populations and to increase resource conservation. The Environmental Defense Fund Web site (Figure 12) contains information for people who would like to help safeguard the environment.

On an international scale, the Environmental Sites on the Internet Web page developed by the Royal Institute of Technology in Stockholm, Sweden, has been rated as one of the better ecological Web sites. Its comprehensive listing of environmental concerns range from aquatic ecology to wetlands.

The U.S. federal government has a number of Web sites devoted to specific environmental concerns. For example, the U.S. Environmental Protection Agency (EPA) provides pollution data, including ozone levels and air pollutants, for specific areas. Its AirData Web site displays air pollution emissions and monitoring data from the entire United States and is the world's most extensive collection of air pollution data.

Environment Web Sites

Name	Web Address
Central African Regional Program for the Environment (CARPE)	carpe.umd.edu
Earthjustice	earthjustice.org
EarthTrends: Environmental Information	earthtrends.wri.org
Environmental Defense Fund	edf.org
Environmental Sites on the Internet	www.ima.kth.se/im/envsite/envsite.htm
EPA AirData — Access to Air Pollution Data	epa.gov/air/data
Global Warming	globalwarming.org
Green Computing Impact Organization	gcio.org
GreenNet	gn.apc.org
New American Dream	newdream.org
University of Wisconsin — Milwaukee Environmental Health and Safety Resources	uwm.edu/Dept/EHSRM/EHSLINKS
USGS Branch of Quality Systems	bqs.usgs.gov/acidrain

For more information about environment Web sites, visit the Computer Concepts CourseMate Web site at www.cengagebrain.com and then navigate to the Making Use of the Web Feature resource for this book.

Figure 11 Environment Web sites provide vast resources for ecological data and action groups.

Figure 12 A visit to the Environmental Defense Fund Web site provides practical advice about protecting the environment.

Environment Web Exercises

1. **The New American Dream Web site encourages consumers to reduce the amount of junk mail sent to their homes.** Using the table in Figure 11, visit the Web site to learn how many trees are leveled each year to provide paper for these mailings and how many garbage trucks are needed to haul this waste. Read the letters used to eliminate names from bulk mail lists. To whom would you mail these letters? How long does it take to stop these unsolicited letters?

2. **Visit the EPA AirData Web site.** What is the highest ozone level recorded in your state this past year? Where are the nearest air pollution monitoring Web sites, and what are their levels? Where are the nearest sources of air pollution? Read two reports about two different topics, such as acid rain and air quality, and summarize their findings. Include information about who sponsored the research, who conducted the studies, when the data was collected, and the impact of this pollution on the atmosphere, water, forests, and human health. Whom would you contact for further information regarding the data and studies?

Finance
Money Matters

Cashing In on Financial Advice

You can manage your money with advice from financial Web sites that offer online banking, tax help, personal finance, and small business and commercial services.

If you do not have a personal banker or a financial planner, consider a Web adviser to guide your investment decisions. The MSN Money Web site (Figure 13) provides financial news and investment information.

If you are ready to ride the ups and downs of the Dow and the NASDAQ, an abundance of Web sites listed in Figure 14, including Reuters and Morningstar, can help you select companies that fit your interests and financial needs.

Claiming to be the fastest, easiest tax publication on the planet, the Internal Revenue Service Web site contains procedures for filing tax appeals and contains IRS forms, publications, and legal regulations.

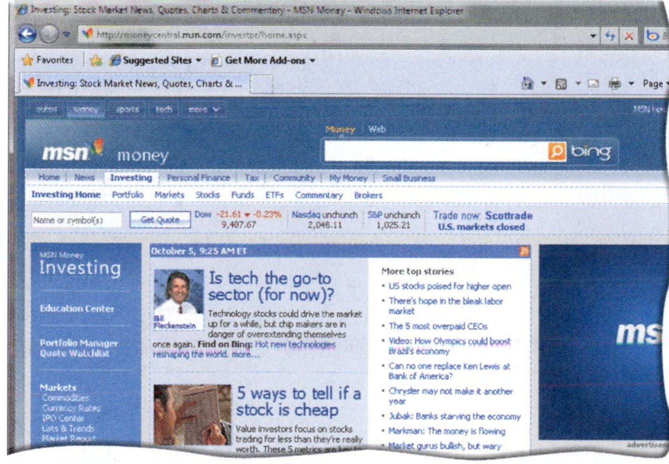

Figure 13 The MSN Money Web site contains features related to college and family finances.

Finance Web Sites

Advice and Education	Web Address
Bankrate	bankrate.com
ING Direct	ingdirect.com
LendingTree	lendingtree.com
Loan.com	loan.com
The Motley Fool	fool.com
MSN Money	moneycentral.msn.com
Wells Fargo	wellsfargo.com
Yahoo! Finance	finance.yahoo.com
Stock Market	**Web Address**
E*TRADE	us.etrade.com
Financial Engines	financialengines.com
Merrill Lynch	ml.com
Morningstar	morningstar.com
Reuters	reuters.com/investing
Valic	valic.com
Vanguard	vanguard.com
Taxes	**Web Address**
H&R Block	hrblock.com
Internal Revenue Service	www.irs.gov
Jackson Hewitt	jacksonhewitt.com
Liberty Tax Service	libertytax.com

For more information about finance Web sites, visit the Computer Concepts CourseMate Web site at www.cengagebrain.com and then navigate to the Making Use of the Web Feature resource for this book.

Figure 14 Financial resources Web sites offer general information, stock market analyses, and tax advice, as well as guidance and money-saving tips.

Finance Web Exercises

1. **Visit three advice and education Web sites listed in Figure 14** and read their top business world reports. Write a paragraph about each, summarizing these stories. Which stocks or mutual funds do these Web sites predict as being sound investments today? What are the current market indexes for the DJIA (Dow Jones Industrial Average), S&P 500, and NASDAQ, and how do these figures compare with the previous day's numbers?

2. **Using two of the stock market Web sites listed in Figure 14,** search for information about Microsoft, Apple, and one other software vendor. Write a paragraph about each of these stocks describing the revenues, net incomes, total assets for the previous year, current stock price per share, highest and lowest prices of each stock during the past year, and other relevant investment information.

Government

Stamp of Approval

Making a Federal Case for Useful Information

When it is time to buy stamps to mail your correspondence, you no longer need to wait in long lines at your local post office. The U.S. Postal Service has authorized several organizations to sell stamps online.

You can recognize U.S. Government Web sites on the Internet by their gov top-level domain. For example, the extensive Library of Congress Web site is loc.gov (Figure 15). Government and military Web sites offer a wide range of information. The Time Service Department Web site will provide you with the correct time. If you are looking for a federal document, FedWorld lists thousands of documents distributed by the government on its Web site. For access to the names of your congressional representatives, visit the extensive HG.org Web site. Figure 16 shows some of the more popular U.S. Government Web sites.

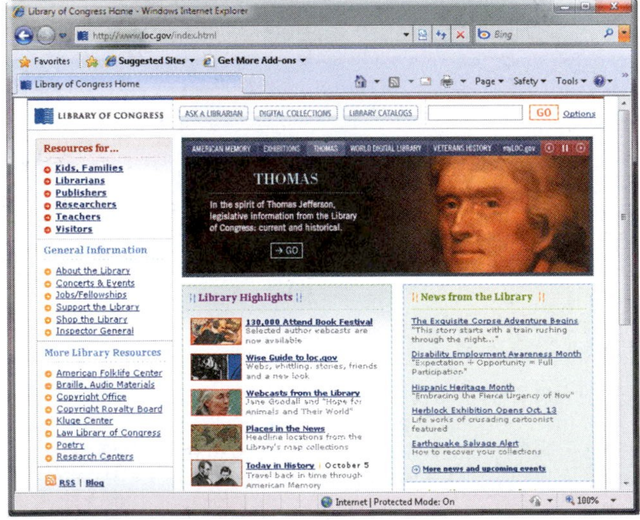

Figure 15 The Library of Congress Web site has resources about American history, world culture, and digital preservation.

Government Resources Web Sites

Postage	Web Address
Endicia	endicia.com
Pitney Bowes	pb.com
Stamps.com	stamps.com
Government	**Web Address**
FedWorld	www.fedworld.gov
HG.org — Worldwide Legal Directories	hg.org
Library of Congress	loc.gov
National Agricultural Library	nal.usda.gov
Smithsonian Institution	smithsonian.org
THOMAS (Library of Congress)	thomas.loc.gov
Time Service Department	tycho.usno.navy.mil
U.S. Department of Education	ed.gov
United States Department of the Treasury	treas.gov
U.S. Government Printing Office	www.access.gpo.gov
United States National Library of Medicine	nlm.nih.gov
United States Patent and Trademark Office	uspto.gov
USAJOBS	usajobs.opm.gov
The White House	whitehouse.gov

For more information about government Web sites, visit the Computer Concepts CourseMate Web site at www.cengagebrain.com and then navigate to the Making Use of the Web Feature resource for this book.

Figure 16 These Web sites offer information about buying U.S.-approved postage online and researching federal agencies.

Government Web Exercises

1. **View the three postage Web sites listed in Figure 16.** Compare and contrast the available services on each one. Consider postage cost, necessary equipment, shipping services, security techniques, and tracking capability. Explain why you would or would not like to use this service.

2. **Visit the HG.org Web site listed in Figure 16.** What are the names, addresses, and phone numbers of your two state senators and your local congressional representative? On what committees do they serve? Who is the chief justice of the Supreme Court, and what has been this justice's opinion on two recently decided cases? Who are the members of the president's cabinet? Then, visit two other Web sites listed in Figure 16. Write a paragraph about each Web site describing its content and features.

Shopping and Auctions

Bargains Galore

Let Your Mouse Do Your Shopping

From groceries to clothing to computers, you can buy just about everything you need with just a few clicks of your mouse. More than one-half of Internet users will make at least one online purchase this year. Books, computer software and hardware, and music are the hottest commodities.

The two categories of Internet shopping Web sites are those with physical counterparts, such as Walmart and Fry's Electronics (Figure 17), and those with only a Web presence, such as Amazon and Buy. Popular Web shopping sites are listed in Figure 18.

Another method of shopping for the items you need, and maybe some you really do not need, is to visit auction Web sites, including those listed in Figure 18. Categories include antiques and collectibles, automotive, computers, electronics, music, sports, sports cards and memorabilia, and toys. Online auction Web sites can offer unusual items, including *Star Wars* memorabilia or a round of golf with Jack Nicklaus. eBay is one of thousands of Internet auction Web sites and is the world's largest personal online trading community. In addition, craigslist is a free online equivalent of classified advertisements.

Figure 17 Fry's is a popular electronic retailer that sells a variety of products.

Shopping and Auctions Web Sites

Auctions	Web Address
craigslist	craigslist.org
eBay	ebay.com
Sotheby's	sothebys.com
uBid	ubid.com
U.S. Treasury — Seized Property Auctions	ustreas.gov/auctions
Books and Music	**Web Address**
Amazon	amazon.com
Barnes & Noble	bn.com
BookFinder	bookfinder.com
Computers and Electronics	**Web Address**
BestBuy	bestbuy.com
Buy	buy.com
Fry's Electronics	frys.com
Miscellaneous	**Web Address**
drugstore	drugstore.com
Google Product Search	google.com/products
SmashBuys	smashbuys.com
Walmart	walmart.com

For more information about shopping and auctions Web sites, visit the Computer Concepts CourseMate Web site at www.cengagebrain.com and then navigate to the Making Use of the Web Feature resource for this book.

Figure 18 Making online purchases can help ease the burden of driving to and fighting the crowds in local malls.

Shopping and Auctions Web Exercises

1. **Visit two of the computers and electronics and two of the miscellaneous Web sites listed in Figure 18.** Write a paragraph describing the features these Web sites offer compared with the same offerings from stores. In another paragraph, describe any disadvantages of shopping at these Web sites instead of actually visiting a store. Then, describe their policies for returning unwanted merchandise and for handling complaints.

2. **Using one of the auction Web sites listed in Figure 18, search for two objects pertaining to your hobbies.** For example, if you are a sports fan, you can search for a complete set of Upper Deck cards. If you are a car buff, search for your dream car. Describe these two items. How many people have bid on these items? Who are the sellers? What are the opening and current bids?

Weather, Sports, and News

What's News?

Weather, Sports, and News Web Sites Score Big Hits

Rain or sun? Hot or cold? Weather is the leading online news item, with at least 10,000 Web sites devoted to this field. Millions of people view The Weather Channel Web site (Figure 19) each month.

Baseball may be the national pastime, but sports aficionados yearn for everything from auto racing to cricket. The Internet has millions of pages of multimedia sports news, entertainment, and merchandise.

The Internet has emerged as a major source for news, with more than one-third of Americans going online at least once a week and 15 percent going online daily for reports of major news events. Many of these viewers are using RSS (Really Simple Syndication) technology to be notified when new stories about their favorite topics are available on the Internet. Popular weather, sports, and news Web sites are listed in Figure 20.

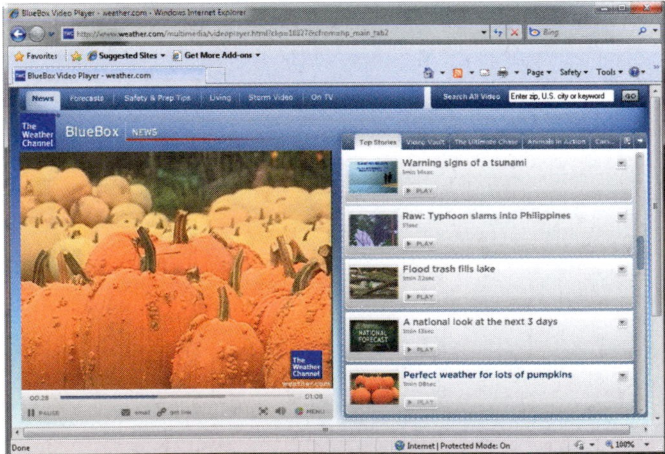

Figure 19 Local, national, and international weather conditions and details about breaking weather stories are available on The Weather Channel Web site.

Weather, Sports, and News Web Sites

Weather	Web Address
AccuWeather	accuweather.com
Infoplease Weather	infoplease.com/weather.html
Intellicast	www.intellicast.com
National Weather Service	www.crh.noaa.gov
The Weather Channel	weather.com
Sports	**Web Address**
CBS Sports	cbssports.com
ESPN	espn.com
NASCAR	nascar.com
International Olympic Committee	www.olympic.org
Sporting News Radio	radio.sportingnews.com
Yahoo! Sports	sports.yahoo.com
News	**Web Address**
FactCheck	factcheck.org
Geek.com	geek.com
Google News	news.google.com
MSNBC	msnbc.com
Onlinenewspapers	onlinenewspapers.com
privacy.org	privacy.org
SiliconValley	siliconvalley.com
starting page	startingpage.com/html/news.html
USA TODAY	usatoday.com
Washington Post	washingtonpost.com

For more information about weather, sports, and news Web sites, visit the Computer Concepts CourseMate Web site at www.cengagebrain.com and then navigate to the Making Use of the Web Feature resource for this book.

Figure 20 Keep informed about the latest weather, sports, and news events with these Web sites.

Weather, Sports, and News Web Exercises

1. Visit two of the sports Web sites in Figure 20 and write a paragraph describing the content these Web sites provide concerning your favorite sport. Visit Google News and then search for stories about this sports team or athlete. Then, create a customized news page with stories about your sports interests. Include RSS feeds to get regularly updated summaries on this subject.

2. Visit the Onlinenewspapers and starting page Web sites listed in Figure 20 and select two newspapers from each site. Write a paragraph describing the top national news story featured in each of these four Web pages. Then, write another paragraph describing the top international news story displayed at each Web site. In the third paragraph, discuss which of the four Web sites is the most interesting in terms of story selection, photos, and Web page design.

Learning

Yearn to Learn

Discover New Worlds Online

While you may believe your education ends when you finally graduate from college, learning is a lifelong process. You can increase your technological knowledge by visiting several Web sites (Figure 21) with tutorials about building your own Web sites, the latest news about the Internet, and resources for visually impaired users.

Learning Web Sites

Learning How To's	Web Address
Bartleby: Great Books Online	bartleby.com
AT&T Knowledge Network Explorer	www.kn.pacbell.com/wired
BBC Learning	bbc.co.uk/learning
CBT Nuggets	cbtnuggets.com
HowStuffWorks	howstuffworks.com
Internet Public Library	ipl.org
Learn the Net	learnthenet.com
ScienceMaster	sciencemaster.com
Search Engine Watch	searchenginewatch.com
Wiredguide	wiredguide.com
Cooking	**Web Address**
Betty Crocker	bettycrocker.com
Chef2Chef	chef2chef.net
Food Network	foodnetwork.com

For more information about learning Web sites, visit the Computer Concepts CourseMate Web site at www.cengagebrain.com and then navigate to the Making Use of the Web Feature resource for this book.

Figure 21 The information gleaned from these Web sites can help you learn about many aspects of our existence.

The HowStuffWorks Web site has won numerous awards for its clear, comprehensive articles that demystify aspects of our everyday life. It includes ratings and reviews of products written by *Consumer Guide* editors.

A consortium of colleges maintains the Internet Public Library, which includes subject collections, reference materials, and a reading room filled with magazines and books. Volunteer librarians will answer your personal questions asked in its Ask an IPL Librarian form.

Enhancing your culinary skills can be a rewarding endeavor. No matter if you are a gourmet chef or a weekend cook, you will be cooking in style with the help of online resources, including those listed in Figure 21.

Have you ever wondered how to make a key lime pie? How about learning how to cook some easy, low-calorie dishes? Are you seeking advice from expert chefs? The Food Network Web site (Figure 22) is filled with information related to cooking, grilling, and healthy eating.

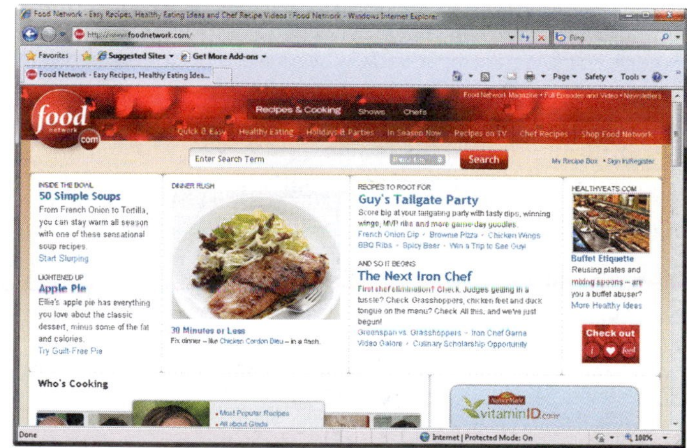

Figure 22 The Food Network Web site provides access to healthy recipes, grilling tips, and cookware.

Learning Web Exercises

1. **Using one of the Learning How To's Web sites listed in Figure 21,** search for information about installing memory in a computer. Write a paragraph about your findings. Then, review the material in the HowStuffWorks Web site listed in Figure 21, and write a paragraph describing articles on this Web site that are pertinent to your major.

2. **Visit one of the cooking Web sites listed in Figure 21** and find two recipes or cooking tips that you can use when preparing your next meal. Write a paragraph about each one, summarizing your discoveries. Which Web sites allow you to create your own online recipe book? What are the advantages and disadvantages of accessing these Web sites on the new appliances and gadgets that might someday be in your kitchen?

Science

$E = mc^2$

Rocket Science on the Web

For some people, space exploration is a hobby. Building and launching model rockets allow these at-home scientists to participate in exploring the great frontier of space. For others, space exploration is their life. Numerous Web sites, including those in Figure 23, provide in-depth information about the universe.

Science Web Sites

Periodicals	Web Address
Archaeology Magazine	archaeology.org
Astronomy Magazine	astronomy.com
New Scientist	newscientist.com
OceanLink	oceanlink.info
Science Magazine	sciencemag.org
Scientific American	sciam.com
Resources	**Web Address**
National Science Foundation (NSF)	nsf.gov
Science.gov: USA.gov for Science	science.gov
Thomson Reuters	scientific.thomson.com/free/
Science Community	**Web Address**
American Scientist	amsci.org
Federation of American Scientists	fas.org
NASA	www.nasa.gov
Sigma Xi, The Scientific Research Society	sigmaxi.org

For more information about science Web sites, visit the Computer Concepts CourseMate Web site at www.cengagebrain.com and then navigate to the Making Use of the Web Feature resource for this book.

Figure 23 Resources available on the Internet offer a wide range of subjects for enthusiasts who want to delve into familiar and unknown territories in the world of science.

NASA's Web site contains information about rockets, space exploration, the International Space Station, space transportation, and communications. Other science resources explore space-related questions about astronomy, physics, the earth sciences, microgravity, and robotics.

Rockets and space are not the only areas to explore in the world of science. Where can you find the latest pictures taken with the Hubble Space Telescope? Do you know how climate change is affecting the human body? You can find the answers to these questions and many others through the New Scientist Web site (newscientist.com) shown in Figure 24.

The National Science Foundation's Web site features overviews of current topics and an extensive Multimedia Gallery with audio and video files, photos, and paintings.

Science.gov is an outstanding resource for scientific databases and thousands of authoritative science Web sites. The U.S. government science information provided offers 200 million pages of research, with search results ranked by relevance and sorted by topic and year.

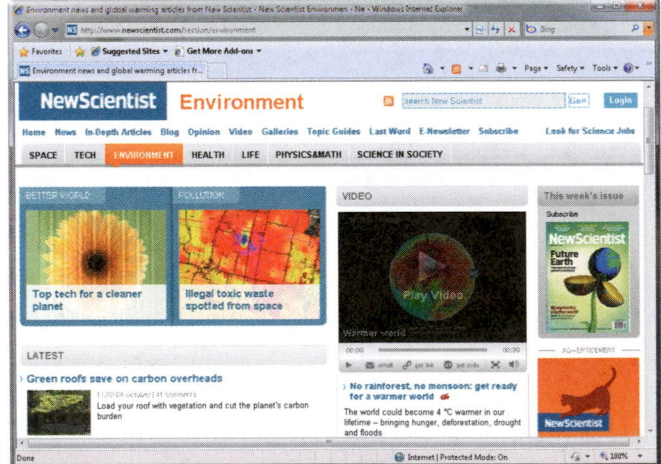

Figure 24 The New Scientist Web site covers news about space exploration, the environment, and technology.

Science Web Exercises

1. **Visit the National Science Foundation Web site listed in the table in Figure 23.** What are the topics of the latest science news and special reports? Which speeches and lectures are featured? What are the titles of image, video, and audio files in the Multimedia Gallery?

2. **Visit the NASA Web site listed in the table in Figure 23.** Click the Missions link and then click the Mission Calendar link. When are the next two launches scheduled? What are the purposes of these missions? Click the Careers @ NASA topic and then write a paragraph describing the internships, cooperative programs, and summer employment opportunities. Then, view two of the science community Web sites listed in Figure 23 and write a paragraph about each of these Web sites describing the information each contains.

Health

No Pain, All Gain

Store Personal Health Records Online

More than 75 million consumers use the Internet yearly to search for health information, so using the Web to store personal medical data is a natural extension of the Internet's capabilities. Internet health services and portals are available to store your personal health history, including prescriptions, lab test results, doctor visits, allergies, and immunizations.

Google Health allows users to create a health profile, import medical records, and locate medical services and doctors. Web sites such as healthfinder.gov (Figure 25) provide free wellness information to consumers. Wise consumers, however, verify the online information they read with their personal physician.

In minutes, you can register with a health Web site by choosing a user name and password. Then, you create a record to enter your medical history. You also can store data for your emergency contacts, primary care physicians, specialists, blood type, cholesterol levels, blood pressure, and insurance plan. No matter where you are in the world, you and medical personnel can obtain records via the Internet or fax machine. Some popular online health databases are shown in Figure 26.

Figure 25 The healthfinder.gov Web site provides advice and tools to prevent illnesses and check drug interactions.

Health Web Sites

Medical History	Web Address
Google Health	google.com/health
Lifestar	mylifestarphr.com
Medem	medem.com
PersonalMD	personalmd.com
Practice Solutions	practicesolutions.ca
Records for Living, Inc — Personal Health and Living Management	recordsforliving.com
WebMD	webmd.com
General Health	**Web Address**
Consumer and Patient Health Information Section (CAPHIS)	caphis.mlanet.org/consumer
Centers for Disease Control and Prevention	cdc.gov
familydoctor	familydoctor.org
healthfinder	healthfinder.gov
KidsHealth	kidshealth.org
LIVESTRONG.COM	livestrong.com
MedlinePlus	medlineplus.gov
PE Central: Health and Nutrition Web Sites	pecentral.org/websites/healthsites.html
Physical Activity Guidelines	health.gov/paguidelines

For more information about health Web sites, visit the Computer Concepts CourseMate Web site at www.cengagebrain.com and then navigate to the Making Use of the Web Feature resource for this book.

Figure 26 These health Web sites allow you to organize your medical information and store it in an online database and also obtain information about a variety of medical conditions and treatments.

Health Web Exercises

1. **Access one of the health Web sites listed in Figure 26.** Register yourself or a family member and then enter the full health history. Create an emergency medical card if the Web site provides the card option. Submit this record and emergency card to your instructor. If you feel uncomfortable disclosing medical information for yourself or a family member, you may enter fictitious information.

2. **Visit three of the health Web sites listed in Figure 26.** Describe the features of each. Which of the three is the most user-friendly? Why? Describe the privacy policies of these three Web sites. Submit your analysis of these Web sites to your instructor.

Careers

In Search of the Perfect Job

Web Helps Career Hunt

While your teachers give you valuable training to prepare you for a career, they rarely teach you how to begin that career. You can broaden your horizons by searching the Internet for career information and job openings.

First, examine some of the job search Web sites. These resources list thousands of openings in hundreds of fields, companies, and locations. For example, the USAJOBS Web site, shown in Figure 27, allows you to find information for Federal jobs. This information may include the training and education required, salary data, working conditions, job descriptions, and more. In addition, many companies advertise careers on their Web sites.

When a company contacts you for an interview, learn as much about it and the industry as possible before the interview. Many of the Web sites listed in Figure 28 include detailed company profiles and links to their corporate Web sites.

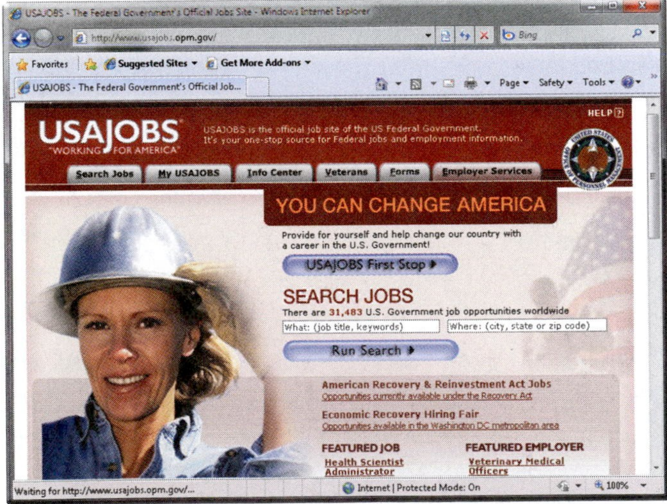

Figure 27 The USAJOBS Web site is the official location for federal jobs and information for job seekers.

Career Web Sites

Job Search	Web Address
BestJobsUSA	bestjobsusa.com
CareerBuilder	careerbuilder.com
Careerjet	careerjet.com
CareerNET	careernet.com
CAREERXCHANGE	careerxchange.com
CollegeGrad.com	collegegrad.com
EmploymentGuide.com	employmentguide.com
Job.com	job.com
Job Bank USA	jobbankusa.com
Job-Hunt	job-hunt.org
Monster	monster.com
USAJOBS	www.usajobs.gov
VolunteerMatch	volunteermatch.org
Yahoo! HotJobs	hotjobs.yahoo.com
Company/Industry Information	**Web Address**
Careers.org	careers.org
Forbes	forbes.com/leadership/careers
Fortune	fortune.com
Hoover's	hoovers.com
Occupational Outlook Handbook	stats.bls.gov/oco

For more information about career Web sites, visit the Computer Concepts CourseMate Web site at www.cengagebrain.com and then navigate to the Making Use of the Web Feature resource for this book.

Figure 28 Career Web sites provide a variety of job openings and information about major companies worldwide.

Careers Web Exercises

1. **Use two of the job search Web sites listed in Figure 28 to find three companies with job openings in your field.** Make a table listing the Web site name, position available, description, salary, location, desired education, and desired experience.

2. **It is a good idea to acquire information before graduation about the industry in which you would like to work.** Are you interested in the automotive manufacturing industry, the restaurant service industry, or the financial industry? Use two of the company/industry information Web sites listed in Figure 28 to research a particular career related to your major. Write a paragraph naming the Web sites and the specific information you found, such as the nature of the work, recommended training and qualifications, employment outlook, and earnings. Then, use two other Web sites to profile three companies with positions available in this field. Write a paragraph about each of these companies, describing the headquarters' location, sales and earnings for the previous year, total number of employees, working conditions, benefits, and competitors.

Literature and Arts

Find Some Culture

Get Ready to Read, Paint, and Dance

Brush up your knowledge of Shakespeare, grab a canvas, and put on your dancing shoes. Literature and arts Web sites, including those in Figure 29, are about to sweep you off your cyberfeet.

Literature and Arts Web Sites

Literature	Web Address
Bartleby	bartleby.com
Bibliomania	bibliomania.com
The Complete Review	www.complete-review.com
eNotes	enotes.com
Fantastic Fiction	fantasticfiction.co.uk
Literary History	literaryhistory.com
Nobel Prize in Literature	nobelprize.org/nobel_prizes/literature/laureates/1909/press.html
Project Gutenberg	gutenberg.org
Project MUSE	muse.jhu.edu
Arts	**Web Address**
absolutearts	absolutearts.com
The Children's Museum of Indianapolis	childrensmuseum.org
ARTINFO Gallery Guide	artinfo.com/galleryguide/
The Getty	getty.edu
Louvre Museum	louvre.fr
Montreal Museum of Fine Arts	mmfa.qc.ca
Museumstuff.com	museumstuff.com
The Museum of Online Museums	coudal.com/moom
National Gallery of Art	nga.gov

For more information about literature and arts Web sites, visit the Computer Concepts CourseMate Web site at www.cengagebrain.com and then navigate to the Making Use of the Web Feature resource for this book.

Figure 29 Discover culture throughout the world by visiting these literature and arts Web sites.

The full text of hundreds of books is available online from the Bibliomania and Project Gutenberg Web sites. The Complete Review provides summaries, reviews, and Web links about a variety of books and their authors. The Bartleby Web site features biographies, definitions, quotations, dictionaries, and indexes.

When you are ready to absorb more culture, you can turn to various art Web sites. Many museums have images of their collections online. Among them are the Getty Museum in Los Angeles, the Montreal Museum of Fine Arts, and the Louvre Museum in Paris (Figure 30).

The absolutearts Web site focuses on contemporary art and includes video interviews with artists, art history research, and artists' blogs.

The Museum of Online Museums Web site provides links to museum and gallery Web sites, such as the Museum of Modern Art, The Bauhaus Archive, and The Art Institute of Chicago.

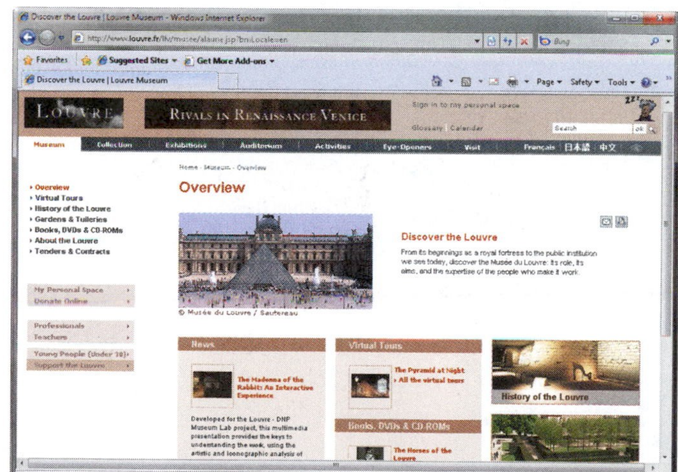

Figure 30 Permanent and temporary exhibitions, educational activities, and a bookstore are featured on the Louvre Museum Web site.

Literature and Arts Web Exercises

1. **Visit the Literary History Web site listed in Figure 29** and view one author in the Twentieth Century Literature, Nineteenth Century Literature, British Poets, and African American Literature sections. Read two literary criticism articles about each of the four authors and write a paragraph describing which of these authors is the most interesting to you. What are the advantages and disadvantages of reading literary criticism electronically?

2. **Using the arts Web sites listed in Figure 29,** search for three temporary exhibitions in galleries throughout the world. Describe the venues, the artists, and the works. Which permanent collections are found in these museums? Some people shop for gifts in the museums' stores. View and describe three items for sale.

Chapter Three

Application Software

Objectives

After completing this chapter, you will be able to:

1. Identify the four categories of application software
2. Differentiate among the seven forms through which software is available: packaged software, custom software, Web application, open source software, shareware, freeware, and public-domain software
3. Explain how the operating system and utility programs work with application software
4. Describe characteristics of a user interface
5. Identify the key features of widely used business programs: word processing, spreadsheet, database, presentation, note taking, personal information manager, business software for phones, business software suite, project management, accounting, document management, and enterprise computing
6. Identify the key features of widely used graphics and multimedia programs: computer-aided design, professional desktop publishing, professional paint/image editing, professional photo editing, professional video and audio editing, multimedia authoring, and Web page authoring
7. Identify the key features of widely used home, personal, and educational programs: personal finance, legal, tax preparation, personal desktop publishing, personal paint/image editing, personal photo editing and photo management, clip art/image gallery, personal video and audio editing, travel and mapping, reference and educational, and entertainment
8. Discuss the advantages of and ways to access Web applications
9. Identify the types of application software used in communications
10. Describe the learning aids available for application software

Application Software

With the proper software, a computer is a valuable tool. Software allows users to create letters, memos, reports, and other documents; develop multimedia presentations; design Web pages and diagrams; draw and alter images; record and enhance audio and video clips; prepare and file taxes; play single player or multiplayer games; compose e-mail messages and instant messages; and much more. To accomplish these and many other tasks, users work with application software. **Application software** consists of programs designed to make users more productive and/or assist them with personal tasks. Application software has a variety of uses:

1. To make business activities more efficient
2. To assist with graphics and multimedia projects
3. To support home, personal, and educational tasks
4. To facilitate communications

The table in Figure 3-1 categorizes popular types of application software by their general use. Although many types of communications software exist, the ones listed in Figure 3-1 are application software oriented.

The categories of application software in Figure 3-1 are not mutually exclusive. Software listed in one category may be used in other categories. For example, desktop publishing programs, which are categorized as graphics and multimedia software, often are used for business or personal reasons.

Application software is available in a variety of forms: packaged, custom, Web application, open source, shareware, freeware, and public domain.

- **Packaged software** is mass-produced, copyrighted retail software that meets the needs of a wide variety of users, not just a single user or company. Packaged software is available in retail stores or on the Web. Figure 3-1 shows some images of packaged software.
- **Custom software** performs functions specific to a business or industry. Sometimes a company cannot find packaged software that meets its unique requirements. In this case, the company may use programmers to develop tailor-made custom software, which usually costs more than packaged software.
- A **Web application** is a Web site that allows users to access and interact with software from any computer or device that is connected to the Internet. Many Web sites provide free access to their programs; some charge a fee. Types of Web applications include e-mail, word processing, tax preparation, and game programs. Web applications are discussed in more depth later in this chapter.

Four Categories of Application Software

Business	Graphics and Multimedia	Home/Personal/Educational
• Word Processing • Spreadsheet • Database • Presentation • Note Taking • Personal Information Manager (PIM) • Business Software for Phones • Business Software Suite • Project Management • Accounting • Document Management • Enterprise Computing	• Computer-Aided Design (CAD) • Desktop Publishing (for the Professional) • Paint/Image Editing (for the Professional) • Photo Editing (for the Professional) • Video and Audio Editing (for the Professional) • Multimedia Authoring • Web Page Authoring	• Software Suite (for Personal Use) • Personal Finance • Legal • Tax Preparation • Desktop Publishing (for Personal Use) • Paint/Image Editing (for Personal Use) • Photo Editing and Photo Management (for Personal Use) • Clip Art/Image Gallery • Video and Audio Editing (for Personal Use) • Home Design/Landscaping • Travel and Mapping • Reference and Educational • Entertainment

Communications

• Web Browser	• E-Mail	• Instant Messaging	• Chat Room	• Text, Picture, Video Messaging	
• RSS Aggregator	• Blogging	• Newsgroup/Message Board	• FTP	• VoIP	• Video Conferencing

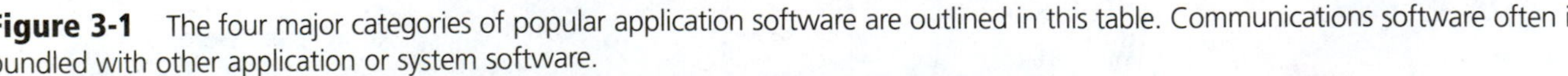

Figure 3-1 The four major categories of popular application software are outlined in this table. Communications software often is bundled with other application or system software.

- **Open source software** is software provided for use, modification, and redistribution. This software has no restrictions from the copyright holder regarding modification of the software's internal instructions and its redistribution. Open source software usually can be downloaded from the Internet, often at no cost.
- **Shareware** is copyrighted software that is distributed at no cost for a trial period. To use a shareware program beyond that period, you send payment to the program developer. Shareware developers trust users to send payment if software use extends beyond the stated trial period. In some cases, a scaled-down version of the software is distributed free, and payment entitles the user to the fully functional product.
- **Freeware** is copyrighted software provided at no cost by an individual or a company that retains all rights to the software. Thus, programmers typically cannot incorporate freeware in applications they intend to sell. The word, free, in freeware indicates the software has no charge.
- **Public-domain software** has been donated for public use and has no copyright restrictions. Anyone can copy or distribute public-domain software to others at no cost.

Thousands of shareware, freeware, and public-domain programs are available on the Internet for users to download. Examples include communications, graphics, and game programs. These programs usually have fewer capabilities than packaged programs. Some packaged programs have trial versions, which you can use at no charge for a limited time, to see if the software meets your needs.

After you purchase or download software, you install it. During installation, the program may ask you to register and/or activate the software. (To learn more about installing software, complete the Learn How To 2 activity on pages 188 and 189.) Registering the software is optional and usually involves submitting your name and other personal information to the software manufacturer or developer. Registering the software often entitles you to product support. *Product activation* is a technique that some software manufacturers use to ensure the software is not installed on more computers than legally licensed. Usually, the software does not function or has limited functionality until you activate it via the Internet or telephone. Thus, activation is a required process for programs requesting it. You can activate some software more than once, for example, to run a program on both a desktop and notebook computer. Registering and/or activating the software also usually entitles you to free program updates for a specified time period, such as a year.

The Role of System Software

System software serves as the interface between the user, the application software, and the computer's hardware (Figure 3-2). To use application software, such as a word processing program, your computer must be running system software — specifically,

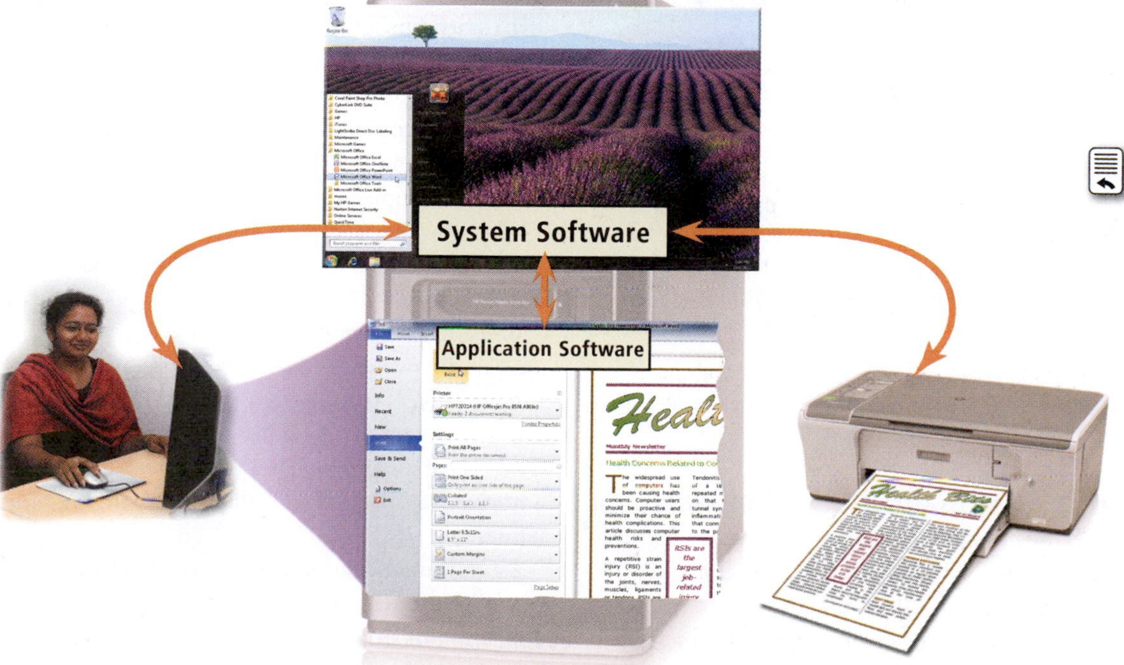

Figure 3-2 A user does not communicate directly with the computer hardware. Instead, system software is the interface between the user, the application software, and the hardware. For example, when a user instructs the application software to print a document, the application software sends the print instruction to the system software, which in turn sends the print instruction to the hardware.

an operating system. Three popular personal computer operating systems are Windows, Mac OS, and Linux.

Each time you start a computer, the operating system is *loaded* (copied) from the computer's hard disk into memory. Once the operating system is loaded, it coordinates all the activities of the computer. This includes starting application software and transferring data among input and output devices and memory. While the computer is running, the operating system remains in memory.

Utility Programs A utility program is a type of system software that assists users with controlling or maintaining the operation of a computer, its devices, or its software. Utility programs typically offer features that provide an environment conducive to successful use of application software. For example, utility programs protect a computer against malicious software and unauthorized intrusions, manage files and disks, compress files, play media files, and burn optical discs. (To learn more about how to compress files, complete the Learn How To 3 activity on page 189.)

One of the more important utility programs protects a computer against malicious software, or *malware*, which is a program that acts without a user's knowledge and deliberately alters the computer's operations. A computer virus is a type of malicious software. For a technical discussion about viruses and other malicious software, read the High-Tech Talk article on page 178. Chapter 8 discusses system software and utility programs in more depth.

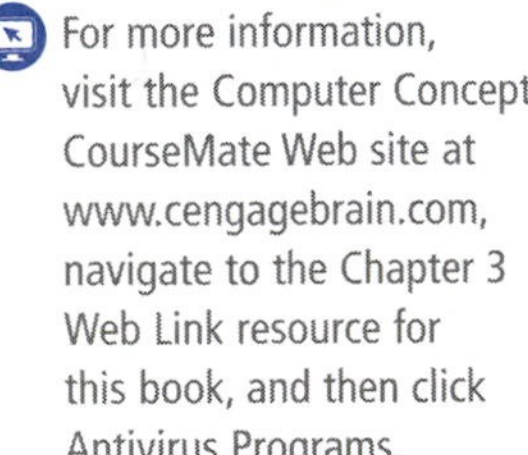

Antivirus Programs

For more information, visit the Computer Concepts CourseMate Web site at www.cengagebrain.com, navigate to the Chapter 3 Web Link resource for this book, and then click Antivirus Programs.

? FAQ 3-1

How many viruses exist on the Internet?

More than one million viruses exist on the Internet. This statistic stresses the importance of protecting your computer from various threats on the Internet, as well as practicing safe Web browsing habits. Not only is it possible to get a computer virus from downloading and opening an infected file or by opening an infected e-mail message, you also can fall victim to a computer virus simply by visiting a malicious Web site.

For more information, visit the Computer Concepts CourseMate Web site at www.cengagebrain.com, navigate to the Chapter 3 FAQ resource for this book, and then click Computer Viruses.

Working with Application Software

To use application software, you must instruct the operating system to start the program. The steps in Figure 3-3 illustrate one way to start and interact with the Paint program, which is included with the Windows operating system. The following paragraphs explain the steps in Figure 3-3.

Personal computer operating systems often use the concept of a desktop to make the computer easier to use. The **desktop** is an on-screen work area that has a graphical user interface. Step 1 of Figure 3-3 shows icons, a button, a pointer, and a menu on the Windows desktop. An **icon** is a small image displayed on the screen that represents a program, a document, or some other object. A **button** is a graphical element that you activate to cause a specific action to occur. One way to activate a button is to click it. To **click** a button on the screen requires moving the pointer to the button and then pressing and releasing a button on the mouse (usually the left mouse button). The **pointer** is a small symbol displayed on the screen that moves as you interact with the mouse or other pointing device. Common pointer shapes are an I-beam (I), a block arrow (↖), and a pointing hand (☝).

The Windows desktop contains a Start button on the lower-left corner of the taskbar. When you click the Start button, the Start menu is displayed on the desktop. A **menu** contains a list of commands from which you make selections. A **command** is an instruction that causes a program to perform a specific action.

As illustrated in Steps 1 and 2 of Figure 3-3, when you click the Start button and then click the All Programs command on the Start menu, the All Programs list is displayed on the Start menu. Clicking the Accessories folder in the All Programs list displays the Accessories list.

To start a program, you can click its program name on a menu or in a list. This action instructs the operating system to start the program, which means the program's instructions load from a storage medium (such as a hard disk) into memory. For example, when you click Paint in the Accessories list, Windows loads the Paint program instructions from the computer's hard disk into memory.

Once loaded into memory, the program appears in a window on the desktop (Step 3 of Figure 3-3). A **window** is a rectangular area of the screen that displays data and information. The top of a window has a **title bar**, which is a horizontal space that contains the window's name.

With the program loaded, you can create a new file or open an existing one. A *file* is a named collection of stored data, instructions, or information. A file can contain text, images, audio, and video. To distinguish among various files, each file has a file name. A *file name* is a unique combination of letters of the alphabet, numbers, and other characters that identifies a file. The title bar of the document window usually displays a document's file name. Step 4 of Figure 3-3 shows the contents of the file, Baby Buffalo, displaying in the Paint window. The file contains an image photographed with a digital camera.

In some cases, when you instruct a program to perform an activity such as print, the program displays a dialog box. A *dialog box* is a window that provides information, presents available options, or requests a response. Dialog boxes, such as the one shown in Step 5 of Figure 3-3, often contain option buttons, text boxes, check boxes, and command buttons. In this case, clicking the Print button in the dialog box instructs the computer to print the photo.

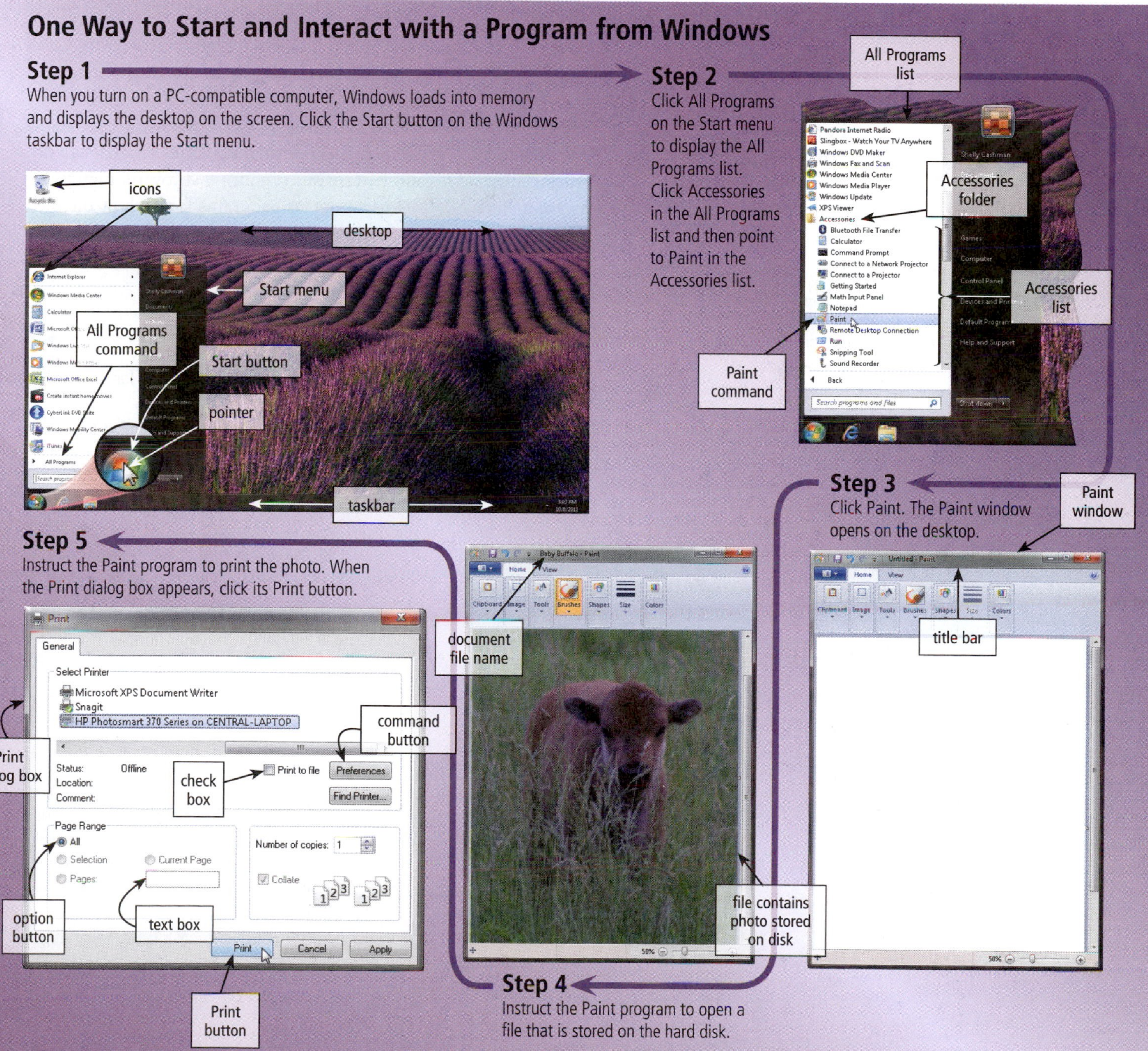

Figure 3-3 This figure shows one way to start and interact with a program from Windows.

✔ QUIZ YOURSELF 3-1

Instructions: Find the true statement below. Then, rewrite the remaining false statements so that they are true.

1. Application software is used to make business activities more efficient; assist with graphics and multimedia projects; support home, personal, and educational tasks; and facilitate communications.
2. Public-domain software is mass-produced, copyrighted retail software that meets the needs of a wide variety of users, not just a single user or company.
3. To use system software, your computer must be running application software.
4. When a program is started, its instructions load from memory into a storage medium.

Quiz Yourself Online: To further check your knowledge of pages 142 through 145, visit the Computer Concepts CourseMate Web site at www.cengagebrain.com, navigate to the Chapter 3 Quiz Yourself resource for this book, and then click Objectives 1 – 4.

Business Software

Business software is application software that assists people in becoming more effective and efficient while performing their daily business activities. Business software includes programs such as word processing, spreadsheet, database, presentation, note taking, personal information manager, business software for phones, business software suites, project management, accounting, document management, and enterprise computing software. Figure 3-4 lists popular programs for each of these categories.

Popular Business Programs

Application Software	Manufacturer	Program Name
Word Processing	Microsoft	Word
	Apple	Pages
	Corel	WordPerfect
Spreadsheet	Microsoft	Excel
	Apple	Numbers
	Corel	Quattro Pro
Database	Microsoft	Access
	Corel	Paradox
	Oracle	Oracle Database
	Sun	MySQL
Presentation	Microsoft	PowerPoint
	Apple	Keynote
	Corel	Presentations
Note Taking	Microsoft	OneNote
	Agilix	GoBinder
	Corel	Grafigo
	SnapFiles	KeyNote
Personal Information Manager (PIM)	Microsoft	Outlook
	Google	Calendar
	IBM	Lotus Organizer
	Palm	Desktop
	Mozilla	Thunderbird
Business Software for Phones	CNetX	Pocket SlideShow
	DataViz	Documents To Go
	Microsoft	Word Mobile Excel Mobile PowerPoint Mobile Outlook Mobile
	Mobile Systems	MobiSystems Office Suite
	Ultrasoft	Money

Application Software	Manufacturer	Program Name
Business Software Suite (for the Professional)	Microsoft	Office Office for Mac
	Apple	iWork
	Google	Google Docs
	Sun	OpenOffice.org StarOffice
	Corel	WordPerfect Office
	IBM	Lotus SmartSuite
Project Management	CS Odessa	ConceptDraw PROJECT
	Microsoft	Project
	Oracle	Primavera SureTrak Project Manager
Accounting	Intuit	QuickBooks
	Microsoft	Accounting
	Sage Software	Peachtree
Document Management	Adobe	Acrobat
	Enfocus	PitStop
	Nuance	PDF Converter
Enterprise Computing	Oracle	PeopleSoft Enterprise Human Capital Management
	Sage Software	Sage MAS 500
	MSC Software	MSC.SimManager
	Oracle	Oracle Manufacturing
	SAP	mySAP Customer Relationship Management
	NetSuite	NetERP
	Syntellect	Syntellect Interaction Management Suite

Figure 3-4 Popular business software.

The following sections discuss the features and functions of business software. Word processing and spreadsheet software have a heavier emphasis because of their predominant use.

Word Processing Software

Word processing software is one of the more widely used types of application software. **Word processing software**, sometimes called a *word processor*, allows users to create and manipulate documents containing mostly text and sometimes graphics (Figure 3-5). Millions of people use word processing software every day to develop documents such as letters, memos, reports, mailing labels, newsletters, and Web pages.

A major advantage of using word processing software is that users easily can change what they have written. For example, you can insert, delete, or rearrange words, sentences, paragraphs, or entire sections. Word processing software also has many features to make documents look professional and visually appealing. For example, you can change the shape, size, and color of characters; apply special effects such as three-dimensional shadows; and organize text in newspaper-style columns. When using colors, however, they print as black or gray unless you have a color printer.

Most word processing software allows users to incorporate graphical images, such as digital photos and clip art, in documents. **Clip art** is a collection of electronic drawings, photos, and other images. Word processing software usually includes public-domain images. You can find additional public-domain and proprietary images on the Web or purchase them on optical disc. In Figure 3-5, a user inserted an image of a baseball player in the document. With word processing software, you easily can modify the appearance of an image after inserting it in the document.

With word processing software, you can define the size of the paper on which to print and specify the *margins* — that is, the portion of the page outside the main body of text, including the top, the bottom, and both sides of the paper. A feature, called *wordwrap*, allows users to type words in a paragraph continually without pressing the ENTER key at the end of each line. When you modify paper size or margins, the word processing software automatically rewraps text so that it fits in the adjusted paper size and margins.

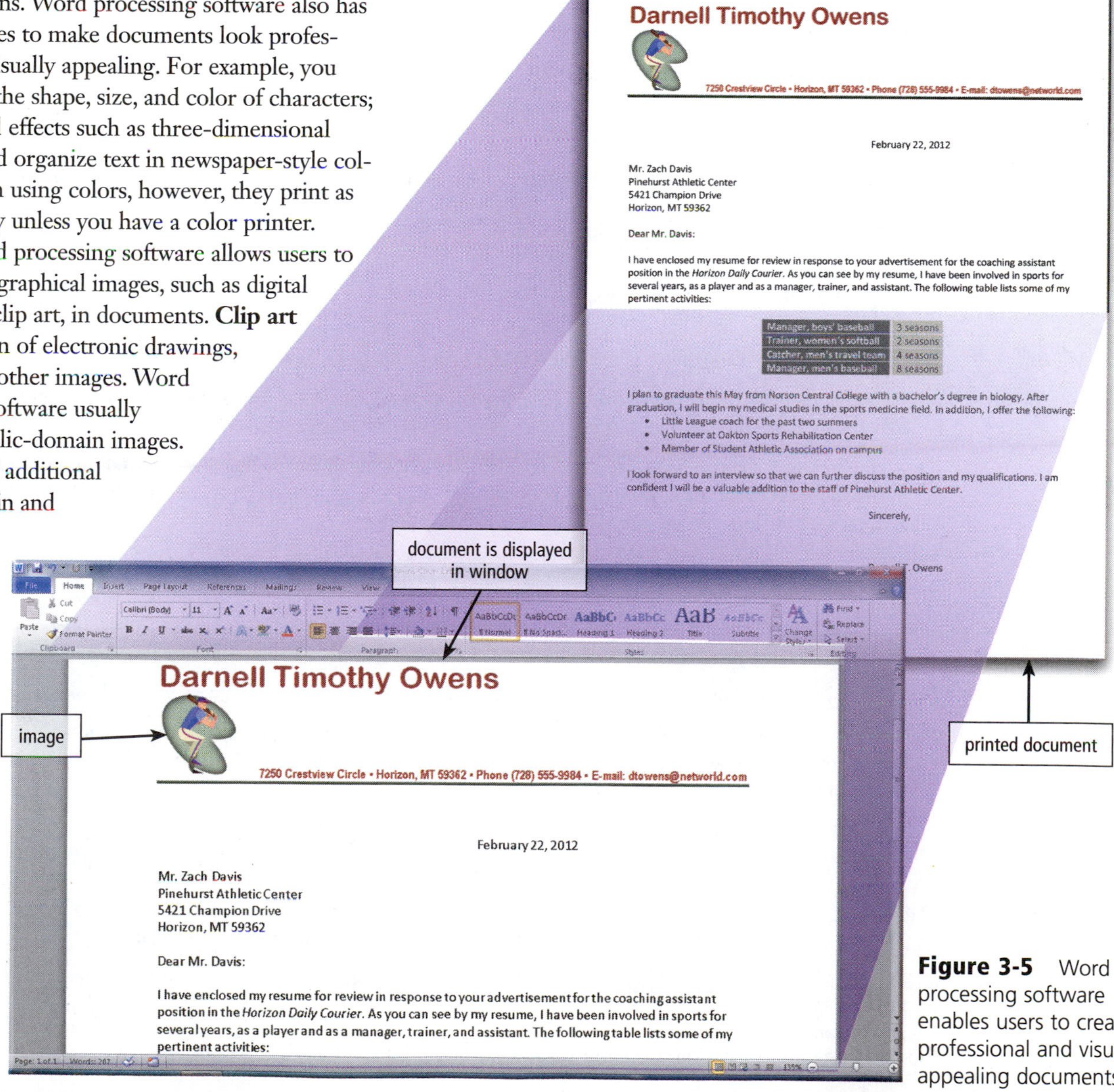

Darnell Timothy Owens

7250 Crestview Circle • Horizon, MT 59362 • Phone (728) 555-9984 • E-mail: dtowens@networld.com

February 22, 2012

Mr. Zach Davis
Pinehurst Athletic Center
5421 Champion Drive
Horizon, MT 59362

Dear Mr. Davis:

I have enclosed my resume for review in response to your advertisement for the coaching assistant position in the *Horizon Daily Courier*. As you can see by my resume, I have been involved in sports for several years, as a player and as a manager, trainer, and assistant. The following table lists some of my pertinent activities:

Manager, boys' baseball	3 seasons
Trainer, women's softball	2 seasons
Catcher, men's travel team	4 seasons
Manager, men's baseball	8 seasons

I plan to graduate this May from Norson Central College with a bachelor's degree in biology. After graduation, I will begin my medical studies in the sports medicine field. In addition, I offer the following:

- Little League coach for the past two summers
- Volunteer at Oakton Sports Rehabilitation Center
- Member of Student Athletic Association on campus

I look forward to an interview so that we can further discuss the position and my qualifications. I am confident I will be a valuable addition to the staff of Pinehurst Athletic Center.

Sincerely,

T. Owens

Figure 3-5 Word processing software enables users to create professional and visually appealing documents.

As you type more lines of text than can be displayed on the screen, the top portion of the document moves upward, or scrolls, off the screen. *Scrolling* is the process of moving different portions of the document on the screen into view.

Word processing software typically includes a *spelling checker*, which reviews the spelling of individual words, sections of a document, or the entire document. The spelling checker compares the words in the document with an electronic dictionary that is part of the word processing software. You can customize the electronic dictionary by adding words such as personal names. Some word processing programs also check for contextual spelling errors, such as a misuse of homophones (words pronounced the same but have different spellings or meanings, such as one and won).

Word processing software also enables you to insert headers and footers in a document. A *header* is text that appears at the top of each page, and a *footer* is text that appears at the bottom of each page. Page numbers, company names, report titles, and dates are examples of items included in headers and footers.

In addition to these basic capabilities, most current word processing programs provide numerous additional features, which are listed in the table in Figure 3-6.

Word Processing Software

For more information, visit the Computer Concepts CourseMate Web site at www.cengagebrain.com, navigate to the Chapter 3 Web Link resource for this book, and then click Word Processing Software.

Additional Word Processing Features	
AutoCorrect	As you type words, the AutoCorrect feature corrects common spelling and capitalization errors.
AutoFormat	As you type, the AutoFormat feature automatically applies formatting to the text. For example, it automatically numbers a list or converts a Web address to a hyperlink.
Collaboration	Collaboration allows multiple users to enter comments in a document and read and reply to each other's comments.
Columns	Most word processing software can arrange text in two or more columns to look like text in a newspaper or magazine. The text from the bottom of one column automatically flows to the top of the next column.
Grammar Checker	The grammar checker proofreads documents for grammar, writing style, sentence structure errors, and reading statistics.
Ink Input	Supports input from a digital pen. Word processing software that supports ink input incorporates user's handwritten text and drawings in a word processing document. Ink input is popular on Tablet PCs.
Macros	A *macro* is a sequence of keystrokes and instructions that a user records and saves. When you want to execute the same series of instructions, execute the macro instead.
Mail Merge	Creates form letters, mailing labels, and envelopes.
Reading Layout	For users who prefer reading on the screen, reading layout increases the readability and legibility of an on-screen document by hiding unnecessary buttons and increasing the size of displayed characters.
Research	Allows you to search through various forms of Internet reference information — based on selected text in a document. Research services available include a thesaurus, English and bilingual dictionaries, encyclopedias, and Web sites that provide information such as stock quotes, news articles, and company profiles.
Search and Replace	The search feature finds all occurrences of a certain character, word, or phrase. The replace feature, which usually works in conjunction with the search feature, substitutes existing characters or words with new ones.
Smart Tags	*Smart tags* automatically appear on the screen when you perform a certain action. For example, typing an address causes a smart tag to appear. Clicking this smart tag provides options to display a map of the address or driving directions to or from the address.
Tables	Tables organize information into rows and columns.
Templates	A *template* is a document that contains the formatting necessary for a specific document type. Templates usually exist for memos, fax cover sheets, and letters. In addition to templates provided with the software, users have access to many online templates through the manufacturer's Web site.
Thesaurus	With a thesaurus, a user looks up a synonym (word with the same meaning) for a word in a document.
Tracking Changes	If multiple users work with a document, the word processing software highlights or color-codes changes made by various users.
Voice Recognition	With some word processing programs, users can speak into the computer's microphone and watch the spoken words appear on the screen as they talk. Users edit and format the document by speaking or spelling an instruction.
Web Page Development	Most word processing software allows users to create, edit, format, and convert documents so that they can be displayed on the Web.

Figure 3-6 Many additional features of word processing software.

Developing a Document

With application software, such as a word processing program, users create, edit, format, save, and print documents. During the process of developing a document, users likely will switch back and forth among all of these activities.

When you **create** a document, you enter text or numbers, insert images, and perform other tasks using an input device such as a keyboard, mouse, digital pen, or microphone. If you are using Microsoft Word to design a flyer, for example, you are creating a document.

To **edit** a document means to make changes to its existing content. Common editing tasks include inserting, deleting, cutting, copying, and pasting. Inserting text involves adding text to a document. Deleting text means that you are removing text or other content. Cutting is the process of removing a portion of the document and storing it in a temporary storage location, sometimes called a *clipboard*. A clipboard also contains items that you copy (duplicate) in a document. *Pasting* is the process of transferring an item from a clipboard to a specific location in a document. Read Ethics & Issues 3-1 for a related discussion.

When users **format** a document, they change its appearance. Formatting is important because the overall look of a document significantly can affect its ability to communicate clearly. Examples of formatting tasks are changing the font, font size, and font style.

A **font** is a name assigned to a specific design of characters. Two basic types of fonts are serif and sans serif. A *serif font* has short decorative lines at the upper and lower ends of some characters. Sans means without. Thus, a *sans serif font* does not have the short decorative lines at the upper and lower ends of the characters. Cambria is an example of a serif font. Calibri is an example of a sans serif font.

Font size indicates the size of the characters in a particular font. Font size is gauged by a measurement system called points. A single *point* is about 1/72 of an inch in height. The text you are reading in this book is about 10 point. Thus, each character is about 5/36 (10/72) of an inch in height. A *font style* adds emphasis to a font. Bold, italic, underline, and color are examples of font styles. Figure 3-7 illustrates fonts, font sizes, and font styles.

Ethics & Issues

For the complete text of the Ethics & Issues boxes found in this chapter, visit the Computer Concepts CourseMate Web site at www.cengagebrain.com and then navigate to the Chapter 3 Ethics & Issues resource for this book.

ETHICS & ISSUES 3-1

How Should Schools Deal with Internet Plagiarism?

A high school teacher failed 28 students for plagiarizing, or copying, material from the Internet. When parents complained, the school board passed the students, and the teacher resigned. Word processing software and the Internet make plagiarism easier than ever. Students can use term paper Web sites, such as CheatHouse.com or Research Papers Online, to copy complete papers on a variety of topics. According to one survey, half of those who responded said that cheating does not or may not matter in the long run, and 60 percent had plagiarized in the past. Students who plagiarize blame peer pressure, classroom competition, the "busy work" nature of some assignments, and the permissive attitude that pervades the Internet. Teachers have several tools to catch plagiarists, including a variety of Internet-based services, such as Turnitin, that compare suspected papers to papers found on the Internet and produce an originality report highlighting text that may have been copied. Some instructors, however, are reluctant to investigate the integrity of a student's work and possibly ruin an academic career.

How should educators deal with plagiarism? Should a school's response to plagiarism depend on such factors as the material copied, the assignment for which it was copied, or the reason it was copied? Why or why not? How would you feel if a paper you wrote was used by a service such as Turnitin to be used as a benchmark against other student's papers? Why? Should schools nationwide be required to use a service such as Turnitin in an attempt to stop cheating? Why or why not?

Figure 3-7 The Cambria and Calibri fonts are shown in two font sizes and a variety of font styles.

During the process of creating, editing, and formatting a document, the computer holds it in memory. To keep the document for future use requires that you save it. When you **save** a document, the computer transfers the document from memory to a storage medium such as a USB flash drive or hard disk. Once saved, a document is stored permanently as a file on the storage medium. To learn more about how to save a file, complete the Learn How To 1 activity on page 188.

When you **print** a document, the computer places the contents of the document on paper or some other medium. You can print the same document many times, with each copy looking just like the first. Instead of printing a document and physically distributing it, some users e-mail the document to others on a network such as the Internet. Read Ethics & Issues 3-2 for a related discussion.

ETHICS & ISSUES 3-2

Are Word Processing Programs Making Students Lazy?

Today, word processing programs fix spelling and grammar mistakes, automatically format documents with templates, help correctly reference works cited in a document, and seem to do everything short of generating an idea for a document. Some educators believe that the proliferation of word processing automation is cheating students of the fundamental ability to perform these tasks on their own. Research shows that as word processing programs became more popular over the past years, the quality of written work done without the aid of this software has dropped dramatically. Opponents of using word processing software for assignments point out the quality of e-mail and instant messages is markedly worse than works written with the aid of modern word processing programs.

Proponents of the use of word processing programs for educational use point out that automation is the way writing should be done now and in the future. The higher quality of works produced using the software is well worth not sacrificing time toward teaching students less modern tactics. Students are more productive and able to focus on the topics at hand, rather than worry about spelling errors.

Are word processing programs making students lazy? Why or why not? Should educators have the ability to turn off time-saving features, such as the AutoCorrect and grammar checker features, in their students' word processing programs? Why? Do students need the ability manually to check spelling and grammar, format a document, and reference cited works in a document, in the same way that students still learn multiplication and long division? Why or why not?

? FAQ 3-2

How often should I save a document?

Saving at regular intervals ensures that the majority of your work will not be lost in the event of a power loss or system failure. Many programs have an AutoSave feature that automatically saves open documents at specified time intervals, such as every 10 minutes.

For more information, visit the Computer Concepts CourseMate Web site at www.cengagebrain.com, navigate to the Chapter 3 FAQ resource for this book, and then click Saving Documents.

Spreadsheet Software

Spreadsheet software is another widely used type of application software. **Spreadsheet software** allows users to organize data in rows and columns and perform calculations on the data. These rows and columns collectively are called a *worksheet*. For years, people used paper to organize data and perform calculations by hand. In an electronic worksheet, you organize data in the same manner, and the computer performs the calculations more quickly and accurately (Figure 3-8). Because of spreadsheet software's logical approach to organizing data, many people use this software to organize and present nonfinancial data, as well as financial data.

Like word processing software, most spreadsheet software has basic features to help users create, edit, and format worksheets. Spreadsheet software also incorporates many of the features found in word processing software such as macros, checking spelling, changing fonts and font sizes, adding colors, tracking changes, inserting audio and video clips, providing research capabilities, recognizing handwritten text and drawings, and creating Web pages from existing spreadsheet documents.

The following sections describe the features of most spreadsheet programs.

Spreadsheet Organization A spreadsheet file is similar to a notebook that can contain more than 1,000 related individual worksheets. Data is organized vertically in columns and horizontally in rows on each worksheet (Figure 3-8). Each worksheet usually can have more than 16,000 columns and 1 million rows. One or more letters identify each column, and a number identifies each row. Only a small fraction of the

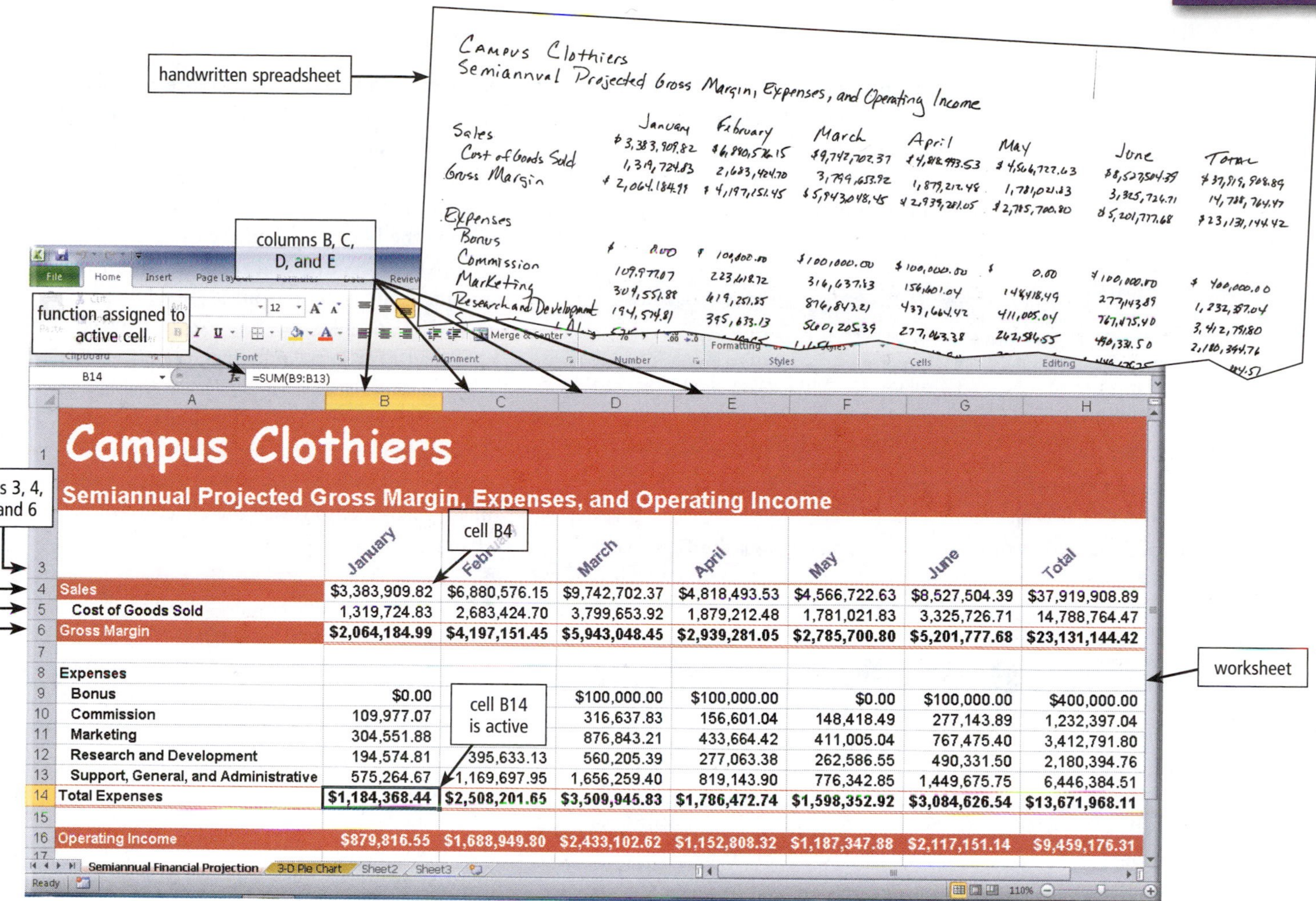

Figure 3-8 With spreadsheet software, you create worksheets that contain data arranged in rows and columns, and you perform calculations on the data in the worksheets.

columns and rows are visible on the screen at one time. Scrolling through the worksheet displays different parts of it on the screen.

A *cell* is the intersection of a column and row. Each worksheet has more than 17 billion cells in which you can enter data. The spreadsheet software identifies cells by the column and row in which they are located. For example, the intersection of column B and row 4 is referred to as cell B4. As shown in Figure 3-8, cell B4 contains the number, $3,383,909.82, which represents the sales for January.

Cells can contain three types of data: labels, values, and formulas. The text, or *label*, entered in a cell identifies the worksheet data and helps organize the worksheet. Using descriptive labels, such as Gross Margin and Total Expenses, helps make a worksheet more meaningful.

Calculations Many of the worksheet cells shown in Figure 3-8 contain a number, called a *value*, that can be used in a calculation. Other cells, however, contain formulas that generate values. A *formula* performs calculations on the data in the worksheet and displays the resulting value in a cell, usually the cell containing the formula. When creating a worksheet, you can enter your own formulas. In Figure 3-8, for example, cell B14 could contain the formula =B9+B10+B11+B12+B13, which would add together (sum) the contents of cells B9, B10, B11, B12, and B13. That is, this formula calculates the total expenses for January. A more efficient way to sum the contents of cells, however, is to use a special type of formula, called a function.

A *function* is a predefined formula that performs common calculations such as adding the values in a group of cells or generating a

Spreadsheet Software
For more information, visit the Computer Concepts CourseMate Web site at www.cengagebrain.com, navigate to the Chapter 3 Web Link resource for this book, and then click Spreadsheet Software.

value such as the time or date. For example, the function =SUM(B9:B13) instructs the spreadsheet program to add all of the numbers in cells B9 through B13. Figure 3-9 lists functions commonly included in spreadsheet programs.

Spreadsheet Functions	
Financial	
FV (rate, number of periods, payment)	Calculates the future value of an investment
NPV (rate, range)	Calculates the net present value of an investment
PMT (rate, number of periods, present value)	Calculates the periodic payment for an annuity
PV (rate, number of periods, payment)	Calculates the present value of an investment
RATE (number of periods, payment, present value)	Calculates the periodic interest rate of an annuity
Date and Time	
DATE	Returns the current date
NOW	Returns the current date and time
TIME	Returns the current time
Mathematical	
ABS (number)	Returns the absolute value of a number
INT (number)	Rounds a number down to the nearest integer
LN (number)	Calculates the natural logarithm of a number
LOG (number, base)	Calculates the logarithm of a number to a specified base
ROUND (number, number of digits)	Rounds a number to a specified number of digits
SQRT (number)	Calculates the square root of a number
SUM (range)	Calculates the total of a range of numbers
Statistical	
AVERAGE (range)	Calculates the average value of a range of numbers
COUNT (range)	Counts how many cells in the range have numeric entries
MAX (range)	Returns the maximum value in a range
MIN (range)	Returns the minimum value in a range
STDEV (range)	Calculates the standard deviation of a range of numbers
Logical	
IF (logical test, value if true, value if false)	Performs a test and returns one value if the result of the test is true and another value if the result is false

Figure 3-9 Functions typically found in spreadsheet software.

Recalculation One of the more powerful features of spreadsheet software is its capability of recalculating the rest of the worksheet when data in a worksheet changes. In Figure 3-8 on the previous page, for example, if you change the bonus for January from $0.00 to $100,000.00, the total expenses in cell B14 automatically change from $1,184,368.44 to $1,284,368.44.

Spreadsheet software's capability of recalculating data also makes it a valuable budgeting, forecasting, and decision making tool. Most spreadsheet software includes *what-if analysis* tools, where you change certain values in a spreadsheet to reveal the effects of those changes.

Charting Another standard feature of spreadsheet software is *charting*, which depicts the data in graphical form. A visual representation of data through charts often makes it easier for users to see at a glance the relationship among the numbers.

Three popular chart types are line charts, column charts, and pie charts. Figure 3-10 shows examples of these charts that were plotted using the five types of expenses for each of the months shown in the worksheet in Figure 3-8 on the previous page. A *line chart* shows a trend during a period of time, as indicated by a rising or falling line. For example, a line chart could show the total expenses for each of the six months. A *column chart*, also called a *bar chart*, displays bars of various lengths to show the relationship of data. The bars can be horizontal, vertical, or stacked on top of one another. For example, a column chart might show the total expenses, with each bar representing a different category of expense in a given month. A *pie chart*, which has the shape of a round pie cut into slices, shows the relationship of parts to a whole. For example, you might use a pie chart to show the percentage each expense category contributed to the total expenditures.

When you modify data in a worksheet, any associated charts automatically update to reflect the worksheet changes. Charts, as well as any other part of a worksheet, can be linked to or embedded in a word processing document.

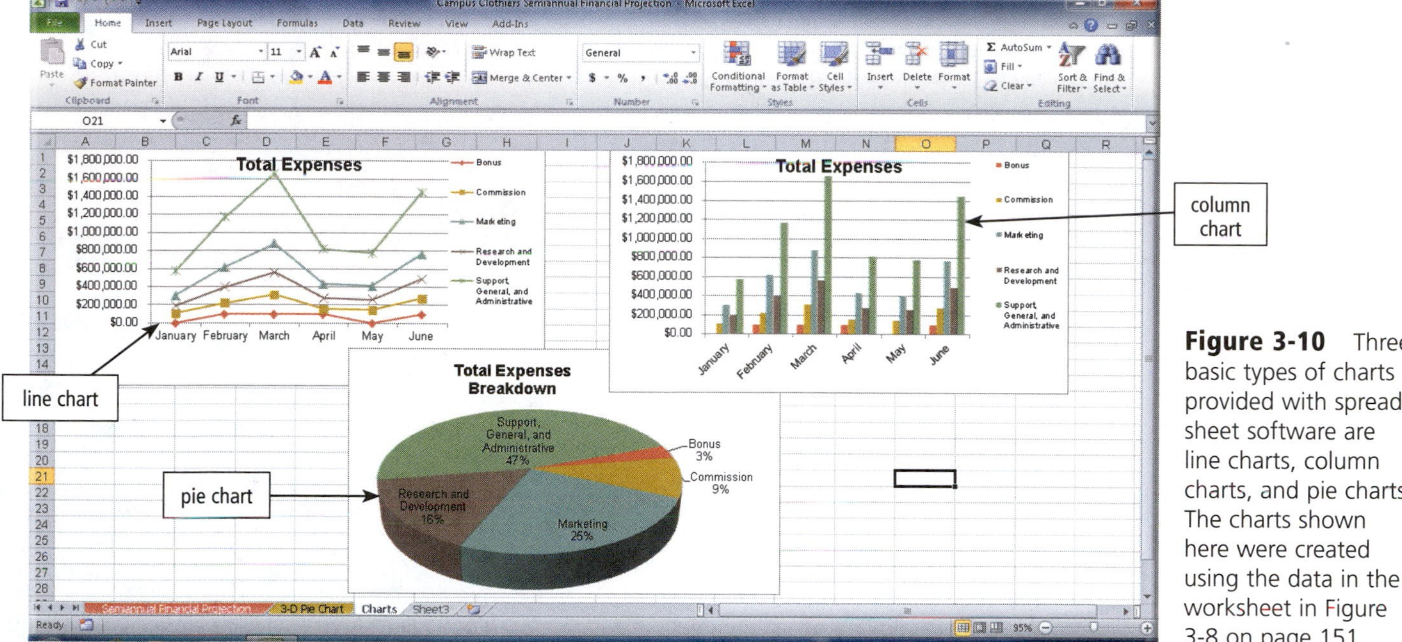

Figure 3-10 Three basic types of charts provided with spreadsheet software are line charts, column charts, and pie charts. The charts shown here were created using the data in the worksheet in Figure 3-8 on page 151.

Database Software

A **database** is a collection of data organized in a manner that allows access, retrieval, and use of that data. In a manual database, you might record data on paper and store it in a filing cabinet. With a computerized database, such as the one shown in Figure 3-11, the computer stores the data in an electronic format on a storage medium such as a hard disk.

Database software is application software that allows users to create, access, and manage a database. Using database software, you can add, change, and delete data in a database; sort and retrieve data from the database; and create forms and reports using the data in the database.

With most personal computer database programs, a database consists of a collection

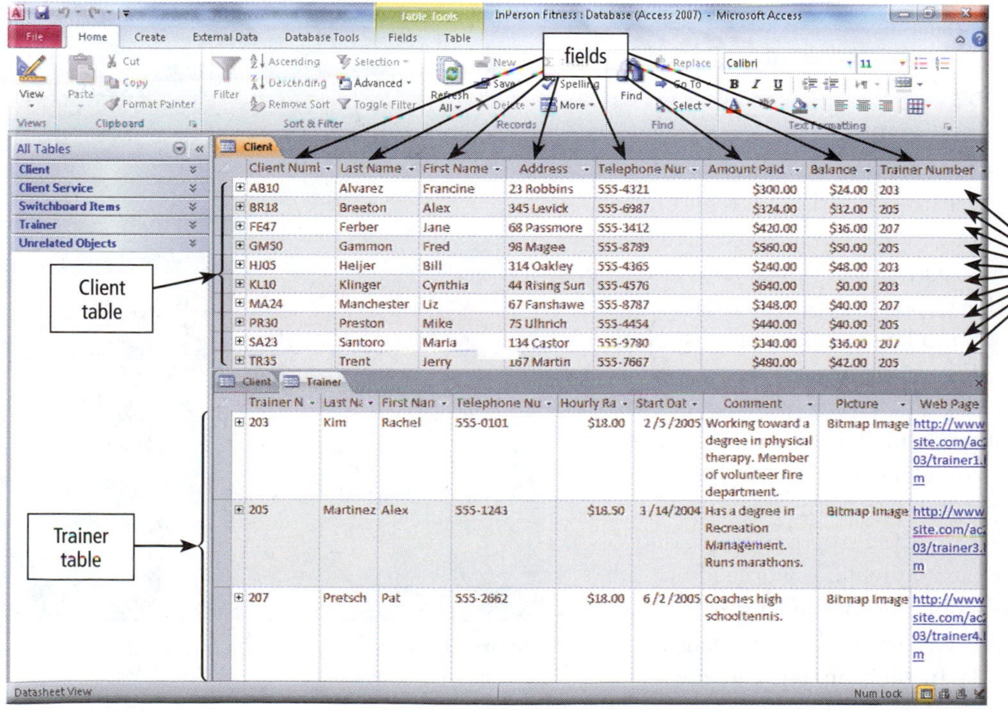

Figure 3-11 This database contains two tables: one for the clients and one for the trainers. The Client table has ten records and eight fields; the Trainer table has three records and eight fields.

of tables, organized in rows and columns. Each row, called a *record*, contains data about a given person, product, object, or event. Each column, called a *field*, contains a specific category of data within a record.

The Fitness database shown in Figure 3-11 on the previous page consists of two tables: a Client table and a Trainer table. The Client table contains ten records (rows), each storing data about one client. The client data is grouped into eight fields (columns): Client Number, Last Name, First Name, Address, Telephone Number, Amount Paid, Balance, and Trainer Number. The Balance field, for instance, contains the balance due from the client. The Client and Trainer tables relate to one another through a common field, Trainer Number.

Users run queries to retrieve data. A *query* is a request for specific data from the database. For example, a query might request clients whose balance is greater than $45. Database software can take the results of a query and present it in a window on the screen or send it to the printer.

Database Software

For more information, visit the Computer Concepts CourseMate Web site at www.cengagebrain.com, navigate to the Chapter 3 Web Link resource for this book, and then click Database Software.

? FAQ 3-3

How big is the largest database?

According to a recent survey, the world's largest database holds more than 6 quadrillion characters. The size of the largest database is expected to rise significantly during the next several years.

For more information, visit the Computer Concepts CourseMate Web site at www.cengagebrain.com, navigate to the Chapter 3 FAQ resource for this book, and then click Enterprise Databases.

Presentation Software

Presentation software is application software that allows users to create visual aids for presentations to communicate ideas, messages, and other information to a group. The presentations can be viewed as slides, sometimes called a *slide show*, that are displayed on a large monitor or on a projection screen (Figure 3-12).

Presentation software typically provides a variety of predefined presentation formats that define complementary colors for backgrounds, text, and graphical accents on the slides. This software also provides a variety of layouts for each individual slide such as a title slide, a two-column slide, and a slide with clip art, a picture, a chart, a table, or a diagram (Figure 3-13). In addition, you can enhance any

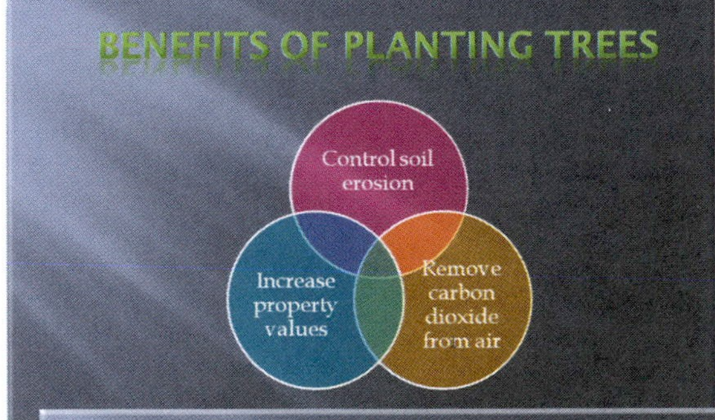

Figure 3-12 This presentation created with presentation software consists of five slides.

text, charts, and graphical images on a slide with 3-D, animation, and other special effects such as shading, shadows, and textures.

When building a presentation, users can set the slide timing so that the presentation automatically displays the next slide after a preset delay. Presentation software allows you to apply special effects to the transition between slides. One slide, for example, might fade away as the next slide appears.

To help organize the presentation, you can view thumbnail versions of all the slides similarly to how 35mm slides look on a photographer's light table.

Presentation software typically includes a clip gallery that provides images, photos, video clips, and audio clips to enhance multimedia presentations. Users with an artistic ability can create their own graphics using paint/image editing software (discussed later in the chapter) and then *import* (bring in) the graphics into a slide. Some audio and video editing programs work with presentation software, providing users with an easy means to record and insert video, music, and audio commentary in a presentation.

You can view or print a finished presentation in a variety of formats, including an outline of text from each slide, audience handouts that show completed slides, and speaker notes for each slide. Current presentation software enables users to work with multiple monitors, for example, displaying the presentation on one monitor and the speaker notes on another.

Presentation software incorporates some of the features found in word processing software such as checking spelling, formatting, providing research capabilities, recognizing handwritten text and drawings, and creating Web pages from existing slide shows.

Presentation Software

For more information, visit the Computer Concepts CourseMate Web site at www.cengagebrain.com, navigate to the Chapter 3 Web Link resource for this book, and then click Presentation Software.

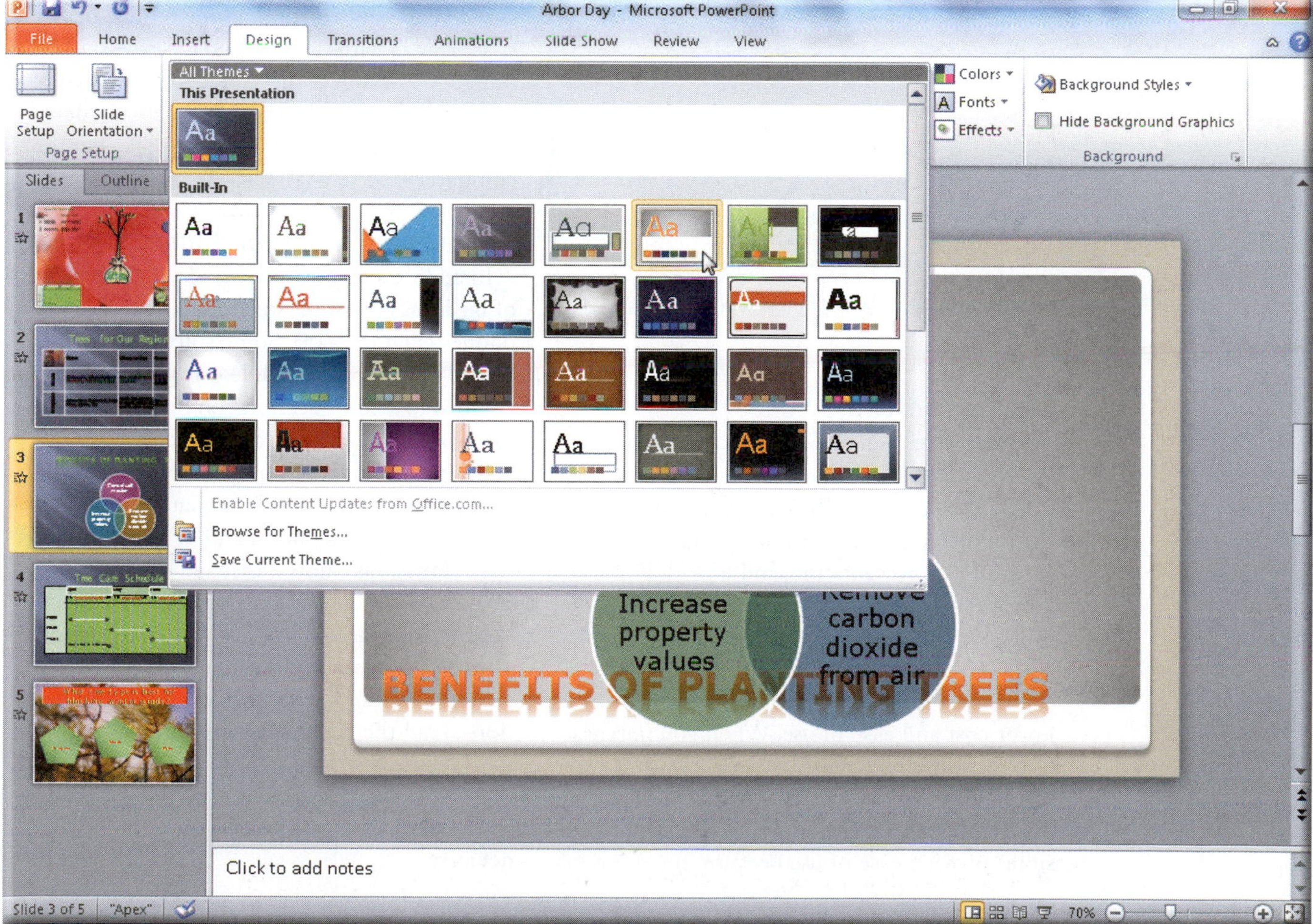

Figure 3-13 In presentation software, users can change the design and layout of any slide in a presentation.

Note Taking Software

Note taking software is application software that enables users to enter typed text, handwritten comments, drawings, or sketches anywhere on a page and then save the page as part of a notebook (Figure 3-14). The software can convert handwritten comments to typed text or store the notes in handwritten form. Users also can include audio recordings as part of their notes.

Users find note taking software convenient during meetings, class lectures, conferences, in libraries, and other settings that previously required a pencil and tablet of paper for recording thoughts and discussions.

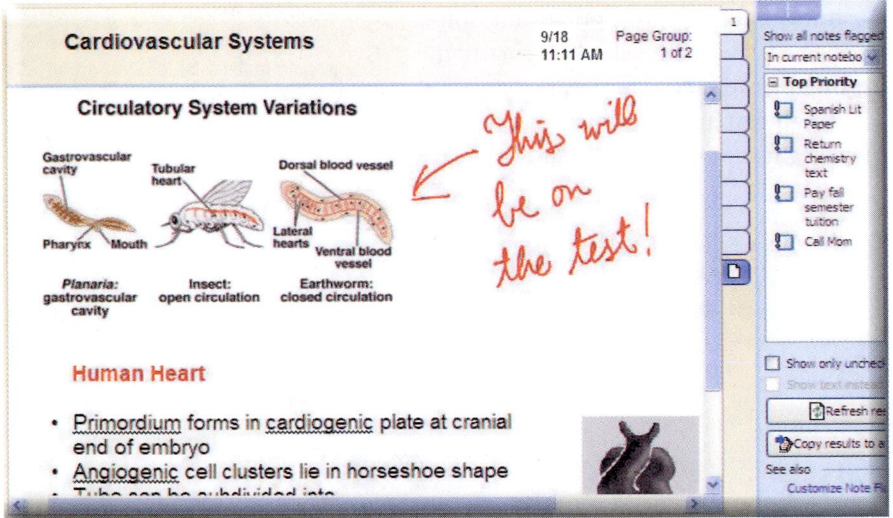

Figure 3-14 With note taking software, mobile users can handwrite notes, draw sketches, and type text.

Business Software Suite

A **software suite** is a collection of individual programs available together as a unit. Business software suites typically include, at a minimum, the following programs: word processing, spreadsheet, presentation, and e-mail. Popular business software suites include Microsoft Office, Apple iWork, Corel WordPerfect Office, and Google Docs.

Software suites offer two major advantages: lower cost and ease of use. When you purchase a collection of programs as a software suite, the suite usually costs significantly less than purchasing the programs individually. Software suites provide ease of use because the programs in the suite normally use a similar interface and share features such as clip art and spelling checker. For example, once you learn how to print using the software suite's word processing program, you can apply the same skill to the spreadsheet and presentation programs in the suite.

Microsoft Office

For more information, visit the Computer Concepts CourseMate Web site at www.cengagebrain.com, navigate to the Chapter 3 Web Link resource for this book, and then click Microsoft Office.

Personal Information Manager Software

A **personal information manager (PIM)** is application software that includes an appointment calendar, address book, notepad, and other features to help users organize personal information. With a PIM, you can take information previously tracked in a weekly or daily calendar, and organize and store it on your computer.

Mobile devices such as smart phones and PDAs include, among many other features, PIM functionality. You can synchronize, or coordinate, information so that both the mobile device and your personal computer and/or organization's server have the latest version of any updated information. Some mobile devices synchronize with the computer wirelessly. With others, you connect the mobile device to the computer with a cable, or you insert the device in a cradle, which has a cable that plugs in the computer.

Business Software for Phones

In addition to PIM software, a huge variety of business and other software is available for phones (Figure 3-15). Some software is preloaded on the phone, while other programs can be downloaded or accessed on memory cards that you insert in a slot on the device.

Business software available for phones enables users to create documents and worksheets, manage databases and lists, create slide shows, take notes, manage budgets and finances, view and edit photos, read electronic books, plan travel routes, compose and read e-mail messages, send instant messages, send text and picture messages, view maps and directions, read the latest news articles, and browse the Web. Many of the programs discussed in this chapter have scaled-down versions that work with smart phones and other mobile devices.

Figure 3-15 In addition to appointment, calendar, address book, and notepad, current phones include business and other software such as e-mail, spreadsheet, presentation, and travel and mapping.

Project Management Software

Project management software allows a user to plan, schedule, track, and analyze the events, resources, and costs of a project. Project management software helps users manage project variables, allowing them to complete a project on time and within budget. An engineer, for example, might use project management software to manage new product development to schedule timing of market analysis, product design, marketing, and public relations activities. A customer service manager might use this software to schedule the process of administering customer surveys, evaluating responses, and presenting recommendations (Figure 3-16).

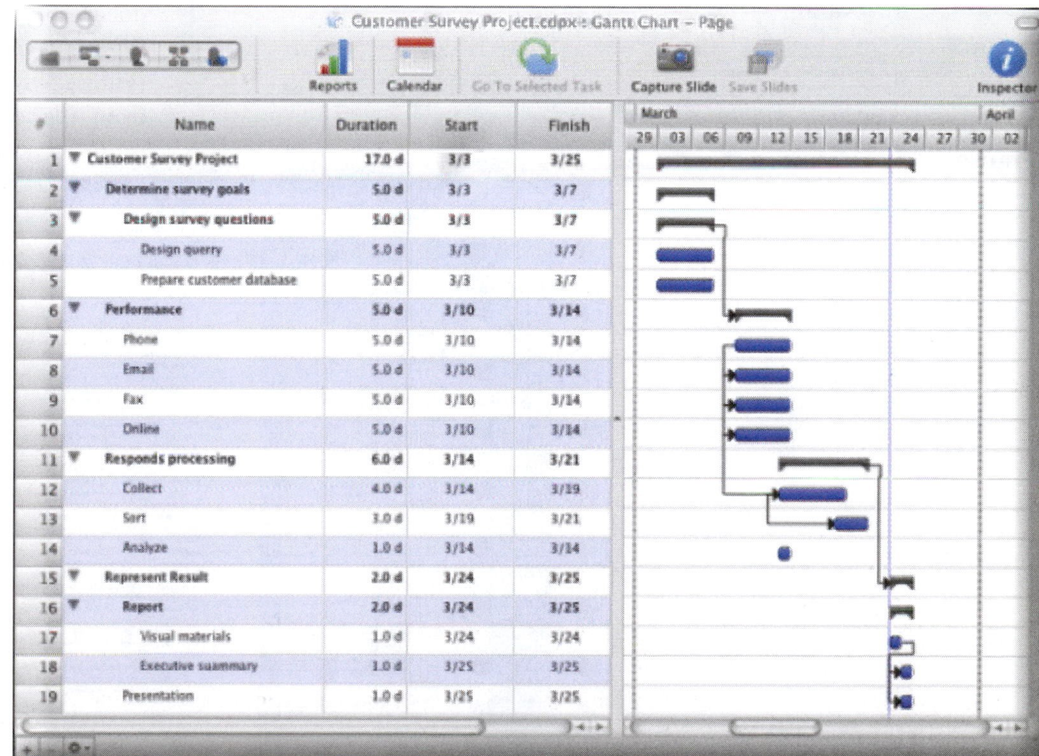

Figure 3-16 With project management software, you can plan and schedule a project.

Accounting Software

Accounting software helps companies record and report their financial transactions (Figure 3-17). With accounting software, business users perform accounting activities related to the general ledger, accounts receivable, accounts payable, purchasing, invoicing, and payroll functions. Accounting software also enables business users to write and print checks, track checking account activity, and update and reconcile balances on demand.

Most accounting software supports online credit checks, invoicing, bill payment, direct deposit, and payroll services. Some accounting software offers more complex features such as job costing and estimating, time tracking, multiple company reporting, foreign currency reporting, and forecasting the amount of raw materials needed for products. The cost of accounting software for small businesses ranges from less than one hundred to several thousand dollars. Accounting software for large businesses can cost several hundred thousand dollars.

Figure 3-17 Accounting software helps companies record and report their financial transactions.

Document Management Software

Document management software provides a means for sharing, distributing, and searching through documents by converting them into a format that can be viewed by any user. The converted document, which mirrors the original document's appearance, can be viewed and printed without the software that created the original document. Some document management software allows users to edit and add comments to the converted document.

A popular file format that document management software uses to save converted documents is *PDF* (Portable Document Format), developed by Adobe Systems. Because of the widespread use of PDF files, some current business programs such as Microsoft Office include a feature that allows users to save their documents as PDF files. To view and print a PDF file, you need Acrobat Reader software (Figure 3-18), which can be downloaded free from Adobe's Web site.

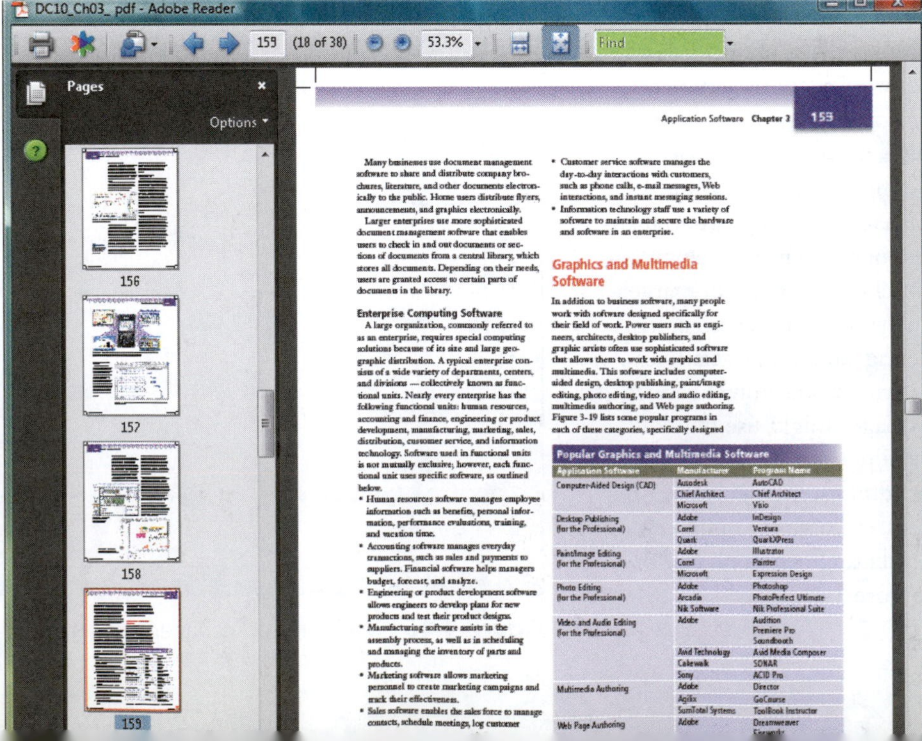

Application Software Chapter 3 159

Many businesses use document management software to share and distribute company brochures, literature, and other documents electronically to the public. Home users distribute flyers, announcements, and graphics electronically.

Larger enterprises use more sophisticated document management software that enables users to check in and out documents or sections of documents from a central library, which stores all documents. Depending on their needs, users are granted access to certain parts of documents in the library.

Enterprise Computing Software

A large organization, commonly referred to as an enterprise, requires special computing solutions because of its size and large geographic distribution. A typical enterprise consists of a wide variety of departments, centers, and divisions — collectively known as functional units. Nearly every enterprise has the following functional units: human resources, accounting and finance, engineering or product development, manufacturing, marketing, sales, distribution, customer service, and information technology. Software used in functional units is not mutually exclusive; however, each functional unit uses specific software, as outlined below.

- Human resources software manages employee information such as benefits, personal information, performance evaluations, training, and vacation time.
- Accounting software manages everyday transactions, such as sales and payments to suppliers. Financial software helps managers budget, forecast, and analyze.
- Engineering or product development software allows engineers to develop plans for new products and test their product designs.
- Manufacturing software assists in the assembly process, as well as in scheduling and managing the inventory of parts and products.
- Marketing software allows marketing personnel to create marketing campaigns and track their effectiveness.
- Sales software enables the sales force to manage contacts, schedule meetings, log customer
- Customer service software manages the day-to-day interactions with customers, such as phone calls, e-mail messages, Web interactions, and instant messaging sessions.
- Information technology staff use a variety of software to maintain and secure the hardware and software in an enterprise.

Graphics and Multimedia Software

In addition to business software, many people work with software designed specifically for their field of work. Power users such as engineers, architects, desktop publishers, and graphic artists often use sophisticated software that allows them to work with graphics and multimedia. This software includes computer-aided design, desktop publishing, paint/image editing, photo editing, video and audio editing, multimedia authoring, and Web page authoring. Figure 3-19 lists some popular programs in each of these categories, specifically designed

Popular Graphics and Multimedia Software

Application Software	Manufacturer	Program Name
Computer-Aided Design (CAD)	Autodesk	AutoCAD
	Chief Architect	Chief Architect
	Microsoft	Visio
Desktop Publishing (for the Professional)	Adobe	InDesign
	Corel	Ventura
	Quark	QuarkXPress
Paint/Image Editing (for the Professional)	Adobe	Illustrator
	Corel	Painter
	Microsoft	Expression Design
Photo Editing (for the Professional)	Adobe	Photoshop
	Arcadia	PhotoPerfect Ultimate
	Nik Software	Nik Professional Suite
Video and Audio Editing (for the Professional)	Adobe	Audition Premiere Pro Soundbooth
	Avid Technology	Avid Media Composer
	Cakewalk	SONAR
	Sony	ACID Pro
Multimedia Authoring	Adobe	Director
	Agilix	GoCourse
	SumTotal Systems	ToolBook Instructor
Web Page Authoring	Adobe	Dreamweaver

Figure 3-18 With Adobe Reader, you can view any PDF file, such as the page from this book shown in this figure.

Many businesses use document management software to share and distribute company brochures, literature, and other documents electronically to the public. Home users distribute flyers, announcements, and graphics electronically.

Larger enterprises use more sophisticated document management software that enables users to check in and out documents or sections of documents from a central library, which stores all documents. Depending on their needs, users are granted access to certain parts of documents in the library.

Enterprise Computing Software

A large organization, commonly referred to as an enterprise, requires special computing solutions because of its size and large geographic distribution. A typical enterprise consists of a wide variety of departments, centers, and divisions — collectively known as functional units. Nearly every enterprise has the following functional units: human resources, accounting and finance, engineering or product development, manufacturing, marketing, sales, distribution, customer service, and information technology. Software used in functional units is not mutually exclusive; however, each functional unit uses specific software, as outlined below.

- Human resources software manages employee information such as benefits, personal information, performance evaluations, training, and vacation time.
- Accounting software manages everyday transactions, such as sales and payments to suppliers. Financial software helps managers budget, forecast, and analyze.
- Engineering or product development software allows engineers to develop plans for new products and test their product designs.
- Manufacturing software assists in the assembly process, as well as in scheduling and managing the inventory of parts and products.
- Marketing software allows marketing personnel to create marketing campaigns and track their effectiveness.
- Sales software enables the sales force to manage contacts, schedule meetings, log customer interactions, manage product information, and take customer orders.
- Distribution software analyzes and tracks inventory and manages product shipping status.
- Customer service software manages the day-to-day interactions with customers, such as phone calls, e-mail messages, Web interactions, and instant messaging sessions.
- Information technology staff use a variety of software to maintain and secure the hardware and software in an enterprise.

Graphics and Multimedia Software

In addition to business software, many people work with software designed specifically for their field of work. Power users such as engineers, architects, desktop publishers, and graphic artists often use sophisticated software that allows them to work with graphics and multimedia. This software includes computer-aided design, desktop publishing, paint/image editing, photo editing, video and audio editing, multimedia authoring, and Web page authoring. Figure 3-19 lists some popular programs in each of these categories, specifically designed

Popular Graphics and Multimedia Software

Application Software	Manufacturer	Program Name
Computer-Aided Design (CAD)	Autodesk	AutoCAD
	Chief Architect	Chief Architect
	Microsoft	Visio
Desktop Publishing (for the Professional)	Adobe	InDesign
	Corel	Ventura
	Quark	QuarkXPress
Paint/Image Editing (for the Professional)	Adobe	Illustrator
	Corel	Painter
	Microsoft	Expression Design
Photo Editing (for the Professional)	Adobe	Photoshop
	Arcadia	PhotoPerfect Ultimate
	Nik Software	Nik Professional Suite
Video and Audio Editing (for the Professional)	Adobe	Audition Premiere Pro Soundbooth
	Avid Technology	Avid Media Composer
	Cakewalk	SONAR
	Sony	ACID Pro
Multimedia Authoring	Adobe	Director
	Agilix	GoCourse
	SumTotal Systems	ToolBook Instructor
Web Page Authoring	Adobe	Dreamweaver Fireworks Flash
	Microsoft	Expression Web SharePoint Designer

Figure 3-19 Popular graphics and multimedia programs — for the professional.

for professional or more technically astute users. These programs often cost several hundred dollars or more.

Many graphics and multimedia programs incorporate user-friendly interfaces and/or have scaled-down versions, making it possible for the home and small business users to create documents using these programs. The following sections discuss the features and functions of graphics and multimedia software. Read Innovative Computing 3-1 to find out how fireworks shows can be produced using multimedia software.

INNOVATIVE COMPUTING 3-1

Fireworks Software Creates a Real Blast

The "oohs" and "aahs" you hear at a fireworks show may be in response to the music and pyrotechnics synchronized with special multimedia software. Major fireworks productions on Independence Day and at theme parks are choreographed with programs designed to fire each shell, sometimes only one-hundredth of a second apart, at a specific beat of the music.

A 20-minute show can take 4 months to plan. Show choreographers estimate they spend at least four hours planning the firing order for each minute of music, not including testing and setting up the equipment. When the fireworks show operator starts the program, the computer sends a signal to the firing module, which connects to each shell.

The multimedia software can cost from $2,000 to $8,000, while the firing hardware that the computer synchronizes wirelessly or with wires can cost between $30,000 and $50,000.

For more information, visit the Computer Concepts CourseMate Web site at www.cengagebrain.com, navigate to the Chapter 3 Innovative Computing resource for this book, and then click Fireworks.

Graphics Software

For more information, visit the Computer Concepts CourseMate Web site at www.cengagebrain.com, navigate to the Chapter 3 Web Link resource for this book, and then click Graphics Software.

Computer-Aided Design

Computer-aided design (CAD) software is a sophisticated type of application software that assists a professional user in creating engineering, architectural, and scientific designs. For example, engineers create design plans for vehicles and security systems. Architects design building structures and floor plans (Figure 3-20). Scientists design drawings of molecular structures.

CAD software eliminates the laborious manual drafting that design processes can require. Three-dimensional CAD programs allow designers to rotate designs of 3-D objects to view them from any angle. Some CAD software even can generate material lists for building designs.

Figure 3-20 Architects use CAD software to design building structures.

Desktop Publishing Software (for the Professional)

Desktop publishing (DTP) software enables professional designers to create sophisticated documents that contain text, graphics, and many colors (Figure 3-21). Professional DTP software is ideal for the production of high-quality color documents such as textbooks, corporate newsletters, marketing literature, product catalogs, and annual reports.

Although many word processing programs have some of the capabilities of DTP software, professional designers and graphic artists use DTP software because it supports page layout. *Page layout* is the process of arranging text and graphics in a document

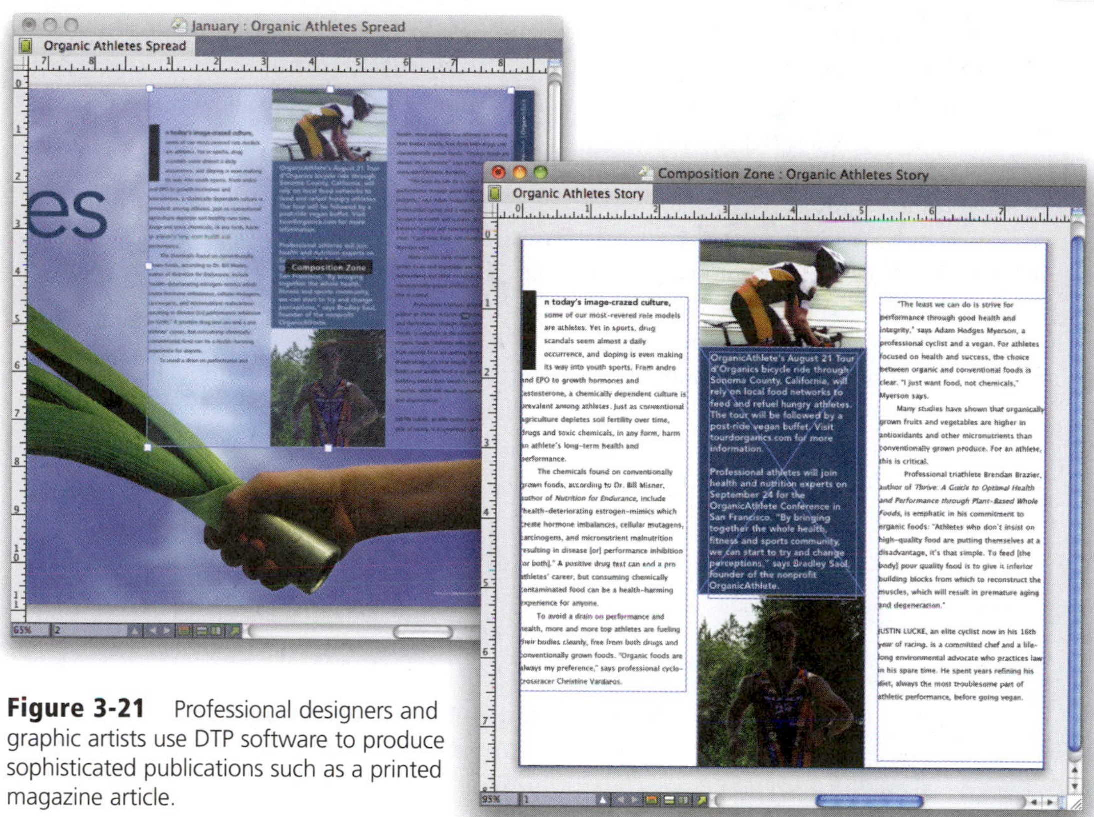

Figure 3-21 Professional designers and graphic artists use DTP software to produce sophisticated publications such as a printed magazine article.

on a page-by-page basis. DTP software includes color libraries to assist in color selections for text and graphics. A *color library* is a standard set of colors used by designers and printers to ensure that colors will print exactly as specified. Designers and graphic artists can print finished publications on a color printer, take them to a professional printer, or post them on the Web in a format that can be viewed by those without DTP software.

Paint/Image Editing Software (for the Professional)

Graphic artists, multimedia professionals, technical illustrators, and desktop publishers use paint software and image editing software to create and modify graphical images such as those used in DTP documents and Web pages. **Paint software**, also called *illustration software*, allows users to draw pictures (Figure 3-22), shapes, and other graphical images with various on-screen tools such as a pen, brush, eyedropper, and paint bucket.

Image editing software provides the capabilities of paint software and also includes the capability to enhance and modify existing images and pictures. Modifications can include adjusting or enhancing image colors, adding special effects such as shadows and glows, creating animations, and *image stitching*, which is the process of combining multiple images into a larger image.

Figure 3-22 This graphic artist uses paint software to draw characters in a computer game.

Photo Editing Software (for the Professional)

Professional photo editing software is a type of image editing software that allows photographers, videographers, engineers, scientists, and other high-volume digital photo users to edit and customize digital photos (Figure 3-23). Professional photo editing software allows users to save images in a wide variety of file formats. With professional photo editing software, users can retouch photos, crop images, remove red-eye, change image shapes, color-correct images, straighten images, remove or rearrange objects in a photo, and apply filters. Read Ethics & Issues 3-3 for a related discussion.

Figure 3-23 With professional photo editing software, users can edit and customize digital photos, such as by adjusting lighting as shown here.

Video and Audio Editing Software (for the Professional)

Video editing software allows professionals to modify a segment of a video, called a clip. For example, users can reduce the length of a video clip, reorder a series of clips, or add special effects such as words that move horizontally across the screen.

Video editing software typically includes audio editing capabilities. **Audio editing software** lets users modify audio clips, produce studio-quality soundtracks, and add audio to video clips (Figure 3-24). Audio editing software usually includes *filters*, which are designed to enhance audio quality. For example, a filter might remove a distracting background noise from the audio clip. Most television shows and movies are created or enhanced using video and audio editing software.

Multimedia Authoring Software

Multimedia authoring software allows users to combine text, graphics, audio, video, and animation in an interactive application (Figure 3-25). With this software, users control the placement of text and images and the duration of sounds, video, and animation. Once created, multimedia presentations often take the form of interactive computer-based presentations or Web-based presentations designed to facilitate learning, demonstrate product functionality, and elicit direct-user participation. Training centers, educational institutions, and online magazine publishers all use multimedia authoring software to develop interactive applications. These applications may be available on an optical disc, over a local area network, or via the Internet.

ETHICS & ISSUES 3-3

Altering Digital Photos — Art or Fraud?

In several recent high-profile cases, major news sources have published purposefully altered photos. The alterations were more than just touching up a bad-hair day; rather, they were attempts to alter the facts. Typically, those responsible for the deception are fired from their jobs. Many commercial artists, photojournalists, and creators of cartoons, book covers, and billboards use photo editing software to alter photos. Real estate agents increasingly are being found to alter photos of homes for online listings. With software, an artist can convert photos to a digital form that can be colorized, stretched, squeezed, texturized, or otherwise altered. For example, tabloid newspapers or dubious online sources may alter a photo by switching a head on a body in a photo with someone else's head. In another situation, several major news sources were duped by a country into publishing pictures of a faked missile test.

The National Press Photographers Association, however, has expressed reservations about digital altering and endorses the following: "As [photo] journalists we believe the guiding principle of our profession is accuracy; therefore, we believe it is wrong to alter the content of a photo in any way … that deceives the public." Yet, some insist that the extent to which a photo "deceives the public" is in the eye of the beholder.

Is it ethical to alter digital photos? Why or why not? Does the answer depend on the reason for the alteration, the extent of the alteration, or some other factor? If some alteration is accepted, can photographic integrity still be guaranteed? Why or why not?

Figure 3-24 With audio editing software, users modify audio clips.

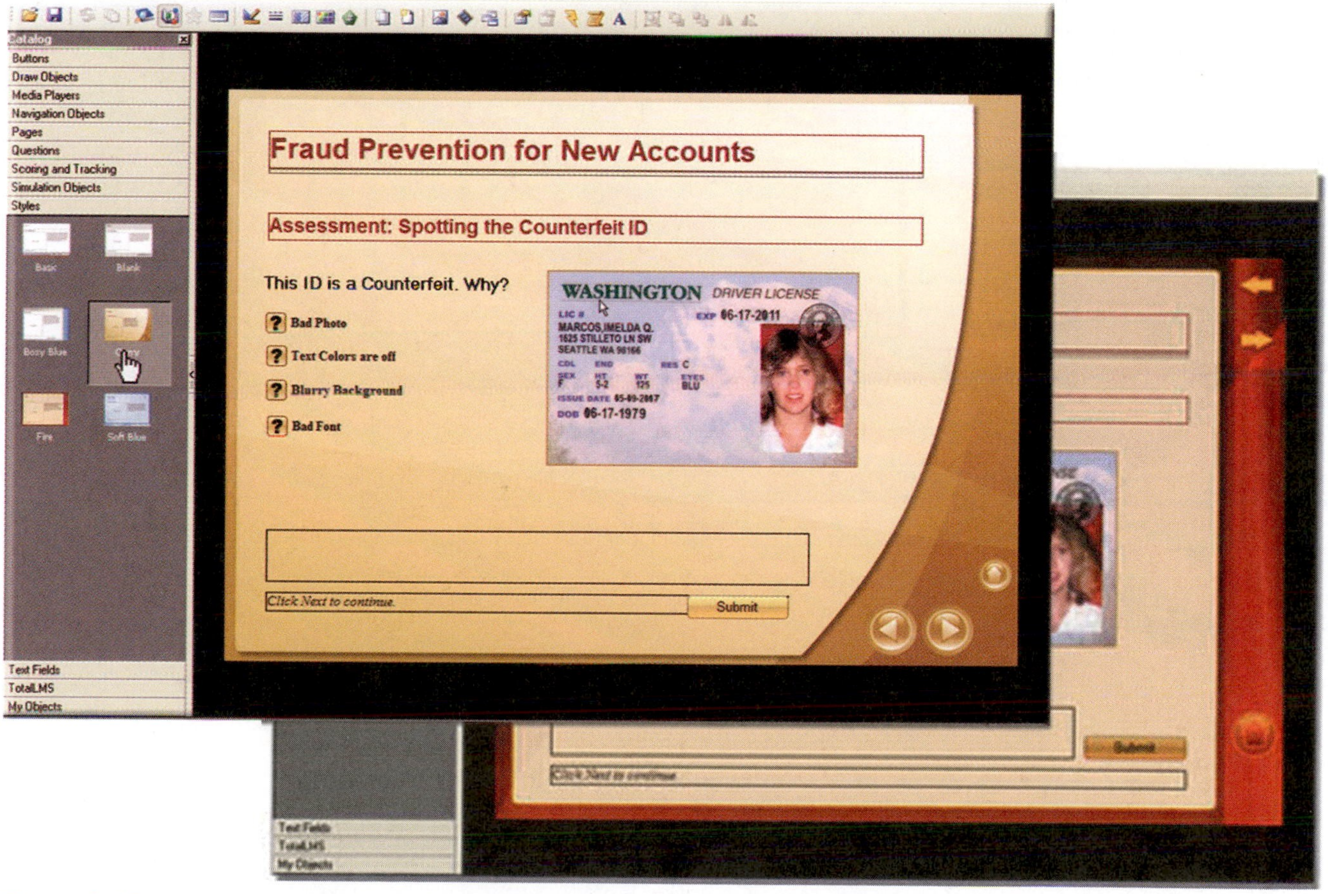

Figure 3-25 Multimedia authoring software allows you to create dynamic presentations that include text, graphics, video, sound, and animation.

Web Page Authoring Software

Web page authoring software helps users of all skill levels create Web pages that include graphical images, video, audio, animation, and other special effects with interactive content (Figure 3-26). In addition, many Web page authoring programs allow users to organize, manage, and maintain Web sites.

Application software, such as Word and Excel, often includes Web page authoring features. This allows home and small business users to create basic Web pages using application software they already own. For more sophisticated Web pages, users work with Web page authoring software. Many Web page developers also use multimedia authoring software along with, or instead of, Web page authoring software for Web page development.

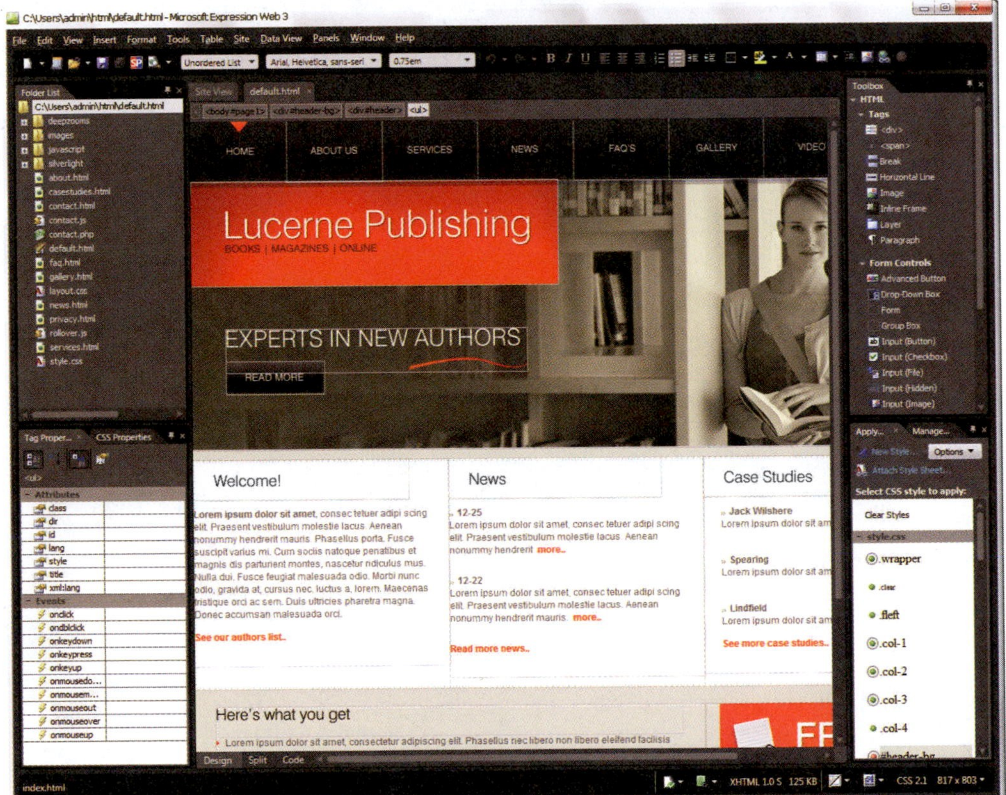

Figure 3-26 With Web page authoring software, users create sophisticated Web pages.

Web Page Authoring Software

For more information, visit the Computer Concepts CourseMate Web site at www.cengagebrain.com, navigate to the Chapter 3 Web Link resource for this book, and then click Web Page Authoring Software.

QUIZ YOURSELF 3-2

Instructions: Find the true statement below. Then, rewrite the remaining false statements so that they are true.

1. Audio editing software typically includes video editing capabilities.
2. Enterprise computing software provides the capabilities of paint software and also includes the capability to modify existing images.
3. Millions of people use spreadsheet software every day to develop documents such as letters, memos, reports, mailing labels, newsletters, and Web pages.
4. Professional accounting software is ideal for the production of high-quality color documents such as textbooks, corporate newsletters, marketing literature, product catalogs, and annual reports.
5. Database software is application software that allows users to create visual aids for presentations to communicate ideas, messages, and other information to a group.
6. Popular CAD programs include Microsoft Office, Apple iWork, Corel WordPerfect Office, and Google Docs.
7. Web page authoring software helps users of all skill levels create Web pages.

Quiz Yourself Online: To further check your knowledge of pages 146 through 164, visit the Computer Concepts CourseMate Web site at www.cengagebrain.com, navigate to the Chapter 3 Quiz Yourself resource for this book, and then click Objectives 5 – 6.

Software for Home, Personal, and Educational Use

A large amount of application software is designed specifically for home, personal, and educational use. Most of the programs in this category are relatively inexpensive, often priced less than $100 and sometimes free. Figure 3-27 lists popular programs for many of these categories. The following pages discuss the features and functions of this application software.

Popular Programs for Home/Personal/Educational Use

Application Software	Manufacturer	Program Names
Personal Finance	IGG Software	iBank
	Intuit	Quicken
Legal	Broderbund	Home and Business Lawyer; WillWriter
	Cosmi	Perfect Attorney
	Nolo	Quicken Legal Business; Quicken WillMaker
Tax Preparation	2nd Story Software	TaxACT
	H&R Block	TaxCut
	Intuit	TurboTax
Desktop Publishing (for Personal Use)	Broderbund	The Print Shop; PrintMaster
	Microsoft	Publisher
Paint/Image Editing (for Personal Use)	Corel	CorelDRAW; Painter Essentials
	The GIMP Team	The Gimp
Photo Editing and Photo Management (for Personal Use)	Adobe	Photoshop Elements; Photoshop Express
	Corel	Paint Shop Pro Photo; Ulead PhotoImpact; MediaOne Plus
	Yahoo!	Flickr
	Google	Picasa
	Microsoft	Windows Live Photo Gallery
	Roxio	PhotoShow
Clip Art/Image Gallery	Broderbund	ClickArt
	Nova Development	Art Explosion
	CoolArchive	CoolArchive
Video and Audio Editing (for Personal Use)	Corel	VideoStudio
	Microsoft	Windows Live Movie Maker
	Pinnacle Systems	Studio
	Roxio	Buzz
Home Design/Landscaping	Broderbund	Instant Architect
	Chief Architect	Better Homes and Gardens Home Designer
	IMSI/Design	TurboFLOORPLAN
Travel and Mapping	DeLorme	Street Atlas
	Microsoft	Streets & Trips
	Google	Earth; Maps
Reference	Fogware Publishing	Merriam-Webster Collegiate Dictionary & Thesaurus
	Encyclopedia Britannica	Britannica Ultimate Reference Suite

Figure 3-27 Many popular programs are available for home, personal, and educational use.

Personal Finance Software

Personal finance software is a simplified accounting program that helps home users and small office/home office users balance their checkbooks, pay bills, track personal income and expenses (Figure 3-28), set up budgets, manage home inventory, track investments, and evaluate financial plans. Personal finance software helps determine where, and for what purpose, you are spending money so that you can manage your finances. Reports can summarize transactions by category (such as dining), by payee (such as the electric company), or by time (such as the last two months). Financial planning features include analyzing home and personal loans, preparing income taxes, and managing retirement savings.

Most of these personal finance programs also offer a variety of online services, which require access to the Internet. For example, users can track investments online, compare insurance rates from leading insurance companies, and bank online. **Online banking** offers access to account balances, provides bill payment services, and allows you to download monthly transactions and statements from the Web directly to your computer.

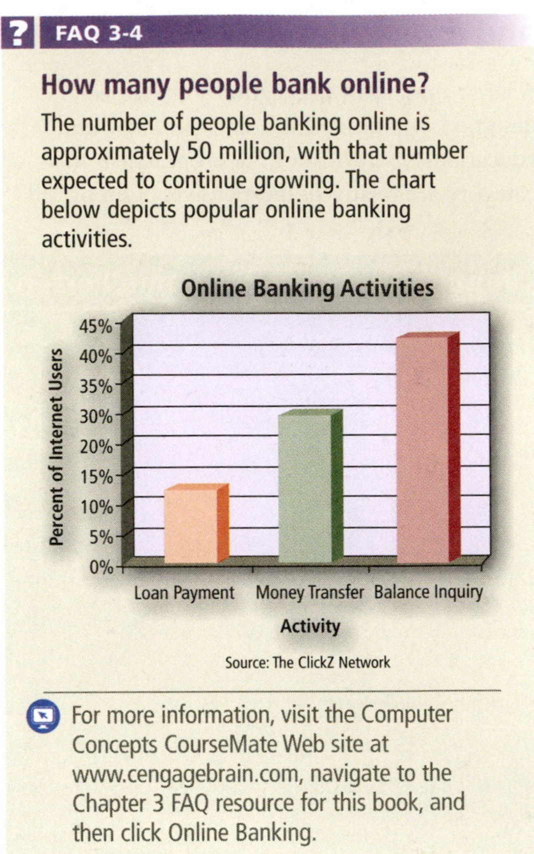

FAQ 3-4

How many people bank online?

The number of people banking online is approximately 50 million, with that number expected to continue growing. The chart below depicts popular online banking activities.

For more information, visit the Computer Concepts CourseMate Web site at www.cengagebrain.com, navigate to the Chapter 3 FAQ resource for this book, and then click Online Banking.

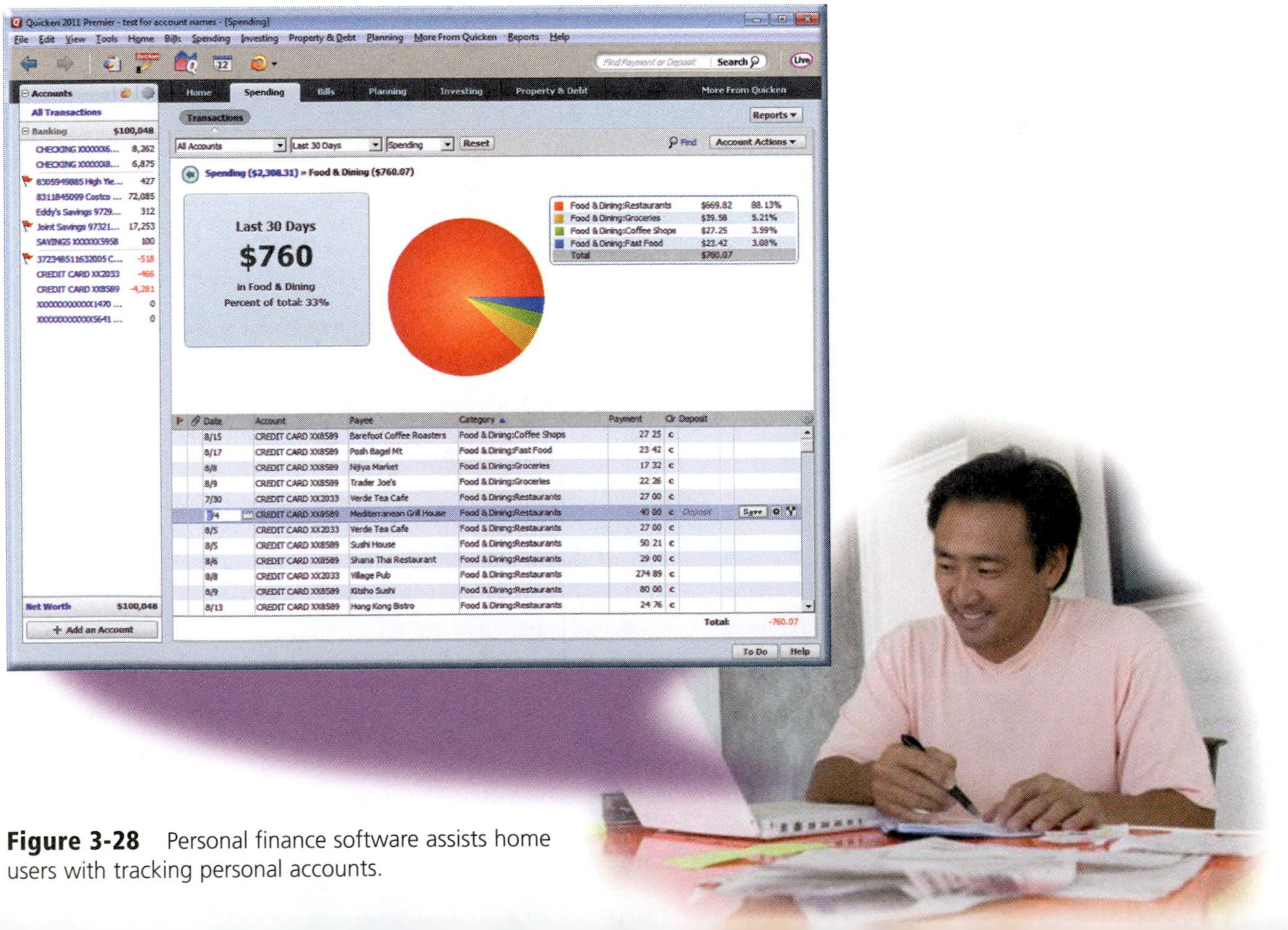

Figure 3-28 Personal finance software assists home users with tracking personal accounts.

Legal Software

Legal software assists in the preparation of legal documents and provides legal information to individuals, families, and small businesses (Figure 3-29). Legal software provides standard contracts and documents associated with buying, selling, and renting property; estate planning; marriage and divorce; and preparing a will or living trust. By answering a series of questions or completing a form, the legal software tailors the legal document to specific needs.

Once the legal document is created, you can file the paperwork with the appropriate agency, court, or office; or take the document to your attorney for his or her review and signature.

? FAQ 3-5

Should I use legal software instead of hiring an attorney?

Although legal software may be approved for creating certain legal documents and can help save time and money in their preparation, you should check with your local bar association for the document's legality before using it.

For more information, visit the Computer Concepts CourseMate Web site at www.cengagebrain.com, navigate to the Chapter 3 FAQ resource for this book, and then click Legal Software.

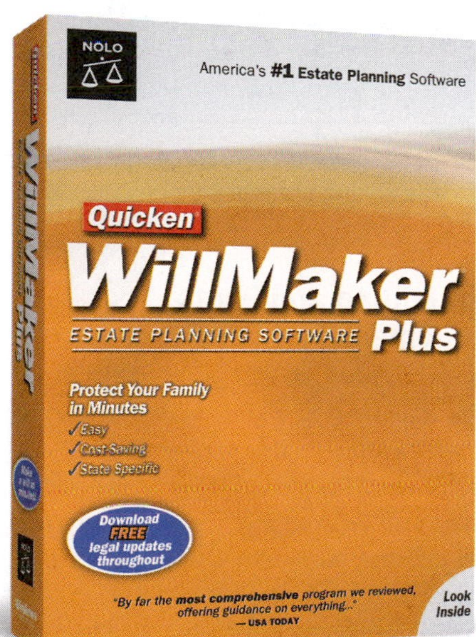

Figure 3-29 Legal software provides legal information to individuals, families, and small businesses and assists in record keeping and the preparation of legal documents.

Tax Preparation Software

Tax preparation software, which is available both as packaged software and as Web applications, can guide individuals, families, or small businesses through the process of filing federal taxes (Figure 3-30). These programs forecast tax liability and offer money-saving tax tips, designed to lower your tax bill. After you answer a series of questions and complete basic forms, the software creates and analyzes your tax forms to search for potential errors and deduction opportunities. Once the forms are complete, you can print any necessary paperwork, and then they are ready for filing. Instead of mailing forms through the postal service, the IRS allows taxpayers to file their state and federal tax returns online, called *e-filing*.

Figure 3-30 Tax preparation software guides individuals, families, or small businesses through the process of filing federal taxes.

Tax Preparation Software

For more information, visit the Computer Concepts CourseMate Web site at www.cengagebrain.com, navigate to the Chapter 3 Web Link resource for this book, and then click Tax Preparation Software.

Desktop Publishing Software (for Personal Use)

Instead of using professional DTP software (as discussed earlier in this chapter), many home and small business users work with simpler, easy-to-understand DTP software designed for smaller-scale desktop publishing projects. **Personal DTP software** helps home and small business users create newsletters, brochures, flyers (Figure 3-31), advertisements, postcards, greeting cards, letterhead, business cards, banners, calendars, logos, and Web pages.

Although many word processing programs include DTP features, users often prefer to create DTP documents using DTP software because of its enhanced features. For example, personal DTP programs provide hundreds of thousands of graphical images. You also can import (bring in) your own digital photos into the documents. These programs typically guide you through the development of a document by asking a series of questions, offering numerous predefined layouts, and providing standard text you can add to documents. Then, you can print a finished publication on a color printer or post it on the Web in a format that can be viewed by those without DTP software.

Many personal DTP programs also include paint/image editing software and photo editing and photo management software.

Desktop Publishing Software

For more information, visit the Computer Concepts CourseMate Web site at www.cengagebrain.com, navigate to the Chapter 3 Web Link resource for this book, and then click Desktop Publishing Software.

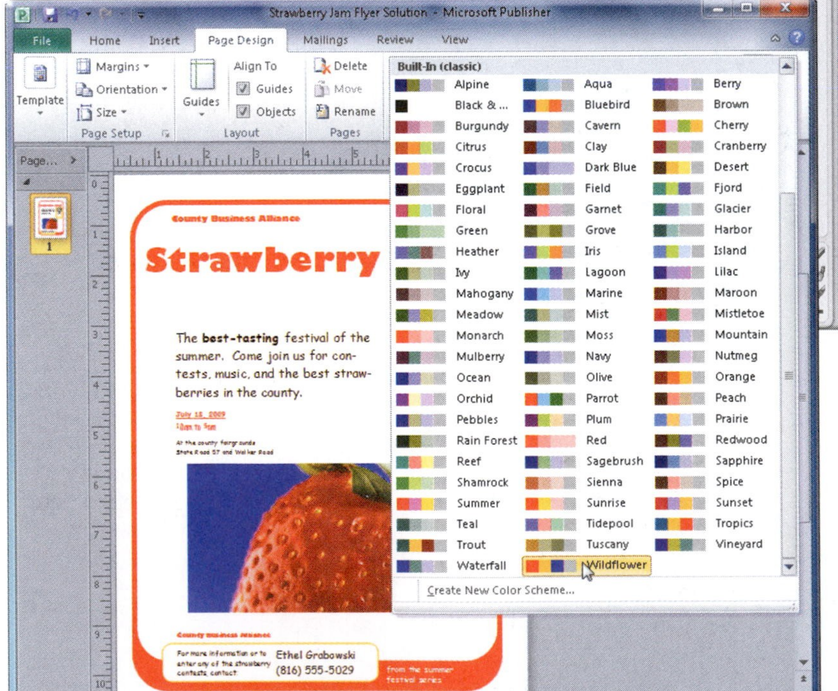

Figure 3-31 With desktop publishing software, home and small business users can create flyers.

Paint/Image Editing Software (for Personal Use)

Personal paint/image editing software provides an easy-to-use interface, usually with more simplified capabilities than its professional counterpart, including functions tailored to meet the needs of the home and small business user.

As with the professional versions, personal paint software includes various simplified tools that allow you to draw pictures (Figure 3-32), shapes, and other images. Personal image editing software provides the capabilities of paint software and the ability to modify existing graphics and photos. These programs also include many templates to assist you in adding images to documents such as greeting cards, banners, calendars, signs, labels, business cards, and letterhead. Some operating systems include a basic paint/image editing program.

Figure 3-32 Home users can purchase affordable paint/image editing programs that enable them to draw images.

Photo Editing and Photo Management Software

Instead of professional photo editing software, many home and small business users work with easier-to-use personal photo editing software, which is available both as packaged software and as Web applications. **Personal photo editing software** allows users to edit digital photos by removing red-eye, erasing blemishes, restoring aged photos, adding special effects, enhancing image quality, or creating electronic photo albums. When you purchase a digital camera, it usually includes photo editing software (Figure 3-33). Some digital cameras

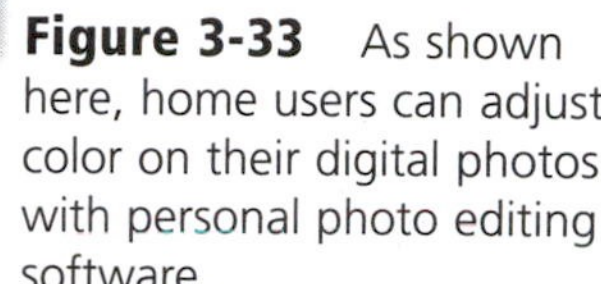

Figure 3-33 As shown here, home users can adjust color on their digital photos with personal photo editing software.

even have basic photo editing software built in so that you can edit the image directly on the camera. You can print edited photos on labels, calendars, business cards, and banners, or you can post them on the Web. Some photo editing software allows users to send digital photos to an online print service, which will deliver high-resolution printed images through the postal service or allow you to pick them up at a local store. Many online print services also have a photo community where users can post photos on the Web for others to view and purchase, if desired.

With *photo management software*, you can view, organize, sort, catalog, print, and share digital photos. Some photo editing software includes photo management functionality (Figure 3-34).

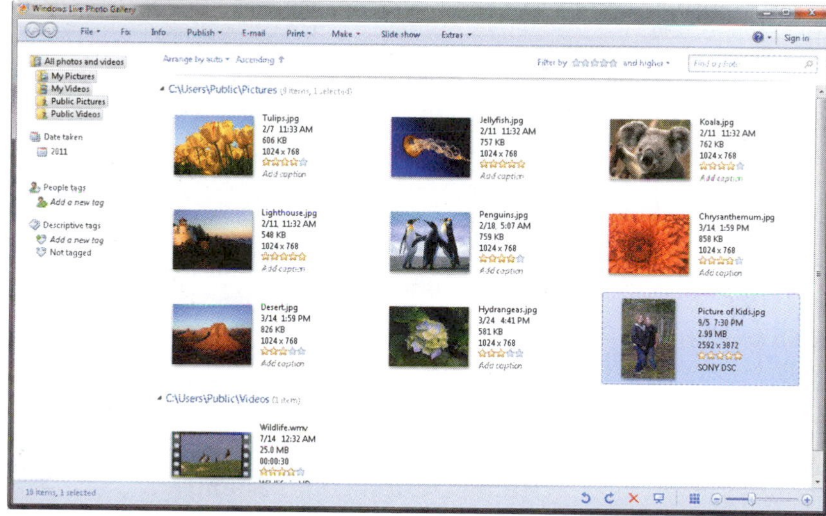

Figure 3-34 Photo management software enables you quickly to view thumbnails of all your digital photos.

Clip Art/Image Gallery

Application software often includes a **clip art/image gallery**, which is a collection of clip art and photos. Some programs have links to additional clips available on the Web or are available as Web applications. You also can purchase clip art/image gallery software that contains thousands of images (Figure 3-35).

In addition to clip art, many clip art/image galleries provide fonts, animations, sounds, video clips, and audio clips. You can use the images, fonts, and other items from the clip art/image gallery in all types of documents, including word processing, desktop publishing, spreadsheet, and presentations.

Figure 3-35 Clip art/image gallery software contains thousands of images.

Video and Audio Editing Software (for Personal Use)

Many home users work with easy-to-use video and audio editing software, which is much simpler to use than its professional counterpart, for small-scale movie making projects (Figure 3-36). With these programs, home users can edit home movies, add music or other sounds to the video, and share their movies on the Web. Some operating systems include video editing and audio editing software.

Figure 3-36 With personal video and audio editing software, home users can edit their home movies.

Home Design/Landscaping Software

Homeowners or potential homeowners can use **home design/landscaping software** to assist them with the design, remodeling, or improvement of a home, deck, or landscape (Figure 3-37).

Figure 3-37 Home design/ landscaping software can help you design or remodel a home, deck, or landscape.

Home design/landscaping software includes hundreds of predrawn plans that you can customize to meet your needs. These programs show changes to home designs and landscapes, allowing homeowners to preview proposed modifications. Once designed, many home design/ landscaping programs print a materials list outlining costs and quantities for the entire project.

Travel and Mapping Software

Travel and mapping software enables users to view maps, determine route directions, and locate points of interest (Figure 3-38). Using travel and mapping software, which is available both as packaged software and as Web applications, you can display maps by searching for an address, postal code, telephone number, or point of interest (such as airports, lodging, and historical sites). This software often provides driving directions when a user enters a starting and destination point. Most programs also allow you to download construction reports and calculate mileage, time, and expenses. Many are compatible with mobile devices such as smart phones and portable media players. Many navigation devices, including those in vehicles, have travel and mapping software. Read Looking Ahead 3-1 for a look at the next generation of navigation software.

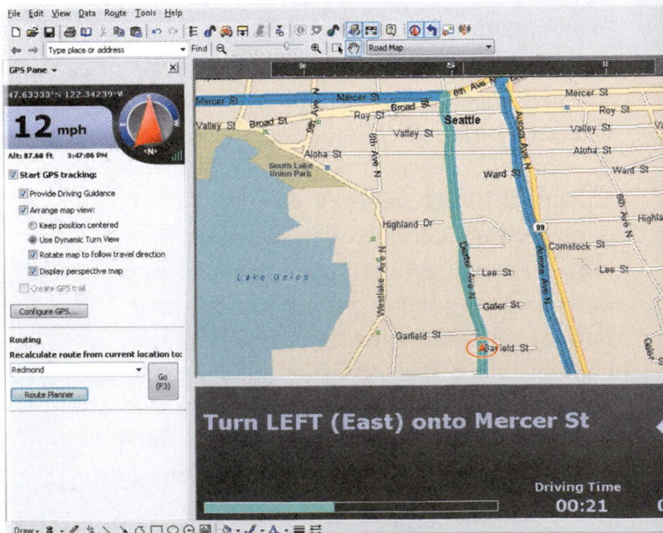

Figure 3-38 This software provides turn-by-turn directions, along with estimated travel times.

LOOKING AHEAD 3-1

Sensors Help Drivers Find Their Way

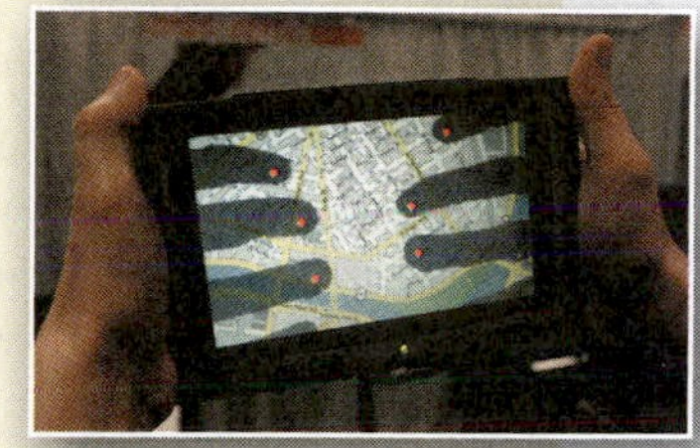

Navigating through town may become less burdensome with products under development at Microsoft. Current devices are touted as being small enough to fit in a pocket, but this size can be a hindrance for people with large hands. When they attempt to place their fingers on the touch screen to press the commands, their fingers cover information they are trying to see. Microsoft's prototype LucidTouch solves this problem by allowing users to place their hands underneath the device, in-between it and a camera attached to the back. The camera captures an image of their hands, and the device overlays a semitransparent shadow of their fingers on the screen.

Microsoft also is developing sensors for a cell phone that collect data as a driver passes through town. These accelerometers sense speed, braking, and even when the driver hits a pothole, and the cell phone's microphone can detect the car's horn. Another potential use of Microsoft's sensors in cell phones is to monitor the behavior and health status of the elderly so that they can lead independent lives.

 For more information, visit the Computer Concepts CourseMate Web site at www.cengagebrain.com, navigate to the Chapter 3 Looking Ahead resource for this book, and then click Mapping.

Reference and Educational Software

Reference software provides valuable and thorough information for all individuals. Popular reference software includes encyclopedias, dictionaries, and health/medical guides.

Educational software is software that teaches a particular skill. Educational software exists for just about any subject, from learning how to type (Figure 3-39) to learning how to cook. Preschool to high-school learners use educational software to assist them with subjects such as reading and math or to prepare them for class or college entrance exams. Educational software often includes games and other content to make the learning experience more fun.

Many educational programs use a computer-based training approach. **Computer-based training (CBT)**, also called computer-aided instruction (CAI), is a type of education in which students learn by using and completing exercises with instructional software. CBT typically consists of self-directed, self-paced instruction about a topic. Beginning athletes, for example, use CBT programs to learn the intricacies of baseball, football, soccer, tennis, and golf. The military and airlines use CBT simulations to train pilots to fly in various conditions and environments (Figure 3-40).

Figure 3-39 Educational software can teach a skill.

Figure 3-40 Military pilots use CBT simulations for flight training.

Entertainment Software

Entertainment software for personal computers, game consoles, and mobile devices includes interactive games, videos, and other programs designed to support a hobby or provide amusement and enjoyment. For example, you might use entertainment software to play games individually (Figure 3-41) or with others online, make a family tree, or fly an aircraft. Many games are available as Web applications, allowing you to play individually or with other online players.

Game Software

For more information, visit the Computer Concepts CourseMate Web site at www.cengagebrain.com, navigate to the Chapter 3 Web Link resource for this book, and then click Game Software.

FAQ 3-6

How popular is entertainment software?

The popularity of entertainment software has increased greatly during the past few years. More than 65 percent of American households play computer or video games. Further, more than 36 percent play games on a mobile device such as a smart phone or PDA.

For more information, visit the Computer Concepts CourseMate Web site at www.cengagebrain.com, navigate to the Chapter 3 FAQ resource for this book, and then click Entertainment Software.

Figure 3-41 Entertainment software can provide hours of recreation on personal computers, game consoles, and mobile devices.

Web Applications

As discussed earlier in this chapter, users can purchase application software from a software vendor, retail store, or Web-based business. Users typically install purchased application software on a computer before they run it. Installed software has two disadvantages: (1) it requires disk space on your computer, and (2) it can be costly to upgrade as vendors release new versions. As an alternative, some users opt to access Web applications.

As previously mentioned, a Web application, or *Web app*, is a Web site that allows users to access and interact with software from any computer or device that is connected to the Internet. Users often interact with Web applications, directly at the Web site, referred to as the host, through their Web browser. Some Web sites, however, require you download the software to your local computer or device. Web application hosts often store users' data and information on their servers, which sometimes is called *cloud storage*. Users concerned with data security may shy away from this type of Web application. Thus, some Web applications provide users with an option of storing data locally on their own personal computer or mobile device.

Many of the previously discussed types of application software are available as Web applications. Figure 3-42 identifies the more popular Web applications. In addition, thousands of games are available as Web applications. Read Ethics & Issues 3-4 for a related discussion.

Many Web application hosts provide free access to their software, such as Google Docs shown in Figure 3-43. Others, such as Google Earth, offer part of their Web application free and charge for access to a more comprehensive program. Some Web applications, such as online tax preparation programs, allow you to use the Web application free and pay a fee when a certain action occurs. For example, you can prepare your tax return free, but if you elect to print it or file it electronically, you pay a minimal fee.

Experts often use the term Web 2.0 to describe Web applications. Recall that Web 2.0 refers to Web sites that provide users with a means to share personal information, allow users to modify Web site content, and/or have application software built into the site for visitors to use.

Popular Web Applications

Program Name	Type of Application Software
Britannica.com	Reference
Dictionary.com	Reference
Flickr	Photo Editing and Photo Management
Gmail	E-Mail
Google Docs	Productivity Suite
Google Earth	Travel and Mapping
Google Maps	Travel and Mapping
MSN Encarta	Reference
Office Web Apps	Productivity Suite
Photoshop Express	Photo Editing
Picnik	Photo Editing
TaxACT Online	Tax Preparation
TurboTax Online	Tax Preparation
Windows Live Calendar	Personal Information Manager
Windows Live Hotmail	E-Mail
YouSendIt	File Transfer and E-Mail

Figure 3-42 Some popular Web applications. For practice using Web applications, complete the last Learn It Online exercise in each chapter.

ETHICS & ISSUES 3-4

Should Online Mapping Services Make You Feel More Secure or More Vulnerable?

Most Internet users find that online maps, such as Google Maps and Bing Maps, provide tremendous convenience and reliability. Instead of searching the house or car for maps or making phone calls for directions, a quick Web search results in a readable map with exact directions. Sometimes, even photos of the route and location are available. Some parents and advocacy groups, however, claim that the services allow predators to locate potential victims quickly. Google Maps, for example, provides photos for neighborhoods of entire cities. The opponents of the services believe that predators may find potential victims in the photos or find likely locations where a crime may be easier to commit. Opponents of this point of view state that mapping services allow known predators and high-crime areas to be more readily identified. The services, therefore, increase personal security because the location of known predators can be pinpointed before the predators find victims. The services also provide much more positive value than any potential problems that they create, and, therefore, should thrive.

Do online mapping services make you feel more secure or more vulnerable? Why? Should parents and neighborhood associations have the legal right to have photos and personal information removed from mapping services? Why or why not? Would you feel comfortable if a service such as Google Maps showed a photo of you walking your normal route from home to work or school? Why?

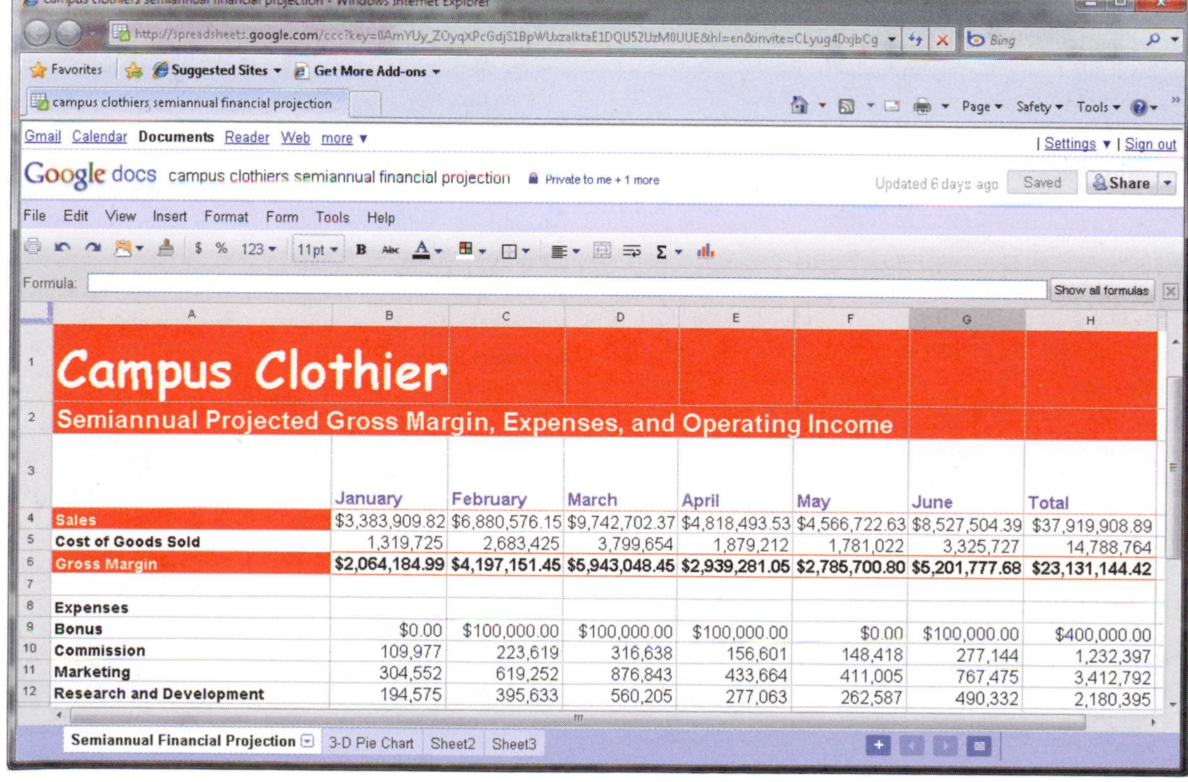

Google Docs
For more information, visit the Computer Concepts CourseMate Web site at www.cengagebrain.com, navigate to the Chapter 3 Web Link resource for this book, and then click Google Docs.

Figure 3-43 The spreadsheet shown here in Google Docs is the same Microsoft Excel spreadsheet that is shown in Figure 3-8 on page 151. Differences between the two figures are due to different features in the two programs.

Application Software for Communications

One of the main reasons people use computers is to communicate and share information with others. Some communications software is considered system software because it works with hardware and transmission media. Other communications software makes users more productive and/or assists them with personal tasks, and thus, is considered application software. Chapter 2 presented a variety of application software for communications, which is summarized in the table in Figure 3-44.

? FAQ 3-7

Does text messaging improve typing skills?

Although some individuals are able to send text messages from their phones quickly, the differences in layout between a phone keypad and a standard computer keyboard might not allow for their typing skills to improve at the same rate. Some individuals are able to send text messages more quickly than they can type. In fact, a 20-year-old college student won $50,000 in a text messaging competition when he typed more than 125 characters in 50 seconds with no mistakes.

For more information, visit the Computer Concepts CourseMate Web site at www.cengagebrain.com, navigate to the Chapter 3 FAQ resource for this book, and then click Text Messaging.

Application Software for Communications

Web Browser
- Allows users to access and view Web pages on the Internet
- Requires a Web browser program
  - Integrated in some operating systems
  - Available for download on the Web free or for a fee

E-Mail
- Messages and files sent via a network such as the Internet
- Requires an e-mail program
  - Integrated in many software suites and operating systems
  - Available free at portals on the Web
  - Included with paid Internet access service
  - Can be purchased separately from retailers

Instant Messaging
- Real-time exchange of messages, files, audio, and/or video with another online user
- Requires instant messenger software
  - Integrated in some operating systems
  - Available for download on the Web, usually at no cost
  - Included with some paid Internet access services

Chat Room
- Real-time, online typed conversation
- Requires chat client software
  - Integrated in some operating systems and Web browsers
  - Available for download on the Web, usually at no cost
  - Included with some paid Internet access services
  - Built into some Web sites

Text, Picture, Video Messaging
- Short text, picture, or video messages sent and received, mainly on mobile devices
- Requires text, picture, video messenger software
  - Integrated in most mobile devices
  - Available for download on the Web, usually at no cost, for personal computers

RSS Aggregator
- Keeps track of changes made to Web sites by checking RSS feeds
- Requires RSS aggregator program
  - Integrated in some e-mail programs and Web browsers
  - Available for download on the Web, usually at no cost

Blogging
- Time-stamped articles, or posts, in a diary or journal format, usually listed in reverse chronological order
- Blogger needs *blog software*, or *blogware*, to create/maintain blog
  - Some Web sites do not require installation of blog software

Newsgroup/Message Board
- Online area where users have written discussions
- Newsgroup may require a newsreader program
  - Integrated in some operating systems, e-mail programs, and Web browsers

FTP
- Method of uploading and downloading files with other computers on the Internet
- May require an FTP program
  - Integrated in some operating systems
  - Available for download on the Web for a small fee

VoIP (Internet Telephony)
- Allows users to speak to other users over the Internet
- Requires Internet connection, Internet telephone service, microphone or telephone, and Internet telephone software or telephone adapter

Video Conferencing
- Meeting between geographically separated people who use a network such as the Internet to transmit video/audio
- Requires video conferencing software, a microphone, speakers, and sometimes a video camera attached to your computer

Figure 3-44 A summary of application software for home and business communications.

Learning Tools for Application Software

Learning how to use application software effectively involves time and practice. To assist in the learning process, many programs include an integrated Help feature. **Online Help** is the electronic equivalent of a user manual (Figure 3-45a). When working with a program, you can use online Help to ask a question or access the Help topics in subject or alphabetical order. Most online Help also links to Web sites that offer *Web-based Help*, which provides updates and more comprehensive resources to respond to technical issues about software (Figure 3-45b). Read Innovative Computing 3-2 to find out about a digital learning resource that can supplement the classroom experience.

If you want to learn more about a particular program from a printed manual, many books are available to help you learn to use the features of personal computer programs. These books typically are available in bookstores and software stores.

Many colleges and schools provide training on several of the programs discussed in this chapter. For more information, contact your local school for a list of class offerings.

Figure 3-45a (online Help)

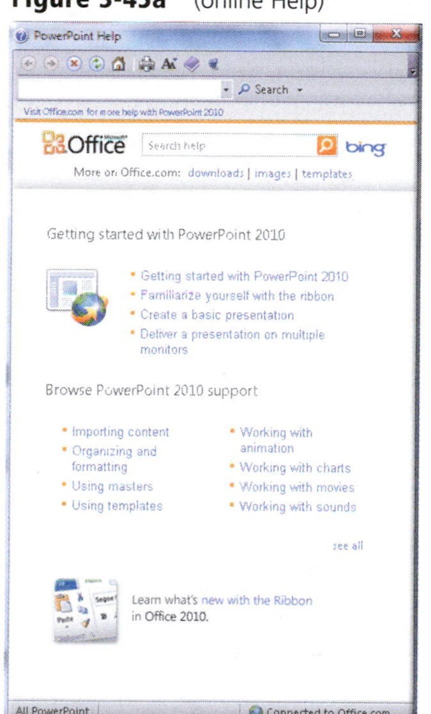

Figure 3-45b (Web-based Help)

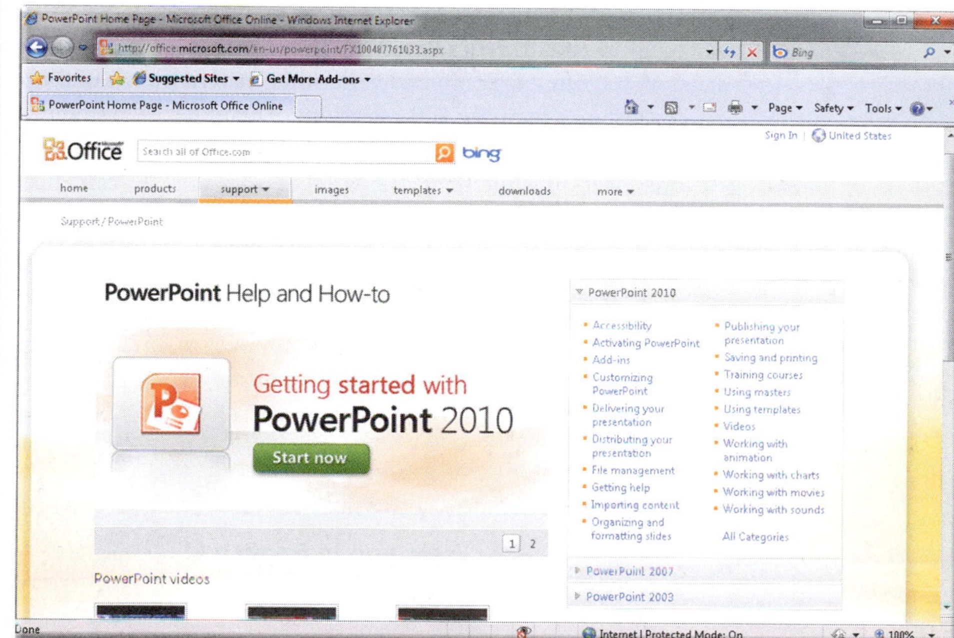

Figure 3-45 Many programs include online Help and Web-based Help.

INNOVATIVE COMPUTING 3-2

iTunes U Supplements Classroom Learning

Your reliable study partner can join you at the gym, on the bus, at dinner, and anywhere you want to go. *iTunes U* is a digital learning resource with a direct connection to lectures, demonstrations, and performances that enrich the classroom experience.

Professors and other educators develop multimedia content for iTunes U, and other organizations add their resources to the Beyond Campus area. For example, PBS, New York's Museum of Modern Art, and the Smithsonian have shared their collections and interviews. All you need to access this treasure trove of free resources is a computer or mobile device and Internet access. You can watch and listen to the iTunes U content on your computer, iPod, and iPhone.

iTunes U content has been downloaded more than four million times since the Web site's inception in 2007. Popular lectures are on the topics of black holes, Mozart, copyright law, and Greek. A world literature lecture was viewed 74,000 times in one month.

For more information, visit the Computer Concepts CourseMate Web site at www.cengagebrain.com, navigate to the Chapter 3 Innovative Computing resource for this book, and then click iTunes U.

Web-Based Training

Web-based training (*WBT*) is a type of CBT (computer-based training) that uses Internet technology and consists of application software on the Web. Similar to CBT, WBT typically consists of self-directed, self-paced instruction about a topic. WBT is popular in business, industry, and schools for teaching new skills or enhancing existing skills of employees, teachers, or students. When using a WBT product, students actively become involved in the learning process instead of remaining passive recipients of information.

Many Web sites offer WBT to the general public. Such training covers a wide range of topics, from how to change a flat tire to creating documents in Word. Many of these Web sites are free. Others require registration and payment to take the complete Web-based course.

WBT often is combined with other materials for distance learning and e-learning. **Distance learning** (**DL**) is the delivery of education at one location while the learning takes place at other locations. DL courses provide time, distance, and place advantages for students who live far from a college campus or work full time. These courses enable students to attend class from anywhere in the world and at times that fit their schedules. Many national and international companies offer DL training. These training courses eliminate the costs of airfare, hotels, and meals for centralized training sessions.

E-learning, short for electronic learning, is the delivery of education via some electronic method such as the Internet, networks, or optical discs. To enhance communications, e-learning systems also may include video conferencing, e-mail, blogs, wikis, newsgroups, chat rooms, and groupware.

E-learning providers often specialize in presenting instructors with the tools for preparation, distribution, and management of DL courses (Figure 3-46). These tools enable instructors to create rich, educational Web-based training sites and allow the students to interact with a powerful Web learning environment. Through the training site, students can check their progress, take practice tests, search for topics, send e-mail messages, and participate in discussions and chats.

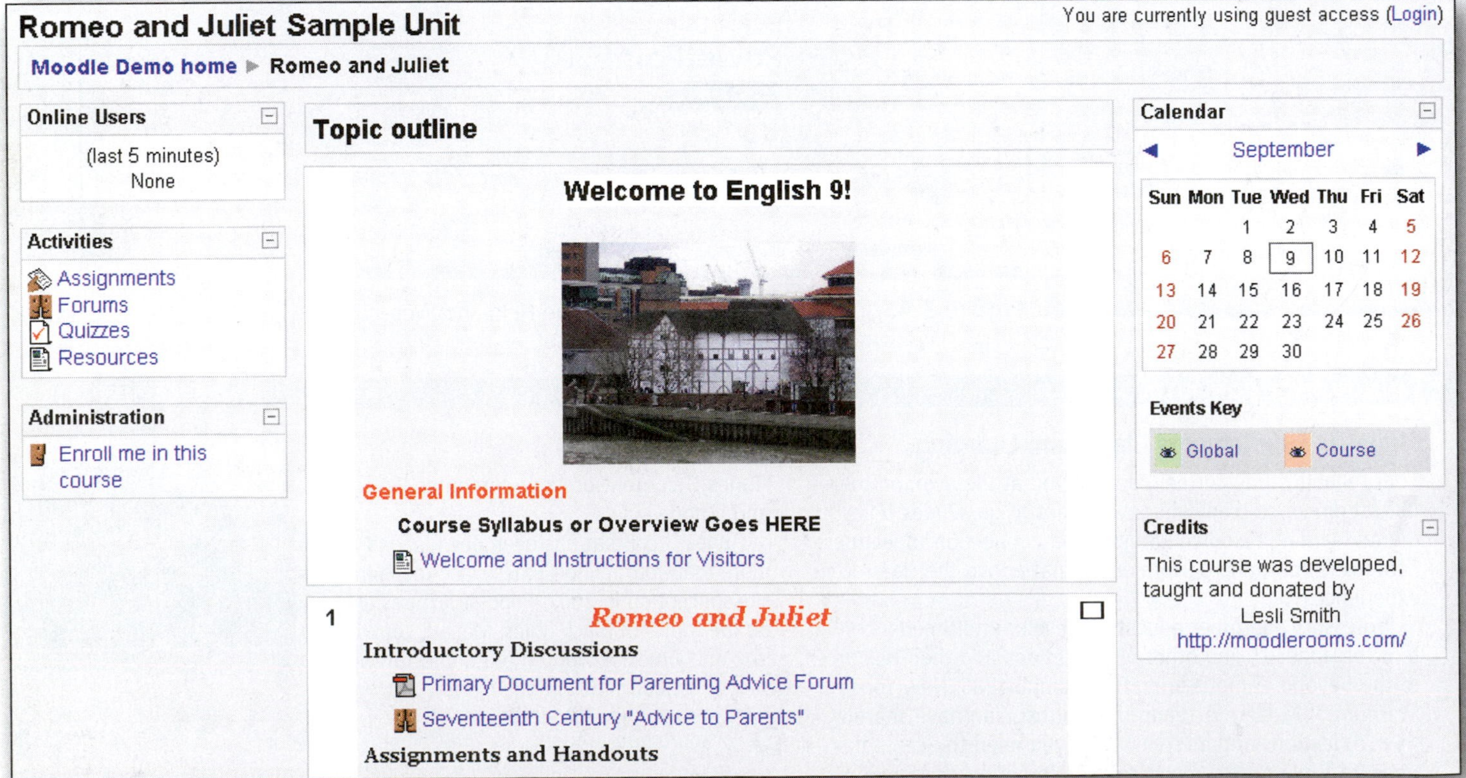

Figure 3-46 E-learning systems enable instructors to post course materials for their students.

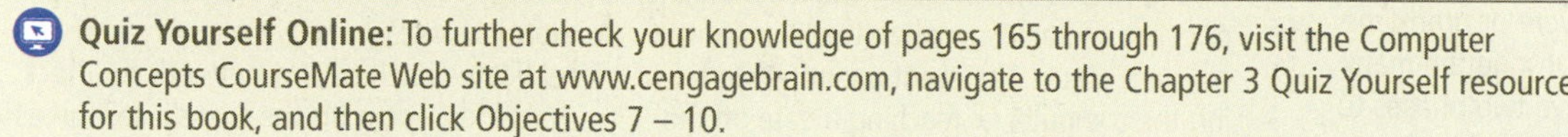

✔ QUIZ YOURSELF 3-3

Instructions: Find the true statement below. Then, rewrite the remaining false statements so that they are true.

1. All Web application hosts provide free access to their software.
2. Computer-based training is a type of Web-based training that uses Internet technology and consists of application software on the Web.
3. E-mail and Web browsers are examples of communications software that are considered application software.
4. Legal software is a simplified accounting program that helps home users and small office/home office users balance their checkbooks, pay bills, track investments, and evaluate financial plans.
5. Personal DTP software is a popular type of image editing software that allows users to edit digital photos.

Quiz Yourself Online: To further check your knowledge of pages 165 through 176, visit the Computer Concepts CourseMate Web site at www.cengagebrain.com, navigate to the Chapter 3 Quiz Yourself resource for this book, and then click Objectives 7 – 10.

Chapter Summary

This chapter illustrated how to start and interact with application software. It then presented an overview of a variety of business software, graphics and multimedia software, and home/personal/educational software.

The chapter also discussed Web applications and application software for communications. Lastly, learning tools for application software and Web-based training were presented.

Computer Usage @ Work

Construction

Walking the streets, you stop to admire a new skyscraper with the most striking architectural features you ever have seen. You think to yourself that those responsible for designing the building are nothing less than brilliant. While a great deal of work goes into the design and construction of a building, computers and technology also play an important role in the process. In fact, the role of computers not only saves time and provides for more accurate results, it also allows us to preview how a building will look before construction even begins.

As mentioned in the chapter, computer-aided design (CAD) software is a sophisticated type of application software that assists a professional user in creating engineering, architectural, and scientific plans. During the preliminary design process, architects and design firms use CAD software to design the appearance and layout of a new building and can provide clients with a three-dimensional walkthrough of a building so that they can determine whether the proposed design will meet their needs. Later, the program can be used to include the placement of support beams, walls, roof shape, and so on, and also conform to building code.

CAD software also allows engineers in various fields, such as mechanical and electrical, to design separate layers in a structure. The software then can superimpose the designs to check for interactions and conflicts, such as if a structural beam in one layer covers a drain in another layer. The CAD software makes it easy to modify and correct the structure before it is built, which can save time and money during the construction process. This software also eliminates most, if not all, of the manual drafting required.

Engineers use computers to determine the type of foundation required to support the building and its occupants; the heating, ventilating, and air conditioning (HVAC); and the electrical requirements, as well as how the building may withstand external threats such as hurricanes and tornadoes.

During construction, contractors and builders are able to use computer software to estimate accurately the amount of materials and time required to complete the job. Without computers, determining materials and time required is a cumbersome and time-consuming task.

The next time you notice a building under construction, stop to think about how computer technology has increased the efficiency of the design and construction process.

For more information, visit the Computer Concepts CourseMate Web site at www.cengagebrain.com, navigate to the Chapter 3 Computer Usage @ Work resource for this book, and then click Construction.

High-Tech Talk

Computer Viruses: Delivery, Infection, and Avoidance

Klez. Melissa. Mydoom. Nimda. Like the common cold, virtually countless variations of computer viruses exist. Unlike the biological viruses that cause the common cold, people create computer viruses. To create a virus, an unscrupulous programmer must code and then test the virus code to ensure the virus can replicate itself, conceal itself, monitor for certain events, and then deliver its *payload* — the destructive event or prank the virus was created to deliver. Despite the many variations of viruses, most have two phases to their execution: infection and delivery.

To start the infection phase, the virus must be activated. Today, the most common way viruses spread is by people running infected programs disguised as e-mail attachments. During the infection phase, viruses typically perform three actions:

1. First, a virus replicates by attaching itself to program files. A *macro virus* hides in the macro language of a program, such as Word. A *boot sector virus* targets the master boot record and executes when the computer starts. A *file virus* attaches itself to program files. The file virus, Win32.Hatred, for example, replicates by first infecting Windows executable files for the Calculator, Notepad, Help, and other programs on the hard disk. The virus then scans the computer to locate .exe files on other drives and stores this information in the system registry. The next time an infected file is run, the virus reads the registry and continues infecting another drive.
2. Viruses also conceal themselves to avoid detection. A *stealth virus* disguises itself by hiding in fake code sections, which it inserts within working code in a file. A *polymorphic virus* actually changes its code as it infects computers. The Win32.Hatred virus uses both concealment techniques. The virus writes itself to the last file section, while modifying the file header to hide the increased file size. It also scrambles and encrypts the virus code as it infects files.
3. Finally, viruses watch for a certain condition or event and activate when that condition or event occurs. The event might be starting the computer or reaching a date on the system clock. A *logic bomb* activates when it detects a specific condition (say, a name deleted from the employee list). A *time bomb* is a logic bomb that activates on a particular date or time. Win32.Hatred, for instance, unleashes its destruction when the computer clock hits the seventh day of any month. If the triggering condition does not exist, the virus simply replicates.

During the delivery phase, the virus unleashes its payload, which might be a harmless prank that displays a meaningless message — or it might be destructive, corrupting or deleting data and files. When the Win32.Hatred virus triggers, it displays the author's message and then covers the screen with black dots. The virus also deletes several antivirus files as it infects the system. The most dangerous viruses do not have an obvious payload; instead they quietly modify files. A virus, for example, could change numbers randomly in an inventory program or introduce delays to slow a computer. One way antivirus software detects computer viruses is by monitoring files for unknown changes, particularly in file size. Because many computer viruses alter system and data files — files that should not change in size — changes in file sizes often are a key indication of an infection.

Other kinds of electronic annoyances exist in addition to viruses. While often called viruses, worms, Trojan horse programs, and rootkits actually are part of a broader category called *malicious-logic programs* or *malware*.

- A *worm*, such as the CodeRed or Sircam worm, resides in active memory and replicates itself over a network to infect machines, using up the system resources and possibly shutting the system down.
- A *Trojan horse* is a destructive program disguised as a real program, such as a screen saver. When a user runs a seemingly innocent program, a Trojan horse hiding inside can capture information, such as user names and passwords, from your system or open up a backdoor that allows a hacker remotely to control your computer. Unlike viruses, Trojan horses do not replicate themselves.
- A *rootkit* is a program that easily can hide and allow someone to take full control of your computer from a remote location, often for nefarious purposes. For example, a rootkit can hide in a folder on your computer, and the folder will appear empty. This is because the rootkit has instructed your computer not to display the contents of the folder. Rootkits can be very dangerous and often require special software to detect and remove. Rootkits are becoming more common. In fact, a recent study has shown that more than 20 percent of computers in the United States are infected with a rootkit. It is extremely important that you use caution when installing software from unknown sources.

Every computer user is susceptible to a computer virus. Studies show that an unprotected computer can be infected by a virus within minutes after being connected to the Internet. Due to the increasing threat of viruses attacking your computer, it is more important than ever to protect your computer from viruses. Figure 3-47 lists steps you can follow to protect your computer from a virus infection.

Steps to Virus Protection
1. Install the latest Microsoft updates.
2. Purchase a reputable antivirus program.
3. After installing an antivirus program, scan your entire computer to be sure it is free of malware.
4. Update your antivirus definitions regularly.
5. Be suspicious of any and all unsolicited e-mail attachments.
6. Stay informed about viruses and virus hoaxes.
7. Install a personal firewall program.
8. Download software only if you are sure the Web site is legitimate.
9. Avoid as best you can visiting unscrupulous Web sites.

Figure 3-47 Guidelines to keep your computer virus free.

For more information, visit the Computer Concepts CourseMate Web site at www.cengagebrain.com, navigate to the Chapter 3 High-Tech Talk resource for this book, and then click Computer Viruses.

Companies on the Cutting Edge

ADOBE SYSTEMS Design Software Leader

Practically all creative professionals involved with art and photography have a copy of Adobe Photoshop on their computer, and the leading computer manufacturers ship their products with a copy of Adobe Reader installed. The worldwide presence of *Adobe Systems* software attests to the company's success in developing programs that help people communicate effectively.

Charles Geschke and John Warnock founded the company in 1982 and named it after a creek that ran behind Warnock's house in California. Creative Suite contains the fundamental tools that help photographers, designers, and publishers develop and maintain their documents and Web sites, and it includes Dreamweaver, Flash, Fireworks, Contribute, InDesign, Illustrator, and Photoshop.

Recently, Adobe was voted one of the 100 Best Companies to Work For.

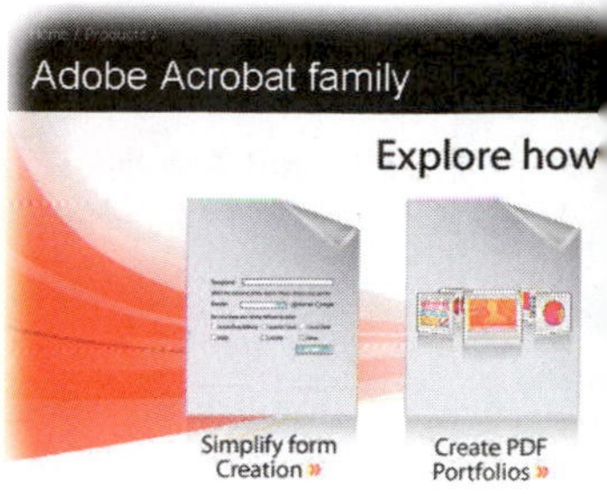

MICROSOFT Computer Technology Innovator

Internet users view *Microsoft*'s Web site more than 2.4 million times each day, attesting to the company's presence as the largest software company in the world. Its Office and Internet Explorer programs dominate the computer industry, and it also has assets in the MSNBC cable television network, the Encarta multimedia encyclopedia, SharePoint, and gaming software, including Flight Simulator and Zoo Tycoon. Microsoft also manufactures hardware, such as the Xbox, Zune, mouse devices, keyboards, fingerprint readers, Web cams, and game controllers.

When Microsoft was incorporated in 1975, the company had three programmers, one product, and revenues of $16,000. The company now employs more than 92,000 people and has annual revenues in excess of $58 billion. Windows 7 is the latest version of Microsoft's flagship operating system.

For more information, visit the Computer Concepts CourseMate Web site at www.cengagebrain.com and then navigate to the Chapter 3 Companies on the Cutting Edge resource for this book.

Technology Trailblazers

DAN BRICKLIN VisiCalc Developer

Dan Bricklin introduced wikiCalc in 2007 as a free software tool for Web pages that have data in lists and tables. This program is an offshoot of a prototype program he had developed 30 years earlier, named VisiCalc, that performed a series of calculations automatically when numbers were entered.

Bricklin and a friend founded a company, Software Arts, to develop VisiCalc, short for Visible Calculator. They programmed the software using Apple Basic on an Apple II computer. This small program was the first type of application software that provided a reason for businesses to buy Apple computers. It included many features found in today's spreadsheet software.

Bricklin founded a small consulting company, Software Garden, to develop and market software such as wikiCalc. The company also distributes resources to help programmers learn about licensing their products and about open source software.

MASAYOSHI SON Softbank President and CEO

In the 1970s, *Masayoshi Son* was convinced that the microchip was going to change people's lives. As an economics major at the University of California, Berkeley, each day he attempted to develop one original use for computer technology. One of these ideas made him a millionaire: a multilingual pocket translating device that he sold to Sharp Corporation.

At age 23, Son founded Softbank, which is one of Japan's largest telecommunications and media corporations. He now is one of the richest men in the world with a net worth of $3.7 billion.

Recently, Softbank partnered with Apple to develop a version of the iPhone for the Japanese market. In addition, Son's company collaborated with Tiffany & Co. to manufacture 10 cell phones, each worth more than $910,000, with 400 diamonds weighing more than 20 karats total.

For more information, visit the Computer Concepts CourseMate Web site at www.cengagebrain.com and then navigate to the Chapter 3 Technology Trailblazers resource for this book.

STUDENT ASSIGNMENTS

Chapter Review

The Chapter Review reinforces the main concepts presented in this chapter.

To listen to an audio version of this Chapter Review, visit the Computer Concepts CourseMate Web site at www.cengagebrain.com and then navigate to the Chapter 3 Chapter Review resource for this book.

1. **What Are the Four Categories of Application Software?** **Application software** consists of programs designed to make users more productive and/or assist them with personal tasks. The major categories of application software are business software; graphics and multimedia software; home, personal, and educational software; and communications software.

2. **What Are the Seven Forms through Which Software Is Available?** Application software is available in a variety of forms. **Packaged software** is mass-produced, copyrighted retail software that meets the needs of a variety of users. **Custom software** performs functions specific to a business or industry. A **Web application** is a Web site that allows users to access and interact with software from any computer or device that is connected to the Internet. **Open source software** is provided for use, modification, and redistribution. **Shareware** is copyrighted software that is distributed free for a trial period. **Freeware** is copyrighted software provided at no cost by an individual or a company that retains all rights to the software. **Public-domain software** is free software donated for public use and has no copyright restrictions.

3. **How Do the Operating System and Utility Programs Work with Application Software?** To use application software, your computer must be running *system software*, specifically an operating system. The system software serves as the interface between the user, the application software, and the computer's hardware. Each time you start a computer, the operating system is *loaded* (copied) from the computer's hard disk into memory. Once loaded, it coordinates all the computer's activities, including starting application software and transferring data among input/output devices and memory. A utility program is a type of system software that assists users with controlling or maintaining the operations of a computer, its devices, or its software.

4. **What Are the Characteristics of a User Interface?** Personal computer operating systems often use the concept of a **desktop**, which is an on-screen work area that has a graphical user interface. One way to start a program in Windows is to move the **pointer** to the Start **button** on the taskbar and **click** the Start button by pressing and releasing a button on the mouse. Then, click the program name on the **menu** or in a list. Once loaded into memory, the program is displayed in a **window** on the desktop.

Visit the Computer Concepts CourseMate Web site at www.cengagebrain.com, navigate to the Chapter 3 Quiz Yourself resource for this book, and then click Objectives 1 – 4.

5. **What Are the Key Features of Widely Used Business Programs?** **Business software** assists people in becoming more effective and efficient while performing daily business activities. Business software includes the following programs. **Word processing software**, sometimes called a *word processor*, allows users to **create** a document by entering text and inserting images, **edit** the document by making changes, and **format** the document by changing its appearance. **Spreadsheet software** allows users to organize data in rows and columns, perform calculations, recalculate when data changes, and chart the data. **Database software** allows users to create, access, and manage a **database**, which is a collection of data organized to allow access, retrieval, and use of that data. **Presentation software** allows users to create a *slide show* that is displayed on a monitor or projection screen. **Note taking software** enables users to enter typed text, handwritten comments, drawings, or sketches on a page and then save the page as part of a notebook. A **personal information manager (PIM)** includes features to help users organize personal information. In addition to PIM software, a huge variety of business and other software for phones is available. A **software suite** is a collection of individual programs available together as a unit. At a minimum, business software suites include word processing, spreadsheet, e-mail, and presentation programs. **Project management software** allows users to plan, schedule, track, and analyze the events, resources, and costs of a project. **Accounting software** helps companies record and report their financial transactions. **Document management software** provides a means for sharing, distributing, and searching through documents by converting them into a format that can be viewed by any user.

6. **What Are the Key Features of Widely Used Graphics and Multimedia Programs?** Graphics and multimedia software includes the following programs. **Computer-aided design (CAD) software** assists in creating engineering, architectural, and scientific designs. **Desktop publishing (DTP) software** enables professional designers to create sophisticated

Chapter Review

documents that contain text, graphics, and colors. **Paint software**, also called *illustration software*, lets users draw graphical images with various on-screen tools. **Image editing software** provides the capabilities of paint software and includes the capability to enhance and modify existing images. **Professional photo editing software** is a type of image editing software that allows high-volume digital photo users to edit and customize digital photos. **Video editing software** allows professionals to modify segments of a video. **Audio editing software** lets users modify audio clips, produce studio-quality soundtracks, and add audio to video clips. **Multimedia authoring software** allows users to combine text, graphics, audio, video, and animation in an interactive application. **Web page authoring software** helps users of all skill levels create Web pages that include graphical images, video, audio, animation, and other special effects with interactive content.

Visit the Computer Concepts CourseMate Web site at www.cengagebrain.com, navigate to the Chapter 3 Quiz Yourself resource for this book, and then click Objectives 5 – 6.

7. **What Are the Key Features of Widely Used Home, Personal, and Educational Programs?** Software for home, personal, and educational use includes the following programs. **Personal finance software** is an accounting program that helps users balance their checkbooks, pay bills, track income and expenses, track investments, and evaluate financial plans. **Legal software** assists in the preparation of legal documents. **Tax preparation software** guides users through filing federal taxes. **Personal DTP software** helps users create newsletters, brochures, flyers, advertisements, greeting and business cards, logos, and Web pages. **Personal paint/image editing software** provides an easy-to-use interface with functions tailored to meet the needs of home and small business users. **Personal photo editing software** is a type of image editing software used to edit digital photos. *Photo management software* helps users view, organize, sort, catalog, and share digital photos. Application software often includes a **clip art/image gallery**, which is a collection of clip art and photos. Video and audio editing software is used to edit home movies, add music or other sounds, and share movies on the Web. **Home design/landscaping software** assists with the design, remodeling, or improvement of a home or landscape. **Travel and mapping software** enables users to view maps, determine route directions, and locate points of interest. **Reference software** provides valuable and thorough information for all individuals. **Educational software** teaches a particular skill. **Entertainment software** includes interactive games, videos, and other programs to support hobbies or provide amusement.

8. **What Are the Advantages of and Ways to Access Web Applications?** A Web application, or *Web app*, requires less disk space on a computer than installed software and is less costly to upgrade. Users often interact with Web applications directly at the Web site, referred to as the host, through their Web browser. Some Web sites require that you download the software to your computer or device.

9. **What Are the Types of Application Software Used in Communications?** Application software for communications includes Web browsers to access and view Web pages; e-mail programs to transmit messages via a network; instant messaging software for real-time exchange of messages or files; chat room software to have real-time, online typed conversations; text, picture, and video messaging software; RSS aggregator program to keep track of changes made to Web sites; *blog software*, or *blogware*, to create and maintain a blog; newsgroup/message board programs that allow online written discussions; FTP programs to upload and download files on the Internet; VoIP (Internet telephony), which allows users to speak to other users over the Internet; and video conferencing software for meetings on a network.

10. **What Learning Aids Are Available for Application Software?** To assist in the learning process, many programs offer Help features. **Online Help** is the electronic equivalent of a user manual. Most online Help links to *Web-based Help*, which provides updates and more comprehensive resources. Popular in business, industry, and schools, **Web-based training** (*WBT*) is a type of computer-based training that uses Internet technology and consists of application software on the Web.

Visit the Computer Concepts CourseMate Web site at www.cengagebrain.com, navigate to the Chapter 3 Quiz Yourself resource for this book, and then click Objectives 7 – 10.

STUDENT ASSIGNMENTS

Key Terms

You should know the Primary Terms and be familiar with the Secondary Terms. The list below helps focus your study.

To see an example of and a definition for each term, and to access current and additional information from the Web, visit the Computer Concepts CourseMate Web site at www.cengagebrain.com and then navigate to the Chapter 3 Key Terms resource for this book.

Primary Terms

(shown in bold-black characters in the chapter)

accounting software (158)
application software (142)
audio editing software (162)
business software (146)
button (144)
click (144)
clip art (147)
clip art/image gallery (169)
command (144)
computer-aided design (CAD) software (160)
computer-based training (CBT) (171)
create (149)
custom software (142)
database (153)
database software (153)
desktop (144)
desktop publishing (DTP) software (160)
distance learning (DL) (176)
document management software (158)
edit (149)
educational software (171)
entertainment software (172)
font (149)
font size (149)
format (149)
freeware (143)
home design/ landscaping software (170)
icon (144)
image editing software (161)
legal software (167)
menu (144)
multimedia authoring software (162)
note taking software (156)
online banking (166)
online Help (175)
open source software (143)
packaged software (142)
paint software (161)
personal DTP software (167)
personal finance software (166)
personal information manager (PIM) (156)
personal paint/image editing software (168)
personal photo editing software (168)
pointer (144)
presentation software (154)
print (150)
professional photo editing software (162)
project management software (157)
public-domain software (143)
reference software (171)
save (150)
shareware (143)
software suite (156)
spreadsheet software (150)
tax preparation software (167)
title bar (144)
travel and mapping software (170)
video editing software (162)
Web application (142)
Web page authoring software (164)
Web-based training (176)
window (144)
word processing software (147)

Secondary Terms

(shown in italic characters in the chapter)

bar chart (152)
blog software (174)
blogware (174)
cell (151)
charting (152)
clipboard (149)
cloud storage (172)
color library (161)
column chart (152)
dialog box (145)
e-filing (167)
e-learning (176)
field (154)
file (144)
file name (145)
filters (162)
font style (149)
footer (148)
formula (151)
function (151)
header (148)
illustration software (161)
image stitching (161)
import (155)
label (151)
line chart (152)
loaded (144)
macro (148)
malware (144)
margins (147)
page layout (160)
pasting (149)
PDF (158)
photo management software (169)
pie chart (152)
point (149)
product activation (143)
query (154)
record (154)
sans serif font (149)
scrolling (148)
serif font (149)
slide show (154)
smart tags (148)
spelling checker (148)
system software (143)
template (148)
value (151)
WBT (176)
Web app (172)
Web-based Help (175)
what-if analysis (152)
word processor (147)
wordwrap (147)
worksheet (150)

computer-aided design (CAD) software (160)

Checkpoint

The Checkpoint exercises test your knowledge of the chapter concepts. The page number containing the answer appears in parentheses after each exercise. The Beyond the Book exercises will help broaden your understanding of the concepts presented in this chapter.

To complete the Checkpoint exercises interactively, visit the Computer Concepts CourseMate Web site at www.cengagebrain.com and then navigate to the Chapter 3 Checkpoint resource for this book.

True/False Mark T for True and F for False.

_____ 1. The categories of application software are mutually exclusive. (142)

_____ 2. Public-domain software is available to the public for a fee. (143)

_____ 3. To click a button on the screen requires moving the pointer to the button and then pressing and holding down a button on the mouse (usually the right mouse button). (144)

_____ 4. A dialog box is a window that provides information, presents available options, or requests a response. (145)

_____ 5. A font is a name assigned to a specific design of characters. (149)

_____ 6. In a spreadsheet program, a function is a predefined formula that performs common calculations such as adding the values in a group of cells or generating a value such as the time or date. (151)

_____ 7. Computer-aided design (CAD) software is a sophisticated type of application software that assists a professional user in creating engineering, architectural, and scientific designs. (160)

_____ 8. Image stitching is the process of adjusting or enhancing image colors and/or adding special effects such as shadows and glows. (161)

_____ 9. Although many word processing programs include desktop publishing (DTP) software features, users often prefer to create DTP documents using DTP software because of its enhanced features. (168)

_____ 10. Some Web sites require you to download software in order to run their Web applications. (172)

_____ 11. Some communications software is considered system software because it works with hardware and transmission media. (174)

_____ 12. An RSS aggregator includes time-stamped articles, or posts, in a diary or journal format, usually listed in reverse chronological order. (174)

Multiple Choice Select the best answer.

1. _____ is mass-produced, copyrighted retail software that meets the needs of a wide variety of users, not just a single user or company. (142)
   a. Packaged software b. A Web application
   c. Open source software d. Custom software

2. _____ is a collection of individual programs available together as a unit. (156)
   a. A software suite b. Shareware
   c. Packaged software d. Custom software

3. _____ allows a user to plan, schedule, track, and analyze the events, resources, and costs of a project. (157)
   a. Accounting software
   b. Project management software
   c. CAD software
   d. Document management software

4. _____ software provides a means for sharing, distributing, and searching through documents by converting them into a format that can be viewed by any user. (158)
   a. Database
   b. Portable Document Format (PDF)
   c. Document management
   d. Word processing

5. _____ helps home and small business users create newsletters, brochures, advertisements, postcards, greeting cards, letterhead, business cards, banners, calendars, logos, and Web pages. (168)
   a. Blogware
   b. A personal information manager
   c. Personal DTP software
   d. Note taking software

6. With _____, you can view, organize, sort, catalog, print, and share digital photos. (169)
   a. spreadsheet software
   b. photo management software
   c. clip art
   d. desktop publishing software

7. A(n) _____ is an online area where users have written discussions. (174)
   a. FTP program
   b. text message
   c. newsgroup/message board
   d. Web browser

8. _____ is the electronic equivalent of a user manual. (175)
   a. Web-based training b. Online Help
   c. E-learning d. Distance learning

STUDENT ASSIGNMENTS

Checkpoint

Matching

Match the terms with their definitions.

_____ 1. button (144)
_____ 2. window (144)
_____ 3. title bar (144)
_____ 4. pasting (149)
_____ 5. cell (151)
_____ 6. database (153)
_____ 7. PDF (158)
_____ 8. personal finance software (166)
_____ 9. online banking (166)
_____ 10. Web app (172)

a. popular file format that document management software uses to save converted documents
b. the process of transferring an item from a clipboard to a specific location in a document
c. Web site that allows users to access and interact with software from any computer or device that is connected to the Internet
d. intersection of a row and column in a spreadsheet
e. rectangular area of the screen that displays data and information
f. small symbol on the screen that moves as you move the mouse
g. simplified accounting program that helps home users and small office/home office users balance their checkbooks, pay bills, track personal income and expenses, set up budgets, manage home inventory, track investments, and evaluate financial plans
h. text that appears at the bottom of every page
i. graphical image activated to cause a specific action to occur
j. horizontal space that contains the window's name
k. offers access to account balances, provides bill payment services, and allows you to download monthly transactions and statements from the Web directly to your computer
l. collection of data organized in a manner that allows access, retrieval, and use of that data

Short Answer

Write a brief answer to each of the following questions.

1. Describe some types of utility programs. ___________ What is malware? ___________
2. What are the features of presentation software? ___________ What types of media might a person use to enhance a presentation? ___________
3. How is travel and mapping software used? ___________ What are some examples of reference software? ___________
4. What is computer-based training (CBT)? ___________ List a few examples of CBT usage. ___________
5. Describe how many Web sites utilize Web-based training. ___________ What are some ways that e-learning enhances communications? ___________

Beyond the Book

Follow the book element instructions below; present your findings (brief report, presentation, discussion, or other means).

1. Ethics & Issues — Select an Ethics & Issues in this chapter (149, 150, 162, 173), find a recent newspaper/magazine article that supports one point of view presented, and then evaluate the article.
2. Computer Usage @ Work — Use the Web or a recent newspaper/magazine to locate three additional unique usages of computer technology in the construction industry (177). What makes the use of these technologies unique to the construction industry?
3. Companies on the Cutting Edge and Technology Trailblazers — Use the Web or a recent business newspaper/magazine to locate an interesting fact about Adobe Systems, Microsoft, Dan Bricklin, or Masayoshi Son that was not presented in the chapter (179).
4. High-Tech Talk — Locate a recent newspaper/magazine article that discusses topics related to Computer Viruses (178). Would you recommend the article you found? Why or why not?
5. FAQs and Web Links — Use the Web or a recent newspaper/magazine to locate three additional facts about an FAQ (144, 150, 154, 166, 167, 172, 174) and Web Link (144, 148, 151, 154, 155, 156, 160, 164, 167, 168, 172, 173) that were not presented in the chapter.
6. Looking Ahead — Use the Web or a recent newspaper/magazine to discover additional uses of the technology presented in Sensors Help Drivers Find Their Way (171).
7. Innovative Computing — Use the Web or a recent newspaper/magazine to locate two additional interesting facts about Fireworks Software Creates a Real Blast (160) and iTunes U Supplements Classroom Learning (175).
8. Making Use of the Web — Visit three of the Blogs sites (127) and outline the information on each Web site and the possible uses for each Web site.
9. Digital Communications — Select a topic discussed in the Digital Communications feature (192) and then present a current issue related to the topic found on the Web or in a magazine article.

Learn It Online

The Learn It Online exercises are interactive Web exercises designed to reinforce and expand your understanding of the chapter concepts. The descriptions below briefly summarize each exercise.

To complete the Learn It Online exercises, visit the Computer Concepts CourseMate Web site at www.cengagebrain.com, navigate to the Chapter 3 resources for this book, click the link for the exercise you want to complete, and then read the instructions.

1 At the Movies — MediaCell Video Converter
Watch a movie to learn how to use the MediaCell Video Converter and then answer questions about the movie.

2 Video and Audio: You Review It — Video Editing Software
Search for, choose, and write a review of a video, podcast, or vodcast that discusses video editing software.

3 Student Edition Labs — Word Processing, Spreadsheets, Databases, and Presentation Software
Enhance your understanding and knowledge about business application software by completing the Word Processing, Spreadsheets, Databases, and Presentation Software Labs.

4 Practice Test
Take a multiple choice test that checks your knowledge of the chapter concepts and review the resulting study guide.

5 Who Wants To Be a Computer Genius^2?
Play the Shelly Cashman Series version of this popular game by answering questions to find out if you are a computer genius. Panic buttons are available to provide assistance during game play.

6 Wheel of Terms
Identify important key terms presented in this chapter by playing the Shelly Cashman Series version of this popular game.

7 You're Hired!
Embark on the path to a career in computers by answering questions and solving puzzles related to concepts discussed in this chapter.

8 Crossword Puzzle Challenge
Complete an interactive crossword puzzle to reinforce concepts presented in this chapter.

9 Windows Exercises
Step through the Windows 7 exercises to learn about working with application programs, creating a word processing document, using WordPad Help, and business software products.

10 Exploring Computer Careers
Read about a career as a help desk specialist, search for related employment advertisements, and then answer related questions.

11 Web Apps — Britannica.com
Learn how to browse world history and search for various encyclopedia articles using Britannica.com.

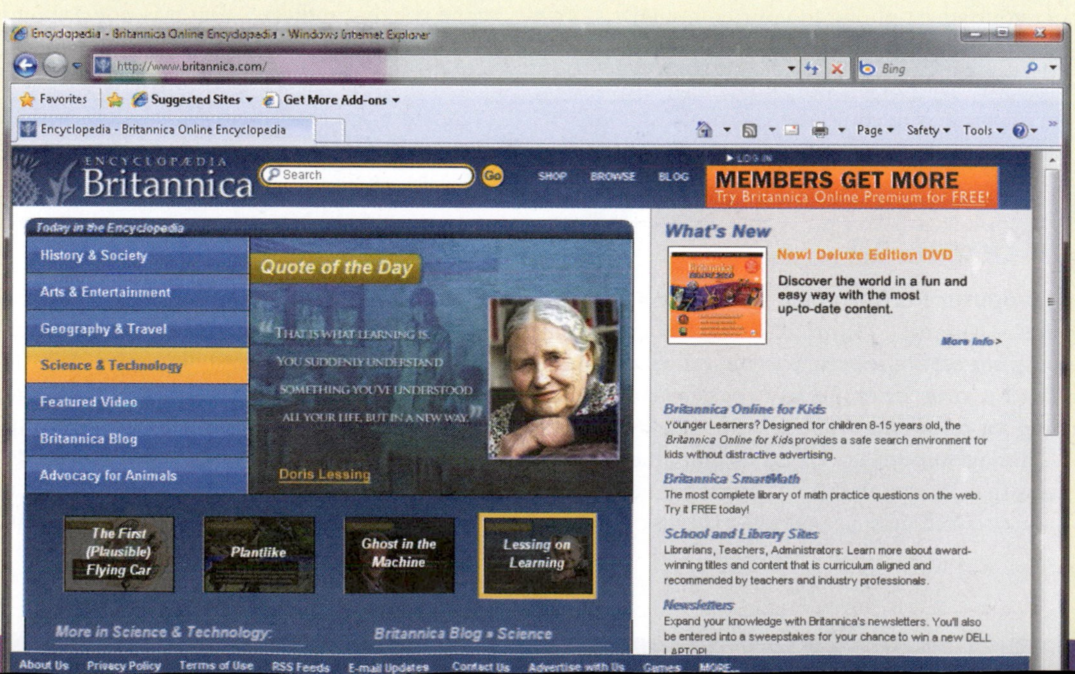

Problem Solving @ Home

The Problem Solving @ Home exercises extend your knowledge of the chapter concepts by seeking solutions to practical computer problems that you may encounter at home or school. The Collaboration exercise should be completed with a team.

In the real world, practical problems often can be solved in multiple ways. Provide one solution to each of the following problems using available resources, such as articles on the Web or in print, blogs, podcasts, videos, television, user guides, other individuals, and electronics and computer stores. You may need to use multiple resources to obtain an answer. Present your solutions in the form requested by your instructor (brief report, presentation, discussion, or other means).

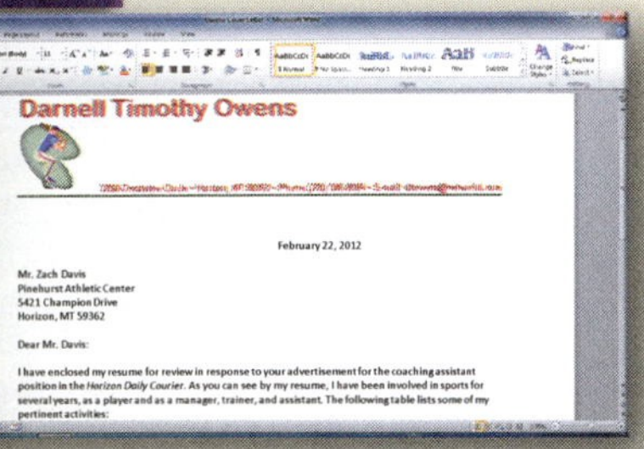

1. **Program Not Responding** While working with a document, Microsoft Word suddenly fails to recognize when you click the mouse or type on the keyboard. The title bar also indicates that the program is not responding. What could be wrong?
2. **Incorrect Calculations** As a teacher's assistant at a local high school, you keep track of students' grades in Microsoft Excel. At semester's end, you use a formula to calculate the final letter grade for each student. The final letter grades, however, do not calculate properly. What might be causing the error?
3. **Unable to Save** You have been using Microsoft Access to maintain a database of your optical discs. Upon attempting to open the database, you receive a message on the screen stating that only a read-only copy of the database could be opened, which means that you are unable to save any changes. What is your next step?
4. **Smart Phone Not Synchronizing** You regularly connect your smart phone to your computer to synchronize your e-mail messages, contacts, and calendar. The last few times you tried to connect the smart phone, the computer did not respond. Before placing a call to technical support, what steps can you take so that the computer will recognize your smart phone?
5. **Unwanted Page** A local charity in which you are active has asked you to design a one-page brochure. Each time you print the brochure, it prints the first page correctly, but a blank second page also comes out. What steps will you take to eliminate the blank second page?
6. **Audio Not Playing** You are attempting for the first time to transfer video from your video recorder directly to your computer. When you save the file on your computer and play it back, the video quality is acceptable, but there is no audio. What is the first step you will take to troubleshoot this problem?
7. **Unusual File Size** You are using photo editing software to remove red eye from a photo. After successfully removing the red eye, you save the file and notice that the size of the file nearly has doubled. What might be causing this?
8. **Program Crashing on Exit** Each time you attempt to quit Microsoft Excel by clicking the Close button, the program does not quit, and the title bar indicates that it is not responding. When you click the Close button again, a dialog box is displayed that states Microsoft Excel has encountered a problem. What steps will you take to solve this problem?

Collaboration

9. **Poor Computer Performance** While working on a class project with a group of friends, you notice that your computer is running exceptionally slowly. In addition, you notice that the light identifying hard disk activity is flashing almost constantly. Your first instincts are that the computer is low on hard disk space, the computer might have a virus, or too many programs are running on the computer. Form a team of three people and begin searching for information about how to isolate the problem. One team member should look for free, up-to-date virus scanning software to scan the computer for viruses, another team member should research ways to find programs that are running (that might not be displayed on the taskbar), and one team member should create a list of ways to free up space on the hard disk. Compile your answers and submit them to your instructor.

Problem Solving @ Work

The Problem Solving @ Work exercises extend your knowledge of the chapter concepts by seeking solutions to practical computer problems that you may encounter at work. The Collaboration exercise should be completed with a team.

In the real world, practical problems often can be solved in multiple ways. Provide one solution to each of the following problems using available resources, such as articles on the Web or in print, blogs, podcasts, videos, television, user guides, other individuals, and electronics and computer stores. You may need to use multiple resources to obtain an answer. Present your solutions in the form requested by your instructor (brief report, presentation, discussion, or other means).

1. **Missing Font** A coworker has sent you a document that was created in Microsoft Word. She asks you to format the heading of the document with a specific font; however, the font name does not appear in your list of fonts. What steps will you take to retrieve the font?
2. **Incorrect File Format** You have been working from your home office creating your company's annual report in Microsoft Word. Upon attempting to open the annual report on a computer at your company's office, an error message is displayed stating that the file format cannot be recognized. What might have caused this?
3. **Insufficient Permission** When reviewing a document in your company's document management system, you attempt to correct a typographical error for the next person who views the file. The document management system prohibits this action and informs you that you do not have the proper permission. What will you do to resolve this problem?
4. **Software Activation Required** Your company has purchased a new netbook to allow you to work from home. After using the computer for about one month, Windows informs you that it must be activated to continue functioning. Why is this happening, and what are your next steps?
5. **Trial Version Expired** New job responsibilities require that you use Adobe Photoshop to create a new company logo. Your boss has been unable to purchase the latest version of the software for you, and recommends that you download and install the trial version until she is able to purchase the software. The trial period now has expired and you are unable to use the program. How might you be able to continue using the software?

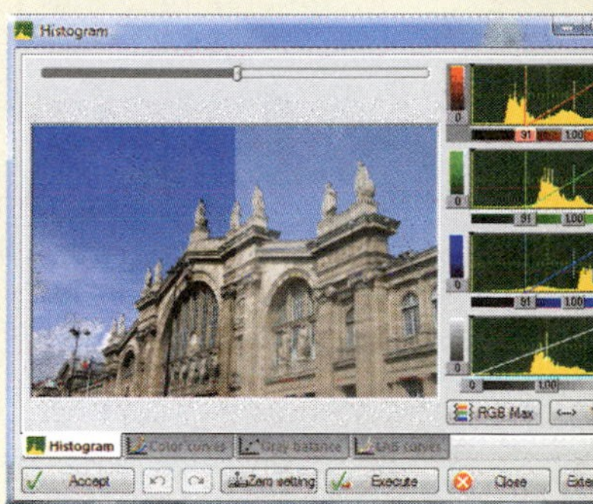

6. **Web-Based Training Difficulties** You have signed up for Web-based training that is designed to teach you how to use your company's new accounting system. During your training, you notice that the Web-based training Web site is not keeping track of your progress. Consequently, you have to start from the beginning of the training program each time you log in to the Web site. What might be causing this?
7. **Installation Media Required** Each time you start Microsoft Excel and attempt to use one of its advanced features, a dialog box appears asking you to insert the installation disc. You are unable to locate the installation disc. What are your next steps so that you can use the advanced features of Microsoft Excel?

Collaboration

8. **Computers in Construction** As a student in a drafting class, your instructor has challenged you to design your dream home by using application software wherever possible. Form a team of three people that will determine how to accomplish this objective. One team member should compare and contrast two programs that can be used to create a two-dimensional floor plan, another team member should compare and contrast two computer-aided design programs that can create a more detailed design of the house, and the third team member should compare and contrast two programs that can assist with other aspects of the design process such as landscaping and interior design.

STUDENT ASSIGNMENTS

Learn How To

The Learn How To activities step you through fundamental technology skills when using a computer. The Learn How To exercises enable you to become more proficient with these skills.

Premium Activity: To relate this Learn How To activity to your everyday life, see a visual demonstration of the activity, and complete a short assessment, visit the Computer Concepts CourseMate Web site at www.cengagebrain.com and then navigate to the Chapter 3 Learn How To resource for this book.

Learn How To 1: Save a File in Application Software

When you use application software, usually you either will create a new file or modify an existing file. If you turn off your computer or lose electrical power while working on the file, the file will not be retained. In order to retain the file, you must save it.

To save a new file, you must complete several tasks:

1. Initiate an action indicating you want to save the file, such as selecting Save on the File menu.
2. Designate where the file should be stored. This includes identifying both the device (such as drive C) and the folder or library.
3. Specify the name of the file.
4. Click the Save button to save the file.

Tasks 2 through 4 normally can be completed using a dialog box such as the one shown in Figure 3-48.

If you close a program prior to saving a new or modified file, the program may display a dialog box asking if you want to save the file. If you click the Yes button, a modified file will be saved using the same file name in the same location. Saving a new file requires that you complete tasks 2 through 4.

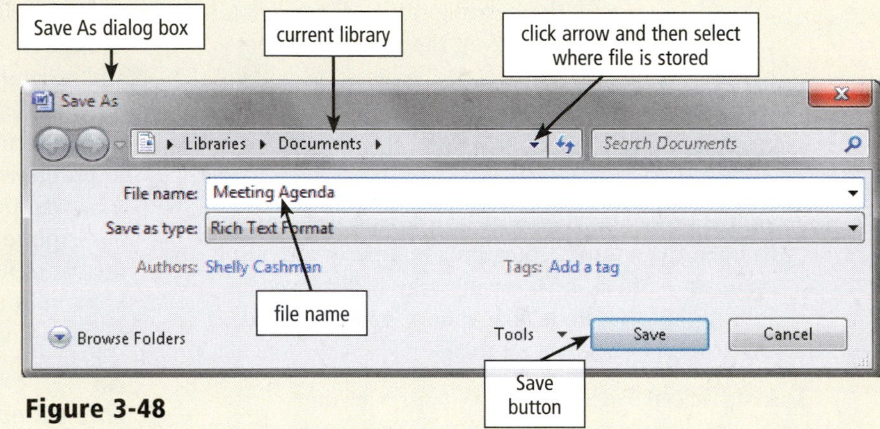

Figure 3-48

Exercise

1a. Start the WordPad program from the Accessories list in the All Programs list. Type `Saving a file is the best insurance against losing work.`

1b. Click the Save button on the Quick Access Toolbar. What dialog box is displayed? Where will the file be saved? What is the default file name? If you wanted to save the file on the desktop, what would you do? Click the Cancel button in the dialog box. Submit your answers to your instructor.

1c. Click the Close button in the WordPad window. What happened? Click the Yes button in the WordPad dialog box. What happened? Connect a USB flash drive to one of the computer's USB ports. Select the USB flash drive as the location for saving the file. Save the file with the name, Chapter 3 Learn How To 1. What happened? Submit your answers to your instructor.

Learn How To 2: Install and Uninstall Application Software

When you purchase application software, you must install the software on the computer where you want to run it. The exact installation process varies with each program, but generally you must complete the following steps:

1. Insert the optical disc containing the application software into a drive.
2. The opening window will appear. If the optical disc contains more than one program, choose the program you want to install. Click the Continue or Next button.
3. Some file extractions will occur and then an Install Wizard will begin. You normally must accomplish the following steps by completing the directions within the wizard:
   a. Accept the terms of the license agreement.
   b. Identify where on your computer the software will be stored. The software usually selects a default location on drive C, and you normally will accept the default location.
   c. Select any default options for the software.
   d. Click a button to install the software.
4. A Welcome/Help screen often will be displayed. Click a button to finish the installation process.

At some point, you may want to remove software. Most software includes an uninstall program that will remove the program and all its software components. To uninstall a program, complete the following steps:

1. Click the Start button on the Windows taskbar.
2. Click Control Panel on the Start menu.

Learn How To

3. Click 'Uninstall a program' to open the Programs and Features window (Figure 3-49).
4. Select the program that you wish to remove. In Figure 3-49, Adobe Acrobat Professional is selected as the program to remove.
5. Click the Uninstall/Change button.
6. A dialog box will be displayed informing you that the software is being prepared for uninstall. You then will be informed that the process you are following will remove the program. You will be asked if you want to continue.

To uninstall the program, click the Yes button. The program will be removed from the computer.

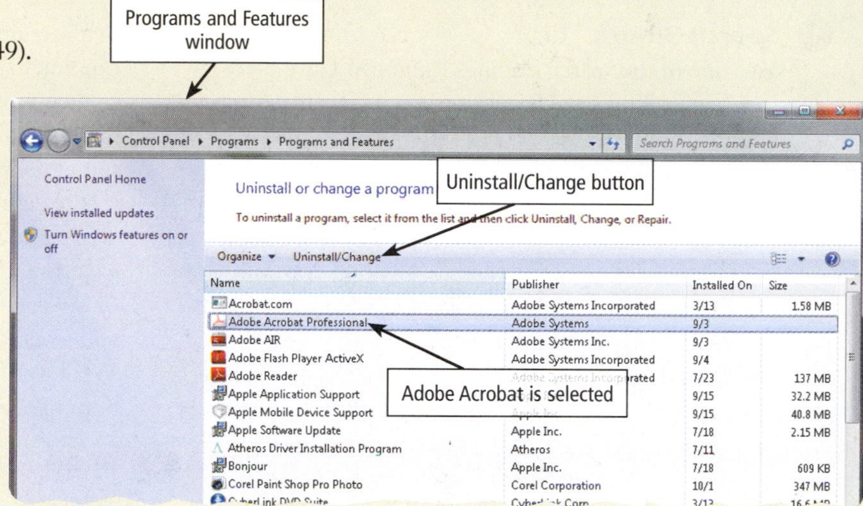

Figure 3-49

Exercises

1. Optional: Insert the optical disc containing the software you want to install into a drive and follow the instructions for installing the software. **Warning: If you are using a computer other than your own, particularly in a school laboratory, do not perform this exercise unless you have specific permission from your instructor.**
2. Optional: Follow the steps above to uninstall software you want to remove. Be aware that if you uninstall software, the software will not be available for use until you reinstall it. **Warning: If you are using a computer other than your own, particularly in a school laboratory, do not perform this exercise unless you have specific permission from your instructor.**

Learn How To 3: Zip/Compress a File

When you zip or compress one or more files in Windows, it attempts to shrink the file size(s) by reducing the amount of unneeded space. Compressing a file is particularly useful when you attach files to an e-mail message and wish to keep the file size as small as possible. It also is useful when you compress multiple files simultaneously, because Windows compresses the multiple files into a single file. You can compress a file or folder by completing the following steps:

1. Locate the file(s) or folder(s) you want to compress. If the files or folders you wish to compress are located in multiple locations, it might be helpful to first move them so that they are in a single location.
2. Select the file(s) or folder(s) you would like to compress. If you are selecting multiple files or folders, click the first one and then hold down the CTRL key while you select the remaining files and/or folders. Once you are finished making your selections, release the CTRL key.
3. Right-click the selection to display a shortcut menu, point to Send to on the shortcut menu to display the Send to submenu (Figure 3-50), and then click Compressed (zipped) folder to create the compressed folder.
4. If necessary, type a new name for the compressed folder and then press the ENTER key.

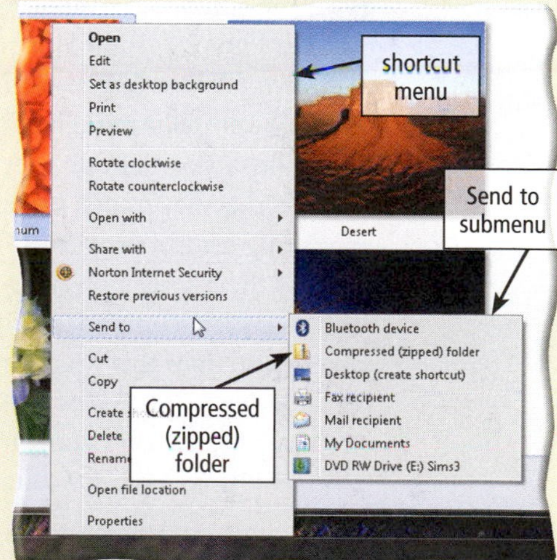

Figure 3-50

Exercise

1. To better organize your hard disk, you decide to compress files you rarely use, but would like to keep as a backup. Click the Start button to display the Start menu, click Pictures to display the Pictures library, and then double-click the Sample Pictures folder to display sample pictures included with Windows 7. Select three pictures and compress them into one compressed folder. Use your first initial and last name as the name of the new compressed folder and then e-mail the folder to your instructor.

Web Research

The Web Research exercises broaden your understanding of the chapter concepts by presenting questions that require you to search the Web for answers.

1 Search Sleuth

Use one of the search engines listed in Figure 2-10 in Chapter 2 on page 85 or your own favorite search engine to find the answers to the following questions. Copy and paste the Web address from the Web page where you found the answer. Some questions may have more than one answer. If required, submit your answers to your instructor. (1) What company did Bruce Artwick form in 1977, and what game did it license to Microsoft in 1982? (2) In what year did the United States Department of Revenue first provide tax forms and booklets in Adobe PDF format on its Web site? (3) What is the latest security incident listed on the United States Computer Emergency Readiness Team (US-CERT) Web site? (4) What is the name of the sans serif font the German Bauhaus movement developed in 1928? (5) What United States president's speech did Peter Norvig turn into a lighthearted PowerPoint presentation?

2 Green Computing

A typical desktop computer and 17-inch monitor that always are turned on release 750 pounds of carbon dioxide in one year, which is the same amount of carbon dioxide released by a car driven 820 miles. Power management software helps conserve a computer's electricity consumption while maintaining acceptable performance. The programs determine when a computer is inactive and, in turn, power down the computer. Use one of the search engines listed in Figure 2-10 in Chapter 2 on page 85 or your own favorite search engine to find information about power management software. What average return-on-investment do they promise? What features do they have, such as generating reports and exempting critical programs from powering down? What is their cost? Powering down the computer stresses critical components, such as the CPU and memory, so does this practice actually result in more waste because these parts must be replaced? Write a report summarizing your findings, and include a table of links to Web sites that you viewed.

3 Social Networking

Career-minded professionals have turned to LinkedIn as a resource for online networking. The more than 45 million registered users, who represent each of the FORTUNE 500 companies, create public profiles that recruiters scour in search of new talent. Users can link to work contacts who, in turn, give access to their work contacts. Visit the LinkedIn Web site (linkedin.com), click the What is LinkedIn? link at the top of the page, and then read the information about reconnecting with current and former colleagues and classmates, job hunting, and obtaining advice from experts. Click the LinkedIn Jobs link at the bottom of the page, type a keyword describing the type of job you would like to have, and then browse the listings. What tips for finding jobs does LinkedIn provide? Summarize the listings and job information you read.

4 Blogs

Vehicle buyers know that the Internet provides a wealth of information that helps direct them toward the best vehicle for their needs. Those consumers who research blogs can obtain price, safety, performance, and maintenance facts and then employ savvy negotiation techniques that help them make the purchase confidently. Visit several automotive blogs, including those from Popular Mechanics (popularmechanics.com/blogs/automotive_news), Autoblog (autoblog.com), Autoblog Green (autobloggreen.com), Autopia (blog.wired.com/cars), and Ask Patty — Car Advice for Women (caradvice.askpatty.com). What new hybrid, luxury, and high-performance vehicles are profiled? Which are promoted as being environmentally friendly? Write a report summarizing the vehicle information you read.

5 Ethics in Action

A hacker is someone who tries to access a computer or network illegally. Although hacking activity sometimes is a harmless prank, at times it causes extensive damage. Some hackers say their activities allow them to test their skills. Others say their activities are a form of civil disobedience that forces companies to make their products more secure. View online sites such as The Ethical Hacker Network (ethicalhacker.net) that provide information about when hackers provide some benefit to the Internet society. Write a report summarizing your findings, and include a table of links to Web sites that provide additional details.

Critical Thinking

The Critical Thinking exercises challenge your assessment and decision-making skills by presenting real-world situations associated with the chapter concepts. The Collaboration exercise should be completed with a team.

To evaluate the situations below, use personal experiences and available resources such as articles on the Web or in print, blogs, podcasts, videos, television, user guides, other individuals, and electronics and computer stores. You may need to use multiple resources to form conclusions and make recommendations.

1. **Class Discussion — Selecting a Spreadsheet Program** Your manager at Dean's Office Supply Outlet intends to choose a spreadsheet program that the entire company will use. He prefers to learn about software using trade books — written textbooks that explain the features of a program and how to use it — rather than using online Help or tutorials. Evaluate the spreadsheet trade books available in online bookstores. Visit an online bookstore and other Web sites that sell books to evaluate the spreadsheet trade books for Microsoft Excel, Lotus, Quattro Pro, and StarOffice Calc. Discuss how difficult it would be to learn each program using the trade books at hand. Include in your discussion which trade book you think is the best. Also discuss which program you would buy if you were going to purchase software solely on the basis of the related trade books. Include the reasons for your recommendation.

2. **Class Presentation — Entertainment Software Recommendations** Karl's Game Den sells new and used computer video games. Karl recently purchased a large quantity of children's games; however, they are not selling as he expected. You recently read that 60 percent of entertainment software purchases are made by males, and the average age of frequent purchasers is 35. You suggest that Karl may be selling to the wrong demographic. Use the Web and/or print media to evaluate the top five selling games in the United States. Determine if males and females favor different types of software, and if software developers adapt their products accordingly. Based on your findings, present your recommendation on what types of games and how many Karl should stock. Discuss the importance of why software developers should modify educational/entertainment software to meet the interests of different groups.

3. **Research — Application Software Comparison** Web applications are becoming increasingly popular, and some people prefer the convenience of using a Web application instead of application software installed on their computer. For example, some prefer to use Google Docs (a Web application) to Microsoft Word. Your boss notices this trend, and asks you whether it will benefit the company to use Web applications instead of application software. Compare application software installed on your computer with a comparable Web application. Are any security risks associated with using the application software? How do the features compare between a Web application and the application software? Would you recommend using a Web application to application software? Why?

Collaboration

4. **Educational Software Effectiveness** The new superintendent of Lisle Elementary School District 205 has recommended that educational software play a major role in the learning process at every grade level. In her presentation to the school board, she claimed that educational software is available for a wide variety of skills and subjects. She also indicated that educational software enables students to learn at their own pace, shows infinite patience, and usually offers an entertaining approach. The president of the school board is not so sure. Unlike human instructors, educational software often does not recognize unique problems, fails to address individual goals, and provides limited feedback. Form a three-member team and investigate the use of educational software. Each member of your team should visit a software vendor's Web site or an educational cooperative's Web site, and list the advantages and disadvantages of using educational software. Select a program on the Web or from your school's education department library and use it. Note the subject being taught, the audience to which the software is directed, the approach used, and any special features. Would you recommend the program you chose? Why or why not? Be sure to consider such factors as initial cost, upgrade costs, online Help, and technical support in your recommendation. Then, meet with your team, discuss your findings, prepare a presentation, and share it with your class.

Digital Communications

DIGITAL COMMUNICATIONS, which factor largely in many people's personal and business lives, include any transmission of information from one computer or mobile device to another (Figure 1). This feature covers many forms of digital communications: e-mail; text messaging, instant messaging, and picture/video messaging; digital voice communications; blogs and wikis; online social networks, chat rooms, and Web conferences; and content sharing.

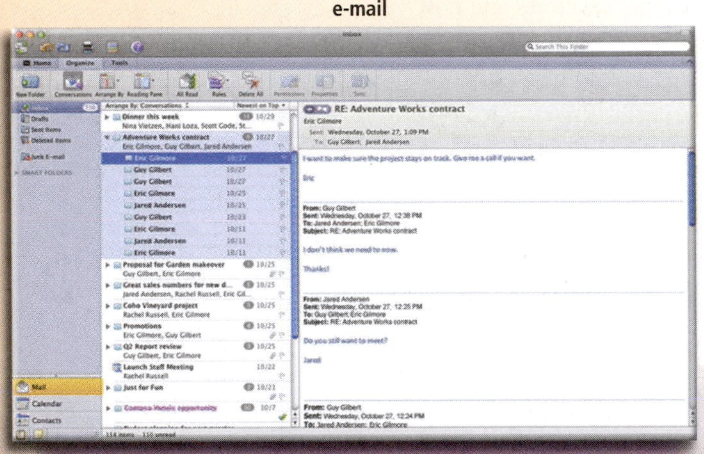

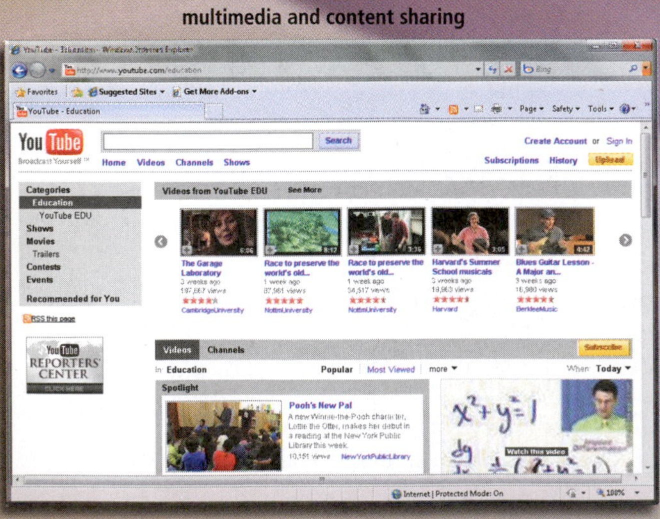

Figure 1 People use a variety of methods in their personal and business lives to engage in digital communications.

With the Internet, cell phone networks, and other wireless networks increasing in size and speed, digital communications have become more and more prevalent. The most common devices used to communicate digitally are desktop computers, mobile computers, smart phones, and other mobile devices.

Successful use of digital communications involves selecting both the proper communications device and the proper mode of communication for a given situation. For example, under what circumstances might sending a text message from a smart phone be more appropriate than sending an e-mail message from a desktop computer? The answer to this question also may depend on whether the situation involves personal or business communications. Each computer or mobile device and communications method has advantages and disadvantages that you should consider.

The following pages describe how people use different types of digital communications in their personal and business lives to enhance collaboration and increase productivity. The final section of the feature includes an example of how you might use digital communications.

digital voice communications

video messaging with smart phone

mobile computer

blog

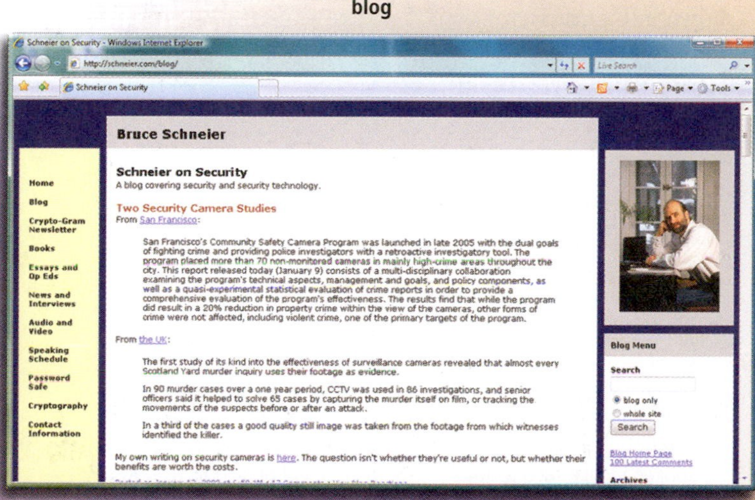

online social network

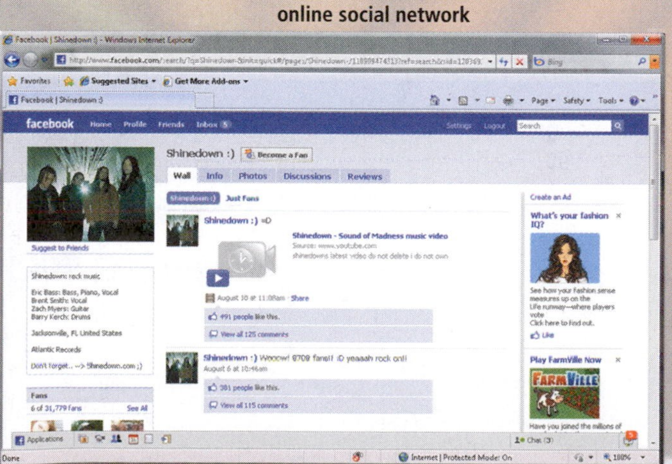

wiki

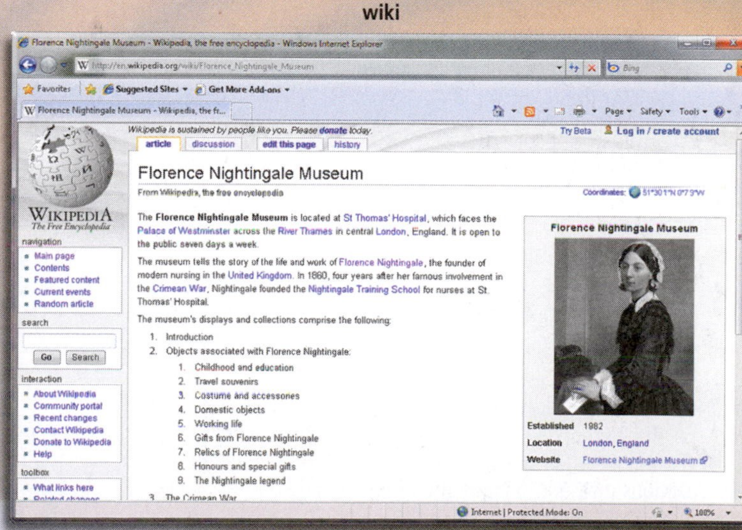

E-Mail

E-mail is the transmission of messages and files via a computer network. E-mail quickly has become one of the more widely used forms of digital communications. Although e-mail is primarily a text-based form of digital communications, it also can be used to share photos, videos, and other types of files by attaching files to e-mail messages.

E-Mail: The Personal Perspective

With a computer or mobile device connected to the Internet, you can use e-mail to keep in contact with friends, family, stores, companies, schools, and government agencies. Some people maintain several different e-mail addresses for use in different situations. Figure 2 lists some advantages, disadvantages, and good practices of personal e-mail use. Some e-mail programs are application programs that run on your computer, while others are Web applications (shown in Figure 3).

Personal E-Mail Use

Advantages

- One of the most preferred methods of online communications.
- Available on nearly any computer or mobile device with Internet access.
- Send files, called attachments, via e-mail messages to others.
- Fast, reliable, and proven technology.
- Allows messages to be sent anywhere free of charge or inexpensively.
- Allows communications with more than one person at a time.
- Provides an electronic forum for communications in which the originator has time to consider a thought before it is sent or spoken, unlike face-to-face meetings or telephone conversations.

Disadvantages

- Number of messages received can become overwhelming and unmanageable.
- Spam can overwhelm your e-mail inbox.
- Message tone can be misunderstood.
- Many computer viruses and other malicious programs are transmitted via e-mail messages.

Good practices

- Keep messages as short as possible.
- Check with the recipient before sending attachments, especially large attachments.
- Respond to messages promptly.
- Use a reputable Internet access provider that uses a spam filter, which is a program that detects and removes spam, and use an e-mail program that includes a spam filter.
- Never respond to unsolicited advertisements or spam.
- Informal language and shortcuts are acceptable when communicating with friends and family (e.g., suitable to use HRU? as a shortcut for How are you?).
- Always include a Subject line.
- Always reread your message and edit it before sending it.
- When replying to questions or comments included with a previous message, include the original message.

Figure 2 Personal e-mail remains one of the more popular reasons to use the Internet.

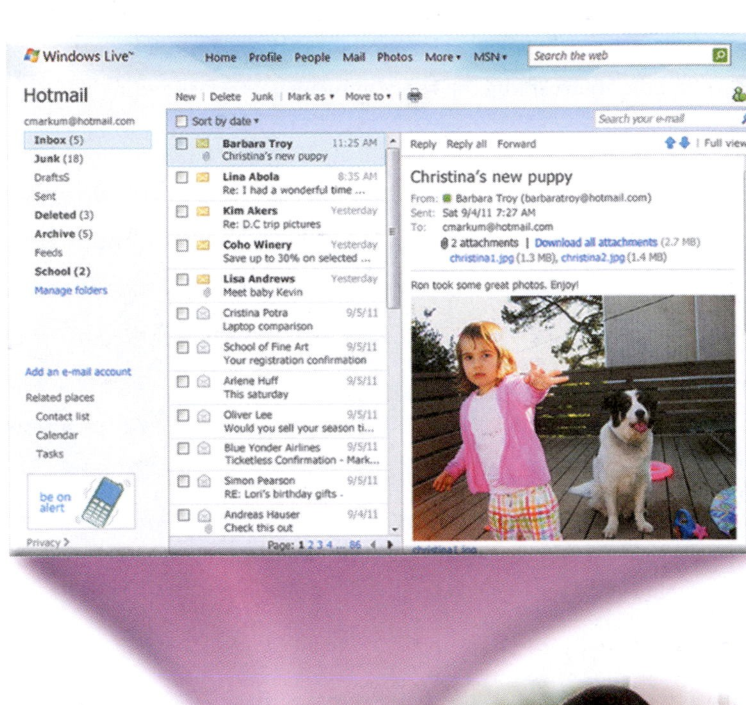

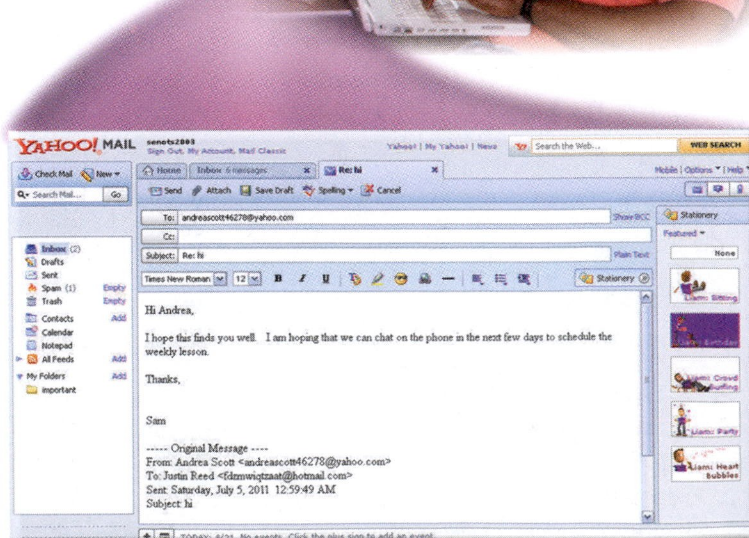

Figure 3 Many home users work with e-mail Web applications.

E-Mail: The Business Perspective

Nearly all businesses use e-mail for internal communications among employees and external communications with customers and business partners. E-mail gradually has replaced typed and copied memos, letters, and faxes while increasing the reliability, cost effectiveness, and speed of the communications. Figure 4 indicates some advantages, disadvantages, and good practices of e-mail use in business. Many of the notes listed in Figure 2 also apply to e-mail communications in business. Figure 5 shows an example of the inbox of a business e-mail program user and an example of an appropriate business e-mail message.

E-Mail Use in Business

Advantages

- Easily archive, or store long-term, all e-mail messages sent from or received by the business.
- Generally can guarantee delivery of any e-mail message that is sent within the business.
- A replacement for memos, letters, faxes, and other internal and external business communications when permitted by company policy.
- Communicate with someone who is not available at the time you need to communicate.

Disadvantages

- Volume of e-mail messages often becomes overwhelming.
- Often leads to overcommunication, which can result in important information being lost because it is ignored.
- Sometimes leads to avoidance of personal contact, such as a meeting or telephone call.

Good practices

- Because most companies archive, or save, all e-mail messages, use e-mail when you want a permanent record of a communication.
- Understand your company's e-mail policies. Many companies prohibit sending personal e-mail messages from a business computer.
- Never include any language that would be considered inappropriate in a business environment.
- Check your e-mail inbox regularly.
- Follow your company's or department's guidelines for formatting messages and including contact information and any appropriate disclaimers.
- In most cases, it is appropriate to send larger attachments in business e-mail messages as compared to those permissible in personal messages.
- Avoid sending messages to many people simultaneously or replying to large groups of people. For example, it is almost always inappropriate to send a message to the entire company.
- Avoid using e-mail messages when the content involves sensitive issues, such as a negotiation, legal matter, or employee review.
- When you need to know that the recipient has read your e-mail message, use the return receipt feature of your e-mail program to receive automatic notification as soon as the message is read.

Figure 4 Most businesses provide written policies and guidelines regarding use of e-mail programs.

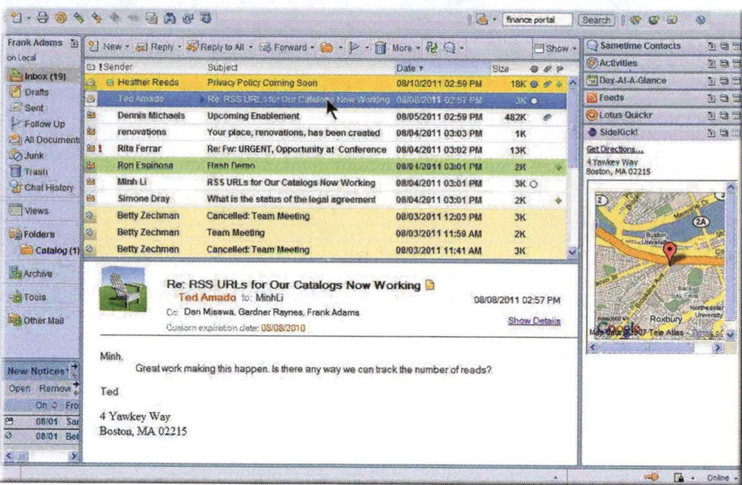

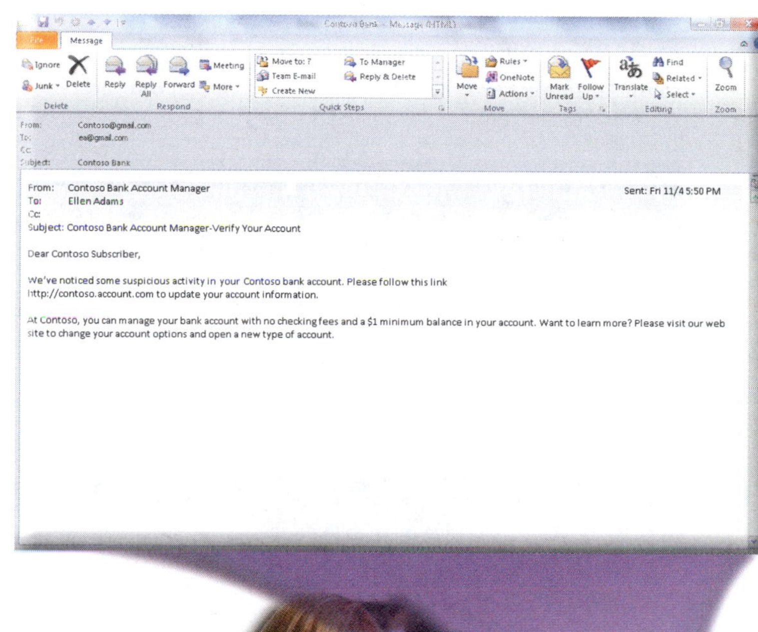

Figure 5 Businesses often use more sophisticated e-mail programs than do home users.

Text Messaging, Instant Messaging, and Picture/Video Messaging

Text messaging, instant messaging, and picture/video messaging allow you to exchange short messages and small multimedia files with other online users. Text messaging is a wireless messaging service that allows users to send and receive short notes on a smart phone or other mobile device. Instant messaging is a real-time Internet communications service that notifies a user when one or more people are online and allows the user to exchange messages or files or join a private chat room with those people. Picture messaging is a wireless messaging service that allows users to send and receive photos and sound files, as well as short text messages, to and from a mobile device or computer. Video messaging is a wireless messaging service that allows users to send and receive short video clips, usually up to 30 seconds, in addition to all picture messaging services.

Text Messaging, Instant Messaging, and Picture/Video Messaging: The Personal Perspective

Text messaging, instant messaging, and picture/video messaging typically are used on smart phones. Instant messaging often is used on desktop and notebook computers. Virtually instantaneous communication is possible with the various forms of messaging. Figure 6 indicates some advantages, disadvantages, and good practices of using text messaging, instant messaging, and picture/video messaging in your personal life. Figure 7 shows some examples of people using messaging.

Personal Text Messaging, Instant Messaging, and Picture/Video Messaging Use

Advantages
- Virtually instantaneous form of digital communications.
- Fast, reliable, and popular method of digital communications.
- Useful when you prefer an immediate response from the recipient.
- Allows you to carry on several conversations at any time.

Disadvantages
- Can be addictive in nature.
- Receiving a constant stream of messages can be distracting.
- May be very expensive on mobile devices.
- Text messaging: Overuse may result in repetitive stress injuries (RSIs).

Good practices
- Know the person with whom you are exchanging messages.
- Keep in mind that any text, picture, or video you send can be sent to others by the recipient.
- When messaging with a new contact, do not share personal information quickly.
- Always reread your text messages and preview your pictures and videos before you send them.
- Respect the status of others when they indicate they are busy.
- Instant messaging: If the program allows you to indicate your status to others, such as "Busy" or "Do not disturb," use these indicators to let others know when you are unavailable.
- Picture/video messaging: When sending picture/video messages, make sure the content is appropriate.

Figure 6 People use various types of messaging for different reasons. (Where noted, some bullet points apply only to particular technologies.)

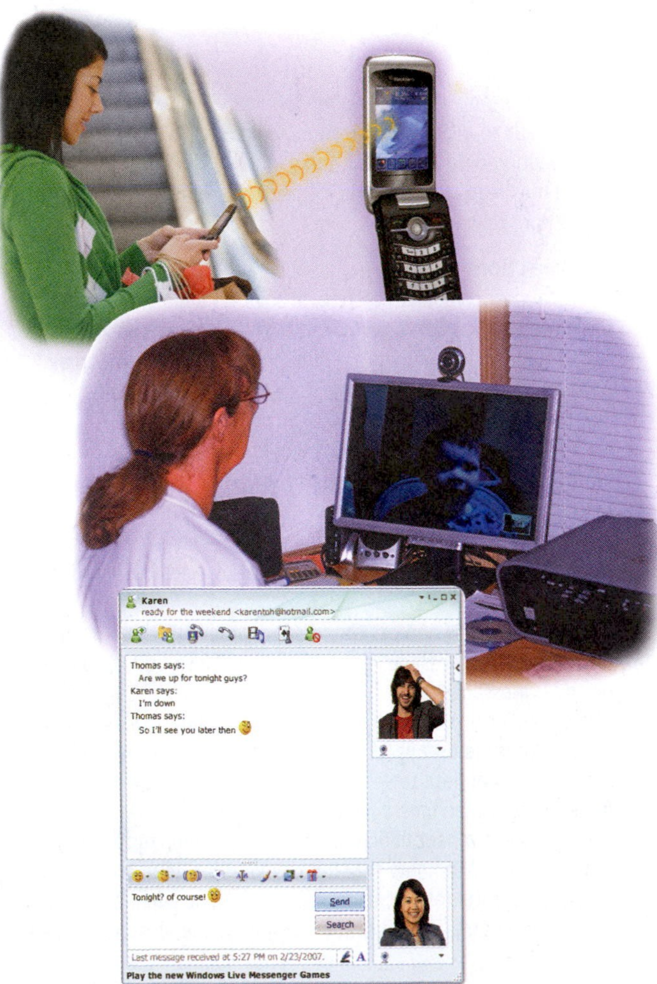

Figure 7 Many people interact with messaging software both at home and while away from home or work.

Text Messaging, Instant Messaging, and Picture/Video Messaging: The Business Perspective

Businesses typically use more secure, feature-rich messaging programs that allow all messages to be archived. Archiving of messages often is required by law and allows old messages to be available for future reference. Messaging allows colleagues to collaborate, or work together, online. Figure 8 indicates some advantages, disadvantages, and good practices of text messaging, instant messaging, and picture/video messaging use in business. Many of the notes listed in Figure 6 also apply to the various forms of messaging in business. Figure 9 shows an example of business-level instant messaging software and video messaging at job sites.

Text Messaging, Instant Messaging, and Picture/Video Messaging Use in Business

Advantages

- When used properly, greatly increases collaboration and communications because users have instantaneous access to each other.
- All messages can be archived for retrieval at a later date or for meeting legal requirements.
- Immediate contact with customers when allowed by company policy and agreed to by the customer.
- Collaboration with geographically separated colleagues.
- Instant messaging: Some programs allow conferences of several people at one time, eliminating the need for scheduling meeting rooms or conference calls.
- Picture/video messaging: Provides instant views of remote locations, such as work sites or company assets.

Disadvantages

- Despite policies, business conversations often lead to personal conversations.
- Often leads to over-reliance on simply messaging a colleague for an answer to a question rather than determining the answer on your own.
- Can lead to a significant decline in important face-to-face contact with coworkers, customers, and business partners.
- Instant messaging: Because all messages can be archived, it can lead to difficult situations when inappropriate content is shared.

Good practices

- When beginning a messaging conversation, make your point quickly and keep messages concise.
- Separate your personal messaging habits from your business messaging habits, avoiding use of emoticons and shortcuts, such as "brb" as a shortcut for "Be right back."
- Use proper spelling, grammar, and punctuation, and avoid colloquialisms.
- Be aware of cultural differences that might arise during casual conversations.
- Acknowledge the end of a messaging conversation.
- Follow your company's policies regarding the type of information that can be conveyed in a message and with whom you may engage in messaging.
- Always try to meet or telephone a person to introduce yourself before sending a first message to him or her.
- Review all messages you send to colleagues to make sure that the contents are appropriate for the workplace.

Figure 8 Businesses use a variety of messaging methods to allow employees to collaborate in a timely and secure manner. (Where noted, some bullet points apply only to particular technologies.)

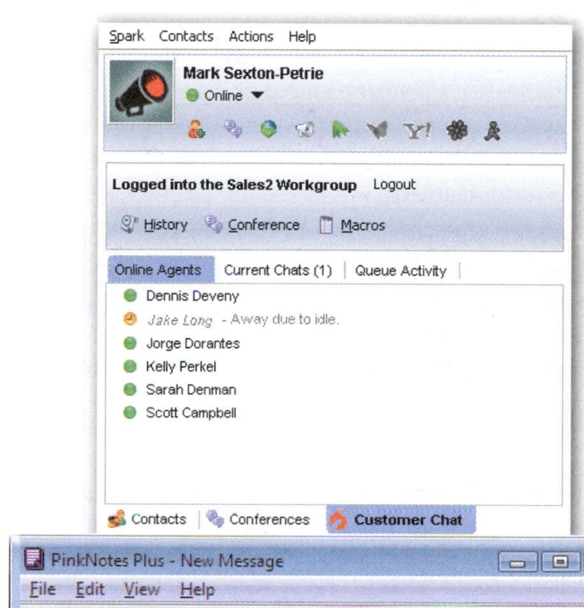

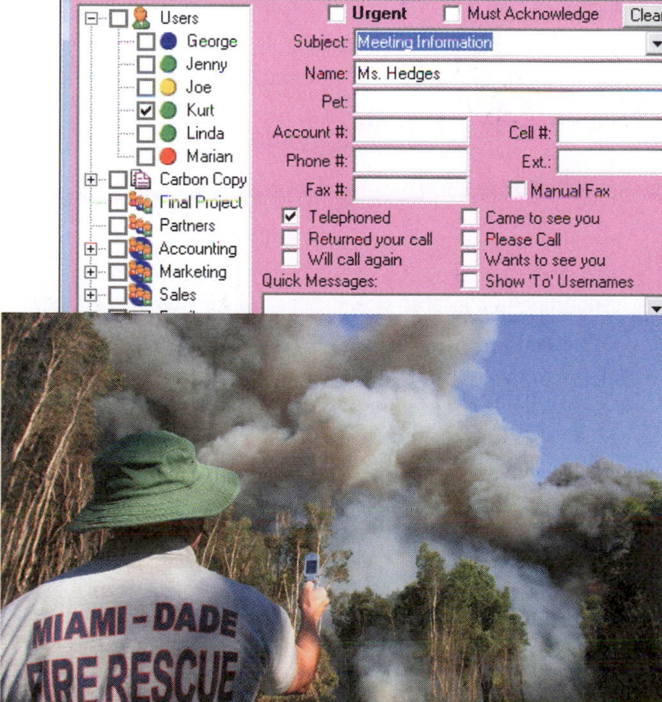

Figure 9 Business users employ instant messaging and video messaging to communicate ideas and multimedia information quickly.

Digital Voice Communications

Digital voice communications includes the use of cell phones, smart phones, and VoIP (Voice over IP). VoIP is a technology that allows users to speak to other users via the Internet. VoIP can be used as a replacement for the traditional telephone at work or in the home.

Digital Voice Communications: The Personal Perspective

With more than 200 million in use in the United States, cell phones are a primary source of digital voice communications. Cell phones can act as a suitable replacement for the traditional, wired, public switched telephone network. Smart phones offer features such as e-mail, text messaging, picture/video messaging, and playing or streaming multimedia.

Figure 10 indicates some advantages, disadvantages, and good practices of digital voice communications in your personal life. Figure 11 shows some examples of digital voice communications, including visual voice mail, which is a service that automatically translates voice mail into text messages or allows you to download voice messages to your smart phone and listen to them at your convenience.

Personal Digital Voice Communications Use

Advantages

- Increase productivity through greater and more timely communications.
- Both cell phones and VoIP offer more choice in providers than the public switched telephone network.
- Cell phones: Widespread coverage of cell phone networks provides voice communications nearly everywhere in the United States.
- Cell phones: Have been instrumental in saving lives in emergency situations.
- VoIP: Often offers free features, such as voice mail, unlimited in-country long distance calling, three-way calling, and call forwarding.
- VoIP: Typically is less expensive for both local and long distance calls than the public switched telephone network.

Disadvantages

- Cell phones: In some situations, such as while driving a car, can contribute to accidents.
- VoIP: Not as strictly regulated as the public switched telephone network, meaning that the quality of service may be lower.
- With many VoIP providers and some cell phone providers, connecting to a local service, such as 911 for emergencies, may be difficult or cumbersome.

Good practices

- Cell phones: Use a headset if you must use a cell phone while driving. Be aware of laws in your area that prohibit or limit cell phone use while driving.
- Cell phones: When using in public, be mindful of and courteous to those around you.
- Cell phones: Be aware of rules or policies at some locations, such as schools, medical facilities, or religious facilities.
- Cell phones: In public locations, use an alternative ring method, such as a vibration setting, to avoid interrupting others.

Figure 10 Cell phones and other forms of digital voice communications have become an essential means of communications throughout the world. (Where noted, some bullet points apply only to particular technologies.)

Figure 11 People use cell phones, VoIP, and visual voice mail in their everyday lives for contact with friends and family.

Digital Voice Communications: The Business Perspective

Businesses embrace digital voice communications because of increased collaboration and productivity, cost savings, and mobility. Figure 12 lists many of the advantages, disadvantages, and good practices of digital voice communications use in business. Many of the notes listed in Figure 10 also apply to the various forms of digital voice communications in business. Figure 13 shows an example of a simple VoIP system.

Digital Voice Communications Use in Business

Advantages

- Increased communications and collaboration can result in increased productivity and cost savings.
- Cell phones: Ability to contact a person almost anywhere at any time.
- VoIP: With some systems, employees can listen to and manage their voice messages on their personal computer.
- VoIP: A computer is not necessary to use a VoIP system.
- VoIP: Allows large companies to consolidate communications between geographically diverse locations.
- VoIP: Implement as an alternative to the public switched telephone network because VoIP allows businesses to use their existing network more efficiently and provides more features than the public switched telephone network.

Disadvantages

- With many VoIP providers and some cell phone providers, connecting to a local service, such as 911 for emergencies, may be difficult or cumbersome.
- The quality of calls may change at times due to excessive network usage.
- Cell phones: Misuse often leads to rude behavior or disruption of meetings.
- Cell phones: Using a cell phone provided by an employer for personal calls may have undesirable tax consequences.
- VoIP: Large companies may find it expensive and difficult to manage.
- VoIP: Unlike a public switched telephone network, many VoIP systems and equipment will not function during a power outage.

Good practices

- Cell phones: Follow company policy regarding the use for business communications. Limit personal calls on your cell phone during business hours.
- Cell phones: Disable the ringer when in meetings or during important discussions.
- Cell phones: Resist the need to answer every call at all times, such as when you are on breaks or when you are not at work.
- Cell phones: Avoid speaking loudly on the phone when walking through others' work areas.
- VoIP: When possible, use a VoIP telephone rather than a cell phone because it generally is less expensive for the company on a per-call basis.

Figure 12 Digital voice communications are used when a more personal form of communications than e-mail or messaging is required in real time. (Where noted, some bullet points apply only to particular technologies.)

Figure 13 VoIP allows businesses to connect their telephone system to their internal network and the Internet for voice telephone calls.

Blogs and Wikis

A **blog** is an informal Web site consisting of time-stamped articles, or posts, in a diary or journal format, usually listed in reverse chronological order. A **wiki** is a collaborative Web site that allows users to create, add to, modify, or delete the Web site content via their Web browser.

Blogs and Wikis: The Personal Perspective

Blog topics often include family life, social life, a personal project, or events during a vacation. You might read and contribute to a wiki regarding classical guitar techniques if your hobbies included playing classical guitar. While blogs can be modified only by the author, a wiki can be authored and edited by any user. Another difference between blogs and wikis is that blog entries typically are not included in search results from search engines, such as Google, while wiki entries are recognized by search engine queries. Figure 14 indicates some advantages, disadvantages, and good practices of using blogs and wikis in your personal life. Figure 15 shows examples of blog and wiki entries.

Personal Blog and Wiki Use

Advantages

- Some blogs and wikis provide secure access so that only a select group of qualified or desired individuals are allowed to read and write entries.
- Blogs: Easy, accessible, and often free method of keeping a group of people informed about events.
- Blogs: Easy way to keep up with an acquaintance or expand your knowledge about political or social points of view.
- Blogs: Often can be read or written using Internet-enabled mobile devices.
- Wikis: Provide free access to concise, almost encyclopedic, information about nearly any topic.

Disadvantages

- Vulnerable to fraudulent or biased entries placed by businesses or special interest groups in an effort to sway public opinion.
- Blogs: Often are biased towards a particular point of view.
- Blogs: Some blogging Web sites are often sources of malicious programs.
- Wikis: Publicly accessible wikis sometimes are vulnerable to vandalism or subject to errors.

Good practices

- Blogs: When writing a blog, be aware that the contents of your blog may be accessible publicly and associated with your identity for a long time.
- Blogs: When reading blogs, be aware of the source of the information and evaluate the credibility of the source.
- Wikis: When performing research using a wiki, check any provided sources and, if possible, check the editorial history of the entries.
- Wikis: If you locate an error, notify the author or editor of the wiki page, or, if possible, edit the page yourself to make the correction.
- Wikis: When possible, contribute your own knowledge to wikis that interest you, being sure to follow the guidelines of the wiki.

Figure 14 While blogs and wikis provide a great deal of information sharing, users and contributors alike should be aware of the risks involved. (Where noted, some bullet points apply only to particular technologies.)

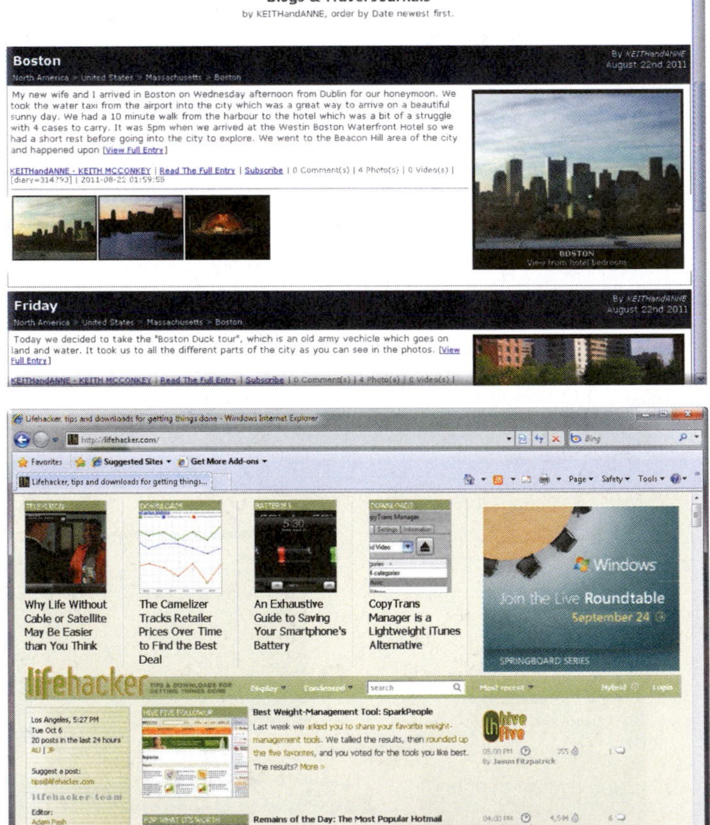

Figure 15 Blogs and wikis allow people to share their knowledge, experience, viewpoints, and personal events on the Internet. People use mobile blogging while away from home or while in interesting locations.

Blogs and Wikis: The Business Perspective

Many businesses use blogs and wikis to share knowledge within the company. One large company claims to maintain more than 300,000 blogs and wikis internally. A key reason that blogs and wikis are so popular in business is that they can be written, read, and searched easily. As the company's resident expert regarding a particular topic, an employee may blog to keep others informed about topics relating to that expertise. A business-oriented wiki may contain a wealth of historical knowledge for a particular department in the company. Figure 16 indicates some advantages, disadvantages, and good practices of using blogs and wikis in business. Many of the notes listed in Figure 14 also apply to using blogs and wikis in business. Figure 17 shows examples of typical business-oriented blog and wiki entries.

Blog and Wiki Use in Business

Advantages

- Provide easy access to gained knowledge and experience.
- Easily can be searched by employees.
- Some may be made available to customers, business partners, or the general public.
- Blogs: Publicly accessible blogs often are used as an effective means to promote products or services.

Disadvantages

- Mistakes, inaccuracies, and inconsistencies in entries can lead to lost productivity and increased costs.
- Internal company blogs and wikis often contain proprietary company information that easily can be leaked to competitors or the press.
- Blogs: When contributing to a blog, some employees become engrossed with capturing every detail of their job.
- Wikis: Information often may become old, or stale, if it is not updated regularly.

Good practices

- Search your company's blogs and wikis for information before telephoning, instant messaging, or e-mailing a colleague with a question.
- If you do not find an answer to a question on your company's blogs or wikis, then contribute to a blog or wiki once you find the answer.
- When contributing to a blog or wiki entry, read your company's policies regarding content, formatting, and style. Some companies employ full-time bloggers and writers who can help you contribute a valuable entry.
- When contributing to a blog or wiki entry, stay on topic and create links within your entry to other related or relevant Web pages, including other blog and wiki entries.
- Blogs: When engaging in personal blogging, do not discredit your employer or potential future employers; many people have lost their jobs as a result of engaging in such behavior.
- Blogs: When engaging in personal blogging, be careful not to divulge proprietary company information.

Figure 16 Business blog and wiki use typically is governed by more guidelines and rules than those for personal blogs and wikis. (Where noted, some bullet points apply only to particular technologies.)

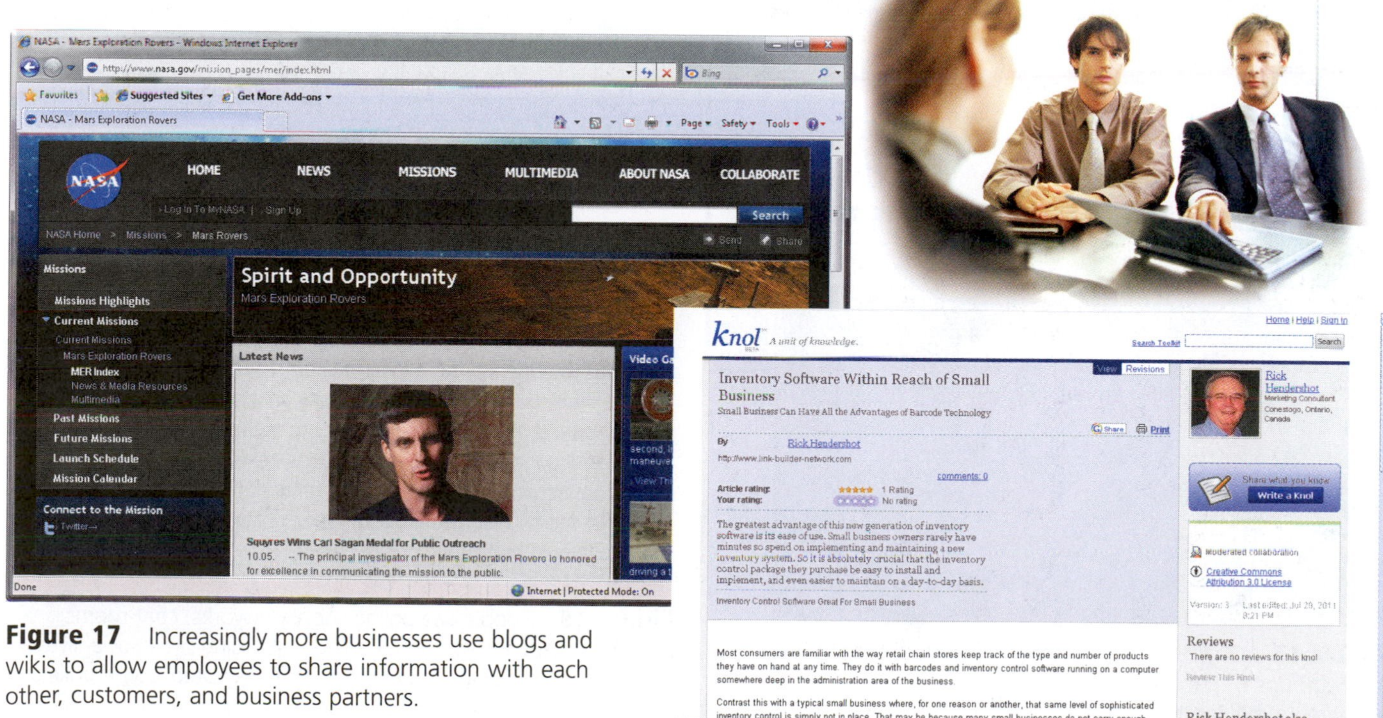

Figure 17 Increasingly more businesses use blogs and wikis to allow employees to share information with each other, customers, and business partners.

Online Social Networks, Chat Rooms, and Web Conferences

An **online social network** is a Web site that encourages members in its online community to share their interest, ideas, stories, photos, music, and videos with other registered users. A **chat room** is a location on the Internet that permits users to chat with one another. A **Web conference** allows two or more people to engage in an online meeting and often allows the attendees to access programs and digital content, such as documents, audio, and video, during the meeting.

Online Social Networks, Chat Rooms, and Web Conferences: The Personal Perspective

The popularity of online social networks such as Facebook continues to skyrocket. Most online social networks allow you to maintain a personal Web site that you can share with other registered users who, after being invited, may view or contribute content to your site. Those invited to your online social network often are known as friends. While chat rooms have decreased in popularity over the years, people often use them for targeted discussions about specific topics. Web conferences often are used by consumers to obtain technical support or assistance from companies and government agencies or in educational settings to engage in online learning. Figure 18 shows an example of an online social network and a virtual chat room.

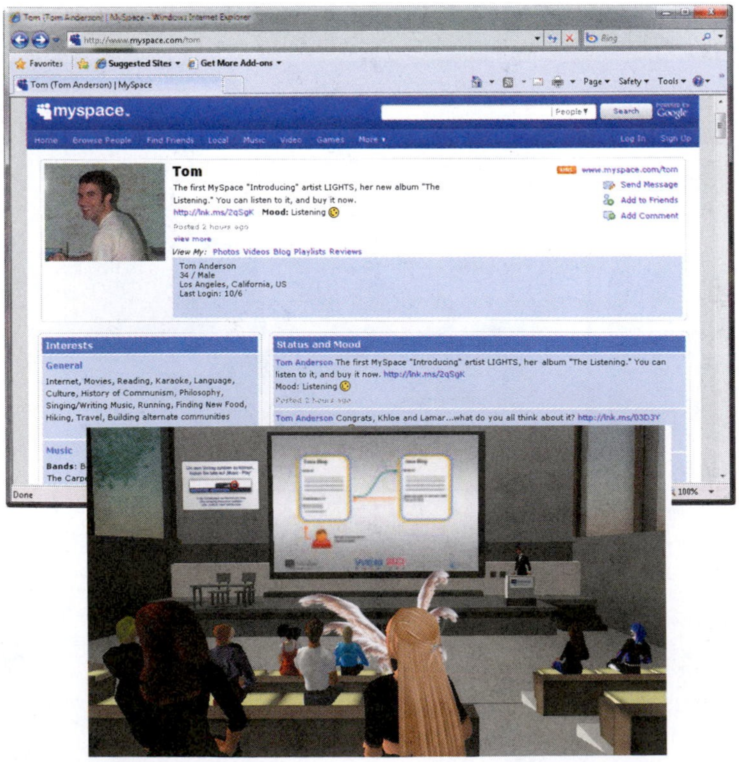

Figure 18 Online social networks and virtual chat rooms allow groups of people with similar interests or lifestyles to enjoy real-time communications.

Figure 19 indicates some advantages, disadvantages, and good practices of using online social networks, chat rooms, and Web conferences in your personal life.

Personal Use of Online Social Networks, Chat Rooms, and Web Conferences

Advantages

- Online social networks/chat rooms: Easily find friends throughout the world with similar interests or traits.
- Online social networks/chat rooms: Can expand your knowledge about political or social points of view.
- Web conferences: Use Web conferencing when offered by a company for technical support issues because the tenor of the interaction is more personal than a telephone call.
- Web conferences: Often effectively provides the necessary communications to avoid a visit to a store location or a visit from a repair technician.

Disadvantages

- Online social networks/chat rooms: Some people are susceptible to overusing these forms of communications in lieu of real, in-person contacts and relationships. Overuse of these forms of communications may lead to addiction.
- Online social networks/chat rooms: People often hide their real identity to lure others into revealing too much personal information.
- Online social networks/chat rooms: Several high-profile incidents occurred in which people engaged in illegal activity using online social networks and chat rooms.

Good practices

- Online social networks: When submitting information, be aware that the information may be accessible publicly and associated with your identity for a long time.
- Online social networks: While many online social networks encourage the practice, do not try to gather too many friends in your social network. Some experts believe that a functional social network is limited to a maximum of 150 people.
- Chat rooms/Web conferences: Be as polite and courteous as you would be to someone in person.

Figure 19 People use online social networks, chat rooms, and Web conferences as a means of extending their social lives beyond their physical surroundings. (Where noted, some bullet points apply only to particular technologies.)

Online Social Networks, Chat Rooms, and Web Conferences: The Business Perspective

Online social networks, chat rooms, and Web conferences allow business users to interact and collaborate as teams. While online social networks have not been as popular as other forms of digital communications in business, their use is showing promise for many companies and groups who use it for business purposes. One company claims to have signed up more than five million business users for its business-oriented online social network. Chat rooms and Web conferences often serve as forums for online meetings. Figure 20 indicates some advantages, disadvantages, and good practices of using online social networks, chat rooms, and Web conferences in business. Many of the notes listed in Figure 6 on page 196 and Figure 19 also apply to these forms of digital communication in business. Figure 21 shows an example of a business-oriented online social network, chat room, and Web conference.

Online Social Network, Chat Room, and Web Conference Use in Business

Advantages

- Online social networks: Encourage people to collaborate with others with whom they typically would not collaborate.
- Online social networks/chat rooms: Often can be accessed using Internet-enabled mobile devices, providing instant collaboration almost anywhere.
- Online social networks/chat rooms: Provide forums for meeting potential customers, employers, and employees.
- Web conferences: Programs often allow application program sharing, which means that all participants can view the contents of one or more participant's computer screen.
- Online social networks/chat rooms: Some are located internally within a company and allow only employees access to the sites.
- Online social networks/chat rooms: Some are subscription-based and allow people to interact freely with others in related fields or industries.

Disadvantages

- Employees often over-rely on these means of online digital communications and do not interact with others in more personal ways.
- Online social networks: Can be cumbersome and expensive to maintain.

Good practices

- When engaging in online social networks, chat rooms, and Web conferences outside of your company, be careful not to divulge proprietary company information.
- Always maintain a professional demeanor. Often, those who use this technology in their personal lives are quick to behave more casually than is appropriate in a business setting.
- Divulge only that information about yourself that is relevant to the reasons you are participating in an online social network or chat room.

Figure 20 Businesses have embraced online social networks, chat rooms, and Web conferences to drive collaboration among geographically separated teams, employees, and other business contacts. (Where noted, some bullet points apply only to particular technologies.)

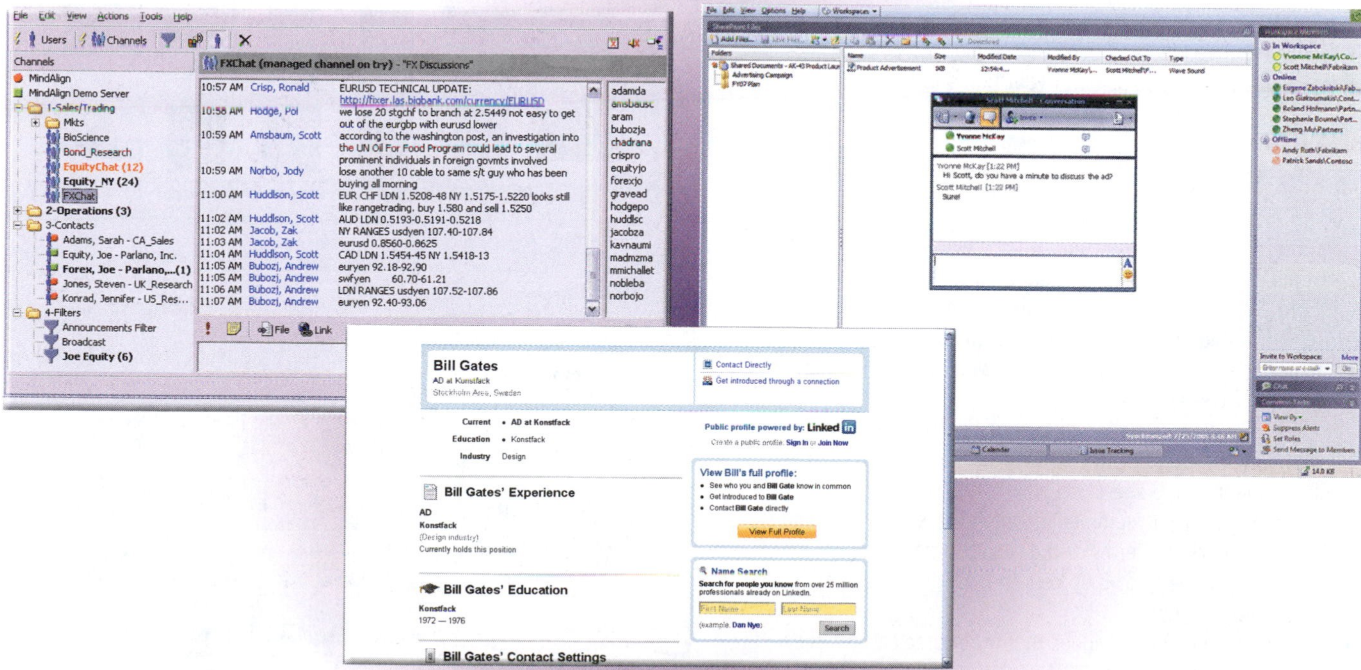

Figure 21 Businesses use online social networks, chat rooms, and Web conferences to allow employees and teams to communicate more effectively.

Content Sharing

Content sharing provides a means by which rich content, such as audio, video, photos, and documents, can be communicated digitally.

Content Sharing: The Personal Perspective

The prolific spread of digital cameras and digital video cameras combined with ever-increasing speeds of home and mobile Internet connections has resulted in the explosive growth of media sharing Web sites, such as YouTube and Flickr. In addition to sharing media, people are sharing documents, spreadsheets, and other content on Web sites. Figure 22 indicates some advantages, disadvantages, and good practices of content sharing in your personal life. Figure 23 shows some examples of a video sharing Web site, a photo sharing group Web site, and a personal photo sharing Web site.

Personal Content Sharing Use

Advantages

- Ability to view broadcasts of events that may not be available through traditional broadcasts in your area.
- Media sharing Web sites provide almost limitless information and entertainment at little or no cost.
- Some services allow you to edit your content or the content of others directly on the site using a Web application.
- View or listen to live broadcasts of sporting events.
- View or listen to news stories.
- Much like online social networks, media sharing Web sites can provide a sense of community to a group of geographically separated individuals.

Disadvantages

- You may find it difficult to locate media and content that interests you.
- When sharing video and photos on a media sharing Web site, you may be giving up some of your rights to the media.
- Many people have been embarrassed by content posted by others to media sharing Web sites.

Good practices

- Before placing your content on a media sharing Web site, make a good effort to edit the content for brevity and clarity. For example, make certain that audio is clear in a video, and use photo editing software to remove red-eye.
- Take advantage of the fact that most media and content sharing Web sites allow you to limit who can access your media and content.
- Before you allow somebody to record video of you or take your picture, remember that the video or photo may end up on a media sharing Web site.
- Before placing your multimedia content on a media sharing Web site, check the terms of the service agreement and make certain you agree to give up certain legal rights to your multimedia content.
- Do not post pictures or videos that are protected by a copyright.

Figure 22 While most people act as consumers of content shared on the Internet, some share their own content.

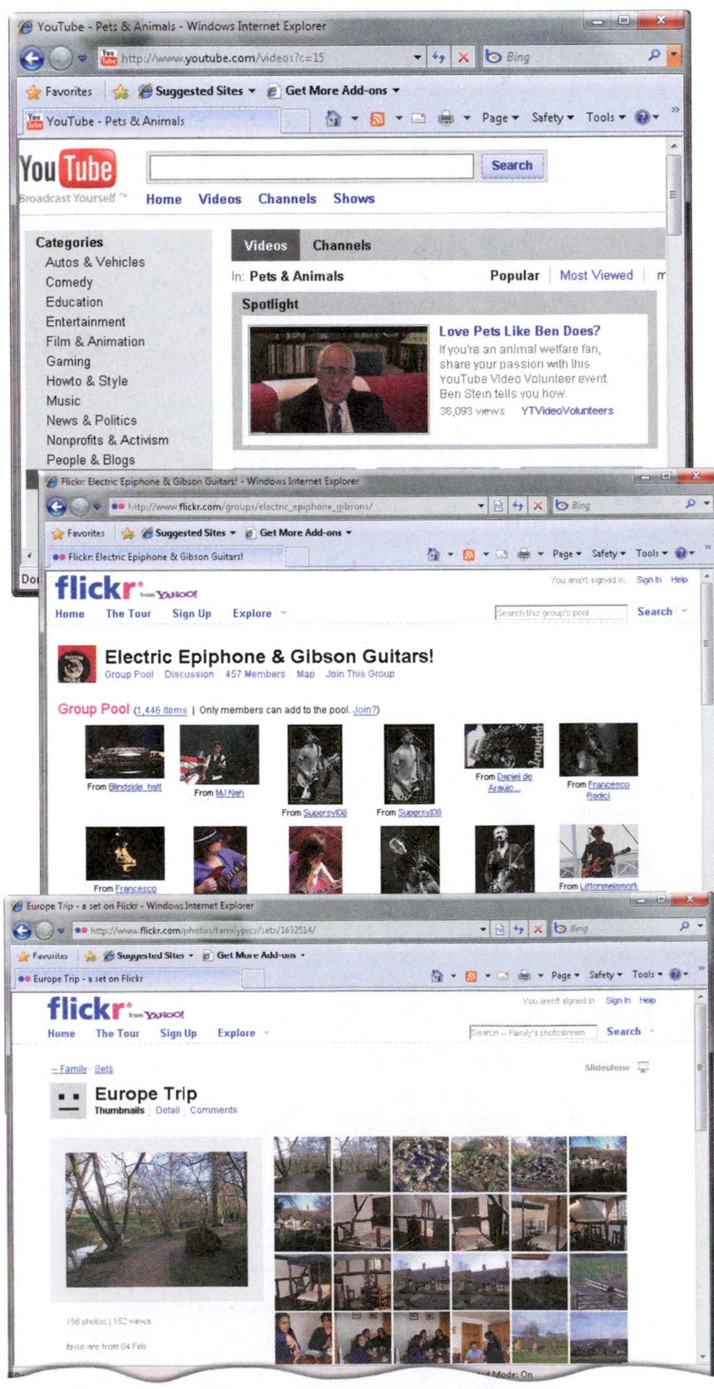

Figure 23 People share and view content on the Internet in a number of ways.

Content Sharing: The Business Perspective

Media sharing Web sites allow business to interact creatively with employees, customers, and prospective customers. Video conferencing is the oldest form of real-time multimedia content sharing in business. Figure 24 outlines some advantages, disadvantages, and good practices of content sharing in business. Many of the notes listed in Figure 22 also apply to content sharing in business. Figure 25 shows examples of content shared in an educational setting and a document management system, which allows for secure storage and management of a company's documents.

Content Sharing Use in Business

Advantages

- Multimedia sharing sites allow companies to archive video conferences, advertisements, employee photos, and other multimedia content.
- Executives and managers create podcasts or vodcasts to spread their vision or message. Vodcasts are podcasts that contain video and usually audio.
- Video conferences allow geographically separate people to transmit audio and video and engage in a meeting remotely.
- Most business-based content sharing software provides for enhanced collaboration by making the content accessible and searchable.
- Multimedia content, such as videos and photos, can be stored in a document management system to archive information about important projects or events.

Disadvantages

- Production and distribution of multimedia content often is more expensive than traditional methods.
- Security on business content sharing systems often frustrates employees who are denied access to information without special approval.

Good practices

- Unless you have permission, do not share company-owned photos and videos on publicly available media sharing Web sites, such as YouTube or Flickr.
- When viewing or sharing photos and videos in the workplace, be certain that the content is appropriate for the workplace. Some businesses have a media department that manages all of the company's multimedia content.

Figure 24 Businesses provide secure content sharing repositories and real-time multimedia.

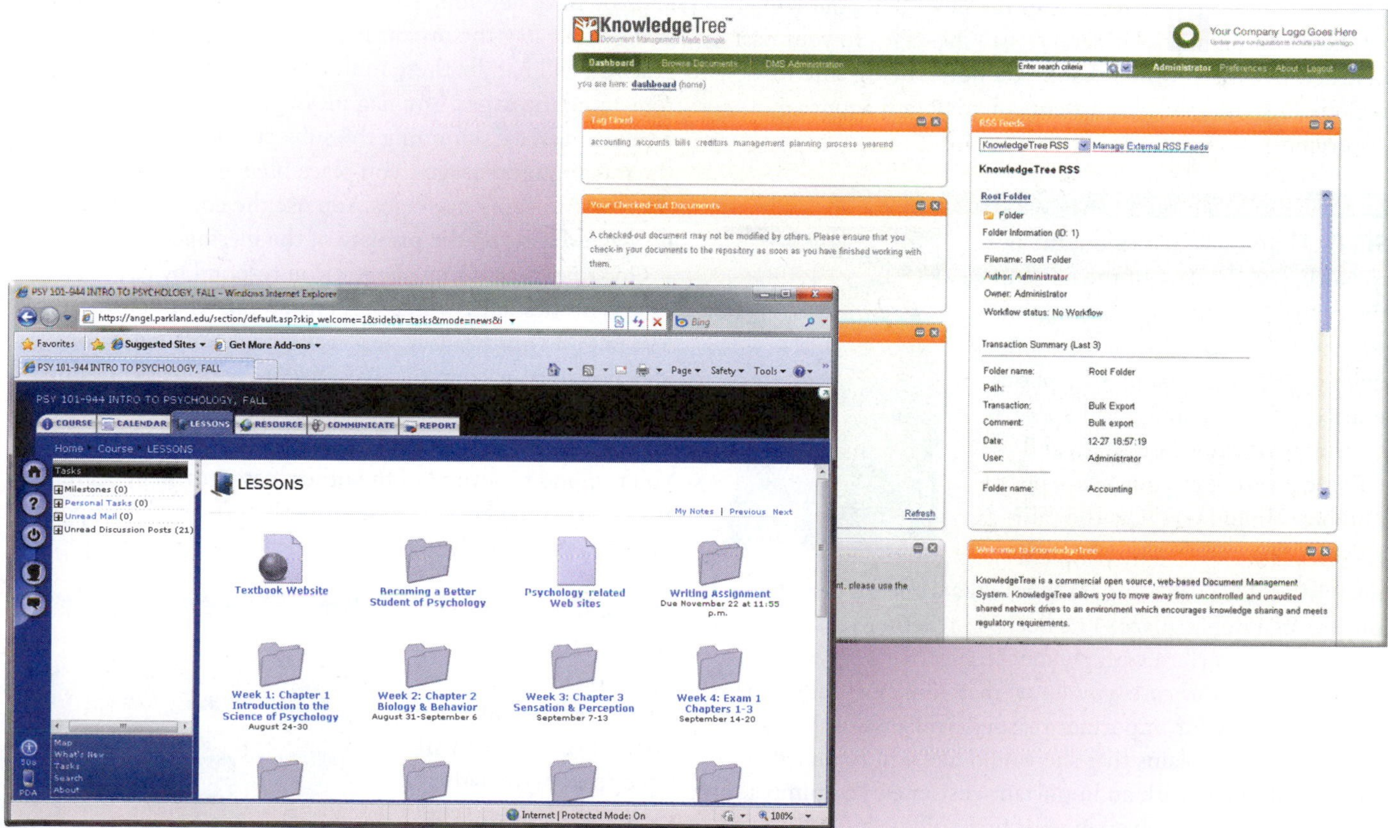

Figure 25 Businesses and other institutions share a variety of digital content in order to facilitate collaboration.

Digital Communications in Your Life

Many people use various forms of digital communications in both their personal and business lives. Imagine you are working in your chosen field and making decisions every day regarding how to communicate best with family, friends, and business contacts. The following scenario presents several situations and decisions regarding digital communications made during a single day.

8:15 a.m.

SITUATION: Before leaving for work, you remember that you are expecting an e-mail confirmation from your travel agent regarding plans for a trip to a friend's birthday party. You also need to send thank-you notes to your past instructors regarding letters of recommendation that they wrote to help you secure the new job.

RESOLUTION: E-mail is a good tool when instant communication is not necessary. Personal business, such as travel arrangements, is negotiated or confirmed easily via e-mail messages, resulting in a permanent record of the communication.

You receive the e-mail message on your personal computer from your travel agent with the news that your trip is booked. You then quickly send e-mail messages to your past instructors with informal thank-you notes, being sure to include links to your blog where you maintain a journal of experiences at your first job.

8:47 a.m.

SITUATION: While riding the bus to work, you drown out the noise of the crowd by using your smart phone to access wirelessly the newest song from your favorite band. The phone number of an incoming call appears on the smart phone's display, and you recognize it as your boss's phone number. Should you take the call?

RESOLUTION: Many people feel uncomfortable answering business calls while on personal time or in a public place. The decision whether to allow work life to interfere with personal life varies with each individual. In your case, you know that your boss calls your cell phone only for important reasons. You answer the call and your boss explains that she would like you to join a video conference with an important customer. You jump at the chance to be involved in your first video conference later in the day. After hanging up the phone, you resume listening to your song.

9:11 a.m.

SITUATION: After arriving at work, your first task is to check e-mail messages. Working at an international firm means that e-mail is a round-the-clock method of communication with coworkers, customers, and business partners. You have more than 30 new e-mail messages since you last checked your e-mail inbox at 5:00 p.m. yesterday.

RESOLUTION: Business e-mail programs usually include several methods for organizing and managing your e-mail inbox. As you view your inbox, a few items have red exclamation marks next to them, indicating that the sender marked them as urgent. Your e-mail program also allows you to mark e-mail messages in your inbox with colored flags, and you have developed a procedure for using these flags. You quickly flag the urgent items with a red flag, meaning that you will handle these immediately after you flag the remaining messages. You flag messages from customers with a yellow flag. By skimming the subject and first few lines of the remaining messages, you place blue, green, and black flags next to some messages. You use the colors to code messages based on the priority of the messages.

Good practices often suggest you respond by telephone to urgent messages or messages from important customers. You put on your headset, and, using your VoIP telephone attached to your computer, you begin the process of calling some of the people whose messages you marked with red and yellow flags. When you are finished talking on the telephone, you respond to several of the other messages, being careful to use a spelling checker and properly format each response before sending it. By 9:45 a.m., your inbox is empty.

10:00 a.m.

SITUATION: By the time you arrive at your office's video conferencing room, five other coworkers already have gathered. After sitting down, you see a large monitor and a camera in front of you.

Instinctively, you check your hair, just as a group of people in another conference room in London appears on the monitor. Your boss whispers that your shirt is a bit bright for the video conference. As the meeting begins, you are asked to introduce yourself. You were not expecting to appear on camera today, but you proceed to introduce yourself and the meeting begins. During the meeting, the cell phone in your pocket buzzes a number of times. Should you take the call?

RESOLUTION: At first, most people find video conferences to be uncomfortable experiences. In comparison to a typical meeting, some people tend to fidget more, tap their fingers, or speak more nervously in a video conference. People tend to recognize those actions when they view others on a monitor in a video conference, so experts suggest keeping these types of actions to a minimum.

You ignore the cell phone calls during the meeting. You have learned that meetings are a time to stay focused and that you would not be invited to the meeting if your presence was not important to someone else. You plan to check your visual voice mail on your cell phone later.

12:19 p.m.

SITUATION: Excited but relieved to be finished with the video conference, you go out for lunch and check your visual voice mail. Your cell phone translates the messages to text so that you can read them on your cell phone rather than listening to them. One personal message from a friend reminds you to sign up for a new online social network. On your way back to the office, you spot a new advertisement for a product from one of your company's competitors. You use your cell phone to take a picture of the advertisement.

RESOLUTION: You instantly use your cell phone to send a picture message to your coworker in your company's marketing department. The coworker sends you a text message thanking you for the advertisement, which she had not seen yet and will be valuable for her research. Later, you decide to sign up for that online social networking Web site recommended by your friend using your work computer. Your company has a liberal attitude toward employees using computers in the office for limited personal use. You also quickly use your cell phone to add an entry to your blog regarding your first video conference today.

3:15 p.m.

SITUATION: Your cell phone rings, indicating that you have a new text message. At the moment, you are engaged in a brief discussion in a colleague's office. When the cell phone rings again, you look at its display and realize that the message is from an important customer. Should you exchange text messages with a customer?

RESOLUTION: Text messaging offers portability and is appropriate for short business and personal contact when responses are not time sensitive. Most businesses restrict employees' use of text messaging to interact with customers or business partners because the messages often are not logged or archived. While looking at the display, you realize that the message is not of a sensitive nature, so you excuse yourself and send a text message to the customer stating that you will research her question. Back at your desk, you search for the answer to the customer's question in your department's wiki. You find that the answer is to send a particular document to the customer that is located in the company's content management system. You locate the document and send it to the customer as an attachment to an e-mail message. Minutes later, you receive a text message from the customer thanking you for the quick reply.

9:15 p.m.

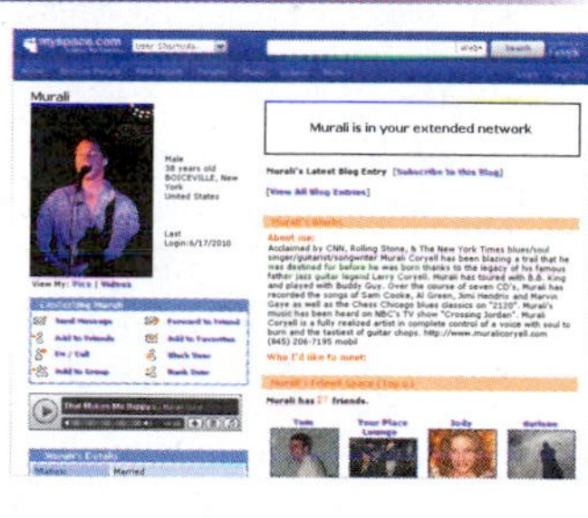

SITUATION: As you end the day at home, you log on to the online social network that you joined earlier in the day. When you add your friend to your list of contacts, you notice that she currently is logged on. You start your instant messaging program and begin instant messaging with your friend. Your friend reminds you that you still have a home page on another online social network from your days in school.

RESOLUTION: You log on to the old online social network that you used when you were in school. You decide to close your home page and ask that the site delete it. People often forget that once they put content on an online social network, in a blog, or on a wiki that it may remain there forever unless they delete or edit it. Periodically, consider checking how others might perceive you based on content you have placed on the Internet.

Digital Communications: Summary

Digital communications are a huge part of our personal and business lives. We make decisions each day when choosing the appropriate method of communication at the right time in the right place. The methods of digital communications involve both the advantages and the disadvantages of instant, archived, and distant collaboration with others.

Chapter Four

The Components of the System Unit

Objectives

After completing this chapter, you will be able to:

1. Differentiate among various styles of system units on desktop computers, notebook computers, and mobile devices
2. Identify chips, adapter cards, and other components of a motherboard
3. Describe the control unit and arithmetic logic unit components of a processor, and explain the four steps in a machine cycle
4. Identify characteristics of various personal computer processors on the market today, and describe the ways processors are cooled
5. Define a bit and describe how a series of bits represents data
6. Explain how program instructions transfer in and out of memory
7. Differentiate among the various types of memory: RAM, cache, ROM, flash memory, and CMOS
8. Describe the purpose and types of expansion slots and adapter cards, and differentiate among slots for various removable flash memory devices
9. Differentiate between a port and a connector, and explain the differences among a USB port, FireWire port, Bluetooth port, SCSI port, eSATA port, IrDA port, serial port, and MIDI port
10. Describe the types of buses in a computer: front side bus, backside bus, and expansion buses (PCI bus, PCIe bus, AGP, USB, FireWire bus, and PC Card bus)
11. Explain the purpose of a power supply and describe how it keeps cool
12. Understand how to clean a system unit on a computer or mobile device

The System Unit

Whether you are a home user or a business user, you most likely will purchase a new computer or upgrade an existing computer at some time in the future. Thus, you should understand the purpose of each component in a computer. As Chapter 1 discussed, a computer includes devices used for input, processing, output, storage, and communications. Many of these components are part of the system unit.

The **system unit** is a case that contains electronic components of the computer used to process data. System units are available in a variety of shapes and sizes. The case of the system unit, sometimes called the *chassis*, is made of metal or plastic and protects the internal electronic components from damage. All computers and mobile devices have a system unit (Figure 4-1).

On desktop personal computers, the electronic components and most storage devices are part of the system unit. Other devices, such as the keyboard, mouse, microphone, monitor, printer, USB flash drive, scanner, Web cam, and speakers, normally occupy space outside the system unit. An all-in-one desktop personal computer is an exception, which houses the monitor and the system unit in the same case. The trend is toward a smaller *form factor*, or size and shape, of the desktop personal computer system unit.

On most notebook computers, including netbooks, the keyboard and pointing device

Figure 4-1 All sizes of computers and mobile devices have a system unit.

often occupy the area on the top of the system unit, and the display attaches to the system unit by hinges. The location of the system unit on a Tablet PC varies, depending on the design of the Tablet PC. With the slate Tablet PC (shown in Figure 4-35 on page 236), which typically does not include a keyboard, the system unit is behind the display. On a convertible Tablet PC (shown in lower-left corner of Figure 4-1), by contrast, the system unit is positioned below a keyboard, providing functionality similar to a traditional notebook computer or netbook. The difference is the display attaches to the system unit with a swivel-type hinge, which enables a user to rotate the display and fold it down over the keyboard to look like a slate Tablet PC. The system unit on an Ultra-Mobile PC, a smart phone, and a PDA usually consumes the entire device. On these mobile computers and devices, the display often is built into the system unit.

With game consoles, the input and output devices, such as controllers and a television, reside outside the system unit. On handheld game consoles, portable media players, and digital cameras, by contrast, the packaging around the system unit houses the input devices and display.

At some point, you might have to open the system unit on a desktop personal computer to replace or install a new electronic component. For this reason, you should be familiar with the electronic components of a system unit. Figure 4-2 identifies some of these components, which include the processor, memory, adapter cards, drive bays, and the power supply.

The processor interprets and carries out the basic instructions that operate a computer. Memory typically holds data waiting to be processed and instructions waiting to be executed. The electronic components and circuitry of the system unit, such as the processor and memory, usually are part of or are connected to a circuit

Figure 4-2 The system unit on a typical personal computer consists of numerous electronic components, some of which are shown in this figure. The sound card and video card are two types of adapter cards.

board called the motherboard. Many current motherboards also integrate sound, video, and networking capabilities.

Adapter cards are circuit boards that provide connections and functions not built into the motherboard or expand on the capability of features integrated into the motherboard. For example, a sound card and a video card are two types of adapter cards found in some desktop personal computers today.

Devices outside the system unit often attach to ports on the system unit by a connector on a cable. These devices may include a keyboard, mouse, microphone, monitor, printer, scanner, USB flash drive, card reader/writer, Web cam, and speakers. A drive bay holds one or more disk drives. The power supply converts electricity from a power cord plugged in a wall outlet into a form that can be used by the computer.

FAQ 4-1

How many PCs are in use worldwide?

A recent study shows that more than one billion personal computers are in use worldwide, with 58 percent of these computers in the United States, Europe, and Japan. This number, expected to double by 2014, is growing rapidly because of developing markets.

For more information, visit the Computer Concepts CourseMate Web site at www.cengagebrain.com, navigate to the Chapter 4 FAQ resource for this book, and then click Personal Computer Use.

The Motherboard

The **motherboard**, sometimes called a *system board*, is the main circuit board of the system unit. Many electronic components attach to the motherboard; others are built into it. Figure 4-3 shows a photo of a current desktop personal computer motherboard and identifies its slots for adapter cards, the processor chip, and memory. Memory chips are installed on memory cards (modules) that fit in a slot on the motherboard.

A computer **chip** is a small piece of semiconducting material, usually silicon, on which integrated circuits are etched. An *integrated circuit* contains many microscopic pathways capable of carrying electrical current. Each integrated circuit can contain millions of elements such as resistors, capacitors, and transistors. A *transistor*, for example, can act as an electronic switch that opens or closes the circuit for electrical charges. Today's computer chips contain millions or billions of transistors. Most chips are no bigger than one-half-inch square. Manufacturers package chips so that the chips can be attached to a circuit board, such as a motherboard or an adapter card. Specific types of processor, memory, and other chips are discussed later in the chapter. Read Innovative Computing 4-1 to find out about chips implanted in animals.

Figure 4-3 Many electronic components attach to the motherboard in a desktop personal computer, including a processor chip, memory modules, and adapter cards.

INNOVATIVE COMPUTING 4-1

Chip Implants Identify Animals

When Fido and Fluffy run away, their safe return home may be based on data stored on a chip that veterinarians have implanted under the skin, usually at the neck or shoulder blades. Other animals can be chipped, including horses, birds, and livestock.

Each chip is numbered uniquely and registered to the owner's name and address. This chip, sometimes called a microchip because it is the size of a grain of rice, contains an antenna and transponder encased in a glass tube. The antenna receives low-frequency radio waves when a scanning device passes over the chip, and the transponder sends a signal with the chip's number back to the scanner.

Shelters and animal control centers routinely scan runaway pets for chips in an attempt to reunite animals with their owners, and some animal hospitals scan pets to determine whether they have been reported lost or stolen. Most shelters require pets to have the implant before the animals are adopted. In addition, breeders, farmers, and animal associations implant the chips to thwart thieves. Researchers also use this technology to track migration of wild animals and fish.

For more information, visit the Computer Concepts CourseMate Web site at www.cengagebrain.com, navigate to the Chapter 4 Innovative Computing resource for this book, and then click ID Chips.

Processor

The **processor**, also called the **central processing unit (CPU)**, interprets and carries out the basic instructions that operate a computer. The processor significantly impacts overall computing power and manages most of a computer's operations. On larger computers, such as mainframes and supercomputers, the various functions performed by the processor extend over many separate chips and often multiple circuit boards. On a personal computer, all functions of the processor usually are on a single chip. Some computer and chip manufacturers use the term *microprocessor* to refer to a personal computer processor chip.

Most processor chip manufacturers now offer multi-core processors. A processor core, or simply core, contains the circuitry necessary to execute instructions. The operating system views each processor core as a separate processor. A **multi-core processor** is a single chip with two or more separate processor cores. Two common multi-core processors are dual-core and quad-core. A **dual-core processor** is a chip that contains two separate processor cores. Similarly, a **quad-core processor** is a chip with four separate processor cores.

Each processor core on a multi-core processor generally runs at a slower clock speed than a single-core processor, but multi-core processors typically increase overall performance. For example, although a dual-core processor does not double the processing speed of a single-core processor, it can approach those speeds. The performance increase is especially noticeable when users are running multiple programs simultaneously such as antivirus software, spyware remover, e-mail program, instant messaging, media player, disc burning software, and photo editing software. Multi-core processors also are more energy efficient than separate multiple processors, requiring lower levels of power consumption and emitting less heat in the system unit.

Processors contain a control unit and an arithmetic logic unit (ALU). These two components work together to perform processing operations. Figure 4-4 illustrates how other devices connected to the computer communicate

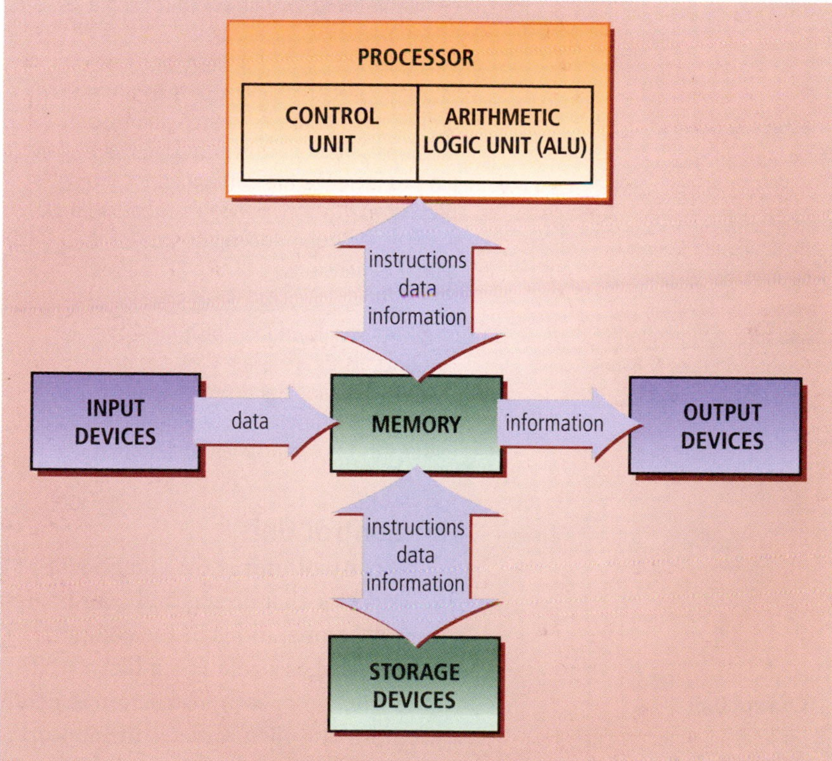

Figure 4-4 Most devices connected to the computer communicate with the processor to carry out a task. When a user starts a program, for example, its instructions transfer from a storage device to memory. Data needed by programs enters memory from either an input device or a storage device. The control unit interprets and executes instructions in memory, and the ALU performs calculations on the data in memory. Resulting information is stored in memory, from which it can be sent to an output device or a storage device for future access, as needed.

with the processor to carry out a task. Read Innovative Computing 4-2 to find out how processors control robots.

INNOVATIVE COMPUTING 4-2

Robots Assist with Everyday Tasks

Be prepared to see a new type of gardener, house cleaner, and receptionist because robots are becoming mainstream. Robotic technology will handle mundane chores as well as provide companionship in both professional and personal worlds.

Approximately 40 percent of the world's robots reside in Japan, where 32 of these machines work alongside every 1,000 workers employed in manufacturing settings. The Japanese accept robots as human replacements and view them as friendly helpers. The machines can greet patients in doctors' offices, print maps when people ask for directions, mow lawns, and check oil and gas pipelines for leaks. They also can feed hospitalized patients and provide companionship for homebound people as well as toddlers.

The United States' military and foreign armed forces are using robots as unmanned drones in combat and search-and-rescue missions. The Department of Defense is planning to increase the unmanned technology's presence with soft, bendable robots that can maneuver through openings smaller than their actual dimensions.

For more information, visit the Computer Concepts CourseMate Web site at www.cengagebrain.com, navigate to the Chapter 4 Innovative Computing resource for this book, and then click Robots.

ETHICS & ISSUES 4-1

Can Computers Think?

Since the dawn of the computing age, people have wondered if a computer ever would be capable of thought. As computer processors and software become more powerful, the question is debated more hotly. People who believe computers can think argue that, if a person had a conversation with a computer and was convinced the computer was really human, then the computer is intelligent. This criteria is known as the Turing Test, named after British mathematician Alan Turing who proposed the test in 1950. If a computer can pass a modern version of the Turing Test, it is considered to be intelligent, and it may win the prestigious $100,000 Loebner Prize. While the $100,000 prize has yet to be claimed, an annual event awards $2,000 to the most human-like computer chat partner.

Opponents to those who believe computers may one day think claim that, if a question written in a foreign language was submitted to a person who can read and write the language and a person who cannot read or write the language but has a list of questions and appropriate answers, it might be impossible to tell the response of one person from the other. But, the person who cannot read or write the language really does not understand it, any more than a computer really can think. Opponents also claim that research towards the Turing Test is a distraction from more beneficial research. Besides, computers lack at least two essential components of human thinking — common sense and emotion.

Can computers think? Why or why not? If computers cannot think now, might they be able to think in the future? Why? How important are common sense and emotion in the ability to think? Are any benefits to be gained if a computer can pass the Turing Test? Why?

Ethics & Issues

For the complete text of the Ethics & Issues boxes found in this chapter, visit the Computer Concepts CourseMate Web site at www.cengagebrain.com and then navigate to the Chapter 4 Ethics & Issues resource for this book.

The Control Unit

The **control unit** is the component of the processor that directs and coordinates most of the operations in the computer. The control unit has a role much like a traffic cop: it interprets each instruction issued by a program and then initiates the appropriate action to carry out the instruction. Types of internal components that the control unit directs include the arithmetic/logic unit, registers, and buses, each discussed later in this chapter. Read Ethics & Issues 4-1 for a related discussion.

Control Unit

For more information, visit the Computer Concepts CourseMate Web site at www.cengagebrain.com, navigate to the Chapter 4 Web Link resource for this book, and then click Control Unit.

The Arithmetic Logic Unit

The **arithmetic logic unit** (*ALU*), another component of the processor, performs arithmetic, comparison, and other operations.

Arithmetic operations include basic calculations such as addition, subtraction, multiplication, and division. *Comparison operations* involve comparing one data item with another to determine whether the first item is greater than, equal to, or less than the other item. Depending on the result of the comparison, different actions may occur. For example, to determine if an employee should receive overtime pay, software instructs the ALU to compare the number of hours an employee worked during the week with the regular time hours allowed (e.g., 40 hours). If the hours worked exceed 40, for example, software instructs the ALU to perform calculations that compute the overtime wage.

Machine Cycle

For every instruction, a processor repeats a set of four basic operations, which comprise a *machine cycle* (Figure 4-5): (1) fetching, (2) decoding, (3) executing, and, if necessary, (4) storing. *Fetching* is the process of obtaining a program instruction or data item from memory. The term *decoding* refers to the process of translating the instruction into signals the computer can execute. *Executing* is the process of carrying out the commands. *Storing*, in this context, means writing the result to memory (not to a storage medium).

In some computers, the processor fetches, decodes, executes, and stores only one instruction at a time. In these computers, the processor waits until an instruction completes all four stages of the machine cycle (fetch, decode, execute, and store) before beginning work on the next instruction.

Most of today's personal computers support a concept called pipelining. With *pipelining*, the processor begins fetching a second instruction before it completes the machine cycle for the first instruction. Processors that use pipelining are faster because they do not have to wait for one instruction to complete the machine cycle before fetching the next. Think of a pipeline as an assembly line. By the time the first instruction is in the last stage of the machine cycle, three

The Steps in a Machine Cycle

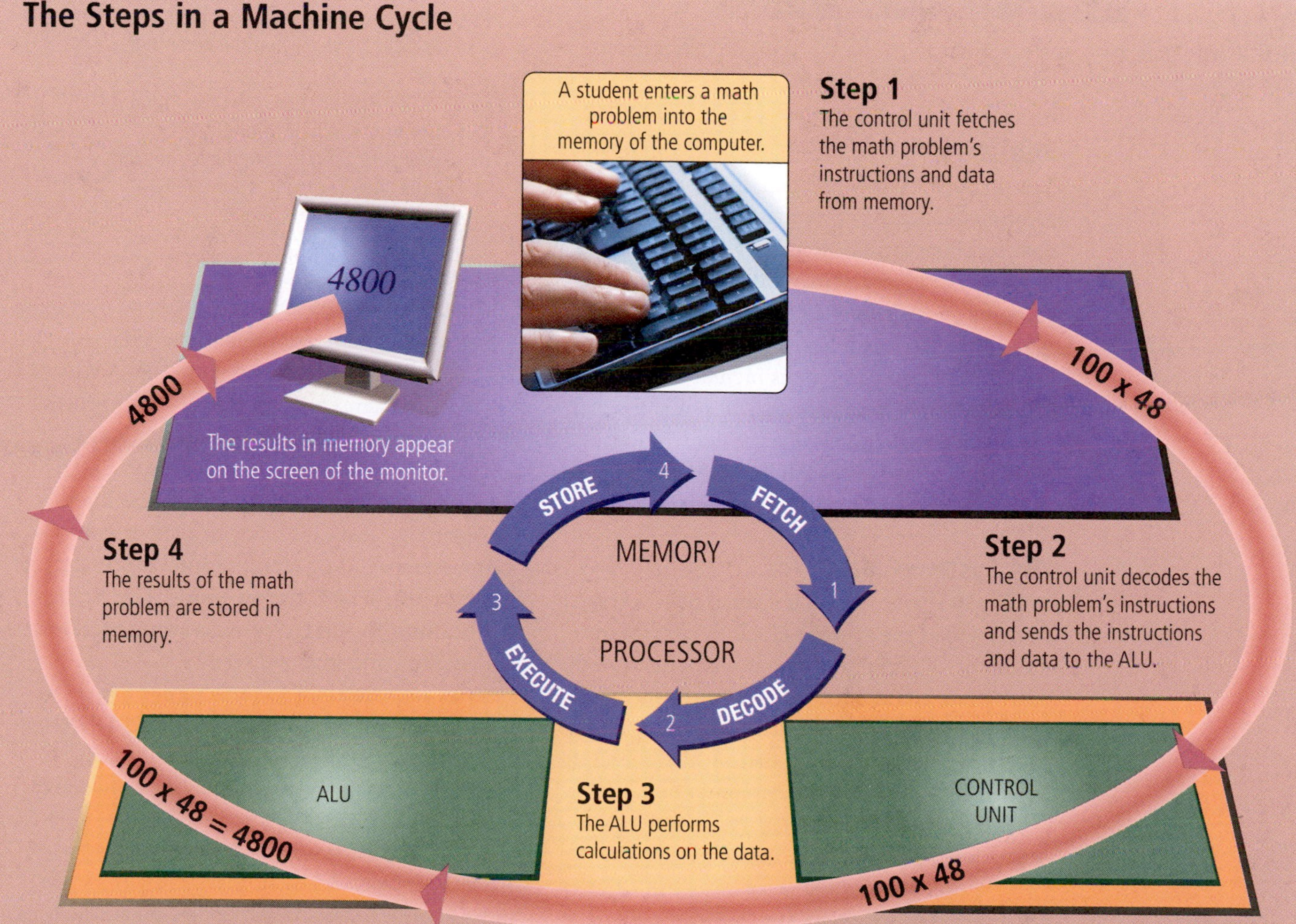

Figure 4-5 This figure shows the steps in a machine cycle.

other instructions could have been fetched and started through the machine cycle (Figure 4-6).

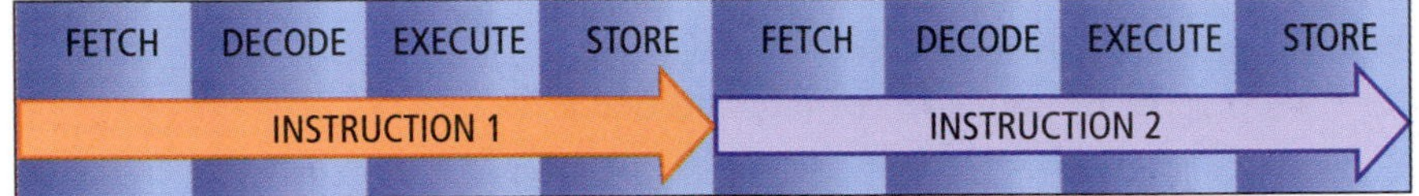

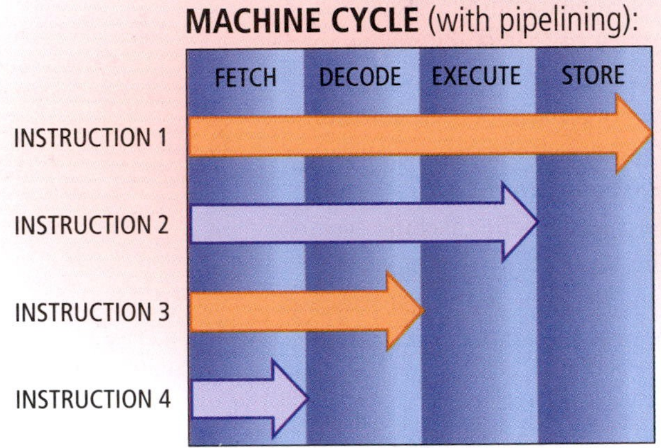

Figure 4-6 With pipelining, the processor fetches a second instruction before the first instruction is completed. The result is faster processing.

Registers

A processor contains small, high-speed storage locations, called *registers*, that temporarily hold data and instructions. Registers are part of the processor, not part of memory or a permanent storage device. Processors have many different types of registers, each with a specific storage function. Register functions include storing the location from where an instruction was fetched, storing an instruction while the control unit decodes it, storing data while the ALU computes it, and storing the results of a calculation.

The System Clock

The processor relies on a small quartz crystal circuit called the **system clock** to control the timing of all computer operations. Just as your heart beats at a regular rate to keep your body functioning, the system clock generates regular electronic pulses, or ticks, that set the operating pace of components of the system unit.

Each tick equates to a *clock cycle*. In the past, processors used one or more clock cycles to execute each instruction. Processors today often are *superscalar*, which means they can execute more than one instruction per clock cycle.

The pace of the system clock, called the **clock speed**, is measured by the number of ticks per second. Current personal computer processors have clock speeds in the gigahertz range. Giga is a prefix that stands for billion, and a *hertz* is one cycle per second. Thus, one **gigahertz (GHz)** equals one billion ticks of the system clock per second. A computer that operates at 3 GHz has 3 billion (giga) clock cycles in one second (hertz).

The faster the clock speed, the more instructions the processor can execute per second. The speed of the system clock has no effect on devices such as a printer or disk drive. The speed of the system clock is just one factor that influences a computer's performance. Other factors, such as the type of processor chip, amount of cache, memory access time, bus width, and bus clock speed, are discussed later in this chapter.

? FAQ 4-2

Does the system clock also keep track of the current date and time?

No, a separate battery-backed chip, called the *real-time clock*, keeps track of the date and time in a computer. The battery continues to run the real-time clock even when the computer is off.

For more information, visit the Computer Concepts CourseMate Web site at www.cengagebrain.com, navigate to the Chapter 4 FAQ resource for this book, and then click Computer Clock.

Comparison of Personal Computer Processors

The leading manufacturers of personal computer processor chips are Intel and AMD. These manufacturers often identify their processor chips by a model name or model number (Figure 4-7). High-performance personal computers today may use a processor in the Intel **Core** family. Less expensive, basic personal computers may use a brand of Intel processor in the **Pentium** or **Celeron** family. The **Xeon** and **Itanium** families of processors are ideal for workstations and low-end servers.

AMD is the leading manufacturer of *Intel-compatible processors*, which have an internal design similar to Intel processors, perform the same functions, and can be as powerful, but often are less expensive.

In the past, chip manufacturers listed a processor's clock speed in marketing literature and advertisements. As previously mentioned, though, clock speed is only one factor that impacts processing speed in today's computers. To help consumers evaluate various processors, manufacturers such as Intel and AMD now use a numbering scheme that more accurately reflects the processing speed of their chips.

Processor chips include technologies to improve processing performance, for example, to improve performance of multimedia and 3-D graphics. Most of Intel's processor chips also include *vPro technology*, which provides the capability to track computer hardware and software, diagnose and resolve computer problems, and secure computers from outside threats. Read Ethics & Issues 4-2 for a related discussion.

As mentioned earlier, many personal computer processors are multi-core, with the processor cores working simultaneously on related instructions. These related instructions, called a thread, can be independent or part of a larger task. Software written to support multiple threads, called a *multi-threaded program*, runs much faster than those in nonthreaded environments.

Processors for traditional notebook computers and Tablet PCs also include technology to optimize and extend battery life, enhance security, and integrate wireless capabilities. For example, Intel's *Centrino 2* mobile technology, which may have a Pro designator depending on its capabilities, integrates wireless functionality in notebook computers and Tablet PCs. Netbooks, smart phones, and other smaller mobile devices often use more compact processors that consume less power, yet offer high performance.

Multi-Core Processors

For more information, visit the Computer Concepts CourseMate Web site at www.cengagebrain.com, navigate to the Chapter 4 Web Link resource for this book, and then click Multi-Core Processors.

Comparison of Currently Available Personal Computer Processors

	Name	Multi-Core Availability	Manufacturer
SERVER PROCESSORS	Xeon	8 Core, 6 Core, Quad Core, Dual Core	Intel
	Itanium	Quad Core, Dual Core	Intel
	Opteron	6 Core, Quad Core	AMD
DESKTOP PERSONAL COMPUTER PROCESSORS	Core i7 Extreme	6 Core, Quad Core	Intel
	Core i7	6 Core, Quad Core	Intel
	Core i5	Quad Core, Dual Core	Intel
	Core i3	Dual Core	Intel
	Celeron	Dual Core	Intel
	Phenom	6 Core, Quad Core, Triple Core	AMD
	Athlon	Quad Core, Triple Core, Dual Core	AMD
	Sempron		AMD
NOTEBOOK COMPUTER PROCESSORS	Core i7 Extreme	Quad Core	Intel
	Core i7	Quad Core, Dual Core	Intel
	Core i5 and i3	Dual Core	Intel
	Atom		Intel
	Phenom	Quad Core, Triple Core, Dual Core	AMD
	Turion	Dual Core	AMD
	Athlon	Dual Core	AMD
	Sempron		AMD

Figure 4-7 Most of today's processors are multi-core.

ETHICS & ISSUES 4-2

Is Government Search and Seizure of Computers Ethical?

In the interest of national security, the Department of Homeland Security may search and seize any mobile computer or device from people arriving in the United States. The sometimes random searches may be done without a warrant or even a reason. Additionally, the government has taken computers from schools and libraries in a similar manner. Computers and mobile devices might be taken away for an off-site inspection for any amount of time. Sometimes, the devices are not returned and little or no reason is given for the seizure.

At airports and other points of entry to the country, the government considers computers and mobile devices to be containers, just as a piece of luggage is a container. Computers, therefore, can be searched and seized similarly to luggage without reasonable suspicion. Opponents claim that the data on a computer is like memories stored in the brain. They claim that the government should be able to inspect the hardware, but not the contents of memory or a hard disk. Librarians and school administrators claim that the government is invading the privacy of patrons and students.

Is government search and seizure of computers without a warrant ethical? Why or why not? Would you allow a government employee to inspect the data on your mobile computer or device? Why or why not? If memories, thoughts, or intentions in one's mind could someday be deciphered by a computer at a security checkpoint, should the government be allowed to scan them? Why?

Another type of processor, called *system-on-a-chip*, integrates the functions of a processor, memory, and a video card on a single chip. Lower-priced personal computers, Tablet PCs, networking devices, portable media players, and game consoles sometimes have a system-on-a-chip processor. The goal of system-on-a-chip manufacturers is to create processors that have faster clock speeds, consume less power, are small, and are cost effective.

Buying a Personal Computer

If you are ready to buy a new computer, the processor you select should depend on how you plan to use the computer (Figure 4-8). To realize greater processing performance, you may want to choose a multi-core processor.

Instead of buying an entirely new computer, you might be able to upgrade your processor to increase the computer's performance. Be certain the processor you buy is compatible with your computer's motherboard; otherwise, you will have to replace the motherboard, too. Replacing a processor is a fairly simple process, whereas replacing a motherboard is much more complicated.

For detailed personal computer and mobile device purchasing guidelines, read the Buyer's Guide feature that follows Chapter 8. Read Ethics & Issues 4-3 for a related discussion.

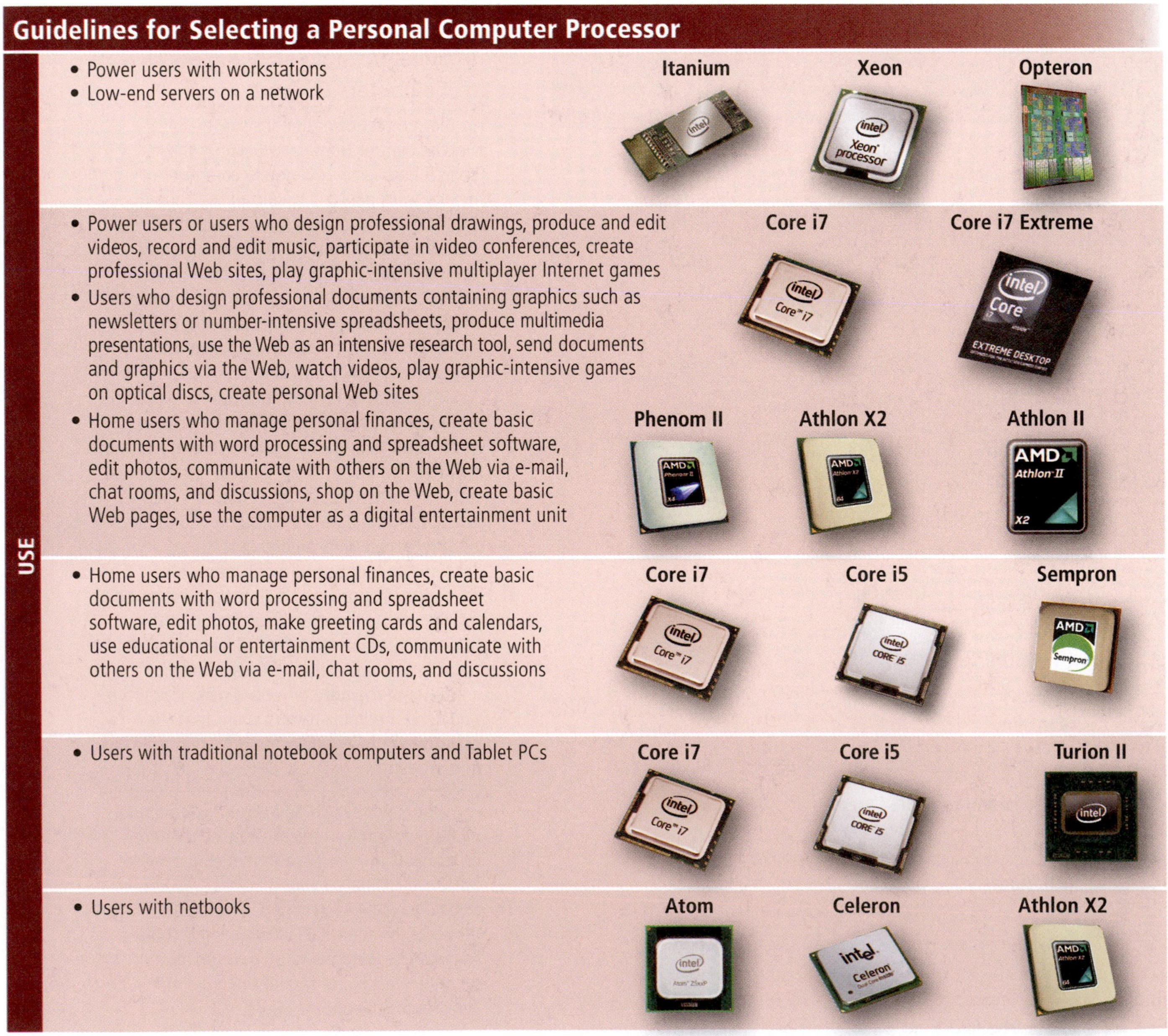

Guidelines for Selecting a Personal Computer Processor

USE	Processors
• Power users with workstations • Low-end servers on a network	Itanium, Xeon, Opteron
• Power users or users who design professional drawings, produce and edit videos, record and edit music, participate in video conferences, create professional Web sites, play graphic-intensive multiplayer Internet games • Users who design professional documents containing graphics such as newsletters or number-intensive spreadsheets, produce multimedia presentations, use the Web as an intensive research tool, send documents and graphics via the Web, watch videos, play graphic-intensive games on optical discs, create personal Web sites	Core i7, Core i7 Extreme
• Home users who manage personal finances, create basic documents with word processing and spreadsheet software, edit photos, communicate with others on the Web via e-mail, chat rooms, and discussions, shop on the Web, create basic Web pages, use the computer as a digital entertainment unit	Phenom II, Athlon X2, Athlon II
• Home users who manage personal finances, create basic documents with word processing and spreadsheet software, edit photos, make greeting cards and calendars, use educational or entertainment CDs, communicate with others on the Web via e-mail, chat rooms, and discussions	Core i7, Core i5, Sempron
• Users with traditional notebook computers and Tablet PCs	Core i7, Core i5, Turion II
• Users with netbooks	Atom, Celeron, Athlon X2

Figure 4-8 Determining which processor to obtain when you purchase a computer depends on computer usage.

ETHICS & ISSUES 4-3

Should Mobile Computers and Devices Be Banned from the Classroom?

Instead of student faces, the view for today's instructors often is a sea of bent necks as students use their notebook computers, netbooks, Tablet PCs, smart phones, and portable media players during lectures. Many students have found that mobile computers and devices provide an ideal place to take notes, make recordings of lectures, and perform lecture-related research. Other students have found that mobile computers and devices provide endless entertainment, instant messaging, and other activities unrelated to course work during a lecture. Some instructors and students find that this inappropriate use of computers during a lecture to be distracting, especially if the computer or device makes sounds such as keyboard clicks or screen taps. Even when used for note taking, some feel that mobile computers are incompatible with a good learning experience. One law professor describes the mobile computers' raised computer screens as a picket fence between an instructor and the student, as students attempt to capture every nuance of the lecture on their computers. This professor is one of a growing number of instructors who have banned the use of mobile computers and devices during lectures. Classroom rules vary by instructor, with some choosing to disallow listening to music, sending text messages, or using a cell phone.

Are mobile computers and devices too distracting in the classroom? Why? Should instructors, departments, or entire schools be able to ban mobile computers and devices in the classroom? Why or why not? What are proper and improper uses of mobile computers and devices in the classroom? Why? Is the use of a mobile computer and devices more of a distraction than taking notes or doodling in a notebook pad during class? Why or why not?

FAQ 4-3

Which PC vendors are the most popular with consumers?

Hewlett-Packard (HP) has the highest market share worldwide at approximately 20 percent, with Dell in second place with nearly 13 percent market share. HP accounts for nearly 21 percent of PC sales in the United States. The chart to the right compares the worldwide market share for various PC vendors.

For more information, visit the Computer Concepts CourseMate Web site at www.cengagebrain.com, navigate to the Chapter 4 FAQ resource for this book, and then click PC Vendor Market.

Worldwide PC Market Share

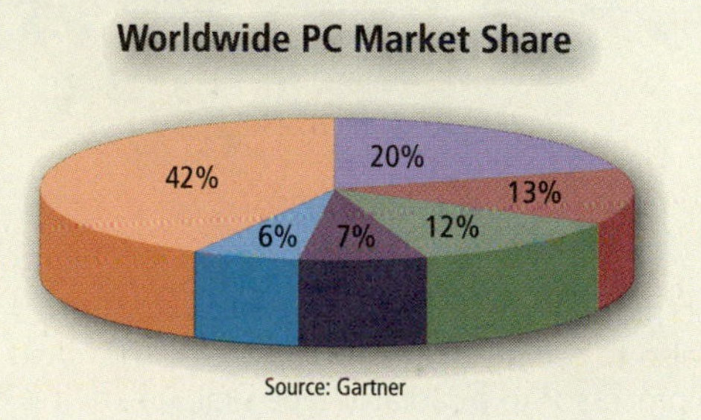

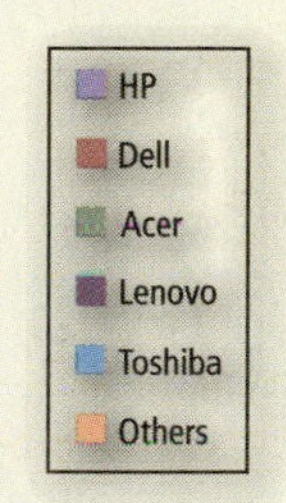

Processor Cooling

Processor chips generate quite a bit of heat, which could cause the chip to burn up. Although the computer's main fan generates airflow, many of today's personal computer processors require additional cooling. Heat sinks/pipes and liquid cooling technologies often are used to help dissipate processor heat.

A *heat sink* is a small ceramic or metal component with fins on its surface that absorbs and disperses heat produced by electrical components such as a processor (Figure 4-9). Some heat sinks are packaged as part of a processor chip. Others are installed on the top or the side of the chip. Because a heat sink consumes extra space, a smaller device called a *heat pipe* cools processors in notebook computers, including netbooks and Tablet PCs.

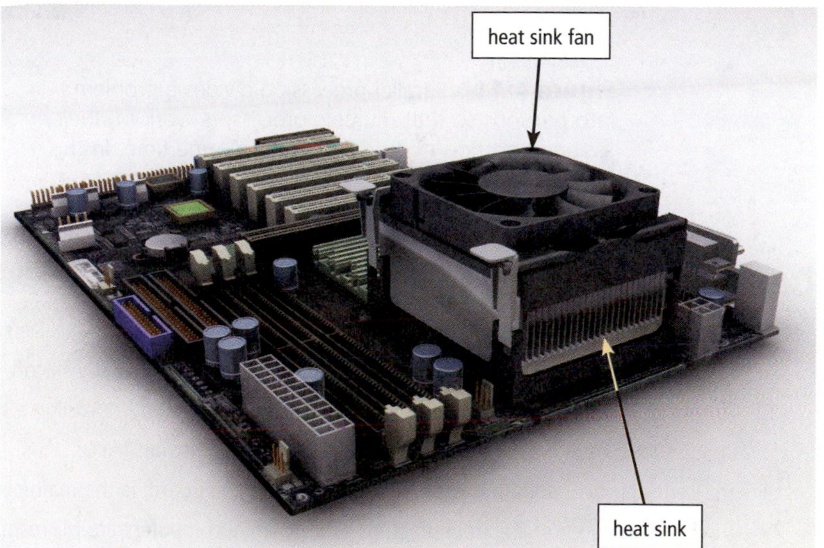

Figure 4-9 A heat sink, which in this photo is attached to the top of a processor, prevents the chip from overheating. The heat sink fan, which attaches to the top of the heat sink, helps distribute air dissipated by the heat sink.

Some computers use liquid cooling technology to reduce the temperature of a processor. *Liquid cooling technology* uses a continuous flow of fluid(s), such as water and glycol, in a process that transfers the heated fluid away from the

Liquid Cooling

For more information, visit the Computer Concepts CourseMate Web site at www.cengagebrain.com, navigate to the Chapter 4 Web Link resource for this book, and then click Liquid Cooling.

processor to a radiator-type grill, which cools the liquid, and then returns the cooled fluid to the processor (Figure 4-10).

Some mobile computers and devices often have Low Voltage or Ultra Low Voltage (ULV) processors, which have such low power demands that they do not require additional cooling.

Figure 4-10 With liquid cooling technology, heat transfers from a processor through a copper plate, which is attached to the processor and also to tubing that contains liquid. The liquid travels away from the processor to a radiator-type grill, where it is cooled before travelling back to the plate attached to the processor.

Parallel Processing

Parallel processing is a method that uses multiple processors simultaneously to execute a single program or task (Figure 4-11). Parallel processing divides a single problem into portions so that multiple processors work on their assigned portion of the problem at the same time. Parallel processing requires special software that recognizes how to divide the problem and then bring the results back together again.

Some personal computers implement parallel processing with dual-core processors or multi-core processors. Others have two or more separate processor chips, respectively called dual processor or multiprocessor computers.

Massively parallel processing is large scale parallel processing that involves hundreds or thousands of processors. Supercomputers use massively parallel processing for applications such as artificial intelligence and weather forecasting.

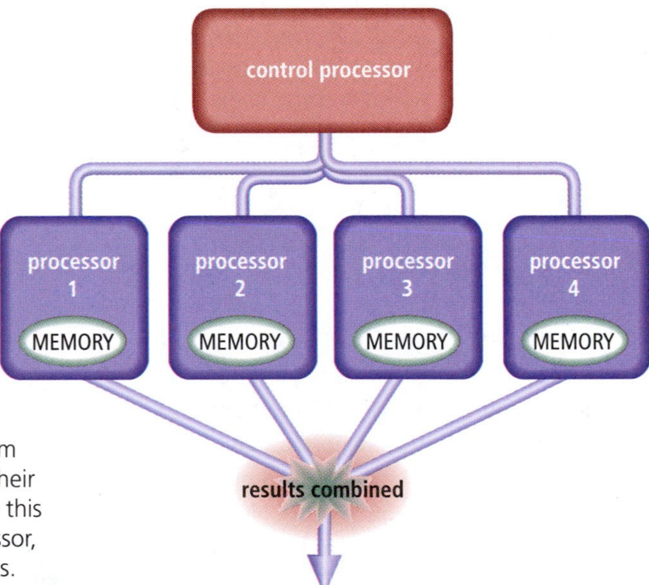

Figure 4-11 Parallel processing divides a problem into portions so that multiple processors work on their assigned portion of a problem at the same time. In this illustration, one processor, called the control processor, is managing the operations of four other processors.

QUIZ YOURSELF 4-1

Instructions: Find the true statement below. Then, rewrite the remaining false statements so that they are true.

1. A computer chip is a small piece of semiconducting material, usually silicon, on which integrated circuits are etched.
2. Four basic operations in a machine cycle are: (1) comparing, (2) decoding, (3) executing, and, if necessary, (4) pipelining.
3. Processors contain a motherboard and an arithmetic logic unit (ALU).
4. The central processing unit, sometimes called a system board, is the main circuit board of the system unit.
5. The leading processor chip manufacturers for personal computers are Microsoft and AMD.
6. The pace of the system clock, called the clock speed, is measured by the number of ticks per minute.
7. The system unit is a case that contains mechanical components of the computer used to process data.

Quiz Yourself Online: To further check your knowledge of pages 210 through 220, visit the Computer Concepts CourseMate Web site at www.cengagebrain.com, navigate to the Chapter 4 Quiz Yourself resource for this book, and then click Objectives 1 – 4.

Data Representation

To understand how a computer processes data, you should know how a computer represents data. People communicate through speech by combining words into sentences. Human speech is **analog** because it uses continuous (wave form) signals that vary in strength and quality. Most computers are **digital**. They recognize only two discrete states: on and off. This is because computers are electronic devices powered by electricity, which also has only two states: on and off.

The two digits, 0 and 1, easily can represent these two states (Figure 4-12). The digit 0 represents the electronic state of off (absence of an electronic charge). The digit 1 represents the electronic state of on (presence of an electronic charge).

When people count, they use the digits in the decimal system (0 through 9). The computer, by contrast, uses a binary system because it recognizes only two states. The **binary system** is a number system that has just two unique digits, 0 and 1, called bits. A **bit** (short for *binary digit*) is the smallest unit of data the computer can process. By itself, a bit is not very informative.

When 8 bits are grouped together as a unit, they form a **byte**. A byte provides enough different combinations of 0s and 1s to represent 256 individual characters. These characters include numbers, uppercase and lowercase letters of the alphabet, punctuation marks, and others, such as the letters of the Greek alphabet.

The combinations of 0s and 1s that represent characters are defined by patterns called a coding scheme. In one coding scheme, the number 4 is represented as 00110100, the number 6 as 00110110, and the capital letter E as 01000101 (Figure 4-13). *ASCII* (pronounced ASK-ee), which stands for American Standard Code for Information Interchange, is the most widely used coding scheme to represent data (Figure 4-14).

The ASCII coding scheme is sufficient for English and Western European languages but is not large enough for Asian and other languages that use different alphabets. *Unicode* is a 16-bit coding scheme that has the capacity of representing more than 65,000 characters and symbols. The Unicode coding scheme is capable of representing almost all the world's current written languages, as well as classic and historical languages. To allow for expansion, Unicode reserves 30,000 codes for future

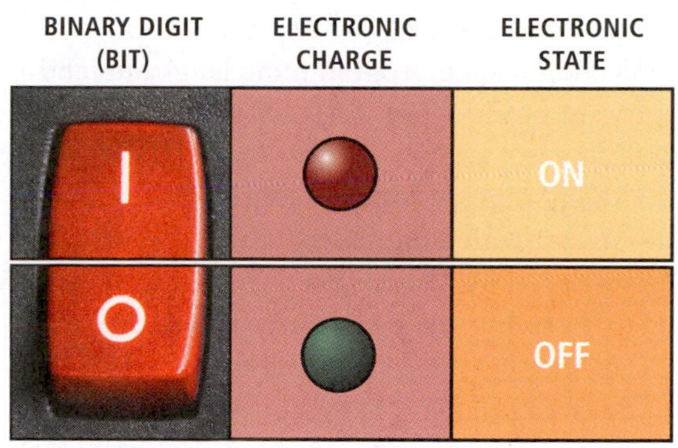

Figure 4-12 A computer circuit represents the 0 or the 1 electronically by the presence or absence of an electronic charge.

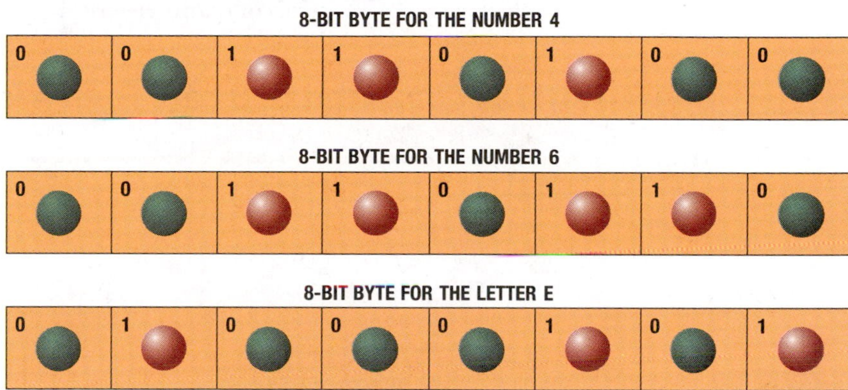

Figure 4-13 Eight bits grouped together as a unit are called a byte. A byte represents a single character in the computer.

ASCII	SYMBOL	ASCII	SYMBOL
00110000	0	01001110	N
00110001	1	01001111	O
00110010	2	01010000	P
00110011	3	01010001	Q
00110100	4	01010010	R
00110101	5	01010011	S
00110110	6	01010100	T
00110111	7	01010101	U
00111000	8	01010110	V
00111001	9	01010111	W
01000001	A	01011000	X
01000010	B	01011001	Y
01000011	C	01011010	Z
01000100	D	00100001	!
01000101	E	00100010	"
01000110	F	00100011	#
01000111	G	00100100	$
01001000	H	00100101	%
01001001	I	00100110	&
01001010	J	00101000	(
01001011	K	00101001	)
01001100	L	00101010	*
01001101	M	00101011	+

Figure 4-14 ASCII is a widely used coding scheme.

use and 6,000 codes for private use. Unicode is implemented in several operating systems, including Windows, Mac OS, and Linux. Unicode-enabled programming languages and software include Java, XML, Microsoft Office, and Oracle.

Coding schemes make it possible for humans to interact with a digital computer that processes only bits. When you press a key on a keyboard, a chip in the keyboard converts the key's electronic signal into a special code that is sent to the system unit. Then, the system unit converts the code into a binary form the computer can process and stores it in memory. Every character is converted to its corresponding byte. The computer then processes the data as bytes, which actually is a series of on/off electrical states. When processing is finished, software converts the byte into a human-recognizable number, letter of the alphabet, or special character that is displayed on a screen or is printed (Figure 4-15). All of these conversions take place so quickly that you do not realize they are occurring.

Standards, such as those defined by ASCII and Unicode, also make it possible for components in computers to communicate with each other successfully. By following these and other standards, manufacturers can produce a component and be assured that it will operate correctly in a computer. Appendix C at the back of this book discusses the ASCII and Unicode schemes in more depth, along with the parity bit and number systems.

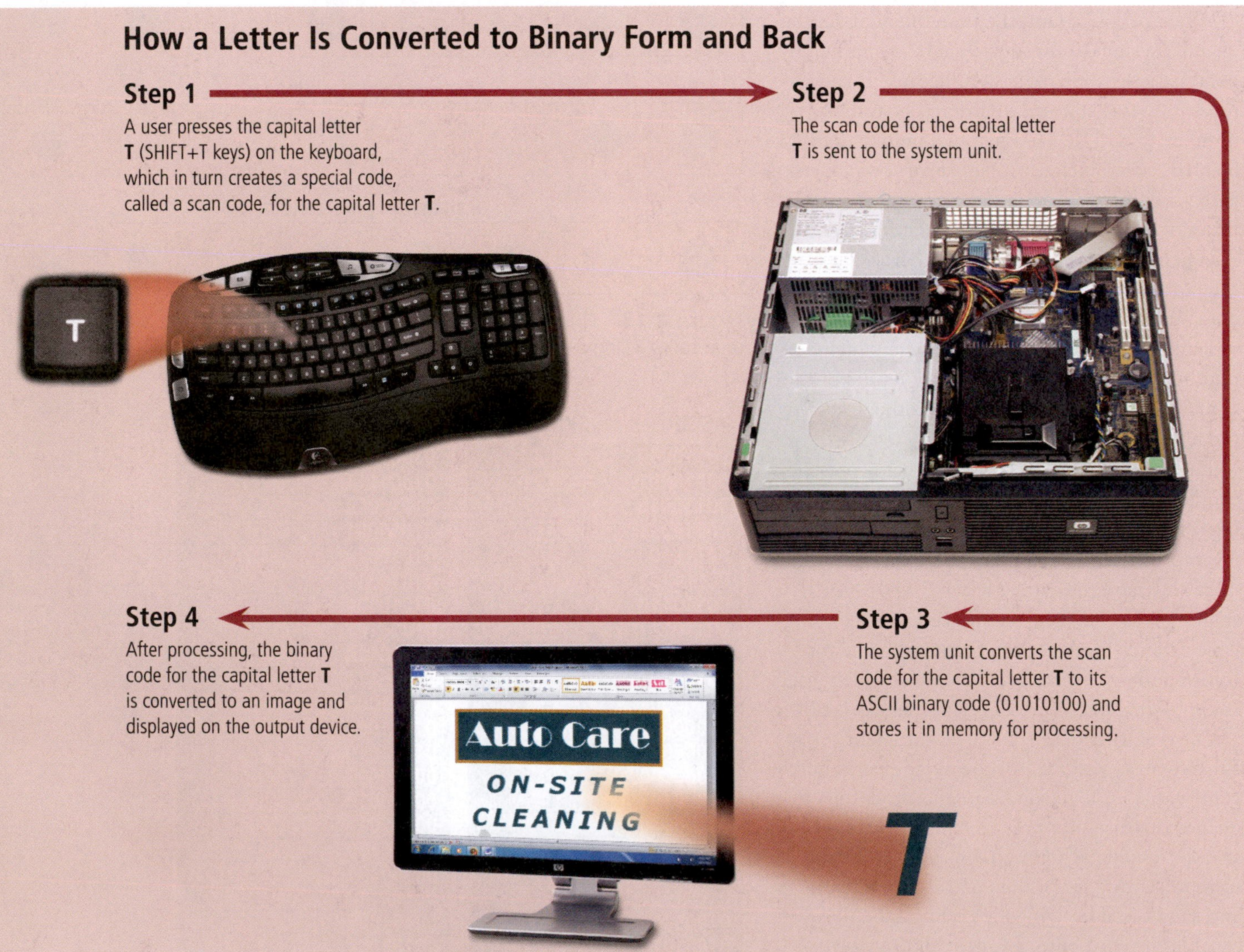

Figure 4-15 This figure shows how a letter is converted to binary form and back.

Memory

Memory consists of electronic components that store instructions waiting to be executed by the processor, data needed by those instructions, and the results of processing the data (information). Memory usually consists of one or more chips on the motherboard or some other circuit board in the computer.

Memory stores three basic categories of items: (1) the operating system and other system software that control or maintain the computer and its devices; (2) application programs that carry out a specific task such as word processing; and (3) the data being processed by the application programs and resulting information. This role of memory to store both data and programs is known as the *stored program concept*.

Bytes and Addressable Memory

A byte (character) is the basic storage unit in memory. When application program instructions and data are transferred to memory from storage devices, the instructions and data exist as bytes. Each byte resides temporarily in a location in memory that has an *address*. An address simply is a unique number that identifies the location of a byte in memory. The illustration in Figure 4-16 shows how seats in an opera house are similar to addresses in memory: (1) a seat, which is identified by a unique seat number, holds one person at a time, and a location in memory, which is identified by a unique address, holds a single byte; and (2) both a seat, identified by a seat number, and a byte, identified by an address, can be empty. To access data or instructions in memory, the computer references the addresses that contain bytes of data.

Figure 4-16 Seats in an opera house are similar to addresses in memory: a seat holds one person at a time, and a location in memory holds a single byte; and both a seat and a byte can be empty.

Memory Sizes

Manufacturers state the size of memory (Figure 4-17) and storage devices in terms of the number of bytes the chip or device has available for storage. Recall that storage devices hold data, instructions, and information for future use, while most memory holds these items temporarily. A **kilobyte** (**KB** or **K**) is equal to exactly 1,024 bytes. To simplify memory and storage definitions, computer users often round a kilobyte down to 1,000 bytes. For example, if a memory chip can store 100 KB, it can hold approximately 100,000 bytes (characters). A **megabyte** (**MB**) is equal to approximately 1 million bytes. A **gigabyte** (**GB**) equals approximately 1 billion bytes. A **terabyte** (**TB**) is equal to approximately 1 trillion bytes.

Memory Sizes

Term	Abbreviation	Approximate Number of Bytes	Exact Number of Bytes	Approximate Number of Pages of Text
Kilobyte	KB or K	1 thousand	1,024	1/2
Megabyte	MB	1 million	1,048,576	500
Gigabyte	GB	1 billion	1,073,741,824	500,000
Terabyte	TB	1 trillion	1,099,511,627,776	500,000,000

Figure 4-17 Terms commonly used to define memory sizes.

Types of Memory

The system unit contains two types of memory: volatile and nonvolatile. When the computer's power is turned off, *volatile memory* loses its contents. *Nonvolatile memory*, by contrast, does not lose its contents when power is removed from the computer. Thus, volatile memory is temporary and nonvolatile memory is permanent. RAM is the most common type of volatile memory. Examples of nonvolatile memory include ROM, flash memory, and CMOS. The following sections discuss these types of memory.

RAM

Users typically are referring to RAM when discussing computer memory. **RAM** (*random access memory*), also called *main memory*, consists of memory chips that can be read from and written to by the processor and other devices. When you turn on power to a computer, certain operating system files (such as the files that determine how the desktop appears) load into RAM from a storage device such as a hard disk. These files remain in RAM as long as the computer has continuous power. As additional programs and data are requested, they also load into RAM from storage.

The processor interprets and executes a program's instructions while the program is in RAM. During this time, the contents of RAM may change (Figure 4-18). RAM can accommodate multiple programs simultaneously.

How Program Instructions Transfer in and out of RAM

Step 1
When you start the computer, certain operating system files are loaded into RAM from the hard disk. The operating system displays the user interface on the screen.

Step 2
When you start a Web browser, the program's instructions are loaded into RAM from the hard disk. The Web browser and certain operating system instructions are in RAM. The Web browser window appears on the screen.

Step 3
When you start a paint program, the program's instructions are loaded into RAM from the hard disk. The paint program, along with the Web browser and certain operating system instructions, are in RAM. The paint program window appears on the screen.

Step 4
When you quit a program, such as the Web browser, its program instructions are removed from RAM. The Web browser no longer is displayed on the screen.

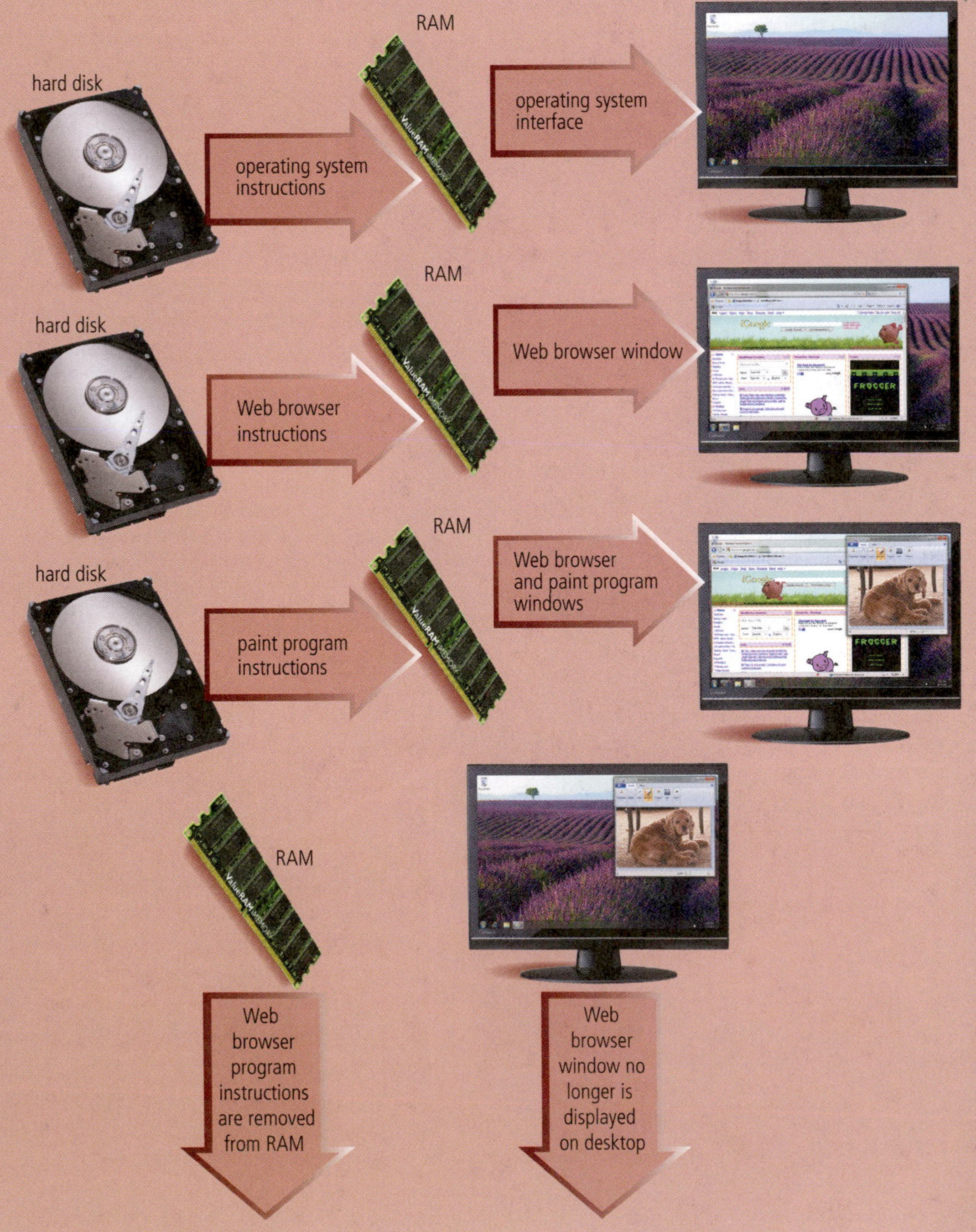

Figure 4-18 This figure shows how program instructions transfer in and out of RAM.

Most RAM is volatile, which means it loses its contents when the power is removed from the computer. For this reason, you must save any data, instructions, and information you may need in the future. Saving is the process of copying data, instructions, and information from RAM to a storage device such as a hard disk.

Three basic types of RAM chips exist: dynamic RAM, static RAM, and magnetoresistive RAM.

- *Dynamic RAM* (*DRAM* pronounced DEE-ram) chips must be re-energized constantly or they lose their contents. Many variations of DRAM chips exist, most of which are faster than the basic DRAM (Figure 4-19). Most personal computers today use some form of SDRAM chips or RDRAM chips.
- *Static RAM* (*SRAM* pronounced ESS-ram) chips are faster and more reliable than any variation of DRAM chips. These chips do not have to be re-energized as often as DRAM chips, thus, the term static. SRAM chips, however, are much more expensive than DRAM chips. Special applications such as cache use SRAM chips. A later section in this chapter discusses cache.
- A newer type of RAM, called *magnetoresistive RAM* (*MRAM* pronounced EM-ram), stores data using magnetic charges instead of electrical charges. Manufacturers claim that MRAM has greater storage capacity, consumes less power, and has faster access times than electronic RAM. Also, MRAM retains its contents after power is removed from the computer, which could prevent loss of data for users. As the cost of MRAM declines, experts predict MRAM could replace both DRAM and SRAM.

RAM chips usually reside on a **memory module**, which is a small circuit board. **Memory slots** on the motherboard hold memory modules (Figure 4-20). Three types of memory modules are SIMMs, DIMMs, and RIMMs. A *SIMM* (*single inline memory module*) has pins on opposite sides of the circuit board that connect together to form a single set of contacts. With a *DIMM* (*dual inline memory module*), by contrast, the pins on opposite sides of the circuit board do not connect and thus form two sets of contacts. SIMMs and DIMMs typically hold SDRAM chips. A *RIMM* (*Rambus inline memory module*) houses RDRAM chips. For a more technical discussion about RAM, read the High-Tech Talk article on page 242 at the end of this chapter. To learn more about how to install RAM in a computer, complete the Learn How To 1 activity on pages 252 and 253.

RAM

For more information, visit the Computer Concepts CourseMate Web site at www.cengagebrain.com, navigate to the Chapter 4 Web Link resource for this book, and then click RAM.

DRAM Variations

Name	Comments
SDRAM (Synchronous DRAM)	• synchronized to the system clock • much faster than DRAM
DDR SDRAM (Double Data Rate SDRAM)	• transfers data twice, instead of once, for each clock cycle • faster than SDRAM
DDR2	• second generation of DDR • faster than DDR
DDR3	• third generation of DDR • designed for computers with multi-core processors • faster than DDR2
RDRAM (Rambus DRAM)	• uses pipelining techniques • much faster than SDRAM

Figure 4-19 This table shows variations of DRAM chips.

Figure 4-20 This photo shows a memory module being inserted in a motherboard.

RAM Configurations The amount of RAM necessary in a computer often depends on the types of software you plan to use. A computer executes programs that are in RAM. Think of RAM as the workspace on the top of your desk. Just as the top of your desk needs a certain amount of space to hold papers, a computer needs a certain amount of memory to store programs, data, and information. The more RAM a computer has, the faster the computer will respond.

Retail software typically indicates the minimum amount of RAM it requires. If you want the software to perform optimally, usually you need more than the minimum specifications for the software.

Figure 4-21 lists guidelines for the amount of RAM for various types of users. Advertisements normally list the type of processor and the amount of RAM in the computer. The amount of RAM in computers purchased today ranges from 1 GB to 128 GB. (A computer with more than 4 GB of RAM should have a 64-bit processor, which is discussed later in this chapter, and an operating system that can utilize the RAM.) In an advertisement, manufacturers typically specify the maximum amount of RAM a computer can hold, for example, 4 GB expandable to 32 GB. Read Ethics & Issues 4-4 for a related discussion.

FAQ 4-4

Can I add more RAM to my computer?

Check your computer documentation to see how much RAM you can add. RAM modules are relatively inexpensive and usually include easy-to-follow installation instructions. Be sure to purchase RAM that is compatible with your brand and model of computer.

For more information, visit the Computer Concepts CourseMate Web site at www.cengagebrain.com, navigate to the Chapter 4 FAQ resource for this book, and then click Upgrading RAM.

ETHICS & ISSUES 4-4

How Much Technology Should Be Provided to Students and Teachers?

Around the country and around the world, local and national governments have begun to supply schoolchildren with inexpensive notebook computers, including netbooks. Many school districts in the United States purchase notebook computers for each student and hope to recoup some of the cost by purchasing lower-cost CD-based textbooks. The United Nations endorses a plan known as *One Laptop per Child* to supply $100 notebook computers to developing countries, some of which already pledged to purchase millions of the devices for schoolchildren. The device, which recharges with a hand crank, includes Wi-Fi networking and a simple, intuitive user interface.

Supporters of these plans maintain that computer literacy and electronic communications are vital skills in today's world, and students should be introduced to computers as early in their school years as possible. Others claim that when students use notebook computers, instructors tend to lecture less, requiring students to engage in more research and independent study. Many people oppose plans to equip every student with a computer because they say that the technology detracts from traditional educational subjects, such as basic reading and math. Some believe that the best approach is to maintain dedicated computer lab rooms rather than allow computers in the classroom. Computers require maintenance, support, and instructional time to teach students how to use the devices. Young children may lack the responsibility to care for and use the computers properly.

Should schools supply computers to all students or teachers or both? Why or why not? What is the appropriate grade level at which to require computer literacy? Why? Should computers be relegated to a dedicated lab room? Why or why not?

RAM	2 GB or less	2 GB to 8 GB	8 GB and up
Use	Home and business users managing personal finances; using standard application software such as word processing; using educational or entertainment optical discs; communicating with others on the Web	Users requiring more advanced multimedia capabilities; running number-intensive accounting, financial, or spreadsheet programs; using voice recognition; working with videos, music, and digital imaging; creating Web sites; participating in video conferences; playing Internet games	Power users creating professional Web sites; running sophisticated CAD, 3-D design, or other graphics-intensive software

Figure 4-21 Determining how much RAM you need depends on the programs you intend to run on your computer.

Cache

Most of today's computers improve their processing times with **cache** (pronounced cash). Two types of cache are memory cache and disk cache. This chapter discusses memory cache. Chapter 7 discusses disk cache.

Memory cache helps speed the processes of the computer because it stores frequently used instructions and data. Most personal computers today have two types of memory cache: L1 cache and L2 cache. Some also have L3 cache.

- *L1 cache* is built directly in the processor chip. L1 cache usually has a very small capacity, ranging from 8 KB to 128 KB. The more common sizes for personal computers are 32 KB or 64 KB.
- *L2 cache* is slightly slower than L1 cache but has a much larger capacity, ranging from 64 KB to 16 MB. When discussing cache, most users are referring to L2 cache. Current processors include *advanced transfer cache* (*ATC*), a type of L2 cache built directly on the processor chip. Processors that use ATC perform at much faster rates than those that do not use it.

  Personal computers today typically have from 512 KB to 12 MB of advanced transfer cache. Servers and workstations have from 12 MB to 16 MB of advanced transfer cache.
- *L3 cache* is a cache on the motherboard that is separate from the processor chip. L3 cache exists only on computers that use L2 advanced transfer cache. Personal computers often have up to 8 MB of L3 cache; servers and workstations have from 8 MB to 24 MB of L3 cache.

Cache speeds up processing time because it stores frequently used instructions and data. When the processor needs an instruction or data, it searches memory in this order: L1 cache, then L2 cache, then L3 cache (if it exists), then RAM — with a greater delay in processing for each level of memory it must search (Figure 4-22). If the instruction or data is not found in memory, then it must search a slower speed storage medium such as a hard disk or optical disc.

Windows users can increase the size of cache through *Windows ReadyBoost*, which can allocate available storage space on removable flash memory devices as additional cache. Examples of removable flash memory include USB flash drives, CompactFlash cards, and SD (Secure Digital) cards. Removable flash memory is discussed in more depth later in the book.

Windows ReadyBoost
For more information, visit the Computer Concepts CourseMate Web site at www.cengagebrain.com, navigate to the Chapter 4 Web Link resource for this book, and then click Windows ReadyBoost.

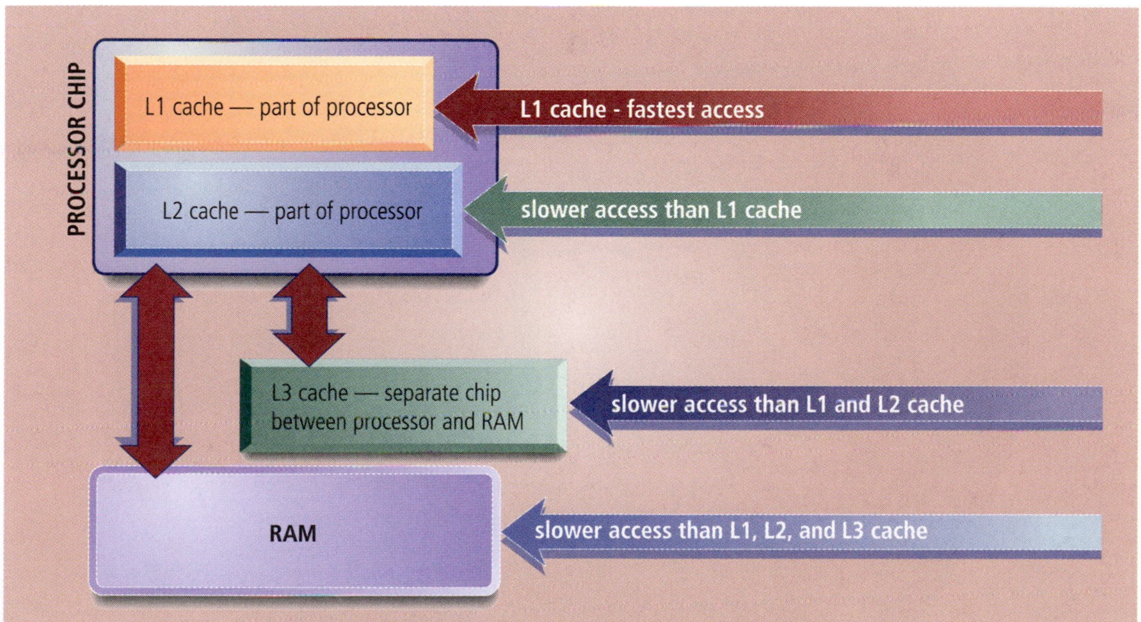

Figure 4-22 Cache helps speed processing times when the processor requests data, instructions, or information.

ROM

Read-only memory (**ROM** pronounced rahm) refers to memory chips storing permanent data and instructions. The data on most ROM chips cannot be modified — hence, the name read-only. ROM is nonvolatile, which means its contents are not lost when power is removed from the computer. In addition to computers, many devices contain ROM chips. For example, ROM chips in printers contain data for fonts.

Manufacturers of ROM chips often record data, instructions, or information on the chips when they manufacture the chips. These ROM chips, called **firmware**, contain permanently written data, instructions, or information.

A *PROM (programmable read-only memory) chip* is a blank ROM chip on which a programmer can write permanently. Programmers use *microcode* instructions to program a PROM chip. Once a programmer writes the microcode on the PROM chip, it functions like a regular ROM chip and cannot be erased or changed.

A variation of the PROM chip, called an *EEPROM* (electrically erasable programmable read-only memory) *chip*, allows a programmer to erase the microcode with an electric signal.

ROM

For more information, visit the Computer Concepts CourseMate Web site at www.cengagebrain.com, navigate to the Chapter 4 Web Link resource for this book, and then click ROM.

Flash Memory

Flash memory is a type of nonvolatile memory that can be erased electronically and rewritten, similar to EEPROM. Most computers use flash memory to hold their startup instructions because it allows the computer easily to update its contents. For example, when the computer changes from standard time to daylight savings time, the contents of a flash memory chip (and the real-time clock chip) change to reflect the new time.

Flash memory chips also store data and programs on many mobile computers and devices, such as smart phones, portable media players, PDAs, printers, digital cameras, automotive devices, digital voice recorders, and pagers. When you enter names and addresses in a smart phone or PDA, a flash memory chip stores the data. Some portable media players store music on flash memory chips (Figure 4-23); others store music on tiny hard disks or flash memory cards. Flash memory cards contain flash memory on a removable device instead of a chip.

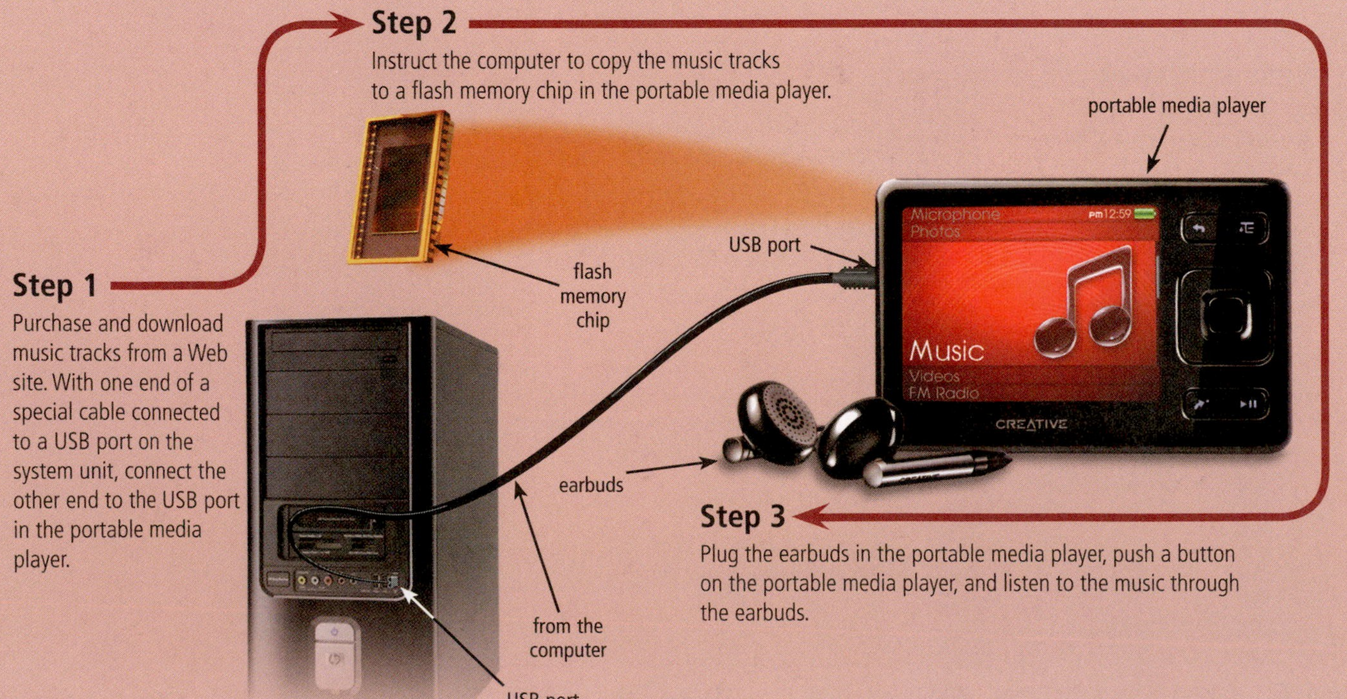

Figure 4-23 This figure shows how a portable media player might store music in flash memory.

FAQ 4-5

How much music can I store on a portable media player?

Portable media players that store music on flash memory chips can hold up to 16,000 songs. Portable media players with tiny hard disks have a much greater storage capacity — from 1,000 to more than 80,000 songs.

For more information, visit the Computer Concepts CourseMate Web site at www.cengagebrain.com, navigate to the Chapter 4 FAQ resource for this book, and then click Portable Media Players.

CMOS

Some RAM chips, flash memory chips, and other memory chips use **complementary metal-oxide semiconductor** (**CMOS** pronounced SEE-moss) technology because it provides high speeds and consumes little power. CMOS technology uses battery power to retain information even when the power to the computer is off. Battery-backed CMOS memory chips, for example, can keep the calendar, date, and time current even when the computer is off. The flash memory chips that store a computer's startup information often use CMOS technology.

Memory Access Times

Access time is the amount of time it takes the processor to read data, instructions, and information from memory. A computer's access time directly affects how fast the computer processes data. Accessing data in memory can be more than 200,000 times faster than accessing data on a hard disk because of the mechanical motion of the hard disk.

Today's manufacturers use a variety of terminology to state access times (Figure 4-24). Some use fractions of a second, which for memory occurs in nanoseconds. A **nanosecond** (abbreviated *ns*) is one billionth of a second. A nanosecond is extremely fast (Figure 4-25). In fact, electricity travels about one foot in a nanosecond.

Other manufacturers state access times in MHz; for example, 800 MHz DDR2 SDRAM. If a manufacturer states access time in megahertz, you can convert it to nanoseconds by dividing 1 billion ns by the megahertz number. For example, 800 MHz equals approximately 1.25 ns (1,000,000,000/800,000,000).

The access time (speed) of memory contributes to the overall performance of the computer. Standard SDRAM chips can have access times up to 133 MHz (about 7.5 ns), and access times of the DDR SDRAM chips reach 266 MHz, DDR2 chips reach 800 MHz, and DDR3 chips reach 1600 MHz. The higher the megahertz, the faster the access time; conversely, the lower the nanoseconds, the faster the access time. The faster RDRAM chips can have access times up to 1600 MHz (about 0.625 ns). ROM access times range from 25 to 250 ns.

While access times of memory greatly affect overall computer performance, manufacturers and retailers usually list a computer's memory in terms of its size, not its access time. Thus, an advertisement might describe a computer as having 2 GB of SDRAM upgradeable to 4 GB.

Access Time Terminology

Term	Abbreviation	Speed
Millisecond	ms	One-thousandth of a second
Microsecond	μs	One-millionth of a second
Nanosecond	ns	One-billionth of a second
Picosecond	ps	One-trillionth of a second

Figure 4-24 Access times are measured in fractions of a second. This table lists the terms used to define access times.

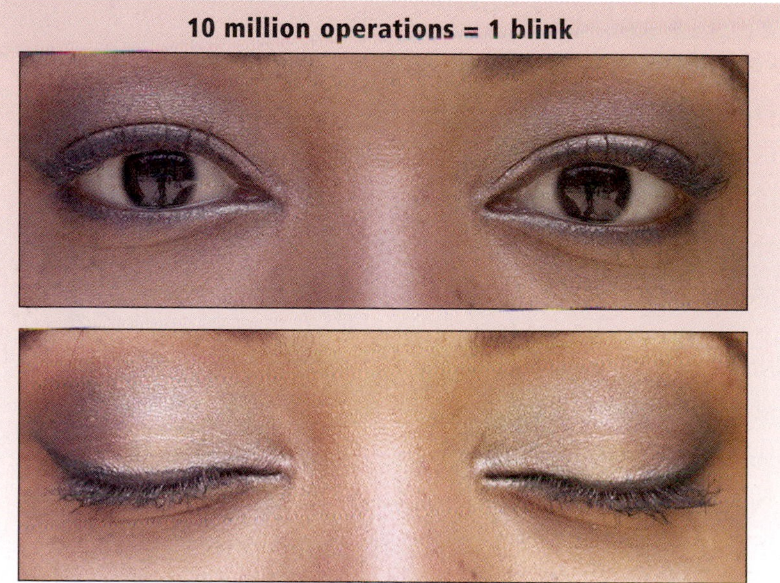

Figure 4-25 It takes about one-tenth of a second to blink your eye, which is the equivalent of 100 million nanoseconds. In the time it takes to blink your eye, a computer can perform some operations 10 million times.

QUIZ YOURSELF 4-2

Instructions: Find the true statement below. Then, rewrite the remaining false statements so that they are true.

1. A computer's memory access time directly affects how fast the computer processes data.
2. A gigabyte (GB) equals approximately 1 trillion bytes.
3. Memory cache helps speed the processes of the computer because it stores seldom used instructions and data.
4. Most computers are analog, which means they recognize only two discrete states: on and off.
5. Most RAM retains its contents when the power is removed from the computer.
6. Read-only memory (ROM) refers to memory chips storing temporary data and instructions.

Quiz Yourself Online: To further check your knowledge of pages 221 through 229, visit the Computer Concepts CourseMate Web site at www.cengagebrain.com, navigate to the Chapter 4 Quiz Yourself resource for this book, and then click Objectives 5 – 7.

Expansion Slots and Adapter Cards

An **expansion slot** is a socket on the motherboard that can hold an adapter card. An **adapter card**, sometimes called an *expansion card*, is a circuit board that enhances functions of a component of the system unit and/or provides connections to peripherals. A **peripheral** is a device that connects to the system unit and is controlled by the processor in the computer. Examples of peripherals are modems, disk drives, printers, scanners, and keyboards.

Video Cards

For more information, visit the Computer Concepts CourseMate Web site at www.cengagebrain.com, navigate to the Chapter 4 Web Link resource for this book, and then click Video Cards.

Figure 4-26 lists currently used types of adapter cards. Sometimes, all functionality is built in the adapter card. With others, a cable connects the adapter card to a device, such as a digital video camera, outside the system unit. Some are a card that you insert in a slot on the computer. Figure 4-27 shows an adapter card being inserted in an expansion slot on a personal computer motherboard.

Some motherboards include all necessary capabilities and do not require adapter cards. Other motherboards may require adapter cards to provide capabilities such as sound and video. A **sound card** enhances the sound-generating capabilities of a personal computer by allowing sound to be input through a microphone and output through external speakers or headphones. A **video card**, also called a *graphics card*, converts computer output into a video signal that travels through a cable to the monitor, which displays an image on the screen.

Types of Adapter Cards

Adapter Card	Purpose
CableCARD	Allows viewing of digital cable television channels
Disk controller	Connects disk drives
FireWire	Connects to FireWire devices
HDTV tuner	Allows viewing of HDTV broadcasts on the monitor
MIDI	Connects musical instruments
Modem	Connects other computers through telephone lines, cable television lines, or other transmission media
Network	Connects other computers and peripherals
PC-to-TV converter	Connects a television
Sound	Connects speakers or a microphone
TV tuner	Allows viewing of television channels on the monitor
USB	Connects to USB devices
Video	Connects a monitor
Video capture	Connects an analog video camera or VCR

Figure 4-26 Currently used adapter cards and their functions.

Figure 4-27 An adapter card being inserted in an expansion slot on the motherboard of a personal computer.

Today's computers support **Plug and Play**, which means the computer automatically can configure adapter cards and other peripherals as you install them. Having Plug and Play support means you can plug in a device, turn on the computer, and then immediately begin using the device.

Removable Flash Memory

Unlike adapter cards that require you to open the system unit and install the card on the motherboard, you can change a removable flash memory device without having to open the system unit or restart the computer. This feature, called *hot plugging*, allows you to insert and remove the removable flash memory and other devices while the computer is running. Removable flash memory includes memory cards, USB flash drives, and PC Cards/ExpressCard modules (Figure 4-28).

- A **memory card** is a removable flash memory device, usually no bigger than 1.5" in height or width, that you insert and remove from a slot in a personal computer, game console, mobile device, or card reader/writer. Many mobile and consumer devices, such as smart phones, digital cameras, and portable media players use memory cards. Some printers and computers have built-in card readers/writers or slots that read memory cards. In addition, you can purchase an external card reader/writer that attaches to any computer.
- A *USB flash drive* is a flash memory storage device that plugs in a USB port on a computer or mobile device. (A later section discusses USB ports.)
- Many desktop computers, traditional notebook computers, and Tablet PCs have a **PC Card slot** or an **ExpressCard slot**, which is a special type of expansion slot that holds a PC Card or an ExpressCard module, respectively. Most netbooks do not have a PC Card slot or ExpressCard slot. A **PC Card** is a thin, credit card-sized removable flash memory device that primarily is used today to enable traditional notebook computers and Tablet PCs to access the Internet wirelessly. ExpressCard modules, about one-half the size of PC Cards, are the next generation of PC Cards. An **ExpressCard module**, which can be used as a removable flash memory device, adds memory, communications, multimedia, and security capabilities to computers.

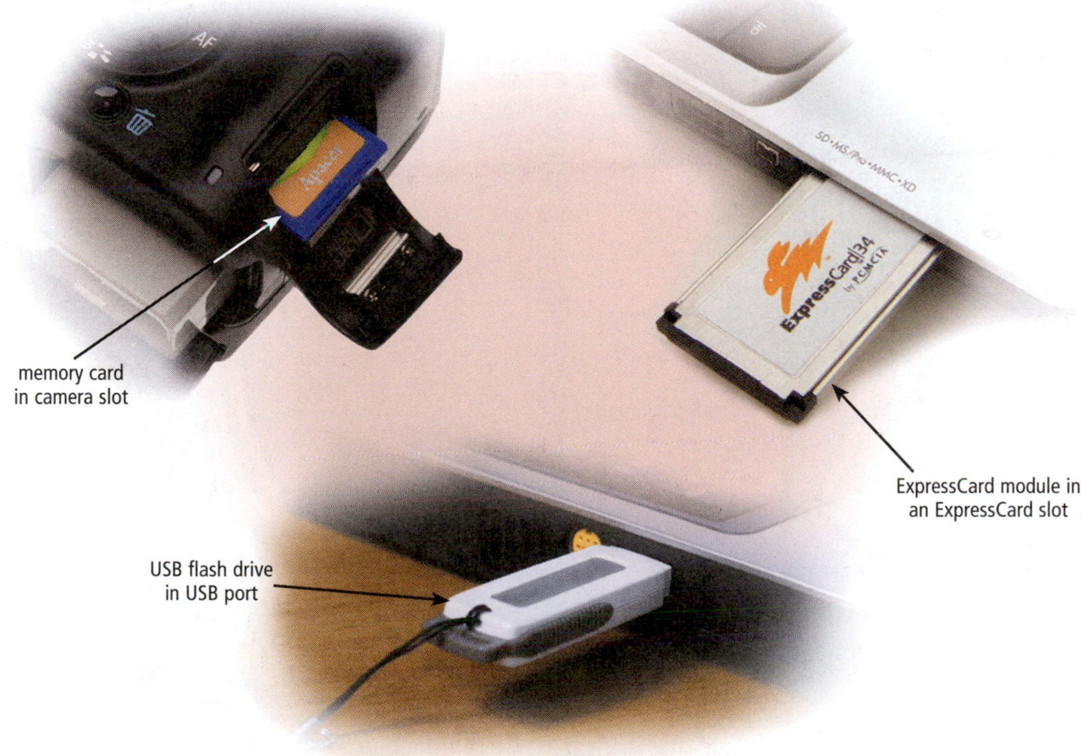

Figure 4-28 Examples of removable flash memory in use.

Ports and Connectors

A **port** is the point at which a peripheral attaches to or communicates with a system unit so that the peripheral can send data to or receive information from the computer. An external device, such as a keyboard, monitor, printer, mouse, and microphone, often attaches by a cable to a port on the system unit. Instead of port, the term **jack** sometimes is used to identify audio and video ports. The front and back of a system unit on a desktop personal computer contain many ports (Figure 4-29). On notebook computers, including netbooks and Tablet PCs, the ports are on the back, front, and/or sides (Figure 4-30).

A **connector** joins a cable to a port. A connector at one end of a cable attaches to a port on the system unit, and a connector at the other end of the cable attaches to a port on the peripheral. Most connectors and ports are available in one of two genders: male or female. Male connectors and ports have one or more exposed pins, like the end of an electrical cord you plug in the wall. Female connectors and ports have matching holes to accept the pins on a male connector or port, like an electrical wall outlet.

Sometimes, you cannot attach a new peripheral to the computer because the port on the system unit is the same gender as the connector on the cable. In this case, purchasing a gender changer solves this problem. A *gender changer* is a device that enables you to join a port and a connector that are both female or both male.

Digital Audio Port

For more information, visit the Computer Concepts CourseMate Web site at www.cengagebrain.com, navigate to the Chapter 4 Web Link resource for this book, and then click Digital Audio Port.

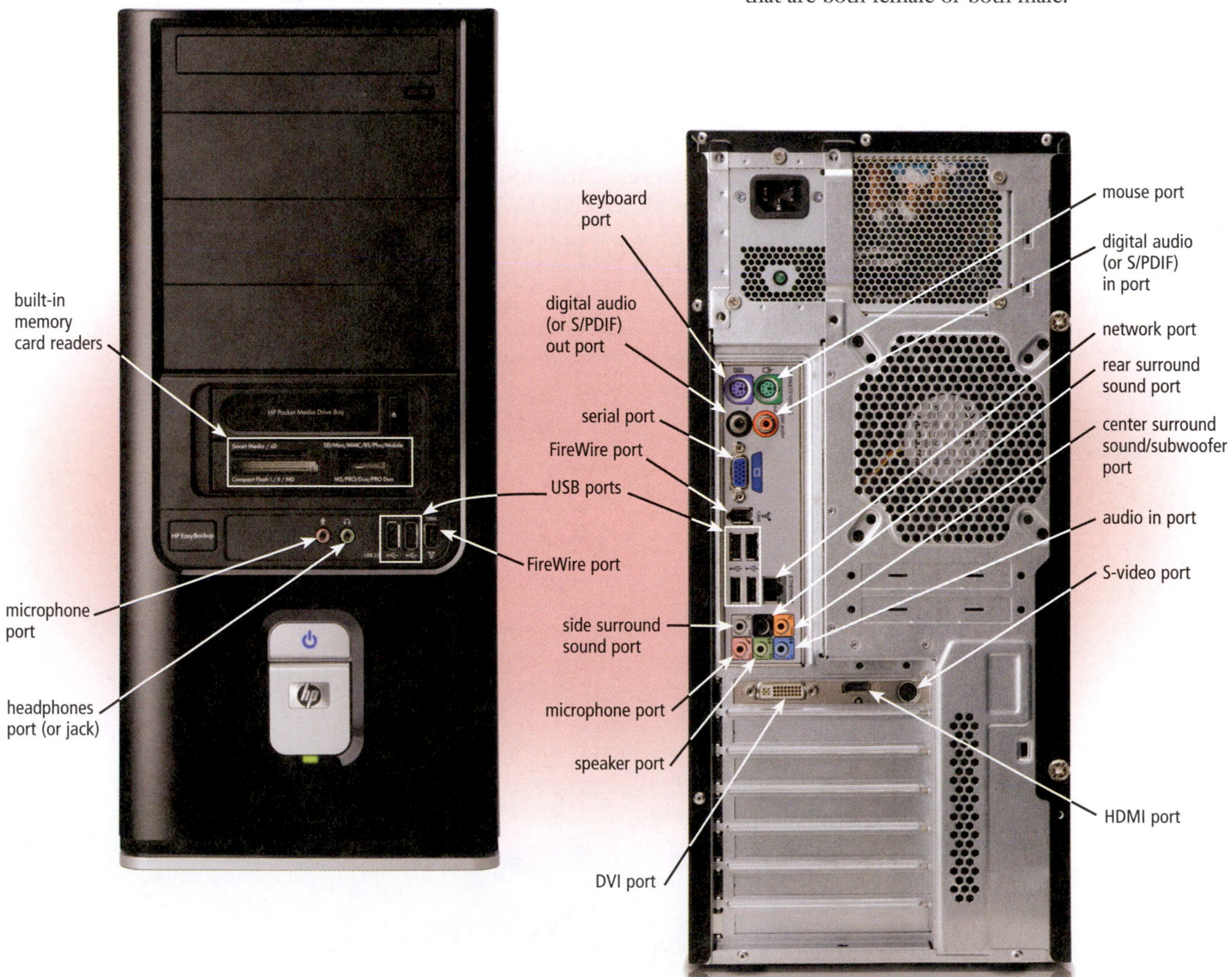

Figure 4-29 A system unit on a desktop personal computer has many ports on its front and back.

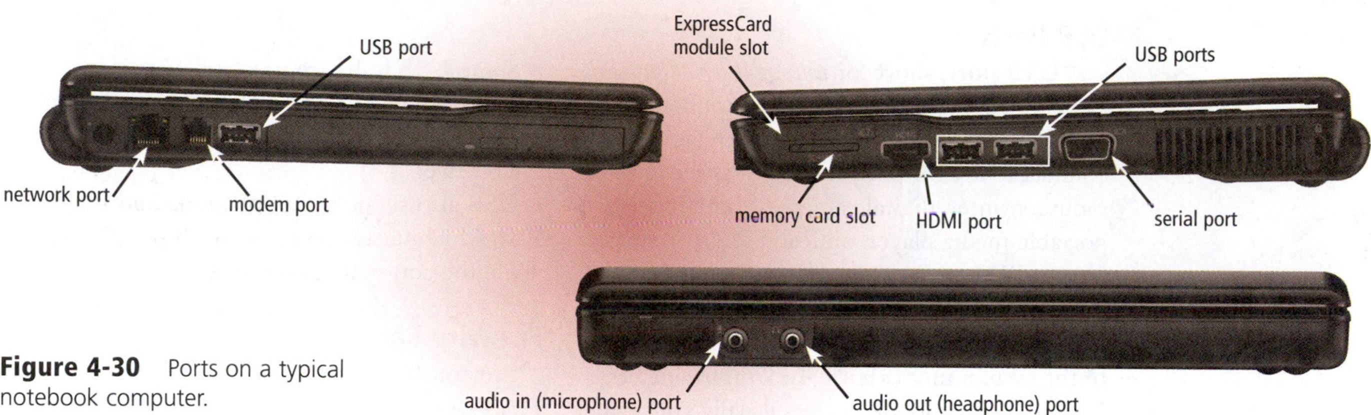

Figure 4-30 Ports on a typical notebook computer.

Manufacturers often identify cables by their connector types to assist you with purchasing a cable to connect a computer to a peripheral port. Figure 4-31 shows the different types of ports you may find on a system unit. Notice that many are color-coded to help you match the connector to the correct port. Some system units include these ports when you buy the computer. You add other ports by inserting adapter cards on the motherboard. Certain adapter cards have ports that allow you to attach a peripheral to the adapter card.

The next section discusses the more widely used ports.

Port Types

Type	Picture	Type	Picture	Type	Picture
Audio in		HDMI port		Serial	
Cable TV		Headphones		Side surround sound	
Center surround sound/subwoofer		Keyboard		S/PDIF in	
Composite video in		Microphone		S/PDIF out	
Digital Video Interface (DVI)		Monitor		Speaker	
eSATA port		Mouse		S-video	
FireWire		Network		Telephone line in	
FM reception		Rear surround sound		USB	

Figure 4-31 Examples of different types of ports on a system unit.

USB Ports

A **USB port**, short for *universal serial bus port*, can connect up to 127 different peripherals together with a single connector. Devices that connect to a USB port include the following: mouse, printer, digital camera, scanner, speakers, portable media player, optical disc drive, smart phone, PDA, game console, and removable hard disk. Personal computers typically have six to eight USB ports on the front and/or back of the system unit (Figure 4-29 on page 232). USB ports on mobile devices usually are smaller than those on personal computers. Figure 4-32 shows a variety of USB ports and connectors.

USB 2.0, also called *Hi-Speed USB*, is a more advanced and faster USB, with speeds 40 times higher than that of its predecessor. *USB 3.0* is approximately 10 times faster than USB 2.0. Both USB 2.0 and USB 3.0 are *backward compatible*, which means they support older USB devices as well as USB 2.0 or USB 3.0 devices. Keep in mind, though, that older USB devices do not run any faster in a newer USB port.

To attach multiple peripherals using a single USB port, you can use a USB hub. A **USB hub** is a device that plugs in a USB port on the system unit and contains multiple USB ports in which you plug cables from USB devices. USB hubs are self-powered or bus-powered. A self-powered USB hub draws power from an electrical outlet, whereas a bus-powered USB hub draws power from the USB bus in the computer. (The USB bus is discussed later in the chapter.) Some devices will work only with a self-powered hub.

USB Ports

For more information, visit the Computer Concepts CourseMate Web site at www.cengagebrain.com, navigate to the Chapter 4 Web Link resource for this book, and then click USB Ports.

USB Connectors and Ports

	Connector	Port	Where Used
Type A			Desktop computers, traditional notebook computers, netbooks, and Tablet PCs
Type B			Peripherals (printers, scanners, external hard disks, etc.)
Mini-B			Mobile devices (cameras, phones, handheld game consoles)

Figure 4-32 A variety of USB ports and connectors are available.

Some USB hubs are wireless. That is, a receiver plugs into a USB port on the computer and the USB hub communicates wirelessly with the receiver.

USB also supports hot plugging and Plug and Play, which means you can attach peripherals while the computer is running.

FireWire Ports

Previously called an *IEEE 1394 port*, a **FireWire port** is similar to a USB port in that it can connect multiple types of devices that require faster data transmission speeds, such as digital video cameras, digital VCRs, color printers, scanners, digital cameras, and DVD drives, to a single connector. A FireWire port allows you to connect up to 63 devices together. The three latest versions, FireWire 800, FireWire 1600, and FireWire 3200, have speeds faster than the original FireWire 400.

You can use a FireWire hub to attach multiple devices to a single FireWire port. A **FireWire hub** is a device that plugs in a FireWire port on the system unit and contains multiple FireWire ports in which you plug cables from FireWire devices. The FireWire port supports Plug and Play.

Other Ports

Some ports not included in typical computers but sometimes used are Bluetooth, SCSI, eSATA, IrDA, serial, and MIDI. For a computer to have these ports, you often must customize the computer purchase order.

Bluetooth Port **Bluetooth** technology uses radio waves to transmit data between two devices. Bluetooth devices have to be within about 33 feet of each other. Many computers, peripherals, smart phones, PDAs, cars, and other consumer electronics are Bluetooth-enabled, which means they contain a small chip that allows them to communicate with other Bluetooth-enabled computers and devices. Bluetooth headsets allow smart phone users to connect their telephone to a headset wirelessly.

If you have a computer that is not Bluetooth enabled, you can purchase a *Bluetooth wireless port adapter* that will convert an existing USB port into a Bluetooth port (Figure 4-33). Also available are Bluetooth PC Cards and ExpressCard modules for traditional notebook computers and Tablet PCs, and Bluetooth cards for smart phones and PDAs.

Figure 4-33 A Bluetooth wireless port adapter, such as the one shown here, converts a USB port into a Bluetooth port.

FAQ 4-6

Can I simultaneously use multiple wireless devices in my house?

Not always. Because some wireless devices may communicate using the same frequency range, they may interfere with each other. For example, a Bluetooth device temporarily may stop working while your cordless phone is in use, or your carbon monoxide detector may sound when your cell phone rings.

For more information, visit the Computer Concepts CourseMate Web site at www.cengagebrain.com, navigate to the Chapter 4 FAQ resource for this book, and then click Wireless Devices.

SCSI Port A special high-speed parallel port, called a **SCSI port**, allows you to attach SCSI (pronounced skuzzy) peripherals such as disk drives and printers. *SAS (serial-attached SCSI)* is a newer type of SCSI that transmits at much faster speeds than parallel SCSI. Depending on the type of *SCSI*, which stands for small computer system interface, you can daisy chain up to either 7 or 15 devices together. Some computers include a SCSI port. Others have a slot that supports a SCSI card.

eSATA Port An **eSATA port**, or *external SATA port*, allows you to connect an external SATA (Serial Advanced Technology Attachment) hard disk to a computer. SATA hard disks are popular because of their fast data transmission speeds. eSATA connections provide up to six times faster data transmission speeds than external hard disks attached to a computer's USB or FireWire port.

IrDA Port Some devices can transmit data via infrared light waves. For these wireless devices to transmit signals to a computer, both the computer and the device must have an **IrDA port** (Figure 4-34). These ports conform to standards developed by the *IrDA* (Infrared Data Association).

To ensure nothing obstructs the path of the infrared light wave, you must align the IrDA port on the device with the IrDA port on the computer, similarly to the way you operate a television remote control. Devices that use IrDA ports include a smart phone, PDA, keyboard, mouse, and printer. Several of these devices use a high-speed IrDA port, sometimes called a *fast infrared port*.

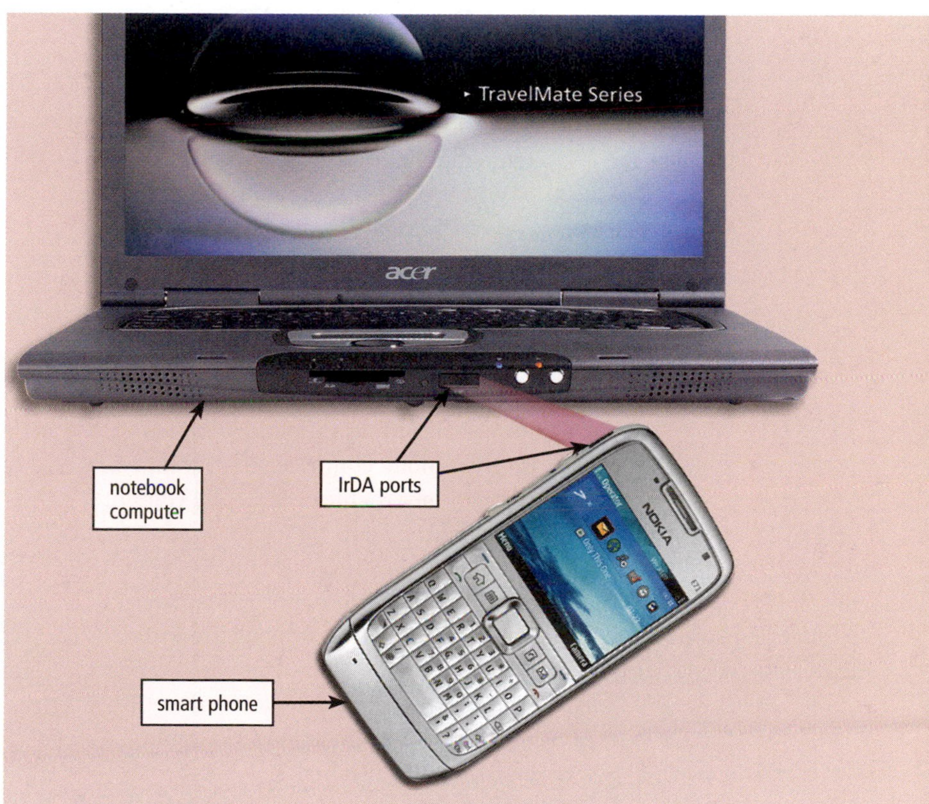

Figure 4-34 Many devices communicate wirelessly with desktop or notebook computers through IrDA ports.

Serial Ports A **serial port** is a type of interface that connects a device to the system unit by transmitting data one bit at a time. Some modems that connect the system unit to a telephone line use a serial port because the telephone line expects the data in a specific frequency.

MIDI Port A special type of serial port that connects the system unit to a musical instrument, such as an electronic keyboard, is called a **MIDI port**. Short for *Musical Instrument Digital Interface*, MIDI (pronounced MID-dee) is the electronic music industry's standard that defines how devices, such as sound cards and synthesizers, represent sounds electronically. A *synthesizer*, which can be a peripheral or a chip, creates sound from digital instructions.

A system unit with a MIDI port has the capability of recording sounds that have been created by a synthesizer and then processing the sounds (the data) to create new sounds. Nearly every sound card supports the MIDI standard, so that you can play and manipulate on one computer sounds that originally were created on another computer.

Port Replicators and Docking Stations

Instead of connecting peripherals directly to ports on a mobile computer, some mobile users prefer the flexibility of port replicators and docking stations. A *port replicator* is an external device that provides connections to peripherals through ports built into the device. The mobile user accesses peripherals by connecting the port replicator to a USB port or a special port on the mobile computer. Port replicators sometimes disable ports on the mobile computer to prevent conflicts among the devices on the computer and port replicator.

A docking station is similar to a port replicator, but it has more functionality. A *docking station*, which is an external device that attaches to a mobile computer or device, contains a power connection and provides connections to peripherals; it usually also includes slots for memory cards, optical disc drives, and other devices (Figure 4-35). With the mobile computer or device in the docking station, users can work with a full-sized keyboard, a mouse, and other desktop peripherals from their traditional notebook computer, netbook, or Tablet PC. Read Looking Ahead 4-1 for a look at the next generation of notebook computers.

Docking Station

For more information, visit the Computer Concepts CourseMate Web site at www.cengagebrain.com, navigate to the Chapter 4 Web Link resource for this book, and then click Docking Station.

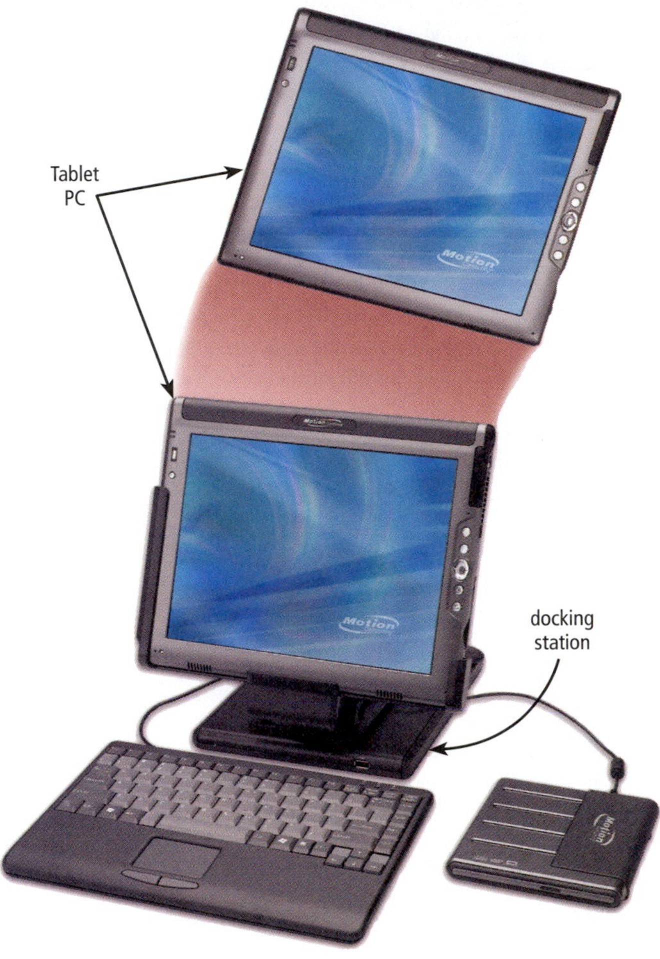

Figure 4-35 To use a slate Tablet PC while working at a desk, insert the Tablet PC in a docking station. Devices such as a keyboard and an optical disc drive can be plugged in the docking station.

LOOKING AHEAD 4-1

Bendable Notebook Computers Will Slip in Your Pocket

Today's notebook computers are light and compact, but they will be enormous compared to what is being planned for the retail marketplace in the next 10 years. Top designers at Lenovo and Intel are designing flexible machines weighing less than one pound that are thin enough to fold and place in a pocket. Battery life will be nearly one week, and the 256-core processors will make current computers with quad-core processors seem like they are running at a snail's pace.

Notebook computer users will speak into a microphone, touch the screen, or type on a virtual keyboard that does not have actual keys but can give feedback that a letter or number has been selected. Thin screens will roll out to any size needed and will be viewed easily outdoors. Users with sight impairments can coat their screens with a synthetic material that will create 3-D shapes for such tactile uses as reading Braille letters and blueprints.

For more information, visit the Computer Concepts CourseMate Web site at www.cengagebrain.com, navigate to the Chapter 4 Looking Ahead resource for this book, and then click Future Notebooks.

Buses

As explained earlier in this chapter, a computer processes and stores data as a series of electronic bits. These bits transfer internally within the circuitry of the computer along electrical channels. Each channel, called a **bus**, allows the various devices both inside and attached to the system unit to communicate with each other. Just as vehicles travel on a highway to move from one destination to another, bits travel on a bus (Figure 4-36).

Buses are used to transfer bits from input devices to memory, from memory to the processor, from the processor to memory, and from memory to output or storage devices. Buses consist of two parts: a data bus and an address bus. The *data bus* is used to transfer actual data and the *address bus* is used to transfer information about where the data should reside in memory.

The size of a bus, called the *bus width*, determines the number of bits that the computer can transmit at one time. For example, a 32-bit bus can transmit 32 bits (4 bytes) at a time. On a 64-bit bus, bits transmit from one location to another 64 bits (8 bytes) at a time. The larger the number of bits handled by the bus, the faster the computer transfers data. Using the highway analogy again, assume that one lane on a highway can carry one bit. A 32-bit bus is like a 32-lane highway. A 64-bit bus is like a 64-lane highway.

If a number in memory occupies 8 bytes, or 64 bits, the computer must transmit it in two separate steps when using a 32-bit bus: once for the first 32 bits and once for the second 32 bits. Using a 64-bit bus, the computer can transmit the number in a single step, transferring all 64 bits at once. The wider the bus, the fewer number of transfer steps required and the faster the transfer of data. Most personal computers today use a 64-bit bus.

In conjunction with the bus width, many computer professionals refer to a computer's word size. **Word size** is the number of bits the processor can interpret and execute at a given time. That is, a 64-bit processor can manipulate 64 bits at a time. Computers with a larger word size can process more data in the same amount of time than computers with a smaller word size. In most computers, the word size is the same as the bus width.

Every bus also has a clock speed. Just like the processor, manufacturers state the clock speed for a bus in hertz. Recall that one megahertz (MHz) is equal to one million ticks per second. Today's processors usually have a bus clock speed of 400, 533, 667, 800, 1066, 1333, or 1600 MHz. The higher the bus clock speed, the faster the transmission of data, which results in programs running faster.

A computer has these basic types of buses: a system bus, possibly a backside bus, and an expansion bus. A *system bus*, also called the *front side bus (FSB)*, is part of the motherboard and connects the processor to main memory. A *backside bus (BSB)* connects the processor to cache. An *expansion bus* allows the processor to communicate with peripherals. When computer professionals use the term bus by itself, they usually are referring to the system bus.

Figure 4-36 Just as vehicles travel on a highway, bits travel on a bus. Buses are used to transfer bits from input devices to memory, from memory to the processor, from the processor to memory, and from memory to output or storage devices.

Expansion Bus

Some peripherals outside the system unit connect to a port on an adapter card, which is inserted in an expansion slot on the motherboard. This expansion slot connects to the expansion bus, which allows the processor to communicate with the peripheral attached to the adapter card. Data transmitted to memory or the processor travels from the expansion slot via the expansion bus and the system bus.

The types of expansion buses on a motherboard determine the types of cards you can add to the computer. Thus, you should understand expansion buses commonly found in today's personal computers: PCI bus, PCI Express bus, AGP bus, USB, FireWire bus, and PC Card bus.

- The *PCI bus* (Peripheral Component Interconnect bus) is a high-speed expansion bus that connects higher speed devices. Types of cards you can insert in a PCI bus expansion slot include video cards, sound cards, SCSI cards, and high-speed network cards.
- The *PCI Express (PCIe) bus* is an expansion bus that expands on and doubles the speed of the original PCI bus. Nearly all video cards today use the PCI Express bus, as well as many hard disks and network cards. The ExpressCard technology used in traditional notebook computers and Tablet PCs also works with the PCI Express bus. Experts predict the PCI Express bus eventually will replace the PCI bus completely.
- The *Accelerated Graphics Port (AGP)* is a bus designed by Intel to improve the speed with which 3-D graphics and video transmit. With an AGP video card in an AGP bus slot, the AGP bus provides a faster, dedicated interface between the video card and memory. Newer processors support AGP technology.
- The USB (universal serial bus) and *FireWire bus* are buses that eliminate the need to install cards in expansion slots. In a computer with a USB, for example, USB devices connect to each other outside the system unit, and then a single cable attaches to the USB port. The USB port then connects to the USB, which connects to the PCI bus on the motherboard. The FireWire bus works in a similar fashion. With these buses, expansion slots are available for devices not compatible with USB or FireWire.
- The expansion bus for a PC Card is the *PC Card bus*. With a PC Card inserted in a PC Card slot, data travels on the PC Card bus to the PCI bus.

FireWire

For more information, visit the Computer Concepts CourseMate Web site at www.cengagebrain.com, navigate to the Chapter 4 Web Link resource for this book, and then click FireWire.

Bays

After you purchase a desktop or notebook computer, you may want to install an additional storage device, such as a disk drive, in the system unit. A **bay** is an opening inside the system unit in which you can install additional equipment. A bay is different from a slot on the motherboard, which is used for the installation of adapter cards. A **drive bay** is a rectangular opening that typically holds disk drives. Other bays house card readers and widely used ports such as USB, FireWire, and audio ports.

An *external bay* allows a user to access openings in the bay from outside the system unit (Figure 4-37). Optical disc drives are examples of devices installed in external bays. An *internal bay* is concealed entirely within the system unit. Hard disk drives are installed in internal bays.

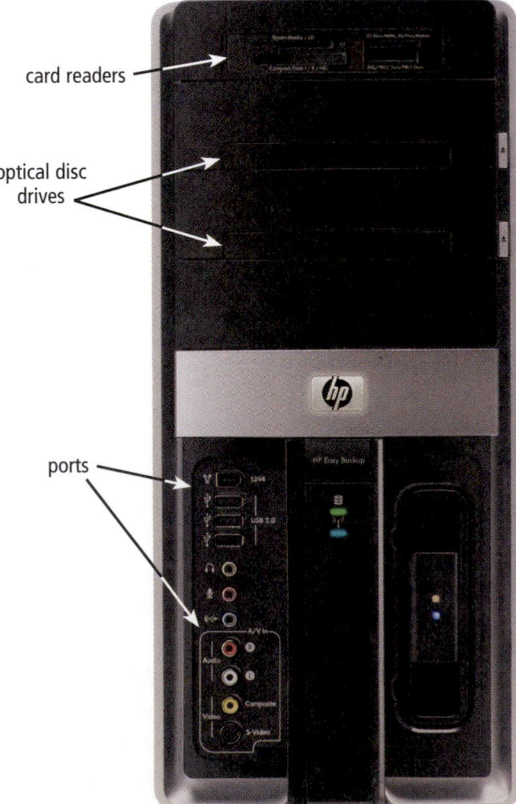

Figure 4-37 External bays usually are located beside or on top of one another.

Power Supply

Many personal computers plug in standard wall outlets, which supply an alternating current (AC) of 115 to 120 volts. This type of power is unsuitable for use with a computer, which requires a direct current (DC) ranging from 5 to more than 15 volts. The **power supply** is the component of the system unit that converts the wall outlet AC power into DC power. Different motherboards and computers require different wattages on the power supply. Notebook computers, including netbooks and Tablet PCs, can run using either batteries or a power supply. If a power supply is not providing the necessary power, the computer will not function properly.

Built into the power supply is a fan that keeps the power supply cool. Some have variable speed fans that change speed or stop running, depending on temperature in the system unit. Many newer computers have additional fans near certain components in the system unit such as the processor, hard disk, and ports. Some users install more fans to help dissipate heat generated by the components of the system unit. Mobile users may place their notebook computer on a cooling pad to help disperse the computer's heat.

Some external peripherals such as a cable modem, speakers, or a printer have an **AC adapter**, which is an external power supply. One end of the AC adapter plugs in the wall outlet and the other end attaches to the peripheral. The AC adapter converts the AC power into DC power that the peripheral requires.

? FAQ 4-7

How many fans are in a system unit?

Most system units have at least three fans: one in the power supply, one in the case, and one on the processor heat sink. In addition, you also may find a fan on a video card or other adapter card. While some computers contain fans that are designed to be quiet or operate in a quiet mode, others allow you to turn off noisy fans until they are needed. You also can purchase utility programs that slow or stop the fan until the temperature reaches a certain level.

For more information, visit the Computer Concepts CourseMate Web site at www.cengagebrain.com, navigate to the Chapter 4 FAQ resource for this book, and then click Computer Fans.

Putting It All Together

Many components of the system unit influence the speed and power of a computer, including the type of processor and the amount of RAM. The table in Figure 4-38 lists the suggested minimum processor and RAM requirements based on the needs of various types of computer users.

Suggested Minimum Configurations by User

User	Processor and RAM
Home	Intel Core i5 or Intel Core i3 or AMD Athlon II or AMD Sempron Minimum RAM: 2 GB
Small Office/ Home Office	Intel Core i7 or Intel Core i7 Extreme or AMD Phenom II or AMD Athlon II Minimum RAM: 4 GB
Mobile	Intel Core i7 Extreme or Intel Core i7 or AMD Phenom II or AMD Turion II Minimum RAM: 2 GB
Power	Intel Xeon or Intel Itanium or AMD Opteron Minimum RAM: 8 GB
Enterprise	Intel Core i7 or Intel Core i7 Extreme or AMD Phenom II or AMD Athlon II Minimum RAM: 4 GB

Figure 4-38 Suggested processor and RAM configurations by user.

Keeping Your Computer or Mobile Device Clean

Over time, the system unit collects dust — even in a clean environment. Built up dust can block airflow in a computer or mobile device, which can cause it to overheat, corrode, or even stop working. By cleaning your computer or mobile device once or twice a year, you can help extend its life. This preventive maintenance task requires a few basic products (Figure 4-39):

- can of compressed air — removes dust and lint from difficult-to-reach areas; removes sticky liquid spilled on keyboards
- lint-free antistatic wipes and swabs
- screen cleaning solution or 50/50 mix of rubbing alcohol and water (do not use ammonia-based solutions)
- small computer vacuum (or small attachments on your house vacuum)
- antistatic wristband — to avoid damaging internal components with static electricity
- small screwdriver (may be required to open the case or remove adapter cards)

Before cleaning the exterior of a computer or mobile device, turn it off, and if necessary, unplug it from the electrical outlet, remove its battery, and disconnect all cables from the ports. Use compressed air to blow away dust from any openings on the computer or device case, such as drives, slots, ports, and fan vents. Then, use an antistatic wipe to clean the exterior of the case and a cleaning solution on a soft cloth to clean the screen.

If you do not feel comfortable cleaning the inside of a desktop or notebook computer case, you can have a local professional or computer company clean it for you (read Ethics & Issues 4-5 for a related discussion). Or, if you are familiar with electronics, you can clean it yourself. While working inside the case, be sure to wear an antistatic wristband. Use the antistatic wipes to clean inside the walls of the case. Vacuum as much dust as possible from the interior of the case, including the wires, chips, adapter cards, and fan blades. Release short blasts of compressed air in areas the vacuum cannot reach. If the motherboard and adapter cards still look dirty, gently clean them with lint-free wipes or swabs lightly dampened with alcohol. When finished, write down the date you cleaned the computer so that you have a record for your next cleaning.

Figure 4-39 With a few products, this computer user keeps his computer clean.

ETHICS & ISSUES 4-5

Should Computer Repair Technicians Be Required to Have a Private Investigator License?

Recently, a state government passed legislation that requires computer repair technicians to obtain a private investigator license if they review or analyze data on computers that they repair. One reason the law was written is that business managers and parents often take computers to technicians to analyze the computer usage habits of employees and children. In this sense, the technician is performing an investigation. To obtain a private investigator license, one must obtain a criminal justice degree or serve as an apprentice for a private investigator. The process takes up to three years and is expensive. Violating the law, however, may result in jail time and a large fine. Many smaller computer repair companies claim that, if enforced, the law certainly will put them out of business. Larger companies sometimes have employees with private investigator licenses. Critics of the law claim that the law is overly broad. For example, parents should have the right to take a computer to a technician to see what their children have been doing on the computer.

Should computer repair technicians be required to have a private investigator license? Why or why not? Should the government consider a different type of certification for computer repair technicians who must review or analyze customer data in the course of their job? If so, what should be required for the certification?

FAQ 4-8

Is it safe to open my computer case?

Yes, as long as you are careful and wear an antistatic wristband. Before opening the case, though, check with the computer manufacturer to be sure you will not void a warranty if you clean the computer or install additional components. Also, do not handle any internal components unless you intend to repair or replace them, as unnecessary handling may decrease the life of the component(s).

For more information, visit the Computer Concepts CourseMate Web site at www.cengagebrain.com, navigate to the Chapter 4 FAQ resource for this book, and then click Computer Cases.

QUIZ YOURSELF 4-3

Instructions: Find the true statement below. Then, rewrite the remaining false statements so that they are true.

1. A bus is the point at which a peripheral attaches to or communicates with a system unit so that the peripheral can send data to or receive information from the computer.
2. An AC adapter is a socket on the motherboard that can hold an adapter card.
3. Built into the power supply is a heater that keeps components of the system unit warm.
4. eSATA ports can connect up to 127 different peripherals together with a single connector.
5. The higher the bus clock speed, the slower the transmission of data.
6. When cleaning the inside of the system unit, wear an antistatic wristband to avoid damaging internal components with static electricity.

Quiz Yourself Online: To further check your knowledge of pages 230 through 240, visit the Computer Concepts CourseMate Web site at www.cengagebrain.com, navigate to the Chapter 4 Quiz Yourself resource for this book, and then click Objectives 8 – 12.

Chapter Summary

Chapter 4 presented the components of the system unit; described how memory stores data, instructions, and information; and discussed the sequence of operations that occur when a computer executes an instruction. The chapter included a comparison of various personal computer processors on the market today. It also discussed how to clean the exterior and interior of a system unit.

Computer Usage @ Work

Sports

While watching your local football team play an out-of-state game on television, you watch various player and game statistics appear on the screen, alerting you to how many yards the offense must travel before making a first down. The camera then focuses on the large, colorful, high-resolution scoreboard at the stadium. While sports such as football have been around for many decades, the integration of computers has added significantly to the viewing experience.

While watching a baseball game, you notice that the scoreboard shows the number of balls and strikes for the player at bat, as well as the speed of each pitch. Behind home plate, an electronic radar gun calculates and records the speed of each pitch. This recorded data, along with the umpire's call (ball or strike) and the player's performance at bat (hit, home run, strike out, etc.) are entered in a computer, which updates the player's batting average automatically. During this entire time, the video display on the stadium's scoreboard plays audio and video to entertain the fans. The computer storing the player and game statistics, audio, and video communicates with the scoreboard and video display using either a wired or wireless connection. (If the computer communicates using wires, the scoreboard and video display connect directly to a port on a system unit. Recall from the chapter that a port is the point at which a peripheral attaches to or communicates with a system unit.) At the same time, these computers send updated scores and statistics to Web pages and mobile devices.

Computers not only are used to keep track of athlete statistics and communicate with scoreboards, but also in NASCAR to help measure a vehicle's performance before a race. Sensors installed on a car can measure throttle inputs, airflow over the body, the distance between the car's frame and the track, and more. The NASCAR teams then can modify the car so that it achieves maximum performance during a race.

Overall, computers add enjoyment to various sporting events for many individuals. While waiting for a pitcher to throw the next ball or for a football team to start its next play, keep in mind that the integration of computers entertains you with interesting statistics and replays between the action.

For more information, visit the Computer Concepts CourseMate Web site at www.cengagebrain.com, navigate to the Chapter 4 Computer Usage @ Work resource for this book, and then click Sports.

High-Tech Talk

Random Access Memory (RAM): The Genius of Memory

Inside your computer, RAM takes the form of separate microchip modules that plug in slots on the computer's motherboard. These slots connect through a line (bus) or set of electrical paths to the computer's processor. Before you turn on a computer, its RAM is a blank slate. As you start and use your computer, the operating system files, programs, and any data currently being used by the processor are written to and stored in RAM so that the processor can access them quickly.

How is this data written to and stored in RAM? In the most common form of RAM, dynamic random access memory (DRAM), *transistors* (in this case, acting as switches) and a *capacitor* (as a data storage element) create a *memory cell*, which represents a single bit of data.

Memory cells are etched onto a silicon wafer in a series of columns (bitlines) and rows (wordlines), known as an *array*. The intersection of a column and row constitutes the *address* of the memory cell (Figure 4-40). Each memory cell has a unique address that can be found by counting across columns and then counting down by row. The address of a character consists of a series of memory cell addresses put together.

To write data to RAM, the processor sends the memory controller the address of a memory cell in which to store data. The *memory controller* organizes the request and sends the column and row address in an electrical charge along the appropriate address lines, which are very thin electrical lines etched into the RAM chip. This causes the transistors along those address lines to close.

These transistors act as a switch to control the flow of electrical current in an either closed or open circuit. While the transistors are closed, the software sends bursts of electricity along selected data lines. When the electrical charge traveling down the data line reaches an address line where a transistor is closed, the charge flows through the closed transistor and charges the capacitor.

A capacitor works as electronic storage that holds an electrical charge. Each charged capacitor along the address line represents a 1 bit. An uncharged capacitor represents a 0 bit. The combination of 1s and 0s from eight data lines forms a single byte of data.

The capacitors used in dynamic RAM, however, lose their electrical charge. The processor or memory controller continuously has to recharge all of the capacitors holding a charge (a 1 bit) before the capacitor discharges. During this *refresh operation*, which happens automatically thousands of times per second, the memory controller reads memory and then immediately rewrites it. This refresh operation is what gives dynamic RAM its name. Dynamic RAM has to be refreshed continually, or it loses the charges that represent bits of data. A specialized circuit called a counter tracks the refresh sequence to ensure that all of the rows are refreshed.

The process of reading data from RAM uses a similar, but reverse, series of steps. When the processor gets the next instruction it is to perform, the instruction may contain the address of a memory cell from which to read data. This address is sent to the memory controller. To locate the memory cell, the memory controller sends the column and row address in an electrical charge down the appropriate address lines.

This electrical charge causes the transistors along the address line to close. At every point along the address line where a capacitor is holding a charge, the capacitor discharges through the circuit created by the closed transistors, sending electrical charges along the data lines.

A specialized circuit called a *sense amplifier* determines and amplifies the level of charge in the capacitor. A capacitor charge over a certain voltage level represents the binary value 1; a capacitor charge below that level represents a 0. The sensed and amplified value is sent back down the address line to the processor.

As long as a computer is running, data continuously is being written to and read from RAM. As soon as you shut down a computer, RAM loses its data. The next time you turn on a computer, operating system files and other data are again loaded into RAM and the read/write process starts all over.

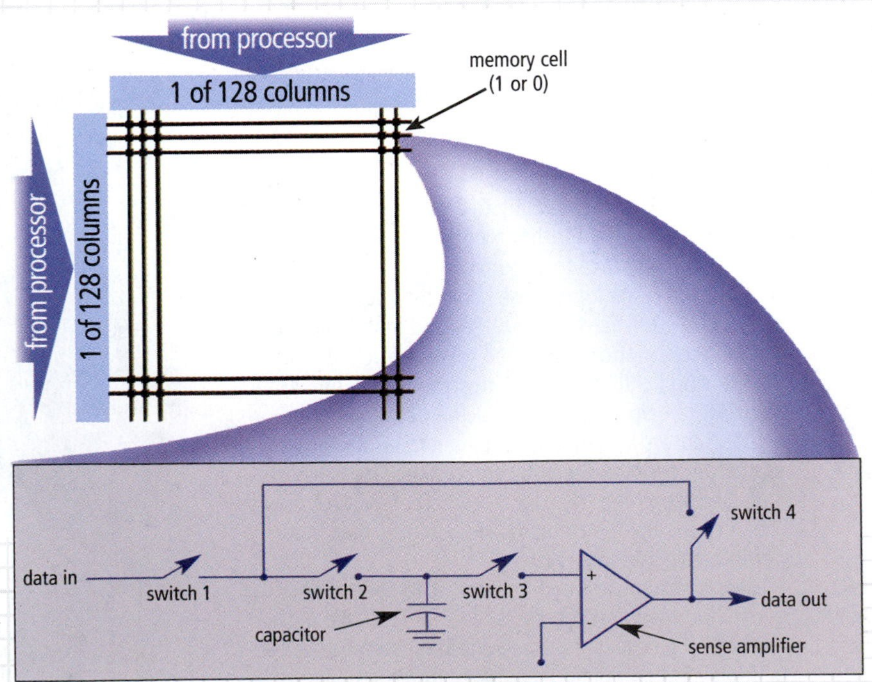

Figure 4-40 An illustration of one type of DRAM. When writing data, switches 1 and 2 in the circuit are closed and switches 3 and 4 are open. When reading data, switches 2, 3, and 4 in the circuit are closed and switch 1 is open. Most DRAM chips actually have arrays of memory cells (upper-left corner of figure) that are 16 rows deep.

For more information, visit the Computer Concepts CourseMate Web site at www.cengagebrain.com, navigate to the Chapter 4 High-Tech Talk resource for this book, and then click Memory.

Companies on the Cutting Edge

NVIDIA Visual Computing Technologies Leader

Serious gamers relish software with ultra-realistic graphics, while film producers need high-definition graphics. Both of these creative types of people likely have used a system unit equipped with an *NVIDIA* processor.

NVIDIA's technological specialty is developing high-performance processors that help generate graphics for personal computers, game consoles, and mobile devices. In the film and entertainment worlds, Sony Pictures, Sportvision, and Weather Central rely on NVIDIA's processor chips to produce imagery and animation. In medicine, the company's processors helped researchers to design a device that stabilizes the heart during bypass surgery and also to develop virtual reality simulations that help burn victims undergoing therapy.

Recently, NVIDIA's CUDA technology was used to enhance the historic *Apollo 11* video of Neil Armstrong walking on the moon.

INTEL World's Leading Chip Manufacturer

Turbochargers have a place in high-performance sports cars, but they have a new home residing in *Intel's* processors. Some of the company's chips have a turbo mode, which turns cores on and off depending upon when programs demand more processing power, all while conserving energy.

The company's chips have set the standard for personal computers since 1980 when IBM chose the Intel 8080 chip for its new product. Intel now is the world's largest chip manufacturer, with its processors found in approximately 80 percent of the world's personal computers.

Recently, Intel completed its acquisition of Wind River Systems, Inc., a leading software vendor in embedded devices. This acquisition will allow Intel to reach customers outside the traditional PC and server market.

 For more information, visit the Computer Concepts CourseMate Web site at www.cengagebrain.com and then navigate to the Chapter 4 Companies on the Cutting Edge resource for this book.

Technology Trailblazers

JACK KILBY Integrated Circuit Inventor

Jack Kilby is credited with being one of the more influential people in the world. He was awarded more than 60 patents during his lifetime, but none changed society as much as the one for his integrated circuit, or microchip, that made microprocessors possible. His Nobel Prize in physics, awarded in 2005, recognized his part in the invention of the integrated circuit.

Kilby started his work with miniature electrical components at Centralab, where he developed transistors for hearing aids. He then took a research position with Texas Instruments and developed a working model of the first integrated circuit, which was patented in 1959. Kilby applied this invention to various industrial, military, and commercial applications, including the first pocket calculator. Kilby died in 2005, but his legacy lives on.

GORDON MOORE Intel Cofounder

Moore's Law is a prediction made in 1965 by one of Intel's founders, *Gordon Moore*, that the number of transistors and resistors placed on a computer chip would double every year. This doubling would have a proportional increase in computing power and decrease in cost. This forecast proved amazingly accurate for 10 years, and then Moore revised the estimate to doubling every two years. A recent breakthrough in chip technology using *photolithography*, which uses light to imprint circuits on a chip, could perpetuate his estimate.

Moore cofounded Intel in 1968 with the conviction that silicon chips would change the world. His lifelong interest in technology is continuing with his contributions to the Large Binocular Telescope, the world's most technologically advanced optical telescope, in southeastern Arizona.

 For more information, visit the Computer Concepts CourseMate Web site at www.cengagebrain.com and then navigate to the Chapter 4 Technology Trailblazers resource for this book.

STUDENT ASSIGNMENTS

Chapter Review

The Chapter Review reinforces the main concepts presented in this chapter.

To listen to the audio version of this Chapter Review, visit the Computer Concepts CourseMate Web site at www.cengagebrain.com and then navigate to the Chapter 4 Chapter Review resource for this book.

1. How Are Various Styles of System Units on Desktop Computers, Notebook Computers, and Mobile Devices Different? The **system unit** is a case that contains electronic components of the computer used to process data. On desktop personal computers, most storage devices also are part of the system unit. On most notebook computers, including netbooks, the keyboard and pointing device often occupy the area on top of the system unit, and the display attaches to the system unit by hinges. The location of the system unit on a Tablet PC varies, depending on the design of the Tablet PC. On mobile computers and devices, the display often is built into the system unit. With game consoles, the input and output devices, such as controllers and a television, reside outside the system unit. On handheld game consoles, portable media players, and digital cameras by contrast, the packaging around the system unit houses the input devices and display.

2. What Are Chips, Adapter Cards, and Other Components of the Motherboard? The **motherboard**, sometimes called a *system board*, is the main circuit board of the system unit. The motherboard contains many electronic components including a processor chip, memory chips, expansion slots, and adapter cards. A computer **chip** is a small piece of semiconducting material, usually silicon, on which integrated circuits are etched. Expansion slots hold adapter cards that provide connections and functions not built into the motherboard.

3. What Are the Control Unit and Arithmetic Logic Unit Components of a Processor, and What Are the Four Steps in a Machine Cycle? The **processor**, also called the **central processing unit** (**CPU**), interprets and carries out the basic instructions that operate a computer. Processors contain a **control unit** that directs and coordinates most of the operations in the computer and an **arithmetic logic unit** (*ALU*) that performs arithmetic, comparison, and other operations. The *machine cycle* is a set of four basic operations — *fetching*, *decoding*, *executing*, and *storing* — that the processor repeats for every instruction.

4. What Are the Characteristics of Various Personal Computer Processors, and How Are Processors Cooled? A **multi-core processor** is a single chip with two or more separate processor cores. Two common multi-core processors are dual-core and quad-core. A **dual-core processor** is a chip that contains two separate processor cores. A **quad-core processor** is a chip with four or more separate processor cores. Intel produces the **Core** processor family for high-performance personal computers, the **Pentium** and **Celeron** processor families for basic personal computers, and the **Xeon** and **Itanium** processor families for workstations and low-end servers. AMD manufactures *Intel-compatible processors*, which have an internal design similar to Intel processors. Some devices have a *system-on-a-chip* processor that integrates the functions of a processor, memory, and a video card on a single chip. Heat sinks/pipes and liquid cooling technologies are used to dissipate processor heat. A *heat sink* is a small ceramic or metal component that absorbs and disperses heat. A smaller device called a *heat pipe* cools processors in notebook computers, including netbooks and Tablet PCs. Some computers use *liquid cooling technology*, which uses a continuous flow of fluid(s) to transfer heated fluid away from the processor.

Visit the Computer Concepts CourseMate Web site at www.cengagebrain.com, navigate to the Chapter 4 Quiz Yourself resource for this book, and then click Objectives 1 – 4.

5. What Is a Bit, and How Does a Series of Bits Represent Data? Most computers are **digital** and recognize only two discrete states: off and on. To represent these states, computers use the **binary system**, which is a number system that has just two unique digits — 0 (for off) and 1 (for on) — called bits. A **bit** (short for *binary digit*), is the smallest unit of data a computer can process. Grouped together as a unit, 8 bits form a **byte**, which provides enough different combinations of 0s and 1s to represent 256 individual characters. The combinations are defined by patterns, called coding schemes, such as *ASCII* and *Unicode*.

6. How Do Program Instructions Transfer in and out of Memory? When a program starts, the program's instructions and data are transferred to memory from storage devices. The program and operating system instructions are in memory, and the program's window appears on the screen. When you quit the program, the program instructions are removed from memory, and the program no longer is displayed on the screen.

Chapter Review

7. What Are the Various Types of Memory? **Memory** usually consists of one or more chips on the motherboard or some other circuit board in the computer. The system unit contains volatile and nonvolatile memory. *Volatile memory* loses its contents when the computer's power is turned off. *Nonvolatile memory* does not lose its contents when the computer's power is turned off. RAM is the most common type of volatile memory. ROM, flash memory, and CMOS are examples of nonvolatile memory. **RAM** (*random access memory*), also called *main memory*, consists of memory chips that can be read from and written to by the processor and other devices. **ROM (read-only memory)** refers to memory chips storing permanent data and instructions that usually cannot be modified. **Flash memory** can be erased electronically and rewritten. **CMOS (complementary metal-oxide semiconductor)** technology uses battery power to retain information even when the power to the computer is turned off.

Visit the Computer Concepts CourseMate Web site at www.cengagebrain.com, navigate to the Chapter 4 Quiz Yourself resource for this book, and then click Objectives 5 – 7.

8. What Are the Purpose and Types of Expansion Slots and Adapter Cards, and What Are the Different Slots for Flash Memory Devices? An **expansion slot** is a socket on the motherboard that can hold an adapter card. An **adapter card**, sometimes called an *expansion card*, is a circuit board that enhances functions of a component of the system unit and/or provides a connection to a **peripheral**. A **sound card** enhances the sound-generating capabilities of a personal computer. A **video card**, also called a *graphics card*, converts computer output into a video signal that displays an image on the screen. A **memory card** is a removable flash memory device that you insert and remove from a slot in a personal computer, a game console, a mobile device, or card reader/writer. A *USB flash drive* plugs in a USB port on a computer or mobile device. A **PC Card slot** or an **ExpressCard slot** holds a **PC Card** or **ExpressCard module**.

9. What Is the Difference between a Port and a Connector, and What Are the Differences among the Various Types of Ports? A **port** is the point at which a peripheral attaches to or communicates with a system unit so that it can send data to or receive information from the computer. A **connector** joins a cable to a port. A **USB port**, short for *universal serial bus port*, can connect up to 127 different peripherals together with a single connector. A **FireWire port** can connect multiple types of devices that require faster data transmission speeds. **Bluetooth** technology uses radio waves to transfer data between two devices. A **SCSI port** attaches the system unit to SCSI peripherals, such as disk drives and printers. An **eSATA port** connects an external SATA hard disk to a computer. An **IrDA port** allows wireless devices to transmit signals to a computer via infrared light waves. A **serial port** transmits data one bit at a time. A **MIDI port** connects the system unit to a musical instrument.

10. What Are the Types of Buses in a Computer? A **bus** is an electrical channel along which bits transfer within the circuitry of a computer, allowing devices both inside and attached to the system unit to communicate. The *data bus* transfers actual data, and the *address bus* transfers information about where the data should reside in memory. The size of a bus, called the *bus width*, determines the number of bits that the computer can transmit at one time. The larger the bus width, the faster the computer transfers data. A computer has a *system bus*, or *front side bus* (*FSB*); possibly a *backside bus* (*BSB*); and an *expansion bus*.

11. What Is the Purpose of a Power Supply, and How Does It Keep Cool? A **power supply** is the component of the system unit that converts wall outlet AC power into DC power for the computer to use. A fan built directly into the power supply keeps it cool. Some have variable speed fans, and many newer computers have additional fans near components in the system unit. Notebook computers, including netbooks and Tablet PCs, can be placed on a cooling pad to help disperse heat.

12. How Do You Clean a System Unit on a Personal Computer or Mobile Device? Before cleaning the exterior of a computer or mobile device, turn it off, and if necessary, unplug it from the electrical outlet, remove the battery, and disconnect all cables from the ports. Use compressed air to blow away dirt from any openings on the case, such as drives, slots, ports, and fan vents. Use an antistatic wipe to clean the exterior of the case and a cleaning solution on a soft cloth to clean the screen. While working inside the case, be sure to wear an antistatic wristband. If you do not feel comfortable cleaning the inside of the case, you can have a professional or computer company clean it for you. Use a vacuum and compressed air to remove dust inside the case.

Visit the Computer Concepts CourseMate Web site at www.cengagebrain.com, navigate to the Chapter 4 Quiz Yourself resource for this book, and then click Objectives 8 – 12.

STUDENT ASSIGNMENTS

Key Terms

You should know the Primary Terms and be familiar with the Secondary Terms. The list below helps focus your study.

To see an example of and a definition for each term, and to access current and additional information from the Web, visit the Computer Concepts CourseMate Web site at www.cengagebrain.com and then navigate to the Chapter 4 Key Terms resource for this book.

Primary Terms

(shown in bold-black characters in the chapter)

AC adapter (239)
access time (229)
adapter card (230)
analog (221)
arithmetic logic unit (214)
bay (238)
binary system (221)
bit (221)
Bluetooth (234)
bus (237)
byte (221)
cache (227)
Celeron (216)
central processing unit (CPU) (213)
chip (212)
clock speed (216)
complementary metal-oxide semiconductor (CMOS) (229)
connector (232)
control unit (214)
Core (216)
digital (221)
drive bay (238)
dual-core processor (213)
eSATA port (235)
expansion slot (230)
ExpressCard module (231)
ExpressCard slot (231)
FireWire hub (234)
FireWire port (234)
firmware (228)
flash memory (228)
gigabyte (GB) (223)
gigahertz (GHz) (216)
IrDA port (235)
Itanium (216)
jack (232)
kilobyte (KB or K) (223)
megabyte (MB) (223)
memory (223)
memory cache (227)
memory card (231)
memory module (225)
memory slots (225)
MIDI port (235)
motherboard (212)
multi-core processor (213)
nanosecond (229)
PC Card (231)
PC Card slot (231)
Pentium (216)
peripheral (230)
Plug and Play (231)
port (232)
power supply (239)
processor (213)
quad-core processor (213)
RAM (224)
read-only memory (ROM) (228)
SCSI port (235)
serial port (235)
sound card (230)
system clock (216)
system unit (210)
terabyte (TB) (223)
USB hub (234)
USB port (234)
video card (230)
word size (237)
Xeon (216)

motherboard (212)

Secondary Terms

(shown in italic characters in the chapter)

Accelerated Graphics Port (AGP) (238)
address (223)
address bus (237)
advanced transfer cache (ATC) (227)
ALU (214)
arithmetic operations (214)
ASCII (221)
backward compatible (234)
backside bus (BSB) (237)
binary digit (221)
Bluetooth wireless port adapter (234)
bus width (237)
Centrino 2 (217)
chassis (210)
clock cycle (216)
comparison operations (214)
data bus (237)
DDR SDRAM (225)
DDR2 (225)
DDR3 (225)
decoding (215)
DIMM (dual inline memory module) (225)
docking station (236)
dynamic RAM (DRAM) (225)
EEPROM chip (228)
executing (215)
expansion bus (237)
expansion card (230)
external bay (238)
external SATA port (235)
fast infrared port (235)
fetching (215)
FireWire bus (238)
form factor (210)
front side bus (FSB) (237)
gender changer (232)
graphics card (230)
heat pipe (219)
heat sink (219)
hertz (216)
Hi-Speed USB (234)
hot plugging (231)
IEEE 1394 port (234)
integrated circuit (212)
Intel-compatible processors (216)
internal bay (238)
IrDA (235)
L1 cache (227)
L2 cache (227)
L3 cache (227)
liquid cooling technology (219)
machine cycle (215)
magnetoresistive RAM (MRAM) (225)
main memory (224)
massively parallel processing (220)
microcode (228)
microprocessor (213)
multi-threaded program (217)
Musical Instrument Digital Interface (235)
nonvolatile memory (223)
ns (229)
parallel processing (220)
PC Card bus (238)
PCI bus (238)
PCI Express (PCIe) bus (238)
pipelining (215)
port replicator (236)
PROM (programmable read-only memory) chip (228)
random access memory (224)
RDRAM (225)
registers (216)
RIMM (Rambus inline memory module) (225)
SAS (serial-attached SCSI) (235)
SCSI (235)
SDRAM (225)
SIMM (single inline memory module) (225)
static RAM (SRAM) (225)
stored program concept (223)
storing (215)
superscalar (216)
synthesizer (236)
system board (212)
system bus (237)
system-on-a-chip (218)
transistor (212)
Unicode (221)
universal serial bus port (234)
USB 2.0 (234)
USB 3.0 (234)
USB flash drive (231)
volatile memory (223)
vPro technology (217)
Windows ReadyBoost (227)

Checkpoint

The Checkpoint exercises test your knowledge of the chapter concepts. The page number containing the answer appears in parentheses after each exercise. The Beyond the Book exercises will help broaden your understanding of the concepts presented in this chapter.

To complete the Checkpoint exercises interactively, visit the Computer Concepts CourseMate Web site at www.cengagebrain.com and then navigate to the Chapter 4 Checkpoint resource for this book.

True/False Mark T for True and F for False.

_____ 1. The system unit is a case that contains electronic components of the computer used to process data. (210)
_____ 2. The processor holds data waiting to be processed and instructions waiting to be executed. (213)
_____ 3. The speed of the system clock is just one factor that influences a computer's performance. (216)
_____ 4. Replacing a motherboard is a fairly complicated process, whereas replacing a processor is much simpler. (218)
_____ 5. A byte is the smallest unit of data the computer can process. (221)
_____ 6. When the computer's power is turned off, volatile memory loses its contents. (223)
_____ 7. Current processors include advanced transfer cache (ATC), a type of L2 cache built directly on the processor chip. (227)
_____ 8. Read-only memory refers to memory chips storing permanent data and instructions. (228)
_____ 9. Hi-Speed USB is a more advanced and faster USB, with speeds 100 times higher than that of its predecessor. (234)
_____ 10. USB 3.0 is more than 10 times faster than USB 2.0. (234)
_____ 11. Both USB 2.0 and USB 3.0 are backward compatible, which means they do not support older USB devices. (234)
_____ 12. SAS (serial-attached SCSI) is a newer type of SCSI that transmits more reliably, but at slower speeds, than parallel SCSI. (235)

Multiple Choice Select the best answer.

1. The processor also is called the _____. (213)
   a. motherboard
   b. central processing unit (CPU)
   c. adapter card
   d. chip

2. The _____ is the component of the processor that directs and coordinates most of the operations in the computer. (214)
   a. control unit
   b. arithmetic logic unit
   c. register
   d. machine cycle

3. A processor contains small, high-speed storage locations, called _____, that temporarily hold data and instructions. (216)
   a. flash drives
   b. registers
   c. jacks
   d. heat sinks

4. Supercomputers use _____ for applications such as artificial intelligence and weather forecasting. (220)
   a. system-on-a-chip technology
   b. massively parallel processing
   c. SCSI
   d. Accelerated Graphics Ports

5. ROM chips, called _____, contain permanently written data, instructions, or information. (228)
   a. memory cache
   b. registers
   c. firmware
   d. transistors

6. A(n) _____ is an external device that provides connections to peripherals through ports built into the device. (236)
   a. expansion bus
   b. port replicator
   c. docking station
   d. synthesizer

7. A(n) _____, which is an external device that attaches to a mobile computer or device, contains a power connection and provides connections to peripherals; it usually also includes slots for memory cards, optical disc drives, and other devices. (236)
   a. docking station b. port replicator
   c. peripheral d. expansion bus

8. A(n) _____ is part of the motherboard and connects the processor to main memory. (237)
   a. expansion bus
   b. system clock
   c. memory module
   d. front side bus

Checkpoint

Matching
Match the terms with their definitions.

_____ 1. motherboard (212)
_____ 2. processor (213)
_____ 3. vPro technology (217)
_____ 4. heat sink (219)
_____ 5. memory (223)
_____ 6. Windows ReadyBoost (227)
_____ 7. flash memory (228)
_____ 8. access time (229)
_____ 9. USB hub (234)
_____ 10. backside bus (237)

a. interprets and carries out the basic instructions that operate a computer
b. small ceramic or metal component with fins on its surface that absorbs and disperses heat produced by electrical components such as a processor
c. amount of time it takes the processor to read data, instructions, and information from memory
d. electronic components that store instructions, data, and results of processed data
e. can allocate available space on removable flash memory devices as additional cache
f. provides the capability to track computer hardware and software, diagnose and resolve computer problems, and secure computers from outside threats
g. nonvolatile memory that can be erased electronically and rewritten
h. main circuit board of the system unit
i. device that plugs in a USB port on the system unit and contains multiple USB ports in which you plug cables from USB devices
j. connects the processor to cache

Short Answer
Write a brief answer to each of the following questions.

1. What are two types of designs of Tablet PCs? ___________ What are the differences in the designs of the two types of Tablet PCs? ___________
2. What is the motherboard? ___________ What is a computer chip? ___________
3. What are the four basic operations in a machine cycle? ___________ What are some functions of registers? ___________
4. What types of devices might be Bluetooth enabled? ___________ Describe three ways in which a computer can become Bluetooth enabled. ___________
5. What is compressed air used for with regards to caring for your computer? ___________ How should you prepare for cleaning your computer? ___________

Beyond the Book
Follow the book element instructions below; present your findings (brief report, presentation, discussion, or other means).

1. Ethics & Issues — Select an Ethics & Issues in this chapter (214, 217, 219, 226, 240), find a recent newspaper/magazine article that supports one point of view presented, and then evaluate the article.
2. Computer Usage @ Work — Use the Web or a recent newspaper/magazine to locate three additional unique usages of computer technology in sports (241). What makes the use of these technologies unique to sports?
3. Companies on the Cutting Edge and Technology Trailblazers — Use the Web or a recent business newspaper/magazine to locate an interesting fact about NVIDIA, Intel, Jack Kilby, or Gordon Moore that was not presented in the chapter (243).
4. High-Tech Talk — Locate a recent newspaper/magazine article that discusses topics related to Random Access Memory (RAM) (242). Would you recommend the article you found? Why or why not?
5. FAQs and Web Links — Use the Web or a recent newspaper/magazine to locate three additional facts about an FAQ (212, 216, 219, 226, 229, 235, 239, 241) and Web Link (214, 217, 220, 225, 227, 228, 230, 232, 234, 236, 238) that were not presented in the chapter.
6. Looking Ahead — Use the Web or a recent newspaper/magazine to discover additional uses of the technology presented in Bendable Notebook Computers Will Slip in Your Pocket (236).
7. Innovative Computing — Use the Web or a recent newspaper/magazine to locate two additional interesting facts about Chip Implants Identify Animals (213) and Robots Assist with Everyday Tasks (214).
8. Making Use of the Web — Visit three of the Online Social Networks and Media Sharing sites (128) and outline the information on each Web site and the possible uses for each Web site.

Learn It Online

The Learn It Online exercises are interactive Web exercises designed to reinforce and expand your understanding of the chapter concepts. The descriptions below briefly summarize each exercise.

To complete the Learn It Online exercises, visit the Computer Concepts CourseMate Web site at www.cengagebrain.com, navigate to the Chapter 4 resources for this book, click the link for the exercise you want to complete, and then read the instructions.

1 At the Movies — The Leopard with a Time Machine
Watch a movie to learn about Apple Computer's "Time Machine" software, which allows users to travel through time by scrolling through different windows that represent days, to help them find the files that they need and then answer questions about the movie.

2 Video and Audio: You Review It — Bluetooth Technology
Search for, choose, and write a review of a video, podcast, or vodcast that discusses Bluetooth technology.

3 Student Edition Labs — Understanding the Motherboard and Binary Numbers
Enhance your understanding and knowledge about the motherboard and binary numbers by completing the Understanding the Motherboard and Binary Numbers Labs.

4 Practice Test
Take a multiple choice test that checks your knowledge of the chapter concepts and review the resulting study guide.

5 Who Wants To Be a Computer Genius²?
Play the Shelly Cashman Series version of this popular game by answering questions to find out if you are a computer genius. Panic buttons are available to provide assistance during game play.

6 Wheel of Terms
Identify important key terms presented in this chapter by playing the Shelly Cashman Series version of this popular game.

7 You're Hired!
Embark on the path to a career in computers by answering questions and solving puzzles related to concepts discussed in this chapter.

8 Crossword Puzzle Challenge
Complete an interactive crossword puzzle to reinforce concepts presented in this chapter.

9 Windows Exercises
Step through the Windows 7 exercises to learn about installing new hardware, setting the system clock, using Calculator to perform number system conversion, and power management.

10 Exploring Computer Careers
Read about a career as a computer engineer, search for related employment advertisements, and then answer related questions.

11 Web Apps — Google Docs
Learn how to create, edit, and share documents, presentations, and spreadsheets using Google Docs.

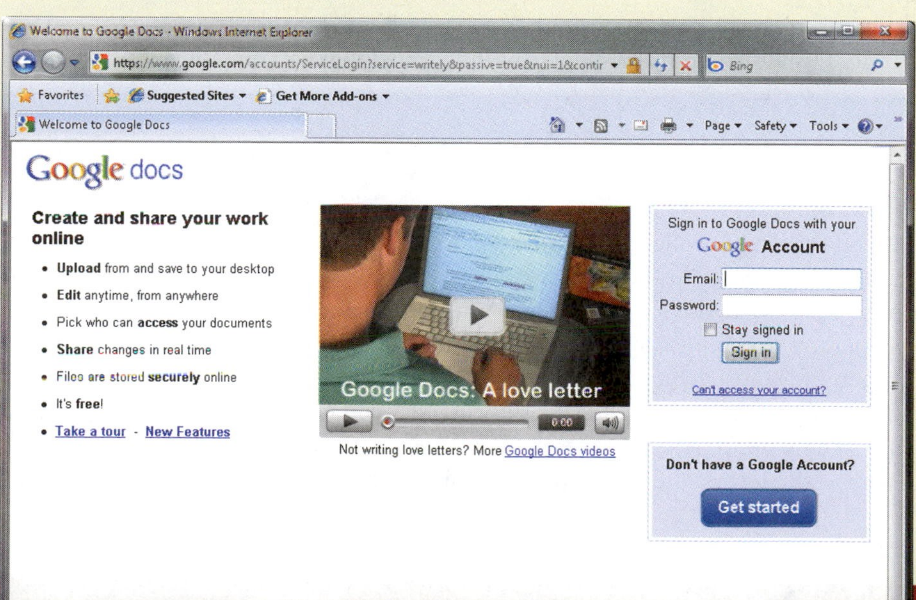

Problem Solving @ Home

The Problem Solving @ Home exercises extend your knowledge of the chapter concepts by seeking solutions to practical computer problems that you may encounter at home or school. The Collaboration exercise should be completed with a team.

In the real world, practical problems often can be solved in multiple ways. Provide one solution to each of the following problems using available resources, such as articles on the Web or in print, blogs, podcasts, videos, television, user guides, other individuals, and electronics and computer stores. You may need to use multiple resources to obtain an answer. Present your solutions in the form requested by your instructor (brief report, presentation, discussion, or other means).

1. **Malfunctioning Speakers** While working on a homework assignment, you decide to listen to one of your favorite music CDs through your computer speakers. The media player program on your computer automatically starts when you insert the CD. Although it looks like the CD is playing, no sound is coming from your speakers. What might be causing this? What is the first step that you will take to correct this problem?
2. **Optical Disc Drive Stuck** While using your computer, you attempt to open the optical disc drive to insert an installation disc for a program you wish to install. The drive, however, does not open when you press the eject button. The drive opened a few minutes prior, when you removed a music CD. What steps will you take to open the drive before calling technical support?

3. **Removing Germs** While recovering from an illness, you realize that by using your computer during your illness, you probably left some germs behind on the keyboard and mouse. How will you clean these devices so that your family members will not become sick?
4. **Computer Will Not Boot** To remedy your computer's slow performance, you installed additional memory. After the installation, you close your computer case, connect the power and all peripheral devices, and turn on the computer. Although your computer turns on, it beeps in rapid succession, it is not responding, and the operating system does not start. What might be causing this?
5. **Numerous Memory Types** You have decided to purchase additional memory for your computer in order to better support the latest version of the Windows operating system. At the local computer store, you notice that not only are different types of memory for sale, but different sizes are available. What will you do to ensure that you get the proper memory for your computer?
6. **Missing Songs** During the past several months, you downloaded more than 1,000 songs to your portable media player. Tonight, when you turn on your portable media player, it is not able to locate any of your songs and an error message displays on the screen. What might be causing this?
7. **Uncommon Memory Card Size** Recently, you purchased a smart phone that is capable of storing pictures, music, and videos on a memory card. The memory card, which you purchased separately, works with your smart phone, but you cannot find a slot on your computer's card reader that will accept the card. Furthermore, you have been unable to find a card reader that can accept this particular type of memory card. Given your predicament, how can you transfer the pictures from your memory card to your computer?

Collaboration

8. **Configuring New Computers** Three of your friends have asked you to configure a new computer for each of them. Each friend has $2,000 budgeted for the computer. One friend likes to play video games, another wants to purchase a computer for his home office (where he works as a travel agent), and the third would like a notebook computer that he can use for schoolwork. You ask two classmates to assist you with this task. Form a team of three people and search for computers that will meet the needs of your three friends. One team member configures a computer for the gamer, another team member configures a computer for the travel agent, and the last team member configures a computer for the student. No team member should exceed the $2,000 budget while configuring a computer that best suits each user's needs. Finally, all team members should discuss the differences among the three computers. Compile the team's findings and submit them to your instructor.

Problem Solving @ Work

The Problem Solving @ Work exercises extend your knowledge of the chapter concepts by seeking solutions to practical computer problems that you may encounter at work. The Collaboration exercise should be completed with a team.

In the real world, practical problems often can be solved in multiple ways. Provide one solution to each of the following problems using available resources, such as articles on the Web or in print, blogs, podcasts, videos, television, user guides, other individuals, and electronics and computer stores. You may need to use multiple resources to obtain an answer. Present your solutions in the form requested by your instructor (brief report, presentation, discussion, or other means).

1. **Update Issue** You just installed some Microsoft updates on your computer, which is running the latest version of the Windows operating system. The updates required you to reboot your computer immediately following their installation. When the desktop appears, the sizes of the icons and other elements on your screen have increased. Why might the update have caused this? What could you do to return the screen elements to their original sizes?
2. **Printer Port Problem** A colleague received a new printer and has delivered her old printer to your desk for your use. When attempting to plug the printer in a port on the back of your computer, you see that the connector will not fit in any of the available ports. You also notice that even the ports that are in use will not accept the connector. What steps will you take so that you can use the printer?
3. **USB Device Not Working** You purchased a new USB external hard disk so that you can take work home. After plugging the hard disk in a USB port on your computer, the other USB devices stopped working, and the external hard disk does not work. You return to the store to exchange the hard disk, but the same problem occurs with the new device. Why might this be happening? What steps will you take to resolve this problem?
4. **Noisy Fan** After moving to a new office, you turn on your computer for the first time and hear a buzzing sound inside the case. You turn off your computer, the noise winds down, and you wait several minutes before turning the computer back on. When you turn on your computer again, however, the noise resumes. What could be causing this?
5. **Slots Unavailable** Your computer is running slowly, and technical support informs you that they will install additional memory to help boost your computer's performance. A technician removes your computer, returns it one hour later, and informs you that no slots are available to accommodate additional memory. What might the technician be able to do to increase your computer's memory?
6. **Incorrect System Date and Time** While using your computer, you notice that the date and time are incorrect. You correct the date and time settings, continue using your computer, and then power it off before leaving work. When you arrive to work the next morning and turn on the computer, the date and time once again are incorrect. What might be causing this, and what is the first step you might take to solve this problem?
7. **Dirty Fan** While using your computer, you notice that the fan that removes the hot air from the inside of the computer has stopped running. You immediately turn off your computer to prevent it from overheating and notice that the fan is coated with dust. How will you clean the fan?

Collaboration

8. **Computers in Sports** You serve as an assistant coach for your former high school's football team. The head coach, who has a computer that is more than five years old, informs you that he would like to create a program that will allow him to keep track of his players' statistics. For instance, he would like to track the quarterback's number of passing yards, rushing yards, and completions. Form a team of three people to determine the requirements for implementing his request. One team member will research the types of application software that can track this data, another team member will determine the specifications for a computer capable of running the software and storing the data, and the other team member will determine the best way to collect the data during the game.

STUDENT ASSIGNMENTS

Learn How To

The Learn How To activities step you through fundamental technology skills when using a computer. The Learn How To exercises enable you to become more proficient with these skills.

Learn How To 1: Purchase and Install Memory in a Computer

One of the less expensive and more effective ways to speed up a computer, make it capable of processing more programs at the same time, and enable it to handle graphics, gaming, and other high-level programs is to increase the amount of memory. The process of increasing memory is accomplished in two phases — purchasing the memory and installing the memory. To purchase memory for a computer, complete the following steps:

1. Determine the amount of memory currently in the computer. The amount of memory in your computer is displayed in the Welcome Center when Windows starts.
2. Determine the maximum amount of memory your computer can contain. This value can change for different computers, based primarily on the number of slots on the motherboard available for memory and the size of the memory modules you can place in each slot. On most computers, different size memory modules can be inserted in slots. A computer, therefore, might allow a 128 MB, 256 MB, 512 MB, 1 GB, or 2 GB memory module to be inserted in each slot. To determine the maximum memory for a computer, in many cases you can multiply the number of memory slots on the computer by the maximum size memory module that can be inserted in each slot.

   For example, if a computer contains four memory slots and is able to accept memory modules of 128 MB, 256 MB, 512 MB, 1 GB, or 2 GB in each of its memory slots, the maximum amount of memory the computer can contain is 8 GB (4 x 2 GB).

   You can find the number of slots and the allowable sizes of each memory module by contacting the computer manufacturer, looking in the computer's documentation, or contacting sellers of memory such as Kingston (kingston.com) or Crucial (crucial.com) on the Web. These sellers have documentation for most computers, and even programs you can download to run on your computer that will specify how much memory your computer currently has and how much you can add.
3. Determine how much memory you want to add, which will be somewhere between the current memory and the maximum memory allowed on the computer.
4. Determine the current configuration of memory on the computer. For example, if a computer with four memory slots contains 1 GB of memory, it could be using one memory module of 1 GB in a single slot and the other three slots would be empty; two memory modules of 512 MB each in two slots with two slots empty; one memory module of 512 MB and two memory modules of 256 MB each in three slots with one slot empty; or four memory modules of 256 MB each in four slots with no slots empty. You may be required to look inside the system unit to make this determination. The current memory configuration on a computer will determine what new memory modules you should buy to increase the memory to the amount determined in Step 3.

   You also should be aware that a few computers require memory to be installed in matching pairs. This means a computer with four slots could obtain 1 GB of memory with two memory modules of 512 MB in two slots, or four memory modules of 256 MB in four slots.
5. Determine the number of available memory slots on your computer and the number and size memory modules you must buy to fulfill your requirement. Several scenarios can occur (in the following examples, assume you can install memory one module at a time).
   a. Scenario 1: The computer has one or more open slots. In this case, you might be able to purchase a memory module that matches the amount of memory increase you desire. For example, if you want to increase memory by 2 GB, you should purchase a 2 GB memory module for insertion in the open slot. Generally, you should buy the maximum size module you can for an open slot. So, if you find two empty slots and wish to increase memory by 2 GB, it is smarter to buy one 2 GB module and leave one empty slot rather than buy two 1 GB memory modules and use both slots. This allows you to increase memory again without removing currently used modules.
   b. Scenario 2: The computer has no open slots. For example, a computer containing 2 GB of memory could have four slots each containing 512 MB memory modules. If you want to increase the memory on the computer to 4 GB, you will have to remove some of the 512 MB memory modules and replace them with the new memory modules you purchase. In this example, you want to increase the memory by 2 GB. You would have several options: (1) You could replace all four 512 MB memory modules with 1 GB memory modules; (2) You could

Learn How To

replace all four 512 MB memory modules with two 2 GB memory modules; (3) You could replace one 512 MB memory module with a 1 GB memory module, and replace a second 512 MB module with a 2 GB memory module. Each of these options results in a total memory of 4 GB. The best option will depend on the price of memory and whether you anticipate increasing the memory size at a later time. The least expensive option probably would be number 3.

c. Scenario 3: Many combinations can occur. You may have to perform calculations to decide the combination of modules that will work for the number of slots on the computer and the desired additional memory.

6. Determine the type of memory to buy for the computer. Computer memory has many types and configurations, and it is critical that you buy the kind of memory for which the computer was designed. It is preferable to buy the same type of memory that currently is found in the computer. That is, if the memory is DDR3 SDRAM with a certain clock speed, then that is the type of additional memory you should place in the computer. The documentation for the computer should specify the memory type. In addition, the Web sites cited in Step 2, and others as well, will present a list of memory modules that will work with your computer. Enough emphasis cannot be placed on the fact that the memory you buy must be compatible with the type of memory usable on your computer. Because so many types and configurations exist, you must be especially diligent to ensure you purchase the proper memory for your computer.
7. Once you have determined the type and size of memory to purchase, buy it from a reputable dealer. Buying poor or mismatched memory is a major reason for a computer's erratic performance and is a difficult problem to troubleshoot.

After purchasing the memory, you must install it on your computer. Complete the following steps to install memory:

1. Unplug the computer, and remove all electrical cords and device cables from the ports on the computer. Open the case of the system unit. You may want to consult the computer's documentation to determine the exact procedure.
2. Ground yourself so that you do not generate static electricity that can cause memory or other components within the system unit to be damaged. To do this, wear an antistatic wristband you can purchase inexpensively in a computer or electronics store; or, before you touch any component within the system unit, touch an unpainted metal surface. If you are not wearing an antistatic wristband, periodically touch an unpainted metal surface to dissipate any static electricity.
3. Within the system unit, find the memory slots on the motherboard. The easiest way to do this is look for memory modules that are similar to those you purchased. The memory slots often are located near the processor. If you cannot find the slots, consult the documentation. A diagram often is available to help you spot the memory slots.
4. Insert the memory module in the next empty slot. Orient the memory module in the slot to match the modules currently installed. A notch or notches on the memory module will ensure you do not install the module backwards.

   If your memory module is a DIMM, insert the module straight down into grooves on the clips and then apply gentle pressure (see Figure 4-20 on page 225). If your memory is SIMM, insert the module at a 45 degree angle and then rotate it to a vertical position until the module snaps into place.
5. If you must remove one or more memory modules before inserting the new memory, carefully release the clips before lifting the memory module out of the memory slot.
6. Plug in the machine and replace all the device cables without replacing the cover.
7. Start the computer. In most cases, the new memory will be recognized and the computer will run normally. If an error message appears, determine the cause of the error.
8. Replace the computer cover.

Exercises

1. Assume you have a computer that contains 1 GB of memory. It contains four memory slots. Each slot can contain 128 MB, 256 MB, 512 MB, 1 GB, or 2 GB memory modules. Two of the slots contain 512 MB memory modules. What memory chip(s) would you buy to increase the memory on the computer to 4 GB? What is the maximum memory on the computer? Submit your answers to your instructor.
2. Assume you have a computer that contains 2 GB of memory. It contains four memory slots. Each slot can contain 128 MB, 256 MB, 512 MB, 1 GB, or 2 GB memory modules. Currently, each slot contains a 512 MB memory module. What combinations of memory modules will satisfy your memory upgrade to 8 GB? Visit a Web site to determine which of these combinations is the least expensive. Submit your answers and recommendations to your instructor.

STUDENT ASSIGNMENTS

Web Research

The Web Research exercises broaden your understanding of the chapter concepts by presenting questions that require you to search the Web for answers.

1 Search Sleuth

Use one of the search engines listed in Figure 2-10 Chapter 2 on page 85 or your own favorite search engine to find the answers to the following questions. Copy and paste the Web address from the Web page where you found the answer. Some questions may have more than one answer. If required, submit your answers to your instructor. (1) In nanometers, what is the current size of a quad-core processor? (2) What company holds the trademark for the term, FireWire? (3) What is the relationship between the names of the Itanium processors and the steamship *Titanic*? (4) What Intel chip powered the Busicom calculator? (5) What is the admission price to visit the Intel Museum in Santa Clara, California? (6) What term did Dr. Werner Buchholz coin while designing the IBM Stretch computer?

2 Green Computing

Greenpeace International's *Guide to Greener Electronics* ranks the major technology hardware companies in their manufacturing and recycling efforts. The goal is to urge these computer, television, mobile devices, and game console manufacturers to reduce the use of toxic chemicals and to implement recycling policies. View the *Guide* (greenpeace.org/electronics) and then use your word processing program to answer the following questions. Then, if required, submit your answers to your instructor. (1) The Guide has been updated every three months since June 2006. What is the version of this most current Guide? (2) Which company is at the top of the list for its better toxic waste, recycling, and climate change practices? What is this company's score, and why did this company receive this ranking? (3) Which company received the lowest ranking? Why? (4) What criteria are used to score the manufacturers? (5) Review the Toxics News links and read the article discussing the rankings from the previous year. Compare the companies' rankings between the past year and the current year. (6) What are Greenpeace's definitions of PVC-free and BFR-free?

3 Social Networking

Business creativity helps drive innovation and invention of new products. Oddpodz is an online meeting place for creative people to share ideas with like-minded professionals. This Web site includes a blog, a marketplace for unique products, job postings, and a forum to discuss current topics. Visit the Oddpodz Web site (Oddpodz.com) and then read the FAQs to get an overview of the Web site. Browse the company profiles in the Creative Services Marketplace. Read the profiles of some new members, who are called citizens, and view some of the creative projects featured. Read several articles in the Cylibrary about advice given to plan a business. Review topics in the blog, especially those discussing current advertising campaigns. Summarize the information you read and viewed.

4 Blogs

Technology news blogs offer information about new products, trends, and issues facing information technology professionals. Visit several technology blogs, including those from CNET (news.cnet.com), Geekzone (geekzone.co.nz/blogindex.asp), Good Morning Silicon Valley (blogs.siliconvalley.com/gmsv), Lifehacker (lifehacker.com), TechnoClicks (technoclicks.com), and WordPress (wordpress.com/tag/technology/). What are bloggers discussing? What top news stories are featured? What products are reviewed? What questions are members asking about computer chips, flash memory, Bluetooth, and green computing products? Which stories have generated more than 20 comments?

5 Ethics in Action

Law enforcement agencies use handheld wireless devices to access commercial databases. For example, Massachusetts state police stationed at Logan International Airport use the LocatePLUS Holdings Corporation's database, which has information on 98 percent of Americans. Police say accessing this information helps them perform their jobs more efficiently. Privacy experts, in contrast, say that information collected for one purpose, such as checking credit or registering motor vehicles, should not be available in other contexts. View online sites that provide information about commercial databases for sale. Write a report summarizing your findings, and include a table of links to Web sites that provide additional details.

Critical Thinking

The Critical Thinking exercises challenge your assessment and decision-making skills by presenting real-world situations associated with the chapter concepts. The Collaboration exercise should be completed with a team.

To evaluate the situations below, use personal experiences and available resources such as articles on the Web or in print, blogs, podcasts, videos, television, user guides, other individuals, and electronics and computer stores. You may need to use multiple resources to form conclusions and make recommendations.

1. **Class Discussion — Technology Purchases** You are the purchasing manager at TechnoInk, a company that specializes in designing and producing logos for local high school and college sports teams. The company has 35 nonnetworked computers that are used throughout the company for common business applications. The computers are four years old, and you would like to replace them. The director of information technology agrees, but he has reservations. Evaluate and compare the cost of new computers, comparing the major features found on system units at three different price levels: less than $1,000; $1,000 to $1,750; and greater than $1,750. Discuss the major features of system units at the various price levels and which computer you would recommend. Include in your discussion recommendations on which system units would meet the company's needs most economically.

2. **Class Presentation — Mac vs. PC** Universal Computing, Inc. has decided to upgrade several hundred PCs used in their offices nationwide. The information technology department has recommended that the company again purchase PCs for approximately $1,500 each. The system units would include Intel Core 2 Quad processors with speeds of 2.4 GHz with 2 GB of RAM. From her days in college, the CFO (chief financial officer) has preferred Apple computers and currently uses an Apple iMac at home. She has hired you as a consultant to analyze purchasing iMacs versus purchasing PCs in the same price range and with similar capabilities. Use the Web and/or print media to select a comparable iMac. Obtain answers to the following questions by analyzing your findings, so that you can present a recommendation on which computer to purchase. Which one starts faster? Which one opens files faster? Which one displays Web pages faster? Is the iMac in the same price range as the PC? Include in your presentation any other advantages and disadvantages of each.

3. **Research — Computer Upgrades** Your boss would like to save money by asking employees to begin performing simple computer upgrades, such as installing additional memory modules, themselves. Your boss informed you that some computers might be easier to upgrade than other computers. For example, smaller form factor computers sometimes can be more difficult to upgrade than towers. Notebook computers, including netbooks and Tablet PCs, can be more difficult to upgrade than desktop computers. Some might find it more difficult to upgrade a Mac than to upgrade a PC because the components inside the system unit are arranged differently. Use the Web to locate copyright-free pictures of the inside of various types of system units. Be sure to include both large and small system units on Macs, PCs, and notebook computers. What type of computer would you find easiest to upgrade? What challenges might you face upgrading a smaller computer? Prepare a brief report for your instructor with your findings, and be sure to include the pictures in your report.

Collaboration

4. **Computers in the Military** Computers have become an integral part of military operations. Many military research projects use simulators that resemble civilian computer games. Your company has been contacted by the Department of Defense for a research project. Form a four-member team, and then form two two-member groups. Assign each group one of the following topics to research: 1) How have notebook computers changed the combat environment, and how have these military uses impacted the design of the personal computer? 2) How can the utilization of microchips worn by soldiers, or wearable computers, be integrated into civilian use? Meet with your team and discuss your findings. Then, prepare a presentation to include both topics and share with your class. Include in your presentation any advantages or disadvantages of introducing these technologies into public use. Discuss any legal ramifications that may arise.

Chapter Five

Input

Objectives

After completing this chapter, you will be able to:

1. Define input and differentiate among a program, command, and user response
2. Identify the keys and buttons commonly found on desktop computer keyboards, and describe how keyboards for mobile computers and devices differ from desktop computer keyboards
3. Describe different mouse types and explain how to use a mouse
4. Describe various types of touch screens and explain how a touch-sensitive pad works
5. Describe various types of pen input, and identify other types of input for smart phones
6. Summarize the purpose of various game controllers: gamepads, joysticks and wheels, light guns, dance pads, and motion-sensing game controllers
7. Explain how resolution affects the quality of a picture captured on a digital camera
8. Describe the uses of voice recognition, Web cams, and video conferencing
9. Discuss how various scanners and reading devices work: optical scanners, optical readers, bar code readers, RFID readers, magnetic stripe card readers, MICR readers, and data collection devices
10. Summarize the various biometric devices: fingerprint reader, face recognition system, hand geometry system, voice verification system, signature verification system, and iris recognition system
11. Discuss how POS terminals, automated teller machines, and DVD kiosks work
12. Identify alternative input devices for physically challenged users

What Is Input?

Input is any data and instructions entered into the memory of a computer. As shown in Figure 5-1, people have a variety of options for entering data and instructions into a computer.

As discussed in Chapter 1, *data* is a collection of unprocessed items, including text, numbers, images, audio, and video. Once data is in memory, the computer interprets and executes instructions to process the data into information. Instructions entered into the computer can be in the form of programs, commands, and user responses.

- A *program* is a series of related instructions that tells a computer what tasks to perform and how to perform them. When a programmer writes a program, he or she enters the program into the computer by using a keyboard, mouse, or other input device. The programmer then stores the program in a file that a user can

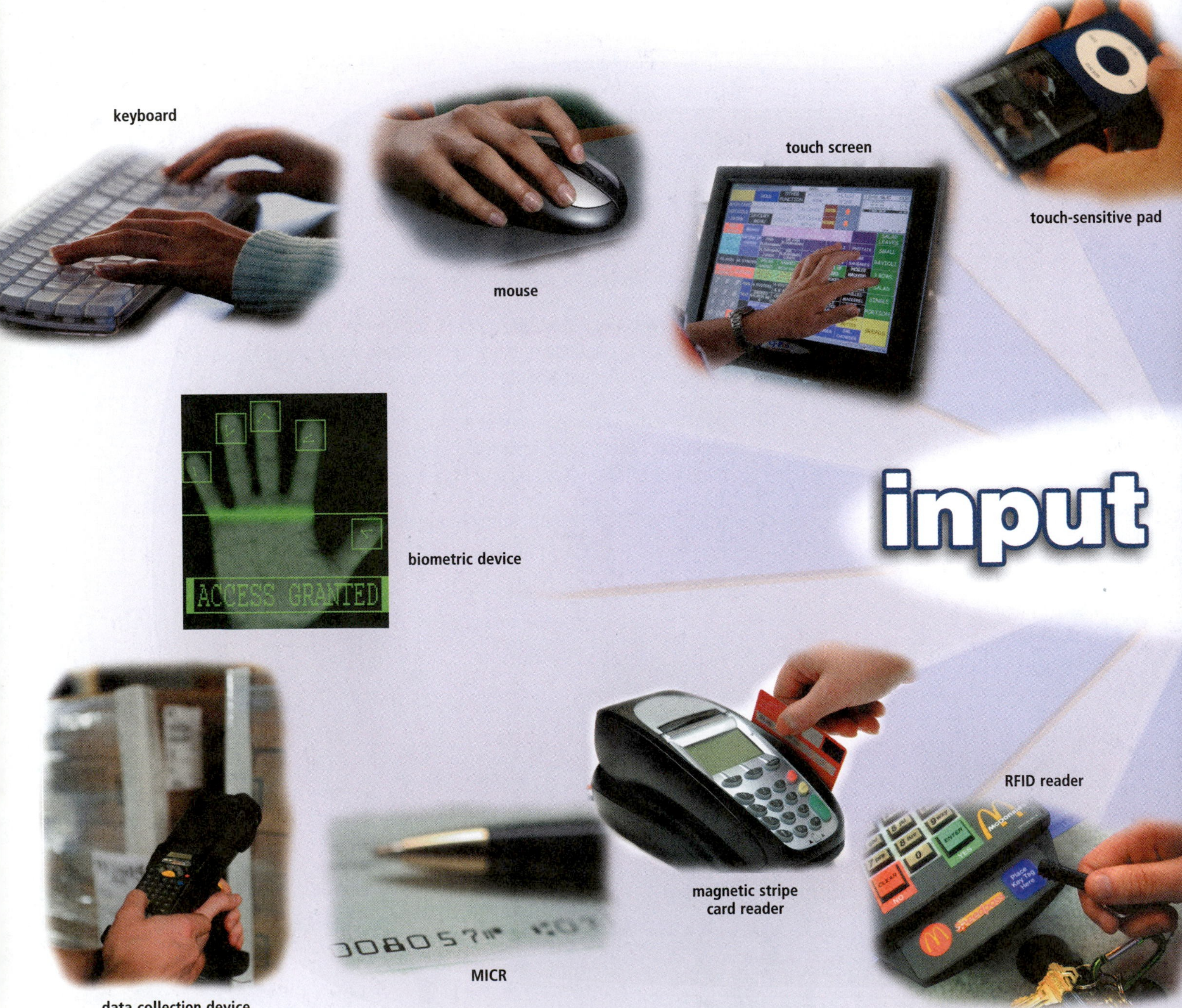

Figure 5-1 Users can enter data and instructions into a computer in a variety of ways.

execute (run). When a user runs a program, the computer loads the program from a storage medium into memory. Thus, a program is entered into a computer's memory.

- Programs respond to commands that a user issues. A *command* is an instruction that causes a program to perform a specific action. Users issue commands by pressing keys on the keyboard, clicking a mouse button, speaking into a microphone, or touching an area on a screen.
- A *user response* is an instruction a user issues by replying to a question displayed by a program. A response to the question instructs the program to perform certain actions. Assume the program asks the question, Is the time card correct? If you answer Yes, the program processes the time card. If you answer No, the program gives you the opportunity to modify the time card entries.

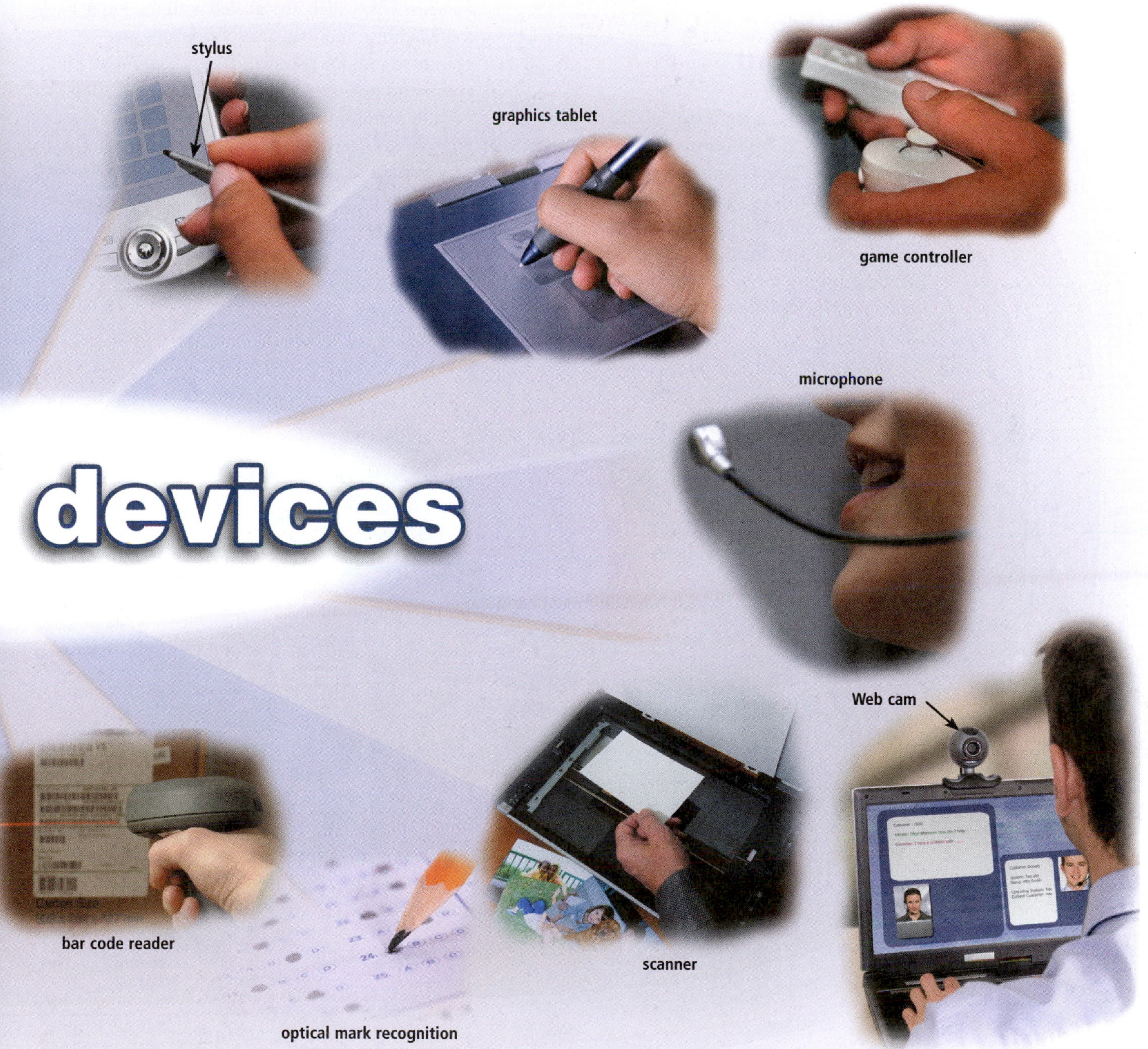

What Are Input Devices?

An **input device** is any hardware component that allows users to enter data and instructions (programs, commands, and user responses) into a computer. Depending on the application and your particular requirements, the input device selected may vary. The following pages discuss a variety of input devices.

Storage devices, such as disk drives, serve as both input and output devices. Chapter 7 discusses storage devices.

The Keyboard

Many people use a keyboard as one of their input devices. A **keyboard** is an input device that contains keys users press to enter data and instructions into a computer (Figure 5-2).

Desktop computer keyboards typically have from 101 to 105 keys. All desktop computer keyboards have a typing area that includes the letters of the alphabet, numbers, punctuation marks, and other basic keys. Many desktop computer keyboards also have a numeric keypad on the right side of the keyboard. A keyboard also contains other keys that allow users to enter data and instructions into the computer. Read Ethics & Issues 5-1 for a related discussion.

Most of today's desktop computer keyboards are enhanced keyboards. An *enhanced keyboard* has twelve or more function keys along the top; it also has two CTRL keys, two ALT keys, and a set of arrow and additional keys between the typing area and the numeric keypad (Figure 5-2). *Function keys*, which are labeled with the letter F followed by a number, are special keys programmed to issue commands to a computer. The command associated with a function key may vary, depending on the program with which you are interacting. For example, the F3 key may issue one command to an operating system and an entirely different command to a word processing program. To issue commands, users often can press a function key in combination with other special keys (SHIFT, CTRL, ALT, and others).

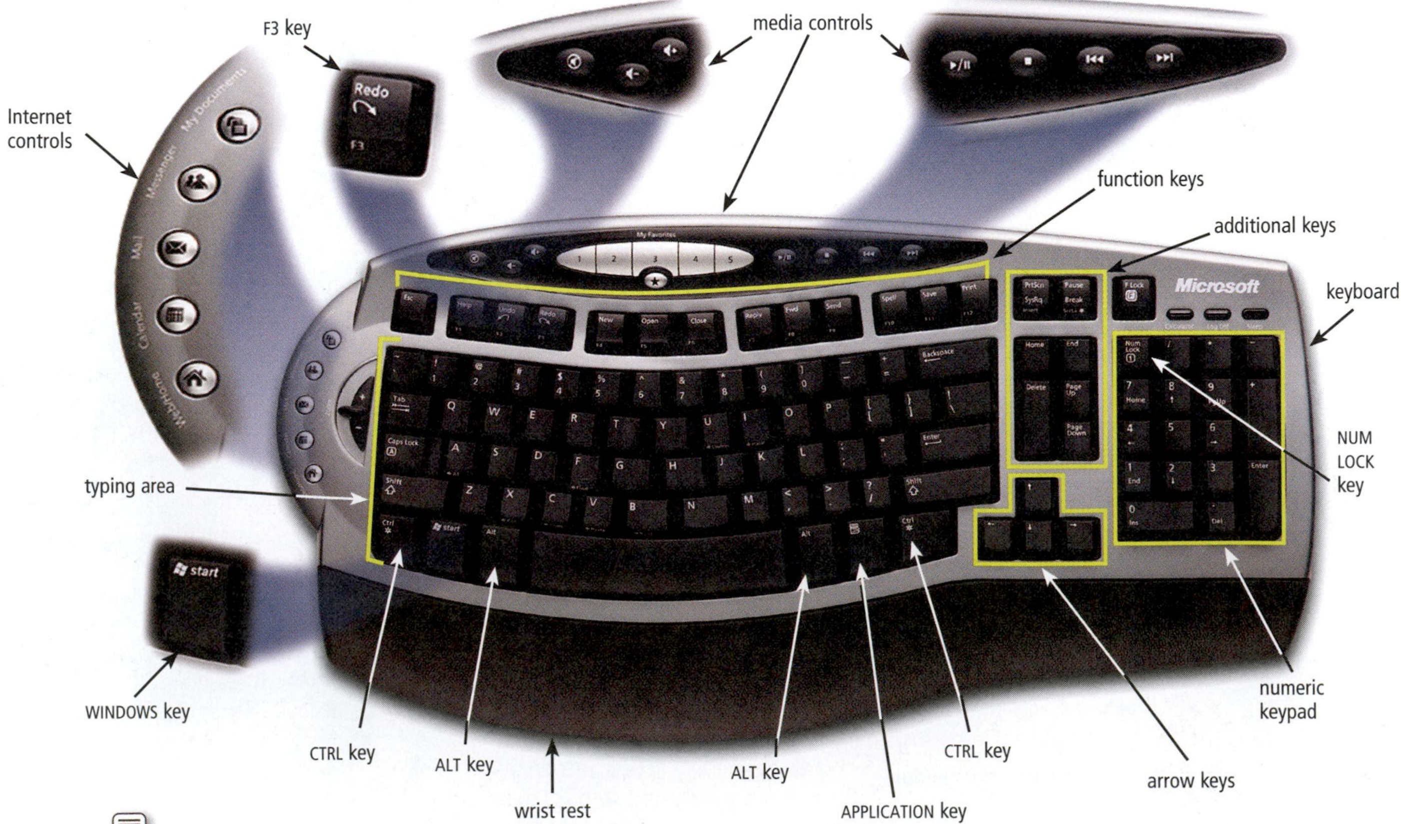

Figure 5-2 On a desktop computer keyboard, you type using keys in the typing area and on the numeric keypad.

FAQ 5-1

What is the rationale for the arrangement of keys in the typing area?

The keys originally were arranged to reduce the frequency of key jams on old mechanical typewriters. Called a *QWERTY keyboard*, the first letters on the top alphabetic line spell QWERTY. A *Dvorak keyboard*, by contrast, places frequently typed letters in the middle of the typing area. Despite the Dvorak keyboard's logical design, most people and computers use a QWERTY keyboard.

For more information, visit the Computer Concepts CourseMate Web site at www.cengagebrain.com, navigate to the Chapter 5 FAQ resource for this book, and then click Keyboards.

Keyboards also often have a WINDOWS key(s) and an APPLICATION key. When pressed, the WINDOWS key displays the Windows Start menu, and the APPLICATION key displays an item's shortcut menu.

Nearly all keyboards have toggle keys. A *toggle key* is a key that switches between two states each time a user presses the key. When you press the NUM LOCK key, for example, it locks the numeric keypad so that you can use the keypad to type numbers. When you press the NUM LOCK key again, the numeric keypad unlocks so that the same keys can serve to move around a document. Many keyboards have status lights that light up when you activate a toggle key.

Users can press the arrow keys and other keys such as PAGE UP and PAGE DOWN on the keyboard to move the insertion point left, right, up, or down. The **insertion point**, also known as a *cursor* in some programs, is a symbol on the screen, usually a blinking vertical bar, that indicates where the next character you type will appear (Figure 5-3).

Keyboards with media control buttons allow you to control your media player program, access the computer's optical disc drive, and adjust speaker volume. Internet control buttons allow you to open an e-mail program, start a Web browser, and search the Internet. Some keyboards have USB ports so that you can plug a USB device directly in the keyboard instead of in the system unit. Some keyboards include a fingerprint reader and/or smart card reader, each of which is discussed later in this chapter.

A *gaming keyboard* is a keyboard designed specifically for users who enjoy playing games on the

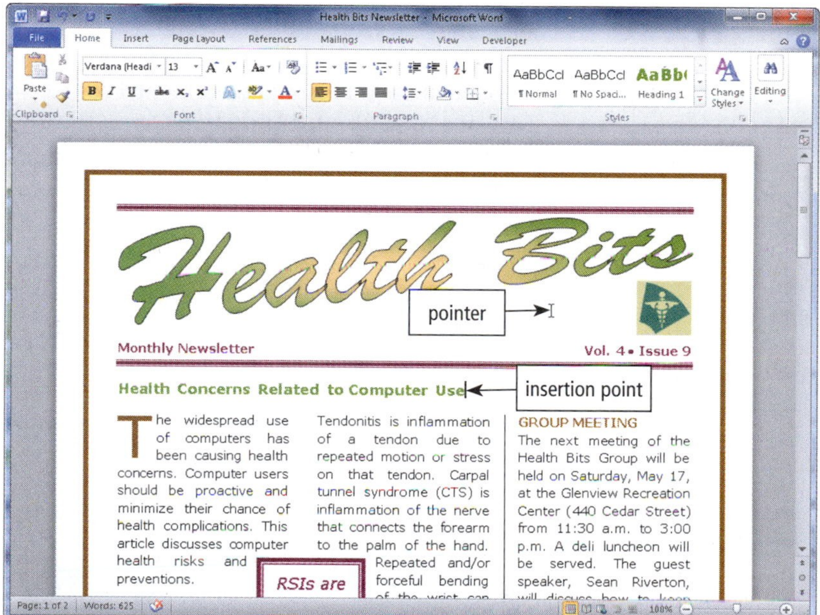

Figure 5-3 In most programs, such as Word, the insertion point is a blinking vertical bar. You use the keyboard or other input device to move the insertion point. The pointer, another symbol that is displayed on the screen, is controlled using a pointing device such as a mouse.

ETHICS & ISSUES 5-1

Keyboard Monitoring — Privacy Risk?

Do you have a feeling that someone is watching everything you type on your computer at work? Are you concerned about your teenager's conversations in Internet chat rooms? Keyboard monitoring software can dispel your doubts. When installed on a computer, *keyboard monitoring software*, also called a *keylogger*, records every keystroke in a hidden file, which later can be accessed by supplying the correct password. With keyboard monitoring software, you can see everything that was typed on a computer keyboard. Some programs also store a record of software used, Web sites visited, user logons, and periodic screen shots. The software can run completely undetected; in fact, recently computer hackers have installed keyloggers in a malicious attempt to capture people's user names and passwords as they sign on to banking and financial Web sites. With keyboard monitoring software, you can discover that an employee is providing sensitive information to a competitor or recognize that your teenager has made a potentially dangerous contact in a chat room. Businesses sometimes use keyboard monitoring software to analyze the efficiency of data entry personnel. Recently, courts ruled that law-enforcement agencies secretly can install keyboard monitoring software on suspects' computers if a proper search warrant is obtained. Many maintain, however, that keyboard monitoring software is an invasion of privacy, even in the workplace, and some states have outlawed the secret installation of such software.

Should keyboard monitoring software ever be used? If so, when? Some marketers of keyboard monitoring software recommend computer users be informed that the software is installed. Is this a good idea? Why or why not?

computer. Gaming keyboards typically include programmable keys so that gamers can customize the keyboard to the game being played. The keys on gaming keyboards light up so that the keys are visible in all lighting conditions. Some have small displays that show important game statistics, such as time or targets remaining.

Desktop computer keyboards often attach via a cable to a USB port on the system unit. Some keyboards, however, do not have any wires connecting the keyboard to the system unit. A *wireless keyboard*, or *cordless keyboard*, is a battery-powered device that transmits data to the system unit using wireless technology, such as radio waves (Bluetooth) or infrared light waves (IrDA).

Keyboard Ergonomics

Many keyboards have a rectangular shape with the keys aligned in straight, horizontal rows. Users who spend a lot of time typing on these keyboards sometimes experience repetitive strain injuries (RSI) of their wrists and hands. For this reason, some manufacturers offer ergonomic keyboards. An *ergonomic keyboard* has a design that reduces the chance of wrist and hand injuries (Figure 5-4). Even keyboards that are not ergonomically designed attempt to offer a user more comfort by including a wrist rest or palm rest (Figure 5-2 on page 260).

Ergonomics

For more information, visit the Computer Concepts CourseMate Web site at www.cengagebrain.com, navigate to the Chapter 5 Web Link resource for this book, and then click Ergonomics.

Figure 5-4 An ergonomic keyboard.

The goal of **ergonomics** is to incorporate comfort, efficiency, and safety in the design of the workplace. Employees can be injured or develop disorders of the muscles, nerves, tendons, ligaments, and joints from working in an area that is not designed ergonomically.

Keyboards for Mobile Computers and Mobile Devices

On notebook computers and some handheld computers, smart phones, and other mobile devices the keyboard is built in the top of the system unit. To fit in these mobile computers and devices, the keyboards usually are smaller and have fewer keys than desktop computer keyboards. A typical notebook computer keyboard usually has only about 85 keys. To provide all of the functionality of a desktop computer keyboard, manufacturers design many of the keys to serve two or three purposes.

A variety of options are available for typing on a smart phone (Figure 5-5). Many can display an on-screen keyboard, where you press the on-screen keys using a stylus or your finger. Some smart phones have one key for each letter of the alphabet, often called a mini-keyboard. Other phones have keypads that contain fewer keys than there are letters in the alphabet. For these phones, each key on the keypad represents multiple characters, which are identified on the key. That is, the 2 key on the phone's keypad displays the letters a, b, and c on the key's face. On many phones, you cycle through the number, letters, and other symbols associated with a particular key by pressing a key on the keypad multiple times. For example, to type the word, hi, on a phone keypad, you would press the 4 key twice to display the letter h, pause momentarily to advance the cursor, and then press the 4 key three times to display the letter i.

Some phones use *predictive text input*, where you press one key on the keypad for each letter in a word, and software on the phone predicts the word you want. Predictive text input saves users time when entering text using the phone's keypad.

FAQ 5-2

What can I do to reduce chances of experiencing repetitive strain injuries?

If possible, use an ergonomic keyboard. Do not rest your wrists on the edge of a desk; use a wrist rest. Keep your forearms and wrists level so that your wrists do not bend. Take a break and do hand exercises every 15 minutes. Keep your shoulders, arms, hands, and wrists relaxed while you work. Maintain good posture. Keep feet flat on the floor, with one foot slightly in front of the other. Immediately stop using the computer if you begin to experience pain or fatigue.

For more information, visit the Computer Concepts CourseMate Web site at www.cengagebrain.com, navigate to the Chapter 5 FAQ resource for this book, and then click Repetitive Strain Injuries.

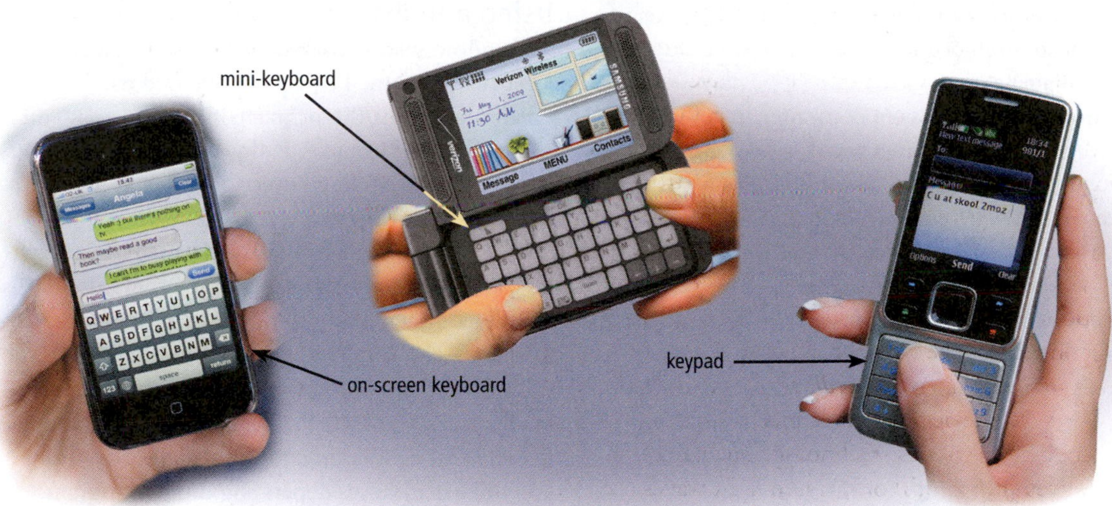

Figure 5-5 Users have a variety of options for typing on a phone.

Pointing Devices

A **pointing device** is an input device that allows a user to control a pointer on the screen. In a graphical user interface, a **pointer** is a small symbol on the screen (Figure 5-3 on page 261) whose location and shape change as a user moves a pointing device. A pointing device can be used to move the insertion point; select text, graphics, and other objects; and click buttons, icons, links, and menu commands. The following sections discuss the mouse and other pointing devices.

Mouse

A **mouse** is a pointing device that fits under the palm of your hand comfortably. The mouse is the most widely used pointing device on desktop computers.

With a mouse, users control the movement of the pointer, often called a *mouse pointer* in this case. As you move a mouse, the pointer on the screen also moves. Generally, you use the mouse to move the pointer on the screen to an object such as a button, a menu, an icon, a link, or text. Then, you press a mouse button to perform a certain action associated with that object. The top and sides of a mouse have one to four buttons; some also have a small wheel. The bottom of a mouse is flat and contains a mechanism that detects movement of the mouse.

Most desktop computer users today have some type of *optical mouse*, which uses devices that emit and sense light to detect the mouse's movement. Some use optical sensors, and others use a laser. The latter, often referred to as a *laser mouse* (Figure 5-6), usually is more expensive than the former. You can place an optical mouse on nearly all types of flat surfaces. Some newer models combine both optical sensors and laser, enabling users to place the mouse on rougher surfaces such as carpeting and park benches. Further, some mouse devices are more sensitive than others for users requiring more precision such as graphic artists, engineers, or game players.

The mobile user who makes presentations may prefer a mouse that has additional buttons for running a slide show and controlling media, similar to a remote control. A newer type of mouse, called an *air mouse*, is a motion-sensing mouse that, in addition to the typical buttons, allows you to control objects, media players, and slide shows by moving the mouse in predetermined directions

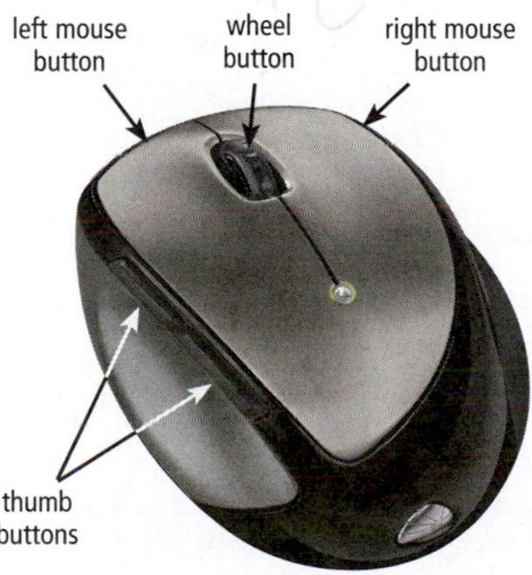

Figure 5-6 This mouse uses a laser to detect movement of the mouse. It also includes buttons you push with your thumb that enable forward and backward navigation through Web pages.

through the air (Figure 5-7). For example, raising the mouse up might increase the volume on your media player.

A mouse connects to a computer in several ways. Many types connect with a cable that attaches to a USB port or a mouse port on the system unit. A *wireless mouse*, or *cordless mouse*, is a battery-powered device that transmits data using wireless technology, such as radio waves (Bluetooth) or infrared light waves (IrDA). Some users prefer a wireless mouse because it frees up desk space and eliminates the clutter of a cord.

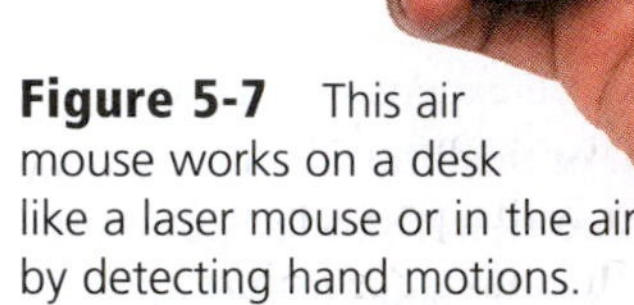

Figure 5-7 This air mouse works on a desk like a laser mouse or in the air by detecting hand motions.

Using a Mouse

Windows users work with a mouse that has at least two buttons. For a right-handed user, the left button usually is the primary mouse button, and the right mouse button is the secondary mouse button. Left-handed people, however, can reverse the function of these buttons.

The table in Figure 5-8 explains how to perform a variety of mouse operations. Some programs also use keys in combination with the mouse to perform certain actions. For example, when you hold down the CTRL key while rolling the wheel, text on the screen becomes larger or smaller based on the direction you roll the wheel. The function of the mouse buttons and the wheel varies depending on the program. Read Ethics & Issues 5-2 for a related discussion.

Some programs support *mouse gestures*, where the user performs certain operations by holding a mouse button while moving the mouse in a particular pattern. For example, moving the mouse down and to the left may close all open windows. Mouse gestures minimize the amount of time users spend navigating through menus or toolbars because users can perform these tasks by simply moving (gesturing) the mouse.

Mouse Operations

Operation	Mouse Action	Example
Point	Move the mouse until the pointer on the desktop is positioned on the item of choice.	Position the pointer on the screen.
Click	Press and release the primary mouse button, which usually is the left mouse button.	Select or deselect items on the screen or start a program or program feature.
Right-click	Press and release the secondary mouse button, which usually is the right mouse button.	Display a shortcut menu.
Double-click	Quickly press and release the left mouse button twice without moving the mouse.	Start a program or program feature.
Triple-click	Quickly press and release the left mouse button three times without moving the mouse.	Select a paragraph.
Drag	Point to an item, hold down the left mouse button, move the item to the desired location on the screen, and then release the left mouse button.	Move an object from one location to another or draw pictures.
Right-drag	Point to an item, hold down the right mouse button, move the item to the desired location on the screen, and then release the right mouse button.	Display a shortcut menu after moving an object from one location to another.
Rotate wheel	Roll the wheel forward or backward.	Scroll vertically (up and down).
Free-spin wheel	Whirl the wheel forward or backward so that it spins freely on its own.	Scroll through hundreds of pages in seconds.
Press wheel	Press the wheel button while moving the mouse.	Scroll continuously.
Tilt wheel	Press the wheel toward the right or left.	Scroll horizontally (left and right).
Press thumb button	Press the button on the side of the mouse with your thumb.	Move forward or backward through Web pages and/or control media, games, etc.

Figure 5-8 Common mouse operations.

ETHICS & ISSUES 5-2

Are Employers Responsible for Computer-Related Repetitive Strain Injuries?

When you consider the causes of workplace injuries, you might not put clicking a mouse or use of a cell phone in the same category with lifting a bag of concrete, but perhaps you should. According to the chairman of a National Academy of Sciences panel that investigated workplace injuries, every year one million Americans lose workdays because of repetitive strain injuries (RSIs), including the latest malady known as cell phone elbow. RSI is caused when muscle groups perform the same actions over and over again. Once, RSIs were common among factory workers who performed the same tasks on an assembly line for hours a day. Today, these injuries, which often result from prolonged use of a computer mouse and keyboard or overuse of cell phones and other mobile devices, are the largest job-related injury and illness problem in the United States and are almost completely avoidable with proper computer and mobile device use. OSHA proposed standards whereby employers would have to establish programs to prevent workplace injuries with respect to computer use. Yet, Congress rejected the standards, accepting the argument that the cost to employers would be prohibitive and unfair. Some argue that it is each employee's responsibility to be aware of preventative measures against RSI.

Should the government establish laws regarding computer use? Why or why not? Are employees, employers, or the government responsible for repetitive strain injuries? Why? Who should be responsible for the costs of prevention and medical care? Why?

Other Pointing Devices

The mouse is the most widely used pointing device today. Some users, however, work with other pointing devices. These include the trackball, touchpad, pointing stick, touch screen, touch-sensitive pads, stylus, pen, signature capture pad, and graphics tablet. The following sections discuss each of these pointing devices.

Trackball

A **trackball** is a stationary pointing device with a ball on its top or side (Figure 5-9). The ball in most trackballs is about the size of a Ping-Pong ball.

To move the pointer using a trackball, you rotate the ball with your thumb, fingers, or the palm of your hand. In addition to the ball, a trackball usually has one or more buttons that work just like mouse buttons.

A trackball requires frequent cleaning because it picks up oils from fingers and dust from the environment. For users who have limited desk space, however, a trackball is a good alternative to a mouse because the device is stationary.

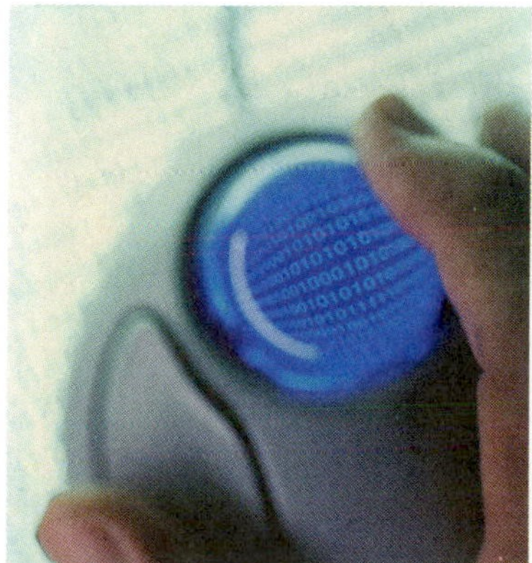

Figure 5-9 A trackball.

Touchpad

A **touchpad** is a small, flat, rectangular pointing device that is sensitive to pressure and motion (Figure 5-10). To move the pointer using a touchpad, slide your fingertip across the surface of the pad. Some touchpads have one or more buttons around the edge of the pad that work like mouse buttons. On most touchpads, you also can tap the pad's surface to imitate mouse operations such as clicking. Touchpads are found most often on notebook computers, including netbooks and many Tablet PCs.

Ethics & Issues
For the complete text of the Ethics & Issues boxes found in this chapter, visit the Computer Concepts CourseMate Web site at www.cengagebrain.com and then navigate to the Chapter 5 Ethics & Issues resource for this book.

Figure 5-10 Most notebook computers have a touchpad that allows users to control the movement of the pointer.

Pointing Stick

A **pointing stick** is a pressure-sensitive pointing device shaped like a pencil eraser that is positioned between keys on a keyboard (Figure 5-11). To move the pointer using a pointing stick, you push the pointing stick with a finger. The pointer on the screen moves in the direction you push the pointing stick. By pressing buttons below the keyboard, users can click and perform other mouse-type operations with a pointing stick. A pointing stick does not require any additional desk space.

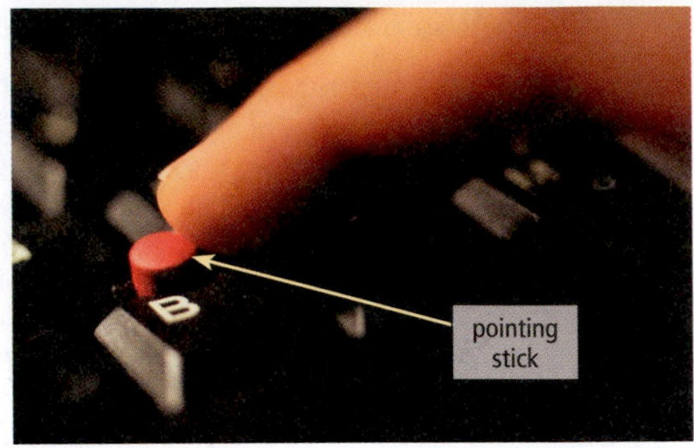

Figure 5-11 Some notebook computers include a pointing stick to allow a user to control the movement of the pointer.

Touch Screens and Touch-Sensitive Pads

A **touch screen** is a touch-sensitive display device. Touch screens that recognize multiple points of contact at the same time are known as *multi-touch*. Users can interact with touch screens by touching areas of the screen. Because touch screens require a lot of arm or hand movements, you do not enter large amounts of data using a touch screen. Instead, you touch words, pictures, numbers, letters, or locations identified on the screen. Some touch screens also respond to finger motions such as sliding your finger to drag an object or pinching your fingers to zoom in or out. The latest version of the Windows operating system provides increased support for computers with touch screens. Support for touch screen makes it easier for users to interact with the operating system.

Multi-Touch Screens
For more information, visit the Computer Concepts CourseMate Web site at www.cengagebrain.com, navigate to the Chapter 5 Web Link resource for this book, and then click Multi-Touch Screens.

Some models of desktop computers and notebook computers, including netbooks and Tablet PCs, and many mobile devices have touch screens (Figure 5-12). With some smart phones, portable media players, and other mobile devices, for example, you can touch the screen to perform tasks such as dialing phone numbers, entering text, and making on-screen selections. Some handheld game consoles also have touch screens.

A *kiosk*, which is a freestanding computer, usually includes a touch screen (Figure 5-13). For example, travelers use kiosks in airports to print tickets ordered online and in hotels for easy check in and check out. To allow easy access of your bank account from a car, many ATMs have touch screens.

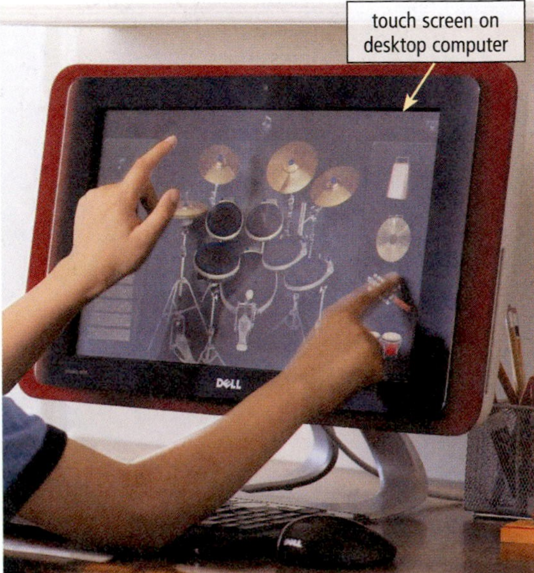

Figure 5-12 Computers and mobile devices have touch screens.

Figure 5-13 This traveler checks in using an airport kiosk.

A recently developed touch screen, called *Microsoft Surface*, is a 30-inch tabletop display that allows one or more people to interact with the screen using their fingers or hands (Figure 5-14). The Microsoft Surface display also allows devices that are not digital, such as an everyday paintbrush, to be used as an input device. Restaurants, hotels, and other public locations provide Microsoft Surface tables to enhance guest services.

Figure 5-14 Guests explore photos of hotel amenities by touching and dragging them across the Microsoft Surface display.

Touch-Sensitive Pads

Portable media players that do not have touch screens typically have a *touch-sensitive pad*, which is an input device that enables users to scroll through and play music, view pictures, watch videos or movies, adjust volume, and/or customize settings. Touch-sensitive pads typically contain buttons and/or wheels that are operated with a thumb or finger. For example, users rotate a *Click Wheel* to browse through the portable media player's song, picture, or movie lists and press the Click Wheel's buttons to play or pause media, display a menu, and perform other actions (Figure 5-15). To learn more about how to download songs to a portable media player, complete the Learn How To 2 activity on pages 298 and 299.

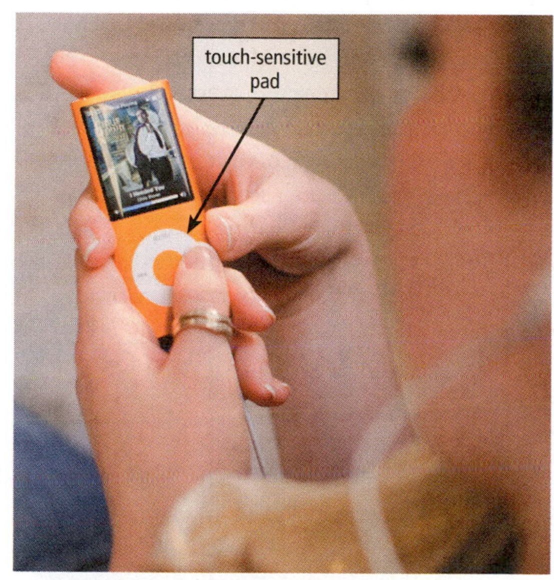

Figure 5-15 You use your thumb to rotate or press buttons on a Click Wheel.

? FAQ 5-3

Which companies sell the most portable media players?

Apple has dominated the portable media player market for several years. A recent study shows that Apple holds 71 percent of the market share, with SanDisk in second place at 11 percent of the market. The chart to the right illustrates the market share for the top four portable media player manufacturers.

For more information, visit the Computer Concepts CourseMate Web site at www.cengagebrain.com, navigate to the Chapter 5 FAQ resource for this book, and then click Portable Media Players.

Portable Media Player Market Share

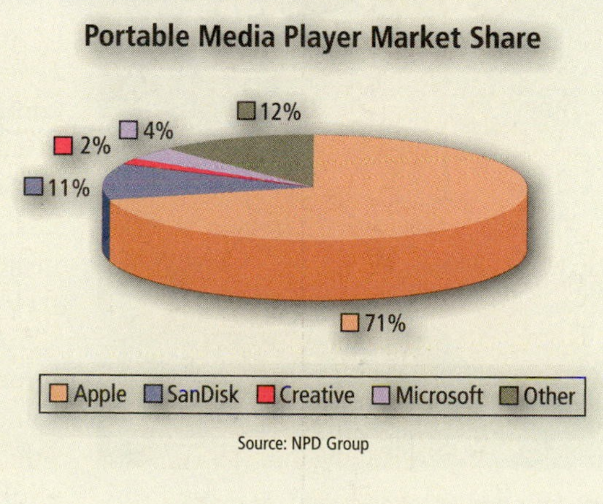

Source: NPD Group

Pen Input

With **pen input**, you touch a stylus or digital pen on a flat surface to write, draw, or make selections. The flat surface may be a screen on a monitor or mobile device, a signature capture pad, or a graphics tablet (Figure 5-16). A **stylus** is a small metal or plastic device that looks like a tiny ink pen but uses pressure instead of ink. A **digital pen**, which is slightly larger than a stylus, typically provides more functionality than a stylus, featuring electronic erasers and programmable buttons. Most digital pens, often simply called pens, are pressure-sensitive.

Some desktop and mobile computers and nearly all mobile devices have touch screens that recognize pen input and thus include a pressure-sensitive digital pen or stylus. Computers and mobile devices often use *handwriting recognition software*, which is a program that translates the handwritten letters and symbols created on the screen with the stylus or pen into characters that the computer or device can process.

Signature Capture Pads
For more information, visit the Computer Concepts CourseMate Web site at www.cengagebrain.com, navigate to the Chapter 5 Web Link resource for this book, and then click Signature Capture Pads.

To capture a handwritten signature, a user writes his or her name on a **signature capture pad** with a stylus or pen that is attached to the device. Software then transmits the signature via a cable connected to a port on the computer. Signature capture pads often include a magnetic stripe card reader and work with POS terminals, both discussed later in the chapter.

To use pen input on a computer that does not have a touch screen, you can attach a graphics tablet to the computer. A **graphics tablet** is a flat, rectangular, electronic, plastic board. Architects, mapmakers, designers, artists, and home users create drawings by using a pressure-sensitive pen on a graphics tablet. Each location on the graphics tablet corresponds to a specific location on the screen. When drawing on the tablet with a pen, the tablet detects and converts the movements into digital signals that are sent in the computer. Large-scale applications sometimes refer to the graphics tablet as a *digitizer*.

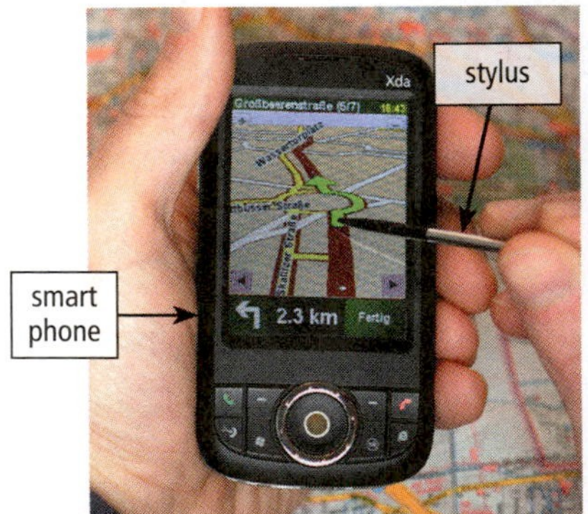

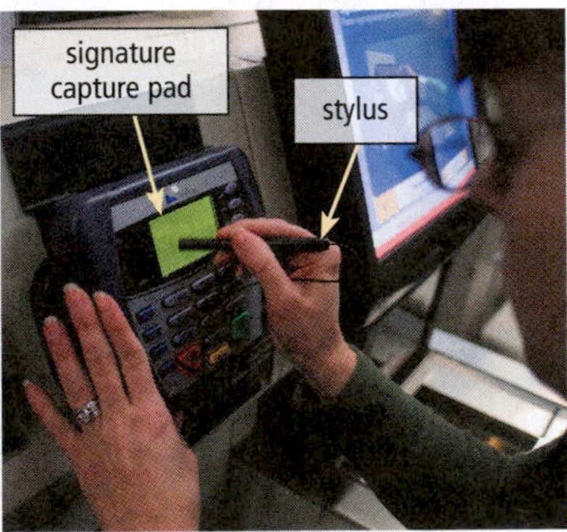

Figure 5-16 You use a stylus or a pen to write, draw, or make selections on a screen, signature capture pad, or graphics tablet.

Other Input for Smart Phones

Previously discussed input devices such as mini-keyboards, keypads, touch screens, and a stylus are used with smart phones. In addition to these input methods, a variety of alternatives for input is available for smart phones (Figure 5-17).

You can talk directly into the smart phone's microphone or into a Bluetooth headset that wirelessly communicates with the phone. Some smart phones have digital cameras that take pictures and touch-sensitive pads that enable you to interact with media, such as music and photos. Others receive navigation signals to provide users with maps and directions. You can purchase a more elaborate stylus that has a ballpoint pen at one end and a stylus at the other.

Instead of typing on a phone's keyboard or keypad, users can enter text via a *portable keyboard*, which is a full-sized keyboard that communicates with a smart phone or PDA. Some portable keyboards physically attach to and remove from the device; others are wireless. Another option is an optical keyboard that projects an image of a keyboard on a flat surface (Figure 5-18).

You also can transfer, or synchronize, data and information from a computer to a phone. With some phones, you synchronize wirelessly; with others, you attach the phone to the computer via a cable or a cradle that has a cable connected to the computer.

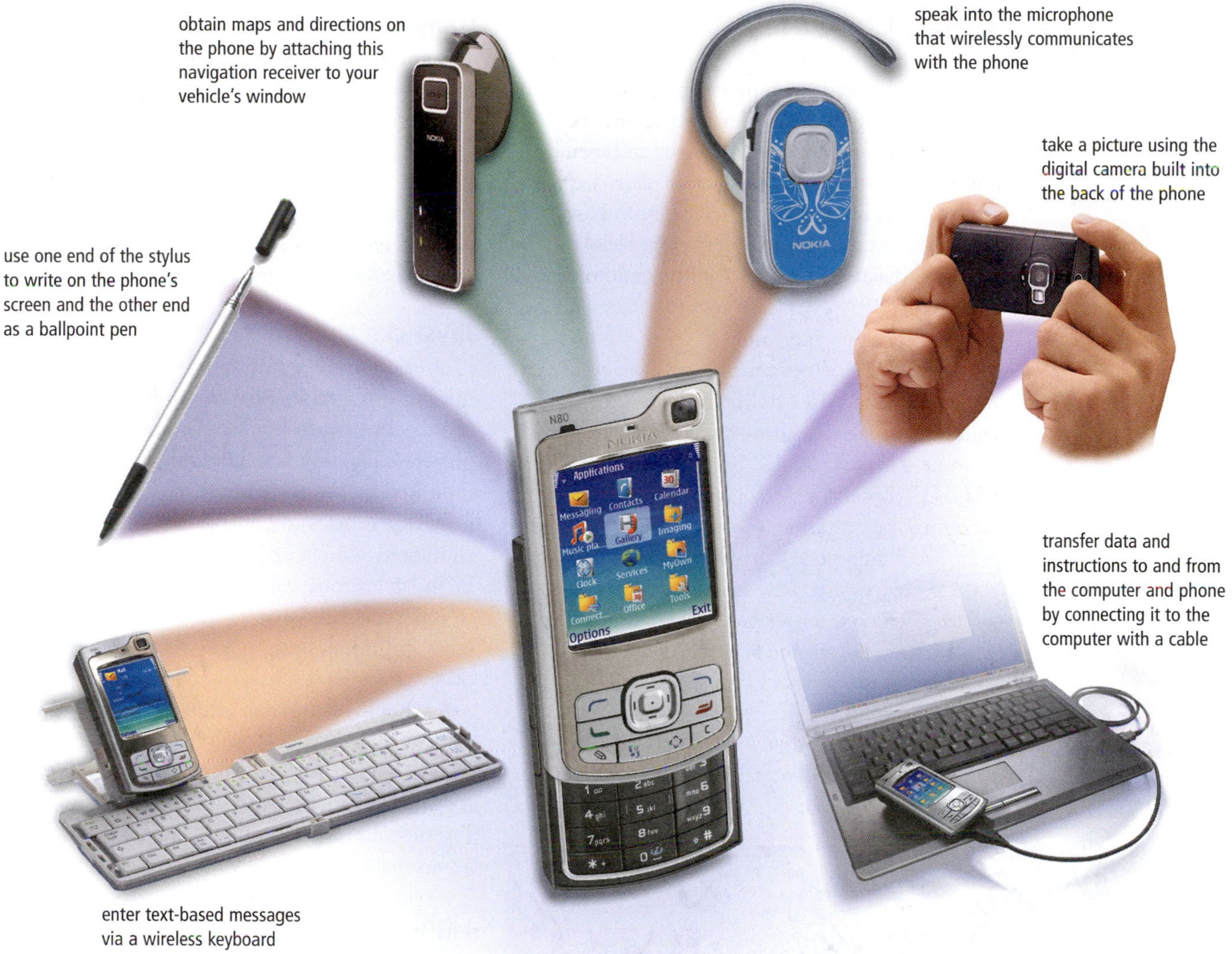

obtain maps and directions on the phone by attaching this navigation receiver to your vehicle's window

speak into the microphone that wirelessly communicates with the phone

take a picture using the digital camera built into the back of the phone

use one end of the stylus to write on the phone's screen and the other end as a ballpoint pen

transfer data and instructions to and from the computer and phone by connecting it to the computer with a cable

enter text-based messages via a wireless keyboard

Figure 5-17 Besides a touch screen and basic stylus, users have a variety of other options for entering data and instructions into a smart phone.

Figure 5-18 The characters you type on this full-sized optical keyboard appear on your smart phone.

FAQ 5-4

What security issues affect mobile computers or devices?

Mobile computers and mobile devices are susceptible to virus threats when you download infected Web pages or open infected e-mail messages. Another risk involves wireless networks, which provide a means for others to connect to your computer or device without your knowledge. One wireless service provider reported that in one year, it cleaned more than 100,000 infections from mobile devices. Once users connect to your computer or device, they may be able to add to, change, or remove your data.

For more information, visit the Computer Concepts CourseMate Web site at www.cengagebrain.com, navigate to the Chapter 5 FAQ resource for this book, and then click Security Threats and Mobile Devices.

Game Controllers

Game Controllers

For more information, visit the Computer Concepts CourseMate Web site at www.cengagebrain.com, navigate to the Chapter 5 Web Link resource for this book, and then click Game Controllers.

Video games and computer games use a **game controller** as the input device that directs movements and actions of on-screen objects. Game controllers include gamepads, joysticks and wheels, light guns, dance pads, and a variety of motion-sensing controllers. The following sections discuss a variety of game controllers (Figure 5-19).

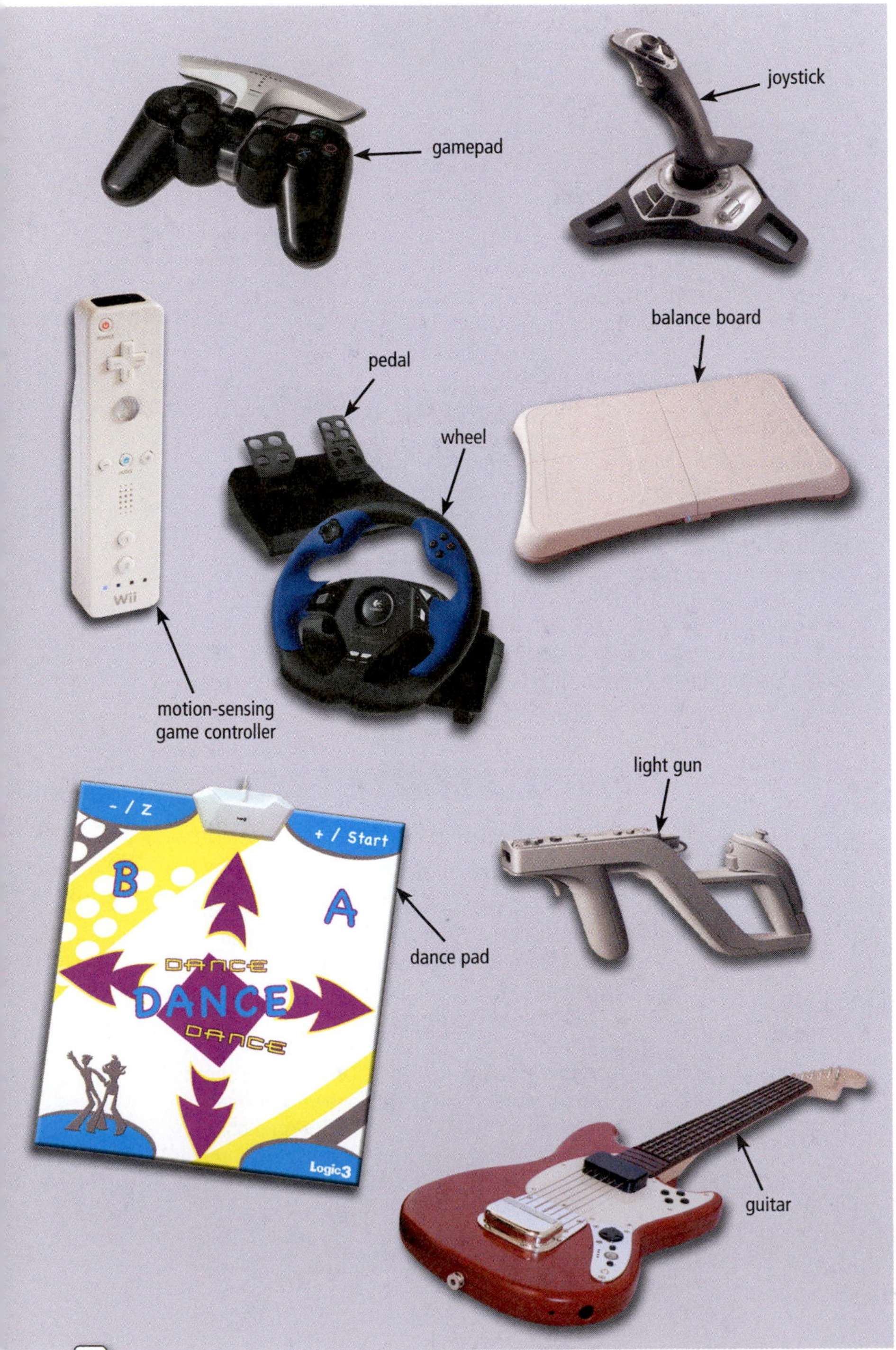

Gamepads

A **gamepad**, which is held with both hands, controls the movement and actions of players or objects in video games or computer games. On the gamepad, users press buttons with their thumbs or move sticks in various directions to trigger events. Gamepads communicate with a game console or a personal computer via wired or wireless technology.

Joysticks and Wheels

Users running game software or flight and driving simulation software often use a joystick or wheel to control an airplane, vehicle, or player. A **joystick** is a handheld vertical lever mounted on a base. You move the lever in different directions to control the actions of the simulated vehicle or player. The lever usually includes buttons, called triggers, that you press to initiate certain events. Some joysticks also have additional buttons you press to perform other actions.

A **wheel** is a steering-wheel-type input device. Users turn the wheel to simulate driving a car, truck, or other vehicle. Most wheels also include foot pedals for acceleration and braking actions. Joysticks and wheels typically attach via a cable to a personal computer or game console.

Light Guns

A **light gun** is used to shoot targets and moving objects after you pull the trigger on the weapon. Instead of emitting light, most light guns work by detecting light. When the user pulls the trigger, the screen uses one of several techniques to send light, which is received by a receptor in the barrel of the gun. Light guns typically attach via a cable to a game console or personal computer.

Dance Pads

A **dance pad** is a flat electronic device divided into panels that users press with their feet in response to instructions from a music video game. These games test the user's ability to step on the correct panel at the correct time, following a pattern that is synchronized with the rhythm or beat of a song. Dance pads communicate with a game console or a personal computer via wired or wireless technology.

Figure 5-19 A variety of game controllers.

Motion-Sensing Game Controllers

Motion-sensing game controllers allow the user to guide on-screen elements by moving a handheld input device in predetermined directions through the air. Some are sold with a particular type of game; others are general purpose. Sports games, for example, use motion-sensing game controllers, such as baseball bats and golf clubs, as their input device. These types of controllers communicate with a game console or a personal computer via wired or wireless technology.

A popular general-purpose, motion-sensing game controller is Nintendo's Wii Remote. Shaped like a television remote control and operated with one hand, the *Wii Remote* is a motion-sensing input device that uses Bluetooth wireless technology to communicate with the Wii game console. Users point the Wii Remote in different directions and rotate it to control on-screen players, vehicles, and other objects.

Other Game Controllers

Other popular game controllers include musical instruments and balance boards. Controllers that resemble musical instruments, such as guitars, drums, and keyboards, work with music video games that enable game players to create sounds and music by playing the instrument. Fitness games often communicate with a balance board, which is shaped like a weight scale and contains sensors that measure a game player's balance and weight (read Ethics & Issues 5-3 for a related discussion). Musical instrument and balance board controllers communicate with game consoles via wired or wireless technology.

ETHICS & ISSUES 5-3

Are Video Game Makers Qualified to Provide Medical Advice?

Video games historically have been considered a couch-potato activity. Recently, however, some video games began providing full workout regimens, including push-ups, sit-ups, yoga, jogging, and even hula hoop. Virtual trainers provide encouragement and guidance. Some critics find fault with these systems, claiming that neither the video game makers nor the games themselves have been evaluated by medical personnel, and as such, are not as qualified as a legitimate human trainer. One game estimated the age of a triathlete to be more than 10 years older than her actual age. Other game players reported that after an hour of an advanced workout with a game, the game reported that only a few calories were burned. In another situation, a game noted that a child was obese, which resulted not only in hurt feelings, but also a lawsuit. Some medical experts note that games do not take a participant's medical history into account when evaluating or recommending activities to a participant. Proponents of fitness-related games state that as long as the games encourage people to be more active, the games are doing what they were designed to do. The games are popular with the elderly and with children who might otherwise not get much physical activity.

Are video game makers qualified to provide medical advice? Why or why not? Can fitness-related video games provide a quality workout similar to an experience at a gym? Why or why not? As long as the games make people more active, should the games' shortcomings be ignored? Why?

QUIZ YOURSELF 5-1

Instructions: Find the true statement below. Then, rewrite the remaining false statements so that they are true.

1. A keyboard is an output device that contains keys users press to enter data in a computer.
2. A stylus is a flat, rectangular, electronic, plastic board.
3. A trackball is a small, flat, rectangular pointing device commonly found on notebook computers, including netbooks and many Tablet PCs.
4. Input is any data or instructions entered into the memory of a computer.
5. Operations you can perform with a wheel include point, click, right-click, double-click, triple-click, drag, right-drag, rotate wheel, free-spin wheel, press wheel button, tilt wheel, and press thumb button.

Quiz Yourself Online: To further check your knowledge of pages 258 through 271, visit the Computer Concepts CourseMate Web site at www.cengagebrain.com, navigate to the Chapter 5 Quiz Yourself resource for this book, and then click Objectives 1 – 6.

Digital Cameras

As discussed in Chapter 1, a **digital camera** is a mobile device that allows users to take pictures and store the photographed images digitally, instead of on traditional film. While many digital cameras look like a traditional camera, many mobile devices such as smart phones, PDAs, and portable media players often have a built-in digital camera. Mobile users such as real estate agents, insurance agents, general contractors, and photojournalists use digital cameras so that they immediately can view photographed images on the camera. Home and business users have digital cameras to save the expense of film developing, duplication, and postage.

The three basic types of digital cameras are studio cameras, field cameras, and point-and-shoot cameras. The most expensive and highest quality of the three is a *studio camera*, which is a stationary camera used for professional studio work. Often used by photojournalists, a *field camera* is a portable camera that has many lenses and other attachments. As with the studio camera, a field camera can be quite expensive. A *point-and-shoot camera* is much more affordable and lightweight and provides acceptable quality photographic images for the home or small business user. Figure 5-20 illustrates how one make of a point-and-shoot digital camera works.

Often users prefer to *download*, or transfer a copy of, the images from the digital camera to the computer's hard disk. With some digital cameras, images download through a cable that connects the digital camera (or the camera's docking station) to a USB port or a FireWire port on the system unit. For cameras that store photos on a memory card, simply insert the media in a reading/writing device that communicates wirelessly or attaches to a port on the system unit.

When you copy photos to the hard disk in a computer, the photos are available for editing with photo editing software, printing, faxing, sending via e-mail, including in another document, or posting to a Web site or photo community for everyone to see. Many users add

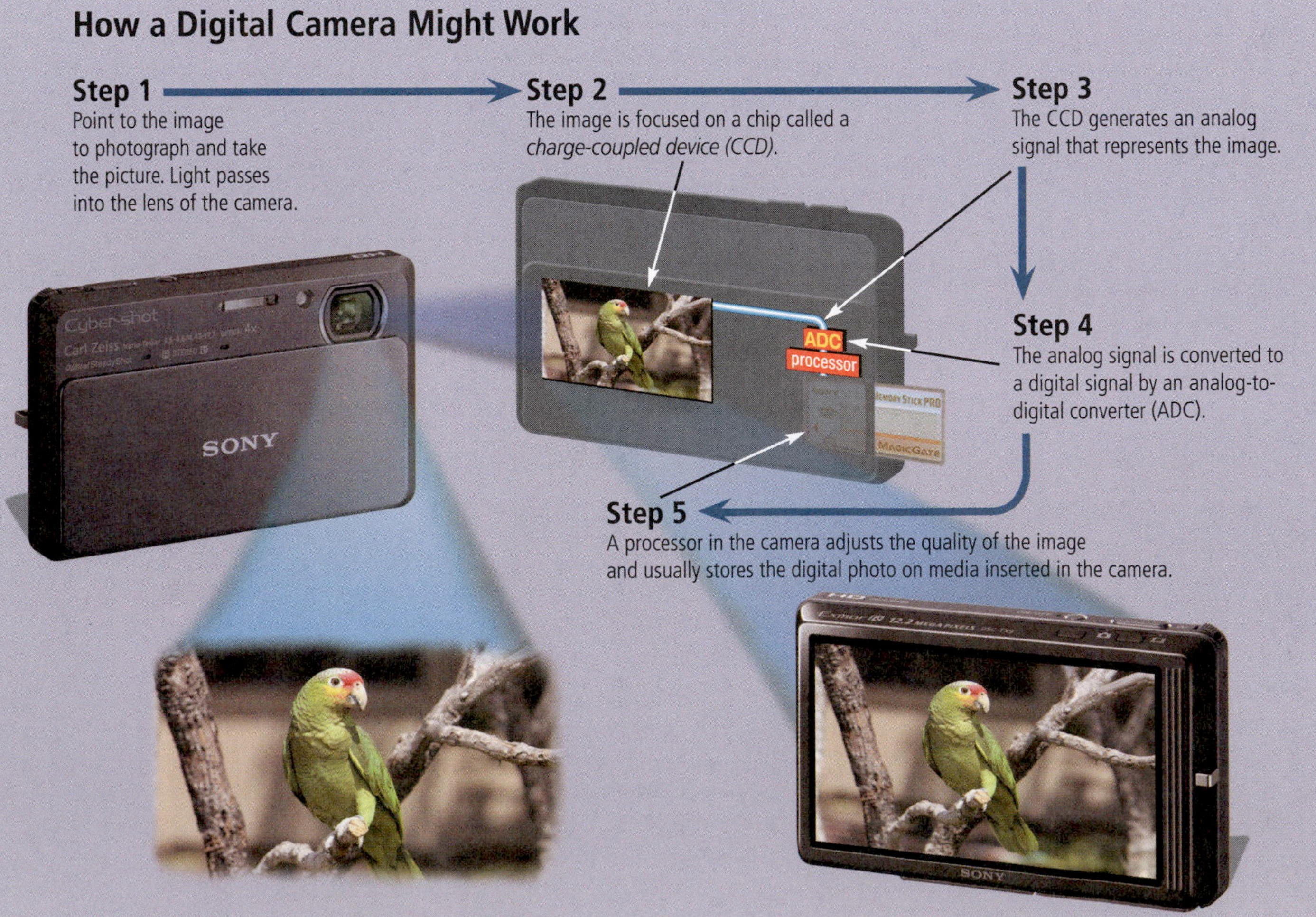

Figure 5-20 This figure shows how a digital camera might work.

photos to greeting cards, a computerized photo album, a family newsletter, certificates, and awards.

Digital Camera Photo Quality

One factor that affects the quality of digital camera photos is its resolution. **Resolution** is the number of horizontal and vertical pixels in a display device. A *pixel* (short for picture element) is the smallest element in an electronic image (Figure 5-21). The greater the number of pixels the camera uses to capture a picture, the better the quality of the picture. Thus, the higher the resolution, the better the picture quality, but the more expensive the camera.

Digital camera resolutions range from approximately 4 million to more than 16 million pixels (*MP*). A camera with a 7.1 MP (7,100,000 pixels) resolution will provide a better quality than one with a 4 MP resolution. As a general rule, a 4 MP camera is fine for photos sent via e-mail or posted on the Web. For good quality printed photos, users should have a 5 MP camera for 4 × 6 inch photos, a 6 MP camera for 8 × 10 photos, and 7 MP or greater camera for larger size prints or more professional results.

Manufacturers often use pixels per inch to represent a digital camera's resolution. *Pixels per inch* (*ppi*) is the number of pixels in one inch of screen display. For example, a 2304 × 1728 (pronounced 2304 by 1728) ppi camera has 2,304 pixels per vertical inch and 1,728 pixels per horizontal inch. Multiplying these two numbers together gives an approximate total number of pixels. For example, 2304 times 1728 equals approximately 4 million, or 4 MP. If just one number is stated, such as 1600 ppi, then both the vertical and horizontal numbers are the same.

Many digital cameras provide a means to adjust the ppi to the desired resolution. With a lower ppi, you can capture and store more images in the camera. For example, a camera set at 1280 × 960 ppi might capture and store 61 photos, if it has sufficient storage capacity. The number of photos may reduce to 24 on the same camera set at 2592 × 1944 ppi, because each photo consumes more storage space.

The actual photographed resolution is known as the *optical resolution*. Some manufacturers state *enhanced resolution*, instead of, or in addition to, optical resolution. Optical resolution is different from enhanced resolution. The enhanced resolution usually is higher because it uses a special formula to add pixels between those generated by the optical resolution. Be aware that some manufacturers compute a digital camera's megapixels from the enhanced resolution, instead of optical resolution.

Figure 5-21 A pixel is a single point in an electronic image.

Another measure of a digital camera's photo quality is the number of bits it stores in a pixel. Each pixel consists of one or more bits of data. The more bits used to represent a pixel, the more colors and shades of gray that can be represented. One bit per pixel is enough for simple one-color images. For multiple colors and shades of gray, each pixel requires more than one bit of data. A point-and-shoot camera should be at least 24 bit.

? FAQ 5-5

Why do some advertisements state camera resolution as dpi?

Some advertisements incorrectly use dpi to mean the same as ppi. The acronym *dpi*, which stands for *dots per inch*, is a measure of a print resolution. For screen resolution, the proper measurement term is ppi (pixels per inch).

For more information, visit the Computer Concepts CourseMate Web site at www.cengagebrain.com, navigate to the Chapter 5 FAQ resource for this book, and then click Resolution.

Voice Input

Voice input is the process of entering input by speaking into a microphone. The microphone may be a stand-alone peripheral that sits on top of a desk, or built in the computer or device, or in a headset. Some external microphones have a cable that attaches to a port on the sound card on the computer. Others communicate using wireless technology such as Bluetooth.

Uses of voice input include instant messaging that supports voice conversations, chat rooms that support voice chats, VoIP, and voice recognition. Recall that VoIP (Voice over IP) enables users to speak to other users over the Internet. **Voice recognition**, also called *speech recognition*, is the computer's capability of distinguishing spoken words. Other popular voice recognition programs for personal computers include IBM ViaVoice and Dragon Naturally Speaking (Figure 5-22).

Voice recognition programs recognize a vocabulary of preprogrammed words, which can range from two words to millions of words. The automated telephone system at your bank may ask you to answer questions by speaking the words Yes or No into the telephone. A voice recognition program on your computer, by contrast, may recognize up to two million words. Some current cell phones and other mobile devices allow you to store voice commands such as "Call Tom at home." Operating systems, such as Windows, also include voice recognition capabilities. Keep in mind that the best voice recognition programs are 90 to 95 percent accurate, which means the software may interpret as many as one in ten words incorrectly.

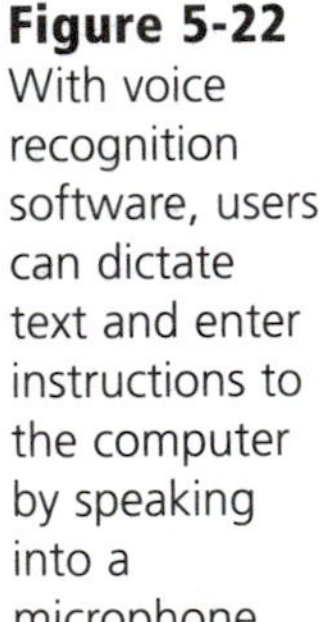

Figure 5-22 With voice recognition software, users can dictate text and enter instructions to the computer by speaking into a microphone.

Audio Input

Voice input is part of a larger category of input called audio input. **Audio input** is the process of entering any sound into the computer such as speech, music, and sound effects. To enter high-quality sound into a personal computer, the computer must have a sound card. Users enter sound into a computer via devices such as microphones, tape players, CD/DVD/Blu-ray Disc players, or radios, each of which plugs in a port on the sound card. Read Innovative Computing 5-1 to find out how software can help you accompany your own songs.

Some users also record live music and other sound effects into a computer by connecting external music devices such as an electronic keyboard (Figure 5-23), guitar, drums, harmonica, and microphones to a port on the system unit. When purchasing a music device, check its specifications for the type(s) of ports to which it connects. Ports that connect music devices to the system unit include USB, FireWire, MIDI, and S/PDIF, each illustrated in the previous chapter.

Music production software allows users to record, compose, mix, and edit music and sounds. For example, you can change the speed, add notes, or rearrange the score to produce an entirely new arrangement.

Figure 5-23 An electronic keyboard can be connected to a computer, allowing users to record and store music in the computer.

INNOVATIVE COMPUTING 5-1

Create Your Vocal Accompaniment Automatically

You never will sing alone again if you use Microsoft's MySong software. This ground-breaking program selects piano chords automatically to accompany vocal melodies. As a result, soloists and composers will hear full musical arrangements for their creations without having to write one note.

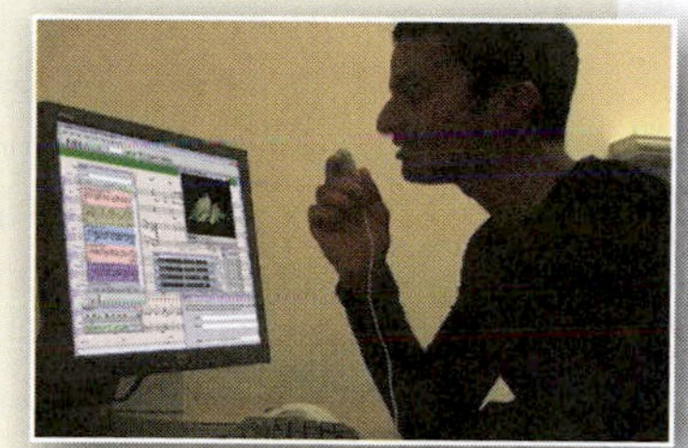

MySong was developed in Microsoft's research lab and at the University of Washington. The programmers asked a person to sing a melody. Then, the researchers created a file of musical notes from the sung melody. Finally, they used an algorithm to match chords with fragments of the melody. Several chord sequences are generated so that the singer can choose the style of accompaniment, such as jazzy or happy.

The software developers intended that novice singers use MySong as a basis to learn how accompaniments are written. In addition, they thought the software would help experienced songwriters explore some possible chords and styles for songs.

For more information, visit the Computer Concepts CourseMate Web site at www.cengagebrain.com, navigate to the Chapter 5 Innovative Computing resource for this book, and then click MySong.

Video Input

Video input is the process of capturing full-motion images and storing them on a computer's storage medium such as a hard disk or optical disc.

Some video devices record video using analog signals. Computers, by contrast, use digital signals. To enter video from an analog device into a personal computer, the analog signal must be converted to a digital signal. To do this, you plug a video camera or other analog video device in a video capture port on the system unit. One type of adapter card that has a video capture port is a *video capture card*, which converts an analog video signal into a digital signal that a computer can process. Most new computers are not equipped with a video capture card because not all users have the need for this type of adapter card.

A **digital video (DV) camera**, by contrast, records video as digital signals instead of analog signals. Many DV cameras can capture still frames, as well as motion. To transfer recorded images to a hard disk or optical disc, users connect DV cameras directly to a USB port or a FireWire port on the system unit. Thus, the computer does not need a video capture card. Simply connect the video device to the computer and begin transferring images. After saving the video on a storage medium, such as a hard disk or optical disc, you can play it or edit it using video editing software on a computer (Figure 5-24).

Figure 5-24 Home users can transfer videos to their computers and then use video editing software to edit the video.

Web Cams

A **Web cam**, also called a *PC video camera*, is a type of digital video camera that enables a home or small business user to capture video and still images, send e-mail messages with video attachments, add live images to instant messages, broadcast live images over the Internet, and make video telephone calls. During a *video telephone call*, both parties see each other as they communicate over the Internet. The cost of Web cams usually is less than $100.

Attached to the computer's USB port or FireWire port, a Web cam usually sits on top of a desktop computer monitor (shown in Figure 5-1 on page 259). Many notebook computers have built-in Web cams, such as the one in Figure 5-25.

You can configure some Web cams to display their output on a Web page. This use of a Web cam attracts Web site visitors by showing images that change regularly. Home or small business users might use Web cams to show a work in-progress, weather and traffic information, employees at work, or as a security system.

Some Web sites have live Web cams that display still pictures and update the displayed image at a specified time or time intervals, such as 15 seconds. A *streaming cam* has the illusion of moving images because it sends a continual stream of still images. To learn more about how to install and use a Web cam, complete the Learn How To 1 activity on page 298.

Web Cams

For more information, visit the Computer Concepts CourseMate Web site at www.cengagebrain.com, navigate to the Chapter 5 Web Link resource for this book, and then click Web Cams.

Figure 5-25 This student uses a notebook computer, which has a built-in Web cam, to watch a video of a lecture for her online class.

Video Conferencing

A **video conference** is a meeting between two or more geographically separated people who use a network or the Internet to transmit audio and video data (Figure 5-26). To participate in a video conference using a computer, you need video conferencing software or use a video conferencing Web application, along with a microphone, speakers, and a video camera attached to or built in to a computer. Examples of video conferencing software include CUworld, Live Meeting, and WebEx.

As you speak, members of the meeting hear your voice on their speakers. Any image in front of the video camera, such as a person's face, appears in a window on each participant's screen. A *whiteboard* is another window on the screen that displays notes and drawings simultaneously on all participants' screens. This window provides multiple users with an area on which they can write or draw.

As the costs of video conferencing hardware and software decrease, increasingly more business meetings, corporate training, and educational classes will be conducted as video conferences. Read Innovative Computing 5-2 to find out how patients conference with their health care providers.

INNOVATIVE COMPUTING 5-2

Monitor Health Status Remotely

As people age, they need to monitor their health regularly. The need for managing and treating their personal medical status is even more critical when their conditions include diabetes or congestive heart failure. Intel has developed the Health Guide to allow patients to measure their own vital signs, interact with health care professionals, and receive information without leaving their homes.

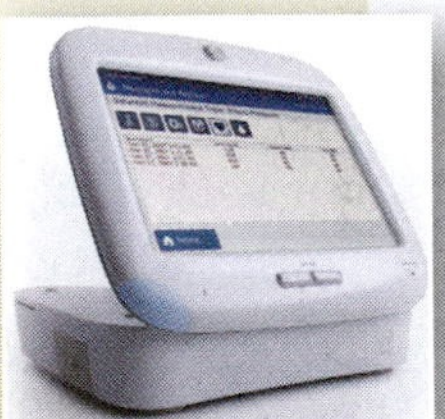

The eight-pound device empowers patients to take a positive role in managing their medical needs. It has a personalized calendar that alerts patients when they need to capture health measurements, such as blood pressure, glucose level, pulse, and weight. Patients input their health data using a touch screen, which also serves as monitor for two-way video conferences that allow caregivers to watch the patients take measurements, give encouragement, and answer questions.

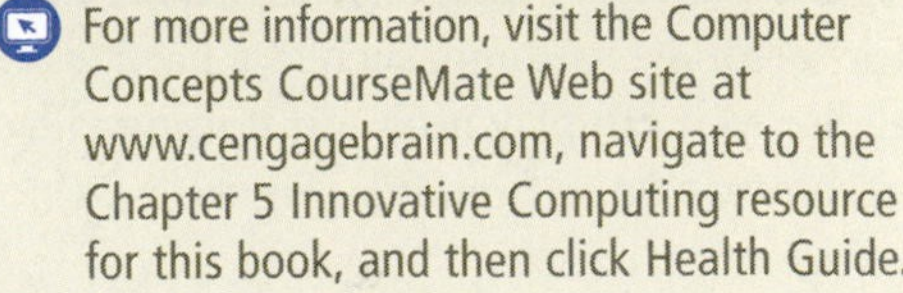

For more information, visit the Computer Concepts CourseMate Web site at www.cengagebrain.com, navigate to the Chapter 5 Innovative Computing resource for this book, and then click Health Guide.

Figure 5-26 To save on travel expenses, many large businesses are turning to video conferencing.

Scanners and Reading Devices

Some input devices save users time by eliminating manual data entry. With these devices, users do not type, speak, or write into the computer. Instead, these devices capture data from a *source document*, which is the original form of the data. Examples of source documents include time cards, order forms, invoices, paychecks, advertisements, brochures, photos, inventory tags, or any other document that contains data to be processed.

Devices that can capture data directly from a source document include optical scanners, optical readers, bar code readers, RFID readers, magnetic stripe card readers, and magnetic-ink character recognition readers. The following pages discuss each of these devices.

Optical Scanners

An *optical scanner*, usually called a **scanner**, is a light-sensing input device that reads printed text and graphics and then translates the results into a form the computer can process. Four types of scanners are flatbed, pen, sheet-fed, and drum (Figure 5-27).

✔ QUIZ YOURSELF 5-2

Instructions: Find the true statement below. Then, rewrite the remaining false statements so that they are true.

1. A digital camera allows users to take pictures and store the photographed images digitally, instead of on traditional film.
2. DV cameras record video as analog signals.
3. Video games and computer games use a Web cam as the input device that directs movements and actions of on-screen objects.
4. Many smart phones today have a built-in camera so that users easily can type text.
5. The lower the resolution of a digital camera, the better the photo quality, but the more expensive the camera.

Quiz Yourself Online: To further check your knowledge of pages 272 through 277, visit the Computer Concepts CourseMate Web site at www.cengagebrain.com, navigate to the Chapter 5 Quiz Yourself resource for this book, and then click Objectives 7 – 8.

Types of Scanners

Scanner	Method of Scanning and Use	Scannable Items
Flatbed 	• Similar to a copy machine • Scanning mechanism passes under the item to be scanned, which is placed on a glass surface	• Single-sheet documents • Bound material • Photos • Some models include trays for slides, transparencies, and negatives
Pen or Handheld 	• Move pen over text to be scanned, then transfer data to computer • Ideal for mobile users, students, and researchers • Some connect to a smart phone	• Any printed text
Sheet-Fed 	• Item to be scanned is pulled into a stationary scanning mechanism • Smaller than a flatbed scanner • A model designed specifically for photos is called a *photo scanner*	• Single-sheet documents • Photos • Slides (with an adapter) • Negatives
Drum 	• Item to be scanned rotates around stationary scanning mechanism • Very expensive • Used in large businesses	• Single-sheet documents • Photos • Slides • Negatives

Figure 5-27 This table describes the various types of scanners.

A **flatbed scanner** works in a manner similar to a copy machine except it creates a file of the document in memory instead of a paper copy (Figure 5-28). Once you scan a document or picture, you can display the scanned object on the screen, modify its appearance, store it on a storage medium, print it, fax it, attach it to an e-mail message, include it in another document, or post it on a Web site or photo community for everyone to see.

As with a digital camera, the quality of a scanner is measured by the number of bits it stores in a pixel and the number of pixels per inch, or resolution. The higher each number, the better the quality, but the more expensive the scanner. Most of today's affordable color desktop scanners for the home or small business range from 30 to 48 bits and have an optical resolution ranging from 600 to 9600 ppi. Commercial scanners designed for power users range from 9600 to 14,000 ppi.

Many scanners include *OCR (optical character recognition) software*, which can read and convert text documents into electronic files. OCR software is useful if you need to modify a document but do not have the original word processing file. For example, if you scan a business report with a flatbed scanner and do not use OCR software, you cannot edit the report because the scanner saves the report as an image. This is because the scanner does not differentiate between text and graphics. OCR software, however, would convert the scanned image into a text file that you could edit, for example, with a word processing program.

Businesses often use scanners for *image processing*, which consists of capturing, storing, analyzing, displaying, printing, and manipulating images. Image processing allows users to convert paper documents such as reports, memos, and procedure manuals into electronic images. Users distribute and publish these electronic documents on networks and the Internet.

Business users typically store and index electronic documents with an image processing system. An *image processing system* is similar to an electronic filing cabinet that provides access to exact reproductions of the original documents. Local governments, for example, use image processing systems to store property deeds and titles to provide the public and professionals, such as lawyers and loan officers, quick access to electronic documents.

? FAQ 5-6

How can I improve the quality of scanned documents?

Place a blank sheet of paper behind translucent papers, newspapers, and other see-through types of paper. If the original image is crooked, draw a line on the back at the bottom of the image. Use that mark to align the original on the scanner. Use photo editing software to fix imperfections in images.

For more information, visit the Computer Concepts CourseMate Web site at www.cengagebrain.com, navigate to the Chapter 5 FAQ resource for this book, and then click Scanning.

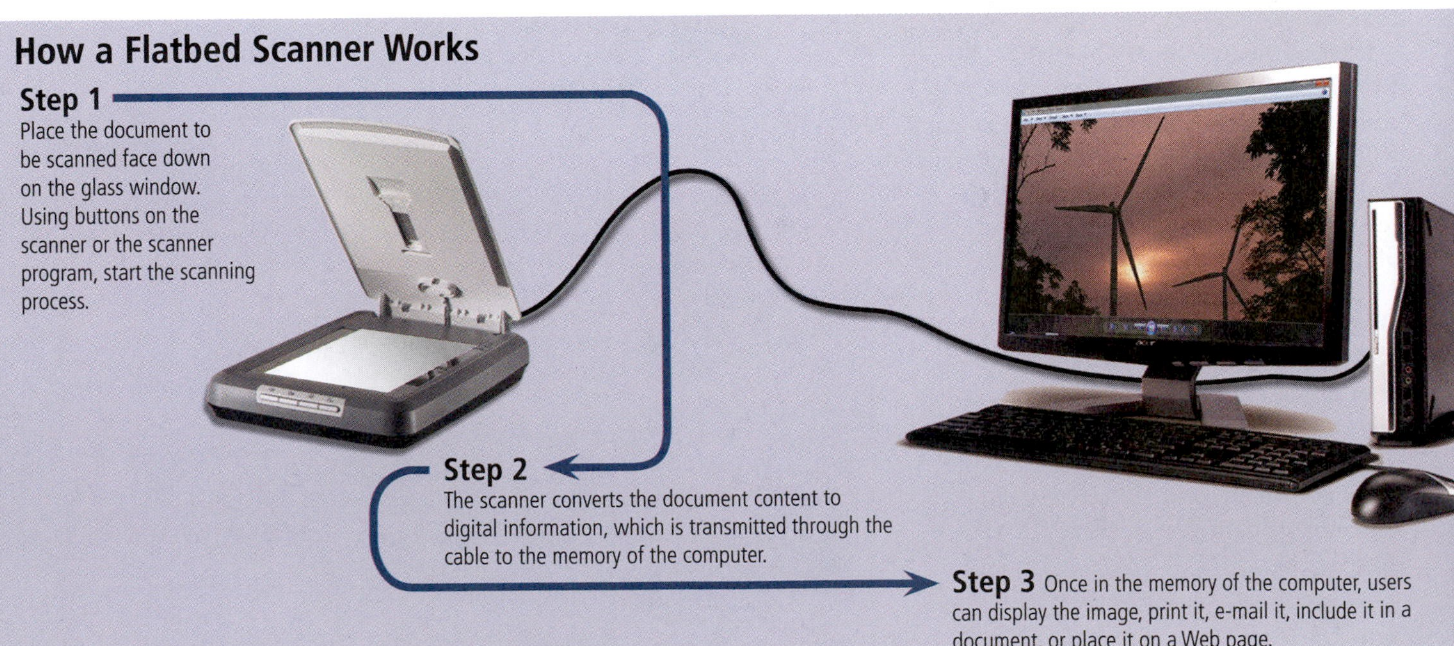

Figure 5-28 This figure shows how a flatbed scanner works.

Optical Readers

An *optical reader* is a device that uses a light source to read characters, marks, and codes and then converts them into digital data that a computer can process. Two technologies used by optical readers are optical character recognition and optical mark recognition.

Optical Character Recognition **Optical character recognition (OCR)** is a technology that involves reading typewritten, computer-printed, or hand-printed characters from ordinary documents and translating the images into a form that the computer can process. Most **OCR devices** include a small optical scanner for reading characters and sophisticated software to analyze what is read.

OCR devices range from large machines that can read thousands of documents per minute to handheld wands that read one document at a time. OCR devices read printed characters in an OCR font. A widely used OCR font is called OCR-A (Figure 5-29). During the scan of a document, an OCR device determines the shapes of characters by detecting patterns of light and dark. OCR software then compares these shapes with predefined shapes stored in memory and converts the shapes into characters the computer can process.

Many companies use OCR characters on turnaround documents. A **turnaround document** is a document that you return (turn around) to the company that creates and sends it. For example, when consumers receive a bill, they often tear off a portion of the bill and send it back to the company with their payment (Figure 5-30). The portion of the bill they return usually has their payment amount, account number, and other information printed in OCR characters.

ABCDEFGHIJKLM

NOPQRSTUVWXYZ

1234567890

- = ■ ; ' , . /

Figure 5-29 A portion of the characters in the OCR-A font. Notice how characters such as the number 0 and the letter O are shaped differently so that the reading device easily can distinguish between them.

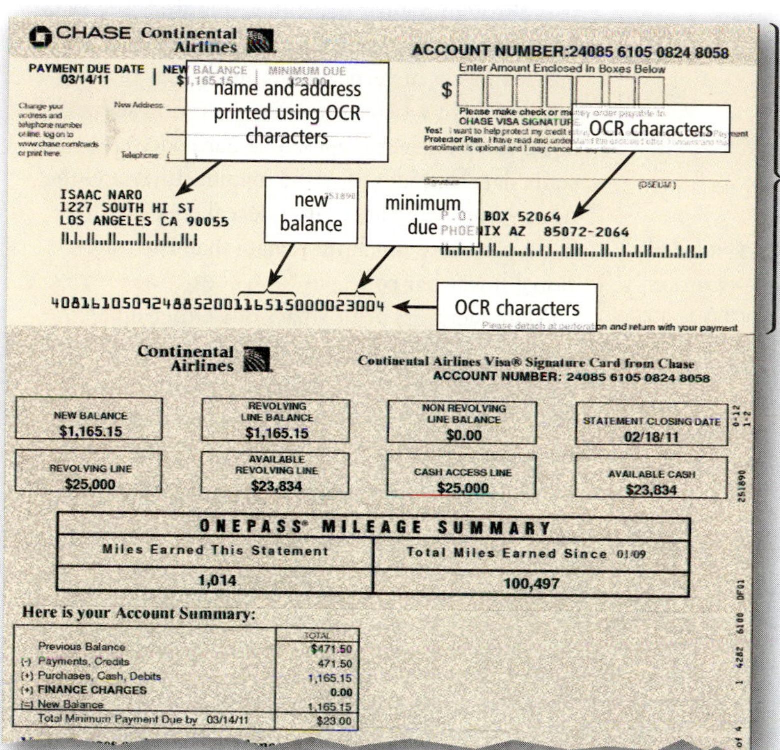

CHASE Continental Airlines

ACCOUNT NUMBER:24085 6105 0824 8058

PAYMENT DUE DATE 03/14/11

Enter Amount Enclosed In Boxes Below

$

ISAAC NARO
1227 SOUTH HI ST
LOS ANGELES CA 90055

P.O. BOX 52064
PHOENIX AZ 85072-2064

4081610509248852001165151500000230041

Continental Airlines

Continental Airlines Visa® Signature Card from Chase
ACCOUNT NUMBER: 24085 6105 0824 8058

NEW BALANCE $1,165.15	REVOLVING LINE BALANCE $1,165.15	NON REVOLVING LINE BALANCE $0.00	STATEMENT CLOSING DATE 02/18/11
REVOLVING LINE $25,000	AVAILABLE REVOLVING LINE $23,834	CASH ACCESS LINE $25,000	AVAILABLE CASH $23,834

ONEPASS® MILEAGE SUMMARY	
Miles Earned This Statement	Total Miles Earned Since 01/09
1,014	100,497

Here is your Account Summary:

	TOTAL
Previous Balance	$471.50
(-) Payments, Credits	471.50
(+) Purchases, Cash, Debits	1,165.15
(+) FINANCE CHARGES	0.00
(=) New Balance	1,165.15
Total Minimum Payment Due by 03/14/11	$23.00

Figure 5-30 OCR characters frequently are used with turnaround documents. With this bill, you tear off the top portion and return it with a payment.

Optical Mark Recognition **Optical mark recognition (OMR)** is a technology that reads hand-drawn marks such as small circles or rectangles (Figure 5-31). A person places these marks on a form, such as a test, survey, or questionnaire answer sheet. With a test, the OMR device first scans the answer key sheet to record correct answers based on patterns of light. The OMR device then scans the remaining documents and matches their patterns of light against the answer key sheet.

Figure 5-31 This person uses a pencil to darken in boxes on this document that can be read by an OMR device.

Bar Code Readers

A **bar code reader**, also called a **bar code scanner**, is an optical reader that uses laser beams to read bar codes by using light patterns that pass through the bar code lines (Figure 5-32). A **bar code** is an identification code that consists either of a set of vertical lines and spaces of different widths or a two-dimensional pattern of dots, squares, and other images. The bar code represents data that identifies the manufacturer and the item. A newer type of bar code, called a 2-D bar code, can store much more data than the traditional linear bar code.

Bar Code Readers
For more information, visit the Computer Concepts CourseMate Web site at www.cengagebrain.com, navigate to the Chapter 5 Web Link resource for this book, and then click Bar Code Readers.

Manufacturers print a bar code either on a product's package or on a label that is affixed to a product. A variety of products such as groceries, books, clothing, vehicles, mail, and packages have bar codes. Some airports now are accepting electronic boarding passes by using a bar code reader to scan a bar code that is displayed on the screen of a smart phone or PDA. Each industry uses its own type of bar code. The United States Postal Service (USPS) uses a POSTNET bar code. Retail and grocery stores use the *UPC* (*Universal Product Code*) bar code.

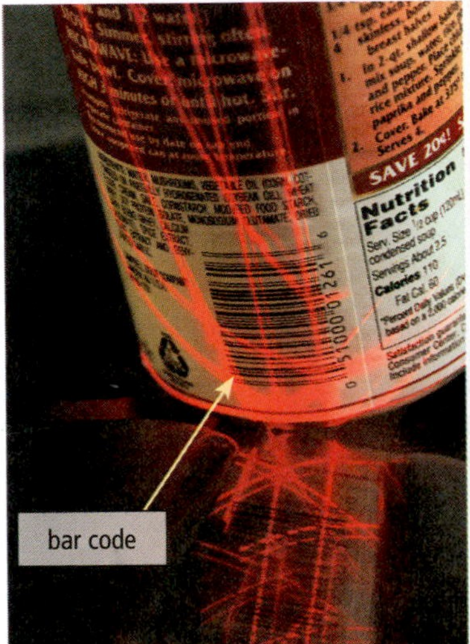

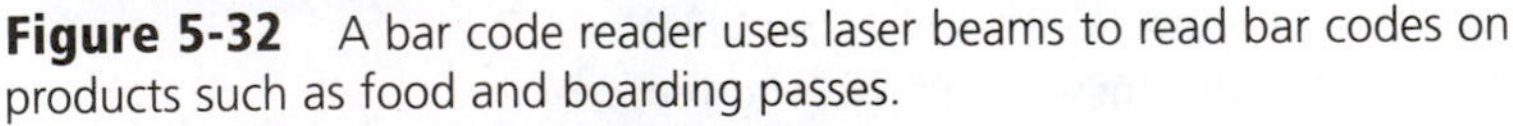
Figure 5-32 A bar code reader uses laser beams to read bar codes on products such as food and boarding passes.

RFID Readers

RFID (*radio frequency identification*) is a technology that uses radio signals to communicate with a tag placed in or attached to an object, an animal, or a person. RFID tags, which contain a memory chip and an antenna, are available in many shapes and sizes and sometimes are embedded in glass, labels, or cards. Some RFID tags are as small as a grain of sand; others are the size of a luggage tag. An **RFID reader** reads information on the tag via radio waves. RFID readers can be handheld devices or mounted in a stationary object such as a doorway.

Many retailers see RFID as an alternative to bar code identification because it does not require direct contact or line-of-site transmission. Each product in a store would contain a tag that identifies the product (Figure 5-33). As consumers remove products from the store shelves and walk through a checkout area, an RFID reader reads the tag(s) and communicates with a computer that calculates the amount due, eliminating the need for checking out each item.

Other uses of RFID include tracking times of runners in a marathon; tracking location of soldiers, employee wardrobes, airline baggage, and misplaced or stolen goods; checking lift tickets of skiers; managing inventory; gauging pressure and temperature of tires on a vehicle; checking out library books; and tracking payment as vehicles pass through booths on tollway systems. Read Ethics & Issues 5-4 for a related discussion.

ETHICS & ISSUES 5-4

Will RFID Track Your Every Move?

The rapid growth of RFID worries some privacy advocates. RFID (radio frequency identification) uses a tiny computer chip that can be mounted on a tag attached to a product, sewn into an article of clothing, or even attached to a document. For merchants, RFID can help to locate items in a warehouse and identify items that need to be replenished. For consumers, RFID can supply detailed product information, and someday let buyers bypass check-out lines and take purchases directly from the store, with the item's cost charged to their card. The federal government started a program to include RFID chips on all passports. Privacy advocates worry, however, that RFID could obliterate a person's anonymity. They fear that with an RFID reader, any individual or organization could track a person's movements and make that information available to marketers or government agencies. Several researchers have shown that current RFID passports can be copied and forged. Further, some fear that the RFID chip in a passport could be copied by a hidden RFID reader and then used for nefarious purposes such as faking one's identity. To protect privacy, privacy advocates insist that merchants should be forced to disable RFID transmitters as soon as buyers leave a store. They also recommend that RFID-enabled documents, such as passports, be kept in special containers made of material that will not allow the chip to be read until it is removed from the container.

Would you be comfortable purchasing a product that includes RFID? Why or why not? Should buyers be allowed to request that RFID transmitters be disabled after they make a purchase, or should merchants be required to render transmitters inoperative when the product leaves the store? Why? Would you feel comfortable carrying a form of identification that is RFID-enabled? Why or why not?

Figure 5-33 RFID readers read information stored on an RFID tag and then communicate this information to computers, which instantaneously compute payments and update inventory records. In this example, the RFID tag is embedded in a label attached to the tire.

Magnetic Stripe Card Readers

A **magnetic stripe card reader**, often called a *magstripe reader*, reads the magnetic stripe on the back of credit cards, entertainment cards, bank cards, and other similar cards. The stripe, which is divided in three horizontal tracks, contains information identifying you and the card issuer (Figure 5-34). Some information stored in the stripe includes your name, account number, the card's expiration date, and a country code.

Information on magnetic card stripes is used to make payments, authenticate users, record attendance, and provide access to secure areas. When a consumer swipes a credit card through a magstripe reader, for example, it reads the information stored on the magnetic stripe on the card. If the magstripe reader rejects the card, it is possible that the magnetic stripe on the card is scratched, dirty, or erased. Exposure to a magnet or magnetic field can erase the contents of a card's magnetic stripe.

In many cases, a magstripe reader is part of a signature capture pad and/or a point-of-sale terminal. Point-of-sale terminals are discussed later in this chapter.

Figure 5-34 A magnetic stripe card reader reads information encoded on the stripe on the back of your credit card.

MICR Readers

MICR (*magnetic-ink character recognition*) devices read text printed with magnetized ink. An **MICR reader** converts MICR characters into a form the computer can process. The banking industry almost exclusively uses MICR for check processing. Each check in your checkbook has precoded MICR characters beginning at the lower-left edge (Figure 5-35). The MICR characters represent the bank routing number, the customer account number, and the check number. These numbers may appear in a different order than the ones shown in the sample in Figure 5-35.

When a bank receives a check for payment, it uses an MICR inscriber to print the amount of the check in MICR characters in the lower-right corner. The check then is sorted or routed to the customer's bank, along with thousands of others. Each check is inserted in an MICR reader, which sends the check information — including the amount of the check — to a computer for processing. When you balance your checkbook, verify that the amount printed in the lower-right corner is the same as the amount written on the check; otherwise, your statement will not balance.

The banking industry has established an international standard not only for bank numbers, but also for the font of the MICR characters. This standardization makes it possible for people to write checks in other countries.

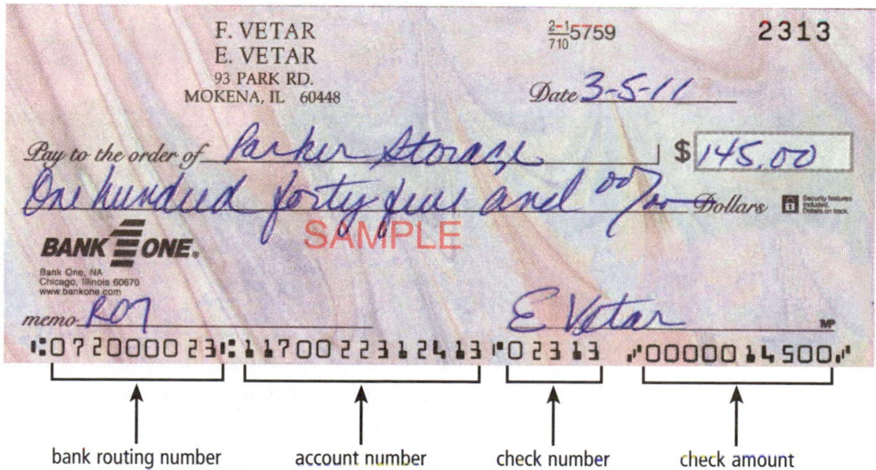

Figure 5-35 The MICR characters preprinted on the check represent the bank routing number, the customer account number, and the check number. The amount of the check in the lower-right corner is added after the check is cashed.

Data Collection Devices

Instead of reading or scanning data from a source document, a *data collection device* obtains data directly at the location where the transaction or event takes place. For example, employees use bar code readers, handheld computers, or other mobile devices to collect data wirelessly (Figure 5-36). These types of data collection devices are used in restaurants, grocery stores, factories, warehouses, the outdoors, or other locations where heat, humidity, and cleanliness are not easy to control. For example, factories and retail stores use data collection devices to take inventory and order products.

Data collection devices and many mobile computers and devices have the capability of wirelessly transmitting data over a network or the Internet. Increasingly more users today send data wirelessly to central office computers using these devices.

Figure 5-36 A warehouse employee uses this rugged handheld computer, which includes a bar code reader, that wirelessly transmits information about the scanned item to the store's inventory system.

Biometric Input

Biometrics is the technology of authenticating a person's identity by verifying a personal characteristic. Biometric devices grant users access to programs, systems, or rooms by analyzing some biometric identifier. A *biometric identifier* is a physiological (related to physical or chemical activities in the body) or behavioral characteristic. Examples include fingerprints, hand geometry, facial features, voice, signatures, and eye patterns.

A *biometric device* translates a personal characteristic (the input) into a digital code that is compared with a digital code stored in the computer. If the digital code in the computer does not match the personal characteristic's code, the computer denies access to the individual.

The most widely used biometric device today is a fingerprint reader. A **fingerprint reader**, or scanner, captures curves and indentations of a fingerprint (Figure 5-37). The reader can be set up to perform different functions for different fingers; for example, one finger starts a program and another finger shuts down the computer. With the cost of fingerprint readers often less than $100, home and small business users install fingerprint readers to authenticate users before they can access a personal computer. External fingerprint readers usually plug into a USB port. To save on desk space, some newer keyboards and notebook computers have a fingerprint reader attached to them, which allows users to log on to programs and Web sites via their fingerprint instead of entering a user name and password. For a technical discussion about fingerprint readers, read the High-Tech Talk article on page 288.

A *face recognition system* captures a live face image and compares it with a stored image to determine if the person is a legitimate user. Some buildings use face recognition systems to secure access to rooms. Law enforcement, surveillance systems, and airports use face recognition to protect the public. Some notebook computers use this security technique to safeguard a computer. The computer will not start unless the user is legitimate. These programs are becoming more sophisticated and can recognize

Figure 5-37 A fingerprint reader.

people with or without glasses, makeup, or jewelry, and with new hairstyles. Read Ethics & Issues 5-5 for a related discussion.

Biometric devices measure the shape and size of a person's hand using a *hand geometry system* (Figure 5-38). Because their cost is more than $1,000, larger companies use these systems as time and attendance devices or as security devices. Colleges use hand geometry systems to verify students' identities. Day-care centers and hospital nurseries use them to verify parents who pick up their children.

A *voice verification system* compares a person's live speech with their stored voice pattern. Larger organizations sometimes use voice verification systems as time and attendance devices. Many companies also use this technology for access to sensitive files and networks. Some financial services use voice verification systems to secure telephone banking transactions.

A *signature verification system* recognizes the shape of your handwritten signature, as well as measures the pressure exerted and the motion used to write the signature. Signature verification systems use a specialized pen and tablet.

High security areas use iris recognition systems. The camera in an *iris recognition system* uses iris recognition technology to read patterns in the iris of the eye (Figure 5-39). These patterns are as unique as a fingerprint. Iris recognition systems are quite expensive and are used by government security organizations, the military, and financial institutions that deal with highly sensitive data. Some organizations use *retinal scanners*, which work similarly but instead scan patterns of blood vessels in the back of the retina.

Biometric Input

For more information, visit the Computer Concepts CourseMate Web site at www.cengagebrain.com, navigate to the Chapter 5 Web Link resource for this book, and then click Biometric Input.

Figure 5-38 A hand geometry system verifies this student's identity before he is allowed access to the school gymnasium.

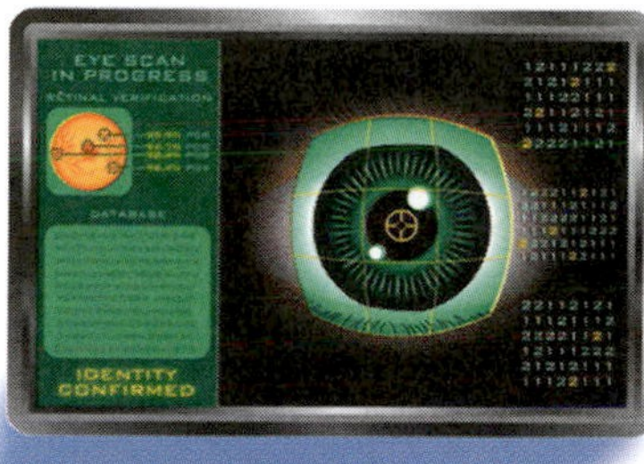

Figure 5-39 An iris recognition system.

ETHICS & ISSUES 5-5

How Often Should You Be Monitored in Public Locations?

Customers with yearly passes for a theme park in Japan enjoy a unique method of entering the park. A biometric face recognition system recognizes the customer's face and allows the visitor entry into the park. At large sporting events, airports, and other public areas, face recognition systems scan visitors' faces and compare the visitors' faces to wanted or known criminals. Those who match a known criminal's face are detained so that authorities can make a final determination if the person should be removed from the location or arrested. Some local governments support placing face recognition systems on streets and scanning everybody who walks by. Supporters state the use of these systems, rather than authorities trying to recognize criminals, is more efficient in finding wanted criminals and allows law enforcement personnel to focus their efforts elsewhere. Opponents of the systems claim that they are an invasion of privacy and even may violate the fourth amendment to the Constitution, which provides protection from unreasonable searches. They also claim that the systems result in an increase in innocent people being detained because the systems are imperfect. In fact, at one large sporting event, more than a dozen people were detained, but none was found to be a match to a known criminal.

Would you mind constant monitoring by face recognition systems? Why? Which types of criminals should face recognition systems be used to locate? Why? How would you react if you were improperly detained due to a mistake made by a face recognition system?

Terminals

A *terminal* is a computer, usually with limited processing power, that enables users to send data to and/or receive information from a host computer. The host computer processes the data and then, if necessary, sends information (output) back to the terminal. The host computer usually is a server or mainframe.

Special-purpose terminals perform specific tasks and contain features uniquely designed for use in a particular industry. Three widely used special-purpose terminals are point-of-sale (POS) terminals, automated teller machines, and DVD kiosks.

Point-of-Sale Terminals

The location in a retail or grocery store where a consumer pays for goods or services is the point of sale (POS). Most retail stores use a **POS terminal** to record purchases, process credit or debit cards, and update inventory.

In a grocery store, the POS terminal is a combination of an electronic cash register, bar code reader, and printer (Figure 5-40). When the checkout clerk or customer scans the bar code on the food product, the computer uses the manufacturer and item numbers to look up the price of the item and the complete product name in a database. Then, the price of the item in the database shows on the display device, the name of the item and its price print on a receipt, and the item being sold is recorded so that the inventory can be updated. Thus, the output from a POS terminal serves as input to other computers to maintain sales records, update inventory, verify credit, and perform other activities associated with the sales transactions that are critical to running the business. Some POS terminals are Web-enabled, which allows updates to inventory at geographically separate locations.

Many POS terminals handle credit card or debit card payments and thus also include a magstripe reader. Some have a fingerprint reader that is linked to a payment method such as a checking account or credit card. After swiping your card through the reader or reading your fingerprint, the POS terminal connects to a system that authenticates the purchase. Once the transaction is approved, the terminal prints a receipt for the customer.

Figure 5-40 Many grocery stores offer self-serve checkouts, where the consumers themselves use the POS terminals to scan purchases, scan their store saver card and coupons, and then pay for the goods.

Automated Teller Machines

An **automated teller machine** (**ATM**) is a self-service banking machine that connects to a host computer through a network (Figure 5-41). Banks place ATMs in convenient locations, including grocery stores, convenience stores, retail outlets, shopping malls, sports and concert venues, and gas stations, so that customers conveniently can access their bank accounts.

Using an ATM, people withdraw cash, deposit money, transfer funds, or inquire about an account balance. Some ATMs have a touch screen; others have special buttons or keypads for entering input. To access a bank account, you insert a plastic bankcard in the ATM's magstripe reader. The ATM asks you to enter a password, called a *personal identification number* (*PIN*), which verifies that you are the holder of the bankcard. When your transaction is complete, the ATM prints a receipt for your records.

Figure 5-41 An ATM is a self-service banking terminal that allows customers to access their bank accounts.

DVD Kiosks

A **DVD kiosk** is a self-service DVD rental machine that connects to a host computer through a network (Figure 5-42). The DVD kiosks, some of which can hold more than 600 DVDs, are located nationwide at retail stores, fast-food restaurants, grocery stores, airports, and other convenient public locations.

A DVD kiosk is associated with a particular vendor. To rent a movie online, for example, a customer visits the vendor's Web site, establishes an account or connects to an existing account, selects the desired movie, and then chooses a nearby DVD kiosk where the movie will be picked up. Customers also usually can select movies directly on the DVD kiosk via a touch screen or some other input device on the kiosk. After presenting identifying information and swiping a credit card through the reader, the DVD kiosk dispenses the rented movie to the customer. When finished viewing the movie, the customer returns it to any of the vendor's nationwide DVD kiosks, at which time the customer's account is charged a fee based on the time elapsed.

Figure 5-42 A DVD kiosk is a self-service DVD rental machine.

Putting It All Together

When you purchase a computer, you should have an understanding of the input devices included with the computer, as well as those you may need that are not included. Many factors influence the type of input devices you may use: the type of input desired, the hardware and software in use, and the desired cost. The type of input devices you require depends on your intended use. Figure 5-43 outlines several suggested input devices for specific computer users.

Suggested Input Devices by User

User	Input Device
Home 	• Enhanced keyboard or ergonomic keyboard • Mouse • Stylus for smart phone or other mobile device • Game controller(s) • 30-bit 600 × 1200 ppi color scanner • 7 MP digital camera • Headphones that include a microphone (headset) • Web cam • Fingerprint reader
Small Office/ Home Office 	• Enhanced keyboard or ergonomic keyboard • Mouse • Stylus and portable keyboard for smart phone or other mobile device, or digital pen for Tablet PC • 36-bit 600 × 1200 ppi color scanner • 8 MP digital camera • Headphones that include a microphone (headset) • Web cam
Mobile 	• Wireless mouse for notebook computer • Touchpad or pointing stick on notebook computer • Stylus and portable keyboard for smart phone or other mobile device, or digital pen for Tablet PC • 7 or 8 MP digital camera • Headphones that include a microphone (headset) • Fingerprint reader for notebook computer
Power 	• Enhanced keyboard or ergonomic keyboard • Mouse • Stylus and portable keyboard for smart phone or other mobile device • Pen for graphics tablet • 48-bit 1200 × 1200 ppi color scanner • 9 to 12 MP digital camera • Headphones that include a microphone (headset) • Web cam
Enterprise 	• Enhanced keyboard or ergonomic keyboard • Mouse • Stylus and portable keyboard for smart phone or other mobile device, or digital pen for Tablet PC • Touch screen • 42-bit 1200 × 1200 ppi color scanner • 9 to 12 MP digital camera • OCR/OMR readers, bar code readers, MICR reader, or data collection devices • Microphone • Video camera for video conferences • Fingerprint reader or other biometric device

Figure 5-43 This table recommends suggested input devices.

Input Devices for Physically Challenged Users

The ever-increasing presence of computers in everyone's lives has generated an awareness of the need to address computing requirements for those who have or may develop physical limitations. The **Americans with Disabilities Act (ADA)** requires any company with 15 or more employees to make reasonable attempts to accommodate the needs of physically challenged workers.

Besides voice recognition, which is ideal for blind or visually impaired users, several other input devices are available. A *keyguard* is a metal or plastic plate placed over the keyboard that allows users to rest their hands on the keyboard without accidentally pressing any keys. A keyguard also guides a finger or pointing device so that a user presses only one key at a time.

Keyboards with larger keys also are available (Figure 5-44). Still another option is the *on-screen keyboard*, in which a graphic of a standard keyboard is displayed on the user's screen.

Figure 5-44 A keyboard with larger keys.

Various pointing devices are available for users with motor disabilities. Small trackballs that the user controls with a thumb or one finger can be attached to a table, mounted to a wheelchair, or held in the user's hand. Another option for people with limited hand movement is a *head-mounted pointer* to control the pointer or insertion point (Figure 5-45). To simulate the functions of a mouse button, a user works with switches that control the pointer. The switch might be a hand pad, a foot pedal, a receptor that detects facial motions, or a pneumatic instrument controlled by puffs of air.

Two exciting developments in this area are gesture recognition and computerized implant devices. Both in the prototype stage, they attempt to provide users with a natural computer interface. With *gesture recognition*, the computer will detect human motions. Computers with gesture recognition capability have the potential to recognize sign language, read lips, track facial movements, or follow eye gazes. For paralyzed or speech impaired individuals, a doctor will implant a computerized device into the brain. This device will contain a transmitter. As the user thinks thoughts, the transmitter will send signals to the computer. Read Looking Ahead 5-1 for a look at a tongue-powered input device.

Gesture Recognition

For more information, visit the Computer Concepts CourseMate Web site at www.cengagebrain.com, navigate to the Chapter 5 Web Link resource for this book, and then click Gesture Recognition.

Figure 5-45 A camera/receiver mounted on the monitor tracks the position of the head-mounted pointer, which is reflective material that this user is wearing on the brim of her hat. As the user moves her head, the pointer on the screen also moves.

LOOKING AHEAD 5-1

Tongue May Become Joystick to Control Devices

Thousands of people are paralyzed from the neck down due to spinal cord damage, but they have full control of their tongue because it is controlled by a cranial nerve, not the spinal cord. For these people, Georgia Institute of Technology's Tongue Drive System may be the input device that helps them control their lives.

In the Georgia Tech prototype, the tongue serves as a joystick. A magnet less than one-eighth of an inch wide is surgically implanted under the tip of the tongue, and when a person moves his or her tongue, sensors on each cheek record the magnet's movements in one of six directions: left, right, forward, backward, single-click, and double-click. This data is sent to a receiver on top of the person's head, which, in turn, transmits a signal wirelessly to a computer that controls an electronic device. For example, if the tongue moves forward and to the left, lights in the room could turn on or a wheelchair could roll forward.

In a future development of the Tongue Drive System, an individual tooth could be designated as a specific letter, so teeth could function, in effect, as a keyboard.

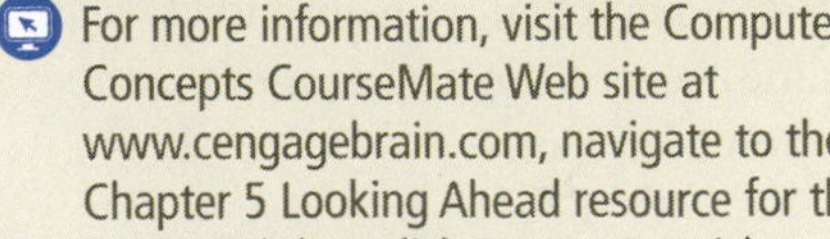
For more information, visit the Computer Concepts CourseMate Web site at www.cengagebrain.com, navigate to the Chapter 5 Looking Ahead resource for this book, and then click Tongue Joystick.

QUIZ YOURSELF 5-3

Instructions: Find the true statement below. Then, rewrite the remaining false statements so that they are true.

1. A fingerprint reader captures curves and indentations of a signature.
2. After swiping a credit card through an MICR reader, a POS terminal connects to a system that authenticates the purchase.
3. ATMs ask you to enter a password, called a biometric identifier, which verifies that you are the holder of the bankcard.
4. Four types of source documents are flatbed, pen, sheet-fed, and drum.
5. Retail and grocery stores use the POSTNET bar code.
6. RFID is a technology that uses laser signals to communicate with a tag placed in an object, an animal, or a person.
7. The Americans with Disabilities Act (ADA) requires any company with 15 or more employees to make reasonable attempts to accommodate the needs of physically challenged workers.

 **Quiz Yourself Online:** To further check your knowledge of pages 277 through 286, visit the Computer Concepts CourseMate Web site at www.cengagebrain.com, navigate to the Chapter 5 Quiz Yourself resource for this book, and then click Objectives 9 – 12.

Chapter Summary

Input is any data and instructions you enter into the memory of a computer. This chapter described the various techniques of entering input and several commonly used input devices. Topics presented included the keyboard, mouse, and other pointing devices; touch screens; pen input; other input for smart phones; game controllers; digital cameras; voice input; video input; scanners and reading devices; biometric input; terminals; and input devices for physically challenged users.

Computer Usage @ Work

Hospitality

Before technology use became widespread in the hospitality industry, the service that customers received was personal but inefficient. For example, most hotel reservations and transactions were recorded manually on paper, which was a time-consuming process. As technology evolved and became more prominent in the hospitality industry, hotels and restaurants began running their businesses more efficiently.

Many hotels now rely on technology to reduce the number of people-hours necessary to perform tasks. For instance, some individuals shop for and reserve hotel rooms online. Many hotel Web sites allow potential guests to take virtual tours of their rooms and read about available amenities. When someone books a reservation online, the information automatically transfers to the hotel's reservation system without intervention from the hotel staff. When guests arrive, an employee verifies their reservation and might hand them an electronic key that opens their room during their stay. After they check out, the key no longer opens the door to that room. During a hotel stay, guests might wish to charge various hotel purchases to their room, which often happens electronically using POS terminals in the hotel's stores and restaurants. An up-to-the-minute listing of all room charges usually is available through the hotel room's television, as well as when the guests check out. Without this technology, employees would complete these transactions manually, which can introduce inaccuracies, causing the hotel to lose money.

In addition to hotels, many restaurants rely on computers for routine tasks. When a server takes a customer's order at a restaurant, the server might enter the order in a computer; the order then is sent directly to a monitor or printer in the kitchen. In this instance, computers can increase accuracy by not requiring cooks and chefs to decipher handwriting. In addition, these computers also store the correct prices for menu items, eliminating the potential for servers to charge customers an incorrect price. When the customer has finished his or her meal, the server prints a check. If the customer pays by credit card, the computer also might process the credit card transaction.

Computers significantly have changed the experience patrons have at restaurants, hotels, and other areas in the hospitality industry. The increased accuracy and efficiency often results in greater guest satisfaction, which can increase sales and justify the investment in the technology.

 For more information, visit the Computer Concepts CourseMate Web site at www.cengagebrain.com, navigate to the Chapter 5 Computer Usage @ Work resource for this book, and then click Hospitality.

High-Tech Talk

Biometrics: Personalized Security

Biometric authentication is based on the measurement of an individual's unique physiological and behavioral characteristics. The most common measurements, described earlier in this chapter, such as fingerprints, hand geometry, facial features, and eye patterns are physiological biometrics. Some of the more novel measurements, such as body odor, brain wave patterns, DNA, ear shape, sweat pores, and vein patterns also fall into the category of physiological biometrics. Voice scan and signature scan are examples of behavioral biometrics.

Any biometric technology process involves two basic steps — enrollment and matching. To illustrate these steps, this High-Tech Talk uses the most common biometric technology, finger-scan technology.

ENROLLMENT Enrollment is the process in which a user presents the fingerprint data to be stored in a template for future use, as shown in the top of Figure 5-46. This initial template is called the *enrollment template*. Creating the enrollment template involves four basic steps: (1) acquire fingerprint, (2) extract fingerprint feature, (3) create enrollment template, and (4) store enrollment template. The enrollment template usually is created only after the user has submitted several samples of the same fingerprint. Most fingerprint images will have false details, usually caused by cuts, scars, or even dirt, which must be filtered out.

The first step, acquire fingerprint, presents a major challenge to finger-scan technology. The quality of a fingerprint may vary substantially from person to person and even finger to finger. The two main methods of acquiring images are optical and silicon. With optical technology, a camera is used to register the fingerprint image against a plastic or glass platen (scanner). Silicon technology uses a silicon chip as a platen, which usually produces a higher quality fingerprint image than optical devices.

The second step, extract fingerprint feature, involves thinning the ridges of the raw image to a minuscule size and then converting the characteristics to binary format. Fingerprints are comprised of ridges and valleys that have unique patterns, such as arches, loops, and swirls. Irregularities and discontinuities in these ridges and valleys are known as *minutiae*. Minutiae are the distinctive characteristics upon which most finger-scan technology is based. The fingerprint-feature extraction process used is highly sophisticated, patented, and a closely-held vendor secret.

In the third step, the binary format is used to create the enrollment template. The fourth and final step involves storing the template on a storage device, such as a hard disk or smart card for future use when the same person attempts to be authenticated.

MATCHING Matching is the process of comparing a match template to an enrollment template. A *match template* is created when the user attempts to gain access through a fingerprint reader. Some biometric systems also include *liveness detection*, which verifies that a living person is creating the match template. For example, a fingerprint reader with liveness detection might monitor a pulse. Most computer and network systems are set up so that the person also must claim an identity, such as a user name, along with the fingerprint. In this case, the match template is compared directly to the enrollment template for that user name. Other systems, such as those used for criminal investigations, will search the entire enrollment template database for a match.

The match template is created in the same fashion as the enrollment template described earlier. Rather than storing the match template on disk, however, it is compared to the user's stored enrollment template, as shown in the bottom of Figure 5-46. The result of the matching process is a score. The score is compared against a threshold. The threshold is a predefined number that can be adjusted depending on the desired level of security.

The scoring process leads to the decision process. The decision process will produce one of three actions: (1) the threshold has been exceeded, thereby resulting in a match; (2) the threshold has not been met, thereby resulting in a nonmatch; or (3) the data may have been insufficient, resulting in the system requesting a new sample from the user to begin a new comparison.

Finger-scan technology has grown to become the centerpiece of the biometric industry, and even is becoming more common as an authentication method on desktop and notebook computers.

For more information, visit the Computer Concepts CourseMate Web site at www.cengagebrain.com, navigate to the Chapter 5 High-Tech Talk resource for this book, and then click Biometrics.

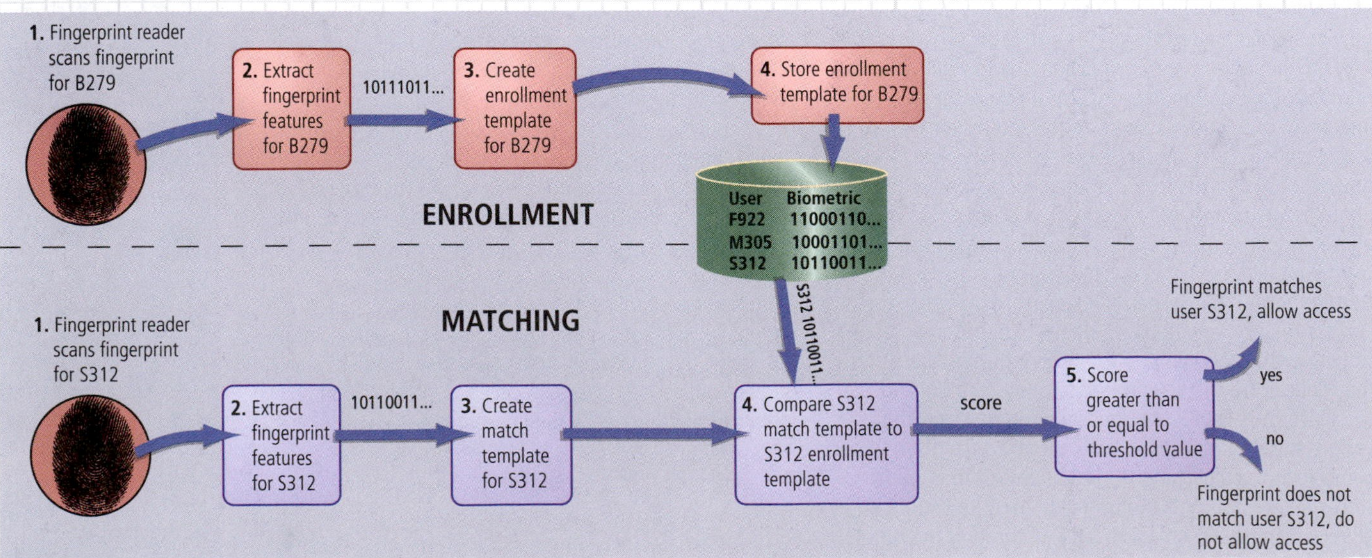

Figure 5-46 The two steps in biometric technology.

Companies on the Cutting Edge

LOGITECH Personal Interface Products Leader

Design and innovation drive the development of *Logitech* products, and the company continues to win top industry awards for its imaginative personal peripheral, Internet communications, home entertainment, gaming, and digital music devices. Logitech has sold millions of mouse devices and wireless products in practically every country in the world.

Stanford computer science students Daniel Borel and Pierluigi Zappacosta, along with Giacomo Marini, founded Logitech in 1981 at Borel's father-in-law's farm in Apples, Switzerland. The company's name is derived from logiciel, which is the French word for software.

Many of Logitech's latest ventures have capitalized on consumers' growing interest in their digital homes. Recently, Logitech announced its one millionth Logitech Vid customer after only three months of being available publicly. Logitech Vid is Logitech's free video conferencing software.

NOKIA Mobile Technology Leader

Approximately four billion people worldwide are using mobile devices, and chances are a majority of them are using a *Nokia* product. This Finnish company is ranked as the number one brand in Asia and Europe and is recognized in the Best Global Brands list as the fifth most valuable brand in the world.

Nokia has a long history in the field of communications. The company began when miner Fredrik Idestam built a wood pulp mill on the Nokianvirta River in Finland in the 1860s and began manufacturing paper. He called his company Nokia Ab. In the next 100 years, the company merged with companies that manufactured rubber and cables. Nokia then focused on the telecommunications industry and became the world's leader in manufacturing mobile phones and cameras.

Recently, Nokia introduced the Nokia Booklet 3G, a netbook boasting a 12-hour battery life. This netbook, slightly thicker than two centimeters, runs the Windows operating system and includes such features as a Web cam, Bluetooth, and an integrated GPS receiver.

For more information, visit the Computer Concepts CourseMate Web site at www.cengagebrain.com and then navigate to the Chapter 5 Companies on the Cutting Edge resource for this book.

Technology Trailblazers

SATORU IWATA Nintendo CEO and President

Being paid to play video games sounds like a dream job, but that activity is all in a day's work for *Satoru Iwata*, Nintendo's fourth president and CEO. The Japanese-born gamer began his career at Nintendo in 2000 as the leader of the company's corporate planning division. Before coming to Nintendo, Iwata served as the coordinator of software production at HAL Laboratory, Inc., where he helped develop the Balloon Flight, EarthBound, and Kirby games. He also freelanced at Nintendo during that time by assisting with some video game development.

At Nintendo, Iwata is credited with leading the GameCube and the Wii technologies. He also has overseen the Zelda, Mario, and Animal Crossing game series. He is commended for persuading third-party companies, including Sega and Electronic Arts, to continue to develop software for the DS and Wii gaming systems.

DOUGLAS ENGELBART Creator of the Mouse

The ubiquitous mouse is a staple for desktop computers, but its evolution to becoming the most widely used pointing device was a slow process. *Douglas Engelbart* conceived the idea of the mouse in 1950 to help humans work more efficiently. Fourteen years later he developed the first prototype with the goal of making it easier for people to move a cursor around a computer screen. In 1974, engineers at Xerox refined Engelbart's prototype and showed the redesigned product to Apple's Steve Jobs, who applied the concept to his graphical Macintosh computer. The final product did not gain worldwide acceptance for another 10 years.

Engelbart is continuing his pursuits of helping people work smarter. His Bootstrap Institute is a California-based company that promotes collaboration, creativity, and competition to solve problems.

For more information, visit the Computer Concepts CourseMate Web site at www.cengagebrain.com and then navigate to the Chapter 5 Technology Trailblazers resource for this book.

STUDENT ASSIGNMENTS

Chapter Review

The Chapter Review reinforces the main concepts presented in this chapter.

To listen to the audio version of this Chapter Review, visit the Computer Concepts CourseMate Web site at www.cengagebrain.com and then navigate to the Chapter 5 Chapter Review resource for this book.

1. **What Is Input, and What Are the Differences among a Program, a Command, and a User Response?** **Input** is any *data* or instructions entered into the memory of a computer. A *program* is a series of related instructions that tells a computer what tasks to perform and how to perform them. A *command* is an instruction that causes a program to perform a specific action. A user issues a *user response* by replying to a question displayed by a program to perform certain actions.

2. **What Keys Are Commonly Found on Desktop Computer Keyboards, and How Do Keyboards for Mobile Computers and Devices Differ from Desktop Computer Keyboards?** A **keyboard** is an input device that contains keys users press to enter data and instructions into a computer. Computer keyboards have a typing area that includes letters of the alphabet, numbers, punctuation marks, and other basic keys. Most keyboards also have *function keys* programmed to issue commands; *toggle keys* that switch between two states when pressed; and keys used to move the **insertion point**, or *cursor*, on the screen. A *gaming keyboard* is a keyboard designed specifically for users who enjoy playing games on the computer. On notebook computers and some other mobile devices, the keyboard is built into the top of the system unit. To fit in these mobile computers and devices, the keyboards usually are smaller and have fewer keys than desktop computer keyboards.

3. **What Are Different Mouse Types, and How Do You Use a Mouse?** A **mouse** is a **pointing device** that fits under the palm of your hand. An *optical mouse* uses devices that emit and sense light to detect the mouse's movement. A *laser mouse* uses a laser and is more expensive than an optical mouse. An *air mouse* allows you to control objects, media players, and slide shows by moving the mouse in predetermined directions through the air. A *wireless mouse*, or *cordless mouse*, transmits data using wireless technology. As you move a mouse, the *mouse pointer* moves on the screen. You then press a mouse button (usually the left) to *click* objects. Some programs support *mouse gestures*, where users can perform certain actions by holding a mouse button while moving the mouse in a particular pattern.

4. **What Are the Various Types of Touch Screens, and How Does a Touch-Sensitive Pad Work?** A **touch screen** is a touch-sensitive display device. Touch screens that recognize multiple points of contact at the same time are known as *multi-touch*. Users interact with touch screens by touching areas of the screen such as pictures, numbers, letters, or locations identified on the screen. A *kiosk* is a freestanding computer that usually includes a touch screen. *Microsoft Surface* is a 30-inch tabletop display that allows one or more people to interact with the screen using their fingers or hands. A *touch-sensitive pad* is an input device that enables users to scroll through and play music, view pictures, watch videos or movies, adjust volume, and/or customize settings on a portable media player or other mobile device.

5. **What Are the Various Types of Pen Input, and What Are Other Types of Input for Smart Phones?** With **pen input**, you touch a stylus or digital pen on a flat surface, such as a screen on a monitor or mobile device, a signature capture pad, or a graphics tablet, to write, draw, or make selections. A **stylus** is a small metal or plastic device that looks like a tiny ink pen but uses pressure instead of ink. A **digital pen**, which is slightly larger than a stylus, features electronic erasers and programmable buttons. *Handwriting recognition software* is a program that translates handwritten letters and symbols into characters a computer or mobile device can process. A **signature capture pad** captures signatures written with a stylus or pen attached to a device. Some smart phones have digital cameras that have touch-sensitive pads. Others have a *portable keyboard* or optical keyboard built in.

6. **What Are the Purposes of Gamepads, Joysticks and Wheels, Light Guns, Dance Pads, and Motion-Sensing Game Controllers?** A **gamepad** controls the movement and actions of players or objects in video games or computer games. A **joystick** is a handheld vertical lever that you move to control a simulated vehicle or player. A **wheel** is a steering-wheel-type device that you turn to simulate driving a vehicle. A **light gun** is used to shoot targets as you pull the trigger on the

Chapter Review

weapon. A **dance pad** is an electronic device, divided into panels, that users press with their feet. *Motion-sensing game controllers*, such as the *Wii Remote*, guide on-screen elements by moving a handheld input device in predetermined directions through the air.

Visit the Computer Concepts CourseMate Web site at www.cengagebrain.com, navigate to the Chapter 5 Quiz Yourself resource for this book, and then click Objectives 1 – 6.

7. How Does Resolution Affect the Quality of a Picture Captured on a Digital Camera? A **digital camera** allows users to take pictures and store the photographed images digitally. **Resolution** is the number of horizontal and vertical pixels in a display device. The greater the number of pixels the camera uses to capture a picture, the better the quality of the picture. Thus, the higher the resolution, the better the picture quality, but the more expensive the camera.

8. How Are Voice Recognition, Web Cams, and Video Conferencing Used? **Voice recognition**, also called *speech recognition*, is the computer's capability of distinguishing spoken words. A **Web cam**, also called a *PC video camera*, is a digital video camera that enables users to capture video and still images and then send or broadcast the images over the Internet. A **video conference** is a meeting between two or more geographically separated people who use a network or the Internet to transmit audio and video data.

Visit the Computer Concepts CourseMate Web site at www.cengagebrain.com, navigate to the Chapter 5 Quiz Yourself resource for this book, and then click Objectives 7 – 8.

9. How Do the Various Types of Scanners and Reading Devices Work? A **scanner**, or *optical scanner*, is a light-sensing input device that reads printed text and graphics and translates the results into a form the computer can process. A **flatbed scanner** works in a manner similar to a copy machine except it creates a file of the document. An *optical reader* uses a light source to read characters, marks, and codes and converts them into digital data that a computer can process. **Optical character recognition** (**OCR**) reads characters from ordinary documents. **Optical mark recognition** (**OMR**) reads hand-drawn marks such as small circles or rectangles. A **bar code reader**, or **bar code scanner**, is an optical reader that uses laser beams to read a **bar code**, or identification code. **RFID** (*radio frequency identification*) uses radio signals to communicate with an embedded tag placed in or attached to an object, an animal, or a person. A **magnetic stripe card reader**, also called a *magstripe reader*, reads the magnetic stripe on the back of credit cards and other similar cards. **MICR** (*magnetic-ink character recognition*) reads text printed with magnetized ink.

10. What Are Various Biometric Devices? A *biometric device* translates a personal characteristic into digital code that is compared with a digital code stored in the computer to identify an individual. A **fingerprint reader** captures curves and indentations of a fingerprint. A *face recognition system* captures a live face image and compares it with a stored image. A *hand geometry system* measures the shape and size of a hand. A *voice verification system* compares live speech with a stored voice pattern. A *signature verification system* recognizes the shape of a signature. An *iris recognition system* reads patterns in the iris of the eye. *Retinal scanners* scan patterns of blood vessels in the back of the retina.

11. How Do POS Terminals, Automated Teller Machines, and DVD Kiosks Work? A *terminal* is a computer, usually with limited processing power, that enables users to send data to and/or receive information from a host computer. POS terminals, ATMs, and DVD kiosks are special-purpose terminals. A **POS** (point-of-sale) **terminal** records purchases, processes credit or debit cards, and updates inventory. An **automated teller machine** (**ATM**) is a self-service banking machine that connects to a host computer through a network. A **DVD kiosk** is a self-service DVD rental machine that connects to a host computer through a network.

12. What Are Alternative Input Devices for Physically Challenged Users? Voice recognition is ideal for visually impaired users. A *keyguard* is a plate placed over the keyboard that allows users with limited hand mobility to rest their hands and press only one key at a time. Keyboards with larger keys or an *on-screen keyboard* displayed on a user's screen also are available. A small trackball or a *head-mounted pointer* helps users with limited hand movement to control the pointer or insertion point. Two developments in the prototype stage are *gesture recognition* and computerized implant devices.

Visit the Computer Concepts CourseMate Web site at www.cengagebrain.com, navigate to the Chapter 5 Quiz Yourself resource for this book, and then click Objectives 9 – 12.

Key Terms

You should know the Primary Terms and be familiar with the Secondary Terms. The list below helps focus your study.

To see an example of and a definition for each term, and to access current and additional information from the Web, visit the Computer Concepts CourseMate Web site at www.cengagebrain.com and then navigate to the Chapter 5 Key Terms resource for this book.

Primary Terms

(shown in bold-black characters in the chapter)

Americans with Disabilities Act (ADA) (286)
audio input (274)
automated teller machine (ATM) (284)
bar code (280)
bar code reader (280)
bar code scanner (280)
dance pad (270)
digital camera (272)
digital pen (268)
digital video (DV) camera (275)
DVD kiosk (285)
ergonomics (262)
fingerprint reader (282)
flatbed scanner (278)
game controller (270)
gamepad (270)
graphics tablet (268)
input (258)
input device (260)
insertion point (261)
joystick (270)
keyboard (260)
light gun (270)
magnetic stripe card reader (281)
MICR (281)
MICR reader (281)
mouse (263)
OCR devices (279)
optical character recognition (OCR) (279)
optical mark recognition (OMR) (279)
pen input (268)
pointer (263)
pointing device (263)
pointing stick (266)
POS terminal (284)
resolution (273)
RFID (280)
RFID reader (280)
scanner (277)
signature capture pad (268)
stylus (268)
touch screen (266)
touchpad (265)
trackball (265)
turnaround document (279)
video conference (276)
video input (275)
voice input (274)
voice recognition (274)
Web cam (275)
wheel (270)

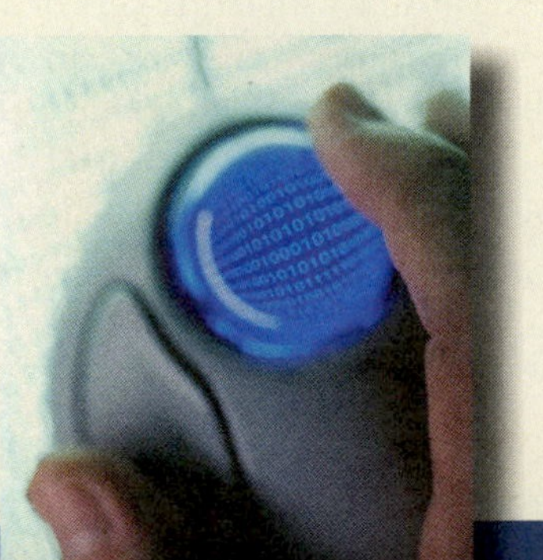

trackball (265)

Secondary Terms

(shown in italic characters in the chapter)

air mouse (263)
biometric device (282)
biometric identifier (282)
biometrics (282)
charge-coupled device (CCD) (272)
Click Wheel (267)
command (259)
cordless keyboard (262)
cordless mouse (264)
cursor (261)
data (258)
data collection device (282)
digitizer (268)
download (272)
enhanced keyboard (260)
enhanced resolution (273)
ergonomic keyboard (262)
face recognition system (282)
field camera (272)
function keys (260)
gaming keyboard (261)
gesture recognition (286)
hand geometry system (283)
handwriting recognition software (268)
head-mounted pointer (286)
image processing (278)
image processing system (278)
iris recognition system (283)
keyguard (286)
kiosk (266)
laser mouse (263)
magnetic-ink character recognition (281)
magstripe reader (281)
Microsoft Surface (267)
motion-sensing game controllers (271)
mouse gestures (264)
mouse pointer (263)
MP (273)
multi-touch (266)
music production software (274)
OCR (optical character recognition) software (278)
on-screen keyboard (286)
optical mouse (263)
optical reader (279)
optical resolution (273)
optical scanner (277)
PC video camera (275)
personal identification number (PIN) (284)
photo scanner (277)
pixel (273)
pixels per inch (ppi) (273)
point-and-shoot camera (272)
portable keyboard (268)
predictive text input (262)
program (258)
radio frequency identification (280)
retinal scanners (283)
signature verification system (283)
source document (277)
speech recognition (274)
streaming cam (276)
studio camera (272)
terminal (284)
toggle key (261)
touch-sensitive pad (267)
UPC (Universal Product Code) (280)
user response (259)
video capture card (275)
video telephone call (275)
voice verification system (283)
whiteboard (276)
Wii Remote (271)
wireless keyboard (262)
wireless mouse (264)

Checkpoint

The Checkpoint exercises test your knowledge of the chapter concepts. The page number containing the answer appears in parentheses after each exercise. The Beyond the Book exercises will help broaden your understanding of the concepts presented in this chapter.

To complete the Checkpoint exercises interactively, visit the Computer Concepts CourseMate Web site at www.cengagebrain.com and then navigate to the Chapter 5 Checkpoint resource for this book.

True/False Mark T for True and F for False.

_____ 1. Once data is in memory, the computer interprets and executes instructions to process the data into information. (258)

_____ 2. An input device is any hardware component that allows users to enter data and instructions into a computer. (260)

_____ 3. The command associated with a function key performs the same task within each program with which you are interacting. (260)

_____ 4. A touchpad is a small, flat, rectangular pointing device that is sensitive to pressure and motion. (265)

_____ 5. Touch-sensitive pads typically contain buttons and/or wheels that are operated with a thumb or finger. (267)

_____ 6. To capture a signature, a user speaks his or her name into a signature capture pad. (268)

_____ 7. Resolution is the smallest element in an electronic image. (273)

_____ 8. A whiteboard is a meeting between two or more geographically separated people who use a network or the Internet to transmit audio and video data. (276)

_____ 9. Scanners capture data from a target document, which is the original form of the data. (277)

_____ 10. A flatbed scanner works in a manner similar to a copy machine except it creates a file of the document in memory instead of a paper copy. (278)

_____ 11. A DVD kiosk is a self-service DVD rental machine that connects to a host computer through a network. (285)

_____ 12. A keyguard is a metal or plastic plate placed over the keyboard that allows users to rest their hands on the keyboard without accidentally pressing any keys. (286)

Multiple Choice Select the best answer.

1. A(n) _____ has a design that reduces the chance of wrist and hand injuries. (262)
   a. gaming keyboard
   b. cordless keyboard
   c. ergonomic keyboard
   d. function key

2. Some phones use _____, where you press one key on the keypad for each letter in a word and software on the phone predicts the word you want. (262)
   a. predictive text input
   b. text messaging
   c. ergonomics
   d. optical character recognition (OCR)

3. Touch screens that recognize multiple points of contact at the same time are known as _____. (266)
   a. touch-sensitive pads
   b. multi-touch
   c. graphics tablets
   d. digitizers

4. Architects, mapmakers, designers, artists, and home users create drawings and sketches on a _____. (268)
   a. trackball
   b. terminal
   c. graphics tablet
   d. touchpad

5. _____ is the computer's capability of distinguishing spoken words. (274)
   a. Voice input
   b. VoIP
   c. MIDI
   d. Voice recognition

6. _____ allows users to record, compose, mix, and edit music and sounds. (274)
   a. Kiosks
   b. Voice input
   c. Music production software
   d. Voice recognition

7. RFID is a technology that uses _____ to communicate with a tag placed in or attached to an object, an animal, or a person. (280)
   a. a thin wire
   b. pixels
   c. radio signals
   d. light waves

8. With _____, the computer will detect human motions. (286)
   a. a head-mounted pointer
   b. an on-screen keyboard
   c. gesture recognition
   d. a computerized implant

STUDENT ASSIGNMENTS

Checkpoint

Matching

Match the terms with their definitions.

_____ 1. insertion point (261)
_____ 2. gaming keyboard (261)
_____ 3. ergonomics (262)
_____ 4. trackball (265)
_____ 5. pointing stick (266)
_____ 6. kiosk (266)
_____ 7. game controller (270)
_____ 8. gamepad (270)
_____ 9. video capture card (275)
_____ 10. data collection device (282)

a. freestanding computer that usually includes a touch screen
b. symbol on the screen that indicates where the next character typed will appear
c. obtains data directly at the location where the transaction or event takes place
d. incorporates comfort, efficiency, and safety in the design of the workplace
e. pressure-sensitive pointing device shaped like a pencil eraser that is positioned between keys on a keyboard
f. controls the movement and actions of players or objects in video games or computer games
g. keyboard designed specifically for users who enjoy playing games on the computer
h. used by video games and computer games as the input device that directs movements and actions of on-screen objects
i. converts an analog video signal to a digital signal that a computer can process
j. stationary pointing device with a ball on its top or side

Short Answer

Write a brief answer to each of the following questions.

1. What are three different types of mouse devices? ____________ What makes them different from each other? ____________
2. Name at least five mouse operations. ____________ Describe and give examples of each of the mouse operations that you chose. ____________
3. What is OCR (optical character recognition)? ____________ What is OMR (optical mark recognition)? ____________
4. What is the most widely used biometric device today? ____________ Describe how the device works. ____________
5. What is the Americans with Disabilities Act (ADA)? ____________ How might gesture recognition and computerized implant devices help physically challenged users in the future? ____________

Beyond the Book

Follow the book element instructions below; present your findings (brief report, presentation, discussion, or other means).

1. Ethics & Issues — Select an Ethics & Issues in this chapter (261, 265, 271, 280, 283), find a recent newspaper/magazine article that supports one point of view presented, and then evaluate the article.
2. Computer Usage @ Work — Use the Web or a recent newspaper/magazine to locate three additional unique usages of computer technology in the hospitality industry (287). What makes the use of these technologies unique to the hospitality industry?
3. Companies on the Cutting Edge and Technology Trailblazers — Use the Web or a recent business newspaper/magazine to locate an interesting fact about Logitech, Nokia, Satoru Iwata, or Douglas Engelbart that was not presented in the chapter (289).
4. High-Tech Talk — Locate a recent newspaper/magazine article that discusses topics related to Biometrics (288). Would you recommend the article you found? Why or why not?
5. FAQs and Web Links — Use the Web or a recent business newspaper/magazine to locate three additional facts about an FAQ (261, 262, 267, 269, 273, 278) and Web Link (262, 266, 268, 270, 276, 280, 283, 286) that were not presented in the chapter.
6. Looking Ahead — Use the Web or a recent newspaper/magazine to discover additional uses of the technology presented in Tongue May Become Joystick to Control Devices (286).
7. Innovative Computing — Use the Web or a recent newspaper/magazine to locate two additional interesting facts about Create Your Vocal Accompaniment Automatically (275) and Monitor Health Status Remotely (276).
8. Making Use of the Web — Visit three of the Travel sites (129) and outline the information on each Web site and the possible uses for each Web site.

Learn It Online

The Learn It Online exercises are interactive Web exercises designed to reinforce and expand your understanding of the chapter concepts. The descriptions below briefly summarize each exercise.

To complete the Learn It Online exercises, visit the Computer Concepts CourseMate Web site at www.cengagebrain.com, navigate to the Chapter 5 resources for this book, click the link for the exercise you want to complete, and then read the instructions.

1 At the Movies — Video Editing on Your Computer
Watch a movie to learn about simple editing tips for converting raw video footage into interesting videos.

2 Video and Audio: You Review It — Voice Recognition
Search for, choose, and write a review of a video, podcast, or vodcast that discusses voice recognition.

3 Student Edition Labs — Working with Audio and Working with Video
Enhance your understanding and knowledge about working with audio and video by completing the Working with Audio and Working with Video Labs.

4 Practice Test
Take a multiple choice test that checks your knowledge of the chapter concepts and review the resulting study guide.

5 Who Wants To Be a Computer Genius^2?
Play the Shelly Cashman Series version of this popular game by answering questions to find out if you are a computer genius. Panic buttons are available to provide assistance during game play.

6 Wheel of Terms
Identify important key terms presented in this chapter by playing the Shelly Cashman Series version of this popular game.

7 You're Hired!
Embark on the path to a career in computers by answering questions and solving puzzles related to concepts discussed in this chapter.

8 Crossword Puzzle Challenge
Complete an interactive crossword puzzle to reinforce concepts presented in this chapter.

9 Windows Exercises
Step through the Windows 7 exercises to learn about locating information about your computer, customizing the keyboard, using the mouse and keyboard to interact with a Web application, mouse keys, and using the on-screen keyboard.

10 Exploring Computer Careers
Read about a career as a data entry clerk, search for related employment advertisements, and then answer related questions.

11 Web Apps — Flickr.com
Learn how to use the Internet to upload and share photos, search for photos, and edit photos online using Flickr.com.

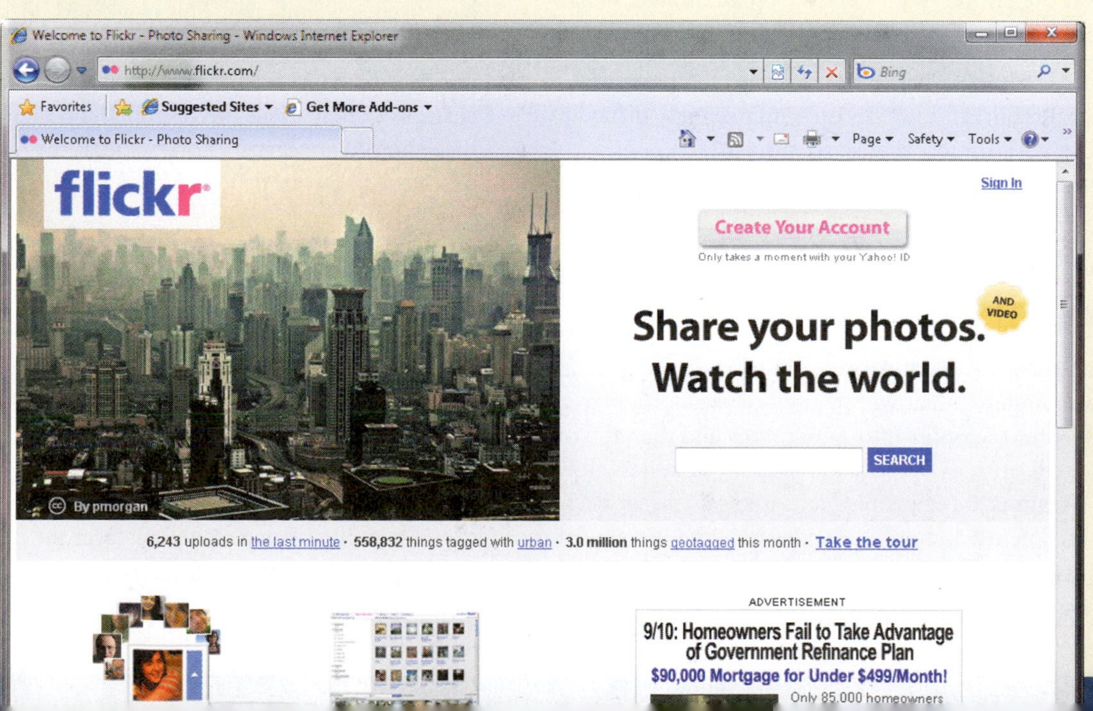

STUDENT ASSIGNMENTS

Problem Solving @ Home

The Problem Solving @ Home exercises extend your knowledge of the chapter concepts by seeking solutions to practical computer problems that you may encounter at home or school. The Collaboration exercise should be completed with a team.

In the real world, practical problems often can be solved in multiple ways. Provide one solution to each of the following problems using available resources, such as articles on the Web or in print, blogs, podcasts, videos, television, user guides, other individuals, and electronics and computer stores. You may need to use multiple resources to obtain an answer. Present your solutions in the form requested by your instructor (brief report, presentation, discussion, or other means).

1. **No Media Controls** You have purchased a new keyboard for your three-year-old computer. When you connect the keyboard to your computer's USB port, you are able to type, but the media controls do not work. What could be the problem?
2. **Unresponsive Keyboard** When you turn on your computer, a message appears on your display that says, "Keyboard Error." You press the ENTER key to bypass the message and continue the startup process, but nothing happens. How will you attempt to troubleshoot the problem before calling technical support?
3. **Arrow Keys Functioning Differently** While typing a report in Microsoft Word, you attempt to use the arrow keys on the keyboard to move the insertion point around the document. When you press the UP and DOWN ARROW keys, instead of moving the insertion point up or down, these keys scroll the entire Word window up and down. What could be causing this?
4. **Optical Mouse Problems** During the past several months, it has become increasingly difficult to use your optical mouse to move the mouse pointer around the screen. For example, when you move the mouse from left to right, the mouse pointer appears to jump randomly around the screen. What could be causing this?
5. **Mouse Keys Reversed** While using your friend's computer, you click the Start button with the left mouse button. Instead of the Start menu, a shortcut menu is displayed. You explain the problem to your friend, and he informs you that he would like this behavior to be corrected. What are your next steps?
6. **Touch Screen Problems** At your bank, you notice that the bank has installed a new ATM with a touch screen. When you insert your bank card to begin the transaction, the ATM asks for your personal identification number (PIN). When you attempt to enter your PIN using the touch screen, you find that the ATM is not recognizing your input. What are your next steps?
7. **Incorrect Calculation** Having resolved the ATM touch screen problem in Exercise 6 (above), you are able to access your bank account using the ATM. You now are ready to deposit the checks that you have been accumulating. This new ATM does not require an envelope; all you do is insert the stack of checks. The ATM reads the amount for which each check is written, totals the amounts, and then displays the sum. You are certain, however, that the ATM is miscalculating your deposit. What are your next steps?

Collaboration

8. **Restaurant Automation** You work in the restaurant industry, and your boss decides that he would like to install new computers that will be used to relay orders to the kitchen. Once a server has taken a customer's order, he or she will enter the order into a computer and then the order will appear on a display device in the kitchen. The computers also will print a check for each guest, as well as allow the managers to generate sales reports at the end of each shift. In a team of three people, determine the input devices that will be necessary for the computers to perform the above tasks. The team should consider how the servers enter orders and how the managers will instruct the computers to print the sales reports. Compile the team's findings into a report and present it to your instructor.

Problem Solving @ Work

The Problem Solving @ Work exercises extend your knowledge of the chapter concepts by seeking solutions to practical computer problems that you may encounter at work. The Collaboration exercise should be completed with a team.

In the real world, practical problems often can be solved in multiple ways. Provide one solution to each of the following problems using available resources, such as articles on the Web or in print, blogs, podcasts, videos, television, user guides, other individuals, and electronics and computer stores. You may need to use multiple resources to obtain an answer. Present your solutions in the form requested by your instructor (brief report, presentation, discussion, or other means).

1. **Fingerprint Not Recognized** To increase security, your company now requires employees to log into their computers using a fingerprint reader instead of entering a user name and password. This past weekend, you cut the finger you use to log in, and your computer now does not recognize your fingerprint. As a result, you are unable to access your computer. What are your next steps?
2. **No Audio** While hosting a video conference from your company's conference room with various remote locations, attendees at one of the locations inform you that they no longer can receive audio from your location. The other locations can hear you without a problem. What could be causing this?
3. **Fuzzy Pictures** Your boss has asked you to take pictures of the office building for the company's new Web site. You take the pictures with a digital camera and then view them on the computer. It appears, however, that distant objects appear fuzzy in the pictures you took. What could be causing this? Why did the pictures not appear fuzzy on the digital camera's display?
4. **Keyboard Not Working** The Bluetooth keyboard for your computer suddenly has stopped working. You have changed the batteries, but the keyboard still does not work. You are sure that the batteries are new, and these same batteries also work in your Bluetooth mouse. What might be wrong with the keyboard, and how can you correct the problem?
5. **Unreadable Bar Code** Your company tracks inventory by placing decals with bar codes on all items that are worth more than $1,000 and then uses a bar code reader to track all items. While performing a semiannual inventory check, you encounter a bar code that the bar code reader is unable to scan. What are your next steps?
6. **Liquid on Keyboard** While enjoying lunch at your desk, you inadvertently spill water on your keyboard. You immediately shut down your computer and unplug it from the wall to prevent further damage. What are your next steps?
7. **Malfunctioning Touchpad** When you attempt to navigate the Windows desktop using the touchpad on your notebook computer, the mouse pointer does not move. The left and right touchpad buttons, however, appear to function without issue. When you connect a mouse to the computer, the pointer moves properly. What might be wrong with the touchpad?
8. **Access Denied** Your company uses security badges with embedded RFID tags to authenticate the rooms to which employees have access. When arriving at work one morning, you wave your badge in front of the RFID reader, but the front door does not open. In addition, a red light blinks on the RFID reader. What are your next steps?

Collaboration

9. **Computers in Hospitality** You work for a bed and breakfast that has 12 guest rooms. You currently record reservations in an appointment book and use traditional door keys to grant access to rooms. Occasionally, your guests check out and forget to turn in their keys. For this reason, you must change the lock to that room so that former guests cannot enter the rooms after their stay has ended. You want to use technology to automate the room keys and other processes at the bed and breakfast. Form a team of three people. One team member should research solutions for a computerized reservation system. Another team member should research solutions for implementing an electronic lock solution, and the last team member should research the costs of creating a Web site that allows guests to reserve rooms online.

Learn How To

The Learn How To activities step you through fundamental technology skills when using a computer. The Learn How To exercises enable you to become more proficient with these skills.

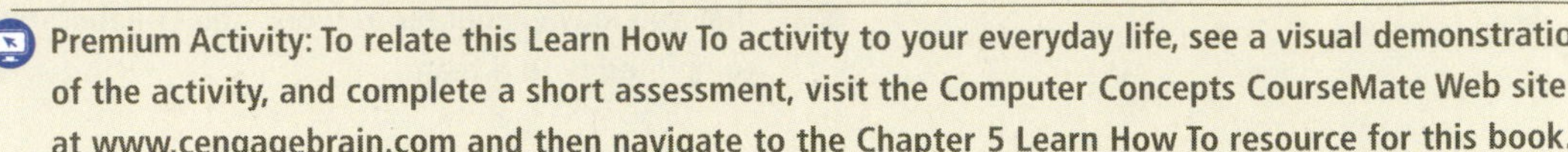

Premium Activity: To relate this Learn How To activity to your everyday life, see a visual demonstration of the activity, and complete a short assessment, visit the Computer Concepts CourseMate Web site at www.cengagebrain.com and then navigate to the Chapter 5 Learn How To resource for this book.

Learn How To 1: Install and Use a Web Cam

A Web cam is a digital video camera that allows you to capture video and still images. The videos can be used in live instant messages or for live images over the Internet. Recordings of the videos can be included on Web pages or in e-mail messages as attachments. In addition, some cameras include software that enables you to establish a visual security environment where the camera can be used to detect and record movement in its general vicinity.

Using a Web cam requires two phases: 1) purchasing and installing the Web cam, and 2) using the Web cam to transmit live video or to record video or digital images.

To purchase and install a Web cam, complete the following steps:

1. Determine how you want to use the camera in order to decide the quality of camera you require and the camera software you need. Web cams range in price from about $25 to more than $125, and vary in picture quality, features, and accompanying software. If you are not sure of all features and prices, search the Web to determine the best camera for your use.
2. After making your purchase, you will find that most cameras are accompanied by an optical disc containing the software that enables the camera to communicate and work with the computer. Often, the instructions with the device will specify that you should place the optical disc in an optical disc drive and follow the on-screen instructions to install the software on the computer.
3. After the software is installed, you likely will be instructed to connect the camera to the computer. You do so by connecting the USB or FireWire cable first to the camera and then to a USB or FireWire port on your computer. When the camera is connected, you will be able to start the camera software from either the All Programs list or the desktop.

Once you have started the camera software, you will be able to use the camera for any of the tasks you require. Each camera and its accompanying software will allow you to create a video, use instant messaging to send live video to your instant messaging contacts, and other uses as well. In addition, you often will be able to control the quality of your video output by modifying brightness, contrast, and clarity. With many cameras, you will be able to zoom in and out and, from your keyboard, enter commands to move the camera lens left, right, up, and down.

On some cameras, you can use a feature called *face tracking*, where the camera will remain focused on your face even when you move. This feature allows you to be more natural and not be concerned with always making sure you are placed exactly right for the camera.

As you can see, once you have purchased and installed a Web cam, you will open an entirely new world of communications right from your computer.

Exercises

1. Assume you have decided to purchase a Web cam to use for instant messaging. Search the Web to find the highest rated cameras available for purchase that can be used for your purposes. What is the most expensive camera you found? The least expensive? What features distinguish the two? Based on your use of the camera for instant messaging, what camera would you choose to buy? Why? Submit your answers to your instructor.
2. Optional: Purchase a Web cam or borrow one from a friend. Install the camera software on a computer. **Warning: If you are using a computer that is not your own, complete this exercise only with the owner's permission.** Connect the camera to the computer. Practice with the camera and the accompanying software. What features does the software provide? Which feature do you find the most compelling? Which features could you do without? Record a video of yourself answering these questions. Submit the video to your instructor.

Learn How To 2: Download Songs to a Portable Media Player

The methods by which you can download a song to a portable media player vary depending upon the type of portable media player you own. Some portable media players connect to your computer, often using a USB connection, and appear as a removable disk in Windows. Some use flash memory mobile media, such as SD cards, that you remove from the portable media player, and then insert into your computer's card reader. Some portable

Learn How To

media players, such as the iPod Touch, can connect to wireless networks and download songs from the Internet without requiring a connection to a computer; others connect directly to your computer and require a special program, such as iTunes, to add songs. This Learn How To exercises describes how to download songs to an iPod from a CD, how to download music to an iPod using iTunes, and how to transfer files to a portable media player that connects directly to your computer.

Using iTunes to Add Songs from a CD to Your iTunes Library

1. If necessary, download and install the latest version of iTunes, which is available at Apple's Web site (apple.com).
2. Click the Start button, click All Programs, click the iTunes folder in the All Programs list, and then click iTunes in the iTunes folder (Figure 5-47).

Figure 5-47

3. If you have not done so already, connect your iPod to a USB port on your computer. When iTunes displays the name of your iPod in the left pane of the iTunes window indicating that your iPod is connected, insert a music CD into an optical disc drive on your computer. **Check the CD's copyright notice before completing the following steps to make sure that you are authorized to copy the CD.**
4. iTunes will download the track names from the CD automatically and display a dialog box asking if you would like to import the entire CD. Click the Yes button to import all songs from the CD. If you wish to select individual songs from the CD, click the No button and select the songs you wish to import.
5. Once the import process is complete, click the Eject button to eject the CD. The songs now are in your iTunes library.
6. If your playlist does not synchronize automatically, right-click the name of your playlist and then click Sync on the shortcut menu. Once the synchronization process is complete, the files are stored on your iPod.

Using iTunes to Add Songs from the iTunes Store

1. If necessary, start iTunes and connect your iPod to your computer.
2. Click iTunes Store in the left pane of the iTunes window to display items available for purchase.
3. Locate the song you wish to purchase in the iTunes Store. If you are looking for a particular song, use the Search iTunes Store box at the top of the iTunes window.
4. Once you locate a song to download, click the Buy Song button. If necessary, enter the information for your iTunes account. If a dialog box is displayed asking if you are sure that you want to buy the song, click the Buy button. iTunes will download the song and charge the credit card or gift card associated with your iTunes account.
5. If your playlist does not synchronize automatically, right-click the name of your playlist and then click Sync on the shortcut menu. Once the synchronization process is complete, the files are stored on your iPod.

Adding a Music File on a Computer to a Portable Media Player

1. Connect your portable media player to an available port on the computer. If the portable media player does not connect to the computer with a cable, remove the memory card from the portable media player and insert it into the card reader on the computer.
2. When Windows displays the AutoPlay dialog box, click the Open device to view files using Windows Explorer button to display a window containing the contents of the portable media player.
3. Locate the song on the computer that you wish to copy to the portable media player and then drag the file to the window containing the contents of the portable media player.
4. Close any open windows and disconnect the portable media player from the computer.

Exercise

1. Locate a music CD that you own and use a program such as Windows Media Player to save the songs as digital files on your hard disk. Once you transfer the songs to your hard disk, connect your portable media player and then transfer the songs from the hard disk to the portable media player. How long did it take to transfer the music from the CD to the computer to the portable media player? Is there an easier way to accomplish this task?

Web Research

The Web Research exercises broaden your understanding of the chapter concepts by presenting questions that require you to search the Web for answers.

1 Search Sleuth

Use one of the search engines listed in Figure 2-10 in Chapter 2 on page 85 or your own favorite search engine to find the answers to the following questions. Copy and paste the Web address from the Web page where you found the answer. Some questions may have more than one answer. If required, submit your answers to your instructor. (1) Which Haruhi Suzumiya games have been released for the Nintendo Wii? (2) What two companies worked in partnership with Kodak to develop kiosks with digital image-making software? (3) Who holds U.S. Patent 4,384,288 issued in 1983 for RFID technology? (4) What object did Tom Cranston, Fred Longstaff, and Kenyton Taylor use as the ball in their trackball, which they invented in 1952? (5) How is the term, disability, defined in the Americans with Disabilities Act? (6) Who are the current MIDI Manufacturers Association (MMA) Executive Board members, and what companies do they represent? (7) Walter Cronkite and Stevie Wonder used the first production version of which machine? (8) According to the Smart Card Alliance, what is the maximum distance a contactless smart card operates?

2 Green Computing

Digital cameras use more battery power than film cameras because they operate electronic image sensors, LCD viewfinders, and flashes. They also write images to storage devices. The battery packs discharge whether you snap photos or not, but you can help extend your digital camera's battery life by following some conservation tips. View online Web sites, including The Battery Bank (batterybank.net), MalekTips (malektips.com/digital_camera_battery_help_and_tips.html), and Associated Content (associatedcontent.com) that provide information about charging battery packs, using cameras, and storing batteries. How do nickel cadmium (Ni-Cd), nickel metal hydride (Ni-MH), and lithium ion (Li-ion) batteries differ in charging time and discharge? How should batteries be stored if cameras are used infrequently? How does conditioning affect "memory effect"? Write a report summarizing your findings, and include a table of links to Web sites that provide additional details.

3 Social Networking

Google's social networking Web site, orkut, enjoys immense popularity in countries outside the United States, with one-half the registered users from Brazil. It won a Pepsi & MTV Youth Icon award for being the largest social networking forum among young users in India. Launched in 2004, the Web site is named after its creator, Orkut Büyükkökten, who is a Turkish software engineer at Google. Visit the orkut Web site (orkut.com) and then click the About orkut link at the bottom of the home page. Click the Demographics link. Which age group has the largest number of registered users? Click the Blog link at the bottom of the page and read several of the entries. Click the Safety Center link and read the Policies, Privacy Features, Security Features, and General Safety Resources sections. Summarize the information you read and viewed.

4 Blogs

Whether you are listening to the radio, watching television, or drinking a beverage at the local coffee shop, the world of sports is likely to surface. People are passionate about their favorite athletes and sporting events, from the community Little League game to the NFL Super Bowl. Visit several sports blogs, including those from Fanblogs (fanblogs.com), BC Sports (blogcritics.org/sports), Deadspin (deadspin.com), Full Throttle (fullthrottle.cranialcavity.net), ESPN (sports.espn.go.com/espn/blog), and Fox Sports (community.foxsports.com/blogs). What are the more popular discussions? Which college football and basketball teams are featured? Who are the professional athletes receiving much discussion? Which NASCAR teams are analyzed?

5 Ethics in Action

Some reports suggest that the Echelon global surveillance system is monitoring more than three billion e-mail messages, telephone calls, and faxes per day. The National Security Agency is forbidden to monitor U.S. citizens, but privacy experts contend that at least 90 percent of U.S. communications is gathered and reviewed. View online sites that provide information about Echelon, including FAS Intelligence Resource Program (fas.org/irp/program/process/echelon.htm) and YouTube videos about Echelon Spy Satellites. Write a report summarizing your findings, and include a table of links to Web sites that provide additional details.

Critical Thinking

The Critical Thinking exercises challenge your assessment and decision-making skills by presenting real-world situations associated with the chapter concepts. The Collaboration exercise should be completed with a team.

To evaluate the situations below, use personal experiences and available resources such as articles on the Web or in print, blogs, podcasts, videos, television, user guides, other individuals, and electronics and computer stores. You may need to use multiple resources to form conclusions and make recommendations.

1. **Class Discussion — Bar Codes vs. RFID** You work in the Efficiency Analysis department of one of the largest retail companies in the world, with multiple stores in every state and many other countries. For the past 25 years, the company has used bar code readers at checkout counters that scan the bar code on products to determine from a database the price to charge customers. The company is considering replacing the bar code readers with radio frequency identification, or RFID. The reader receives the code identifying the product via a chip with an antenna that is part of the box or label on the outside of the product. Analyze and discuss the impact such a change would have on the company, its suppliers, and its customers.

2. **Class Presentation — Carpal Tunnel Syndrome** While attending college part-time for the past two years, you have worked as a data entry clerk for Salmon Mirror. Recently, you began to feel an unusual pain in your right wrist. Your doctor diagnosed the problem as carpal tunnel syndrome, which is the most well-known of a series of musculoskeletal disorders that fall under the umbrella of repetitive strain injuries (RSIs). Your doctor made several recommendations to relieve the pain, one of which was to find a new job. Before you begin job hunting, however, you want to learn more about this debilitating injury. Use the Web and/or print media to investigate carpal tunnel syndrome. Prepare a presentation to include information about carpal tunnel syndrome warning signs, risk factors, suggestions about proper workstation ergonomics, and procedures for healing the injury.

3. **Research — Advantages of Video Conferencing** An electronics company where you are employed as an analyst spends hundreds of thousands of dollars each year on travel to the multiple locations where they operate around the country. In an effort to curb the ever-increasing costs of travel, the chief financial officer has asked you to research the feasibility of adopting video conferencing at all of its major locations. Use the Web and/or print media to determine the advantages and disadvantages of video conferencing. Prepare a brief report that answers the following questions. Can the technology replace all or most face-to-face meetings? What are the costs of common video conferencing systems and the recurring costs their use incurs? Compare those costs to the cost of travel for a team of three people making six trips per year between New York and Los Angeles, including hotel, rental car, airline, and food expenses.

Collaboration

4. **Professional Photography**

You currently work for a small professional photography company that wants to transition from using traditional film cameras to using digital cameras. The company, however, does not want to sacrifice quality because of this change, and they want to keep the cost associated with purchasing new digital cameras reasonable. Your boss has asked you, along with two coworkers, to look for digital cameras that will meet the company's needs for a reasonable price. One team member should research the resolution requirements for the camera, as well as the prices of various digital cameras with that resolution. It might be necessary to research other photography Web sites to determine the acceptable resolution for professional photography. Another team member should determine the type of memory card the cameras should support. Be sure to select a camera that uses a memory card that can hold as many high-quality photos as possible. The third team member should research the type of lens and optical zoom that are required to take professional pictures. The team should compile its findings and make a recommendation to the instructor about which digital camera will meet the needs of the business.

Chapter Six

Output

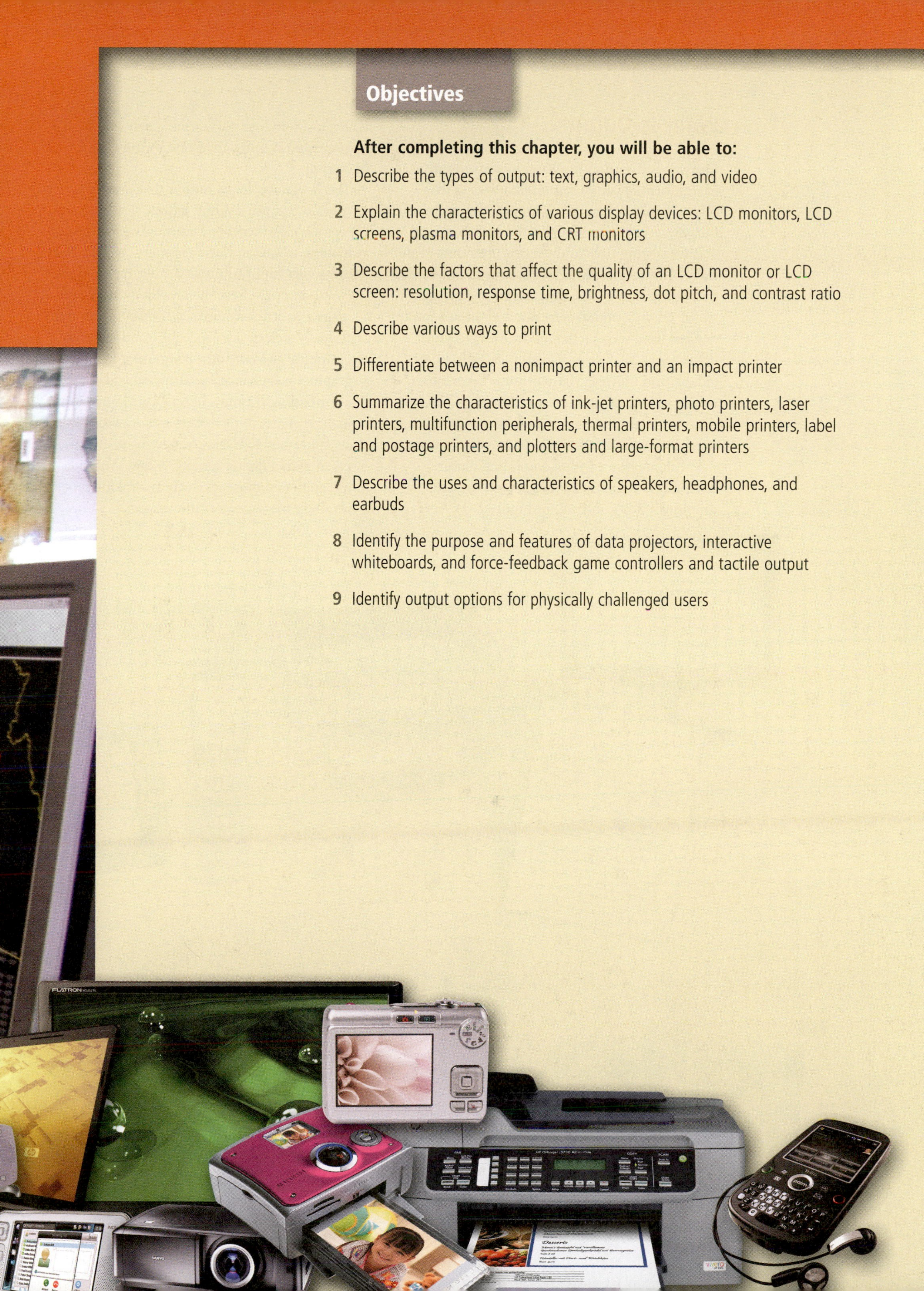

Objectives

After completing this chapter, you will be able to:

1. Describe the types of output: text, graphics, audio, and video
2. Explain the characteristics of various display devices: LCD monitors, LCD screens, plasma monitors, and CRT monitors
3. Describe the factors that affect the quality of an LCD monitor or LCD screen: resolution, response time, brightness, dot pitch, and contrast ratio
4. Describe various ways to print
5. Differentiate between a nonimpact printer and an impact printer
6. Summarize the characteristics of ink-jet printers, photo printers, laser printers, multifunction peripherals, thermal printers, mobile printers, label and postage printers, and plotters and large-format printers
7. Describe the uses and characteristics of speakers, headphones, and earbuds
8. Identify the purpose and features of data projectors, interactive whiteboards, and force-feedback game controllers and tactile output
9. Identify output options for physically challenged users

What Is Output?

Output is data that has been processed into a useful form. That is, computers process data (input) into information (output). The form of output varies, depending on the hardware and software being used and the requirements of the user. Monitors, traditional notebook computers, netbooks, Tablet PCs, portable media players, smart phones, digital cameras, and other mobile devices have screens that allow users to view documents, Web sites, e-mail messages, photos, videos, and movies. Many printers enable users to print color documents and photos. Through the computer's speakers, headphones, or earbuds, users listen to sounds, music, and voice messages.

While working with a computer, a user encounters four basic types of output: text, graphics, audio, and video (Figure 6-1). Very often, a single form of output, such as a Web page, includes more than one of these types of output.

- Text — Examples of output that primarily contain text are memos, letters, press releases, reports, classified advertisements, envelopes, mailing labels, and text messages. On the Web, users view and print many other types of text-based output. These include blogs, news and magazine articles, books, television show transcripts, stock quotes, speeches, and lectures.
- Graphics — Many forms of output include graphics to enhance visual appeal and convey information. Business letters have logos. Reports include charts. Newsletters use drawings, clip art, and photos. Users print high-quality photos taken with a digital camera. Many Web sites use animated graphics, such as blinking icons, scrolling messages, or simulations.

Figure 6-1 Four types of output are text, graphics, audio, and video.

- Audio — Users download their favorite songs from iTunes and listen to the music while working on the computer. Software such as games, encyclopedias, and simulations often have musical accompaniments for entertainment and audio clips, such as narrations and speeches, to enhance understanding. On the Web, users tune into radio and television stations and listen to audio clips, podcasts, or live broadcasts of interviews, talk shows, sporting events, news, music, and concerts. They also use the Internet to conduct real-time conversations with friends, coworkers, or family members, just as if they were speaking on the telephone.
- Video — As with audio, software and Web sites often include video clips to enhance understanding. Vodcasts and video blogs, for example, add a video component to the traditional podcast and blog. Users watch a live or prerecorded news report, view a replay while attending a live sporting event, observe weather conditions, or enjoy a live performance of their favorite musician or musical group on a computer or mobile device. Instead of renting a movie, users can download movie content from a Web site for a fee and then watch the entire movie on a computer or mobile device. Attaching a video camera to the computer allows users to watch home movies on the computer. They also can attach a television's antenna or cable to the computer and watch a television program on the computer screen.

An **output device** is any type of hardware component that conveys information to one or more people. Commonly used output devices include display devices; printers; speakers, headphones, and earbuds; data projectors; interactive whiteboards; and force-feedback game controllers and tactile output. This chapter discusses each of these output devices.

Display Devices

A **display device**, or simply *display*, is an output device that visually conveys text, graphics, and video information. Information on a display device, sometimes called *soft copy*, exists electronically and appears for a temporary period. Read Ethics & Issues 6-1 for a related discussion.

Display devices consist of a screen and the components that produce the information on the screen. Desktop computers typically use a monitor as their display device. A **monitor** is a display device that is packaged as a separate peripheral. Some monitors have a tilt-and-swivel base that allows users to adjust the angle of the screen to minimize neck strain and reduce glare from overhead lighting. With some, you can rotate the screen. Adjustable monitor stands allow you to adjust the height of the monitor. Monitor controls permit users to adjust the brightness, contrast, positioning, height, and width of images. Some have integrated speakers and/or a built-in Web cam.

Most mobile computers and devices integrate the display and other components into the same physical case. Some have touch screens. Traditional notebook computers and netbooks have a display that attaches with a hinge to the system unit. Tablet PCs are available with two types of displays: one that attaches with a hinge and one built into the top of the case. Some smart phone and digital camera displays also attach with a hinge to the device. On other smart phones and most PDAs, portable media players, digital cameras, and handheld game consoles, the display is built into the case. Newer vehicles integrate a display in the dashboard, enabling drivers to control audio, video, navigation, temperature, and other settings.

Most display devices show text, graphics, and video information in color. Some, however, are monochrome. *Monochrome* means the information appears in one color (such as white, amber, green, black, blue, or gray) on a different color background (such as black or grayish-white). Some mobile devices use monochrome displays because they require less battery power.

Two types of display devices are flat-panel displays and CRT monitors. A *flat-panel display* is a lightweight display device with a shallow depth and flat screen that typically uses LCD (liquid crystal display) or gas plasma technology. Types of flat-panel displays include LCD monitors, LCD screens, and plasma monitors. All flat-panel displays and some CRT monitors have a flat screen. The term, flat screen, means the screen is not curved. The following sections discuss a variety of display devices.

Ethics & Issues

For the complete text of the Ethics & Issues boxes found in this chapter, visit the Computer Concepts CourseMate Web site at www.cengagebrain.com and then navigate to the Chapter 6 Ethics & Issues resource for this book.

FAQ 6-1

What can I do to ease eyestrain while using my computer?

Position the computer screen about 20 degrees below eye level. Clean the screen regularly. Blink your eyes every five seconds. Adjust the room lighting. Face into an open space beyond the computer screen. Use larger fonts or zoom a display. Take an eye break every 30 minutes: look into the distance and focus on an object for 20 to 30 seconds, roll your eyes in a complete circle, and then close your eyes for at least 30 seconds. If you wear glasses, ask your doctor about computer glasses.

For more information, visit the Computer Concepts CourseMate Web site at www.cengagebrain.com, navigate to the Chapter 6 FAQ resource for this book, and then click Eye Strain.

ETHICS & ISSUES 6-1

Are Digital Billboards a Public Safety Hazard?

A company that sells advertising space on billboards recently upgraded seven static billboards in an area to digital billboards at a cost of more than $3 million. In the first year alone, the seven billboards nearly paid for themselves by increasing advertising revenue tenfold from $300,000 to $3 million per year. *Digital billboards* display advertisements that often change every six seconds and can include video content. While advertising industry funded research shows no correlation between the location of digital billboards and vehicle accidents, other research proves otherwise. Supporters of the billboards claim that the billboards are no more of a distraction than anything else visible near a roadway. Some research shows a significant increase in accident rates where digital billboards replace static billboards. Government agencies that control zoning issues for the billboards often are torn between the tax and lease revenue generated by the billboards and the need for public safety. Some states and municipalities have banned digital billboards, while others welcome them. The billboards often display public service advertisements, Amber Alerts, or other valuable information.

Are digital billboards any more of a distraction than other driving distractions? Why or why not? Should the government regulate digital billboards? What types of regulations, if any, should governments apply to digital billboards, and which level of government should regulate them? Have you seen a digital billboard, and, if so, do you feel that the billboard was distracting?

LCD Monitors and LCD Screens

An **LCD monitor** is a desktop monitor that uses a liquid crystal display to produce images. These monitors produce sharp, flicker-free images. LCD monitors have a small footprint; that is, they do not take up much desk space. For additional space savings, some LCD monitors are wall mountable. LCD monitors are available in a variety of sizes, with the more common being 19, 20, 22, 24, 26, 27, and 30 inches — some are 45 or 65 inches. Most are *widescreen*, which are wider than they are tall (Figure 6-2). You measure a monitor the same way you measure a television, that is, diagonally from one corner to the other.

Determining which size monitor to purchase depends on your intended use. A large monitor allows you to view more information on the screen at once, but usually is more expensive. You may want to invest in a 30-inch monitor if you use multiple programs at one time or do a lot of research on the Web. Users working with intense graphics programs, such as desktop publishing and engineering, typically have larger monitors.

For an even wider screen area, some users position two or more monitors side by side or stacked. For example, the left monitor can show the left side of a wide document, such as a spreadsheet, with the right monitor showing the right side. Or, you can run multiple programs simultaneously with some programs showing on one monitor and other program(s) on a second monitor (Figure 6-3). Users of side-by-side or stacked monitors include music editors, video editors, network administrators, gamers, researchers, Web developers, graphic designers, and engineers.

Mobile computers and mobile devices have built-in LCD screens (Figure 6-4). Many are widescreen; some are touch screen.

Notebook computer screens are available in a variety of sizes, with the more common

Widescreen LCD Monitors

For more information, visit the Computer Concepts CourseMate Web site at www.cengagebrain.com, navigate to the Chapter 6 Web Link resource for this book, and then click Widescreen LCD Monitors.

Figure 6-2 This widescreen LCD monitor has built-in speakers.

Figure 6-3 Users sometimes have multiple monitors stacked or side by side to increase their viewing area.

Figure 6-4 Many people use their computers and mobile devices to view photos or watch downloaded videos and home movies. To learn about creating and uploading videos to YouTube, complete the Learn How To 1 activity on pages 340 and 341.

being 14.1, 15.4, 17, and 20.1 inches. Netbook screens typically range in size from 7 inches to 12.1 inches, and Tablet PC screens range from 8.4 inches to 14.1 inches. Portable media players usually have screen sizes from 1.5 inches to 3.5 inches. On smart phones, screen sizes range from 2.5 inches to 4.1 inches. Digital camera screen sizes usually range from 2.5 inches to 4 inches. Read Innovative Computing 6-1 to find out about another use of LCD screens.

INNOVATIVE COMPUTING 6-1

Get the Picture with Digital Frames

Put away your photo albums filled with vacation pictures, baby portraits, and wedding reception candids. With *digital photo frames*, you constantly can display all the photos that capture the best times of your life.

Digital photo frames are becoming mainstream as they drop in price and increase in quality. A correlation exists between price, photo quality, and features, so the higher priced frames generally have clearer displays with accurate color. They also have adjustments for brightness, contrast, tint, and color and may use rechargeable batteries instead of electricity to power the display and dissolve from one photo to the next. Look for frames with a resolution of at least 640 × 480.

Some frames integrate Wi-Fi so that you can send your photos to the frame via your home network or download them from photo sharing Web sites. Once the photos are stored, you can add transitions and set the mood by timing the presentation to your favorite songs.

For more information, visit the Computer Concepts CourseMate Web site at www.cengagebrain.com, navigate to the Chapter 6 Innovative Computing resource for this book, and then click Digital Frames.

LCD Technology

A **liquid crystal display (LCD)** uses a liquid compound to present information on a display device. Computer LCDs typically contain fluorescent tubes that emit light waves toward the liquid-crystal cells, which are sandwiched between two sheets of material. When an electrical charge passes through the cells, the cells twist. This twisting causes some light waves to be blocked and allows others to pass through, creating images on the display.

LCD monitors and LCD screens typically produce color using either active-matrix or passive-matrix technology. An *active-matrix display*, also known as a *TFT* (*thin-film transistor*) *display*, uses a separate transistor to apply charges to each liquid crystal cell and thus displays high-quality color that is viewable from all angles. A newer type of TFT technology, called *organic LED* (*OLED*), uses organic molecules that produce an even brighter, easier-to-read display than standard TFT displays. OLEDs are less expensive to produce, consume less power, and can be fabricated on thin, flexible surfaces. A newer use of OLED technology is in the *head-mounted display* (HMD), which is a display in a helmet, goggles, or glasses. HMDs are used by pilots, military and law enforcement personnel, engineers, scientists, travelers, and video game players. Some newer LCD screens, known as LCD LED screens, use LEDs to light the screen. LCD LED screens offer better picture quality than traditional LCD screens. LCD LED screens also are thinner and consume approximately 40 percent less power than LCD screens.

A *passive-matrix display* uses fewer transistors, requires less power, and is less expensive than an active-matrix display. The color on a passive-matrix display often is not as bright as an active-matrix display. Users view images on a passive-matrix display best when working directly in front of it.

LCD Quality

The quality of an LCD monitor or LCD screen depends primarily on its resolution, response time, brightness, dot pitch, and contrast ratio.

- **Resolution** is the number of horizontal and vertical pixels in a display device. For example, a monitor that has a 1440 × 900 resolution displays up to 1440 pixels per horizontal row and 900 pixels per vertical row, for a total of 1,296,000 pixels to create a screen image. Recall that a *pixel* (short for picture element) is a single point in an electronic image. A higher resolution uses a greater number of pixels and thus provides a smoother, sharper, and clearer image. As you increase the resolution, however, some items on the screen appear smaller (Figure 6-5).

  With LCD monitors and screens, resolution generally is proportional to the size of the device. For example, a widescreen 19-inch LCD monitor typically has a resolution of 1440 × 900, while a widescreen 22-inch LCD monitor has a resolution of 1680 × 1050. LCDs are geared for a specific resolution, called the *native resolution*. Although you can change the resolution to any setting, for optimal results, use the monitor's native resolution setting.
- *Response time* of an LCD monitor or screen is the time in milliseconds (ms) that it takes to turn a pixel on or off. LCD monitors' and screens' response times range from 3 to 16 ms. The lower the number, the faster the response time.

Figure 6-5a (screen resolution at 1024 × 768)

fewer Ribbon commands are displayed at a lower resolution

fewer spreadsheet cells are displayed at a lower resolution (only columns A through I are displayed)

more Ribbon commands are displayed at higher resolution

Figure 6-5b (screen resolution at 1366 × 768)

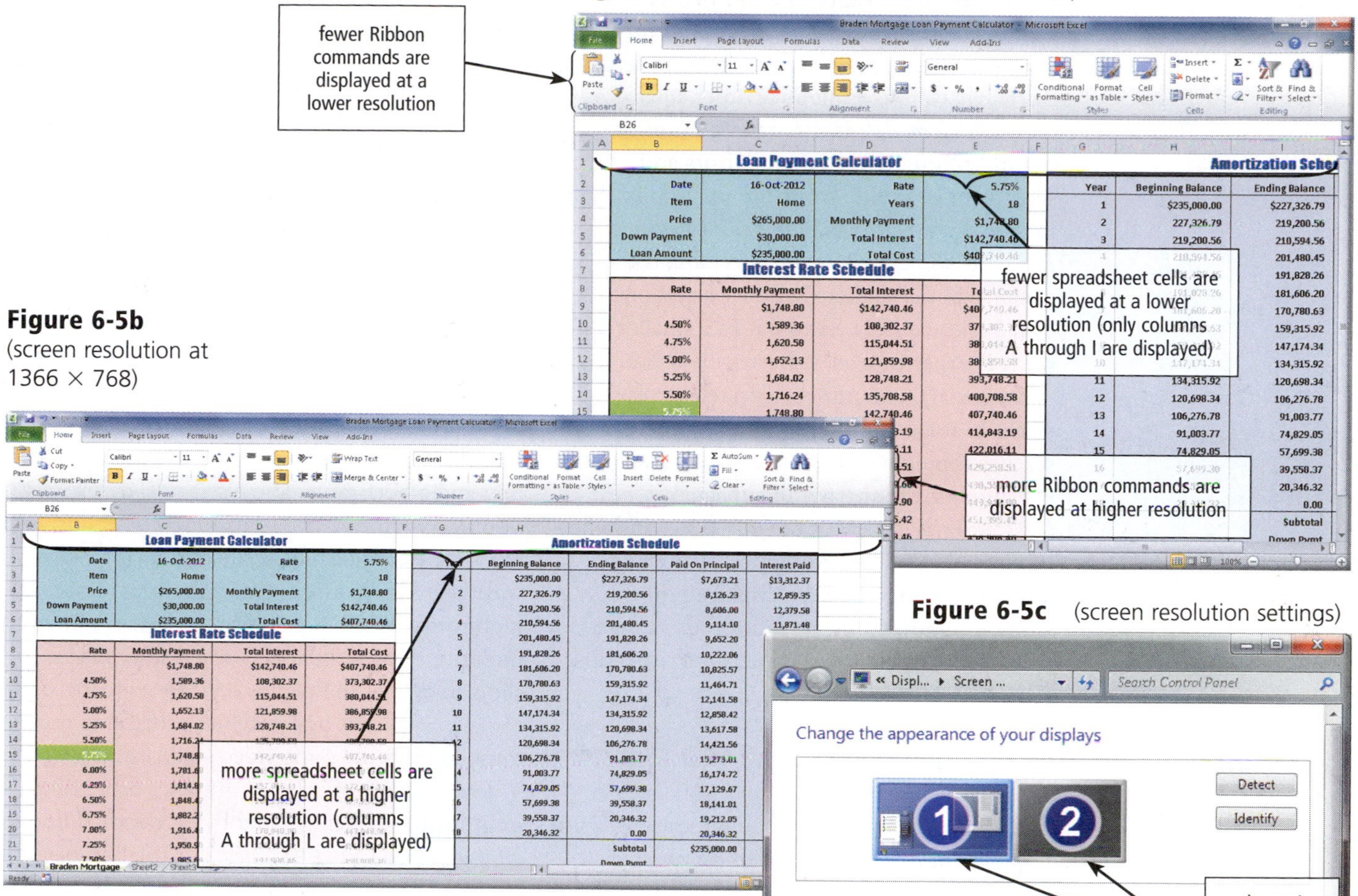

more spreadsheet cells are displayed at a higher resolution (columns A through L are displayed)

Figure 6-5c (screen resolution settings)

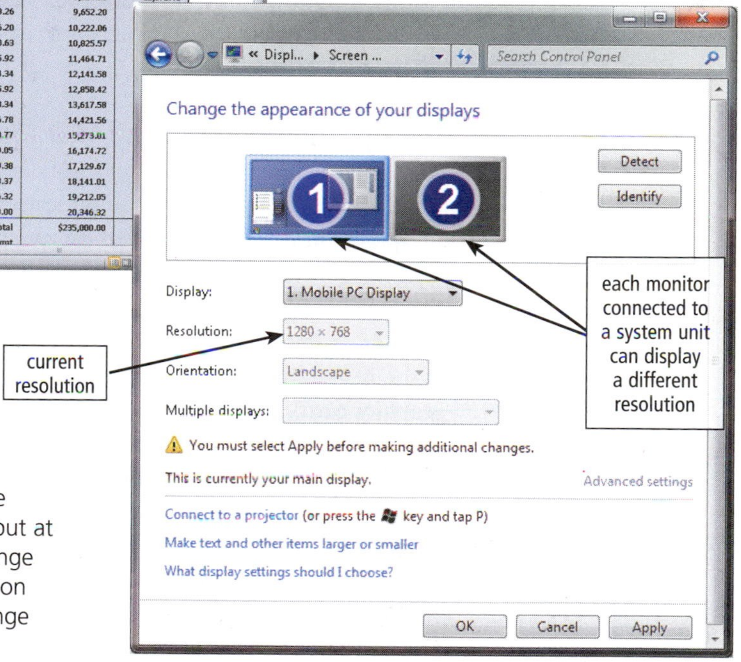

current resolution

each monitor connected to a system unit can display a different resolution

Figure 6-5 Elements on the screen become smaller when the resolution is increased from 1024 × 768 (a) to 1366 × 768 (b) but at the higher resolution more content shows on the screen. To change screen resolution, right-click the desktop, click Screen resolution on the shortcut menu, and then make desired changes in the 'Change the appearance of your displays' window (c).

FAQ 6-2

Which screen resolution currently is the most popular?

A recent study has shown that more than 93 percent of computer users configure their display device with a 1024 x 768 resolution or higher. The chart to the right lists some common resolutions, along with the percentage of users for each resolution.

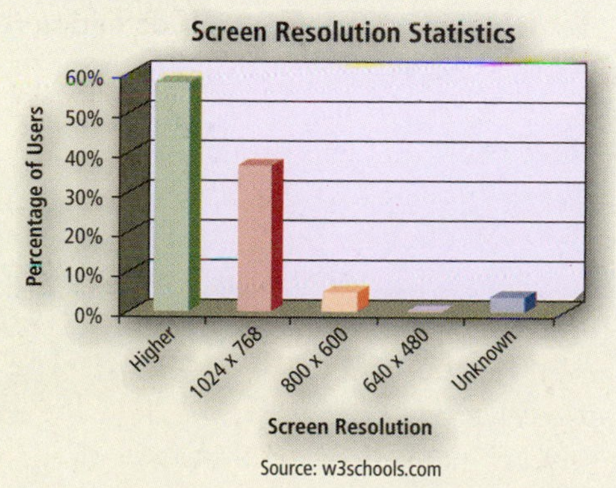

For more information, visit the Computer Concepts CourseMate Web site at www.cengagebrain.com, navigate to the Chapter 6 FAQ resource for this book, and then click Screen Resolution.

- Brightness of an LCD monitor or LCD screen is measured in nits. A *nit* is a unit of visible light intensity equal to one candela (formerly called candlepower) per square meter. The *candela* is the standard unit of luminous intensity. LCD monitors and screens today range from 250 to 550 nits. The higher the nits, the brighter the images.
- *Dot pitch*, sometimes called *pixel pitch*, is the distance in millimeters between pixels on a display device. Text created with a smaller dot pitch is easier to read. Advertisements normally specify a monitor's dot pitch or pixel pitch. Average dot pitch on LCD monitors and screens should be .30 mm or lower. The lower the number, the sharper the image.
- *Contrast ratio* describes the difference in light intensity between the brightest white and darkest black that can be displayed on an LCD monitor. Contrast ratios today range from 500:1 to 2000:1. Higher contrast ratios represent colors better.

Graphics Chips, Ports, and LCD Monitors

A cable on a monitor plugs in a port on the system unit, which enables communications from a graphics chip. This chip, called the *graphics processing unit (GPU)*, controls the manipulation and display of graphics on a display device. The graphics processing unit either is integrated on the motherboard or resides on a video card (graphics card) in a slot in the motherboard. Video cards usually contain a fan or heat sink to keep this and other chips from overheating.

LCD monitors use a digital signal to produce a picture. To display the highest quality images, an LCD monitor should plug in a DVI port, an HDMI port, or a DisplayPort. A *DVI (Digital Video Interface) port* enables digital signals to transmit directly to the LCD monitor. An *HDMI (High-Definition Media Interface) port* combines DVI with high-definition (HD) television and video. The *DisplayPort* is an alternative to DVI that also supports HDMI. Current models of system units either have an integrated DVI chip or contain a video card that has one or more DVI ports, HDMI ports, and/or DisplayPorts. They also may have a standard monitor port and an *S-video port*, allowing users to connect external analog devices such as a television, DVD/Blu-ray Disc player, or video recorder, to the computer (Figure 6-6).

DVI

For more information, visit the Computer Concepts CourseMate Web site at www.cengagebrain.com, navigate to the Chapter 6 Web Link resource for this book, and then click DVI.

Over the years, several video standards have been developed to define the resolution, number of colors, and other display properties. The table in Figure 6-7 identifies some video standards available today, along with their typical resolution and aspect ratio. The *aspect ratio* defines a display's width relative to its height. A 2:1 aspect ratio, for example, means the display is twice as wide as it is tall. The aspect ratio for widescreen monitors is 16:10. Some display devices support multiple video standards. For a display device to show images as defined by a video standard, both the display device and graphics processing unit must support the same video standard.

The number of colors a graphics processing unit displays is determined by bit depth. The *bit depth*, also called *color depth*, is the number of bits used to store information about each pixel. For example, a video card with a 24-bit depth uses 24 bits to store information about each pixel. Thus, this video card can display 2^{24} or 16.7 million colors. The greater the number of bits, the better the resulting image. Today's video cards use a pipelining technique that enables them to display in excess of one billion colors.

A video card or motherboard, in the case of integrated video, must have enough video memory to generate the resolution and number

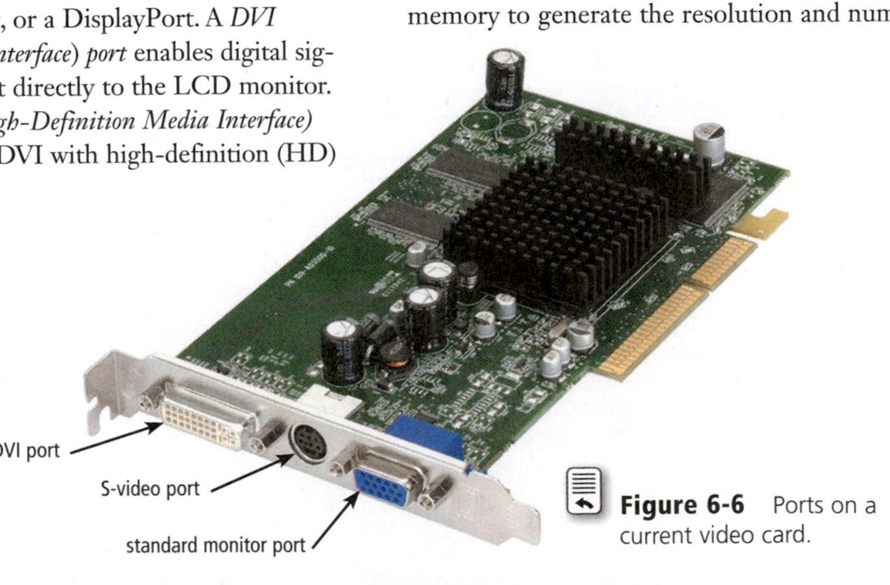

Figure 6-6 Ports on a current video card.

Popular Video Standards

Video Standard		Typical Resolution	Aspect Ratio
SVGA	Super Video Graphics Array	800 × 600	4:3
XGA	Extended Graphics Array	1024 × 768	4:3
SXGA	Super XGA	1280 × 1024	5:4
WXGA	Wide XGA	1280 × 1024 or 1366 × 768	16:10 or 16:9
UXGA	Ultra XGA	1600 × 1200	4:3
WSXGA	Wide Super XGA	1680 × 1050	16:10
WUXGA	Wide Ultra XGA	1920 × 1200	16:10
WQXGA	Wide Quad XGA	2560 × 1600	16:10

Figure 6-7 Wide (widescreen) video standard formats are preferable for users who watch movies and play video games on the computer.

of colors you want to display. This memory, which often is between 128 MB and 512 MB on typical video cards, stores information about each pixel. Users with intense graphics or gaming requirements may opt for more video memory, such as 1 GB. For a more technical discussion about the manipulation and display of graphics on a display device, read the High-Tech Talk article on page 330.

Plasma Monitors

A **plasma monitor** is a display device that uses gas plasma technology, which sandwiches a layer of gas between two glass plates (Figure 6-8). When voltage is applied, the gas releases ultraviolet (UV) light. This UV light causes the pixels on the screen to glow and form an image.

Plasma monitors offer screen sizes up to 150 inches wide and richer colors than LCD monitors but are more expensive. Like LCD monitors, plasma monitors can hang directly on a wall.

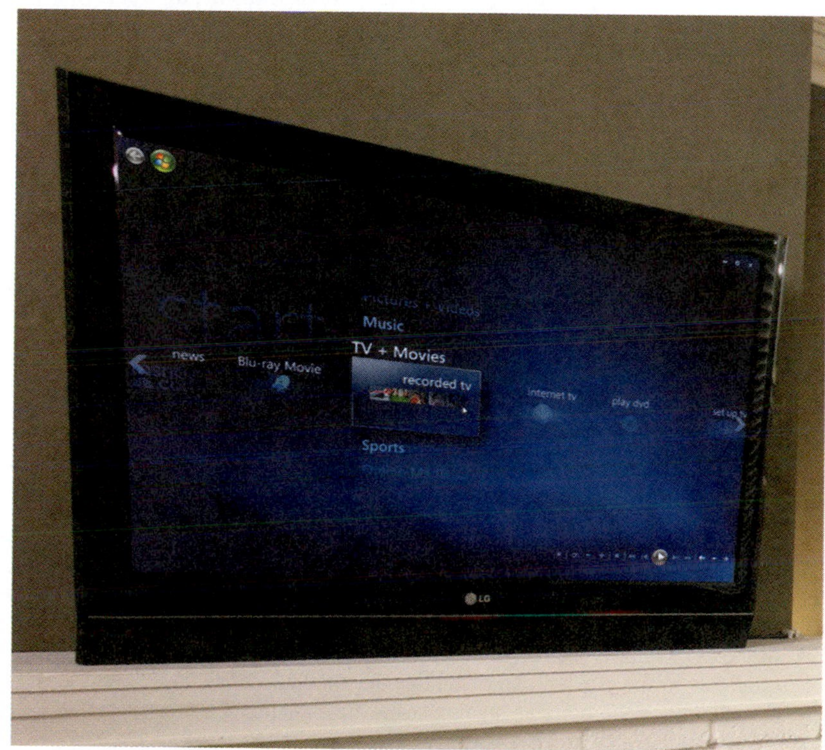

Figure 6-8 Large plasma monitors can measure up to 150 inches wide.

FAQ 6-3

What type of video content do users view on display devices?

Music videos and newscasts are the most widely viewed video content on display devices, as shown in the chart to the right.

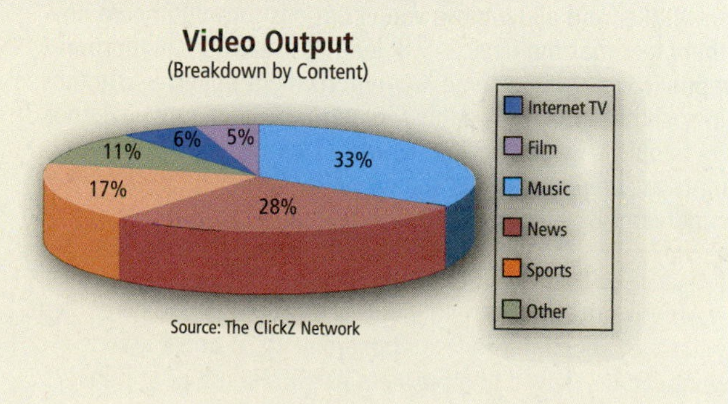

For more information, visit the Computer Concepts CourseMate Web site at www.cengagebrain.com, navigate to the Chapter 6 FAQ resource for this book, and then click Video Output Content.

Televisions

Home users sometimes use their television as a display device. Connecting a computer to an analog television requires a converter that translates the digital signal from the computer into an analog signal that the television can display. The best analog televisions have a resolution of only 520 × 400 pixels. Thus, users are turning to *digital television* (*DTV*) for crisper, higher-quality output on their LCD or plasma televisions.

Digital television signals provide two major advantages over analog signals. First, digital signals produce a higher-quality picture. Second, many programs can be broadcast on a single digital channel, whereas only one program can be broadcast on an analog channel. Today, all broadcast stations must transmit digital signals, as mandated by the FCC. Read Ethics & Issues 6-2 for a related discussion.

HDTV (*high-definition television*) is the most advanced form of digital television, working with digital broadcast signals, transmitting digital sound, supporting wide screens, and providing resolutions up to 1920 × 1080 pixels. With HDTV, the broadcast signals are digitized when they are sent via over-the-air (OTA) broadcasts from local television networks, satellite, or cable. To receive the HDTV signals via OTA broadcasts, you need a VHF/UHF antenna; via satellite, you need an HDTV-compatible satellite receiver/tuner; and via cable, you need an HDTV-compatible cable box.

With game consoles, such as Microsoft's Xbox 360, Nintendo's Wii, and Sony's PlayStation 3, the output device often is a television (Figure 6-9). Users plug one end of a cable in the game console and the other end in the video port on the television. Home users often prefer the larger television displays for game playing, watching movies, and browsing the Internet on a television connected to a game console.

ETHICS & ISSUES 6-2

Should People Be Allowed to Watch Inappropriate Movies in Public?

While seated with their small child on a cross-country flight, parents are shocked when the person seated across from them begins to watch a violent movie projected from a handheld device onto the seatback in front of them. Situations like this occur every day, and the problem continues to grow due to the proliferation of multimedia-enabled mobile devices, such as cell phones and portable media players. The situation, however, promises to become more controversial as new miniature digital projectors become prevalent. The new generation of digital projectors allows any multimedia-enabled mobile device to display a movie on any flat surface, such as the side of a home or the inside wall of a restaurant. Manufacturers of such devices claim that they enhance productivity for business people because the devices are smaller and allow more venue options for multimedia presentations. Others feel that the devices will lead to even more inappropriate content in public view. While some law-enforcement agencies cite those who engage in such behavior with minor violations of laws, most overlook the issue. Some people engaging in the behavior claim First Amendment free speech rights as the reason that they should be allowed to view their movies when and wherever they like.

Should people be allowed to view what some consider inappropriate movies in public? Why or why not? Who should judge what is inappropriate content and why? In what way should business or governments, if at all, assert control over what can be viewed in a business establishment or in public?

? FAQ 6-4

What is the largest high-definition display to date?

The new Dallas Cowboys stadium in Texas has a more than 11,000 square foot display, measuring about 160 feet wide and 70 feet tall.

For more information, visit the Computer Concepts CourseMate Web site at www.cengagebrain.com, navigate to the Chapter 6 FAQ resource for this book, and then click Largest High-Definition Display.

Figure 6-9 Video game players often use a television as their game console's output device.

CRT Monitors

A **CRT monitor** is a desktop monitor that contains a cathode-ray tube (Figure 6-10). A *cathode-ray tube* (*CRT*) is a large, sealed glass tube. The front of the tube is the screen. Tiny dots of phosphor material coat the screen on a CRT. Inside the CRT, an electron beam moves back and forth across the back of the screen. This causes the dots on the front of the screen to glow, which produces an image on the screen.

CRT monitors have a much larger footprint than do LCD monitors; that is, they take up more desk space and thus are not used much today. A CRT monitor's *viewable size* is the diagonal measurement of the actual viewing area provided by the screen in the CRT monitor. A 21-inch monitor, for example, may have a viewable size of 20 inches.

Figure 6-10 The popularity of CRT monitors is declining.

✔ QUIZ YOURSELF 6-1

Instructions: Find the true statement below. Then, rewrite the remaining false statements so that they are true.

1. A lower resolution uses a greater number of pixels and thus provides a smoother image.
2. An output device is any type of software component that conveys information to one or more people.
3. Documents often include text to enhance their visual appeal and convey information.
4. Types of pixels include LCD monitors, LCD screens, and plasma monitors.
5. You measure a monitor diagonally from one corner to the other.

Quiz Yourself Online: To further check your knowledge of pages 304 through 313, visit the Computer Concepts CourseMate Web site at www.cengagebrain.com, navigate to the Chapter 6 Quiz Yourself resource for this book, and then click Objectives 1 – 3.

Printers

A **printer** is an output device that produces text and graphics on a physical medium such as paper. Printed information, called *hard copy*, exists physically and is a more permanent form of output than that presented on a display device (soft copy).

A hard copy, also called a *printout*, is either in portrait or landscape orientation (Figure 6-11). A printout in *portrait orientation* is taller than it

Figure 6-11a (portrait orientation)

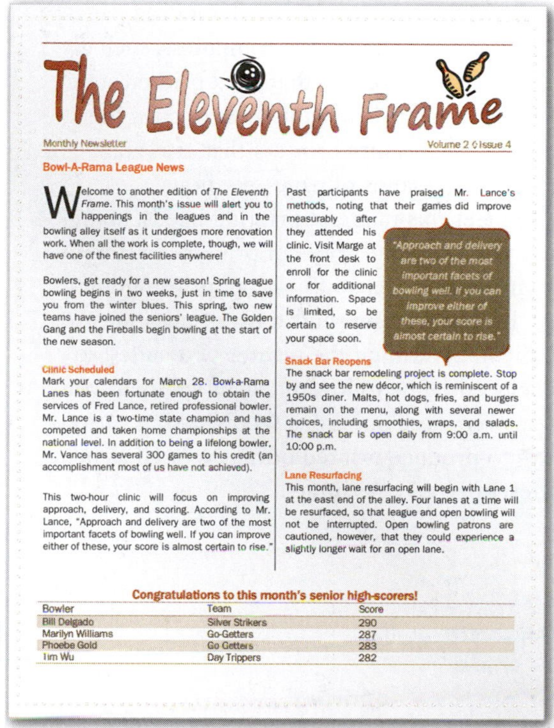

The Eleventh Frame

Monthly Newsletter — Volume 2 ◊ Issue 4

Bowl-A-Rama League News

Welcome to another edition of *The Eleventh Frame*. This month's issue will alert you to happenings in the leagues and in the bowling alley itself as it undergoes more renovation work. When all the work is complete, though, we will have one of the finest facilities anywhere!

Bowlers, get ready for a new season! Spring league bowling begins in two weeks, just in time to save you from the winter blues. This spring, two new teams have joined the seniors' league. The Golden Gang and the Fireballs begin bowling at the start of the new season.

Clinic Scheduled

Mark your calendars for March 28. Bowl-a-Rama Lanes has been fortunate enough to obtain the services of Fred Lance, retired professional bowler. Mr. Lance is a two-time state champion and has competed and taken home championships at the national level. In addition to being a lifelong bowler, Mr. Vance has several 300 games to his credit (an accomplishment most of us have not achieved).

This two-hour clinic will focus on improving approach, delivery, and scoring. According to Mr. Lance, "Approach and delivery are two of the most important facets of bowling well. If you can improve either of these, your score is almost certain to rise."

Past participants have praised Mr. Lance's methods, noting that their games did improve measurably after they attended his clinic. Visit Marge at the front desk to enroll for the clinic or for additional information. Space is limited, so be certain to reserve your space soon.

"Approach and delivery are two of the most important facets of bowling well. If you can improve either of these, your score is almost certain to rise."

Snack Bar Reopens

The snack bar remodeling project is complete. Stop by and see the new décor, which is reminiscent of a 1950s diner. Malts, hot dogs, fries, and burgers remain on the menu, along with several newer choices, including smoothies, wraps, and salads. The snack bar is open daily from 9:00 a.m. until 10:00 p.m.

Lane Resurfacing

This month, lane resurfacing will begin with Lane 1 at the east end of the alley. Four lanes at a time will be resurfaced, so that league and open bowling will not be interrupted. Open bowling patrons are cautioned, however, that they could experience a slightly longer wait for an open lane.

Congratulations to this month's senior high-scorers!

Bowler	Team	Score
Bill Delgado	Silver Strikers	290
Marilyn Williams	Go-Getters	287
Phoebe Gold	Go Getters	283
Tim Wu	Day Trippers	282

Figure 6-11b (landscape orientation)

Figure 6-11 Portrait orientation is taller than it is wide. Landscape orientation is wider than it is tall.

is wide, with information printed across the shorter width of the paper. A printout in *landscape orientation* is wider than it is tall, with information printed across the widest part of the paper. Letters, reports, and books typically use portrait orientation. Spreadsheets, slide shows, and graphics often use landscape orientation. To learn about controlling printing on a computer, complete the Learn How To 2 activity on page 341. Read Looking Ahead 6-1 for a look at a future type of paper.

Home computer users might print fewer than a hundred pages a week. Small business computer users might print several hundred pages a day. Users of mainframe computers, such as large utility companies that send printed statements to hundreds of thousands of customers each month, require printers that are capable of printing thousands of pages per hour.

To meet this range of printing needs, many different types and styles of printers exist with varying speeds, capabilities, and printing methods. Figure 6-12 presents a list of questions to help you determine the printer best suited to your needs. The following pages will help you to answer these questions by discussing various ways to produce printed output, as well as many different types of printers.

1. What is my budget?
2. How fast must my printer print?
3. Do I need a color printer?
4. What is the cost per page for printing?
5. Do I need multiple copies of documents?
6. Will I print graphics?
7. Do I want to print photos?
8. Do I want to print directly from a memory card?
9. What types of paper does the printer use?
10. What sizes of paper does the printer accept?
11. Do I want to print on both sides of the paper?
12. How much paper can the printer tray hold?
13. Will the printer work with my computer and software?
14. How much do supplies such as ink, toner, and paper cost?
15. Can the printer print on envelopes?
16. How many envelopes can the printer print at a time?
17. How much do I print now, and how much will I be printing in a year or two?
18. Will the printer be connected to a network?
19. Do I want wireless printing capability?

Figure 6-12 Questions to ask when purchasing a printer.

LOOKING AHEAD 6-1

Reusable Paper May Become a Disappearing Act

If you want that stack of papers on your desk to disappear, Xerox may have the solution. The company is developing paper that allows print on it to disappear in a short period of time, generally no more than one day.

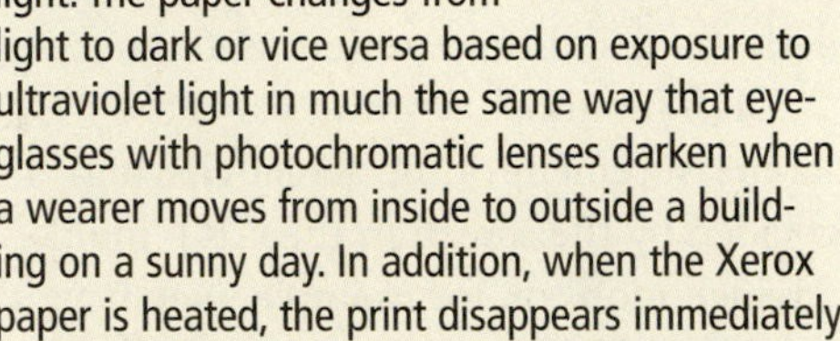

The paper's molecular compound changes color when it is exposed to a particular wavelength of light. The paper changes from light to dark or vice versa based on exposure to ultraviolet light in much the same way that eyeglasses with photochromatic lenses darken when a wearer moves from inside to outside a building on a sunny day. In addition, when the Xerox paper is heated, the print disappears immediately.

Although the erasable paper will cost three times more than conventional paper, it can be reused approximately 30 times. Xerox estimates that 40 percent of paper is looked at only once and then discarded, so the erasable paper product should reduce drastically the 20 trillion pieces of paper that will be used by 2018.

For more information, visit the Computer Concepts CourseMate Web site at www.cengagebrain.com, navigate to the Chapter 6 Looking Ahead resource for this book, and then click Erasable Paper.

Producing Printed Output

Until a few years ago, printing a document required connecting a computer to a printer with a cable. Although many users today continue to print using this method, a variety of printing options are available, as shown in Figure 6-13.

Today, wireless printing technology makes the task of printing from a notebook computer, smart phone, or digital camera much easier. As discussed in Chapter 4, two wireless technologies for printing are Bluetooth and infrared. With *Bluetooth printing*, a computer or other device transmits output to a printer via radio waves. The computer or other device and the printer do not have to be aligned with each other; rather, they need to be within an approximate 30-foot range. With *infrared printing*, a printer communicates with a computer or other device using infrared light waves. To print from a smart phone, for example, a user lines up the IrDA port on the smart phone with the IrDA port on the printer.

Instead of downloading photos from a digital camera to a computer, users can print these digital photos using a variety of techniques. Some cameras connect directly to a printer via a cable. Others store photos on memory cards that can be removed and inserted in the printer. Some printers have a docking station, into which the user inserts the camera to print photos stored in the camera.

Finally, many home and business users print to a central printer on a network. Their computer may communicate with the network printer via cables or wirelessly.

Nonimpact Printers

A **nonimpact printer** forms characters and graphics on a piece of paper without actually striking the paper. Some spray ink, while others use heat or pressure to create images.

Commonly used nonimpact printers are ink-jet printers, photo printers, laser printers, thermal printers, mobile printers, label and postage printers, plotters, and large-format printers. The following pages discuss each of these printer types.

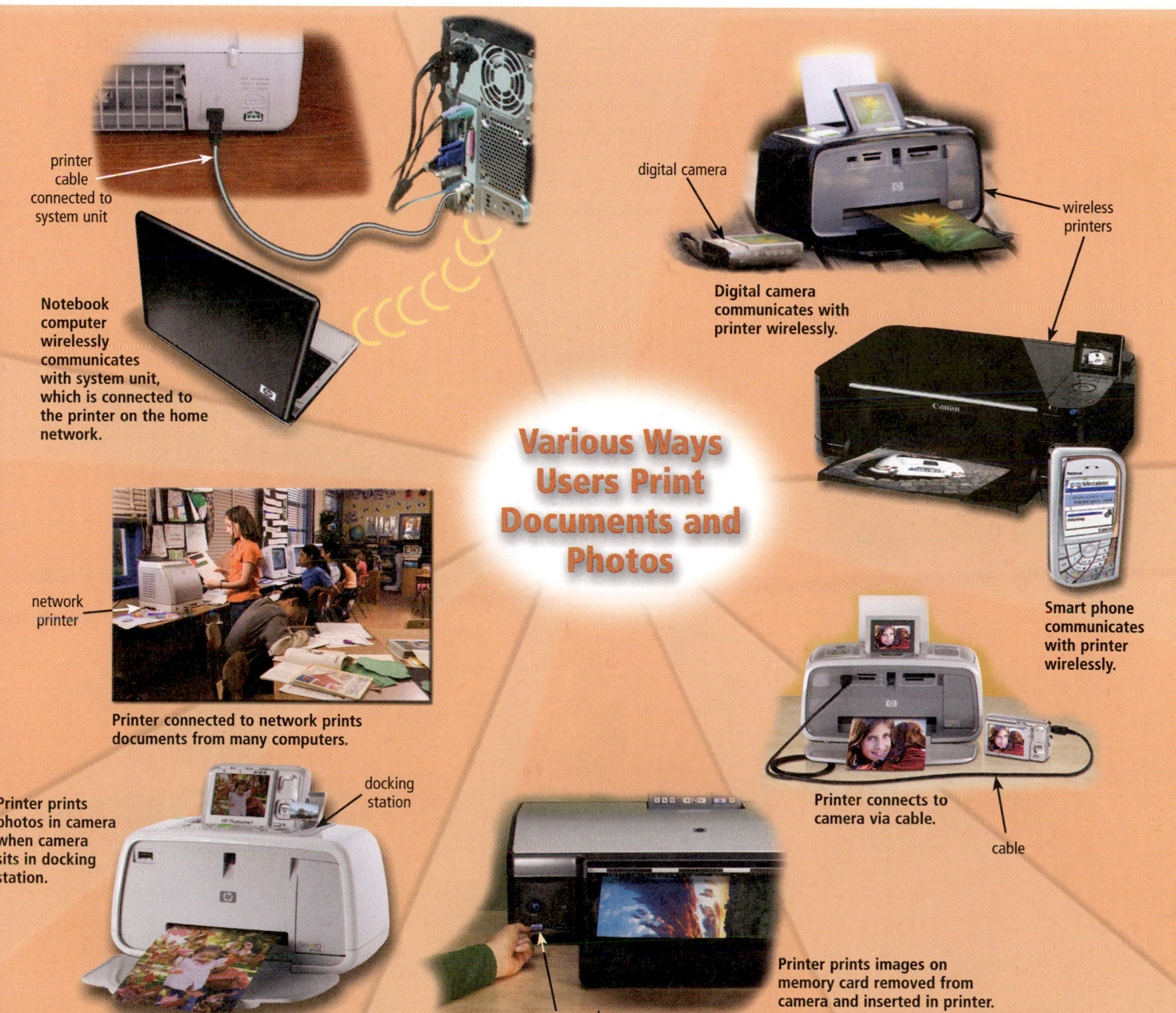

Figure 6-13 Users print documents and photos using a variety of printing methods.

Ink-Jet Printers

An **ink-jet printer** is a type of nonimpact printer that forms characters and graphics by spraying tiny drops of liquid ink onto a piece of paper. Ink-jet printers have become a popular type of color printer for use in the home. A reasonable quality ink-jet printer costs less than $100.

Ink-jet printers produce text and graphics in both black-and-white and color on a variety of paper types (Figure 6-14). These printers normally use individual sheets of paper stored in one or two removable or stationary trays. Ink-jet printers accept papers in many sizes, ranging from 3 × 5 inches to 8½ × 14 inches. Available paper types include plain paper, ink-jet paper, photo paper, glossy paper, and banner paper. Most ink-jet printers can print photographic-quality images on any of these types of paper.

Ink-jet printers also print on other materials such as envelopes, labels, index cards, greeting card paper (card stock), transparencies, and iron-on T-shirt transfers. Many ink-jet printers include software for creating greeting cards, banners, business cards, and letterhead.

As with many other input and output devices, one factor that determines the quality of an ink-jet printer is its resolution. Printer resolution is measured by the number of *dots per inch* (*dpi*) a printer can print. With an ink-jet printer, a dot is a drop of ink. A higher dpi means the drops of ink are smaller. Most ink-jet printers can print from 1200 to 4800 dpi.

As shown in Figure 6-15, the higher the dpi, the better the print quality. The difference in quality becomes noticeable when the size of the printed image increases. That is, a wallet-sized image printed at 1200 dpi may look similar in quality to one printed at 2400 dpi. When you increase the size of the image, to 8 × 10 for example, the printout of the 1200 dpi resolution may look grainier than the one printed using a 2400 dpi resolution.

Figure 6-14 Ink-jet printers are a popular type of color printer used in the home.

The speed of an ink-jet printer is measured by the number of pages per minute (ppm) it can print. Most ink-jet printers print from 12 to 36 ppm. Graphics and colors print at a slower rate. For example, an ink-jet printer may print 36 ppm for black text and only 27 ppm for color and/or graphics.

The print head mechanism in an ink-jet printer contains ink-filled cartridges. Each cartridge has fifty to several hundred small ink holes, or nozzles. The steps in Figure 6-16 illustrate how a drop of ink appears on a page. The ink propels through any combination of the nozzles to form a character or image on the paper.

Figure 6-15 You will notice a higher quality output with printers that can print at a higher dpi.

When the cartridge runs out of ink, you simply replace the cartridge. Most ink-jet printers use two or more ink cartridges: one containing black ink and the other(s) containing colors. Some color cartridges contain a variety of ink colors; others contain only a single color. Consider the number of ink cartridges a printer requires, along with the cost of the cartridges, when purchasing a printer. Cartridges with black ink cost $10 to $40 each. Color ink cartridge prices range from $15 to $45 each. The number of pages a single cartridge can print varies by manufacturer and the type of documents you print. For example, black ink cartridges typically print from 200 to 800 pages, and color ink cartridges from 125 to 450 pages. To reduce the expense of purchasing cartridges, some users opt to purchase refilled cartridges or have empty cartridges refilled by a third party vendor.

Ink-Jet Printers

For more information, visit the Computer Concepts CourseMate Web site at www.cengagebrain.com, navigate to the Chapter 6 Web Link resource for this book, and then click Ink-Jet Printers.

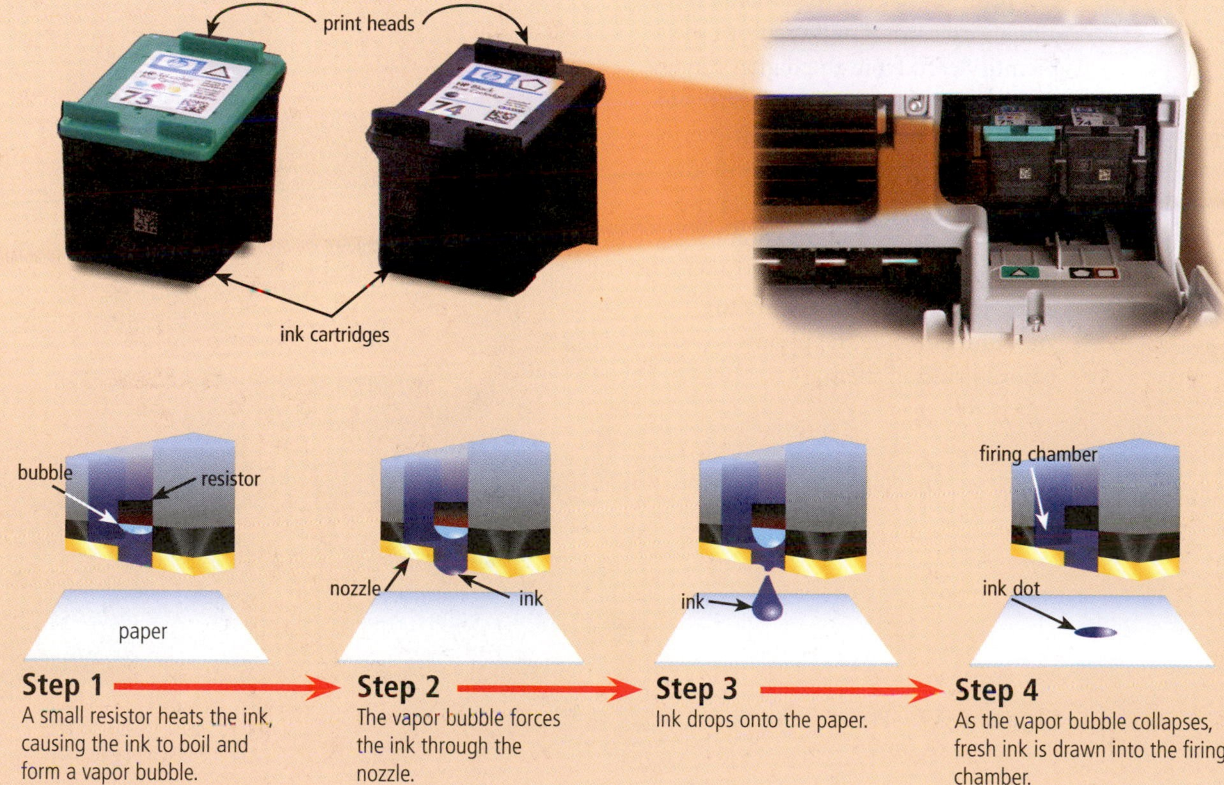

Figure 6-16 This figure shows how an ink-jet printer works.

Photo Printers

A **photo printer** is a color printer that produces photo-lab-quality pictures (Figure 6-17). Some photo printers print just one or two sizes of photos, for example, 3 × 5 inches and 4 × 6 inches. Others print up to letter size, legal size, or even larger. Some even print panoramic photos. Generally, the more sizes the printer prints, the more expensive the printer.

Many photo printers use ink-jet technology. With models that can print letter-sized documents, users connect the photo printer to their computer and use it for all their printing needs. For a few hundred dollars, this type of photo printer is ideal for the home or small business user. Other photo printer technologies are discussed later in the chapter.

Most photo printers are PictBridge enabled, so that you can print photos without a computer. *PictBridge* is a standard technology that allows you to print photos directly from a digital camera by connecting a cable from the digital camera to a USB port on the printer.

Photo printers also usually have a built-in card slot(s) so that the printer can print digital photos directly from a memory card. Simply remove the memory card from the digital camera and insert it in the printer's card slot. Then, push buttons on the printer to select the desired photo, specify the number of copies, and indicate the size of the printed photo. Some photo printers have built-in LCD color screens, allowing users to view and enhance the photos before printing them.

Photo Printers

For more information, visit the Computer Concepts CourseMate Web site at www.cengagebrain.com, navigate to the Chapter 6 Web Link resource for this book, and then click Photo Printers.

? FAQ 6-5

How long do photos printed on a photo or ink-jet printer last?

Recent studies indicate that depending on the combination of paper and ink you use to print photos, some photos might begin to fade after several months. To ensure that your photos retain the best possible quality, you should use high-quality paper, as well as ink that is supplied by the printer's manufacturer.

For more information, visit the Computer Concepts CourseMate Web site at www.cengagebrain.com, navigate to the Chapter 6 FAQ resource for this book, and then click Photo Paper.

Figure 6-17 Photo printers print in a range of sizes.

Laser Printers

A **laser printer** is a high-speed, high-quality nonimpact printer (Figure 6-18). Laser printers are available in both black-and-white and color models. A laser printer for personal computers ordinarily uses individual 8½ × 11-inch sheets of paper stored in one or more removable trays that slide in the printer case. Some laser printers have built-in trays that accommodate different sizes of paper, while others require separate trays for letter- and legal-sized paper. Most laser printers have a manual feed slot where you can insert individual sheets and envelopes.

Laser printers print text and graphics in high-quality resolutions, usually 1200 dpi for black-and-white printers and up to 2400 dpi for color printers. While laser printers usually cost more than ink-jet printers, many models are available at affordable prices for the home user. Laser printers usually print at faster speeds than ink-jet printers. Printer manufacturers state that a laser printer for the home and small office user typically prints black-and-white text at speeds of 15 to 62 ppm. Color laser printers print 8 to 40 ppm. Laser printers for large business users print more than 150 ppm.

Depending on the quality, speed, and type of laser printer, the cost ranges from a few hundred to a few thousand dollars for the home and small office user, and several hundred thousand dollars for the large business user. Color laser printers are slightly higher priced than otherwise equivalent black-and-white laser printers.

When printing a document, laser printers process and store the entire page before they actually print it. For this reason, laser printers sometimes are called page printers. Storing a page before printing requires that the laser printer has a certain amount of memory in the device. The more memory in the printer, the faster it usually can print.

Depending on the amount of graphics you intend to print, a laser printer for the small business user can have up to 1 GB of memory and an 80 GB hard disk. To print a full-page 1200-dpi photo, for instance, you might need 64 MB of memory in the printer. If the printer does not have enough memory to print the photo, either it will print as much of the photo as its memory will allow, or it will display an error message and not print any of the photo.

Laser printers use software that enables them to interpret a *page description language* (*PDL*), which tells the printer how to arrange the contents of a printed page. When you purchase a laser printer, it comes with at least one of two common page description languages: PCL or PostScript. Developed by HP, a leading printer manufacturer, *PCL* (*Printer Control Language*) is a standard printer language that supports the fonts and layout used in standard office documents. Professionals in the desktop publishing and graphic art fields commonly use *PostScript* because it is designed for complex documents with intense graphics and colors.

Figure 6-18 Laser printers are available in both black-and-white and color models.

Operating in a manner similar to a copy machine, a laser printer creates images using a laser beam and powdered ink, called *toner*. The laser beam produces an image on a special drum inside the printer. The light of the laser alters the electrical charge on the drum wherever it hits. When this occurs, the toner sticks to the drum and then transfers to the paper through a combination of pressure and heat (Figure 6-19).

When the toner runs out, you replace the toner cartridge. Toner cartridge prices range from $40 to more than $200 for about 5,000 printed pages.

Laser Printers

For more information, visit the Computer Concepts CourseMate Web site at www.cengagebrain.com, navigate to the Chapter 6 Web Link resource for this book, and then click Laser Printers.

? FAQ 6-6

How do I dispose of toner cartridges?

Do not throw them in the garbage. The housing contains iron, metal, and aluminum that is not biodegradable. The ink toner inside the cartridges contains toxic chemicals that pollute water and soil if discarded in dumps. Instead, recycle empty toner cartridges. Many stores that sell new toner cartridges also allow you to recycle your old ones. Recycling programs in which some schools and organizations participate offer discounts or cash to customers who bring in depleted cartridges. If you are unable to find a recycling program in your area, contact your printer manufacturer to see if it has a recycling program.

For more information, visit the Computer Concepts CourseMate Web site at www.cengagebrain.com, navigate to the Chapter 6 FAQ resource for this book, and then click Recycling Toner Cartridges.

Multifunction Peripherals

A **multifunction peripheral** (MFP), also called an *all-in-one device*, is a single device that looks like a printer or a copy machine but provides the functionality of a printer, scanner, copy machine, and perhaps a fax machine (Figure 6-20). A fax machine is a device that codes and encodes documents so that they can be transmitted over telephone lines. The documents can contain text, drawings or photos, or can be handwritten.

The features of these devices vary. For example, some use color ink-jet printer technology, while others include a black-and-white or color laser printer.

Small offices and home office (SOHO) users have multifunction peripherals because these devices require less space than having a separate printer, scanner, copy machine, and fax machine. Another advantage of these devices is they are significantly less expensive than if you purchase each device separately. If the device breaks down, however, you lose all four functions, which is the primary disadvantage.

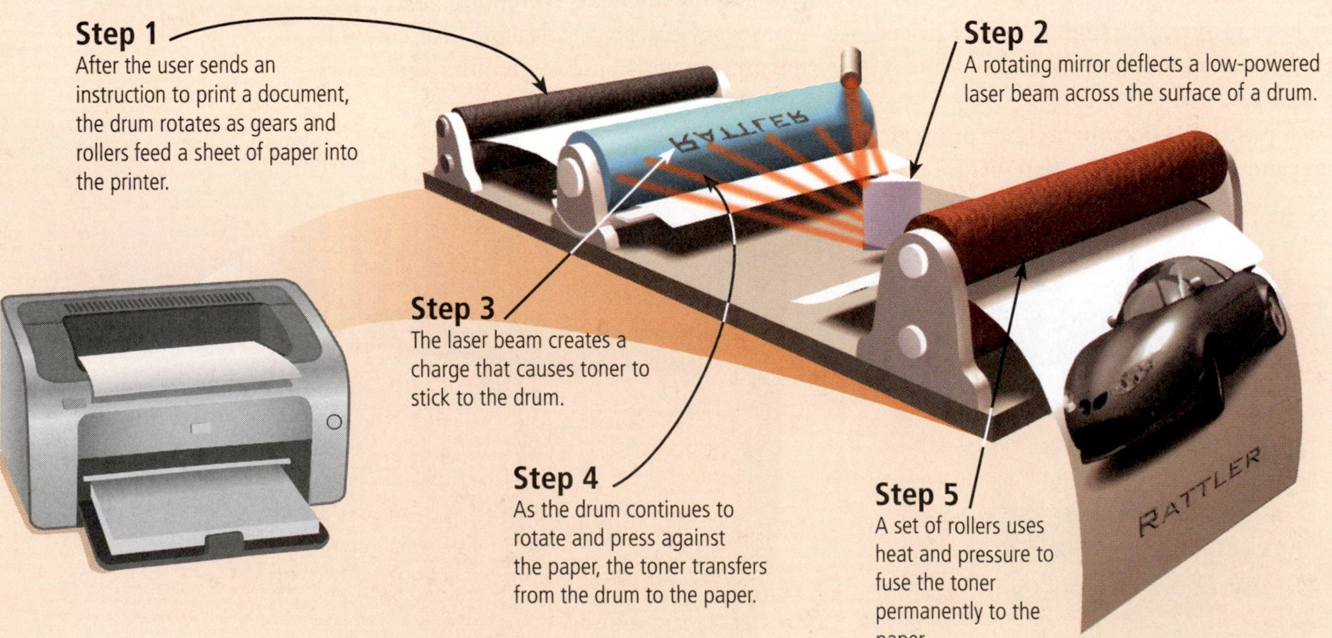

Figure 6-19 This figure shows how a black-and-white laser printer works.

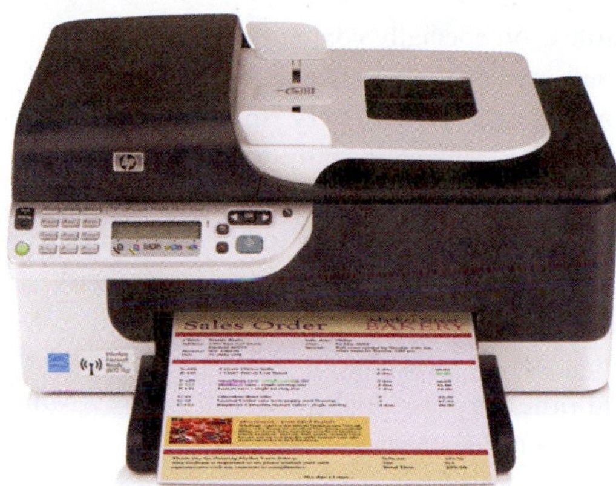

Figure 6-20 This multifunction peripheral is a color printer, scanner, copy machine, and fax machine.

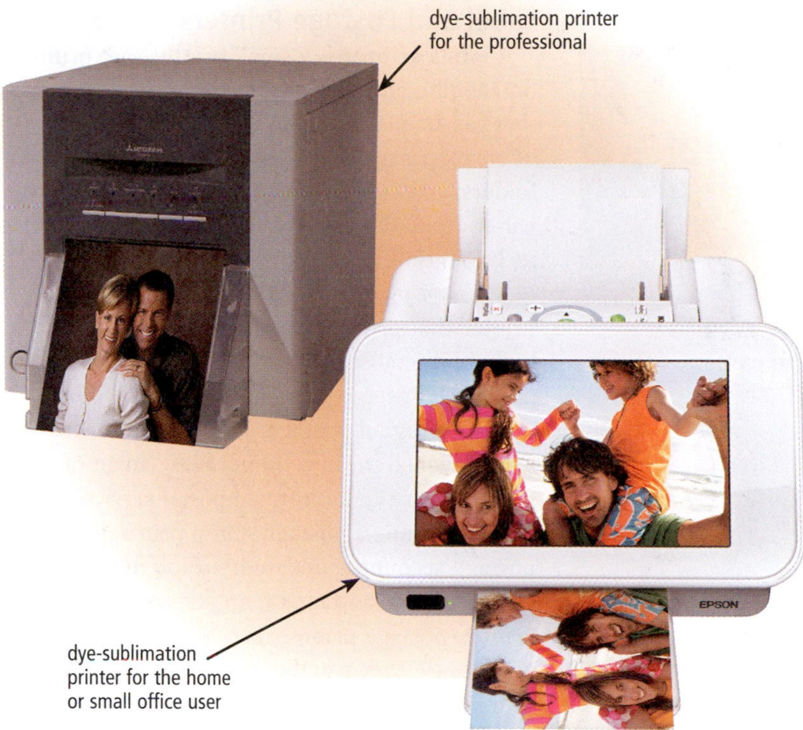

Figure 6-21 The printers shown in this figure use dye-sublimation technology to create photographic-quality output.

Thermal Printers

A **thermal printer** generates images by pushing electrically heated pins against heat-sensitive paper. Basic thermal printers are inexpensive, but the print quality is low and the images tend to fade over time. Self-service gas pumps often print gas receipts using a built-in lower-quality thermal printer. Many point-of-sale terminals in retail and grocery stores also print purchase receipts on thermal paper.

Two special types of thermal printers have high print quality and can print at much faster rates than ink-jet and laser printers. A *thermal wax-transfer printer* generates rich, nonsmearing images by using heat to melt colored wax onto heat-sensitive paper. Thermal wax-transfer printers are more expensive than ink-jet printers, but less expensive than many color laser printers.

A *dye-sublimation printer*, sometimes called a *digital photo printer*, uses heat to transfer colored dye to specially coated paper. Most dye-sublimation printers create images that are of photographic quality (Figure 6-21). Professional applications requiring high image quality, such as photography studios, medical labs, and security identification systems, use dye-sublimation printers. These high-end printers cost thousands of dollars and print images in a wide range of sizes. Most dye-sublimation printers for the home or small business user, by contrast, typically print images in only one or two sizes and are much slower than their professional counterparts. These lower-end dye-sublimation printers are comparable in cost to a photo printer based on ink-jet technology. Some are small enough for the mobile user to carry the printer in a briefcase.

Mobile Printers

A **mobile printer** is a small, lightweight, battery-powered printer that allows a mobile user to print from a notebook computer, smart phone, or other mobile device while traveling (Figure 6-22). Barely wider than the paper on which they print, mobile printers fit easily in a briefcase alongside a notebook computer.

Mobile printers mainly use ink-jet, thermal, thermal wax-transfer, or dye-sublimation technology. Many of these printers connect to a USB port. Others have a built-in wireless port through which they communicate with the computer wirelessly.

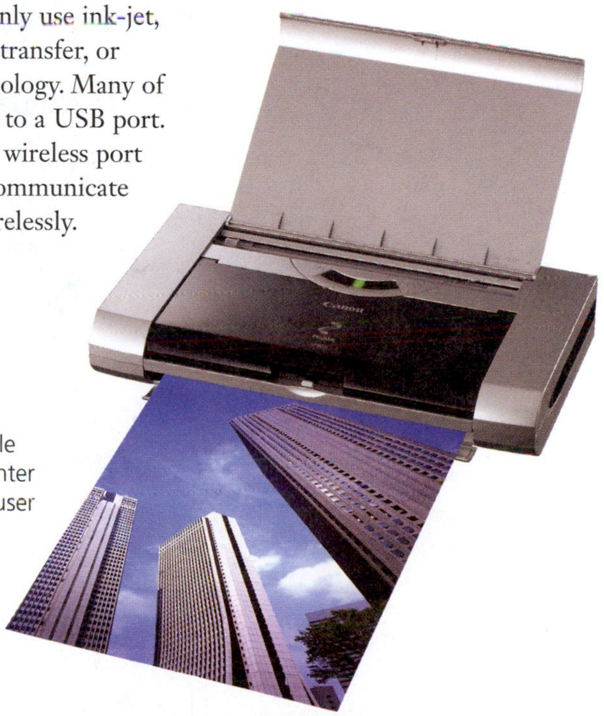

Figure 6-22 A mobile printer is a compact printer that allows the mobile user to print from a mobile computer or device.

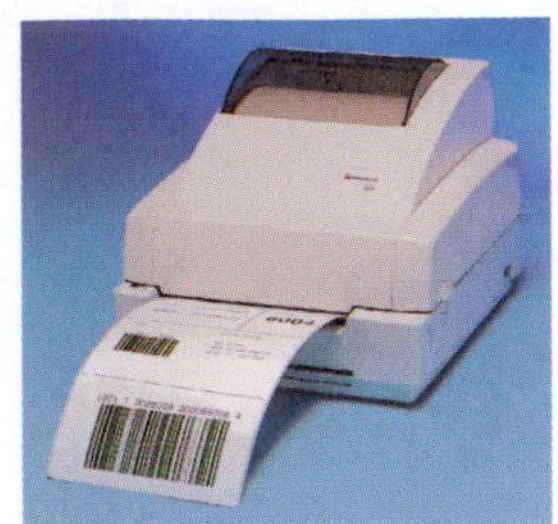

Figure 6-23
A label printer.

Label and Postage Printers

A **label printer** is a small printer that prints on an adhesive-type material (Figure 6-23) that can be placed on a variety of items such as envelopes, packages, optical discs, photos, file folders, and toys. Most label printers also print bar codes. Label printers typically use thermal technology.

A *postage printer* is a special type of label printer that prints postage stamps. Some have built-in digital scales for weighing letters and packages. Postage printers allow users to buy and print digital postage, often called *Internet postage*, which means you purchase an amount of postage from an authorized postal service Web site. Each time a postage stamp prints, your postage account is updated. Although you can print Internet postage on an ink-jet or photo printer, postage printers can be more economical because they use thermal technology instead of ink cartridges.

Large-Format Printers
For more information, visit the Computer Concepts CourseMate Web site at www.cengagebrain.com, navigate to the Chapter 6 Web Link resource for this book, and then click Large-Format Printers.

Plotters and Large-Format Printers

Plotters are sophisticated printers used to produce high-quality drawings such as blueprints, maps, and circuit diagrams. These printers are used in specialized fields such as engineering and drafting and usually are very costly. Current plotters use a row of charged wires (called styli) to draw an electrostatic pattern on specially coated paper and then fuse toner to the pattern. The printed image consists of a series of very small dots, which provides high-quality output.

Using ink-jet printer technology, but on a much larger scale, a **large-format printer** creates photo-realistic-quality color prints. Graphic artists use these high-cost, high-performance printers for signs, posters, and other professional quality displays (Figure 6-24).

Plotters and large-format printers can accommodate paper with widths up to 98 inches because blueprints, maps, signs, posters and other such drawings and displays can be quite large. Some plotters and large-format printers use individual sheets of paper, while others take large rolls.

Impact Printers

An **impact printer** forms characters and graphics on a piece of paper by striking a mechanism against an inked ribbon that physically contacts the paper. Impact printers characteristically are noisy because of this striking activity. These printers commonly produce *near letter quality* (*NLQ*) output, which is print quality slightly less clear than what is acceptable for business letters. Companies may use impact printers for routine jobs such

Figure 6-24 Graphic artists use large-format printers to print signs, posters, and other professional quality displays.

as printing labels. Impact printers are ideal for printing multipart forms because they easily print through many layers of paper. Factories, warehouses, and retail counters may use impact printers because these printers withstand dusty environments, vibrations, and extreme temperatures. Two commonly used types of impact printers are dot-matrix printers and line printers.

A **dot-matrix printer** produces printed images when tiny wire pins on a print head mechanism strike an inked ribbon (Figure 6-25). When the ribbon presses against the paper, it creates dots that form characters and graphics. Most dot-matrix printers use *continuous-form paper*, in which thousands of sheets of paper are connected together end to end. The pages have holes along the sides to help feed the paper through the printer.

The speed of a dot-matrix printer is measured by the number of characters per second (cps) it can print. The speed of most dot-matrix printers ranges from 375 to 1100 characters per second (cps), depending on the desired print quality.

A **line printer** is a high-speed impact printer that prints an entire line at a time. The speed of a line printer is measured by the number of lines per minute (lpm) it can print. Some line printers print as many as 3,000 lpm. Mainframes, servers, or networked applications, such as manufacturing, distribution, or shipping, often use line printers. These printers typically use 11 × 17-inch continuous-form paper.

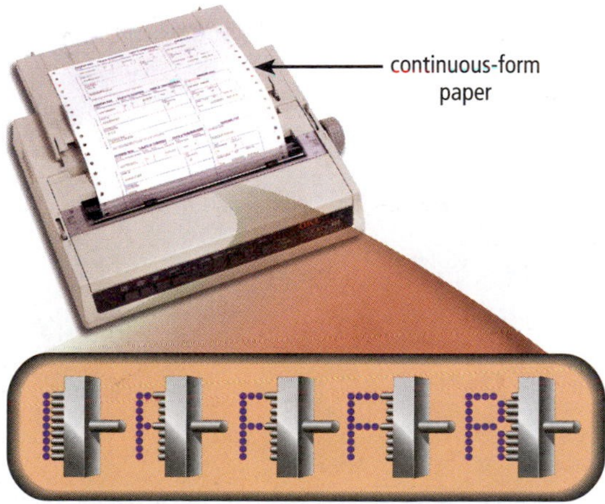

Figure 6-25 A dot-matrix printer produces printed images when tiny pins strike an inked ribbon.

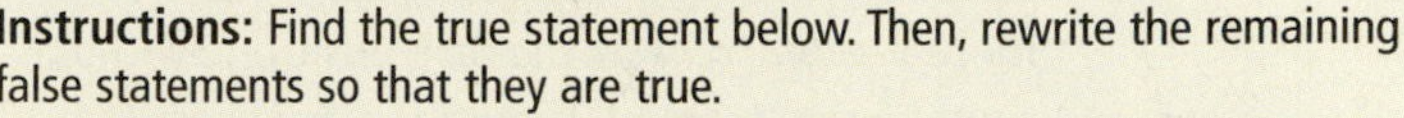

QUIZ YOURSELF 6-2

Instructions: Find the true statement below. Then, rewrite the remaining false statements so that they are true.

1. A laser printer generates images by pushing electrically heated pins against heat-sensitive paper.
2. A photo printer creates images using a laser beam and powdered ink, called toner.
3. An ink-jet printer is a type of impact printer that forms characters and graphics by spraying tiny drops of liquid nitrogen onto a piece of paper.
4. Printed information is called soft copy.
5. With Bluetooth printing, a computer or other device transmits output to a printer via radio waves.

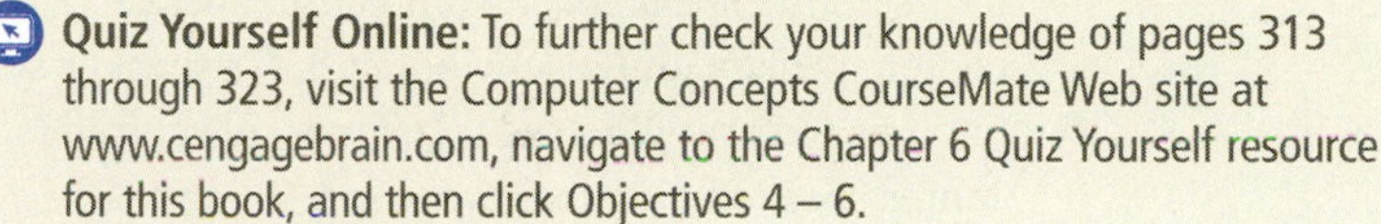

Quiz Yourself Online: To further check your knowledge of pages 313 through 323, visit the Computer Concepts CourseMate Web site at www.cengagebrain.com, navigate to the Chapter 6 Quiz Yourself resource for this book, and then click Objectives 4 – 6.

Speakers, Headphones, and Earbuds

An **audio output device** is a component of a computer that produces music, speech, or other sounds, such as beeps. Three commonly used audio output devices are speakers, headphones, and earbuds.

Most personal computers and mobile devices have a small internal speaker that usually emits only low-quality sound. Thus, many users attach surround sound **speakers** or speaker systems to their computers, including game consoles and mobile devices, to generate higher-quality sounds for playing games, interacting with multimedia presentations, listening to music, and viewing movies (Figure 6-26).

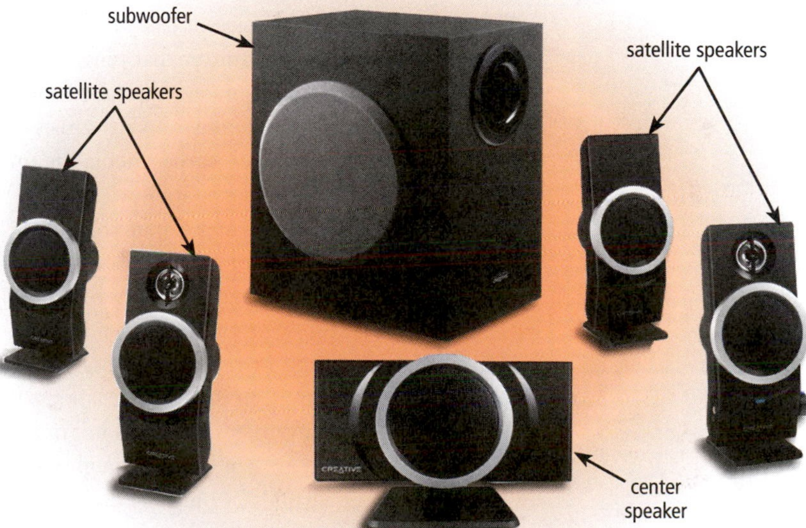

Figure 6-26 Most personal computer users attach high-quality surround sound speaker systems to their computers.

Most surround sound computer speaker systems include one or two center speakers and two or more *satellite speakers* that are positioned so that sound emits from all directions. Speakers typically have tone and volume controls, allowing users to adjust settings. To boost the low bass sounds, surround sound speaker systems also include a *subwoofer*.

Surround sound systems are available in a variety of configurations. For example, a 2.1 speaker system contains two speakers and a subwoofer. A 5.1 speaker system has four satellite speakers, a center speaker, and a subwoofer. A 6.1 speaker system has four satellite speakers, a front center speaker, a rear center speaker, and a subwoofer. A 7.1 speaker system has four satellite speakers, two side speakers, a center speaker, and a subwoofer.

In many cases, a cable connects the speakers or the subwoofer to a port on the sound card. With wireless speakers, however, a transmitter connects to the sound card, which wirelessly communicates with the speakers. To take full advantage of high-end surround sound speaker systems, be sure the sound card in the computer is compatible with the speaker system.

Audio resolution, which is the number of bytes that represent sound in a given time, is stated as a bit rate such as 8-bit, 16-bit, or 24-bit. A sound card using 8-bit resolution, for example, represents a sound with any 1 of 256 values (2^8), and a 16-bit sound card uses any 1 of 65,536 values (2^{16}). Higher resolutions result in better sound quality. With 8-bit resolution, the sound quality is similar to an AM radio; 16-bit resolution yields optical disc-quality sound; and 24-bit resolution is used for high-quality digital audio editing.

Many users opt for a wireless music system, which includes a USB transmitter that plugs in a computer, a receiver that connects to a television or stereo system, and a remote control. With this system, you can play any optical disc or media file on your computer and transmit the audio to a home or office stereo or television at a distance of up to about 330 feet. You also can plug a portable media player, such as an iPod, into the computer to hear its songs on the stereo or television speakers.

Earbuds

For more information, visit the Computer Concepts CourseMate Web site at www.cengagebrain.com, navigate to the Chapter 6 Web Link resource for this book, and then click Earbuds.

When using speakers, anyone in listening distance can hear the output. In a computer laboratory or other crowded environment, speakers might not be practical. Instead, users can listen through wireless headphones or earbuds or plug the device in a port on the sound card, in a speaker, or on the front of the system unit. With headphones or earbuds, only the individual wearing the headphones or earbuds hears the sound from the computer. The difference is that **headphones** cover or are placed outside of the ear (Figure 6-27), whereas **earbuds**, or *earphones* (shown in Figure 6-1 on page 304), rest inside the ear canal. Both headphones and earbuds usually include noise-cancelling technology to reduce the interference of sounds from the surrounding environment.

A *headset* is a device that functions as both headphones and a microphone. Computer and smart phone users wear a headset to free their hands for typing and other activities while talking or listening to audio output.

Portable media players usually include a set of earbuds. As an alternative, you can listen to audio from the portable media player through speakers in a vehicle or on a stereo system at home or work. Or, you can purchase speakers specifically designed to play audio from a portable media player (Figure 6-28).

Figure 6-27 In a crowded environment where speakers are not practical, users can wear headphones to hear audio output.

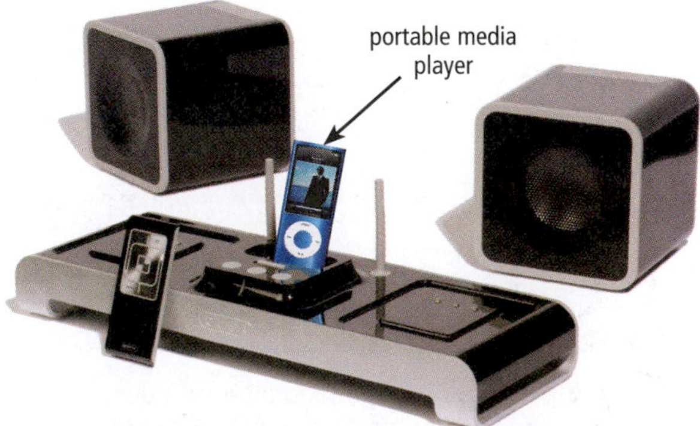

Figure 6-28 Instead of listening to your portable media player through earbuds, you can purchase separate speakers for the device, such as the wireless speakers shown here.

Electronically produced voice output is growing in popularity. **Voice output** occurs when you hear a person's voice or when the computer talks to you through the speakers on the computer. In some programs, the computer can speak the contents of a document through voice output.

On the Web, you can listen to (or download and then listen to) interviews, talk shows, sporting events, news, recorded music, and live concerts from many radio and television stations. Some Web sites and programs, such as media players, dedicate themselves to providing voice output, such as those that allow you to listen to and then purchase and download songs.

Very often, voice output works with voice input. For example, when you call an airline to check the status of gates, terminals, and arrival times, your voice interacts with a computer-generated voice output. Another example is *VoIP*, which allows users to speak and listen to others over the Internet using their desktop computer, mobile computer, or mobile device.

Sophisticated programs enable the computer to converse with you. Talk into the microphone and say, "I'd like today's weather report." The computer replies, "For which city?" You reply, "Chicago." The computer says, "Sunny and 80 degrees."

Other Output Devices

In addition to display devices, printers, and speakers, other output devices are available for specific uses and applications such as data projectors, interactive whiteboards, and force-feedback game controllers and tactile output.

Data Projectors

A **data projector** is a device that takes the text and images displaying on a computer screen and projects them on a larger screen so that an audience can see the image clearly (Figure 6-29). For example, many classrooms use data projectors so that all students easily can see an instructor's presentation on the screen. Read Ethics & Issues 6-3 for a related discussion.

Some data projectors are large devices that attach to a ceiling or wall in an auditorium. Some operating systems allow projectors to be part of the network, which enables a presenter to operate the projector remotely via a network connection. Others, designed for the mobile user, are small portable devices that can be transported easily. Two types of smaller, lower-cost units are LCD projectors and DLP projectors.

An *LCD projector*, which uses liquid crystal display technology, attaches directly to a computer, and uses its own light source to display the information shown on the computer screen.

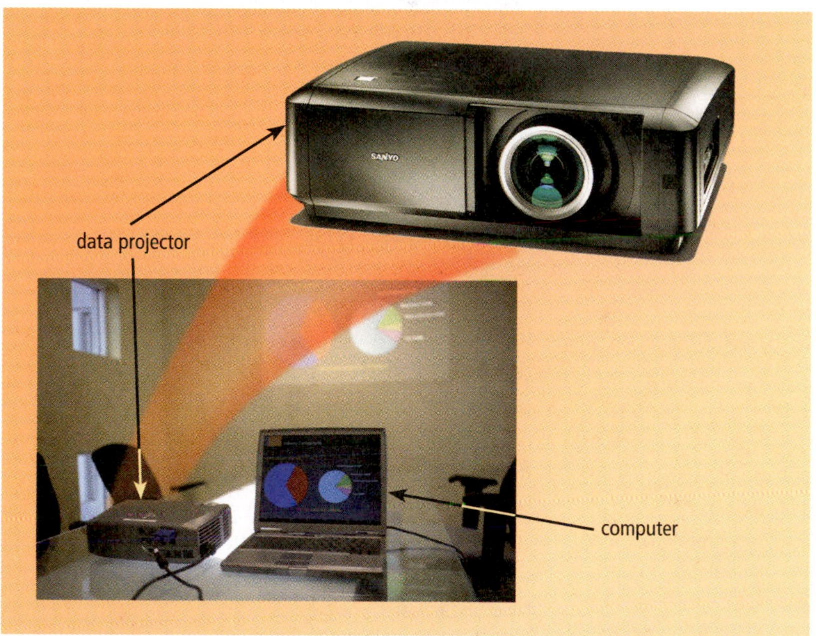

Figure 6-29 A data projector projects an image from a computer screen on a larger screen so that an audience easily can see the image.

ETHICS & ISSUES 6-3

Is Green Graffiti an Acceptable Form of Free Speech?

Around the world, activists paint protest graffiti across historical landmarks and public structures, such as the Coliseum of Rome or the Brooklyn Bridge. Artists paint their works across skyscrapers. More and more, however, the "paint" is in the form of light or laser beams, not the traditional, indelible spray paint. Use of digital projectors or laser beams is part of the growing practice known as *green graffiti*. When used for graffiti, the practice also is known as laser tagging. Sometimes, the devices used for green graffiti also are used for creative advertising. Proponents of green graffiti state that the practice is an environmentally friendly form of free speech and is no more damaging than writing "Wash Me" with one's finger on a dusty car. Opponents claim that the graffiti is as much an eyesore as traditional graffiti, especially when the message or art interferes with the view of landmarks and other interesting vistas.

Is green graffiti an acceptable form of free speech? Why or why not? Should protesters and artists be required to receive permission from the owners or caretakers of their venues before they engage in the practice? Why or why not? If you spent a large sum of money on a vacation to see a historic location only to find it covered in green graffiti on the evening of your visit, how would you react? Would you engage in green graffiti to make a political statement or create art? Is green graffiti an acceptable form of advertising? Why or why not?

Because LCD projectors tend to produce lower-quality images, users often prefer DLP projectors for their sharper, brighter images.

A *digital light processing (DLP) projector* uses tiny mirrors to reflect light, which produces crisp, bright, colorful images that remain in focus and can be seen clearly even in a well-lit room. Some newer televisions use DLP instead of LCD or plasma technology.

As an alternative to data projectors, some users work with an LCD or plasma display.

Interactive Whiteboards

An **interactive whiteboard** is a touch-sensitive device, resembling a dry-erase board, that displays the image on a connected computer screen. A presenter controls the computer program by clicking a remote control, touching the whiteboard, drawing on or erasing the whiteboard with a special digital pen and eraser, or writing on a special tablet. Notes written on the interactive whiteboard can be saved directly on the computer. Interactive whiteboards are used frequently in classrooms as a teaching tool (Figure 6-30), during meetings as a collaboration tool, and to enhance delivery of presentations.

SMART Board

For more information, visit the Computer Concepts CourseMate Web site at www.cengagebrain.com, navigate to the Chapter 6 Web Link resource for this book, and then click SMART Board.

Three basic technologies exist for displaying computer images on an interactive whiteboard: (1) front projection: separate projector displays an image from the computer screen on the interactive whiteboard; (2) rear projection: a projector built into the back of the interactive whiteboard displays an image from the computer screen on the whiteboard; and (3) an interactive whiteboard fits over an LCD screen or a plasma display. Front projection and rear projection interactive whiteboards, which are hung on the wall or mounted on a stand, range in size from 48 to 94 inches. A widely used interactive whiteboard is the SMART Board.

Force-Feedback Game Controllers and Tactile Output

As discussed in Chapter 5, joysticks, wheels, gamepads, and motion-sensing game controllers are input devices used to control movement and actions of a player or object in computer games, simulations, and video games. Today's joysticks, wheels, gamepads, and motion-sensing game controllers also include *force feedback*, which is a technology that sends resistance to the device in response to actions of the user (Figure 6-31). For example, as you use the simulation software to drive from a smooth road onto a gravel alley, the steering wheel trembles or vibrates, making the driving experience as realistic as possible.

Figure 6-30 Teachers and students can write directly on an interactive whiteboard, or they can write on a wireless slate that communicates with the whiteboard.

Figure 6-31 Gaming devices often provide force feedback, giving the user a realistic experience.

These devices also are used in practical training applications such as in the military and aviation.

Some input devices, such as a mouse, and mobile devices, such as a smart phone, include *tactile output* that provides the user with a physical response from the device. For example, users may sense a bumping feeling on their hand while scrolling through a smart phone's contact list.

Putting It All Together

Many factors influence the type of output devices you should use: the type of output desired, the hardware and software in use, and the anticipated cost. Figure 6-32 outlines several suggested monitors, printers, and other output devices for various types of computer users.

Suggested Output Devices by User

User	Monitor	Printer	Other
Home	• 19- or 20-inch LCD monitor, or 17-inch LCD screen on notebook computer	• Ink-jet color printer; or • Photo printer	• Speakers • Headphones or earbuds or headset • Force-feedback game controller or tactile output
Small Office/Home Office	• 20- or 22-inch LCD monitor • LCD screen smart phone or other mobile device	• Multifunction peripheral; or • Ink-jet color printer; or • Laser printer (black-and-white or color) • Label printer • Postage printer	• Speakers
Mobile	• 17-inch LCD screen on notebook computer • 8.9-inch screen on a netbook • LCD screen on smart phone or other mobile device	• Mobile color printer • Ink-jet color printer; or • Laser printer for in-office use (black-and-white or color) • Photo printer	• Headphones or earbuds or headset • DLP data projector
Power	• 30-inch LCD monitor	• Laser printer (black-and-white or color) • Plotter or large-format printer; or • Photo printer; or • Dye-sublimation printer	• Speakers • Headphones or earbuds or headset
Enterprise	• 20- or 22-inch LCD monitor • LCD screen on smart phone or other mobile device	• High-speed laser printer • Laser printer, color • Line printer (for large reports from a mainframe) • Label printer	• Speakers • Headphones or earbuds or headset • Networked DLP data projector • Interactive whiteboard

Figure 6-32 This table recommends suggested output devices for various types of users.

Output Devices for Physically Challenged Users

As Chapter 5 discussed, the growing presence of computers has generated an awareness of the need to address computing requirements for those with physical limitations. Read Ethics & Issues 6-4 for a related discussion.

For users with mobility, hearing, or vision disabilities, many different types of output devices are available. Hearing-impaired users, for example, can instruct programs to display words instead of sounds. With the latest Windows operating systems, users also can set options to make programs easier to use. The Magnifier, for example, enlarges text and other items in a window on the screen (Figure 6-33).

ETHICS & ISSUES 6-4

Should Web Sites Be Held Accountable for Accessibility Levels for Physically Challenged People?

The World Wide Web Consortium (W3C) has published accessibility guidelines for Web sites. The guidelines specify measures that Web site designers can take to increase accessibility for physically challenged users. Among its guidelines, the W3C urges Web site designers to provide equivalent text for audio or visual content, include features that allow elements to be activated and understood using a variety of input and output devices, and make the user interface follow principles of accessible design. A recent report found that most Web sites do not meet all of the W3C guidelines. This failure is disappointing, because many physically challenged users could benefit from the Web's capability to bring products and services into the home. Ironically, a survey discovered that more than 50 percent of the Web sites hosted by disability organizations also fail to meet the W3C guidelines. Critics contend that these Web sites neglect the needs of their users and fail to lead by example. The Web site supporters contend, however, that many sponsoring organizations lack the funding necessary to comply with the guidelines.

Should the government require that all Web sites meet the W3C accessibility guidelines? Why or why not? Do Web sites hosted by disability organizations have a moral obligation to meet the guidelines? Why? What can be done to encourage people and organizations to make their Web sites more accessible?

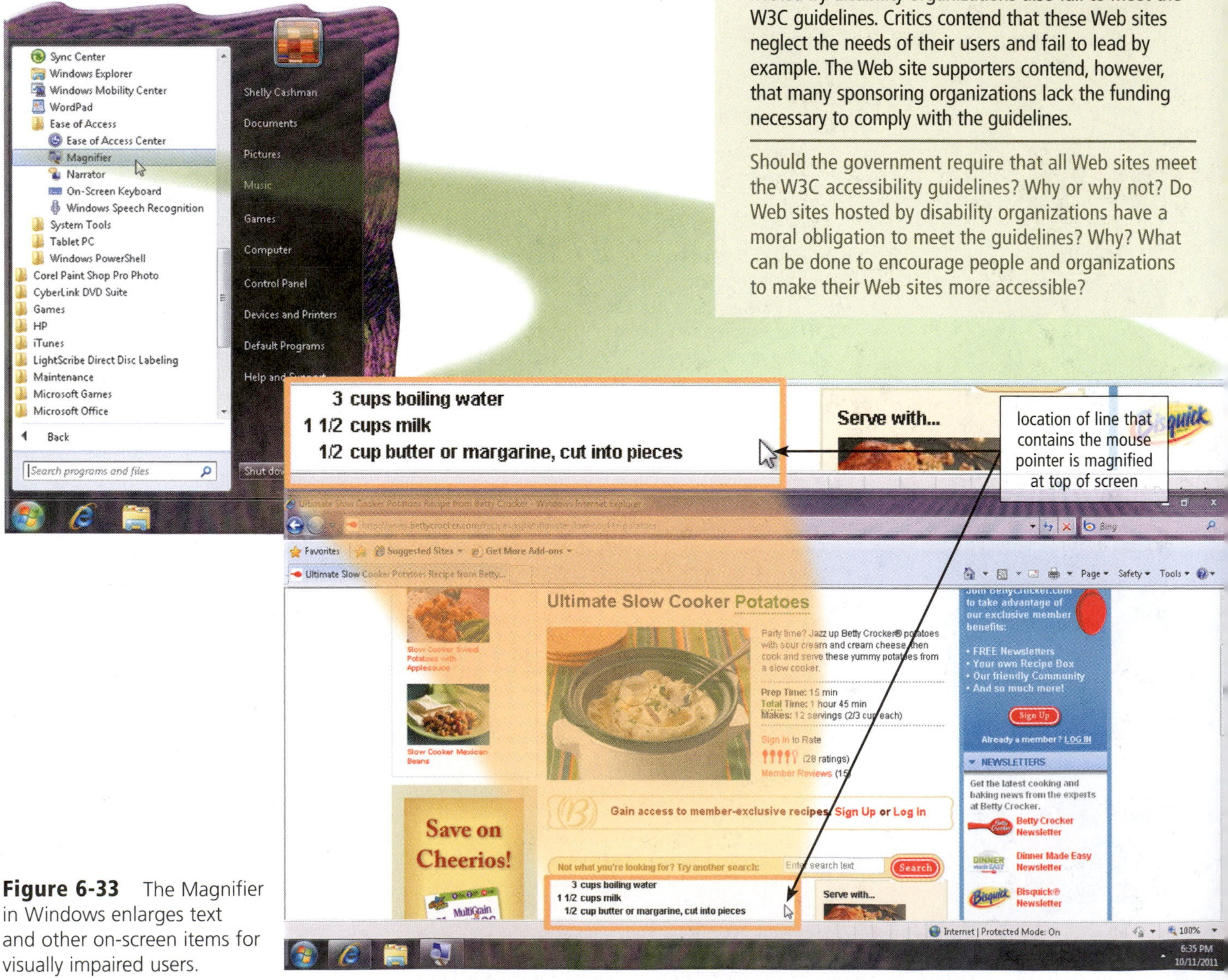

Figure 6-33 The Magnifier in Windows enlarges text and other on-screen items for visually impaired users.

Visually impaired users can change Windows settings, such as increasing the size or changing the color of the text to make the words easier to read. Instead of using a monitor, blind users can work with voice output via Windows Narrator. That is, the computer reads the information that is displayed on the screen. Another alternative is a *Braille printer*, which prints information on paper in Braille (Figure 6-34).

Figure 6-34
A Braille printer.

QUIZ YOURSELF 6-3

Instructions: Find the true statement below. Then, rewrite the remaining false statements so that they are true.

1. A digital light processing (DLP) projector uses tiny lightbulbs to reflect light.
2. Many personal computer users attach surround sound printer systems to their computers to generate a higher-quality sound.
3. Multifunction peripherals require less space than having a separate printer, scanner, copy machine, and fax machine.
4. Some game controllers and mobile devices include real-time action, which is a technology that sends resistance to the device in response to actions of the user.

Quiz Yourself Online: To further check your knowledge of pages 323 through 329, visit the Computer Concepts CourseMate Web site at www.cengagebrain.com, navigate to the Chapter 6 Quiz Yourself resource for this book, and then click Objectives 7 – 9.

Chapter Summary

Computers process and organize data (input) into information (output). This chapter described the various methods of output and several commonly used output devices. Output devices presented were display devices; printers; speakers, headphones, and earbuds; data projectors; interactive whiteboards; and force-feedback game controllers and tactile output.

Computer Usage @ Work

Space Exploration

Watching the television closely, you hear the announcer count the seconds until the spacecraft lifts off from its launch pad: "Three, two, one, and we have liftoff." The engines ignite and the glow from the burning fuel illuminates the night sky as it begins its journey toward the International Space Station. As you sit back and watch, mesmerized by the thought that a group of astronauts are accomplishing something of which you only could dream, hundreds of individuals and computers are working behind the scenes to ensure a safe mission.

Because space exploration is fraught with danger, it is extremely important that all decisions be made with precision and that personnel become aware of problems before the problems become too serious. For instance, space vehicles contain a plethora of sensors that measure environmental variables such as temperature, velocity, position, and altitude. If the sensors return readings outside an acceptable range, computers correct any problems or notify mission managers as necessary. Employees work around the clock monitoring the output from the spacecraft sensors while it is in flight and communicating to astronauts any actions required to ensure a continued safe mission.

In addition to keeping the spacecraft safe while in orbit, computers also help guide the spacecraft into and out of orbit. To reach the International Space Station, spacecraft can be launched safely only during specified launch time frames. Once the spacecraft is launched, it must travel in a precise direction at an exact velocity to ensure a successful mission. As the mission nears completion and a capsule containing the astronauts reenters the atmosphere, onboard computers position the capsule precisely so that the extreme temperatures at the reentry interface do not cause catastrophic damage. Furthermore, these onboard computers help to ensure that the capsule touches down in a safe location.

With billions of dollars spent on space travel, computers play a vital role in guaranteeing the safety of the space vehicle, the astronauts, and those of us on Earth.

For more information, visit the Computer Concepts CourseMate Web site at www.cengagebrain.com, navigate to the Chapter 6 Computer Usage @ Work resource for this book, and then click Space Exploration.

High-Tech Talk

3-D Graphics: Creating a Realistic Experience

Three-dimensional (3-D) graphics, which appear to have height, width, and depth, give realistic qualities to objects in computer programs, particularly computer games. Although you view computer games on a two-dimensional (2-D) computer screen, modern technology creates a 3-D experience by adding the appearance of depth. A game programmer can give single objects or an entire virtual world a 3-D appearance.

Creating a 3-D appearance first requires that you create a wireframe. A *wireframe* is a series of lines, curves, and shapes arranged to resemble an object in a 3-D world (Figure 6-35a). Most 3-D wireframes, for example, consist of a series of polygons. A completed wireframe enables you to identify the shape of the object, although it appears to be hollow. To transform the appearance of the 3-D object from hollow to solid, you add a surface to the wireframe (Figure 6-35b). Some 3-D graphics are composed of more than one wireframe. When adding a surface, it is important to make the object look as realistic as possible by adding color, texture, and reflectance. *Reflectance* refers to the amount of light the object's surface reflects.

With the surface added to a wireframe, you next consider how the object will be lit from one or more lighting sources. Some people create 3-D graphics using a technique called ray-tracing. *Ray-tracing* involves drawing an imaginary path that rays of light follow as they leave their source and then land on an object. The light intensity will be greater on some portions of the object and less on other portions. In addition, the object also might cast a shadow once it is lit from a particular angle.

When creating a 3-D world, the next considerations are perspective and depth of field. *Perspective* refers to differences in how objects appear in relation to one another when they are close to you, versus farther away. Objects appearing close may seem to be spaced apart. As they move farther away from you, they become closer to one another. A technique for calculating which objects appear in front of or behind one another is called the *Z-Buffer*, named after the imaginary axis from the screen to the distant horizon. *Depth of field* gives the appearance that objects farther from you are less focused than closer objects.

Anti-aliasing is the final technique in creating 3-D objects that appear in a 3-D world. *Anti-aliasing* makes curved and diagonal lines appear straight. When computers render graphics with curved and diagonal lines, they often appear jagged. Anti-aliasing inserts additional colored pixels that give the appearance of a smooth edge. All these techniques combined create a realistic 3-D graphic (Figure 6-35c).

The complex nature of 3-D technology requires more computing power in order to render a graphic in an acceptable period of time. For example, computer gamers often buy computers designed for gaming so that a lack of performance does not slow their game. Gaming computers often have faster processors, several gigabytes of RAM, and one or more video cards containing at least 256 MB of RAM. These video cards also might support *DirectX*, which is a programming interface that allows game programmers direct access to enhanced hardware features. For some computer games to work properly, they require a video card that supports a specific version of DirectX. For example, if a game is programmed using the DirectX 11 standard, the video card also must support DirectX 11 for the game to work.

Although game programmers spend many hours creating 3-D graphics for programs such as computer games, the results are rewarding when a player faces an experience so realistic that it is difficult to differentiate between the game and reality.

For more information, visit the Computer Concepts CourseMate Web site at www.cengagebrain.com, navigate to the Chapter 6 High-Tech Talk resource for this book, and then click 3-D Graphics.

Figure 6-35b (adding surface)

Figure 6-35a (wireframe)

Figure 6-35c (completed 3-D graphic)

Figure 6-35
The development of a 3-D graphic.

Companies on the Cutting Edge

HP Hardware and Software Products Leader

One of the more famous real estate parcels in the United States is the birthplace of the Silicon Valley: the garage where Stanford University friends William Hewlett and David Packard developed various electronic products. Their first success in 1938 was an oscillator used to test sound equipment.

Today *HP* (*Hewlett-Packard*) has become the world's top manufacturer of ink-jet and laser printers, multifunction peripherals, desktop and notebook computers, and servers. It also is a leading software company with products for networking and storage management.

In 2009, HP introduced the first workstation with a six-core AMD Opteron processor, delivering high productivity for multi-threaded programs. HP also ranked ninth in the 2009 FORTUNE 500 ranking.

SAMSUNG ELECTRONICS Top Consumer Electronics Manufacturer

Products branded as "Wow, Simple, Inclusive" are part of *SAMSUNG Electronics*' presence as the world's leading consumer electronics company. Based in Seoul, South Korea, SAMSUNG manufactures more than 60 categories of products including flash memory, plasma monitors, mobile devices, laser printers, and home appliances.

The company was founded in 1969 and originally manufactured electronic home appliances such as televisions, refrigerators, washers, and air conditioners. It merged with Samsung Semiconductor & Communications in 1988 and has grown to become the world's second largest cell phone manufacturer.

The company introduced the world's slimmest watch-phone device in 2009. This device features a full touch screen that allows users to stay connected. By 2013, Samsung Electronics plans to be a leading eco-friendly company.

 For more information, visit the Computer Concepts CourseMate Web site at www.cengagebrain.com and then navigate to the Chapter 6 Companies on the Cutting Edge resource for this book.

Technology Trailblazers

STEVE JOBS Apple and Pixar Cofounder

Apricot orchards once grew in the area known today as California's Silicon Valley. *Steve Jobs* was raised in this area, but he has found his fruit of choice to be an Apple. As Apple's CEO, Jobs continues to use his charismatic personality and motivational skills to lead the company and lists himself on patent applications as the coinventor of more than 100 Apple products.

Jobs cofounded Apple in 1976 in his parents' garage with Steve Wozniak. Five years later, he was worth $200 million and on the cover of *Time* magazine at the age of 26. By that time he had helped build the first desktop personal computer, marketed an innovative operating system, and cofounded the Apple Computer Corporation.

Jobs also cofounded Pixar Animation Studios, which merged with The Walt Disney Company in 2006. Pixar and its employees have received more than 100 awards and nominations.

URSULA BURNS Xerox Chairman and CEO

When *Ursula Burns* was nominated to chair Xerox Corporation in 2010, two milestones were reached: she became the first African-American woman to lead a major American company and the first woman to succeed another woman in that role.

She began working at Xerox 30 years earlier as a mechanical engineering summer intern. After earning her bachelor's and master's degrees in that field, she worked in various areas of the corporation, including office network printing, global research, product development, manufacturing, and planning. When Burns was named Xerox's president in 2007, her leadership role expanded to include the information technology, corporate marketing, and human resources departments.

Forbes and *Fortune* have named Burns as one of the most powerful women in the world. She serves as advisor to several educational and community organizations, including FIRST (For Inspiration and Recognition of Science and Technology) and the White House's STEM (Science, Technology, Engineering, and Math) program.

 For more information, visit the Computer Concepts CourseMate Web site at www.cengagebrain.com and then navigate to the Chapter 6 Technology Trailblazers resource for this book.

Chapter Review

The Chapter Review reinforces the main concepts presented in this chapter.

To listen to an audio version of this Chapter Review, visit the Computer Concepts CourseMate Web site at www.cengagebrain.com and then navigate to the Chapter 6 Chapter Review resource for this book.

1. **What Are the Four Types of Output?** **Output** is data that has been processed into a useful form. Computers process data (input) into information (output). Four categories of output are text, graphics, audio, and video. An **output device** is any hardware component that conveys information to one or more people. Commonly used output devices include display devices; printers; speakers, headphones, and earbuds; data projectors; interactive whiteboards; and force-feedback game controllers and tactile output.

2. **What Are the Characteristics of Various Display Devices?** A **display device**, or simply *display*, is an output device that visually conveys text, graphics, and video information and consists of a screen and the components that produce the information on the screen. Desktop computers typically use a **monitor** as their display device; most mobile computers and devices integrate the display into the same physical case. LCD monitors, LCD screens, and plasma monitors are types of flat-panel displays. A *flat-panel display* is a lightweight display device with a shallow depth that typically uses LCD or gas plasma technology. An **LCD monitor** is a desktop monitor that uses a liquid crystal display to produce images. A **plasma monitor** is a display device that uses gas plasma technology, which substitutes a layer of gas for the liquid crystal material in an LCD monitor. A **CRT monitor** is a desktop monitor that contains a *cathode-ray tube* (*CRT*). CRT monitors take up more desk space and thus are not used much today.

3. **What Factors Affect the Quality of an LCD monitor or LCD screen?** The quality of an LCD monitor or LCD screen depends primarily on its resolution, response time, brightness, dot pitch, and contrast ratio. **Resolution** is the number of horizontal and vertical pixels in a display device; a higher resolution uses a greater number of pixels and provides a sharper image. *Response time* is the time in milliseconds that it takes to turn a pixel on or off. Brightness of an LCD monitor or LCD screen is measured in nits; the higher the nits, the brighter the image. A *nit* is a unit of visible light intensity equal to one *candela* per square meter. *Dot pitch*, or *pixel pitch*, is the distance in millimeters between pixels on a display device. *Contrast ratio* describes the difference in light intensity between the brightest white and darkest black that can be displayed on a monitor.

Visit the Computer Concepts CourseMate Web site at www.cengagebrain.com, navigate to the Chapter 6 Quiz Yourself resource for this book, and then click Objectives 1 – 3.

4. **What Are the Various Ways to Print?** Users can print by connecting a computer to a printer with a cable that plugs in a port on the computer. *Bluetooth printing* uses radio waves to transmit output to a printer. With *infrared printing*, a computer or other device communicates with the printer via infrared light waves. Some digital cameras connect directly to a printer via a cable; others store images on memory cards that can be removed and inserted in the printer. Networked computers can communicate with the network printer via cables or wirelessly.

5. **How Is a Nonimpact Printer Different from an Impact Printer?** A **printer** is an output device that produces text and graphics on a physical medium, such as paper. A **nonimpact printer** forms characters and graphics on a piece of paper without actually striking the paper. Some spray ink, while others use heat or pressure to create images. Commonly used nonimpact printers are ink-jet printers, photo printers, laser printers, thermal printers, mobile printers, label and postage printers, plotters, and large-format printers. An **impact printer** forms characters and graphics on a piece of paper by striking a mechanism against an inked ribbon that physically contacts the paper. These printers commonly produce *near letter quality* (*NLQ*) output, which is print quality slightly less clear than what is acceptable for business letters. Two commonly used types of impact printers are a **dot-matrix printer** and a **line printer**.

6. **What Are Ink-Jet Printers, Photo Printers, Laser Printers, Multifunction Peripherals, Thermal Printers, Mobile Printers, Label and Postage Printers, and Plotters and Large-Format Printers?** An **ink-jet printer** is a type of nonimpact printer that forms characters and graphics by spraying tiny drops of liquid ink onto a piece of paper. One factor that influences the quality of an ink-jet printer is its resolution. Printer resolution is measured

Chapter Review

by the number of *dots per inch* (*dpi*) a printer can print. A **photo printer** is a color printer that produces photo-lab-quality pictures. A **laser printer** is a high-speed, high-quality nonimpact printer that operates in a manner similar to a copy machine, creating images using a laser beam and powdered ink, called *toner*. Laser printers usually print at faster speeds than ink-jet printers. A **multifunction peripheral** (MFP), or *all-in-one device*, is a single device that looks like a printer or a copy machine but provides the functionality of a printer, scanner, copy machine, and perhaps a fax machine. Some MFPs use color ink-jet printer technology; others include a black-and-white or color laser printer. The primary disadvantage of these devices is that if the device breaks down, you lose all four functions. A **thermal printer** generates images by pushing electrically heated pins against heat-sensitive paper. They are inexpensive, but the print quality is low and the images tend to fade over time. A **mobile printer** is a small, lightweight, battery-powered printer that allows a mobile user to print from a notebook computer or other mobile device. A **label printer** is a small printer that prints on an adhesive-type material that can be placed on a variety of items. Most label printers also print bar codes. A *postage printer* is a special type of label printer that has a built-in scale and prints postage stamps. **Plotters** are sophisticated printers used to produce high-quality drawings, such as blueprints, maps, and circuit diagrams. A **large-format printer** uses ink-jet technology on a large scale to create photo-realistic-quality color prints.

Visit the Computer Concepts CourseMate Web site at www.cengagebrain.com, navigate to the Chapter 6 Quiz Yourself resource for this book, and then click Objectives 4 – 6.

7. What Are the Uses and Characteristics of Speakers, Headphones, and Earbuds? Speakers, headphones, and earbuds are three commonly used audio output devices. An **audio output device** is a component of a computer that produces music, speech, or other sounds. Many personal computer users add stereo **speakers** to their computers, including game consoles and mobile devices, to generate higher-quality sounds. With headphones or earbuds, only the individual wearing the headphones or earbuds hears the sound from the computer. The difference is that **headphones** cover or are placed outside of the ear, whereas **earbuds**, or *earphones*, rest inside the ear canal. A *headset* is a device that functions as both headphones and a microphone, so that users' hands are free for typing or other activities while listening to audio output.

8. What Are the Purposes and Features of Data Projectors, Interactive Whiteboards, and Force-Feedback Game Controllers and Mobile Devices? A **data projector** is a device that takes the text and images displaying on a computer screen and projects them onto a larger screen so that an audience of people can see the image clearly. An *LCD projector* attaches directly to a computer and uses its own light source to display information shown on the computer screen. A *digital light processing* (*DLP*) *projector* uses tiny mirrors to reflect light. An **interactive whiteboard** is a touch-sensitive device, resembling a dry-erase board, that displays the image on a connected computer screen. Joysticks, wheels, gamepads, and motion-sensing game controllers are input devices used to control actions of a player or object in computer games, simulations, and video games. Today's joysticks, wheels, gamepads, and motion-sensing game controllers also include *force feedback*, which is a technology that sends resistance to the device in response to actions of the user. Some input devices include *tactile output* that provides the user with a physical response from the device.

9. What Output Options Are Available for Physically Challenged Users? Hearing-impaired users can instruct programs to display words instead of sound. The Magnifier in Windows enlarges text and other items in a window on the screen. Visually impaired users can enlarge items on the screen and change other settings, such as increasing the size or changing the color of text to make words easier to read. Blind users can work with voice output instead of a monitor via Windows Narrator. Another alternative is a *Braille printer*, which prints information in Braille on paper.

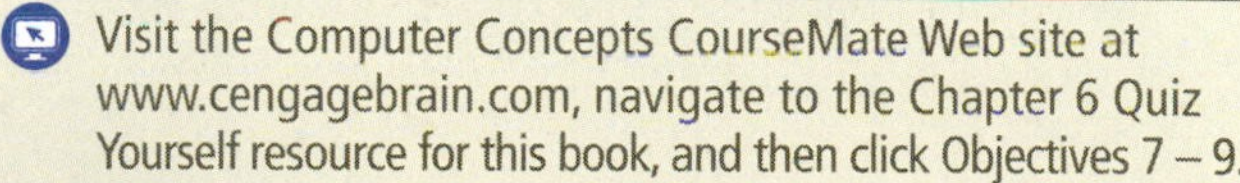
Visit the Computer Concepts CourseMate Web site at www.cengagebrain.com, navigate to the Chapter 6 Quiz Yourself resource for this book, and then click Objectives 7 – 9.

Key Terms

You should know the Primary Terms and be familiar with the Secondary Terms. The list below helps focus your study.

To see an example of and a definition for each term, and to access current and additional information from the Web, visit the Computer Concepts CourseMate Web site at www.cengagebrain.com and then navigate to the Chapter 6 Key Terms resource for this book.

Primary Terms

(shown in bold-black characters in the chapter)

audio output device (323)
CRT monitor (313)
data projector (325)
display device (306)
dot-matrix printer (323)
earbuds (324)
HDTV (312)
headphones (324)
impact printer (322)
ink-jet printer (316)
interactive whiteboard (326)
label printer (322)
large-format printer (322)
laser printer (319)
LCD monitor (307)
line printer (323)
liquid crystal display (LCD) (308)
mobile printer (321)
monitor (306)
multifunction peripheral (320)
nonimpact printer (315)
output (304)
output device (305)
photo printer (318)
plasma monitor (311)
plotters (322)
printer (313)
resolution (308)
speakers (323)
thermal printer (321)
voice output (325)

photo printer (318)

Secondary Terms

(shown in italic characters in the chapter)

active-matrix display (308)
all-in-one device (320)
aspect ratio (310)
bit depth (310)
Bluetooth printing (314)
Braille printer (329)
candela (310)
cathode-ray tube (CRT) (313)
color depth (310)
continuous-form paper (323)
contrast ratio (310)
digital light processing (DLP) projector (326)
digital photo printer (321)
digital television (DTV) (312)
display (306)
DisplayPort (310)
dot pitch (310)
dots per inch (dpi) (316)
DVI (Digital Video Interface) port (310)
dye-sublimation printer (321)
earphones (324)
flat-panel display (306)
force feedback (326)
graphics processing unit (GPU) (310)
hard copy (313)
HDMI (High-Definition Media Interface) port (310)
head-mounted display (308)
headset (324)
high-definition television (312)
infrared printing (314)
Internet postage (322)
landscape orientation (314)
LCD projector (325)
monochrome (306)
native resolution (308)
near letter quality (NLQ) (322)
nit (310)
organic LED (OLED) (308)
page description language (PDL) (319)
passive-matrix display (308)
PCL (Printer Control Language) (319)
PictBridge (318)
pixel (308)
pixel pitch (310)
portrait orientation (313)
postage printer (322)
PostScript (319)
printout (313)
response time (308)
satellite speakers (324)
soft copy (306)
subwoofer (324)
S-video port (310)
SVGA (311)
SXGA (311)
tactile output (327)
TFT (thin-film transistor) display (308)
thermal wax-transfer printer (321)
toner (320)
UXGA (311)
viewable size (313)
VoIP (325)
widescreen (307)
WQXGA (311)
WSXGA (311)
WUXGA (311)
WXGA (311)
XGA (311)

Checkpoint

The Checkpoint exercises test your knowledge of the chapter concepts. The page number containing the answer appears in parentheses after each exercise. The Beyond the Book exercises will help broaden your understanding of the concepts presented in this chapter.

To complete the Checkpoint exercises interactively, visit the Computer Concepts CourseMate Web site at www.cengagebrain.com and then navigate to the Chapter 6 Checkpoint resource for this book.

True/False Mark T for True and F for False.

_____ 1. The form of output generated by a computer varies depending on the hardware and software being used and the requirements of the user. (304)

_____ 2. Information on a display device sometimes is called soft copy. (306)

_____ 3. Most mobile computers and devices do not integrate the display and other components into the same physical case. (306)

_____ 4. Widescreen LCD monitors are wider than they are tall. (307)

_____ 5. Brightness describes the difference in light intensity between the brightest white and darkest black that can be displayed on an LCD monitor. (310)

_____ 6. An HDMI (High-Definition Media Interface) port combines S-video with high-definition (HD) television and video. (310)

_____ 7. With game consoles, the output device often is a television. (312)

_____ 8. A printout in landscape orientation is taller than it is wide. (313)

_____ 9. With Bluetooth printing, a computer or other device transmits output to a printer via infrared light waves. (314)

_____ 10. An all-in-one device is a single device that looks like a printer or a copy machine but provides the functionality of a printer, scanner, copy machine, and perhaps a fax machine. (320)

_____ 11. An impact printer forms characters and graphics on a piece of paper without actually striking the paper. (322)

_____ 12. A headset is a device that functions as both headphones and a Web cam. (324)

_____ 13. An LCD projector uses tiny mirrors to reflect light, which produces crisp, bright, colorful images that remain in focus and can be seen clearly even in a well lit room. (326)

Multiple Choice Select the best answer.

1. Examples of output that primarily contain text-based documents are _____. (304)
   a. drawings, clip art, and photos
   b. music, narrations, and speeches
   c. home movies and live performances
   d. letters, reports, and e-mail messages

2. _____ uses organic molecules that produce an even brighter, easier-to-read display than standard TFT displays. (308)
   a. HDTV b. OLED
   c. LCD d. LED

3. The _____ is an alternative to DVI that also supports HDMI. (310)
   a. DisplayPort
   b. Digital Video Interface
   c. S-video port
   d. standard monitor port

4. A CRT monitor's viewable size is the _____ measurement of the actual viewing area provided by the screen in the monitor. (313)
   a. horizontal b. vertical
   c. three-dimensional d. diagonal

5. Ink-jet printer resolution is measured by the number of _____ a printer can print. (316)
   a. pages per minute (ppm) b. pixels per inch (ppi)
   c. lines per minute (lpm) d. dots per inch (dpi)

6. The primary disadvantage of multifunction peripherals is that _____. (320)
   a. they require more space than having separate devices
   b. if the multifunction peripheral breaks down, all functions are lost
   c. they are significantly more expensive than purchasing each device separately
   d. all of the above

7. A(n) _____ is a touch-sensitive device, resembling a dry-erase board, that displays the image on a connected computer screen. (326)
   a. flatbed scanner b. data projector
   c. interactive whiteboard d. video conference

8. _____ is a technology that sends resistance to a device in response to actions of the user. (326)
   a. An interactive whiteboard b. A CRT
   c. A dance pad d. Force feedback

Checkpoint

Matching Match the terms with their definitions.

_____ 1. display device (306)
_____ 2. LCD monitor (307)
_____ 3. head-mounted display (HMD) (308)
_____ 4. nit (310)
_____ 5. candela (310)
_____ 6. aspect ratio (310)
_____ 7. hard copy (313)
_____ 8. nonimpact printer (315)
_____ 9. audio output device (323)
_____ 10. tactile output (327)

a. printed information that exists physically and is a more permanent form of output
b. component of a computer that produces music, speech, or other sounds, such as beeps
c. defines a display's width relative to its height
d. an output device that visually conveys text, graphics, and video information
e. forms characters and graphics on a piece of paper without actually striking the paper
f. standard unit of luminous intensity
g. a display in a helmet, goggles, or glasses
h. unit of visible light intensity equal to one candela per square meter
i. provides the user with a physical response from a device
j. a desktop monitor that uses a liquid crystal display to produce images

Short Answer Write a brief answer to each of the following questions.

1. How does resolution affect images displayed on a monitor? ____________ How does resolution relate to the size of an LCD monitor or screen? ____________
2. Describe some of the features of HDTV. __________ How do game console users set up the output for the consoles? __________
3. What are two types of wireless printing technology? ____________ How do they differ in how they communicate with a computer or other device? ____________
4. How does an ink-jet printer work? ____________ What are the differences between dye-sublimation printers used by professionals as compared to home or small business users? ____________
5. What might be included with a surround sound system for a computer? ____________ What is audio resolution, and what are three examples of audio resolutions? ____________

Beyond the Book Follow the book element instructions below; present your findings (brief report, presentation, discussion, or other means).

1. Ethics & Issues — Select an Ethics & Issues in this chapter (306, 312, 325, 328), find a recent newspaper/magazine article that supports one point of view presented, and then evaluate the article.
2. Computer Usage @ Work — Use the Web or a recent newspaper/magazine to locate three additional unique usages of computer technology in the space exploration industry (329). What makes the use of these technologies unique to the space exploration industry?
3. Companies on the Cutting Edge and Technology Trailblazers — Use the Web or a recent business newspaper/magazine to locate an interesting fact about HP, SAMSUNG Electronics, Steve Jobs, or Anne Mulcahy that was not presented in the chapter (331).
4. High-Tech Talk — Locate a recent newspaper/magazine article that discusses topics related to 3-D Graphics (330). Would you recommend the article you found? Why or why not?
5. FAQs and Web Links — Use the Web or a recent newspaper/magazine to locate three additional facts about an FAQ (306, 309, 311, 312, 318, 320) and Web Link (307, 310, 317, 318, 320, 322, 324, 326) that were not presented in the chapter.
6. Looking Ahead — Use the Web or a recent newspaper/magazine to discover additional uses of the technology presented in Reusable Paper May Become a Disappearing Act (314).
7. Innovative Computing — Use the Web or a recent newspaper/magazine to locate two additional interesting facts about Get the Picture with Digital Frames (308).
8. Making Use of the Web — Visit three of the Environment sites (130) and outline the information on each Web site and the possible uses for each Web site.
9. Digital Video Technology — Select a topic from the Digital Video Technology feature (344) and then create a presentation about the topic using the Web or a newspaper/magazine article.

Learn It Online

The Learn It Online exercises are interactive Web exercises designed to reinforce and expand your understanding of the chapter concepts. The descriptions below briefly summarize each exercise.

To complete the Learn It Online exercises, visit the Computer Concepts CourseMate Web site at www.cengagebrain.com, navigate to the Chapter 6 resources for this book, click the link for the exercise you want to complete, and then read the instructions.

1 At the Movies — SID: Size Matters
Watch a movie to learn about 100-inch HD screens and dual-imaging screens making appearances at a technology trade show and applications of two-way viewing, and then answer questions about the movie.

2 Video and Audio: You Review It — HDTV
Search for, choose, and write a review of a video, podcast, or vodcast that discusses HDTV.

3 Student Edition Labs — Peripheral Devices and Working with Graphics
Enhance your understanding and knowledge about the motherboard and binary numbers by completing the Peripheral Devices and Working with Graphics Labs.

4 Practice Test
Take a multiple choice test that checks your knowledge of the chapter concepts and review the resulting study guide.

5 Who Wants To Be a Computer Genius^2?
Play the Shelly Cashman Series version of this popular game by answering questions to find out if you are a computer genius. Panic buttons are available to provide assistance during game play.

6 Wheel of Terms
Identify important key terms presented in this chapter by playing the Shelly Cashman Series version of this popular game.

7 You're Hired!
Embark on the path to a career in computers by answering questions and solving puzzles related to concepts discussed in this chapter.

8 Crossword Puzzle Challenge
Complete an interactive crossword puzzle to reinforce concepts presented in this chapter.

9 Windows Exercises
Step through the Windows 7 exercises to learn about your computer, Accessibility options, Magnifier, and adjusting the sound on a computer.

10 Exploring Computer Careers
Read about a career as a graphic designer/illustrator, search for related employment advertisements, and then answer related questions.

11 Web Apps — YouSendIt
Learn how to use YouSendIt to create an e-mail message with an attachment and add options such as premium delivery, password-protected secure delivery, certified delivery with tracking, and return receipt.

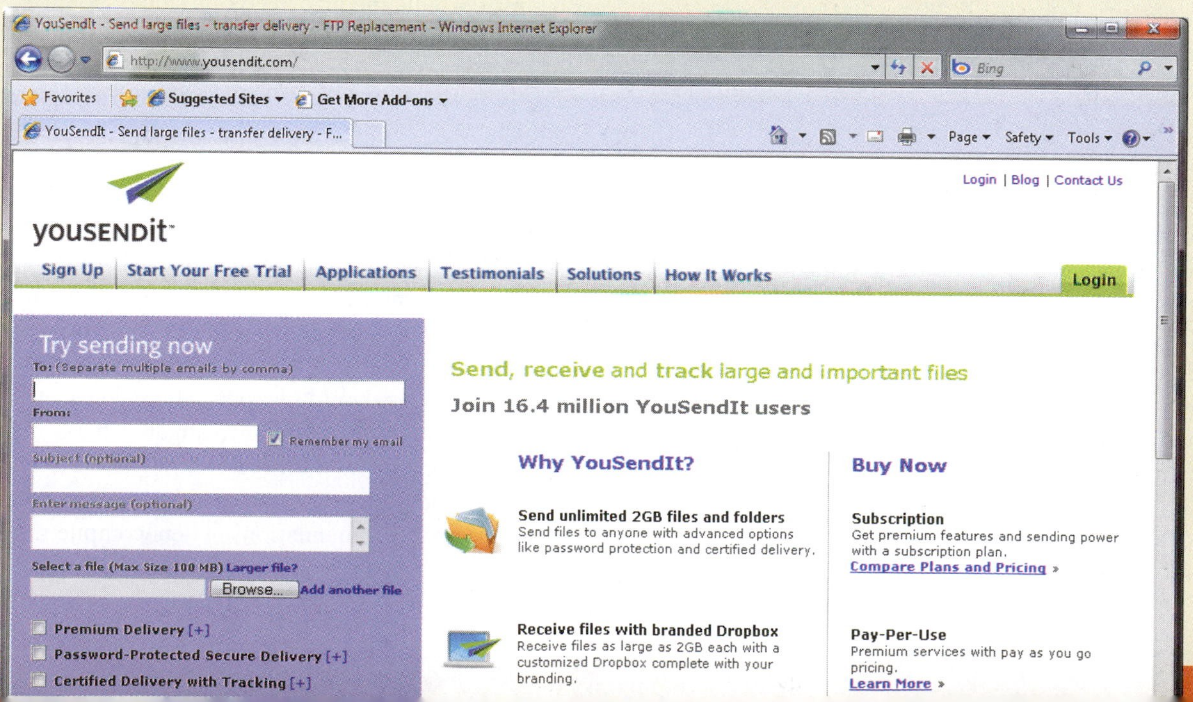

STUDENT ASSIGNMENTS

Problem Solving @ Home

The Problem Solving @ Home exercises extend your knowledge of the chapter concepts by seeking solutions to practical computer problems that you may encounter at home or school. The Collaboration exercise should be completed with a team.

In the real world, practical problems often can be solved in multiple ways. Provide one solution to each of the following problems using available resources, such as articles on the Web or in print, blogs, podcasts, videos, television, user guides, other individuals, and electronics and computer stores. You may need to use multiple resources to obtain an answer. Present your solutions in the form requested by your instructor (brief report, presentation, discussion, or other means).

1. **Smeared Printouts** Each time you print a picture on photo paper using your photo printer, the photo comes out of the printer smeared. What is one step you can take that might prevent the ink from smearing while the photo is printing?
2. **Damaged Monitor** You have just moved into a new house. After unpacking your notebook computer and turning it on, you notice that the center of the screen contains a dark spot, about the size of a quarter. You try cleaning the monitor, but the dark spot does not go away. What might have caused this?
3. **Image Not Displaying** When you turn on your computer and monitor, the monitor's power light is flashing orange and no image is displayed. Normally, when your monitor is on, an image is displayed, and the power light is green. What might be wrong?
4. **Monitor Not Working** You just purchased a second monitor for your computer. When you plug in the monitor, turn on the computer, and start Windows, the new monitor does not display an image. What steps will you take to display an image correctly on your new, second monitor?
5. **Incorrect Resolution** You installed a new video card that supports higher resolutions. After installing the video card and turning on the computer, the components of the Windows desktop (taskbar, icons, and gadgets) appear larger than normal. You attempt to change the resolution, but Windows will not allow the resolution to be set any higher than 640 × 480. You know that your new video card can support higher resolutions. What are your next steps?
6. **Paper Loading Incorrectly** Having depleted your supply of business cards, you decide to print temporary business cards to use until you receive the new cards from your company. You use Microsoft Publisher to design your business cards and then print them on business card paper. When you print the cards, however, the printer loads the paper unevenly. As a result, the printing on the business cards is crooked. What steps will you take to correct this?
7. **Dim Screen** While using your notebook computer, the screen suddenly becomes dim. You set the brightness to its highest setting before it dimmed, and wonder why it suddenly changed. After resetting the brightness to its highest setting, you continue working. What might have caused the screen to dim?
8. **Malfunctioning Earbud** While listening to music on your portable media player, one side of your earbuds suddenly stops working. What might have caused this?

Collaboration

9. **Allocating Printers** You and two of your classmates volunteered at a new private school in your community. A local technology company has donated five printers to the school, including a color laser printer, a black-and-white laser printer, a line printer, and two ink-jet printers. The school, however, is having difficulty deciding where the printers should be placed to be the most effective. The school has asked you and your classmates to recommend locations for the printers. In a team of three people, determine where these printers should be placed in a small private school. One team member should research where color and black-and-white laser printers might be used most effectively, one team member should investigate where line printers would be used, and one team member should provide a recommendation regarding where the ink-jet printers should be placed. After each team member has completed his or her research, the teammates should present their findings to each other and offer any suggestions or recommendations. Then, compile the team's findings in a report and submit it to your instructor.

Problem Solving @ Work

The Problem Solving @ Work exercises extend your knowledge of the chapter concepts by seeking solutions to practical computer problems that you may encounter at work. The Collaboration exercise should be completed with a team.

In the real world, practical problems often can be solved in multiple ways. Provide one solution to each of the following problems using available resources, such as articles on the Web or in print, blogs, podcasts, videos, television, user guides, other individuals, and electronics and computer stores. You may need to use multiple resources to obtain an answer. Present your solutions in the form requested by your instructor (brief report, presentation, discussion, or other means).

1. **Junk Faxes** Your company has a fax machine that sometimes receives faxes advertising low software prices and low mortgage rates at various times throughout the day. These faxes not only are a nuisance, they also are wasting toner and paper. What actions might you take to eliminate or minimize this problem?
2. **Misaligned Printer** While working at your job fulfilling orders in a warehouse, you notice that each time an invoice prints on the dot-matrix printer, the customer and order information does not align properly with the rows and columns on the preprinted forms. What steps will you take to correct this?
3. **Problem with Printouts** You have printed slide handouts on your color printer to distribute during a presentation you are giving later in the day. When you retrieve the printouts from the printer, you notice that the colors do not look right. In fact, anything that was a shade of blue on your monitor did not print on handout. What might be wrong?
4. **Speaker Interference** You work in a cubicle located in a room containing several other cubicles. Whenever a nearby coworker's cell phone rings, a strange sound comes from your computer speakers. You turn the speaker volume lower, but still hear the sound. Why might this be happening? What can you do to resolve the problem?
5. **Unrecognizable Characters** You and your coworkers print to a printer connected to the company network. You started to print a 40-page document, but realized immediately that the document needed one more change, so you cancelled the print job. After making the change and printing the document again, you walk to the printer and find the printer printing many pages with unrecognizable characters. What might be wrong?
6. **Printer Not Ready** While attempting to print an expense report to submit to your supervisor, your computer displays an error message stating that your printer is not ready. What could be causing this?
7. **Monitors Reversed** You have two monitors set up on your desk at work: the monitor on the left is your primary monitor and displays the taskbar, and you typically use the monitor on the right to display your e-mail program. When you arrive at work and log into Windows, you realize that the monitor on the right is now the primary monitor. What might have happened?
8. **Printer Error** Your printer is displaying an error message stating that the toner needs to be replaced; however, the print quality is acceptable each time you print a document. Why might the printer ask you to change the toner when it still is printing acceptable copies?

Collaboration

9. **Computers in Space Exploration** The space tourism industry is gaining worldwide attention. Many more people might express interest in experiencing outer space if prices become more reasonable and safety concerns are minimized. Computers help ensure safety by helping the space vehicles to fly with great precision, but human intervention also is necessary. Form a team of three people and determine how computer output can provide enough information to ensure a safe experience. One team member should research current space exploration and data returned from space vehicles that proves useful. Another team member should research how space vehicles collect this data and present it in a useful form, and the other team member should think of additional ways that computer output can assist in space exploration. Write a brief report summarizing your findings.

Learn How To

The Learn How To activities step you through fundamental technology skills when using a computer. The Learn How To exercises enable you to become more proficient with these skills.

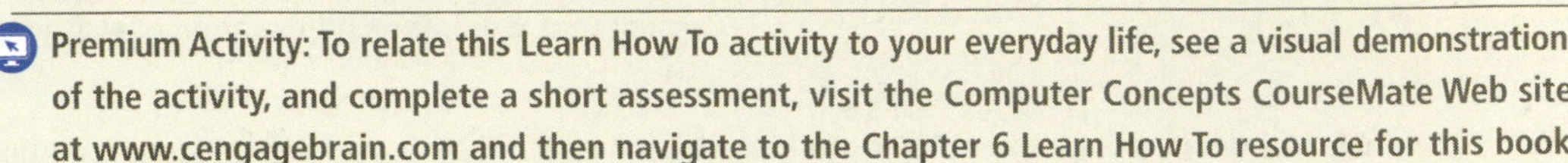
Premium Activity: To relate this Learn How To activity to your everyday life, see a visual demonstration of the activity, and complete a short assessment, visit the Computer Concepts CourseMate Web site at www.cengagebrain.com and then navigate to the Chapter 6 Learn How To resource for this book.

Learn How To 1: Make a Video and Upload It to YouTube

As digital video cameras become smaller and more affordable, many individuals are choosing to create digital recordings of everyday events. In the past, video cameras were bulky, expensive, and required big VCR tapes. Video cameras now are digital and small enough to take anywhere. They also have the capability to transfer video footage to a computer, allowing you to reuse tapes. The increase in individuals storing videos on their computer has prompted companies to develop media sharing Web sites, such as YouTube, for people to post their videos online for others to view. This is especially helpful when you would like to share a video of a memorable event, such as your child's first steps, with a relative across the country who was unable to experience it in person.

Transferring a Video from a Digital Video Camera to a Computer

1. Connect the digital video camera to the computer using the provided USB or FireWire cable. If the camera does not have a cable and stores the digital video on a memory card, remove the memory card from the camera and then insert it into your computer.
2. You can transfer the video from a digital video camera to a computer in one or more of the following ways, depending upon the type of camera you own:
   a. Start the program that came with the digital video camera and follow the manufacturer's instructions for importing the video to a hard disk.
   b. When the digital video camera or memory card is displayed as a removable disk in Windows, copy the video file(s) to the hard disk.
   c. Open Windows Live Movie Maker and click the 'Import from device' command on the Movie Maker menu to import video from the digital video camera.
3. Your video should be less than 10 minutes, less than 2 GB in size, and one of the following file formats: .AVI, .MOV, .WMV, or .MPG. If your video does not meet these requirements, you either should create your video again or use software such as Windows Live Movie Maker to change its file format or reduce its length or size.
4. Double-click the video on the computer to make sure that it plays in its entirety and that you can hear audio.
5. If you would like to free space on the digital camera's media, delete the original video file(s) from the digital video camera or memory card.
6. Disconnect the digital video camera from the computer or remove the memory card from the computer.

Log into YouTube

1. Start a Web browser, type `youtube.com` in the Address bar, and then press the ENTER key to display the YouTube — Broadcast Yourself Web page.
2. Click the Sign In link.
3. Type your user name and password, and then click the Sign In button. If you do not have a YouTube account, click the Sign up for YouTube! link and follow the instructions to sign up for a new YouTube account.

Upload the Video

1. Click the Upload button to display the Video File Upload Web page.
2. Click the Upload Video button to display the 'Select file to upload' dialog box. Locate the video on your computer that you wish to upload and then click the Open button.
3. If necessary, change the title of the video to one you prefer.
4. Enter the description and tags for this video. If you would like to make it easy for people to find your video, enter a detailed description and several tags.
5. Select a video category from the Category drop-down list.
6. If you want to make the video private, click the 'Private (Viewable by you and up to 25 people)' option button.
7. Click the Save Changes button.
8. YouTube will save your changes once the video is finished uploading.

View the Video

1. Point to your user name at the top of the Video File Upload Web page and then click My Videos.
2. Click the Play button to preview the video. Once the video has finished playing, click the Sign Out link to sign out of YouTube.

Learn How To

Exercise

1. Use a digital video camera to create a short video that is less than 20 seconds in length. Save the video to your computer and then sign into YouTube. Upload the video you just created (if you do not have a digital video camera, upload a sample video that is included with Windows or another video on your computer that is not protected by copyright). Once the video has finished uploading, preview it and then send the Web address to your instructor.

Learn How To 2: Control Printing on Your Computer

When you print using a computer, you control printing at two different points: first, before the printing actually begins, and second, after the document has been sent to the printer and either is physically printing or is waiting to be printed. To set the parameters for printing and then print the document, complete the following steps:

1. Click File on the menu bar of the program that will be used for printing and then click Print on the File menu to display the Print dialog box (Figure 6-36). The Print dialog box will vary somewhat depending on the program used. If you are using a program without a menu bar, locate and click the Print command.
2. In the Print dialog box, make the selections for which printer will be used, which pages will be printed, the number of copies to be printed, and any other choices available. For further options, click the Preferences button (or, sometimes, the Properties button) or click the Options button.
3. Click the OK button or the Print button. The document to be printed is sent to a print queue, which is an area on disk storage from which documents actually are printed.

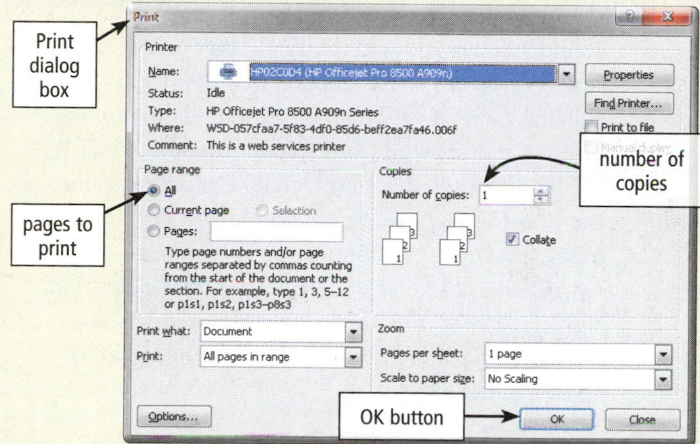

Figure 6-36

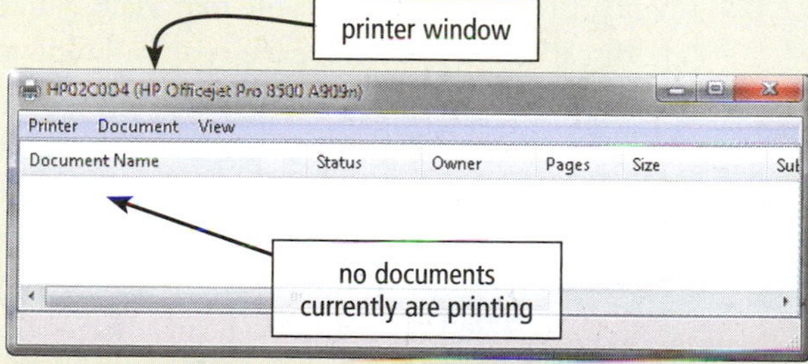

Figure 6-37

When you click the Print button to send the document to the print queue, a printer icon may appear on the Windows taskbar. To see the print queue and control the actual printing of documents on the printer, complete the following steps:

1. If the printer icon appears on the Windows taskbar, double-click it; otherwise, click the Start button on the Windows taskbar, click Control Panel on the Start menu, click the Devices and Printers link, and then double-click the printer icon with the checkmark. The checkmark indicates the default printer. A window opens with the name of the printer on the title bar (Figure 6-37). All documents either printing or waiting to be printed are listed in the window. The Status column indicates whether the document is printing or waiting. In addition, the owner of the file, number of pages, size, date and time submitted, and printer port are listed.
2. If you click Printer on the menu bar in the printer window, you can set printing preferences from the Printer menu. In addition, you can pause all printing and cancel all printing jobs from the Printer menu.
3. If you select a document in the document list and then click Document on the menu bar, you can cancel the selected document for printing, or you can pause the printing for the selected document. To continue printing for the selected document, click Document on the menu bar and then click Resume on the Document menu.

Exercises

1. Start WordPad from the Accessories list. Type `Click Print on the File menu to display the Print dialog box.`
2. Display the Print dialog box and then click the Preferences button. What choices do you have in the Layout sheet? Close the Printing Preferences dialog box. How do you select the number of copies you want to print? How would you print pages 25–35 of a document? Submit your answers to your instructor.

Web Research

The Web Research exercises broaden your understanding of the chapter concepts by presenting questions that require you to search the Web for answers.

1 Search Sleuth

Use one of the search engines listed in Figure 2-10 in Chapter 2 on page 85 or your own favorite search engine to find the answers to the following questions. Copy and paste the Web address from the Web page where you found the answer. Some questions may have more than one answer. If required, submit your answers to your instructor. (1) Which countries have adopted the ENERGY STAR program? (2) What is the function of a Bayer filter in a digital camera? (3) What invention relating to the printing industry did Lord Kelvin patent in 1867? (4) Which output devices did Donald Bitzer design for the PLATO IV computer assisted instruction system at the University of Illinois? (5) Which television network was the first to broadcast a high-definition signal in 1997? (6) Which country has imposed a maximum limit of 100 decibels on all headphones and earbuds sold?

2 Green Computing

Nearly all printer toner and ink-jet cartridges are made of recyclable or reusable materials. Millions are discarded in the trash each year and ultimately reach landfills. One method of reducing the environmental impact of disposing these oil-based products is to buy locally remanufactured cartridges and to refill empty cartridges yourself at office supply stores. View online Web sites that provide information about recycling printer cartridges. Which stores give a credit toward a purchase for returning an empty cartridge? What is the cost of refilling a cartridge compared to buying a comparable new cartridge? What steps are involved in the cartridge remanufacturing process? Do schools in your community sponsor a fundraising opportunity for recycling cartridges? Write a report summarizing your findings, and include a table of links to Web sites that provide additional details.

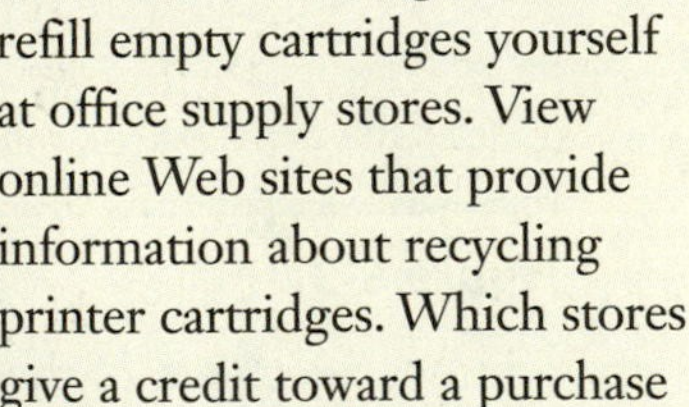

3 Social Networking

Each day, more than 100,000 people register for Friendster, which is one of the top three online social networking Web sites in the world. The San Francisco-based company is popular in more than 75 countries, particularly in Asia. Its mobile Web site, m.friendster.com, allows the more than 110 million registered users to receive and send messages using their smart phones. Visit the Friendster Web site (friendster.com). Follow the instructions to create a Friendster account, log in, and then click the Explore link at the top of the home page. Who are some musicians, athletes, and artists featured in the Fan Profiles section? Click the Classifieds link and then select a city in the Location area. What types of computer listings are shown in the Services area? Click the About Us link at the bottom of the page and then click the Testimonials link. What do members like about Friendster? Summarize the information you read and viewed.

4 Blogs

One of the foremost online music entertainment companies is MTV Networks. Its Web sites feature music and entertainment from throughout the world, including Europe, Asia, and Latin America. MTV has a news blog (newsroom.mtv.com) and a video games blog (multiplayerblog.mtv.com). Visit these two sites and read the blogs. What are the top news stories? Which games are reviewed? VH1.com and CMT.com are the Networks' more popular Web sites, and each has its own blog: blog.vh1.com and blog.cmt.com. Visit these sites and read the blogs. Who is the intended audience? Which musicians and celebrities are featured in the first three posts?

5 Ethics in Action

"Netomania" is not a recognized disorder, but this popular name for Internet Addiction Disorder (IAD) may be affecting some Internet users who spend many hours gaming, blogging, shopping, and social networking. People may be addicted when they spend up to 10 hours a day online, they occasionally binge for extended Internet sessions, and they suffer withdrawal symptoms when they have not been online for some time. Some researchers, however, believe the Internet problem is just a symptom of other psychiatric disorders, such as manic depression. View online sites that provide information about IAD, including the Center for Internet Addiction Recovery (netaddiction.com). Write a report summarizing your findings, and include a table of links to Web sites that provide additional details.

Critical Thinking

The Critical Thinking exercises challenge your assessment and decision-making skills by presenting real-world situations associated with the chapter concepts. The Collaboration exercise should be completed with a team.

To evaluate the situations below, use personal experiences and available resources such as articles on the Web or in print, blogs, podcasts, videos, television, user guides, other individuals, and electronics and computer stores. You may need to use multiple resources to form conclusions and make recommendations.

1. Class Discussion — Music in the Workplace
Your company is purchasing new computers for all employees, and your supervisor asks you if it is necessary to purchase a set of speakers with each computer. Standard job duties do not require speakers, but employees enjoy listening to music quietly at their desk. The added cost of including speakers with the new computers is minimal, but your supervisor is concerned that listening to music while working can decrease job performance. Do you feel that listening to music can increase or decrease your job performance? Is the increase in employee morale worth the cost of purchasing speakers? Could the speakers from employees' old computers work on their new computers? If your supervisor chooses not to include speakers, how else would you recommend he spend the money to improve the computers?

2. Class Presentation — Printer Comparison
Printing requirements vary greatly among users. The local insurance agency where you are employed part time is having their IT person shop for a printer. The owner is aware that you are taking a computer class and has asked you to assist her in deciding which printer to buy. Figure 6-12 on page 314 lists several questions to consider when choosing a printer. Use what you learned in class to answer the questions posed in Figure 6-12. Answer each question according to what you believe to be your employer's needs. Then, use the Web and/or print media to research at least two printers that meet the requirements. Prepare a presentation that identifies the printers you researched, describes their features, and evaluates their advantages and disadvantages. Include in your presentation a recommendation for which printer you would buy and reasons supporting your recommendation.

3. Research — Recurring Costs for Plotters
While printers produce an image on a page from top to bottom, plotters can draw on any part of a page at random and then move on to any other part. This capability, coupled with their capacity to use large sheets of paper, make plotters particularly valuable to people who produce maps or blueprints. A local engineering firm that has used hand drawings for the past 50 years has hired you to assist the head of their drafting department in purchasing three 42-inch plotters with a maximum print length of 300 feet and at least 1200 × 600 dpi. Use the Web and/or print media to research both the initial and recurring costs (ink, paper, maintenance, etc.) of plotters that meet the stated requirements from three different manufacturers. Include in your research how long each plotter takes to produce an image and other noteworthy information. What are the advantages or disadvantages of using a plotter compared to simply creating a drawing by hand? Prepare a report summarizing your findings.

Collaboration

4. Recommending Output Devices
Three accountants at the company where you work want to branch off independently and open a small accounting office with approximately 20 to 25 employees. They have hired your team as consultants to help with the setup. The goal is to determine the type of output devices they will need within the office. Consider the types and number of printers, types and number of display devices, audio devices, microphones, LCD projectors, accommodations or specialized devices for the physically challenged, and whether multifunction peripherals are needed. Form a three-member team and assign each team member one or more categories of output devices. Each team member should use the Web and/or print media to research his or her assignments. Prepare a presentation that combines all team members' findings. List the advantages and disadvantages of the various devices. Include your team's recommendations on which devices would be appropriate and a short explanation of why the team selected each device.

Digital Video Technology

Everywhere you look, people are capturing moments they want to remember. They shoot movies of their vacations, birthday parties, activities, accomplishments, sporting events, weddings, and more. Because of the popularity of digital video cameras and mobile devices with built-in digital cameras, increasingly more people desire to capture their memories digitally, instead of on film. As shown in Figure 1, people have the ability to modify and share the digital videos they create. When you use special hardware and/or software, you can copy, manipulate, and distribute digital videos using your personal computer and the Internet. Amateurs can achieve professional quality results by using more sophisticated hardware and software. This feature describes how to select a video camera, record a video, transfer and manage videos, edit a video, and distribute a video.

Digital recordings deliver significant benefits over film-based movie making. With digital video cameras, recordings reside on storage media such as a hard disk, optical disc, or memory card. Unlike film, storage media can be reused, which reduces costs, saves time, and provides immediate results. Digital technology allows greater control over the creative process, both while recording video and in the editing process. You can check results immediately after recording video to determine whether it meets your expectations. If you are dissatisfied with a video, you can erase it and recapture it, again and again. Today, many mobile devices, such as smart phones and PDAs, allow you to capture video.

Figure 1 A variety of input, output, and storage devices are used by home users to process and edit digital video.

As shown in Figure 1, digital video cameras and mobile devices function as input devices when they transmit video to a personal computer. You can transmit video by connecting the video camera or mobile device to your personal computer using a USB or FireWire port, or by placing the storage media used on the camera or mobile device in the computer. Some cameras and devices also can transmit wirelessly to a computer or to the media sharing Web sites.

When you transmit video that was captured with a digital video camera or mobile device to a computer, you can edit the video using video editing software. If desired, you often can preview the video during the editing process on a television. Finally, you save the finished result to the desired media, such as an optical disc or, perhaps, e-mail the edited video or post it to a media sharing Web site. In this example, an optical disc drive also can be used to input video from an optical disc. Also in the example shown in Figure 1, a mobile device that includes a video camera sends a video directly to a media sharing Web site.

Digital video technology allows you to input, edit, manage, publish, and share your videos using a personal computer. With digital video technology, you can transform home videos into Hollywood-style movies by enhancing the videos with scrolling titles and transitions, cutting out or adding scenes, and adding background music and voice-over narration. The following sections outline the steps involved in the process of using digital video technology.

1 Select a Video Camera

Video cameras record in either analog or digital format. **Analog formats** include 8mm, Hi8, VHS-C, and Super VHS-C. **Digital formats** include Mini-DV, MICROMV, Digital8, DVD, Blu-ray, and HDV (high-definition video format). Some digital video cameras record on an internal hard disk. Others may allow you to record directly on an optical disc drive. Digital video cameras fall into three general categories: high-end consumer,

consumer, and webcasting and monitoring (Figure 2). Consumer digital video cameras are by far the most popular type among consumers. High-end consumer models may support the Blu-ray or HDV standards. A video recorded in high-definition can be played back on a high-definition display. Many mobile devices allow you to record video that you later can transmit to your computer or e-mail from the device. Some devices allow you to upload video directly to video sharing Web sites. Digital video cameras provide more features than analog video cameras, such as a higher level of zoom, better sound, or greater control over color and lighting.

Figure 2 The high-end consumer digital video camera can produce professional-grade results. The consumer digital video camera produces amateur-grade results. The webcasting and monitoring digital video camera is appropriate for webcasting and security monitoring.

2 Record a Video

Most video cameras provide you with a choice of recording programs, which sometimes are called automatic settings. Each recording program includes a different combination of camera settings, so that you can adjust the exposure and other functions to match the recording environment. Usually, several different programs are available, such as point-and-shoot, point-and-shoot with manual adjustment, sports, portrait, spotlit scenes, and low light. You also have the ability to select special digital effects, such as fade, wipe, and black and white. If you are recording outside on a windy day, then you can enable the windscreen to prevent wind noise. If you are recording home videos or video meant for a Web site, then the point-and-shoot recording program is sufficient.

3 Transfer and Manage Videos

After recording the video, the next step is to transfer the video to your personal computer or to the Internet. Most video cameras connect directly to a USB or FireWire port on a personal computer (Figure 3). Transferring video with a digital camera or mobile device is easy, because the video already is in a digital format that the computer can recognize. Many mobile devices include a special cable used to connect the device to a personal computer or allow you to transfer the videos to a media sharing Web site or your own Web site.

Some people own analog format video tapes that require additional hardware to convert the analog signals to a digital format before the video can be manipulated on a personal computer. The additional hardware includes a special video capture card using a standard RCA video cable or an S-video cable (Figure 4). *S-video* cables provide sharper images and greater overall quality. A personal computer also can record video to an optical disc, or it can be connected to an external DVD/Blu-ray Disc recorder to record videos. Video conversion services often specialize in converting older analog video to a variety of digital formats.

Figure 3 A digital video camera is connected to the personal computer or DVD/Blu-ray Disc recorder via a USB or FireWire port. No additional hardware is needed.

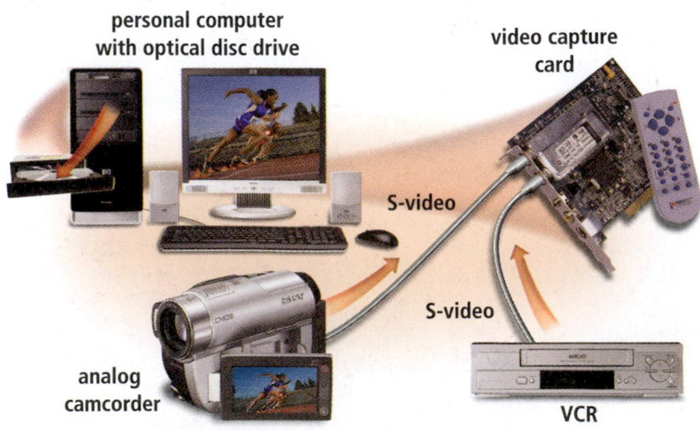

Figure 4 An analog camcorder or VCR is connected to the personal computer via an S-video port on a video capture card.

When transferring video, plan to use approximately 15 to 30 GB of hard disk storage per hour of digital video. High-definition formats may require much more storage per hour. A typical video project requires about four times the amount of raw footage as the final product. At the high end, therefore, a video that lasts an hour may require up to 120 GB of storage for the raw footage, editing process, and final video. This storage requirement can vary depending on the software you use to copy the video from the video camera to the hard disk and the format you select to save the video. For example, Microsoft's Windows Live Movie Maker can save 15 hours of video in 10 GB when creating video for playback on a computer, but saves only 1 hour of video in 10 GB when creating video for playback on a DVD. A high-definition video file may require more than 10 GB per hour.

The video transfer requires application software on the personal computer (Figure 5). The Windows Live Movie Maker software, available as a free download from Microsoft's Web site, allows you to transfer the video from a video camera. Depending on the length of video and the type of connection used, the video may take a long time to transfer. Make certain that no other programs are running on your personal computer while transferring the video.

The frame rate of a video refers to the number of frames per second (fps) that are captured in the video. The most widely used frame rate is 30 fps. A smaller frame rate results in a smaller file size for the video, but playback of the video will not be as smooth as one recorded with a higher frame rate.

When transferring video, the software may allow you to choose a file format and a codec to store the video. A video **file format** holds the video information in a manner specified by a vendor, such as Apple or Microsoft. Six of the more popular file formats are listed in Figure 6. The 3GP format is widely used on mobile devices.

Figure 5 Some video editing software allows you to transfer a video from any video source to a hard disk.

File formats support codecs to encode the audio and video into the file formats. A **codec** specifies how the audio and video is compressed and stored within the file. A particular file format may be able to store audio and video in a number of different codecs. Figure 7 shows some options available for specifying a file format and video quality settings in a video capture program. The file format and codec you choose often is based on what you plan to do with the movie. For example, if you plan to upload your video to the YouTube video sharing Web site, the best choices are DivX and MPEG-4 file formats. Many users find that they are unable to play their own or others' videos, and the problem often is that the proper codec is not installed on the user's personal computer. Video conversion software often allows the user to convert a video in a less popular format to a better supported format. Many of these programs are available as freeware.

After transferring the video to a personal computer or the Internet, and before manipulating the video, you should store the video files in appropriate folders, named correctly, and backed up. Most video transfer application software helps manage these tasks.

Popular Video File Formats

File Format	File Extensions
Apple QuickTime	.MOV or .QT
DivX	.DIVX
Microsoft Windows Media Video	.WMV or .ASF
MPEG-4 Part 4	.MP4
Real RealMedia	.RM or .RAM
3GP	.3GP or .3G2

Figure 6 Apple, DivX, Microsoft, and Real offer the more popular video file formats.

Figure 7 Video editing software allows you to specify a combination of file format and video quality settings when saving a video.

4 Edit a Video

Once the video is stored on your hard disk or the Internet, the next step is to edit, or manipulate, the video. If you used a video capture card to transfer analog video to the computer (Figure 4 on page 346), the files may require extra initial processing. Some Web sites allow you to perform minor editing and other tasks on the Web site. When you use a video capture card, some of the video frames may be lost in the transfer process. Some video editing programs allow you to fix this problem with **frame rate correction** tools.

The first step in the editing process is to split the video into smaller pieces, or *scenes*, that you can manipulate more easily. This process is called *splitting*. Most video software automatically splits the video into scenes, thus sparing you the task. After splitting, you should delete unwanted scenes or portions of scenes. This process is called *pruning*.

After creating the scenes you want to use in the final production, you edit each individual scene. You can *crop*, or change the size of, scenes. That is, you may want to delete the top or a side of a scene that is irrelevant. You also can resize the scene. For example, you may be creating a video that will be displayed on a media sharing Web site. Making a smaller video, such as 320 × 200 pixels instead of 640 × 480 pixels, results in a smaller file that transmits faster over the Internet. Some media sharing Web sites recommend smaller video resolutions, such as 320 × 200 pixels, and some will perform the conversion for you automatically.

If a video has been recorded over a long period, using different cameras or under different lighting conditions, the video may need color correction. *Color correction tools* analyze your video and match brightness, colors, and other attributes of video clips to ensure a smooth look to the video (Figure 8).

You can add logos, special effects, or titles to scenes. You can place a company logo or personal logo in a video to identify yourself or the company producing the video. Logos often are added on the lower-right corner of a video and remain for the duration of the video. Special effects include warping, changing from color to black and white, morphing, or zoom motion. *Morphing* is a special effect in which one video image is transformed into another image over the course of several frames of video, creating the illusion of metamorphosis. You usually add titles at the beginning and ending of a video to give the video context. A training video may have titles throughout the video to label a particular scene, or each scene may begin with a title.

The next step in editing a video is to add audio effects, including voice-over narration and background music. Many video editing programs allow you to add additional tracks, or *layers*, of sound to a video in addition to the sound that was

Figure 8 Color correction tools in video editing software allow a great deal of control over the mood of your video creation.

recorded on the video camera or mobile device. You also can add special audio effects.

The final step in editing a video is to combine the scenes into a complete video (Figure 9). This process involves ordering scenes and adding transition effects between scenes. Video editing software allows you to combine scenes and separate each scene with a transition. *Transitions* include fading, wiping, blurry, bursts, ruptures, erosions, and more.

5 Distribute the Video

After editing the video, the final step is to distribute it or save it on an appropriate medium. You can save video in a variety of formats. Video recorded on a mobile device often requires conversion to a more widely accepted format.

Video also can be stored in digital formats in any of several optical disc formats or on a media sharing Web site. *Optical disc creation software*, which often is packaged with video editing software, allows you to create, or *master*, optical discs. You can add interactivity to your optical disc creations. For example, you can allow viewers to jump to certain scenes using a menu.

You also can save your video creation in electronic format for distribution over the Web, via e-mail, or to a mobile device. Some cameras include a button that allows users to upload directly to a media sharing Web site. Popular media sharing Web sites, such as YouTube (Figure 10), have recommendations for the best file format and codecs to use for video that you upload to them (Figure 11). Your video editing software must support the file format and codec you want to use. For example, Apple's iMovie software typically saves files in the QuickTime file format.

Professionals use hardware and software that allow them to create a film version of digital video that can be played in movie theaters. This technology is becoming increasingly popular. The cost of professional video editing software ranges from thousands to hundreds of thousands of dollars. Video editing software for the home user is available for a few hundred dollars or less. Some Hollywood directors believe that eventually all movies will be recorded and edited digitally.

After creating your final video for distribution or for your personal video collection, you should back up the final video file. You can save your scenes for inclusion in other video creations or create new masters using different effects, transitions, and ordering of scenes.

Figure 9 Scenes are combined into a sequence on the bottom of the screen.

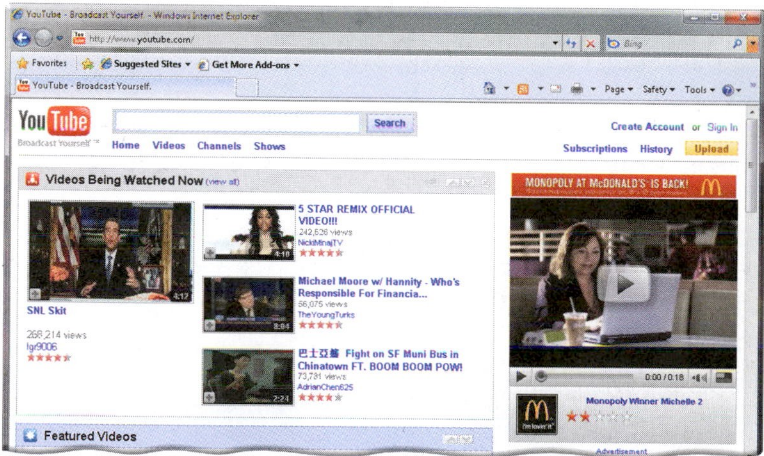

Figure 10 Media sharing Web sites allow you to share your videos with acquaintances or the entire world.

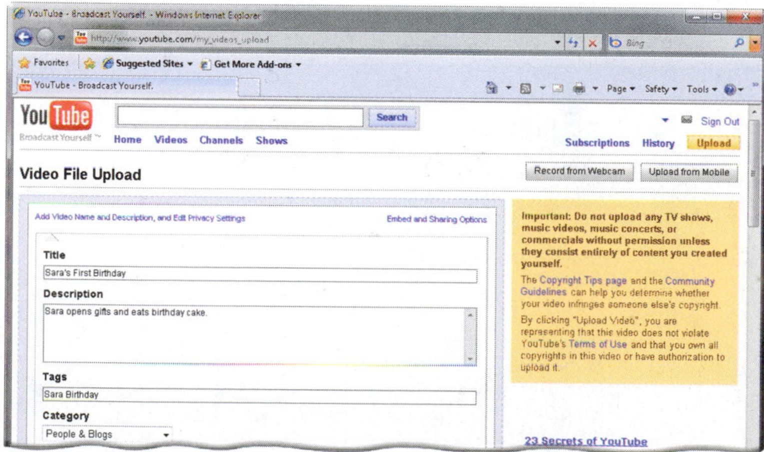

Figure 11 Media sharing Web sites, such as YouTube, provide tools that simplify the process of uploading videos to the site.

Chapter Seven

Storage

Objectives

After completing this chapter, you will be able to:

1. Differentiate between storage devices and storage media
2. Describe the characteristics of an internal hard disk including capacity, platters, read/write heads, cylinders, sectors and tracks, revolutions per minute, transfer rate, and access time
3. Discuss the purpose of network attached storage devices, external and removable hard disks, and hard disk controllers
4. Describe the various types of flash memory storage: solid state drives, memory cards, USB flash drives, and ExpressCard modules
5. Describe cloud storage and explain its advantages
6. Describe the characteristics of optical discs
7. Differentiate among various types of optical discs: CDs, archive discs and Picture CDs, DVDs, and Blu-ray Discs
8. Identify the uses of tape, magnetic stripe cards, smart cards, microfilm and microfiche, and enterprise storage

Storage

Storage holds data, instructions, and information for future use. Every computer stores system software and application software. To start up, a computer locates an operating system (system software) in storage, usually a hard disk, and loads it into memory (RAM). When a user issues a command to start application software, such as a word processing program or a Web browser, the operating system locates the program in storage, such as on a hard disk or optical disc, and loads it into memory (RAM).

In addition to programs, users store a variety of data and information on mainframe computers, servers, desktop computers, notebook computers (including netbooks and Tablet PCs), smart phones, portable media players, and other mobile devices. For example, all types of users store digital photos; appointments, schedules, and contact/address information; correspondence, such as letters and e-mail messages; tax records; and Web pages.

A home user also might store budgets, bank statements, a household inventory, records of stock purchases, tax information, homework assignments, recipes, music, and videos. In addition or instead, a business user stores reports, financial records, travel records, customer

Figure 7-1 A variety of storage options.

orders and invoices, vendor payments, payroll records, inventory records, presentations, quotations, and contracts. Other users store diagrams, drawings, blueprints, designs, marketing literature, corporate newsletters, and product catalogs.

Storage requirements among users vary greatly. Home users, small office/home office users, and mobile users typically have much smaller storage requirements than enterprise users. For example, a home user may need 320 GB (billion bytes) of storage, while enterprises may require 50 PB (quadrillion bytes).

A **storage medium** (media is the plural), also called *secondary storage*, is the physical material on which a computer keeps data, instructions, and information. Examples of storage media are hard disks, solid state drives, memory cards, USB flash drives, ExpressCard modules, optical discs, smart cards, magnetic stripe cards, and microfilm. Cloud storage is another storage option, in which the actual storage media used is transparent to the user. Figure 7-1 shows a variety of storage options. Memory (RAM), by contrast, typically consists of one or more chips on the motherboard or some other circuit board in the computer.

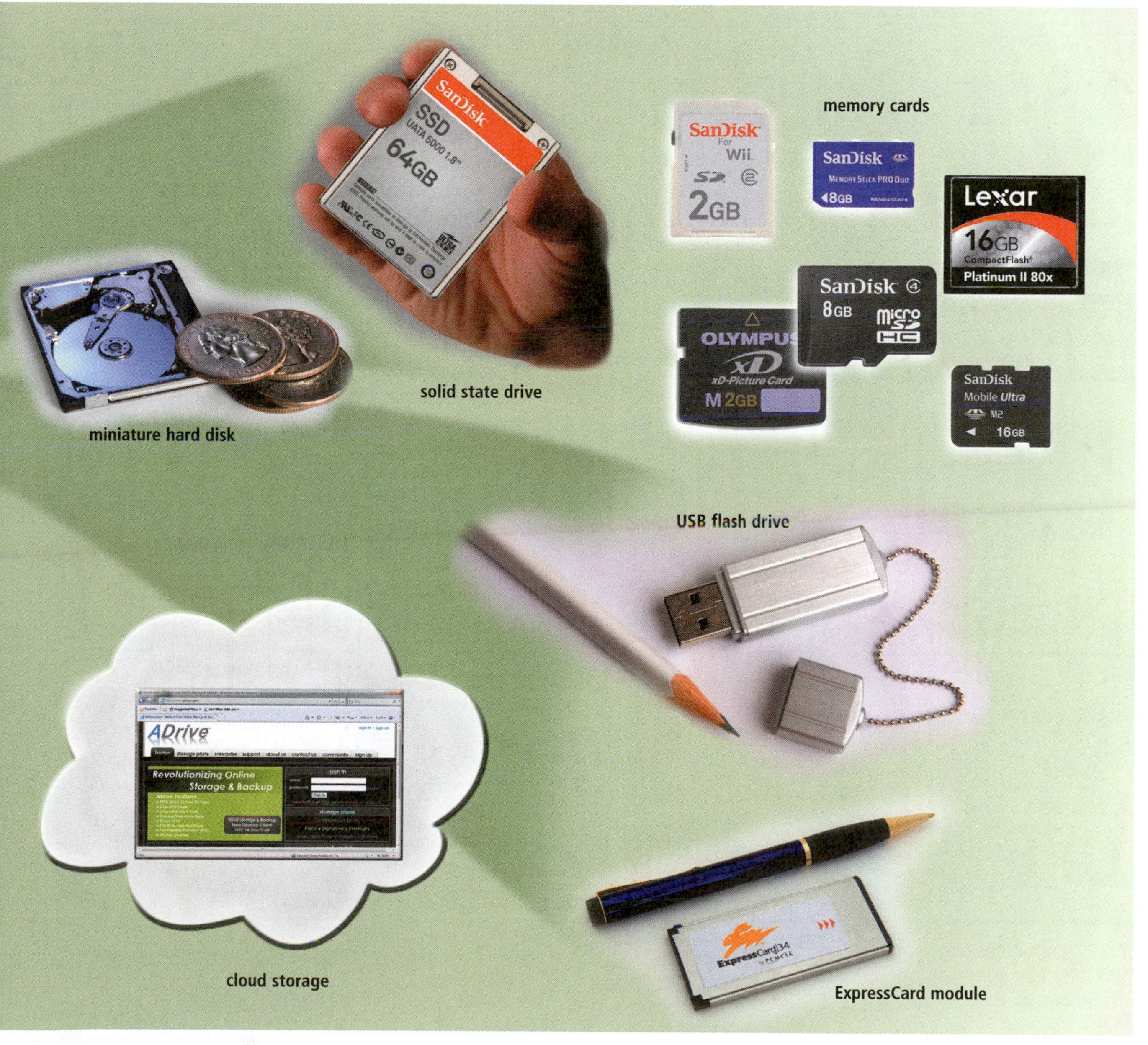

Capacity is the number of bytes (characters) a storage medium can hold. Figure 7-2 identifies the terms manufacturers use to define the capacity of storage media. For example, a reasonably priced USB flash drive can store up to 4 GB of data (approximately four billion bytes) and a typical hard disk has 320 GB (approximately 320 billion bytes) of storage capacity.

Items on a storage medium remain intact even when power is removed from the computer. Thus, a storage medium is nonvolatile. Most memory (i.e., RAM), by contrast, holds data and instructions temporarily and thus is volatile. Figure 7-3 illustrates the concept of volatility. For an analogy, think of a filing cabinet that holds file folders as a storage medium, and the top of your desk as memory. When you want to work with a file, you remove it from the filing cabinet (storage medium) and place it on your desk (memory). When you are finished with the file, you remove it from your desk (memory) and return it to the filing cabinet (storage medium).

A **storage device** is the computer hardware that records and/or retrieves items to and from storage media. **Writing** is the process of transferring data, instructions, and information from memory to a storage medium. **Reading** is the process of transferring these items from a storage medium into memory. When storage devices write data on storage media, they are creating

Storage Terms

Storage Term	Approximate Number of Bytes	Exact Number of Bytes
Kilobyte (KB)	1 thousand	2^{10} or 1,024
Megabyte (MB)	1 million	2^{20} or 1,048,576
Gigabyte (GB)	1 billion	2^{30} or 1,073,741,824
Terabyte (TB)	1 trillion	2^{40} or 1,099,511,627,776
Petabyte (PB)	1 quadrillion	2^{50} or 1,125,899,906,842,624
Exabyte (EB)	1 quintillion	2^{60} or 1,152,921,504,606,846,976
Zettabyte (ZB)	1 sextillion	2^{70} or 1,180,591,620,717,411,303,424
Yottabyte (YB)	1 septillion	2^{80} or 1,208,925,819,614,629,174,706,176

Figure 7-2 The capacity of a storage medium is measured by the number of bytes it can hold.

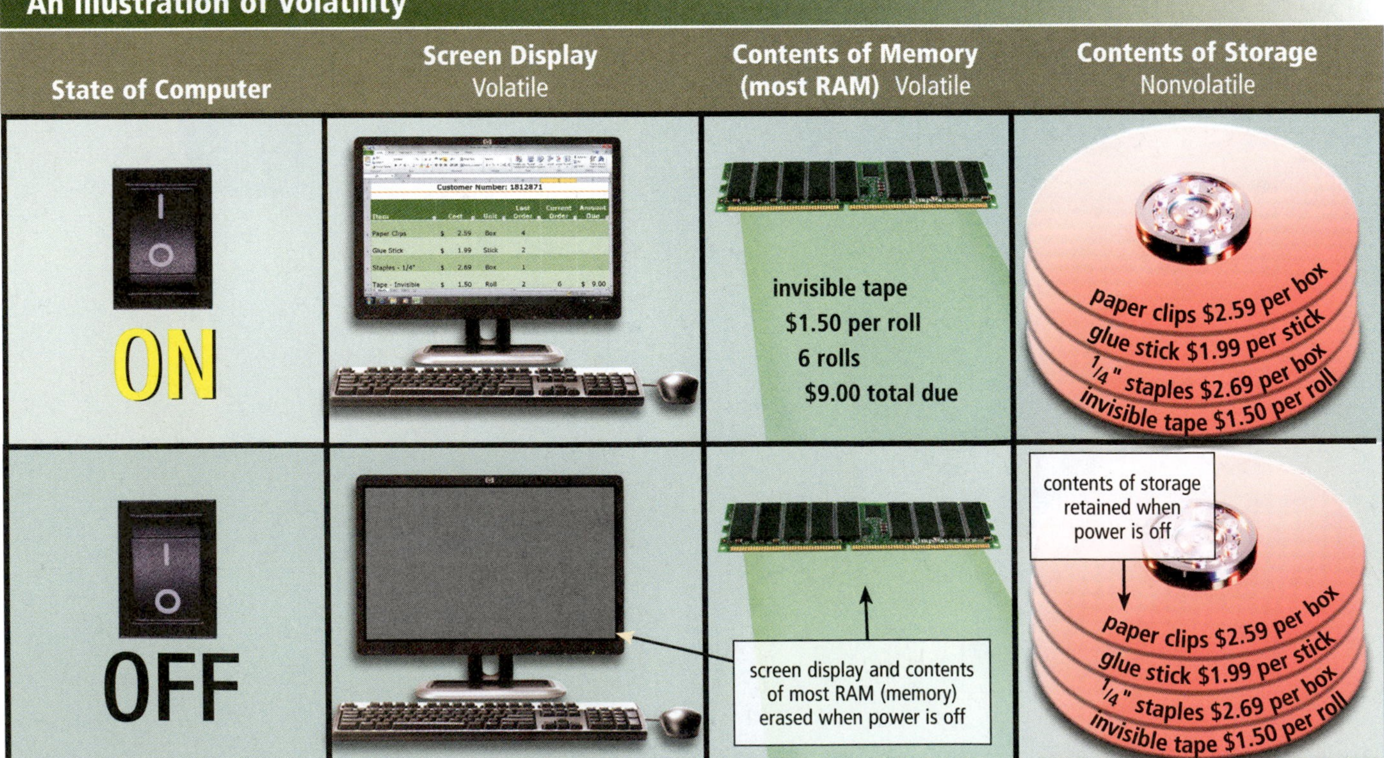

Figure 7-3 A screen display is considered volatile because its contents disappear when power is removed. Likewise, most RAM chips are volatile. That is, their contents are erased when power is removed from the computer. Storage, by contrast, is nonvolatile. Its contents remain when power is off.

output. Similarly, when storage devices read from storage media, they function as a source of input. Nevertheless, they are categorized as storage devices, not as input or output devices.

The speed of storage devices and memory is defined by access time. **Access time** measures (1) the amount of time it takes a storage device to locate an item on a storage medium or (2) the time required to deliver an item from memory to the processor. The access time of storage devices is slow, compared with the access time of memory. Memory (chips) accesses items in billionths of a second (nanoseconds). Storage devices, by contrast, access items in thousandths of a second (milliseconds) or millionths of a second (microseconds).

Instead of, or in addition to access time, some manufacturers state a storage device's transfer rate because it affects access time. *Transfer rate* is the speed with which data, instructions, and information transfer to and from a device. Transfer rates for storage are stated in *KBps* (kilobytes per second), *MBps* (megabytes per second), and *GBps* (gigabytes per second).

Numerous types of storage media and storage devices exist to meet a variety of users' needs. Figure 7-4 shows how different types of storage media and memory compare in terms of transfer rates and uses. This chapter discusses these and other storage media.

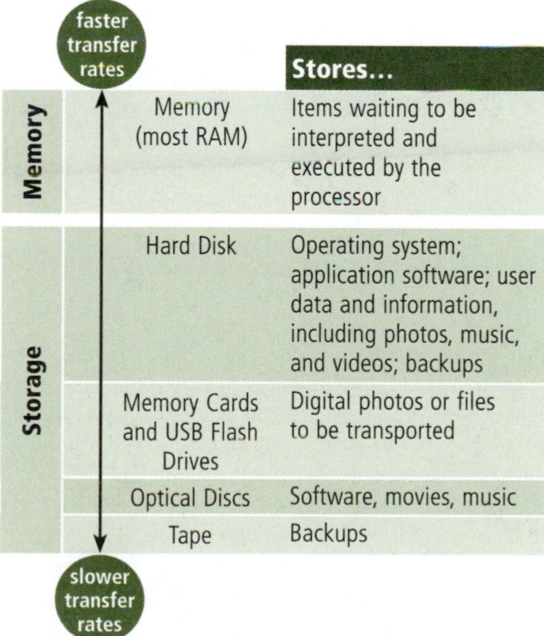

faster transfer rates

		Stores...
Memory	Memory (most RAM)	Items waiting to be interpreted and executed by the processor
Storage	Hard Disk	Operating system; application software; user data and information, including photos, music, and videos; backups
	Memory Cards and USB Flash Drives	Digital photos or files to be transported
	Optical Discs	Software, movies, music
	Tape	Backups

slower transfer rates

Figure 7-4 A comparison of different types of storage media and memory in terms of relative speed and uses. Memory is faster than storage but is expensive and not practical for all storage requirements. Storage is less expensive but is slower than memory.

Hard Disks

A **hard disk**, also called a *hard disk drive* or hard drive, is a storage device that contains one or more inflexible, circular platters that use magnetic particles to store data, instructions, and information. Depending on how the magnetic particles are aligned, they represent either a 0 bit or a 1 bit. Recall from Chapter 4 that a bit (binary digit) is the smallest unit of data a computer can process. Thus, the alignment of the magnetic particles represents the data.

The system unit on most desktop and notebook computers contains at least one hard disk. The entire device is enclosed in an airtight, sealed case to protect it from contamination. A hard disk that is mounted inside the system unit sometimes is called a *fixed disk* because it is not portable (Figure 7-5). With respect to a storage medium, the term *portable* means you can remove the medium from one computer and carry it to another computer. Portable hard disks are discussed later in this chapter.

Current personal computer hard disks have storage capacities from 160 GB to 2 TB and more. Home users store documents, spreadsheets, presentations, databases, e-mail messages,

Figure 7-5 The hard disk in a desktop personal computer is enclosed inside an airtight, sealed case inside the system unit. (In this and other hard disk photos in the book, the top plate is removed from the hard disk for illustration purposes.)

Web pages, digital photos, music, videos, and software on hard disks. Businesses also store correspondence, reports, financial records, customer orders and invoices, payroll records, inventory records, contracts, marketing literature, schedules, and Web sites.

Traditionally, hard disks stored data using *longitudinal recording*, which aligned the magnetic particles horizontally around the surface of the disk. With *perpendicular recording*, by contrast, hard disks align the magnetic particles vertically, or perpendicular to the disk's surface, making much greater storage capacities possible. Figure 7-6 shows the difference between longitudinal and perpendicular recording. Experts estimate that hard disks using perpendicular recording provide storage capacities about 10 times greater than disks that use longitudinal recording.

Perpendicular Recording

For more information, visit the Computer Concepts CourseMate Web site at www.cengagebrain.com, navigate to the Chapter 7 Web Link resource for this book, and then click Perpendicular Recording.

Hard disks are read/write storage media. That is, you can read from and write on a hard disk any number of times. If the computer contains only one hard disk, the operating system designates it as drive C. Additional hard disks are assigned the next available drive letter. Some people use a second hard disk to duplicate the contents of the first hard disk, in case the first is damaged or destroyed. Read Ethics & Issues 7-1 for a related discussion.

FAQ 7-1

To what degree are hard disk capacities increasing?

Hard disk capacities have increased at an exponential rate. Advancements in technology, such as perpendicular recording and enhanced read/write heads that can read and write denser areas on the platter, have resulted in a hard disk's capability of storing increasing amounts of data and information in a fixed amount of space. The chart below illustrates that the maximum hard disk size is growing.

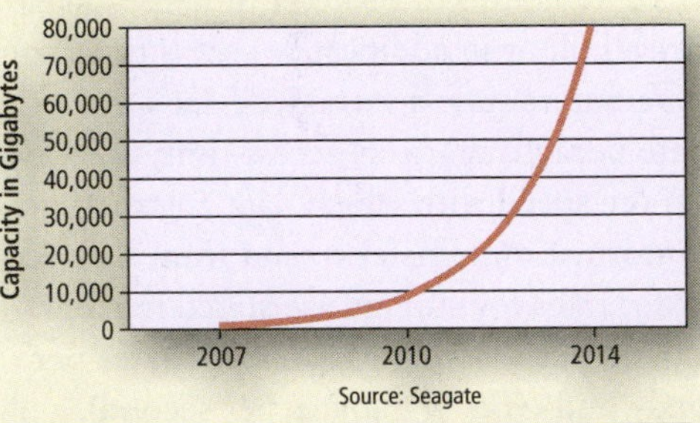

For more information, visit the Computer Concepts CourseMate Web site at www.cengagebrain.com, navigate to the Chapter 7 FAQ resource for this book, and then click Hard Disk Capacity.

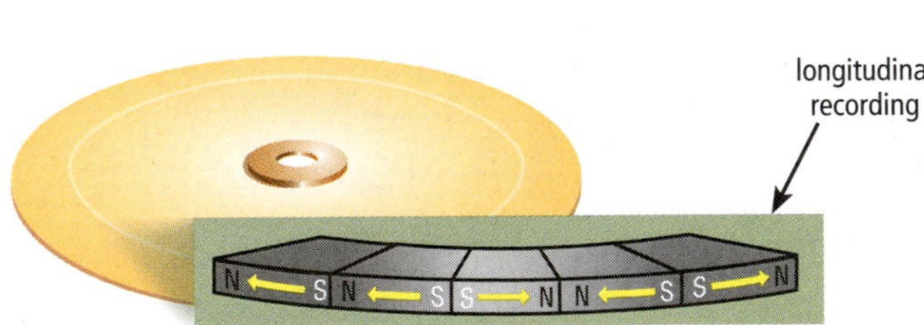

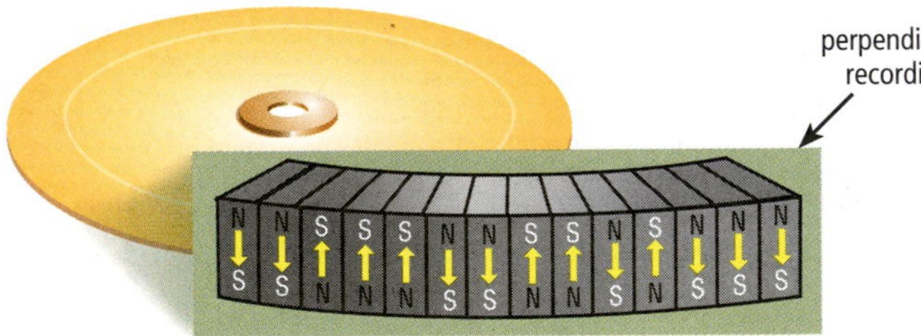

Figure 7-6 Magnetic particles are aligned horizontally in longitudinal recording and vertically in perpendicular recording.

ETHICS & ISSUES 7-1

Should the Government Require Hard Disks to Be Cleaned?

An IT professional recently purchased a hard disk on an auction Web site only to find private banking records of several million people. Fortunately, the purchaser notified authorities, rather than use the data for nefarious purposes. In other incidents, taxpayer data and secret police tactics appeared on hard disks purchased on auction Web sites, donated to charitable organizations, or recovered from discarded computers. Most people do not realize that deleting files from a computer does not render the data permanently inaccessible. Deleted files can be recovered easily by a smart criminal or digital forensics examiner.

Experts recommend that special utility software, known as a *wiping utility*, be used to clean the contents of a hard disk before it leaves possession of the owner. The government sets various disk wiping standards. For example, one standard requires that the software wipe the drive seven times, while a more stringent standard requires fourteen. Experts also recommend the use of full disk encryption, which is the process of encoding data and information into an unreadable form. Others recommend that any hard disk that at any time contained sensitive information be destroyed by a service company that specializes in hard disk destruction. Some companies now offer a service that allows you to keep a hard disk if it fails while covered by a warranty. Typically, companies require that you return the damaged hard disk when you receive the replacement. Some people are not comfortable with this service, for fear of confidential information on the damaged hard disk falling into the wrong hands.

Should the government require that hard disks on sold, donated, or discarded computers be cleaned, encrypted, or destroyed? Why or why not? Would you make an extra effort to clean or encrypt the contents of hard disks on sold, donated, or discarded computers? Why or why not?

Characteristics of a Hard Disk

Characteristics of a hard disk include its capacity, platters, read/write heads, cylinders, sectors and tracks, revolutions per minute, transfer rate, and access time. Figure 7-7 shows characteristics of a sample 1 TB hard disk that uses perpendicular recording. The following paragraphs discuss each of these characteristics.

The capacity of a hard disk is determined from whether it uses longitudinal or perpendicular recording, the number of platters it contains, and the composition of the magnetic coating on the platters. A *platter* is made of aluminum, glass, or ceramic and is coated with an alloy material that allows items to be recorded magnetically on its surface. The coating usually is three millionths of an inch thick.

Before any data can be read from or written on a hard disk, the disk must be formatted. **Formatting** is the process of dividing the disk into tracks and sectors (Figure 7-8), so that the operating system can store and locate data and information on the disk. A *track* is a narrow recording band that forms a full circle on the surface of the disk. The disk's storage locations consist of pie-shaped sections, which break the tracks into small arcs called *sectors*. On a hard disk, a sector typically stores up to 512 bytes of data. Sometimes, a sector has a flaw and cannot store data. When you format a disk, the operating system marks these bad sectors as unusable.

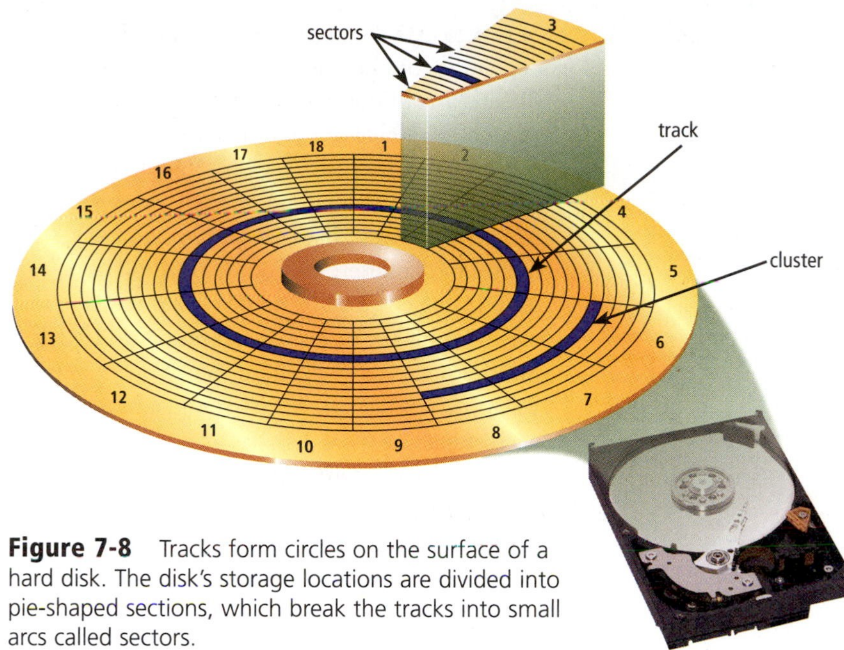

Figure 7-8 Tracks form circles on the surface of a hard disk. The disk's storage locations are divided into pie-shaped sections, which break the tracks into small arcs called sectors.

For reading and writing purposes, sectors are grouped into clusters. A *cluster* is the smallest unit of disk space that stores data and information. Each cluster, also called an *allocation unit*, consists

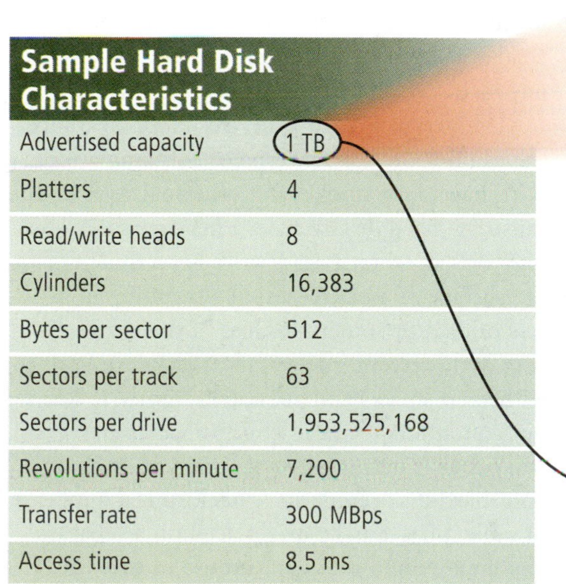

Sample Hard Disk Characteristics	
Advertised capacity	1 TB
Platters	4
Read/write heads	8
Cylinders	16,383
Bytes per sector	512
Sectors per track	63
Sectors per drive	1,953,525,168
Revolutions per minute	7,200
Transfer rate	300 MBps
Access time	8.5 ms

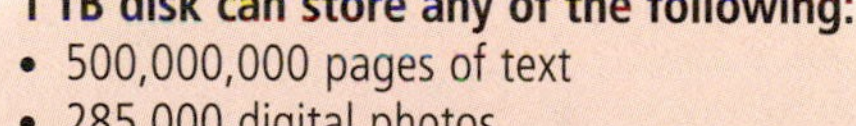

1 TB disk can store any of the following:
- 500,000,000 pages of text
- 285,000 digital photos
- 250,000 songs
- 120 hours of digital video

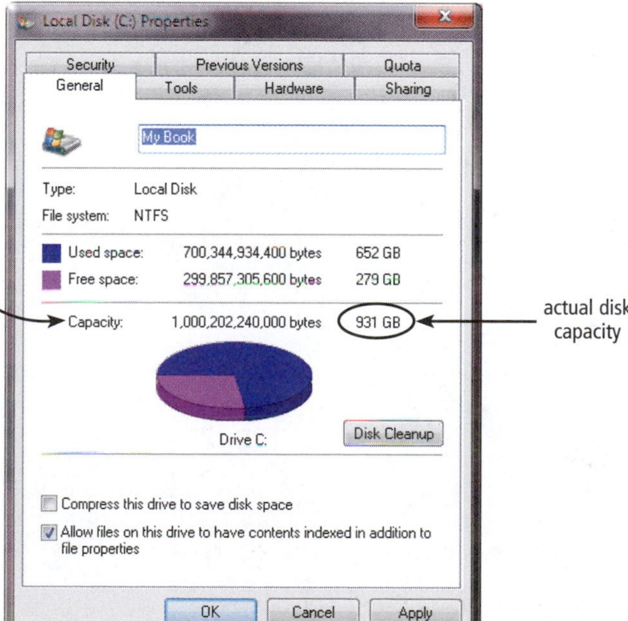

Figure 7-7 Characteristics of a sample 1 TB hard disk. The actual disk's capacity sometimes is different from the advertised capacity because of bad sectors on the disk.

of two to eight sectors (the number varies depending on the operating system). Even if a file consists of only a few bytes, it uses an entire cluster. Each cluster holds data from only one file. One file, however, can span many clusters.

On desktop computers, platters most often have a *form factor*, or size, of approximately 3.5 inches in diameter; on notebook computers, mobile devices, and some servers, the form factor is 2.5 inches or less. A typical hard disk has multiple platters stacked on top of one another. Each platter has two read/write heads, one for each side. The hard disk has arms that move the read/write heads to the proper location on the platter (Figure 7-9). A *read/write head* is the mechanism that reads items and writes items in the drive as it barely touches the disk's recording surface.

The location of the read/write heads often is referred to by its cylinder. A *cylinder* is the vertical section of a track that passes through all platters (Figure 7-10). A single movement of the read/write head arms accesses all the platters in a cylinder. If a hard disk has two platters

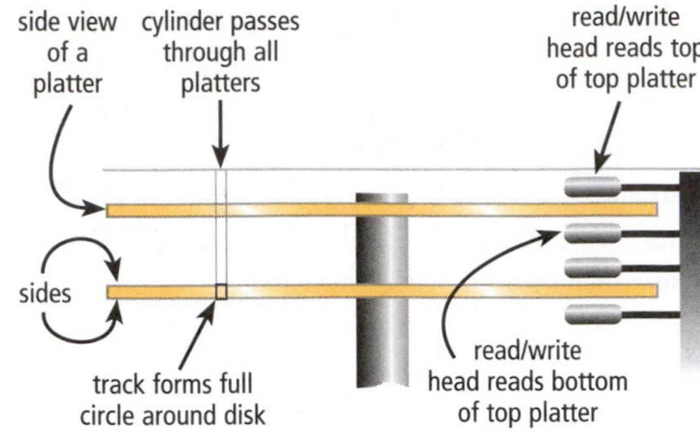

Figure 7-10 A cylinder is the vertical section of track through all platters on a hard disk.

(four sides), each with 1,000 tracks, then it will have 1,000 cylinders with each cylinder consisting of 4 tracks (2 tracks for each platter).

While the computer is running, the platters in the hard disk rotate at a high rate of speed. This spinning, which usually is 5,400 to 15,000 *revolutions per minute* (*rpm*), allows nearly instant access to all tracks and sectors on the platters. The platters may continue to spin until power is removed from the computer, or more commonly today, they stop spinning or slow down after a specified time to save power. The spinning motion creates a cushion of air between the platter and its read/write head. This cushion ensures that the read/write head floats above the platter instead of making direct contact with the platter surface. The distance between the read/write head and the platter is about two millionths of one inch.

As shown in Figure 7-11, this close clearance leaves no room for any type of contamination. Dirt, hair, dust, smoke, and other particles could cause the hard disk to have a head crash. A *head crash* occurs when a read/write head touches the surface of a platter, usually resulting in a loss of data or sometimes loss of the entire disk. Although current internal hard disks are built to withstand shocks and are sealed tightly to keep out contaminants, head crashes occasionally do still occur. Thus, it is crucial that you back up your hard disk regularly. A **backup** is a duplicate of a file, program, or disk placed on a separate storage medium that you can use in case the original is lost, damaged, or destroyed. Chapter 8 discusses backup techniques.

Depending on the type of hard disk, transfer rates range from 15 MBps to 320 MBps. Access time for today's hard disks ranges from about 3 to 12 ms (milliseconds).

Figure 7-9 This figure shows how a hard disk works.

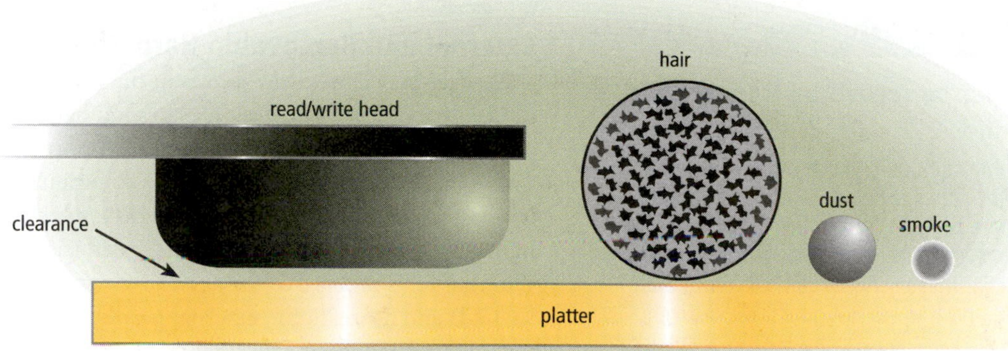

Figure 7-11 The clearance between a disk read/write head and the platter is about two millionths of an inch. A smoke particle, dust particle, human hair, or other contaminant could render the disk unusable.

Hard disks improve their access time by caching, specifically using disk cache. *Disk cache* (pronounced cash), sometimes called a buffer, consists of a memory chip(s) on a hard disk that stores frequently accessed items such as data, instructions, and information (Figure 7-12). Disk cache and memory cache work in a similar fashion. When a processor requests data, instructions, or information from the hard disk, the hard disk first checks its disk cache — before moving any mechanical parts to access the platters. If the requested item is in disk cache, the hard disk sends it to the processor. If the hard disk does not find the requested item in the disk cache, then the processor must wait for the hard disk to locate and transfer the item from the disk to the processor. Hard disks today contain between 2 MB and 64 MB of disk cache. The greater the disk cache, the faster the hard disk.

Density is the number of bits in an area on a storage medium. A higher density means more storage capacity.

How Disk Cache Works

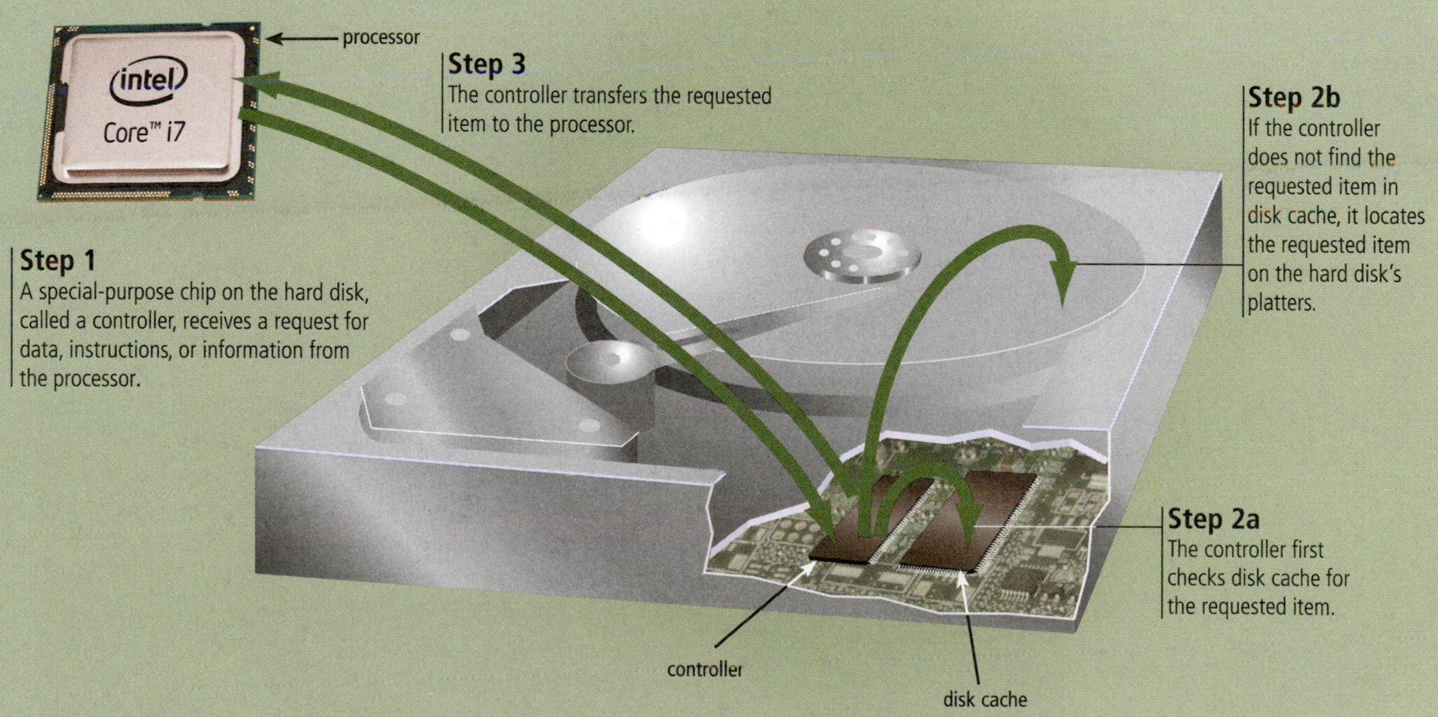

Figure 7-12 This figure shows how disk cache works.

? FAQ 7-2

Can files be recovered from a failed hard disk?

Yes. Some companies, such as DriveSavers, specialize in retrieving data and information from hard disks that have failed mechanically or have sustained other damage to the physical media. These services can cost more than $1,000, and they do not guarantee recovery of specific lost files. For this reason, it still is critical that you back up important files.

For more information, visit the Computer Concepts CourseMate Web site at www.cengagebrain.com, navigate to the Chapter 7 FAQ resource for this book, and then click Hard Disk Recovery.

RAID

Some personal computer manufacturers provide a hard disk configuration that connects multiple smaller disks into a single unit that acts like a single large hard disk. A group of two or more integrated hard disks is called a **RAID** (redundant array of independent disks). RAID is an ideal storage solution for users who must have the data available when they attempt to access it.

NAS

A **network attached storage** (*NAS*) device is a server connected to a network with the sole purpose of providing storage (Figure 7-13). Any user or device connected to the network can access files on the NAS device. These devices often use a RAID configuration. In the past, enterprises were the primary users of NAS. With the introduction of smaller, less expensive NAS devices, however, some home and small business users opt to add up to 6 TB or more of hard disk storage space to their network with a NAS device.

Network Attached Storage

For more information, visit the Computer Concepts CourseMate Web site at www.cengagebrain.com, navigate to the Chapter 7 Web Link resource for this book, and then click Network Attached Storage.

Figure 7-13 A network attached storage device.

External and Removable Hard Disks

An **external hard disk,** shown in the top photo in Figure 7-14, is a separate freestanding hard disk that connects with a cable to a USB port or FireWire port on the system unit or communicates wirelessly. As with the internal hard disk, the entire hard disk is enclosed in an airtight, sealed case. External hard disks have storage capacities of up to 4 TB and more. Some external hard disk units include multiple hard disks that you can use for different purposes, if desired.

A **removable hard disk** is a hard disk that you insert and remove from a drive. Sometimes the drive is built in the system unit. Others are external devices that connect with a cable to a USB port or FireWire port on the system unit. A removable hard disk drive, shown in the bottom photo in Figure 7-14, reads from and writes on the removable hard disk. Removable hard disks have storage capacities up to 1 TB or more.

Figure 7-14 Examples of external and removable hard disks.

Although the transfer rate of external and removable hard disks usually is slower than that of internal hard disks, they do offer many advantages over internal hard disks (fixed disks):

- Transport a large number of files
- Back up important files or an entire internal hard disk (several external hard disk models allow you to back up simply by pushing a button on the disk)
- Easily store large audio and video files
- Secure your data; for example, at the end of a work session, remove the hard disk and lock it up, leaving no data in the computer
- Add storage space to a notebook computer, including netbooks and Tablet PCs
- Add storage space to a desktop computer without having to open the system unit or connect to a network

Miniature Hard Disks

Both internal and external hard disks are available in miniature sizes. These tiny hard disks have form factors of 1.8 inch, 1 inch, and 0.85 inch. Devices such as portable media players, digital cameras, and smart phones often have internal miniature hard disks, which provide greater storage capacities than flash memory (Figure 7-15). External hard disks that are smaller in size and capacity, which also contain miniature hard disks, are sometimes called a *pocket hard drive* because they enable mobile users easily to transport photos and other files from one computer to another (Figure 7-16).

When a device containing a miniature hard disk is connected to a computer, the user can read from and write on the device as a separate drive. Miniature hard disks have storage capacities that range from 1 GB to 320 GB. Miniature hard disks with the greater storage capacities typically use perpendicular recording.

Figure 7-15 This miniature hard disk is used in portable media players and other small devices, enabling users to store music, videos, movies, and any other type of files on the disk.

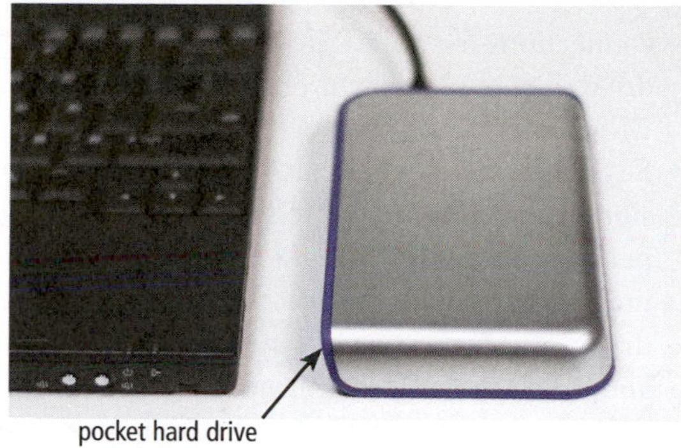

Figure 7-16 Users easily can transport data from one computer to another with a pocket hard drive.

Hard Disk Controllers

A *disk controller* consists of a special-purpose chip and electronic circuits that control the transfer of data, instructions, and information from a disk to and from the system bus and other components in the computer. That is, it controls the interface between the hard disk and the system bus. A disk controller for a hard disk, called the hard disk controller, may be part of a hard disk or the motherboard, or it may be a separate adapter card inside the system unit.

In their personal computer advertisements, vendors usually state the type of hard disk interface supported by the hard disk controller. Thus, you should understand the types of available hard disk interfaces. In addition to USB and FireWire, which can function as external hard disk interfaces, four other types of hard disk interfaces for use in personal computers are SATA, EIDE, SCSI, and SAS.

- *SATA* (*Serial Advanced Technology Attachment*) uses serial signals to transfer data, instructions, and information. The primary advantage of SATA interfaces is their cables are thinner, longer, more flexible, and less susceptible to interference than cables used by hard disks that use parallel signals. SATA interfaces have data transfer rates of up to 300 MBps and higher. In addition to hard disks, SATA interfaces support connections to optical disc drives. External disks can use the *eSATA* (external SATA) interface, which is much faster than USB and FireWire.
- *EIDE* (*Enhanced Integrated Drive Electronics*) is a hard disk interface that uses parallel signals to transfer data, instructions, and information. EIDE interfaces can support up to four hard disks at 137 GB per disk. These interfaces have data transfer rates up to 133 MBps. EIDE interfaces also provide

eSATA

For more information, visit the Computer Concepts CourseMate Web site at www.cengagebrain.com, navigate to the Chapter 7 Web Link resource for this book, and then click eSATA.

connections for optical disc drives and tape drives. Some manufacturers market their EIDE interfaces as Fast ATA or Ultra ATA.

- *SCSI* interfaces, which also use parallel signals, can support up to eight or fifteen peripheral devices. Supported devices include hard disks, optical disc drives, tape drives, printers, scanners, network cards, and much more. Recall from Chapter 4 that SCSI is an acronym for Small Computer System Interface. Some computers have a built-in SCSI interface, while others use an adapter card to add a SCSI interface. SCSI interfaces provide up to 640 MBps data transfer rates.
- *SAS* (*serial-attached SCSI*) is a newer type of SCSI that uses serial signals to transfer data, instructions, and information. Advantages of SAS over parallel SCSI include thinner, longer cables; reduced interference; less expensive; support for many more connected devices at once; and faster speeds. SAS interfaces have data transfer rates of 750 MBps and higher. In addition to hard disks, SAS interfaces support connections to optical disc drives, printers, scanners, digital cameras, and other devices. SAS interfaces usually are compatible with devices that have parallel SCSI and SATA interfaces. Experts predict that SAS eventually will replace parallel SCSI.

Maintaining Data Stored on a Hard Disk

Most manufacturers guarantee their hard disks to last approximately three to five years. Many last much longer with proper care. To prevent the loss of items stored on a hard disk, you regularly should perform preventive maintenance such as defragmenting or scanning the disk for errors. To learn more about how to maintain a hard disk, complete the Learn How To 1 activity on pages 392 and 393. Chapter 8 discusses these and other utilities in depth.

QUIZ YOURSELF 7-1

Instructions: Find the true statement below. Then, rewrite the remaining false statements so that they are true.

1. Disk recording consists of a memory chip(s) on a hard disk that stores frequently accessed items.
2. Hard disks contain one or more inflexible, circular platters that magnetically store data, instructions, and information.
3. SATA is a hard disk interface that uses parallel signals to transfer data, instructions, and information.
4. Storage media is the computer hardware that records and/or retrieves items to and from a storage device.
5. Users can move an internal hard disk from computer to computer as needed by connecting the disk to a USB port or FireWire port on the system unit.

Quiz Yourself Online: To further check your knowledge of pages 352 through 362, visit the Computer Concepts CourseMate Web site at www.cengagebrain.com, navigate to the Chapter 7 Quiz Yourself resource for this book, and then click Objectives 1 – 3.

Flash Memory Storage

As discussed in Chapter 4, flash memory is a type of nonvolatile memory that can be erased electronically and rewritten. Flash memory chips are a type of *solid state media*, which means they consist entirely of electronic components, such as integrated circuits, and contain no moving parts. The lack of moving parts makes flash memory storage more durable and shock resistant than other types of media such as magnetic hard disks or optical discs.

Types of flash memory storage include solid state drives, memory cards, USB flash drives, and ExpressCard modules.

FAQ 7-3

How can I improve the performance of my hard disk?

Windows includes many tools that can be used to improve the performance of your hard disk, including Disk Cleanup and Disk Defragmenter. Disk Cleanup removes unused files from a hard disk so that the computer does not have to spend time searching through and accessing unneeded files, and Disk Defragmenter reorganizes the data on a hard disk so that the data can be accessed more quickly. The next chapter further describes these two tools.

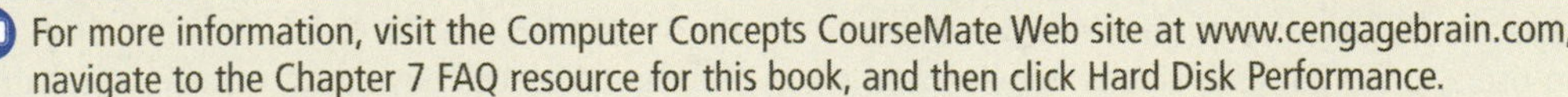

For more information, visit the Computer Concepts CourseMate Web site at www.cengagebrain.com, navigate to the Chapter 7 FAQ resource for this book, and then click Hard Disk Performance.

Solid State Drives

A **solid state drive (SSD)** is a storage device that typically uses flash memory to store data, instructions, and information (Figure 7-17). With available form factors of 3.5 inches, 2.5 inches, and 1.8 inches, SSDs are used in all types of computers including servers, desktop computers, and mobile computers and devices such as portable media players and digital video cameras. Storage capacities of current SSDs range from 16 GB to 256 GB and more.

SSDs have several advantages over magnetic hard disks.

- Access times of SSDs are about 0.1 ms, which is more than 80 times faster than a hard disk.
- Transfer rates of SSDs are faster than comparable hard disks. For example, SSD transfer rates range from 80 to 100 MBps, while transfer rates of a typical 2.5-inch hard disk is about 60 MBps.
- SSDs generate less heat and consume less power than hard disks.
- Manufacturers claim that SSDs will last more than 50 years, which is much greater than the 3 to 5 year hard disk stated lifespan.

The disadvantages of SSDs are they currently have a higher failure rate than hard disks, and their cost is much higher per gigabyte. As the price of SSDs drops, experts estimate that increasingly more users will purchase computers and devices that use this media.

? FAQ 7-4

Are data transfer speeds on solid state technology increasing?

IBM's Project Quicksilver is breaking new ground by achieving data transfer speeds of more than one million input/output operations per second. Significant increases in data transfer speeds on solid state devices eventually may result in more solid state storage devices replacing storage devices with moving components, such as hard disks and optical disc drives.

For more information, visit the Computer Concepts CourseMate Web site at www.cengagebrain.com, navigate to the Chapter 7 FAQ resource for this book, and then click Project Quicksilver.

Solid State Drives

For more information, visit the Computer Concepts CourseMate Web site at www.cengagebrain.com, navigate to the Chapter 7 Web Link resource for this book, and then click Solid State Drives.

Figure 7-17 As the price of SSDs drops, experts estimate that increasingly more users will purchase computers and devices that use this media.

Memory Cards

Memory cards enable mobile users easily to transport digital photos, music, or files to and from mobile devices and computers or other devices. As mentioned in Chapter 4, a **memory card** is a removable flash memory device, usually no bigger than 1.5 inches in height or width, that you insert and remove from a slot in a computer, mobile device, or card reader/writer (Figure 7-18).

Common types of memory cards include *CompactFlash* (*CF*), *Secure Digital* (*SD*), *Secure Digital High Capacity* (*SDHC*), *microSD*, *microSDHC*, *xD Picture Card*, *Memory Stick*, and *Memory Stick Micro* (*M2*). The table in Figure 7-19 compares storage capacities and uses of these media.

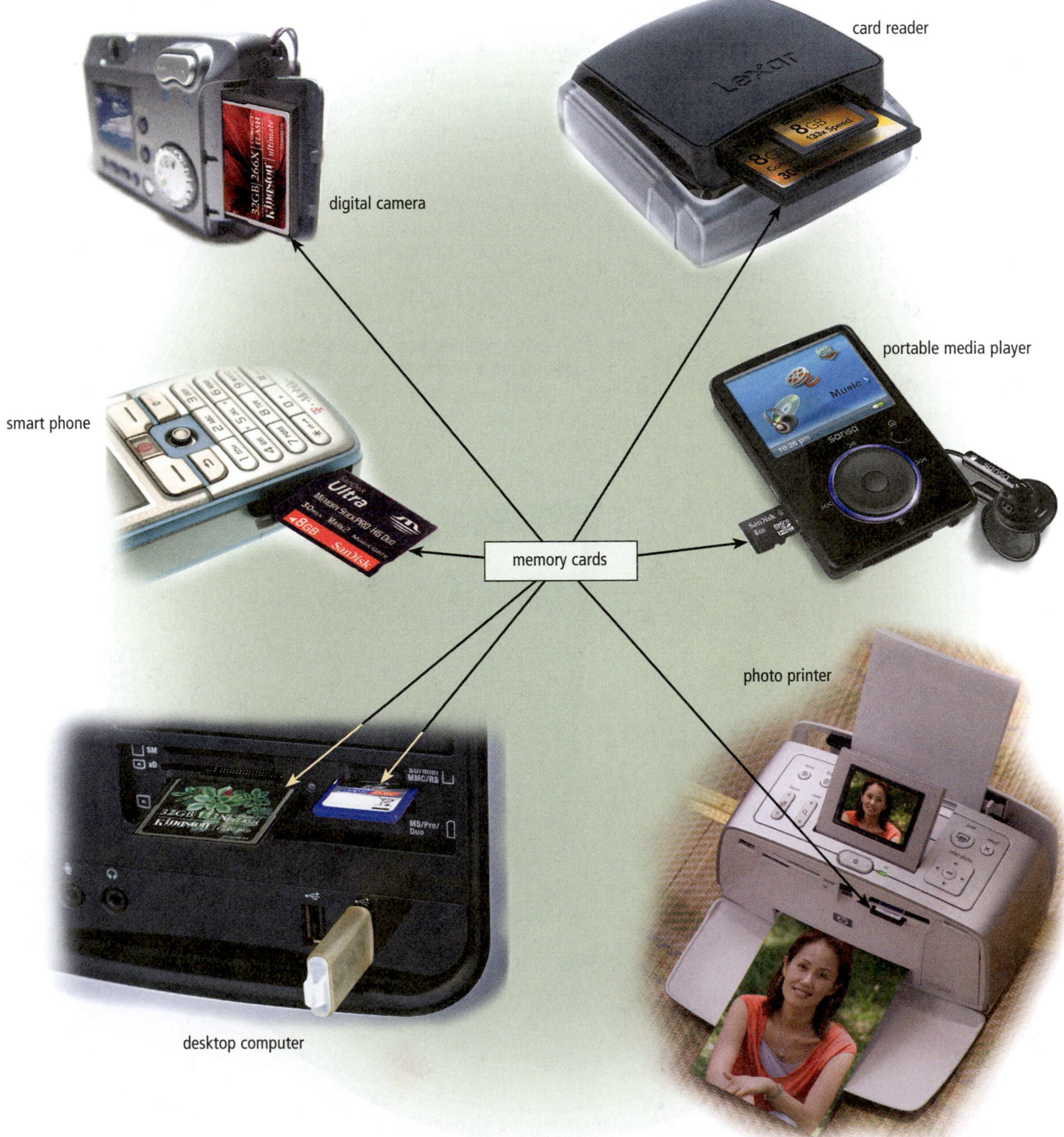

Figure 7-18 Many types of computers and devices have slots for memory cards.

Depending on the device, manufacturers claim memory cards can last from 10 to 100 years. Transfer rates range from about 1 MBps to 20 MBps or more, depending on the device. Memory cards are quite expensive compared to other storage media with equivalent capacity. For example, the cost of a 16 GB CompactFlash card can be the same as a 1 TB external hard disk.

To view, edit, or print images and information stored on memory cards, you transfer the contents to your desktop computer or other device. Some printers have slots to read memory cards. If your computer or printer does not have a built-in slot, you can purchase a *card reader/writer*, which is a device that reads and writes data, instructions, and information stored on memory cards. Card reader/writers usually

SDHC Cards

For more information, visit the Computer Concepts CourseMate Web site at www.cengagebrain.com, navigate to the Chapter 7 Web Link resource for this book, and then click SDHC Cards.

Various Memory Cards

Media Type	Storage Capacity	Use
CompactFlash (CF)	512 MB to 100 GB	Digital cameras, smart phones, PDAs, photo printers, portable media players, notebook computers, desktop computers
Secure Digital (SD)	512 MB to 8 GB	Digital cameras, digital video cameras, smart phones, PDAs, photo printers, portable media players
SDHC	4 to 32 GB	Digital cameras
microSD	1 to 2 GB	Smart phones, portable media players, handheld game consoles, handheld navigation devices
microSDHC	4 to 16 GB	Smart phones, portable media players, handheld game consoles, handheld navigation devices
xD Picture Card	256 MB to 2 GB	Digital cameras, photo printers
Memory Stick PRO Duo	1 to 16 GB	Digital cameras, smart phones, handheld game consoles
Memory Stick Micro (M2)	1 to 16 GB	Smart phones

Figure 7-19 A variety of memory cards.

connect to the USB port or FireWire port on the system unit. The type of card you have will determine the type of card reader/writer needed. Figure 7-20 shows how one type of memory card works with a card reader/writer. Read Ethics & Issues 7-2 for a related discussion.

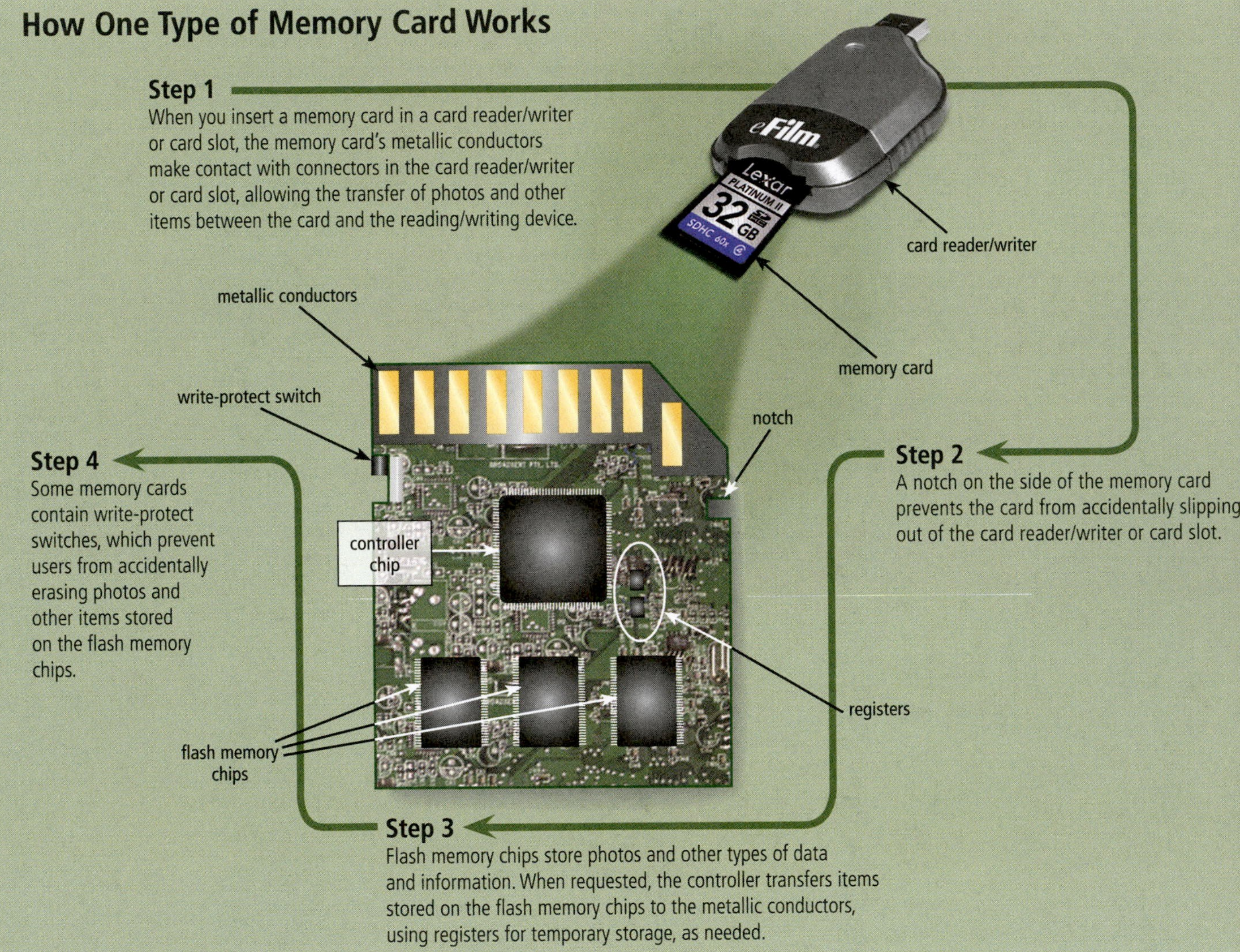

Figure 7-20 This figure shows how one type of memory card works.

ETHICS & ISSUES 7-2

Is the Large Variety of Options for Flash Memory Mobile Media Good?

When you buy a new mobile device, such as a cell phone, digital camera, or GPS device, you probably consider how much flash memory you will be able to use on the device. Too often, though, people do not consider the type of flash memory mobile media that the device supports. With more than 50 types of memory cards and USB flash drives available, consumers find their devices cannot share media, resulting in frustration and additional costs for adapters and readers. One company sells a card reader that reads 56 types of memory cards and USB flash drives. While companies in the flash memory mobile media business failed at developing a smaller set of standards in the past, a new attempt by some companies looks promising for frustrated consumers. The proposed standard, known as *Universal Flash Storage* (*UFS*), would be faster, use less power, allow for higher capacities, and eliminate the need for the array of adapters and readers currently used by consumers. Some analysts remain skeptical, noting that many of the larger manufacturers do not support the standard and that the effort, therefore, is doomed to fail. These manufacturers claim that more choices for consumers are good, and multiple standards are necessary to support various device storage capacities and usages of flash memory.

Is the large variety of options for flash memory mobile media an advantage or disadvantage for consumers? Why? Should manufacturers join forces to develop fewer standards, or should the free market be allowed to run its course over time with the best formats winning the format war? Why?

USB Flash Drives

As discussed in Chapter 4, a **USB flash drive**, sometimes called a *thumb drive*, is a flash memory storage device that plugs in a USB port on a computer or mobile device (Figure 7-21). USB flash drives are convenient for mobile users because they are small and lightweight enough to be transported on a keychain or in a pocket. With a USB flash drive, users easily transfer documents, photos, music, and videos from one computer to another. Current USB flash drives have data transfer rates of about 12 MBps and storage capacities ranging from 512 MB to 100 GB, with the latter being extremely expensive.

A special type of USB flash drive, called a *U3 smart drive*, includes pre-installed software accessed through a Windows-type interface. Some USB flash drives include fingerprint readers, restricting access to authenticated users.

The drive designation of a USB flash drive usually follows alphabetically after all other disks. For example, if the computer has one internal hard disk (drive C) and an optical disc drive (drive D) and no other disk drives, then the USB flash drive probably will be drive E.

? FAQ 7-5

Can airport security screening equipment damage or erase the data on my mobile media or hard disk?

The Transportation Security Administration's Web site states that their screening (X-ray) equipment will not damage or erase the data stored on flash memory mobile media, optical discs, or hard disks. Although your media is equally safe whether you carry it onto the airplane or leave it in checked baggage, packing it with your carry-on items is a better safeguard against physical damage. If you are uneasy about your media passing through the airport screening equipment, you may be able to request that the items be manually (hand) searched. It is important to note that the equipment used to screen checked baggage will not harm electronic media, but it may damage undeveloped film. As a safeguard, you should carry all film onto the airplane and request a manual search.

For more information, visit the Computer Concepts CourseMate Web site at www.cengagebrain.com, navigate to the Chapter 7 FAQ resource for this book, and then click Airport Screening Equipment.

Figure 7-21 A close-up of the flash memory and circuitry inside a USB flash drive.

ExpressCard Modules

As discussed in Chapter 4, an **ExpressCard module** is a removable device, about 75 mm long and 34 mm wide or L-shaped with a width of 54 mm, that fits in an ExpressCard slot (Figure 7-22). ExpressCard modules can be used to add memory, storage, communications, multimedia, and security capabilities to a computer. Developed by the PCMCIA (Personal Computer Memory Card International Association), ExpressCard modules commonly are used in notebook computers.

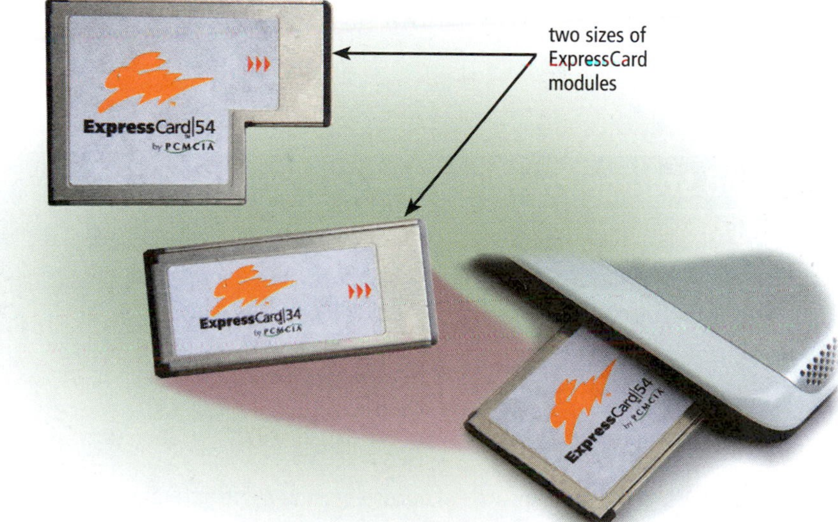

Figure 7-22 ExpressCard modules are available in two sizes.

Cloud Storage

Some users choose cloud storage instead of storing data locally on a hard disk or other media. **Cloud storage** is an Internet service that provides storage to computer users (Figure 7-23).

Types of services offered by cloud storage providers vary. Some provide storage for specific types of files, such as photos or e-mail messages, whereas others store any type of file. Many cloud storage providers offer additional services such as encryption, passwords, Web applications, and Web services. Figure 7-24 identifies a variety of cloud storage providers. Read Innovative Computing 7-1 to find out about another type of cloud storage.

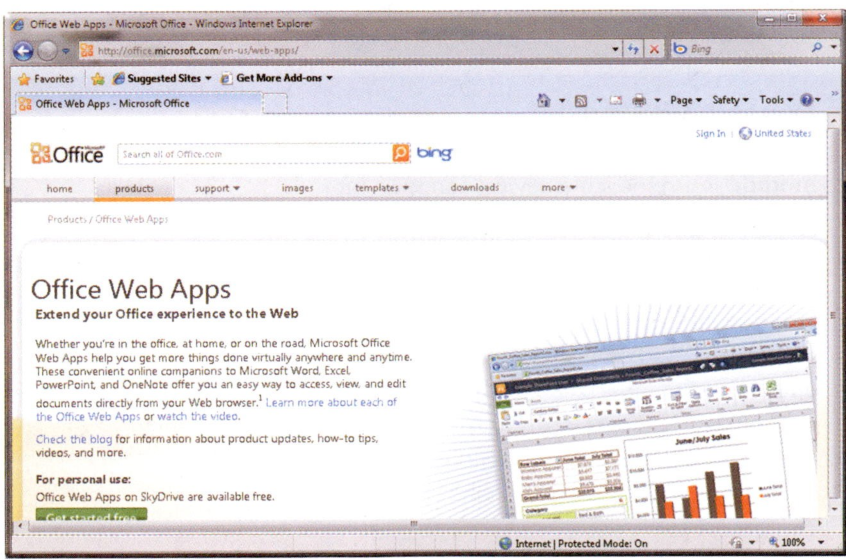

Figure 7-23 An example of one Web site that provides cloud storage.

INNOVATIVE COMPUTING 7-1

Digital Books Are a Good Read

It is time to dust off your library card because thousands of libraries are stocking their digital shelves with electronic books that you can download from anywhere you have computer access. Just locate a participating library's Web site, download the desired book files to your personal computer, and then transfer the files to your portable media player or smart phone. For patrons who do not want to download files, some libraries are lending a Playaway, which is a small device that stores 80 hours of digitized audio books.

Another set of books is available for reading at the British Library's Online Gallery. Software called Turning the Pages allows readers to browse some of the rarest books in the world and magnify details on the pages. The books include the *Gutenberg Bible*, Lewis Carroll's original *Alice in Wonderland*, and *The Diamond Sutra*, the oldest book in existence, printed in China in 868 A.D.

For more information, visit the Computer Concepts CourseMate Web site at www.cengagebrain.com, navigate to the Chapter 7 Innovative Computing resource for this book, and then click Online Libraries.

Cloud Storage Providers

Web Site Names	Type of Storage Provided	Other Services
Box.net, IDrive, Windows Live SkyDrive	Backup or additional storage for any type of file	
Flickr, Picasa	Digital photos	Photo editing and photo management
YouTube	Digital videos	
Facebook, MySpace	Digital photos, digital videos, messages, and personal information	Social networking
Google Docs, Office Web Apps	Documents, spreadsheets, presentations	Productivity suite
Gmail, Windows Live Hotmail, Yahoo! Mail	E-mail messages	
Amazon EC2, Amazon S3, Nirvanix	Enterprise-level storage	Web services, data center services

Figure 7-24 Some of the more widely used cloud storage providers.

Cloud storage is available for all sizes of users, with various degrees of storage services available for home and business users. Cloud storage fee arrangements vary, depending on the user's storage requirements. For example, one cloud storage service provides 25 GB of storage free to registered users; another charges $5 per month for 150 GB of storage. For enterprises, cloud storage services typically charge for storage on a per gigabyte basis, such as 15 cents per gigabyte. Some also charge an additional per gigabyte fee for data transferred to and from the cloud storage service. Read Ethics & Issues 7-3 for a related discussion.

Users subscribe to cloud storage for a variety of reasons:

- To access files on the Internet from any computer or device that has Internet access
- To store large audio, video, and graphics files on the Internet instantaneously, instead of spending time downloading to a local hard disk or other media
- To allow others to access their files on the Internet so that others can listen to an audio file, watch a video clip, or view a photo — instead of e-mailing the file to them
- To view time-critical data and images immediately while away from the main office or location; for example, doctors can view X-ray images from another hospital, home, or office, or while on vacation
- To store offsite backups of data (Chapter 8 presents this and other backup strategies)
- To provide data center functions, relieving enterprises of this task

Cloud Storage
For more information, visit the Computer Concepts CourseMate Web site at www.cengagebrain.com, navigate to the Chapter 7 Web Link resource for this book, and then click Cloud Storage.

ETHICS & ISSUES 7-3

Is Data Stored in the Cloud Free from Prying Eyes?

At an ever increasing rate, companies and individuals store Web sites and data in the cloud. For example, those who utilize Web-based e-mail store their sent and received e-mail messages in the e-mail provider's cloud environment. Those who use corporate or private e-mail servers do not store their communications in the cloud. Important legal rulings highlight the differences between the two approaches for storing e-mail messages. Law enforcement agencies consider e-mail stored in the cloud to belong to the company that owns the cloud service, often an Internet access provider.

E-mail stored on a private e-mail server, however, is the property of the company or individual who owns the server. When the law enforcement officials need to read someone's e-mail on a private e-mail server, they must obtain a warrant that outlines exactly the information being sought. In the cloud, however, law enforcement officials simply may need to request the information from the company that owns the cloud service. The user might not be notified of the search until up to 90 days later; further, the search may occur without limitations and may include continuous monitoring of an individual's e-mail. While the government takes a liberal approach to viewing one's e-mail in the cloud, individuals who secretly read others' e-mail messages may be subject to felony computer crimes.

Should data kept in the cloud be treated the same way legally as items that are kept in one's home? Why? Should the government be able to access your data in the cloud without your knowledge or permission? Why or why not? What types and amount of personal data are you comfortable storing in the cloud? Why?

QUIZ YOURSELF 7-2

Instructions: Find the true statement below. Then, rewrite the remaining false statements so that they are true.

1. Cloud storage is a storage device that typically uses flash memory to store data, instructions, and information.
2. A USB flash drive is a flash memory storage device that plugs in a parallel port on a computer or mobile device.
3. Flash memory cards are a type of magnetic media, which means they consist entirely of electronic components and contain no moving parts.
4. An ExpressCard module is a removable device that fits in an ExpressCard slot.

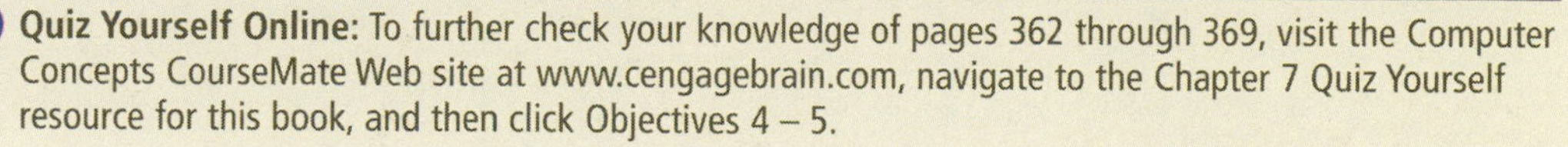

Quiz Yourself Online: To further check your knowledge of pages 362 through 369, visit the Computer Concepts CourseMate Web site at www.cengagebrain.com, navigate to the Chapter 7 Quiz Yourself resource for this book, and then click Objectives 4 – 5.

Optical Discs

An *optical disc* is a type of storage media that consists of a flat, round, portable disc made of metal, plastic, and lacquer that is written and read by a laser. (The spelling, disk, is used for magnetic and flash memory media, and disc is used for optical media.) Optical discs used in personal computers are 4.75 inches in diameter and less than one-twentieth of an inch thick. Smaller computers, game consoles, and mobile devices, however, often use *mini discs* that have a diameter of 3 inches or less.

Optical discs primarily store software, data, digital photos, movies, and music. Some optical disc formats are read only, meaning users cannot write (save) on the media. Others are read/write, which allows users to save on the disc just as they save on a hard disk.

Figure 7-25
A slot-loaded optical disc drive.

Nearly every personal computer today has some type of optical disc drive installed in a drive bay. On some, you push a button to slide out a tray, insert the disc, and then push the same button to close the tray; others are slot loaded, which means you insert the disc in a narrow opening on the drive (Figure 7-25). When you insert the disc, the operating system automatically may start the program, music, or video on the disc.

With some discs, you can read and/or write on one side only. Manufacturers usually place a silk-screened label on the top layer of these single-sided discs. You insert a single-sided disc in the drive with the label side up. Other discs are double-sided. Simply remove the disc from the drive, flip it over, and reinsert it in the drive to use the other side of the disc. Double-sided discs often have no label; instead, each side of the disc is identified with small writing around the center of the disc. Some drives use *LightScribe technology*, which works with specially coated optical discs, to etch labels directly on the disc (as opposed to placing an adhesive label on the disc).

The drive designation of an optical disc drive usually follows alphabetically after that of all the hard disks. For example, if the computer has one internal hard disk (drive C) and an external hard disk (drive D), then the first optical disc drive is drive E. A second optical disc drive would be drive F.

Optical discs store items by using microscopic pits (indentations) and lands (flat areas) that are in the middle layer of the disc (Figure 7-26).

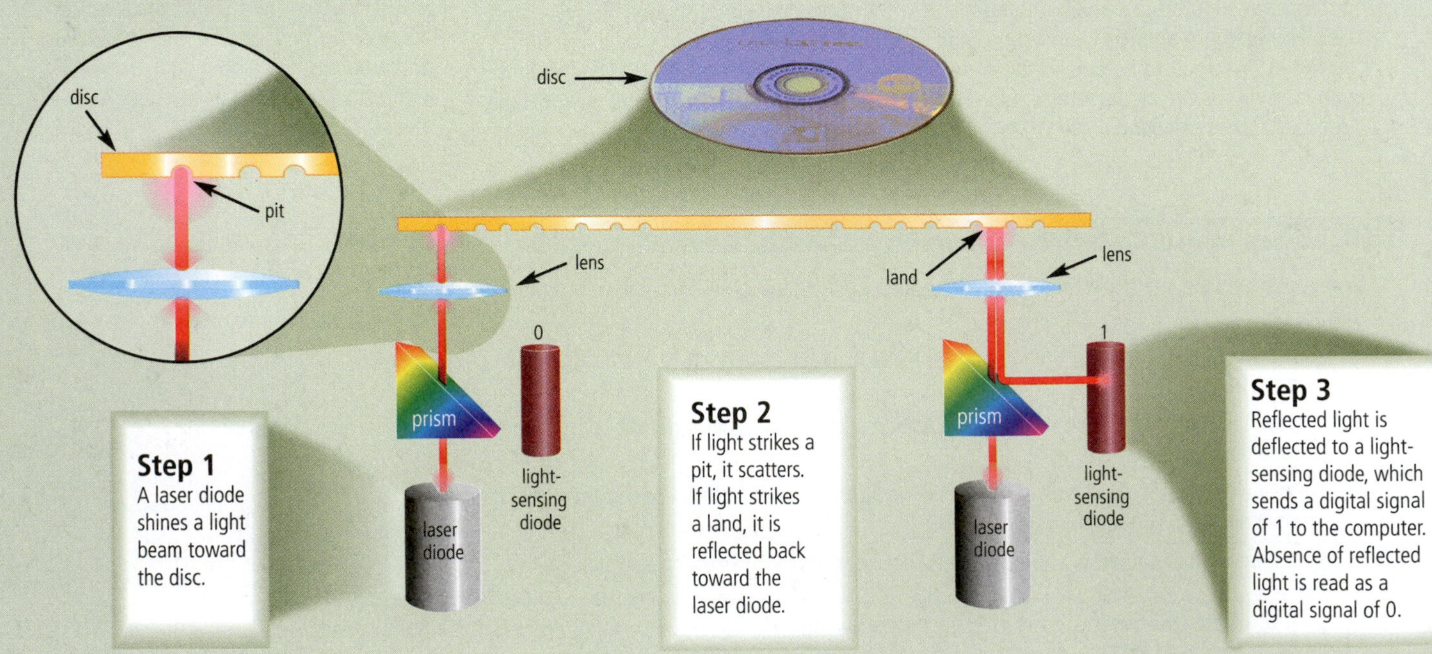

Figure 7-26 This figure shows how a laser reads data on an optical disc.

A high-powered laser light creates the pits. A lower-powered laser light reads items from the disc by reflecting light through the bottom of the disc. The reflected light is converted into a series of bits the computer can process. A land causes light to reflect, which is read as binary digit 1. Pits absorb the light; this absence of light is read as binary digit 0.

Optical discs commonly store items in a single track that spirals from the center of the disc to the edge of the disc. As with a hard disk, this single track is divided into evenly sized sectors on which items are stored (Figure 7-27).

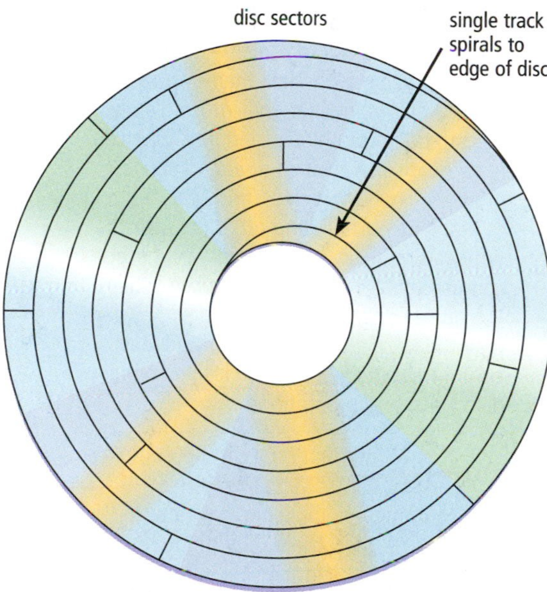

Figure 7-27 An optical disc typically stores data, instructions, and information in a single track that spirals from the center of the disc to the edge of the disc.

Care of Optical Discs

Manufacturers claim that a properly cared for high-quality optical disc will last 5 years but could last up to 100 years. Figure 7-28 offers some guidelines for the proper care of optical discs. Never bend a disc; it may break. Do not expose discs to extreme temperatures or humidity. The ideal temperature range for disc storage is 50 to 70 degrees Fahrenheit. Stacking discs, touching the underside of discs, or exposing them to any type of contaminant may scratch a disc. Place an optical disc in its protective case, called a *jewel box*, when you are finished using it and store in an upright (vertical) position.

FAQ 7-6

Can I clean a disc?

Yes, you can remove dust, dirt, smudges, and fingerprints from the surface of an optical disc. Moisten a nonabrasive cloth with warm water or rubbing alcohol (do not use ammonia-based solutions) and then wipe the disc in straight lines from the center outward. You also can repair scratches on the surface with a specialized disc repair kit.

For more information, visit the Computer Concepts CourseMate Web site at www.cengagebrain.com, navigate to the Chapter 7 FAQ resource for this book, and then click Cleaning and Repairing Discs.

Figure 7-28 Some guidelines for the proper care of optical discs.

Types of Optical Discs

Many different formats of optical discs exist today. Figure 7-29 identifies a variety of optical disc formats and specifies whether a user can read from the disc, write to the disc, and/or erase the disc. The following sections describe characteristics unique to each of these disc formats. Read Innovative Computing 7-2 to find out about a new use for optical discs.

Optical Disc Formats

Optical Disc	Read	Write	Erase
CD-ROM	Y	N	N
CD-R	Y	Y	N
CD-RW	Y	Y	Y
DVD-ROM BD-ROM	Y	N	N
DVD-R DVD+R BD-R	Y	Y	N
DVD-RW DVD+RW DVD-RAM BD-RE	Y	Y	Y

Figure 7-29 Manufacturers sell CD-ROM, DVD-ROM, and BD-ROM media prerecorded (written) with audio, video, and software. Users cannot change the contents of these discs. Users, however, can purchase the other formats of optical discs as blank media and record (write) their own data, instructions, and information on these discs.

INNOVATIVE COMPUTING 7-2

The Perfect Gift for Buying and Marketing

The one-size-fits-all gift card is the gift of choice for more than 60 percent of shoppers. Consumers now find store racks filled with a wide variety of cards, and marketers are searching for unique methods of persuading consumers to buy a particular merchant's gift card instead of a competitor's card.

One way to stand out from the rest is to use a multimedia card on an optical disc. EnXnet has developed an interactive gift card for companies to use as a marketing tool, one being a physical therapy and personal training provider. The card is distributed to doctors, athletes, and fans who can play the disc on their computers and view printable coupons, videos, and special offers.

Marketers are finding other uses for the optical disc gift cards. For example, hotels can use the product as a room key. When the guests open their hotel doors, they can play the key on their computer and view content about the hotel, exclusive online discounts, and promotions.

For more information, visit the Computer Concepts CourseMate Web site at www.cengagebrain.com, navigate to the Chapter 7 Innovative Computing resource for this book, and then click Optical Discs.

CDs

A **CD-ROM**, or *compact disc read-only memory*, is a type of optical disc that users can read but not write (record) or erase — hence, the name read-only. Manufacturers write the contents of standard CD-ROMs. A standard CD-ROM is called a *single-session disc* because manufacturers write all items on the disc at one time. Software manufacturers often distribute their programs using CD-ROMs (Figure 7-30).

A typical CD-ROM holds from 650 MB to 1 GB of data, instructions, and information. To read a CD-ROM, insert the disc in a **CD-ROM drive** or a CD-ROM player. Because audio CDs and CD-ROMs use the same laser technology, you may be able to use a CD-ROM drive to listen to an audio CD while using the computer.

Figure 7-30 Encyclopedias, games, simulations, and many other programs are distributed on CD-ROM.

The speed of a CD-ROM drive determines how fast it installs programs and accesses the disc. Original CD-ROM drives were single-speed drives with transfer rates of 150 KBps. Manufacturers measure all optical disc drives relative to this original CD-ROM drive. They use an X to denote the original transfer rate of 150 KBps. For example, a 48X CD-ROM drive has a data transfer rate of 7,200 (48 × 150) KBps, or 7.2 MBps.

Current CD-ROM drives have transfer rates, or speeds, ranging from 48X to 75X or faster. The higher the number, the faster the CD-ROM drive. Faster CD-ROM drives are more expensive than slower drives.

CD-Rs and CD-RWs A **CD-R** (*compact disc-recordable*) is a multisession optical disc on which users can write, but not erase, their own items such as text, graphics, and audio. *Multisession* means you can write on part of the disc at one time and another part at a later time. Each part of a CD-R, however, can be written on only one time, and the disc's contents cannot be erased.

A **CD-RW** (*compact disc-rewritable*) is an erasable multisession disc you can write on multiple times. CD-RW overcomes the major disadvantage of CD-R because it allows users to write and rewrite data, instructions, and information on the CD-RW disc multiple times — instead of just once. Reliability of the disc tends to drop, however, with each successive rewrite.

To write on a CD-RW disc, you must have CD-RW software and a **CD-RW drive**. These drives have write speeds of 52X or more, rewrite speeds of 32X or more, and read speeds of 52X or more. Manufacturers state the speeds in this order; that is, write speed, rewrite speed, and read speed is stated as 52/32/52. Most CD-RW drives can read audio CDs, CD-ROMs, CD-Rs, and CD-RWs.

Many personal computers today include either a CD-R or CD-RW drive, or a combination drive that includes CD-R or CD-RW capabilities, as a standard feature so that users can burn their own discs. The process of writing on an optical disc is called *burning*. Some operating systems, such as Windows, include the capability of burning discs.

A popular use of CD-RW and CD-R discs is to create audio CDs. For example, users can record their own music and save it on a CD, purchase and download songs from the Web, or rearrange tracks on a purchased music CD. The process of copying audio and/or video data from a purchased disc and saving it on digital media is called *ripping*.

Archive Discs and Picture CDs

Many people use archive discs or Picture CDs to preserve their photos. When you post and share photos online on a photo sharing community, you can choose to save your collection of online photos on an archive disc (Figure 7-31). An **archive disc** stores photos from an online photo center in the jpg file format, usually at a maximum resolution of 7200 pixels per photo. The cost of archive discs is determined by the number of photos being stored. One service, for example, charges $9.99 for the first hundred pictures.

A Kodak **Picture CD** is a single-session CD-ROM that stores digital versions of film using a jpg file format at a lower resolution, typically 1024 × 1536 pixels. Many photo centers offer Picture CD service for consumers when they drop off film to be developed. The average cost for a Picture CD is about $3 per roll of film.

Most optical disc drives can read an archive disc and a Picture CD. Using photo editing software and photos on these discs, you can remove red eye, crop the photo, enhance colors, trim away edges, adjust the lighting, and edit just about any aspect of a photo. In addition, you can print copies of the photos from the disc on glossy paper with an ink-jet printer. If you do not have a printer to print the images, many stores have kiosks at which you can print pictures from an archive disc, a Picture CD, or other media.

How an Archive Disc Works

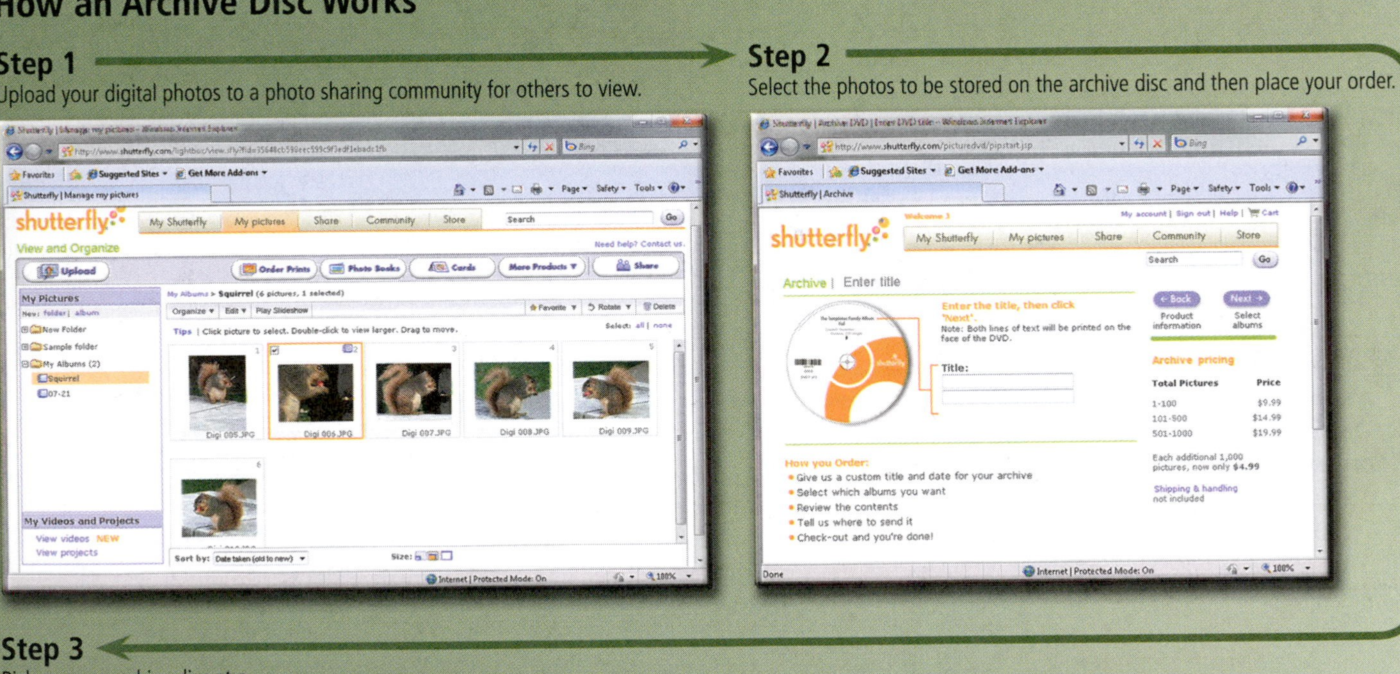

Figure 7-31 This figure shows how an archive disc works.

DVDs and Blu-ray Discs

Although the size and shape of a CD and DVD are similar, a DVD stores data, instructions, and information in a slightly different manner and thus achieves a higher storage capacity. DVD quality also far surpasses that of CDs because images are stored at higher resolution.

Widely used DVDs are capable of storing 4.7 GB to 17 GB, depending on the storage techniques used. The first storage technique involves making the disc denser by packing the pits closer together. The second involves using two layers of pits. For this technique to work, the lower layer of pits is semitransparent so that the laser can read through it to the upper layer. This technique doubles the capacity of the disc. Finally, some DVDs are double-sided.

A **DVD-ROM** (*digital versatile disc-read-only memory* or *digital video disc-read-only memory*) is a high-capacity optical disc on which users can read but not write or erase. Manufacturers write the contents of DVD-ROMs and distribute them to consumers. DVD-ROMs store movies, music, music videos, huge databases, and complex software (Figure 7-32).

To read a DVD-ROM, you need a **DVD-ROM drive** or DVD player. Most DVD-ROM drives also can read audio CDs, CD-ROMs, CD-Rs, and CD-RWs. DVD-ROM drives can read DVDs at speeds of 16X or more and CDs at speeds of 52X or more. Some drives, called DVD/CD-RW drives, are combination drives that read and write DVD and CD media. Many of today's computers include these combination drives.

A newer, more expensive DVD format is Blu-ray, which has a higher capacity and better quality than standard DVDs, especially for high-definition audio and video. A *Blu-ray Disc-ROM (BD-ROM)* has storage capacities of 100 GB, with expectations of exceeding 200 GB in the future. Blu-ray Disc (BD) drives and players are backward compatible with DVD and CD formats. Some game consoles include a Blu-ray drive. Original Blu-ray Disc drives had read speeds of 4.5 MBps, designated as 1X. Current read/write speeds of Blu-ray Discs range from 9 MBps (2X) to 36 Mbps (8X) in the future. Figure 7-33 compares the current storage capacities of DVD and Blu-ray media.

Another high density format, called HD VMD, recently emerged as a competitor to Blu-ray. With future technology, an *HD VMD* (*Versatile Multilayer Disc*) potentially will contain up to 20 layers, each with a capacity of 5 GB. Current HD VMDs have capacities of 40 GB and more.

A mini-DVD that has grown in popularity is the UMD, which works specifically with the PlayStation Portable (PSP) handheld game console. The *UMD* (Universal Media Disc), which has a diameter of about 2.4 inches, can store up to 1.8 GB of games, movies, or music (Figure 7-34). Similarly, the mini Blu-ray Disc, which is used primarily in digital video recorders, stores approximately 7.5 GB.

Blu-ray
For more information, visit the Computer Concepts CourseMate Web site at www.cengagebrain.com, navigate to the Chapter 7 Web Link resource for this book, and then click Blu-ray.

DVD and Blu-ray Storage Capacities

Sides	Layers	DVD	Blu-ray
1	1	4.7 GB	25 GB
1	2	8.5 GB	50 GB
2	1	9.4 GB	50 GB
2	2	17 GB	100 GB

Figure 7-33 Storage capacities of DVDs and Blu-ray Discs.

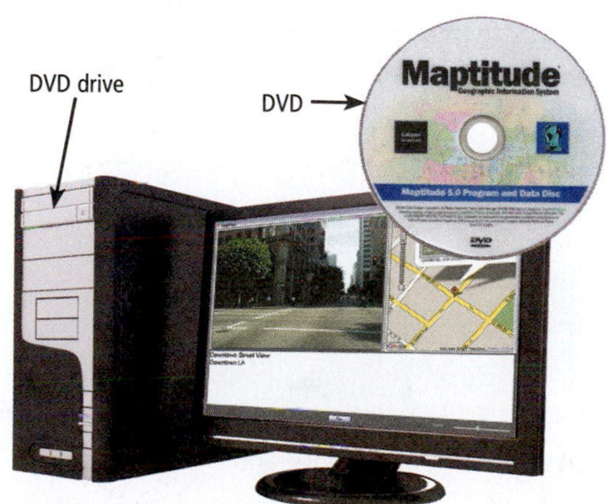

Figure 7-32 A DVD-ROM is a high-capacity optical disc.

Figure 7-34 The PSP handheld game console plays games stored on a UMD.

Recordable and Rewritable DVDs Many types of recordable and rewritable DVD formats are available. *DVD-R* and *DVD+R* are competing DVD-recordable formats, each with up to 4.7 GB storage capacity. Similarly, *BD-R* is a high-capacity DVD-recordable format. Each of these formats allows users to write on the disc once and read (play) it many times.

Instead of recordable DVDs, however, most users work with rewritable DVDs because these discs can be written on multiple times and also erased. Three competing rewritable DVD formats, each with storage capacities up to 4.7 GB per side are **DVD-RW, DVD+RW**, and **DVD+RAM**. Likewise, *BD-RE* is a high-capacity rewritable DVD format. To write on these discs, you must have a compatible drive or recorder. Rewritable drives usually can read a variety of DVD and CD media. Before investing in equipment, check to be sure it is compatible with the media on which you intend to record.

? FAQ 7-7

Is it a good idea to transfer movies from older media, such as VHS, to an optical disc or cloud storage?

Older media, especially magnetic disks and tapes, have a relatively short lifespan and can be damaged easily. For this reason, many people prefer to transfer their older recordings to newer storage media, such as an optical disc or cloud storage. While it might be safe to copy movies to which you own the rights entirely, you should check applicable copyright laws in your area before making a copy of a movie to which someone else owns the rights.

For more information, visit the Computer Concepts CourseMate Web site at www.cengagebrain.com, navigate to the Chapter 7 FAQ resource for this book, and then click Transferring Movies.

Other Types of Storage

In addition to the previously discussed types of storage, other options are available for specific uses and applications. These include tape, magnetic stripe cards and smart cards, microfilm and microfiche, and enterprise storage.

Tape

One of the first storage media used with mainframe computers was tape. **Tape** is a magnetically coated ribbon of plastic capable of storing large amounts of data and information at a low cost. Tape no longer is used as a primary method of storage. Instead, business users utilize tape most often for long-term storage and backup.

Comparable to a tape recorder, a **tape drive** reads and writes data and information on a tape. Although older computers used reel-to-reel tape drives, today's tape drives use tape cartridges. A *tape cartridge* is a small, rectangular, plastic housing for tape (Figure 7-35). Tape cartridges that contain quarter-inch-wide tape are slightly larger than audiocassette tapes. Business users sometimes back up personal computer hard disks to tape, often using an external tape drive. On larger computers, tape cartridges are mounted in a separate cabinet called a *tape library*. Often, a tape robot automatically retrieves tape cartridges, which are identified by location or bar code. Transfer rates of tape drives range from 1.25 MBps to 6 MBps.

Tape storage requires *sequential access*, which refers to reading or writing data consecutively. As with a music tape, you must forward or rewind the tape to a specific point to access a specific piece of data. For example, to access item W requires passing through items A through V sequentially.

Hard disks, flash memory storage, and optical discs all use direct access. *Direct access*, also called *random access*, means that the device can locate a particular data item or file immediately, without having to move consecutively through items stored in front of the desired data item or file. When writing or reading specific data, direct access is much faster than sequential access.

Figure 7-35 A tape drive and a tape cartridge.

Magnetic Stripe Cards and Smart Cards

A **magnetic stripe card** is a credit card, entertainment card, bank card, or other similar card, with a stripe that contains information identifying you and the card (shown in Figure 7-1 on page 352). Information stored in the stripe includes your name, account number, and the card's expiration date. A magnetic stripe card reader reads information stored on the stripe.

A **smart card**, which is similar in size to a credit card or ATM card, stores data on a thin microprocessor embedded in the card. Smart cards contain a processor and have input, process, output, and storage capabilities. When you insert the smart card in a specialized card reader, the information on the smart card is read and, if necessary, updated. Some credit cards are smart cards, and some store biometric data such as fingerprints to authenticate a user (Figure 7-36).

Uses of smart cards include storing medical records, vaccination data, and other health care and identification information; tracking information, such as employee attendance or customer purchases; storing a prepaid amount of money, such as for student purchases on campus; and authenticating users, such as for Internet purchases or building access. In addition, a smart card can double as an ID card. Read Ethics & Issues 7-4 for a related discussion.

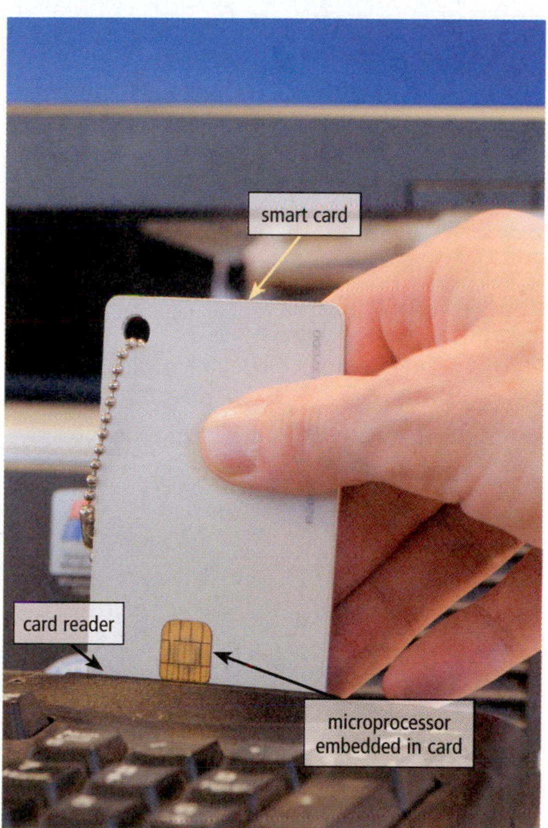

Figure 7-36 This user inserts the smart card to access the computer.

Smart Cards

For more information, visit the Computer Concepts CourseMate Web site at www.cengagebrain.com, navigate to the Chapter 7 Web Link resource for this book, and then click Smart Cards.

ETHICS & ISSUES 7-4

Should the World Become a Cashless Society?

Do you toss your loose change in a jar with the hopes of making a special purchase with the savings someday? This habit may become futile if the world goes cashless. Some forecasters say that the world is moving toward a cashless society. One form of payment that could end the need for cash is the smart card, which can store a dollar amount on a thin microprocessor and update the amount whenever a transaction is made. Advocates claim that smart cards would eliminate muggings and robberies, make it difficult to purchase illegal goods, and reduce taxes by identifying tax cheats. Also, payment using biometrics, such as fingerprints, is becoming more common. Several high-profile security breaches at credit reporting and credit card companies, however, have heightened concerns over privacy. In a recent survey, most Americans said that they would not use a smart card even if privacy was guaranteed. Another survey shows that most Americans believe that fingerprints are a trustworthy form of identification. A cash purchase usually is anonymous. Yet, a smart card purchase preserves a record of the transaction that could become available to other merchants, advertisers, government agencies, or hackers.

Should the world become a cashless society? Why or why not? Would you be comfortable using a smart card or fingerprint instead of cash for all transactions? Why?

Ethics & Issues

For the complete text of the Ethics & Issues boxes found in this chapter, visit the Computer Concepts CourseMate Web site at www.cengagebrain.com and then navigate to the Chapter 7 Ethics & Issues resource for this book.

Microfilm and Microfiche

Microfilm and microfiche store microscopic images of documents on roll or sheet film. **Microfilm** is a 100- to 215-foot roll of film. **Microfiche** is a small sheet of film, usually about 4 × 6 inches. A *computer output microfilm recorder* is the device that records the images on the film. The stored images are so small that you can read them only with a microfilm or microfiche reader (Figure 7-37).

Microfilm and microfiche use is widespread, with many companies allowing you to search through and view microfilm images online. Libraries use these media to store back issues of newspapers, magazines, and genealogy records. Some large organizations use microfilm and microfiche to archive inactive files. Some banks use them to store transactions and canceled checks. The U.S. Army uses them to store personnel records.

The use of microfilm and microfiche provides a number of advantages. They greatly reduce the amount of paper firms must handle. They are inexpensive and have the longest life of any storage media (Figure 7-38). Read Looking Ahead 7-1 for a look at long-term storage.

Figure 7-37 Images on microfilm can be read only with a microfilm reader.

Media Life Expectancies* (when using high-quality media)		
Media Type	**Guaranteed Life Expectancy**	**Potential Life Expectancy**
Magnetic disks	3 to 5 years	20 to 30 years
Optical discs	5 to 10 years	50 to 100 years
Solid state drives	50 years	140 years
Microfilm	100 years	500 years
* according to manufacturers of the media		

Figure 7-38 Microfilm is the medium with the longest life.

LOOKING AHEAD 7-1

Rosetta Project a Storage Solution

The Rosetta Stone unlocked the secret of understanding Egyptian hieroglyphics. Created in 186 B.C., the carved stone contains translations of one hieroglyphic passage into three languages. Today, more than 2,500 human languages exist, but 50 to 90 percent of them are expected to become extinct by the end of this century. In an effort to preserve these languages using long-term storage technology, thousands of people collaborated on the Rosetta Project to create the Rosetta Disk.

Measuring only 3 inches wide, the nickel Rosetta Disk contains 15,000 etched pages documenting more than 1,000 known languages in the world. Each page is .019 inches wide, approximately the width of 5 human hairs. The pages are readable when the Disk is magnified 1,000 times. For protection, the Disk is housed in a 4-inch spherical container.

Five prototype Disks were created. The original Disk is attached to the European Space Agency's Rosetta Space Probe that was launched in 2004 and is expected to land on a comet in 2014. The Probe will measure the comet's molecular composition and then orbit the sun for millions of years.

For more information, visit the Computer Concepts CourseMate Web site at www.cengagebrain.com, navigate to the Chapter 7 Looking Ahead resource for this book, and then click Long-Term Storage.

Enterprise Storage

A large business, commonly referred to as an enterprise, has hundreds or thousands of employees in offices across the country or around the world. Enterprises use computers and computer networks to manage and store huge volumes of data and information about customers, suppliers, and employees (Figure 7-39).

To meet their large-scale needs, enterprises use special hardware geared for heavy use, maximum availability, and maximum efficiency. One or more servers on the network have the sole purpose of providing storage to connected users. For high-speed storage access, entire networks are dedicated exclusively to connecting devices that provide storage to other servers. (For a technical discussion about a particular type of Internet server, read the High-Tech Talk article on page 382.) In an enterprise, some storage systems can provide more than 185 TB of storage capacity. Optical disc servers hold hundreds of optical discs.

An enterprise's storage needs usually grow daily. Thus, the storage solutions an enterprise chooses must be able to store its data and information requirements today and tomorrow.

Enterprise Storage

For more information, visit the Computer Concepts CourseMate Web site at www.cengagebrain.com, navigate to the Chapter 7 Web Link resource for this book, and then click Enterprise Storage.

Figure 7-39 An enterprise uses high-capacity storage devices.

Categories of Users

User	Typical Storage Devices
Home 	• 500 GB hard disk • Cloud storage • Optical disc drive • Card reader/writer • USB flash drive
Small Office/Home Office 	• 1 TB hard disk • Cloud storage • Optical disc drive • External hard disk for backup • USB flash drive
Mobile 	• 250 GB hard disk • Cloud storage • Optical disc drive • Card reader/writer • Portable hard disk for backup • USB flash drive
Power 	• 2.5 TB hard disk • Cloud storage • Optical disc drive • Portable hard disk for backup • USB flash drive
Enterprise 	• Desktop Computer - 1 TB hard disk - Optical disc drive - Smart card reader - Tape drive - USB flash drive • Server or Mainframe - Network storage server - 40 TB hard disk system - Optical disc server - Microfilm or microfiche

Figure 7-40 Recommended storage devices for various users.

Putting It All Together

Many factors influence the type of storage devices you should use: the amount of data, instructions, and information to be stored; the hardware and software in use; and the desired cost. The table in Figure 7-40 outlines several suggested storage devices for various types of computer users. Read Ethics & Issues 7-5 for a related discussion.

ETHICS & ISSUES 7-5

Who Should Be Looking at Your Medical Records?

A medical transcriber based in a foreign country and hired by a U.S. medical center threatened to post private medical records to the Internet if she was not paid more. With the widespread use of computers and an explosion in data storage capacity around the world, private information, such as medical records, requires increased diligence by companies, governments, and individuals to maintain this privacy. The government would like most Americans' health care records available in privacy-protected electronic format by 2014. Although these records will be stored by a corporation or the government, individuals probably will have complete control, or ownership, of these electronic records.

The Health Insurance Portability and Accountability Act (HIPAA) sets rigorous standards for medical record privacy. The law does not cover financial records, education records, or employment records — each of which may contain medical information about you. Your medical information also may be examined by insurance companies, government agencies, the Medical Information Bureau (MIB), employers, and the courts. You also inadvertently may pass on medical information to direct marketers when you participate in informal health screenings or surveys. Some people have found that discussing medical conditions via Internet chat rooms or newsgroups has resulted in unwanted attention, and they later regret the disclosures. Proponents of greater electronic access to medical records claim that more access means that physicians can be better prepared when they see patients, physicians will make fewer errors, and insurance companies can better root out fraud.

Should more limits be placed on what other people can do with your medical information? Why or why not? What are the advantages of increased access to medical records? What are the disadvantages?

✔ QUIZ YOURSELF 7-3

Instructions: Find the true statement below. Then, rewrite the remaining false statements so that they are true.

1. A CD-RW is a type of optical disc on which users can read but not write (record) or erase.
2. A DVD-RAM is a single-session disc that stores digital versions of film using a jpg file format.
3. DVDs have the same storage capacities as CDs.
4. Optical discs are written and read by mirrors.
5. Single session means you can write on part of the disc at one time and another part at a later time.
6. Microfilm and microfiche have the longest life of any media.

Quiz Yourself Online: To further check your knowledge of pages 370 through 380, visit the Computer Concepts CourseMate Web site at www.cengagebrain.com, navigate to the Chapter 7 Quiz Yourself resource for this book, and then click Objectives 6 – 8.

Chapter Summary

Storage holds data, instructions, and information, which includes pictures, music, and videos, for future use. Users depend on storage devices to provide access to their storage media for years and decades to come.

This chapter identified and discussed various storage media and storage devices. Storage media covered included internal hard disks; external and removable hard disks; solid state drives; memory cards; USB flash drives; ExpressCard modules; cloud storage; CDs, DVDs, and Blu-ray Discs; tape; smart cards; and microfilm and microfiche.

Computer Usage @ Work

Meteorology

With the television tuned to the local weather station, you anxiously are awaiting to see the projected path of a hurricane in the tropics. Having experienced hurricanes in the past, you rely heavily on the accuracy of weather forecasts so that you can adequately prepare if a storm travels through the area. Computers allow meteorologists to better estimate the severity and path of storms, enabling people to make potentially life-saving preparations.

The National Hurricane Center uses multiple computer models to determine a storm's path. These models consider factors such as the storm's current strength, the effects of nearby weather systems, the storm's central pressure, and whether the storm may travel over land. These models also may consider previous storms that traveled a similar path. Historical weather and storm data are stored on large storage devices by the National Weather Service. While these models are not 100 percent accurate, they do ensure that everyone who may be affected by the storm has enough time to prepare.

Violent, rotating thunderstorms potentially can spawn tornadoes, which sometimes cause catastrophic damage. For this reason, it is important for everyone to closely watch or listen to the weather during the storm. Meteorologists can monitor weather systems on multiple radars and send additional severe weather warnings automatically to weather radios. Computer technology enables these messages to be broadcast automatically only to weather radios in areas that may be affected.

In addition to computers helping us stay safe during severe storms, they also assist with day-to-day weather forecasting. Several years ago, meteorologists could predict the weather for only a few days into the future. Beyond that point, the forecast was very uncertain. Meteorologists presently are able to predict the weather, including temperature and chance of precipitation, one week or more into the future with much greater accuracy because computers create models using historical weather data and behavior to predict the future path of various weather systems.

News and weather stations also post their weather forecasts online. In fact, several Web sites have interactive radars that allow visitors to zoom in and view how weather is affecting their immediate neighborhood.

The meteorology field has made significant advancements because of computer technologies. Weather forecasts are more meaningful, which not only helps us prepare on land but also helps to protect those traveling by air or by sea.

For more information, visit the Computer Concepts CourseMate Web site at www.cengagebrain.com, navigate to the Chapter 7 Computer Usage @ Work resource for this book, and then click Meteorology.

High-Tech Talk

DNS Servers: How Devices on the Internet Easily Locate Each Other

Domain name system (DNS) servers, also called name servers, play an important role for Internet users who visit Web sites and send e-mail messages. DNS is a service on the Internet that converts domain names into Internet protocol (IP) addresses. Recall that a domain name is the text version of an IP address; for example, www.google.com is the domain name for the IP address of 72.14.207.99. Because the DNS stores IP addresses for each domain name, it is one of the largest databases stored across servers worldwide. In fact, some view DNS databases as nothing more than large address books. The absence of DNS servers would require users to remember IP addresses for Web sites.

To visit a Web site on the Internet, you begin by starting a Web browser and typing the Web address (which includes a domain name) in the Address bar. Once you press the ENTER key, the Web browser initiates a request for the IP address associated with the Web address. If the DNS server on your network or your Internet access provider's network knows the IP address, it will answer the request. Otherwise, it will ask another DNS server for this information or return an error message indicating that the domain name does not exist. If a DNS server is able to return an IP address to the Web browser, the Web browser contacts the Web server located at that IP address and requests a Web page. In some cases, DNS servers cache IP addresses for frequently requested domain names for a specified period of time, called the *Time To Live* (TTL). Because IP addresses are cached for certain domain names, it can take several days or more for updates to be reflected on DNS servers worldwide. For example, if the google.com Web server (accessible at www.google.com) is replaced with a new Web server with a new IP address, it might take several days for other DNS servers to acquire the new IP address.

If a DNS server does not know the IP address for a requested domain name, it will contact a root name server. A *root name server* stores a list of IP addresses for all DNS servers that handle a specific top-level domain, such as com or edu. For example, if you are attempting to reach www.google.com and your DNS server does not know the IP address, the root name server forwards the request to one of the DNS servers that handle the top-level domain of com. Your request will travel from one root server to the next until one can fulfill it. At that time, it requests the IP address associated with the Web address – in this case, www.google.com – from the COM root name server. Figure 7-41 illustrates a simple example of a DNS request.

The DNS has built-in redundancy. Network administrators typically set up multiple DNS servers on their network so that if one becomes overburdened or stops functioning, the other one(s) can continue filling requests. Similarly, multiple root name servers exist for each top-level domain.

Domain name servers also play an important role in e-mail communications. If you send an e-mail message to kbarnhill@esite.com, the DNS servers will locate the mail exchange (MX) record for the esite.com domain. The *MX record* identifies the location, or IP address, of the SMTP server accepting e-mail messages.

DNS servers often process billions of requests each day; each time you send an e-mail message or view a Web site, you are creating a request for a DNS server. While the average user might generate around 20 requests each day, those who primarily work with computers may generate hundreds of requests per day. Consequently, the millions of users connected to the Internet at any given time are generating billions of DNS requests each day.

For more information, visit the Computer Concepts CourseMate Web site at www.cengagebrain.com, navigate to the Chapter 7 High-Tech Talk resource for this book, and then click DNS Servers.

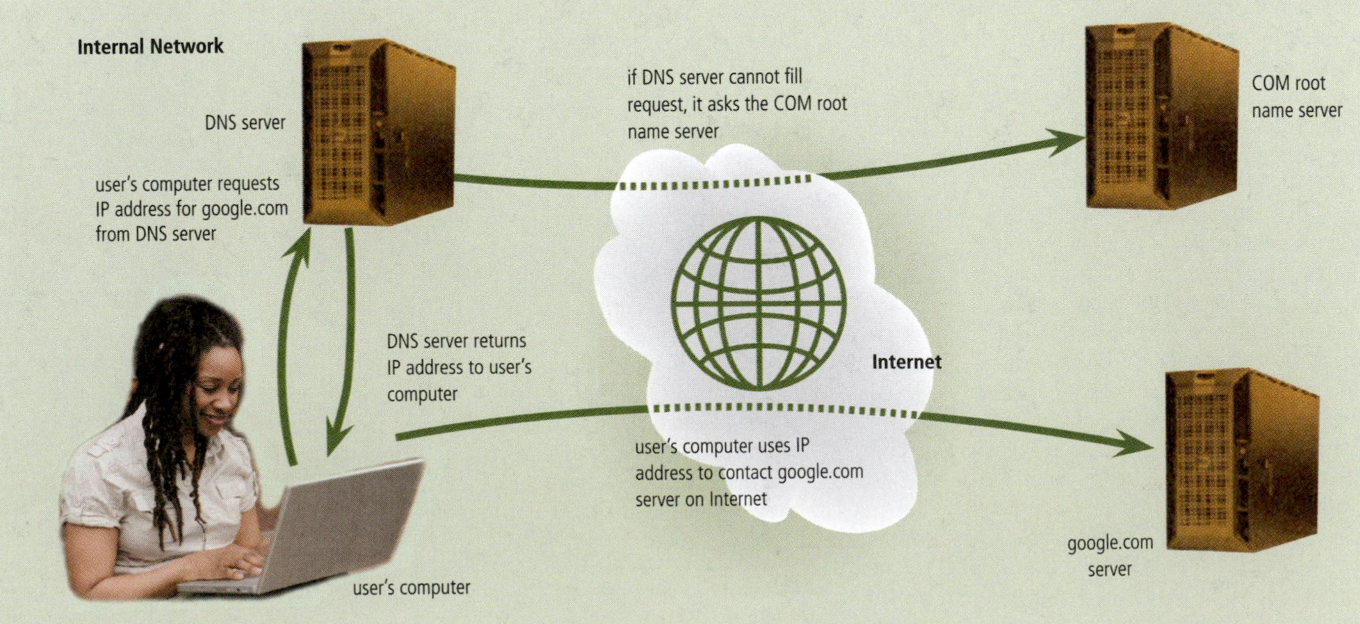

Figure 7-41 A simple DNS request.

Companies on the Cutting Edge

SEAGATE TECHNOLOGY Storage Solutions Supplier

The average household with a broadband Internet connection will need nearly 1 TB of storage for its personal media collections, and *Seagate* has the storage solutions for practically every digital need. The company offers more than 40 products for the personal computing, consumer electronics, and enterprise computing fields.

Seagate has been at the forefront of the digital storage world since it developed the first 5.25-inch hard disk for the personal computer in 1980. In 2008 it shipped its one billionth hard disk, making the company's production for the past 30 years a total of 79 million terabytes. Seagate expects to ship its two billionth hard disk by 2013.

Seagate recently introduced the FreeAgent DockStar network adapter. This device allows users to access their digital media from anywhere in the world and share these files with anyone. The FreeAgent DockStar network adapter also enables users to link their digital content to online social networks such as Facebook, Twitter, and MySpace.

SANDISK CORPORATION Flash Memory Storage Supplier

The number of flash memory card formats is growing, and only one company has the rights to design, develop, manufacture, and market every one of them: *SanDisk*. The company is the world's largest supplier of flash memory storage products and also has lines of portable media players.

The company was founded in 1988, and one of its earliest flash drives was used on a U.S. space shuttle three years later. Today SanDisk is developing rewritable 3-D memory products that will store data vertically, and company executives believe this technology will replace flash products in the next decade.

SanDisk recently introduced the world's fastest 32 GB SDHC card. The 32 GB SanDisk Extreme SDHC card boasts read and write speeds of 30 megabytes per second. The increased speeds enable photographers to take pictures quickly without having to wait long for the card to record the images. In addition, computer users also are able to transfer data to and from the card quickly.

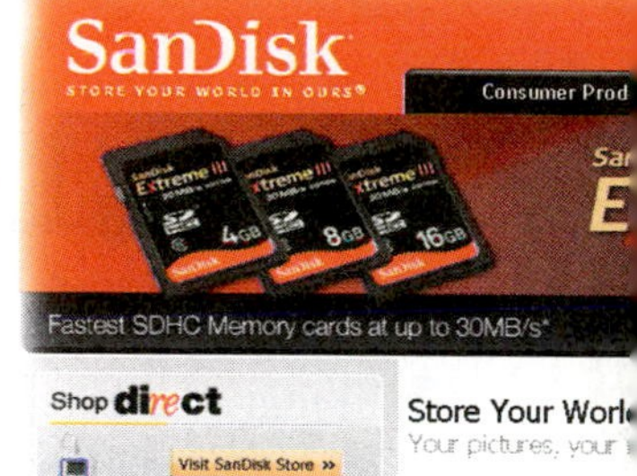

For more information, visit the Computer Concepts CourseMate Web site at www.cengagebrain.com and then navigate to the Chapter 7 Companies on the Cutting Edge resource for this book.

Technology Trailblazers

AL SHUGART Storage Expert

Al Shugart said that his real goal in life was to have fun, and he spent his life doing the things that gave him the most pleasure. The day after receiving his bachelor's degree in engineering physics in 1951, he landed a job at IBM doing what he loved to do: fixing broken items and developing new technology. He was promoted to supervisor of the product development team that developed the first removable hard disk drive.

Shugart then left IBM, became vice president of Memorex, and then started Shugart Associates and began developing floppy disks. In 1979 he founded Seagate Technology with a friend. As his company grew to become the world's largest hard disk manufacturer, he had fun placing his dog, Ernest, on the ballot for a Congressional seat.

Shugart served as president and CEO of Al Shugart International, a venture capital firm in California, until his death in 2006.

MARK DEAN IBM Inventor

Web 2.0 applications demand large, inexpensive storage, and *Mark Dean* is hard at work helping to meet this need. As vice president of IBM's Almaden Research Center lab in California, Dean is responsible for developing innovative products.

Dean joined IBM after graduating from Stanford University with a degree in electrical engineering. He led a team that developed the first CMOS microprocessor to operate at one gigahertz and has more than 40 patents or patents pending that are used in more than 40 million personal computers manufactured each year. Three of his patents are among the nine registered for the architecture of the original personal computer.

Dean is the first African-American to be appointed to IBM Fellow, the company's highest level of technical merit. He also was inducted in the National Inventors Hall of Fame.

For more information, visit the Computer Concepts CourseMate Web site at www.cengagebrain.com and then navigate to the Chapter 7 Technology Trailblazers resource for this book.

STUDENT ASSIGNMENTS

Chapter Review

The Chapter Review reinforces the main concepts presented in this chapter.

To listen to an audio version of this Chapter Review, visit the Computer Concepts CourseMate Web site at www.cengagebrain.com and then navigate to the Chapter 7 Chapter Review resource for this book.

1. How Are Storage Devices Different from Storage Media? A **storage medium** is the physical material on which a computer keeps data, instructions, and information. The number of bytes (characters) a storage medium can hold is its **capacity**. A **storage device** is the computer hardware that records and/or retrieves items to and from storage media. **Writing** is the process of transferring items from memory to a storage medium, and **reading** is the process of transferring these items from a storage medium into memory.

2. What Are the Characteristics of an Internal Hard Disk? A **hard disk**, also called a *hard disk drive* or hard drive, is a storage device that contains one or more inflexible, circular platters that use magnetic particles to store data, instructions, and information. Traditionally, hard disks stored data using *longitudinal recording*, which aligned the magnetic particles horizontally. With *perpendicular recording*, hard disks align the particles vertically, making much greater storage capacities possible. The capacity of a hard disk is determined from whether it uses longitudinal or perpendicular recording, the number of platters it contains, and the composition of the magnetic coating on the platters. A *platter* is made of aluminum, glass, or ceramic and is coated with a material that allows items to be recorded magnetically on its surface. Each platter has two read/write heads, one for each side. The location of a *read/write head* often is referred to by its *cylinder*, which is the vertical section of a track that passes through all platters. **Formatting** is the process of dividing the disk into tracks and sectors. A *track* is a narrow recording band that forms a full circle on the surface of the disk. The disk's storage locations are divided into pie-shaped sections, which break the tracks into small arcs called *sectors*. While the computer is running, the platters in the hard disk rotate at 5,400 to 15,000 *revolutions per minute* (*rpm*), which allows nearly instant access to all tracks and sectors on the platters. *Transfer rate* is the speed with which data, instructions, and information transfer to and from a storage device. **Access time** measures the amount of time it takes a storage device to locate an item on a storage medium, or the time required to deliver an item from memory to the processor.

3. What Is the Purpose of Network Attached Storage Devices, External and Removable Hard Disks, and Hard Disk Controllers? A **network attached storage** (*NAS*) device is a server connected to a network with the sole purpose of providing storage. NAS devices often use a **RAID** configuration. An **external hard disk** is a separate freestanding hard disk that connects with a cable to a USB or FireWire port on the system unit or communicates wirelessly. External hard disks have storage capacities up to 4 TB and more. A **removable hard disk** can be inserted or removed from a built-in or external drive. Removable hard disks have storage capacities up to 1 TB. A *disk controller* consists of a special-purpose chip and electronic circuits that control the transfer of data, instructions, and information from a disk to and from the system bus and other components in a computer. A hard disk controller may be part of the hard disk on the motherboard, or it may be a separate adapter card inside the system unit.

Visit the Computer Concepts CourseMate Web site at www.cengagebrain.com, navigate to the Chapter 7 Quiz Yourself resource for this book, and then click Objectives 1 – 3.

4. What Are the Various Types of Flash Memory Storage? Flash memory chips are a type of *solid state media*, which means they consist entirely of electronic components and contain no moving parts. A **solid state drive** (**SSD**) typically uses flash memory to store data, instructions, and information. A **memory card** is a removable flash memory device that you insert and remove from a slot in a computer, mobile device, or *card reader/writer*. Common memory cards include *CompactFlash* (*CF*), *Secure Digital* (*SD*), *Secure Digital High Capacity* (*SDHC*), *microSD*, *microSDHC*, *xD Picture Card*, *Memory Stick*, and *Memory Stick Micro* (*M2*). A **USB flash drive**, sometimes called a *thumb drive*, is a flash memory storage device that plugs in a port on a computer or mobile

Chapter Review

device. An **ExpressCard module** is a removable device that fits in an ExpressCard slot. ExpressCard modules can add memory, storage, communications, or other capabilities to a computer.

5. What Is Cloud Storage, and What Are Its Advantages? **Cloud storage** is an Internet service that provides storage for computer users. Available for all sizes of users, with various degrees of storage services available for home and business users, cloud storage fees vary, depending on the user's storage requirements. Advantages include accessing files on the Internet from any computer or device with Internet access; storing large audio, video, and graphics files on the Internet instantaneously; allowing others to access their files on the Internet; viewing time-critical data and images immediately; storing off-site backups of data; and providing data center functions.

Visit the Computer Concepts CourseMate Web site at www.cengagebrain.com, navigate to the Chapter 7 Quiz Yourself resource for this book, and then click Objectives 4 – 5.

6. What Are the Characteristics of Optical Discs? An *optical disc* is a type of storage media that consists of a flat, round, portable disc made of metal, plastic, and lacquer that is written and read by a laser. Optical discs, which primarily store software, data, digital photos, movies, and music, contain microscopic pits (indentations) and lands (flat areas) in their middle layer. Optical discs commonly store items in a single track that spirals from the center of the disc to its edge. Like a hard disk, the single track is divided into evenly sized sectors.

7. How Are the Various Types of Optical Discs Different? A **CD-ROM**, or *compact disc read-only memory*, is a type of optical disc that uses laser technology to store items. Users can read the contents of standard CD-ROMs but cannot erase or modify their contents. A **CD-R** (*compact disc-recordable*) is a *multisession* disc on which users can record their own items, such as text, graphics, and audio. Each part of a CD-R can be written on only one time, and the disc's contents cannot be erased. A **CD-RW** (*compact disc-rewritable*) is an erasable disc that can be written on multiple times. An **archive disc** stores photos from an online photo center in the jpg file format. A **Picture CD** is a *single-session* CD-ROM that stores digital versions of film using the jpg format at a lower resolution than an archive disc. A **DVD-ROM** (*digital versatile disc-read-only memory* or *digital video disc-read-only memory*) is a high capacity optical disc that you can read but not write on or erase. A newer, more expensive DVD format is *Blu-ray Disc-ROM* (*BD-ROM*), with higher capacity and better quality than standard DVDs. Many types of recordable and rewritable DVD formats are available. *DVD-R* and *DVD+R* are DVD-recordable formats. *BD-R* is a high-capacity DVD-recordable format. **DVD-RW**, **DVD+RW**, and **DVD+RAM** are rewritable DVD formats that allow users to erase and record multiple times. *BD-RE* is a high-capacity rewritable DVD format.

8. How Are Tape, Magnetic Stripe Cards, Smart Cards, Microfilm and Microfiche, and Enterprise Storage Used? **Tape** is a magnetically coated ribbon of plastic capable of storing large amounts of data and information at a low cost. A **tape drive** reads and writes data and information on tape. Business users utilize tape most often for long-term storage and backup. A **magnetic stripe card** is a credit card, entertainment card, bank card, or other similar card with a stripe that contains information identifying you and the card. A magnetic stripe card reader reads the information stored on the stripe. A **smart card**, which is similar in size to a credit or ATM card, stores data on a thin microprocessor embedded in the card. A smart card reader reads the information on the smart card and updates it if necessary. **Microfilm** is a 100- to 215-foot roll of film. **Microfiche** is a small sheet of film, usually about 4 × 6 inches. Microfilm and microfiche reduce the amount of paper firms must handle, are inexpensive, and have the longest life of any storage media. Enterprises use computers, servers, and networks to manage and store huge volumes of data and information. In an enterprise, some storage systems can provide more than 185 TB of storage, and optical disc servers hold hundreds of optical discs.

Visit the Computer Concepts CourseMate Web site at www.cengagebrain.com, navigate to the Chapter 7 Quiz Yourself resource for this book, and then click Objectives 6 – 8.

STUDENT ASSIGNMENTS

Key Terms

You should know the Primary Terms and be familiar with the Secondary Terms. The list below helps focus your study.

To see an example of and a definition for each term, and to access current and additional information from the Web, visit the Computer Concepts CourseMate Web site at www.cengagebrain.com and then navigate to the Chapter 7 Key Terms resource for this book.

Primary Terms

(shown in bold-black characters in the chapter)

access time (355)
archive disc (374)
backup (358)
capacity (354)
CD-R (373)
CD-ROM (372)
CD-ROM drive (372)
CD-RW (373)
CD-RW drive (373)
cloud storage (368)
DVD+RAM (376)
DVD-ROM (375)
DVD-ROM drive (375)
DVD+RW (376)
DVD-RW (376)
ExpressCard module (367)
external hard disk (360)
formatting (357)
hard disk (355)
magnetic stripe card (377)
memory card (364)
microfiche (378)
microfilm (378)
network attached storage (360)
Picture CD (374)
RAID (360)
reading (354)
removable hard disk (360)
smart card (377)
solid state drive (SSD) (363)
storage device (354)
storage medium (353)
tape (376)
tape drive (376)
USB flash drive (367)
writing (354)

Secondary Terms

(shown in italic characters in the chapter)

allocation unit (357)
BD-R (376)
BD-RE (376)
Blu-ray Disc-ROM (BD-ROM) (375)
burning (373)
card reader/writer (365)
cluster (357)
compact disc read-only memory (372)
compact disc-recordable (373)
compact disc-rewritable (373)
CompactFlash (CF) (364)
computer output microfilm recorder (378)
cylinder (358)
density (359)
digital versatile disc-read-only memory (375)
digital video disc-read-only memory (375)
direct access (376)
disk cache (359)
disk controller (361)
DVD+R (376)
DVD-R (376)
EIDE (Enhanced Integrated Drive Electronics) (361)
eSATA (361)
fixed disk (355)
form factor (358)
GBps (355)
hard disk drive (355)
HD VMD (Versatile Multilayer Disc) (375)
head crash (358)
jewel box (371)
KBps (355)
LightScribe technology (370)
longitudinal recording (356)
MBps (355)
Memory Stick (364)
Memory Stick Micro (M2) (364)
microSD (364)
microSDHC (364)
mini discs (370)
multisession (373)
NAS (360)
optical disc (370)
perpendicular recording (356)
platter (357)
pocket hard drive (361)
portable (355)
random access (376)
read/write head (358)
revolutions per minute (rpm) (358)
ripping (373)
SAS (serial-attached SCSI) (362)
SATA (Serial Advanced Technology Attachment) (361)
SCSI (362)
secondary storage (353)
sectors (357)
Secure Digital (SD) (364)
Secure Digital High Capacity (SDHC) (364)
sequential access (376)
single-session disc (372)
solid state media (362)
storage (352)
tape cartridge (376)
tape library (376)
thumb drive (367)
track (357)
transfer rate (355)
U3 smart drive (367)
UMD (375)
xD Picture Card (364)

external hard disk (360)

Checkpoint

The Checkpoint exercises test your knowledge of the chapter concepts. The page number containing the answer appears in parentheses after each exercise. The Beyond the Book exercises will help broaden your understanding of the concepts presented in this chapter.

To complete the Checkpoint exercises interactively, visit the Computer Concepts CourseMate Web site at www.cengagebrain.com and then navigate to the Chapter 7 Checkpoint resource for this book.

True/False Mark T for True and F for False.

_____ 1. A storage medium, also called secondary storage, is the physical material on which a computer keeps data, instructions, and information. (353)

_____ 2. Reading is the process of transferring data, instructions, and information from memory to a storage medium. (354)

_____ 3. Formatting is the process of dividing the disk into clusters and cylinders. (357)

_____ 4. A cluster can hold data from many files. (358)

_____ 5. A typical hard disk contains only one platter. (358)

_____ 6. A removable hard disk is a separate, freestanding hard disk that connects with a cable to a port on the system unit or communicates wirelessly. (360)

_____ 7. microSD and miniSDHC are common types of removable hard disks. (364)

_____ 8. ExpressCard modules can be used to add memory, storage, communications, multimedia, and security capabilities to a computer. (367)

_____ 9. The process of writing on an optical disc is called ripping. (373)

_____ 10. HD VMDs have a capacity of 40 GB and more. (375)

_____ 11. BD-R is an older low-capacity DVD-recordable format. (376)

_____ 12. Rewritable drives usually can read one type of media. (376)

_____ 13. Direct access means that the device can locate a particular data item or file immediately, without having to move consecutively through items stored in front of the desired data item or file. (376)

Multiple Choice Select the best answer.

1. _____ is the speed with which data, instructions, and information transfer to and from a device. (355)
   a. Access time
   b. Transfer rate
   c. Formatting
   d. Reading

2. Traditionally, hard disks stored data using _____, which aligned the magnetic particles horizontally around the surface of the disk. (356)
   a. LightScribe technology
   b. RAID
   c. longitudinal recording
   d. perpendicular recording

3. A group of two or more integrated hard disks is called a _____. (360)
   a. backup
   b. disk cache
   c. portable hard disk
   d. RAID

4. Users subscribe to a cloud storage service to _____. (369)
   a. save time by storing large files instantaneously
   b. allow others to access their files
   c. store offsite backups of data
   d. all of the above

5. A(n) _____ is a type of storage media that consists of a flat, round, portable disc made of metal, plastic, and lacquer that is written and read by a laser. (370)
   a. optical disc
   b. hard disk
   c. memory card
   d. thumb drive

6. _____ technology works with specially coated optical discs to etch labels directly on the disc. (370)
   a. SCSI
   b. SATA
   c. LightScribe
   d. LightSaber

7. On larger computers, tape cartridges are mounted in a separate cabinet called a(n) _____. (376)
   a. SATA (Serial Advanced Technology Attachment)
   b. tape library
   c. tape cartridge
   d. HD VMD

8. A _____ card is a credit card, entertainment card, bank card, or other similar card, with a stripe that contains information identifying you and the card. (377)
   a. Secure Digital High Capacity
   b. magnetic stripe
   c. Secure Digital
   d. microSDHC

Checkpoint

Matching
Match the terms with their definitions.

_____ 1. capacity (354)
_____ 2. cluster (357)
_____ 3. cylinder (358)
_____ 4. head crash (358)
_____ 5. backup (358)
_____ 6. disk cache (359)
_____ 7. disk controller (361)
_____ 8. eSATA (361)
_____ 9. solid state media (362)
_____ 10. solid state drive (363)

a. vertical section of a track that passes through all platters
b. external disk interface that is much faster than USB and FireWire
c. smallest unit of disk space that stores data and information
d. special-purpose chip and electronic circuits that control the transfer of items to and from the system bus
e. occurs when a read/write head touches the surface of a platter on a hard disk
f. duplicate of a file, program, or disk placed on a separate storage medium that you can use in case the original is lost, damaged, or destroyed
g. a storage device that typically uses flash memory to store data, instructions, and information
h. the number of bytes (characters) a storage medium can hold
i. media which consist entirely of electronic components, such as integrated circuits, and contain no moving parts
j. memory chips that the processor uses to store frequently accessed items

Short Answer
Write a brief answer to each of the following questions.

1. What is network attached storage? ___________ How much hard disk storage can home and small business users add to their network with a NAS device? ___________
2. What are the advantages of SAS (serial-attached SCSI)? ___________ What types of devices can be connected to SAS interfaces? ___________
3. How is a single-session disc different from a multisession disc? ___________ What is the purpose of archive discs and Picture CDs? ___________
4. Why do users use memory cards? ___________ Name five types of memory cards and describe some of the characteristics of each card. ___________
5. What is one difference between microfilm and microfiche? ___________ What are some uses of microfilm and microfiche? ___________

Beyond the Book
Follow the book element instructions below; present your findings (brief report, presentation, discussion, or other means).

1. Ethics & Issues — Select an Ethics & Issues in this chapter (356, 366, 369, 377, 380), find a recent newspaper/magazine article that supports one point of view presented, and then evaluate the article.
2. Computer Usage @ Work — Use the Web or a recent newspaper/magazine to locate three additional unique usages of computer technology in the meteorology field (381). What makes the use of these technologies unique to the meteorology field?
3. Companies on the Cutting Edge and Technology Trailblazers — Use the Web or a recent business newspaper/magazine to locate an interesting fact about Seagate Technology, SanDisk Corporation, Al Shugart, or Mark Dean that was not presented in the chapter (383).
4. High-Tech Talk — Locate a recent newspaper/magazine article that discusses topics related to DNS Servers (382). Would you recommend the article you found? Why or why not?
5. FAQs and Web Links — Use the Web or a recent newspaper/magazine to locate three additional facts about an FAQ (356, 360, 362, 363, 367, 371, 376) and Web Link (356, 360, 361, 363, 365, 369, 375, 377, 379) that were not presented in the chapter.
6. Looking Ahead — Use the Web or a recent newspaper/magazine to discover additional uses of the technology presented in Rosetta Project a Storage Solution (379).
7. Innovative Computing — Use the Web or a recent newspaper/magazine to locate two additional interesting facts about Digital Books Are a Good Read (368) and The Perfect Gift for Buying and Marketing (372).
8. Making Use of the Web — Visit three of the Finance sites (131) and outline the information on each Web site and the possible uses for each Web site.

Learn It Online

The Learn It Online exercises are interactive Web exercises designed to reinforce and expand your understanding of the chapter concepts. The descriptions below briefly summarize each exercise.

To complete the Learn It Online exercises, visit the Computer Concepts CourseMate Web site at www.cengagebrain.com, navigate to the Chapter 7 resources for this book, click the link for the exercise you want to complete, and then read the instructions.

1 At the Movies — Thumb-drive (USB Flash Drive) Encryption
Watch a movie to learn how people who store personal and confidential information on USB flash drives can use third-party programs to password-protect the files so that others cannot access them, and then answer questions about the movie.

2 Video and Audio: You Review It — Blu-ray Disc-ROM (BD-ROM)
Search for, choose, and write a review of a video, podcast, or vodcast that discusses Blu-ray Disc-ROMs.

3 Student Edition Labs — Maintaining a Hard Drive (Hard Disk) and Managing Files and Folders
Enhance your understanding and knowledge about maintaining a hard disk and managing files and folders by completing the Maintaining a Hard Drive and Managing Files and Folders Labs.

4 Practice Test
Take a multiple choice test that checks your knowledge of the chapter concepts and review the resulting study guide.

5 Who Wants To Be a Computer Genius^2?
Play the Shelly Cashman Series version of this popular game by answering questions to find out if you are a computer genius. Panic buttons are available to provide assistance during game play.

6 Wheel of Terms
Identify important key terms presented in this chapter by playing the Shelly Cashman Series version of this popular game.

7 You're Hired!
Embark on the path to a career in computers by answering questions and solving puzzles related to concepts discussed in this chapter.

8 Crossword Puzzle Challenge
Complete an interactive crossword puzzle to reinforce concepts presented in this chapter.

9 Windows Exercises
Step through the Windows 7 exercises to learn about the Recycle Bin, working with files, the hard disk, and Disk Cleanup.

10 Exploring Computer Careers
Read about a career as a computer technician, search for related employment advertisements, and then answer related questions.

11 Web Apps — TurboTax Online
Learn how to use TurboTax Online to create an account, start a new tax return from scratch, review your tax return, and then print and file your tax return.

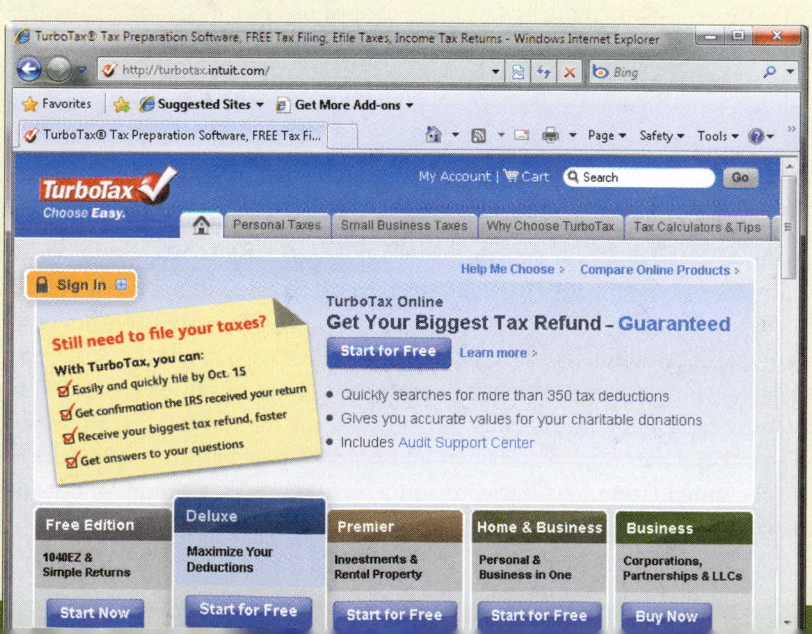

Problem Solving @ Home

The Problem Solving @ Home exercises extend your knowledge of the chapter concepts by seeking solutions to practical computer problems that you may encounter at home or school. The Collaboration exercise should be completed with a team.

In the real world, practical problems often can be solved in multiple ways. Provide one solution to each of the following problems using available resources, such as articles on the Web or in print, blogs, podcasts, videos, television, user guides, other individuals, and electronics and computer stores. You may need to use multiple resources to obtain an answer. Present your solutions in the form requested by your instructor (brief report, presentation, discussion, or other means).

1. **Old Movies** During the past two decades, you have been recording home movies on VHS tapes. It is becoming more difficult to locate blank VHS tapes, and you are worried that if your current VCR breaks, it will be hard to find a new one. A friend suggests that you copy these movies to an optical disc. What steps will you take to convert these movies?
2. **Possible Head Crash** When you turn on your computer, you hear a clicking sound coming from inside the computer. Furthermore, you realize that Windows is not starting automatically. You talk to a friend who said that your hard disk might have experienced a head crash. What might have caused this?
3. **Missing Cable** You are attempting to install a new 1 TB hard disk in your computer. You have found the empty bay for the new hard disk, but you cannot locate the cable that connects it to the computer. What are your next steps?
4. **Different Disk Capacity** After successfully connecting the secondary hard disk that you purchased, you turn on your computer. You click the Computer icon in Windows and then display the properties for the new hard disk. To your surprise, the hard disk capacity that Windows displays is lower than the capacity of the hard disk you have purchased. What might be wrong?
5. **No Space Available** You are attempting to copy some files to an optical disc. After starting the program to burn an optical disc and attempting to start the copy process, the program informs you that not enough space is available on the optical disc. The optical disc that is in the drive is brand new and contains no files of any type. What could be causing this?
6. **Memory Card Problems** For the past two years, you have been using the same Secure Digital (SD) memory card to take pictures with your digital camera. When you insert the SD memory card in your computer's card reader to transfer the pictures, your computer does not display the contents of the card. When you put the card back into your digital camera, you can see that the pictures still are stored on the card. What might be wrong?
7. **Unreadable Credit Card** Lately, the magnetic stripe readers at some store check-out registers are having increasing difficulty reading your credit card. In fact, many merchants now enter your credit card information manually, because the card cannot be read. What might be the problem?

Collaboration

8. **Backup Strategies** You and two of your coworkers have been tasked with determining an effective backup strategy for your company. Specifically, your supervisor would like to know what storage medium is best for the backed up data. You work for a company that sells electronics, and it is important that all data is backed up at the end of each business day. You inform your supervisor that he can back up his data to a hard disk, an optical disc, or cloud storage. He would like more information about each, as well as your recommendation about which medium best suits the needs of the company. Form a team of three classmates. Each team member should research the pros and cons of using one of the three mentioned backup media (hard disk, optical disc, and cloud storage). Each team member should report his or her findings to the other members. As a team, formulate a recommendation for your company's backup media. Compile the team's findings in a report and then submit it to your instructor.

Problem Solving @ Work

The Problem Solving @ Work exercises extend your knowledge of the chapter concepts by seeking solutions to practical computer problems that you may encounter at work. The Collaboration exercise should be completed with a team.

In the real world, practical problems often can be solved in multiple ways. Provide one solution to each of the following problems using available resources, such as articles on the Web or in print, blogs, podcasts, videos, television, user guides, other individuals, and electronics and computer stores. You may need to use multiple resources to obtain an answer. Present your solutions in the form requested by your instructor (brief report, presentation, discussion, or other means).

1. **Disc Will Not Eject** You just installed the newest version of Microsoft Office on your computer. When you attempt to eject the installation disc from the slot-loaded optical disc drive, the disc will not eject from the drive, and you still can hear it spinning inside. You want to remove this disc so that you can insert another disc with photos from the last company party. What steps will you take before calling technical support?
2. **Low Disk Space** While using your computer, Windows displays a message in the notification area indicating that you are very low on disk space. You have not installed any programs or saved any files recently. What could be causing this?
3. **RAID Failure** Your office computer has two hard disks configured as a redundant array of independent disks (RAID) to increase performance. Windows reports that there is a problem with the RAID configuration; specifically, one of your hard disks might be ready to fail. What are your next steps?
4. **Moving Files between Computers** A company policy dictates that employees are not allowed to connect USB flash drives to their office computers for fear of infecting the computer with a virus. After spending the weekend creating PowerPoint presentations for a meeting, you are unsure of how to transfer these files to your office computer. What are your next steps?
5. **Disk Not Recognized** The information technology manager at your company has purchased external hard disks for employees to use to back up their files. When you connect the external hard disk to the USB port on your computer, the computer displays a message stating that it cannot recognize the device. What might you do to correct this problem?
6. **File Will Not Open** Your computer is unable to open a file on an optical disc that you just inserted into the optical disc drive. You have been able to access other files on the same disc, but one file in particular is not opening. What might be causing this?

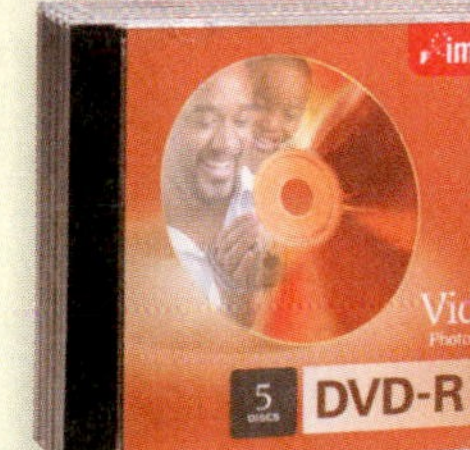

7. **Backing Up Data** It has been several years since your office computer was upgraded, and you just received an e-mail message stating that you finally will receive a new computer next week. The e-mail message also stated that all employees will be responsible for backing up their data. What files will you back up?
8. **Optical Disc Problem** Your colleague gives you an optical disc containing some video files. When you insert the disc in your computer, the disc burning software asks if you would like to finalize the disc. How will you respond?

Collaboration

9. **Computers in Meteorology** Your environmental sciences instructor is teaching a lesson about how computers have advanced the meteorology field. Form a team of three people to prepare a brief report about how computers and meteorology are connected. One team member should research how meteorologists predicted weather patterns before computer use became mainstream. Another team member should create a timeline illustrating when and how computers were introduced to the meteorology field, and the third team member should research the types of computer hardware and software required for a typical news station to forecast and present the weather.

Learn How To

The Learn How To activities step you through fundamental technology skills when using a computer. The Learn How To exercises enable you to become more proficient with these skills.

Premium Activity: To relate this Learn How To activity to your everyday life, see a visual demonstration of the activity, and complete a short assessment, visit the Computer Concepts CourseMate Web site at www.cengagebrain.com and then navigate to the Chapter 7 Learn How To resource for this book.

Learn How To 1: Maintain a Hard Disk

A computer's hard disk is used for the majority of storage requirements. It is important, therefore, to ensure that each hard disk on a computer is operating at peak efficiency.

Three tasks that maximize disk operations are detecting and repairing disk errors by using the Check Disk utility program; removing unused or unnecessary files and folders by using the Disk Cleanup utility program; and consolidating files and folders into contiguous storage areas using the Disk Defragmenter utility program.

A. Check Disk

To detect and repair disk errors using the Check Disk utility program, complete the following steps:

1. Click the Start button on the Windows taskbar and then click Computer on the Start menu.
2. When the Computer window opens, right-click the hard disk icon for drive C (or any other hard disk you want to select) and then click Properties on the shortcut menu.
3. In the Properties dialog box, if necessary, click the Tools tab to display the Tools sheet. The Tools sheet contains buttons to start the Check Disk program, the Defragment program, and the Backup program (Figure 7-42).
4. Click the Check now button to display the Check Disk dialog box.
5. To do a complete scan of the disk and correct any errors that are found, place a checkmark in the 'Scan for and attempt recovery of bad sectors' check box, and then click the Start button. Four phases of checking the disk will occur. While the checking is in progress, the disk being checked cannot be used for any purpose whatsoever; furthermore, once it has started, the process cannot be stopped. If the Check Disk program cannot check the disk because it is in use, you can schedule the disk check to run next time you start the computer.
6. When the four phases are complete (this may take more than one-half hour, depending on the size of the hard disk and how many corrections must occur), a dialog box is displayed with the message, Disk Check Complete. Click the OK button in the dialog box.

B. Cleanup Disk

After checking the disk, your next step can be to clean up the disk by removing any programs and data that are not required for the computer. To do so, complete the following steps:

1. Click the General tab (Figure 7-42) in the disk drive Properties dialog box to display the General sheet.
2. Click the Disk Cleanup button in the General sheet to display the Disk Cleanup Options dialog box.
3. The Disk Cleanup dialog box is displayed and contains a message that indicates the amount of space that can be freed up is being calculated.
4. After the calculation is complete, the Disk Cleanup dialog box specifies the amount of space that can be freed up and the files to delete, some of which are selected automatically (Figure 7-43). Select those items from which you wish to delete files.

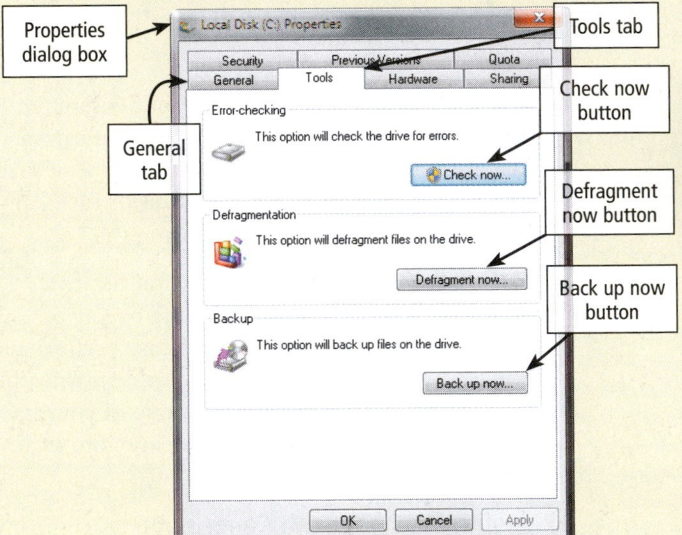

Figure 7-42

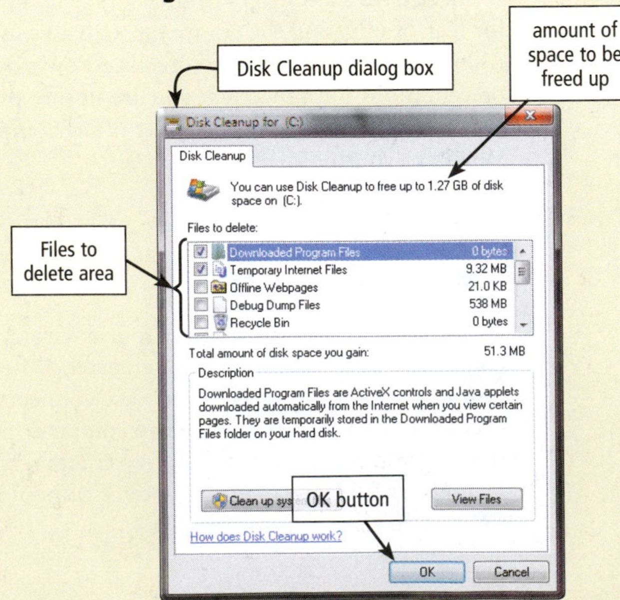

Figure 7-43

Learn How To

5. Click the OK button in the Disk Cleanup dialog box.
6. A dialog box asks if you are sure you want to perform these actions. Click the Delete Files button. The Disk Cleanup dialog box illustrates the progress of the cleanup. When the cleanup is complete, the dialog box closes.

C. Defragment Disk

The next step in disk maintenance is to defragment all the files on the disk. When a file is stored on disk, the data in the file sometimes is stored contiguously, and other times is stored in a noncontiguous manner. When a file is stored in a noncontiguous manner, it can take significantly longer to find and retrieve data from the file. One of the more useful utilities to speed up disk operations, therefore, is the defragmentation program, which combines all files so that no files are stored in a noncontiguous manner. To use the defragmentation program, complete the following steps:

1. If necessary, click the Tools tab (Figure 7-42) in the Properties dialog box for the hard disk to be defragmented.
2. Click the Defragment now button in the Tools sheet to open the Disk Defragmenter window (Figure 7-44). This window displays the Disk Defragmenter schedule, when Disk Defragmenter was run last, and when Disk Defragmenter is scheduled to run next.
3. Click the Defragment disk button to begin the defragmentation process. During the defragmentation process, the Stop operation button replaces the Defragment disk button. The defragmentation process can consume more than one hour in some cases. You can cancel the operation at any time by clicking the Stop operation button in the Disk Defragmenter window.
4. When the process is complete, the Defragment disk button will replace the Stop operation button.
5. Click the Close button to close the Disk Defragmenter window.

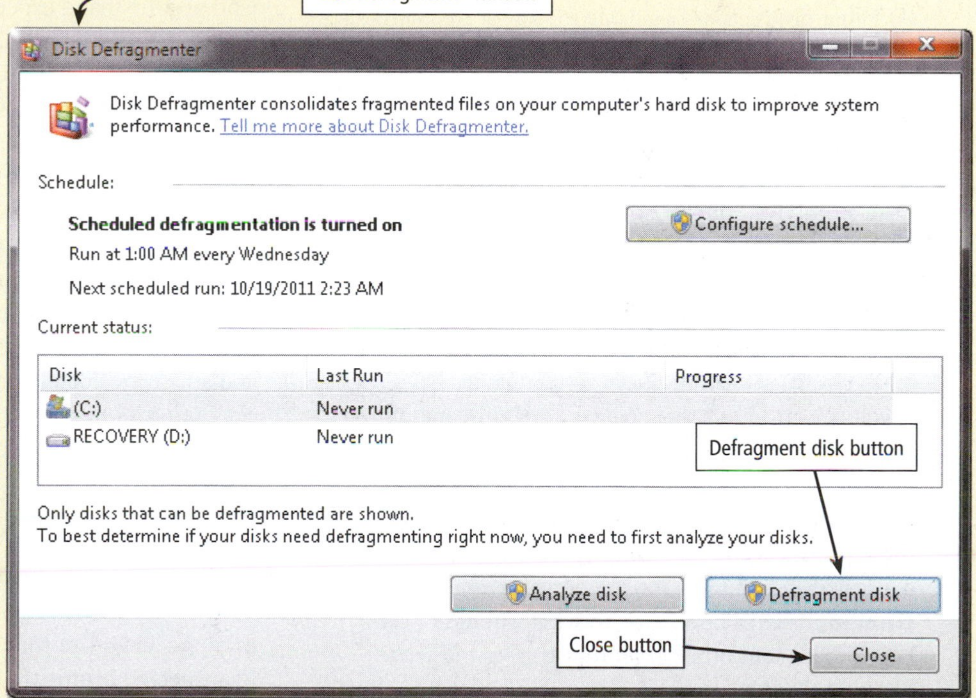

Figure 7-44

Exercises

Caution: The exercises for this chapter that require actual disk maintenance are optional. If you are performing these exercises on a computer that is not your own, obtain explicit permission to complete these exercises. Keep in mind that these exercises can require significant computer time and the computer may be unusable during this time.

1. Display the Properties dialog box for a hard disk found on the computer. Display the Tools sheet. Click the Check now button and then place a check mark in the 'Scan for and attempt recovery of bad sectors' check box. Click the Start button. How long did it take to complete the check of the hard disk? Were any errors discovered and corrected? Submit your answers to your instructor.
2. Display the Properties dialog box for a hard disk found on the computer. Display the General sheet. What is the capacity of the hard disk? How much space is used? How much free space is available? Click the Disk Cleanup button. How much space can be freed up if you use the Disk Cleanup program? Click the OK button to clean up the disk. How long did it take to perform the disk cleanup? Submit your answers to your instructor.
3. Display the Properties dialog box for a hard disk found on the computer. Display the Tools sheet. Click the Defragment now button. In the Disk Defragmenter window, click the Defragment disk button. How could you tell when the defragmentation process completes? How long did defragmentation require? Submit your answers to your instructor.

STUDENT ASSIGNMENTS

Web Research

The Web Research exercises broaden your understanding of the chapter concepts by presenting questions that require you to search the Web for answers.

1 Search Sleuth

Use one of the search engines listed in Figure 2-10 in Chapter 2 on page 85 or your own favorite search engine to find the answers to the following questions. Copy and paste the Web address from the Web page where you found the answer. Some questions may have more than one answer. If required, submit your answers to your instructor. (1) What album did Hillsong United release in 2008 on a flash drive embedded in a rubber wristband? (2) What country uses the MyKad smart card for national identification? (3) What product did HP develop in 2004 based on the efforts of engineer Daryl Anderson? (4) What products are available for sale at the SanDisk Plaza? (5) For what storage medium are phase change alloys used? (6) What company introduced using a hard disk for accounting projects in 1956?

2 Green Computing

Data storage is doubling every 18 months according to some computer industry experts, and consumers and businesses are turning to environmentally sound methods of backing up and storing files. Accessing hard disks consumes 80 percent of a storage system's electrical consumption, so companies have developed products that reduce a system's energy usage. Businesses invest in cooling systems that dissipate the heat generated when servers and storage hardware operate. Locate Web sites that describe these products and how they operate efficiently to conserve energy. How much energy savings do they claim to make in one year? To what extent are carbon dioxide and other greenhouse gases reduced? How do they maximize the use of power and cooling resources? Review your search results and then write a 50-word summary of your findings.

3 Social Networking

Privacy on social networking Web sites such as MySpace and Facebook is an international concern, and the Electronic Privacy Information Center (epic .org/privacy/socialnet) features news, policies, and resources discussing safeguarding and controlling personal information. At least one-fourth of hiring managers admit to researching job applicants' "digital dirt" by searching social networks and blogs, and some employers search social networking Web sites for profiles of current employees. Visit the Reputation Defender (reputationdefender.com) and Defend My Name (defendmyname.com) Web sites and read about the services offered. Then view the standards posted on the MySpace and Facebook Web sites regarding privacy and allowable content. Summarize the information you read and viewed.

4 Blogs

Exercise and nutrition advice is available from experts who post firsthand experiences in their blogs. These authorities may be people who share a particular experience, such as losing weight or training for a marathon, or who have specialized training in the fitness field. For example, noted author Lou Schuler discusses nutrition, weight training, and issues of particular interest to men (malepatternfitness.com). Other popular fitness blogs are featured by The Families.com (fitness.families.com/blog) and Diet-Blog (diet-blog.com). Athlete Blog Central (yardbarker.com/athletes) lists blogs that professional and amateur athletes and their fans write. Visit these sites and read the posts. Which stories received more than 25 comments? Which food, exercises, and programs are featured?

5 Ethics in Action

The United States Federal Bureau of Investigation used a controversial program until January 2005 to monitor and store the e-mail and Internet activity of suspected criminals. Originally called Carnivore, the surveillance program was renamed DCS1000. The program was designed to track the activities of potential terrorists, spies, drug traffickers, and organized crime ring members. FBI agents needed to obtain a court order to monitor an individual, but privacy advocates claim the software tracked people not covered under the court order. View online sites that provide information about DCS1000 or Carnivore, including HowStuffWorks (howstuffworks.com/carnivore.htm). What commercial software has replaced Carnivore? Write a report summarizing your findings, and include a table of links to Web sites that provide additional details.

Critical Thinking

The Critical Thinking exercises challenge your assessment and decision-making skills by presenting real-world situations associated with the chapter concepts. The Collaboration exercise should be completed with a team.

To evaluate the situations below, use personal experiences and available resources such as articles on the Web or in print, blogs, podcasts, videos, television, user guides, other individuals, and electronics and computer stores. You may need to use multiple resources to form conclusions and make recommendations.

1. Class Discussion — Cloud Storage

The owner of the motorcycle repair shop where you are employed as a part-time office manager is seeking alternatives to continually upgrading the company's computers. After attending a seminar about how small businesses can make use of the Internet, she asked you to look into the feasibility of using cloud storage, rather than purchasing additional storage for the company's computer. Analyze and discuss the advantages and disadvantages of using cloud storage. Include in your discussion a comparison between Box.net and Windows Live SkyDrive cloud storage offerings. Which company offers the best arrangement? Why?

2. Class Presentation — Increasing Storage Capacity

An old aphorism claims, "You never can have too much money." Many computer users support a similar maxim, "You never can have too much storage." Your manager at MJ National Bank where you are employed as an analyst, however, would prefer other options to buying more hardware to meet the bank's storage needs. She wants you to investigate alternative ways to increase storage capacity. Use the Web and/or print media to learn more about hard disk partitions and data compression as a means of increasing storage capacity. Evaluate the differences among various data compression algorithms. Prepare a presentation that shows how partitions and compression increase the capacity of hard disks. Include the following in your presentation: What kind of data compression is most suitable for storage devices? What are the most well known data compression algorithms? How can compression ratios of different algorithms be compared? What are some formats for data compression archives?

3. Research — Permanently Removing Data

Many companies and government agencies make extensive efforts to protect the data and information stored on their computers. When a computer reaches the end of its useful life, it either is recycled or thrown away. Although the obsolete computer does not perform well, if at all, the data on the hard disk often is intact. For this reason, companies and government agencies take precautionary measures to remove the data and information so that someone else cannot recover it and use it for malicious purposes. Use the Internet to find ways that some companies currently destroy their data before discarding their computers. Next, locate at least three programs that permanently can destroy data on a hard disk. Finally, prepare a report recommending to your instructor which method or program is the best for destroying data so that nobody can recover it.

Collaboration

4. Computers in Telemarketing Your team has been assigned to perform IT research for a new local magazine-subscription telemarketing company that is about to open for business. The company's business plan calls for 150 telemarketers to make a minimum of 100 calls a day. If a telemarketer does not meet the minimum number of calls, then he or she is required to finish the calls from home. The company plans to buy used computers for each telemarketer to use at home. The company also must decide on the type of storage device to provide the telemarketers so that when they have to make calls from home, they have a way to take the necessary data home with them. Senior management has narrowed down their choice to three storage devices — rewritable optical discs, cloud storage, or USB flash drives. Form a three-member team. Each team member should choose and research a different storage device. Using the Web and/or print media, each team member should evaluate the advantages and disadvantages of their chosen device. Include features such as capacity, access time, durability of media, ease of transporting between home and office, and cost. As a team, merge your findings and prepare a presentation to share your recommendations with your class.

Chapter Eight

Operating Systems and Utility Programs

Objectives

After completing this chapter, you will be able to:

1 Define system software and identify the two types of system software

2 Describe each of these functions of an operating system: starting and shutting down a computer, providing a user interface, managing programs, managing memory, coordinating tasks, configuring devices, establishing an Internet connection, monitoring performance, providing file management and other utilities, updating automatically, controlling a network, and administering security

3 Summarize the startup process on a personal computer

4 Summarize the features of several stand-alone operating systems: Windows, Mac OS, UNIX, and Linux

5 Briefly describe various server operating systems: Windows Server, UNIX, Linux, Solaris, and NetWare

6 Summarize the features of several embedded operating systems: Windows Embedded CE, Windows Phone, Palm OS, iPhone OS, BlackBerry, Google Android, Embedded Linux, and Symbian OS

7 Explain the purpose of several utility programs: file manager, search utility, image viewer, uninstaller, disk cleanup, disk defragmenter, backup and restore utilities, screen saver, personal firewall, antivirus programs, spyware and adware removers, Internet filters, file compression, media player, disc burning, and personal computer maintenance

System Software

When you purchase a personal computer, it usually has system software installed on its hard disk. **System software** consists of the programs that control or maintain the operations of the computer and its devices. System software serves as the interface between the user, the application software, and the computer's hardware.

Two types of system software are operating systems and utility programs. This chapter discusses the operating system and its functions, as well as several types of utility programs for personal computers.

Operating Systems

An **operating system** (**OS**) is a set of programs containing instructions that work together to coordinate all the activities among computer hardware resources. Most operating systems perform similar functions that include starting and shutting down a computer, providing a user interface, managing programs, managing memory, coordinating tasks, configuring devices, establishing an Internet connection, monitoring performance, providing file management and other utilities, and automatically updating itself and certain utility programs. Some operating

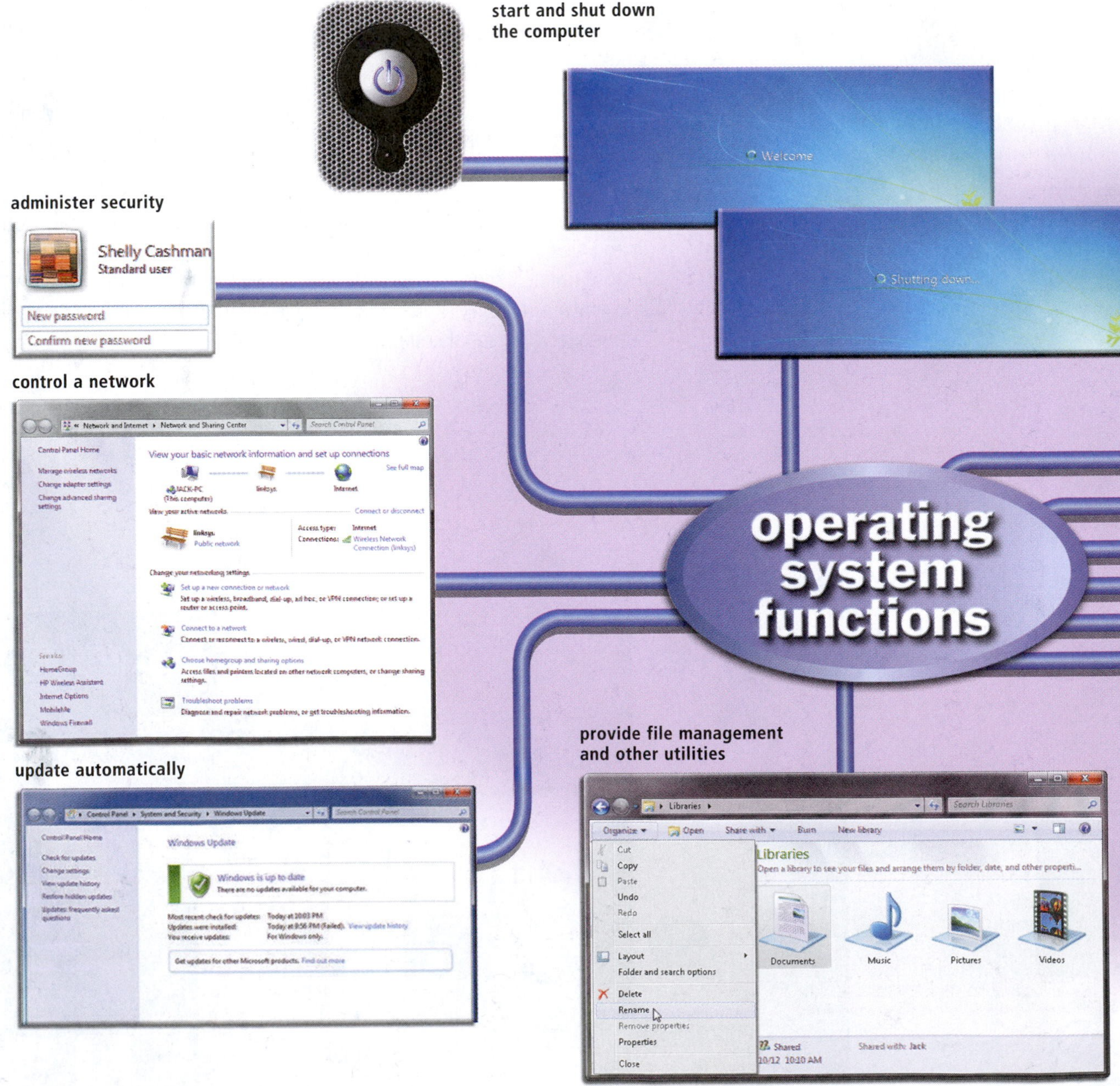

Figure 8-1 Most operating systems perform similar functions, which are illustrated with the latest version of Windows in this figure.

systems also allow users to control a network and administer security (Figure 8-1).

Although an operating system can run from an optical disc and/or flash memory mobile media, in most cases, the operating system is installed and resides on the computer's hard disk. On handheld computers and many mobile devices such as smart phones, the operating system may reside on a ROM chip.

Different sizes of computers typically use different operating systems because operating systems generally are written to run on a specific type of computer. For example, a mainframe computer does not use the same operating system as a personal computer. Even the same types of computers, such as desktop computers, may not use the same operating system. Some, however, can run multiple operating systems. When purchasing application software, you must ensure that it works with the operating system installed on your computer or mobile device.

The operating system that a computer uses sometimes is called the *platform*. With purchased application software, the package or specifications identify the required platform (operating system). A *cross-platform* program is one that runs the same on multiple operating systems.

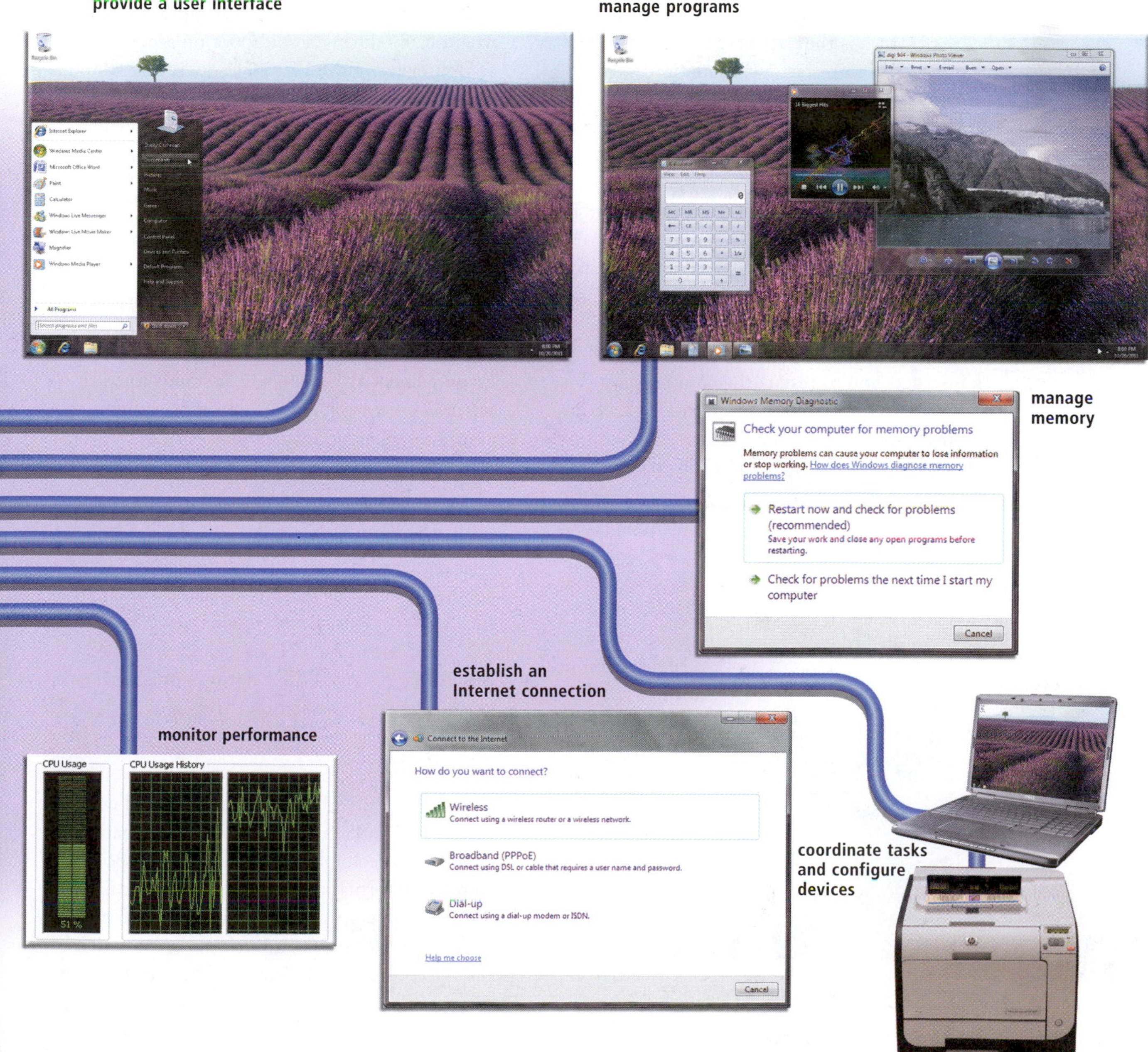

Operating System Functions

Many different operating systems exist, designed for all types of computers. Regardless of the size of the computer, however, most operating systems provide similar functions. The following sections discuss functions common to most operating systems. The operating system handles many of these functions automatically, without requiring any instructions from a user.

Starting and Shutting Down a Computer

The process of starting or restarting a computer is called **booting**. When turning on a computer that has been powered off completely, you are performing a **cold boot**. A **warm boot**, by contrast, is the process of using the operating system to restart a computer. A warm boot properly closes any running processes and programs; however, it does not save any unsaved work. Thus, always remember to save your work before rebooting (restarting) a computer.

With Windows, you can perform a warm boot by clicking the Start button on the taskbar, clicking the arrow next to the Shut down button on the Start menu, and then clicking Restart (Figure 8-2).

When you install new software or update existing software, often an on-screen prompt instructs you to restart the computer. In this case, a warm boot is appropriate. If the computer stops responding, try pressing and holding down the power button to turn off the computer. As a last resort, remove power from the computer and then restart the computer. On newer computers, pressing the power button momentarily is the same as a warm boot, whereas pressing and holding the power button does not properly close running processes and programs.

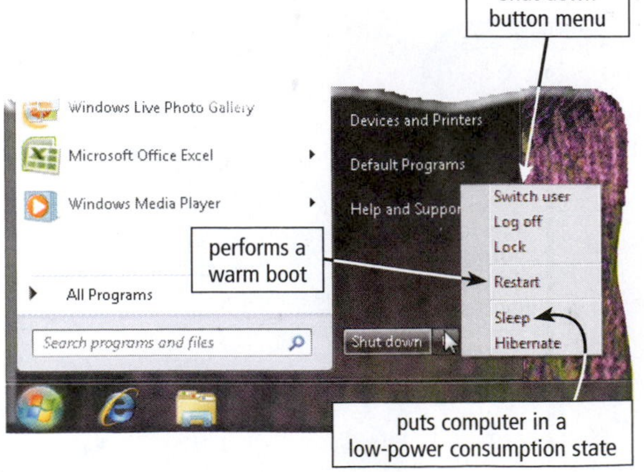

Figure 8-2 To reboot a running computer, click the Shut down button arrow and then click Restart.

Each time you boot a computer, the kernel and other frequently used operating system instructions are loaded, or copied, from storage into the computer's memory (RAM). The *kernel* is the core of an operating system that manages memory and devices, maintains the computer's clock, starts programs, and assigns the computer's resources, such as devices, programs, data, and information. The kernel is *memory resident*, which means it remains in memory while the computer is running. Other parts of the operating system are *nonresident*, that is, these instructions remain on a storage medium until they are needed.

When you boot a computer, a series of messages may appear on the screen. The actual information displayed varies depending on the make and type of the computer and the equipment installed. The boot process, however, is similar for large and small computers.

The steps in the following paragraphs explain what occurs during a cold boot on a personal computer using the Windows operating system. The steps in Figure 8-3 illustrate and correspond to the steps discussed in the following paragraphs.

Step 1: When you turn on the computer, the power supply sends an electrical signal to the components in the system unit.

Step 2: The charge of electricity causes the processor chip to reset itself and find the ROM chip(s) that contains the BIOS. The **BIOS** (pronounced BYE-ose), which stands for *basic input/output system*, is firmware that contains the computer's startup instructions.

Step 3: The BIOS executes a series of tests to make sure the computer hardware is connected properly and operating correctly. The tests, collectively called the *power-on self test (POST)*, check the various system components including the buses, system clock, adapter cards, RAM chips, mouse, keyboard, and drives. As the POST executes, LEDs (tiny lights) flicker on devices such as the disk drives and keyboard. Beeps also may sound, and messages may appear on the screen.

Step 4: The POST results are compared with data in a CMOS chip. As discussed in Chapter 4, CMOS is a technology that uses battery power to retain information when the computer is off. The CMOS chip stores configuration information about the computer, such as the amount of memory; type of disk drives, keyboard, and monitor; the current date and time; and other startup information. It also detects any new devices connected to the computer. If any problems are

Live Movie Maker program is in the foreground, and three other programs are running in the background (Windows Media Player, Microsoft PowerPoint and Chess Titans). For example, Windows Media Player can play music while you create a movie.

The foreground program typically displays on the desktop, and the background programs are hidden partially or completely behind the foreground program. You easily can switch between foreground and background programs. To make a program active (in the foreground) in Windows, click its program button on the taskbar. This causes the operating system to place all other programs in the background.

In addition to application programs, an operating system manages other processes. These processes include utilities or routines that provide support to other programs or hardware. Some are memory resident. Others run as they are required. Figure 8-7 shows a list of some processes running on a Windows computer. The list contains the applications programs running, as well as other programs and processes.

Some operating systems use preemptive multitasking to prevent any one process from monopolizing the computer's resources. With *preemptive multitasking*, the operating system interrupts a program that is executing and passes control to another program waiting to be executed. An advantage of preemptive multitasking is the operating system regains control if one program stops operating properly.

A *multiuser* operating system enables two or more users to run programs simultaneously. Networks, servers, mainframes, and supercomputers allow hundreds to thousands of users to connect at the same time, and thus are multiuser.

A *multiprocessing* operating system supports two or more processors running programs at the same time. Multiprocessing involves the coordinated processing of programs by more than one processor. Multiprocessing increases a computer's processing speed.

A computer with separate processors also can serve as a fault-tolerant computer. A *fault-tolerant computer* continues to operate when one of its components fails, ensuring that no data is lost. Fault-tolerant computers have duplicate components such as processors, memory, and disk drives. If any one of these components fails, the computer switches to the duplicate component and continues to operate. Airline reservation systems, communications networks, automated teller machines, and other systems that must be operational at all times use fault-tolerant computers.

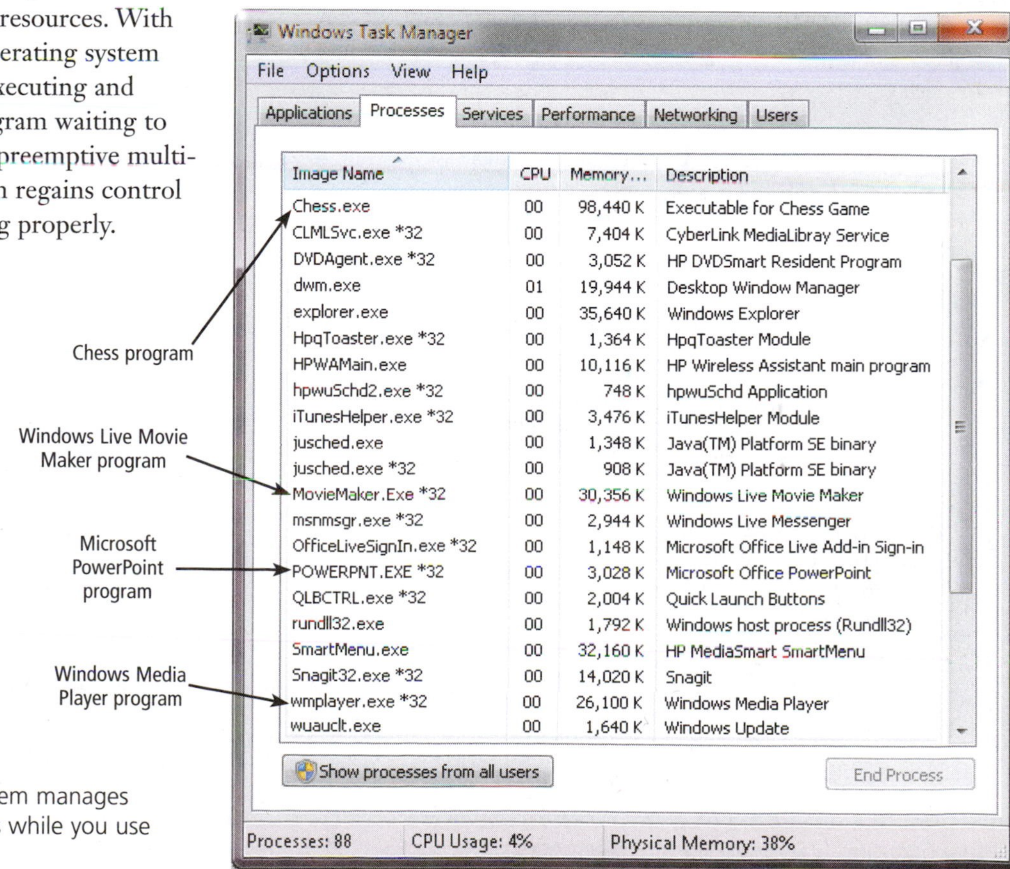

Figure 8-7 An operating system manages multiple programs and processes while you use the computer.

Managing Memory

The purpose of **memory management** is to optimize the use of random access memory (RAM). As Chapter 4 discussed, RAM consists of one or more chips on the motherboard that hold items such as data and instructions while the processor interprets and executes them. The operating system allocates, or assigns, data and instructions to an area of memory while they are being processed. Then, it carefully monitors the contents of memory. Finally, the operating system releases these items from being monitored in memory when the processor no longer requires them.

If you have multiple programs running simultaneously, it is possible to run out of RAM. For example, assume an operating system requires 512 MB of RAM, an antivirus program — 256 MB of RAM, a Web browser — 128 MB of RAM, a business software suite — 512 MB of RAM, and a photo editing program — 256 MB of RAM. With all these programs running simultaneously, the total RAM required would be 1664 MB of RAM (512 + 256 + 128 + 512 + 256). If the computer has only 1 GB of RAM, the operating system may have to use virtual memory to solve the problem.

With **virtual memory**, the operating system allocates a portion of a storage medium, usually the hard disk, to function as additional RAM (Figure 8-8). As you interact with a program, part of it may be in physical RAM, while the rest of the program is on the hard disk as virtual memory. Because virtual memory is slower than RAM, users may notice the computer slowing down while it uses virtual memory.

The area of the hard disk used for virtual memory is called a *swap file* because it swaps (exchanges) data, information, and instructions between memory and storage. A *page* is the amount of data and program instructions that can swap at a given time. The technique of swapping items between memory and storage, called *paging*, is a time-consuming process for the computer.

When an operating system spends much of its time paging, instead of executing application software, it is said to be *thrashing*. If application software, such as a Web browser, has stopped responding and the hard disk's LED blinks repeatedly, the operating system probably is thrashing.

Instead of using a hard disk as virtual memory, Windows users can increase the size of memory through *Windows ReadyBoost*, which can allocate

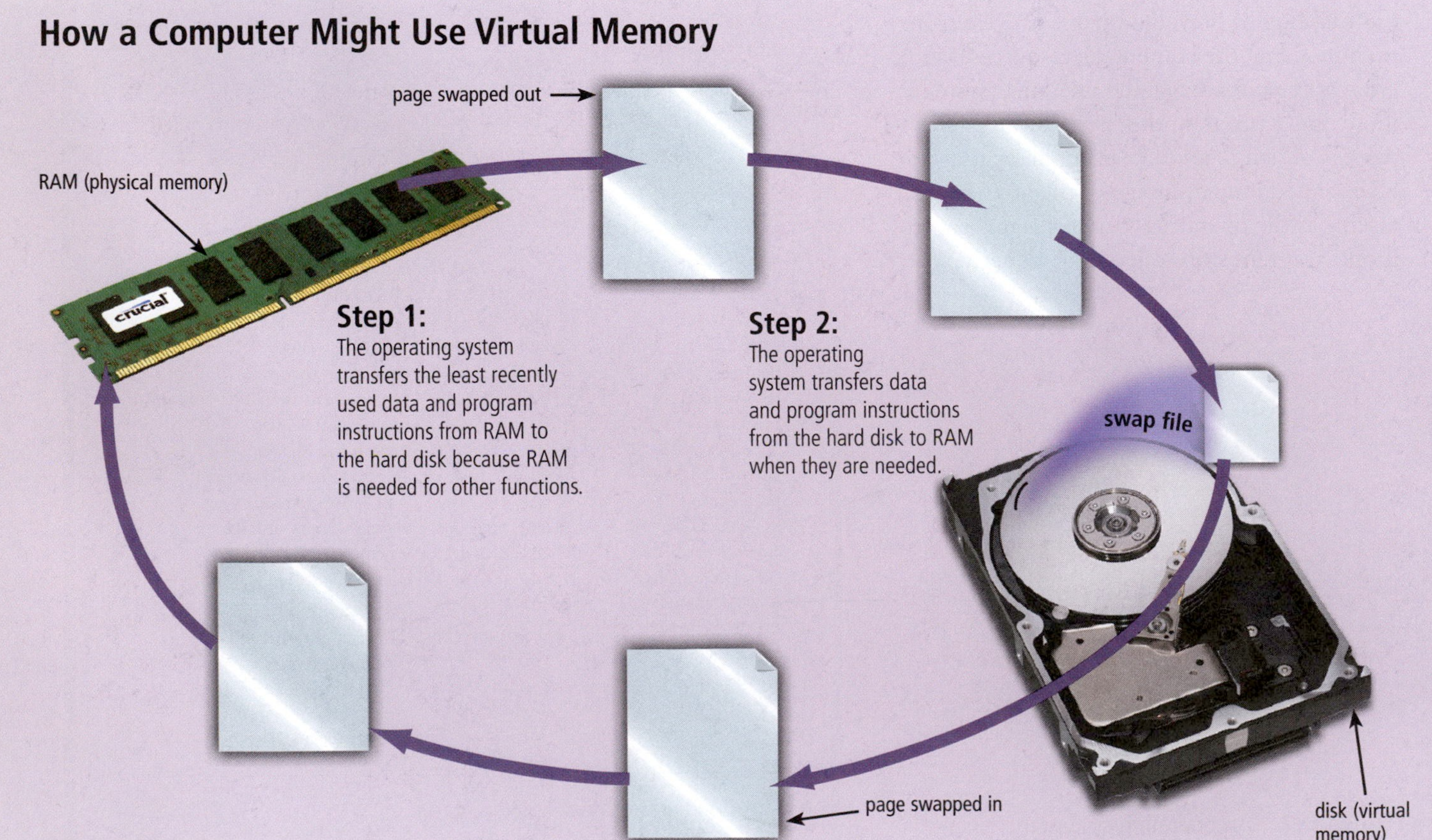

Figure 8-8 This figure shows how a computer might use virtual memory.

available storage space on removable flash memory devices as additional memory cache. Users notice better peformance with Windows ReadyBoost versus hard disk virtual memory because the operating system accesses a flash memory device, such as a USB flash drive or SD memory card, more quickly than it accesses a hard disk.

? FAQ 8-2

How can I stop a computer from thrashing?

Try to quit the program that stopped responding. If the computer does not respond and continues to thrash, do a warm boot. When the computer reboots, check whether the available hard disk space is less than 200 MB. If it is, remove unnecessary files from the hard disk and if possible uninstall seldom used programs. Defragment the hard disk (discussed later in this chapter). If thrashing continues to occur, you may need to install more RAM in the computer.

For more information, visit the Computer Concepts CourseMate Web site at www.cengagebrain.com, navigate to the Chapter 8 FAQ resource for this book, and then click Optimizing Memory.

Coordinating Tasks

The operating system determines the order in which tasks are processed. A task, or job, is an operation the processor manages. Tasks include receiving data from an input device, processing instructions, sending information to an output device, and transferring items from storage to memory and from memory to storage.

A mulituser operating system does not always process tasks on a first-come, first-served basis. Sometimes, one user may have a higher priority than other users. In this case, the operating system adjusts the schedule of tasks.

Sometimes, a device already may be busy processing one task when it receives a second task. This occurs because the processor operates at a much faster rate of speed than peripheral devices. For example, if the processor sends five documents to a printer, the printer can print only one document at a time and store as many documents as its memory can handle.

While waiting for devices to become idle, the operating system places items in buffers. A **buffer** is a segment of memory or storage in which items are placed while waiting to be transferred from an input device or to an output device.

The operating system commonly uses buffers with printed documents. This process, called **spooling**, sends documents to be printed to a buffer instead of sending them immediately to the printer. If a printer does not have its own internal memory or if its memory is full, the operating system's buffer holds the documents waiting to print while the printer prints from the buffer at its own rate of speed. By spooling documents to a buffer, the processor can continue interpreting and executing instructions while the printer prints. This allows users to work on the computer for other activities while a printer is printing. Multiple documents line up in a **queue** (pronounced Q) in the buffer. A program, called a *print spooler*, intercepts documents to be printed from the operating system and places them in the queue (Figure 8-9).

Spooling

For more information, visit the Computer Concepts CourseMate Web site at www.cengagebrain.com, navigate to the Chapter 8 Web Link resource for this book, and then click Spooling.

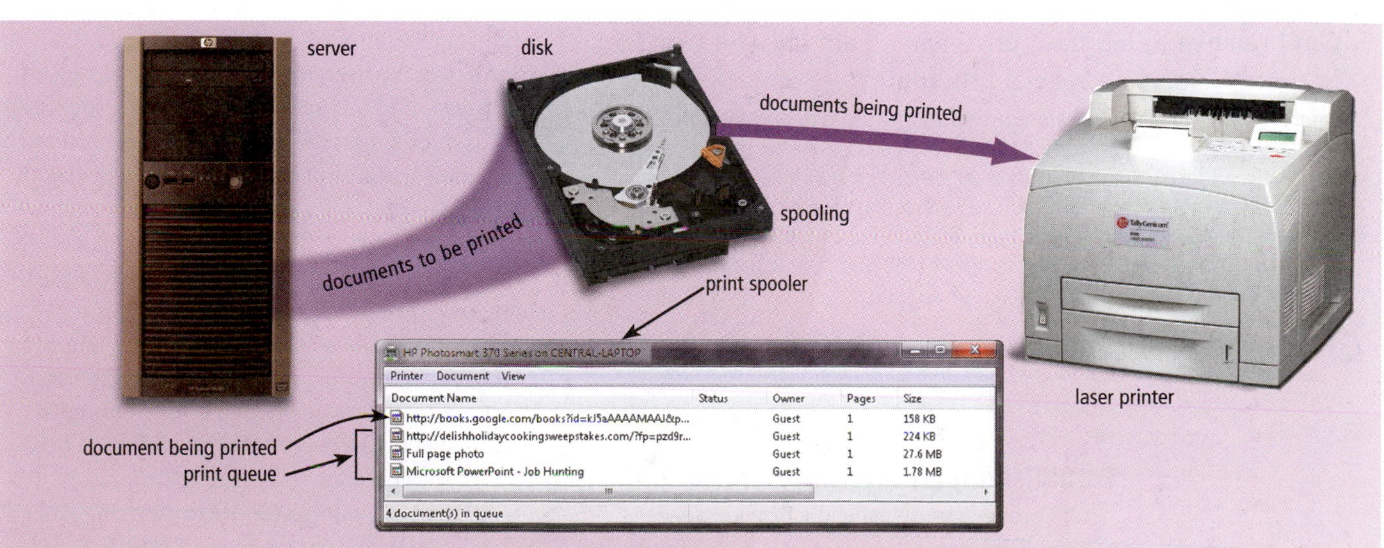

Figure 8-9 Spooling increases both processor and printer efficiency by placing documents to be printed in a buffer on disk before they are printed. This figure illustrates three documents in the queue with one document printing.

Configuring Devices

A **driver**, short for *device driver*, is a small program that tells the operating system how to communicate with a specific device. Each device on a computer, such as the mouse, keyboard, monitor, printer, card reader/writer, and scanner, has its own specialized set of commands and thus requires its own specific driver. When you boot a computer, the operating system loads each device's driver. These devices will not function without their correct drivers.

If you attach a new device to a computer, such as a printer or scanner, its driver must be installed before you can use the device. Today, most devices and operating systems support Plug and Play. As discussed in Chapter 4, **Plug and Play** means the operating system automatically configures new devices as you install them. Specifically, it assists you in the device's installation by loading the necessary drivers automatically and checking for conflicts with other devices. With Plug and Play, a user plugs in a device, turns on the computer, and then uses the device without having to configure the system manually. Devices that connect to a USB port on the system unit typically are Plug and Play.

Plug and Play

For more information, visit the Computer Concepts CourseMate Web site at www.cengagebrain.com, navigate to the Chapter 8 Web Link resource for this book, and then click Plug and Play.

Manufacturers often update a device's driver. For example, the update may enable the device to work with a new operating system, or it may improve the reliability of the device. You can visit the manufacturer's Web site to determine if a driver has been updated. In some cases, you may be notified that a driver has been updated. Always be sure to install updated drivers.

? FAQ 8-3

Can I remove a USB flash drive when I am finished with it, or should I follow a special procedure?

Before removing an external storage device from the USB port, you first should close all programs and files you have opened from the device. To avoid any chance of losing some or all data on the device, operating systems usually provide a means to ensure you can remove the device safely. In Windows, for example, if the Safely Remove Hardware and Eject Media icon appears on the taskbar, click it (or right-click the drive in the Computer window) and then click the appropriate Eject command on the menu.

For more information, visit the Computer Concepts CourseMate Web site at www.cengagebrain.com, navigate to the Chapter 8 FAQ resource for this book, and then click USB Flash Drives.

Establishing an Internet Connection

Operating systems typically provide a means to establish Internet connections. For example, Windows automatically configures some broadband Internet connections as soon as you connect to the broadband line. Otherwise, Windows includes a Set Up a Connection or Network wizard that guides users through the process of setting up a connection between a computer and an Internet access provider (Figure 8-10).

Some operating systems also include a Web browser and an e-mail program, enabling you to begin using the Web and communicate with others as soon as you set up the Internet connection. Some also include utilities to protect computers from unauthorized intrusions and unwanted software such as viruses and spyware.

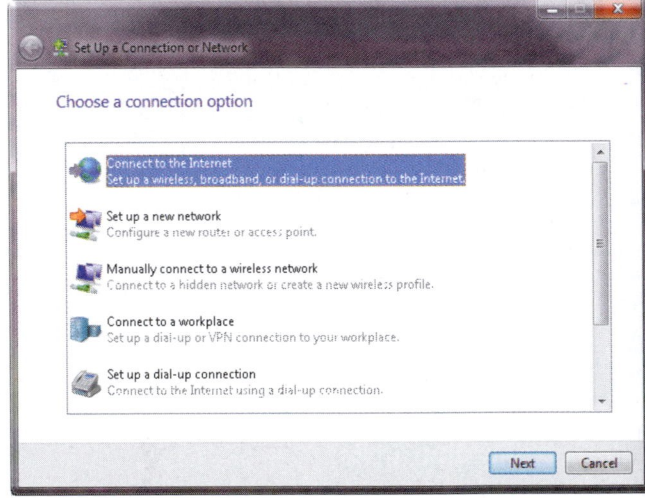

Figure 8-10 To connect to a network using Windows, click the Start button, click Control Panel, click Network and Internet, click Network and Sharing Center, and then click 'Set up a new connection or network' to open the window shown here.

Monitoring Performance

Operating systems typically contain a performance monitor. A **performance monitor** is a program that assesses and reports information about various computer resources and devices (Figure 8-11). For example, users can monitor the processor, disks, network, and memory usage.

The information in performance reports helps users and administrators identify a problem with resources so that they can try to resolve any problems. If a computer is running extremely slow, for example, the performance monitor may determine that the computer's memory is being used to its maximum. Thus, you might consider installing additional memory in the computer. Read Looking Ahead 8-1 for a look at a future type of health-based performance monitor.

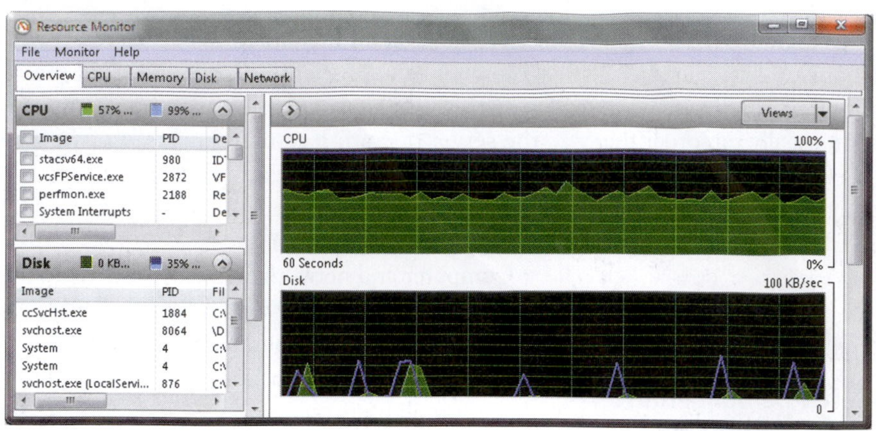

Figure 8-11 The Windows Resource Monitor above is tracking CPU (processor), disk, network, and memory usage.

Providing File Management and Other Utilities

Operating systems often provide users with the capability of managing files, searching for files, viewing images, securing a computer from unauthorized access, uninstalling programs, cleaning up disks, defragmenting disks, diagnosing problems, backing up files and disks, and setting up screen savers. A later section in the chapter discusses these and other utilities in depth. To learn about installing and maintaining a computer, complete the Learn How To 1 exercise on page 440.

Updating Software Automatically

Many popular programs, including most operating systems, include an **automatic update** feature that automatically provides updates to the program. With an operating system, these updates can include fixes to program *bugs*, or errors, enhancements to security, modifications to device drivers, access to new or expanded components such as desktop themes or games, and even updates to application software on the computer such as a Web browser or an e-mail program (Figure 8-12).

Many software makers provide free downloadable updates, sometimes called a *service pack*, to users who have registered and/or activated their software. With operating systems, the automatic update feature automatically alerts users when an update is

LOOKING AHEAD 8-1

Contact Lenses Monitor Glaucoma

The future looks good for contact lenses that will help study and treat glaucoma. Biomedical engineers at the University of California – Davis are developing lenses that measure eye pressure and then flow if the readings are abnormal.

Glaucoma occurs when the fluid pressure inside the eye increases. This intraocular pressure can result in total blindness if the optic nerve, which sends messages from the eyes to the brain, is damaged. Doctors can measure the amount of pressure and then perform surgery to correct the blockage in the back of the eye that prevents the fluid from draining. As an alternative to the pressure measurement, the new contact lenses can perform the fluidic resistance evaluation for the drainage network of the eye, which prevents dangerously high levels in the early glaucomatous eyes.

Lasers, too, are expected to become part of a doctor's means of detecting glaucoma. A high-resolution laser can measure 28 million areas of the optic nerve, and then software can create a 3-D view of the eye and assess signs of the disease.

For more information, visit the Computer Concepts CourseMate Web site at www.cengagebrain.com, navigate to the Chapter 8 Looking Ahead resource for this book, and then click Contact Lenses.

Figure 8-12 With Windows Update, you can download and install important operating system and utility updates.

available; further, it can be configured to download and install the update automatically. Read Ethics & Issues 8-1 for a related discussion. Users without an Internet connection usually can order the updates on an optical disc for a minimal shipping fee. To learn about keeping Windows up-to-date, complete the Learn How To 3 exercise on pages 440 and 441.

ETHICS & ISSUES 8-1

Is Operating System Automatic Update Software Dangerous?

When the feature is enabled, Microsoft Windows automatically downloads updates to a computer. One recent automatic update was installed even on computers that had the feature disabled. Microsoft claimed that the update was harmless and was for the benefit of its customers. Only later did some customers realize that this stealth update caused serious problems. Ironically, one problem was that updates no longer could be installed on the affected computers. Customers not only were furious about the problems, but many were angry that Microsoft was making changes to computers without the knowledge of the owners of the computers. One of the consequences of the ensuing outrage was that many people turned off the automatic update feature on their computers, fearing that future updates might cause even more damage. This action may backfire because these users may not receive critical security updates. Many people believe that Microsoft should be more forthcoming about its automatic update feature.

Should software companies be able to send automatic updates to your computer without your knowledge? Why or why not? How should software companies be held accountable when automatic software updates cause serious problems? Why? Who should determine actions to be taken against software companies that cause serious problems with automatic updates? Why?

Ethics & Issues

For the complete text of the Ethics & Issues boxes found in this chapter, visit the Computer Concepts CourseMate Web site at www.cengagebrain.com and then navigate to the Chapter 8 Ethics & Issues resource for this book.

Controlling a Network

Some operating systems are designed to work with a server on a network. A **server operating system** is an operating system that organizes and coordinates how multiple users access and share resources on a network. Resources include hardware, software, data, and information. For example, a server operating system allows multiple users to share a printer, Internet access, files, and programs.

Some operating systems have network features built into them. In other cases, the server operating system is a set of programs separate from the operating system on the client computers that access the network. When not connected to the network, the client computers use their own operating system. When connected to the network, the server operating system may assume some of the operating system functions.

The *network administrator*, the person overseeing network operations, uses the server operating system to add and remove users, computers, and other devices to and from the network. The network administrator also uses the server operating system to install software and administer network security.

Administering Security

Computer and network administrators typically have an *administrator account* that enables them to access all files and programs on the computer or network, install programs, and specify settings that affect all users on a computer or network. Settings include creating user accounts and establishing permissions. These *permissions* define who can access certain resources and when they can access those resources.

For each user, the computer or network administrator establishes a user account, which enables a user to access, or **log on** to, a computer or a network (Figure 8-13). Each user account typically consists of a user name and password. A **user name**, or **user ID**, is a unique combination of characters, such as letters of the alphabet or numbers, that identifies one specific user. Many users select a combination of their first and last names as their user name. A user named Henry Baker might choose H Baker as his user name.

A **password** is a private combination of characters associated with the user name that allows access to certain computer resources. Some operating systems allow the computer or network administrator to assign passwords to files and commands, restricting access to only authorized users.

Figure 8-13 Most multiuser operating systems allow each user to log on, which is the process of entering a user name and a password into the computer.

To prevent unauthorized users from accessing computer resources, keep your password confidential. While users type a password, most computers hide the actual password characters by displaying some other characters, such as asterisks (*) or dots. After entering a user name and password, the operating system compares the user's entry with a list of authorized user names and passwords. If the entry matches the user name and password kept on file, the operating system grants the user access. If the entry does not match, the operating system denies access to the user.

The operating system records successful and unsuccessful logon attempts in a file. This allows the computer or network administrator to review who is using or attempting to use the computer. The administrators also use these files to monitor computer usage.

To protect sensitive data and information further as it travels over a network, the operating system may encrypt it. *Encryption* is the process of encoding data and information into an unreadable form. Administrators can specify that data be encrypted as it travels over a network to prevent unauthorized users from reading the data. When an authorized user attempts to read the data, it automatically is decrypted, or converted back into a readable form.

FAQ 8-4

What are the guidelines for selecting a good password?

Choose a password that is easy to remember, and that no one could guess. Do not use any part of your first or last name, your spouse's or child's name, telephone number, street address, license plate number, Social Security number, birthday, and so on. Be sure your password is at least eight characters long, mixed with uppercase and lowercase letters, numbers, and special characters. You also should avoid using single-word passwords that are found in the dictionary. Security experts also recommend using a *passphrase*, which is similar to a password, but comprised of several words separated by spaces.

For more information, visit the Computer Concepts CourseMate Web site at www.cengagebrain.com, navigate to the Chapter 8 FAQ resource for this book, and then click Passwords.

QUIZ YOURSELF 8-1

Instructions: Find the true statement below. Then, rewrite the remaining false statements so that they are true.

1. A buffer is a small program that tells the operating system how to communicate with a specific device.
2. A cold boot is the process of using the operating system to restart a computer.
3. A password is a public combination of characters associated with the user name that allows access to certain computer resources.
4. Firmware that contains the computer's startup instructions is called the kernel.
5. The program you currently are using is in the background, and the other programs running but not in use are in the foreground.
6. Two types of system software are operating systems and application programs.
7. With virtual memory, the operating system allocates a portion of a storage medium, usually the hard disk, to function as additional RAM.

Quiz Yourself Online: To further check your knowledge of pages 398 through 411, visit the Computer Concepts CourseMate Web site at www.cengagebrain.com, navigate to the Chapter 8 Quiz Yourself resource for this book, and then click Objectives 1 – 3.

Types of Operating Systems

Many of the first operating systems were device dependent and proprietary. A *device-dependent* program is one that runs only on a specific type or make of computer. *Proprietary software* is privately owned and limited to a specific vendor or computer model. Some operating systems still are device dependent. The trend today, however, is toward *device-independent* operating systems that run on computers provided by a variety of manufacturers. The advantage of device-independent operating systems is you can retain existing application software and data files even if you change computer models or vendors.

When you purchase a new computer or mobile device, it typically has an operating system preinstalled. As new versions of the operating system are released, users upgrade their existing computers and mobile devices to incorporate features of the new version. Purchasing an operating system upgrade usually costs less than purchasing the entire operating system.

New versions of an operating system usually are backward compatible. That is, they recognize and work with application software written for an earlier version of the operating system (or platform). The application software, by contrast, may or may not be upward compatible, meaning it may or may not run on new versions of the operating system.

The three basic categories of operating systems that exist today are stand-alone, server, and embedded. The table in Figure 8-14 lists specific names of operating systems in each category. The following pages discuss a variety of operating systems.

Categories of Operating Systems

Category	Operating System Name
Stand-alone	• DOS • Early Windows versions (Windows 3.x, Windows 95, Windows NT Workstation, Windows 98, Windows 2000 Professional, Windows Millennium Edition, Windows XP, Windows Vista) • Windows 7 • Mac OS X • UNIX • Linux
Server	• Early Windows Server versions (Windows NT Server, Windows 2000 Server, Windows Server 2003) • Windows Server 2008 • UNIX • Linux • Solaris • NetWare
Embedded	• Windows Embedded CE • Windows Phone 7 • Palm OS • iPhone OS • BlackBerry • Google Android • Embedded Linux • Symbian OS

Figure 8-14 Examples of stand-alone, server, and embedded operating systems. Some stand-alone operating systems include the capability of configuring small home or office networks.

FAQ 8-5

Which operating systems have the most market share?

The Windows operating system family currently dominates the operating system market with more than 93 percent market share. The Mac operating system is in second place with nearly 5 percent market share. The chart to the right illustrates the market share for various operating systems.

For more information, visit the Computer Concepts CourseMate Web site at www.cengagebrain.com, navigate to the Chapter 8 FAQ resource for this book, and then click Operating System Market Share.

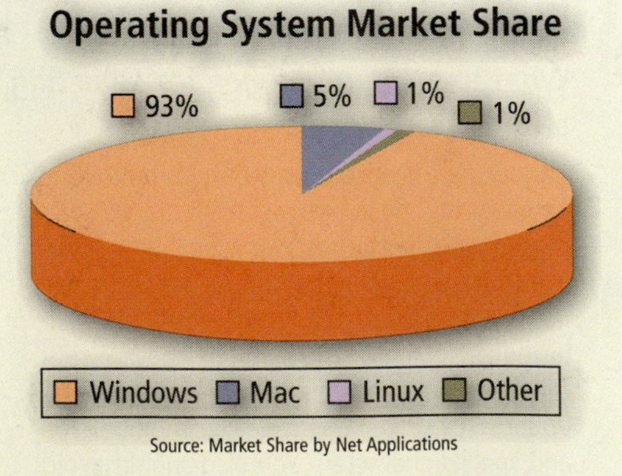

Stand-Alone Operating Systems

A **stand-alone operating system** is a complete operating system that works on a desktop computer, notebook computer, or mobile computing device. Some stand-alone operating systems are called *client operating systems* because they also work in conjunction with a server operating system. Client operating systems can operate with or without a network. Other stand-alone operating systems include networking capabilities, allowing the home and small business user to set up a small network.

Examples of currently used stand-alone operating systems are Windows 7, Mac OS X, UNIX, and Linux. The following pages briefly discuss these operating systems.

Windows 7

In the mid-1980s, Microsoft developed its first version of Windows, which provided a graphical user interface (GUI). Since then, Microsoft continually has updated its Windows operating system, incorporating innovative features and functions with each subsequent version (Figure 8-15). **Windows 7** is Microsoft's fastest, most efficient operating system to date, offering quicker program start up, built-in

Highlights of Stand-Alone Windows Versions

Windows Version	Year Released	Highlights
Windows 3.x	1990	• Provided a GUI • An operating environment only — worked in combination with DOS
Windows NT 3.1	1993	• Client OS that connected to a Windows NT Advanced Server • Interface similar to Windows 3.x
Windows 95	1995	• True multitasking operating system • Improved GUI • Included support for networking, Plug and Play technology, longer file names, and e-mail
Windows NT Workstation 4.0	1996	• Client OS that connected to a Windows NT Server • Interface similar to Windows 95 • Network integration
Windows 98	1998	• Upgrade to Windows 95 • More integrated with the Internet; included *Internet Explorer* (a Web browser) • Faster system startup and shut down, better file management, support for multimedia technologies (e.g., DVDs), and USB connectivity
Windows Millennium Edition	2000	• Upgrade to Windows 98 • Designed for the home user who wanted music playing, video editing, and networking capabilities
Windows 2000 Professional	2000	• Upgrade to Windows NT Workstation 4.0 • Complete multitasking client OS designed for business personal computers • Certified device drivers, faster performance, adaptive Start menu, image viewer, enhanced for mobile users
Windows XP	2001	• Upgrade to Windows Millennium Edition called Windows XP Home Edition • Upgrade to Windows 2000 Professional called Windows XP Professional • Windows XP Tablet PC Edition designed for Tablet PC users • Windows XP Media Center Edition designed for PCs used for home entertainment • Windows XP Professional x64 Edition designed for workstations that use 64-bit processors • Improved interface and increased performance in all editions
Service Pack 2	2004	• More built-in security technologies, improved firewall utility, and automatic blocking of Internet pop-up advertisements
Service Pack 3	2008	• Improved security and Network Access Protection restricts computers that do not meet specified requirements
Windows Vista	2006/2007	• Upgrade to Windows XP • Easier to navigate user interface, simplified customization techniques, and improved performance and reliability • Enhanced administration of user accounts and improved firewall • New Instant Search improves searching capabilities • New Documents Explorer, Pictures Explorer, and Music Explorer improve organizing capabilities
Service Pack 1	2008	• Improved Instant Search feature, increased support for devices and drivers, compatibility with more application software, and enhanced security
Service Pack 2	2009	• Support for new hardware, increased performance, and increased security
Windows 7	2009	• Upgrade to Windows Vista • Improved desktop interface and navigation • Simplified home and wireless networking • Enhanced searching capabilities • Improved performance for both desktop and notebook computers • Support for touch screen computers • Access to free, downloadable programs through the Windows Live Web site

Figure 8-15 Microsoft has released many versions of Windows.

diagnostics, automatic recovery, improved security, enhanced searching and organizing capabilities, and an easy-to-use interface (Figure 8-16).

Windows 7 includes several programs to enhance user experiences. Home and small office users easily can set up a network and secure it from hackers with *Windows Firewall*. With *Windows DVD Maker*, users easily can create DVDs from digital videos. *Windows Media Player* allows users to listen to Internet radio stations, play MP3 and other music formats, copy music and data to CDs, and watch movies.

Using the *Desktop Gadget Gallery*, users can display a variety of gadgets on the Windows desktop. A *gadget*, also known as a *widget*, is a mini-program with minimal functionality that connects to another program or provides information. Examples of gadgets included with Windows 7 include a calendar, clock, CPU meter, currency converter, news headlines, picture puzzle, picture slide show, weather, and a Windows Media Center gadget.

Most users choose one of these Windows 7 editions: Windows 7 Starter, Windows 7 Home Premium, Windows 7 Ultimate, or Windows 7 Professional.

Windows 7

For more information, visit the Computer Concepts CourseMate Web site at www.cengagebrain.com, navigate to the Chapter 8 Web Link resource for this book, and then click Windows 7.

- *Windows 7 Starter*, designed for netbooks and other small notebook computers, uses the Windows 7 Basic interface and allows users easily to search for files, connect to printers and devices, browse the Internet, join home networks, and connect to wireless networks. This edition of Windows typically is preinstalled on new computers and not available for purchase in retail stores.
- *Windows 7 Home Premium* includes all the capabilities of Windows 7 Starter and also includes Windows Aero with its *Aero Flip 3D* feature (Figure 8-17). It also provides tools to create and edit high-definition movies, record and watch television shows, connect to a game console, and read from and write on Blu-ray Discs.
- *Windows 7 Ultimate*, which includes all features of Windows 7 Home Premium, provides additional features designed to keep your files secure and support for 35 languages.
- With *Windows 7 Professional*, users in all sizes of businesses are provided a secure operating environment that uses Windows Aero where they easily can search for files, protect their computers from unauthorized intruders and unwanted programs, use improved backup technologies, securely connect to Wi-Fi networks, quickly view messages on a powered-off, specially equipped notebook computer, easily share documents and collaborate with other users, and watch and record live television.

Additional Windows 7 features are summarized in Figure 8-18. To run Windows 7 Home Premium, your computer must have at least 1 GB of RAM. If you are installing Windows on a 64-bit computer, 2 GB of RAM is required. Windows 7 adapts to the hardware configuration on which it is installed. Thus, two users with the same edition of Windows 7 may experience different functionality and interfaces.

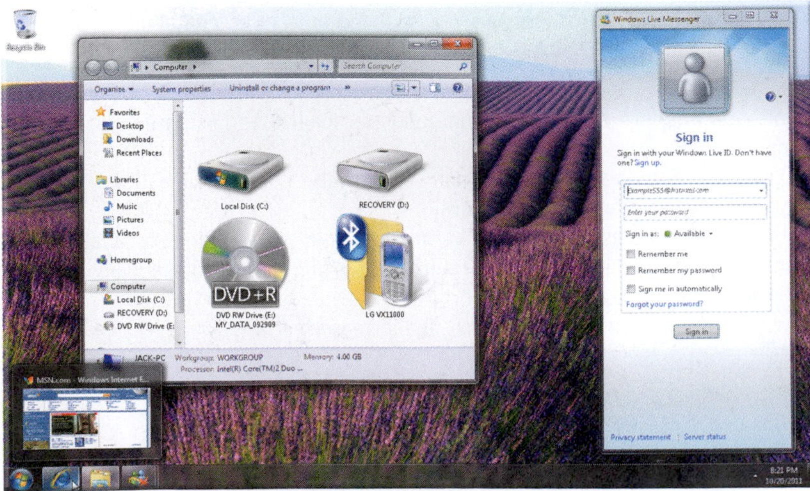

Figure 8-16 Windows 7 has a new interface, easier navigation and searching techniques, and improved security.

Figure 8-17 With Windows 7 Aero Flip 3D, users flip through windows by rolling the wheel on their mouse.

Additional Windows 7 Features	
Reliability and Performance	• Low-powered Sleep state allows you to resume work quickly when you return to the computer • Programs start faster with Windows SuperFetch technology • Automatically detects and fine-tunes performance problems • Built-in hardware diagnostics detect and repair problems automatically • Automatically recovers from failures, including restoring an unbootable computer to a usable state
Security	• User Account Control allows administrators to restrict permissions • Protects users from dangerous Web sites • Improved firewall and *Windows Defender* protects your computer from external threats • Parental controls allow parents to monitor and control computer usage
Information Management	• Improved and redesigned windows help users locate files by showing thumbnails that preview content • Use Search to locate files based on file name or any other property saved with the file • Coordinate your schedule with others' schedules in *Windows Calendar* • Use the *Snipping Tool* to copy screen elements to a file on your computer • Easily share files with other users
Appearance and Navigation	• Easy-to-navigate user interface with translucent windows • Display a preview of windows open in a particular program when you point to that program button on the taskbar • Windows Snap and Aero Shake make it easier to manage the appearance of open windows • Jump Lists make it easier to open recent files quickly in their respective program • *Windows Touch* supports computers with multi-touch technology
Communications and the Internet	• Enhanced Internet Explorer • Free access to *Windows Live Essentials*, which includes programs such as *Windows Live Messenger* for instant messaging, *Windows Live Photo Gallery* for photo editing and sharing, *Windows Live Mail* for e-mail, *Windows Live Writer* for blogging, and *Windows Live Movie Maker* for video editing and sharing • Consistent and secure wireless network connections • Speech recognition allows you to interact with the computer by voice

Figure 8-18 Some additional features of Windows 7.

Mac OS X

Since it was released in 1984 with Macintosh computers, Apple's **Macintosh operating system** has set the standard for operating system ease of use and has been the model for most of the new GUIs developed for non-Macintosh systems. The latest version, **Mac OS X**, is a multitasking operating system available only for computers manufactured by Apple (Figure 8-19).

Mac OS X includes features from previous versions of the Macintosh operating system such as large photo-quality icons, built-in networking support, e-mail, chat, online shopping, enhanced speech recognition, optical disc burning, and enhanced multimedia capabilities. In addition, Mac OS X includes these features:

- New desktop search technology
- Dashboard, a desktop area for mini-programs called widgets
- Built-in, fast Web browser
- Parental controls
- Improved backup utility, called Time Machine
- Accessibility interface reads e-mail messages
- 3-D personal video and audio conferencing
- Filter to eliminate junk e-mail messages
- Contact lists synchronized with Bluetooth-enabled smart phone or other mobile device
- Latest version of QuickTime to listen to music and view videos on the Internet
- Easy networking of computers and devices
- Windows network connection and shared Windows documents

Mac OS X

For more information, visit the Computer Concepts CourseMate Web site at www.cengagebrain.com, navigate to the Chapter 8 Web Link resource for this book, and then click Mac OS X.

Figure 8-19 Mac OS X is the operating system used with Apple Macintosh computers.

UNIX

UNIX (pronounced YOU-nix) is a multitasking operating system developed in the early 1970s by scientists at Bell Laboratories. Bell Labs (a subsidiary of AT&T) was prohibited from actively promoting UNIX in the commercial marketplace because of federal regulations. Bell Labs instead licensed UNIX for a low fee to numerous colleges and universities, where UNIX obtained a wide following. UNIX was implemented on many different types of computers. After deregulation of the telephone companies in the 1980s, UNIX was licensed to many hardware and software companies.

Several versions of this operating system exist, each slightly different. When programmers move application software from one UNIX version to another, they sometimes have to rewrite some of the programs. Although some versions of UNIX have a command-line interface, most versions of UNIX offer a graphical user interface (Figure 8-20).

Today, a version of UNIX is available for most computers of all sizes. Power users often work with UNIX because of its flexibility and power. Manufacturers such as Sun and IBM sell personal computers and workstations with a UNIX operating system.

Figure 8-20 Many versions of UNIX have a graphical user interface.

Linux

Linux is one of the faster growing operating systems. **Linux** (pronounced LINN-uks), introduced in 1991, is a popular, multitasking UNIX-type operating system. In addition to the basic operating system, Linux also includes many free programming languages and utility programs.

Linux is not proprietary software like the operating systems discussed thus far. Instead, Linux is *open source software*, which means its code is provided for use, modification, and redistribution. It has no restrictions from the copyright holder regarding modification of the software's internal instructions and redistribution of the software. Many programmers have donated time to modify and redistribute Linux to make it the best possible version of UNIX. Promoters of open source software state two main advantages: users who modify the software share their improvements with others, and customers can personalize the software to meet their needs. Read Ethics & Issues 8-2 for a related discussion.

Linux is available in a variety of forms, known as distributions. Some distributions of Linux are command-line. Others are GUI (Figure 8-21).

ETHICS & ISSUES 8-2

Closed Source vs. Open Source Operating Systems

One of the features that make Linux different from other operating systems is that Linux is open source and its source code, along with any changes, remains public. Often, when closed source operating system developers refuse to share some or all of the operating system code, third-party software developers become hindered when developing application software for the operating system. Supporters of open source maintain that source code should be open to the public so that it can be scrutinized, corrected, and enhanced. In light of concerns about security and fears of possible virus problems, however, some people are not sure open source software is a good idea. Besides, they argue, companies and programmers should be able to control, and profit from, the operating systems they create. On the other hand, open source software can be scrutinized for errors by a much larger group of people and changes can be made immediately, resulting in better software.

Are open source operating systems a good idea? Why or why not? How can the concerns about open source operating systems be addressed? What might be some of the advantages and disadvantages of open versus closed source operating systems? Does the open source model lead to better software? Why or why not?

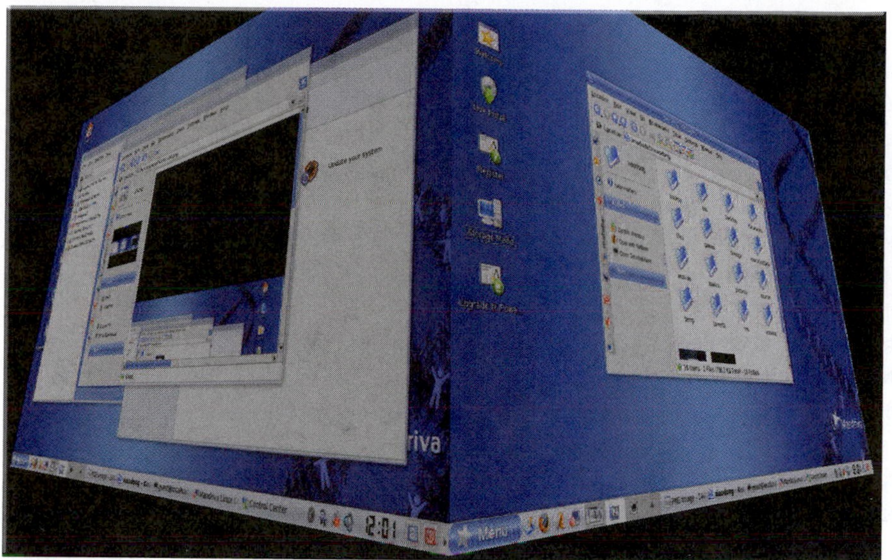

Figure 8-21 This distribution of Linux has a graphical user interface.

Linux

For more information, visit the Computer Concepts CourseMate Web site at www.cengagebrain.com, navigate to the Chapter 8 Web Link resource for this book, and then click Linux.

The two most popular GUIs available for Linux are GNOME and KDE. Some companies such as Red Hat market software that runs on their own distribution of Linux. Many application programs, utilities, and plug-ins have Linux distributions, including OpenOffice.org, StarOffice, Mozilla, Yahoo! Messenger, RealPlayer, QuickTime, and Acrobat Reader.

Users obtain Linux in a variety of ways. Some download it free from the Web. Others purchase it from vendors such as Red Hat or IBM, who bundle their own software with the operating system. Linux optical discs are included in many Linux books and also are available for purchase from vendors. Some retailers such as Dell will preinstall Linux on a new computer's hard disk on request. If you want to preview the Linux operating system, you can obtain a Live CD or Live USB.

Server Operating Systems

As discussed earlier in this chapter, a server operating system is an operating system that is designed specifically to support a network. A server operating system typically resides on a server. The client computers on the network rely on the server(s) for resources.

Many of the stand-alone operating systems discussed in the previous section function as clients and work in conjunction with a server operating system. Some of these stand-alone operating systems do include networking capability; however, server operating systems are designed specifically to support all sizes of networks, including medium- to large-sized businesses and Web servers. Examples of server operating systems include Windows Server 2008, UNIX, Linux, Solaris, and NetWare.

Windows Server 2008

Windows Server 2008 is an upgrade to Windows Server 2003. Windows Server 2008, which includes features of previous Windows Server versions, offers the following capabilities:

- Improved Web server management, enabling users to share data
- Enhanced server security
- Network Access Protection restricts computers that do not meet specified requirements
- Protection against malicious software attacks
- Shares many technologies with Windows
- Client support using Windows, Mac OS, UNIX, and Linux

To meet the needs of all sizes of businesses, the **Windows Server 2008 family** includes many editions, with the more common listed below:

- *Windows Server 2008 Standard* for the typical small- to medium-sized business network
- *Windows Server 2008 Enterprise* for medium- to large-sized businesses, including those with e-commerce operations
- *Windows Server 2008 Datacenter* for businesses with huge volumes of transactions and large-scale databases

- *Windows Web Server 2008* for Web server and Web hosting businesses
- *Windows Server 2008 for Itanium-Based Systems* for computers with 64-bit processors that function as a Web server

Most editions of Windows Server 2008 include Hyper-V, which is a virtualization technology. *Virtualization* is the practice of sharing or pooling computing resources, such as servers. Through virtualization, for example, operating systems such as Windows Server 2008 can separate a physical server into several virtual servers. Each virtual server then can perform an independent, separate function, such as running a different operating system.

Virtualization

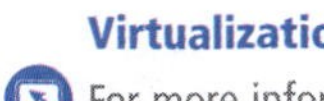
For more information, visit the Computer Concepts CourseMate Web site at www.cengagebrain.com, navigate to the Chapter 8 Web Link resource for this book, and then click Virtualization.

UNIX

In addition to being a stand-alone operating system, UNIX also is a server operating system. That is, UNIX is capable of handling a high volume of transactions in a multiuser environment and working with multiple processors using multiprocessing. For this reason, some computer professionals call UNIX a *multipurpose operating system* because it is both a stand-alone and server operating system. Many Web servers use UNIX as their operating system.

Linux

Some network servers use Linux as their operating system. Thus, Linux also is a multipurpose operating system. With Linux, a network administrator can configure the network, administer security, run a Web server, and process e-mail. Clients on the network can run Linux, UNIX, or Windows. Distributions of Linux include the Mozilla Web browser.

Solaris

Solaris, a version of UNIX developed by Sun Microsystems, is a server operating system designed specifically for e-commerce applications. Solaris manages high-traffic accounts and incorporates security necessary for Web transactions. Client computers often use a desktop program, such as GNOME desktop, that communicates with the Solaris operating system.

NetWare

Novell's *NetWare* is a server operating system designed for client/server networks. NetWare has a server portion that resides on the network server and a client portion that resides on each client computer connected to the network. NetWare supports open source software and runs on all types of computers from mainframes to personal computers. Client computers also can have their own stand-alone operating system such as a Windows, Mac OS, or Linux.

Embedded Operating Systems

The operating system on mobile devices and many consumer electronics, called an **embedded operating system**, resides on a ROM chip. Popular embedded operating systems today include Windows Embedded CE, Windows Phone 7, Palm OS, iPhone OS, BlackBerry, Google Android, embedded Linux, and Symbian OS. The following sections discuss these operating systems, most of which work on smart phones. Read Ethics & Issues 8-3 for a related discussion.

ETHICS & ISSUES 8-3

Should the Smart Phone Industry Adopt a Standard?

When you purchase a new personal computer, typically you choose between a Windows or Mac operating system. When you purchase a smart phone, however, you probably spend little time considering the operating system running on the phone. More than 10 operating systems currently run the functions of an increasing number of available smart phones. The many choices result in considerable frustration for third-party program developers who want their programs to operate on all possible smart phones. Today, developers must rewrite code, often in different programming languages, to provide their programs on a variety of phones. The situation results in *user lockdown,* meaning that users of smart phones often are forced to stay with the same brand of mobile phone, because changing to a different brand results in losing access to their favorite programs. Third-party program developers, consumers, and enterprises increasingly demand that the industry create a standard operating system for smart phones. They state that smart phone manufacturers would retain control of the phones' graphical user interface, input and output technology, and built-in utility programs in order to differentiate their phones from the competition. The manufacturers claim, however, that competition eventually will solve the issue.

Should the smart phone industry adopt a standard development platform? Why or why not? Should competition, a group of companies, or a standards-setting body decide the best operating system for smart phones? Why?

Windows Embedded CE

Windows Embedded CE is a scaled-down Windows operating system designed for use on communications, entertainment, and computing devices with limited functionality. Examples of devices that use Windows Embedded CE include VoIP telephones, industrial control devices, digital cameras, point-of-sale terminals, automated teller machines, digital photo frames, fuel pumps, security robots, handheld navigation devices, portable media players, ticket machines, and computerized sewing machines (Figure 8-22).

Windows Embedded CE is a GUI that supports color, sound, multitasking, multimedia, e-mail, Internet access, and Web browsing. A built-in file viewer allows users to view files created in popular programs such as Word, Excel, and PowerPoint.

Devices equipped with Windows Embedded CE can communicate wirelessly with computers and other devices using Bluetooth or other wireless technologies, as long as the device is equipped with the necessary communications hardware.

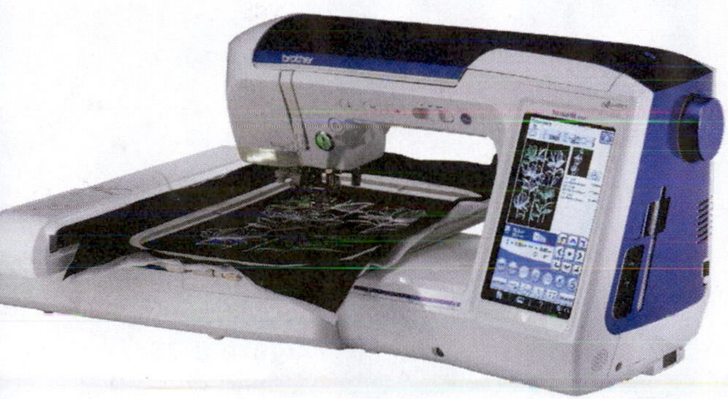

Figure 8-22 This sewing machine uses Windows Embedded CE to assist with stitching quilts, garments, crafts, decorations, and embroidery.

Windows Phone 7

Windows Phone 7, which is a successor to Windows Mobile, includes functionality, programs, and a user interface designed for specific types of smart phones (Figure 8-23). Windows Phone 7 supports multi-touch screens, which are touch screens that recognize multiple points of contact at the same time.

With the Windows Phone 7 operating system and a compatible device, users have access to all the basic PIM (personal information manager) functions such as contact lists, schedules, tasks, calendars, and notes. Information on the mobile device easily synchronizes with a personal computer [illegible] a cable or a [illegible]

Windows Ph[illegible] provides numero[illegible] tional features that [illegible] users to check e-mail, browse the Web, listen to music, take pictures or record video, watch a video, send and receive text messages and instant messages, record a voice message, manage finances, view a map, read an e-book, or play a game. Many programs, such as Word, Excel, Outlook, and Internet Explorer, have scaled-down versions that run with Windows Phone 7. Some devices with Windows Phone 7 also support voice input.

Figure 8-23 A smart phone that uses the Windows Phone 7 operating system, which uses tiles on the home screen to link to various programs and functions.

Palm OS

A competing operating system to Windows Phone 7 is *Palm OS*, which runs on smart phones (Figure 8-24) and PDAs. With Palm OS devices, users manage schedules and contacts, phone messages, notes, task and address lists, and appointments. Information on the mobile device easily synchronizes with a personal computer or prints on a printer using a cable or a wireless technology.

Many Palm OS devices allow users to connect wirelessly to the Internet; browse the Web; send and receive e-mail messages, text messages, and instant messages; listen to music; record voice messages; and view digital photos. Most have touch screens. The latest version of Palm OS allows for biometric identification and supports the use of smart cards.

Figure 8-24 A smart phone that uses the Palm OS operating system.

iPhone OS

...Apple, is an operating ...iPod touch, Apple's ...) and touch screen ... respectively. These devices ...ning they recognize multiple ... This feature enables users to ...hone OS devices using finger ... as tapping a button on the screen, ...r finger to drag an object, and pinching ...ching your fingers to zoom in or out. ...th the iPhone OS, users can manage contacts ...d notes, send and receive e-mail and text messages, take pictures, record videos, record voice messages, view a compass, connect to the Internet wirelessly and browse the Web, check stocks, access maps and obtain directions, listen to music, watch movies and videos, and display photos. It also provides Wi-Fi access to the iTunes Music Store.

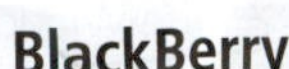

iPhone OS
For more information, visit the Computer Concepts CourseMate Web site at www.cengagebrain.com, navigate to the Chapte... Web Link resource f... book, and then cli... iPhone OS.

Figure 8-25 The iPhone OS runs on Apple's iPhone.

BlackBerry

The *BlackBerry* operating system runs on handheld devices supplied by RIM (Research In Motion). BlackBerry devices provide PIM capabilities such as managing schedules, contacts, and appointments, as well as phone capabilities. They also provide wireless functionality that includes sending e-mail messages, text messages, and instant messages; connecting to the Internet and browsing the Web; and accessing Bluetooth devices. Some BlackBerry devices allow users to take pictures, play music, and access maps and directions.

Information on the device easily synchronizes wirelessly with a computer or other BlackBerry device. Many BlackBerry devices include a mini-keyboard; some have touch screens (Figure 8-26). For a technical discussion about touch screens, read the High-Tech Talk article on page 430.

BlackBerry
For more information, visit the Computer Concepts CourseMate Web site at www.cengagebrain.com, navigate to the Chapter 8 Web Link resource for this book, and then click BlackBerry.

Figure 8-26 A smart phone that uses the BlackBerry operating system.

Google Android

Google Android is an operating system designed by Google for mobile devices. Used on more than 20 different types of mobile devices, Google Android allows programmers to design programs specifically for devices supporting this operating system. Google Android contains features such as access to e-mail accounts, an alarm clock, video capture, access to Google Apps, Wi-Fi access, and easy Web browsing.

Embedded Linux

Embedded Linux is a scaled-down Linux operating system designed for smart phones, PDAs, portable media players, Internet telephones, and many other types of devices and computers requiring an embedded operating system. Devices with embedded Linux offer calendar and address book and other PIM functions, touch screens, and handwriting recognition. Many also allow you to connect to the Internet, take pictures, play videos, listen to music, and send e-mail and instant messages. Devices that use embedded Linux synchronize with desktop computers using a variety of technologies including Bluetooth.

Symbian OS

Symbian OS is an open source multitasking operating system designed for smart phones. In addition to making phone calls, users of Symbian OS can maintain contact lists; save appointments; browse the Web; and send and receive text and picture messages, e-mail messages, and faxes using a smart phone. Users enter data by pressing keys on the keypad or keyboard, touching the screen, writing on the screen with a stylus, or speaking into the smart phone. Symbian OS allows users to communicate wirelessly.

QUIZ YOURSELF 8-2

Instructions: Find the true statement below. Then, rewrite the remaining false statements so that they are true.

1. BlackBerry devices use Palm OS as their operating system.
2. Examples of embedded operating systems include Windows Server 2008, UNIX, Linux, Solaris, and NetWare.
3. Windows 7 Starter uses Windows Aero.
4. Mac OS X is a multitasking operating system available only for computers manufactured by Apple.
5. Aero Flip 3D is a UNIX-type operating system that is open source software.

Quiz Yourself Online: To further check your knowledge of pages 411 through 421, visit the Computer Concepts CourseMate Web site at www.cengagebrain.com, navigate to the Chapter 8 Quiz Yourself resource for this book, and then click Objectives 4 – 6.

Utility Programs

A **utility program**, also called a **utility**, is a type of system software that allows a user to perform maintenance-type tasks, usually related to managing a computer, its devices, or its programs. Most operating systems include several built-in utility programs (Figure 8-27). Users often buy stand-alone utilities, however, because they offer improvements over those included with the operating system.

Functions provided by utility programs include the following: managing files, searching for files, viewing images, uninstalling programs, cleaning up disks, defragmenting disks, backing up files and disks, setting up screen savers, securing a computer from unauthorized access, protecting against viruses, removing spyware and adware, filtering Internet content, compressing files, playing media files, burning optical discs, and maintaining a personal computer. The following sections briefly discuss each of these utilities. Read Innovative Computing 8-1 to find out about utility programs that can help you recover deleted files.

INNOVATIVE COMPUTING 8-1

Utility Programs Locate Deleted Files

If you delete a file mistakenly from a USB flash drive, removable flash memory device, or hard disk, you easily can recover that erased file with utility programs. A few of the more popular utility programs have names that explain their purpose: Recuva, Recover My Files, FreeUndelete, FileMakerRecovery, R-Studio, and Recovery Toolbox. Most can be downloaded from the Web, often free of charge.

Data recovery experts offer advice on actions to take immediately when you realize you have erased files, even if you have emptied the Recycle Bin. Although the file name does not appear in the list of files on that storage medium, the file actually remains intact on the storage medium. The computer marks the space on the disk as free so that another file can overwrite the contents of the deleted file. As long as you do not save any file, no matter how small, the utility program generally can locate the marked space and then retrieve the contents of the file.

For more information, visit the Computer Concepts CourseMate Web site at www.cengagebrain.com, navigate to the Chapter 8 Innovative Computing resource for this book, and then click Recovering Deleted Files.

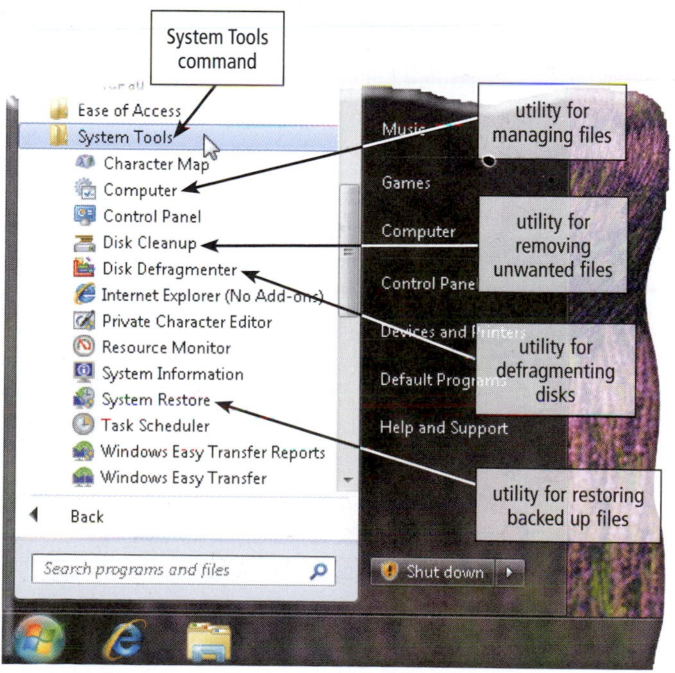

Figure 8-27 To display the utilities available in the Windows System Tools list, click the Start button, click All Programs, click Accessories, and then click System Tools.

File Manager

A **file manager** is a utility that performs functions related to file management. Some of the file management functions that a file manager performs are displaying a list of files on a storage medium (Figure 8-28); organizing files in folders; copying, renaming, deleting, moving, and sorting files and folders; and creating shortcuts. A **folder** is a specific named location on a storage medium that contains related documents. A **shortcut** is an icon on the desktop or in a folder that provides a user with immediate access to a program or file.

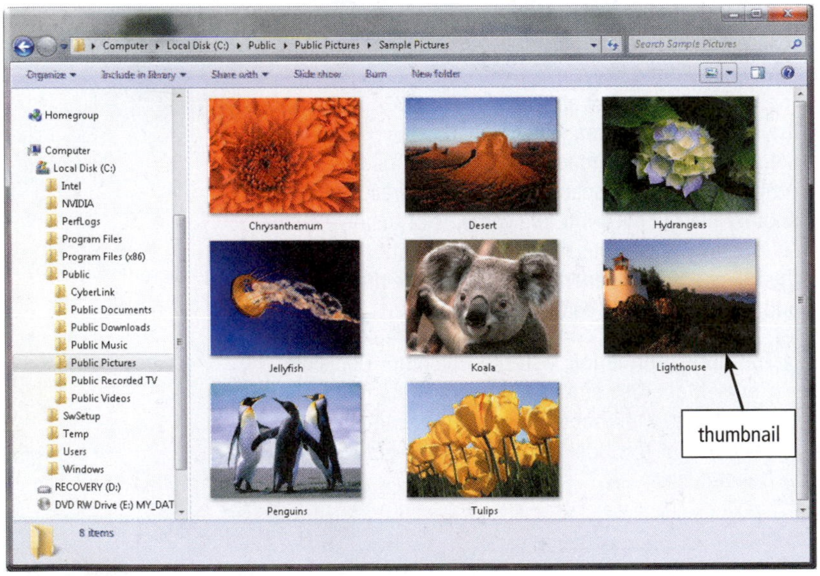

Operating systems typically include a file manager. Windows, for example, includes Windows Explorer, which displays links to files and folders, as well as previews of folder contents and certain types of files.

Figure 8-28 Windows includes file managers that allow you to view documents, photos, and music. In this case, thumbnails of photos are displayed.

Search Utility

A **search utility** is a program that attempts to locate a file on your computer based on criteria you specify (Figure 8-29). The criteria could be a word or words contained in a file, date the file was created or modified, size of the file, location of the file, file name, author/artist, and other similar properties. Search utilities can look through documents, photos, music, and other files on your computer and/or on the Internet, combining search results in a single location.

Search utilities typically use an index to assist with locating files quickly. An *index* stores a variety of information about a file, including its name, date created, date modified, author name, and so on. When you enter search criteria, instead of looking through every file and folder on the storage medium, the search utility looks through the index first to find a match. Each entry in the index contains a link to the actual file on the disk for easy retrieval. Operating systems typically include a built-in search utility. In Windows, all the Explorer windows, as well as the Start menu, contain a Search box where you enter the search criteria.

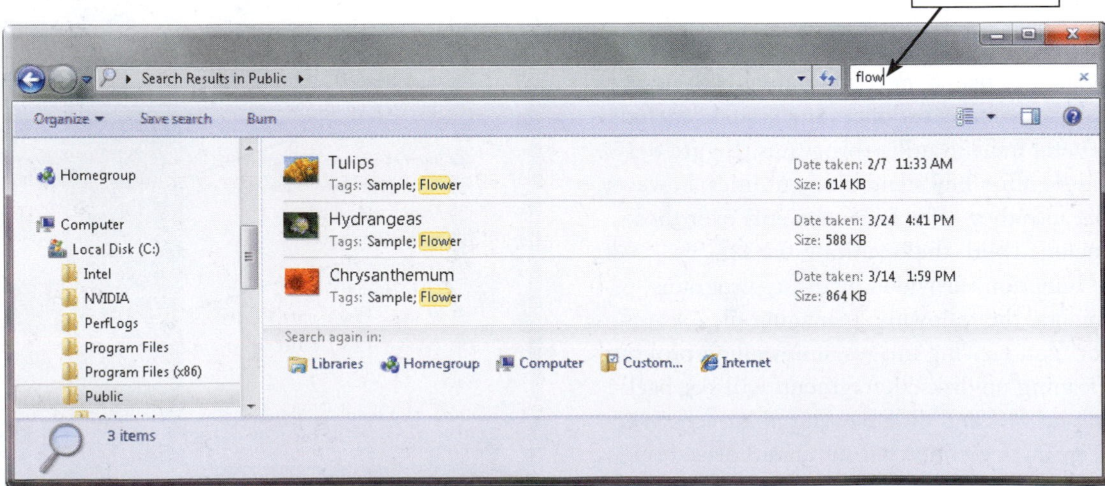

Figure 8-29 This search displays files whose name or contents contain the text, flow.

Image Viewer

An **image viewer** is a utility that allows users to display, copy, and print the contents of a graphics file, such as a photo. With an image viewer, users can see images without having to open them in a paint or image editing program. Most operating systems include an image viewer. Windows image viewer is called *Windows Photo Viewer*, which also allows you to print and e-mail photos (Figure 8-30).

Figure 8-30 Windows Photo Viewer allows users to see the contents of a photo file.

Uninstaller

An **uninstaller** is a utility that removes a program, as well as any associated entries in the system files. When you install a program, the operating system records the information it uses to run the software in the system files. The uninstaller deletes files and folders from the hard disk, as well as removes program entries from the system files. Operating systems usually provide an uninstaller.

In Windows, you are able to access the uninstaller for many installed programs through the 'Uninstall a program' command in the Control Panel. You also can access the uninstaller for some program's through that programs folder on the Start menu, or on the program's installation media.

FAQ 8-6

Should I use Windows Explorer to delete a program?

No! If you remove software from a computer by deleting the files and folders associated with the program without running the uninstaller, the system file entries are not updated. This may cause the operating system to display error messages when you start the computer. If a program has an uninstaller, always use it to remove software.

For more information, visit the Computer Concepts CourseMate Web site at www.cengagebrain.com, navigate to the Chapter 8 FAQ resource for this book, and then click Uninstalling Programs.

Disk Cleanup

A *disk cleanup* utility searches for and removes unnecessary files. Unnecessary files may include downloaded program files, temporary Internet files, deleted files, and unused program files. Operating systems, such as Windows, include a disk cleanup utility (Figure 8-31).

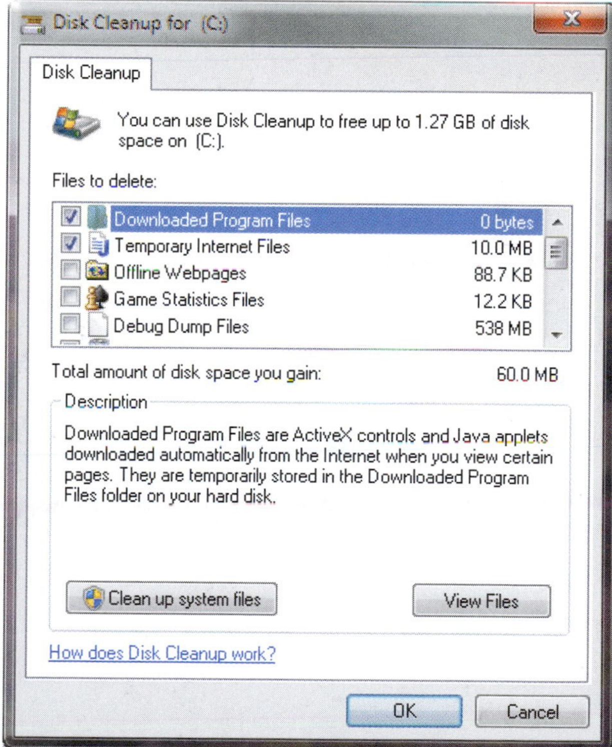

Figure 8-31 Disk Cleanup searches for and removes unnecessary files.

Disk Defragmenter

A **disk defragmenter** is a utility that reorganizes the files and unused space on a computer's hard disk so that the operating system accesses data more quickly and programs run faster. When an operating system stores data on a disk, it places the data in the first available sector on the disk. It attempts to place data in sectors that are contiguous (next to each other), but this is not always possible. When the contents of a file are scattered across two or more noncontiguous sectors, the file is *fragmented*.

Fragmentation slows down disk access and thus the performance of the entire computer. **Defragmenting** the disk, or reorganizing it so that the files are stored in contiguous sectors, solves this problem (Figure 8-32). Operating systems usually include a disk defragmenter. Windows Disk Defragmenter is available in the System Tools list.

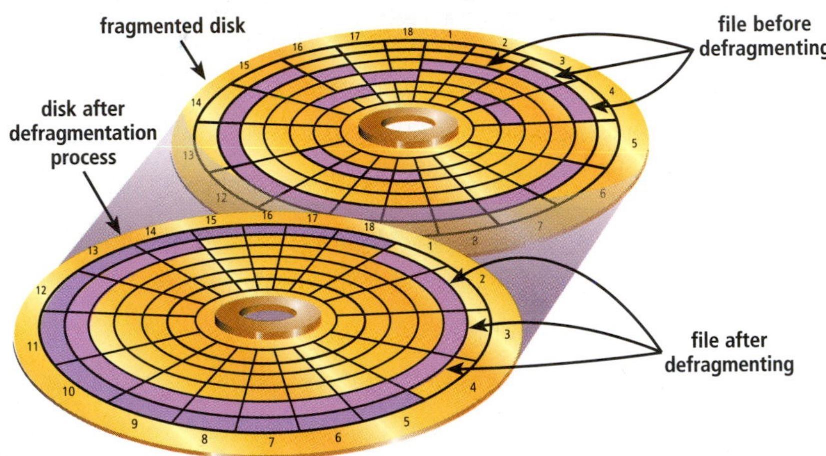

Figure 8-32 A fragmented disk has many files stored in noncontiguous sectors. Defragmenting reorganizes the files so that they are located in contiguous sectors, which speeds access time.

Backup and Restore Utilities

A **backup utility** allows users to copy, or *back up*, selected files or an entire hard disk to another storage medium such as another hard disk, optical disc, USB flash drive, or tape. During the backup process, the utility monitors progress and alerts you if it needs additional media, such as another disc. Many backup programs *compress*, or shrink the size of, files during the backup process. By compressing the files, the backup program requires less storage space for the backup files than for the original files.

Because they are compressed, you usually cannot use backup files in their backed up form. In the event you need to use a backup file, a **restore utility** reverses the process and returns backed up files to their original form. Backup utilities work with a restore utility.

You should back up files and disks regularly in the event your originals are lost, damaged, or destroyed. Most backup and restore utilities include a scheduler, which instructs the computer to perform a backup automatically on a regularly scheduled basis. Operating systems, such as Windows, include a backup and restore utility (Figure 8-33). When you purchase an external hard disk, it also usually includes a backup and restore utility. Instead of backing up to a local disk storage device, some users opt to use cloud storage to back up their files. As described in Chapter 7, cloud storage is a service on the Web that provides storage to computer users, usually for free or for a minimal monthly fee.

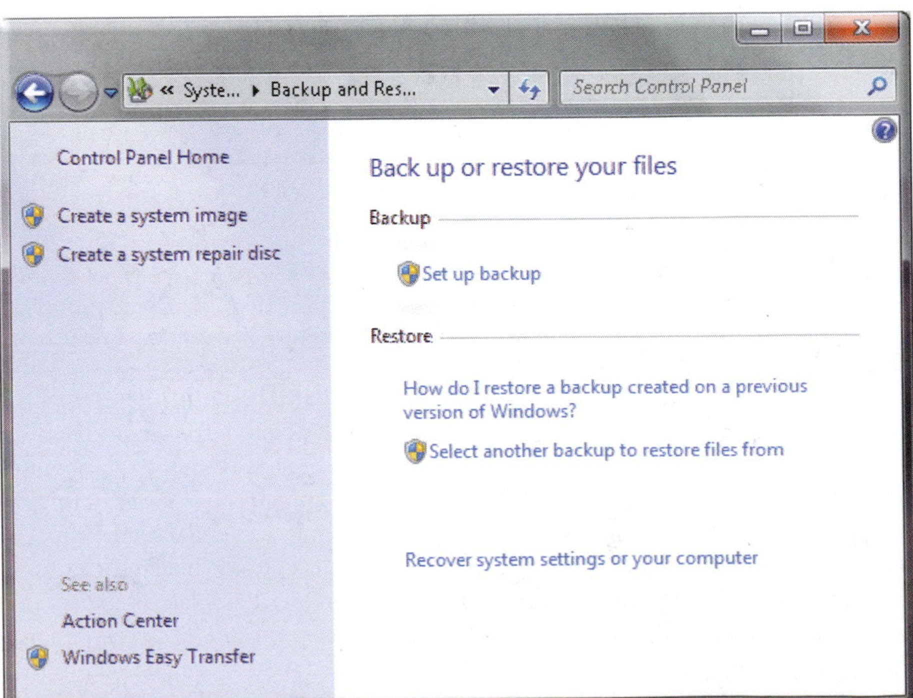

Figure 8-33 A backup utility allows users to copy files or an entire hard disk to another storage medium.

Screen Saver

A **screen saver** is a utility that causes a display device's screen to show a moving image or blank screen if no keyboard or mouse activity occurs for a specified time. When you press a key on the keyboard or move the mouse, the screen saver disappears and the screen returns to the previous state.

Screen savers originally were developed to prevent a problem called *ghosting*, in which images could be etched permanently on a monitor's screen. Although ghosting is not as severe of a problem with today's displays, manufacturers continue to recommend that users install screen savers for this reason. Screen savers also are popular for security, business, and entertainment purposes. To secure a computer, users configure their screen saver to require a password to deactivate. In addition to those included with the operating system, many screen savers are available in stores (Figure 8-34) and on the Web for free or a minimal fee.

Figure 8-34 With this screen saver software, you can create your own screen savers.

Personal Firewall

A **personal firewall** is a utility that detects and protects a personal computer from unauthorized intrusions. Personal firewalls constantly monitor all transmissions to and from a computer.

When connected to the Internet, your computer is vulnerable to attacks from a hacker. A *hacker* is someone who tries to access a computer or network illegally. Users with broadband Internet connections, such as through DSL and cable Internet service, are even more susceptible than those with dial-up access because the Internet connection always is on.

Operating systems often include a personal firewall. Windows automatically enables its built-in personal firewall, called Windows Firewall, upon installation of the operating system. If your operating system does not include a personal firewall or you want additional protection, you can purchase a stand-alone personal firewall utility (Figure 8-35) or a hardware firewall, which is a device such as a router that has a built-in firewall.

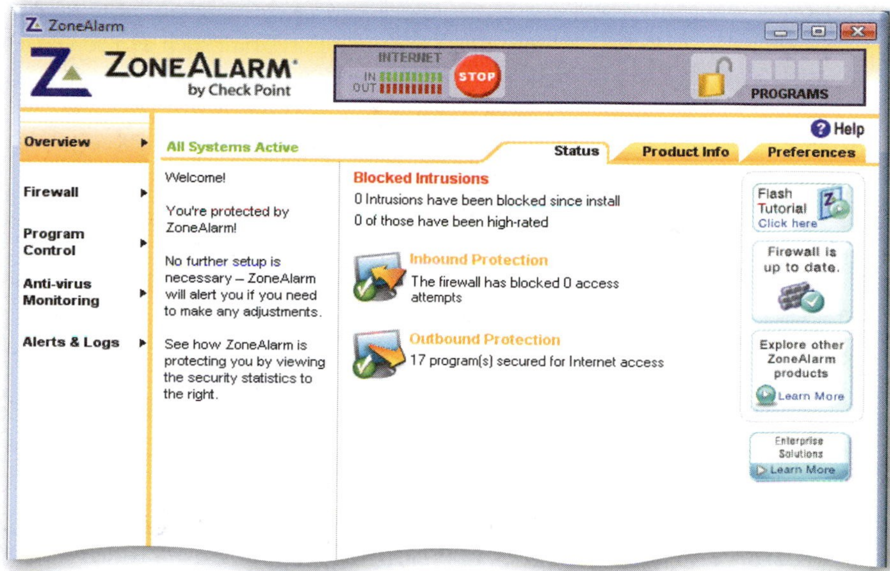

Figure 8-35 A stand-alone personal firewall utility.

Antivirus Programs

The term, computer **virus**, describes a potentially damaging computer program that affects, or infects, a computer negatively by altering the way the computer works without the user's knowledge or permission. Once the virus is in a computer, it can spread throughout and may damage your files and operating system.

Computer viruses do not generate by chance. The programmer of a virus, known as a *virus author*, intentionally writes a virus program. Some virus authors find writing viruses a challenge. Others write virus programs to cause destruction. Writing a virus program usually requires significant programming skills.

Some viruses are harmless pranks that simply freeze a computer temporarily or display sounds or messages. The Music Bug virus, for example, instructs the computer to play a few chords of music. Other viruses destroy or corrupt data stored on the hard disk of the infected computer. If you notice any unusual changes in your computer's performance, it may be infected with a virus (Figure 8-36).

Signs of Virus Infection

- An unusual message or image is displayed on the computer screen
- An unusual sound or music plays randomly
- The available memory is less than what should be available
- A program or file suddenly is missing
- An unknown program or file mysteriously appears
- The size of a file changes without explanation
- A file becomes corrupted
- A program or file does not work properly
- System properties change
- The computer operates much slower than usual

Figure 8-36 Viruses attack computers in a variety of ways. This list indicates some of the more common signs of virus infection.

Viruses are just one type of malicious software. *Malware* (short for malicious software) is software that acts without a user's knowledge and deliberately alters the computer's operations. In addition to viruses, worms and Trojan horses are malware.

A **worm**, such as Sasser or Klez, copies itself repeatedly, for example, in memory or over a network, using up system resources and possibly shutting down the system. A **Trojan horse** (named after the Greek myth) hides within or looks like a legitimate program such as a screen saver. A certain condition or action usually triggers the Trojan horse. Unlike a virus or worm, a Trojan horse does not replicate itself to other computers. Currently, more than one million known threats to your computer exist. For a more technical discussion about computer viruses, read the High-Tech Talk article in Chapter 3 on page 178.

To protect a computer from virus attacks, users should install an antivirus program and update it frequently. An **antivirus program** protects a computer against viruses by identifying and removing any computer viruses found in memory, on storage media, or on incoming files. Most antivirus programs also protect against worms and Trojan horses. When you purchase a new computer, it often includes antivirus software.

Three more popular antivirus programs are McAfee VirusScan, Norton AntiVirus (Figure 8-37), and Windows Live OneCare, most of which also contains spyware removers, Internet filters, and other utilities. As an alternative to purchasing these products on disc, both McAfee and Norton offer Web-based antivirus programs.

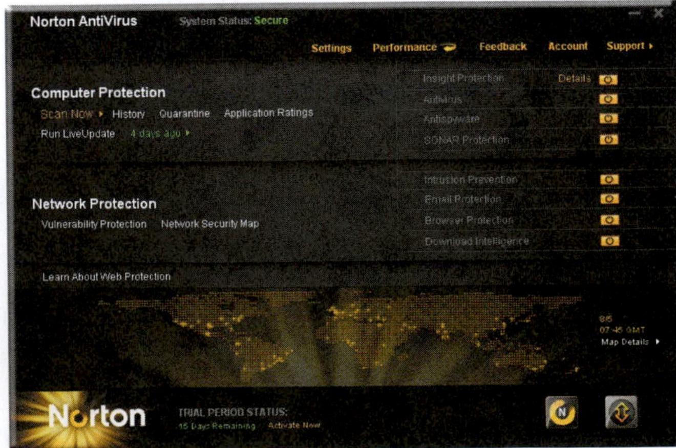

Figure 8-37 An antivirus program scans memory, disks, and incoming e-mail messages and attachments for viruses and attempts to remove any viruses it finds.

? FAQ 8-7

What steps should I take to prevent virus infections on my computer?

Set up the antivirus program to scan on a regular basis. Update your virus definitions regularly. Never open an e-mail attachment unless you are expecting the attachment and it is from a trusted source. If you use Windows, install the latest Microsoft updates. Set macro security in programs such as word processing and spreadsheet so that you can enable or disable macros. Back up files regularly.

For more information, visit the Computer Concepts CourseMate Web site at www.cengagebrain.com, navigate to the Chapter 8 FAQ resource for this book, and then click Preventing Virus Infections.

Spyware and Adware Removers

Spyware is a program placed on a computer without the user's knowledge that secretly collects information about the user, often related to Web browsing habits. Spyware can enter a computer as a virus or as a result of a user installing a new program. The spyware program communicates information it collects to an outside source while you are online.

Adware is a program that displays an online advertisement in a banner or pop-up window on Web pages, e-mail, or other Internet services. Sometimes, spyware is hidden in adware.

A **spyware remover** is a program that detects and deletes spyware and other similar programs. An *adware remover* is a program that detects and deletes adware. Most spyware and adware removers cost less than $50; some are available on the Web at no cost. Some operating systems and antivirus programs include spyware and adware removers. Popular stand-alone spyware and adware removers include Ad-Aware, Spy Sweeper, Spybot - Search and Destroy, and Windows Defender.

Internet Filters

Filters are programs that remove or block certain items from being displayed. Four widely used Internet filters are Web filters, anti-spam programs, phishing filters, and pop-up blockers.

Web Filters **Web filtering software** is a program that restricts access to certain material on the Web. Some restrict access to specific Web sites; others filter sites that use certain words or phrases. Many businesses use Web filtering software to limit employee's Web access. Some schools, libraries, and parents use this software to restrict access to minors. Windows 7 contains parental controls, which allow parents to record and control the types of content their children can access on the Internet.

Anti-Spam Programs *Spam* is an unsolicited e-mail message or newsgroup posting sent to many recipients or newsgroups at once. Spam is Internet junk mail. The content of spam ranges from selling a product or service, to promoting a business opportunity, to advertising offensive material. An **anti-spam program** is a filtering program that attempts to remove spam before it reaches your inbox. If your e-mail program does not filter spam, many anti-spam programs are available at no cost on the Web. Internet access providers often filter spam as a service for their subscribers.

? FAQ 8-8

Where does spam originate?

Research indicates that spam originates from various countries throughout the world. Symantec Corporation found that in a 30-day period, the United States was responsible for more spam than any other country. The following chart illustrates the countries responsible for the most spam worldwide.

Spam Origin

39% 23% 12% 5% 3% 4% 2% 4% 3% 3% 2%

United States
Brazil
South Korea
Turkey
India
Colombia
Poland
China
Vietnam
Argentina
Other

Source: Symantec

For more information, visit the Computer Concepts CourseMate Web site at www.cengagebrain.com, navigate to the Chapter 8 FAQ resource for this book, and then click Spam.

Phishing Filters *Phishing* is a scam in which a perpetrator attempts to obtain your personal and/or financial information. A **phishing filter** is a program that warns or blocks you from potentially fraudulent or suspicious Web sites. Some Web browsers include phishing filters.

Pop-Up Blockers A *pop-up ad* is an Internet advertisement that suddenly appears in a new window in the foreground of a Web page displayed in your browser. A **pop-up blocker** is a filtering program that stops pop-up ads from displaying on Web pages. Many Web browsers include a pop-up blocker. You also can download pop-up blockers from the Web at no cost.

File Compression

A **file compression utility** shrinks the size of a file(s). A compressed file takes up less storage space than the original file. Compressing files frees up room on the storage media and improves system performance. Attaching a compressed file to an e-mail message, for example, reduces the time needed for file transmission. Uploading and downloading compressed files to and from the Internet reduces the file transmission time.

Two types of compression are lossy and lossless. With *lossy* compression, because the quality of a file decreases slightly each time the file is compressed, you will be unable to restore the file to its exact original state. With audio and video files, small degradations in quality usually are not recognizable; thus, lossy compression often is used on these types of files. With *lossless* compression, by contrast, a compressed file can be returned to its exact original state. Text files typically use lossless compression.

Compressed files, sometimes called **zipped files**, usually have a .zip extension. When you receive or download a compressed file, you must uncompress it. To **uncompress**, or *unzip*, a file, you restore it to its original form. Some operating systems such as Windows include file compression and uncompression capabilities. Two popular stand-alone file compression utilities are PKZIP and WinZip.

WinZip

For more information, visit the Computer Concepts CourseMate Web site at www.cengagebrain.com, navigate to the Chapter 8 Web Link resource for this book, and then click WinZip.

Media Player

A **media player** is a program that allows you to view images and animation, listen to audio, and watch video files on your computer (Figure 8-38). Media players may also include

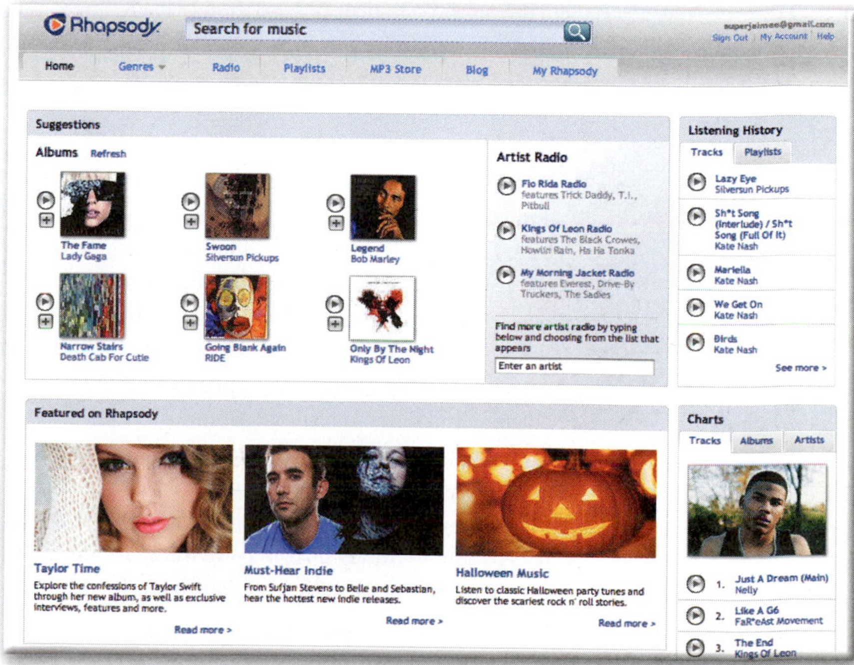

Figure 8-38 A popular media player.

the capability to organize media files, convert them to different formats, connect to and purchase media from an online media store, download podcasts and vodcasts, burn audio CDs, and transfer media to portable media players. Windows includes Windows Media Player. Three other popular media players are iTunes, RealPlayer, and Rhapsody. Read Ethics & Issues 8-4 for a related discussion.

ETHICS & ISSUES 8-4

Should the Government Tax Media Downloads?

When you purchase a DVD or Blu-ray Disc that contains a season or two of your favorite television show, chances are that you also pay a state and/or local sales tax. If you purchase and download the same material online in a digital format, however, chances are that you do not pay a sales tax. Some government taxing bodies seek to change that discrepancy. Two main reasons for the pressure to tax include: state and local governments feeling the pinch of lost revenue to legally downloaded digital content because consumers purchase less taxable, physical media; and pressure from the media industry to recoup lost sales due to illegally downloaded digital content. Some governments go as far as funneling collected taxes directly to the multimedia industry as compensation for illegally downloaded content that occurs in a region. Critics of the new taxes claim that government should not tax the greenest form of media purchases. Digitally downloaded content eliminates packaging, optical discs, trips to the store, and use of delivery vehicles. Critics also claim that governments single out multimedia content due to pressure from the multimedia industry. For example, some governments tax the purchase of newspapers, magazines and books, but often the same content is sold online and is not taxed. Typically, government taxing bodies tax goods, but not food and services.

Should the government tax media downloads, such as music, video, e-books, newspaper articles, and magazine articles? Why or why not? Should digital content delivery be considered a service rather than a good by taxing bodies? Why?

Disc Burning

Disc burning software writes text, graphics, audio, and video files on a recordable or rewritable CD, DVD, or Blu-ray Disc. This software enables the home user easily to back up contents of their hard disk on an optical disc and make duplicates of uncopyrighted music or movies. Disc burning software usually also includes photo editing, audio editing, and video editing capabilities (Figure 8-39). To learn about burning files to a disc, complete the Learn How To 2 exercise on page 440.

Burning Discs
For more information, visit the Computer Concepts CourseMate Web site at www.cengagebrain.com, navigate to the Chapter 8 Web Link resource for this book, and then click Burning Discs.

When you buy a recordable or rewritable disc, it typically includes burning software. You also can buy stand-alone disc burning software for a cost of less than $100.

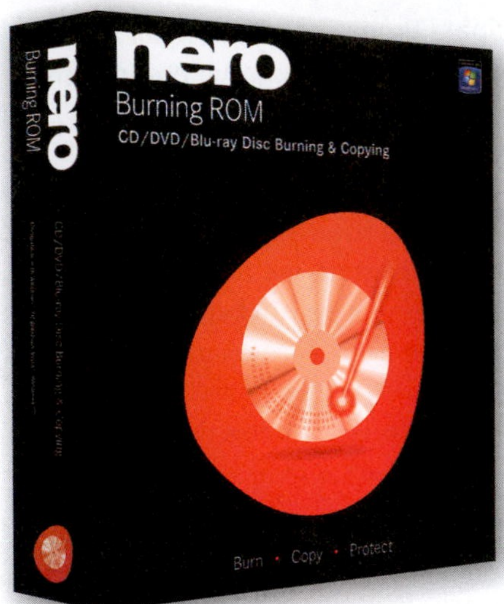

Figure 8-39 You can copy text, graphics, audio, and video files to discs using the digital media suite shown here, provided you have the correct type of drive and media.

Personal Computer Maintenance

Operating systems typically include a diagnostic utility that diagnoses computer problems but does not repair them. A **personal computer maintenance utility** identifies and fixes operating system problems, detects and repairs disk problems, and includes the capability of improving a computer's performance. Additionally, some personal computer maintenance utilities continuously monitor a computer while you use it to identify and repair problems before they occur. Norton SystemWorks is a popular personal computer maintenance utility designed for Windows operating systems (Figure 8-40).

Figure 8-40 A popular maintenance program for Windows users.

QUIZ YOURSELF 8-3

Instructions: Find the true statement below. Then, rewrite the remaining false statements so that they are true.

1. A pop-up blocker shrinks the size of a file(s).
2. An anti-spam program protects a computer against viruses by identifying and removing any computer viruses found in memory, on storage media, or on incoming files.
3. A personal firewall is a utility that detects and protects a personal computer from unauthorized intrusions.
4. You should uninstall files and disks regularly in the event your originals are lost, damaged, or destroyed.
5. Web filtering software writes text, graphics, audio, and video files to a recordable or rewritable disc.
6. Fragmenting a disk is the process of reorganizing it so that the files are stored in contiguous sectors.

Quiz Yourself Online: To further check your knowledge of pages 421 through 428, visit the Computer Concepts CourseMate Web site at www.cengagebrain.com, navigate to the Chapter 8 Quiz Yourself resource for this book, and then click Objective 7.

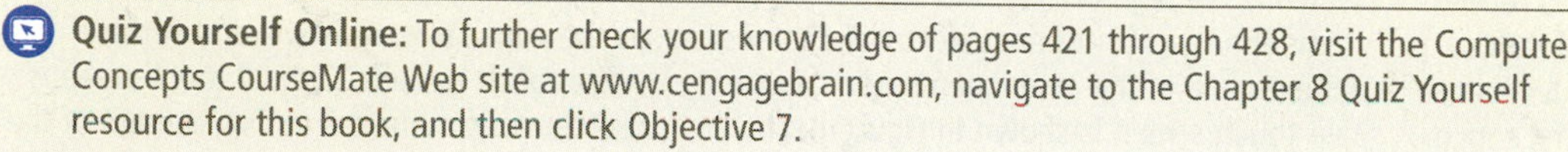

Chapter Summary

This chapter defined an operating system and then discussed the functions common to most operating systems. The chapter introduced a variety of stand-alone operating systems, server operating systems, and embedded operating systems. Finally, the chapter described several utility programs.

Computer Usage @ Work

Education

Teachers and students have been using computers in education for many years. Teachers have been taking advantage of advances in computer technology to help provide a better educational experience for their students.

Many grade schools throughout the United States, as well as other countries, enable parents to track their child's performance online. In the past, parents would rely solely on their child bringing home graded assignments and tests to know how he or she was doing. In some cases, parents would be surprised when they saw their child's grades on report cards every two to three months. Teachers now have the opportunity to engage parents in their child's education not only by giving them an up-to-the-minute snapshot of grades, but also by posting lesson plans online so that parents know what their child is learning.

Computers and technology also benefit students in the classroom. Schools now have one or more computers in almost every classroom, enabling students to access the Internet to do research that they otherwise would have had to visit the library to perform. Schools also are able to offer additional technology courses such as Web page design, digital media, and computer programming.

At the college level, many instructors today rely heavily on e-learning systems to provide students with Web-based access to course materials and assessments, discussion forums, chat rooms, and e-mail. Once used mainly in online classes, e-learning systems provide instructors with an easy way to allow students access to the class at any time of the day.

Most instructors go beyond e-learning systems and use additional technologies to enhance their classes. For example, digital media instructors might require students to upload their assignments to a photo sharing community, and an English instructor might save paper by requiring students to upload research papers to Google Docs and share them with the instructor.

Computer use in education not only enhances the teaching experience for instructors and learning experience for students, it also provides students with technological knowledge that will benefit them for the rest of their lives.

For more information, visit the Computer Concepts CourseMate Web site at www.cengagebrain.com, navigate to the Chapter 8 Computer Usage @ Work resource for this book, and then click Education.

High-Tech Talk

Touch Screen Technology: How the Screen Is So Smart

Touch screen technology is becoming a larger part of everyday life for many individuals. As presented in Chapter 5, a touch screen is a touch-sensitive display device that users can interact with by touching areas of the screen. People have been using touch screens for more than 30 years, and this technology now is being used in more places, such as in smart phones, point-of-sale terminals, automated teller machines, remote controls, GPS receivers, home security systems, and Tablet PCs.

Touch screen technology has evolved since its creation in the late 1960s. The first touch screens developed allowed users to press only one area at a time with the tip of their finger, and they were much less accurate than today's touch screens. As the technology is advancing, users are able to perform additional tasks, such as dragging their finger across the screen and touching more than one area of the screen at a time. For example, the iPhone and iPod touch allow you to zoom in pictures or other objects on the screen by placing two fingers close together on the screen, and then slowly moving them apart. Three types of touch screens most in use today are capacitive, resistive, and surface wave touch screens.

A *capacitive touch screen* has a layer of material that stores electrical charges coating the surface. When a finger touches the screen, it conducts a small amount of the electrical charge, reducing the charge on the capacitive layer. Circuits located at each corner of the capacitive touch screen measure the change in electrical charge. The circuits then send this data to the touch screen controller, or software that is running on the computer. The controller then uses the data to calculate the location where the finger is touching the screen. Capacitive touch screens typically are high-quality and unaffected by items that do not conduct electrical charges. An example of the components of a capacitive touch screen is shown in Figure 8-41.

The second type of touch screen is a resistive touch screen. A metallic conductive and resistive layer held apart by spacers cover a *resistive touch screen*. When a user touches a resistive touch screen, the conductive and resistive layers connect in the location of the touch. An electronic current runs between the two layers, and the interruption in the current enables the touch screen controller to calculate the exact location of the touch. Although resistive touch screens usually are more affordable than capacitive touch screens, they are not as clear and can be damaged more easily.

The third type of touch screen uses surface wave technology. *Surface wave technology* passes ultrasonic waves over the touch screen. Touching the screen absorbs portions of the waves, which then allows the touch screen controller to calculate the position at which the object touched the screen. Because ultrasonic waves pass over the touch screen, it is easy for outside elements to damage the device. Touch screens using surface wave technology are the most advanced and often the most expensive of the three types.

Additional types of touch screen technologies exist, but they are not used as widely as the capacitive, resistive, and surface wave touch screens. *Optical touch screens* use cameras mounted at two corners of the screen to detect objects close to the surface. *Infrared touch screens* use light emitting diodes and light detectors at the edges of the touch screen to detect objects that break the beams of light traveling across the screen.

As touch screen prices continue to decrease, they most likely will be incorporated in an increasing number of computers and devices. Touch screens have increased productivity by allowing people to interact with devices more quickly than they can with a mouse or keyboard.

For more information, visit the Computer Concepts CourseMate Web site at www.cengagebrain.com, navigate to the Chapter 8 High-Tech Talk resource for this book, and then click Touch Screen Technology.

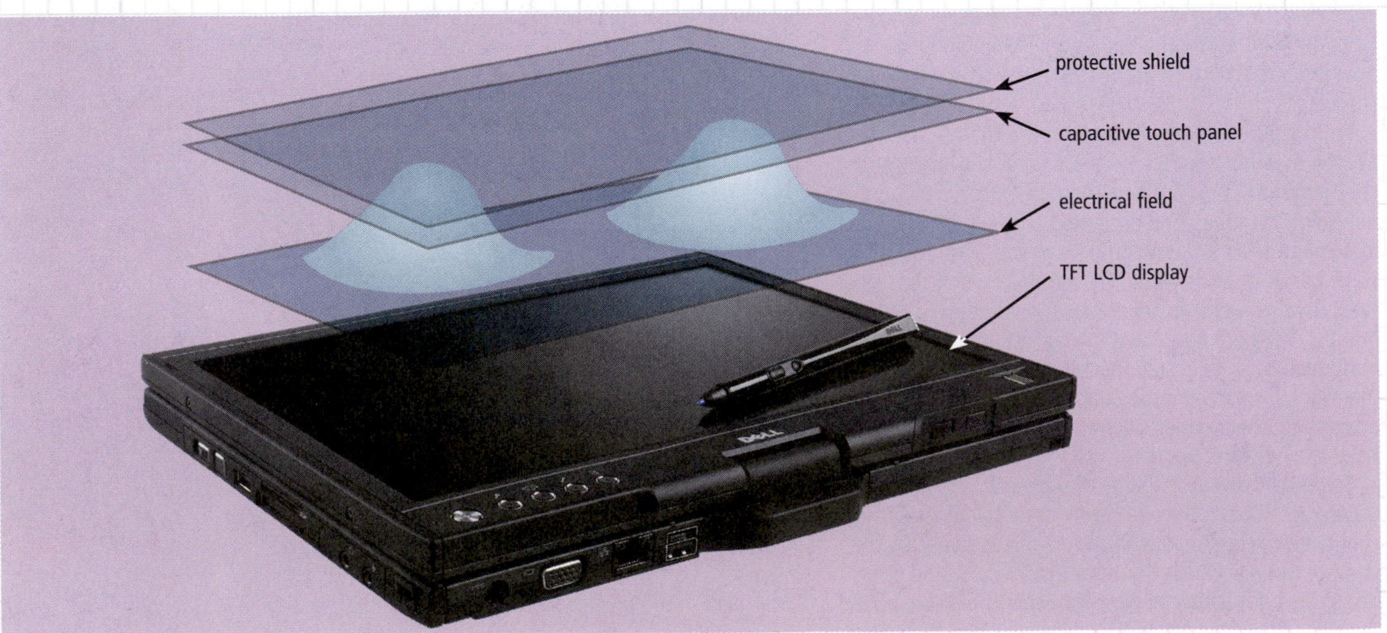

Figure 8-41 A capacitive touch screen identifies where someone touches the screen by measuring differences in electrical charges.

Companies on the Cutting Edge

VERISIGN Internet Infrastructure Services

Technology users desire immediate access to information and services. Their ability to communicate and conduct commerce securely is aided in large part by *VeriSign*. More than 30 billion times a day, people interact on the Internet, and their purchases, text messages, downloads, and other transactions are enabled and protected by VeriSign's infrastructure services.

Computer security company Semantic acquired VeriSign's Authentication division business in 2010 to strengthen encryption and identity services and help protect businesses and consumers by protecting information and detecting online fraud. Its domain name services department registers all .com, .net, .cc, and .tv domain names. The VeriSign Secured Seal, which has been issued to more than 100,000 domains in 145 countries, ensures companies and consumers that the Web site is secure.

The California-based company was founded in 1995 and has more than 2,200 employees worldwide.

RESEARCH IN MOTION (RIM) Wireless Mobile Communications Devices Manufacturer

By 2012, 800 million people worldwide are expected to access social networking Web sites on smart phones, up from 82 million in 2007. *Research in Motion (RIM)* helped fuel this networking frenzy by partnering with MySpace in 2008 to help connect networkers on the go. They can access MySpace Mobile on a BlackBerry smart phone, which is RIM's key product.

The Canadian company was founded in 1984 by Mike Lazaridis, who serves as its president and co-CEO. Lazaridis's vision for wireless technology developed in high school when he was a member of the local amateur radio and television club. He developed RIM's first major product, the Inter@active Pager, which was integrated in the first BlackBerry product in 1998. The BlackBerry gained attention for having the capability to combine a wireless mailbox with a corporate mailbox so that users could assess e-mail continuously.

Recently, Research in Motion launched BlackBerry App World, an application store that allows BlackBerry users to download personal and business programs.

For more information, visit the Computer Concepts CourseMate Web site at www.cengagebrain.com and then navigate to the Chapter 8 Companies on the Cutting Edge resource for this book.

Technology Trailblazers

STEVE WOZNIAK Apple Cofounder

Mixing fun with work comes naturally for *Steve Wozniak*. As Apple's cofounder, he says his computer designing career began and still continues to be a hobby filled with creativity, humor, games, and education. In his opinion, Apple's success evolved because he designed computers that had minimal parts and maximum performance.

Wozniak designed the original Apple computer in 1975 with Apple's current CEO, Steve Jobs, and wrote most of the software. Ten years later he cofounded Pixar, the award winning animation studio. He left Apple in 1985 to spend time with his family, work on community projects, and teach, but he still serves as an advisor to the corporation.

Wozinak was inducted into the Consumer Electronics Hall of Fame and the National Inventors Hall of Fame. One of his current passions is applying artificial intelligence to the area of robotics. He also is a member of the Silicon Valley Aftershocks, a polo team that plays using Segway electric transportation devices.

LINUS TORVALDS Linux Creator

Inductees to the Computer History Museum in Mountain View, CA, are noted for their contribution to computer technology. *Linus Torvalds* joined the Museum's Hall of Fellows in 2008 for his creation of the open source operating system, Linux.

When he developed an operating system in 1991, he announced his project in an Internet newsgroup. He made the source code available and asked readers for suggestions to enhance the product. Computer users responded by reviewing the system and offering enhancements. Three years later he released a greatly enhanced version he called Linux.

Torvalds developed this innovative operating system when he was a 21-year-old computer science student in Finland. Today, he leads the development of Linux as a fellow at OSDL (Open Source Development Labs), a not-for-profit consortium of companies dedicated to developing and promoting the operating system. Torvalds says his daily involvement with Linux involves coordinating and merging the lines of code submitted by users so that the software runs smoothly.

For more information, visit the Computer Concepts CourseMate Web site at www.cengagebrain.com and then navigate to the Chapter 8 Technology Trailblazers resource for this book.

Chapter Review

The Chapter Review reinforces the main concepts presented in this chapter.

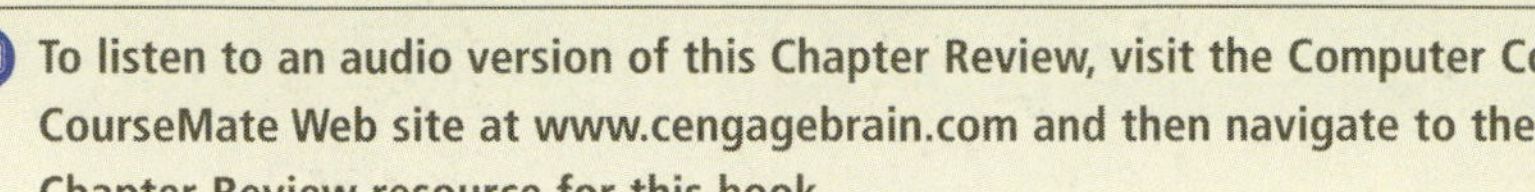

To listen to an audio version of this Chapter Review, visit the Computer Concepts CourseMate Web site at www.cengagebrain.com and then navigate to the Chapter 8 Chapter Review resource for this book.

1. **What Is System Software, and What Are the Two Types of System Software?** **System software** consists of the programs that control or maintain the operations of a computer and its devices. Two types of system software are operating systems and utility programs. An **operating system (OS)** is a set of programs containing instructions that work together to coordinate all the activities among computer hardware resources. A **utility program**, also called a **utility**, performs maintenance-type tasks, usually related to managing a computer, its devices, or its programs.

2. **What Are the Functions of an Operating System?** The operating system starts and shuts down a computer, provides a user interface, manages programs, manages memory, coordinates tasks, configures devices, establishes an Internet connection, monitors performance, provides utilities, updates automatically, controls a network, and administers security. The **user interface** controls how data and instructions are entered and how information is displayed on the screen. Two types of user interfaces are a *graphical user interface* (*GUI*) and a *command-line interface*. Managing programs refers to how many users, and how many programs, an operating system can support at one time. An operating system can be *single user/single tasking*, *single user/multitasking*, *multiuser*, or *multiprocessing*. **Memory management** optimizes the use of random access memory (RAM). If memory is insufficient, the operating system may use **virtual memory**, which allocates a portion of a storage medium to function as additional RAM. Coordinating tasks determines the order in which tasks are processed. Tasks include receiving data from an input device, processing instructions, sending information to an output device, and transferring items between storage and memory. Configuring devices involves loading each device's driver when a user boots the computer. A **driver**, short for *device driver*, is a small program that tells the operating system how to communicate with a specific device. Establishing an Internet connection sets up a connection between a computer and an Internet access provider. A **performance monitor** is an operating system program that assesses and reports information about computer resources and devices. Operating systems often provide the capability of managing and searching for files, viewing images, securing a computer from unauthorized access, uninstalling programs, and other tasks. Most operating systems also include an **automatic update** feature that provides updates to the program. A **server operating system** is an operating system that organizes and coordinates how multiple users access and share network resources. Network administrators typically have an *administrator account* that enables them to access files, install programs, and specify network settings, including creating user accounts and establishing *permissions*.

3. **What Is the Startup Process on a Personal Computer?** **Booting** is the process of starting or restarting a computer. When a user turns on a computer, the power supply sends a signal to the system unit. The processor chip finds the ROM chip(s) that contains the **BIOS** (*basic input/output system*), which is firmware with the computer's startup instructions. The BIOS performs the *power-on self test* (*POST*) to check system components and compares the results with data in a CMOS chip. If the POST completes successfully, the BIOS searches for the *system files* and the *kernel* of the operating system, which manages memory and devices, and loads them into memory from storage. Finally, the operating system loads configuration information, requests any necessary user information, and displays the desktop on the screen. The operating system executes programs in the *Startup folder*, which contains a list of programs that open automatically when you boot the computer.

Visit the Computer Concepts CourseMate Web site at www.cengagebrain.com, navigate to the Chapter 8 Quiz Yourself resource for this book, and then click Objectives 1 – 3.

4. **What Are Features of Windows 7, Mac OS X, UNIX, and Linux Operating Systems?** A **stand-alone operating system** is a complete operating system that works on a desktop computer, notebook computer, or mobile computing device. **Windows 7** is Microsoft's fastest, most efficient operating system to date, offering quicker program start up, built-in diagnostics, automatic recovery, improved security, enhanced searching and

Chapter Review

organizing capabilities, and an easy-to-use interface. Most users choose from *Windows 7 Starter*, *Windows 7 Home Premium*, *Windows 7 Ultimate*, or *Windows 7 Professional* editions. **Mac OS X** is a multitasking operating system available only for Apple computers. **UNIX** is a multitasking operating system developed at Bell Laboratories. **Linux** is a popular, multitasking UNIX-type operating system that is *open source software*, which means its code is available to the public for use, modification, and redistribution.

5. **What Are Various Server Operating Systems?** Server operating systems include Windows Server 2008, UNIX, Linux, Solaris, and NetWare. **Windows Server 2008** is an upgrade to Windows Server 2003 and includes features of previous Windows Server versions. UNIX, like Linux, is a *multipurpose operating system* because it is both a stand-alone and server operating system. *Solaris*, a version of UNIX developed by Sun Microsystems, is a server operating system designed specifically for e-commerce applications. Novell's *NetWare* is a server operating system designed for client/server networks.

6. **What Are the Features of Several Embedded Operating Systems?** Mobile devices and many consumer electronics have an **embedded operating system** that resides on a ROM chip. Popular embedded operating systems include Windows Embedded CE, Windows Phone 7, Palm OS, iPhone OS, BlackBerry, Google Android, embedded Linux, and Symbian OS. **Windows Embedded CE** is a scaled-down Windows operating system designed for use on communications, entertainment, and computing devices with limited functionality. **Windows Phone 7**, which is a successor to Windows Mobile, provides a user interface designed for specific types of smart phones. *Palm OS* is an operating system used on smart phones and PDAs. **iPhone OS**, developed by Apple, is an operating system for the iPhone and iPod touch. The *BlackBerry* operating system runs on handheld devices supplied by RIM. *Google Android* is an operating system developed by Google for mobile devices. *Embedded Linux* is a scaled-down Linux operating system for smart phones, PDAs, portable media players, and other devices requiring an embedded operating system. *Symbian OS* is an open source multitasking operating system designed for smart phones.

Visit the Computer Concepts CourseMate Web site at www.cengagebrain.com, navigate to the Chapter 8 Quiz Yourself resource for this book, and then click Objectives 4 – 6.

7. **What Is the Purpose of Several Utility Programs?** Most operating systems include several built-in utility programs. A **file manager** performs functions related to file management. A **search utility** attempts to locate a file on your computer based on criteria you specify. An **image viewer** displays, copies, and prints the contents of a graphics file, such as photos. An **uninstaller** removes a program and any associated entries in the system files. A *disk cleanup utility* searches for and removes unnecessary files. A **disk defragmenter** reorganizes the files and unused space on a computer's hard disk. A **backup utility** is used to copy, or *back up*, selected files or an entire hard disk to another storage medium. A **restore utility** reverses the backup process and returns backed up files to their original form. A **screen saver** displays a moving image or blank screen if no keyboard or mouse activity occurs for a specified time. A **personal firewall** detects and protects a personal computer from unauthorized intrusions. An **antivirus program** protects computers against a **virus**, or potentially damaging computer program, by identifying and removing any computer viruses. A **spyware remover** detects and deletes *spyware* and other similar programs. An *adware remover* detects and deletes *adware*. Internet filter programs can include **Web filtering software**, an **anti-spam** program, a **phishing filter**, and a **pop-up blocker**. A **file compression utility** shrinks the size of a file so that it takes up less storage space. A **media player** allows you to view images and animation, listen to audio, and watch video files on a computer. **Disc burning software** writes text, graphics, audio, and video files on a recordable or rewritable CD, DVD, or Blu-ray Disc. A **personal computer maintenance utility** identifies and fixes operating system problems and improves a computer's performance.

Visit the Computer Concepts CourseMate Web site at www.cengagebrain.com, navigate to the Chapter 8 Quiz Yourself resource for this book, and then click Objective 7.

STUDENT ASSIGNMENTS

Key Terms

You should know the Primary Terms and be familiar with the Secondary Terms. The list below helps focus your study.

To see an example of and a definition for each term, and to access current and additional information from the Web, visit the Computer Concepts CourseMate Web site at www.cengagebrain.com and then navigate to the Chapter 8 Key Terms resource for this book.

Primary Terms

(shown in bold-black characters in the chapter)

anti-spam program (427)
antivirus program (426)
automatic update (409)
backup utility (424)
BIOS (400)
boot disk (402)
boot drive (402)
booting (400)
buffer (407)
cold boot (400)
defragmenting (424)
disc burning software (428)
disk defragmenter (423)
driver (408)
embedded operating system (418)
file compression utility (427)
file manager (422)
folder (422)
image viewer (423)
iPhone OS (420)
Linux (416)
log on (410)
Mac OS X (415)
Macintosh operating system (415)
media player (427)
memory management (406)
operating system (OS) (398)
password (410)
performance monitor (408)
personal computer maintenance utility (428)
personal firewall (425)
phishing filter (427)
Plug and Play (408)
pop-up blocker (427)
queue (407)
recovery disk (402)
restore utility (424)
screen saver (425)
search utility (422)
server operating system (410)
shortcut (422)
spooling (407)
spyware remover (426)
stand-alone operating system (412)
system software (398)
Trojan horse (426)
uncompress (427)
uninstaller (423)
UNIX (416)
user ID (410)
user interface (402)
user name (410)
utility (421)
utility program (421)
virtual memory (406)
virus (425)
warm boot (400)
Web filtering software (426)
Windows 7 (413)
Windows Embedded CE (419)
Windows Phone 7 (419)
Windows Server 2008 (417)
Windows Server 2008 family (417)
worm (426)
zipped files (427)

Aero Flip 3D (414)

Secondary Terms

(shown in italic characters in the chapter)

administrator account (410)
adware (426)
adware remover (426)
Aero Flip 3D (414)
back up (424)
background (404)
basic input/output system (400)
BlackBerry (420)
bugs (409)
client operating systems (412)
command language (403)
command-line interface (403)
compress (424)
cross-platform (399)
Desktop Gadget Gallery (414)
device driver (408)
device-dependent (411)
device-independent (411)
disk cleanup (423)
embedded Linux (420)
encryption (411)
fault-tolerant computer (405)
foreground (404)
fragmented (423)
gadget (414)
ghosting (425)
Google Android (420)
graphical user interface (GUI) (402)
hacker (425)
hibernate (402)
index (422)
Internet Explorer (413)
kernel (400)
lossless (427)
lossy (427)
malware (426)
memory resident (400)
multiprocessing (405)
multipurpose operating system (418)
multiuser (405)
NetWare (418)
network administrator (410)
nonresident (400)
open source software (416)
page (406)
paging (406)
Palm OS (419)
permissions (410)
phishing (427)
platform (399)
pop-up ad (427)
power-on self test (POST) (400)
preemptive multitasking (405)
print spooler (407)
proprietary software (411)
registry (401)
service pack (409)
single user/multitasking (404)
single user/single tasking (404)
sleep mode (402)
Snipping Tool (415)
Solaris (418)
spam (427)
spyware (426)
Startup folder (401)
swap file (406)
Symbian OS (420)
system files (401)
thrashing (406)
unzip (427)
virtualization (418)
virus author (425)
widget (414)
Windows 7 Home Premium (414)
Windows 7 Professional (414)
Windows 7 Starter (414)
Windows 7 Ultimate (414)
Windows Aero (402)
Windows Calendar (415)
Windows Defender (415)
Windows DVD Maker (414)
Windows Firewall (414)
Windows Live Essentials (415)
Windows Live Mail (415)
Windows Live Messenger (415)
Windows Live Movie Maker (415)
Windows Live Photo Gallery (415)
Windows Live Writer (415)
Windows Media Player (414)
Windows Photo Viewer (423)
Windows ReadyBoost (406)
Windows Server 2008 Datacenter (417)
Windows Server 2008 Enterprise (417)
Windows Server 2008 for Itanium-Based Systems (418)
Windows Server 2008 Standard (417)
Windows Touch (415)
Windows Web Server 2008 (418)

Checkpoint

The Checkpoint exercises test your knowledge of the chapter concepts. The page number containing the answer appears in parentheses after each exercise. The Beyond the Book exercises will help broaden your understanding of the concepts presented in this chapter.

 **To complete the Checkpoint exercises interactively, visit the Computer Concepts CourseMate Web site at www.cengagebrain.com and then navigate to the Chapter 8 Checkpoint resource for this book.**

True/False Mark T for True and F for False.

_____ 1. All sizes of computers typically use the same operating system because operating systems generally are written to run on any type of computer. (399)

_____ 2. Booting is the process of permanently removing a computer from operation. (400)

_____ 3. Permissions define who can access certain resources and when they can access those resources. (410)

_____ 4. A device-independent program is one that runs only on a specific type or make of computer. (411)

_____ 5. Users can control and customize a variety of gadgets on the Windows desktop. (414)

_____ 6. Linux is open source software, which means its code can be modified and redistributed. (416)

_____ 7. BlackBerry devices provide PIM capabilities such as managing schedules, contacts, and appointments, as well as phone capabilities. (420)

_____ 8. Windows allows you to manage your documents, pictures, music, and other files using Windows Explorer. (422)

_____ 9. An adware remover is a program that detects and deletes spam. (426)

_____ 10. Phishing is a scam in which a perpetrator attempts to obtain your personal and/or financial information. (427)

Multiple Choice Select the best answer.

1. The _____ chip, which uses battery power, stores configuration information about the computer. (400)
   a. BIOS
   b. CMOS
   c. POST
   d. RAM

2. Windows users can increase the size of memory through _____, which can allocate available storage space on removable flash memory devices as additional memory cache. (406)
   a. Windows Aero
   b. Windows ReadyBoost
   c. Plug and Play
   d. a disk defragmenter

3. A _____ is a mini-program with minimal functionality that connects to another program or provides information. (414)
   a. service pack
   b. search utility
   c. gadget
   d. swap file

4. When you enter search criteria, instead of looking through every file and folder on the storage medium, the search utility looks through the _____ first to find a match. (422)
   a. index
   b. buffer
   c. file manager
   d. driver

5. Defragmenting reorganizes the files on a disk so that they are located in _____ access time. (424)
   a. noncontiguous sectors, which slows
   b. contiguous sectors, which slows
   c. contiguous sectors, which speeds
   d. noncontiguous sectors, which speeds

6. _____ is a utility that detects and protects a personal computer from unauthorized intrusions. (425)
   a. Automatic updates
   b. Sleep mode
   c. Windows Explorer
   d. Windows Firewall

7. _____ is a program that displays an online advertisement in a banner or pop-up window on Web pages, e-mail, or other Internet services. (426)
   a. Spyware
   b. A Trojan horse
   c. Adware
   d. Spam

8. A(n) _____ is a program that warns or blocks you from potentially fraudulent or suspicious Web sites. (427)
   a. phishing filter
   b. Web filter
   c. adware remover
   d. Trojan horse

Checkpoint

Matching
Match the terms with their definitions.

	Term		Definition
_____	1. sleep mode (402)	a.	the practice of sharing or pooling computing resources, such as servers
_____	2. hibernate (402)	b.	server operating system designed for client/server networks
_____	3. page (406)	c.	saves any open documents and programs to a hard disk before removing power from the computer
_____	4. user name (410)	d.	unique combination of characters that identifies one specific user
_____	5. Aero Flip 3D (414)	e.	works with the mouse to flip through windows by rolling the wheel on the mouse
_____	6. UNIX (416)	f.	saves any open documents and programs to RAM, turns off all unneeded functions, and then places the computer in a low-power state
_____	7. virtualization (418)	g.	with virtual memory, the amount of data and program instructions that can be swapped at a given time
_____	8. NetWare (418)	h.	multitasking operating system developed in the early 1970s by scientists at Bell Laboratories
_____	9. Google Andriod (420)	i.	operating system for mobile devices
_____	10. shortcut (422)	j.	an icon on the desktop or in a folder that provides a user with immediate access to a program or file

Short Answer
Write a brief answer to each of the following questions.

1. How is a cold boot different from a warm boot? ____________ How is a memory-resident part of an operating system different from a nonresident part of an operating system? ____________
2. What is a user interface? ____________ How are graphical and command-line user interfaces different? ____________
3. What is the purpose of an automatic update feature? ____________ Why and when might a user receive a service pack? ____________
4. What happens during a backup? ____________ What is the purpose of a restore utility? ____________
5. Describe four embedded operating systems. ____________ What are the uses for each of the four types? ____________

Beyond the Book
Follow the book element instructions below; present your findings (brief report, presentation, discussion, or other means).

1. Ethics & Issues — Select an Ethics & Issues in this chapter (410, 416, 418, 428), find a recent newspaper/magazine article that supports one point of view presented, and then evaluate the article.
2. Computer Usage @ Work — Use the Web or a recent newspaper/magazine to locate three additional unique usages of computer technology in the education field (429). What makes the use of these technologies unique to the education field?
3. Companies on the Cutting Edge and Technology Trailblazers — Use the Web or a recent business newspaper/magazine to locate an interesting fact about VeriSign, Research in Motion (RIM), Steve Wozniak, or Linus Torvalds that was not presented in the chapter (431).
4. High-Tech Talk — Locate a recent newspaper/magazine article that discusses topics related to Touch Screen Technology (430). Would you recommend the article you found? Why or why not?
5. FAQs and Web Links — Use the Web or a recent newspaper/magazine to locate three additional facts about an FAQ (402, 407, 408, 411, 412, 423, 426, 427) and Web Link (401, 402, 407, 408, 414, 415, 417, 418, 420, 427, 428) that were not presented in the chapter.
6. Looking Ahead — Use the Web or a recent newspaper/magazine to discover additional uses of the technology presented in Contact Lenses Monitor Glaucoma (409).
7. Innovative Computing — Use the Web or a recent newspaper/magazine to locate two additional interesting facts about Utility Programs Locate Deleted Files (421).
8. Making Use of the Web — Visit three of the Government sites (132) and outline the information on each Web site and the possible uses for each Web site.
9. Buyers Guide: How to Purchase Computers and Mobile Devices — Use the Buyers Guide feature (444) to determine the configuration for a desktop computer, notebook computer, smart phone, portable media player, or digital camera that you would like to purchase, then create a presentation about the reasons you made your choices using the suggested Web sites or advertisements in magazines.

Learn It Online

The Learn It Online exercises are interactive Web exercises designed to reinforce and expand your understanding of the chapter concepts. The descriptions below briefly summarize each exercise.

To complete the Learn It Online exercises, visit the Computer Concepts CourseMate Web site at www.cengagebrain.com, navigate to the Chapter 8 resources for this book, click the link for the exercise you want to complete, and then read the instructions.

1 At the Movies — Free Online Antivirus
Watch a movie to learn why it is important to run antivirus software on your computer and how to scan your computer for malware online for no cost and then answer questions about the movie.

2 Video and Audio: You Review It — Spyware
Search for, choose, and write a review of a video, podcast, or vodcast that discusses spyware.

3 Student Edition Labs — Installing and Uninstalling Software and Keeping Your Computer Virus Free
Enhance your understanding and knowledge about installing and uninstalling software and keeping your computer virus free by completing the Installing and Uninstalling Software and Keeping Your Computer Virus Free Labs.

4 Practice Test
Take a multiple choice test that checks your knowledge of the chapter concepts and review the resulting study guide.

5 Who Wants To Be a Computer Genius^2?
Play the Shelly Cashman Series version of this popular game by answering questions to find out if you are a computer genius. Panic buttons are available to provide assistance during game play.

6 Wheel of Terms
Identify important key terms presented in this chapter by playing the Shelly Cashman Series version of this popular game.

7 You're Hired!
Embark on the path to a career in computers by answering questions and solving puzzles related to concepts discussed in this chapter.

8 Crossword Puzzle Challenge
Complete an interactive crossword puzzle to reinforce concepts presented in this chapter.

9 Windows Exercises
Step through the Windows 7 exercises to learn about Windows, using a screen saver, changing desktop colors, customizing the desktop for multiple users, and backing up a computer.

10 Exploring Computer Careers
Read about a career as a systems programmer, search for related employment advertisements, and then answer related questions.

11 Web Apps — PhotoshopExpress
Learn how to use PhotoshopExpress to upload new photos as well as photos stored on other photo sharing communities, edit photos, create new pictures, and share them with others.

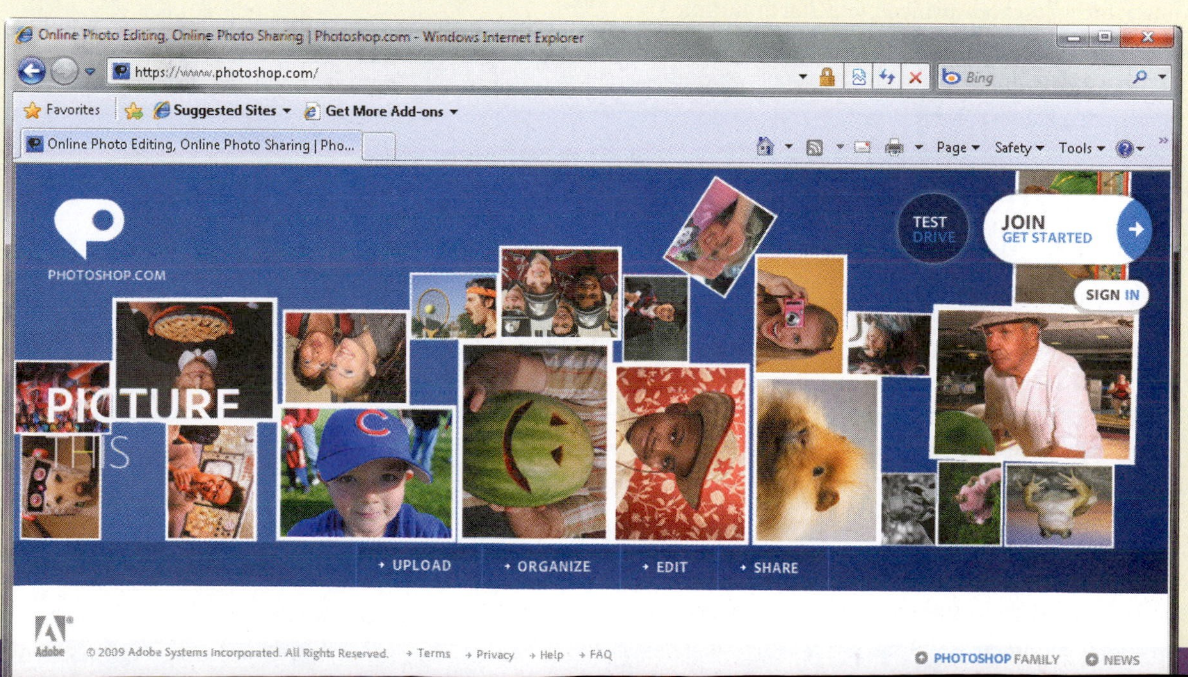

Problem Solving @ Home

The Problem Solving @ Home exercises extend your knowledge of the chapter concepts by seeking solutions to practical computer problems that you may encounter at home or school. The Collaboration exercise should be completed with a team.

In the real world, practical problems often can be solved in multiple ways. Provide one solution to each of the following problems using available resources, such as articles on the Web or in print, blogs, podcasts, videos, television, user guides, other individuals, and electronics and computer stores. You may need to use multiple resources to obtain an answer. Present your solutions in the form requested by your instructor (brief report, presentation, discussion, or other means).

1. **Computer Cannot Boot** You recently purchased a computer from a friend. When you turn on the computer, a message displays that says, "Operating system not found." What steps will you take before calling technical support?
2. **Improper Shut Down** During the startup process, your computer displays a message indicating that the computer did not shut down properly. You are certain that you shut down the computer properly when you last used it. The message also lists options to start Windows normally or start Windows in safe mode. How will you respond? Why?
3. **Incorrect Display Settings** You recently turned on your computer and noticed that the screen resolution, desktop background, and color scheme had changed, even though you have not changed the display settings since purchasing the computer several months ago. What might have caused Windows to change the display settings? What are your next steps?

4. **Unreadable Taskbar Buttons** While using your computer for a research project, you start multiple programs. With so many programs running, you are unable to determine which buttons correspond to each program. How can you determine which button to click to access the desired program?
5. **Poor Computer Performance** Your friend sends you an e-mail message stating that her computer is running slowly. She asks if you know of any programs that are included with Windows that will help increase her computer's performance. How will you respond?
6. **Maximum CPU Usage** Because your computer is performing slowly, you start the Windows Task Manager to investigate. You see that the CPU usage is near 100%. You are not aware of any other programs currently running. What might be causing this?
7. **Command Not Displaying** While using a computer in your school's computer lab, you decide to use the Control Panel to change the desktop background. When you click the Start button, the Control Panel command does not display on the Start menu. What could be the reason for this?
8. **Unwanted Programs** The new computer that you ordered online arrived today. You anxiously unpack it, connect all components, and then turn it on. After answering a series of questions to set up the computer, you notice it includes programs that you do not want. How will you remove these unwanted programs?

Collaboration

9. **Slow Computer** A fellow classmate has been complaining that his computer does not seem to be working properly. He complains that Windows takes too long to start and that it runs very slowly. You would like more practice troubleshooting computer problems, so you offer to look at his computer. When you start Windows, you notice that the hard disk has less than 100 MB of free space, many icons appear in the notification area, no antivirus software is installed, and more than 50 Windows updates are available for the computer. Form a team of three people and determine how to use the software that is included with Windows, in addition to any third-party software that may be needed, to resolve these computer problems. Compile your findings and submit them to your instructor.

Problem Solving @ Work

The Problem Solving @ Work exercises extend your knowledge of the chapter concepts by seeking solutions to practical computer problems that you may encounter at work. The Collaboration exercise should be completed with a team.

In the real world, practical problems often can be solved in multiple ways. Provide one solution to each of the following problems using available resources, such as articles on the Web or in print, blogs, podcasts, videos, television, user guides, other individuals, and electronics and computer stores. You may need to use multiple resources to obtain an answer. Present your solutions in the form requested by your instructor (brief report, presentation, discussion, or other means).

1. **Long Defragmentation Process** You started the Disk Defragmenter in Windows and clicked the Defragment now button. Several hours have elapsed, and Disk Defragmenter reports that it still is defragmenting the hard disk, despite its initial message that the defragmenting process may take from a few minutes to a few hours. With your computer tied up in the defragmenting process, you are unable to use it to complete a report that is due to your supervisor tomorrow. How should you proceed?
2. **Password Required** After turning on your computer, it prompts you to type a password to continue the boot process; however, you forgot the password. What are your next steps to allow the computer to continue the boot process, start Windows, and access the files on the hard disk?
3. **Frozen Manufacturer Logo** After turning on your computer, the computer manufacturer's logo displays on the monitor for several minutes. Suspecting that your computer might be frozen, you turn it off. Three minutes later, you turn the computer on and the same problem arises. What might be wrong?
4. **Automatic Updates** Two or three times per month, your coworker receives a notification on his computer that the computer recently has been updated. You ask your coworker about these messages, and he says that Microsoft periodically installs updates automatically to protect the computer from various threats, as well as to improve performance. You never have seen this message appear on your computer. Does this mean that your computer does not update automatically? How can you configure your computer to update automatically?
5. **Configuring Updates** After an employee from your company's technical support department configures your computer to download and install updates automatically, you want to change the schedule so that your computer checks for and installs new updates every day instead of once per week. Your computer, however, does not allow you to change the settings for Windows Update. What could be causing this?

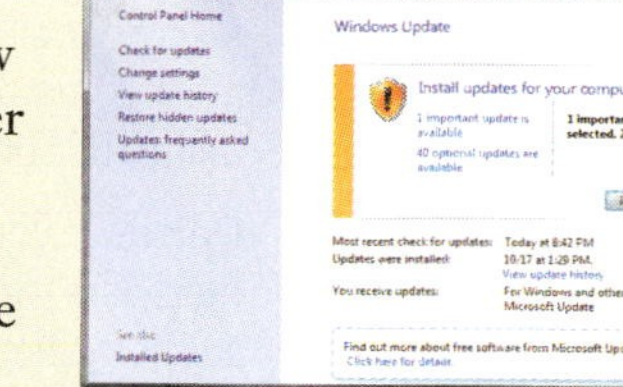

6. **Antivirus Schedule** You recently changed your work schedule so that you work until 6:00 p.m. instead of 5:00 p.m. At 5:00 p.m. each day, you notice that the antivirus program on your computer automatically begins scanning all files on your hard disk. This process slows your computer, and the program usually still is scanning when you leave the office. How can you change the configuration so that the antivirus program does not start until after you leave?
7. **Minimum Battery Power** When you use your notebook computer and it is not plugged in, the battery lasts for only one hour, but the documentation states that the computer can last for two hours on battery power. What are some ways that you can increase the battery life?

Collaboration

8. **Computers in Education** A private elementary school in your neighborhood has received a grant to create a computer lab with Internet access so that students can learn about computers and related technologies. Your neighbor, who also is a teacher at the school, asks for advice regarding how they should spend the grant money. Form a team of three people to determine the best configuration for the lab. One team member should research whether a PC or Mac is more beneficial. Another team member should research the application software that should be installed on these computers, and the other team member should determine what, if any, peripheral devices should be attached to the computers in the lab. Compile your findings and submit them to your instructor.

STUDENT ASSIGNMENTS

Learn How To

The Learn How To activities step you through fundamental technology skills when using a computer. The Learn How To exercises enable you to become more proficient with these skills.

Premium Activity: To relate this Learn How To activity to your everyday life, see a visual demonstration of the activity, and complete a short assessment, visit the Computer Concepts CourseMate Web site at www.cengagebrain.com and then navigate to the Chapter 8 Learn How To resource for this book.

Learn How To 1: Install and Maintain a Computer

Once you have purchased a computer, you must install it for use, and then maintain it. Based on years of experience, a set of guidelines for installing and maintaining your computer has been developed. To examine these guidelines, complete the following steps:

1. Start the browser on your computer.
2. Type the Web address `www.cengagebrain.com` in the Address bar and then press the ENTER key.
3. Navigate to the Chapter 8 Learn How To Install and Maintain a Computer resource for this book.
4. Read the material presented about how to install and maintain a computer.

Exercises

1. Using your Web search skills, research the latest recommendations with respect to proper ergonomics for using a computer. What information did you find that you did not know before? What changes would you make to your current computer setup that might make you more productive? Submit your answers to your instructor.
2. Many people report illnesses or injuries from using computers. Perform research in a library or on the Web to discover the five most common ailments associated with using a computer. Determine the actions people can take to minimize or eliminate these ailments. Submit a report to your instructor describing your findings.
3. On either your computer or the computer on which you are working, perform a hardware and software inventory of at least five hardware devices and five application programs. List the vendor, product, vendor Web address, vendor e-mail address, and vendor support telephone number. Submit the inventory to your instructor.

Learn How To 2: Burn Files to an Optical Disc

Many people use USB flash drives to transport files from one location to another. If they wish to share files with someone else, however, they might choose to distribute these files on an optical disc. To learn how to burn files to an optical disc using Windows 7, complete the following steps:

1. Insert a blank optical disc into the optical disc drive.
2. When the AutoPlay dialog box is displayed, click the Burn files to disc using Windows Explorer link.
3. If necessary, change the Disc title, click the 'Like a USB flash drive' option button, and then click the Next button in the Burn a Disc dialog box to prepare the blank disc.
4. Drag the files you wish to burn to the empty window that opens.
5. Click the 'Burn to disk' button.
6. Click the Next button to burn the files to the disc. When the disc has finished burning, remove the disc from the optical disc drive.

Exercise

1. Locate photos on your computer that you are willing to share with others. If you are unable to locate any photos or are using someone else's computer, download at least three photos from the Internet. Insert a blank optical disc into your optical disc drive and then burn the photos to the disc. Once you have finished burning the disc, eject it, write your name on it, and then submit it to your instructor.

Learn How To 3: Keep Windows Up-to-Date

Keeping Windows up-to-date is a critical part of keeping your computer in working order. The updates made available by Microsoft for no charge over the Internet can help to keep errors from occurring on your computer and attempt to ensure that all security safeguards are in place. To update Windows, complete the next steps:

Learn How To

1. Click the Start button on the Windows taskbar, click All Programs, and then click Windows Update in the All Programs list (Figure 8-42) to display the Windows Update window.
2. Click the link indicating that updates are available.
3. If necessary, select those updates you wish to install and then click the OK button. Be aware that some updates might take 20 minutes or more to download and install, based primarily on your Internet access speed.
4. Often, after installation of updates, you must restart your computer to allow those updates to take effect. Be sure to save any open files before restarting your computer.

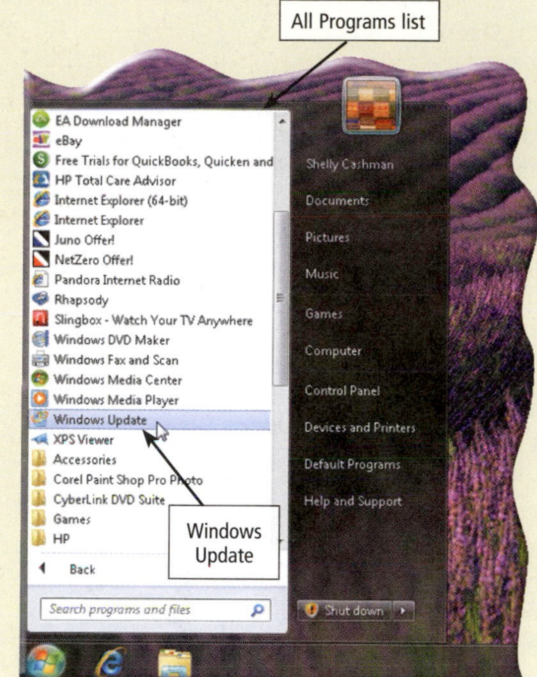

Figure 8-42

You also can schedule automatic updates for your computer. To do so, complete the following steps:

1. Click the Start button on the Windows taskbar and then click Control Panel on the Start menu.
2. In the Control Panel window, click System and Security to open the System and Security window.
3. In the System and Security window, click 'Turn automatic updating on or off' to open the Change settings window (Figure 8-43).
4. Select the option you want to use for Windows updates. Microsoft, together with all security and operating system experts, strongly recommends you select 'Install updates automatically' so that updates will be installed on your computer automatically. Notice that if you select 'Install updates automatically', you also should select a time when your computer will be on and be connected to the Internet. A secondary choice is to download the suggested updates and then choose when you want to install them, and a third choice allows you to check for updates and then choose when you want to download and install them.
5. When you have made your selection, click the OK button in the Change settings window.

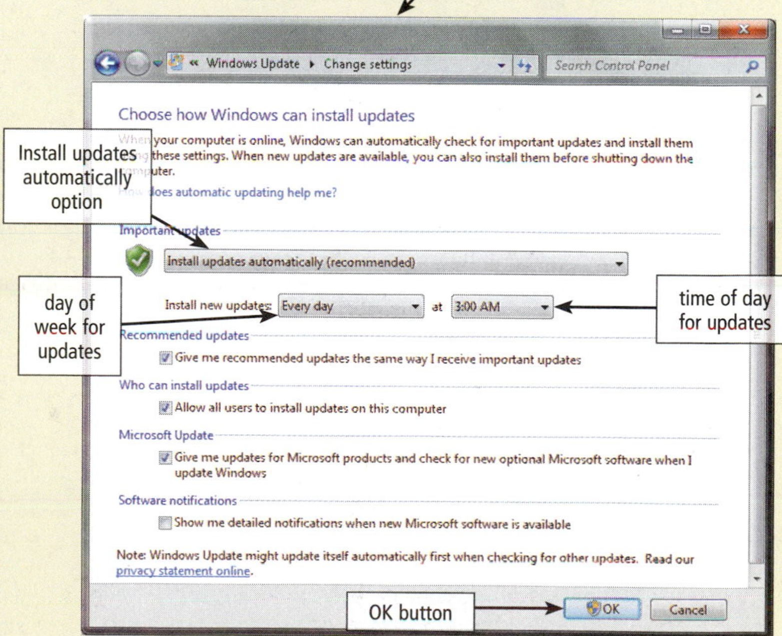

Figure 8-43

Updating Windows on your computer is vital to maintain security and operational integrity.

Exercises

1. Open the Windows Update window. Make a list of the important updates to Windows on the computer you are using. Add to the list the optional updates that are available. If you are using your own computer, install the updates of your choice on your computer. Submit the list of updates to your instructor.
2. **Optional: If you are not using your own computer, do not complete this exercise.** Open the Control Panel, click System and Security, and then click 'Turn automatic updating on or off'. Select the level of automatic updates you want to use. Write a report justifying your choice of automatic updates and then submit the report to your instructor.

Web Research

The Web Research exercises broaden your understanding of the chapter concepts by presenting questions that require you to search the Web for answers.

1 Search Sleuth

Use one of the search engines listed in Figure 2-10 in Chapter 2 on page 85 or your own favorite search engine to find the answers to the following questions. Copy and paste the Web address from the Web page where you found the answer. Some questions may have more than one answer. If required, submit your answers to your instructor. (1) Who are the "goons" who attend DEFCON? What color shirts do they wear? (2) Which product does IBM propose in its "Reincarnating PCs with Portable SoulPads" paper? (3) Which bird is the mascot for Linux? What is the mascot's name? (4) Why do some computer experts consider the term, spool, a backronym? (5) Who invented the Control-Alt-Delete (CTRL+ALT+DEL) key combination used to reboot a computer? (6) Which virus did the Farooq Alvi brothers invent? (7) Why are UNIX programmers concerned about the "Year 2038 problem"?

2 Green Computing

Operating systems can help monitor computer energy use and suggest methods of reducing electricity through efficient power management. Experts claim monitoring systems can save each computer user at least $60 per year in electricity costs. Suggestions include not using a screen saver, turning down a monitor's brightness level, and using a high performance power setting that balances processing power with notebook computer battery life. View online Web sites that provide information about power management. Which methods are effective in reducing power consumption, especially for notebook computers? Which sleep state setting gives significant power savings? Which power management settings are recommended for balanced, power saver, and high performance? Write a report summarizing your findings, and include a table of links to Web sites that provide additional details.

3 Social Networking

Social networking Web site advertisers in the United States spent $108 million in 2009, an increase of 119 percent in one year. Millions of registered online social networking users have posted demographic information about themselves, including age, gender, and geographical location. This data helps marketing managers deliver specific advertisements to each user in an attempt to raise revenue. Adknowledge (adknowledge.com) is one of the primary companies that gathers and studies data regarding online users and then sells targeted ads on social networking, e-mail, and gaming Web sites. Visit the Adknowledge Web site, view the information about targeting social network consumers, and then read articles in the About Us and Press Room sections. How are advertisers using virtual currency? How do traffic networks help advertisers create marketing campaigns? View the posts in the Adverblog Web site (adverblog.com) to read about interactive marketing trends. Summarize the information you read and viewed.

4 Blogs

A number of the search engine Web sites feature blogs describing popular search topics. Ask.com's blog (blog.ask.com), for example, lists its Blogroll, which gives recommended research and search engine Web sites. The Yahoo! Search blog (ysearchblog .com) includes news about consumer search trends (Yahoo! Buzz) and innovations in Web search technology. Google Blog Search (blogsearch.google.com) has search engines to help users find blogs about particular topics, including technology and business. Visit these sites and read the posts. What topics are discussed? Compose search queries about issues and products discussed in this chapter, such as personal firewalls or antivirus programs, and read a few of the blogs describing these topics. Summarize the information you read.

5 Ethics in Action

Several automobile insurers, including Progressive Casualty Insurance Company, are promising drivers insurance premium discounts up to 25 percent if they install a data recorder in their cars voluntarily to track their driving and then exercise good driving behavior. Privacy experts predict more insurance companies will offer this monitoring system and that it eventually will become mandatory. These critics fear that negative data will be used against poor drivers. View online sites that provide information about vehicle monitoring devices. Write a report summarizing your findings, and include a table of links to Web sites that provide additional details.

Critical Thinking

The Critical Thinking exercises challenge your assessment and decision-making skills by presenting real-world situations associated with the chapter concepts. The Collaboration exercise should be completed with a team.

To evaluate the situations below, use personal experiences and available resources such as articles on the Web or in print, blogs, podcasts, videos, television, user guides, other individuals, and electronics and computer stores. You may need to use multiple resources to form conclusions and make recommendations.

1. **Class Discussion — Downloading Music** Many students at the local college have been using the college's computers to download music from the Internet. You have been asked to serve on a student committee to analyze and discuss this questionable use of the college's computers based on the following questions. Is it the college's responsibility to block music downloads? Why or why not? How would the college prevent students from downloading music? What is the difference between recording a song from the radio and downloading music from the Internet? Should violators be expelled, fined, required to attend a seminar on the ethical use of computers, or given a verbal warning? What recommendations would you give to the committee regarding the downloading of music?

2. **Class Presentation — Windows 7 Editions** Your cousin is buying a new computer both for personal use and for operating his consulting business, which he runs out of his home. He is undecided about which edition of the Windows 7 operating system to purchase with his new computer. Windows 7 Professional is intended for business users. Windows 7 Home Premium is designed for home computing. Windows 7 Ultimate contains features both for home and business users. He has asked you to review the differences between each edition and help him decide which he should buy. Prepare a presentation comparing the similarities and contrasting the differences among the three editions. Be sure to include items such as features that are included with one edition that are not available in another and cost differences. At the end of your presentation, provide a recommendation and the reasons why the edition you chose would be best.

3. **Research — Complete Security Solutions** Your neighbor started a new construction business and opened an office several blocks from your house. He is impressed by your computer knowledge and would like to hire you to set up his new computers. He mentions that because of the increasing security concerns on the Internet, he first would like you to install a program or programs designed to protect his computers from various security threats. What types of security threats exist on the Internet? Write a brief report describing two programs that provide a comprehensive security solution. What are the programs' functions? What computer requirements, if any, exist? Do the programs appear to be easy to install? What is their cost? Are subscription fees charged in order to receive automatic updates? In your opinion, are the programs worth the price? Why or why not?

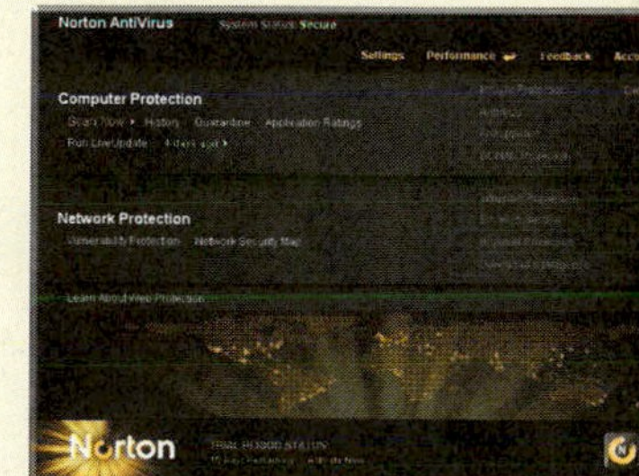

Collaboration

4. **Operating Systems** Your team members are employed as analysts at Soap-n-Suds, an international manufacturer of laundry soaps. The company currently uses an early version of the Windows operating system on its 5,000 desktop computers. This year, the company plans to upgrade the operating system and, if necessary, its desktop computers. The vice president of information technology has asked your team to compare the latest desktop versions of the Windows operating system, Mac OS, and the Linux operating system. Assign each member of your team an operating system. Each member should use the Web and/or print media to develop a feature/benefit analysis along with the answers to the following questions. What is the initial cost of the operating system per computer? What are the memory and storage requirements? Will the operating system require the company to purchase new computers? Are training costs involved? Which operating system is best at avoiding viruses, spam, and spyware? Which operating system is easier to use? Why? Can the latest version of Microsoft Office run with the operating system? As a team, merge your findings into a team presentation and share your findings and recommendation with the class.

Buyer's Guide: How to Purchase Computers and Mobile Devices

AT SOME POINT, perhaps while you are taking this course, you may decide to buy a computer or mobile device (Figure 1). The decision is an important one and will require an investment of both time and money. Like many buyers, you may have little experience with technology and find yourself unsure of how to proceed. You can start by talking to your friends, coworkers, and instructors about their computers and mobile devices. What type of computers and mobile devices did they buy? Why? For what purposes do they use their computers and mobile devices?

desktop computer

notebook computer

portable media player

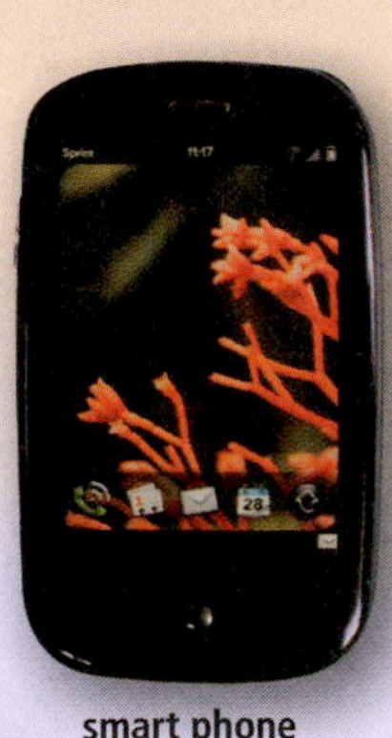

smart phone

digital camera

Figure 1 Computers and mobile devices.

How to Purchase a Desktop Computer

A desktop computer sits on or below a desk or table in a stationary location such as a home, office, or dormitory room. Desktop computers are a good option if you work mostly in one place and have plenty of space in a work area. Desktop computers generally provide more performance for your money. Today, manufacturers are placing more emphasis on style by offering bright colors, stylish displays, and theme-based displays so that the computer looks attractive if it is in an area of high visibility. Once you have decided that a desktop computer is most suited to your computing needs, the next step is to determine specific software, hardware, peripheral devices, and services to purchase, as well as where to buy the computer.

1 Determine the specific software to use on your computer.

Before deciding to purchase software, be sure it contains the features necessary for the tasks you want to perform. Rely on the computer users in whom you have confidence to help you decide on the software to use. In addition, consider purchasing software that might help you perform tasks at home that you otherwise would perform at another location, such as at school or at work. The minimum requirements of the software you select may determine the operating system (Microsoft Windows, Mac OS, Linux) you need. If you decide to use a particular operating system that does not support software you want to use, you may be able to purchase similar software from other manufacturers.

Many Web sites and trade magazines provide reviews of software products. These Web sites frequently have articles that rate computers and software on cost, performance, and support.

Your hardware requirements depend on the minimum requirements of the software you will run on your computer. Some software requires more memory and disk space than others, as well as additional input, output, and storage devices. For example, suppose you want to run software that can copy one optical disc's contents directly to another optical disc, without first copying the data to the hard disk. To support that, you should consider a desktop computer or a high-end notebook computer, because the computer will need two optical disc drives: one that reads from an optical disc, and one that writes on an optical disc. If you plan to run software that allows your computer to function as an entertainment system, then you will need an optical disc drive, quality speakers, and an upgraded sound card.

2 Know the system requirements of the operating system.

After determining the software you want to run on your new computer, the next step is to determine the operating system to use. If, however, you purchase a new computer, chances are it will have the latest version of your preferred operating system (Windows, Mac OS, Linux).

3 Look for bundled software.

When you purchase a computer, it may include bundled software. Some sellers even let you choose which software you want. Remember, however, that bundled software has value only if you would have purchased the software even if it had not been included with the computer. At the very least, you probably will want word processing software and an antivirus program. If you need additional programs, such as a spreadsheet, a database, or presentation software, consider purchasing or downloading Microsoft Office, Microsoft Works, OpenOffice.org, or Sun StarOffice, which include several programs at a reduced price or at no cost.

4 Avoid buying the least powerful computer available.

Once you know the application software you want to use, then consider the following important criteria about the computer's components: (1) processor speed, (2) size and types of memory (RAM) and storage, (3) types of input/output devices, (4) types of ports and adapter cards, and (5) types of communications devices. You also should consider if the computer is upgradeable and to what extent you are able to upgrade. For example, all manufacturers limit the amount of memory you can add. The information in Figure 2 on pages 446 and 447 can help you determine which computer components are best for you and outlines considerations for specific hardware components. For a sample Base Components worksheet that lists PC recommendations for each category of user discussed in this

Considerations for Hardware Components

Card Reader/Writer: A card reader/writer is useful for transferring data directly to and from a memory card, such as the type used in a digital camera, smart phone, or portable media player. Make sure the card reader/writer can read from and write on the memory cards that you use.

Digital Video Capture Device: A digital video capture device allows you to connect a computer to a video camera or VCR and record, edit, manage, and then write video back on an optical disc or VCR tape. To create quality video (true 30 frames per second, full-sized TV), the digital video capture device should have a USB or FireWire port.

External Hard Disk: An external hard disk can serve many purposes: it can serve as extra storage for your computer, provide a way to store and transport large files or large quantities of files, and provide a convenient way to back up data on other internal and external hard disks. External hard disks can be purchased with the same capacity as any internal disk.

Fingerprint Reader: For added security, you may want to consider purchasing a fingerprint reader. It helps prevent unauthorized access to your computer and also allows you to log onto Web sites quickly via your fingerprint, rather than entering a user name and password each time you access the site. Most use a USB connection and require software installation.

Hard Disk: It is recommended that you buy a computer with at least a 320 GB hard disk if your primary interests are browsing the Web and using e-mail and Office suite-type programs; 1 TB if you also want to edit digital photos or if you plan to edit digital video or manipulate large audio files even occasionally; and 2 TB if you will edit digital video, movies, or photos often; store audio files and music; or consider yourself to be a power user. Internal hard disk controllers are available with the RAID option for added data protection.

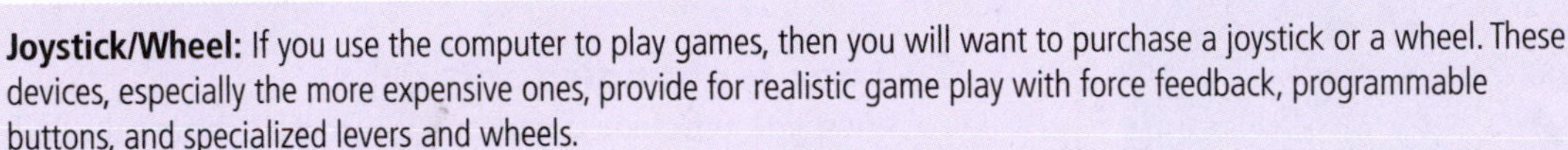

Joystick/Wheel: If you use the computer to play games, then you will want to purchase a joystick or a wheel. These devices, especially the more expensive ones, provide for realistic game play with force feedback, programmable buttons, and specialized levers and wheels.

Keyboard: The keyboard is one of the more important devices used to communicate with the computer. For this reason, make sure the keyboard you purchase has 101 to 105 keys, is comfortable and easy to use, and has a USB connection. A wireless keyboard should be considered, especially if you have a small desk area.

Microphone: If you plan to record audio or use speech recognition to enter text and commands, then purchase a close-talk headset with gain adjustment support.

Modem: Most computers include a modem so that you can use a telephone line to access the Internet. Some modems also have fax capabilities. Your modem should be rated at 56 Kbps.

Monitor: The monitor is where you will view documents, read e-mail messages, and view pictures. A minimum of a 19" LCD flat-panel monitor is recommended, but if you plan to use the computer for graphic design or game playing, then you may want to purchase a 22" or 27" monitor. Instead of a single large, widescreen monitor, you may want to consider a side-by-side monitor setup.

Mouse: While working with a desktop computer, you use the mouse constantly. Make sure the mouse has a wheel, which acts as a third button in addition to the top two buttons on the left and right. An ergonomic design also is important because your hand is on the mouse most of the time when you are using the computer. A wireless mouse should be considered to eliminate the cord and allow you to work at short distances from the computer.

Optical Disc Drives: Most computers include a DVD±RW combination drive and/or DVD/Blu-ray Disc drive. A DVD±RW or a Blu-ray Disc drive allows you to read optical discs and to write data on (burn) an optical disc. It also will allow you to store and share video files, digital photos, and other large files with other people who have access to a DVD/Blu-ray Disc drive. A Blu-ray Disc has a capacity of at least 25 GB, and a DVD has a capacity of at least 4.7 GB, versus the 650 MB capacity of a CD.

Figure 2 Hardware guidelines.

Considerations for Hardware Components

Ports: Depending on how you are using the computer, you may need anywhere from 4 to 10 USB ports. USB ports have become the connection of choice in the computer industry. They offer an easy way to connect peripheral devices such as printers, digital cameras, and portable media players. Many computers intended for home or professional audio/video use have built-in FireWire ports. Most personal computers include a minimum of six USB ports, two FireWire ports, and an Ethernet port.

Printer: Your two basic printer choices are ink-jet and laser. Color ink-jet printers cost on average between $50 and $300. Laser printers cost from $200 to $2,000. In general, the less expensive the printer, the lower the resolution and speed, and the more often you are required to change the ink cartridges or toner. Laser printers print faster and with a higher quality than an ink-jet, and their toner on average costs less.

Processor: For a personal computer, an Intel Core i7 processor at 2.93 GHz is more than enough processor power for most home and small office/home office users. Game home, enterprise, and power users should upgrade to faster, more powerful processors.

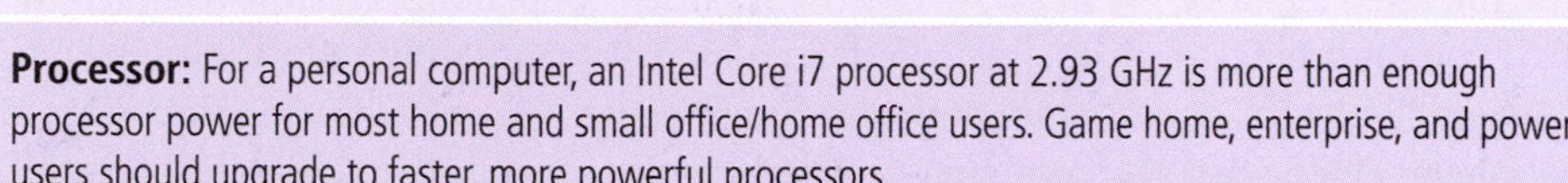

RAM: RAM plays a vital role in the speed of a computer. Make sure the computer you purchase has at least 2 GB of RAM. If you have extra money to invest in a computer, consider increasing the RAM. The extra money for RAM will be well spent because more RAM typically translates into more speed.

Scanner: The most popular scanner purchased with a computer today is the flatbed scanner. When evaluating a flatbed scanner, check the color depth and resolution. Do not buy anything less than a color depth of 48 bits and a resolution of 1200 x 2400 dpi. The higher the color depth, the more accurate the color. A higher resolution picks up the more subtle gradations of color.

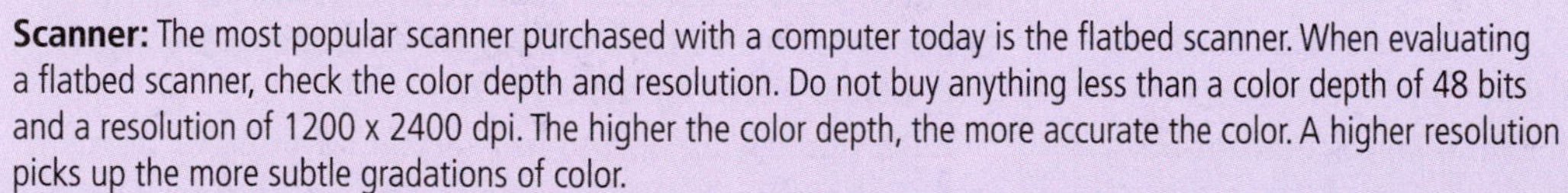

Sound Card: Many computers include a standard sound card that supports Dolby 5.1 surround and are capable of recording and playing digital audio. Make sure they are suitable in the event you decide to use the computer as an entertainment or gaming system.

Speakers: Once you have a good sound card, quality speakers and a separate subwoofer that amplifies the bass frequencies of the speakers can turn the computer into a premium stereo system.

USB Flash Drive: If you work on different computers and need access to the same data and information, then this portable flash memory device is ideal. USB flash drive capacity varies from 1 GB to 16 GB.

USB Hub: If you plan to connect several peripheral devices to the computer at the same time, then you need to be concerned with the number of ports available on the computer. If the computer does not have enough ports, then you should purchase a USB hub. A USB hub plugs into a single USB port and provides several additional ports.

Video Card: Most standard video cards satisfy the monitor display needs of most home and small office users. If you are a game home user or a graphic designer, you will want to upgrade to a higher quality video card. The higher refresh rates will further enhance the display of games, graphics, and movies.

Web Cam: A Web cam is a small digital video camera that can capture and display live video on a Web page. You also can capture, edit, and share video and still photos. Recommended minimum specifications include 640 x 480 resolution, a video with a rate of 30 frames per second, and a USB or FireWire port. Some Web cams are built into computer monitors.

Wireless LAN Access Point: A wireless LAN access point allows you to network several computers, so that multiple users can share files and access the Internet through a single broadband connection. Each device that you connect requires a wireless card. A wireless LAN access point can offer a range of operations up to several hundred feet, so be sure the device has a high-powered antenna.

Figure 2 Hardware guidelines. *(continued)*

book, visit the Computer Concepts CourseMate Web site at www.cengagebrain.com and then navigate to the Buyer's Guide Feature resource for this book. In the worksheet, the Home User category is divided into two groups: Application Home User and Game Home User.

Computer technology changes rapidly, meaning a computer that seems powerful enough today may not serve your computing needs in several years. In fact, studies show that many users regret not buying a more powerful computer. To avoid this, plan to buy a computer that will last for at least two to three years. You can help delay obsolescence by purchasing the fastest processor, the most memory, and the largest hard disk you can afford. If you must buy a less powerful computer, be sure you can upgrade it with additional memory, components, and peripheral devices as your computer requirements grow.

5 Consider upgrades to the mouse, keyboard, monitor, printer, microphone, and speakers.

You use these peripheral devices to interact with the computer, so make sure they are up to your standards. Review the peripheral devices listed in Figure 2 and then visit both local computer dealers and large retail stores to test the computers and devices on display. Ask the salesperson which input and output devices would be best for you and whether you should upgrade beyond the standard product. Consider purchasing a wireless keyboard and wireless mouse to eliminate wires on your desktop. A few extra dollars spent on these components when you initially purchase a computer can extend its usefulness by years.

6 Determine whether to use a broadband or dial-up connection to access the Internet.

If your computer has a modem, you can access the Internet using a standard telephone line. Ordinarily, you call a local or toll-free 800 number to connect to an Internet access provider. Using a dial-up Internet connection usually is relatively inexpensive but slow.

Broadband connections provide much faster Internet connections, which are ideal if you want faster file download speeds for software, digital photos, digital video, and music. As you would expect, they can be more expensive than a dial-up connection. If you want to use a broadband connection, your computer should have an Ethernet card installed, unless you are using a wireless broadband connection such as WiMax or 3G. If you will be using a dial-up connection, your computer should have a modem installed.

7 Use a worksheet to compare computers, services, and other considerations.

You can use a separate sheet of paper to take notes about each vendor's computer and then summarize the information on a worksheet. For a sample worksheet that compares prices for a PC or a Mac, visit the Computer Concepts CourseMate Web site at www.cengagebrain.com and then navigate to the Buyer's Guide Feature resource for this book. Most companies advertise a price for a base computer that includes components housed in the system unit (processor, RAM, sound card, video card, network card), hard disks, optical disc drives, a keyboard, mouse, monitor, printer, speakers, and modem. Be aware, however, that some advertisements list prices for computers with only some of these components. Monitors and printers, for example, often are not included in a base computer's price. Depending on how you plan to use the computer, you may want to invest in additional or more powerful components. When comparing the prices of computers, make sure you are comparing identical or similar configurations.

8 If you are buying a new computer, you have several purchasing options: buying from a school bookstore, a local computer dealer, a local large retail store, or ordering by mail via telephone or the Web.

Each purchasing option has certain advantages. Many college bookstores, for example, sign exclusive pricing agreements with computer manufacturers and, thus, can offer student discounts. Local dealers and local large retail stores, however, more easily can provide hands-on support. Mail-order companies that sell computers by telephone or online via the Web (Figure 3) often provide the lowest prices, but extend less personal service. Some major mail-order companies, however, have started to provide next-business-day, on-site services. A credit card usually is required to buy from a mail-order company.

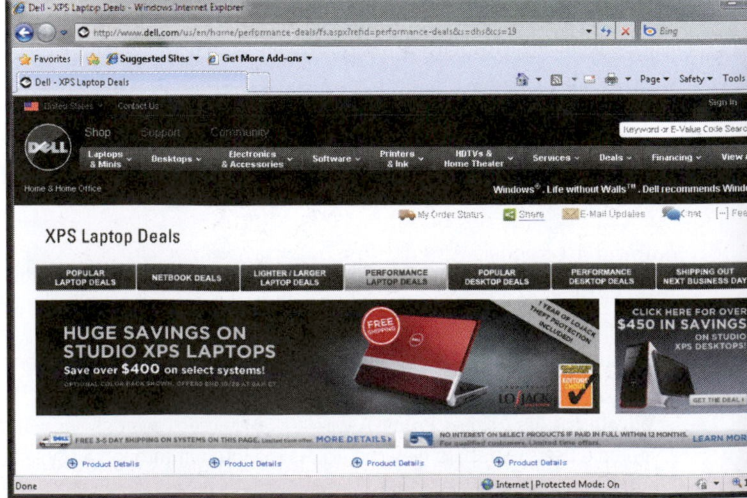

Figure 3 Mail-order companies, such as Dell, sell computers online.

9 If you are buying a used computer, stay with name brands such as Dell, Apple, HP, and Gateway.

Although brand-name equipment can cost more, most brand-name computers have longer, more comprehensive warranties, are better supported, and have more authorized centers for repair services. As with new computers, you can purchase a used computer from local computer dealers, local large retail stores, or mail order via the telephone or the Web. Classified ads and used computer sellers offer additional outlets for purchasing used computers.

10 If you have a computer and are upgrading to a new one, then consider selling or trading in the old one.

If you are a replacement buyer, your older computer still may have value. If you cannot sell the computer through the classified ads, via a Web site, or to a friend, then ask if the computer dealer will buy your old computer.

An increasing number of companies are taking trade-ins, but do not expect too much money for your old computer. Other companies offer to recycle your old computer free or for a fee.

11 Be aware of hidden costs.

Before purchasing, be sure to consider any additional costs associated with buying a computer, such as an additional telephone line, a broadband modem, an uninterruptible power supply (UPS), computer furniture, a USB flash drive, paper, and computer training classes you may want to take. Depending on where you buy the computer, the seller may be willing to include some or all of these in the computer purchase price.

12 Consider more than just price.

The lowest-cost computer may not be the best long-term buy. Consider such intangibles as the vendor's time in business, regard for quality, and reputation for support. If you need to upgrade a computer often, you may want to consider a leasing arrangement, in which you pay monthly lease fees, but can upgrade or add on to your computer as your equipment needs change. No matter what type of buyer you are, insist on a 30-day, no-questions-asked return policy on the computer.

13 Avoid restocking fees.

Some companies charge a restocking fee of 10 to 20 percent as part of their money-back return policy. In some cases, no restocking fee for hardware is applied, but it is applied for software. Ask about the existence and terms of any restocking policies before you buy.

14 Use a credit card to purchase a new computer.

Many credit cards offer purchase protection and extended warranty benefits that cover you in case of loss of or damage to purchased goods. Paying by credit card also gives you time to install and use the computer before you have to pay for it. Finally, if you are dissatisfied with the computer and are unable to reach an agreement with the seller, paying by credit card gives you certain rights regarding withholding payment until the dispute is resolved. Check your credit card terms for specific details.

15 Consider purchasing an extended warranty or service plan.

If you use your computer for business or require fast resolution to major computer problems, consider purchasing an extended warranty or a service plan through a local dealer or third-party company. Most extended warranties cover the repair and replacement of computer components beyond the standard warranty. Most service plans ensure that your technical support calls receive priority response from technicians. You also can purchase an on-site service plan that states that a technician will arrive at your home, work, or school within 24 hours. If your computer includes a warranty and service agreement for a year or less, consider extending the service for two or three years when you buy the computer.

CENTURY COMPUTERS

Performance Guarantee

(See reverse for terms & conditions of this contract)

Invoice #: 1984409
Invoice Date: 10/12/11

Effective Date: 10/12/11
Expiration Date: 10/12/14

Customer Name: Leon, Richard
Date: 10/12/11
Address: 1123 Roxbury
Sycamore, IL 60178
Day phone: (815) 555-0303
Evening Phone: (728) 555-0203

System & Serial Numbers
IMB computer
S/N: US759290C

John Smith
Print Name of Century's Authorized Signature

10/12/11
Date

How to Purchase a Notebook Computer

If you need computing capability when you travel or to use in lectures or meetings, you may find a notebook computer to be an appropriate choice. The guidelines mentioned in the previous section also apply to the purchase of a notebook computer. The following are additional considerations unique to notebook computers, including netbooks and Tablet PCs.

1 Determine which computer fits your mobile computing needs.

Before purchasing a notebook computer, you need to determine whether a traditional notebook computer, netbook, or Tablet PC will meet your needs. If you spend most of your time working on spreadsheets, writing and/or editing documents, e-mail, or using the Internet, then a traditional notebook computer will suffice. If your primary use will be to access the Internet while traveling and you are not concerned as much with processing power or hard disk capacity, consider a netbook. If you find yourself in need of a computer in class or that you spend more time in meetings than in your office, then the Tablet PC may be the answer. Before you invest money in a Tablet PC, however, determine which programs you plan to use on it. You should not buy a Tablet PC simply because it is an interesting type of computer.

2 Purchase a notebook computer with a sufficiently large screen.

Active-matrix screens display high-quality color that is viewable from all angles. Less expensive, passive-matrix screens sometimes are difficult to see in low-light conditions and cannot be viewed from an angle.

Notebook computers typically include a 12.1-inch, 13.3-inch, 14.1-inch, 15.4-inch, or 17-inch display. Netbooks have screens as small as 7 inches. For most users, a 14.1-inch display is satisfactory. If you intend to use the notebook computer as a desktop computer replacement, however, you may opt for a 15.4-inch or 17-inch display. The WSXGA+ standard (1680 × 1050) is popular with 17-inch displays, so if you intend to watch HD movies on the computer, take this into consideration. Dell offers a notebook computer with a 20.1-inch display that looks like a briefcase when closed. Some notebook computers with these larger displays weigh more than 10 pounds, however, so if you travel a lot and portability is essential, you might want a lighter computer with a smaller display. The lightest notebook computers, which weigh less than 3 pounds, are equipped with a 12.1-inch display.

Regardless of size, the resolution of the display should be at least 1024 × 768 pixels. To compare the screen size on various notebook computers, including netbooks and Tablet PCs, visit the company Web sites. Tablet PCs use a digitizer below a standard 10.4-inch motion-sensitive LCD display to make the writing experience on the screen feel like writing on paper. To ensure you experience the maximum benefits from the ClearType technology, make sure the LCD display has a resolution of 800 × 600 in landscape mode and a 600 × 800 in portrait mode.

3 Experiment with different keyboards, pointing devices, and digital pens.

Notebook computer keyboards, especially netbook keyboards, are far less standardized than those for desktop computers. Some notebook computers, for example, have wide wrist rests, while others have none, and keyboard layouts on notebook computers often vary. Notebook computers also use a range of pointing devices, including touchpads, pointing sticks, trackballs, and, in the case of Tablet PCs, digital pens.

Before purchasing a notebook computer, try various types of keyboards and pointing devices to determine which is easiest for you to use. Regardless of the device you select, you also may want to purchase a standard mouse to use when you are working at a desk or other large surface. Figure 4 compares the standard point-and-click of a mouse with the gestures made with a digital pen. Other gestures with the digital pen replicate some of the commonly used keys on a keyboard.

Mouse and Digital Pen Operations

Mouse	Digital Pen
Point	Point
Click	Tap
Double-click	Double-tap
Right-click	Tap and hold
Click and drag	Drag

Figure 4 Standard point-and-click of a mouse compared with the gestures made with a digital pen.

4 Make sure the notebook computer you purchase has an optical disc drive.

Most mobile computers include an optical disc drive. Although DVD/Blu-ray Disc drives are slightly more expensive, they allow you to play CDs, DVDs, and Blu-ray Discs using your notebook computer and hear the sound through earbuds. If you decide to purchase a netbook, it might not include an optical disc drive. Instead, you might need to purchase an external optical disc drive.

5 If necessary, upgrade the processor, memory, and disk storage at the time of purchase.

As with a desktop computer, upgrading a notebook computer's memory and disk storage usually is less expensive at the time of initial purchase. Some disk storage is custom designed for notebook computer manufacturers, meaning an upgrade might not be available in the future. If you are purchasing a lightweight notebook computer or Tablet PC, then it should include at least an Intel Core 2 Quad processor, 2 GB RAM, and 250 GB of storage. If you are purchasing a netbook, it should have an Intel Atom processor, at least 1 GB RAM, and 120 GB of storage.

6 The availability of built-in ports and slots and a USB hub on a notebook computer is important.

A notebook computer does not have much room to add adapter cards. If you know the purpose for which you plan to use the notebook computer, then you can determine the ports you will need. Netbooks typically have fewer ports than traditional notebook computers and Tablet PCs. Most notebook computers include common ports, such as a video port, audio port, network port, FireWire port, and multiple USB ports. If you plan to connect the notebook computer to a television, however, then you will need a PC to TV port. To optimize television viewing, you may want to consider DisplayPort, DVI, or HDMI ports. If you want to connect to networks at school or in various offices via a network cable, make sure the notebook computer you purchase has a network port. If the notebook computer does not contain a network port, you will have to purchase an external network card that slides into an expansion slot in your computer, as well as a network cable. You also may want to consider adding a card reader.

7 If you plan to use your notebook computer for note-taking at school or in meetings, consider a convertible Tablet PC.

Some computer manufacturers have developed convertible Tablet PCs that allow the screen to rotate 180 degrees on a central hinge and then fold down to cover the keyboard (Figure 5). You then can use a digital pen to enter text or drawings into the computer by writing on the screen. Some notebook computers have wide screens for better viewing and editing, and some even have a screen on top of the unit in addition to the regular screen. If you spend much of your time attending lectures or meetings, then the slate Tablet PC is ideal. With a slate Tablet PC, users can attach a removable keyboard.

Figure 5
A convertible Tablet PC.

8 If you purchase a Tablet PC, determine whether you require multi-touch technology.

Newer operating systems now support hardware with multi-touch technology. If you choose an operating system that supports this technology, the Tablet PC also must support this technology.

9 Purchase a notebook computer with an integrated Web cam.

If you will be using a notebook computer to connect to the Internet and chat with friends online, consider purchasing one with an integrated Web cam.

10 Check with your wireless carrier to see if it offers netbooks for sale.

Most wireless carriers now offer wireless data plans allowing you to connect to the Internet from almost anywhere with a cell phone signal. Some wireless carriers now are selling netbooks with built-in capability to connect wirelessly to the Internet using a wireless data plan.

11 Purchase a notebook computer with a built-in wireless network connection.

A wireless network connection (Bluetooth, Wi-Fi a/b/g/n, WiMAX, etc.) can be useful when you travel or as part of a home network. Increasingly more airports, hotels, schools, and cafés have wireless networks that allow you to connect to the Internet. Many users today are setting up wireless home networks. With a wireless home network, your notebook computer can access the Internet, as well as other computers in the house, from any location to share files and hardware, such as a printer, and browse the Web. Most home wireless networks allow connections from distances of 150 to 800 feet.

12 If you plan to use your notebook computer for long periods without access to an electrical outlet, purchase a second battery.

The trend among notebook computer users today is power and size over battery life. Many notebook computer users today are willing to give up longer battery life for a larger screen, faster processor, and more storage. In addition, some manufacturers typically sell the notebook computer with the lowest capacity battery. For this reason, be careful in choosing a notebook computer if you plan to use it without access to electrical outlets for long periods, such as an airplane flight. You also might want to purchase a second battery as a backup. If you anticipate running the notebook computer on batteries frequently, choose a computer that uses lithium-ion batteries, which last longer than nickel cadmium or nickel hydride batteries.

13 Purchase a well-padded and well-designed carrying case.

An amply padded carrying case will protect your notebook computer from the bumps it will receive while traveling. A well-designed carrying case will have room for accessories such as spare optical discs, pens, and paperwork (Figure 6). Although a netbook may be small enough to fit in a handbag, make sure that the bag has sufficient padding to protect the computer.

Figure 6 A well-designed notebook computer carrying case.

14 If you plan to connect your notebook computer to a video projector, make sure the notebook computer is compatible with the video projector.

You should check, for example, to be sure that your notebook computer will allow you to display an image on the computer screen and projection device at the same time. Also, ensure that the notebook computer has the ports required to connect to the video projector. You also may consider purchasing a notebook computer with a built-in Web cam for video conferencing purposes.

15 For improved security and convenience, consider a fingerprint reader.

More than half a million notebook computers are stolen or lost each year. If you have critical information stored on your notebook computer, consider purchasing one with a fingerprint reader (Figure 7) to protect the data if your computer is stolen or lost. Fingerprint security offers a level of protection that extends well beyond the standard password protection. If your notebook computer is stolen, the odds of recovering it improve dramatically with anti-theft tracking software. Manufacturers claim recovery rates of 90 percent or more for notebook computers using their product. For convenience, fingerprint readers also allow you to log onto several Web sites in lieu of entering user name and password information.

Figure 7 Fingerprint reader technology offers greater security than passwords.

16 Review the docking capabilities of the Tablet PC.

The Tablet Technology in the Windows operating system supports a grab-and-go form of docking, so that you can pick up and take a docked Tablet PC with you, just as you would pick up a notepad on your way to a meeting (Figure 8).

Figure 8 A Tablet PC docked to create a desktop computer with the Tablet PC as the monitor.

How to Purchase a Smart Phone

You probably will use a smart phone more often than other mobile devices. For this reason, it is important to choose a phone that is available through your preferred wireless carrier, available in your price range, and offers access to the features you will use most frequently. This section lists guidelines you should consider when purchasing a smart phone.

1 Choose a wireless carrier and plan that satisfies your needs and budget.

Multiple wireless carriers exist today, and each one offers a different line of smart phones. For example, the Samsung Alias is available only through Verizon Wireless. Alternatively, some smart phones, such as the BlackBerry line of smart phones, are available from multiple wireless carriers. Before deciding on a smart phone, you first should research the wireless carriers in your area, and be sure to ascertain whether the coverage is acceptable. Additionally, compare the calling plans for the various carriers and determine which one best meets your needs. Once you have determined the wireless carrier to use, you then can choose from one of their available smart phones. Once you purchase a smart phone, most carriers allow you to perform a risk-free evaluation for 30 days. If you are not satisfied with the phone or its performance, you can return the phone and pay only for the service you have used.

2 Decide on the size, style, and weight of the smart phone that will work best for you.

Smart phones are available in various sizes, weights, shapes, and colors. Some people prefer larger, heavier phones because they feel that they are more durable, while others prefer smaller, lightweight phones for easy portability. Some smart phones are flip phones, meaning that you have to open the phone (like a clamshell) to display the screen and keypad, some open by sliding the phone, and others do not need to be opened to use them. Figure 9 shows the various smart phone styles.

Figure 9
Various smart phone styles.

3 Determine whether you prefer a touch screen, keypad, or mini-keyboard.

Modern smart phones provide various ways to enter text. During the past several years, smart phones with touch screens as their primary input device have been penetrating the market. Some smart phone users prefer touch screens because the phone does not require additional space for a keypad or mini-keyboard, but others find it more difficult to type on a touch screen. Most newer smart phones with touch screens also include handwriting recognition. Smart phones with keypads might make it easier to type for some users, but others do not like the unfamiliar feeling of keys arranged in alphabetical order. In addition, you often have to press the keys multiple times before reaching the letter you want to type. Mini-keyboards are available on some smart phones, such as the BlackBerry and Samsung Alias. Mini-keyboards provide a key for each letter, but the keys are significantly smaller than those on a standard keyboard. Most smart phone users type on mini-keyboards using their thumbs.

4 If you will be synchronizing your smart phone with a program on your computer, select a smart phone that is compatible with the program you wish to use.

Programs such as Microsoft Outlook allow you to synchronize your e-mail messages, contacts, and calendar with your smart phone. If you would like this functionality, purchase a smart phone that can synchronize with Microsoft Outlook. Similarly, if your company uses a BlackBerry Enterprise server or Microsoft Exchange server, you should consider purchasing a smart phone that can synchronize, either using wires or wirelessly, with those servers.

5 Compare battery life.

Any smart phone is useful only if it has the power required to run. Talking and using the Internet on your smart phone will shorten battery life more quickly than when the phone is powered on but not in use. If you have a choice, be sure to purchase a battery that will allow the phone to function all day. Pay particular attention to the talk time and standby time. If you plan to talk on the phone more than the advertised talk time, you might consider purchasing a second battery or an extended battery if your phone supports it.

6 Make sure your smart phone has enough memory and storage.

If you are using the smart phone to send and receive picture, video, and e-mail messages, and to store music, purchase a memory card that not only is compatible with your computer and smart phone, but also has adequate storage space for your messages and files. If you purchase a memory card and eventually fill it, you easily can transfer the data to a larger memory card.

7 Check out the accessories.

Determine which accessories you want for the smart phone. Accessories include carrying cases, screen protectors, synchronization cradles and cables, and car chargers.

How to Purchase a Portable Media Player

Portable media players are becoming the preferred device for listening to music and watching videos on the go. When choosing a portable media player, it is important to consider features and characteristics other than the physical size and amount of storage space. This section lists guidelines you should consider when purchasing a portable media player.

1 Choose a device with sufficient storage capacity.

Audio and video files can consume a great deal of storage space, so be sure to purchase a portable media player that has enough capacity to store your audio and video files. You also should consider approximately how many media files you acquire each year, and make sure that your device has enough storage space to accommodate these files for years to come.

2 Determine which file formats your new portable media player should support and how you will add files to your library.

Some portable media players are designed to accept new audio and video files only through a program installed on a computer. For example, it is easiest to add media files to an iPod using the iTunes program. Other portable media players connect to a computer using a cable and are displayed in Windows as a removable disk. You then can add files to the media player by dragging the files to the removable disk icon in Windows. The portable media player must support the file formats you are using. You can determine the file format by looking at the file extension on the media files you wish to transfer to your portable media player. Before purchasing a portable media player, make sure that it can support the file formats you are using.

3 Consider a portable media player that can play video.

Some users prefer to watch videos on their portable media player in addition to playing music. You typically can download videos for portable media players less expensively than purchasing the movie on a DVD/Blu-ray Disc. Although the display on a portable media player is small, many still find entertainment value because they are able to watch videos and stay occupied while waiting for a bus, on an airplane, or at other locations where they otherwise might not have anything to occupy them.

4 Read reviews about the sound quality on the portable media players you are considering.

Sound quality may vary greatly among portable media players. If you are unable to try the portable media player before buying it, read reviews and make sure that those reviewing the devices find the sound quality to be acceptable. You also may consider purchasing higher-quality earbuds or headphones to enhance the sound quality.

5 Select a size and style that works best for you.

Portable media players are available in various shapes and styles. For example, Apple offers the iPod shuffle, iPod nano, iPod classic, and iPod touch (Figure 10). Each type of iPod varies in size and style, and some have capabilities (such as video) that others do not. Choose a size and style that meets your needs and fits your personality.

Figure 10 Portable media players are available in different shapes, styles, and colors.

6 Check out additional memory cards.

Most portable media players have internal storage for your media files. If you wish to increase the available storage, consider purchasing a portable media player that allows you to increase storage capacity by inserting memory cards. Similar to most computers, it is less expensive initially to purchase the largest amount of storage that you can afford, but it is helpful to be able to increase your storage at a later date.

7 Consider rechargeable batteries.

Although most portable media players include rechargeable batteries, some still use traditional alkaline batteries. Portable media players sometimes can last for only a few hours on alkaline batteries, and battery replacement can be costly. Rechargeable batteries often last longer and create less waste. If you are not near a power source, you are unable to recharge the batteries when they die. With alkaline batteries, you simply can insert new ones and continue enjoying your player.

8 Stay within your budget.

As previously mentioned, portable media players are available in a variety of shapes and sizes, and they also are available with various storage capacities. When shopping for a portable media player, be realistic when you consider how you will use the device, as well as how much storage you require. Purchasing the latest and greatest device is not always the best option, and the cost can exceed what you care to spend.

How to Purchase a Digital Camera

Both amateur and professional photographers now are mostly purchasing digital cameras to meet their photography needs. Because digital cameras with new and improved features regularly are introduced to the marketplace, consumers should know how to compare the differences among the multiple cameras that are available. This section lists guidelines you should consider when purchasing a digital camera.

1 Determine the type of digital camera that meets your needs.

Various types of digital cameras exist, including point-and-shoot cameras, field cameras, and studio cameras. Point-and-shoot cameras typically fit in your pocket and meet the needs of most general consumers. Field cameras, which often are used by photojournalists, are portable but flexible. Field cameras allow photographers to change lenses and use other attachments, and also are more customizable than point-and-shoot cameras. Studio cameras are used in photo studios and are stationary. These cameras give you the widest range of lenses and settings.

2 The digital camera with the highest resolution is not always the best.

Many consumers mistakenly believe that the digital camera with the highest resolution is the best camera for their needs. A higher resolution increases quality and clarity of your photos, as well as the size at which you can print the photos before noticing degradation in quality. If you never plan to print photos larger than 8" × 10", for example, you do not need a camera with a resolution greater than 5-megapixels. Many cameras available today advertise higher resolutions, but taking pictures at these high resolutions can use valuable storage space. Just because your camera can take a 10-megapixel photo does not mean that you always should set the resolution to 10 megapixels.

3 Consider size and weight.

Digital cameras are available in various sizes and weights. Some people prefer smaller, lighter cameras because they are easier to transport and take up less space. Others prefer bulkier, heavier cameras because the weight helps steady them to take a clearer picture. Many digital cameras also include an image stabilization feature that reduces the possibility of a blurry picture if you move your hands slightly while taking the picture. Some also believe that heavier cameras are of better quality, although that seldom is true. When choosing a digital camera, practice taking pictures with it and select one that feels comfortable and natural.

4 Different cameras require different memory cards.

When purchasing a digital camera, pay careful attention to the type of memory card the camera uses. Many use SD cards, some use xD Picture cards, and some use CompactFlash memory cards. Some memory cards are more expensive to replace than others, and some have a higher capacity than other cards. If you take a lot of pictures, purchase a camera that supports a memory card with a higher storage capacity so that you can avoid carrying multiple memory cards. You also might consider purchasing a camera that uses a memory card that is compatible with your other mobile devices.

5 Photo editing features can save you time.

Some digital cameras have integrated tools that allow you to edit photos directly from the camera. For instance, you may be able to crop photos, change the brightness, or remove red eye effects. Editing photos directly on the camera after taking them can save you from editing multiple photos at once when you transfer them to a computer. The photo editing capabilities available on digital cameras are limited when compared to photo editing programs, but in many cases they can edit a photo to your satisfaction.

6 Make sure that you can see the LCD screen easily.

LCD screens on digital cameras allow you to configure the settings, frame a shot before taking it, and preview photos after taking them. LCD screens vary by inches, so select a camera with a screen that does not require you to strain your eyes to view. This is especially important if the camera you are considering does not have a viewfinder, because you then will be required to use the display to frame your shots.

7 Determine whether your pictures will require you to zoom.

If you plan to take pictures of people or objects that require you to zoom in, select a digital camera that has a high optical zoom. An optical zoom enlarges the subject by adjusting the camera lens, whereas a digital zoom uses algorithms built into the camera to magnify images. Optical zooms, as opposed to digital zooms, often result in a higher quality photo. While a digital zoom might be capable of magnifying objects that are 100 feet away, the photo will suffer a loss of quality.

8 Price is important.

As with all other devices, locate a digital camera that does not exceed your budget. If you find a great camera that is available for more than you are willing to spend, consider locating a camera with a slightly lower resolution, an alternate brand, or a smaller screen. Digital cameras can last well beyond five years if properly maintained, so consider this a longer-term investment that will create memories lasting you a lifetime.

9 Know your batteries.

Some digital cameras require replaceable alkaline or rechargeable batteries (often AA or AAA), and others have a rechargeable battery. Similar to batteries in portable media players, using disposable batteries in digital cameras can get expensive, and they may not last as long as rechargeable battery packs. Digital camera battery life is not measured in hours (as is the case with smart phones and portable media players); instead, it is measured in how many pictures can be taken on a single charge or set of batteries. Turning off the LCD screen and flash when you take pictures can help to extend battery life.

10 Purchase accessories.

Accessories that are available for digital cameras include carrying cases, extra batteries and battery chargers, and extra memory cards (Figure 11). Carrying cases can help protect your digital camera, especially while traveling, and the extra batteries and chargers can stay inside your carrying case so that they are readily available should you need them. Screen protectors can help protect the LCD screen on your digital camera.

Figure 11 Digital camera accessories include memory cards, cases, batteries, and battery chargers.

Multiple Web sites on the Internet allow you to purchase computers and mobile devices (Figure 12). Some Web sites even post reviews for you to read before you commit to making a purchase.

Web Site	Web Address	Desktop Computers	Notebook Computers	Smart Phones	Portable Media Players	Digital Cameras
Acer	acer.com	X	X			
Amazon.com	amazon.com	X	X	X	X	X
Apple	apple.com	X	X	X	X	
Best Buy	bestbuy.com	X	X	X	X	X
BlackBerry	blackberry.com			X		
Canon	canon.com					X
CNET Shopper	shopper.cnet.com	X	X	X	X	X
Dell	dell.com	X	X		X	X
Fry's Electronics	frys.com	X	X	X	X	X
Gateway	gateway.com	X	X			
hhgregg	hhgregg.com	X	X	X	X	X
HP	hp.com	X	X	X		
Lenovo	lenovo.com	X	X		X	X
LG	lge.com			X		
MSN Shopping	shopping.msn.com	X	X	X	X	X
Nokia	nokia.com			X		
Panasonic	panasonic.com		X			X
RadioShack	radioshack.com	X	X	X	X	X
SAMSUNG	samsung.com			X	X	X
Sony	sony.com	X	X	X	X	X
Target	target.com	X	X	X	X	X
Walmart	walmart.com	X	X	X	X	X
Yahoo! Computers	shopping.yahoo.com	X	X	X	X	X

For an updated list of companies and their Web addresses, visit the Computer Concepts CourseMate Web site at www.cengagebrain.com and then navigate to the Buyer's Guide Feature resource for this book.

Figure 12 Web sites that sell computers and mobile devices.

Notes

Chapter Nine

Communications and Networks

Objectives

After completing this chapter, you will be able to:

1. Discuss the purpose of the components required for successful communications (sending device, communications device, communications channel, and receiving device) and identify various sending and receiving devices
2. Describe these uses of computer communications: wireless messaging services, wireless Internet access points, cybercafés, global positioning systems, collaboration, groupware, voice mail, and Web services
3. List advantages of using a network, and differentiate among LANs, MANs, and WANs
4. Differentiate between client/server and peer-to-peer networks, and describe how a P2P network works
5. Differentiate among a star network, bus network, and ring network
6. Describe the various network communications standards: Ethernet, token ring, TCP/IP, Wi-Fi, Bluetooth, UWB, IrDA, RFID, WiMAX, and WAP
7. Explain the purpose of communications software
8. Describe various types of lines for communications over the telephone network: dial-up, ISDN, DSL, FTTP, T-carrier, and ATM
9. Describe commonly used communications devices: dial-up modems, digital modems, wireless modems, network cards, wireless access points, routers, and hubs and switches
10. Discuss different ways to set up a home network
11. Describe various physical and wireless transmission media: twisted-pair cable, coaxial cable, fiber-optic cable, infrared, broadcast radio, cellular radio, microwaves, and communications satellite

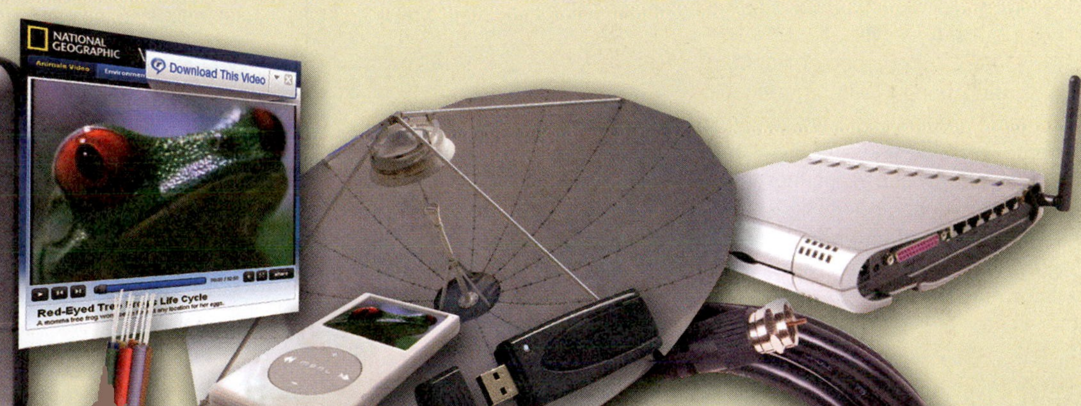

Communications

Computer **communications** describes a process in which two or more computers or devices transfer data, instructions, and information. Today, even the smallest computers and devices can communicate directly with one another, with hundreds of computers on a company network, or with millions of other computers around the globe — often via the Internet.

Figure 9-1 shows a sample communications system. Some communications involve cables and wires; others are sent wirelessly through the air. For successful communications, you need the following:

- A **sending device** that initiates an instruction to transmit data, instructions, or information.
- A communications device that connects the sending device to a communications channel.
- A **communications channel**, or transmission media on which the data, instructions, or information travel.
- A communications device that connects the communications channel to a receiving device.
- A **receiving device** that accepts the transmission of data, instructions, or information.

Figure 9-1 An example of a communications system. Some devices that serve as sending devices and receiving devices are (a) mainframe computers, (b) servers, (c) desktop computers, (d) notebook computers, (e) smart phones, (f) Internet-enabled portable media players, (g) handheld game consoles, and (h) GPS receivers. The communications channel consists of telephone and power lines, cable television and other underground lines, microwave stations, and satellites.

As shown in Figure 9-1, all types of computers and mobile devices serve as sending and receiving devices in a communications system. This includes mainframe computers, servers, desktop computers, notebook computers, smart phones, portable media players, handheld game consoles, and GPS receivers. One type of communications device that connects a communications channel to a sending or receiving device such as a computer is a modem. Two examples of communications channels are cable television lines and telephone lines.

This chapter presents various uses of communications, discusses different types of networks, and then examines several types of communications devices and communications channels.

Uses of Computer Communications

Computer communications are everywhere. Many require that users subscribe to an Internet access provider. With other computer communications, an organization such as a business or school provides communications services to employees, students, or customers. The following pages discuss a variety of computer communications.

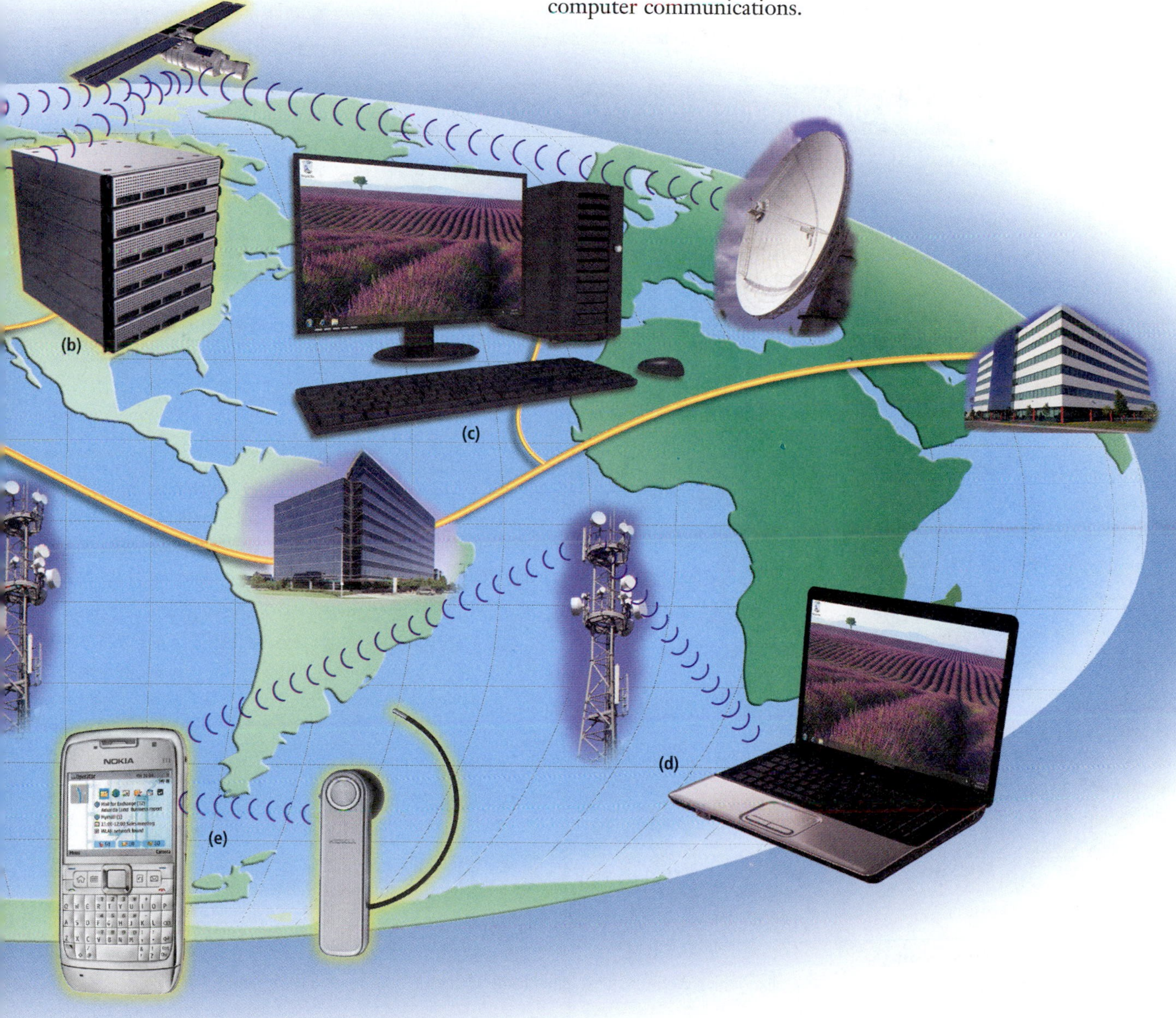

Blogs, Chat Rooms, E-Mail, Fax, FTP, Instant Messaging, Internet, Newsgroups, RSS, Video Conferencing, VoIP, Web, Web 2.0, Web Folders, and Wikis

Previous chapters discussed many uses of computer communications as they related to a particular topic. In the course of a day, it is likely you use, or use information generated by, one or more of these previously discussed communications technologies. The list in Figure 9-2 reviews the features of these modes of communications.

The following pages discuss a variety of other uses of communications that have not been discussed in depth previously. These include wireless messaging services, wireless Internet access points, cybercafés, global positioning systems, collaboration, groupware, voice mail, and Web services.

Wireless Messaging Services

Users can send and receive wireless messages to and from smart phones, cell phones, handheld game consoles, and other mobile devices and computers using three techniques: text messaging, picture/video messaging, and wireless instant messaging (Figure 9-3). The type of messaging you use depends primarily on the services offered by the wireless Internet service provider (WISP) that works with the cell phone or other mobile device you select. In most cases, you can receive these messages at no cost but pay a per use or monthly fee to send messages to others.

Summary of Communications Discussed in Previous Chapters

Communications Type	Brief Description
Blogs	Time-stamped articles on a network that reflect the author's interests, opinions, and personality
Chat Rooms	Real-time typed conversation among two or more people that takes place on a computer connected to a network that also may allow the exchange of messages, photos, files, audio, and video
E-Mail	Transmission of messages and files via a computer network
Fax	Transmits and receives documents over telephone lines
FTP	Internet standard that permits users to upload and download files to and from FTP servers on the Internet
Instant Messaging	Real-time one-on-one Internet communications service that notifies you when one or more people are online and then allows you to exchange messages, photos, files, audio, and video
Internet	Worldwide collection of networks that links millions of businesses, government agencies, educational institutions, and individuals
Newsgroups	Online areas in which users have written discussions about a particular subject
RSS	Specification that enables Web content to be distributed to subscribers
Video Conferencing	Real-time meeting between two or more geographically separated people who use a network to transmit audio and video data
VoIP	Conversation that takes place over the Internet using a telephone connected to a computer, mobile device, or telephone adapter
Web	Worldwide collection of electronic documents on the Internet that users access through a Web browser
Web 2.0	Web sites that provide a means for users to share personal information, allow users to modify Web site content, and/or have application software built into the site for visitors to use
Web Folders	Location on a Web server to which users publish documents and other files
Wikis	Collaborative Web sites that allow users to create, add to, modify, or delete Web site content

Figure 9-2 Uses of communications discussed in earlier chapters.

Wikis
For more information, visit the Computer Concepts CourseMate Web site at www.cengagebrain.com, navigate to the Chapter 9 Web Link resource for this book, and then click Wikis.

FAQ 9-1

How many households are using cell phones as their primary telephone?

A recent study indicates that approximately 20 percent of households use cell phones as their primary telephone. Some families choose to save money by disconnecting their home telephone and using their cell phone for all calls, although they tend to make more telephone calls than families with a traditional telephone line.

For more information, visit the Computer Concepts CourseMate Web site at www.cengagebrain.com, navigate to the Chapter 9 FAQ resource for this book, and then click Wireless Households.

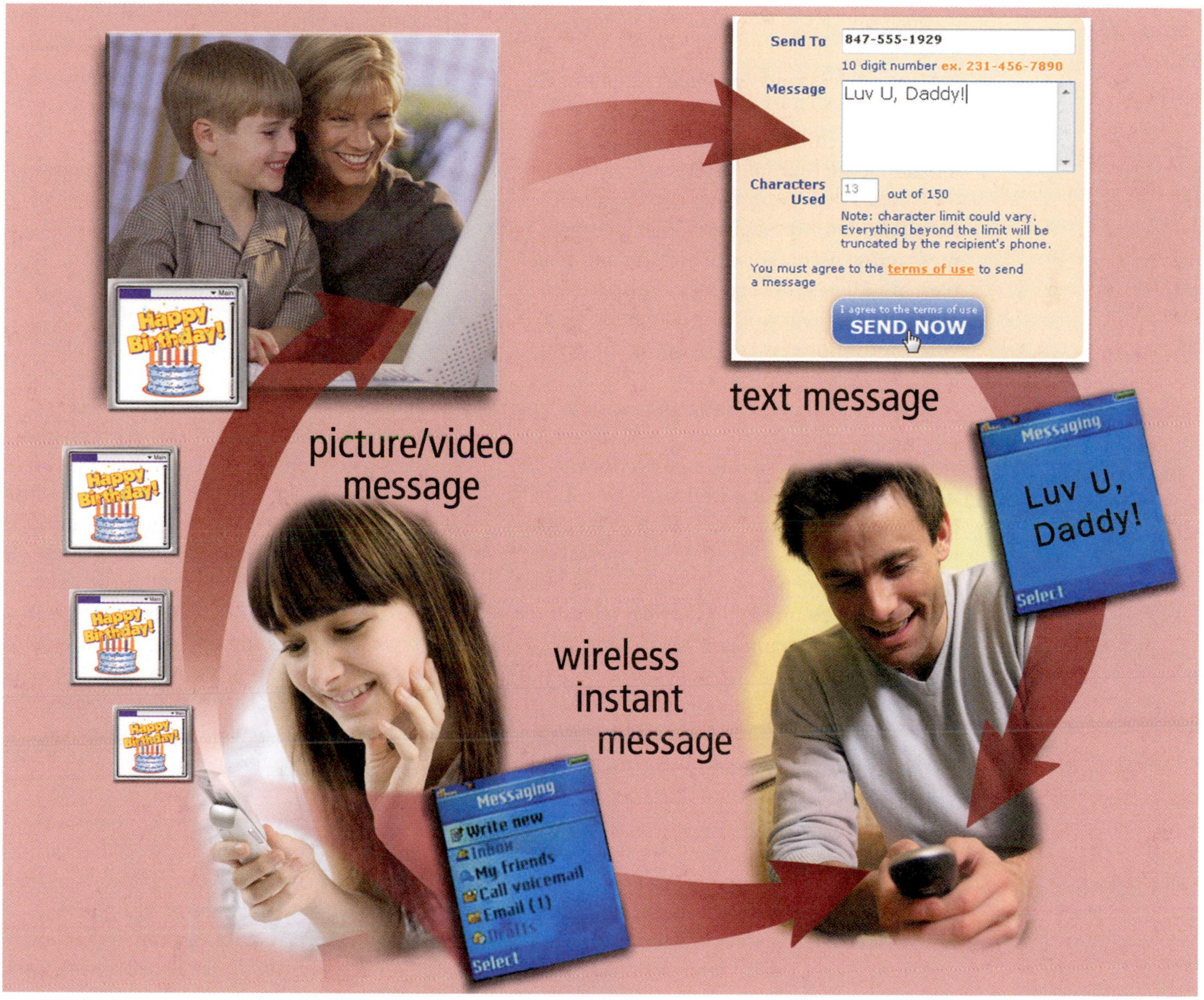

Figure 9-3 Users can send and receive text messages, picture/video messages, and wireless instant messages to and from their smart phones and other computers and devices.

Text Messaging A mobile device with **text messaging**, also called **SMS** (*short message service*), capability allows users to send and receive short text messages, typically fewer than 300 characters, on a phone or other mobile device or computer. Text messaging services typically provide users with several options for sending and receiving messages:

- Mobile to Mobile: send a message from your mobile device to another mobile device
- Mobile to E-Mail: send a message from your mobile device to an e-mail address anywhere in the world
- Web to Mobile: send a message from a text messaging Web site to a mobile device, or

request that a Web site alert a mobile device with messages of breaking news and other updates, such as sports scores, stock prices, and weather forecasts
- Mobile to Provider: send a message by entering a *common short code (CSC)*, which is a four- or five-digit number assigned to a specific content or wireless service provider, followed by the message, such as a vote for a television program contestant or an entry for a sweepstakes

Most services store incoming text messages for a limited amount of time, such as five days. After the specified time, the WISP deletes any unread messages from its server.

Picture/Video Messaging With **picture messaging**, users can send pictures and sound files, as well as short text messages, to a phone or other mobile device, or a computer. With **video messaging**, users can send short video clips, usually about 30 seconds in length, in addition to all picture messaging services. Smart phones and other mobile devices with picture/video messaging, also called *MMS* (*multimedia message service*), capability typically have a digital camera built into the device. Users who expect to receive numerous picture/video messages should verify the phone has sufficient memory.

Picture/video messaging services typically provide users these options for sending and receiving messages:
- Mobile to Mobile: send the picture/video from your mobile device to another mobile device
- Mobile to E-Mail: send the picture/video from your mobile device to an e-mail address anywhere in the world

Video Messaging
For more information, visit the Computer Concepts CourseMate Web site at www.cengagebrain.com, navigate to the Chapter 9 Web Link resource for this book, and then click Video Messaging.

If you send a picture message to a phone that does not have picture/video messaging capability, the phone usually displays a text message directing the user to a Web page that contains the picture/video message. Some online social networks allow you to send a picture/video message to an assigned number to post the message automatically to your online profile.

Wireless Instant Messaging Wireless instant messaging (IM) is a real-time Internet communications service that allows wireless mobile devices to exchange messages with one or more mobile devices or online users. Some WISPs partner with IM services so that you can use your smart phone or other mobile device to send and receive wireless instant messages. AT&T's wireless service, for example, allows communications through various instant messengers such as AIM (AOL Instant Messenger), Windows Live Messenger, and Yahoo! Messenger. With a compatible IM service, users have these IM options:
- Mobile to Mobile: use a wireless instant messenger to communicate between two mobile devices
- Mobile to Personal Computer: use a wireless instant messenger to communicate between a mobile device and a desktop or notebook computer
- Web to Mobile: send or forward messages from a desktop or notebook computer's instant messenger to a mobile device

Wireless Internet Access Points

At home, work, school, and in many public locations, people connect wirelessly to the Internet through a **wireless Internet access point** using notebook computers, smart phones, handheld game consoles, or other devices. Users access wireless Internet access points with computers or devices that have the necessary built-in wireless capability or the appropriate wireless network card, USB network adapter, ExpressCard module, or PC Card (Figure 9-4). Two types of wireless Internet access points are hot spots and mobile wireless networks.

A *hot spot* is a wireless network that provides Internet connections to mobile computers and devices. Through the hot spot, mobile users check e-mail, browse the Web, and access any service on the Internet. Three hot spot technologies are Wi-Fi, WiMAX, and Bluetooth. Wi-Fi hot spots provide wireless network connections to users in public locations such as airports and airplanes, train stations, hotels, convention centers, schools, campgrounds, marinas, shopping malls, bookstores, libraries, restaurants, and coffee shops. The coverage range for WiMAX hot spots can be much wider than Wi-Fi; for example, they can cover an entire city. Bluetooth hot spots provide location-based services, such as sending coupons or menus, to users whose enabled devices enter the coverage range. Sections later in this chapter discuss Wi-Fi, WiMAX, and Bluetooth in more detail.

Some hot spots provide free Internet access, some charge a per-use fee, and others require users to subscribe to a WISP, to which they pay per-access fees, daily fees, or a monthly fee.

Per-access fees average $3, daily fees range from $5 to $20, and monthly fees range from $20 to $60 for unlimited access, with the higher monthly fee providing greater coverage areas. Read Ethics & Issues 9-1 for a related discussion.

Instead of hot spots, some users access the Internet through mobile wireless networks that provide users with high-speed wireless Internet connections, as long as they are in the network's range. A mobile wireless network usually covers most major cities and airports. Subscription fees for unlimited monthly Internet access to a mobile wireless network through a cell phone usually range from $30 to $50. Fees for notebook computer access are higher, usually ranging from $60 to $80 per month. Two types of mobile wireless networks are 3G and 4G, which are discussed later in this chapter.

Figure 9-4 Mobile users in this hot spot access the Internet through their notebook computers. One computer uses a wireless USB network adapter; another uses a wireless PC Card. Others have Intel's built-in wireless Centrino 2 mobile technology.

ETHICS & ISSUES 9-1

Will Widespread Wireless Broadband Connections Kill Print Media?

Airlines around the world recently started offering Wi-Fi hot spots on some flights. Communications companies also began offering WiMax coverage throughout entire cities. Even smart phones deliver high-speed Web browsing. With the proliferation of high-speed wireless Internet access, some experts believe that the end is near for print media, such as newspapers and magazines. The traditional airport and city newspaper and magazine stands' days may be numbered. Instead of buying a newspaper and a couple of magazines before a flight, travelers choose from thousands of searchable publications on their mobile devices while traveling. Even the morning newspaper delivery is at risk as more people choose to use mobile devices to access wirelessly their favorite newspapers from home. Some experts dispute this claim, stating that the print media industry perfected the centuries-old hard copy delivery of newspapers and magazines, and that, when given the choice, most people prefer print reading. For now, people prefer the style, quality, and portability of print media.

Will widespread wireless broadband connections, such as Wi-Fi, put an end to printed newspapers and magazines? Why or why not? Would you prefer to read newspapers and magazines in print or on a mobile device that provides similar or better readability as compared to print media? Why or why not? How can the media industry take advantage of the wireless Internet trend?

Cybercafés

When mobile users travel without their notebook computer or Internet-enabled mobile device, they can visit a cybercafé to access e-mail, the Web, and other Internet services. A **cybercafé**, or Internet cafe, is a coffeehouse, restaurant, or other location that provides personal computers with Internet access to its customers (Figure 9-5). Cybercafés exist in cities around the world. Although some provide free Internet access, most charge a per-hour or per-minute fee. Some cybercafés also are hot spots, providing wireless Internet connections to users with mobile computers and devices.

Figure 9-5 People using Internet-connected computers in a cybercafé.

Global Positioning Systems

A **global positioning system (GPS)** is a navigation system that consists of one or more earth-based receivers that accept and analyze signals sent by satellites in order to determine the receiver's geographic location (Figure 9-6). A *GPS receiver* is a handheld, mountable, or embedded device that contains an antenna, a radio receiver, and a processor. Many include a screen display that shows an individual's location on a map. Some also function as a portable media player allowing you, for example, to play music and view pictures on the device.

Many mobile devices such as smart phones have GPS capability built into the device or as an add-on feature. Some users carry a handheld GPS receiver; others mount a receiver to an object such as an automobile, boat, airplane, farm and construction equipment, or computer.

The first and most used application of GPS technology is to assist people with determining where they are located. The data obtained from a GPS, however, can be applied to a variety of other uses: creating a map, ascertaining the best route between two points, locating a lost person or stolen object, monitoring the movement of a person or object, determining altitude, and calculating speed.

Many vehicles use GPSs to provide drivers with directions or other information, such as alternate traffic routes, automatically call for help if the airbag is deployed, dispatch roadside assistance, unlock the driver's side door if keys are locked in the car, and track the vehicle if it is stolen. Newer GPS receivers also give drivers information about nearby points of interest, such as gas stations, restaurants, and hotels. Hikers and remote campers may carry GPS receivers in case they need emergency help or directions. Read Innovative Computing 9-1 to find out about a hobby that uses GPS technology.

Some GPS receivers work in conjunction with a cellular wireless network. Parents, for example, can locate a child's whereabouts through a cell phone equipped with a GPS receiver.

GPS

For more information, visit the Computer Concepts CourseMate Web site at www.cengagebrain.com, navigate to the Chapter 9 Web Link resource for this book, and then click GPS.

INNOVATIVE COMPUTING 9-1

Geocaching for Hidden Treasure

Treasure hunting for all ages has gone high-tech. *Geocaching* is a form of outdoor recreation, discovery, and fun, and the only requirements are a GPS receiver, Internet access, and a sense of adventure.

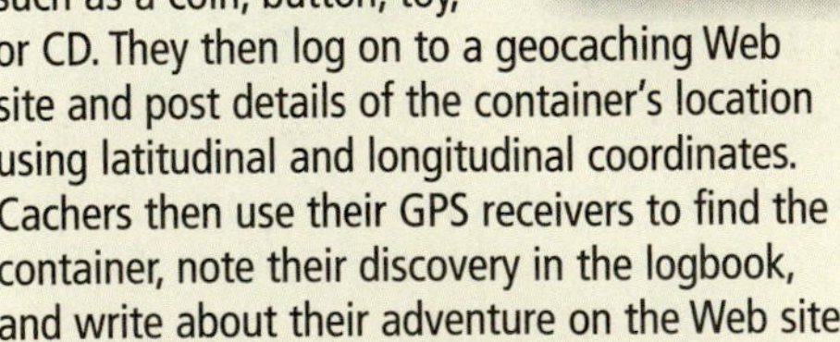

Participants bury or hide a small container, called a *cache*, that has a logbook and writing instrument and usually small novelty trinkets such as a coin, button, toy, or CD. They then log on to a geocaching Web site and post details of the container's location using latitudinal and longitudinal coordinates. Cachers then use their GPS receivers to find the container, note their discovery in the logbook, and write about their adventure on the Web site.

The first cache with GPS coordinates was documented in 2000. Today, more than 900,000 geocaches in more than 100 countries and on all 7 continents are registered on a variety of Web sites, such as geocaching.com. The locations range from under water to mountain peaks. Cachers generally follow the Geocacher's Creed, which encourages ethical behavior and preservation of natural resources.

For more information, visit the Computer Concepts CourseMate Web site at www.cengagebrain.com, navigate to the Chapter 9 Innovative Computing resource for this book, and then click Geocaching.

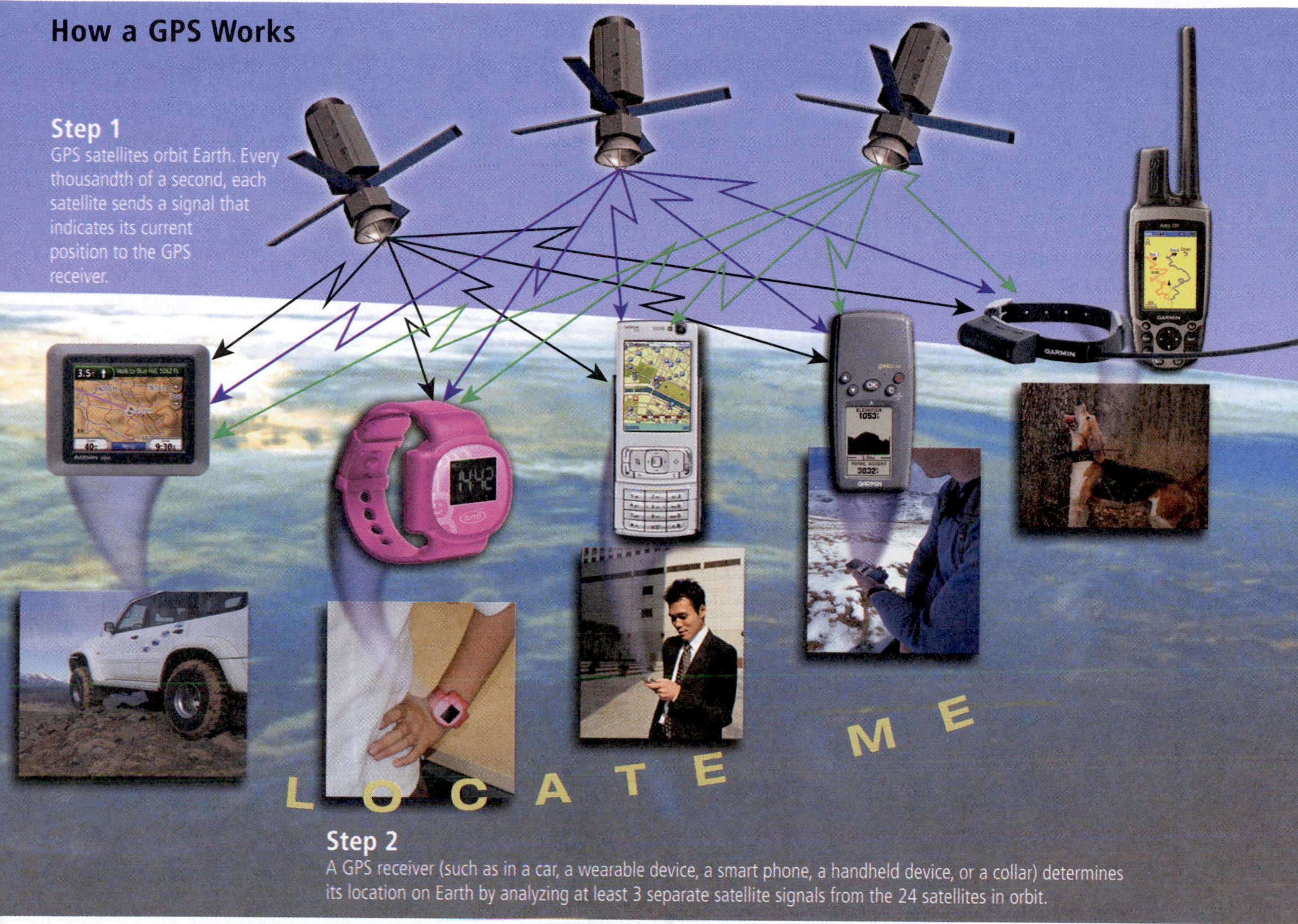

Figure 9-6 This figure shows how a GPS works.

Groupware

Groupware is software that helps groups of people work together on projects and share information over a network. Groupware is a component of a broad concept called *workgroup computing*, which includes network hardware and software that enables group members to communicate, manage projects, schedule meetings, and make group decisions. To assist with these activities, most groupware provides personal information manager (PIM) functions, such as an electronic appointment calendar, an address book, and a notepad. A major feature of groupware is group scheduling, in which a group calendar can track the schedules of multiple users and help coordinate appointments and meeting times.

Voice Mail

Voice mail, which functions much like an answering machine, allows someone to leave a voice message for one or more people. Unlike answering machines, however, a computer in the voice mail system converts an analog voice message into digital form. Once digitized, the message is stored in a voice mailbox. A *voice mailbox* is a storage location on a hard disk in the voice mail system. To help users manage voice mail messages, some systems offer visual voice mail. With *visual voice mail*, users can view message details such as the length of calls and, in some cases, read message contents instead of listening to them.

Some voice mail systems can send audio voice mail files to e-mail addresses. Others can convert a voice mail message to a text message for display on a computer or mobile device such as a smart phone, which you then can manage like any other text message.

Collaboration

Many programs provide a means to **collaborate**, or work online, with other users connected to a server. Three methods of collaboration include collaborative software, reviewing via e-mail, and document management systems.

Collaborative software includes tools that enable users to share documents via online meetings and communicate with other connected users. An *online meeting* allows users to share documents with others in real time (Figure 9-7). When the online meeting takes place on the Web, it is called a **Web conference**. In an online meeting, all participants see a document(s) at the same time. As someone changes the document, everyone in the meeting sees the changes being made. During the online meeting, participants have the ability to open a chat window and type messages to one another. Collaborative software often has whiteboard and video/audio conferencing capabilities. Examples of collaborative software include Acrobat Connect, GoToMeeting, Microsoft SharePoint Workspace, Microsoft Office Live Meeting, Google Wave, and WebEx. Microsoft Office SharePoint Server contains a suite of programs, one of which is collaborative software.

Instead of interacting in a live meeting, users often collaborate via e-mail. For example, if users want others to review a document, they can e-mail the document for review. When the recipients (reviewers) receive the document, they may add comments to the document. As the reviewers make changes to the document, both the original text and the changes are displayed. When the originator receives the document back from all reviewers, he or she can merge all comments and changes into a single document.

Some organizations use document management systems to make collaboration possible among employees. A *document management system* provides for storage and management of a company's documents, such as word processing documents, presentations, and spreadsheets. Users then access these documents, depending on their needs. A document management system can track all changes made to a document. It also can store additional information such as the document's creation date, the user who created the document, a summary of the document, and any keywords associated with the document. Google Docs is a Web-based document management system with basic services available to subscribers at no cost and premium services available for a fee. With Google Docs, multiple users can work on the same document at the same time, viewing each other's edits as they are entered.

Microsoft SharePoint Workspace

For more information, visit the Computer Concepts CourseMate Web site at www.cengagebrain.com, navigate to the Chapter 9 Web Link resource for this book, and then click Microsoft SharePoint Workspace.

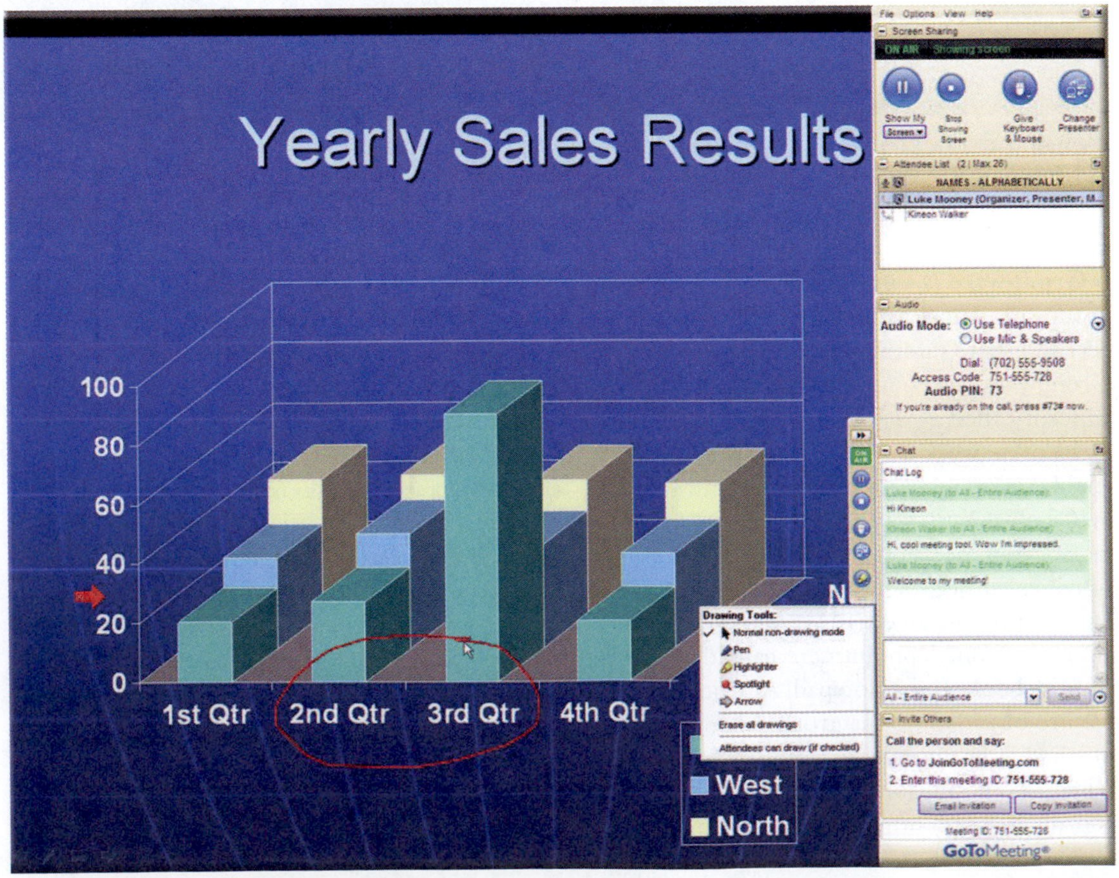

Figure 9-7 Through an online meeting, all participants see a document at the same time.

Web Services

Web services describe standardized software that enables programmers to create applications that communicate with other remote computers over the Internet or on an internal business network (Figure 9-8). Businesses use Web services because this technology provides a means for departments to communicate with each other, suppliers, vendors, and with clients. For example, third-party vendors can use Web services to communicate with their online retailer's Web site to manage their inventory levels.

Web services often provide content for mashups. A *mashup* is a Web application that combines services from two or more sources, creating a new application. An e-commerce business, for example, might determine the address of its closest retail store from its Web site and combine (mash) the location with a map from a travel and mapping Web site to provide a Web site visitor with driving directions.

Web services do not require a specific programming language, operating system, or Web browser. Different applications from different platforms can communicate with each other by sending properly formatted *XML* (Extensible Markup Language) files to the Web services. A Windows application, for example, can communicate with a UNIX application. Web services do not have a user interface because the application's user interface interacts with the Web service.

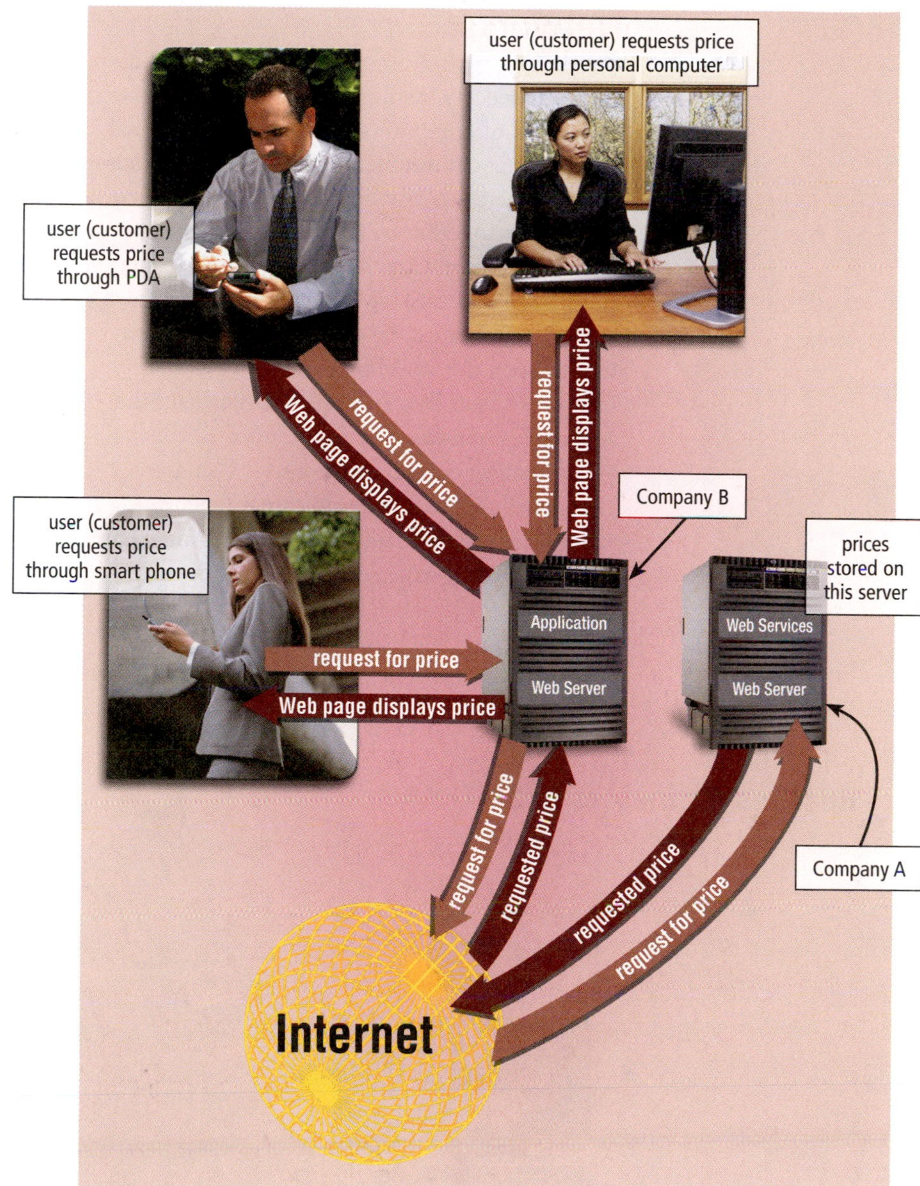

Figure 9-8 An example of Web services.

QUIZ YOURSELF 9-1

Instructions: Find the true statement below. Then, rewrite the remaining false statements so that they are true.

1. A cybercafé is a wireless network that provides Internet connections to mobile computers and other devices.
2. A Web folder is a navigation system that consists of one or more earth-based receivers that accept and analyze signals sent by satellites in order to determine the receiver's geographic location.
3. Web services describe standardized software that enables programmers to create applications that communicate with other remote computers over the Internet or on an internal business network.
4. Receiving devices initiate an instruction to transmit data, instructions, or information.
5. Users can send pictures and sound files, as well as short text messages, with text messaging.

To further check your knowledge of pages 460 through 469, visit the Computer Concepts CourseMate Web site at www.cengagebrain.com, navigate to the Chapter 9 Quiz Yourself resource for this book, and then click Objectives 1 – 2.

Networks

As discussed in Chapter 1, a **network** is a collection of computers and devices connected together via communications devices and transmission media. Many businesses network their computers together to facilitate communications, share hardware, share data and information, share software, and transfer funds (Figure 9-9). A network can be internal to an organization or span the world by connecting to the Internet. The following paragraphs explain the advantages of using a network.

- Facilitating communications — Using a network, people communicate efficiently and easily via e-mail, instant messaging, chat rooms, blogs, wikis, online social networks, video telephone calls, online meetings, video conferencing, VoIP, wireless messaging services, and groupware. Some of these communications, such as e-mail, occur within a business's internal network. Other times, they occur globally over the Internet.
- Sharing hardware — In a networked environment, each computer on the network can have access to hardware on the network. Business and home users network their hardware to save money. That is, it may be too costly to provide each user with the same piece of hardware such as a printer. If the computers and a laser printer are connected to a network, the computer users each access the laser printer on the network, as they need it.

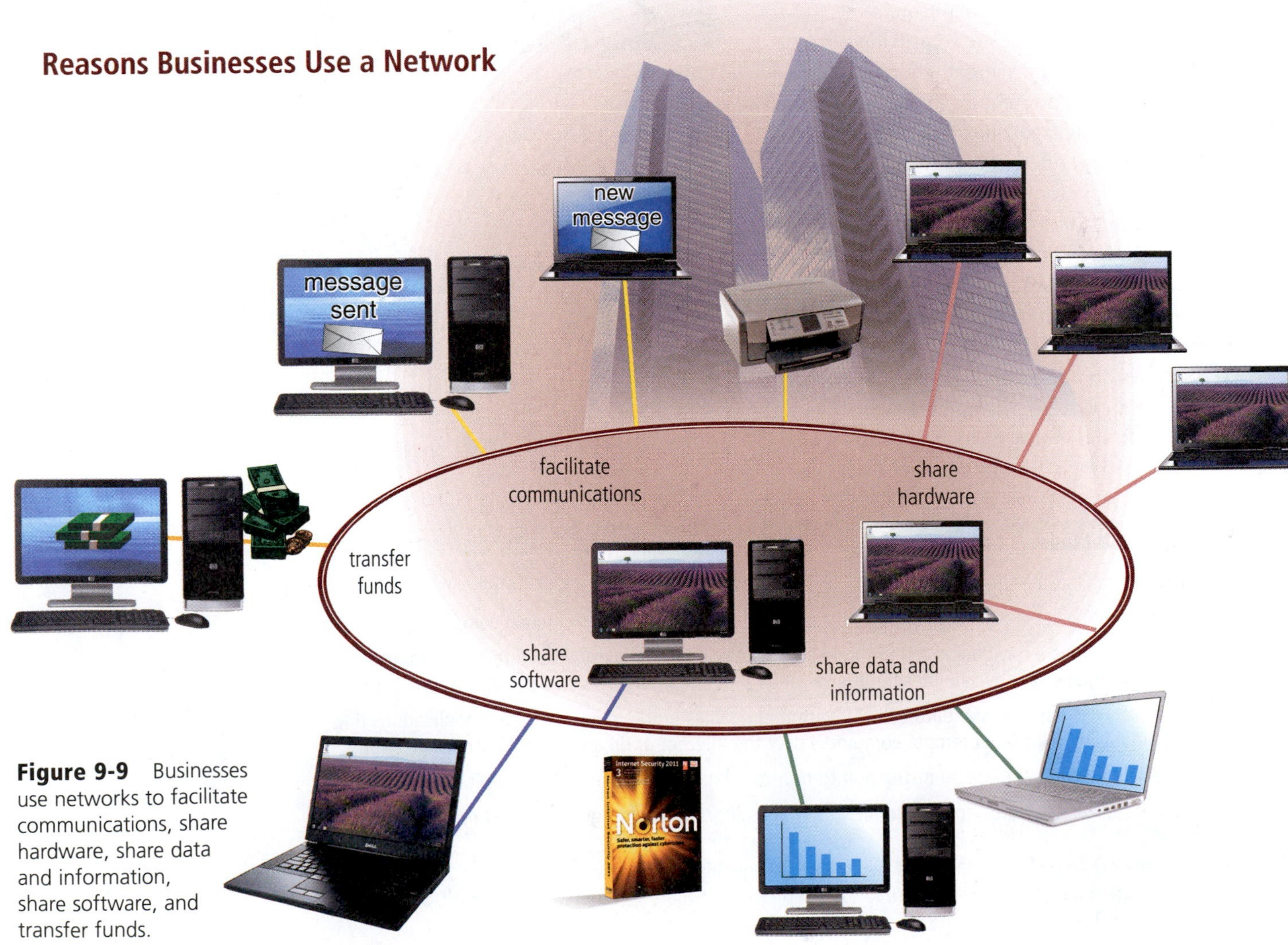

Figure 9-9 Businesses use networks to facilitate communications, share hardware, share data and information, share software, and transfer funds.

- Sharing data and information — In a networked environment, any authorized computer user can access data and information stored on other computers on the network. A large company, for example, might have a database of customer information. Any authorized person, including a mobile user with a smart phone or other device connected to the network, has access to the database.

  Most businesses use a standard, such as *EDI* (*electronic data interchange*), that defines how data transmits across telephone lines or other means. For example, companies use EDI to handle product catalog distribution, bids, requests for quotations, proposals, order placement, shipping notifications, invoicing, and payment processing. EDI enables businesses to operate with a minimum amount of paperwork.

  Another popular data sharing standard is XML, briefly described earlier in this chapter. Using XML, Web programmers can create one version of a Web page that then can be displayed in a form appropriate for a variety of display devices. XML also is used in RSS, which is used to distribute content, such as news, to subscribers.
- Sharing software — Users connected to a network have access to software on the network. To support multiple users' access of software, most vendors sell network versions or site licenses of their software, which usually cost less than buying individual copies of the software for each computer. A *network license* is a legal agreement that allows multiple users to access the software on a server simultaneously. The network license fee usually is based on the number of users or the number of computers attached to the network. A *site license* is a legal agreement that permits users to install the software on multiple computers — usually at a volume discount.
- Transferring funds — Called *electronic funds transfer* (*EFT*), it allows users connected to a network to transfer money from one bank account to another via transmission media. Both businesses and consumers use EFT. Consumers use an ATM to access their bank account. Businesses deposit payroll checks directly in employees' bank accounts. Consumers use credit cards to make purchases from a retail Web site. Businesses use EFT to purchase and pay for goods purchased from vendors. Both businesses and consumers pay bills online, with which they instruct a bank to use EFT to pay creditors.

Instead of using the Internet or investing in and administering an internal network, some companies hire a value-added network provider for network functions. A *value-added network* (*VAN*) is a third-party business that provides networking services such as secure data and information transfer, storage, e-mail, and management reports. Some VANs charge an annual or monthly fee; others charge by service used.

For a technical discussion about networks, read the High-Tech Talk article on page 498.

LANs, MANs, and WANs

Networks usually are classified as a local area network, metropolitan area network, or wide area network. The main differentiation among these classifications is their area of coverage, as described in the following pages. Read Looking Ahead 9-1 for a look at another type of network.

LOOKING AHEAD 9-1

Body Area Networks Sense Intentions

Local area networks literally can move over when a *body area network* (BAN) makes the scene in a few years. This set of wearable or implanted body sensors will turn the body into a human router. The devices will communicate wirelessly and transmit data from the body to another device that performs an action.

For example, you can save a word processing document to a device on your wrist, walk to a printer, and just touch the printer with your hand to print. Or, merely by shaking hands, you can transfer information from a business card stored on your wrist device to another device worn by a business colleague.

Researchers actively are pursuing the BAN architecture and applications. Many of the uses are being developed for physical rehabilitation, interactive games, and human interaction with computers. Each year experts in the fields of computer science, electrical engineering, biomedical engineering, and medicine meet at the BodyNet conference to exchange ideas.

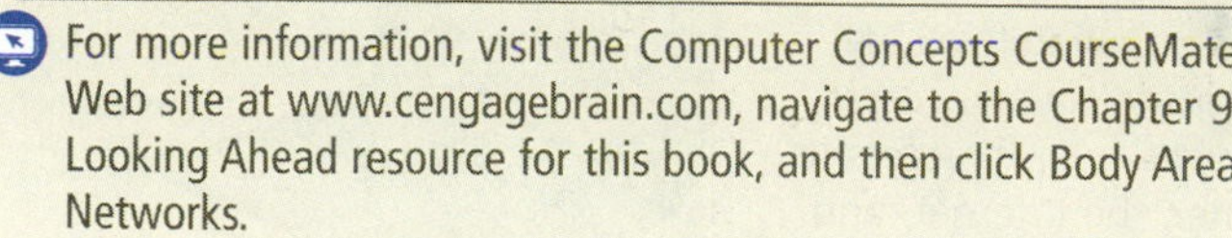

For more information, visit the Computer Concepts CourseMate Web site at www.cengagebrain.com, navigate to the Chapter 9 Looking Ahead resource for this book, and then click Body Area Networks.

LAN A **local area network (LAN)** is a network that connects computers and devices in a limited geographical area such as a home, school computer laboratory, office building (Figure 9-10), or closely positioned group of buildings. Each computer or device on the network, called a *node*, often shares resources such as printers, large hard disks, and programs. Often, the nodes are connected via cables.

A **wireless LAN (WLAN)** is a LAN that uses no physical wires. Computers and devices that access a wireless LAN must have built-in wireless capability or the appropriate wireless network card, USB network adapter, ExpressCard module, PC Card, or flash card. Very often, a WLAN communicates with a wired LAN for access to its resources, such as software, hardware, and the Internet (Figure 9-11).

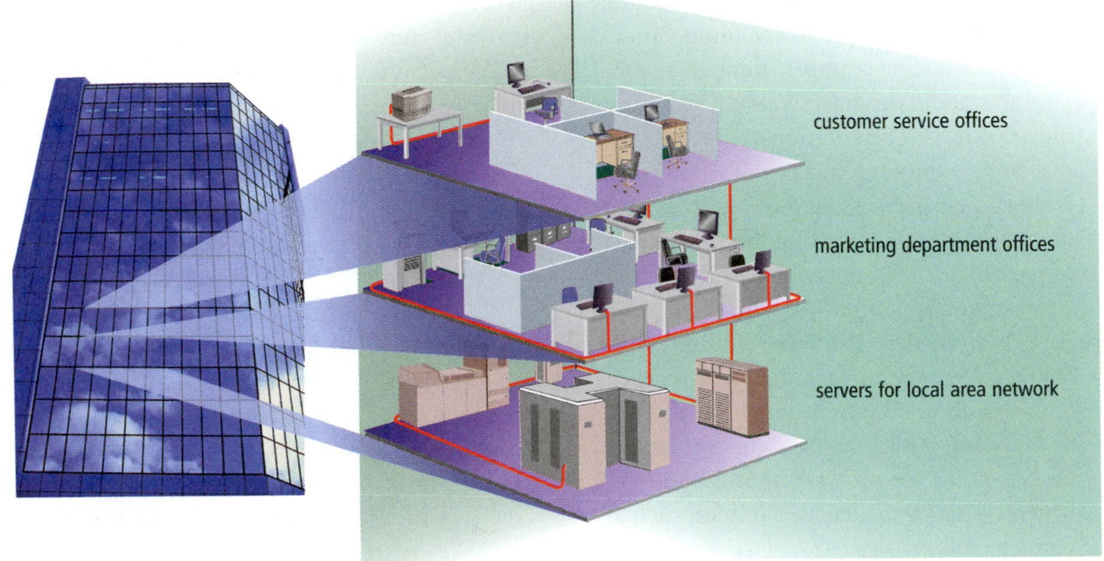

Figure 9-10 Computers on different floors access the same local area network (LAN) in an office building.

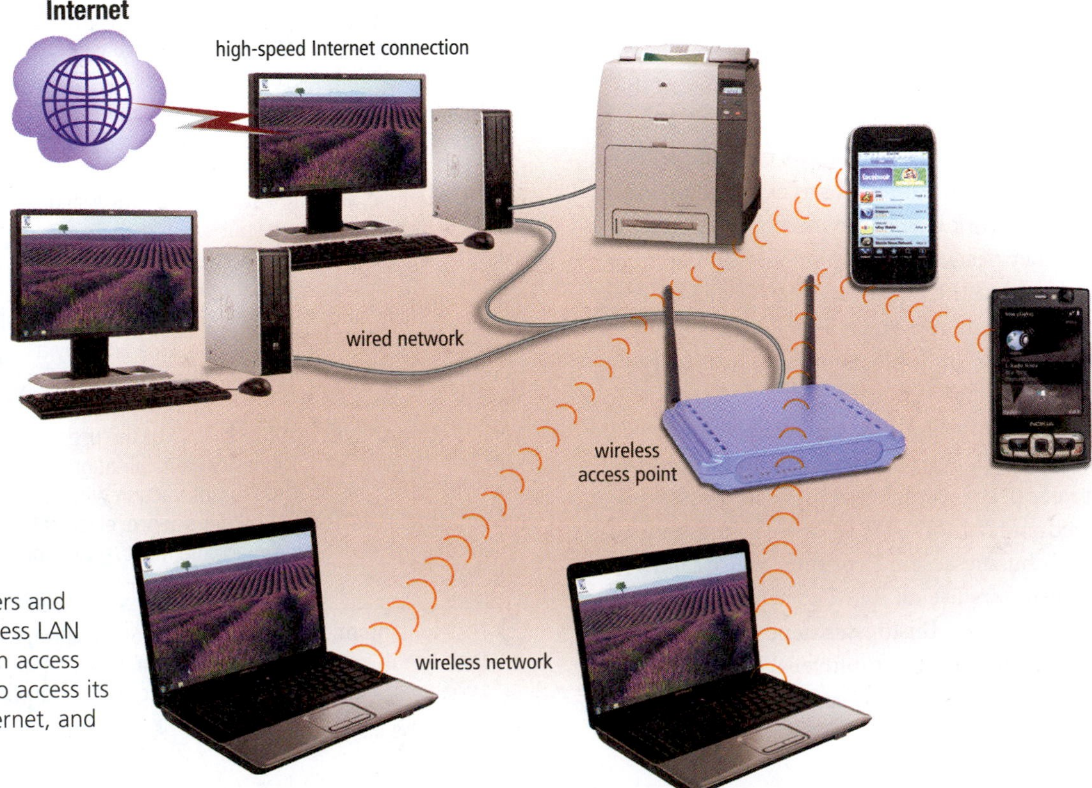

Figure 9-11 Computers and mobile devices on a wireless LAN often communicate via an access point with a wired LAN to access its software, printer, the Internet, and other resources.

MAN A *metropolitan area network* (*MAN*) is a high-speed network that connects local area networks in a metropolitan area such as a city or town and handles the bulk of communications activity across that region. A MAN typically includes one or more LANs, but covers a smaller geographic area than a WAN.

A MAN usually is managed by a consortium of users or by a single network provider that sells the service to the users. Local and state governments, for example, regulate some MANs. Telephone companies, cable television operators, and other organizations provide users with connections to the MAN.

WAN A **wide area network** (**WAN**) is a network that covers a large geographic area (such as a city, country, or the world) using a communications channel that combines many types of media such as telephone lines, cables, and radio waves (Figure 9-12). A WAN can be one large network or can consist of two or more LANs connected together. The Internet is the world's largest WAN.

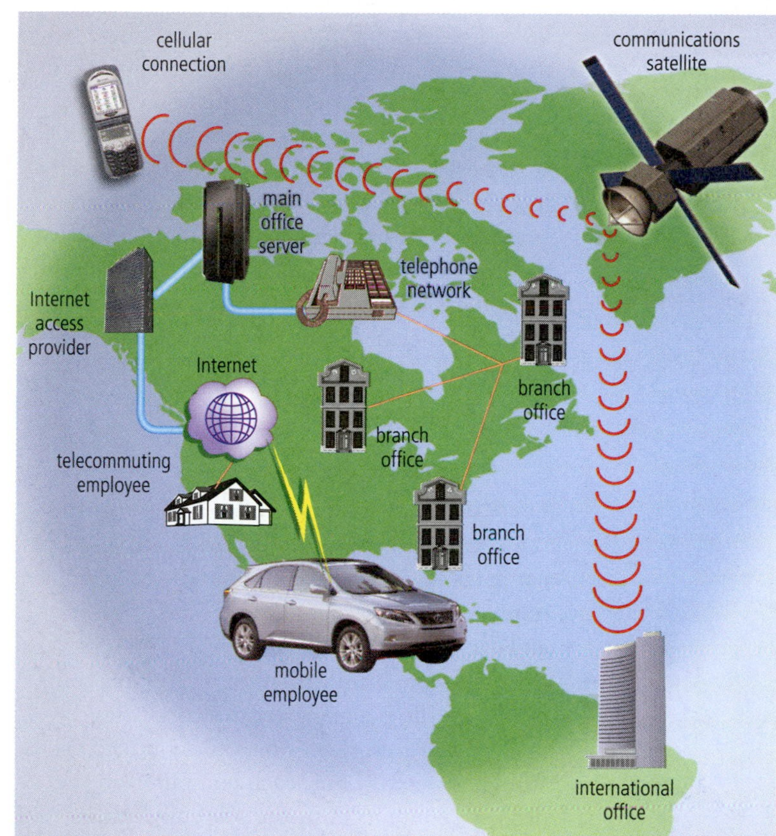

Figure 9-12 An example of a WAN.

Network Architectures

The design of computers, devices, and media in a network, sometimes called the *network architecture*, is categorized as either client/server or peer-to-peer. The following sections discuss these network architectures.

Client/Server On a **client/server network**, one or more computers act as a server, and the other computers on the network request services from the server (Figure 9-13). A **server**, sometimes called a *host computer*, controls access to the hardware, software, and other resources on the network and provides a centralized storage area for programs, data, and information. The **clients** are other computers and mobile devices on the network that rely on the server for its resources. For example, a server might store a database of customers. Clients on the network (company employees) access the customer database on the server.

Some servers, called *dedicated servers*, perform a specific task and can be placed with other dedicated servers to perform multiple

Figure 9-13 On a client/server network, one or more computers act as a server, and the clients access the server(s).

tasks. For example, a *file server* stores and manages files. A *print server* manages printers and documents being printed. A *database server* stores and provides access to a database. A *network server* manages network traffic (activity). A *Web server* is a computer that delivers requested Web pages to your computer.

Although it can connect a smaller number of computers, a client/server network typically provides an efficient means to connect 10 or more computers. Most client/server networks require a person to serve as a network administrator because of the large size of the network.

Peer-to-Peer One type of *peer-to-peer network* is a simple, inexpensive network that typically connects fewer than 10 computers. Each computer, called a *peer*, has equal responsibilities and capabilities, sharing hardware (such as a printer), data, or information with other computers on the peer-to-peer network (Figure 9-14). Each computer stores files on its own storage devices. Thus, each computer on the network contains both the server operating system and application software. All computers on the network share any peripheral device(s) attached to any computer. For example, one computer may have a laser printer and a scanner, while another has an ink-jet printer and an external hard disk.

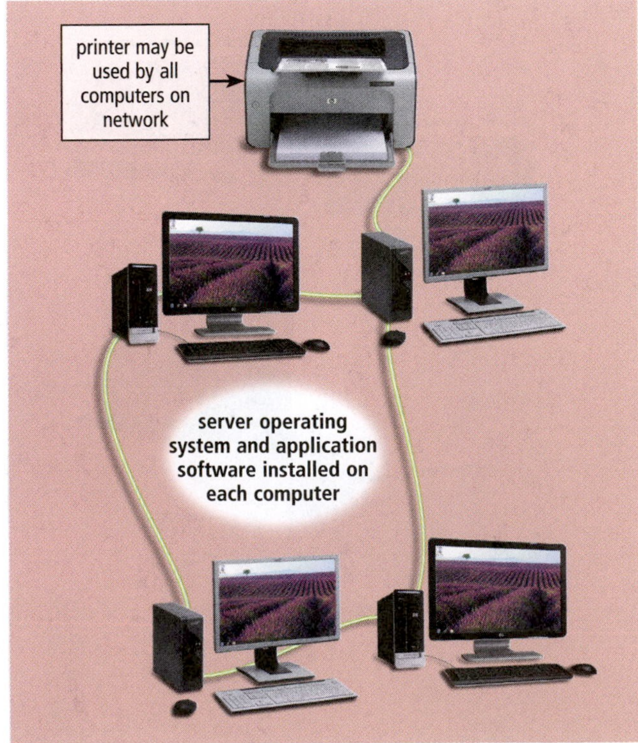

Figure 9-14 Each computer on a peer-to-peer network shares its hardware and software with other computers on the network.

Peer-to-peer networks are ideal for very small businesses and home users. Some operating systems, such as Windows, include a peer-to-peer networking utility that allows users to set up a peer-to-peer network. Read Ethics & Issues 9-2 for a related discussion.

ETHICS & ISSUES 9-2

Should Internet Access Providers Be Allowed to Control Your Internet Usage?

People often compare the anything-goes early days of the Internet and Web to a wild frontier. Internet access providers simply offered customers an Internet connection and exerted no control over how the customer chose to use the connection, in much the same way that a telephone company does not control who a customer calls, the length of a call, or the reason for the call. A provision of telecommunications law, known as safe harbor, provides immunity to telecommunications companies if illegal activity occurs over their networks, as long as the company is not examining the content of any activity on its network or content stored by customers on its servers.

With the increase in peer-to-peer networking, some Internet access providers' customers are stretching the providers' networks to their limits by sharing large files. Often, the files are illegal copies of music, movies, and software. Some providers have begun controlling peer-to-peer Internet usage by sabotaging peer-to-peer Internet connections without notice. The Internet access providers argue that they are not examining the content of the shared files but simply are controlling certain types of Internet usage to the benefit of their other customers. Limiting such sharing allows other users to share the provider's resources fairly. Critics argue that Internet access provider meddling is illegal and, if allowed, could lead providers to implement further control over Internet usage.

Should Internet access providers be allowed to control your Internet usage? Why or why not? Should Internet access providers or telephone companies be allowed to monitor how you use your Internet or telephone connection? Why or why not?

Internet Peer-to-Peer Another type of peer-to-peer, called *P2P*, describes an Internet network on which users access each other's hard disks and exchange files directly over the Internet (Figure 9-15). This type of peer-to-peer network sometimes is called a *file sharing network* because users with compatible software and an Internet connection copy files from someone else's hard disk to their hard disks. As more users connect to the network, each user has access to shared files on other users' hard disks. When users log off the network, others no longer have access to their hard disks. To maintain an acceptable speed for communications, some implementations of P2P limit the number of users.

Examples of networking software that support P2P are BitTorrent, Gnutella, Kazaa, and LimeWire, which allow users to swap music and other files via the Web. For example, when one user requests a song, the program searches through lists of shared files — which are stored on one or more connected computers, called supernodes. If a match is found, the music file is copied from the computer on which it resides to the requesting computer. These programs initially stirred much controversy with respect to copyright infringement of music because they allowed users easily to copy music and movie files free from one computer to another. To help reduce copyright infringement, today's music and movie sharing services typically are fee based, and music and movie files often are encrypted as they travel across the Internet.

Many businesses also see an advantage to using P2P. That is, companies and employees can exchange files using P2P, freeing the company from maintaining a network server for this purpose. Business-to-business e-commerce Web sites find that P2P easily allows buyers and sellers to share company information such as product databases.

P2P

For more information, visit the Computer Concepts CourseMate Web site at www.cengagebrain.com, navigate to the Chapter 9 Web Link resource for this book, and then click P2P.

Network Topologies

A **network topology** refers to the layout of the computers and devices in a communications network. Three commonly used network topologies are star, bus, and ring. Most networks, including the Internet, use combinations of these topologies.

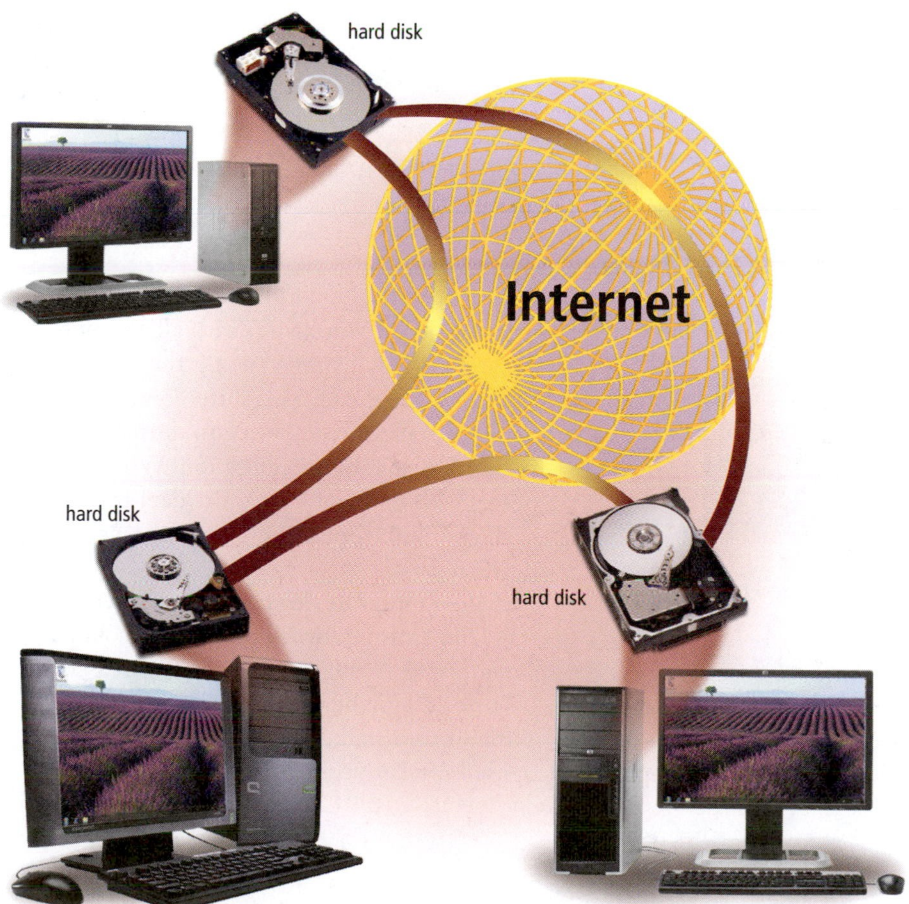

Figure 9-15 P2P describes an Internet network on which users connect to each other's hard disks and exchange files directly.

Star Network On a *star network*, all of the computers and devices (nodes) on the network connect to a central device, thus forming a star (Figure 9-16). Two types of devices that provide a common central connection point for nodes on the network are a *hub* and a *switch*. All data that transfers from one node to another passes through the hub or switch.

Star networks are fairly easy to install and maintain. Nodes can be added to and removed from the network with little or no disruption to the network.

On a star network, if one node fails, only that node is affected. The other nodes continue to operate normally. If the hub or switch fails, however, the entire network is inoperable until the device is repaired. Most large star networks, therefore, keep backup hubs or switches available in case the primary one fails.

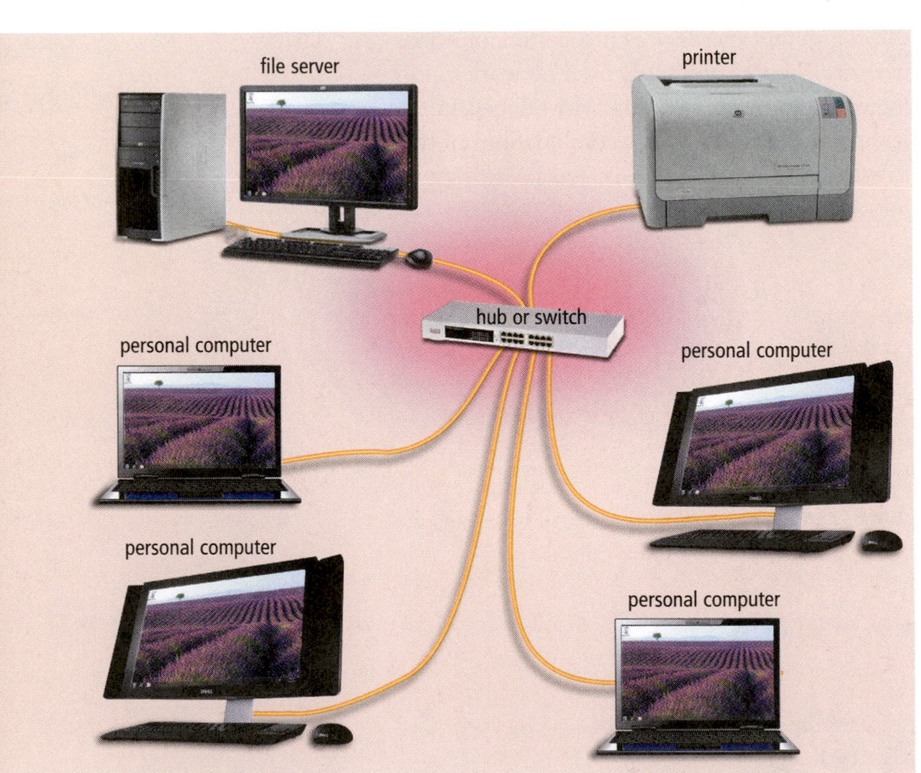

Figure 9-16 A star network contains a single, centralized hub or switch through which all the devices in the network communicate.

Bus Network A *bus network* consists of a single central cable, to which all computers and other devices connect (Figure 9-17). The *bus* is the physical cable that connects the computers and other devices. The bus in a bus network transmits data, instructions, and information in both directions. When a sending device transmits data, the address of the receiving device is included with the transmission so that the data is routed to the appropriate receiving device.

Bus networks are popular on LANs because they are inexpensive and easy to install. One advantage of the bus network is that computers and other devices can be attached and detached at any point on the bus without disturbing the rest of the network. Another advantage is that failure of one device usually does not affect the rest of the bus network. The greatest risk to a bus network is that the bus itself might become inoperable. If that happens, the network remains inoperative until the bus is back in working order.

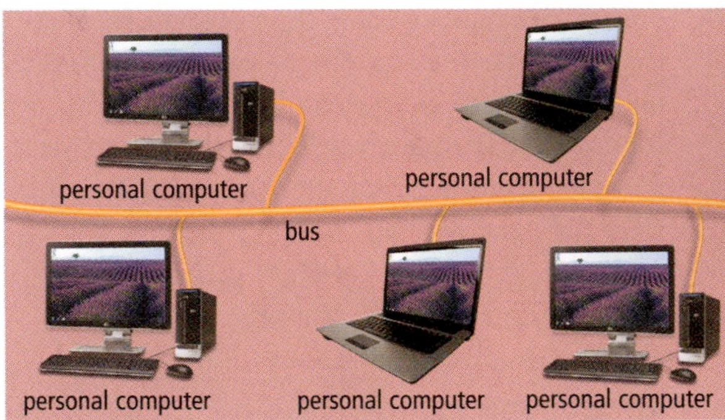

Figure 9-17 Devices in a bus network share a single data path.

Ring Network On a *ring network*, a cable forms a closed loop (ring) with all computers and devices arranged along the ring (Figure 9-18). Data transmitted on a ring network travels from device to device around the entire ring, in one direction. When a computer or device sends data, the data travels to each computer on the ring until it reaches its destination.

If a computer or device on a ring network fails, the entire network potentially could stop functioning. A ring network can span a larger distance than a bus network, but it is more difficult to install. The ring topology primarily is used for LANs, but also is used in WANs.

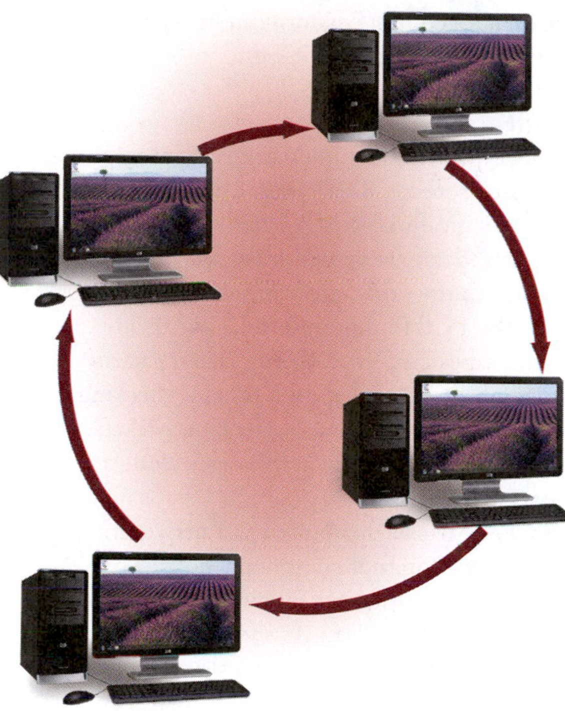

Figure 9-18 On a ring network, all connected devices form a continuous loop.

Intranets

Recognizing the efficiency and power of the Internet, many organizations apply Internet and Web technologies to their internal networks. An *intranet* (intra means within) is an internal network that uses Internet technologies. Intranets generally make company information accessible to employees and facilitate working in groups.

Simple intranet applications include electronic publishing of organizational materials such as telephone directories, event calendars, procedure manuals, employee benefits information, and job postings. Additionally, an intranet typically includes a connection to the Internet. More sophisticated uses of intranets include groupware applications such as project management, chat rooms, group scheduling, and video conferencing.

An intranet essentially is a small version of the Internet that exists within an organization. It has a Web server, supports Web pages containing multimedia, and is accessible via a Web browser such as Internet Explorer, Firefox, Opera, Safari, and Google Chrome. Users update information on the intranet by creating and posting a Web page, using a method similar to that used on the Internet.

Sometimes a company uses an *extranet*, which allows customers or suppliers to access part of its intranet. Package shipping companies, for example, allow customers to access their intranet to print air bills, schedule pickups, and even track shipped packages as the packages travel to their destinations.

Network Communications Standards

Today's networks connect terminals, devices, and computers from many different manufacturers across many types of networks, such as wide area, local area, and wireless. For the different devices on various types of networks to be able to communicate, the network must use similar techniques of moving data through the network from one application to another. For example, an IBM mainframe computer cannot communicate directly with an Apple Macintosh network — some form of translation must occur for devices on these two types of networks to communicate.

To alleviate the problems of incompatibility and ensure that hardware and software components can be integrated into any network, various organizations such as ANSI and IEEE (pronounced I triple E) propose, develop, and approve network standards. A *network standard* defines guidelines that specify the way computers access the medium to which they are attached, the type(s) of medium used, the speeds used on different types of networks, and the type(s) of physical cable and/or the wireless technology used. A standard that outlines characteristics of how two network devices communicate is called a *protocol*. Specifically, a protocol may define data format, coding schemes, error handling, and sequencing techniques. Hardware and software manufacturers design their products to meet the guidelines specified in a particular standard, so that their devices can communicate with the network.

The following pages discuss some of the more widely used network communications standards and protocols for both wired and wireless networks including Ethernet, token ring, TCP/IP, Wi-Fi, Bluetooth, UWB, IrDA, RFID, WiMAX, and WAP. Oftentimes, these network standards and protocols work together to move data through a network. Some of these standards define how a network is arranged physically;

others specify how messages travel along a network, and so on. Thus, as data moves through a network from one program to another, it may use one or more of these standards.

Ethernet

Ethernet is a network standard that specifies no central computer or device on the network (nodes) should control when data can be transmitted; that is, each node attempts to transmit data when it determines the network is available to receive communications. If two computers on an Ethernet network attempt to send data at the same time, a collision will occur, and the computers must attempt to send their messages again.

Ethernet is based on a bus topology, but Ethernet networks can be wired in a star pattern. The Ethernet standard defines guidelines for the physical configuration of a network, e.g., cabling, network cards, and nodes. Today, Ethernet is the most popular network standard for LANs because it is relatively inexpensive and easy to install and maintain.

Ethernet networks often use cables to transmit data. At a 10 Mbps (million bits per second) data transfer rate, the original Ethernet standard is not very fast by today's standards. A more recent Ethernet standard, called *Fast Ethernet*, has a data transfer rate of 100 Mbps, ten times faster than the original standard. *Gigabit Ethernet* provides an even higher speed of transmission, with transfer rates of 1 Gbps (1 billion bits per second). The *10-Gigabit Ethernet* standard supports transfer rates up to 10 Gbps, *40-Gigabit Ethernet* up to 40 Gbps, and *100-Gigabit Ethernet* up to 100 Gbps.

Ethernet
For more information, visit the Computer Concepts CourseMate Web site at www.cengagebrain.com, navigate to the Chapter 9 Web Link resource for this book, and then click Ethernet.

Token Ring

The **token ring** standard specifies that computers and devices on the network share or pass a special signal, called a token, in a unidirectional manner and in a preset order. A *token* is a special series of bits that function like a ticket. The device with the token can transmit data over the network. Only one token exists per network. This ensures that only one computer transmits data at a time.

Token ring is based on a ring topology (although it can use a star topology). The token ring standard defines guidelines for the physical configuration of a network, e.g., cabling, network cards, and devices. Some token ring networks connect up to 72 devices. Others use a special type of wiring that allows up to 260 connections. The data transfer rate on a token ring network can be 4 Mbps, 16 Mbps, 100 Mbps, or 1 Gbps.

TCP/IP

Short for Transmission Control Protocol/ Internet Protocol, **TCP/IP** is a network standard, specifically a protocol, that defines how messages (data) are routed from one end of a network to the other, ensuring the data arrives correctly. TCP/IP describes rules for dividing messages into small pieces, called *packets*; providing addresses for each packet; checking for and detecting errors; sequencing packets; and regulating the flow of messages along the network.

TCP/IP has been adopted as a network standard for Internet communications. Thus, all hosts on the Internet follow the rules defined in this standard. As shown in Figure 9-19, Internet communications also use other standards, such as the Ethernet standard, as data is routed to its destination.

When a computer sends data over the Internet, the data is divided into packets. Each packet contains the data, as well as the recipient (destination), the origin (sender), and the sequence information used to reassemble the data at the destination. Each packet travels along the fastest individual available path to the recipient's computer via communications devices called routers.

This technique of breaking a message into individual packets, sending the packets along the best route available, and then reassembling the data is called *packet switching*.

? FAQ 9-2

Can IP addresses be used to determine a computer or device's location?

In many cases, you can determine a computer's or a device's location from its IP address. For example, if an IP address begins with 132.170, a small amount of research will discover that the University of Central Florida assigns IP addresses beginning with these numbers; however, additional research would be necessary to determine where the computer or mobile device is located on the network. Web sites such as IP2Location allow visitors to find a location by entering an IP address.

For more information, visit the Computer Concepts CourseMate Web site at www.cengagebrain.com, navigate to the Chapter 9 FAQ resource for this book, and then click IP Addresses.

Example of How Communications Standards Work Together

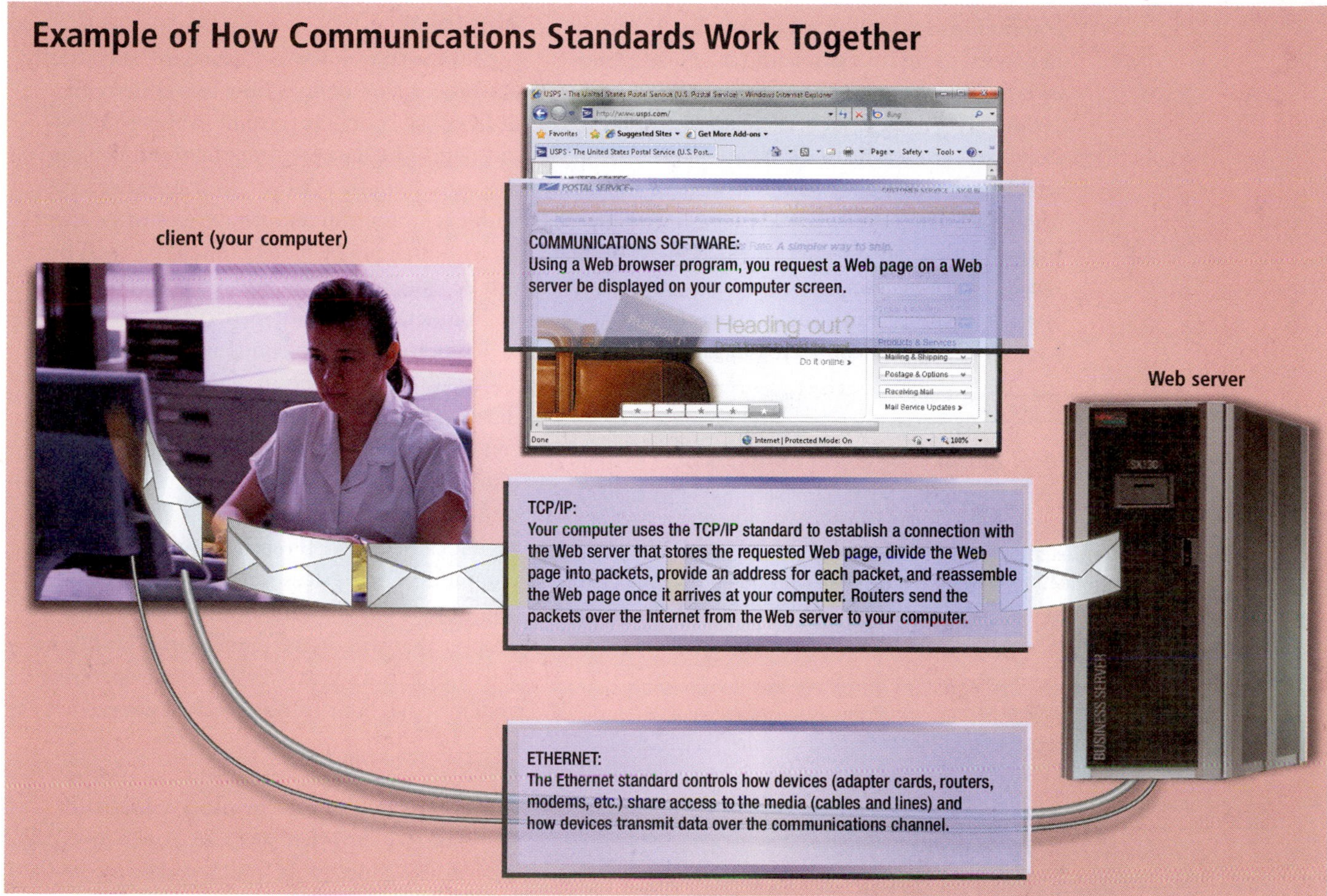

Figure 9-19 Network communications use a variety of standards to ensure that data travels correctly to its destination. Some standards used in Internet communications include the TCP/IP and Ethernet standards, as shown in this figure.

Wi-Fi

Computers and devices that have the appropriate wireless capability can communicate via radio waves with other computers or devices using **Wi-Fi** (wireless fidelity), which identifies any network based on the 802.11 standards. Developed by IEEE, **802.11** is a series of network standards that specifies how two wireless devices communicate over the air with each other. The table in Figure 9-20 outlines various 802.11 standards and their data transfer rates. A designation of 802.11 a/b/g on a computer or device indicates it supports those three standards (a, b, and g). The newest standard, 802.11n, uses multiple transmitters and receivers, known as *MIMO* (multiple-input multiple-output), to reach speeds from 2 to 10 times faster than 802.11g.

Wi-Fi sometimes is referred to as wireless Ethernet because it uses techniques similar to the Ethernet standard to specify how physically to configure a wireless network. Thus, Wi-Fi networks easily can be integrated with wired Ethernet networks. When a Wi-Fi network accesses the Internet, it works in conjunction with the TCP/IP network standard.

Wi-Fi Certified products are guaranteed to be able to communicate with each other. Most of today's computers and many mobile devices, such as smart phones and handheld game consoles, are Wi-Fi enabled.

One popular use of the Wi-Fi network standard is in hot spots (discussed earlier in this chapter) that offer mobile users the ability to connect to the Internet with their Wi-Fi enabled wireless computers and devices. Many homes and small businesses also use Wi-Fi to network computers and devices wirelessly. In open or outdoor areas free from interference, the computers or devices should be within 300 feet of each other. In closed areas, the wireless network range is about 100 feet. To obtain

802.11 Series of Standards

Standard	Transfer Rates
802.11	1 or 2 Mbps
802.11a	Up to 54 Mbps
802.11b	Up to 11 Mbps
802.11g	54 Mbps and higher
802.11n	108 Mbps and higher

Figure 9-20 A comparison of standards in the 802.11 series.

communications at the maximum distances, you may need to install extra hardware. Read Ethics & Issues 9-3 for a related discussion.

Some large areas, such as college or business campuses, are set up as a *Wi-Fi mesh network*, in which each mesh node routes its data to the next available node until the data reaches its destination — usually an Internet connection. A Wi-Fi mesh network is more flexible than a hot spot because each node in a mesh network does not have to be directly connected to the Internet.

? FAQ 9-3

How do I know where hot spots exist?

If your computer has wireless capability that is enabled, Windows automatically will search for hot spots. If a hot spot exists, Windows will display an indication in the notification area on the taskbar. New notebook computers also may have a switch that allows you to determine if a hot spot exists, without turning on the computer.

For more information, visit the Computer Concepts CourseMate Web site at www.cengagebrain.com, navigate to the Chapter 9 FAQ resource for this book, and then click Hot Spots.

ETHICS & ISSUES 9-3

Would You Connect to an Unsecured Wireless Network?

Police raided a home and detained a man suspected of using his computer for a serious crime. Upon further analysis, an unknown individual had used the man's unsecured home wireless network to cover up his or her involvement in the crime. If you turn on your wireless notebook computer only to see that you can connect to a nearby home or business's wireless network and access the Internet for free, you may find yourself in an ethical quandary. Because of a lack of knowledge about how to secure wireless home networks, many people accidentally leave their networks open to use by anybody in the area or driving or walking past. One study found that 12 percent of consumers have accessed unsecured wireless connections. Some people are canceling their own costly service and secretly using the stolen connections full-time. In most areas, the law is unclear or nonexistent regarding such unauthorized use, while some areas ban any unauthorized access. Some lawmakers even support punishing those who leave their networks unsecured.

Would you use your neighbor's unsecured wireless home network? Why or why not? What would you do if you found out that someone was using your wireless home network? How should the law handle such abuse, and how should violators be punished? Should those leaving their networks unsecured be punished as well? Why?

Bluetooth

Bluetooth is a network standard, specifically a protocol, that defines how two Bluetooth devices use short-range radio waves to transmit data. The data transfers between devices at a rate of up to 3 Mbps. To communicate with each other, Bluetooth devices often must be within about 10 meters (about 33 feet) but can be extended to 100 meters with additional equipment.

A Bluetooth device contains a small chip that allows it to communicate with other Bluetooth devices. Examples of Bluetooth-enabled devices can include desktop computers, notebook computers, handheld computers, smart phones, headsets, keyboards, mouse devices, microphones, digital cameras, GPS receivers, and printers. For computers and devices not Bluetooth-enabled, you can purchase a Bluetooth wireless port adapter that will convert an existing USB port into a Bluetooth port. Most current operating systems have built-in Bluetooth support.

UWB

UWB, which stands for **ultra-wideband**, is a network standard that specifies how two UWB devices use short-range radio waves to communicate at high speeds with each other. At distances of 10 meters (about 33 feet), the data transfer rate is 110 Mbps. At closer distances, such as 2 meters (about 6.5 feet), the transfer rate is at least 480 Mbps. UWB can transmit signals through doors and other obstacles. Because of its high transfer rates, UWB is best suited for transmission of large files such as video, graphics, and audio. Examples of UWB uses include wirelessly transferring video from a digital video camera, printing pictures from a digital camera, downloading media to a portable media player, or displaying a slide show on a projector.

IrDA

As discussed in Chapter 4, some computers and devices use the **IrDA** standard to transmit data wirelessly to each other via infrared (IR) light waves. The devices transfer data at rates from 115 Kbps (thousand bits per second) to 4 Mbps between their IrDA ports.

Infrared requires a *line-of-sight transmission*; that is, the sending device and the receiving device must be in line with each other so that nothing obstructs the path of the infrared light wave. Because Bluetooth and UWB do not require line-of-sight transmission, some industry experts predict that these technologies will replace infrared.

RFID

RFID (*radio frequency identification*) is a standard, specifically a protocol, that defines how a network uses radio signals to communicate with a tag placed in or attached to an object, an animal, or a person. The tag, called a transponder, consists of an antenna and a memory chip that contains the information to be transmitted via radio waves. Through an antenna, an RFID reader, also called a transceiver, reads the radio signals and transfers the information to a computer or computing device.

RFID tags are passive or active. An active RFID tag contains a battery that runs the chip's circuitry and broadcasts a signal to the RFID reader. A passive RFID tag does not contain a battery and thus cannot send a signal until the reader activates the tag's antenna by sending out electromagnetic waves. Because passive RFID tags contain no battery, these can be small enough to be embedded in skin.

Depending on the type of RFID reader, the distance between the tag and the reader ranges from 5 inches to 15 feet. Readers can be handheld or embedded in an object such as a doorway or the tollbooth shown in Figure 9-21.

RFID
For more information, visit the Computer Concepts CourseMate Web site at www.cengagebrain.com, navigate to the Chapter 9 Web Link resource for this book, and then click RFID.

How Electronic RFID Toll Collection Works

Step 1
Motorist purchases an RFID transponder or RFID tag and attaches it to the vehicle's windshield.

Step 2
As the vehicle approaches the tollbooth, the RFID reader in the tollbooth sends a radio wave that activates the windshield-mounted RFID tag. The activated tag sends vehicle information to the RFID reader.

high-speed camera

RFID reader

RFID tag

Step 3
The RFID reader sends the vehicle information to the lane controller. The lane controller, which is part of a local area network, transmits the vehicle information to a central computer that subtracts the toll from the motorist's account. If the vehicle does not have an RFID tag, a high-speed camera takes a picture of the license plate and the computer prints a violation notice, which is mailed to the motorist.

Figure 9-21 This figure shows how electronic RFID toll collection works.

WiMAX

WiMAX (Worldwide Interoperability for Microwave Access), also known as **802.16**, is a network standard developed by IEEE that specifies how wireless devices communicate over the air in a wide area. Using the WiMAX standard, computers or devices with the appropriate WiMAX wireless capability communicate via radio waves with other computers or devices via a WiMAX tower. The WiMAX tower, which can cover up to a 30-mile radius, connects to the Internet or to another WiMAX tower.

Two types of WiMAX specifications are fixed wireless and mobile wireless. With fixed wireless WiMAX, a customer accesses the Internet from a desktop computer at home or other permanent location. Mobile wireless WiMAX, by contrast, enables users to access the WiMAX network with mobile computers and mobile devices such as smart phones. Fixed wireless WiMAX has data transfer rates up to 40 Mbps, while mobile wireless WiMAX has data transfer rates up to 15 Mbps.

The WiMAX standard provides wireless broadband Internet access at a reasonable cost over long distances to business and home users, including rural and remote areas. WiMAX, similar to Wi-Fi, connects mobile users to the Internet via hot spots. Many computers and mobile devices such as smart phones have built-in WiMAX capability. Some game consoles also support the WiMAX standard.

Figure 9-22
A WAP-enabled smart phone.

WAP

The **Wireless Application Protocol (WAP)** is a standard, specifically a protocol, that specifies how some mobile devices such as smart phones can display the content of Internet services such as the Web, e-mail, and chat rooms (Figure 9-22). To display a Web page on a smart phone, the phone should contain a microbrowser. WAP works in conjunction with the TCP/IP network standard.

WAP uses a client/server network. The wireless device contains the client software, which connects to the Internet access provider's server.

Communications Software

Communications software consists of programs that (1) help users establish a connection to another computer or network; (2) manage the transmission of data, instructions, and information; and (3) provide an interface for users to communicate with one another. The first two are system software and the third is application software. Chapter 3 presented a variety of examples of application software for communications: e-mail, FTP, Web browser, newsgroup/message boards, chat rooms, instant messaging, video conferencing, and VoIP.

Sometimes, communications devices are preprogrammed to accomplish communications tasks. Other communications devices require separate communications software to ensure proper transmission of data. Communications software works with the network standards and protocols just discussed to ensure data moves through the network or the Internet correctly. Communications software usually is bundled with the operating system or purchased network devices.

Often, a computer has various types of communications software, each serving a different purpose. One type of communications software, for example, helps users establish an Internet connection using wizards, dialog boxes, and other on-screen messages. Another allows home and small office users to configure wired and wireless networks and connect devices to an existing network.

Communications over the Telephone Network

The *public switched telephone network* (*PSTN*) is the worldwide telephone system that handles voice-oriented telephone calls (Figure 9-23). Nearly the entire telephone network today uses digital technology, with the exception of the final link from the local telephone company to a home, which often is analog.

The telephone network is an integral part of computer communications. Data, instructions, and information are transmitted over the telephone network using dial-up lines or dedicated lines. The following sections discuss various types of lines that use the telephone network for data communications.

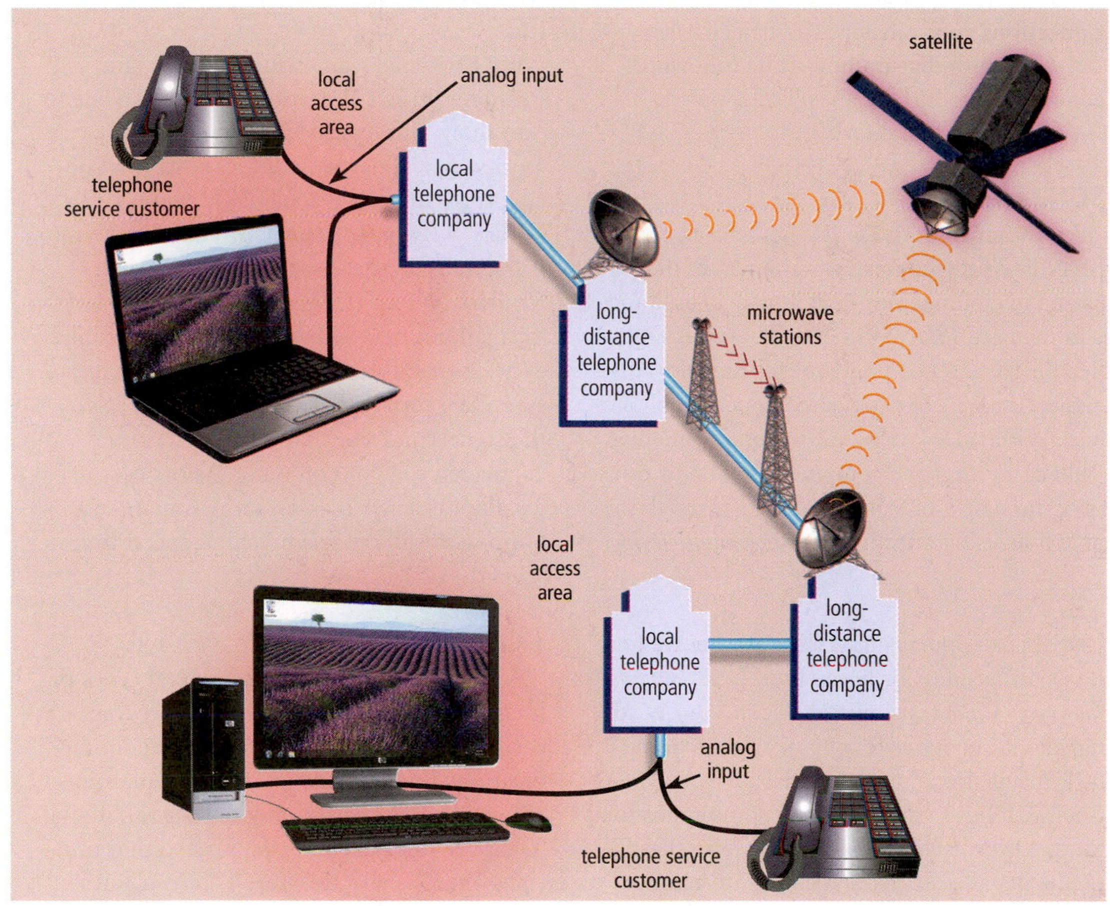

Figure 9-23
A sample telephone network configuration.

Dial-Up Lines

A **dial-up line** is a temporary connection that uses one or more analog telephone lines for communications. A dial-up connection is not permanent. Using a dial-up line to connect computers costs no more than making a regular telephone call.

Dedicated Lines

A **dedicated line** is a type of always-on connection that is established between two communications devices (unlike a dial-up line where the connection is reestablished each time it is used). The quality and consistency of the connection on a dedicated line are better than a dial-up line because dedicated lines provide a constant connection.

Businesses often use dedicated lines to connect geographically distant offices. Dedicated lines can be either analog or digital. Digital lines increasingly are connecting home and business users to networks around the globe because they transmit data and information at faster rates than analog lines.

Five types of digital dedicated lines are ISDN lines, DSL, FTTP, T-carrier lines, and ATM. Although cable television (CATV) lines and fixed wireless are not a type of telephone line, they are very popular ways for the home user to connect to the Internet. Fixed wireless Internet connections use an antenna on your house or business to communicate with a tower location via radio signals. Later sections in this chapter discuss the use of CATV lines and radio signals to connect to the Internet.

The table in Figure 9-24 lists the approximate monthly costs of various types of Internet

Speeds of Various Internet Connections

Type of Line	Approximate Monthly Cost	Transfer Rates
Dial-up	Local or long-distance rates	Up to 56 Kbps
ISDN	\$10 to \$40	Up to 1.54 Mbps
DSL	\$13 to \$70	128 Kbps to 8.45 Mbps
Cable TV (CATV)	\$20 to \$50	128 Kbps to 52 Mbps
FTTP	\$35 to \$180	5 Mbps to 100 Mbps
Fixed wireless	\$35 to \$80	256 Kbps to 10 Mbps
Fractional T1	\$200 to \$700	128 Kbps to 768 Kbps
T1	\$400 to \$1,600	1.544 Mbps
T3	\$5,000 to \$15,000	44.736 Mbps
ATM	\$3,000 or more	155 Mbps to 622 Mbps, can reach 10 Gbps

Figure 9-24 The speeds of various lines that can be used to connect to the Internet.

connections and transfer rates (speeds), as compared with dial-up lines. The following sections discuss ISDN lines, DSL, FTTP, T-carrier lines, and ATM.

ISDN Lines

For the small business and home user, an ISDN line provides faster transfer rates than dial-up telephone lines. Not as widely used today as in the past, *ISDN* (Integrated Services Digital Network) is a set of standards for digital transmission of data over standard copper telephone lines. With ISDN, the same telephone line that could carry only one computer signal now can carry three or more signals at once through the same line, using a technique called *multiplexing*.

DSL

DSL is a popular digital line alternative for the small business or home user. **DSL** (*Digital Subscriber Line*) transmits at fast speeds on existing standard copper telephone wiring. Some DSL installations include a dial tone, providing users with both voice and data communications. These DSL installations often require that filters be installed to reduce noise interference when voice communications share the same line.

ADSL is one of the more popular types of DSLs. As shown in Figure 9-25, *ADSL* (*asymmetric digital subscriber line*) is a type of DSL that supports faster transfer rates when receiving data (the *downstream rate*) than when sending data (the *upstream rate*). ADSL is ideal for Internet access because most users download more information from the Internet than they upload.

DSL

For more information, visit the Computer Concepts CourseMate Web site at www.cengagebrain.com, navigate to the Chapter 9 Web Link resource for this book, and then click DSL.

FTTP

FTTP, which stands for **Fiber to the Premises**, uses fiber-optic cable to provide extremely high-speed Internet access to a user's physical permanent location. Two specific types of FTTP are FTTH and FTTB. *FTTH* (*Fiber to the Home*) provides home users with Internet access via fiber-optic cable. Similarly, *FTTB* (*Fiber to the Building*) refers to small businesses that use fiber-optic cables to access the Internet. With FTTP service, an optical terminal at your location receives the signals and transfers them to a router connected to your computer. As the cost of installing fiber decreases, more homes and businesses will opt for this high-speed Internet access.

T-Carrier Lines

A **T-carrier line** is any of several types of long-distance digital telephone lines that carry multiple signals over a single communications line. Whereas a standard dial-up telephone line carries only one signal, digital T-carrier lines use multiplexing so that multiple signals share the line. T-carrier lines provide very fast data transfer rates. Only medium to large companies usually can afford the investment in T-carrier lines because these lines are so expensive.

The most popular T-carrier line is the *T1 line*. Businesses often use T1 lines to connect to the Internet. Many Internet access providers use T1 lines to connect to the Internet backbone. Home and small business users purchase

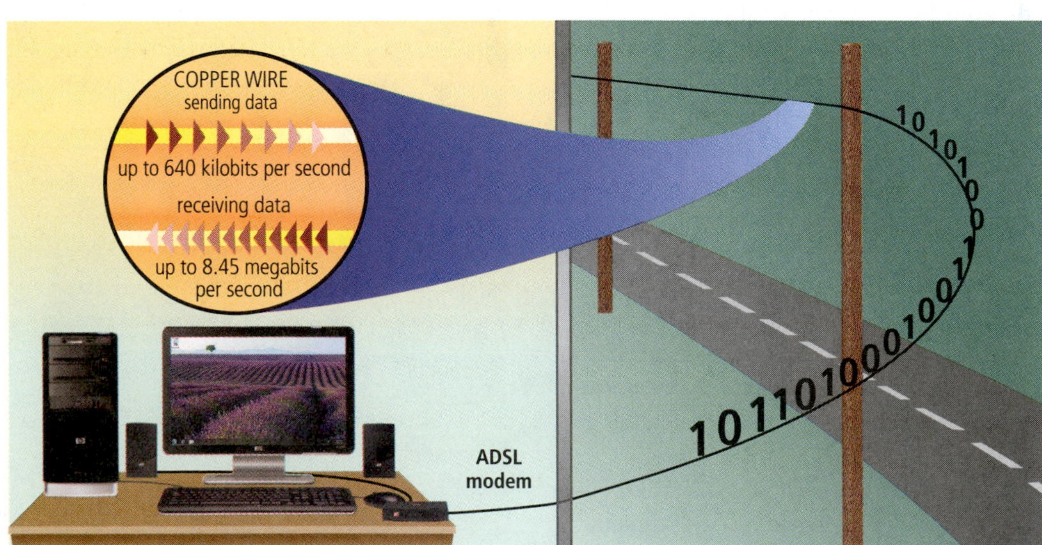

Figure 9-25 ADSL connections transmit data downstream (receiving) at a much faster rate than upstream (sending).

fractional T1, in which they share a connection to the T1 line with other users. Fractional T1 is slower than a dedicated T1 line, but it also is less expensive. Users who do not have other high-speed Internet access in their areas can opt for fractional T1. With fractional T1 lines, the data transfer rates become slower as additional users are added.

A *T3 line* is equal in speed to 28 T1 lines. T3 lines are quite expensive. Main users of T3 lines include large corporations, telephone companies, and Internet access providers connecting to the Internet backbone. The Internet backbone itself also uses T3 lines.

ATM

ATM (Asynchronous Transfer Mode) is a service that carries voice, data, video, and multimedia at very high speeds. Telephone networks, the Internet, and other networks with large amounts of traffic use ATM. Some experts predict that ATM eventually will become the Internet standard for data transmission, replacing T3 lines.

✔ QUIZ YOURSELF 9-2

Instructions: Find the true statement below. Then, rewrite the remaining false statements so that they are true.

1. A wireless LAN is a LAN that uses physical wires.
2. An intranet is an internal network that uses video conferencing technologies.
3. Five types of digital dial-up lines are ISDN lines, DSL, FTTP, T-carrier lines, and ATM.
4. In a client/server network, servers on the network access resources on the client.
5. In a networked environment, any unauthorized computer user can access data and information stored on other computers on the network.
6. P2P describes an Internet network on which users access each other's hard disks and exchange files directly over the Internet.

Quiz Yourself Online: To further check your knowledge of pages 470 through 485, visit the Computer Concepts CourseMate Web site at www.cengagebrain.com, navigate to the Chapter 9 Quiz Yourself resource for this book, and then click Objectives 3 – 8.

Communications Devices

A **communications device** is any type of hardware capable of transmitting data, instructions, and information between a sending device and a receiving device. At the sending end, a communications device sends the data, instructions, or information from the sending device to a communications channel. At the receiving end, a communications device receives the signals from the communications channel.

One type of communications device that connects a communications channel to a sending or receiving device such as a computer is a modem. Computers process data as digital signals. Data, instructions, and information travel along a communications channel in either analog or digital form, depending on the communications channel.

The following pages describe these types of communications devices: dial-up modems, digital modems, wireless modems, network cards, wireless access points, routers, and hubs and switches.

Dial-Up Modems

A *dial-up modem* is a communications device that can convert digital signals to analog signals and analog signals to digital signals, so that data can travel along an analog telephone line. Recall that an analog signal consists of a continuous electrical wave, and a digital signal consists of individual electrical pulses that represent bits grouped together into bytes. For example, a dial-up modem connected to a sending computer converts the computer's digital signals into analog signals. The analog signals then can travel over a standard telephone line. At the receiving end, if necessary, another dial-up modem converts the analog signals back into digital signals that a receiving computer can process.

A dial-up modem usually is in the form of an adapter card that you insert in an expansion slot on a computer's motherboard. One end of a standard telephone cord attaches to a port on the modem card and the other end plugs into a telephone outlet. Devices other than computers also use modems. A stand-alone fax machine, for example, has a modem that converts a scanned digitized image into an analog signal that is sent to a recipient's fax machine.

Digital Modems: ISDN, DSL, and Cable

A *digital modem* is a communications device that sends and receives data and information to and from a digital line. Three types of digital modems are ISDN modems, DSL modems, and cable modems. These modems typically include built-in Wi-Fi connectivity.

An *ISDN modem* sends digital data and information from a computer to an ISDN line and receives digital data and information from an ISDN line. A **DSL modem** sends digital data and information from a computer to a DSL line and receives digital data and information from a DSL line. ISDN and DSL modems usually are external devices, in which one end connects to the telephone line and the other end connects to a port on the system unit.

A **cable modem**, sometimes called a *broadband modem*, is a digital modem that sends and receives digital data over the cable television (CATV) network (Figure 9-26). With more than 110 million homes wired for cable television, cable modems provide a faster Internet access alternative to dial-up for the home user and can have speeds similar to DSL. Some users install an amplifier to improve the signal strength, which can fluctuate depending on many factors such as tasks you are performing and number of other connected users.

Cable Modems

For more information, visit the Computer Concepts CourseMate Web site at www.cengagebrain.com, navigate to the Chapter 9 Web Link resource for this book, and then click Cable Modems.

As shown in Figure 9-27, CATV service enters your home through a single line. To access the Internet using the CATV service, the CATV company installs a splitter inside your house. From the splitter, one part of the cable runs to your televisions and the other part connects to the cable modem. Many CATV operators provide a cable modem as part of the installation; some offer a rental plan, and others require that you purchase one separately. A cable modem usually is an external (separate) device, in which one end of a cable connects to a CATV wall outlet and the other end plugs in a port, such as on an Ethernet card, in the system unit. An Ethernet card is a type of network card. A later section discusses network cards.

FAQ 9-4

Which is better, DSL or cable Internet service?

Each has its own advantages. DSL uses a line that is not shared with other users in the neighborhood. With cable Internet service, by contrast, users might share the node with up to hundreds of other cable Internet users. Simultaneous access by many users can cause the cable Internet service to slow down. Cable Internet service, however, has widespread availability.

For more information, visit the Computer Concepts CourseMate Web site at www.cengagebrain.com, navigate to the Chapter 9 FAQ resource for this book, and then click DSL and Cable Internet Service.

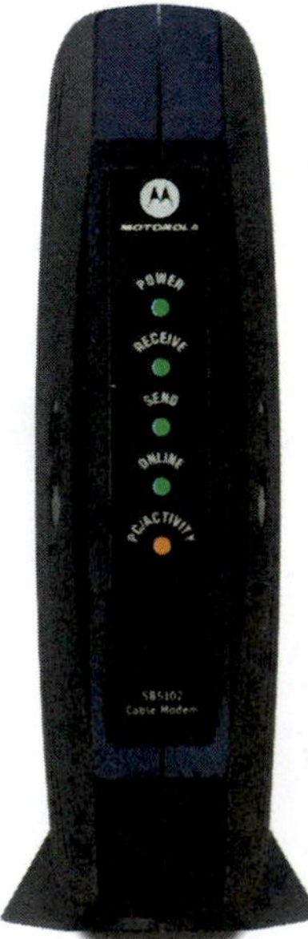

Figure 9-26 A cable modem.

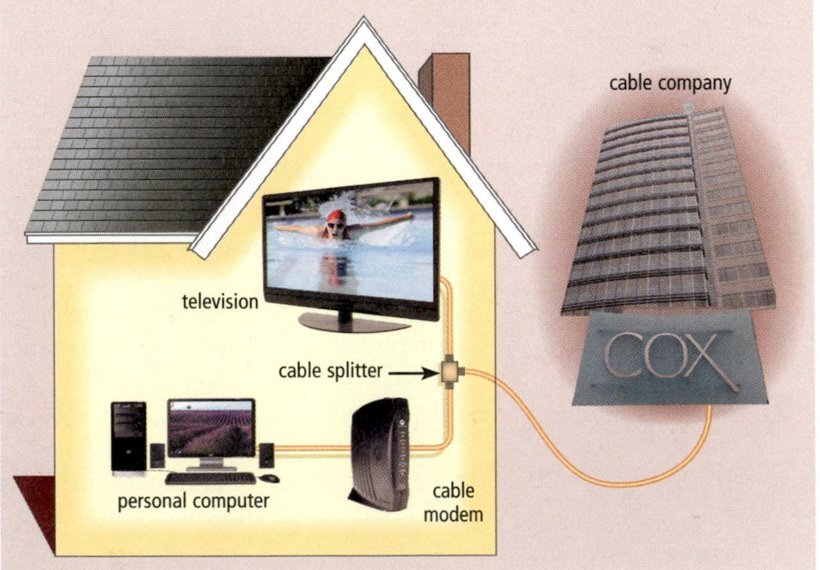

Figure 9-27 A typical cable modem installation.

Wireless Modems

Some mobile users have a **wireless modem** that uses the cell phone network to connect to the Internet wirelessly from a notebook computer, a smart phone, or other mobile device (Figure 9-28). Wireless modems, which have an external or built-in antenna, are available as USB flash drives, ExpressCard modules, PC Cards, and memory cards. Some smart phones also can function as a wireless modem when connected with a special cable to a personal computer.

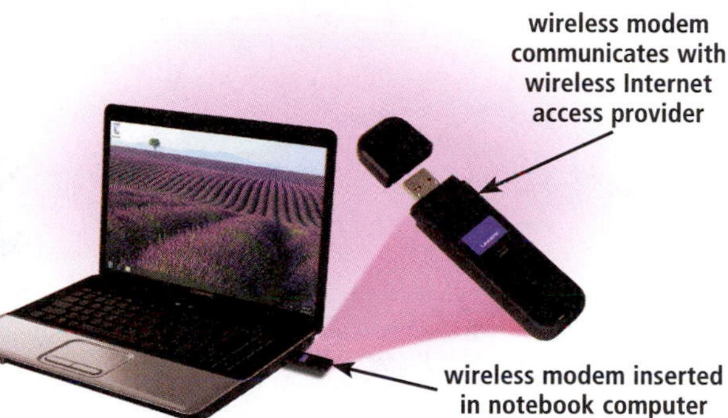

Figure 9-28 Wireless modems allow users to access the Internet wirelessly using the cell phone network.

Network Cards

A **network card**, sometimes called a *network interface card* (*NIC* pronounced nick), is a communications device that enables a computer or device that does not have built-in networking capability to access a network. The network card coordinates the transmission and receipt of data, instructions, and information to and from the computer or device containing the network card.

Network cards are available in a variety of styles (Figure 9-29). A network card for a desktop computer is an adapter card that has a port to which a cable connects. A network card for mobile computers and devices is in the form of a USB network adapter, ExpressCard module, PC Card, or a memory card.

Figure 9-29
Network cards are available for both desktop and notebook computers.

Network cards that provide wireless data transmission also are available. This type of card, called a *wireless network card*, often has an antenna. Sometimes the antenna is detachable, allowing the user to position it in a location with the best signal strength. Users also can install an amplifier to increase and/or stabilize the signal strength. Some network cards include support for both wired and wireless networks.

A network card follows the guidelines of a particular network communications standard, such as Ethernet or token ring. An Ethernet card is the most common type of network card. Ethernet cards may support multiple speeds.

Wireless Access Points

A *wireless access point* is a central communications device that allows computers and devices to transfer data wirelessly among themselves or to transfer data wirelessly to a wired network (Figure 9-30). Wireless access points have high-quality antennas for optimal signals. For the best signal, some manufacturers suggest positioning the wireless access point at the highest possible location and the use of an amplifier.

Figure 9-30 Wireless access points around campus allow students to access the school network wirelessly from their classrooms, the library, dorms, and other campus locations. To access the network, the notebook computer or mobile device must have built-in wireless capability or a wireless network card.

Routers

A *router* is a communications device that connects multiple computers or other routers together and transmits data to its correct destination on a network. A router can be used on any size of network. On the largest scale, routers along the Internet backbone forward data packets to their destination using the fastest available path. For smaller business and home networks, a router allows multiple computers to share a single high-speed Internet connection such as through a cable modem or DSL modem (Figure 9-31). These routers connect from 2 to 250 computers.

To prevent unauthorized users from accessing files and computers, many routers are protected by a built-in firewall, called a *hardware firewall*. Some also have built-in antivirus protection. Routers also support wireless communications, eliminating the need for a separate wireless access point in a wireless network. If the network has a separate wireless access point, it connects to the router via a cable. Some routers also include additional functionality such as including a built-in print server. Today's routers or combination wireless access point/routers are easy to configure and secure against unauthorized access.

Wireless Routers
For more information, visit the Computer Concepts CourseMate Web site at www.cengagebrain.com, navigate to the Chapter 9 Web Link resource for this book, and then click Wireless Routers.

Figure 9-31 Through a router, home and small business networks can share access to a high-speed Internet connection such as through a cable or DSL modem.

FAQ 9-5

Where is the best location in my home for a wireless router?

If you experience slow wireless network connections or frequently lose the wireless network connection in your home, you may need to change the location of the wireless router. To obtain the best wireless coverage and minimize the number of dropped network connections in your home, place the wireless router in a central location. In addition, do not place the wireless router on the floor or near walls and metal objects. Also, make sure that the antennas are connected properly to, and fully extended from, the wireless router. In larger homes, it may be necessary to install a *wireless repeater*, which can extend the range of a wireless network.

For more information, visit the Computer Concepts CourseMate Web site at www.cengagebrain.com, navigate to the Chapter 9 FAQ resource for this book, and then click Wireless Routers.

Hubs and Switches

Today, thousands of computer networks exist, ranging from small networks operated by home users to global networks operated by numerous telecommunications firms. Interconnecting these many types of networks requires various types of communications devices. A hub or switch is a device that provides a central point for cables in a network (Figure 9-32). Larger networks typically use a hub, while smaller networks use a switch. Some hubs and/or switches include routers. That is, the hub or switch receives data from many directions and then forwards it to one or more destinations.

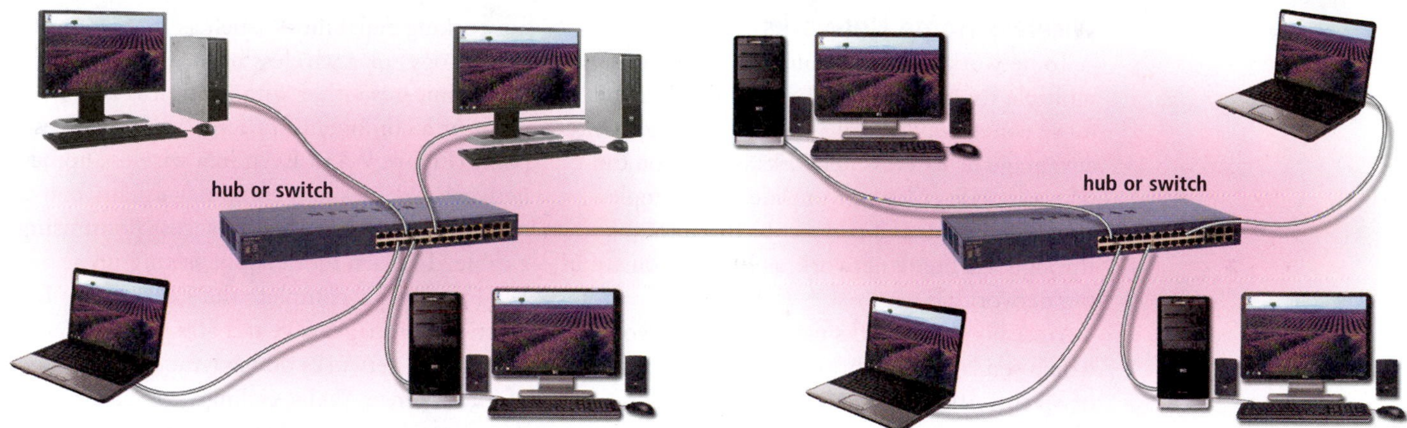

Figure 9-32 A hub or switch is a central point that connects several devices in a network together.

Home Networks

Many home users are connecting multiple computers and devices together in a **home network**. Home networking saves the home user money and provides many conveniences. Each networked computer in the house has the following capabilities:

- Connect to the Internet at the same time
- Share a single high-speed Internet connection
- Access files and programs on the other computers in the house
- Share peripherals such as a printer, scanner, external hard disk, or optical disc drive
- Play multiplayer games with players on other computers in the house
- Connect game consoles to the Internet
- Subscribe to and use VoIP

Many vendors offer home networking packages that include all the necessary hardware and software to network your home using wired or wireless techniques. Some of these packages also offer intelligent networking capabilities. An *intelligent home network* extends the basic home network to include features such as lighting control, thermostat adjustment, and a security system. You no longer need extensive knowledge of networks to set up a home network. For example, the latest version of Windows allows you to connect all computers in your house to a home network easily.

Wired Home Networks

As with other networks, a home network can use wires, be wireless, or use a combination of wired and wireless. Three types of wired home networks are Ethernet, powerline cable, and phoneline.

Ethernet Network As discussed earlier in this chapter, traditional Ethernet networks require that each computer have built-in network capabilities or contain a network card, which connects to a central network hub or similar device with a physical cable. This may involve running cable through walls, ceilings, and floors in the house. For the average home user, the hardware and software of an Ethernet network can be difficult to configure.

Powerline Cable Network A home *powerline cable network* is a network that uses the same lines that bring electricity into the house. This network requires no additional wiring. One end of a cable plugs in the computer's USB port and the other end of the cable plugs in a wall outlet. The data transmits through the existing power lines in the house.

Phoneline Network A *phoneline network* is an easy-to-install and inexpensive network that uses existing telephone lines in the home. With this network, one end of a cable connects to an adapter card or PC Card in the computer and the other end plugs in a wall telephone jack. The phoneline network does not interfere with voice and data transmissions on the telephone lines. That is, you can talk on the telephone and use the same line to connect to the Internet.

Home Networks
For more information, visit the Computer Concepts CourseMate Web site at www.cengagebrain.com, navigate to the Chapter 9 Web Link resource for this book, and then click Home Networks.

Wireless Home Networks

To network computers and devices that span multiple rooms or floors in a home, it may be more convenient to use a wireless strategy. One advantage of wireless networks is that you can take a mobile computer outside, for example in the backyard, and connect to the Internet through the home network, as long as you are in the network's range.

Most home networks use a Wi-Fi network, which sends signals through the air at distances of up to 1,500 feet in some configurations. Wi-Fi networks are fairly easy to configure. Each computer accessing the network must have the appropriate built-in wireless networking capabilities (such as Intel's Centrino technology) or a wireless network card, which communicates either with a wireless access point or a combination router/wireless access point (Figure 9-33). Even in a wireless home network, one desktop computer usually connects to the router/wireless access point using a cable. To learn more about setting up a Wi-Fi network, complete the Learn How To 1 activity on pages 508 and 509.

Wireless networks do have the disadvantage of interference. Walls, ceilings, and electrical devices such as cordless telephones and microwave ovens can disrupt wireless network communications.

How to Set Up Hardware for a Wi-Fi Home Network

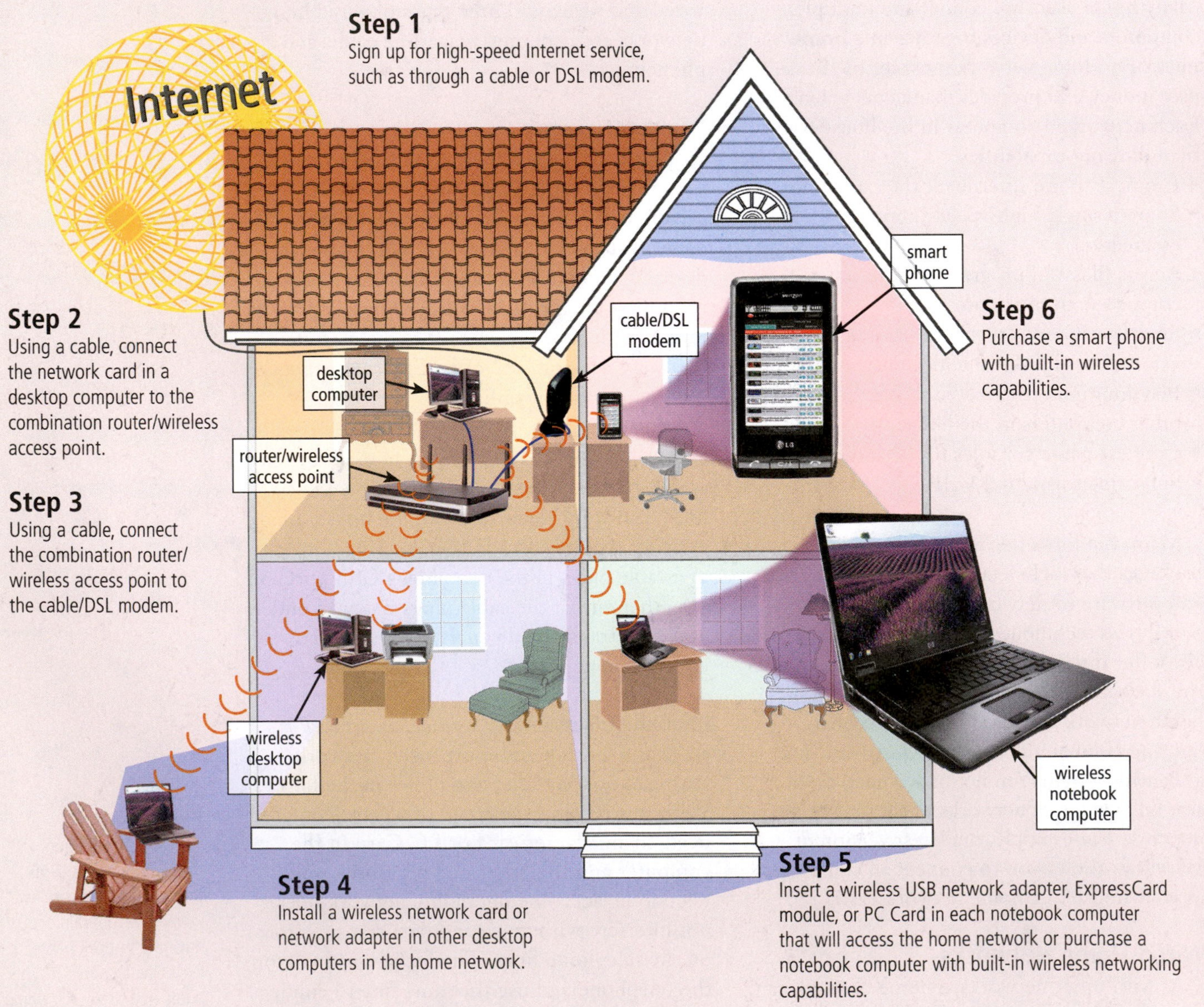

Figure 9-33 This figure shows how to set up hardware for a Wi-Fi home network.

Communications Channel

As described at the beginning of the chapter, a communications channel is the transmission media on which data, instructions, or information travel in a communications system. The amount of data, instructions, and information that can travel over a communications channel sometimes is called the **bandwidth**. The higher the bandwidth, the more the channel transmits. For example, a cable modem has more bandwidth than a dial-up modem.

For transmission of text only, a lower bandwidth is acceptable. For transmission of music, graphics, photos, virtual reality images, or 3-D games, however, you need a higher bandwidth. When the bandwidth is too low for the application, you will notice a considerable slowdown in system performance.

Latency is the time it takes a signal to travel from one location to another on a network. Several factors that negatively can affect latency include the distance between the two points, the type of transmission media, and the number of nodes through which the data must travel over the communications channel. For best performance, bandwidth should be high and latency low.

A communications channel consists of one or more transmission media. **Transmission media** consist of materials or substances capable of carrying one or more signals. When you send data from a computer, the signal that carries the data may travel over various transmission media. This is especially true when the transmission spans a long distance.

Figure 9-34 illustrates a typical communications channel and shows the variety of transmission media used to complete the connection. Although many media and devices are involved, the entire communications process could take less than one second.

Broadband media transmit multiple signals simultaneously. In many cases, download transfer rates of broadband are faster than its upload transfer rates. Home and business users today opt for broadband Internet access because of the fast transfer rates. Two previously discussed services that offer broadband transmission

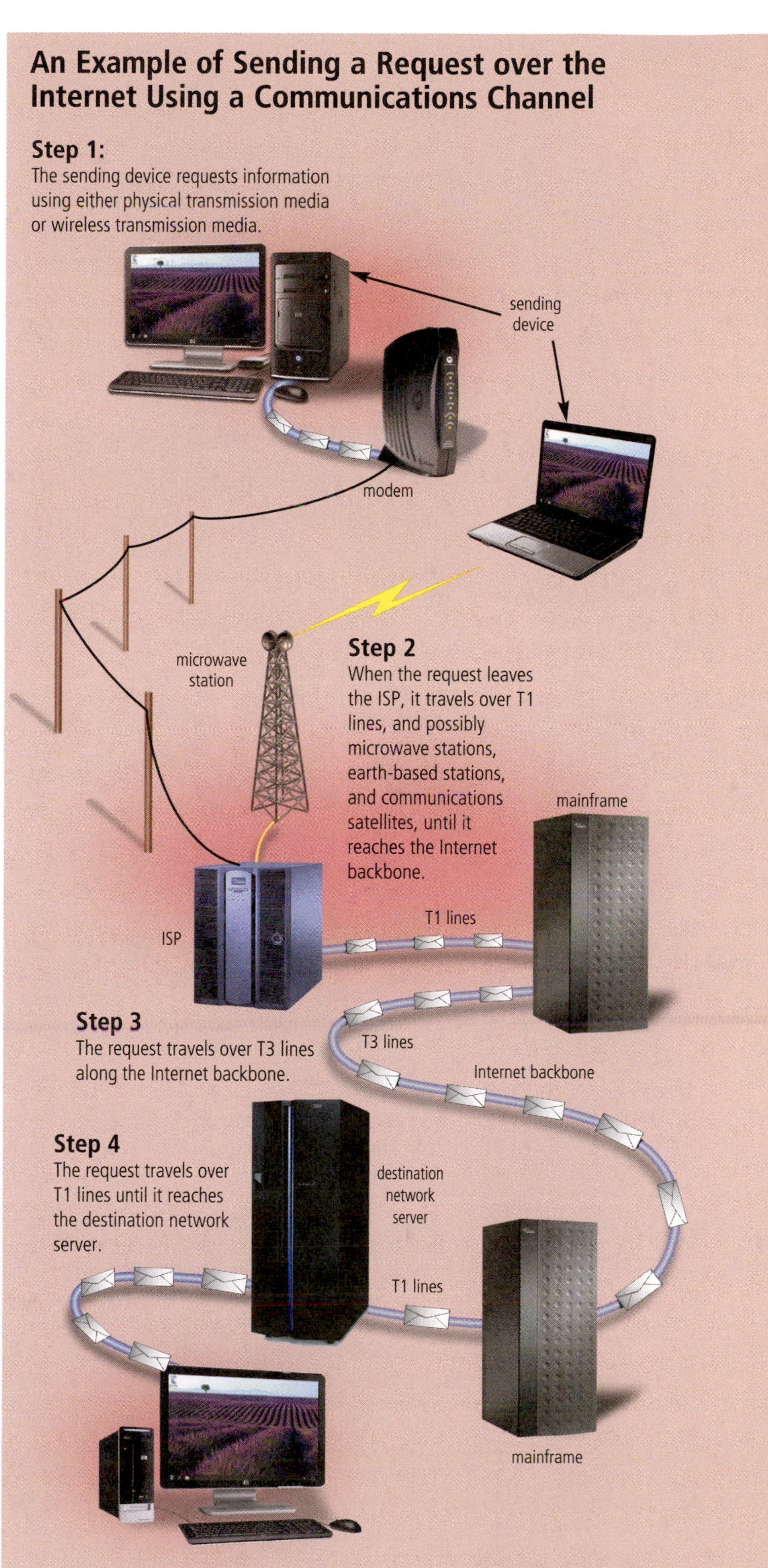

Figure 9-34 This figure shows an example of sending a request over the Internet using a communications channel.

are DSL and the cable television Internet service. Satellites also offer broadband transmission. Read Ethics & Issues 9-4 for a related discussion.

Transmission media are one of two types: physical or wireless. *Physical transmission media* use wire, cable, and other tangible materials to send communications signals. *Wireless transmission media* send communications signals through the air or space using radio, microwave, and infrared signals. The following sections discuss these types of media.

FAQ 9-6

Is home broadband adoption increasing?

Home broadband Internet is increasing overall. The following chart illustrates broadband adoption for various categories of users.

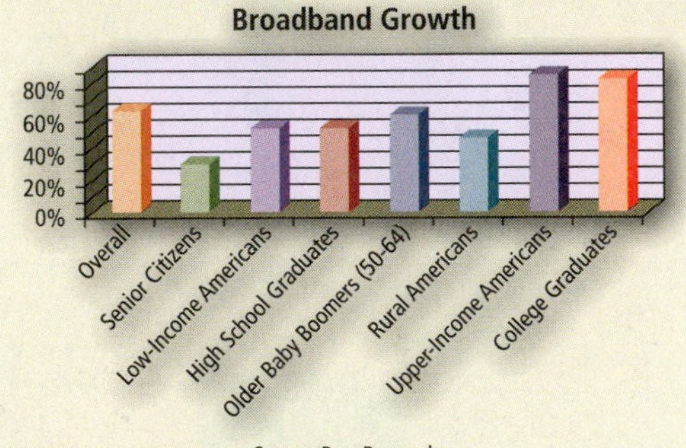

For more information, visit the Computer Concepts CourseMate Web site at www.cengagebrain.com, navigate to the Chapter 9 FAQ resource for this book, and then click Broadband Adoption.

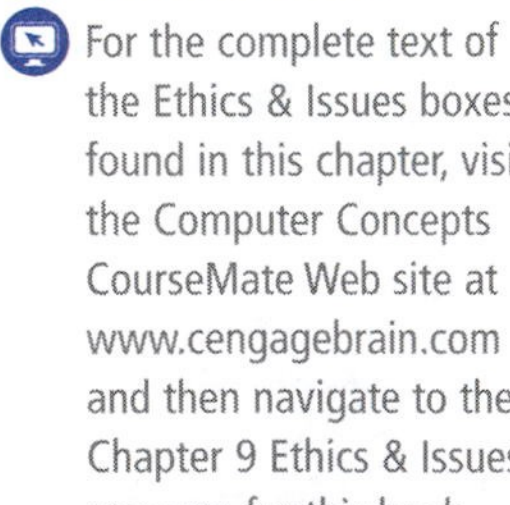

Ethics & Issues

For the complete text of the Ethics & Issues boxes found in this chapter, visit the Computer Concepts CourseMate Web site at www.cengagebrain.com and then navigate to the Chapter 9 Ethics & Issues resource for this book.

Physical Transmission Media

Physical transmission media used in communications include twisted-pair cable, coaxial cable, and fiber-optic cable. These cables typically are used within or underground between buildings. Ethernet and token ring LANs often use physical transmission media. The table in Figure 9-35 lists the transfer rates of LANs using various physical transmission media. The following sections discuss each of these types of cables.

Transfer Rates for Various Types of LANs Using Physical Transmission Media

Type of Cable and LAN	Maximum Transfer Rate
Twisted-Pair Cable	
• 10Base-T (Ethernet)	10 Mbps
• 100Base-T (Fast Ethernet)	100 Mbps
• 1000Base-T (Gigabit Ethernet)	1 Gbps
• Token ring	4 Mbps to 16 Mbps
Coaxial Cable	
• 10Base2 (ThinWire Ethernet)	10 Mbps
• 10Base5 (ThickWire Ethernet)	10 Mbps
Fiber-Optic Cable	
• 10Base-F (Ethernet)	10 Mbps
• 100Base-FX (Fast Ethernet)	100 Mbps
• FDDI (Fiber Distributed Data Interface) token ring	100 Mbps
• Gigabit Ethernet	1 Gbps
• 10-Gigabit Ethernet	10 Gbps
• 40-Gigabit Ethernet	40 Gbps
• 100-Gigabit Ethernet	100 Gbps

Figure 9-35 The speeds of various physical communications media when they are used in LANs.

ETHICS & ISSUES 9-4

Are Internet Access Providers Truthful about Internet Connection Speeds?

When choosing an Internet access provider, speed, or bandwidth, remains one of the most important features to consumers. Internet access providers often focus their advertising efforts on the bandwidth of their services. A provider may offer 2 Mbps, 4 Mbps, and 8 Mbps speeds at different price levels. When savvy consumers test their Internet connection speed at Web sites such as speedtest.com, however, often they become disillusioned with their provider's claims because the speed test does not reflect the provider's claims. Internet speed tests often vary for consumers depending on the time of day or day of the week. Internet access providers state that a customer's experience often depends on the Web sites they visit, and if a Web site is slow because it is experiencing heavy demand, then blame cannot be placed on the provider. Internet access providers claim that they advertise the maximum speed possible under a service plan, in the same way that cars may be advertised with high gas mileage. The advertised gas mileage, however, is attainable only under ideal driving conditions. Critics claim that Internet access providers simply mislead customers to gain a competitive advantage, and customers pay for more than they actually receive.

Should Internet access providers be forced to be more upfront about Internet connection speeds? Why or why not? Should the government regulate how Internet speeds are advertised or stated to customers, in much the same way that food products are labeled? Why or why not? Should ISPs provide average Internet speeds for a customer's geographical area on demand? Why?

Twisted-Pair Cable

One of the more widely used transmission media for network cabling and telephone systems is twisted-pair cable. **Twisted-pair cable** consists of one or more twisted-pair wires bundled together (Figure 9-36). Each *twisted-pair wire* consists of two separate insulated copper wires that are twisted together. The wires are twisted together to reduce noise. **Noise** is an electrical disturbance that can degrade communications.

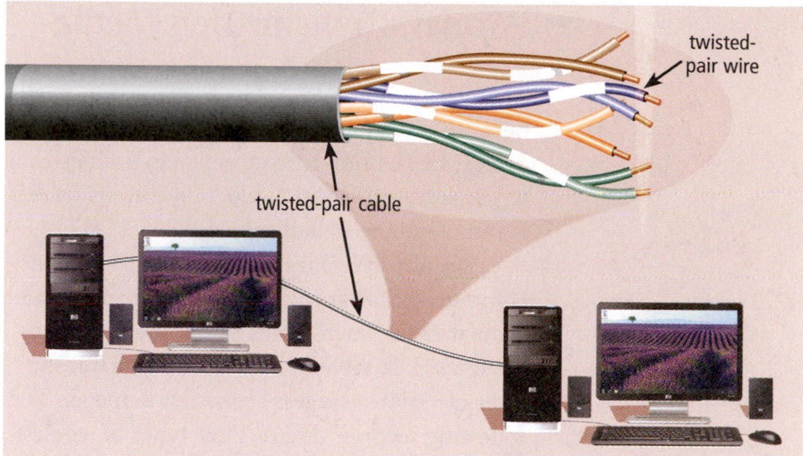

Figure 9-36 A twisted-pair cable consists of one or more twisted-pair wires. Each twisted-pair wire usually is color coded for identification. Telephone networks and LANs often use twisted-pair cable.

Coaxial Cable

Coaxial cable, often referred to as *coax* (pronounced KO-ax), consists of a single copper wire surrounded by at least three layers: (1) an insulating material, (2) a woven or braided metal, and (3) a plastic outer coating (Figure 9-37).

Cable television (CATV) network wiring often uses coaxial cable because it can be cabled over longer distances than twisted-pair cable. Most of today's computer networks, however, do not use coaxial cable because other transmission media such as fiber-optic cable transmit signals at faster rates.

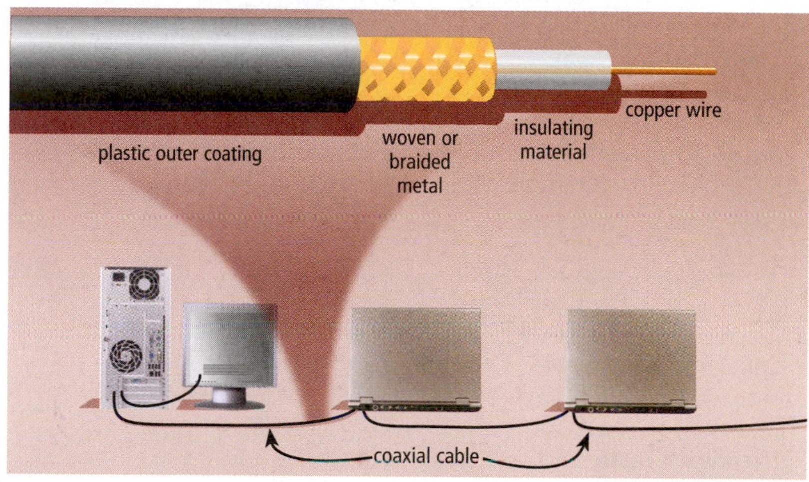

Figure 9-37 On a coaxial cable, data travels through a copper wire. This illustration shows computers networked together with coaxial cable.

Fiber-Optic Cable

The core of a **fiber-optic cable** consists of dozens or hundreds of thin strands of glass or plastic that use light to transmit signals. Each strand, called an *optical fiber*, is as thin as a human hair. Inside the fiber-optic cable, an insulating glass cladding and a protective coating surround each optical fiber (Figure 9-38).

Fiber-optic cables have the following advantages over cables that use wire, such as twisted-pair and coaxial cables:

- Capability of carrying significantly more signals than wire cables
- Faster data transmission
- Less susceptible to noise (interference) from other devices such as a copy machine
- Better security for signals during transmission because they are less susceptible to noise
- Smaller size (much thinner and lighter weight)

Disadvantages of fiber-optic cable are it costs more than twisted-pair or coaxial cable and can be difficult to install and modify. Despite these limitations, many local and long-distance telephone companies are replacing existing telephone lines with fiber-optic cables, enabling them to offer fiber Internet access to home and business users. Businesses also are using fiber-optic cables in high-traffic networks or as the backbone in a network.

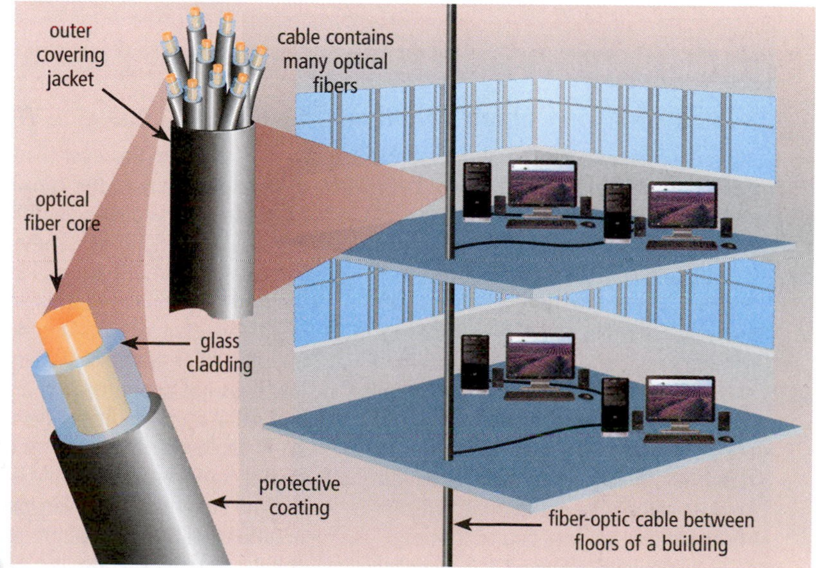

Figure 9-38 A fiber-optic cable consists of hair-thin strands of glass or plastic that carry data as pulses of light.

Wireless Transmission Media

Many users opt for wireless transmission media because it is more convenient than installing cables. In addition to convenience, businesses use wireless transmission media in locations where it is impossible to install cables.

Types of wireless transmission media used in communications include infrared, broadcast radio, cellular radio, microwaves, and communications satellites. The table in Figure 9-39 lists transfer rates of various wireless transmission media. The following sections discuss these types of wireless transmission media. Read Ethics & Issues 9-5 for a related discussion.

Transfer Rates for Various Types of Wireless Transmission Media

Medium		Maximum Transfer Transmission Rate
Infrared		115 Kbps to 4 Mbps
Broadcast radio	• Bluetooth	1 Mbps to 2 Mbps
	• HomeRF	1.6 Mbps to 10 Mbps
	• 802.11b	11 Mbps
	• 802.11a	54 Mbps
	• 802.11g	54 Mbps
	• 802.11n	108 Mbps
	• UWB	110 Mbps to 480 Mbps
Cellular radio	• 2G	9.6 Kbps to 19.2 Kbps
	• 3G	144 Kbps to 2.4 Mbps
	• 4G	Up to 15 Mbps
Microwave radio		150 Mbps
Communications satellite		1 Gbps

Figure 9-39 The transfer rates of various wireless transmission media.

Infrared

As discussed earlier in the chapter, infrared (IR) is a wireless transmission medium that sends signals using infrared light waves. Mobile computers and devices, such as a mouse, printer, and smart phone, often have an IrDA port that enables the transfer of data from one device to another using infrared light waves.

Broadcast Radio

Broadcast radio is a wireless transmission medium that distributes radio signals through the air over long distances such as between cities, regions, and countries and short distances such as within an office or home.

For radio transmissions, you need a transmitter to send the broadcast radio signal and a receiver to accept it. To receive the broadcast radio signal, the receiver has an antenna that is located in the range of the signal. Some networks use a transceiver, which both sends and receives signals from wireless devices. Broadcast radio is slower and more susceptible to noise than physical transmission media but it provides flexibility and portability.

Bluetooth, UWB, Wi-Fi, and WiMAX communications technologies discussed earlier in this chapter use broadcast radio signals. Bluetooth and UWB are alternatives to infrared communications, with the latter designed for high bandwidth transmissions. Hot spots use Wi-Fi, WiMAX, and Bluetooth networks.

ETHICS & ISSUES 9-5

Should You Worry about Cell Phone, Cellular Antenna, and Wi-Fi Device Radiation?

Billions of people use cell phones, and more than 80 percent of the world's population has access to cell phone service from cellular antennas. Wi-Fi signals permeate businesses, public areas, and homes everywhere. The number of wireless devices is expected to rise sharply in coming years, and many are concerned about potential health effects from cell phones, cellular antennas, and Wi-Fi devices. Some cell phone users who suffered rare illnesses have filed lawsuits against cell phone companies, but the cases usually are lost due to lack of scientific evidence linking the use of the phones to the illnesses. While debates rage in communities over placement of cellular antennas, the consideration of health effects on residents is muted because the federal government's Telecommunications Act of 1996 prohibits local governments from considering health effects when making decisions about cellular antenna placement. The law does not apply to Wi-Fi antennas, and some municipalities reject municipal Wi-Fi deployments due to residents' health concerns. It generally is agreed that no studies conclusively demonstrate negative health effects from cell phones, cellular antennas, and Wi-Fi devices, but skeptics claim that the technology is too new to have endured long-term studies on humans. Long-term studies that are underway may not provide results for decades.

Are you concerned about cell phone, cellular antenna, and Wi-Fi radiation? Why or why not? Do you or does anyone you know minimize use of cell phones or other wireless devices due to health concerns? Should governments be required to consider health concerns when making decisions about wireless deployments? Why? Would you live next to a cellular antenna? Why or why not?

Cellular Radio

Cellular radio is a form of broadcast radio that is used widely for mobile communications, specifically wireless modems and cell phones (Figure 9-40). A cell phone is a telephone device that uses high-frequency radio waves to transmit voice and digital data messages. Because only a limited number of radio frequencies exist, cellular network providers reuse frequencies so that they can accommodate the large number of users. Some users install an amplifier or booster to improve the signal strength.

Some mobile users connect their notebook computer or other mobile computer to a cell phone to access the Web, send and receive e-mail messages, enter a chat room, or connect to an office or school network while away from a standard telephone line. Others watch *mobile TV*, which is a service that provides television programs over the cellular network. Read Innovative Computing 9-2 to find out about watching television programs remotely.

Several categories of cellular transmissions exist, defining the development of cellular networks. Although the definitions of these categories may vary by cellular providers, below are some general guides.

- *1G* (first generation) transmitted analog data
- *2G* (second generation) transmit digital data at speeds from 9.6 Kbps to 19.2 Kbps
- *3G* (third generation) transmit digital data at speeds from 144 Kbps to 2.4 Mbps
- *4G* (fourth generation) transmit digital data at speeds up to 15 Mbps

Examples of 3G standards include *GSM* (Global System for Mobile Communications), *UMTS* (Universal Mobile Telecommunications System), *GPRS* (General Packet Radio Service), *CDMA* (Code Division Multiple Access), *EDGE* (Enhanced Data GSM Environment), and *EVDO* (Evolution Data Optimized). These 3G standards allow users quickly to display multimedia and graphics, browse the Web, watch television or a video, have a video conference, and transfer data on a cellular device. Providers that offer 3G service include Sprint, Verizon, and AT&T.

The most recent cellular network category, the 4G network, uses the mobile wireless WiMAX communication standard. Several major communications companies have worked together to develop a nationwide 4G network.

Mobile TV

For more information, visit the Computer Concepts CourseMate Web site at www.cengagebrain.com, navigate to the Chapter 9 Web Link resource for this book, and then click Mobile TV.

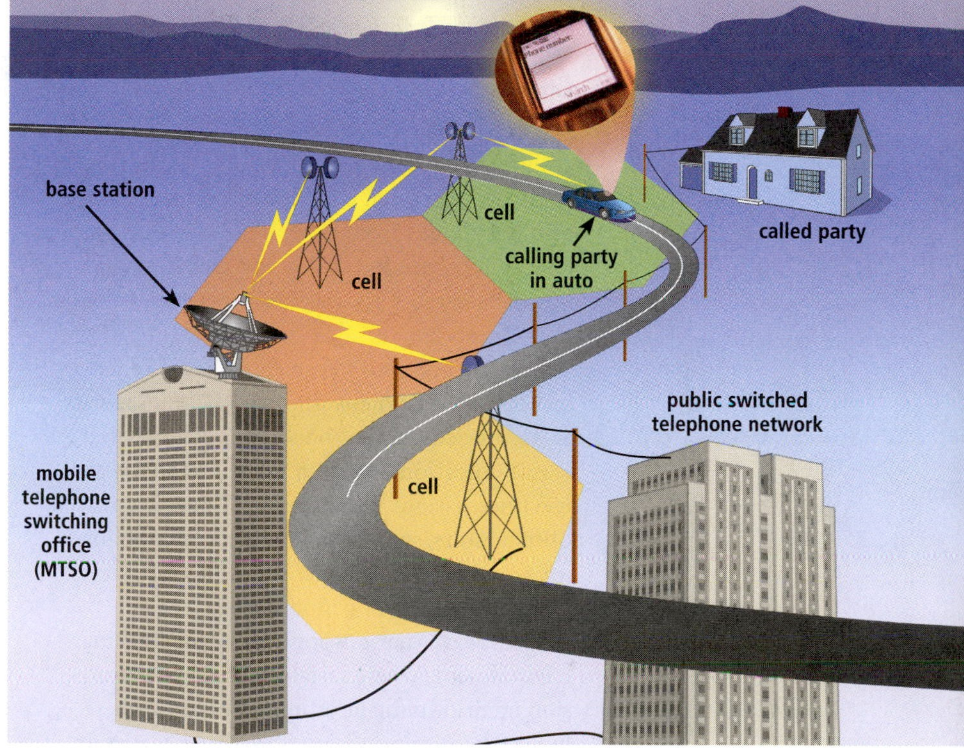

Figure 9-40 As a person with a cell phone drives from one cell to another, the radio signals transfer from the base station (microwave station) in one cell to a base station in another cell.

INNOVATIVE COMPUTING 9-2

Watch Your Television Wherever You Go

If you cannot endure missing an episode of your favorite soap opera or talk show when you are on vacation or at work, then a *Slingbox* may be the perfect device to bring television to your computer or smart phone. This hardware redirects signals from your home cable, satellite, or digital video recorder (DVR) to any computer or portable media player with a broadband Internet connection. The virtual remote displayed on your monitor controls the video source. It allows you to change channels, program your DVR, and adjust the contrast.

The Slingbox is a product of Sling Media, a San Francisco-based company. Its SlingCatcher reverses the process and sends signals from a computer to a television so that you can, for example, view YouTube videos in your home theater. It also allows you to send a signal from the main television to a second television in the house, eliminating the need for two set-top boxes.

For more information, visit the Computer Concepts CourseMate Web site at www.cengagebrain.com, navigate to the Chapter 9 Innovative Computing resource for this book, and then click Slingbox.

Personal Communications Services (*PCS*) is the term used by the U.S. Federal Communications Commission (FCC) to identify all wireless digital communications. Devices that use PCS include cell phones, PDAs, pagers, and fax machines. These devices have voice mail, call forwarding, fax capability, caller ID, and wireless modems for Internet and e-mail access.

Microwaves

Microwaves are radio waves that provide a high-speed signal transmission. Microwave transmission, often called *fixed wireless*, involves sending signals from one microwave station to another (Figure 9-41). Microwaves can transmit data at rates up to 4,500 times faster than a dial-up modem.

A *microwave station* is an earth-based reflective dish that contains the antenna, transceivers, and other equipment necessary for microwave communications. As with infrared, microwaves use line-of-sight transmission. To avoid possible obstructions, such as buildings or mountains, microwave stations often sit on the tops of buildings, towers, or mountains.

Microwave transmission typically is used in environments where installing physical transmission media is difficult or impossible and where line-of-sight transmission is available. For example, microwave transmission is used in wide-open areas such as deserts or lakes, between buildings in a close geographic area, or to communicate with a satellite. Current users of microwave transmission include universities, hospitals, city governments, cable television providers, and telephone companies. Homes and small businesses that do not have other high-speed Internet connections available in their area also opt for lower-cost fixed wireless plans.

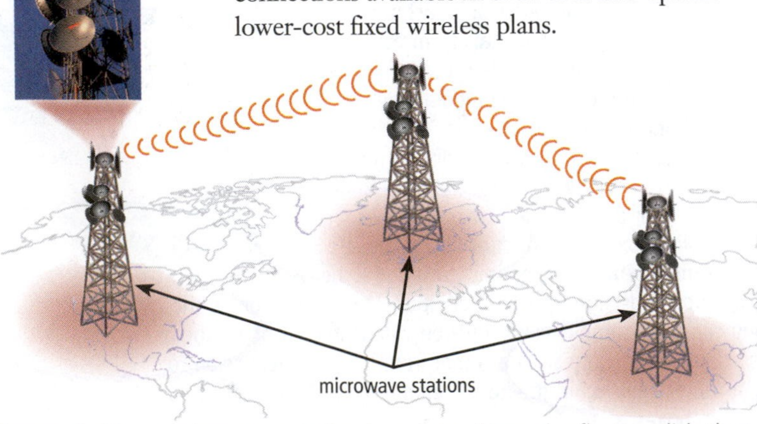

Figure 9-41 A microwave station is a ground-based reflective dish that contains the antenna, transceivers, and other equipment necessary for microwave communications.

Communications Satellite

A **communications satellite** is a space station that receives microwave signals from an earth-based station, amplifies (strengthens) the signals, and broadcasts the signals back over a wide area to any number of earth-based stations (Figure 9-42).

These earth-based stations often are microwave stations. Other devices, such as smart phones and GPS receivers, also can function as earth-based stations. Transmission from an earth-based station to a satellite is an *uplink*. Transmission from a satellite to an earth-based station is a *downlink*.

Applications such as air navigation, television and radio broadcasts, weather forecasting, video conferencing, paging, global positioning systems, and Internet connections use communications satellites. With the proper satellite dish and a satellite modem card, consumers can access the Internet using satellite technology. With satellite Internet connections, however, uplink transmissions usually are slower than downlink transmissions. This difference in speeds usually is acceptable to most Internet satellite users because they download much more data than they upload. Although a satellite Internet connection is more expensive than cable Internet or DSL connections, sometimes it is the only high-speed Internet option in remote areas.

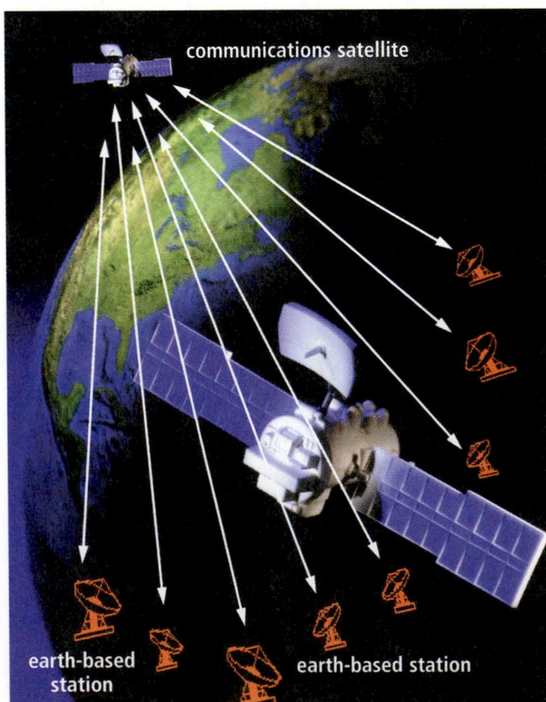

Figure 9-42 Communications satellites are placed about 22,300 miles above the Earth's equator.

QUIZ YOURSELF 9-3

Instructions: Find the true statement below. Then, rewrite the remaining false statements so that they are true.

1. A cable modem converts a computer's digital signals to analog signals before they are transmitted over standard telephone lines.
2. A hardware firewall is a communications device that allows computers and devices to transfer data wirelessly among themselves or to transfer data wirelessly to a wired network.
3. A network card is an adapter card, USB network adapter, ExpressCard module, PC Card, or flash card that enables the computer or device to access a network.
4. Analog signals consist of individual electrical pulses that represent bits grouped together into bytes.
5. Physical transmission media send communications signals through the air or space using radio, microwave, and infrared signals.
6. The lower the bandwidth, the more data, instructions, and information the channel transmits.
7. Most wireless home networks use powerline cables.

Quiz Yourself Online: To further check your knowledge of pages 485 through 496, visit the Computer Concepts CourseMate Web site at www.cengagebrain.com, navigate to the Chapter 9 Quiz Yourself resource for this book, and then click Objectives 9 – 11.

Chapter Summary

This chapter provided an overview of communications terminology and applications. It also discussed how to join computers into a network, allowing them to communicate and share resources such as hardware, software, data, and information. It also explained various communications devices, media, and procedures as they relate to computers.

Computer Usage @ Work

Agriculture

The world's dependence on the agriculture industry is enormous. The demand to keep food prices affordable encourages those working in this industry to operate as efficiently as possible. Although people have worked in agriculture for more than 10,000 years, advances in technology assist with maintaining and protecting land, crops, and animals.

Almost all companies in this industry have many acres of land that they must maintain, and it is not always feasible for farmers to take frequent trips around the property to perform basic tasks such as watering soil in the absence of rain. The number of people-hours required to water soil manually on several thousand acres of land might result in businesses spending thousands of dollars in labor and utility costs. If an irrigation system is installed instead, one or more individuals still are responsible for deciding when to water and how long to water. If the irrigation process is automated, sensors detect how much rain has fallen recently, as well as whether the soil is in need of watering. The sensors then send this data to a computer that processes it and decides when and how much to water. Many automated home irrigation systems also are programmable and use rain sensors, which keep the irrigation system from turning on, or turn it off when rainfall occurs.

In addition to keeping the soil moist and reducing maintenance costs, computers also can utilize sensors to analyze the condition of crops in the field and determine whether pests or diseases are affecting the crops. If sensors detect pests and/or diseases, computers send a notification to the appropriate individual to take corrective action. In some cases, the discovery of pests might trigger a pesticide to discharge in the affected area automatically.

Until recently, the lack of adequate cellular and wireless network signals in the fields made communications difficult for farmers. Mobile cellular antennas and amplifiers stretch mobile broadband coverage across entire farms, enabling farmers to receive wireless signals up to eight times farther from the cellular tower than they would without the antennas and amplifiers. Wireless access throughout the farm also allows farmers to monitor their farms and communicate with colleagues from remote locations.

The next time you take a bite of a delicious carrot or juicy cucumber, you can appreciate how technology has helped to maintain an ideal environment for these vegetables to grow and protected them from unwanted pests, all for a reasonable price when you purchase them from your local supermarket.

For more information, visit the Computer Concepts CourseMate Web site at www.cengagebrain.com, navigate to the Chapter 9 Computer Usage @ Work resource for this book, and then click Agriculture.

High-Tech Talk

OSI Reference Model: The Driving Force behind Network Communications

Every message sent over a network — even the simplest e-mail message — must be divided into discrete packages of data and routed via transmission media such as telephone lines. While traveling from the sending computer to the receiving computer, each data package can take a different path over the network. How do these messages get to their destination, intact and accurate?

The *Open Systems Interconnection (OSI) reference model*, a communications standard developed by the International Organization for Standardization (ISO), offers an answer. The OSI reference model describes the flow of data in a network through seven layers, from the user's application to the physical transmission media.

A simple way to understand the OSI reference model is to think of it as an elevator (Figure 9-43). On the sending end, data enters at the top floor (the application layer) and travels to the bottom floor (the physical layer). Each layer communicates with the layers immediately above and below it. When a layer receives data, it performs specific functions, adds control information to the data, and passes it to the next layer. The control information contains error-checking, routing, and other information needed to ensure proper transmission along the network.

The top layer, the *application layer*, serves as the interface between the user and the network. Using application software, such as an e-mail program, a user can type a message and specify a recipient. The application then prepares the message for delivery by converting the message data into bits and attaching a header identifying the sending and receiving computers.

The *presentation layer* translates the converted message data into a language the receiving computer can process (from ASCII to EBCDIC, for example) and also may compress or encrypt the data. Finally, the layer attaches another header specifying the language, compression, and encryption schemes.

The next layer, called the *session layer*, establishes and maintains communications sessions. A *session* is the period between establishment of a connection, transmission of the data, and termination of the connection.

The *transport layer*, also called the end-to-end layer, ensures that data arrives correctly and in proper sequence. The transport layer divides the data into segments and creates a *checksum*, a mathematical sum based on the data, and puts this information in the transport header. The checksum later is used to determine if the data was scrambled during transmission.

The *network layer* routes the message from sender to receiver. This layer splits the data segments from the transport layer into smaller groups of bits called *packets*. Next, it adds a header containing the packet sequence, the receiving computer address, and routing information. The network layer also manages network problems by rerouting packets to avoid network congestion.

The *data link layer* supervises the transmission of the message to the next network node by specifying the network technology (such as Ethernet or token ring) and grouping data accordingly. The data link layer also calculates the checksum and keeps a copy of each packet until it receives confirmation that the packet arrived undamaged at the next node.

Finally, the *physical layer* encodes the packets into a signal recognized by the medium that will carry them — such as an analog signal to be sent over a telephone line — and sends the packets along that medium to the receiving computer.

At the receiving computer, the process is reversed and the data moves back through the seven layers from the physical layer to the application layer, which identifies the recipient, converts the bits into readable data, removes some of the error-checking and control information from the data, and directs it to the appropriate application. A modified 5-layer model is used for data sent using the Transmission Control Protocol (TCP) and/or the Internet Protocol (IP). This model includes the physical, data link, network, transport, and application layers. The next time you send an e-mail message to a friend, consider the network communications processes described by the OSI reference model, which ensure that your message travels safely over many networks to your friend's computer.

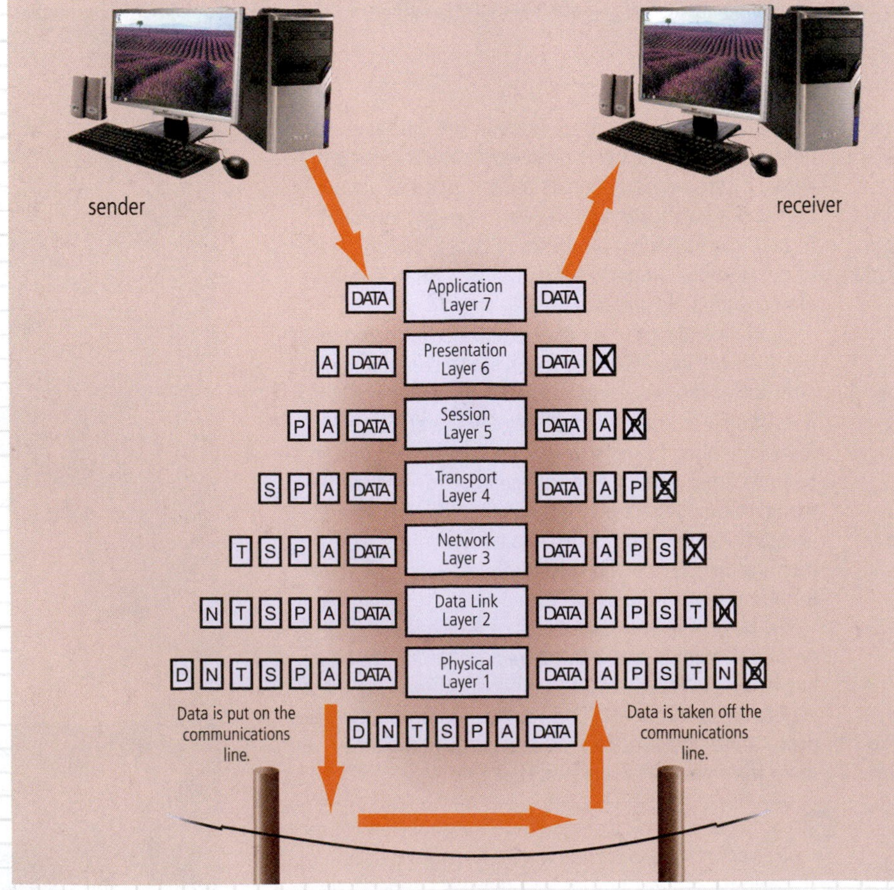

Figure 9-43 The seven layers of the OSI model.

For more information, visit the Computer Concepts CourseMate Web site at www.cengagebrain.com, navigate to the Chapter 9 High-Tech Talk resource for this book, and then click OSI Reference Model.

Companies on the Cutting Edge

CISCO SYSTEMS Networking the Internet

Green networking practices have given *Cisco Systems* top ranking on the Vendor Matrix, a research tool used to assess companies' innovation and implementation of environmentally sound initiatives. Low power consumption, green power supplies and switching tools, and sound recycling efforts are part of the reason for Cisco's high marks and for the company's success.

Cisco manufactures a broad line of networking equipment for transporting data within a building, across a campus, and across the globe. A group of computer scientists at Stanford University founded Cisco in 1984. From the start, the company focused on communicating over networks. Today, Cisco's Internet Protocol-based (IP) networking equipment is the basis of the Internet and most private networks.

The company's TelePresence video conferencing system is installed in more than 100 cities worldwide and serves a variety of audiences, ranging from corporate board members to soldiers stationed at military bases overseas. More than 2.5 million students in 160 countries have received certification credentials through the company's Cisco Academy.

VERIZON Communications Network Leader

One of the largest mergers in United States' history occurred when Bell Atlantic acquired GTE in 2000. The company was renamed *Verizon*, a combination of the words Veritas, the Roman goddess of truth, and horizon. Verizon's famous "Can you hear me now?" tagline has become synonymous with the cell phone industry's connectivity issues.

More than 87 million customers nationwide subscribe to Verizon's wireless network, which is managed through the company's Wireless division. Its other units are Verizon Telecom and Verizon Business, which offer local telephone, nationwide long distance, broadband Internet services, networking, and security services. The company's global fiber-optic network serves more than 150 countries on 6 continents, and its United States network, FiOS, was the first in the country to offer Internet, television, and telephone service.

Verizon is the only telecommunications company that has been named repeatedly to *Working Mother* magazine's 100 Best Companies for Working Mothers list. Recently, it was ranked 17th among FORTUNE 500 companies. Verizon Wireless also boasts the highest customer loyalty, profitability, and cost efficiency.

For more information, visit the Computer Concepts CourseMate Web site at www.cengagebrain.com and then navigate to the Chapter 9 Companies on the Cutting Edge resource for this book.

Technology Trailblazers

ROBERT METCALFE Ethernet Inventor

Robert Metcalfe promised to eat his words if his prediction of the Internet's collapse in 1996 was wrong. During his keynote speech at the WWW International Conference in 1997, he placed the paper containing his prediction in a blender, mixed it with liquid, and drank the pulp. Metcalfe certainly has been correct in predicting many other aspects of the Internet, however, primarily the vision that his Ethernet invention would one day connect millions of computers worldwide.

Metcalfe's fascination with linking computers developed while he was in college. At Harvard's Project MAC, he connected the university's computers to the ARPANET. Then, at Xerox's Palo Alto Research Center (PARC), he coinvented Ethernet in 1973. Xerox managers did not see how the Ethernet fit with the company's primary business of photocopying, so he left the company in 1979 to found 3Com Corporation and make Ethernet the standard for computer communications.

After his retirement from 3Com, he became a general partner in Polaris Venture Partners, a venture capital firm that invests in the early stages of information technology and life sciences companies.

PATRICIA RUSSO Communications Industry Leader

The ability to lead teams and solve problems is important for any top corporate leader, and *Patricia Russo* has used these skills in her career in the communications industry.

After graduating from Georgetown University, she held positions in sales and marketing at IBM and then in management at AT&T for more than 20 years. She also served as CEO and president of Eastman Kodak. Forbes.com has listed Russo as one of the most powerful women in the world and noted that she has the skills to lead a company through difficult financial times.

Russo was instrumental in forming Lucent Technologies in 1996 and was appointed CEO in 2002. Under her leadership, Lucent merged with Alcatel in 2006 to become a major worldwide communications services equipment manufacturer. She served as CEO until 2008, and during her tenure Alcatel-Lucent was one of the largest corporations in the world run by a woman.

For more information, visit the Computer Concepts CourseMate Web site at www.cengagebrain.com and then navigate to the Chapter 9 Technology Trailblazers resource for this book.

STUDENT ASSIGNMENTS

Chapter Review

The Chapter Review reinforces the main concepts presented in this chapter.

To listen to an audio version of this Chapter Review, visit the Computer Concepts CourseMate Web site at www.cengagebrain.com and then navigate to the Chapter 9 Chapter Review resource for this book.

1. What Is the Purpose of the Components Required for Successful Communications, and What Are Various Sending and Receiving Devices? Computer **communications** describes a process in which two or more computers or devices transfer data, instructions, and information. Successful communications requires a **sending device** that initiates a transmission instruction, a communications device that connects the sending device to a communications channel, a **communications channel** on which the data travels, a communications device that connects the communications channel to a receiving device, and a **receiving device** that accepts the transmission of data, instructions, or information. All types of computers and mobile devices serve as sending and receiving devices in a communications system.

2. How Are Computer Communications Used? Communications technologies include blogs, chat rooms, e-mail, fax, FTP, instant messaging, newsgroups, RSS, video conferencing, VoIP, Web, Web folders, and wikis. Users can send and receive wireless messages to and from smart phones, cell phones, handheld game consoles, and other mobile devices using **text messaging**, **picture messaging** and **video messaging**, and wireless instant messaging. People connect wirelessly to the Internet through a **wireless Internet access point**. A *hot spot* is a wireless network that provides Internet connections to mobile computers and devices. A **cybercafé** is a coffeehouse, restaurant, or other location that provides computers with Internet access. A **global positioning system (GPS)** analyzes signals sent by satellites to determine an earth-based receiver's geographic location. Many software products provide a means to **collaborate**, or work online with other users connected to a server. **Groupware** is software that helps groups of people work on projects or share information over a network. **Voice mail** allows someone to leave a voice message for one or more people. *Web services* describe standardized software that enables programmers to create applications that communicate with other remote computers.

Visit the Computer Concepts CourseMate Web site at www.cengagebrain.com, navigate to the Chapter 9 Quiz Yourself resource for this book, and then click Objectives 1 – 2.

3. What Are the Advantages of Using a Network, and How Are LANs, MANs, and WANs Different? A **network** is a collection of computers and devices connected together via communications devices and transmission media. Advantages of using a network include facilitating communications, sharing hardware, sharing data and information, sharing software, and transferring funds. Networks typically are classified as a **local area network (LAN)**, which connects computers in devices in a limited geographical area; a *metropolitan area network (MAN)*, which is a high-speed network that connects local area networks in a larger area, such as city or town; or a **wide area network (WAN)**, which covers a large geographic area using a communications channel that combines many types of media.

4. How Are a Client/Server and Peer-to-Peer Networks Different, and How Does a P2P Network Work? On a **client/server network**, one or more computers acts as a **server**, sometimes called a *host computer*, which controls access to network resources and provides a centralized storage area, while the other computers and devices on the network are **clients** that rely on the server for resources. A *peer-to-peer network* is a simple network that typically connects fewer than 10 computers that have equal responsibilities and capabilities. *P2P* is an Internet peer-to-peer network on which users access each other's hard disks directly and exchange files over the Internet.

5. How Are a Star Network, Bus Network, and Ring Network Different? A **network topology** refers to the layout of computers and devices in a communications network. Three commonly used network topologies are the star, bus, and ring. On a *star network*, all computers and devices on the network connect to a central device, thus forming a star. A *bus network* consists of a single central cable to which all computers and other devices connect. On a *ring network*, a cable forms a closed loop (ring) with all computers and devices arranged along the ring.

6. What Are Various Network Communications Standards? A *network standard* defines guidelines that specify the way computers access a medium, the type(s) of medium, the speeds on different types of networks, and the type of physical cable or wireless technology used. Network communications standards include the following. **Ethernet** specifies that no central computer or device on the network should control when data can be transmitted. **Token ring** requires devices to share or pass a special

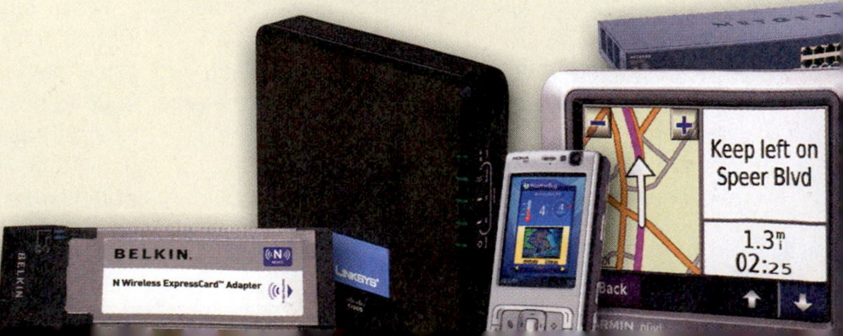

Chapter Review

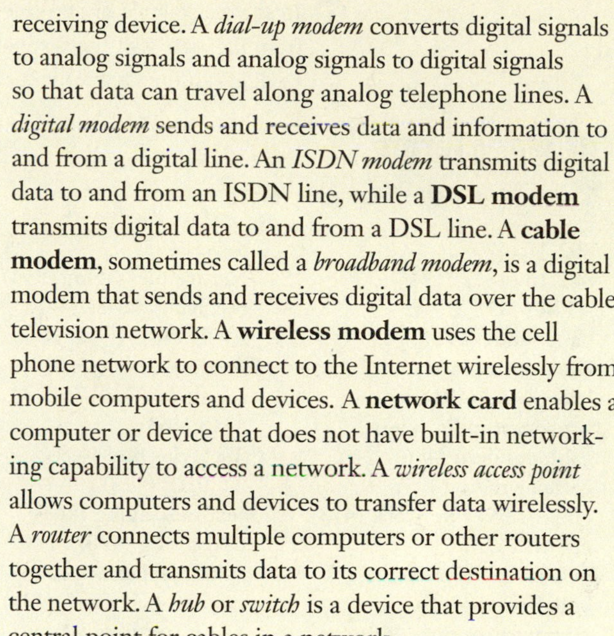

signal, called a *token*. **TCP/IP** divides data into *packets*. **Wi-Fi** identifies any network based on the **802.11** standards for wireless communications. **Bluetooth** uses short-range radio waves to transmit data. **UWB** specifies how two UWB devices use short-range radio waves to communicate at high speeds. **IrDA** transmits data wirelessly via infrared light waves. **RFID** uses radio signals for communications. **WiMAX** is a network standard developed by IEEE that specifies how wireless devices communicate over the air in a wide area. The **Wireless Application Protocol (WAP)** specifies how some mobile devices can display Internet content.

7. What Is the Purpose of Communications Software? **Communications software** helps users establish a connection to another computer or network; manages the transmission of data, instructions, and information; and provides an interface for users to communicate with one another.

8. What Are Various Types of Lines for Communications over the Telephone Network? The telephone network uses dial-up lines or dedicated lines. A **dial-up line** is a temporary connection that uses one or more analog telephone lines for communications. A **dedicated line** is an always-on connection established between two communications devices. Dedicated lines include the following. *ISDN* is a set of standards for digital transmission of data over standard copper telephone lines. **DSL** transmits at fast speeds on existing standard copper telephone wiring. **FTTP**, or **Fiber to the Premises**, uses fiber-optic cable to provide extremely high-speed Internet access to a user's physical permanent location. Two specific types of FTTP are *FTTH* (*Fiber to the Home*) and *FTTB* (*Fiber to the Building*). A **T-carrier line** is a long-distance digital telephone line that carries multiple signals over a single communications line. **ATM** is a service that carries voice, data, video, and multimedia at extremely high speeds.

Visit the Computer Concepts CourseMate Web site at www.cengagebrain.com, navigate to the Chapter 9 Quiz Yourself resource for this book, and then click Objectives 3 – 8.

9. What Are Commonly Used Communications Devices? A **communications device** is hardware capable of transmitting data between a sending device and a receiving device. A *dial-up modem* converts digital signals to analog signals and analog signals to digital signals so that data can travel along analog telephone lines. A *digital modem* sends and receives data and information to and from a digital line. An *ISDN modem* transmits digital data to and from an ISDN line, while a **DSL modem** transmits digital data to and from a DSL line. A **cable modem**, sometimes called a *broadband modem*, is a digital modem that sends and receives digital data over the cable television network. A **wireless modem** uses the cell phone network to connect to the Internet wirelessly from mobile computers and devices. A **network card** enables a computer or device that does not have built-in networking capability to access a network. A *wireless access point* allows computers and devices to transfer data wirelessly. A *router* connects multiple computers or other routers together and transmits data to its correct destination on the network. A *hub* or *switch* is a device that provides a central point for cables in a network.

10. How Can a Home Network Be Set Up? A **home network** connects multiple computers and devices in a home. An Ethernet network connects each computer to a hub with a physical cable. A home *powerline cable network* uses the same lines that bring electricity into the house. A *phoneline network* uses existing telephone lines in a home. Most home networks use a Wi-Fi network.

11. What Are Various Physical and Wireless Transmission Media? **Transmission media** consist of materials or substances capable of carrying one or more signals. *Physical transmission media* use tangible materials to send communications signals. **Twisted-pair cable** consists of one or more twisted-pair wires bundled together. **Coaxial cable** consists of a single copper wire surrounded by at least three layers: an insulating material, a woven or braided metal, and a plastic outer coating. **Fiber-optic cable** consists of thin strands of glass or plastic that use light to transmit signals. *Wireless transmission media* send communications signals through the air or space. Infrared (IR) sends signals using infrared light waves. **Broadcast radio** distributes radio signals through the air over long and short distances. **Cellular radio** is a form of broadcast radio that is used widely for mobile communications. **Microwaves** are radio waves that provide a high-speed signal transmission. A **communications satellite** is a space station that receives microwave signals from an earth-based station, amplifies the signals, and broadcasts the signals back over a wide area.

Visit the Computer Concepts CourseMate Web site at www.cengagebrain.com, navigate to the Chapter 9 Quiz Yourself resource for this book, and then click Objectives 9 – 11.

Key Terms

You should know the Primary Terms and be familiar with the Secondary Terms. The list below helps focus your study.

To see an example of and a definition for each term, and to access current and additional information from the Web, visit the Computer Concepts CourseMate Web site at www.cengagebrain.com and then navigate to the Chapter 9 Key Terms resource for this book.

Primary Terms

(shown in bold-black characters in the chapter)

802.11 (479)
802.16 (482)
ATM (485)
bandwidth (491)
Bluetooth (480)
broadband (491)
broadcast radio (494)
cable modem (486)
cellular radio (495)
client/server network (473)
clients (473)
coaxial cable (493)
collaborate (468)
communications (460)
communications channel (460)
communications device (485)
communications satellite (496)
communications software (482)
cybercafé (466)
dedicated line (483)
dial-up line (483)
DSL (484)
DSL modem (486)
Ethernet (478)
fiber-optic cable (493)
FTTP (Fiber to the Premises) (484)
global positioning system (GPS) (466)
groupware (467)
home network (489)
IrDA (480)
latency (491)
local area network (LAN) (472)
microwaves (496)
network (470)
network card (487)
network topology (475)
noise (493)
picture messaging (464)
receiving device (460)
RFID (481)
sending device (460)
server (473)
SMS (463)
T-carrier line (484)
TCP/IP (478)
text messaging (463)
token ring (478)
transmission media (491)
twisted-pair cable (493)
UWB (ultra-wideband) (480)
video messaging (464)
voice mail (467)
Web conference (468)
wide area network (WAN) (473)
Wi-Fi (479)
WiMAX (482)
Wireless Application Protocol (WAP) (482)
wireless Internet access point (464)
wireless LAN (WLAN) (472)
wireless modem (487)

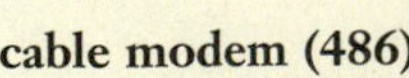

cable modem (486)

Secondary Terms

(shown in italic characters in the chapter)

10-Gigabit Ethernet (478)
40-Gigabit Ethernet (478)
100-Gigabit Ethernet (478)
1G (495)
2G (495)
3G (495)
4G (495)
ADSL (asymmetric digital subscriber line) (484)
broadband modem (486)
bus (476)
bus network (476)
CDMA (495)
coax (493)
collaborative software (468)
common short code (CSC) (464)
database server (474)
dedicated servers (473)
dial-up modem (485)
digital modem (486)
Digital Subscriber Line (484)
document management system (468)
downlink (496)
downstream rate (484)
EDGE (495)
EDI (electronic data interchange) (471)
electronic funds transfer (EFT) (471)
EVDO (495)
extranet (477)
Fast Ethernet (478)
file server (474)
file sharing network (475)
fixed wireless (496)
fractional T1 (485)
FTTB (Fiber to the Building) (484)
FTTH (Fiber to the Home) (484)
Gigabit Ethernet (478)
GPRS (495)
GPS receiver (466)
GSM (495)
hardware firewall (488)
host computer (473)
hot spot (464)
hub (476)
intelligent home network (489)
intranet (477)
ISDN (484)
ISDN modem (486)
line-of-sight transmission (480)
mashup (469)
metropolitan area network (MAN) (473)
microwave station (496)
MIMO (479)
MMS (multimedia message service) (464)
mobile TV (495)
multiplexing (484)
network architecture (473)
network interface card (NIC) (487)
network license (471)
network server (474)
network standard (477)
node (472)
online meeting (468)
optical fiber (493)
P2P (475)
packet switching (478)
packets (478)
PCS (496)
peer (474)
peer-to-peer network (474)
phoneline network (489)
physical transmission media (492)
powerline cable network (489)
print server (474)
protocol (477)
public switched telephone network (PSTN) (482)
radio frequency identification (481)
ring network (476)
router (488)
short message service (463)
site license (471)
star network (476)
switch (476)
T1 line (484)
T3 line (485)
token (478)
twisted-pair wire (493)
UMTS (495)
uplink (496)
upstream rate (484)
value-added network (VAN) (471)
visual voice mail (467)
voice mailbox (467)
Web server (474)
Web services (469)
Wi-Fi mesh network (480)
wireless access point (487)
wireless network card (487)
wireless transmission media (492)
workgroup computing (467)
XML (469)

Checkpoint

The Checkpoint exercises test your knowledge of the chapter concepts. The page number containing the answer appears in parentheses after each exercise. The Beyond the Book exercises will help broaden your understanding of the concepts presented in this chapter.

To complete the Checkpoint exercises interactively, visit the Computer Concepts CourseMate Web site at www.cengagebrain.com and then navigate to the Chapter 9 Checkpoint resource for this book.

True/False Mark T for True and F for False.

_____ 1. A communications channel is the media on which data, instructions, or information travel. (460)

_____ 2. With video messaging, users can send short video clips, usually about 15 minutes, in addition to all picture messaging services. (464)

_____ 3. A network is a collection of computers and devices connected together via communications devices and transmission media. (470)

_____ 4. A local area network (LAN) is a network that covers a large geographic area using a communications channel that combines many types of media such as telephone lines, cables, and radio waves. (472)

_____ 5. A Web server is a computer that delivers requested Web pages to your computer. (474)

_____ 6. An intranet is an internal network that uses Internet technologies. (477)

_____ 7. The 40-Gigabit Ethernet standard is the fastest of the Ethernet standards. (478)

_____ 8. Bluetooth does not require line-of-sight transmission. (480)

_____ 9. At distances of 10 meters (about 33 feet), the data transfer rate for UWB devices is 480 Mbps. (480)

_____ 10. Fiber to the Premises (FTTP) uses fiber-optic cable to provide extremely high-speed Internet access to a user's physical permanent location. (484)

_____ 11. Latency is the time it takes a signal to travel from one location to another on a network. (491)

Multiple Choice Select the best answer.

1. With _____, users can view message details such as the length of calls and, in some cases, read message contents instead of listening to them. (467)
   a. Web services
   b. Internet telephony
   c. visual voice mail
   d. video messaging

2. When an online meeting takes place on the Web, it is called _____. (468)
   a. video messaging
   b. a peer-to-peer network
   c. a Web conference
   d. a Web meeting

3. A document management system _____. (468)
   a. allows users to share documents with other users in real time
   b. provides personal information manager functions
   c. provides for storage and management of a company's documents
   d. prints to a Web address associated with a particular printer

4. A _____ is a Web application that combines services from two or more sources, creating a new application. (469)
   a. document management system
   b. peer-to-peer network
   c. Web service
   d. mashup

5. _____ are devices that provide a common central connection point for nodes on the network. (476)
   a. Packets and tokens
   b. Hubs and switches
   c. T1 and T3 lines
   d. Routers and digital modems

6. _____ is a standard, specifically a protocol, that defines how a network uses radio signals to communicate with a tag placed in or attached to an object, an animal, or a person. (481)
   a. RFID
   b. WiMAX
   c. Bluetooth
   d. UWB

7. _____ consists of a single copper wire surrounded by at least three layers. (493)
   a. Fiber-optic cable
   b. Infrared
   c. Twisted-pair cable
   d. Coaxial cable

8. _____ is a service that provides television programs over the cellular network. (495)
   a. Cellular radio
   b. Mobile TV
   c. Video messaging
   d. UWB

STUDENT ASSIGNMENTS

Checkpoint

Matching Match the terms with their definitions.

_____ 1. picture messaging (464)
_____ 2. groupware (467)
_____ 3. extranet (477)
_____ 4. IrDA (480)
_____ 5. ATM (485)
_____ 6. dial-up modem (485)
_____ 7. digital modem (486)
_____ 8. bandwidth (491)
_____ 9. transmission media (491)
_____ 10. noise (493)

a. communications device that can convert digital signals to analog signals and analog signals to digital signals, so that data can travel along an analog telephone line
b. amount of data, instructions, and information that can travel over a communications channel
c. materials or substances capable of carrying one or more signals
d. specification to transmit data wirelessly among computers and devices via infrared light waves
e. allows users to send pictures and sound files, as well as short text messages, to a phone or other mobile device, or a computer
f. service that carries voice, data, video, and multimedia at very high speeds
g. communications device that sends and receives data and information to and from a digital line
h. allows customers or suppliers to access part of a company's intranet
i. electrical disturbance that can degrade communications
j. software that helps groups of people share information over a network

Short Answer Write a brief answer to each of the following questions.

1. What is text messaging? ____________ What are some options for sending and receiving text messages? ____________
2. Describe how the global positioning system (GPS) works. ____________ How do individuals use GPS technology? ____________
3. How are a local area network (LAN), a metropolitan area network (MAN), and a wide area network (WAN) different? ____________ What is a wireless LAN? ____________
4. What is a network topology? ____________ What are the five types of digital dedicated lines? ____________
5. What are three different types of digital modems? ____________ How does each one function? ____________

Beyond the Book Follow the book element instructions below; present your findings (brief report, presentation, discussion, or other means).

1. Ethics & Issues — Select an Ethics & Issues in this chapter (465, 474, 480, 492, 494), find a recent newspaper/magazine article that supports one point of view presented, and then evaluate the article.
2. Computer Usage @ Work — Use the Web or a recent newspaper/magazine to locate three additional unique usages of computer technology in the agriculture field (497). What makes the use of these technologies unique to the agriculture field?
3. Companies on the Cutting Edge and Technology Trailblazers — Use the Web or a recent newspaper/magazine to locate an interesting fact about Cisco Systems, Verizon, Robert Metcalfe, or Patricia Russo that was not presented in the chapter (499).
4. High-Tech Talk — Locate a recent newspaper/magazine article that discusses topics related to OSI Reference Model (498). Would you recommend the article you found? Why or why not?
5. FAQs and Web Links — Use the Web or a recent newspaper/magazine to locate three additional facts about an FAQ (463, 478, 480, 486, 488, 492) and Web Link (462, 464, 466, 468, 475, 478, 481, 484, 486, 488, 489, 495) that were not presented in the chapter.
6. Looking Ahead — Use the Web or a recent newspaper/magazine to discover additional uses of the technology presented in Body Area Networks Sense Intentions (471).
7. Innovative Computing — Use the Web or a recent newspaper/magazine to locate two additional interesting facts about Geocaching for Hidden Treasure (466) or Watch Your Television Wherever You Go (495).
8. Making Use of the Web — Visit three of the Shopping and Auctions sites (133) and outline the information on each Web site and the possible uses for each Web site.

Learn It Online

The Learn It Online exercises are interactive Web exercises designed to reinforce and expand your understanding of the chapter concepts. The descriptions below briefly summarize each exercise.

To complete the Learn It Online exercises, visit the Computer Concepts CourseMate Web site at www.cengagebrain.com, navigate to the Chapter 9 resources for this book, click the link for the exercise you want to complete, and then read the instructions.

1 At the Movies — Got Your Video Right Here

Watch a movie to see why the Sling Media Slingbox is the best way to beam your favorite shows to any broadband-connected computer or Windows Mobile device in the world and then answer questions about the movie.

2 Video and Audio: You Review It — Wireless Instant Messaging

Search for, choose, and write a review of a video, podcast, or vodcast that discusses wireless instant messaging.

3 Student Edition Labs — Networking Basics and Wireless Networking

Enhance your understanding and knowledge about networking basics and wireless networking by completing the Networking Basics and Wireless Networking Labs.

4 Practice Test

Take a multiple choice test that checks your knowledge of the chapter concepts and review the resulting study guide.

5 Who Wants To Be a Computer Genius^2?

Play the Shelly Cashman Series version of this popular game by answering questions to find out if you are a computer genius. Panic buttons are available to provide assistance during game play.

6 Wheel of Terms

Identify important key terms presented in this chapter by playing the Shelly Cashman Series version of this popular game.

7 You're Hired!

Embark on the path to a career in computers by answering questions and solving puzzles related to concepts discussed in this chapter.

8 Crossword Puzzle Challenge

Complete an interactive crossword puzzle to reinforce concepts presented in this chapter.

9 Windows Exercises

Step through the Windows 7 exercises to learn about understanding your modem, Windows Firewall, viewing network connections, and using Help and Support to understand networks.

10 Exploring Computer Careers

Read about a career as a network specialist, search for related employment advertisements, and then answer related questions.

11 Web Apps — Gmail

Learn how to use Gmail to send and receive e-mail messages, label e-mail messages, chat with others, and search for e-mail messages.

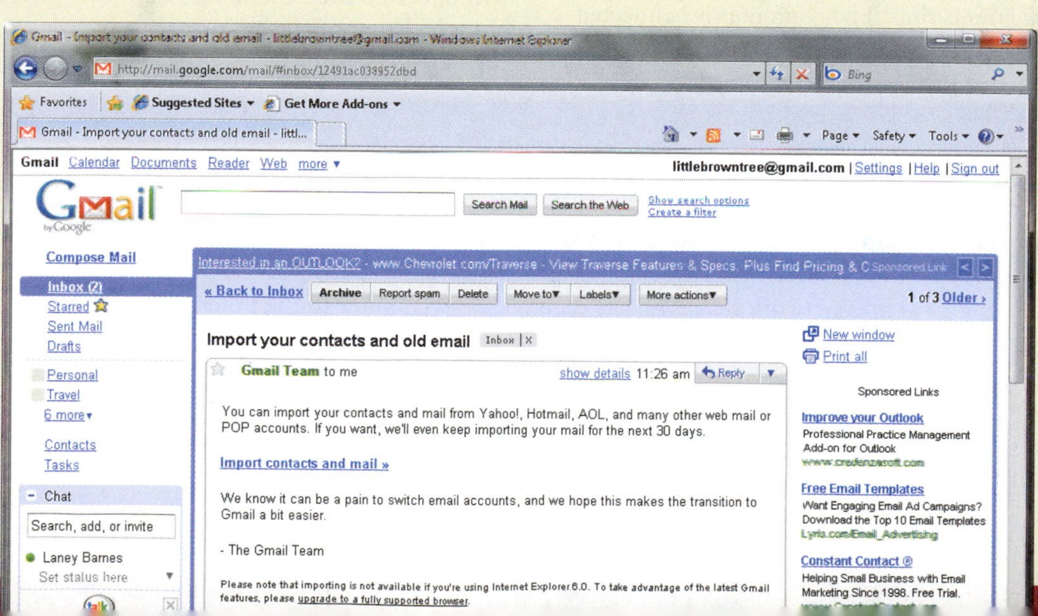

STUDENT ASSIGNMENTS

Problem Solving @ Home

The Problem Solving @ Home exercises extend your knowledge of the chapter concepts by seeking solutions to practical computer problems that you may encounter at home or school. The Collaboration exercise should be completed with a team.

In the real world, practical problems often can be solved in multiple ways. Provide one solution to each of the following problems using available resources, such as articles on the Web or in print, blogs, podcasts, videos, television, user guides, other individuals, and electronics and computer stores. You may need to use multiple resources to obtain an answer. Present your solutions in the form requested by your instructor (brief report, presentation, discussion, or other means).

1. **Headset Does Not Synchronize** You are attempting to synchronize a Bluetooth-enabled cell phone with a Bluetooth headset. When the cell phone searches for nearby devices, it does not recognize the Bluetooth headset. What might be causing this?
2. **Bluetooth Headset Static** After successfully synchronizing your Bluetooth-enabled cell phone with the Bluetooth headset from Exercise 1, you experience a significant amount of static when you use the headset in certain locations inside your house. What might be causing this interference?

3. **Text Messages Not Received** Although you have sent your friend multiple text messages from a cell phone, he is not receiving them. What might be the problem?
4. **Cannot Determine Location** Recently, you purchased cell phones with GPS capabilities for your children, which allows you to use the Internet to determine their location. You attempt to determine your child's location, but the location does not display. Why is this happening?
5. **Intermittent Network Connection** While using your computer, you intermittently lose the network connection. The computer is connected to a wired network using an Ethernet cable. What might be causing this loss of connection?
6. **Telephone Noise** Recently, you installed DSL service in your house. Your computers can connect to the Internet successfully, but your home telephone now has a lot of noise. Before the DSL service was installed, your telephone had no noise problem. What steps will you take to eliminate the noise?
7. **No Network Activity** Your computer has a network card installed to access the wired network in your house. Upon plugging the Ethernet cable into the network card and the network port on the wall, the activity lights on the network card do not illuminate. What might be causing this?
8. **Instant Messaging Problems** While staying in a hotel, you attempt to use your notebook computer to connect to the hotel's wireless network. You start AIM (AOL Instant Messenger) to chat with your friends, but the computer has difficulty connecting to AIM. You then try to use Yahoo! Messenger, but a similar problem occurs. What steps will you take before calling technical support?
9. **Offline Game Console** You are attempting to connect a new Nintendo Wii game console to your wireless home network. After configuring the game console with all necessary information about your network, it still does not connect. Your netbook and other wireless devices in your house connect without issue from the same location as the game console. What might be wrong?

Collaboration

10. **Multiplayer Game Setup** You, along with two of your friends, decide to play multiplayer computer games at your house. In order to play multiplayer computer games from the same location, however, you learn that you must set up a local area network that connects each player's computer to the other computers. Form a team of three people. One team member should research what software (if any) is required, besides the game itself, to connect the computers to the local area network. Another team member should research what additional hardware is required to set up this local area network. Finally, the last team member should research how to configure the computers to connect to one another. Compile your findings and then submit them to your instructor.

Problem Solving @ Work

The Problem Solving @ Work exercises extend your knowledge of the chapter concepts by seeking solutions to practical computer problems that you may encounter at work. The Collaboration exercise should be completed with a team.

In the real world, practical problems often can be solved in multiple ways. Provide one solution to each of the following problems using available resources, such as articles on the Web or in print, blogs, podcasts, videos, television, user guides, other individuals, and electronics and computer stores. You may need to use multiple resources to obtain an answer. Present your solutions in the form requested by your instructor (brief report, presentation, discussion, or other means).

1. **Network Not Found** To take advantage of your employer's Wi-Fi services, you brought your notebook computer to work. When you turn on the computer, it does not recognize the available wireless networks. What steps will you take to determine why your computer is not recognizing the wireless networks?

2. **Slow Network Connection** You subscribed to an Internet service for your home business. After performing several tests, you realize that the Internet connection speed you were promised by your Internet access provider is higher than the speed you currently are experiencing. What might be causing this? What are your next steps?

3. **Phone Cannot Access E-Mail Messages** After purchasing a new smart phone so that you can check your work e-mail account from remote locations, you are unable to configure it to access your e-mail account. What are your next steps?

4. **Cannot Send E-Mail Messages** You successfully have configured your smart phone to access your work e-mail account from Exercise 3 and now can receive e-mail messages successfully. You find, however, that you are unable to send e-mail messages. What might be causing this?

5. **WEP Key Required** The information technology team has provided you with a new notebook computer. When you attempt to connect to the wireless network, Windows asks you for a WEP key. How will you proceed?

6. **Trouble Accessing Wired Network** In an effort to save money spent in commuting to and from your office, your boss has agreed to provide you with a notebook computer so that you can work from home. When you work in the office, you bring the notebook computer and regularly retrieve files from your desktop computer. When you attempt to use the corporate network to connect the notebook computer to the desktop computer, an error message appears stating that the connection is unsuccessful. What might be wrong?

7. **No GPS Signal** As a traveling sales representative for a startup company, your boss provided you with a GPS receiver so that you can locate your customers when driving to meet them at various locations. When you travel to certain areas, the GPS receiver has a difficult time receiving signals from the GPS satellites. What might be wrong? How can you make sure that you are able to locate your customers' addresses?

8. **Bad Network Cable** Each time you move your office computer slightly, it loses the network connection. You check the network port on the back of the computer and realize that the Ethernet cable does not snap into the port, making it easy for it to become dislodged. What will you do to resolve this problem?

Collaboration

9. **Computers in Agriculture** Your employer owns hundreds of acres of orange groves and realizes labor and utility costs can be decreased by installing automated systems to manage the property. As a computer-literate employee of the organization, your supervisor asks you to research automated systems that can help decrease expenses. Form a team of three people to research automated agricultural solutions. One team member should research automated irrigation systems that water the trees only as needed. Another team member should research solutions that can keep the trees healthy and free from pests, and the third team member should create a list of reasons why these automated systems can decrease costs, bolster efficiency, and increase profit. Compile your findings and submit them to your instructor.

Learn How To

The Learn How To activities step you through fundamental technology skills when using a computer. The Learn How To exercises enable you to become more proficient with these skills.

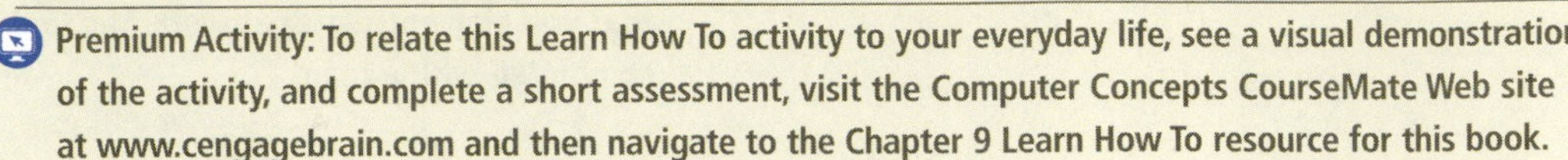

Premium Activity: To relate this Learn How To activity to your everyday life, see a visual demonstration of the activity, and complete a short assessment, visit the Computer Concepts CourseMate Web site at www.cengagebrain.com and then navigate to the Chapter 9 Learn How To resource for this book.

Learn How To 1: Set Up and Install a Wi-Fi Home Network

In this chapter you learned about home networks and their advantages (see page 489, Home Networks). Creating a Wi-Fi home network consists of four phases: 1) subscribe to a high-speed Internet access provider, 2) purchase the Wi-Fi equipment, 3) connect the physical devices, and 4) create the network through the use of software.

Subscribe to a High-Speed Internet Access Provider A high-speed Internet access provider is advisable to connect all computers on the home network to the Internet. The three primary ways for home users to obtain a fast connection to the Internet are DSL, cable, and satellite. DSL is provided by telephone companies, cable is provided by cable TV companies, and satellite connections are provided by satellite TV providers. Each has its advantages and disadvantages, including the minimum and maximum speed of Internet access, cost, and availability.

Determining the optimal high-speed Internet access provider depends largely on where the network will be located, local costs, and service availability. The way to obtain the best high-speed Internet access provider is to research the options available in your area.

Exercise

1. Assume you live near Coeur d'Alene, Idaho. You have decided that a high-speed Internet access provider and a Wi-Fi network would be advantageous for your at-home business. Find answers to the following questions for this Idaho town or a town specified by your instructor: What high-speed Internet access providers are available? Which provides the best service? Which is the cheapest? Based on the information you gather, write a plan for subscribing to a high-speed Internet access provider. Submit the answers to the questions and your plan to your instructor.

Purchase the Wi-Fi Equipment As part of the service when you subscribe to a high-speed Internet access provider, you receive a modem that is capable of connecting to the Internet. In most cases, the modem is not a wireless transmitter. So, in order to establish a wireless connection between the Internet and the home network, you will need a wireless router that establishes the wireless access point.

You can visit any retail electronics store and find a wide variety of wireless routers. A key to purchasing the correct router is to ensure it will work with your modem and Internet access provider. Some Internet access providers support only certain brands of routers and, while it is true that other routers may work, you might be taking a risk if you purchase an unsupported router. With the popularity of wireless home networks, though, some Internet access providers now provide a wireless router as part of the subscription service, often for an additional fee. You should investigate closely the needs for the Wi-Fi router to ensure compatibility with your Internet access provider.

In addition to the router, each computer that is to be part of the Wi-Fi network needs a wireless network adapter. This device allows the computers to communicate with one another. Most external wireless network adapters plug in either a PC Card slot, ExpressCard slot, or a USB connection. Many notebook computers have a built-in wireless network adapter.

Finally, some home networks have a combination of wired and wireless devices. In these networks, the modem connects to the wireless router, and computers on the network connect to the wireless router using either a wireless or wired connection.

Once the Wi-Fi equipment is assembled, you are ready to connect your home network.

Exercise

1. Using your Web research skills, determine the type of IEEE 802.11 standard used by modems available from Internet access providers. What percentage use 802.11b? What percentage use 802.11g? What percentage use 802.11n? If your modem uses 802.11b but your wireless network router is 802.11n, what happens? Based on your research, which router do you recommend? Submit your answers to your instructor.

Connect the Physical Devices Once you have assembled your equipment, you can connect the devices in the network. Usually, the modem will be connected to the source of the Internet transmission (DSL, cable, or satellite). Then the modem is connected to the wireless router, which in turn is connected to the computers on your network.

After these connections are completed, each of the computers that will be used in the network that do not have

Learn How To

a built-in wireless network adapter must have the adapter attached, often by using a USB connection. Once these connections are made, the computers can join the network. Follow the remaining instructions in the wizard to finish creating the network configuration. Once the network is created, follow the network adapter's instructions to join the network. When Windows prompts you to select a location for the network, select Home network. If you do not select Home network, you will be unable to complete the steps in the next section. If the computer you are connecting is in a public place and you are concerned about its security, you either should select Work network or Public network and not complete the following steps.

Create the Homegroup To establish a homegroup and share files with other computers on your network, complete the following steps:

1. Click the Start button on the Windows taskbar and then click Control Panel on the Start menu.
2. Click the 'Choose homegroup and sharing options' link below the Network and Internet heading to display the HomeGroup dialog box.
3. Click the 'Create a homegroup' button to display the Create a Homegroup dialog box.
4. In the Create a Homegroup dialog box, place a check mark next to each item you wish to share with other computers connected to the same homegroup and then click the Next button.
5. Once Windows sets up the homegroup, it will display a password that other computer users will need to know to join your homegroup.
6. Click the 'Print password and instructions' link to open the 'View and print your homegroup password' window, which contains your homegroup password and instructions about how other computers on your network can join your homegroup (Figure 9-44).
7. Ready the printer according to the printer instructions and then click the 'Print this page' button to display the Print dialog box. Select the printer to which you want to print and then click the Print button to print these instructions.
8. Click the Close button on the title bar to close the 'View and print your homegroup password' window.
9. Click the Finish button to open the HomeGroup window (Figure 9-45).
10. If necessary, make changes to your homegroup settings and then click the Save changes button. If you have no changes, click the Close button on the title bar to close the HomeGroup window.
11. Follow the instructions you printed in Step 7 to join other computers to the homegroup.

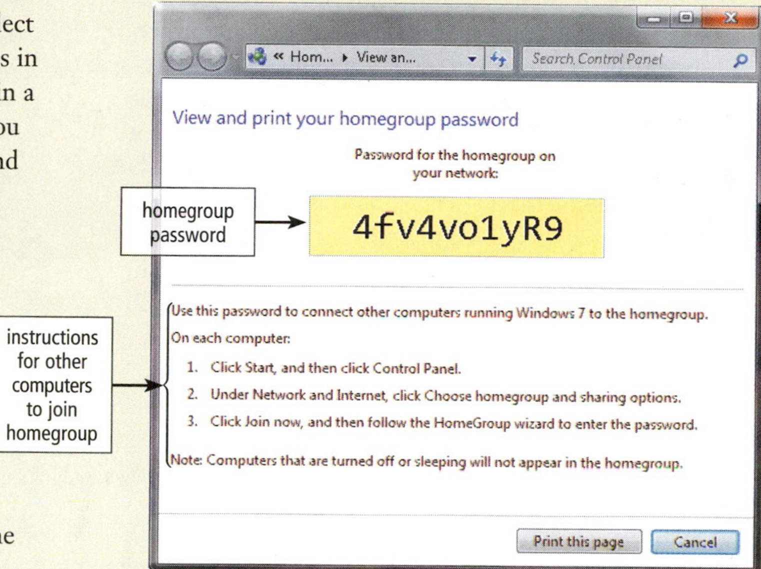

Figure 9-44

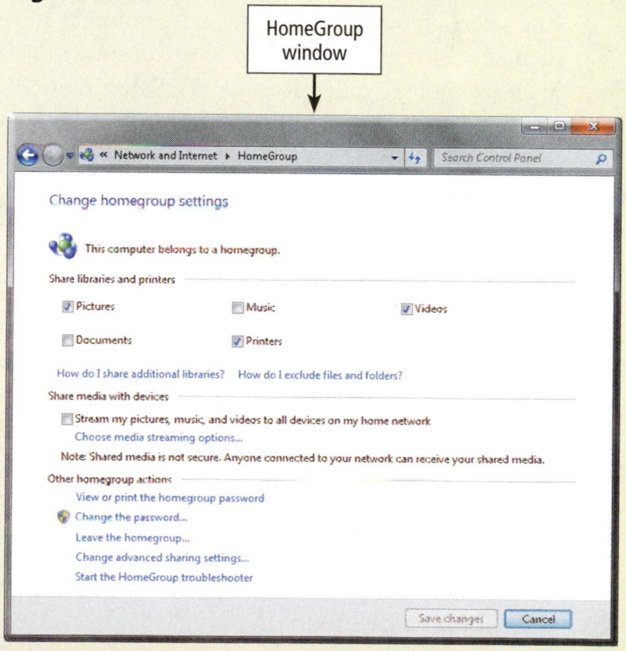

HomeGroup window

Figure 9-45

Exercise

1. Form a three-person team whose responsibility is to create a Wi-Fi network for a small business in your local area. Assign tasks to each member of the team. Write a detailed plan for creating the Wi-Fi network, including the brand and type of equipment to be purchased, costs, and a schedule for completing the work. Explain why your team made each choice, and be prepared to defend your choices. Submit the plan to your instructor.

Web Research

The Web Research exercises broaden your understanding of the chapter concepts by presenting questions that require you to search the Web for answers.

1 Search Sleuth

Use one of the search engines listed in Figure 2-10 in Chapter 2 on page 85 or your own favorite search engine to find the answers to the following questions. Copy and paste the Web address from the Web page where you found the answer. Some questions may have more than one answer. If required, submit your answers to your instructor. (1) Which product is manufactured in the modified chemical vapor deposition (MCVD) process? (2) In what city is the IrDA corporate office located? How many companies are IrDA members? (3) Which agency funds and controls the global positioning system? In how many hours does one satellite orbit the earth? (4) Which California county built a crime lab in 2008 that uses passive RFID tags to track evidence? (5) Who is the author of the scientific paper, "A Mathematical Theory of Communication"? Which elements comprise the communications system described in this paper? (6) Who sent the first text message in 1989?

2 Green Computing

As the speed of Ethernet routers, switches, and servers increases, so does the amount of electricity consumed. Engineers are working to reduce the power requirements by increasing efficiency in various ways, including a technology called Rapid PHY Selection (RPS), which could save $1.2 billion during computer systems' lifetimes. Critics say such measures would slow the networks' performance and cause connectivity problems. Consumers, too, can benefit from using green Wi-Fi routers that adjust power consumption and shut down automatically. View online Web sites that provide information about reducing networks' electricity consumption. How does RPS adjust Ethernet speed and power usage? What technological challenges are engineers facing when developing this RPS technology? Which companies are manufacturing Wi-Fi routers for home networks? How much energy do they claim to save? Write a report summarizing your findings, and include a table of links to Web sites that provide additional details.

3 Social Networking

Conversations, experiences, photos, videos, and other aspects of a person's life can be preserved for future generations using LifeNaut, an online social network funded by the Terasem Movement Foundation, Inc. More than 9,000 people have created a personal space, called a mindfile, to create a profile, build a 3-D virtual avatar, upload files, and then share these personal life memories with other users. Members can meet new people by browsing the online mindfiles. As biotechnology advances, scientists predict that these preserved memories could be added to a person's mind, not necessarily the mind of the person who originally created these mindfiles. Visit the LifeNaut Web site (lifenaut.com) and then click the About and FAQ links on the left side of the home page. Could viewing the LifeNaut mindfiles be useful to people who have lost their memory? Would parents desire to preserve aspects of their lives for their children to view and hear? Would you desire to record your life? Summarize the information you read and viewed.

4 Blogs

Avoiding information overload is difficult in today's world, with more than 80 million live Web sites available at all times of the day. Managing blogs, news feeds, and podcasts can be accomplished by subscribing to Bloglines, a free service that tracks Web sites tailored to specific interests. More than 10,000 subscribers monitor an average of 20 news feeds, which are updated hourly. Visit Bloglines (bloglines.com) and then read the information in the About link at the bottom of the home page. What are Bloglines' key features? How does Bloglines examine RSS feeds? How does the Web site help readers organize their subscriptions? What is the purpose of a Clip Blog? Summarize the information you read and viewed.

5 Ethics in Action

Consumers may welcome customized advertisements, but they may be unaware of how they have become targeted to receive these marketing messages. When people visit some Web sites, their IP address, browser software, operating system, date, time, and viewing habits are tracked and recorded along with their wish lists and purchase histories. These details are collected and shared among advertisers without the computer users' consent. The Center for Digital Democracy (CDD) filed a complaint with the Federal Trade Commission stating that these targeted advertisements and user profiles can constitute an invasion of privacy. Visit the CDD Web site (democraticmedia.org) and other Web sites discussing online ads and privacy concerns. How are the CDD and other organizations working to protect consumers from being exploited by digital advertisers? What steps can Web users take to avoid sharing personal data with marketers? Write a report summarizing your findings, and include a table of links to Web sites that provide additional details.

Critical Thinking

The Critical Thinking exercises challenge your assessment and decision-making skills by presenting real-world situations associated with the chapter concepts. The Collaboration exercise should be completed with a team.

To evaluate the situations below, use personal experiences and available resources such as articles on the Web or in print, blogs, podcasts, videos, television, user guides, other individuals, and electronics and computer stores. You may need to use multiple resources to form conclusions and make recommendations.

1. Class Discussion — Online Collaboration
Your aunt owns a major development firm in the Southeast. The company specializes in designing and constructing retirement communities throughout the United States. One of her biggest expenses is the cost of her project management team traveling to meetings with on-site personnel. She recently learned about the collaboration features of Microsoft Office. She is aware that you are taking computer classes and has asked you to examine online collaboration as an alternative to some or all of the face-to-face meetings with on-site personnel. Discuss the advantages and disadvantages of collaborating online. Be sure to address the following questions in your discussion: What is a whiteboard? How are online meetings set up? What is NetMeeting? Does collaboration require additional hardware?

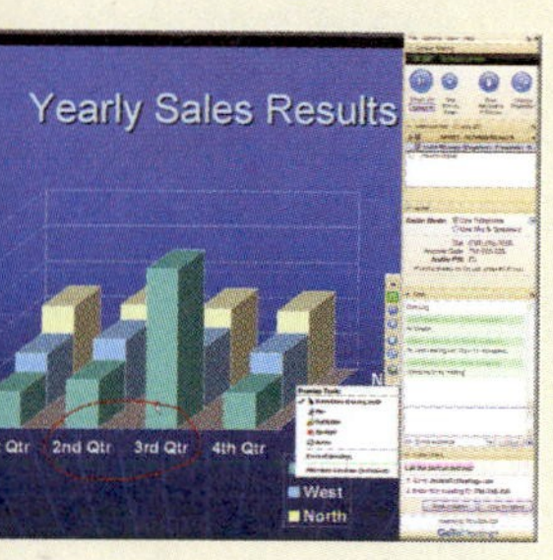

2. Class Presentation — Transmission Media
You work as an intern in the information technology department for the *Star Journal*, a local newspaper. The newspaper's board of directors recently approved a budget for redesigning the interior of its century-old building as part of an urban rehabilitation project. Your manager has been asked to recommend the type of transmission media (wired or wireless) to use for the newspaper's local area network. He has asked you to prepare a presentation that summarizes the advantages of wired versus wireless transmission media for the building. He also requested that you include the following information in your presentation: Which transmission media would have a greater startup cost? Which transmission media do you think is the most secure? Do the walls in the building present a problem for a wireless network? Does a wireless network present any health hazards?

3. Research — Wireless Networking Standards
Several networking standards exist for wireless networks, including 802.11a, 802.11b, 802.11g, and 802.11n. You wish to install a wireless network in your house and want to ensure that you choose the standard that best meets your needs. Research the various wireless networking standards and answer the following questions: Which standard was developed first? Are any of the standards more susceptible to interference from other wireless devices in your home, such as alarm systems and cell phones? Which standard is the fastest? Is the fastest standard always the best, or do other factors on your wireless network or on the Internet affect performance? Is equipment to support one standard more expensive than the equipment that supports the other standards? Address the answers to those questions, as well as any other information you find pertinent to deciding upon the best standard for your use, and then submit a report to your instructor.

Collaboration

4. Internet Access Providers Your school offers free student-intern assistance to the county government. The county in turn assigns a manager to each team of students. The manager is responsible for defining the project assigned to the student team and ensuring that dates are met. Your team has been assigned to the manager of communications in the information technology department. Next year, he plans to select an Internet access provider — DSL, cable, or wireless — to handle all Internet communications in the county buildings. He has asked your group to prepare a report recommending which type of Internet access provider to use. Form a three-member team. Each team member should choose a different type of Internet access provider. Using the Web and/or print media, each team member should analyze the advantages and disadvantages of their chosen access provider. Include such features as startup costs, installation time, e-mail disk storage, speed, online protection, and recurring costs. As a team, merge your findings into a team report and share your recommendations with your class.

Chapter Ten

Database Management

Objectives

After completing this chapter, you will be able to:

1. Define the term, database, and explain how a database interacts with data and information
2. Define the term, data integrity, and describe the qualities of valuable information
3. Discuss the terms character, field, record, and file
4. Describe file maintenance techniques (adding records, modifying records, deleting records) and validation techniques
5. Differentiate between a file processing approach and the database approach
6. Discuss the functions common to most database management systems: data dictionary, file retrieval and maintenance, data security, and backup and recovery
7. Describe characteristics of relational, object-oriented, and multidimensional databases
8. Explain how to access Web databases
9. Identify database design guidelines and discuss the responsibilities of database analysts and administrators

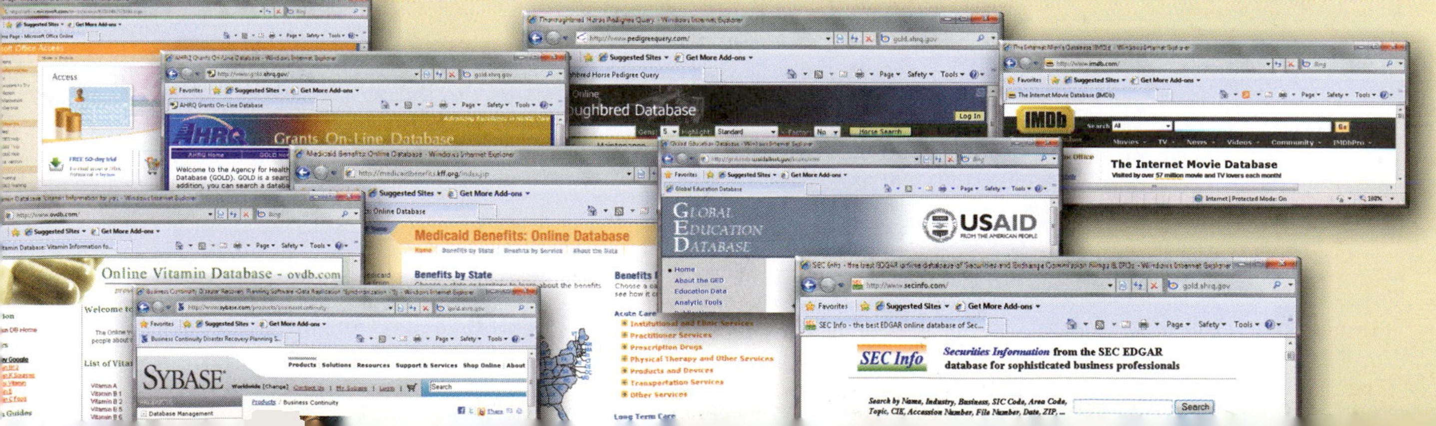

Databases, Data, and Information

As presented in Chapter 3, a **database** is a collection of data organized in a manner that allows access, retrieval, and use of that data. *Data* is a collection of unprocessed items, which can include text, numbers, images, audio, and video. For example, you can type text on a keyboard, talk into a computer's microphone, transfer photos taken with a digital camera to a computer, and capture motion and sounds with a video camera and store the recordings on a computer.

Information is processed data; that is, it is organized, meaningful, and useful. In addition to documents, information can be in the form of audio, images, and video. For example, voice communications can be sent in an e-mail message for a family member, friend, or coworker to hear. You can post photos taken with a digital camera on a Web page for others to view. With a Web cam, others can see you in real time during a conference call.

Computers process data in a database into information. A database at a school, for example, contains data about its students and classes. When a student is admitted to a school, an admissions department clerk enters several data items into a computer. The clerk also uses a digital camera to photograph the new student. This photo, along with the other entered data, is

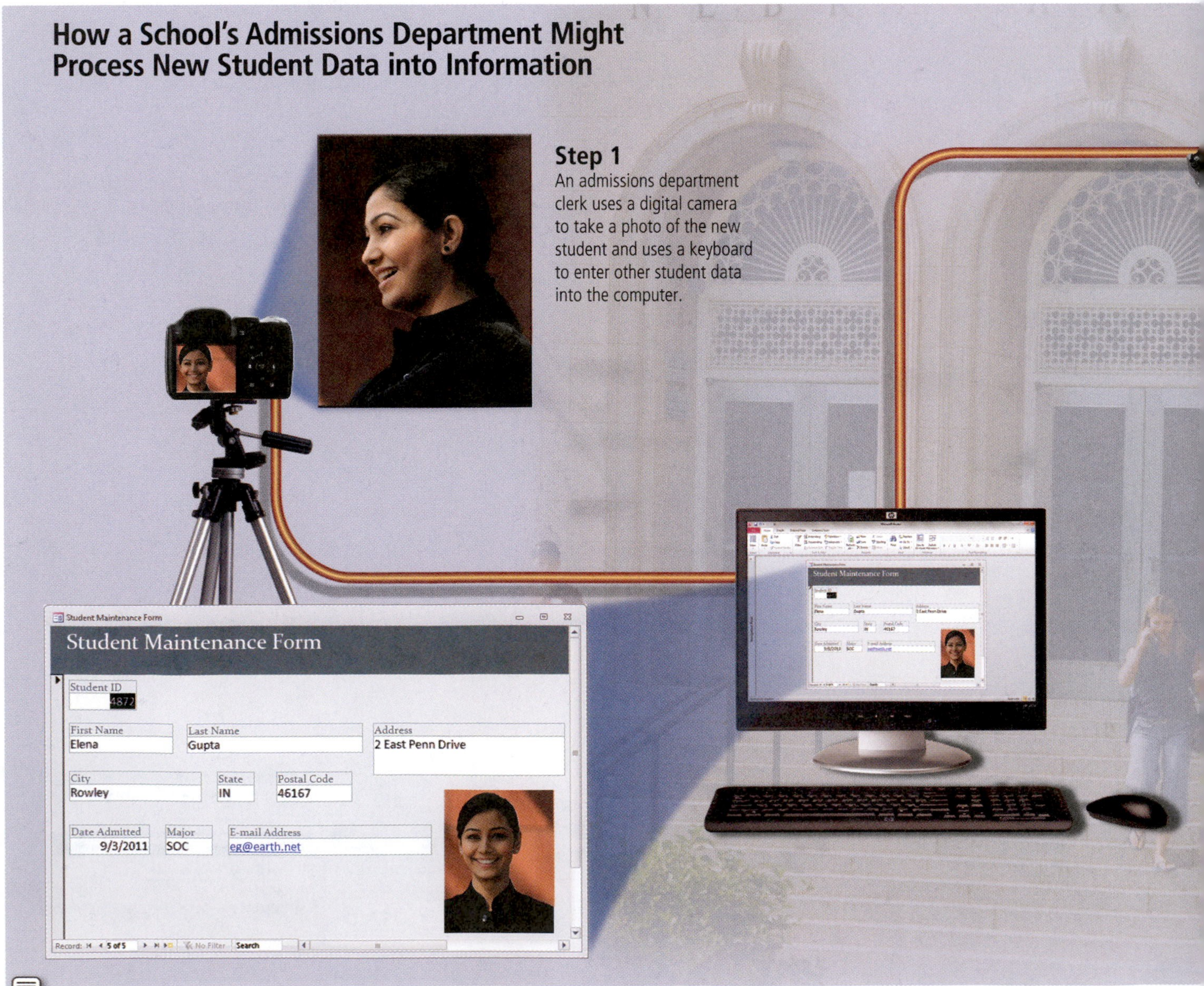

How a School's Admissions Department Might Process New Student Data into Information

Step 1
An admissions department clerk uses a digital camera to take a photo of the new student and uses a keyboard to enter other student data into the computer.

Student Maintenance Form
Student ID 4872
First Name Elena
Last Name Gupta
Address 2 East Penn Drive
City Rowley
State IN
Postal Code 46167
Date Admitted 9/3/2011
Major SOC
E-mail Address eg@earth.net
Record: 5 of 5 No Filter Search

Figure 10-1 This figure shows how a school's admissions department might process new student data into information.

stored in a database on a server's hard disk. A computer at the school then processes the new student data and sends advising appointment information to a laser printer and student ID card information to an ID card printer (Figure 10-1). The student ID is encoded on a magnetic stripe on the back of the ID card.

With **database software**, often called a **database management system (DBMS)**, users create a computerized database; add, modify, and delete data in the database; sort and retrieve data from the database; and create forms and reports from the data in the database. Database software includes many powerful features, as you will discover later in this chapter.

Most organizations realize that data is one of their more valuable assets — because data is used to generate information. Many business transactions take less time when employees have instant access to information. For example, if admissions department clerks at a school have instant access to the advisor records, they can schedule advising appointments while admitting students. When employees are more productive, customers (students, in this case) usually are more satisfied. When customers are happy, typically they become loyal to that organization. Loyal customers can lead to referrals and an increase in profits.

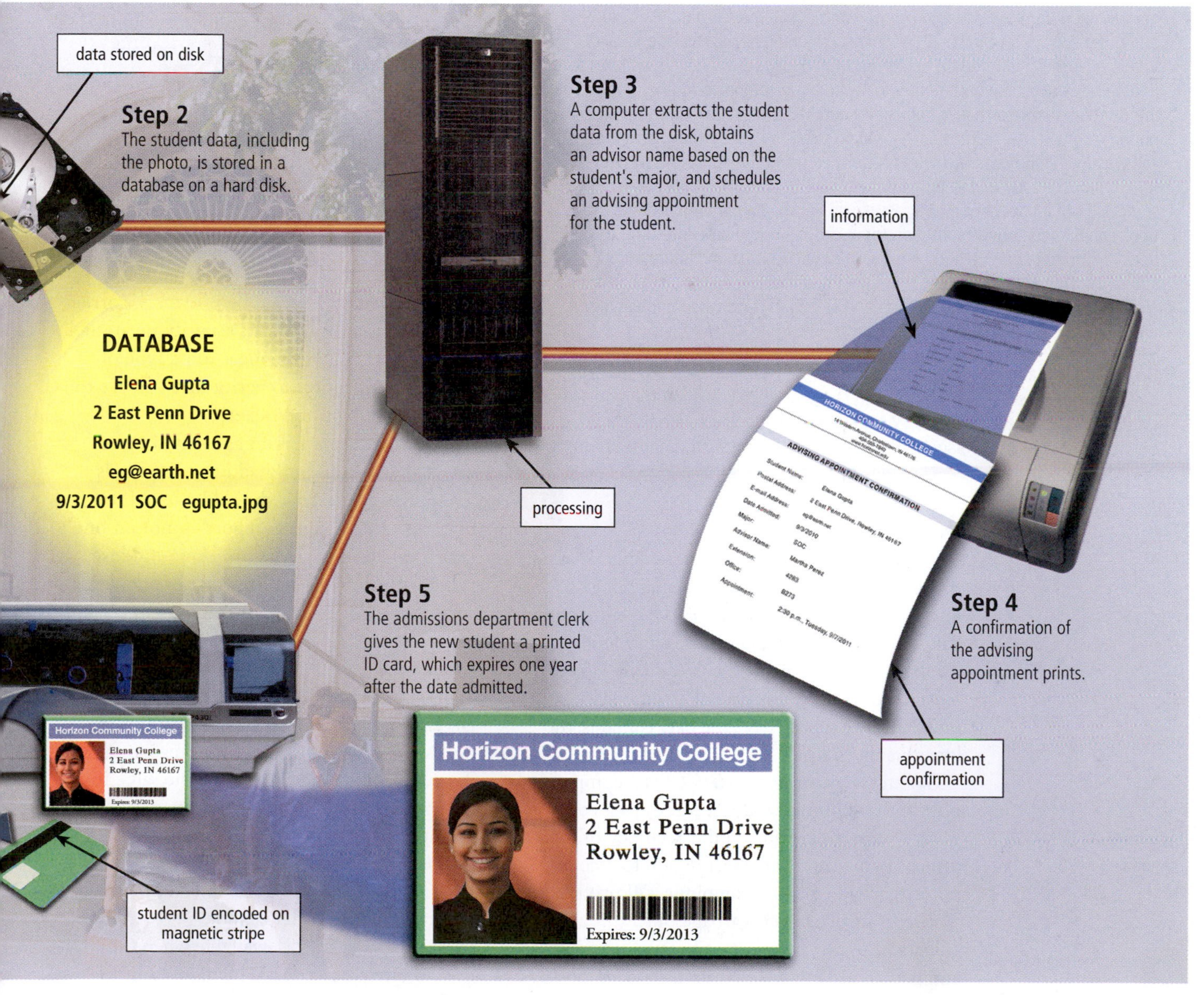

Ethics & Issues

For the complete text of the Ethics & Issues boxes found in this chapter, visit the Computer Concepts CourseMate Web site at www.cengagebrain.com and then navigate to the Chapter 10 Ethics & Issues resource for this book.

To ensure that data is accessible on demand, an organization must manage and protect its data just as it would any other resource. Thus, it is vital that the data has integrity and is kept secure. For example, data in a database often is encrypted, or encoded in an unreadable form, to prevent unauthorized users from reading its contents. Chapter 11 discusses encryption and other forms of data security. Read Ethics & Issues 10-1 for a related discussion.

ETHICS & ISSUES 10-1

Do Internet Databases Mean the End of Privacy?

The amount of data and information about individuals that is stored anywhere on the Internet increases every day. Photos, financial records, employment history, personal relationship details, and purchases are just a few of the types of data and information available to others for free or for a fee. Any type of data and information placed on the Internet is almost instantly indexed, and often copied, by a vast number of search engines, such as Google and Yahoo!. Older data stored on paper is scanned, digitized, indexed, and stored in databases available on the Internet. Marketing companies gather and sell information about consumer habits and detailed transaction information. Cell phone records can track not only a person's calls but also from where the call was made and other activities performed using the phone. Many people find it almost impossible to purge details about themselves from any of these sources. Even incorrect or embarrassing information regarding past indiscretions can damage one's reputation for decades. Privacy advocates fear that because of the pervasive and permanent nature of data and information stored on the Internet, nobody can expect privacy. They encourage people not to share personal information online and to be judicious when engaging in financial transactions.

Do Internet databases mean the end of privacy? Why or why not? Should the government enact laws to prevent the sale of personal information gathered in Internet databases? Why? How can people change their behaviors so that less personal data is available in Internet databases?

Data Integrity

For a computer to produce correct information, the data that is entered into a database must have integrity. *Data integrity* identifies the quality of the data. An erroneous student address in a student database is an example of incorrect data. When a database contains this type of error, it loses integrity. The more errors the data contains, the lower its integrity.

Garbage in, garbage out (*GIGO*) is a computing phrase that points out the accuracy of a computer's output depends on the accuracy of the input. If you enter incorrect data into a computer (garbage in), the computer will produce incorrect information (garbage out).

Data Integrity

For more information, visit the Computer Concepts CourseMate Web site at www.cengagebrain.com, navigate to the Chapter 10 Web Link resource for this book, and then click Data Integrity.

Data integrity is important because computers and people use information to make decisions and take actions. When you register for classes and pay with a credit card, a process begins that charges an amount to your credit card. If the per credit fee is not correct in the school database, an incorrect amount will be billed to your credit card. This type of error costs both you and the registration clerk extra time and effort to remedy.

Qualities of Valuable Information

The information that data generates also is an important asset. People make decisions daily using all types of information such as receipts, bank statements, pension plan summaries, stock analyses, transcripts, and credit reports. At school, students use grade reports and degree audits to make decisions. In a business, managers make decisions based on sales trends, competitors' products and services, production processes, and even employee skills.

To assist with sound decision making, information must have value. For it to be valuable, information should be accurate, verifiable, timely, organized, accessible, useful, and cost-effective.

- *Accurate information* is error free. Inaccurate information can lead to incorrect decisions. For example, consumers assume their credit report is accurate. If your credit report incorrectly shows past due payments, a bank may not lend you money for a car or house.
- *Verifiable information* can be proven as correct or incorrect. For example, security personnel at an airport usually request some type of photo identification to verify that you are the person named on the ticket.
- *Timely information* has an age suited to its use. A decision to build additional schools in a particular district should be based on the most recent census report — not on one that is 20 years old. Most information loses value with time. Some information, however, such as information about trends, gains value as time passes and more information is obtained. For example, your transcript gains value as you take more classes.
- *Organized information* is arranged to suit the needs and requirements of the decision maker. Two different people may need the same information presented in a different manner. For example, an inventory manager may want an inventory report to list out-of-stock items first. The purchasing agent, instead, wants the report alphabetized by vendor.
- *Accessible information* is available when the decision maker needs it. Having to wait for information may delay an important decision. For example, a sales manager cannot decide

which sales representative deserves the award for highest annual sales if the December sales have not yet been placed in the database.

- *Useful information* has meaning to the person who receives it. Most information is important only to certain people or groups of people. Always consider the audience when collecting and reporting information. Avoid distributing useless information. For example, an announcement of an alumni association meeting is not useful to students not yet graduated.
- *Cost-effective information* should give more value than it costs to produce. An organization occasionally should review the information it produces to determine if it still is cost-effective to produce. Sometimes, it is not easy to place a value on information. For this reason, some organizations create information only on demand, that is, as people request it, instead of on a regular basis. Many make information available online. Users then can access and print online information as they need it. For example, sending a printed benefits manual to each employee could be quite costly. Instead, employees can access an online benefits manual, when they need to review it.

FAQ 10-1

How can I verify the accuracy of my credit report?

The three credit reporting agencies (Equifax, Experian, and TransUnion) developed a central Web site at annualcreditreport.com. Through this Web site, you can request a free copy of your credit report from each credit reporting agency every 12 months. You also can request the reports by mailing a form or calling a toll-free number. If you would like constant monitoring of the activity on your credit report, you can subscribe to a credit monitoring service for a minimal fee. The service will contact you if any unusual or suspicious activity occurs on your credit report.

For more information, visit the Computer Concepts CourseMate Web site at www.cengagebrain.com, navigate to the Chapter 10 FAQ resource for this book, and then click Verifying Credit Report Accuracy.

The Hierarchy of Data

Data is organized in layers. In the computer profession, data is classified in a hierarchy. Each higher level of data consists of one or more items from the lower level. For example, a student has an address, and an address consists of letters and numbers. Depending on the application and the user, different terms describe the various levels of the hierarchy.

As shown in Figure 10-2, a database contains files (sometimes called tables), a file contains records, a record contains fields, and a field is made up of one or more characters. This sample School database contains four files: Student, Instructor, Schedule of Classes, and Student Schedule. The Student file contains records about enrolled students. The Instructor file contains records about current instructors. The Schedule of Classes file contains records about class offerings in a particular semester, and the Student Schedule file contains records about the classes in which a student is enrolled for a given semester. Each field in a record contains many characteristics, one of which is the field size.

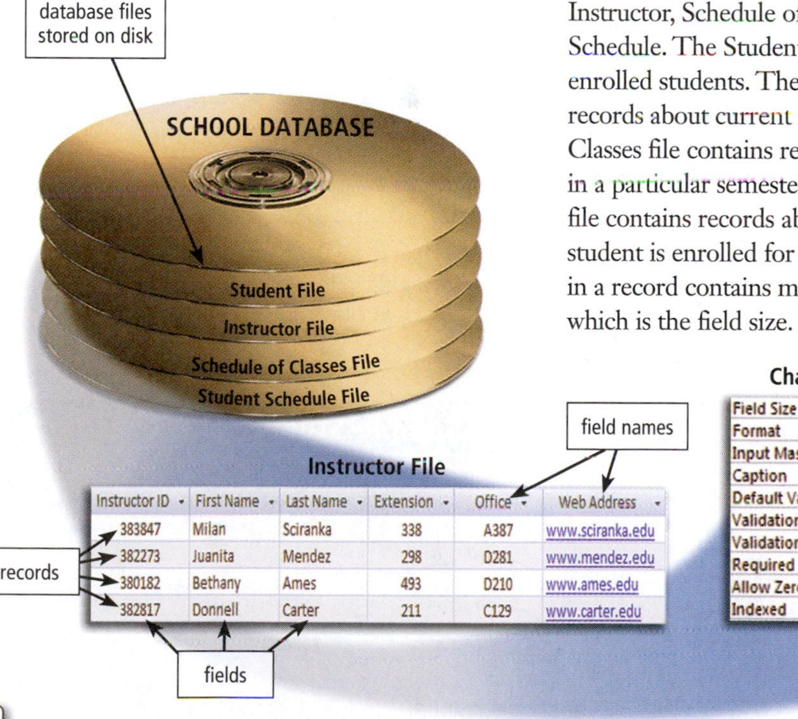

Instructor ID	First Name	Last Name	Extension	Office	Web Address
383847	Milan	Sciranka	338	A387	www.sciranka.edu
382273	Juanita	Mendez	298	D281	www.mendez.edu
380182	Bethany	Ames	493	D210	www.ames.edu
382817	Donnell	Carter	211	C129	www.carter.edu

Characteristics of Instructor ID Field

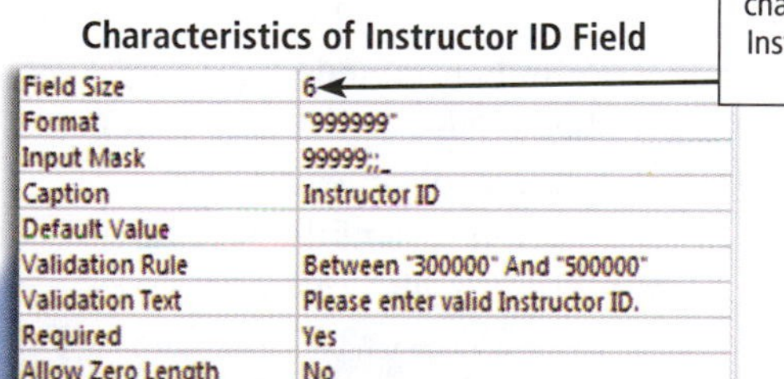

Field Size	6
Format	"999999"
Input Mask	99999;;_
Caption	Instructor ID
Default Value	
Validation Rule	Between "300000" And "500000"
Validation Text	Please enter valid Instructor ID.
Required	Yes
Allow Zero Length	No
Indexed	Yes (No Duplicates)

Figure 10-2 A sample school database with four files: Student, Instructor, Schedule of Classes, and Student Schedule. The sample Instructor file contains four records. Each record contains six fields. The Instructor ID field can contain a maximum of six characters (bytes).

Characters

As discussed in Chapter 4, a bit is the smallest unit of data the computer can process. Eight bits grouped together in a unit comprise a byte. In the ASCII coding scheme, each byte represents a single **character**, which can be a number (4), letter (R), space, punctuation mark (?), or other symbol (&). The Unicode coding scheme, by contrast, uses one or two bytes to represent a character. (Read Appendix C for more information about coding schemes.)

Fields

A **field** is a combination of one or more related characters or bytes and is the smallest unit of data a user accesses. A **field name** uniquely identifies each field. When searching for data in a database, you often specify the field name. Field names for the data in the Instructor file are Instructor ID, First Name, Last Name, Extension, Office, and Web Address.

A database uses a variety of characteristics, such as field size and data type, to define each field. The **field size** defines the maximum number of characters a field can contain. For example, the Instructor ID field contains 6 characters and thus has a field size of 6 (shown in Figure 10-2 on the previous page).

The type of data in a field is an important consideration. Figure 10-3 identifies the data types for fields in the Instructor and Student files. The **data type** specifies the kind of data a field can contain and how the field is used. Common data types include:

- Text (also called *alphanumeric*) — letters, numbers, or special characters
- Numeric (also called number) — numbers only
- AutoNumber — unique number automatically assigned by the DBMS to each added record
- Currency — dollar and cent amounts or numbers containing decimal values
- Date (also called date/time) — month, day, year, and sometimes time
- Memo — lengthy text entries
- Yes/No (also called *Boolean*) — only the values Yes or No (or True or False)
- Hyperlink — E-mail address or Web address that links to a Web page on the Internet or document on a local network
- Object (also called *BLOB* for binary large object) — photo, audio, video, or a document created in other programs, such as word processing or spreadsheet, stored as a bitmap in the database
- Attachment — document or image that is attached to the field, which can be opened in the program that created the document or image (functioning similarly to e-mail attachments)

In the Instructor file, four fields (Instructor ID, First Name, Last Name, and Office) have a text data type; another field (Extension) has a number (numeric) data type; and the last field (Web Address) has a hyperlink data type (Figure 10-3). In the Student file, the Student ID field has an autonumber data type. The First Name, Last Name, Address, City, State, and Major

Instructor file

Instructor ID	Text
First Name	Text
Last Name	Text
Extension	Number
Office	Text
Web Address	Hyperlink

data types

Student file

Student ID	AutoNumber
First Name	Text
Last Name	Text
Address	Text
City	Text
State	Text
Postal Code	Number
E-mail Address	Hyperlink
Date Admitted	Date/Time
Major	Text
Photo	Attachment

Figure 10-3 Data types of fields in the Instructor and Student files.

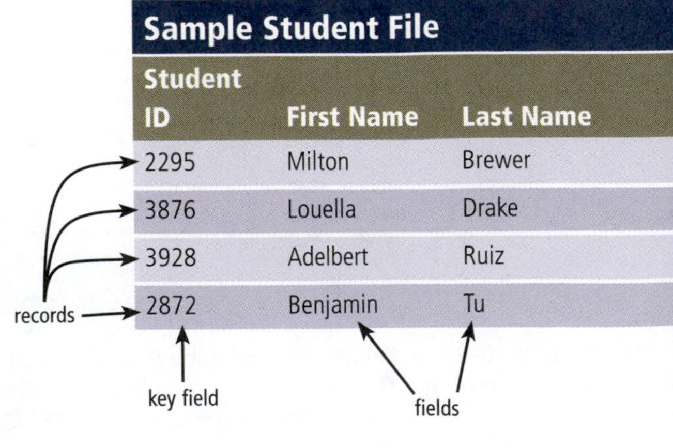

Sample Student File

Student ID	First Name	Last Name
2295	Milton	Brewer
3876	Louella	Drake
3928	Adelbert	Ruiz
2872	Benjamin	Tu

fields have a text data type; the Postal Code field has a number (numeric) data type. The E-mail Address field has a hyperlink data type, Date Admitted a date/time data type, and Photo an attachment data type.

Records

A **record** is a group of related fields. For example, a student record includes a set of fields about one student. A **primary key** is a field that uniquely identifies each record in a file. The data in a primary key is unique to a specific record. For example, the Student ID field uniquely identifies each student because no two students can have the same Student ID. In some tables, the primary key consists of multiple fields, called a *composite key*. For example, the primary key for the Schedule of Classes file could consist of the fields Semester Code, Class Code, and Class Section, which together would uniquely identify each class listed in a schedule.

Files

A **data file** is a collection of related records stored on a storage medium such as a hard disk or optical disc. A Student file at a school might consist of thousands of individual student records. Each student record in the file contains the same fields. Each field, however, contains different data. Figure 10-4 shows a small sample Student file that contains four student records, each with eleven fields. Typical fields about people often include First Name, Last Name, Address, City, State, Postal Code, and E-mail Address.

A database includes a group of related data files. With a DBMS, users access data and set relationships among the data in data files. Read Ethics & Issues 10-2 for a discussion related to a use of databases.

FAQ 10-2

When should I use a database instead of a spreadsheet?

Databases are ideal when you have a large amount of related data to store and quickly need to be able to add to, update, query, and create reports about the data. Use a spreadsheet instead of a database when you have less data to store but frequently need to perform calculations with the data, create charts, and review statistics.

For more information, visit the Computer Concepts CourseMate Web site at www.cengagebrain.com, navigate to the Chapter 10 FAQ resource for this book, and then click Databases and Spreadsheets.

ETHICS & ISSUES 10-2

Should Government Databases Be Used for Dragnets?

In the past several years, the federal government began collecting vast amounts of data about citizens and foreigners who travel to the United States. The data includes fingerprints, DNA samples, travel records, and financial records. Several federal agencies attempt to bring as much of this data together in an effort to locate criminals and prevent future criminal activity. Sometimes, however, these agencies attempt to extract names from the databases based on profiles of known criminals. That is, based on past activities of known criminals, the agencies attempt to predict who is likely to engage in criminal activity in the future. This practice is known as a dragnet. In one case, the FBI performed a dragnet on 250,000 visitors to Las Vegas based on data gathered from airlines, hotels, rental car companies, and other businesses.

As the government gathers more data and links various databases, civil liberties activists claim that dragnets will infringe on the rights of more and more citizens. People may find themselves pulled from flights, banned from checking into hotels, or questioned by law enforcement based on little or no evidence. Law enforcement officials state that the law allows them to perform such acts using the data available and that the dragnets are necessary to prevent criminal activity.

Should the government be allowed to engage in dragnets with available databases? Why or why not? Would you feel that your rights had been violated if you were targeted by law enforcement and had done nothing wrong? Why?

Address	City	State	Postal Code	E-mail Address	Date Admitted	Major	Photo
54 Lucy Court	Charlestown	IN	46176		6/10/2010	EE	mbrewer.jpg
33 Timmons Place	Bonner	IN	45208	lou@world.com	8/9/2010	BIO	ldrake.jpg
99 Tenth Street	Sheldon	IN	46033		10/8/2010	CT	aruiz.jpg
2204 Elm Court	Rowley	IN	46167	tu@indi.net	11/6/2010	GEN	btu.jpg

fields

Figure 10-4 A sample data file, stored on a hard disk, that contains four records, each with eleven fields.

Maintaining Data

File maintenance refers to the procedures that keep data current. File maintenance procedures include adding records to, modifying records in, and deleting records from a file.

Adding Records

Users add new records to a file when they obtain new data. If a new student is admitted to the school, an admissions department clerk adds a new record to the Student file. The process required to add this record to the file might include the following steps:

1. An admissions department clerk uses the database management system (DBMS) to display a Student Maintenance Form that gives him or her access to the Student file. The clerk then clicks the New button, which begins the process of adding a record to the Student file.
2. The clerk fills in the fields of the student record with data (except for the Student ID, which automatically is assigned by the DBMS). In this example, the data entered is kept to a minimum.
3. The clerk takes a picture of the student using a digital camera. The DBMS stores this picture as an attachment to the Student file and prints it on a Student ID card.
4. The admissions department clerk verifies the data on the screen and then instructs the DBMS to add the new student record to the Student file. The system software determines where to write the record on the disk, depending on the location of enough free space on the disk. In some cases, it writes the new record at the end of the file. In other cases, such as illustrated in Figure 10-5, it writes the new record for Elena Gupta between existing records in the file.

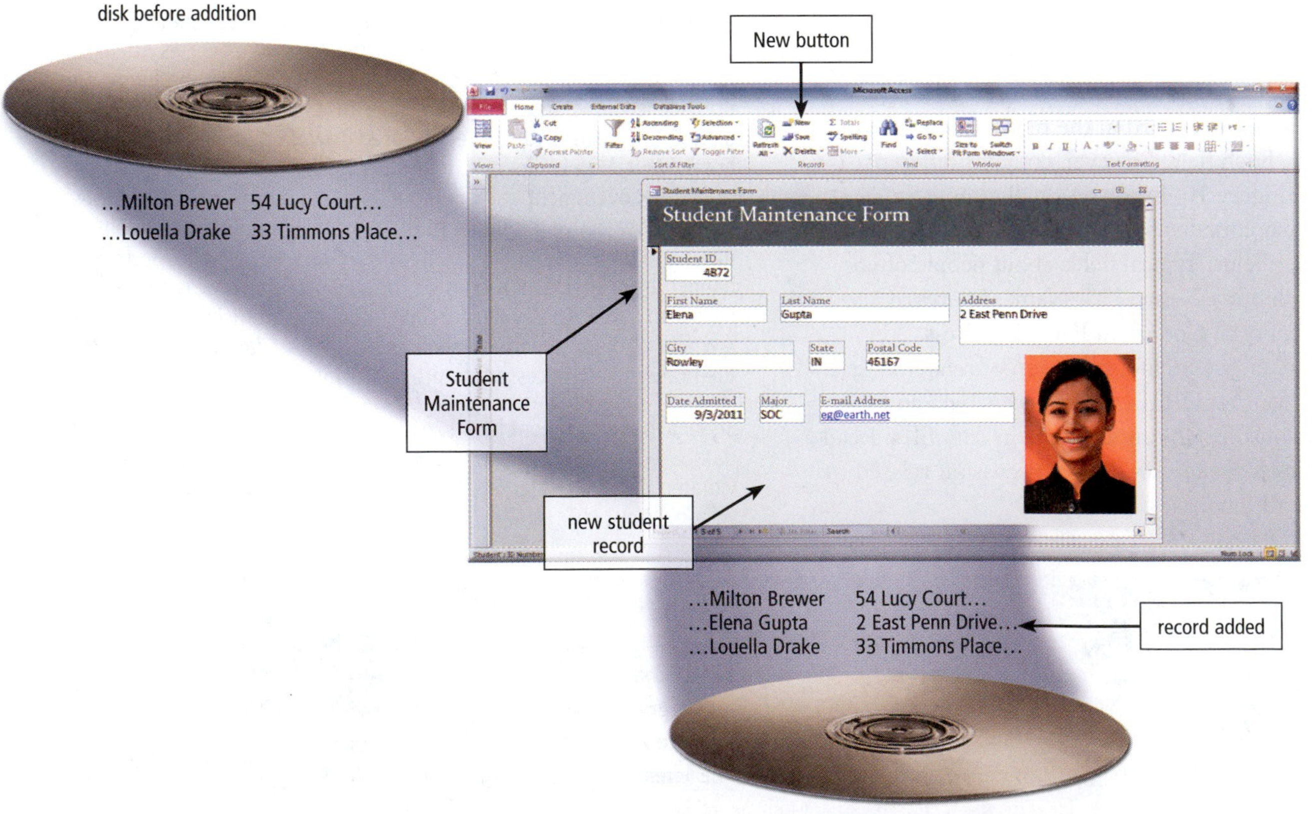

Figure 10-5 Using the Student Maintenance Form, an admissions department clerk adds a new student record for Elena Gupta. After the clerk takes the photo with the digital camera and confirms the data is correct, he or she adds the record to the database file.

Modifying Records

Generally, users modify a record in a file for two reasons: (1) to correct inaccurate data or (2) to update old data with new data.

As an example of the first type of change, assume that an admissions department clerk enters a student's e-mail address as ge@earth.net, instead of eg@earth.net. The student notices the error when she reviews her advising appointment confirmation at home. The next time she visits school, she requests that an admissions department clerk correct her e-mail address.

A more common reason to modify a record is to update old data with new data. Suppose, for example, that Elena Gupta moves from 2 East Penn Drive to 76 Ash Street. The process to change the address and update Elena Gupta's record might include the following steps:

1. The admissions department clerk displays the Student Maintenance Form.
2. Assuming Elena Gupta is present, the clerk inserts Elena's student ID card in a card reader to display her student record on the screen. If Elena did not have her ID card or was not present, the clerk could enter Elena's student ID number — if Elena knew it. Otherwise, the clerk could enter Gupta in the Last Name field, which would retrieve all students with that same last name. The clerk then would scroll through all of the retrieved records to determine which one is Elena's.
3. The DBMS displays data about Elena Gupta so that the clerk can confirm the correct student record is displayed.
4. The clerk enters the new street address, 76 Ash Street.
5. The admissions department clerk verifies the data on the screen and then, if required, clicks the Save button to modify the record in the Student file. The DBMS modifies the record on the disk (Figure 10-6).

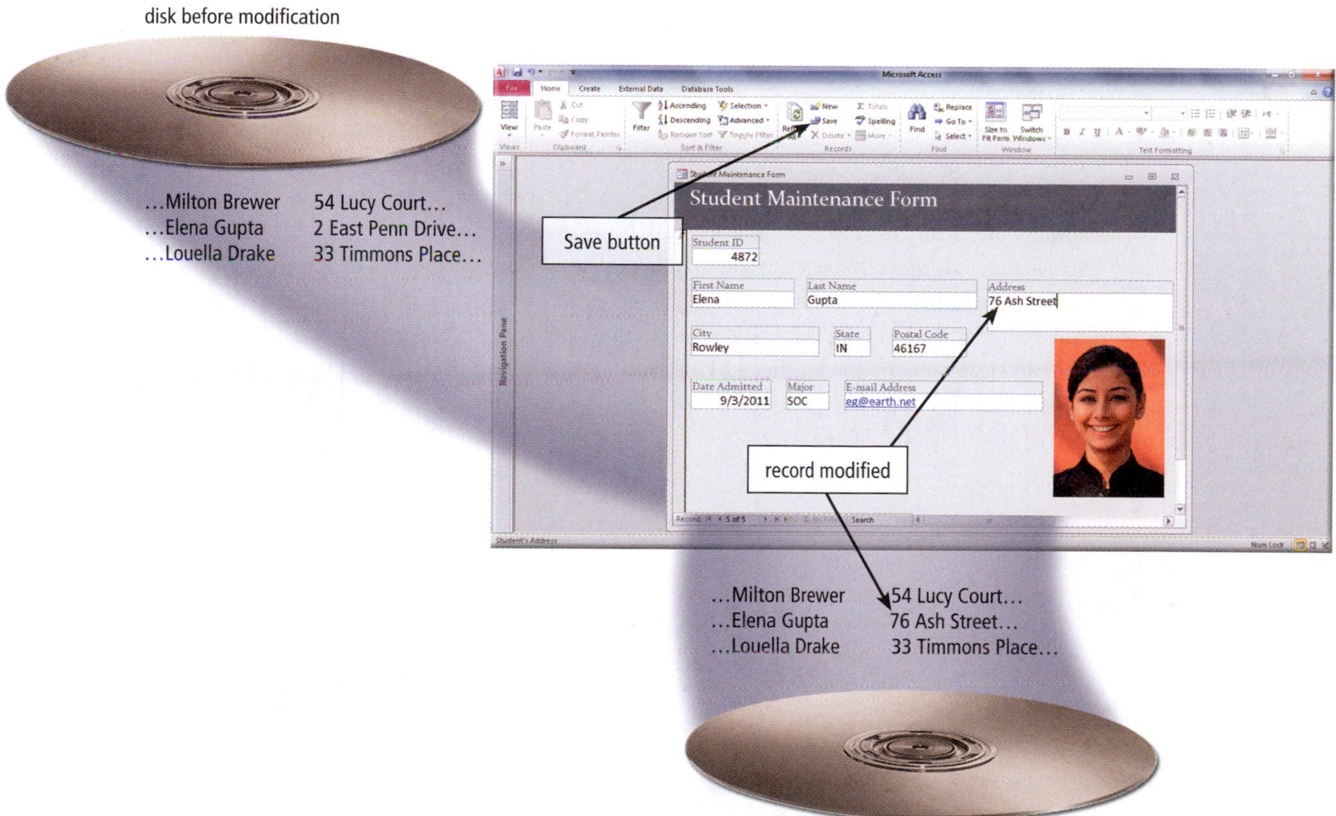

Figure 10-6 The admissions department clerk scans the student ID card to display the student's record. After looking at the photo on the screen to confirm that the correct student record is displayed, the clerk modifies the student's address.

Deleting Records

When a record no longer is needed, a user deletes it from a file. Assume a student named Benjamin Tu is moving out of the country. The process required to delete a record from a file includes the following steps:

1. The admissions department clerk displays the Student Maintenance Form.
2. The clerk displays Benjamin Tu's student record on the screen.
3. The clerk confirms the correct student record is displayed. Then, the clerk clicks the Delete button to delete the record from the Student file and then, if required, clicks the Save button to save the modified file.

DBMSs use a variety of techniques to manage deleted records. Sometimes, the DBMS removes the record from the file immediately, which means the deleted record cannot be restored. Other times, the record is flagged, or marked, so that the DBMS will not process it again. In this case, the DBMS places an asterisk (*) or some other character at the beginning of the record (Figure 10-7).

DBMSs that maintain inactive data for an extended period commonly flag records. For example, a school might flag inactive students. When a DBMS flags a deleted record, the record remains physically on the disk. The record, however, is deleted logically because the DBMS will not process it. DBMSs will ignore flagged records unless an instruction is issued to process them.

From time to time, users should run a utility program that removes flagged records and reorganizes current records. For example, the school may remove from disk any students who have not taken classes in five years. Deleting unneeded records reduces the size of files and frees up storage space.

Validating Data

Validation is the process of comparing data with a set of rules or values to find out if the data is correct. Many programs perform a *validity check* that analyzes data, either as you enter it or after you enter it, to help ensure that it is correct. For instance, when an admissions department clerk adds or modifies data in a student record, the DBMS tests the entered data.

With per credit hour fee, you would expect to see numbers before and after a decimal point. For example, a valid per credit hour fee is 220.25. An entry of 2DW.8I clearly is not correct. If the data fails a validity check, the computer either should not allow the invalid data to be entered, or it should display an error message that instructs the user to enter the data again. Validity checks, sometimes called *validation rules*, reduce data entry errors and thus enhance the data's integrity. Read Innovative Computing 10-1 to find out how data validation is used in baseball.

Various types of validity checks include alphabetic checks, numeric checks, range checks, consistency checks, and completeness checks. Check digits also validate data accuracy. The following paragraphs describe the purpose of these validity checks. The table in Figure 10-8 illustrates several of these validity checks and shows valid data that passes the check and invalid data that fails the check.

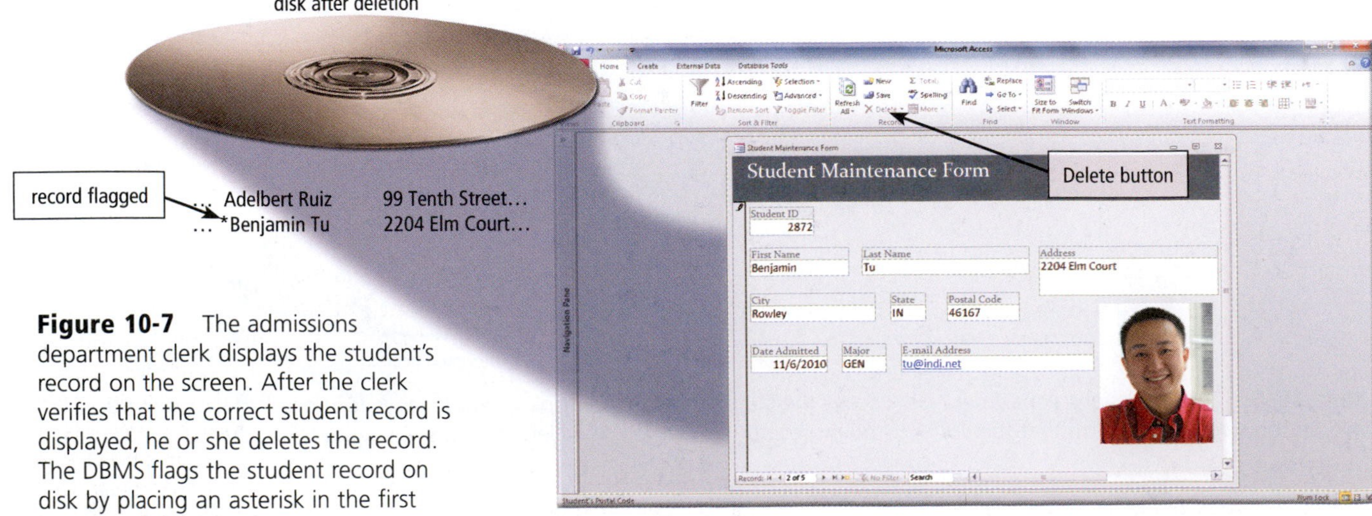

Figure 10-7 The admissions department clerk displays the student's record on the screen. After the clerk verifies that the correct student record is displayed, he or she deletes the record. The DBMS flags the student record on disk by placing an asterisk in the first position of the record.

INNOVATIVE COMPUTING 10-1

America's Favorite Pastime Adds Authentic Twist

Validating baseball memorabilia has been simplified with the help of holograms and an online database. Each game uniform, bat, and other licensed Major League Baseball (MLB) merchandise is issued a specific hologram with a tracking number. More than 135 carefully trained authenticators enter this number and other data into the database's fields for all 30 MLB teams.

Obtaining data for significant home run balls is a bit more challenging. MLB authenticators are assigned to the bleachers where they must track the home run ball and identify the person who caught it. They immediately glue a hologram to the ball and record the specific details in the database.

Another innovative use of databases in baseball is found in Baseball Boss, a free game that meshes players from the past with today's stars. Each gamer becomes a manager who randomly is assigned 40 players. This team is paired with another team, and the computer determines, in an inning-by-inning contest, the final score in minutes. The score is determined by analyzing actual player statistics in the database's fields and with chance. Ultimately, gamers will be able to determine how Babe Ruth would fare against today's power pitchers.

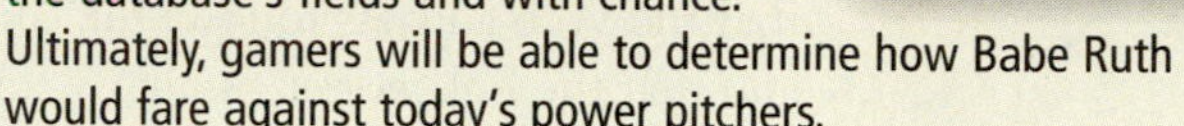

For more information, visit the Computer Concepts CourseMate Web site at www.cengagebrain.com, navigate to the Chapter 10 Innovative Computing resource for this book, and then click Baseball Databases.

Sample Valid and Invalid Data

Validity Check	Field(s) Being Checked	Valid Data	Invalid Data
Alphabetic Check	First Name	Karen	Ka24n
Numeric Check	Postal Code	46322	4tr22
Range Check	Per Credit Hour Fee	$220.25	$2,120.00
Consistency Check	Date Admitted and Birth Date	9/20/2010 8/27/1985	9/20/2010 8/27/2011
Completeness Check	Last Name	Gupta	

Figure 10-8 In this table of sample valid and invalid data, the first column lists commonly used validity checks. The second column lists the name of the field that contains data being checked. The third column shows valid data that passes the validity checks. The fourth column shows invalid data that fails the validity checks.

Alphabetic/Numeric Check An *alphabetic check* ensures that users enter only alphabetic data into a field. A *numeric check* ensures that users enter only numeric data into a field. For example, data in a First Name field should contain only characters from the alphabet. Data in a Postal Code field should contain numbers (with the exception of the special characters such as a hyphen).

Range Check A *range check* determines whether a number is within a specified range. Assume the lowest per credit hour fee at the school is $75.00 and the highest is $370.75. A range check for the Credit Hour Fee field ensures it is a value between $75.00 and $370.75.

Consistency Check A *consistency check* tests the data in two or more associated fields to ensure that the relationship is logical and their data is in the correct format. For example, the value in a Date Admitted field cannot occur earlier in time than a value in a Birth Date field.

Completeness Check A *completeness check* verifies that a required field contains data. For example, some fields cannot be left blank; others require a minimum number of characters. One completeness check can ensure that data exists in a Last Name field. Another can ensure that a day, month, and year are included in a Birth Date field.

Check Digit A *check digit* is a number(s) or character(s) that is appended to or inserted in a primary key value. A check digit often confirms the accuracy of a primary key value. Bank account, credit card, and other identification numbers often include one or more check digits.

A program determines the check digit by applying a formula to the numbers in the primary key value. An oversimplified illustration of a check digit formula is to add the numbers in the primary key. For example, if the primary key is 1367, this formula would add these numbers (1 + 3 + 6 + 7) for a sum of 17. Next, the formula would add the numbers in the result (1 + 7) to generate a check digit of 8. The primary key then is 13678.

When a data entry clerk enters the primary key of 13678, for example, to look up an existing record, the program determines whether the check digit is valid. If the clerk enters an incorrect primary key, such as 13778, the check digit entered (8) will not match the computed check

Data Validation

For more information, visit the Computer Concepts CourseMate Web site at www.cengagebrain.com, navigate to the Chapter 10 Web Link resource for this book, and then click Data Validation.

digit (9). In this case, the program displays an error message that instructs the user to enter the primary key value again.

Other Checks DBMSs that include the hyperlink and attachment data types can perform validity checks on data entered in those fields. Hyperlink entries can be tested to ensure that the Web address follows the correct format and that the link works. Similarly, an attachment entry can be validated by confirming that the file exists.

QUIZ YOURSELF 10-1

Instructions: Find the true statement below. Then, rewrite the remaining false statements so that they are true.

1. A coding scheme is a number(s) or character(s) that is appended to or inserted in a primary key value.
2. A database is a combination of one or more related characters or bytes and is the smallest unit of data a user accesses.
3. A record is a collection of data organized in a manner that allows access, retrieval, and use of that data.
4. Data is processed information.
5. Hierarchy of data procedures include adding records to, modifying records in, and deleting records from a file.
6. To be valuable, information should be accurate, verifiable, timely, organized, accessible, useful, and cost-effective.

Quiz Yourself Online: To further check your knowledge of pages 514 through 524, visit the Computer Concepts CourseMate Web site at www.cengagebrain.com, navigate to the Chapter 10 Quiz Yourself resource for this book, and then click Objectives 1 – 4.

File Processing versus Databases

Almost all application programs use the file processing approach, the database approach, or a combination of both approaches to store and manage data. The next sections discuss these two approaches.

File Processing Systems

In the past, many organizations exclusively used file processing systems to store and manage data. In a typical **file processing system**, each department or area within an organization has its own set of files. The records in one file may not relate to the records in any other file.

Organizations have used file processing systems for many years. Many of these systems, however, have two major weaknesses: they have redundant data and they isolate data.

- Data Redundancy — Each department or area in an organization has its own files in a file processing system. Thus, the same fields are stored in multiple files. If a file processing system is used at a school, for example, the Student file and the Student Schedule file both might store the same students' names and addresses.

  Duplicating data in this manner wastes resources such as storage space and people's time. When new students are added or student data is modified, file maintenance tasks consume additional time because people must update multiple files that contain the same data.

  Data redundancy also can increase the chance of errors. If a student changes his or her address, for example, the school must update the address wherever it appears. If the Address field is not changed in all the files where it is stored, then discrepancies among the files exist.
- Isolated Data — Often it is difficult to access data stored in separate files in different departments. Assume that the student e-mail addresses exist in the Student files, and class room numbers (locations) are in the Schedule of Classes file. To send an e-mail message informing students about a room change, data is needed from both the Student file and the Schedule of Classes file. Sharing data from multiple, separate files to generate such a list in a file processing system often is a complicated procedure and usually requires the experience of a computer programmer.

The Database Approach

When an organization uses a **database approach**, many programs and users share the data in the database. A school's database most likely at a minimum contains data about students, instructors, schedule of classes, and student schedules. As shown in Figure 10-9, various areas within the school share and interact with the data in this database. The database does secure its data, however, so that only authorized users can access certain data items.

While a user is working with the database, the DBMS resides in the memory of the computer. Instead of working directly with the DBMS,

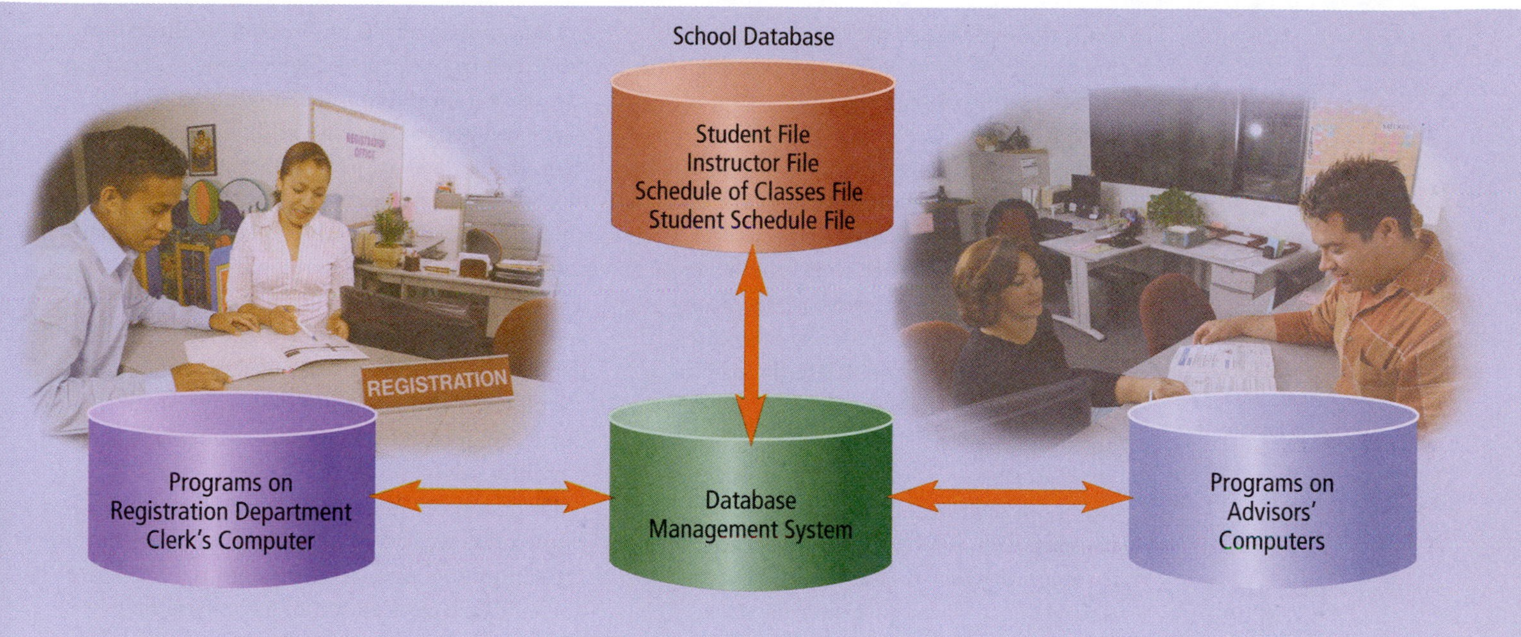

Figure 10-9 In a school that uses a database, the computer used by a registration department clerk and the computers used by advisors access data in a single database through the DBMS.

some users interact with a front end. A *front end* is a program that generally has a more user-friendly interface than the DBMS. For example, a registration department clerk interacts with the Class Registration program. This front-end program interacts with the DBMS, which in turn, interacts with the database. Many programs today have a Web page as their front end. An application that supports a front-end program sometimes is called the *back end*. In this case, the DBMS is the back end.

The database approach addresses many of the weaknesses associated with file processing systems. The following paragraphs present some strengths of the database approach.

- Reduced Data Redundancy — Most data items are stored in only one file, which greatly reduces duplicate data. For example, a school's database would record a student's name and address only once. When student data is entered or changed, one employee makes the change once. Figure 10-10 demonstrates the differences between how a file processing application and a database application might store data.
- Improved Data Integrity — When users modify data in the database, they make changes to one file instead of multiple files.

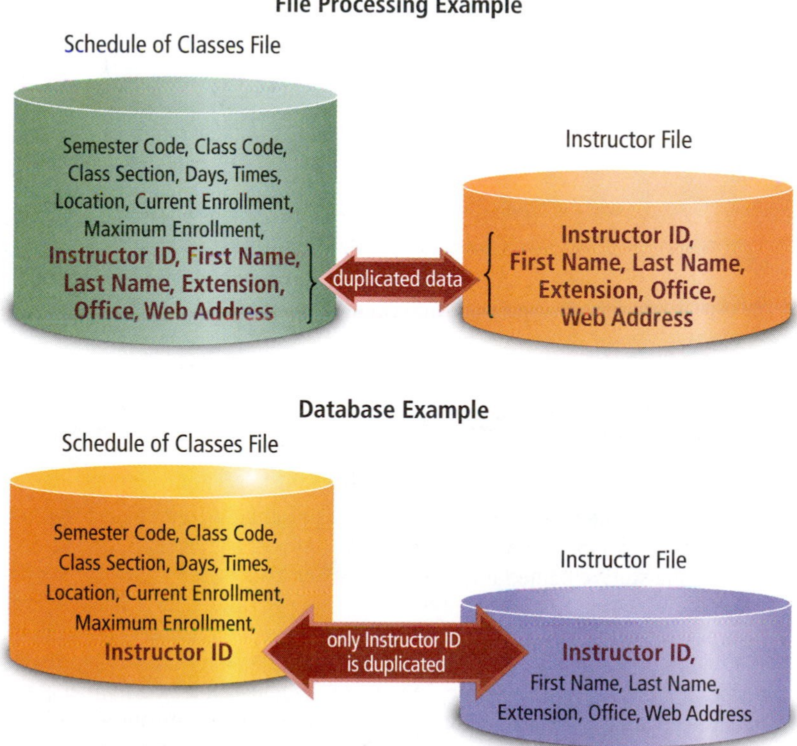

Figure 10-10 In the file processing environment, both files contain all six instructor data fields. In a database environment, only the Instructor file contains the First Name, Last Name, Extension, Office, and Web Address fields. Other files, however, such as the Schedule of Classes file, contain the Instructor ID, which links to the Instructor file when instructor data is needed.

Thus, the database approach increases the data's integrity by reducing the possibility of introducing inconsistencies.

- Shared Data — The data in a database environment belongs to and is shared, usually over a network, by the entire organization. This data is independent of, or separate from, the programs that access the data. Organizations that use databases typically have security settings to define who can access, add, modify, and delete the data in a database. Read Ethics & Issues 10-3 for a related discussion.
- Easier Access — The database approach allows nontechnical users to access and maintain data, providing they have the necessary privileges. Many computer users also can develop smaller databases themselves, without professional assistance.
- Reduced Development Time — It often is easier and faster to develop programs that use the database approach. Many DBMSs include several tools to assist in developing programs, which further reduces the development time. The next section discusses these tools and other DBMS features.

Databases also have some disadvantages. A database can be more complex than a file processing system. People with special training usually develop larger databases and their associated applications. Databases also require more memory, storage, and processing power than file processing systems.

Data in a database can be more vulnerable than data in file processing systems. A database can store a lot of data in a single file. Many users and programs share and depend on this data. If the database is not operating properly or is damaged or destroyed, users may not be able to perform their jobs. Furthermore, unauthorized users potentially could gain access to a single database file that contains personal and confidential data. To protect their valuable database resource, individuals and companies should establish and follow security procedures. Chapter 11 discusses a variety of security methods.

Despite these limitations, many business and home users work with databases because of their tremendous advantages. Although the hardware and software costs to set up a database may seem expensive, long-term benefits exceed the initial costs.

? FAQ 10-3

Can a database eliminate redundant data completely?

No, a database reduces redundant data — it does not eliminate it. Key fields link data together in a database. For example, a Student ID field will exist in any database table that requires access to student data. Thus, a Student ID is duplicated (exists in many tables) in the database.

For more information, visit the Computer Concepts CourseMate Web site at www.cengagebrain.com, navigate to the Chapter 10 FAQ resource for this book, and then click Database Relationships.

ETHICS & ISSUES 10-3

Should States Share Criminal Databases?

California was the first state to employ a controversial database. Based on Megan's Law — the statute named for a seven-year-old girl who was violated and killed by a paroled felon — the database listed the names and addresses of people convicted of crimes against children. Today, all states employ similar databases and are required to share the information with a national database. Most states now allow you to use these databases to find out if these felons live near you. In some communities, when an offender moves in, the police inform the local school system, which in turn sends parents a notification that includes a history, address, and photo of the wrongdoer. Some states share information with each other regarding almost all criminals, and some allow citizens to search for these offenders by name. Touted as a valuable tool in crime prevention, some feel that publishing this information makes it impossible for an offender to lead a normal life and can result in vigilantism — including those on the lists suffering bodily harm and being forced to leave their homes and jobs.

Should a database of people paroled or released for crimes be made public? Why or why not? What about those who have committed other types of crimes? Who should have access to the database? Why?

Database Management Systems

As previously discussed, a database management system (DBMS), or database program, is software that allows you to create, access, and manage a database. DBMSs are available for many sizes and types of computers (Figure 10-11). Whether designed for a small or large computer, most DBMSs perform common functions. The following pages discuss functions common to most DBMSs.

Popular Database Management Systems

Database	Manufacturer	Computer Type
Access	Microsoft Corporation	Personal computer, server, mobile devices
Adabas	Software AG	Server, mainframe
D^3	Raining Data	Personal computer, server
DB2	IBM Corporation	Personal computer, server, mainframe
Essbase	Oracle Corporation	Personal computer, server, mobile devices
FastObjects	Versant Corporation	Personal computer, server
FileMaker	FileMaker, Inc.	Personal computer, server
GemFire	GemStone Systems	Server
Informix	IBM Corporation	Personal computer, server, mainframe
Ingres	Ingres Corporation	Personal computer, server, mainframe
InterBaseSMP	Embarcadero Technologies	Personal computer, server
KE Texpress	KE Software, Inc.	Personal computer, server
MySQL	Oracle Corporation	Personal computer, server
ObjectStore	Progress Software Corporation	Personal computer, server
Oracle Database	Oracle Corporation	Personal computer, server, mainframe, mobile devices
SQL Server	Microsoft Corporation	Server, personal computer
SQL Server Compact Edition	Microsoft Corporation	Mobile devices
Sybase	Sybase Inc.	Personal computer, server, mobile devices
Teradata Database	Teradata	Server
Versant	Versant Corporation	Personal computer, server
Visual FoxPro	Microsoft Corporation	Personal computer, server

Figure 10-11 Many database management systems run on multiple types of computers.

MySQL
For more information, visit the Computer Concepts CourseMate Web site at www.cengagebrain.com, navigate to the Chapter 10 Web Link resource for this book, and then click MySQL.

FAQ 10-4

Which database vendors have the largest revenue market share?

As shown in the chart to the right, Oracle has the largest market share in terms of revenue, followed by IBM and Microsoft.

For more information, visit the Computer Concepts CourseMate Web site at www.cengagebrain.com, navigate to the Chapter 10 FAQ resource for this book, and then click Database Market Share.

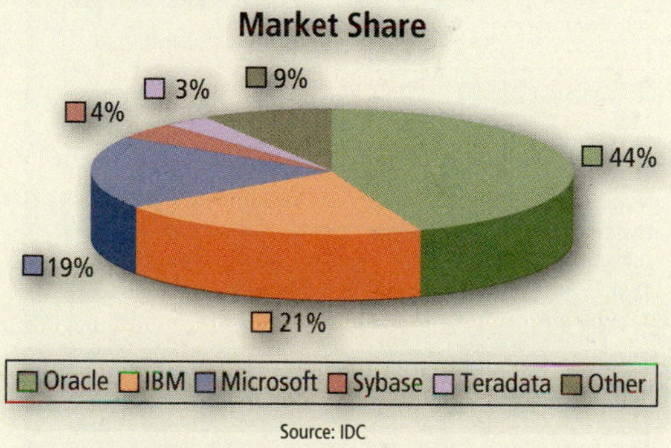

Data Dictionary

A **data dictionary**, sometimes called a *repository*, contains data about each file in the database and each field in those files. For each file, it stores details such as the file name, description, the file's relationship to other files, and the number of records in the file. For each field, it stores details such as the field name, description, field type, field size, default value, validation rules, and the field's relationship to other fields. Figure 10-12 shows how a data dictionary might list data for a Student file.

Because the data dictionary contains details about data, some call it *metadata* (meta means more comprehensive). Sometimes, a data dictionary also contains data about programs and users. It might keep track of who accessed data and when they accessed it. The data dictionary is a crucial backbone to a DBMS. Thus, only skilled professionals should update the contents of a data dictionary.

A DBMS uses the data dictionary to perform validation checks. When users enter data, the data dictionary verifies that the entered data matches the field's data type. For example, the data dictionary allows only dates to be entered in a Date Admitted field. The data dictionary also can limit the type of data that can be entered, often allowing a user to select from a list. For example, the data dictionary ensures that the State field contains a valid two-letter state code, such as IN, by presenting a list of valid state codes to the user. By validating data, the data dictionary helps to maintain the integrity of the data.

A data dictionary allows users to specify a default value for a field. A *default value* is a value that the DBMS initially displays in a field. If most students who attend the school live in Indiana, then the DBMS initially could display IN in the State field. The user does not have to type in a default value. Displaying a default value reduces the possibility of errors. A user typically can override a default value if it does not apply for a certain record. For example, you can change the value from IN to OH if the student lives in Ohio.

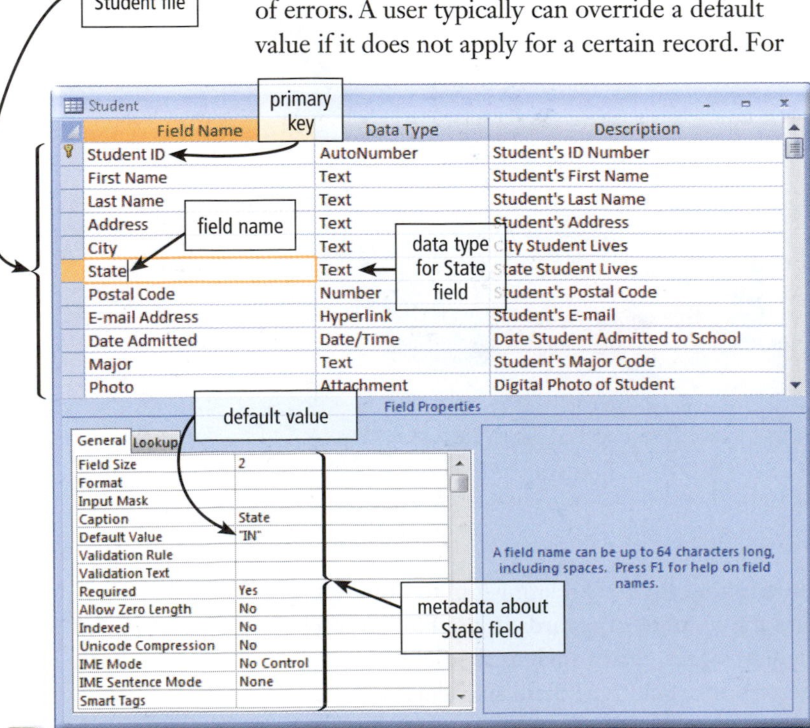

Figure 10-12 A sample data dictionary entry shows the fields in the Student file and the properties of the State field.

File Retrieval and Maintenance

A DBMS provides several tools that allow users and programs to retrieve and maintain data in the database. As discussed earlier in this chapter, file maintenance involves adding new records, modifying data in existing records, and removing unwanted records from the database.

To retrieve or select data in a database, you query it. A **query** is a request for specific data from the database. Users can instruct the DBMS to display, print, or store the results of a query. The capability of querying a database is one of the more powerful database features.

To meet the needs of a wide variety of database users, from trained experts to nontechnical staff, a DBMS offers several methods to retrieve and maintain its data. The four more commonly used are query languages, query by example, forms, and report generators. The following paragraphs describe each of these methods.

Query Language A **query language** consists of simple, English-like statements that allow users to specify the data to display, print, or store. Each query language has its own grammar and vocabulary. A person without a programming background usually can learn a query language in a short time.

Although a query language can be used to maintain (add, modify, and delete) data, most users only retrieve (query) data with a query language. Users can retrieve actual data in a query or display the results of calculations performed on the data. For example, to display a monthly payment instead of a stored annual payment, you would instruct the query to display the results of the annual payment divided by 12.

To simplify the query process, many DBMSs provide wizards to guide users through the steps of creating a query. Figure 10-13 shows how to use the Simple Query Wizard in Microsoft Access to display the First Name, Last Name, and E-mail Address fields from the Student file.

Instead of using the Simple Query Wizard, you could enter the query language statement shown in Figure 10-13 directly in the DBMS to display the results shown in Step 3. SQL, which is a widely used query language, is discussed later in the chapter.

Query by Example Most DBMSs include **query by example (QBE)**, a feature that has a graphical user interface to assist users with retrieving data. Figure 10-14 shows a sample QBE screen

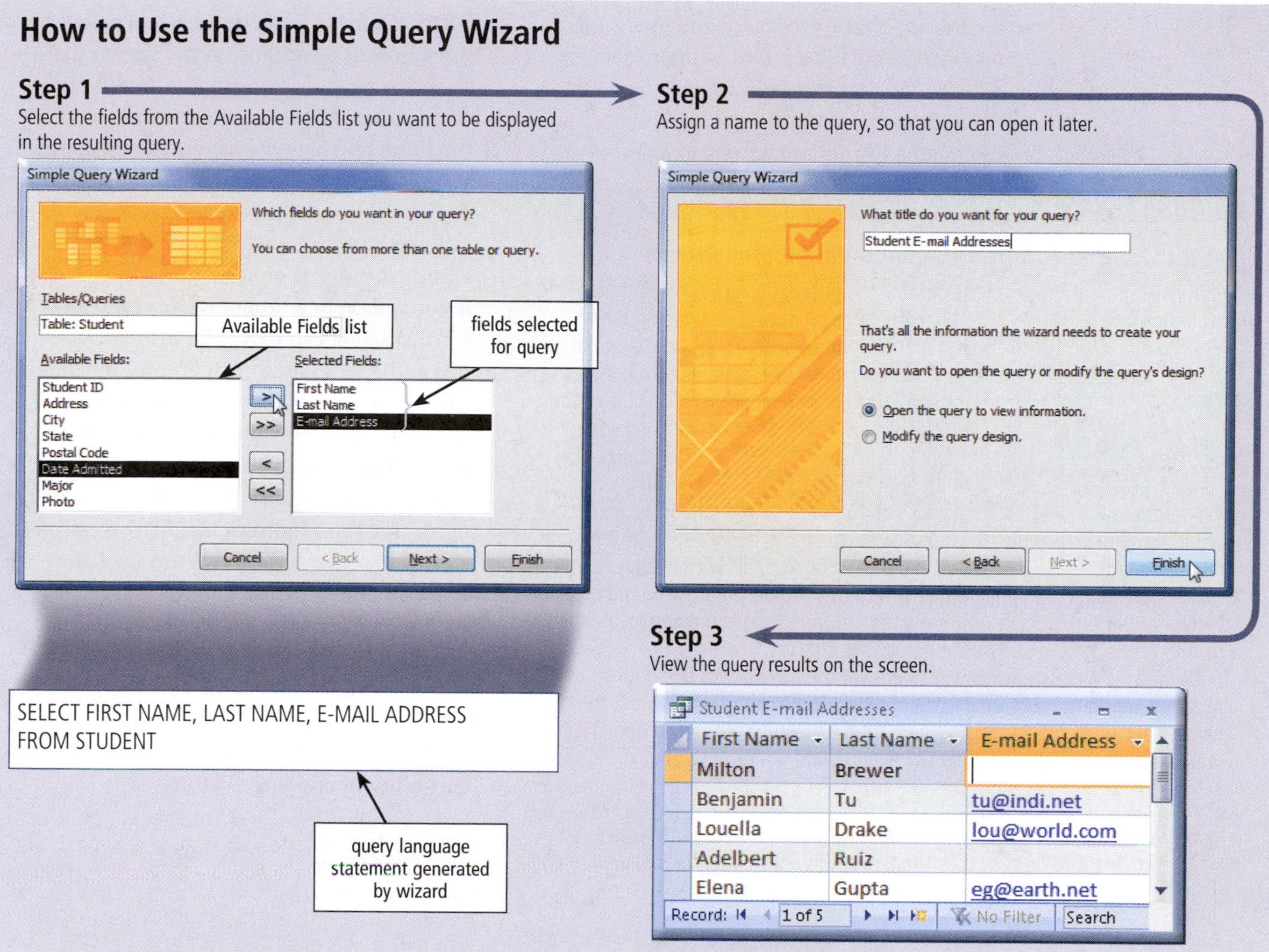

How to Use the Simple Query Wizard

Step 1
Select the fields from the Available Fields list you want to be displayed in the resulting query.

Simple Query Wizard
Which fields do you want in your query?
You can choose from more than one table or query.
Tables/Queries
Table: Student
Available Fields: Student ID, Address, City, State, Postal Code, Date Admitted, Major, Photo
Selected Fields: First Name, Last Name, E-mail Address
Cancel | < Back | Next > | Finish

Available Fields list

fields selected for query

SELECT FIRST NAME, LAST NAME, E-MAIL ADDRESS
FROM STUDENT

query language statement generated by wizard

Step 2
Assign a name to the query, so that you can open it later.

Simple Query Wizard
What title do you want for your query?
Student E-mail Addresses
That's all the information the wizard needs to create your query.
Do you want to open the query or modify the query's design?
Open the query to view information.
Modify the query design.
Cancel | < Back | Next > | Finish

Step 3
View the query results on the screen.

Student E-mail Addresses

First Name	Last Name	E-mail Address
Milton	Brewer	
Benjamin	Tu	tu@indi.net
Louella	Drake	lou@world.com
Adelbert	Ruiz	
Elena	Gupta	eg@earth.net

Record: 1 of 5 No Filter Search

Figure 10-13 This figure shows how to use the Simple Query Wizard.

Figure 10-14a (all records in Student table)

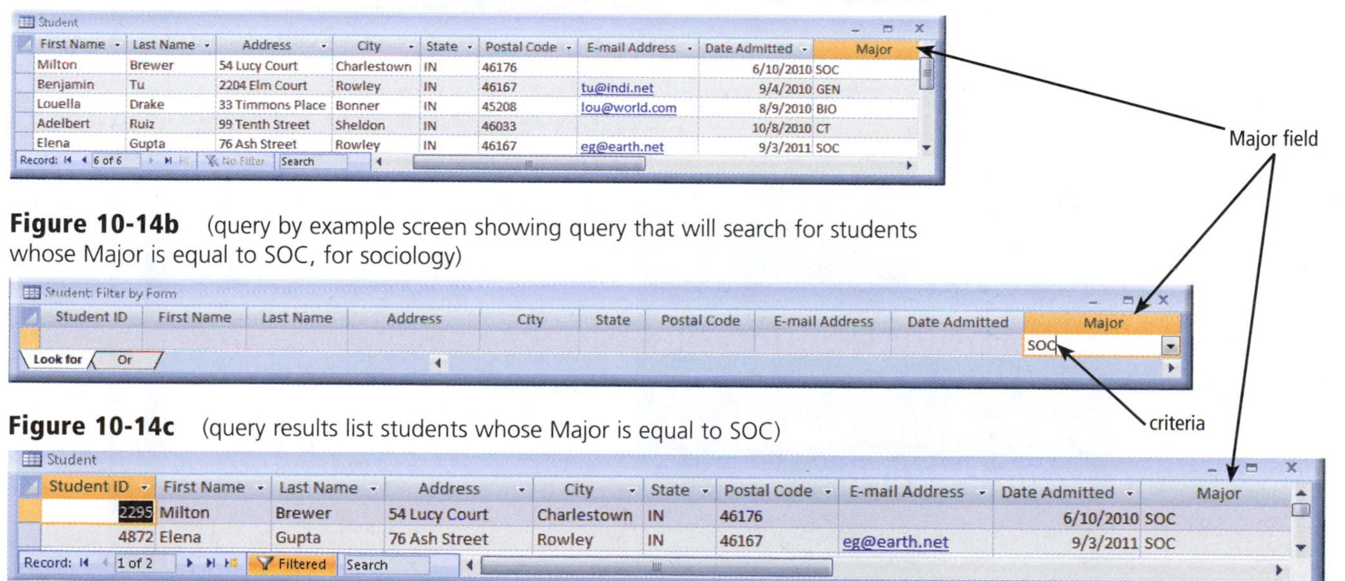

Figure 10-14b (query by example screen showing query that will search for students whose Major is equal to SOC, for sociology)

Figure 10-14c (query results list students whose Major is equal to SOC)

Figure 10-14 Access has many QBE capabilities. One QBE technique is Filter by Form, which uses a form to show available fields. The database program retrieves records that match criteria you enter in the form fields. This example searches for students whose major is sociology.

for a query that searches for and lists students majoring in sociology; that is, their Major field value is equal to SOC. Read Innovative Computing 10-2 to find out how political campaigns use and query databases.

INNOVATIVE COMPUTING 10-2

Voter Databases Target Likely Candidate Supporters

Political campaigners use vast databases containing records of voters' party affiliations, voting history, and personal preferences to locate and target likely candidate supporters. One major political party, for example, spent more than $8 million to build a database consisting of millions of records that contain hundreds of fields per record. The public and commercial data includes details such as marital status, age, pets, children, union affiliations, and hunting licenses.

The database can handle more than 40 queries simultaneously, and campaigners compose searches to target specific records. For example, a female who own cats and is married with small children is likely to belong to a particular political party, so a woman fitting this profile probably would receive campaign literature from that party. This data mining is proving invaluable to find and contact voters from across the country.

Database administrators need to ensure the accuracy of this data so that likely voters do not receive a flood of mail, telephone calls, and door-to-door canvassers. Incorrect addresses, disconnected telephones, and changed job status all must remain current to provide reliable query results.

For more information, visit the Computer Concepts CourseMate Web site at www.cengagebrain.com, navigate to the Chapter 10 Innovative Computing resource for this book, and then click Voter Databases.

Form A **form**, sometimes called a *data entry form*, is a window on the screen that provides areas for entering or modifying data in a database. You use forms (such as the Student Maintenance Form in Figure 10-5 on page 520) to retrieve and maintain the data in a database.

To reduce data entry errors, well-designed forms should validate data as it is entered. When designing a form using a DBMS, you can make the form attractive and easy to use by incorporating color, shading, lines, boxes, and graphics; varying the fonts and font styles; and using other formatting features.

A form that sends entered data across a network or the Internet is called an *e-form*, short for *electronic form* (Figure 10-15). E-forms generally use a means to secure the data while it is transported across the network. Often, the data in the e-form automatically enters in, or updates existing data in, a database on the network or the Internet. Thus, many DBMSs include the capability of creating e-forms.

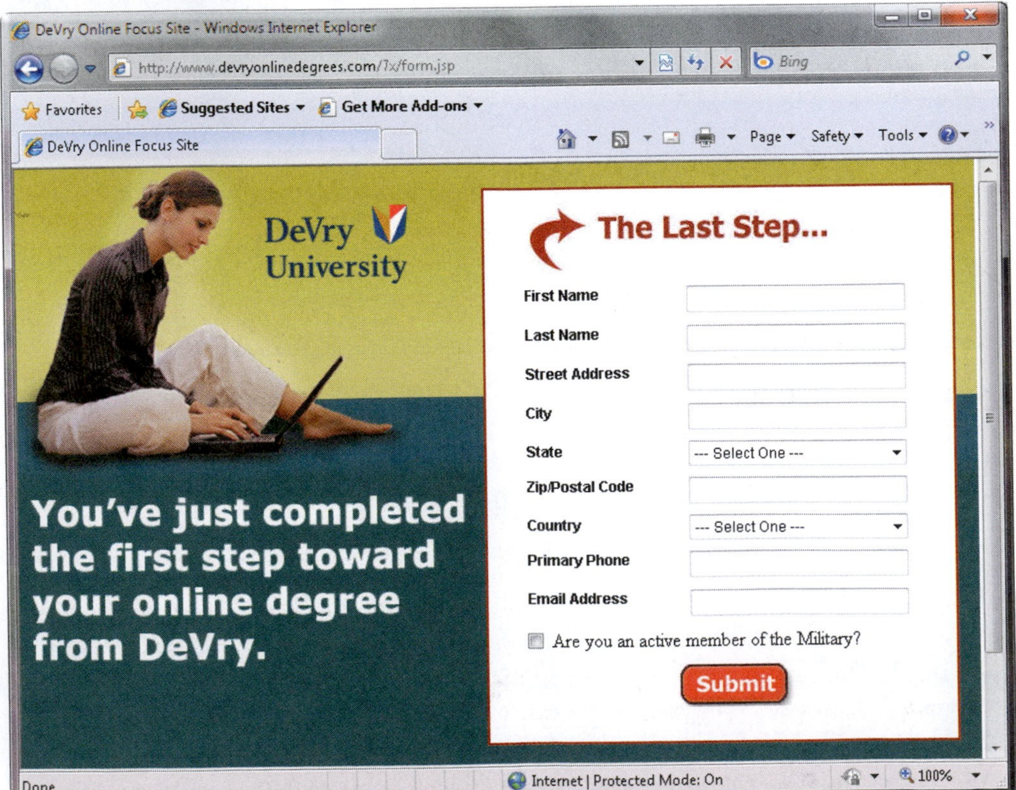

Figure 10-15 Prospective students can submit this e-form to learn more about online degrees.

E-Form
For more information, visit the Computer Concepts CourseMate Web site at www.cengagebrain.com, navigate to the Chapter 10 Web Link resource for this book, and then click E-Form.

Report Generator A **report generator**, also called a *report writer*, allows users to design a report on the screen, retrieve data into the report design, and then display or print the report (Figure 10-16). Unlike a form, you use a report generator only to retrieve data. Report generators usually allow you to format page numbers and dates; titles and column headings; subtotals and totals; and fonts, font sizes, color, and shading. Many allow you to include images, for example, a product catalog with photos and descriptions of products. Some report generators allow you to create a report as a Web page, which can be interactive.

Student List by Major

Major	Last Name	Student ID	First Name	Address	City	Date Admitted
BIO						
	Drake	3876	Louella	33 Timmons Place	Bonner	8/9/2010
CT						
	Ruiz	3928	Adelbert	99 Tenth Street	Sheldon	10/8/2010
GEN						
	Tu	2928	Benjamin	2204 Elm Court	Rowley	9/4/2010
SOC						
	Brewer	2295	Milton	54 Lucy Court	Charlestown	6/10/2010
	Gupta	4872	Elena	76 Ash Street	Rowley	9/3/2011

Figure 10-16 This report, created in Microsoft Access, displays student information by major.

Data Security

A DBMS provides means to ensure that only authorized users access data at permitted times. In addition, most DBMSs allow different levels of access privileges to be identified for each field in the database. These access privileges define the actions that a specific user or group of users can perform.

Access privileges for data involve establishing who can enter new data, modify existing data, delete unwanted data, and view data. In the Schedule of Classes file, the student would have read-only privileges. That is, the student could view the list of classes offered in a semester, but cannot change them. A department head, by contrast, would have full-update privileges to classes offered during a particular semester, meaning he or she can view and modify the data. Finally, some users have no access privileges to the data; that is, they cannot view or modify any data in the database. Many organizations adopt the *principle of least privilege* policy, where users' access privileges are limited to the lowest level necessary to perform required tasks. Chapter 11 discusses access privileges and other security techniques in more depth. Read Ethics & Issues 10-4 for a related discussion.

ETHICS & ISSUES 10-4

Should People Be Punished for Accidently Accessing Stolen Data?

A university student discovered a file containing private student data, including Social Security numbers and student grades, on a publicly accessible area of a university computer. Instead of notifying authorities, he took the file to the student newspaper in the hopes of making sure that the security breach was made public. After the newspaper published an article about the situation, the student was nearly expelled and the newspaper's adviser was fired for violating the university's computer policies. Some privacy advocates felt that the outcome was a case of shooting the messenger. More and more often, institutions attempt to resolve security breaches as quietly as possible, fearing that publicity may cause financial loss and loss of public confidence, and may encourage hackers to target the institution. In some cases, an institution may file lawsuits against those who make security breaches public, including reporters. Some states require computer technicians to report illegally obtained data that they encounter in the course of their jobs.

If you find a USB flash drive left behind by someone that contains inappropriate or illegally obtained data, should you be required to report the incident to pertinent authorities? Why or why not? In the situation described above, should the student and newspaper be praised or punished for making the security breach public knowledge? Why? Should people who inadvertently receive illegal photos or videos on their cell phones be prosecuted? Why or why not?

Backup and Recovery

Occasionally a database is damaged or destroyed because of hardware failure, a problem with the software, human error, or a catastrophe such as fire or flood. A DBMS provides a variety of techniques to restore the database to a usable form in case it is damaged or destroyed.

- A **backup**, or copy, of the entire database should be made on a regular basis. Some

DBMSs have their own built-in backup utilities. Others require users to purchase a separate backup utility, or use one included with the operating system.

- More complex DBMSs maintain a **log**, which is a listing of activities that modify the contents of the database. If a registration department clerk modifies a student's address, for example, the change appears in the log. The DBMS places the following in the log: (1) a copy of the student record prior to the change, called the *before image* (Figure 10-17a); (2) the actual change of address data (Figure 10-17b); and (3) a copy of the student record after the change, called the *after image* (Figure 10-17c). The log also might store who made the change, when it was made, and from which computer it was made.

Figure 10-17a (before image)

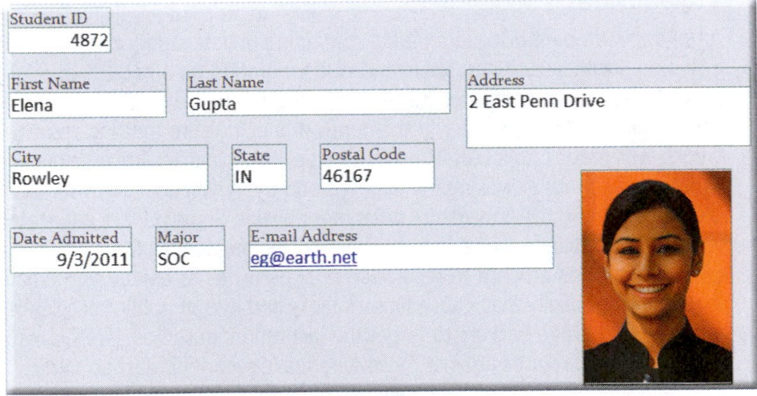

Figure 10-17b (change)

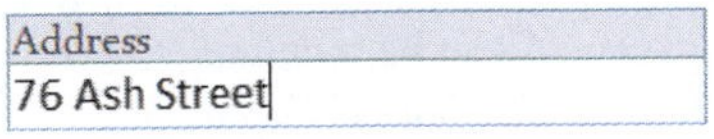

Address
76 Ash Street

Figure 10-17c (after image)

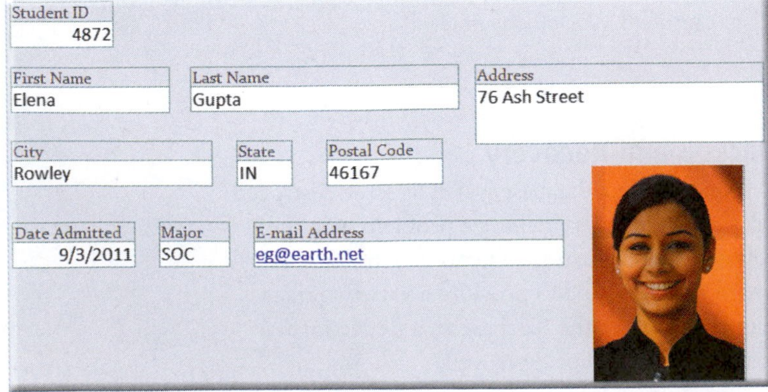

Figure 10-17 When the contents of a record are modified, the DBMS places three items in the log: the before image of the record, the actual change, and the after image of the record.

- A DBMS that creates a log usually provides a recovery utility. A **recovery utility** uses the logs and/or backups to restore a database when it becomes damaged or destroyed. The recovery utility restores the database using rollforward and rollback techniques. In a *rollforward*, also called *forward recovery*, the DBMS uses the log to reenter changes made to the database since the last save or backup. In a *rollback*, also called *backward recovery*, the DBMS uses the log to undo any changes made to the database during a certain period. The rollback restores the database to its condition prior to the failure. Depending on the type of failure, the DBMS determines which type of recovery technique to use. For example, if the database is destroyed by a lightning strike, the DBMS would rollforward from the last backup. Assume, however, that a power failure happens at 3:15 p.m. and shuts down all computers, but does not destroy any data. Because some users may have been in the middle of entering transactions, the DBMS would rollback the database to 3:00 p.m. and send a message to all users that they need to reenter any transactions made after that time.
- *Continuous backup* is a backup plan in which all data is backed up whenever a change is made. This backup technique can cost more than other backup strategies but is growing in popularity because of its benefits. Continuous backup provides recovery of damaged data in a matter of seconds.

✔ QUIZ YOURSELF 10-2

Instructions: Find the true statement below. Then, rewrite the remaining false statements so that they are true.

1. A DBMS is hardware that allows you to create, access, and manage an operating system.
2. A query contains data about files and fields in the database.
3. Backup and recovery procedures for data involve establishing who can enter new data, modify existing data, delete unwanted data, and view data.
4. To reduce data entry errors, well-designed forms should rollback data as it is entered.
5. Two major weaknesses of file processing systems are data redundancy and isolated data.

Quiz Yourself Online: To further check your knowledge of pages 524 through 532, visit the Computer Concepts CourseMate Web site at www.cengagebrain.com, navigate to the Chapter 10 Quiz Yourself resource for this book, and then click Objectives 5 – 6.

Relational, Object-Oriented, and Multidimensional Databases

Every database and DBMS is based on a specific data model. A **data model** consists of rules and standards that define how the database organizes data. A data model defines how users view the organization of the data. It does not define how the operating system actually arranges the data on the disk.

Three popular data models in use today are relational, object-oriented, and multidimensional. A database typically is based on one data model. For example, when using a relational database, users work with the relational data model. Some databases are called *object-relational databases* because they combine features of the relational and object-oriented data models.

The table in Figure 10-18 lists some popular DBMSs and the data model on which they are based. The following sections discuss the features of relational, object-oriented, and multidimensional databases.

Relational Databases

A **relational database** is a database that stores data in tables that consist of rows and columns. Each row has a primary key and each column has a unique name.

As discussed earlier in this chapter, a file processing environment uses the terms file, record, and field to represent data. A relational database uses terms different from a file processing system. A developer of a relational database refers to a file as a *relation*, a record as a *tuple*, and a field as an *attribute*. A user of a relational database, by contrast, refers to a file as a **table**, a record as a **row**, and a field as a **column**. Figure 10-19 summarizes this varied terminology.

In addition to storing data, a relational database also stores data relationships. A **relationship** is a link within the data. In a relational database, you can set up a relationship between tables at any time. The tables must have a common column (field). For example, you would relate the Schedule of Classes table and the Instructor table using the Instructor ID column. Figure 10-20 illustrates these relational database concepts. In a relational

Data Models for Popular DBMSs

Data Model	Popular DBMSs		Data Model	Popular DBMSs	
Relational	Access Adabas FileMaker Informix Ingres InterBase MySQL	SQL Server Sybase Teradata	Object-relational	DB2 Oracle Polyhedra PostgreSQL Visual FoxPro Teradata	
Object-oriented	FastObjects GemFire KE Texpress	ObjectStore Versant	Multi-dimensional	D^3 Essbase	Oracle Express Edition

Figure 10-18 Most DBMSs are based on a particular data model.

Data Terminology

File Processing Environment	Relational Database Developer	Relational Database User
File	Relation	Table
Record	Tuple	Row
Field	Attribute	Column

Figure 10-19 Varied terminology for relational databases.

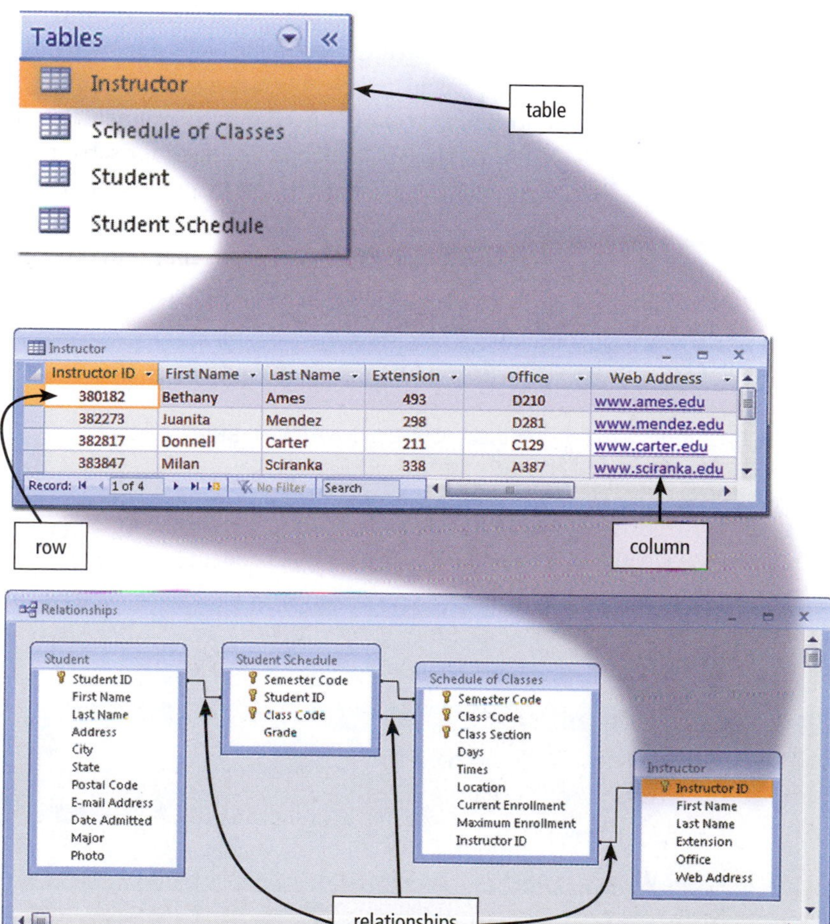

Figure 10-20 This figure shows relationships among some tables in the School database. For example, the Schedule of Classes table is related to the Instructor table through the Instructor ID column.

database, the only data redundancy (duplication) exists in the common columns (fields). The database uses these common columns for relationships.

Applications best suited for relational databases are those whose data can be organized into a two-dimensional table. Many organizations use relational databases for payroll, accounts receivable, accounts payable, general ledger, inventory, order entry, invoicing, and other business-related functions.

A developer of relational databases uses normalization to organize the data in a database. *Normalization* is a process designed to ensure the data within the relations (tables) contains the least amount of duplication. For a technical discussion about normalization, read the High-Tech Talk article on page 540.

SQL **Structured Query Language (SQL)** is a popular query language that allows users to manage, update, and retrieve data. SQL has special keywords and rules that users include in SQL statements. For example, the SQL statement in Figure 10-21a shows how to write the join operation that creates the results shown in Figure 10-21b. The statement displays the Class Title, Class Section, and Seats Remaining fields in alphabetical order by class title for all records in the Schedule of Classes table. The seats remaining are calculated by subtracting the current enrollment from the maximum enrollment.

Most relational database products for servers and mainframes include SQL. Many personal computer databases also include SQL. The structure and wording in SQL statements may differ slightly among database management systems.

SQL
For more information, visit the Computer Concepts CourseMate Web site at www.cengagebrain.com, navigate to the Chapter 10 Web Link resource for this book, and then click SQL.

Figure 10-21a (SQL statement)

```
SELECT CLASS_TITLE, CLASS_CODE, MAXIMUM_ENROLLMENT -
  CURRENT_ENROLLMENT AS SEATS_REMAINING
FROM SCHEDULE_OF_CLASSES, CLASS_CATALOG
WHERE SCHEDULE_OF_CLASSES.CLASS_CODE =
  CLASS_CATALOG.CLASS_CODE
ORDER BY CLASS_TITLE
```

Figure 10-21b (SQL statement results)

Class Title	Class Section	Seats Remaining
Algebra 1	51	14
Art Appreciation	52	19
English Composition 1	02	5
Introduction to Sociology	01	14

Figure 10-21 A sample SQL statement and its results.

Object-Oriented Databases

An **object-oriented database (OODB)** stores data in objects. An **object** is an item that contains data, as well as the actions that read or process the data. A Student object, for example, might contain data about a student such as Student ID, First Name, Last Name, Address, and so on. It also could contain instructions about how to print a student transcript or the formula required to calculate a student's grade point average. A record in a relational database, by contrast, would contain only data about a student.

Object-oriented databases have several advantages compared with relational databases: they can store more types of data, access this data faster, and allow programmers to reuse objects. An object-oriented database stores unstructured data more efficiently than a relational database. Unstructured data can include photos, video clips, audio clips, and documents. When users query an object-oriented database, the results often are displayed more quickly than the same query of a relational database. If an object already exists, programmers can reuse it instead of recreating a new object — saving on program development time.

Examples of applications appropriate for an object-oriented database include the following:

- A *multimedia database* stores images, audio clips, and/or video clips. For example, a *GIS* (geographic information system) database stores maps and other geographic data (Figure 10-22). A voice mail system database stores audio messages. A television news station database stores audio and video clips.
- A *groupware database* stores documents such as schedules, calendars, manuals, memos, and reports. Users perform queries to search the document contents. For example, you can search people's schedules for available meeting times.
- A *computer-aided design* (*CAD*) *database* stores data about engineering, architectural, and scientific designs. Data in the database includes a list of components of the item being designed, the relationship among the components, and previous versions of the design drafts.
- A *hypertext database* contains text links to other types of documents. A *hypermedia database* contains text, graphics, video, and sound. The Web contains a variety of hypertext and hypermedia databases. You can search these databases for items such as documents, graphics, audio and video clips, and links to Web pages.

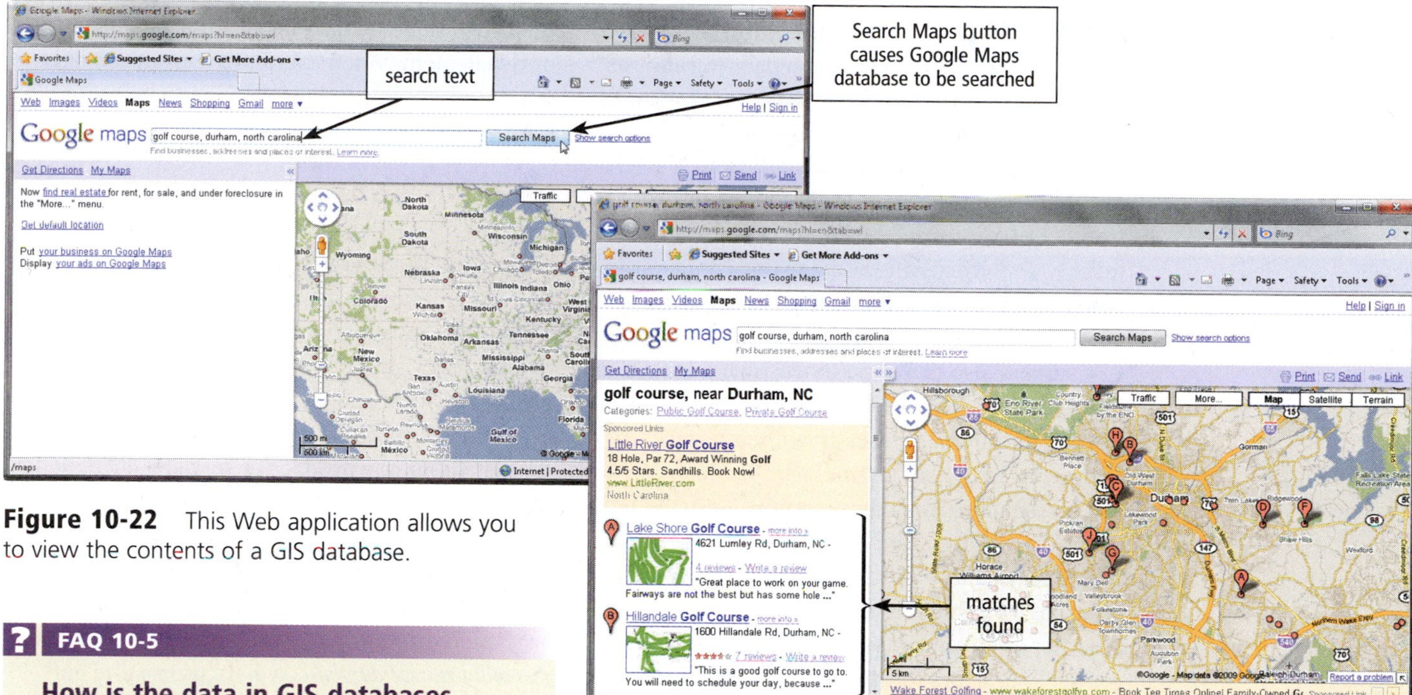

Figure 10-22 This Web application allows you to view the contents of a GIS database.

FAQ 10-5

How is the data in GIS databases obtained?

Although GIS database data sometimes is created from hard copy maps that are digitized using special software, much of the data is collected by teams who drive from location to location and record the data by hand. Satellite imagery also can be used to collect data from locations worldwide. Some computer databases developed by government and nongovernment agencies are able to feed data directly into a GIS database.

For more information, visit the Computer Concepts CourseMate Web site at www.cengagebrain.com, navigate to the Chapter 10 FAQ resource for this book, and then click GIS Databases.

Object Query Language Object-oriented and object-relational databases often use a query language called *object query language* (*OQL*) to manipulate and retrieve data. OQL is similar to SQL. OQL and SQL use many of the same rules, grammar, and keywords. Because OQL is a relatively new query language, not all object databases support it.

Multidimensional Databases

A **multidimensional database** stores data in dimensions. Whereas a relational database is a two-dimensional table, a multidimensional database can store more than two dimensions of data. These multiple dimensions, sometimes known as a *hypercube*, allow users to access and analyze any view of the database data.

A Webmaster at a retail business may want information about product sales and customer sales for each region spanning a given time. A manager at the same business may want information about product sales by department for each sales representative spanning a given time. A multidimensional database can consolidate this type of data from multiple dimensions at very high rates of speed.

The number of dimensions in a multidimensional database varies. A retail business might have four dimensions: products, customers, regions, and time. A multidimensional database for a hospital procedure could have six dimensions: time, procedure type, patient, hospital, physician, and diagnosis. A multidimensional database for an insurance policy may include five dimensions: time, policy type, agent, customer, and coverage. Nearly every multidimensional database has a dimension of time. The content of other dimensions varies depending on the subject.

The key advantage of the multidimensional database is that it can consolidate data much faster than a relational database. A relational database typically does not process and summarize large numbers of records efficiently. With a multidimensional database, users obtain summarized results very quickly. For example, a query that takes minutes or hours to execute in a relational database will take only seconds to execute in a multidimensional database.

No standard query language exists for multidimensional databases. Each database uses its own language. Most are similar to SQL.

Data Warehouses One application that uses multidimensional databases is a data warehouse. A **data warehouse** is a huge database that stores and manages the data required to analyze historical and current transactions. Through a data warehouse, managers and other users access transactions and summaries of transactions quickly and efficiently. Some major credit card companies monitor and manage customers' credit card transactions using a data warehouse. Consumers also can access their own transactions in the data warehouse via the Web. A data warehouse typically has a user-friendly interface, so that users easily can interact with its data.

The database in a data warehouse usually is quite large. Often, the database is distributed. The data in a *distributed database* exists in many separate locations throughout a network or the Internet. The data is accessible through a single server. The data's location is transparent to the user, who usually is unaware that the data is stored in multiple servers.

Data warehouses often use a process called *data mining* to find patterns and relationships among data. A state government could mine through data to check if the number of births has a relationship to income level. Many e-commerce sites use data mining to determine customer preferences.

A smaller version of a data warehouse is the *data mart*. A data mart contains a database that helps a specific group or department make decisions. Marketing and sales departments may have their own separate data marts. Individual groups or departments often extract data from the data warehouse to create their data marts.

Data Warehouses
For more information, visit the Computer Concepts CourseMate Web site at www.cengagebrain.com, navigate to the Chapter 10 Web Link resource for this book, and then click Data Warehouses.

Web Databases

One of the more profound features of the Web is the vast amount of information it provides. The Web offers information about jobs, travel destinations, television programming, photos, movies, videos, local and national weather, sporting events, and legislative information. You can shop for just about any product or service, buy or sell stocks, search for a job, make airline reservations, register for college classes, and check semester grades. Much of this and other information exists in databases that are stored on the Web or are accessible through the Web. Some Web databases are *collaborative databases*, where users store and share photos, videos, recordings, and other personal media with other registered users (Figure 10-23). Read Ethics & Issues 10-5 for a related discussion.

To access data in a Web database, you fill in a form or enter search text on a Web page. The Web page is the front end to the database. Many search engines such as Yahoo! use databases to store Web site descriptions. Thus, the search engine's home page is the front end to the database. To access the database, you enter search text into the search engine.

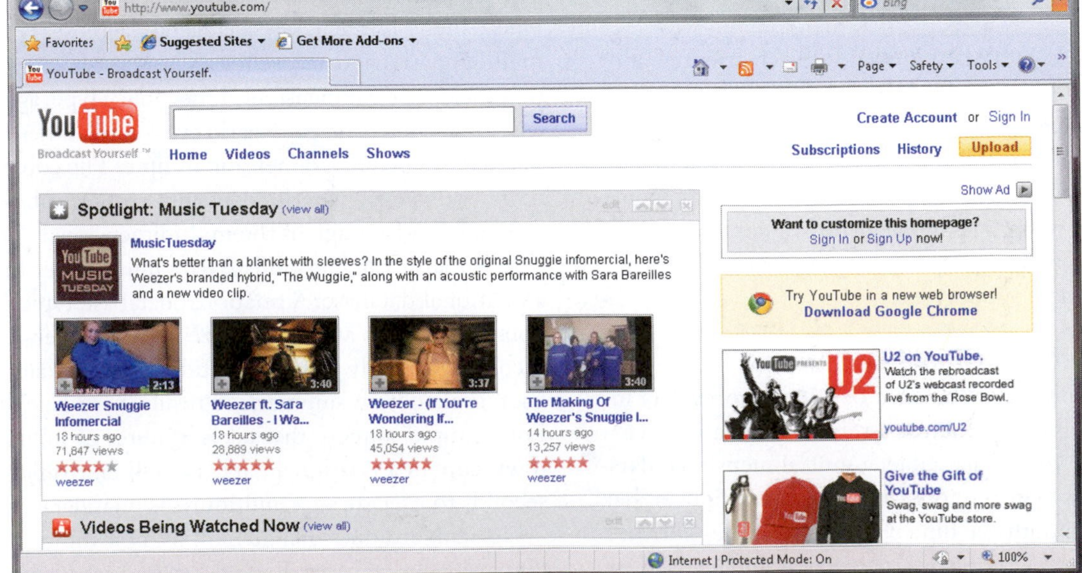

Figure 10-23 Media sharing Web sites store users' digital videos, photos, and other media in a collaborative database, the contents of which are shared with other registered users.

ETHICS & ISSUES 10-5

Who Should Be Held Accountable for the Rash of Database Security Breaches?

Over the course of three years, a privacy advocacy group documented the fact that more than 160 million records that contain personal information were accessed illegally or stolen. The records were allowed to be accessed because of carelessness by government agencies, educational institutions, and corporations. Often database software is not updated properly with security-related bug fixes. Information such as credit card numbers, credit history, and employment information often are involved in such security breaches. In one case, a security breach resulted in more than 45 million customer records being stolen with an estimated cost to the company of more than $4 billion. Institutions typically have their own set of guidelines to manage the security of such information, yet the number of security breaches is escalating.

While some have proposed laws requiring stricter controls for how institutions handle private data and provide for harsher penalties for those not properly securing data, corporations resist such efforts. They claim that the costs involved in such measures would hurt their capability of competing with corporations in other states and countries that are not bound by the same rules. Many institutions voluntarily notify individuals whose information was breached, and some even compensate victims; for example, some provide credit monitoring for free.

Who should be held accountable for the rash of database security breaches? Why? Should the government enact stronger laws regarding data security? Why or why not? Should institutions be required to notify individuals whose data has been breached? Why or why not?

A Web database usually resides on a database server. A *database server* is a computer that stores and provides access to a database. One type of program that manages the sending and receiving of data between the front end and the database server is a *CGI* (*Common Gateway Interface*) *script*. CGI scripts run automatically — as soon as you click the button to send or receive information. Writing a CGI script requires computer programming skills.

In addition to accessing information, users provide information to Web databases. Many Web sites request that users enter personal information, such as name, address, telephone number, and preferences, into an e-form. The database then stores this personal information for future use. An organization, for example, may send e-mail messages to certain groups of customers. If you are a frequent flyer, you may receive travel information.

For smaller databases, many personal computer database programs provide a variety of Web publishing tools that enable users without computer programming experience to create a home or small office database.

FAQ 10-6

Are my portable media player's playlists stored in a database?

Most programs that manage your playlist, such as iTunes and Windows Media Player, use a database to store details about your playlists. Storing this data in a database makes it easier and faster for you to search for songs that you wish to play or add to a playlist.

For more information, visit the Computer Concepts CourseMate Web site at www.cengagebrain.com, navigate to the Chapter 10 FAQ resource for this book, and then click Media Player Databases.

Database Administration

Managing a company's database requires a great deal of coordination. The role of coordinating the use of the database belongs to the database analysts and administrators. To carry out their responsibilities, these IT (information technology) professionals follow database design guidelines and need cooperation from all database users. To learn about organizing and searching for files and folders on a computer, complete the Learn How To 1 and 2 activities on pages 550 and 551.

Database Design Guidelines

A carefully designed database makes it easier for a user to query the database, modify its data, and create reports. The guidelines shown in Figure 10-24 apply to databases of all sizes.

Database Design Guidelines

For more information, visit the Computer Concepts CourseMate Web site at www.cengagebrain.com, navigate to the Chapter 10 Web Link resource for this book, and then click Database Design Guidelines.

Database Design Guidelines
1. Determine the purpose of the database.
2. Design the tables or files. - Design tables or files on paper first. - Each table or file should contain data about one subject. The Student table, for example, contains data about students.
3. Design the records and fields for each table or file. - Be sure every record has a unique primary key. - Use separate fields for logically distinct items. For example, a name could be stored in six fields: Title (Mr., Mrs., Dr., etc.), First Name, Middle Name, Last Name, Suffix (Jr., Sr., etc.), and Nickname. - Do not create fields for information that can be derived from entries in other fields. For example, do not include a field for Age. Instead, store the birth date and compute the age. - Allow enough space for each field. - Set default values for frequently entered data.
4. Determine the relationships among the tables or files.

Figure 10-24 Guidelines for designing a database.

Role of the Database Analysts and Administrators

The database analysts and administrators are responsible for managing and coordinating all database activities. The **database analyst (DA)**, or *data modeler*, focuses on the meaning and usage of data. The DA decides on the proper placement of fields, defines the relationships among data, and identifies users' access privileges. The **database administrator (DBA)** requires a more technical inside view of the data. The DBA creates and maintains the data dictionary, manages security of the database, monitors the performance of the database, and checks backup and recovery procedures.

Database Administrators

For more information, visit the Computer Concepts CourseMate Web site at www.cengagebrain.com, navigate to the Chapter 10 Web Link resource for this book, and then click Database Administrators.

In small companies, one person often is both the DA and DBA. In larger companies, the responsibilities of the DA and DBA are split among two or more people.

Role of the Employee as a User

Employees should learn how to use the data in the database effectively. The amount of information available often amazes first-time database users. Instant access to information helps employees perform their jobs more effectively. For example, assume you want to change your class schedule. You call your advisor to find out other sections that have seats available. The advisor reads to you a list of available classes and enrolls you in the one you prefer. Today, employees access databases from their office desktop computers, notebook computers, or even smart phones and other mobile devices.

Employees in most retail stores interact with databases related to inventory (Figure 10-25). For example, when a customer purchases an item, the inventory level that is stored in a database is updated. If the inventory level is at or below the reorder point, a program automatically orders more items from the supplier. The reorder point and supplier data also are stored in the database.

Figure 10-25 This bookstore employee scans the bar codes before placing the products on the shelf, so that the inventory accurately reflects book availability.

Employees also must take an active role in identifying new data for the database. For example, maybe an advisor does not have access to the list of classes on the computer. Instead, the advisor looks them up in a printed class catalog. The advisor's job would be much easier if this information was available on the computer.

The maintenance of a database is an ongoing task that organizations measure constantly against their overall goals. Users can take part in designing the database that will help them achieve those goals. Read Looking Ahead 10-1 for a look at a future use of databases.

LOOKING AHEAD 10-1

DNA Barcoding Identifies World's Species

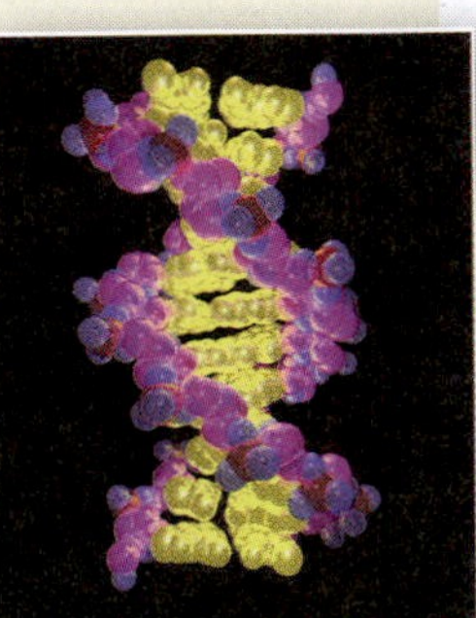

Taxonomists have been collecting and cataloging the world's 1.7 million known species of plants, animals, and microbes for the past 300 years. Each of these species has a unique DNA sequence, called the barcode of life, that researchers can extract from tissue samples.

The Consortium for the Barcode of Life is attempting to build three separate databases with data obtained from analyzing the tissues: GenBank at the National Institutes of Health in the United States, the European Molecular Biology Laboratory (EMBL) in Germany, and the DNA Data Bank of Japan (DDBJ). These global databases will contain records with the DNA sequence, data on the specimen, and the species' name. The data will be available to researchers worldwide free of charge.

Researchers hope the databases will help protect endangered species, provide basic research in taxonomy, sustain natural resources, explore marine biodiversity, control agricultural pests, monitor environmental quality, and stop the spread of disease-bearing mosquitoes.

For more information, visit the Computer Concepts CourseMate Web site at www.cengagebrain.com, navigate to the Chapter 10 Looking Ahead resource for this book, and then click DNA Barcode.

✔ QUIZ YOURSELF 10-3

Instructions: Find the true statement below. Then, rewrite the remaining false statements so that they are true.

1. Data warehouses often use a process called OQL to find patterns and relationships among data.
2. Object-oriented databases store data in tables.
3. One type of program that manages the sending and receiving of data between the front end and the database server is a CGI script.
4. Relational database users refer to a file as a table, a record as a column, and a field as a row.
5. SQL is a data modeling language that allows users to manage, update, and retrieve data.
6. The database analyst requires a more technical inside view of the data than does the database administrator.

Quiz Yourself Online: To further check your knowledge of pages 533 through 538, visit the Computer Concepts CourseMate Web site at www.cengagebrain.com, navigate to the Chapter 10 Quiz Yourself resource for this book, and then click Objectives 7 – 9.

Chapter Summary

This chapter discussed how data and information are valuable assets to an organization. The chapter also presented methods for maintaining high-quality data and assessing the quality of valuable information. It then discussed the advantages of organizing data in a database and described various types of databases. It also presented the roles of the database analysts and administrators.

Computer Usage @ Work

Health Sciences

During an intramural volleyball game, you suffer an injury that requires a trip to the emergency room. Upon check-in, you notice that the emergency room is extremely crowded, so the employee at the front desk uses a computer to record your personal data and symptoms. She also uses the computer to verify that your insurance coverage is current and informs you of your co-payment amount. After waiting several minutes, a triage nurse takes your temperature and blood pressure and then asks a series of questions about your symptoms. The nurse also records this data in a computer and asks you to remain in the waiting room until someone from the radiology department is available to perform a CT scan. The radiology department is located in a different area of the hospital, so the technicians watch a computer monitor that displays a list of patients who currently are waiting for their services.

About 30 minutes later, a technician calls your name and escorts you to the radiology department for your CT scan. As she is performing the scan, a computer records the images that later will be reviewed by a physician. When the CT scan is complete, you return to the waiting room until a physician reviews the results. Once he receives the results and reviews them, a hospital employee takes you to a consultation room.

The physician informs you that other than a few bumps and bruises, he believes that you have sustained no permanent damage and prescribes medication to help ease the pain. He then returns to a computer at the nurse's station and adds his diagnosis to the database that stores your medical records. He also sends your prescription electronically to the hospital's pharmacy. Once discharged, you visit the cashier to pay the bill. You then sign an electronic version of your discharge paperwork using a Tablet PC so that the hospital can store it electronically. The hospital bills your insurance company electronically. If you owe a balance after the insurance company has paid its portion, a computer at the hospital will generate a bill that will be mailed to you.

After purchasing your medication and leaving the hospital, you realize that despite the hospital being busy, computers decreased the time of your visit by automating processes that otherwise would have been performed manually.

For more information, visit the Computer Concepts CourseMate Web site at www.cengagebrain.com, navigate to the Chapter 10 Computer Usage @ Work resource for this book, and then click Health Sciences.

High-Tech Talk

Normalization: Ensuring Data Consistency

Normalization organizes a database into one of several normal forms to remove ambiguous relationships between data and minimize data redundancy. In *zero normal form* (*0NF*), the database is completely nonnormalized, and all of the data fields are included in one relation or table. Repeating groups are listed within parentheses (Figure 10-26a). The table has large rows due to the repeating groups and wastes disk space when an order has only one item.

To normalize the data from 0NF to *1NF* (*first normal form*), you remove the repeating groups (fields 3 through 7 and 8 through 12) and place them in a second table (Figure 10-26b). You then assign a primary key to the second table (Line Item), by combining the primary key of the nonrepeating group (Order #) with the primary key of the repeating group (Product #), called a composite key. Primary keys are underlined to distinguish them from other fields.

To further normalize the database from 1NF to *2NF* (*second normal form*), you remove partial dependencies. A *partial dependency* exists when fields in the table depend on only part of the primary key. In the Line Item table (Figure 10-26b), Product Name is dependent on Product #, which is only part of the primary key. Second normal form requires you to place the product information in a separate Product table to remove the partial dependency (Figure 10-26c).

To move from 2NF to *3NF* (*third normal form*), you remove transitive dependencies. A *transitive dependency* exists when a nonprimary key field depends on another nonprimary key field. As shown in Figure 10-26c, Vendor Name is dependent on Vendor #, both of which are nonprimary key fields. If Vendor Name is left in the Line Item table, the database will store redundant data each time a product is ordered from the same vendor.

Third normal form requires Vendor Name to be placed in a separate Vendor table, with Vendor # as the primary key. The field that is the primary key in the new table — in this case, Vendor # — also remains in the original table as a *foreign key* and is identified by a dotted underline (Figure 10-26d). In 3NF, the database now is logically organized in four separate tables and is easier to maintain. For instance, to add, delete, or modify a Vendor or Product Name, you make the change in just one table.

For more information, visit the Computer Concepts CourseMate Web site at www.cengagebrain.com, navigate to the Chapter 10 High-Tech Talk resource for this book, and then click Normalization.

Order Table

Order #	Order Date	Product #	Product Name	Qty Ordered	Vendor #	Vendor Name	Product #	Product Name	Qty Ordered	Vendor #	Vendor Name
		repeating group I					repeating group II				
1001	6/8/2011	605	8.5" x 11" White Copy Paper	2	321	Hammermill	203	Jewel Cases	5	110	Fellowes
1002	6/10/2011	751	Ballpoint Pens	6	166	Pilot					
1003	6/10/2011	321	1" Ring Binder, Blue	12	450	Globe					
1004	6/11/2011	605	8.5" x 11" White Copy Paper	2	321	Hammermill	102	Interior File Folders	2	450	Globe

(a) Zero Normal Form (0NF)
(Order #, Order Date, (Product #, Product Name, Quantity Ordered, Vendor #, Vendor Name))

(b) First Normal Form (1NF)
Order (Order #, Order Date)
Line Item (Order # + Product #, Product Name, Quantity Ordered, Vendor #, Vendor Name)

(c) Second Normal Form (2NF)
Order (Order #, Order Date)
Line Item (Order # + Product #, Quantity Ordered, Vendor #, Vendor Name)
Product (Product #, Product Name)

(d) Third Normal Form (3NF)
Order (Order #, Order Date)
Line Item (Order # + Product #, Quantity Ordered, Vendor #)
Product (Product #, Product Name)
Vendor (Vendor #, Vendor Name)

Order

Order #	Order Date
1001	6/8/2011
1002	6/10/2011
1003	6/10/2011
1004	6/11/2011

Line Item

Order # + Product #	Qty Ordered	Vendor #
1001605	2	321
1001203	5	110
1002751	6	166
1003321	12	450
1004605	2	321
1004102	2	450

Product

Product #	Product Name
102	Interior File Folders
203	Jewel Cases
321	1" Ring Binder, Blue
605	8.5" x 11" White Copy Paper
751	Ballpoint Pens

Vendor

Vendor #	Vendor Name
110	Fellowes
166	Pilot
321	Hammermill
450	Globe

Figure 10-26 The process of normalizing a database.

Companies on the Cutting Edge

ORACLE Database Software Developer

One hundred terabytes of data may seem impossible to manage, but *Oracle* can handle a database of this size with its recent products. The company is the world's second largest independent software company and is the world's largest enterprise software company.

Larry Ellison, the company's CEO, founded Oracle in 1977 with the help of two partners. They envisioned developing a commercially viable relational database, and their efforts were an instant success. Their first Oracle database changed the way companies stored and managed information because, for the first time, users could connect separate data tables by using a common field.

More than one-half of the FORTUNE 100 companies use an Oracle database. Its latest products feature online social networking and collaboration. Oracle's acquisitions and growth dominate the database community. Recently, Oracle acquired Sun Microsystems, another pioneer in the IT industry, for $7.4 billion.

SYBASE Unwired Enterprise Database and Services Leader

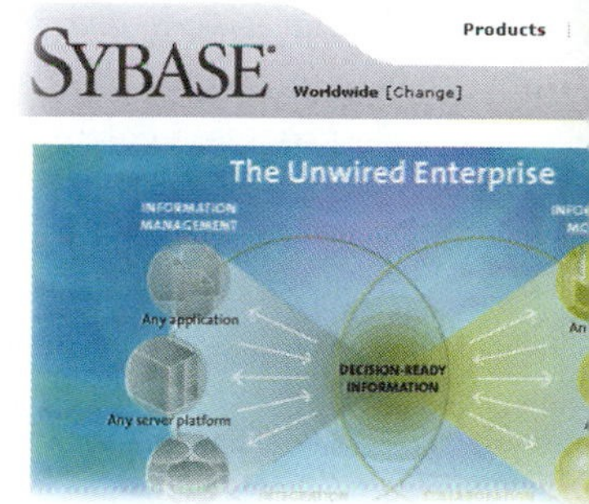

Wireless banking and messaging technology are two areas in demand today, and *Sybase* is helping companies meet consumers' demands for these services. The company provides mobile software for wireless applications and services, especially in the customer service and emergency response areas of the financial, telecommunications, health care, and government sectors.

Mark Hoffman and Bob Epstein founded Sybase more than 25 years ago out of Epstein's Berkeley, CA, home. Their company was the first to develop a client/server relational database; one of the first tests of this product was for the Human Genome Project, a 13-year study sponsored by the U.S. Department of Energy and the National Institutes of Health to identify more than 20,000 genes in human DNA and then store the findings in a database.

Sybase recently made the *InformationWeek* 500 list for the fifth year in a row. The *InformationWeek* 500 lists the most innovative technology users, including companies such as Kimberly-Clark, National Semiconductor, and Hilton Hotels.

For more information, visit the Computer Concepts CourseMate Web site at www.cengagebrain.com and then navigate to the Chapter 10 Companies on the Cutting Edge resource for this book.

Technology Trailblazers

E. F. CODD Relational Database Model Inventor

Organized data is the key to effective database design, and the normalization process that helps structure data and eliminate redundancy is credited to *Edgar Frank (E. F.) Codd.* His relational database design is the structure for most of the small and large databases used today, and this concept is considered one of the greatest technological inventions of the twentieth century.

After attending college in England and serving in the Royal Air Force, he immigrated to New York and began working at IBM as a programming mathematician. He developed and promoted his relational model in a series of research papers beginning with his 1969 IBM report, "Derivability, Redundancy, and Consistency of Relations Stored in Large Data Banks." As a result of his research, IBM introduced in 1982 the first version of Structured Query Language (SQL).

Among his achievements is earning the prestigious A. M. Turing Award, which is the Association for Computing Machinery's highest technical achievement honor given to an individual.

LARRY ELLISON Oracle Cofounder and CEO

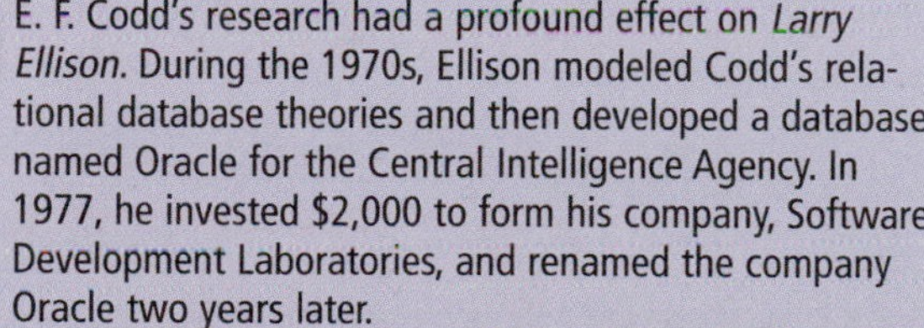

E. F. Codd's research had a profound effect on *Larry Ellison.* During the 1970s, Ellison modeled Codd's relational database theories and then developed a database named Oracle for the Central Intelligence Agency. In 1977, he invested $2,000 to form his company, Software Development Laboratories, and renamed the company Oracle two years later.

Ellison called his company's first database Oracle 2. He hoped this name gave the impression that an earlier version of the software had existed and that the second edition eliminated programming errors. This relational database system used IBM's Structured Query Language (SQL).

His compensation from Oracle and investments have made him one of the wealthiest men in the United States with an estimated net worth of $22.5 billion. In 2000, he was considered the richest man in the world. Among his hobbies are racing sailboats, flying jet planes, and playing guitar and tennis. He sits on the board of the Dian Fossey Gorilla Fund.

For more information, visit the Computer Concepts CourseMate Web site at www.cengagebrain.com and then navigate to the Chapter 10 Technology Trailblazers resource for this book.

STUDENT ASSIGNMENTS

Chapter Review

The Chapter Review reinforces the main concepts presented in this chapter.

To listen to an audio version of this Chapter Review, visit the Computer Concepts CourseMate Web site at www.cengagebrain.com and then navigate to the Chapter 10 Chapter Review resource for this book.

1. What Is a Database, and How Does a Database Interact with Data and Information? A **database** is a collection of data organized in a manner that allows access, retrieval, and use of that data. **Database software**, often called a **database management system (DBMS)**, allows users to create a computerized database; add, modify, and delete the data; sort and retrieve the data; and create forms and reports from the data. *Data* is a collection of unprocessed items, which can include text, numbers, images, audio, and video. Computers process data into information. *Information* is processed data; that is, it is organized, meaningful, and useful. In addition to documents, information can be in the form of audio, images, and video.

2. What Is Data Integrity, and What Are the Qualities of Valuable Information? Because data is used to generate information, many organizations realize that data is one of their more valuable assets. *Data integrity* identifies the quality of data. Data integrity is important because computers and people use information to make decisions and take actions. For a computer to produce correct information, the data that is entered in a database must have integrity. For information to be valuable, it should be accurate, verifiable, timely, organized, accessible, useful, and cost-effective. *Accurate information* is error free. *Verifiable information* can be proven as correct or incorrect. *Timely information* has an age suited to its use. *Organized information* is arranged to suit the needs and requirements of the decision maker. *Accessible information* is available when the decision maker needs it. *Useful information* has meaning to the person who receives it. *Cost-effective information* should give more value than it costs to produce.

3. What Is Meant by Character, Field, Record, and File? Data is classified in a hierarchy, with each level of data consisting of one or more items from the lower level. A bit is the smallest unit of data a computer can process. Eight bits grouped together in a unit form a byte, and each byte represents a single **character**, which can be a number, letter, space, punctuation mark, or other symbol. A **field** is a combination of one or more related characters or bytes and is the smallest unit of data a user accesses. A **record** is a group of related fields. A **data file** is a collection of related records stored on a storage medium such as a hard disk or optical disc.

4. What Are File Maintenance Techniques and Validation Techniques? **File maintenance** refers to the procedures that keep data current. File maintenance procedures include adding records when new data is obtained, modifying records to correct inaccurate data or to update old data with new data, and deleting records when they no longer are needed. **Validation** is the process of comparing data with a set of rules or values to find out if the data is correct. Many programs perform a *validity check* that analyzes data, either as you enter it or after you enter it, to help ensure that it is correct. Types of validity checks include an *alphabetic check*, a *numeric check*, a *range check*, a *consistency check*, a *completeness check*, and a *check digit*.

Visit the Computer Concepts CourseMate Web site at www.cengagebrain.com, navigate to the Chapter 10 Quiz Yourself resource for this book, and then click Objectives 1 – 4.

5. How Is a File Processing Approach Different from the Database Approach? In a **file processing system**, each department or area within an organization has its own set of data files. The records in one file may not relate to the records in any other file. Two major weaknesses of file processing systems are redundant data (duplicated data) and isolated data. With a **database approach**, many programs and users share the data in a database. The database approach reduces data redundancy, improves data integrity, shares data, permits easier access, and reduces development time. A database, however, can be more complex than a file processing system, requiring special training and more computer memory, storage, and processing power than file processing systems. Data in a database also can be more vulnerable than data in file processing systems.

6. What Functions Are Common to Most Database Management Systems? Database management systems (DBMSs) are available for many sizes and types of computers. Whether designed for a small or large computer, most DBMSs perform common functions.

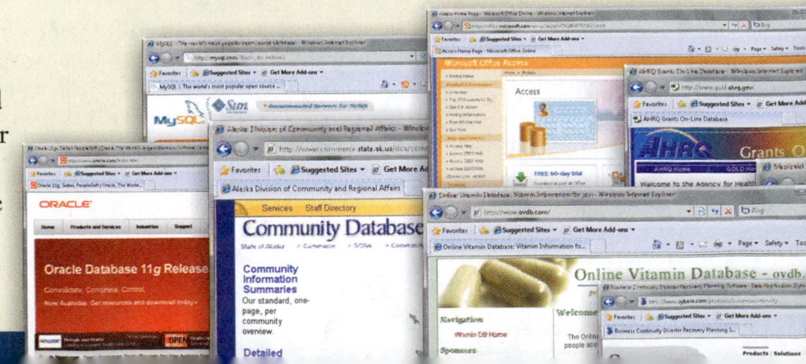

Chapter Review

A **data dictionary**, sometimes called a *repository*, contains data about each file in the database and each field in those files. A DBMS offers several methods to retrieve and maintain data in the database, such as query languages, query by example, forms, and report generators. A **query language** consists of simple, English-like statements that allow users to specify the data to display, print, or store. **Query by example (QBE)** has a graphical user interface that assists users with retrieving data. A **form**, sometimes called a *data entry form*, is a window on the screen that provides areas for entering or modifying data in a database. A **report generator**, also called a *report writer*, allows users to design a report on the screen, retrieve data into the report design, and then display or print the report. To supply security, most DBMSs can identify different levels of *access privileges* that define the actions a specific user or group of users can perform for each field in a database. If a database is damaged or destroyed, a DBMS provides techniques to return the database to a usable form. A **backup** is a copy of the database. A **log** is a listing of activities that modify the contents of the database. A **recovery utility** uses the logs and/or backups to restore the database using rollforward or rollback techniques. In a *rollforward*, also called *forward recovery*, the DBMS uses the log to reenter changes made to the database since the last save or backup. In a *rollback*, also called *backward recovery*, the DBMS uses the log to undo any changes made to the database during a certain period. *Continuous backup* is a backup plan in which all data is backed up whenever a change is made.

Visit the Computer Concepts CourseMate Web site at www.cengagebrain.com, navigate to the Chapter 10 Quiz Yourself resource for this book, and then click Objectives 5 – 6.

7. What Are Characteristics of Relational, Object-Oriented, and Multidimensional Databases? A **data model** consists of rules and standards that define how the database organizes data. Three popular data models are relational, object-oriented, and multidimensional. A **relational database** stores data in tables that consist of rows and columns. A relational database developer refers to a file as a *relation*, a record as a *tuple*, and a field as an *attribute*. A relational database user refers to a file as a **table**, a record as a **row**, and a field as a **column**. A **relationship** is a link within the data in a relational database. **Structured Query Language (SQL)** allows users to manage, update, and retrieve data in a relational database. An **object-oriented database (OODB)** stores data in objects. An **object** is an item that contains data, as well as the actions that read or process the data. Applications appropriate for an object-oriented database include a *multimedia database*, a *groupware database*, a *computer-aided design (CAD) database*, a *hypertext database*, and a *hypermedia database*. Object-oriented databases often use an *object query language (OQL)* to manipulate and retrieve data. A **multidimensional database** stores data in dimensions. These multiple dimensions, sometimes known as a *hypercube*, allow users to access and analyze any view of the database data. No standard query language exists for multidimensional databases. One application that uses multidimensional databases is a **data warehouse**, which is a huge database that stores and manages the data required to analyze historical and current transactions. A smaller version of a data warehouse is the *data mart*, which contains a database that helps a specific group or department make decisions.

8. How Are Web Databases Accessed? To access data in a Web database, you fill in a form or enter search text on a Web page, which is the *front end* to the database. A Web database usually resides on a *database server*, which is a computer that stores and provides access to a database. One type of program that manages the sending and receiving of data between the front end and the database server is a *CGI (Common Gateway Interface) script*.

9. What Are the Responsibilities of Database Analysts and Administrators? A **database analyst (DA)**, or *data modeler*, focuses on the meaning and usage of data. The DA decides on the placement of fields, defines data relationships, and identifies users' access privileges. A **database administrator (DBA)** requires a more technical inside view of the data. The DBA creates and maintains the data dictionary, manages database security, monitors database performance, and checks backup and recovery procedures. In small companies, one person often is both the DA and DBA. In larger companies, the responsibilities of the DA and DBA are split among two or more people.

Visit the Computer Concepts CourseMate Web site at www.cengagebrain.com, navigate to the Chapter 10 Quiz Yourself resource for this book, and then click Objectives 7 – 9.

Key Terms

You should know the Primary Terms and be familiar with the Secondary Terms. The list below helps focus your study.

To see an example of and a definition for each term, and to access current and additional information from the Web, visit the Computer Concepts CourseMate Web site at www.cengagebrain.com and then navigate to the Chapter 10 Key Terms resource for this book.

Primary Terms

(shown in bold-black characters in the chapter)

backup (531)
character (518)
column (533)
data dictionary (527)
data file (519)
data model (533)
data type (518)
data warehouse (536)
database (514)
database administrator (DBA) (538)
database analyst (DA) (538)
database approach (524)
database management system (DBMS) (515)
database software (515)
field (518)
field name (518)
field size (518)
file maintenance (520)
file processing system (524)
form (530)
log (532)
multidimensional database (535)
object (534)
object-oriented database (OODB) (534)
primary key (519)
query (528)
query by example (QBE) (528)
query language (528)
record (519)
recovery utility (532)
relational database (533)
relationship (533)
report generator (531)
row (533)
Structured Query Language (SQL) (534)
table (533)
validation (522)

Secondary Terms

(shown in italic characters in the chapter)

access privileges (531)
accessible information (516)
accurate information (516)
after image (532)
alphabetic check (523)
alphanumeric (518)
attribute (533)
back end (525)
backward recovery (532)
before image (532)
BLOB (518)
Boolean (518)
CGI (Common Gateway Interface) script (537)
check digit (523)
collaborative databases (536)
completeness check (523)
composite key (519)
computer-aided design (CAD) database (534)
consistency check (523)
continuous backup (532)
cost-effective information (517)
data (514)
data entry form (530)
data integrity (516)
data mart (536)
data mining (536)
data modeler (538)
database server (537)
default value (528)
distributed database (536)
e-form (530)
electronic form (530)
forward recovery (532)
front end (525)
garbage in, garbage out (GIGO) (516)
GIS (534)
groupware database (534)
hypercube (535)
hypermedia database (534)
hypertext database (534)
information (514)
metadata (528)
multimedia database (534)
normalization (534)
numeric check (523)
object query language (OQL) (535)
object-relational databases (533)
organized information (516)
principle of least privilege (531)
range check (523)
relation (533)
report writer (531)
repository (527)
rollback (532)
rollforward (532)
timely information (516)
tuple (533)
useful information (517)
validation rules (522)
validity check (522)
verifiable information (516)

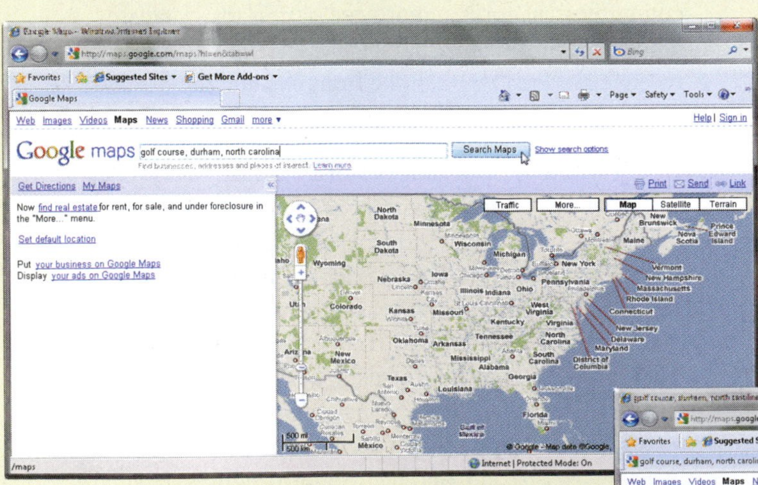

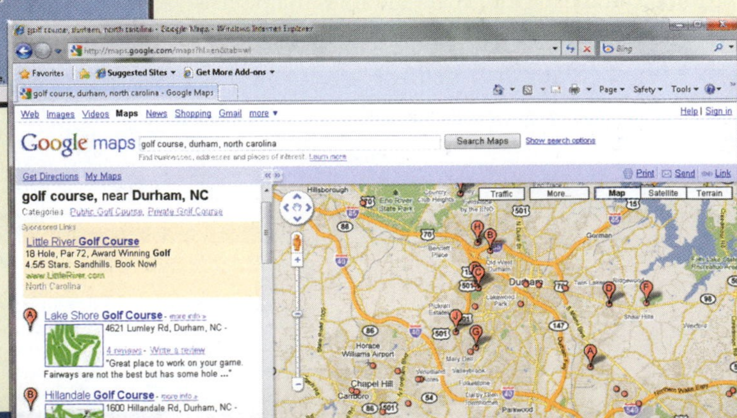

GIS (534)

Checkpoint

The Checkpoint exercises test your knowledge of the chapter concepts. The page number containing the answer appears in parentheses after each exercise. The Beyond the Book exercises will help broaden your understanding of the concepts presented in this chapter.

To complete the Checkpoint exercises interactively, visit the Computer Concepts CourseMate Web site at www.cengagebrain.com and then navigate to the Chapter 10 Checkpoint resource for this book.

True/False Mark T for True and F for False.

_____ 1. Data is a collection of unprocessed items, which can include text, numbers, images, audio, and video. (514)

_____ 2. A database management system allows users to create forms and reports from the data in the database. (515)

_____ 3. A range check ensures users enter only numeric data in a field. (523)

_____ 4. A check digit often confirms the accuracy of a primary key value. (523)

_____ 5. Databases require less memory, storage, and processing power than a file processing system. (526)

_____ 6. A report is a window on the screen that provides areas for entering or modifying data in a database. (530)

_____ 7. Continuous backup is a backup plan in which all data is backed up whenever a change is made. (532)

_____ 8. A relationship is a link within the data in a database. (533)

_____ 9. Normalization is a process designed to ensure the data within the relations (tables) is duplicated so that it is not lost. (534)

_____ 10. The data in a distributed database exists in many separate locations throughout a network or the Internet. (536)

Multiple Choice Select the best answer.

1. _____ information has an age suited to its use. (516)
   a. Organized
   b. Timely
   c. Cost-effective
   d. Verifiable

2. In some tables, the primary key consists of multiple fields, called a _____. (519)
   a. composite key
   b. secondary key
   c. key field
   d. column

3. _____ procedures include adding records to, modifying records in, and deleting records from a file. (520)
   a. Backup
   b. Range check
   c. Validation
   d. File maintenance

4. A range check _____. (523)
   a. ensures that users enter only alphabetic data into a field
   b. determines whether a number is within a specified range
   c. ensures that users enter only numeric data into a field
   d. verifies that a required field contains data

5. All of the following are strengths of the database approach, except _____. (525)
   a. less complexity
   b. improved data integrity
   c. easier access
   d. reduced development time

6. Because the _____ contains details about data, some call it metadata (meta means more comprehensive). (528)
   a. data mart
   b. data dictionary
   c. data modeler
   d. data warehouse

7. Many organizations adopt the _____ policy, where users' access privileges are limited to the lowest level necessary to perform required tasks. (531)
   a. golden rule
   b. principle of least privilege
   c. principle of highest access
   d. least order

8. The database analyst (DA) _____. (538)
   a. decides on the proper placement of fields
   b. creates and maintains the data dictionary
   c. monitors the performance of the database
   d. checks backup and recovery procedures

Checkpoint

Matching Match the terms with their definitions.

_____ 1. field name (518)
_____ 2. field size (518)
_____ 3. data type (518)
_____ 4. primary key (519)
_____ 5. query language (528)
_____ 6. log (532)
_____ 7. recovery utility (532)
_____ 8. GIS (534)
_____ 9. data modeler (538)
_____ 10. database administrator (538)

a. listing of activities that modify the contents of a database
b. field that uniquely identifies each record in a file
c. specifies the kind of data a field can contain and how the field is used
d. database that stores maps and other geographic data
e. uniquely identifies each field
f. creates and maintains the data dictionary, manages security of the database, monitors the performance of the database, and checks backup and recovery procedures
g. defines the maximum number of characters a field can contain
h. person who focuses on the meaning and usage of data
i. uses the logs and/or backups to restore a database when it becomes damaged or destroyed
j. consists of simple, English-like statements that allow users to specify the data to display, print, or store

Short Answer Write a brief answer to each of the following questions.

1. What is validation? ___________ What are five types of validity checks? ___________
2. Why is data redundancy a weakness of file processing systems? ___________ Why is isolated data a weakness of file processing systems? ___________
3. What is the database approach? ___________ Describe five strengths of the database approach. ___________
4. Describe how you might use a Simple Query Wizard. ___________ What is query by example? ___________
5. What are the advantages of object-oriented databases? ___________ Describe four examples of object-oriented databases. ___________

Beyond the Book Follow the book element instructions below; present your findings (brief report, presentation, discussion, or other means).

1. Ethics & Issues — Select an Ethics & Issues in this chapter (516, 519, 526, 531, 537), find a recent newspaper/magazine article that supports one point of view presented, and then evaluate the article.
2. Computer Usage @ Work — Use the Web or a recent newspaper/magazine to locate three additional unique usages of computer technology in the health sciences field (539). What makes the use of these technologies unique to the health sciences field?
3. Companies on the Cutting Edge and Technology Trailblazers — Use the Web or a recent business newspaper/magazine to locate an interesting fact about Oracle, Sybase, E. F. Codd, or Larry Ellison that was not presented in the chapter (541).
4. High-Tech Talk — Locate a recent newspaper/magazine article that discusses topics related to Normalization: Ensuring Data Consistency (540). Would you recommend the article you found? Why or why not?
5. FAQs and Web Links — Use the Web or a recent newspaper/magazine to locate three additional facts about an FAQ (517, 519, 526, 527, 535, 537) and Web Link (516, 523, 527, 530, 534, 536, 537, 538) that were not presented in the chapter.
6. Looking Ahead — Use the Web or a recent newspaper/magazine to discover additional uses of the technology presented in DNA Barcoding Identifies World's Species (538).
7. Innovative Computing — Use the Web or a recent newspaper/magazine to locate two additional interesting facts about America's Favorite Pastime Adds Authentic Twist (523) or Voter Databases Target Likely Candidate Supporters (530).
8. Making Use of the Web — Visit three of the Weather, Sports, and News sites (134) and outline the information on each Web site and the possible uses for each Web site.

Learn It Online

The Learn It Online exercises are interactive Web exercises designed to reinforce and expand your understanding of the chapter concepts. The descriptions below briefly summarize each exercise.

To complete the Learn It Online exercises, visit the Computer Concepts CourseMate Web site at www.cengagebrain.com, navigate to the Chapter 10 resources for this book, click the link for the exercise you want to complete, and then read the instructions.

1 At the Movies — How a Photo Sharing Site Keeps Its Data
Watch a movie to visit Equinix, the data storage site for Smugmug.com, and learn how photos are uploaded and shared on the Web, and then answer questions about the movie.

2 Video and Audio: You Review It — Web Databases
Search for, choose, and write a review of a video, podcast, or vodcast that discusses Web databases.

3 Student Edition Labs — Advanced Databases and Advanced Spreadsheets
Enhance your understanding and knowledge about advanced databases and advanced spreadsheets by completing the Advanced Databases and Advanced Spreadsheets Labs.

4 Practice Test
Take a multiple choice test that checks your knowledge of the chapter concepts and review the resulting study guide.

5 Who Wants To Be a Computer Genius^2?
Play the Shelly Cashman Series version of this popular game by answering questions to find out if you are a computer genius. Panic buttons are available to provide assistance during game play.

6 Wheel of Terms
Identify important key terms presented in this chapter by playing the Shelly Cashman Series version of this popular game.

7 You're Hired!
Embark on the path to a career in computers by answering questions and solving puzzles related to concepts discussed in this chapter.

8 Crossword Puzzle Challenge
Complete an interactive crossword puzzle to reinforce concepts presented in this chapter.

9 Windows Exercises
Step through the Windows 7 exercises to learn about managing files and folders, creating folders, and moving and deleting files.

10 Exploring Computer Careers
Read about a career as a database administrator, search for related employment advertisements, and then answer related questions.

11 Web Apps — Windows Live Calendar
Learn how to use Windows Live Calendar to create events, display a list of recent and upcoming events, share your calendar, and display items in your to-do list.

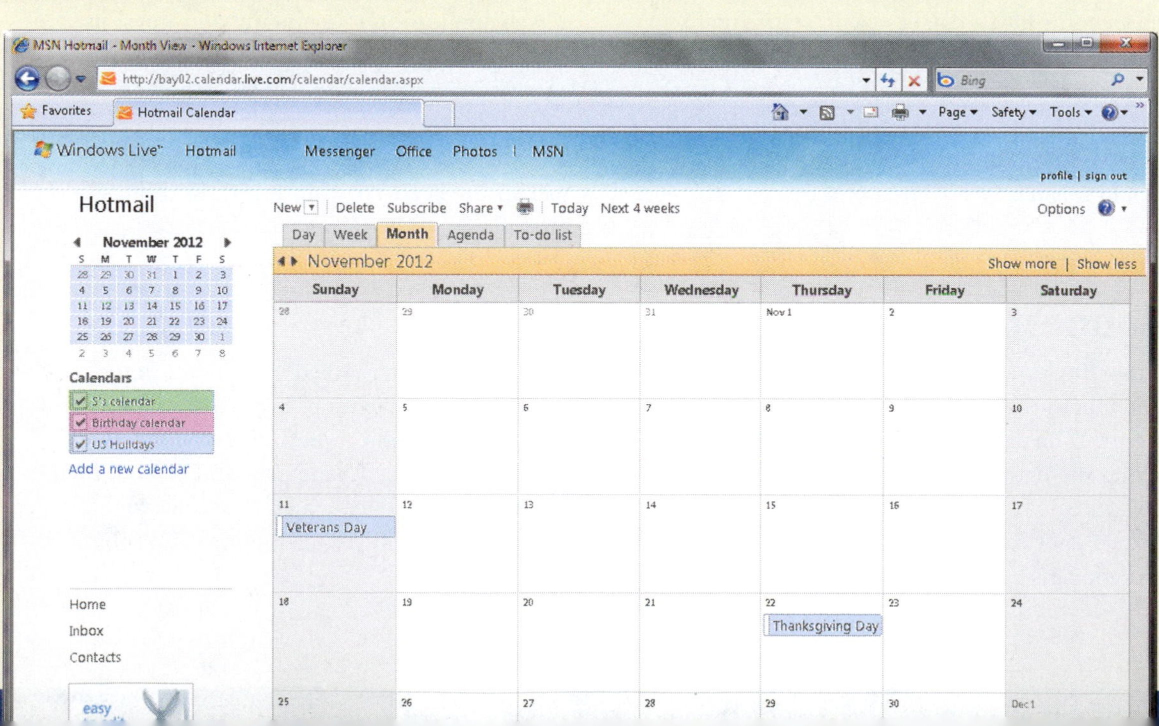

STUDENT ASSIGNMENTS

Problem Solving @ Home

The Problem Solving @ Home exercises extend your knowledge of the chapter concepts by seeking solutions to practical computer problems that you may encounter at home or school. The Collaboration exercise should be completed with a team.

In the real world, practical problems often can be solved in multiple ways. Provide one solution to each of the following problems using available resources, such as articles on the Web or in print, blogs, podcasts, videos, television, user guides, other individuals, and electronics and computer stores. You may need to use multiple resources to obtain an answer. Present your solutions in the form requested by your instructor (brief report, presentation, discussion, or other means).

1. **Blocked E-Mail Attachment** Your friend sent you an e-mail message. Attached to the message is a copy of a database containing the contact information for each member in a student organization to which you belong. When you receive the e-mail message, a message appears stating that your e-mail program has blocked the attachment. What are your next steps?
2. **Missing Frequent Flyer Credit** You set up a frequent flyer account with a major airline. On the last statement you received, the airline did not credit you for two recent flights; however, you are sure that you presented your frequent flyer card when you checked in at the counter. What might be the problem?
3. **Value Too Long** As a teacher's assistant at a local high school, you keep track of student grades in a Microsoft Access database. When you enter the last name of one of the students, you receive an error message stating that the value is too long for the field. What are your next steps?
4. **Nonsequential AutoNumber Values** While entering records into a database, you realize that you entered the same record two times. You delete the record with the duplicate information and then add a new record. It now appears, however, that the values in the AutoNumber field are not sequential. How could this be?
5. **Invalid Telephone Number** While editing a database, you change the value in the telephone number field in one of the records. After editing the field and moving to the next record, the DBMS informs you that you have entered an invalid value. What might have caused this error message to appear, and what will you do first to fix this problem?
6. **No Results Returned** You have written a query to display a list of customers in a database who reside in the state of Florida. When you run the query, the DBMS displays no records. You know at least 10 customers reside in Florida, and those records should have been displayed. What might have caused this?
7. **Account Already Exists** While registering for an account at an online photo sharing community, you receive an error message stating that an account with your e-mail address already exists. You are unable to remember whether you have registered for an account on that Web site previously and want to access the other account, if it exists. What are your next steps?
8. **Cannot Access Web Database** To prepare for your upcoming wedding, you have been using a Web application to maintain your guest list. This Web application stores each guest's name, contact information, and whether he or she will attend. Today when you attempt to access this information, the Web site is unavailable. How can you ensure access to your guest list if the site is unavailable in the future?

Collaboration

9. **Database Backup Plan** Your boss at your part-time job in a retail store has asked you to determine how and when to back up the database containing the company's sales information. Form a team of three classmates. Your team should research various backup strategies and determine whether it would be best to back up the data continuously or perform backups on a set schedule. Discuss the pros and cons of each backup strategy. If your team decides to back up the database on a set schedule, which schedule would work best? Once your team has formulated a backup strategy, summarize and justify your findings and submit them to your instructor.

Problem Solving @ Work

The Problem Solving @ Work exercises extend your knowledge of the chapter concepts by seeking solutions to practical computer problems that you may encounter at work. The Collaboration exercise should be completed with a team.

In the real world, practical problems often can be solved in multiple ways. Provide one solution to each of the following problems using available resources, such as articles on the Web or in print, blogs, podcasts, videos, television, user guides, other individuals, and electronics and computer stores. You may need to use multiple resources to obtain an answer. Present your solutions in the form requested by your instructor (brief report, presentation, discussion, or other means).

1. **Error Opening Database** While attempting to open a database, you receive an error message stating that the database is damaged. What are your next steps?
2. **Insufficient Access Permissions** A customer has called to inform you of his change of address. When you open the customer database to enter this change, an error message appears stating that you do not have sufficient access to update the customer's record. What might have caused this error message to appear? What steps will you take to resolve this problem?
3. **Accidentally Deleted Records** While working in Microsoft Access, you select all records to copy them to another table in the database. Instead of copying the records, you accidentally press another key combination that removes all records from the table. Your attempt to paste the records back into the table is unsuccessful, and the records appear to have been removed permanently. What steps will you take to restore the records?
4. **Incorrect Password** At work, your company's database requires a password to access it. When you attempt to open the database, a dialog box requesting the database password is displayed. After typing your password and pressing the ENTER key, an error message states that your password is invalid. The same message appears on your next attempt. What are your next steps?
5. **Copying Contacts to Smart Phone** Your employer purchased a new smart phone for you, and you wish to copy the contacts from your company's database to the smart phone's address book. What are your first steps to accomplish this task?
6. **Inconsistent Search Performance** When you search a customer database, you notice that the search performance is inconsistent. For example, searching for a customer by his or her customer number or last name displays search results quickly. Searching for a customer by his or her first name, however, takes considerably longer. Why might this be?

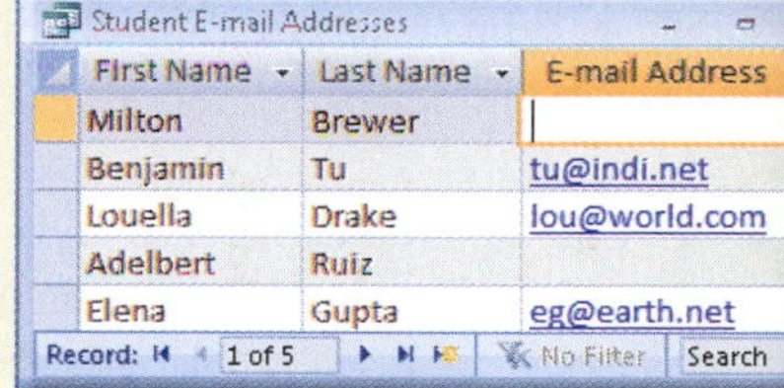

7. **Read-Only Database** While attempting to open a database, a dialog box appears stating that the database is read-only and any changes you make will not be saved. What steps will you take to open the database in a way that will allow you to make changes?
8. **Duplicate Records Exist** A search of your company's employee database reveals that duplicate records exist for multiple employees. You notice minor differences between each record and believe that you should remove duplicate records to decrease data redundancy; however, you do not want to lose data that might be valuable. What steps will you take to back up the database before removing the duplicate records?

Collaboration

9. **Computers in Health Sciences** Your physician, who once shared an office with three other physicians, has decided to open his own practice. Because his former colleagues will not allow him to take patient data to his new office, he needs to establish a method of recording and tracking patient data. Form a team of three people to determine a strategy to collect and maintain data. One team member should research various database management systems and provide a recommendation for the most useful one for this practice. Another team member should research which specific patient data the database should store, and the third team member should research the computer hardware necessary to store, update, maintain, and properly back up the data. Compile your findings in a report and submit it to your instructor.

Learn How To

The Learn How To activities step you through fundamental technology skills when using a computer. The Learn How To exercises enable you to become more proficient with these skills.

Premium Activity: To relate this Learn How To activity to your everyday life, see a visual demonstration of the activity, and complete a short assessment, visit the Computer Concepts CourseMate Web site at www.cengagebrain.com and then navigate to the Chapter 10 Learn How To resource for this book.

Learn How To 1: Organize and Manage Files on a Computer

Introduction In Learn How To 1 in Chapter 3 (page 188), you learned the procedure for saving a file. In this Learn How To activity, you will learn how to manage files using folders and how to find a file if you cannot remember where you saved it.

Folders A folder is a virtual container where you can store a file on media. When you store any file, the file must be stored in a folder. The folder symbol, together with the folder name, identifies a folder.

You can create folders in a variety of ways. To create a folder on the desktop, complete the following steps:

1. Right-click the desktop in a location that does not contain an icon or toolbar.
2. Point to New on the shortcut menu that is displayed (Figure 10-27).
3. Click Folder on the New submenu.
4. When the folder icon is displayed on the desktop, type the name you want to assign to the folder and then press the ENTER key. You should choose a name that identifies the contents of the folder.

A folder can contain other folders. This allows you to organize your files in a hierarchical manner so that the highest-level folder contains all the folders for a given subject, and lower-level folders contain more specific files and folders. For example, your highest-level folder could be named Fall Semester. For each class, such as Computer Information Systems 110, you could define a folder within the Fall Semester folder. Within each class folder, you could define folders for each week of the class, or for each project or assignment within the class. In this manner, you would have a set of folders, each designated for a specific use. You then would save your files in the appropriate folder.

To create a folder within a folder, complete the following steps:

1. Double-click the folder name either on the desktop or in the window or dialog box in which the folder name appears.
2. Click the New folder button.
3. When the folder icon is displayed, type the name you want to assign to the folder, and then press the ENTER key.

To delete a folder, complete the following steps:

1. Right-click the folder.
2. On the shortcut menu that is displayed (Figure 10-28), click Delete.
3. In the Delete Folder dialog box, click the Yes button.

When you delete a folder, all the files and folders contained in the folder you are deleting, together with all files and folders on the lower hierarchical levels, are deleted. If you accidentally delete a folder, complete the following steps:

1. Double-click the Recycle Bin icon on the desktop.
2. In the Recycle Bin window, select the folder you wish to restore.
3. Click the 'Restore this item' button.

Using folders effectively will aid you in keeping track of files you create for your classes.

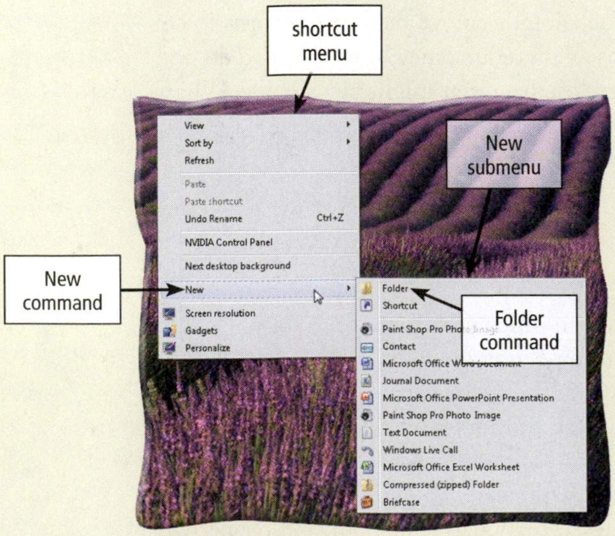

Figure 10-27

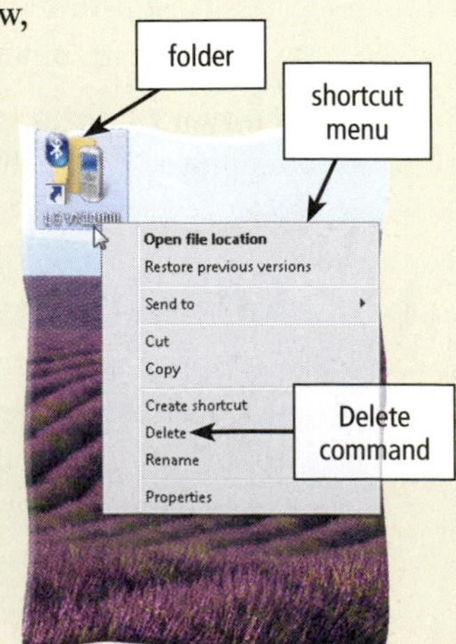

Figure 10-28

Learn How To

Exercises

1. Assume you are taking the following courses: Computer Information Systems 120, History 210, English 145, Marketing 221, and Business Law 120. Define the hierarchy of folders you would create for these classes. In which folder would you store an assignment from English 145 that was assigned in the sixth week of class? Submit your answers to your instructor.
2. Windows creates a collection of folders that is associated with each user account. For example, each user might have a My Pictures folder that stores pictures, and a My Documents folder that stores documents. What subfolders exist in your My Documents folder? In addition to the subfolders already present, what subfolders might you add in the future to help organize your files? What subfolders, if any, exist in your My Pictures folder? What is your hierarchy of subfolders in the My Pictures folder? Finally, explain why organizing your files is important.

Learn How To 2: Search for Files and Folders

At times, you might store a file in a folder and then forget where you stored the file. The Search feature in Windows enables you to search storage media on a computer to find the file. To use the Search feature, complete the following steps:

1. Click the Start button on the Windows taskbar.
2. In the Search box, type the name of the file for which you are searching. If you do not know the entire file name, enter as much of the file name as you can remember.
3. Windows will search as you type your search criteria into the Search box.
4. All items containing the file name or partial file name will be displayed on the Start menu so that you can open the displayed file in the appropriate program by clicking it.
5. If the file for which you are searching is displayed, click the file name on the Start menu to open the file in the appropriate program.
6. If the file for which you are searching is not displayed, click the 'See more results' command on the Start menu to open the Search Results window (Figure 10-29).
7. If you are unable to find the file you are seeking, scroll to the bottom of the Search Results window and select another location to search.
8. Before you close the Search Results window, make a note of the location of the file. If this is not the location where you want the file to be stored, store the file in the correct location.

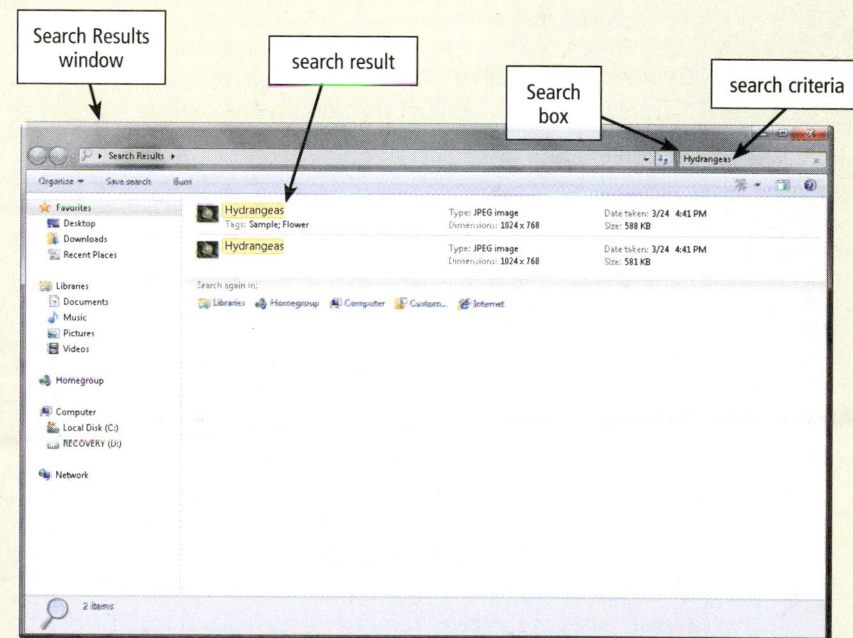

Figure 10-29

Exercises

1. Using the Windows Search feature, locate the file named Lighthouse. How many file names were displayed? Which folder contains the Lighthouse file? Submit your answers to your instructor.
2. On the computer you are using, create a hierarchy of folders for your classes. Create a WordPad file that contains the following text: `This file will be found using the Search feature.` Save the file in one of the folders using a file name of your choice. Using the Search feature, search for the file you just created. How many files were displayed from your search? Delete all folders and files you created in this exercise. Write a paragraph describing the steps you will take to organize your files for the coming semester. Submit your responses to your instructor.

Web Research

The Web Research exercises broaden your understanding of the chapter concepts by presenting questions that require you to search the Web for answers.

1 Search Sleuth

Use one of the search engines listed in Figure 2-10 in Chapter 2 on page 85 or your own favorite search engine to find the answers to the following questions. Copy and paste the Web address from the Web page where you found the answer. Some questions may have more than one answer. If required, submit your answers to your instructor. (1) How many seconds did it take for Google's 1,000 computers to sort 1 TB of data in 2008? (2) Which company has built data centers in Kronstorf, Austria; Goose Creek, South Carolina; and Dalles, Oregon? (3) Which energy source do Ormat and Raser Technologies use? (4) What is the name of the database system Charles Bachman helped create? (5) What geographic information system (GIS) functions does ArcExplorer perform? (6) What are the ACID rules for executed transactions?

2 Green Computing

Corporations are building eco-friendly data centers to help reduce power consumption while they are exploring alternative energy sources. AMD, Intel, IBM, Sun Microsystems, and Microsoft have formed The Green Grid to explore data center efficiency worldwide. Google has publicized its commitment to develop clean energy solutions for its power-hungry data centers. The U.S. Green Building Council awards certifications to data centers meeting rigorous energy-efficiency standards. View online Web sites that provide information about companies that are making strides to reduce their data centers' power consumption. Which companies are developing geothermal power plants to run the data centers? Where is Google exploring and building data centers to take advantage of favorable geographical and environmental factors? Which companies are planning to build data centers driven by tidal and wave power? Which companies have earned a U.S. Green Building Council certification? Write a report summarizing your findings, and include a table of links to Web sites that provide additional details.

3 Social Networking

Bebo is the third largest online social network and is popular in the United Kingdom. It has an active instant messaging partnership with Microsoft Windows Live Messenger and AOL's AIM. The online social network also partners with iTunes to allow Bebo users to buy music directly from the 700,000 musicians with a Bebo profile and whose music is available on iTunes. Visit the Bebo site (bebo.com) and view several profiles in the Video, Music, Authors, Groups, and Applications categories. Which features, news, and polls are listed in the More Fun Stuff group? Which weekly highlights from the Gap Year are available? Click the Safety link at the bottom of the home page and read the advice. Summarize the information you read and viewed.

4 Blogs

Dave Winer developed the Scripting News Web site in 1997 before the term "Weblog" had been coined, and he continues to post to his blog regularly. Scripting News is the longest-running blog on the Internet. Visit the Scripting News blog (scripting.com) and read Winer's biographical information. What technological breakthroughs did he develop? What are his employment and educational backgrounds? What are the three most recent topics discussed? Locate the article posted on or closest to your most recent birthday and then summarize the article. Which podcasts are listed in the Morning Coffee Notes? Click the Archive link at the top of the page and then click the year and month three years ago from today. What topics were posted? Summarize the information you read and viewed.

5 Ethics in Action

Businesses automatically store data about you and your transactions in a marketing database when you shop online, enter contests, and complete warranty registration cards. They often use this data to analyze sales and develop advertising campaigns. Unbeknownst to many consumers, some companies also sell this data to third parties for financial gain. Consumers can refuse to receive targeted e-mail messages and marketing materials, but they actively must search the Web sites or paper forms for check boxes to indicate these opt-out preferences. Some privacy experts, however, view this practice as unethical and urge businesses to default to not adding consumers' information to databases unless the consumer opts in to receive additional materials. View online sites that include opt-in or opt-out provisions. Write a report summarizing your findings, and include a table of links to Web sites that provide additional details.

Critical Thinking

The Critical Thinking exercises challenge your assessment and decision-making skills by presenting real-world situations associated with the chapter concepts. The Collaboration exercise should be completed with a team.

To evaluate the situations below, use personal experiences and available resources such as articles on the Web or in print, blogs, podcasts, videos, television, user guides, other individuals, and electronics and computer stores. You may need to use multiple resources to form conclusions and make recommendations.

1. **Class Discussion — Online Movie Reviews** Reviews of movies on a video store's new release shelf are fairly easy to find, but critiques of other movies in stock may be less accessible. To help film buffs, information about more than 100,000 movie titles is available from a database on the Web. The Internet Movie Database Ltd. can be searched using a movie's title, cast members, year produced, characters, genre, awards, or other criteria. Each movie's page offers a brief description and rating and includes links to such items as stars, summary, trivia, reviews, quotes, and recommendations. Visit the movie database at imdb.com and search for several movies. Discuss how visitors can query the movie database, how complete the information provided was, and who would benefit most from using the movie database and why.

2. **Class Presentation — Spreadsheets vs. Databases** Some individuals and small organizations prefer using spreadsheets instead of databases to maintain data. People who use spreadsheets might argue that similar to databases, spreadsheets have rows and columns, and you can keep track of different sets of data in individual worksheets, similar to how you would use tables in a database to store different data sets. In addition, some find it easier to install, use, and maintain spreadsheet software than database software. After reading this chapter, you become convinced that storing data in a database can offer the same advantages as storing data in spreadsheets, as well as additional advantages, such as the capability to store more data and more quickly search for data. In addition, you use knowledge from previous chapters to determine that spreadsheets are best used for storing data that will be used in simple and/or complex calculations, charting, and additional analysis. Prepare a presentation aimed toward individuals who prefer spreadsheets to databases. Your presentation should include reasons why it is not advisable to store large amounts of data in spreadsheets, as well as the reasons why databases are a more appropriate solution. In addition, your presentation should include mention of database management systems that are easy to use for people with limited database software knowledge.

3. **Research — Normalization** You recently were hired as a student intern to assist a local insurance agency in reorganizing their customer files. The agency employs a file processing system to maintain three distinct customer files — billing, claims, and promotions. The manager indicates that data entry has become unwieldy because of unclear relationships between data and data redundancy. Furthermore, customers are complaining about inconsistencies in the information they receive. The problem is beginning to affect business in a negative way. As a first step, she has asked you to prepare a report analyzing the benefits of normalizing the data in the three files. Use the Web and/or print media and the High-Tech Talk article on page 540 to research the normalization process. Be sure to answer the following questions in your report: What is zero normal form? First normal form? Second normal form? Third normal form? Also, define and give an example of each of the following terms: data redundancy, primary key, and repeating group.

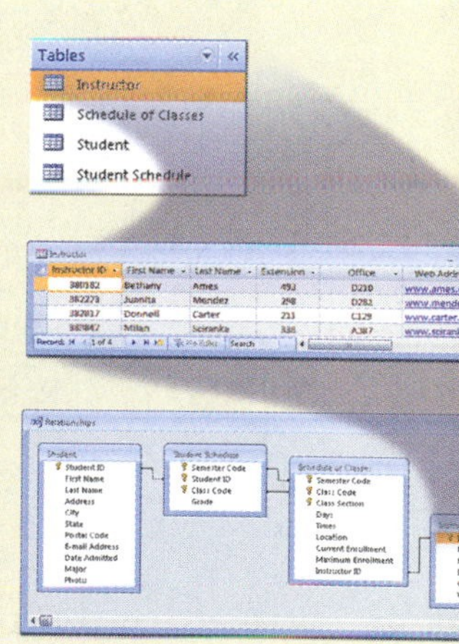

Collaboration

4. **Data Models** A major retail company has hired your team as database specialists to determine the data model — relational, object-oriented, or multidimensional — best suited for its applications. Form a three-member team and have each team member choose a different data model. Each member should use the Web and/or print media to research each data model. As a team, merge your findings, evaluate the information you have gathered, and prepare a team report that addresses the following questions: Does the data model allow for query by example? How does the data model allow users to manage, update, and retrieve data?

Chapter Eleven

Computer Security and Safety, Ethics, and Privacy

Objectives

After completing this chapter, you will be able to:

1. Define the term, computer security risks, and briefly describe the types of cybercrime perpetrators: hacker, cracker, script kiddie, corporate spy, unethical employee, cyberextortionist, and cyberterrorist
2. Describe various types of Internet and network attacks (computer viruses, worms, Trojan horses, rootkits, botnets, denial of service attacks, back doors, and spoofing), and identify ways to safeguard against these attacks, including firewalls, intrusion detection software, and honeypots
3. Discuss techniques to prevent unauthorized computer access and use
4. Identify safeguards against hardware theft and vandalism
5. Explain the ways software manufacturers protect against software piracy
6. Discuss how encryption works, and explain why it is necessary
7. Discuss the types of devices available that protect computers from system failure
8. Explain the options available for backing up computer resources
9. Identify risks and safeguards associated with wireless communications
10. Discuss ways to prevent health-related disorders and injuries due to computer use
11. Recognize issues related to information accuracy, intellectual property rights, codes of conduct, and green computing
12. Discuss issues surrounding information privacy, including electronic profiles, cookies, spyware and adware, spam, phishing, privacy laws, social engineering, employee monitoring, and content filtering

Computer Security Risks

Today, people rely on computers to create, store, and manage critical information. Thus, it is important that computers and the data they store are accessible and available when needed. It also is crucial that users take measures to protect their computers and data from loss, damage, and misuse. For example, organizations must ensure that sensitive data and information such as credit records, employee and customer data, and purchase information is secure. Home users must ensure that their credit card number is secure when they use it for online purchases.

A **computer security risk** is any event or action that could cause a loss of or damage to computer hardware, software, data, information, or processing capability. While some breaches to computer security are accidental, many are intentional. Some intruders do no damage; they merely access data, information, or programs on the computer before logging off. Other intruders indicate some evidence of their presence either by leaving a message or by deliberately altering or damaging data.

An intentional breach of computer security often involves a deliberate act that is against the law. Any illegal act involving a computer generally is referred to as a **computer crime**. The term **cybercrime** refers to online or Internet-based illegal acts. Software used by cybercriminals sometimes is called *crimeware*. Today, cybercrime is one of the FBI's top three priorities.

Perpetrators of cybercrime and other intrusions fall into seven basic categories: hacker, cracker, script kiddie, corporate spy, unethical employee, cyberextortionist, and cyberterrorist.

- The term **hacker**, although originally a complimentary word for a computer enthusiast, now has a derogatory meaning and refers to someone who accesses a computer or network illegally. Some hackers claim the intent of their security breaches is to improve security.
- A **cracker** also is someone who accesses a computer or network illegally but has the intent of destroying data, stealing information, or other malicious action. Both hackers and crackers have advanced computer and network skills.
- A **script kiddie** has the same intent as a cracker but does not have the technical skills and knowledge. Script kiddies often use prewritten hacking and cracking programs to break into computers.
- Some corporate spies have excellent computer and networking skills and are hired to break into a specific computer and steal its proprietary data and information, or to help identify security risks in their own organization. Unscrupulous companies hire corporate spies, a practice known as corporate espionage, to gain a competitive advantage.
- Unethical employees may break into their employers' computers for a variety of reasons. Some simply want to exploit a security weakness. Others seek financial gains from selling confidential information. Disgruntled employees may want revenge.

- A **cyberextortionist** is someone who uses e-mail as a vehicle for extortion. These perpetrators send an organization a threatening e-mail message indicating they will expose confidential information, exploit a security flaw, or launch an attack that will compromise the organization's network — if they are not paid a sum of money.
- A **cyberterrorist** is someone who uses the Internet or network to destroy or damage computers for political reasons. The cyberterrorist might target the nation's air traffic control system, electricity-generating companies, or a telecommunications infrastructure. The term, *cyberwarfare*, describes an attack whose goal ranges from disabling a government's computer network to crippling a country. Cyberterrorism and cyberwarfare usually require a team of highly skilled individuals, millions of dollars, and several years of planning.

Business and home users must protect, or safeguard, their computers from breaches of security and other computer security risks. Some organizations hire individuals previously convicted of computer crimes to help identify security risks and implement safeguards because these individuals know how criminals attempt to breach security.

The more common computer security risks include Internet and network attacks, unauthorized access and use, hardware theft, software theft, information theft, and system failure (Figure 11-1). The following pages describe these computer security risks and also discuss safeguards users might take to minimize or prevent their consequences.

Figure 11-1 Computers and computer users are exposed to several types of security risks.

Internet and Network Attacks

Information transmitted over networks has a higher degree of security risk than information kept on an organization's premises. In an organization, network administrators usually take measures to protect a network from security risks. On the Internet, where no central administrator is present, the security risk is greater.

To determine if your computer is vulnerable to an Internet or network attack, you could use an online security service. An **online security service** is a Web site that evaluates your computer to check for Internet and e-mail vulnerabilities (Figure 11-2). The service then provides recommendations of how to address the vulnerabilities.

Companies and individuals requiring assistance or information about Internet security breaches can contact or visit the Web site for the *Computer Emergency Response Team Coordination Center*, or *CERT/CC*, which is a federally funded Internet security research and development center.

Computer Emergency Response Team Coordination Center

For more information, visit the Computer Concepts CourseMate Web site at www.cengagebrain.com, navigate to the Chapter 11 Web Link resource for this book, and then click Computer Emergency Response Team Coordination Center.

Internet and network attacks that jeopardize security include computer viruses, worms, Trojan horses, and rootkits; botnets; denial of service attacks; back doors; and spoofing. The following pages address these computer security risks and suggest measures organizations and individuals can take to protect their computers while on the Internet or connected to a network.

Popular Online Security Services for Personal Computers

Name of Online Service	Web Address
Audit My PC	http://www.auditmypc.com/firewall-test.asp
McAfee FreeScan	http://home.mcafee.com/Downloads/FreeScan.aspx
Symantec Security Check	http://security.symantec.com/sscv6/home.asp
Trend Micro House Call	http://housecall.trendmicro.com/

Figure 11-2 Some popular online security services.

Computer Viruses, Worms, Trojan Horses, and Rootkits

Every unprotected computer is susceptible to the first type of computer security risk — a computer virus, worm, Trojan horse, and/or rootkit.

- A computer **virus** is a potentially damaging computer program that affects, or infects, a computer negatively by altering the way the computer works without the user's knowledge or permission. Once the virus infects the computer, it can spread throughout and may damage files and system software, including the operating system.
- A **worm** is a program that copies itself repeatedly, for example in memory or on a network, using up resources and possibly shutting down the computer or network.
- A **Trojan horse** (named after the Greek myth) is a program that hides within or looks like a legitimate program. A certain condition or action usually triggers the Trojan horse. Unlike a virus or worm, a Trojan horse does not replicate itself to other computers.
- A **rootkit** is a program that hides in a computer and allows someone from a remote location to take full control of the computer. Once the rootkit is installed, the rootkit author can execute programs, change settings, monitor activity, and access files on the remote computer. Although rootkits can have legitimate uses, such as in law enforcement, their use in nefarious and illegal activities is growing rapidly.

Computer viruses, worms, Trojan horses, and rootkits are classified as *malware* (short for *malicious software*), which are programs that act without a user's knowledge and deliberately alter the computer's operations. Other classes of malware include back doors and spyware, which are discussed later in this chapter. Although malware often falls in one of these classes (virus, worm, Trojan horse, rootkit, back door, or spyware), some malware has characteristics of two or more classes. For example, MyDoom and Blaster are worms; Melissa has elements of a virus, worm, and Trojan horse.

Unscrupulous programmers write malware and then test it to ensure it can deliver its payload. The *payload* is the destructive event or prank the program is intended to deliver.

A computer infected by a virus, worm, Trojan horse, or rootkit often has one or more of the following symptoms:

- Operating system runs much slower than usual
- Available memory is less than expected
- Files become corrupted
- Screen displays unusual message or image
- Music or unusual sound plays randomly

- Existing programs and files disappear
- Programs or files do not work properly
- Unknown programs or files mysteriously appear
- System properties change
- Operating system does not start up
- Operating system shuts down unexpectedly

Malware delivers its payload on a computer in a variety of ways: when a user (1) opens an infected file, (2) runs an infected program, (3) boots the computer with infected removable media inserted in a drive or plugged in a port, (4) connects an unprotected computer to a network, or (5) when a certain condition or event occurs, such as the computer's clock changing to a specific date. Today, a common way computers become infected with viruses and other malware is through users opening infected e-mail attachments (Figure 11-3).

Currently, more than 300,000 Web sites can infect your computer with known viruses, worms, Trojan horses, rootkits, and other malware. Many Web sites maintain lists of all known malware. For a more technical discussion about these types of malware, read the High-Tech Talk article on page 178 in Chapter 3.

FAQ 11-1

Can multimedia files be infected with a virus?

Yes. The increase in popularity of media sharing Web sites provides a great opportunity to distribute malicious programs. During one year, approximately 500,000 people downloaded what they thought was a media file from the Internet. In fact, the file was a Trojan horse that infected many computers with spyware. For this reason, it is important to scan all media files for malware before playing them.

For more information, visit the Computer Concepts CourseMate Web site at www.cengagebrain.com, navigate to the Chapter 11 FAQ resource for this book, and then click Infected Media Files.

Figure 11-3 This figure shows how a virus can spread through an e-mail message.

Safeguards against Computer Viruses and Other Malware

Methods that guarantee a computer or network is safe from computer viruses and other malware simply do not exist. Users can take several precautions, however, to protect their home and work computers and mobile devices from these malicious infections. The following paragraphs discuss these precautionary measures.

Do not start a computer with removable media inserted in the drives or plugged in the ports. For example, optical disc drives should be empty, and a USB port should not contain a USB flash drive. During the startup process, a computer may attempt to execute the boot sector on media in certain drives and ports. Even if the attempt is unsuccessful, a virus on the boot sector of removable media can infect the computer's hard disk. If you must start the computer with media in a drive or port, be certain the media are uninfected or from a trusted source. A **trusted source** is an organization or person you believe will not send a virus infected file knowingly.

Never open an e-mail attachment unless you are expecting the attachment *and* it is from a trusted source. If the e-mail message is from an unknown source or untrusted source, delete the e-mail message immediately — without opening or executing any attachments. If the e-mail message is from a trusted source, but you were not expecting an attachment, carefully check the spelling of the e-mail address and contents of the message for errors because perpetrators often make typographical errors. If the message is error-free, verify with the source that he or she intended to send you an attachment — before opening it.

Some viruses are hidden in *macros*, which are instructions saved in software such as a word processing or spreadsheet program. In programs that allow users to write macros, you should set the macro security level so that the application software warns users that a document they are attempting to open contains a macro (Figure 11-4). From this warning, a user chooses to disable or enable the macro. If the document is from a trusted source, the user can enable the macro. Otherwise, it should be disabled.

Users should install an antivirus program and update it frequently. As Chapter 8 discussed, an **antivirus program** protects a computer against viruses by identifying and removing any computer viruses found in memory, on storage media, or on incoming files. Most antivirus programs also protect against other malware. When you purchase a new computer, it often includes antivirus software. Many e-mail servers also have antivirus programs installed to check incoming and outgoing e-mail messages for malware. The table in Figure 11-5 lists popular antivirus programs.

An antivirus program scans for programs that attempt to modify the boot program, the operating system, and other programs that normally are read from but not modified. In addition, many antivirus programs automatically scan files downloaded from the Web, e-mail attachments, opened files, and all types of removable media inserted in the computer.

One technique that antivirus programs use to identify a virus is to look for virus signatures. A **virus signature**, also called a **virus definition**, is a known specific pattern of virus code. Computer users should update their antivirus program's signature files regularly (Figure 11-6). This

Macro Settings

For macros in documents not in a trusted location:

- ○ Disable all macros without notification
- ◉ Disable all macros with notification
- ○ Disable all macros except digitally signed macros
- ○ Enable all macros (not recommended; potentially dangerous code can run)

Developer Macro Settings

☐ Trust access to the VBA project object model

Figure 11-4 Many application programs, such as Microsoft Word, can be configured to display a warning if a user attempts to open a file that contains a macro.

Popular Antivirus Programs
• AVG Anti-Virus
• avast! antivirus
• CA Anti-Virus
• F-Secure Anti-Virus
• Kaspersky Anti-Virus
• McAfee VirusScan
• Norton AntiVirus
• Trend Micro AntiVirus
• Vexira AntiVirus

Figure 11-5 Popular antivirus programs.

important activity allows the antivirus program to protect against viruses written since the antivirus program was released and/or its last update. Most antivirus programs contain an automatic update feature that regularly prompts users to download the virus signature, usually at least once a week. The vendor usually provides this service to registered users at no cost for a specified time.

Another technique that antivirus programs use to detect viruses is to inoculate existing program files. To **inoculate** a program file, the antivirus program records information such as the file size and file creation date in a separate inoculation file. The antivirus program then uses this information to detect if a virus tampers with the data describing the inoculated program file.

If an antivirus program identifies an infected file, it attempts to remove the malware. If the antivirus program cannot remove the infection, it often quarantines the infected file. A **quarantine** is a separate area of a hard disk that holds the infected file until the infection can be removed. This step ensures other files will not become infected. Users also can quarantine suspicious files themselves. Quarantined files remain on your computer until you delete them or restore them. Restore a quarantined file only if you are certain the antivirus program has removed the infection from the quarantined file.

In extreme cases, you may need to reformat the hard disk to remove malware from an infected computer. Having uninfected, or clean, backups of all files is important. In addition to an antivirus program, users often install a personal firewall program to protect a computer and its data from unauthorized intrusions. Later sections in this chapter discuss backup techniques and firewalls.

Finally, stay informed about new virus alerts and virus hoaxes. A **virus hoax** is an e-mail message that warns users of a nonexistent virus or other malware. Often, these hoaxes are in the form of a chain letter that requests the user to send a copy of the e-mail message to as many people as possible. The content of the hoax message, for example, may inform users that an important operating system file on their computer is a virus and encourage them to delete the file, which could make their computer unusable. Instead of forwarding the message, visit a Web site that publishes a list of virus alerts and virus hoaxes.

The list in Figure 11-7 summarizes important tips for protecting your computer from viruses and other malware.

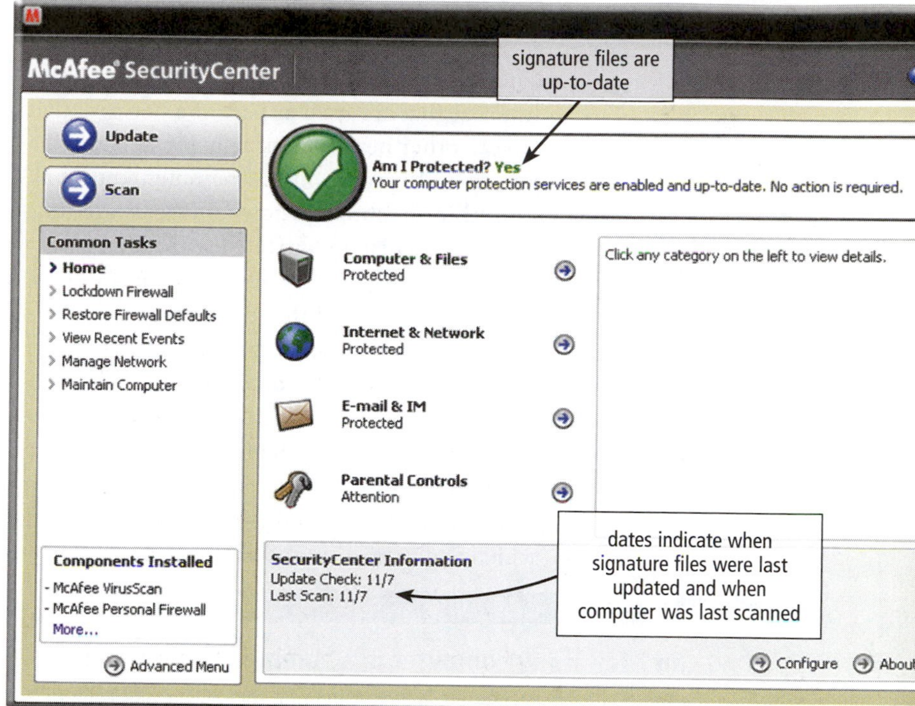

Figure 11-6 This antivirus program, which protects a computer from a variety of malware, regularly checks for the latest virus signatures and other important updates.

Tips for Preventing Viruses and Other Malware

1. Never start a computer with removable media inserted in the drives or plugged in the ports, unless the media are uninfected.
2. Never open an e-mail attachment unless you are expecting it *and* it is from a trusted source.
3. Set the macro security in programs so that you can enable or disable macros. Enable macros only if the document is from a trusted source and you are expecting it.
4. Install an antivirus program on all of your computers. Update the software and the virus signature files regularly.
5. Scan all downloaded programs for viruses and other malware.
6. If the antivirus program flags an e-mail attachment as infected, delete or quarantine the attachment immediately.
7. Before using any removable media, scan the media for malware. Follow this procedure even for shrink-wrapped software from major developers. Some commercial software has been infected and distributed to unsuspecting users.
8. Install a personal firewall program.
9. Stay informed about new virus alerts and virus hoaxes.

Figure 11-7 With the growing number of new viruses and other malware, it is crucial that users take steps to protect their computers.

Botnets

A **botnet** is a group of compromised computers connected to a network such as the Internet that are used as part of a network that attacks other networks, usually for nefarious purposes. A compromised computer, known as a **zombie**, is one whose owner is unaware the computer is being controlled remotely by an outsider.

A *bot* is a program that performs a repetitive task on a network. Cybercriminals install malicious bots on unprotected computers to create a botnet, also called a *zombie army*. The perpetrator then uses the botnet to send spam via e-mail, spread viruses and other malware, or commit a distributed denial of service attack, which is discussed in the next section.

? FAQ 11-2

How can I tell if my computer is a zombie or in a botnet?

The number of zombie computers is increasing at a rapid rate. Your computer may be a zombie or part of a botnet if you notice unusually high disk activity, a slower than normal Internet connection, or devices connected to your computer becoming increasingly unresponsive. The chances of your computer becoming a zombie or part of a botnet greatly increase if you do not have an effective firewall.

For more information, visit the Computer Concepts CourseMate Web site at www.cengagebrain.com, navigate to the Chapter 11 FAQ resource for this book, and then click Zombies and Botnets.

Denial of Service Attacks

A **denial of service attack**, or **DoS attack**, is an assault whose purpose is to disrupt computer access to an Internet service such as the Web or e-mail. Perpetrators carry out a DoS attack in a variety of ways. For example, they may use an unsuspecting computer to send an influx of confusing data messages or useless traffic to a computer network. The victim computer network slows down considerably and eventually becomes unresponsive or unavailable, blocking legitimate visitors from accessing the network.

A more devastating type of DoS attack is the *DDoS (distributed DoS) attack*, in which a zombie army is used to attack computers or computer networks. DDoS attacks have been able to stop operations temporarily at numerous Web sites, including powerhouses such as Yahoo!, eBay, Amazon.com, and CNN.com. Read Ethics & Issues 11-1 for a related discussion.

DoS Attacks

For more information, visit the Computer Concepts CourseMate Web site at www.cengagebrain.com, navigate to the Chapter 11 Web Link resource for this book, and then click DoS Attacks.

The damage caused by a DoS or DDoS attack usually is extensive. During the outage, retailers lose sales from customers, news sites and search engines lose revenue from advertisers, and time-sensitive information may be delayed. Repeated attacks could tarnish reputations, causing even greater losses.

Perpetrators have a variety of motives for carrying out a DoS or DDoS attack. Those who disagree with the beliefs or actions of a particular organization claim political anger motivates their attacks. Some perpetrators use the attack as a vehicle for extortion. Others simply want the recognition, even though it is negative.

ETHICS & ISSUES 11-1

How Should Cybercriminals Be Punished?

Recently, a hacker was sentenced to 41 months in jail for illegally using hundreds of a company's computers as part of a money-making botnet. The punishment is about the same for auto theft, despite the hundreds of thousands of dollars in damages caused in addition to the thousands of dollars the scheme netted the criminal. Viruses, DDoS attacks, adware, and other malware continue to disrupt businesses and cause damages that are difficult to estimate.

Many experts and computer administrators claim that the punishment for cybercrime often is out of proportion with the damages caused by the crime. Some legal experts claim that lax security on the part of Internet users is to blame, and perhaps those who practice lax security should be punished as well. Others claim that many organizations provide exorbitant estimates of true damages that cybercriminals cause and that these alleged damages provoke an emotional overreaction to the crimes. The types of crimes and international extent of possible damages are relatively new territories in criminal law.

Should the government create new laws specifically aimed at punishing cybercriminals? Why or why not? Should cybercriminals be punished in proportion to the alleged damages that they cause? Why or why not? Who should decide the extent of the true damages caused by a cybercrime? Why?

Back Doors

A **back door** is a program or set of instructions in a program that allow users to bypass security controls when accessing a program, computer, or network. Once perpetrators gain access to unsecure computers, they often install a back door or modify an existing program to include a back door, which allows them to continue to access the computer remotely without the user's knowledge. A rootkit can be a back door. Some worms leave back doors, which have been used to spread other worms or to distribute junk e-mail from the unsuspecting victim computers.

Programmers often build back doors into programs during system development. These back doors save development time because the programmer can bypass security controls while writing and testing programs. Similarly, a computer repair technician may install a back door while troubleshooting problems on a computer. If a programmer or computer repair technician fails to remove a back door, a perpetrator could use the back door to gain entry to a computer or network.

Spoofing

Spoofing is a technique intruders use to make their network or Internet transmission appear legitimate to a victim computer or network. Several types of spoofing schemes exist. One type, called *e-mail spoofing*, occurs when the sender's address or other components of the e-mail header are altered so that it appears the e-mail originated from a different sender. E-mail spoofing commonly is used for virus hoaxes, spam, and phishing scams; the latter two are discussed later in the chapter.

Another type, called *IP spoofing*, occurs when an intruder computer fools a network into believing its IP address is associated with a trusted source. Perpetrators of IP spoofing trick their victims into interacting with the phony Web site. For example, the victim may provide confidential information or download files containing viruses, worms, or other malware.

Safeguards against Botnets, DoS/DDoS Attacks, Back Doors, and Spoofing

Some of the latest antivirus programs include provisions to protect a computer from DoS and DDoS attacks. To further defend against these and other Internet and network attacks, users can implement firewall solutions, install intrusion detection software, and set up honeypots.

Firewalls

A **firewall** is hardware and/or software that protects a network's resources from intrusion by users on another network such as the Internet (Figure 11-8). All networked and online computer users should implement a firewall solution.

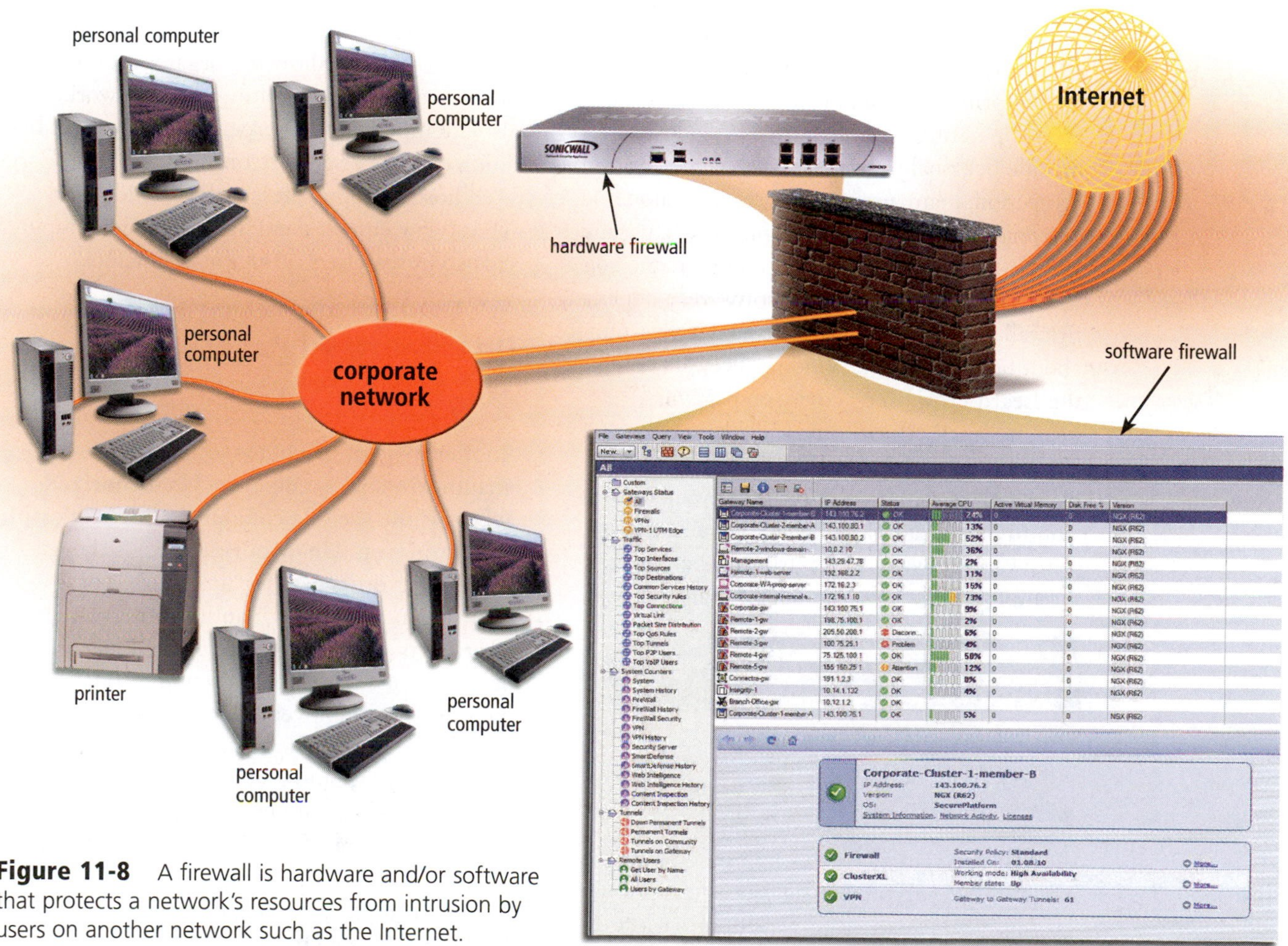

Figure 11-8 A firewall is hardware and/or software that protects a network's resources from intrusion by users on another network such as the Internet.

Organizations use firewalls to protect network resources from outsiders and to restrict employees' access to sensitive data such as payroll or personnel records. They can implement a firewall solution themselves or outsource their needs to a company specializing in providing firewall protection.

Large organizations often route all their communications through a proxy server, which typically is a component of the firewall. A *proxy server* is a server outside the organization's network that controls which communications pass into the organization's network. That is, a proxy server carefully screens all incoming and outgoing messages. Proxy servers use a variety of screening techniques. Some check the domain name or IP address of the message for legitimacy. Others require that the messages have digital signatures. A section later in this chapter discusses digital signatures.

Home and small office/home office users often protect their computers with a personal firewall. As discussed in Chapter 8, a **personal firewall** is a utility program that detects and protects a personal computer and its data from unauthorized intrusions. Personal firewalls constantly monitor all transmissions to and from the computer and may inform a user of any attempted intrusion. Some operating systems, such as Windows, include personal firewalls. For enhanced firewall protection, many users purchase stand-alone personal firewall software (Figure 11-9), usually for less than $50. Many new computers include a free trial version of antivirus software, a personal firewall, and other similar software. To learn more about how to use the Windows firewall, complete the Learn How To 2 activity on page 603.

Some small office/home office users purchase a hardware firewall, such as a router or other device that has a built-in firewall, in addition to or instead of personal firewall software. Hardware firewalls stop intrusions before they attempt to affect your computer maliciously.

Firewalls

For more information, visit the Computer Concepts CourseMate Web site at www.cengagebrain.com, navigate to the Chapter 11 Web Link resource for this book, and then click Firewalls.

Stand-Alone Personal Firewall Software
BitDefender Internet Security
CA Personal Firewall
McAfee Internet Security
Norton Personal Firewall
Webroot Desktop Firewall
ZoneAlarm Pro

Figure 11-9 Popular personal firewall software.

Intrusion Detection Software

To provide extra protection against hackers and other intruders, large organizations may use intrusion detection software to identify possible security breaches. *Intrusion detection software* automatically analyzes all network traffic, assesses system vulnerabilities, identifies any unauthorized intrusions, and notifies network administrators of suspicious behavior patterns or system breaches.

To utilize intrusion detection software requires the expertise of a network administrator because the programs are complex and difficult to use and interpret. These programs also are quite expensive. This software, however, when combined with a firewall, provides an added layer of protection to companies with highly sensitive data such as credit card databases.

Honeypots

Some organizations use honeypots so that they can analyze an attack being perpetrated. A *honeypot* is a vulnerable computer that is set up to entice an intruder to break into it. These computers, which appear real to the intruder, actually are separated safely from the organization's network. Honeypots allow the organization to learn how intruders are exploiting their network and also attempt to catch perpetrators who have been doing damage elsewhere on their network. Large Web hosting companies, such as Yahoo! and AT&T, law enforcement agencies, and computer security researchers often use honeypots.

Unauthorized Access and Use

Another type of computer security risk is unauthorized access and use. **Unauthorized access** is the use of a computer or network without permission. **Unauthorized use** is the use of a computer or its data for unapproved or possibly illegal activities. Unauthorized use includes a variety of activities: an employee using an organization's computer to send personal e-mail messages, an employee using the organization's word processing software to track his or her child's soccer league scores, or someone gaining access to a bank computer and performing an unauthorized transfer. For the home user, most unauthorized use occurs on computers that have always-on Internet connections, such as through Internet cable or DSL.

Safeguards against Unauthorized Access and Use

Organizations take several measures to help prevent unauthorized access and use. At a minimum, they should have a written acceptable use policy (AUP) that outlines the computer activities for which the computer and network may and may not be used. An organization's AUP should specify the acceptable use of computers by employees for personal reasons. Some organizations prohibit such use entirely. Others allow personal use on the employee's own time such as a lunch hour. Whatever the policy, an organization should document and explain it to employees.

To protect your personal computer from unauthorized intrusions, you should disable file and printer sharing on your Internet connection (Figure 11-10). This security measure attempts to ensure that others cannot access your files or your printer. To open the window shown in Figure 11-10 in Windows 7, click the Start button on the taskbar, click Control Panel on the Start menu, and then click the 'Choose homegroup and sharing options' link in the Network and Internet area of the dialog box.

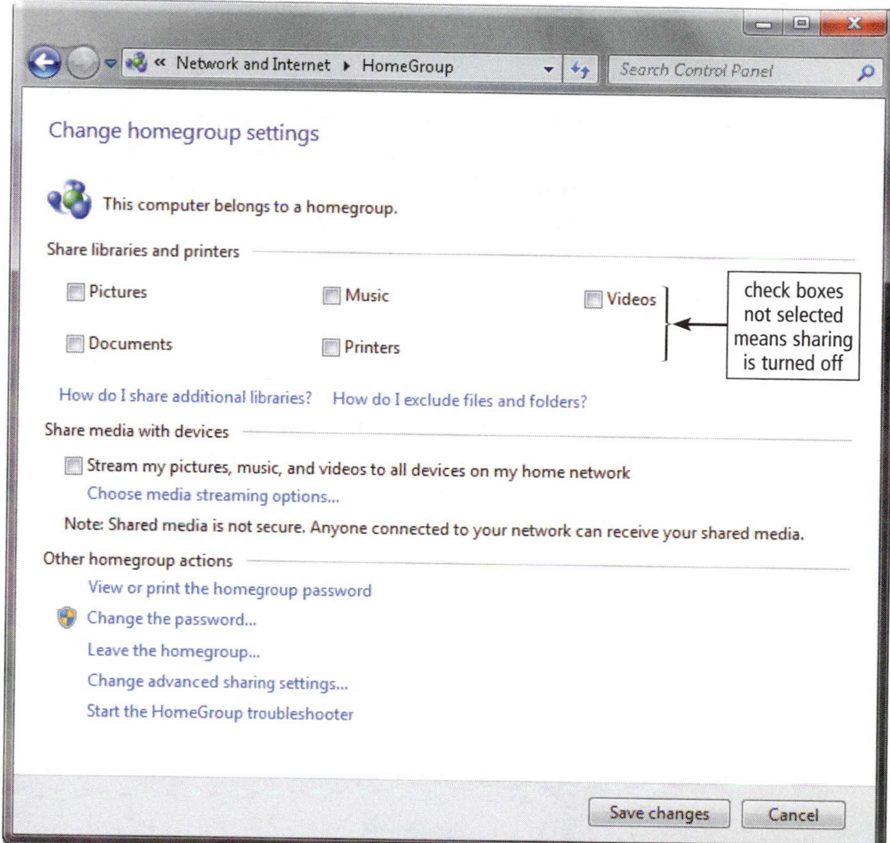

Figure 11-10 To protect files on your local hard disk from hackers and other intruders, turn off file and printer sharing on your Internet connection.

Other measures that safeguard against unauthorized access and use include firewalls and intrusion detection software, which were discussed in the previous section, and identifying and authenticating users.

Identifying and Authenticating Users

Many organizations use access controls to minimize the chance that a perpetrator intentionally may access or an employee accidentally may access confidential information on a computer. An *access control* is a security measure that defines who can access a computer, when they can access it, and what actions they can take while accessing the computer. In addition, the computer should maintain an **audit trail** that records in a file both successful and unsuccessful access attempts. An unsuccessful access attempt could result from a user mistyping his or her password, or it could result from a hacker trying thousands of passwords.

Organizations should investigate unsuccessful access attempts immediately to ensure they are not intentional breaches of security. They also should review successful access for irregularities, such as use of the computer after normal working hours or from remote computers. In addition, an organization regularly should review users' access privilege levels to determine whether they still are appropriate.

Many systems implement access controls using a two-phase process called identification and authentication. *Identification* verifies that an individual is a valid user. *Authentication* verifies that the individual is the person he or she claims to be. Three methods of identification and authentication include user names and passwords, possessed objects, and biometric devices. The technique(s) an organization uses should correspond to the degree of risk that is associated with the unauthorized access. The next sections discuss each of the identification and authentication methods.

User Names and Passwords A **user name**, or *user ID* (identification), is a unique combination of characters, such as letters of the alphabet or numbers, that identifies one specific user. A **password** is a private combination of characters associated with the user name that allows access to certain computer resources.

Most multiuser (networked) operating systems require that users correctly enter a user name and a password before they can access the data, information, and programs stored on a computer or network. Many other systems that maintain financial, personal, and other confidential information also require a user name and password as part of their logon procedure (Figure 11-11).

Some systems assign a user name or user ID to each user. For example, a school may use the student identification number as a user ID. Some Web sites use your e-mail address as the user ID. With other systems, users select their own user name or user ID. Many users select a combination of their first and last names.

Figure 11-11 Many Web sites that maintain personal and confidential data require a user to enter a user name and password.

Most systems require that users select their own passwords. If a program or device has a default or preset password, such as admin, be sure to change it to prevent unauthorized access. Users typically choose an easy-to-remember word or series of characters for passwords. If your password is too obvious, however, such as your initials or birthday, others can guess it easily.

Easy passwords make it simple for hackers and other intruders to break into a system. Hackers often use computer automated tools to assist them with guessing passwords. Thus, you should select a password carefully. Longer passwords provide greater security than shorter ones. Each character added to a password significantly increases the number of possible combinations and the length of time it might take for someone or for a hacker's computer to guess the password (Figure 11-12). Passwords typically range from 6 to 16 characters.

In addition to a user name and password, some systems ask users to enter one of several pieces of personal information. Such items can include a spouse's first name, a birth date, a place of birth, or a mother's maiden name. As with a password, if the user's response does not match information on file, the system denies access.

Instead of passwords, some organizations use passphrases to authenticate users. A *passphrase* is a private combination of words, often containing mixed capitalization and punctuation, associated with a user name that allows access to certain computer resources. Passphrases, which

Password Protection

Number of Characters	Possible Combinations	AVERAGE TIME TO DISCOVER Human	Computer
1	36	3 minutes	.000018 second
2	1,300	2 hours	.00065 second
3	47,000	3 days	.02 second
4	1,700,000	3 months	1 second
5	60,000,000	10 years	30 seconds
10	3,700,000,000,000,000	580 million years	59 years

- *Possible characters include the letters A–Z and numbers 0–9*
- *Human discovery assumes 1 try every 10 seconds*
- *Computer discovery assumes 1 million tries per second*
- *Average time assumes the password would be discovered in approximately half the time it would take to try all possible combinations*

Figure 11-12 This table shows the effect of increasing the length of a password that consists of letters and numbers. The longer the password, the more effort required to discover it. Long passwords, however, are more difficult for users to remember.

often can be up to 100 characters in length, are more secure than passwords, yet can be easy to remember because they contain words.

Some Web sites use a CAPTCHA to further protect a user's password. A *CAPTCHA*, which stands for Completely Automated Public Turing test to tell Computers and Humans Apart, is a program developed at Carnegie Mellon University to verify that user input is not computer generated. A CAPTCHA displays a series of distorted characters and requires the user enter the characters correctly to continue using the Web site (Figure 11-13). For visually impaired users, the CAPTCHA text can be read aloud. Because unscrupulous individuals attempt to circumvent or decode CAPTCHAs, developers continually are seeking ways to make them more secure or develop alternative authentication techniques. Read Innovative Computing 11-1 to find out how CAPTCHA digitizes newspapers and books.

INNOVATIVE COMPUTING 11-1

RECAPTCHAs Help Digitize Newspapers, Books

More than 47,000 editions of *The New York Times* were published from 1851 to 1980, and a major movement is underway to digitize each paper by scanning every page. Occasionally, the computer cannot decipher a faded or blurry word. When this occurs, the actual image, called a RECAPTCHA, is given an identification number and placed on a Web site such as Ticketmaster, Craigslist, Twitter, LastFM, and Facebook. Visitors must type the correct letters that appear in two images in order to enter the site. When they do, the deciphered words are placed back in their original location in the article being digitized.

Carnegie-Mellon Professor Luis von Ahn created RECAPTCHAs to digitize the millions of words printed in the *Times'* archives. He estimates that people worldwide type up to 16 million RECAPTCHAs each day in 1.9 seconds with 100 percent accuracy. Each word has six to eight characters.

In 2000, von Ahn developed single-word CAPTCHAs in an effort to prevent spammers from attacking the Yahoo! Web site. He expanded the venture to help various humanitarian projects, including the Internet Archive, which uses RECAPTCHAs to digitize books.

For more information, visit the Computer Concepts CourseMate Web site at www.cengagebrain.com, navigate to the Chapter 11 Innovative Computing resource for this book, and then click RECAPTCHA.

FAQ 11-3

How can I protect my password?

Once you select a password, change it frequently. Do not disclose it to anyone or write it on a slip of paper kept near the computer, especially taped to the monitor or under the keyboard. E-mail and telemarketing scams often ask unsuspecting users to disclose their password, so be wary if you did not initiate the inquiry or telephone call. One research study indicates that having too many passwords might compromise security. The average person can remember approximately two secure passwords. Using more than two passwords results in an increased number of calls to the Help desk to reset lost or forgotten passwords.

For more information, visit the Computer Concepts CourseMate Web site at www.cengagebrain.com, navigate to the Chapter 11 FAQ resource for this book, and then click Protecting Passwords.

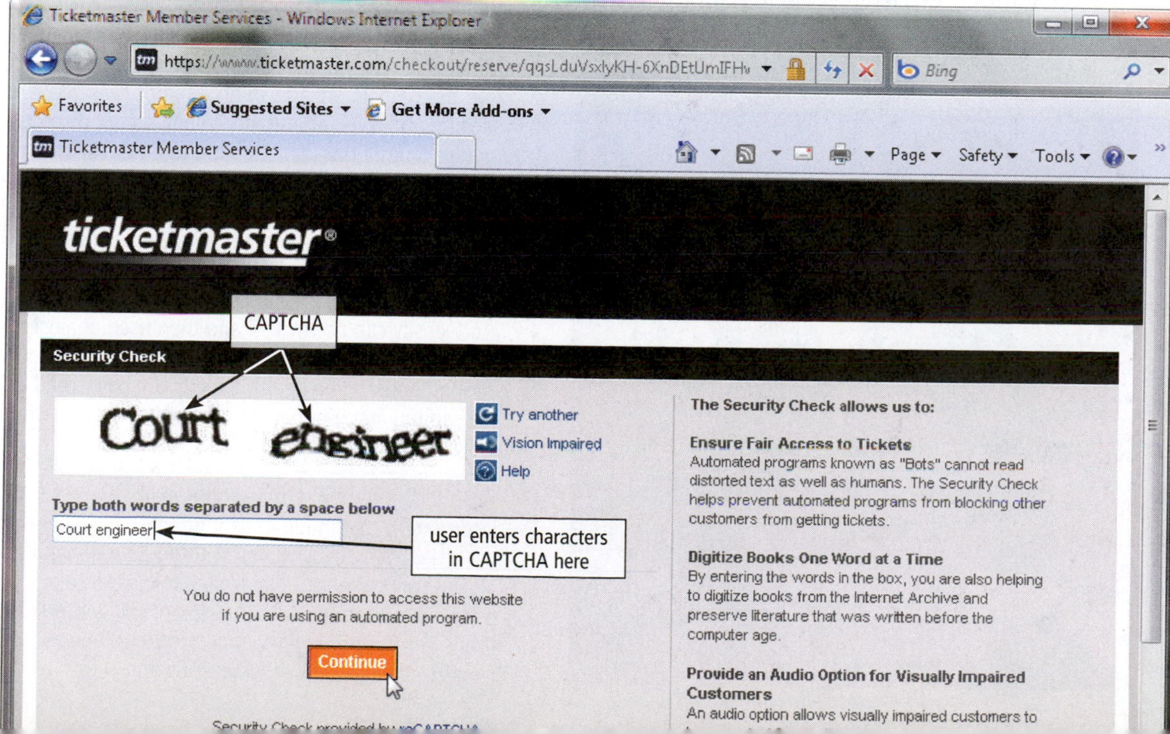

Figure 11-13 To continue with the ticket order process at this Web site, the user must enter the characters in the CAPTCHA, which consists of the letters, Court engineer, in this case.

Possessed Objects A *possessed object* is any item that you must carry to gain access to a computer or computer facility. Examples of possessed objects are badges, cards, smart cards, and keys. The card you use in an automated teller machine (ATM) is a possessed object that allows access to your bank account.

Possessed objects often are used in combination with personal identification numbers. A **personal identification number (PIN)** is a numeric password, either assigned by a company or selected by a user. PINs provide an additional level of security. An ATM card typically requires a four-digit PIN. Most debit cards and some credit cards use PINs. If someone steals these cards, the thief must enter the user's PIN to access the account. PINs are passwords. Select them carefully and protect them as you do any other password.

Biometric Devices As Chapter 5 discussed, a **biometric device** authenticates a person's identity by translating a personal characteristic, such as a fingerprint, into a digital code that is compared with a digital code stored in the computer verifying a physical or behavioral characteristic. If the digital code in the computer does not match the personal characteristic code, the computer denies access to the individual.

Biometric devices grant access to programs, computers, or rooms using computer analysis of some biometric identifier. Examples of biometric devices and systems include fingerprint readers (Figure 11-14), hand geometry systems, face recognition systems, voice verification systems, signature verification systems, iris recognition systems, and retinal scanners. For a more technical discussion about biometrics, specifically fingerprint readers, read the High-Tech Talk article on page 288 in Chapter 5.

Biometric Devices
For more information, visit the Computer Concepts CourseMate Web site at www.cengagebrain.com, navigate to the Chapter 11 Web Link resource for this book, and then click Biometric Devices.

Figure 11-14
A fingerprint reader verifies this traveler's identity.

Biometric devices are gaining popularity as a security precaution because they are a virtually foolproof method of identification and authentication (read Ethics & Issues 11-2 for a related discussion). For example, many grocery stores, retail stores, and gas stations now use *biometric payment*, where the customer's fingerprint is read by a fingerprint reader that is linked to a payment method such as a checking account or credit card. Users can forget their user names and passwords. Possessed objects can be lost, copied, duplicated, or stolen. Personal characteristics, by contrast, are unique and cannot be forgotten or misplaced.

Biometric devices do have disadvantages. If you cut your finger, a fingerprint reader might reject you as a legitimate user. Hand geometry readers can transmit germs. If you are nervous, a signature might not match the one on file. If you have a sore throat, a voice recognition system might reject you. Many people are uncomfortable with the thought of using an iris scanner.

ETHICS & ISSUES 11-2

Should You Be Concerned about the Use of Biometric Devices in Public Places?

Hundreds of thousands of students use a biometric thumbprint to pay for their school lunches each day. School administrators cite the need for biometrics to better track the number of free and subsidized lunches that the schools provide. In an attempt to increase security and track attendance, many school districts require thumbprint identification to enter classrooms or participate in school activities. Retail stores, theme parks, and even physicians' offices use biometric devices to identify customers and patients. Some privacy advocates believe that the devices store too much personal information. Many are concerned that individuals' habits more easily can be tracked and then used against them in the future, or that the information could end up in the wrong hands. Some health experts are concerned about the sanitary issue of people passing germs to each other over the biometric devices.

Should children be required to provide biometric information to engage in common public school-related activities? Why or why not? Should anyone who provides products and services be allowed to collect biometric information from a customer? Why or why not? What are the privacy and sanitary issues involved and should they be a concern?

FAQ 11-4

How many people are victims of identity theft each year?

Studies reveal that identity theft is the fastest growing crime in the United States. In fact, identity theft costs banks, victims, and the government millions of dollars each year, with that amount continually increasing. The chart to the right illustrates the reported number of identity theft cases grouped by age.

Identity Theft — Complaints by Victim Age

Under 18	5%
18–29	29%
30–39	24%
40–49	20%
50–59	13%
60 and over	9%

Source: FTC.gov

For more information, visit the Computer Concepts CourseMate Web site at www.cengagebrain.com, navigate to the Chapter 11 FAQ resource for this book, and then click Identity Theft.

Digital Forensics

Digital forensics, also called *computer forensics*, *network forensics*, or *cyberforensics*, is the discovery, collection, and analysis of evidence found on computers and networks. Digital forensics involves the examination of computer media, programs, data and log files on computers, servers, and networks. Many areas use digital forensics, including law enforcement, criminal prosecutors, military intelligence, insurance agencies, and information security departments in the private sector.

A digital forensics examiner must have knowledge of the law, technical experience with many types of hardware and software products, superior communication skills, familiarity with corporate structures and policies, a willingness to learn and update skills, and a knack for problem solving. For more information about digital forensics, read the Digital Forensics Special Feature that follows this chapter. For a look at the next generation of forensics, read Looking Ahead 11-1.

LOOKING AHEAD 11-1

Brain Waves, Behavior Tracked to Prevent and Solve Crimes

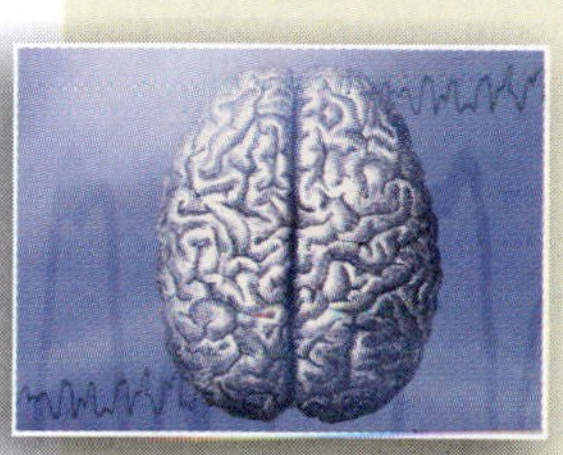

The brain may one day become part of a crime scene investigation. When a person has committed a criminal or fraudulent act, his brain generates unique waves involuntarily when confronted with pictures, sounds, and words related to the crime scene. Computers can capture and analyze this brain fingerprint of distinctive brain waves to determine if a person has stored critical details of a particular felony or misdemeanor situation.

Similarly, behavior detection systems study a person's body language, facial expressions, speech, and emotions to isolate specific patterns that criminals commonly exhibit. The surveillance systems can recognize microexpressions, which are the split-second emotions lasting one-fifteenth of a second, on a person's face.

The U.S. Department of Homeland Security is testing its Future Attribute Screening Technologies (FAST) program, which uses cameras, infrared heat sensors, and lasers to measure pulse and breathing rates. The trial technology is being tested for use at airports and sporting and music events.

For more information, visit the Computer Concepts CourseMate Web site at www.cengagebrain.com, navigate to the Chapter 11 Looking Ahead resource for this book, and then click Brain Fingerprinting.

QUIZ YOURSELF 11-1

Instructions: Find the true statement below. Then, rewrite the remaining false statements so that they are true.

1. A back door attack is an assault whose purpose is to disrupt computer access to an Internet service such as the Web or e-mail.

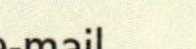

2. All networked and online computer users should implement a firewall solution.
3. A biometric device translates a personal characteristic into an analog code that is compared with a digital code stored in the computer.
4. Computer viruses, worms, Trojan horses, and rootkits are malware that acts with a user's knowledge.
5. Perpetrators of cybercrime and other intrusions fall into seven basic categories: hacker, cracker, CERT/CC, corporate spy, unethical employee, trusted source, and cyberterrorist.
6. Shorter passwords provide greater security than longer ones.
7. Updating an antivirus program's quarantine protects a computer against viruses written since the antivirus program was released.

Quiz Yourself Online: To further check your knowledge of pages 556 through 569, visit the Computer Concepts CourseMate Web site at www.cengagebrain.com, navigate to the Chapter 11 Quiz Yourself resource for this book, and then click Objectives 1 – 3.

Hardware Theft and Vandalism

Hardware theft and vandalism are other types of computer security risks. **Hardware theft** is the act of stealing computer equipment. **Hardware vandalism** is the act of defacing or destroying computer equipment. Hardware vandalism takes many forms, from someone cutting a computer cable to individuals breaking into a business or school computer lab and aimlessly smashing computers.

Hardware theft and vandalism do not really pose a threat to the home desktop computer user. Companies, schools, and other organizations that house many computers, however, are at risk of hardware theft and vandalism, especially those that have smaller system units that easily can fit in a backpack or briefcase.

Mobile users also are susceptible to hardware theft. It is estimated that more than 600,000 notebook computers are stolen each year. The size and weight of these computers, especially netbooks, make them easy to steal. Thieves often target notebook computers of company executives, so that they can use the stolen computer to access confidential company information illegally. In this case, hardware theft is combined with software and information theft.

Safeguards against Hardware Theft and Vandalism

To help reduce the chances of theft, companies and schools use a variety of security measures. Physical access controls, such as locked doors and windows, usually are adequate to protect the equipment. Many businesses, schools, and some homeowners install alarm systems for additional security. School computer labs and other areas with a large number of semifrequent users often attach additional physical security devices such as cables that lock the equipment to a desk (Figure 11-15), cabinet, or floor. Small locking devices also exist that require a key to access a hard disk or optical disc drive.

RTLS
For more information, visit the Computer Concepts CourseMate Web site at www.cengagebrain.com, navigate to the Chapter 11 Web Link resource for this book, and then click RTLS.

Some businesses use a *real time location system (RTLS)* to track and identify the location of high-risk or high-value items. One implementation of RTLS places RFID tags in items to be tracked.

Mobile computer users must take special care to protect their equipment. The best preventive measures are common sense and a constant awareness of the risk. Some users attach a physical device such as a cable to lock a mobile computer temporarily to a stationary object. For example, a hotel guest could lock a notebook computer to a desk or table in a hotel room when he or she leaves the room. Other mobile users install a mini-security system in the notebook computer. Some of these security systems shut down the computer and sound an alarm if the computer moves outside a specified distance. Others can be configured to photograph the thieves when they use the computer. Notebook computer security systems and tracking software also can track the location of a stolen notebook computer.

Some notebook computers use passwords, possessed objects, and biometrics as methods of security. When you start up these computers, you must enter a password, slide a card in a card reader, or press your finger on a fingerprint reader before the hard disk unlocks. This type of security does not prevent theft, but it renders the computer useless if it is stolen.

You also can password-protect many portable storage devices such as USB flash drives, smart phones, and other mobile devices. This allows only authorized users to access the device's data. Some can be set to destroy data if an incorrect password is entered a certain number of times. You usually can instruct the password screen to display your name and telephone number, so that a Good Samaritan can return it to you if lost. Several models also allow you to encrypt data in the device. A later section in this chapter discusses encryption.

Figure 11-15 Using cables to lock computers can help prevent the theft of computer equipment.

Software Theft

Another computer security risk is software theft. **Software theft** occurs when someone (1) steals software media, (2) intentionally erases programs, (3) illegally copies a program, or (4) illegally registers and/or activates a program.

The first type of software theft involves a perpetrator physically stealing the media that contain the software or the hardware that contains the media, as described in the previous section. For example, an unscrupulous library patron might steal the Encyclopedia Britannica optical disc.

The second type of software theft can occur when a programmer is terminated from, or stops working for, a company. Although the programs are company property, some dishonest programmers intentionally remove or disable the programs they have written from company computers.

The third type of software theft occurs when software is stolen from software manufacturers. This type of theft, called piracy, is by far the most common form of software theft. Software **piracy** is the unauthorized and illegal duplication of copyrighted software.

The fourth type of software theft involves users illegally obtaining registration numbers and/or activation codes. A program called a *keygen*, short for key generator, creates software registration numbers and sometimes activation codes. Some unscrupulous individuals create and post keygens so that users can install software without legally purchasing it.

Safeguards against Software Theft

To protect software media from being stolen, owners should keep original software boxes and media in a secure location, out of sight of prying eyes. All computer users should back up their files and disks regularly, in the event of theft. When some companies terminate a programmer or if the programmer quits, they escort the employee off the premises immediately. These companies believe that allowing terminated employees to remain on the premises gives them time to sabotage files and other network procedures.

To protect themselves from software piracy, software manufacturers issue users license agreements. A **license agreement** is the right to use the software. That is, you do not own the software. The license agreement provides specific conditions for use of the software, which a user must accept before using the software (Figure 11-16). These terms usually are displayed when you install the software. Use of the software constitutes acceptance of the terms on the user's part.

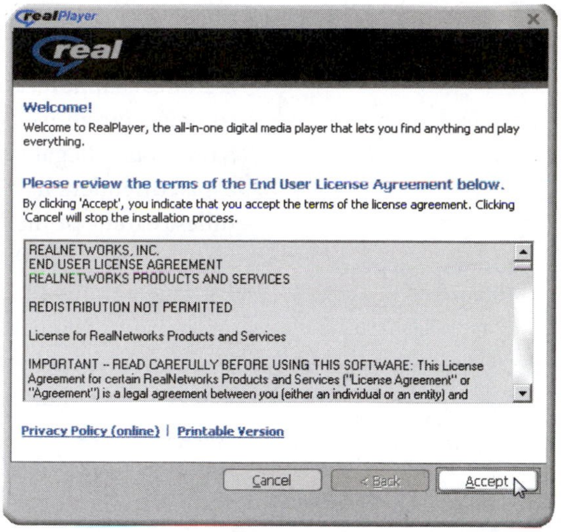

The most common type of license included with software purchased by individual users is a *single-user license agreement*, also called an *end-user license agreement (EULA)*. A single-user license agreement typically includes many of the following conditions that specify a user's responsibility upon acceptance of the agreement.

Users are permitted to:

- Install the software on only one computer. (Some license agreements allow users to install the software on one desktop computer and one notebook computer.)
- Make one copy of the software as a backup.
- Give or sell the software to another individual, but only if the software is removed from the user's computer first.

Users are not permitted to:

- Install the software on a network, such as a school computer lab.
- Give copies to friends and colleagues, while continuing to use the software.
- Export the software.
- Rent or lease the software.

Unless otherwise specified by a license agreement, you do not have the right to copy, loan, borrow, rent, or in any way distribute software. Doing so is a violation of copyright law. It also is a federal crime. Despite this, some experts estimate for every authorized copy of software in use, at least one unauthorized copy exists.

Software piracy continues for several reasons. In some countries, legal protection for software does not exist. In other countries, laws rarely are enforced. In addition, many buyers believe they have the right to copy the software for which they pay hundreds, even thousands, of dollars. Finally, software piracy is a fairly simple crime to commit.

Software piracy, however, is a serious offense. For one, it introduces a number of risks into

Figure 11-16 A user must accept the terms in the license agreement before using the software.

the software market. It increases the chance of spreading viruses, reduces your ability to receive technical support, and drives up the price of software for all users. Further, software companies take illegal copying seriously. In some cases, offenders have been prosecuted to the fullest extent of the law with penalties including fines up to $250,000 and five years in jail. Read Ethics & Issues 11-3 for a related discussion.

Business Software Alliance

For more information, visit the Computer Concepts CourseMate Web site at www.cengagebrain.com, navigate to the Chapter 11 Web Link resource for this book, and then click Business Software Alliance.

To promote a better understanding of software piracy problems and, if necessary, to take legal action, a number of major worldwide software companies formed the *Business Software Alliance* (*BSA*). The BSA operates a Web site and antipiracy hotlines in the United States and more than 40 other countries.

In an attempt to prevent software piracy, Microsoft and other manufacturers have incorporated an activation process into many of their consumer products. During the **product activation**, which is conducted either online or by telephone, users provide the software product's 25-character identification number to receive an installation identification number unique to the computer on which the software is installed. Usually, the software does not function or has limited functionality until you activate it via the Internet or telephone.

Many organizations and businesses also have strict written policies governing the installation and use of software and enforce their rules by checking networked or online computers periodically to ensure that all software is licensed properly. If you are not completely familiar with your school or employer's policies governing installation of software, check with the information technology department or your school's technology coordinator.

Information Theft

Information theft is yet another type of computer security risk. **Information theft** occurs when someone steals personal or confidential information. If stolen, the loss of information can cause as much damage as (if not more than) hardware or software theft.

Both business and home users can fall victim to information theft. An unethical company executive may steal or buy stolen information to learn about a competitor. A corrupt individual may steal credit card numbers to make fraudulent purchases. Information theft often is linked to other types of computer crime. For example, an individual first might gain unauthorized access to a computer and then steal credit card numbers stored in a firm's accounting department.

Information transmitted over networks offers a higher degree of risk because unscrupulous users can intercept it during transmission. Every computer along the path of your data can see what you send and receive. Ironically, though, studies show that the biggest threat to a business's information is its internal employees.

Safeguards against Information Theft

Most organizations will attempt to prevent information theft by implementing the user identification and authentication controls discussed earlier in this chapter. These controls are best suited for protecting information on computers located on an organization's premises.

To protect information on the Internet and networks, organizations and individuals use a variety of encryption techniques.

ETHICS & ISSUES 11-3

Should Online Auctions Be Liable for Pirated Software Sales?

Currently, software companies patrol online auction sites looking for pirated copies of their software that might be for sale. When they find such activity, the software company takes legal action against the seller of the pirated software. With the explosion of online auctions, however, the companies are fighting an uphill battle given the amount of time it takes to discover the sales, find the perpetrators, and then individually bring each perpetrator to justice. Many software companies have joined forces to demand that auction sites, such as eBay, legally be held liable for pirated software sold on their Web sites, and they have offered more than 20 suggestions as to how auction sites could better police their Web sites for pirated software. Online auction Web sites claim that the law clearly states they are not responsible for such sales, but that the software companies legally are responsible for controlling pirated sales. For its part, eBay claims already to enforce more than 13,000 rules to check for suspicious activity on its Web site, and offers trademark holders a special program in which they can enroll and have additional rules enforced.

Should online auctions be liable for pirated software sales on their Web sites? Why or why not? Should new or clearer laws be written to force online auctions to check whether software for sale on their Web sites is pirated? Why? Would you purchase software at an online auction being sold at a substantial discount to prices offered elsewhere? Why or why not?

Encryption

Encryption is a process of converting readable data into unreadable characters to prevent unauthorized access. You treat encrypted data just like any other data. That is, you can store it or send it in an e-mail message. To read the data, the recipient must **decrypt**, or decipher, it into a readable form.

In the encryption process, the unencrypted, readable data is called *plaintext*. The encrypted (scrambled) data is called *ciphertext*. An *encryption algorithm*, or *cypher*, is a set of steps that can convert readable plaintext into unreadable ciphertext. Figure 11-17 shows examples of some simple encryption algorithms. Encryption programs typically use more than one encryption algorithm, along with an encryption key. An *encryption key* is a set of characters that the originator of the data uses to encrypt the plaintext and the recipient of the data uses to decrypt the ciphertext.

Two basic types of encryption are private key and public key. With *private key encryption*, also called *symmetric key encryption*, both the originator and the recipient use the same secret key to encrypt and decrypt the data. *Public key encryption*, also called *asymmetric key encryption*, uses two encryption keys: a public key and a private key (Figure 11-18). Public key encryption software generates both the private key and the public key. A message encrypted with a public key can be

Simple Encryption Algorithms

Name	Algorithm	Plaintext	Ciphertext	Explanation
Transposition	Switch the order of characters	SOFTWARE	OSTFAWER	Adjacent characters swapped
Substitution	Replace characters with other characters	INFORMATION	WLDIMXQUWIL	Each letter replaced with another
Expansion	Insert characters between existing characters	USER	UYSYEYRY	Letter Y inserted after each character
Compaction	Remove characters and store elsewhere	ACTIVATION	ACIVTIN	Every third letter removed (T, A, O)

Figure 11-17 This table shows four simple encryption algorithms. Most encryption keys use a combination of algorithms.

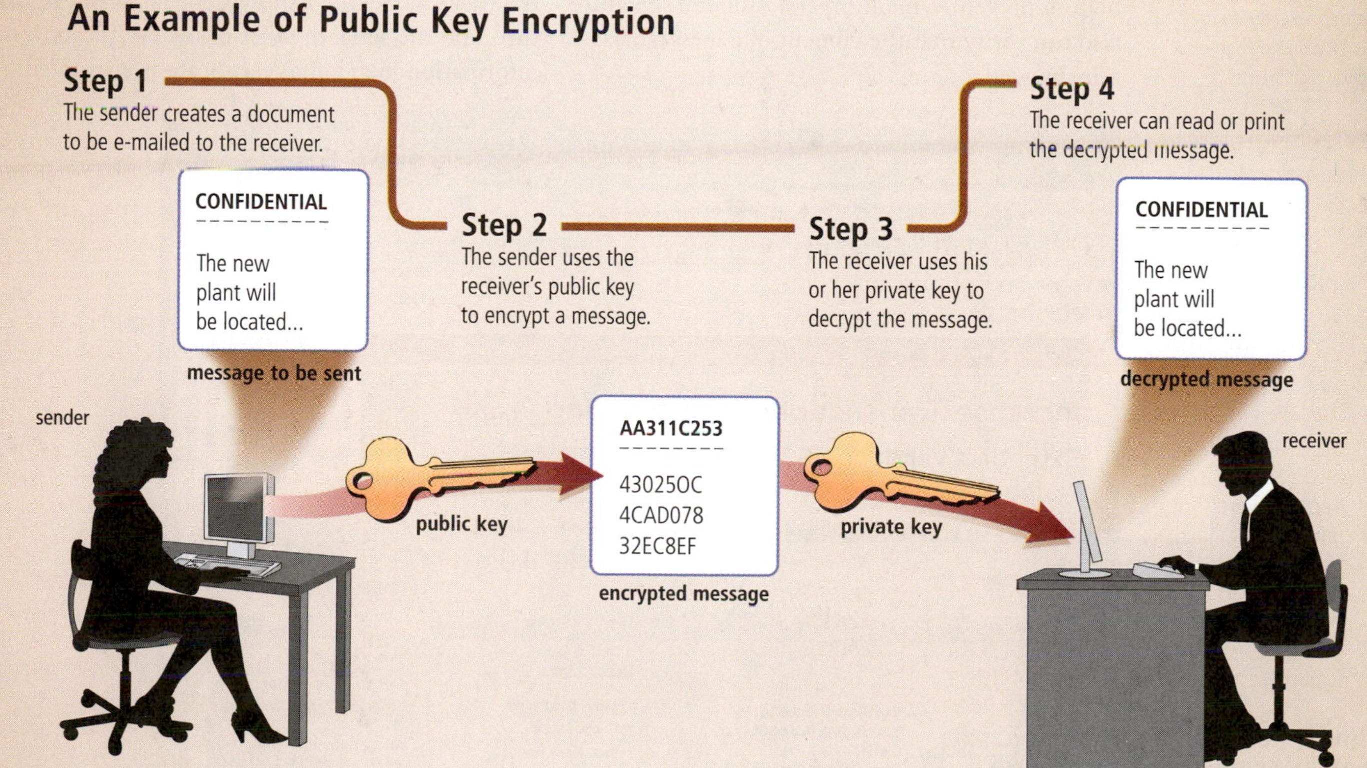

Figure 11-18 This figure shows an example of public key encryption.

decrypted only with the corresponding private key, and vice versa. The public key is made known to message originators and recipients. For example, public keys may be posted on a secure Web page or a public-key server, or they may be e-mailed. The private key, by contrast, should be kept confidential. For a more technical discussion about encryption algorithms and keys, read the High-Tech Talk article on page 592.

Some operating systems and e-mail programs allow you to encrypt the contents of files and messages that are stored on your computer. You also can purchase an encryption program, such as *Pretty Good Privacy* (*PGP*).

A **digital signature** is an encrypted code that a person, Web site, or organization attaches to an electronic message to verify the identity of the message sender. The code usually consists of the user's name and a hash of all or part of the message. A *hash* is a mathematical formula that generates a code from the contents of the message. Thus, the hash differs for each message. Receivers of the message decrypt the digital signature. The recipient generates a new hash of the received message and compares it with one in the digital signature to ensure they match.

Digital Certificates

For more information, visit the Computer Concepts CourseMate Web site at www.cengagebrain.com, navigate to the Chapter 11 Web Link resource for this book, and then click Digital Certificates.

Digital signatures often are used to ensure that an impostor is not participating in an Internet transaction. That is, digital signatures help to prevent e-mail forgery. A digital signature also can verify that the content of a message has not changed.

Many Web browsers also use encryption. Some browsers offer a protection level known as *40-bit encryption*. Many also offer *128-bit encryption* and *1024-bit encryption*, which are even higher levels of protection because they have longer encryption keys. Applications requiring more security, such as banks, brokerage firms, or online retailers that use credit card or other financial information, require 128-bit or 1024-bit encryption.

A Web site that uses encryption techniques to secure its data is known as a **secure site**. Secure sites use digital certificates along with a security protocol. Two popular security protocols are Transport Layer Security and Secure HTTP. Organizations often use VPNs. The following paragraphs briefly discuss security techniques.

Digital Certificates A **digital certificate** is a notice that guarantees a user or a Web site is legitimate. E-commerce applications commonly use digital certificates. Web browsers, such as Internet Explorer, often display a warning message if a Web site does not have a valid digital certificate.

A *certificate authority* (*CA*) is an authorized person or a company that issues and verifies digital certificates. Users apply for a digital certificate from a CA (Figure 11-19). A digital certificate typically contains information such as the user's name, the issuing CA's name and signature, and the serial number of the certificate. The information in a digital certificate is encrypted.

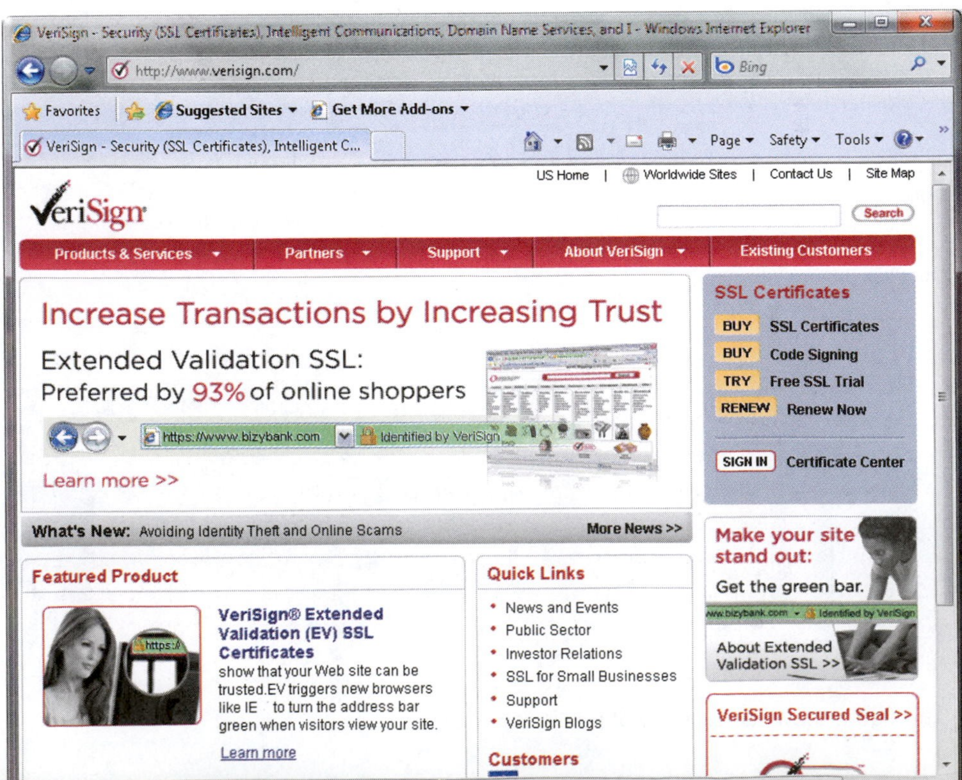

Figure 11-19 A certificate authority issues and verifies digital certificates.

Transport Layer Security *Transport Layer Security (TLS)*, a successor to *Secure Sockets Layer (SSL)*, provides encryption of all data that passes between a client and an Internet server. TLS requires the client have a digital certificate. Once the server has a digital certificate, the Web browser communicates securely with the client. TLS prevents perpetrators from accessing or tampering with communications. Web addresses of pages that use TLS typically begin with https, instead of http (Figure 11-20). TLS is available in 128-bit encryption and higher.

Secure HTTP *Secure HTTP (S-HTTP)* allows users to choose an encryption scheme for data that passes between a client and a server. With S-HTTP, the client and server both must have digital certificates. S-HTTP is more difficult to use than TLS, but it is more secure. Applications that must verify the authenticity of a client, such as for online banking, use S-HTTP.

VPN Mobile users today often access their company networks through a virtual private network. When a mobile user connects to a main office using a standard Internet connection, a *virtual private network (VPN)* provides the mobile user with a secure connection to the company network server, as if the user has a private line. VPNs help ensure that data is safe from being intercepted by unauthorized people by encrypting data as it transmits from a notebook computer, smart phone, or other mobile device.

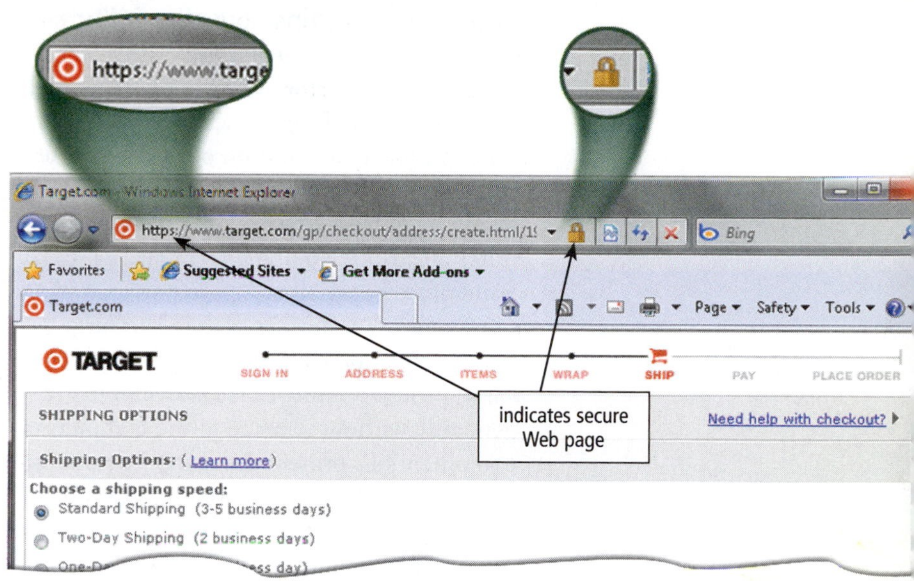

Figure 11-20 Web addresses of secure sites often begin with https instead of http. Browsers also often display a lock symbol in the window.

System Failure

System failure is yet another type of computer security risk. A *system failure* is the prolonged malfunction of a computer. System failure also can cause loss of hardware, software, data, or information. A variety of causes can lead to system failure. These include aging hardware; natural disasters such as fires, floods, or hurricanes; random events such as electrical power problems; and even errors in computer programs.

One of the more common causes of system failure is an electrical power variation. Electrical power variations can cause loss of data and loss of equipment. If the computer equipment is networked, a single power disturbance can damage multiple systems. Electrical disturbances include noise, undervoltages, and overvoltages.

Noise is any unwanted signal, usually varying quickly, that is mixed with the normal voltage entering the computer. Noise is caused by external devices such as fluorescent lighting, radios, and televisions, as well as by components within the computer itself. Noise generally is not a risk to hardware, software, or data. Computer power supplies, however, do filter out noise.

An **undervoltage** occurs when the electrical supply drops. In North America, a wall plug usually supplies electricity at approximately 120 volts. An undervoltage occurs when the voltage drops, often defined as more than five percent, below the normal volts. A *brownout* is a prolonged (more than a minute) undervoltage. A *blackout* is a complete power failure. Undervoltages can cause data loss but generally do not cause equipment damage.

An **overvoltage**, or **power surge**, occurs when the incoming electrical power increases, often defined as more than five percent, above the normal volts. A momentary overvoltage, which is called a *spike*, occurs when the increase in power lasts for less than one millisecond (one thousandth of a second). Uncontrollable disturbances such as lightning bolts can cause spikes. Overvoltages can cause immediate and permanent damage to hardware.

Safeguards against System Failure

To protect against electrical power variations, use a surge protector. A **surge protector**, also called a *surge suppressor*, uses special electrical components to smooth out minor noise, provide a stable current flow, and keep an overvoltage from reaching the computer and other electronic equipment (Figure 11-21). Sometimes resembling a power strip, the computer and other devices plug in the surge protector, which plugs in the power source. The surge protector absorbs small overvoltages — generally without damage to the computer and equipment. To protect the computer and other equipment from large overvoltages, such as those caused by a lightning strike, some surge protectors completely stop working when an overvoltage reaches a certain level. Surge protectors also usually protect the computer from undervoltages.

No surge protectors are 100 percent effective. Large power surges can bypass the protector. Repeated small overvoltages can weaken a surge protector permanently. Some experts recommend replacing a surge protector every two to three years. Typically, the amount of protection offered by a surge protector is proportional to its cost. That is, the more expensive, the more protection the protector offers. Be sure to review the manufacturer's guarantee when purchasing a surge protector. Some will replace equipment damaged by a power surge, if the equipment was connected to their surge protector.

Surge Protectors
For more information, visit the Computer Concepts CourseMate Web site at www.cengagebrain.com, navigate to the Chapter 11 Web Link resource for this book, and then click Surge Protectors.

The surge protector you purchase should meet the safety specification for surge suppression products. This specification, which is called the *Underwriters Laboratories (UL) 1449 standard*, allows no more than 500 maximum volts to pass through the line. The response time of the surge protector should be less than one nanosecond. The surge protector also should have a Joule rating of at least 200. A *Joule* is the unit of energy a surge protection device can absorb before it can be damaged. The higher the Joule rating, the better the protection.

If your computer connects to a network or the Internet, also be sure to have protection for your modem, telephone lines, DSL lines, Internet cable lines, and network lines. Many surge protectors include plug-ins for telephone lines and other cables. If yours does not, you can purchase separate devices to protect these lines.

For additional electrical protection, some users connect an uninterruptible power supply to the computer. An **uninterruptible power supply (UPS)** is a device that contains surge protection circuits and one or more batteries that can provide power during a temporary or permanent loss of power (Figure 11-22). A UPS connects between your computer and a power source.

Two types of UPS devices are standby and online. A *standby UPS*, sometimes called an *offline UPS*, switches to battery power when a problem occurs in the power line. The amount of time a standby UPS allows a user to continue working depends on the electrical requirements of the computer and the size of the batteries in the UPS. A UPS for a personal computer should provide from 10 to 50 minutes of use in the event of a total power loss. This should

Figure 11-21 Circuits inside a surge protector safeguard against electrical power variations.

Figure 11-22 If power fails, an uninterruptible power supply (UPS) uses batteries to provide electricity for a limited amount of time.

be enough time to save current work and shut down the computer properly. An *online UPS* always runs off the battery, which provides continuous protection. An online UPS is much more expensive than a standby UPS.

Some companies use duplicate components or computers to protect against system failure. A *fault-tolerant computer* has duplicate components so that it can continue to operate when one of its main components fail. Companies that must have their computers operational at all times may have two separate duplicate computers running simultaneously. Airline reservation systems, communications networks, and automated teller machines are examples of systems that duplicate components or computers to ensure that no data is lost in the event of a system failure.

? FAQ 11-5

Should I use a surge protector on electronic equipment, appliances, or even my entire house?

It is a good idea to use a surge protector on high-end, expensive electronic equipment such as entertainment systems, DVD/Blu-ray Disc players, computers, and copy machines, and on any household appliance or device that includes a circuit board or computer such as a stove, dishwasher, and microwave. You also can hire an electrician to install a surge protector that protects your entire house. This type of surge protector is installed where the power lines connect to your house's electrical system. A lightning strike or other substantial power surge could damage electrical devices in your house. In addition to protecting the equipment in your house, it also is a good idea to carry a portable surge protector when you travel, so that you can protect your cell phone and other mobile devices when you plug them in to charge.

For more information, visit the Computer Concepts CourseMate Web site at www.cengagebrain.com, navigate to the Chapter 11 FAQ resource for this book, and then click Surge Protectors.

Backing Up — The Ultimate Safeguard

To protect against data loss caused by system failure or hardware/software/information theft, computer users should back up files regularly. A **backup** is a duplicate of a file, program, or disk that can be used if the original is lost, damaged, or destroyed. Thus, to **back up** a file means to make a copy of it. In the case of system failure or the discovery of corrupted files, you **restore** the files by copying the backed up files to their original location on the computer.

You can use just about any media to store backups. Be sure to use high-quality media. A good choice for a home user might be optical discs or external hard disks. Some home users also set up a RAID configuration, as described in Chapter 7, to automatically back up the contents of a disk.

Keep backup copies in a fireproof and heatproof safe or vault, or offsite. *Offsite* means in a location separate from the computer site. Home and business users keep backup copies offsite so that a single disaster, such as a fire, does not destroy both the original and the backup copy of the data. An offsite location can be a safe deposit box at a bank or a briefcase. A growing trend is to use cloud storage as an offsite location. As discussed in Chapter 7, cloud storage is an Internet service that provides storage to computer users. To learn more about how to back up files using an Internet service, complete the Learn How To 1 activity on pages 602 and 603.

Most backup programs for the home user provide for a full backup and a selective backup. A *full backup* copies all of the files in the computer. With a *selective backup*, users choose which folders and files to include in a backup.

Some users implement a *three-generation backup* policy to preserve three copies of important files. The *grandparent* is the oldest copy of the file. The *parent* is the second oldest copy of the file. The *child* is the most recent copy of the file. Others use RAID to duplicate the contents of a disk. Instead of multiple backup copies, some users choose continuous backup, where data is backed up whenever a change is made.

Backup programs are available from many sources. Most operating systems include a backup program. Backup devices, such as external disk drives, also include backup programs. Numerous stand-alone backup utilities exist. Many of these can be downloaded from the Web at no cost.

Wireless Security

Wireless technology has made dramatic changes in the way computer users communicate worldwide. Billions of home and business users have notebook computers, smart phones, and other mobile devices to access the Internet, send e-mail and instant messages, chat online, or share network connections — all without wires. Home users set up wireless home networks. Mobile users access wireless networks in hot spots at airports, hotels, shopping malls, bookstores, restaurants, and coffee shops. Schools have wireless networks so that students can access the school network using their mobile computers and devices as they move from building to building.

Although wireless access provides many conveniences to users, it also poses additional security risks. One study showed that about 80 percent of wireless networks have no security protection. Some perpetrators connect to other's wireless networks to gain free Internet access; others may try to access an organization's confidential data.

To access the network, the individual must be in range of the wireless network. Some intruders intercept and monitor communications as they transmit through the air. Others connect to a network through an unsecured wireless access point (WAP). In one technique, called *war driving* or *access point mapping*, individuals attempt to detect wireless networks via their notebook computer or mobile device while driving a vehicle through areas they suspect have a wireless network. Some individuals instead use *war flying*, where they use airplanes instead of vehicles to detect unsecured wireless networks. Once located, some individuals use a GPS device to add the WAP to a war driving access point map on the Internet (Figure 11-23), making the wireless network vulnerable.

War Driving

For more information, visit the Computer Concepts CourseMate Web site at www.cengagebrain.com, navigate to the Chapter 11 Web Link resource for this book, and then click War Driving.

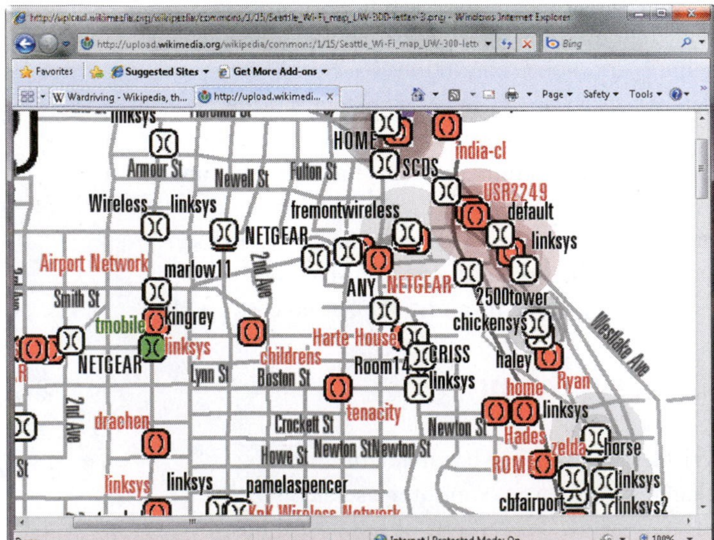

Figure 11-23 This Web site marks all unsecured wireless networks located during a war drive.

In addition to using firewalls, some safeguards that improve the security of wireless networks include reconfiguring the wireless access point and ensuring equipment uses one or more wireless security standards such as Wi-Fi Protected Access and 802.11i.

- A wireless access point (WAP) should be configured so that it does not broadcast a network name, known as an *SSID* (service set identifier). Users should change the default SSID to prevent unauthorized users from accessing their wireless network. The WAP also can be programmed so that only certain devices can access it.
- *Wi-Fi Protected Access* (*WPA*) is a security standard that improves on older security standards by authenticating network users and providing more advanced encryption techniques.
- An *802.11i* network, sometimes called WPA2, the most recent network security standard, conforms to the government's security standards and uses more sophisticated encryption techniques than WPA.

By implementing these security measures, you can help to prevent unauthorized access to wireless networks.

? FAQ 11-6

Can you detect if someone is accessing your wireless home network?

Yes. If you notice that the speed of your wireless network connection is slower than normal, it may be a sign that someone else is accessing your network. You also may notice indicator lights on your wireless router flashing rapidly when you are not connected to your wireless network. Most wireless routers have a built-in utility that allows you to view the computers currently connected to your network. If you notice a computer that does not belong to you, consult your wireless router's documentation to determine how to remove it from the network.

For more information, visit the Computer Concepts CourseMate Web site at www.cengagebrain.com, navigate to the Chapter 11 FAQ resource for this book, and then click Wireless Home Networks.

QUIZ YOURSELF 11-2

Instructions: Find the true statement below. Then, rewrite the remaining false statements so that they are true.

1. An end-user license agreement (EULA) permits users to give copies to friends and colleagues, while continuing to use the software.
2. Encryption is a process of converting ciphertext into plaintext to prevent unauthorized access.
3. Mobile users are not susceptible to hardware theft.
4. Overvoltages can cause immediate and permanent damage to hardware.
5. Two backup security standards are Wi-Fi Protected Access and 802.11i.
6. To protect against data loss caused by a system failure, computer users should restore files regularly.

Quiz Yourself Online: To further check your knowledge of pages 570 through 578, visit the Computer Concepts CourseMate Web site at www.cengagebrain.com, navigate to the Chapter 11 Quiz Yourself resource for this book, and then click Objectives 4 – 9.

Health Concerns of Computer Use

Users are a key component in any information system. Thus, protecting users is just as important as protecting hardware, software, and data.

The widespread use of computers has led to some important user health concerns. Users should be proactive and minimize their chance of risk. The following sections discuss health risks and preventions, along with measures users can take to keep the environment healthy.

Computers and Health Risks

A **repetitive strain injury (RSI)** is an injury or disorder of the muscles, nerves, tendons, ligaments, and joints. Computer-related RSIs include tendonitis and carpal tunnel syndrome. RSIs are the largest job-related injury and illness problem in the United States today. For this reason, OSHA (Occupational Safety and Health Administration) has developed industry-specific and task-specific guidelines designed to prevent workplace injuries with respect to computer usage.

Tendonitis is inflammation of a tendon due to repeated motion or stress on that tendon. *Carpal tunnel syndrome* (*CTS*) is inflammation of the nerve that connects the forearm to the palm of the wrist. Repeated or forceful bending of the wrist can cause CTS or tendonitis of the wrist. Symptoms of tendonitis of the wrist include extreme pain that extends from the forearm to the hand, along with tingling in the fingers. Symptoms of CTS include burning pain when the nerve is compressed, along with numbness and tingling in the thumb and first two fingers.

Long-term computer work can lead to tendonitis or CTS. Factors that cause these disorders include prolonged typing, prolonged mouse usage, or continual shifting between the mouse and the keyboard. If untreated, these disorders can lead to permanent physical damage.

You can take many precautions to prevent these types of injuries. Take frequent breaks during the computer session to exercise your hands and arms (Figure 11-24). To prevent injury due to typing, place a wrist rest between the keyboard and the edge of your desk. To prevent injury while using a mouse, place the mouse at least six inches from the edge of the desk. In this position, your wrist is flat on the desk. Finally, minimize the number of times you switch between the mouse and the keyboard, and avoid using the heel of your hand as a pivot point while typing or using the mouse.

Another type of health-related condition due to computer usage is **computer vision syndrome** (*CVS*). You may have CVS if you have sore, tired, burning, itching, or dry eyes; blurred or double vision; distance blurred vision after prolonged

Hand Exercises

- **Spread fingers apart for several seconds while keeping wrists straight.**
- **Gently push back fingers and then thumb.**
- **Dangle arms loosely at sides and then shake arms and hands.**

Figure 11-24 To reduce the chance of developing tendonitis or carpal tunnel syndrome, take frequent breaks during computer sessions to exercise your hands and arms.

staring at a display device; headache or sore neck; difficulty shifting focus between a display device and documents; difficulty focusing on the screen image; color fringes or after-images when you look away from the display device; and increased sensitivity to light. Eyestrain associated with CVS is not thought to have serious or long-term consequences. Figure 11-25 outlines some techniques you can follow to ease eyestrain.

Techniques to Ease Eyestrain

- **Every 10 to 15 minutes, take an eye break.**
  - **Look into the distance and focus on an object for 20 to 30 seconds.**
  - **Roll your eyes in a complete circle.**
  - **Close your eyes and rest them for at least one minute.**
- **Blink your eyes every five seconds.**
- **Place your display device about an arm's length away from your eyes with the top of the screen at eye level or below.**
- **Use large fonts.**
- **If you wear glasses, ask your doctor about computer glasses.**
- **Adjust the lighting.**

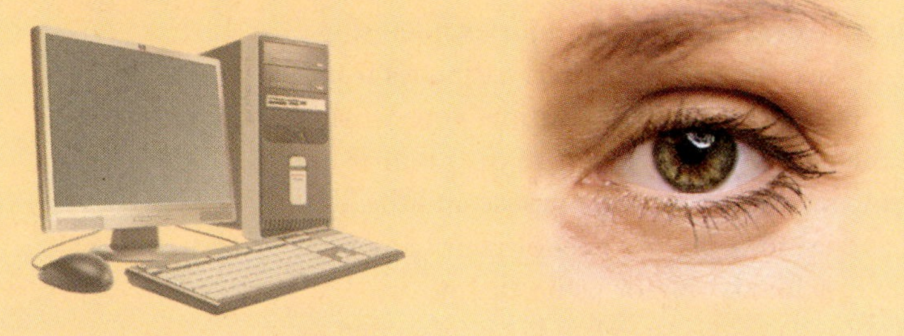

Figure 11-25 Following these tips may help reduce eyestrain while working on a computer.

People who spend their workday using the computer sometimes complain of lower back pain, muscle fatigue, and emotional fatigue. Lower back pain sometimes is caused from poor posture. Always sit properly in the chair while you work. To alleviate back pain, muscle fatigue, and emotional fatigue, take a 15- to 30-minute break every 2 hours — stand up, walk around, stretch, and relax. Another way to help prevent these injuries is to be sure your workplace is designed ergonomically.

Ergonomics and Workplace Design

Ergonomics is an applied science devoted to incorporating comfort, efficiency, and safety into the design of items in the workplace. Ergonomic studies have shown that using the correct type and configuration of chair, keyboard, display device, and work surface helps users work comfortably and efficiently and helps protect their health. For the computer work space, experts recommend an area of at least two feet by four feet. Figure 11-26 illustrates additional guidelines for setting up the work area.

Figure 11-26 A well-designed work area should be flexible to allow adjustments to the height and build of different individuals. Good lighting and air quality also are important considerations.

Computer Addiction

Computers can provide entertainment and enjoyment. Some computer users, however, become obsessed with the computer and the Internet. **Computer addiction** occurs when the computer consumes someone's entire social life. Computer addiction is a growing health problem but can be treated through therapy and support groups.

Symptoms of a user with computer addiction include the following:

- Craves computer time
- Overjoyed when at the computer
- Unable to stop computer activity
- Irritable when not at the computer
- Neglects family and friends
- Problems at work or school

Ethics and Society

As with any powerful technology, computers can be used for both good and bad intentions. The standards that determine whether an action is good or bad are known as ethics.

Computer ethics are the moral guidelines that govern the use of computers and information systems. Seven frequently discussed areas of computer ethics are unauthorized use of computers and networks, software theft (piracy), information accuracy, intellectual property rights, codes of conduct, information privacy, and green computing. The questionnaire in Figure 11-27 raises issues in each of these areas.

Previous sections in this chapter discussed unauthorized use of computers and networks, and software theft (piracy). The following sections

Your Thoughts?

	Ethical	Unethical
1. An organization requires employees to wear badges that track their whereabouts while at work.	☐	☐
2. A supervisor reads an employee's e-mail.	☐	☐
3. An employee uses his computer at work to send e-mail messages to a friend.	☐	☐
4. An employee sends an e-mail message to several coworkers and blind copies his supervisor.	☐	☐
5. An employee forwards an e-mail message to a third party without permission from the sender.	☐	☐
6. An employee uses her computer at work to complete a homework assignment for school.	☐	☐
7. The vice president of your Student Government Association (SGA) downloads a photo from the Web and uses it in a flyer recruiting SGA members.	☐	☐
8. A student copies text from the Web and uses it in a research paper for his English Composition class.	☐	☐
9. An employee sends political campaign material to individuals on her employer's mailing list.	☐	☐
10. As an employee in the registration office, you have access to student grades. You look up grades for your friends, so that they do not have to wait for delivery of grade reports from the postal service.	☐	☐
11. An employee makes a copy of software and installs it on her home computer. No one uses her home computer while she is at work, and she uses her home computer only to finish projects from work.	☐	☐
12. An employee who has been laid off installs a computer virus on his employer's computer.	☐	☐
13. A person designing a Web page finds one on the Web similar to his requirements, copies it, modifies it, and publishes it as his own Web page.	☐	☐
14. A student researches using only the Web to write a report.	☐	☐
15. In a society in which all transactions occur online (a cashless society), the government tracks every transaction you make and automatically deducts taxes from your bank account.	☐	☐
16. Someone copies a well-known novel to the Web and encourages others to read it.	☐	☐
17. A person accesses an organization's network and reports to the organization any vulnerabilities discovered.	☐	☐
18. Your friend uses a neighbor's wireless network to connect to the Internet and check e-mail.	☐	☐
19. A company uses recycled paper to print a 50-page employee benefits manual that is distributed to 425 employees.	☐	☐
20. Your friend donates her old computers and mobile devices to local schools when she purchases newer models.	☐	☐

Figure 11-27 Indicate whether you think the situation described is ethical or unethical. Discuss your answers with your instructor and other students.

discuss issues related to information accuracy, intellectual property rights, codes of conduct, green computing, and information privacy.

Information Accuracy

Information accuracy today is a concern because many users access information maintained by other people or companies, such as on the Internet. Do not assume that because the information is on the Web that it is correct. As Chapter 2 discussed, users should evaluate the value of a Web page before relying on its content. Be aware that the organization providing access to the information may not be the creator of the information.

In addition to concerns about the accuracy of computer input, some individuals and organizations raise questions about the ethics of using computers to alter output, primarily graphical output such as a retouched photo. Using graphics equipment and software, users easily can digitize photos and then add, change, or remove images (Figure 11-28).

One group that completely opposes any manipulation of an image is the National Press Photographers Association. It believes that allowing even the slightest alteration eventually could lead to misrepresentative photos. Others believe that digital photo retouching is acceptable as long as the significant content or meaning of the photo does not change. Digital retouching is an area in which legal precedents so far have not been established.

Digital Rights Management

For more information, visit the Computer Concepts CourseMate Web site at www.cengagebrain.com, navigate to the Chapter 11 Web Link resource for this book, and then click Digital Rights Management.

Figure 11-28 A digitally altered photo shows the movie character Forrest Gump (1994) meeting President John F. Kennedy (who died in 1963).

Intellectual Property Rights

Intellectual property (*IP*) refers to unique and original works such as ideas, inventions, art, writings, processes, company and product names, and logos. **Intellectual property rights** are the rights to which creators are entitled for their work. Certain issues arise surrounding IP today because many of these works are available digitally.

A **copyright** gives authors and artists exclusive rights to duplicate, publish, and sell their materials. A copyright protects any tangible form of expression.

A common infringement of copyright is piracy. People pirate (illegally copy) software, movies, and music. Many areas are not clear-cut with respect to the law, because copyright law gives the public fair use to copyrighted material. The issues surround the phrase, fair use, which allows use for educational and critical purposes. This vague definition is subject to widespread interpretation and raises many questions:

- Should individuals be able to download contents of your Web site, modify it, and then put it on the Web again as their own?
- Should a faculty member have the right to print material from the Web and distribute it to all members of the class for teaching purposes only?
- Should someone be able to scan photos or pages from a book, publish them to the Web, and allow others to download them?
- Should someone be able to put the lyrics of a song on the Web?
- Should students be able to post term papers they have written on the Web, making it tempting for other students to download and submit them as their own work?

These issues with copyright law led to the development of *digital rights management* (*DRM*), a strategy designed to prevent illegal distribution of movies, music, and other digital content.

Codes of Conduct

Recognizing that individuals need specific standards for the ethical use of computers, a number of computer-related organizations have established IT (information technology) codes of conduct (Figure 11-29). An IT **code of conduct** is a written guideline that helps determine whether a specific computer action is ethical or unethical.

IT Code of Conduct
1. Computers may not be used to harm other people.
2. Employees may not interfere with others' computer work.
3. Employees may not meddle in others' computer files.
4. Computers may not be used to steal.
5. Computers may not be used to bear false witness.
6. Employees may not copy or use software illegally.
7. Employees may not use others' computer resources without authorization.
8. Employees may not use others' intellectual property as their own.
9. Employees shall consider the social impact of programs and systems they design.
10. Employees always should use computers in a way that demonstrates consideration and respect for fellow humans.

Figure 11-29 Sample IT code of conduct employers may distribute to employees.

Green Computing

Green computing involves reducing the electricity and environmental waste while using a computer. People use, and often waste, resources such as electricity and paper while using a computer. Society has become aware of this waste and is taking measures to combat it.

Personal computers, display devices, and printers should comply with guidelines of the ENERGY STAR program. The United States Department of Energy (DOE) and the United States Environmental Protection Agency (EPA) developed the *ENERGY STAR program* to help reduce the amount of electricity used by computers and related devices. This program encourages manufacturers to create energy-efficient devices that require little power when they are not in use. For example, many devices switch to sleep or power save mode after a specified number of inactive minutes or hours. Computers and devices that meet the ENERGY STAR guidelines display an ENERGY STAR label.

A recent study showed that organizational computer facilities, or data centers, in the United States consumed as much power as about six million households, and if no measures are taken to reduce consumption, the number is expected to continue rising quickly. Data center resources that consume power include computer hardware and associated devices, uninterruptible power supplies, and utilities such as air conditioning, coolers, lighting, etc. Organizations can implement a variety of measures to reduce electrical waste.

- Consolidate servers by using virtualization (discussed in Chapter 8)
- Purchase high-efficiency equipment, such as uninterruptible power supplies and storage devices
- Use sleep modes and other power management features for computers and devices
- Buy computers with low power consumption processors and power supplies
- When possible, use outside air to cool the data center

Some organizations continually review their *power usage effectiveness* (PUE), which is a ratio that measures how much power enters the computer facility, or data center, against the amount of power required to run the computers.

Users should not store obsolete computers and devices in their basement, storage room, attic, warehouse, or any other location. Computers, monitors, and other equipment contain toxic materials and potentially dangerous elements including lead, mercury, and flame retardants. In a landfill, these materials release into the environment. Recycling and refurbishing old equipment are much safer alternatives for the environment. Manufacturers can use the millions of pounds of recycled raw materials to make products such as outdoor furniture and automotive parts.

Experts estimate that more than 700 million personal computers are obsolete. Because of the huge volumes of electronic waste, the U.S. federal government has proposed a bill that would require computer recycling across the country. Many state and local governments have methods in place to make it easy for consumers to recycle this type of equipment. Many computer manufacturers, office supply stores, and other agencies offer free recycling to consumers and organizations.

To reduce the environmental impact of computing further, users simply can alter a few habits. Figure 11-30 lists the ways you can contribute to green computing. To learn more about green computing, complete the Green Computing exercise on the Web Research page in each chapter of this book.

Green Computing Suggestions

1. Use computers and devices that comply with the ENERGY STAR program.
2. Do not leave the computer running overnight.
3. Turn off the monitor, printer, and other devices when not in use.
4. Use LCD monitors instead of CRT monitors.
5. Use paperless methods to communicate.
6. Recycle paper.
7. Buy recycled paper.
8. Recycle toner cartridges.
9. Recycle old computers, printers, and other devices.
10. Telecommute to save gas.
11. Use video conferencing and VoIP for meetings.

Figure 11-30 A list of suggestions to make computing healthy for the environment.

Information Privacy

Information privacy refers to the right of individuals and companies to deny or restrict the collection and use of information about them. In the past, information privacy was easier to maintain because information was kept in separate locations. Each retail store had its own credit files. Each government agency maintained separate records. Doctors had their own patient files.

Today, huge databases store this data online. Much of the data is personal and confidential and should be accessible only to authorized users. Many individuals and organizations, however, question whether this data really is private. That is, some companies and individuals collect and use this information without your authorization. Web sites often collect data about you, so that they can customize advertisements and send you personalized e-mail messages. Some employers monitor your computer usage and e-mail messages.

Figure 11-31 lists measures you can take to make your personal data more private. The following sections address techniques companies and employers use to collect your personal data. Read Innovative Computing 11-2 to find out how merchants watch shoppers' behaviors.

How to Safeguard Personal Information

1. Fill in only necessary information on rebate, warranty, and registration forms.
2. Do not preprint your telephone number or Social Security number on personal checks.
3. Have an unlisted or unpublished telephone number.
4. If Caller ID is available in your area, find out how to block your number from displaying on the receiver's system.
5. Do not write your telephone number on charge or credit receipts.
6. Ask merchants not to write credit card numbers, telephone numbers, Social Security numbers, and driver's license numbers on the back of your personal checks.
7. Purchase goods with cash, rather than credit or checks.
8. Avoid shopping club and buyer cards.
9. If merchants ask personal questions, find out why they want to know before releasing the information.
10. Inform merchants that you do not want them to distribute your personal information.
11. Request, in writing, to be removed from mailing lists.
12. Obtain your credit report once a year from each of the three major credit reporting agencies (Equifax, Experian, and TransUnion) and correct any errors.
13. Request a free copy of your medical records once a year from the Medical Information Bureau.
14. Limit the amount of information you provide to Web sites. Fill in only required information.
15. Install a cookie manager to filter cookies.
16. Clear your history file when you are finished browsing.
17. Set up a free e-mail account. Use this e-mail address for merchant forms.
18. Turn off file and printer sharing on your Internet connection.
19. Install a personal firewall.
20. Sign up for e-mail filtering through your Internet access provider or use an anti-spam program such as Brightmail.
21. Do not reply to spam for any reason.
22. Surf the Web anonymously with a program such as Freedom WebSecure or through an anonymous Web site such as Anonymizer.com.

Figure 11-31 Techniques to keep personal data private.

INNOVATIVE COMPUTING 11-2

Customers' Behavior, Conversations Monitored

Deciding whether to display peanut butter next to jelly on a supermarket shelf is made easier with consumer-monitoring technology. Leading stores, including Best Buy, Walmart, Walgreens, Office Depot, and Abercrombie & Fitch, have installed video cameras and recorders, heat sensors, and sometimes microphones to track customers' movement throughout the store and their buying patterns.

One system, called Smartlane, counts the number of people, known as "hot blobs," entering and exiting the store and records how quickly clerks are completing transactions at cash registers. It alerts management when many hot blobs are waiting in checkout lanes or have entered the store in a short period of time so that additional clerks can be made available to reduce checkout waiting times.

Another system, BehaviorIQ, collects data on where customers walk throughout the store, when and for how long they stop to browse, and what they take from shelves and racks.

Some stores claim information gleaned from these monitoring systems has increased sales 300 percent.

Privacy experts warn that consumers might object to being recorded and analyzed. The monitoring companies, however, dispel these concerns by explaining that the data actually resembles audio recordings made when calling customer-service hotlines and when being observed for loss prevention purposes.

For more information, visit the Computer Concepts CourseMate Web site at www.cengagebrain.com, navigate to the Chapter 11 Innovative Computing resource for this book, and then click Shopping Behavior.

Electronic Profiles

When you fill out a form such as a magazine subscription, product warranty registration card, or contest entry form, the merchant that receives the form usually enters it into a database. Likewise, every time you click an advertisement on the Web or register software online, your information and preferences enter a database. Merchants then sell the contents of their databases to national marketing firms and Internet advertising firms. By combining this data with information from public sources such as driver's licenses and vehicle registrations, these firms create an electronic profile of individuals. The information in these electronic profiles includes personal details such as your age, address, telephone number, spending habits, marital status, number of dependents, ages of dependents, and so on.

Direct marketing supporters say that using information in this way lowers overall selling costs, which lowers product prices. Critics contend that the information in an electronic profile reveals more about an individual than anyone has a right to know. They claim that companies should inform people if they plan to provide personal information to others, and people should have the right to deny such use. Many companies today allow people to specify whether they want their personal information distributed (Figure 11-32).

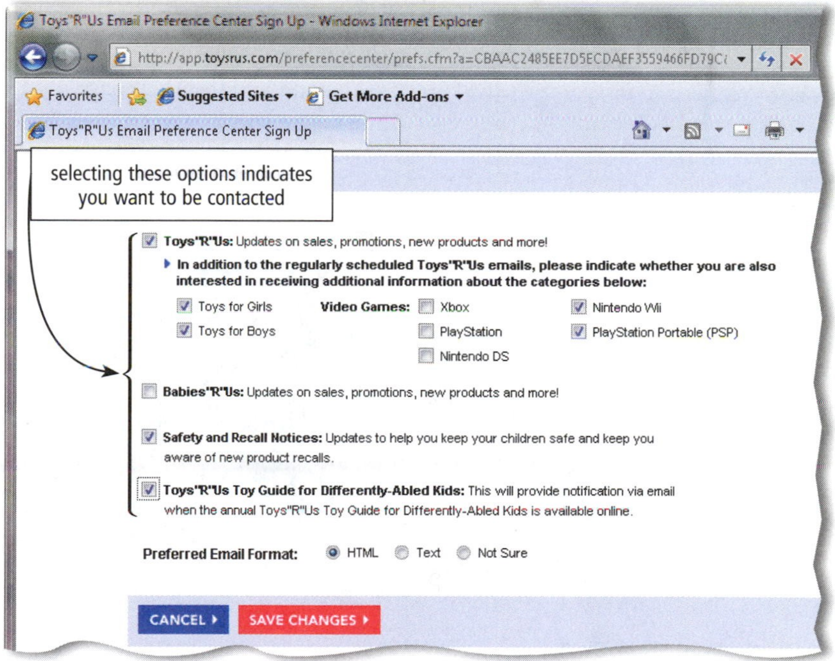

Figure 11-32 Many companies today allow people to specify whether they want their personal information distributed.

Cookies

E-commerce and other Web applications often rely on cookies to identify users and customize Web pages. A **cookie** is a small text file that a Web server stores on your computer. Cookie files typically contain data about you, such as your user name or viewing preferences.

Web sites use cookies for a variety of purposes:

- Most Web sites that allow for personalization use cookies to track user preferences. On such sites, users may be asked to fill in a form requesting personal information, such as their name, postal code, or site preferences. A news Web site, for example, might allow users to customize their viewing preferences to display certain stock quotes or the local weather forecast. The Web site stores their preferences in a cookie on the users' hard disks.
- Some Web sites use cookies to store users' passwords, so that they do not need to enter it every time they log in to the Web site.
- Online shopping sites generally use a *session cookie* to keep track of items in a user's shopping cart. This way, users can start an order during one Web session and finish it on another day in another session. Session cookies usually expire after a certain time, such as a week or a month.
- Some Web sites use cookies to track how often users visit a site and the Web pages they visit while at the site.
- Web sites may use cookies to target advertisements. These sites store a user's interests and browsing habits in the cookie.

Many commercial Web sites send a cookie to your browser, and then your computer's hard disk stores the cookie. The next time you visit the Web site, your browser retrieves the cookie from your hard disk and sends the data in the cookie to the Web site. Figure 11-33 illustrates how Web sites work with cookies. A Web site can read data only from its own cookie file stored on your hard disk. That is, it cannot access or view any other data on your hard disk — including another cookie file.

Some Web sites do sell or trade information stored in your cookie to advertisers — a practice many believe to be unethical. If you do not want your personal information distributed, you should limit the amount of information you provide to a Web site.

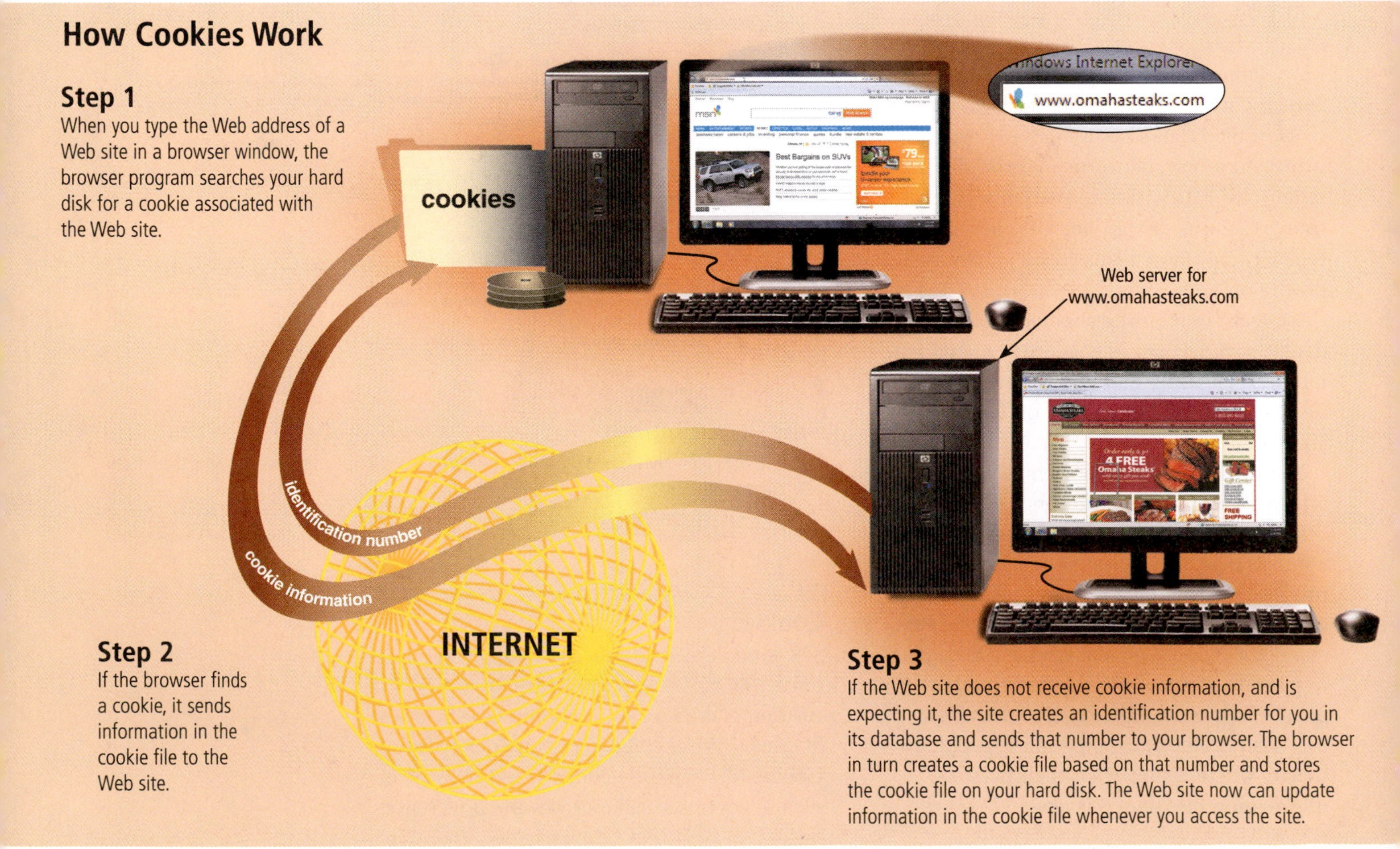

Cookies

For more information, visit the Computer Concepts CourseMate Web site at www.cengagebrain.com, navigate to the Chapter 11 Web Link resource for this book, and then click Cookies.

How Cookies Work

Step 1
When you type the Web address of a Web site in a browser window, the browser program searches your hard disk for a cookie associated with the Web site.

cookies

Windows Internet Explorer
www.omahasteaks.com

Web server for www.omahasteaks.com

identification number

cookie information

INTERNET

Step 2
If the browser finds a cookie, it sends information in the cookie file to the Web site.

Step 3
If the Web site does not receive cookie information, and is expecting it, the site creates an identification number for you in its database and sends that number to your browser. The browser in turn creates a cookie file based on that number and stores the cookie file on your hard disk. The Web site now can update information in the cookie file whenever you access the site.

Figure 11-33 This figure shows how cookies work.

You can set your browser to accept cookies automatically, prompt you if you want to accept a cookie, or disable cookie use altogether. Keep in mind if you disable cookie use, you may not be able to use many of the e-commerce Web sites. As an alternative, you can purchase software that selectively blocks cookies.

Spam

Spam is an unsolicited e-mail message or newsgroup posting sent to many recipients or newsgroups at once. Spam is Internet junk mail (Figure 11-34). The content of spam ranges from selling a product or service, to promoting a business opportunity, to advertising offensive material. One study indicates more than 92 percent of e-mail is spam. Instead of via e-mail, some spam is sent through an instant messaging system and, thus, is called *spim*. Another type, called *spit*, is spam sent via VoIP.

Users can reduce the amount of spam they receive with a number of techniques. Some e-mail programs have built-in settings that allow users to delete spam automatically. Users also can sign up for e-mail filtering from their Internet access provider. **E-mail filtering** is a service that blocks e-mail messages from designated sources. These services typically collect the spam in a central location that users can view at any time. An alternative to e-mail filtering is to purchase an **anti-spam program** that attempts to remove spam before it reaches your inbox. The disadvantage of e-mail filters and anti-spam programs is that sometimes they remove valid e-mail messages. Thus, users should review the contents of the spam messages periodically to ensure they do not contain valid messages.

Phishing

Phishing is a scam in which a perpetrator sends an official looking e-mail message that attempts to obtain your personal and financial information (Figure 11-35). Some phishing e-mail messages ask you to reply with your information; others direct you to a phony Web site, or a pop-up window that looks like a Web site, that collects the information.

If you receive an e-mail message that looks legitimate and requests you update credit card numbers, Social Security numbers, bank account numbers, passwords, or other private information, the FTC recommends you visit the Web site directly to determine if the request is valid.

? FAQ 11-7

How prevalent is spam?

The amount of spam on the Internet has continued to increase for several years. One research study indicates that during one three-month period, more than 92 percent of all e-mail messages were spam. The study also estimates that the United States relays more spam than any other country.

For more information, visit the Computer Concepts CourseMate Web site at www.cengagebrain.com, navigate to the Chapter 11 FAQ resource for this book, and then click Spam.

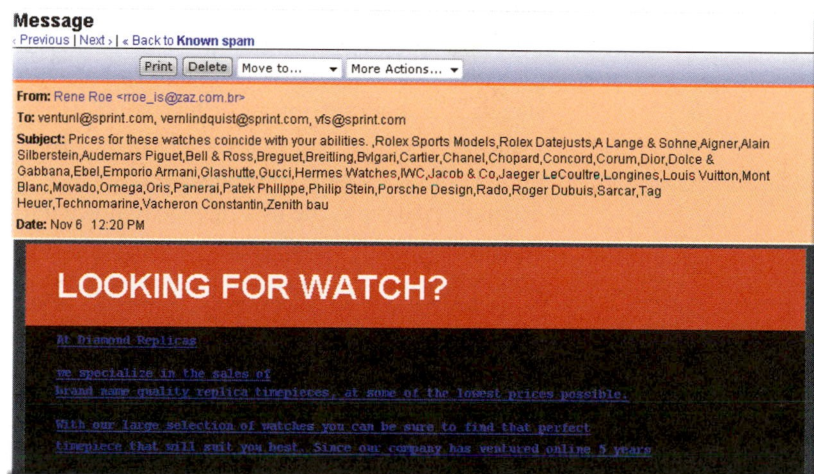

Figure 11-34 An example of spam.

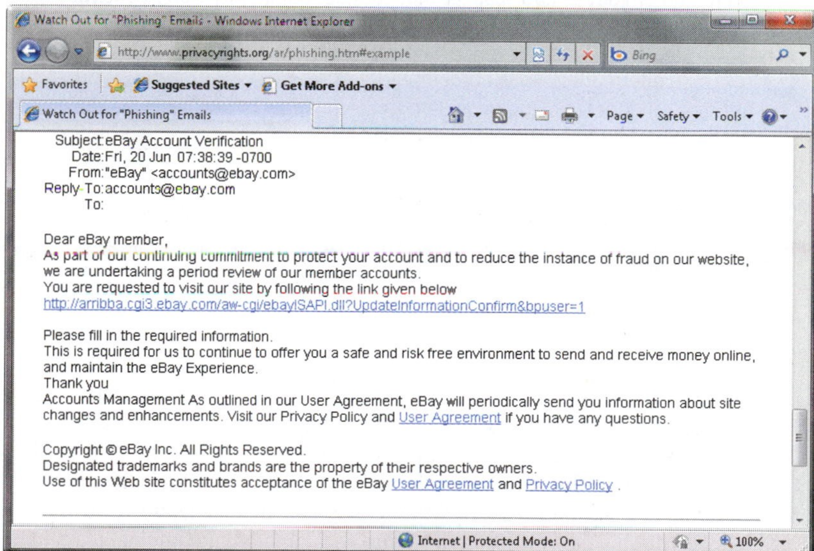

Figure 11-35 An example of a phishing e-mail message.

Never click a link in an e-mail message; instead, retype the Web address in your browser.

A *phishing filter* is a program that warns or blocks you from potentially fraudulent or suspicious Web sites. Some Web browsers include phishing filters. To further help deter spam and phishing scams, Microsoft and others are developing standards that require e-mail messages contain sender identification so that recipients can verify the legitimacy of messages. Read Ethics & Issues 11-4 for a related discussion.

Pharming is a scam, similar to phishing, where a perpetrator attempts to obtain your personal and financial information, except they do so via spoofing. That is, when you type a Web address in the Web browser, you are redirected to a phony Web site that looks legitimate. The phony Web site requests you enter confidential information.

Clickjacking is yet another similar scam. With *clickjacking*, an object that can be clicked on a Web site, such as a button, image, or link, contains a malicious program. When a user clicks the disguised object, a variety of nefarious events may occur. For example, the user may be redirected to a phony Web site that requests personal information, or a virus may download to the computer.

? FAQ 11-8

What do I do if I have been caught in a phishing scam?

If you have been trapped in a phishing scam, immediately change any passwords that may have been compromised. If you have disclosed your debit or credit card numbers, contact your financial institutions. You also should visit http://www.ftc.gov or call the FTC help line at this number: 1-877-FTC-HELP. If you are an employee and suspect that confidential information about your organization has been compromised, immediately notify your supervisor.

For more information, visit the Computer Concepts CourseMate Web site at www.cengagebrain.com, navigate to the Chapter 11 FAQ resource for this book, and then click Phishing Scams.

ETHICS & ISSUES 11-4

Who Should Protect You from Phishing Scams?

If you respond to a phishing attempt, the information you submit ends up in the hands of a scammer, who then either uses the information to access your accounts and take money or sells and trades the information with other criminals. Sadly, the result often is identity theft. Law enforcement agencies believe that many of the phishing schemes are related to organized crime. Some phishing operations result in up to 20 percent of those targeted providing the requested information. More than $2 billion is lost to phishing attacks each year, and the figure is on the rise as the growing amount of ill-gained profits emboldens the scammers. Law enforcement agencies claim that these scams are difficult to stop and that people simply need to learn to ignore the requests for information. Computer users find that the scams often are impossible to distinguish from legitimate requests for information, and that the fault lies with Internet access providers or the makers of e-mail programs and Web browsers. Many modern Web browsers include tools that fight phishing.

Who should be responsible for stopping the phishing phenomenon? What can a person do to protect against phishing when e-mail messages are received from what appear to be legitimate organizations? What can be done to limit or stop the practice of phishing? Are companies and/or consumers to share in the blame for the success of phishing? Why or why not?

Spyware and Adware

Recall from Chapter 8 that *spyware* is a program placed on a computer without the user's knowledge that secretly collects information about the user. Some vendors or employers use spyware to collect information about program usage or employees. Internet advertising firms often collect information about users' Web browsing habits by hiding spyware in adware. *Adware* is a program that displays an online advertisement in a banner or pop-up window on Web pages, e-mail messages, or other Internet services.

Another type of spyware, called a *Web bug*, is hidden on Web pages or in e-mail messages in the form of graphical images. Web businesses use Web bugs to monitor online habits of Web site visitors. Often, Web bugs link to a cookie stored on the hard disk. (Cookies are not considered spyware because you know they exist.)

To remove spyware and adware, you can obtain spyware and adware removers that can detect and delete spyware and adware. Some operating systems and Web browsers include spyware removers.

Privacy Laws

The concern about privacy has led to the enactment of federal and state laws regarding the storage and disclosure of personal data (Figure 11-36). Common points in some of these laws are outlined at the top of the next page.

1. Information collected and stored about individuals should be limited to what is necessary to carry out the function of the business or government agency collecting the data.
2. Once collected, provisions should be made to restrict access to the data to those employees within the organization who need access to it to perform their job duties.
3. Personal information should be released outside the organization collecting the data only when the person has agreed to its disclosure.
4. When information is collected about an individual, the individual should know that the data is being collected and have the opportunity to determine the accuracy of the data.

One law with an apparent legal loophole is the 1970 **Fair Credit Reporting Act**. The act limits the rights of others viewing a credit report to only those with a legitimate business need. The problem is that it does not define a legitimate business need. The result is that just about anyone can claim a legitimate business need and gain access to your credit report.

Date	Law	Purpose
2006	**Telephone Records and Privacy Protection Act**	Makes it illegal to use fraudulent means to obtain someone's telephone records.
2003	**CAN-SPAM Act**	Gives law enforcement the right to impose penalties on people using the Internet to distribute spam.
2002	**Sarbanes-Oxley Act**	Requires corporate officers, auditors, and attorneys of publicly-traded companies follow strict financial reporting guidelines.
2001	**Children's Internet Protection Act (CIPA)**	Protects minors from inappropriate content when accessing the Internet in schools and libraries.
2001	**Provide Appropriate Tools Required to Intercept and Obstruct Terrorism (PATRIOT) Act**	Gives law enforcement the right to monitor people's activities, including Web and e-mail habits.
1999	**Gramm-Leach-Bliley Act (GLBA) or Financial Modernization Act**	Protects consumers from disclosure of their personal financial information and requires institutions to alert customers of information disclosure policies.
1998	**Children's Online Privacy Protection Act (COPPA)**	Requires Web sites protect personal information of children under 13 years of age.
1998	**Digital Millennium Copyright Act (DMCA)**	Makes it illegal to circumvent antipiracy schemes in commercial software; outlaws sale of devices that copy software illegally.
1997	**No Electronic Theft (NET) Act**	Closes a narrow loophole in the law that allowed people to give away copyrighted material (such as software) on the Internet without legal repercussions.
1996	**Health Insurance Portability and Accountability Act (HIPAA)**	Protects individuals against the wrongful disclosure of their health information.
1996	**National Information Infrastructure Protection Act**	Penalizes theft of information across state lines, threats against networks, and computer system trespassing.
1994	**Computer Abuse Amendments Act**	Amends 1984 act to outlaw transmission of harmful computer code such as viruses.
1992	**Cable Act**	Extends the privacy of the Cable Communications Policy Act of 1984 to include cellular and other wireless services.
1991	**Telephone Consumer Protection Act**	Restricts activities of telemarketers.
1988	**Computer Matching and Privacy Protection Act**	Regulates the use of government data to determine the eligibility of individuals for federal benefits.
1988	**Video Privacy Protection Act**	Forbids retailers from releasing or selling video-rental records without customer consent or a court order.
1986	**Electronic Communications Privacy Act (ECPA)**	Provides the same right of privacy protection for the postal delivery service and telephone companies to the new forms of electronic communications, such as voice mail, e-mail, and cell phones.
1984	**Cable Communications Policy Act**	Regulates disclosure of cable television subscriber records.
1984	**Computer Fraud and Abuse Act**	Outlaws unauthorized access of federal government computers.
1978	**Right to Financial Privacy Act**	Strictly outlines procedures federal agencies must follow when looking at customer records in banks.
1974	**Privacy Act**	Forbids federal agencies from allowing information to be used for a reason other than that for which it was collected.
1974	**Family Educational Rights and Privacy Act**	Gives students and parents access to school records and limits disclosure of records to unauthorized parties.
1970	**Fair Credit Reporting Act**	Prohibits credit reporting agencies from releasing credit information to unauthorized people and allows consumers to review their own credit records.

Figure 11-36 Summary of the major U.S. government laws concerning privacy.

Social Engineering

As related to the use of computers, **social engineering** is defined as gaining unauthorized access or obtaining confidential information by taking advantage of the trusting human nature of some victims and the naivety of others. Some social engineers trick their victims into revealing confidential information such as user names and passwords on the telephone, in person, or on the Internet. Techniques they use include pretending to be an administrator or other authoritative figure, feigning an emergency situation, or impersonating an acquaintance. Social engineers also obtain information from users who do not destroy or conceal information properly. These perpetrators sift through company dumpsters, watch or film people dialing telephone numbers or using ATMs, and snoop around computers looking for openly displayed confidential information.

Social Engineering

For more information, visit the Computer Concepts CourseMate Web site at www.cengagebrain.com, navigate to the Chapter 11 Web Link resource for this book, and then click Social Engineering.

Employee Monitoring

Employee monitoring involves the use of computers to observe, record, and review an employee's use of a computer, including communications such as e-mail messages, keyboard activity (used to measure productivity), and Web sites visited. Many programs exist that easily allow employers to monitor employees. Further, it is legal for employers to use these programs.

A frequently debated issue is whether an employer has the right to read employee e-mail messages. Actual policies vary widely. Some companies declare that they will review e-mail messages regularly, and others state that e-mail messages are private. In some states, if a company does not have a formal e-mail policy, it can read e-mail messages without employee notification. One survey discovered that more than 73 percent of companies search and/or read employee files, voice mail, e-mail messages, Web connections, and other networking communications. Several lawsuits have been filed against employers because many believe that such internal communications should be private. Read Ethics & Issues 11-5 for a related discussion.

Another controversial issue relates to the use of cameras to monitor employees, customers, and the public. Many people feel that this use of video cameras is a violation of privacy.

Content Filtering

One of the more controversial issues that surround the Internet is its widespread availability of objectionable material, such as racist literature, violence, and obscene pictures. Some believe that such materials should be banned. Others believe that the materials should be filtered, that is, restricted. **Content filtering** is the process of restricting access to certain material on the Web. Content filtering opponents argue that banning any materials violates constitutional guarantees of free speech and personal rights.

Many businesses use content filtering to limit employees' Web access. These businesses argue that employees are unproductive when visiting inappropriate or objectionable Web sites. Some schools, libraries, and parents use content filtering to restrict access to minors.

One approach to content filtering is through a rating system of the *Internet Content Rating Association* (*ICRA*), which is similar to those used for movies and videos. Major Web sites such as

ETHICS & ISSUES 11-5

Should Text Messages Sent by Employees Be Private?

When an employee sends or receives an e-mail message using his or her employer's e-mail server, the company most likely retains a backup of the message, which can be used as evidence against the employee if the employee is suspected of engaging in unscrupulous activity. When an employee sends a text message using a company-issued smart phone for such activity, however, the smart phone provider may store a record of the message. If an employer's workplace policy requires an employee to disclose all text message communications with customers, vendors, and competitors, the employee is required legally to divulge those communications. The U.S. Supreme Court ruled that an employer can read workers' text messages if there is reason to believe the texts violate workplace rules. The Court held that employees can purchase their own cell phones if they need to make personal calls or text messages. Employees may believe they have an expectation of privacy and the right of self-expression when they use an employer's cell phone. Employers argue, however, that because they provide the devices and service to the employee, they should have a right to view the content of the messages.

Should text messages sent by employees be private? Why or why not? How can employers create and enforce policies regarding the content of text messages sent on employer-issued smart phones? Should employers demand that smart phone providers offer the option to send all employee text message communications to the company on a monthly basis? Why or why not?

Ethics & Issues

For the complete text of the Ethics & Issues boxes found in this chapter, visit the Computer Concepts CourseMate Web site at www.cengagebrain.com and then navigate to the Chapter 11 Ethics & Issues resource for this book.

Yahoo!, AOL, and MSN use the rating system established by the ICRA. If content at the Web site goes beyond the rating limits set in the Web browser software, a user cannot access the Web site. Concerned parents can set the rating limits and prevent these limits from being changed by using a password.

Another approach to content filtering is to use filtering software. **Web filtering software** is a program that restricts access to specified Web sites. Some also filter sites that use specific words. Others allow you to filter e-mail messages, chat rooms, and programs. Many Internet security programs include a firewall, antivirus program, and filtering capabilities combined (Figure 11-37).

Figure 11-37 Many Internet security programs include content filtering capabilities, where users can block specified Web sites and applications.

✔ QUIZ YOURSELF 11-3

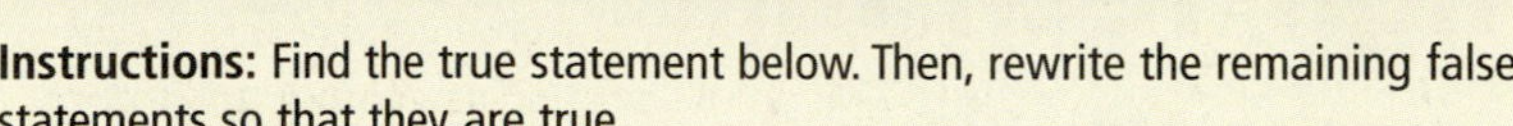

Instructions: Find the true statement below. Then, rewrite the remaining false statements so that they are true.

1. A code of conduct gives authors and artists exclusive rights to duplicate, publish, and sell their materials.
2. Factors that cause CVS include prolonged typing, prolonged mouse usage, or continual shifting between the mouse and the keyboard.
3. Phishing is the discovery, collection, and analysis of evidence found on computers and networks.
4. Spam is Internet junk mail.
5. Users should store obsolete computers and devices in their basement or attic.
6. You can assume that information on the Web is correct.

Quiz Yourself Online: To further check your knowledge of pages 579 through 591, visit the Computer Concepts CourseMate Web site at www.cengagebrain.com, navigate to the Chapter 11 Quiz Yourself resource for this book, and then click Objectives 10 – 12.

Chapter Summary

This chapter identified some potential computer risks and the safeguards that organizations and individuals can implement to minimize these risks. Wireless security risks and safeguards also were discussed.

The chapter presented computer-related health issues and their preventions. The chapter ended with a discussion about ethical issues surrounding information accuracy, intellectual property rights, codes of conduct, green computing, and information privacy.

Computer Usage @ Work

National and Local Security

Since 2001, the federal government, local governments, businesses, and individuals have been implementing aggressive new security measures because of the increase in terrorist activity. A security threat can exist anywhere, and it is nearly impossible for humans alone to protect the country. As a result, computers now assist governments, law enforcement officials, business owners, and other individuals with monitoring and maintaining security.

Advancements in computer vision enable computers to monitor indoor and outdoor areas that might be subject to a high amount of criminal activity. For example, some cities are installing cameras in problematic areas. A computer program analyzes the output from the camera and can determine whether two or more people in close proximity to one another might be engaged in a physical confrontation. If the computer detects suspicious behavior, it automatically notifies local law enforcement.

Computers also use facial recognition to identify individuals who do not belong in a particular area. For example, one theme park in Florida often takes a picture of individuals they escort out of and ban from the park. As visitors walk from their cars to the park, surveillance cameras positioned in strategic locations scan visitors' faces and compare them to the database containing images of those who are banned from the park. If the computer finds a match, it alerts a security officer who then can investigate the situation. Thousands of people visit theme parks each day, and computers make it easier to perform the otherwise impossible task of identifying those who might be trespassing.

The federal government, particularly the Department of Homeland Security, uses a computerized No Fly List to track individuals who are not authorized to travel on commercial flights within the United States. When an individual makes a reservation, a computer compares his or her name to the names on the No Fly List. If the computer finds a match, the individual must prove that he or she is not the person on the list before being allowed to board an aircraft.

Whether you are walking outside, visiting an attraction, or traveling, the chances are good that computers are, in some way, ensuring your safety.

For more information, visit the Computer Concepts CourseMate Web site at www.cengagebrain.com, navigate to the Chapter 11 Computer Usage @ Work resource for this book, and then click National and Local Security.

High-Tech Talk

Encryption Algorithms: The Brains behind Encryption

As mentioned in this chapter, encryption is a process of converting readable data into unreadable characters to prevent unauthorized access. Various encryption algorithms are used to encrypt data, with some more secure than others. The chapter showed a few simple encryption algorithms. Individuals and organizations often desire more secure encryption, which requires a complex encryption algorithm. Thousands of encryption algorithms exist, and it even is possible to write your own. Commonly used secure encryption algorithms include Blowfish, DES, 3DES, and IDEA.

The Blowfish encryption algorithm was introduced in 1993 as a free alternative to other encryption algorithms that were available at that time. *Blowfish*, which has been thoroughly tested since its development and has proven to be a strong algorithm, uses a key length varying between 32 and 448 bits and is applied to a block of data as opposed to single bits of data.

The *DES* (Data Encryption Standard) encryption algorithm in the late 1970s was developed by the United States government and IBM. This standard uses a 56-bit key to encrypt 64-bit blocks of data at a time. The encryption process requires that each block of the message go through 16 different stages, adding to the strength of the algorithm. Advancements in technology, however, made it easier and faster for computers with increased processing capabilities to decrypt these 56-bit keys, which were only 7 characters long. As a result, the Triple-DES (*3DES*) encryption algorithm was developed. This algorithm uses the original Data Encryption Standard to encrypt the data with the first 56-bit key and then decrypts the data with another 56-bit key. Finally, a third 56-bit key encrypts the data once again. This process creates a total key length of 168 bits, which is significantly more difficult to compromise.

IDEA (International Data Encryption Algorithm) was developed in the early 1990s to replace the DES encryption algorithm. This algorithm uses the same key for encryption and decryption on blocks of data that are 64 bits long. Unlike the DES algorithm, IDEA uses a 128-bit key, greatly increasing the complexity and security of the encrypted data.

The U.S. government uses the Advanced Encryption Standard (*AES*), mostly for unclassified data. In addition, various other organizations use AES. Windows 7 Ultimate edition includes *BitLocker Drive Encryption* (Figure 11-38), a security feature using the Encrypting File System (*EFS*) to encrypt data. EFS uses the Advanced Encryption Standard to protect files and data from almost any method of unauthorized access. When a user encrypts a file, EFS generates a random number for the file that EFS calls the file's FEK (file encryption key) to encrypt the data. EFS then uses FEK to encrypt the file's contents with the encryption algorithm. The user's public key then encrypts the FEK using the RSA public-key-based encryption algorithm, and the encrypted FEK then is stored with the file. The entire encryption process happens behind the scenes for the user, who simply completes a few mouse clicks to encrypt a folder or file. That is part of the elegance of EFS: while it is simple for a user, it is very difficult for any unauthorized user without the correct keys to crack the encryption. In the end, that is the key to keeping your data safe and sound.

For more information, visit the Computer Concepts CourseMate Web site at www.cengagebrain.com, navigate to the Chapter 11 High-Tech Talk resource for this book, and then click Encryption Algorithms.

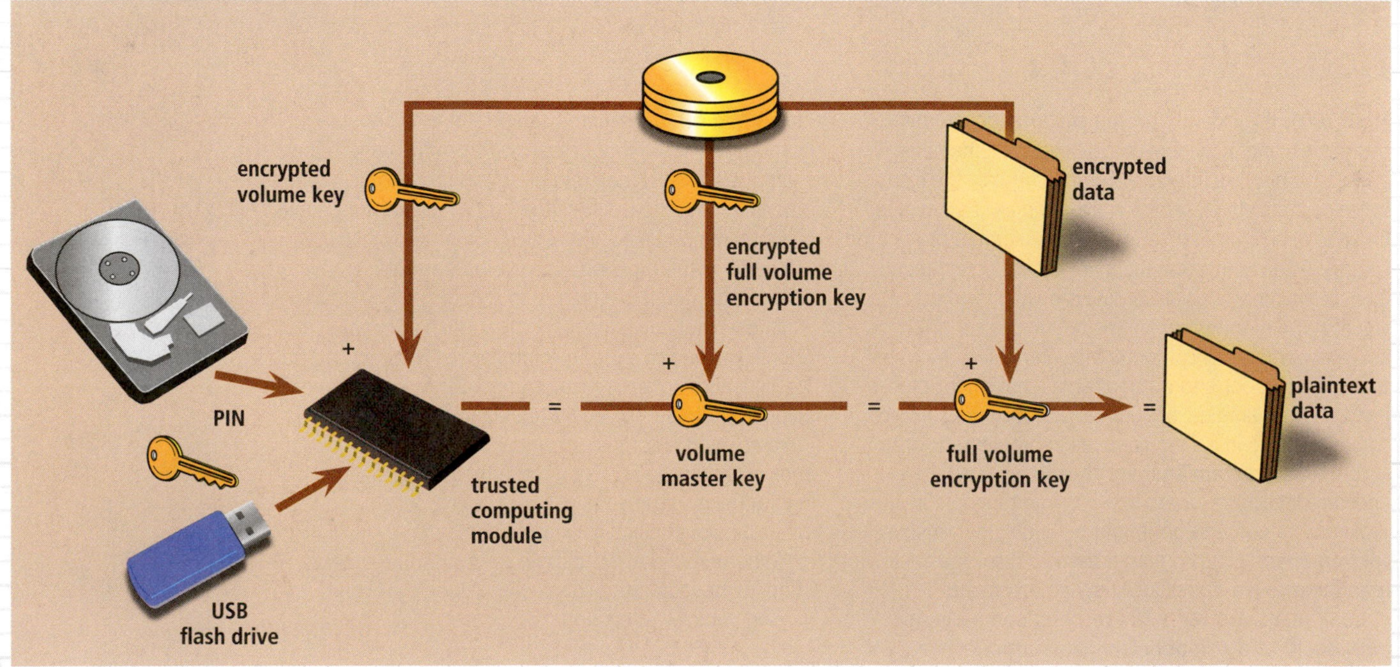

Figure 11-38 One authentication scenario in BitLocker Drive Encryption.

Companies on the Cutting Edge

MCAFEE Intrusion Prevention Products Developer

The *McAfee* Initiative to Fight Cybercrime is a global effort to thwart security threats and criminal activity. The world's largest dedicated security technology company has partnered with experts in law enforcement, education, government, and society to investigate, prosecute, and attempt to prevent security breaches.

McAfee products protect more than 60 million consumers, small- and medium-sized businesses, governmental agencies, and large corporations from malware, spam, and unauthorized access. In addition, more than 100 million mobile devices are protected with McAfee software. The corporation takes its name from its founder, John McAfee, who started the company in 1987 from his Santa Clara, California, home.

Recently, McAfee launched a new online backup service with unlimited capacity that allows consumers to back up and encrypt their important files such as documents, photos, music, and e-mail messages.

SYMANTEC Computer Security Solutions Leader

Symantec's programmers analyzed every line of code, rewrote programs, and developed a new security model to create its latest versions of Norton AntiVirus and Norton Internet Security. The results are programs that use less hard disk space, decrease starting and scanning time, and average less than 7 MB of memory. The more than 100 performance improvements offer advanced protection for millions of computer users worldwide.

The California-based company is one of the ten largest software corporations in the world. It was founded in 1982 and has offices in more than 40 countries. Its primary manufacturing facility is located in Dublin, Ireland.

Symantec recently released the latest version of its Norton Internet Security software. A rating service tested the level of protection provided by 10 different security products and gave Norton Internet Security the only perfect score.

For more information, visit the Computer Concepts CourseMate Web site at www.cengagebrain.com and then navigate to the Chapter 11 Companies on the Cutting Edge resource for this book.

Technology Trailblazers

RICHARD STALLMAN Software Freedom Advocate

The relationship between software and freedom is key to *Richard Stallman*'s philosophy. Since his days as a physics student at Harvard University, he has advocated free software and campaigned against software patents and copyright laws. His pioneering work developed the concept of *copyleft*, which gives each person who has purchased a software product the ability to copy, adapt, and distribute the program as long as the new software also has the same lack of restrictions.

Stallman began the GNU/Linux Project in 1983 as an effort to develop and use the copyleft concept. Linux is an outgrowth of this project, which continues to be a forum for software development, ethical practices, and political campaigning. He also started the Free Software Foundation (FSF) in 1985 to promote writing free software for the GNU Project. The Free Software Directory catalogs more than 5,300 packages that run on the Linux and GNU operating systems.

GENE SPAFFORD Computer Security Expert

The Morris Worm, also called the MBDF virus, is considered the first computer worm distributed on the Internet, and *Gene Spafford* gained fame for deconstructing and analyzing this 1988 attack. His work led to the conviction of a Cornell University student, Robert Morris. Today, Spafford, who also is known as Spaf, is recognized as one of the world's foremost experts in the computer security, intelligence, cybercrime, and software engineering fields.

For 30 years, he has advised major corporations, including Microsoft, Intel, and Unisys, the U.S. Air Force, the Federal Bureau of Investigation, and two U.S. presidents. He is noted for several firsts in the computer security field. For example, he defined the terms, software forensics and firewall, wrote the first English-language book on the topics of viruses and malware, and founded the world's first multidisciplinary academic security awareness group: the Center for Education and Research in Information Assurance and Security (CERIAS).

For more information, visit the Computer Concepts CourseMate Web site at www.cengagebrain.com and then navigate to the Chapter 11 Technology Trailblazers resource for this book.

STUDENT ASSIGNMENTS

Chapter Review

The Chapter Review reinforces the main concepts presented in this chapter.

To listen to an audio version of this Chapter Review, visit the Computer Concepts CourseMate Web site at www.cengagebrain.com and then navigate to the Chapter 11 Chapter Review resource for this book.

1. **What Are Computer Security Risks, and What Are the Types of Cybercrime Perpetrators?** A **computer security risk** is any event or action that could cause a loss of or damage to computer hardware, software, data, information, or processing capability. Any illegal act involving a computer is a **computer crime**; the term **cybercrime** refers to online or Internet-based illegal acts. Perpetrators of cybercrime include: **hacker**, **cracker**, **script kiddie**, corporate spy, unethical employee, **cyberextortionist**, and **cyberterrorist**.

2. **What Are Various Internet and Network Attacks, and How Can Users Safeguard against These Attacks?** A computer **virus** is a potentially damaging program that affects, or infects, a computer negatively by altering the way the computer works without the user's knowledge or permission. A **worm** is a program that copies itself repeatedly, using up resources and possibly shutting down the computer or network. A **Trojan horse** is a program that hides within or looks like a legitimate program. A **rootkit** is a program that hides in a computer and allows someone from a remote location to take full control of the computer. To take precautions against this *malware*, do not start a computer with removable media in the drives or ports. Never open an e-mail attachment unless you are expecting the attachment and it is from a **trusted source**. Disable *macros* in documents that are not from a trusted source. Install an **antivirus program** and a personal firewall. Stay informed about any new virus alert or **virus hoax**. To defend against a **botnet**, a **denial of service attack**, improper use of a **back door**, and **spoofing**, users can install a **firewall**, install *intrusion detection software*, and set up a *honeypot*.

3. **What Are Techniques to Prevent Unauthorized Computer Access and Use?** **Unauthorized access** is the use of a computer or network without permission. **Unauthorized use** is the use of a computer or its data for unapproved or illegal activities. Organizations can take measures such as implementing a written acceptable use policy (AUP), a **firewall**, *intrusion detection software*, an *access control*, and an **audit trail**. Access controls include a **user name** and **password** or *passphrase*, a *CAPTCHA*, a *possessed object*, and a **biometric device**.

Visit the Computer Concepts CourseMate Web site at www.cengagebrain.com, navigate to the Chapter 11 Quiz Yourself resource for this book, and then click Objectives 1 – 3.

4. **What Are Safeguards against Hardware Theft and Vandalism?** **Hardware theft** is the act of stealing computer equipment. **Hardware vandalism** is the act of defacing or destroying computer equipment. The best preventive measures against hardware theft and vandalism are common sense and a constant awareness of the risk. Physical devices and practical security measures, such as locked doors and windows, can help protect equipment. Passwords, possessed objects, and biometrics can reduce the risk of theft or render a computer useless if it is stolen.

5. **How Do Software Manufacturers Protect against Software Piracy?** Software **piracy** is the unauthorized and illegal duplication of copyrighted software. To protect themselves from software piracy, manufacturers issue a **license agreement** and require **product activation**.

6. **How Does Encryption Work, and Why Is It Necessary?** **Encryption** prevents information theft and unauthorized access by converting readable data into unreadable characters. To read the data, a recipient must **decrypt**, or decipher, it into a readable form. An *encryption algorithm*, or *cypher*, converts readable *plaintext* into unreadable *ciphertext*. Encryption is used to protect information on the Internet and networks.

7. **What Types of Devices Are Available to Protect Computers from System Failure?** A *system failure* is the prolonged malfunction of a computer. A common cause of system failure is an electrical power variation such as **noise**, an **undervoltage**, or an **overvoltage**. A **surge protector**, also called a *surge suppressor*, uses special electrical components to smooth out minor noise, provide a stable current flow, and keep an overvoltage from reaching the computer and other electronic equipment.

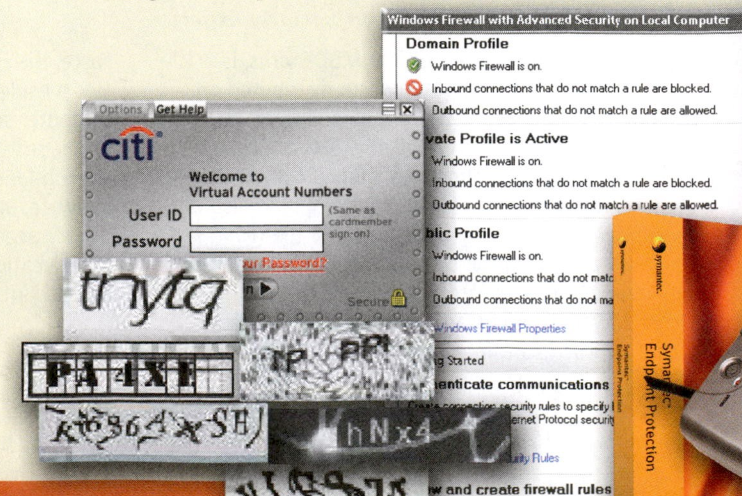

Chapter Review

An **uninterruptible power supply (UPS)** contains surge protection circuits and one or more batteries that can provide power during a temporary loss of power.

8. What Are Options for Backing Up Computer Resources? A **backup** is a duplicate of a file, program, or disk that can be used to **restore** the file if the original is lost, damaged, or destroyed. Users can opt for a *full backup* or a *selective backup*. Some users implement a *three-generation backup* policy that preserves three copies of important files: the *grandparent*, the *parent*, and the *child*. Others use RAID or continuous backup. Most operating systems and backup devices include a backup program.

9. What Risks and Safeguards Are Associated with Wireless Communications? Wireless access poses additional security risks. Intruders connect to other wireless networks to gain free Internet access or an organization's confidential data. Some individuals intercept and monitor communications as they transmit. Others connect to a network through an unsecured wireless access point (WAP), sometimes using the techniques of *war driving* or *war flying*. Some safeguards include firewalls, reconfiguring the WAP, and ensuring equipment uses a wireless security standard, such as *Wi-Fi Protected Access* (*WPA*) and *802.11i*.

Visit the Computer Concepts CourseMate Web site at www.cengagebrain.com, navigate to the Chapter 11 Quiz Yourself resource for this book, and then click Objectives 4 – 9.

10. How Can Health-Related Disorders and Injuries Due to Computer Use Be Prevented? A computer-related **repetitive strain injury (RSI)** can include *tendonitis* and *carpal tunnel syndrome* (*CTS*). Another health-related condition is eyestrain associated with **computer vision syndrome** (*CVS*). To prevent health-related disorders, take frequent breaks, use precautionary exercises and techniques, and use *ergonomics* when planning the workplace. **Computer addiction** occurs when the computer consumes someone's entire social life.

11. What Are Issues Related to Information Accuracy, Intellectual Property Rights, Codes of Conduct, and Green Computing? **Computer ethics** govern the use of computers and information systems. Issues in computer ethics include the responsibility for information accuracy and the **intellectual property rights** to which creators are entitled for their works. An IT (information technology) **code of conduct** helps determine whether a specific computer action is ethical or unethical. **Green computing** reduces the electricity and environmental waste while using a computer.

12. What Are Issues Surrounding Information Privacy? **Information privacy** is the right of individuals and companies to deny or restrict the collection and use of information about them. Issues surrounding information privacy include the following. An electronic profile combines data about an individual's Web use with data from public sources, which then is sold. A **cookie** is a file that a Web server stores on a computer to collect data about the user. *Spyware* is a program placed on a computer that secretly collects information about the user. *Adware* is a program that displays an online advertisement in a banner or pop-up window. **Spam** is an unsolicited e-mail message or newsgroup posting sent to many recipients or newsgroups at once. **Phishing** is a scam in which a perpetrator attempts to obtain personal or financial information. The concern about privacy has led to the enactment of many federal and state laws regarding the disclosure of data. As related to the use of computers, **social engineering** is defined as gaining unauthorized access or obtaining confidential information by taking advantage of the trusting human nature of some victims and the naivety of others. **Employee monitoring** uses computers to observe, record, and review an employee's computer use. **Content filtering** restricts access to certain materials on the Web.

Visit the Computer Concepts CourseMate Web site at www.cengagebrain.com, navigate to the Chapter 11 Quiz Yourself resource for this book, and then click Objectives 10 – 12.

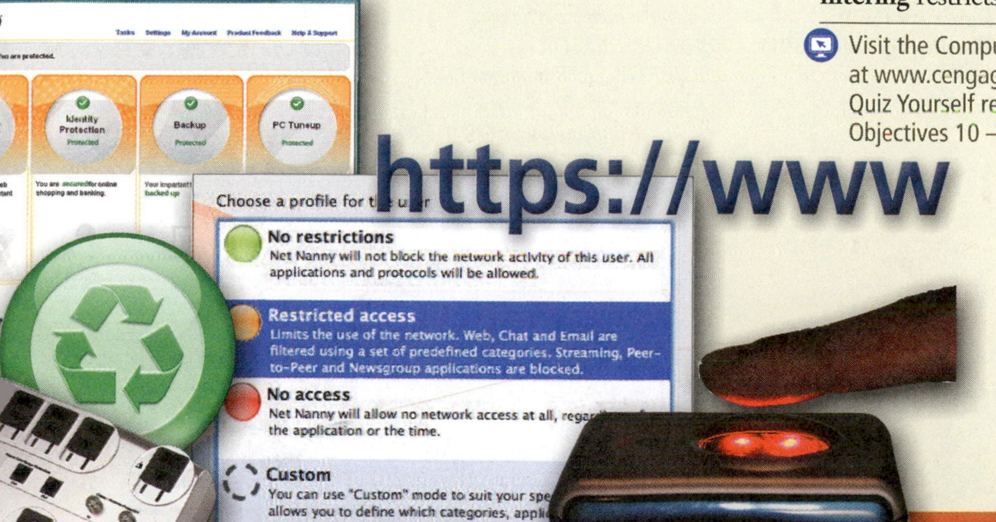

STUDENT ASSIGNMENTS

Key Terms

You should know the Primary Terms and be familiar with the Secondary Terms. The list below helps focus your study.

To see an example of and a definition for each term, and to access current and additional information from the Web, visit the Computer Concepts CourseMate Web site at www.cengagebrain.com and then navigate to the Chapter 11 Key Terms resource for this book.

Primary Terms

(shown in bold-black characters in the chapter)

anti-spam program (587)
antivirus program (560)
audit trail (565)
back door (562)
back up (577)
backup (577)
biometric device (568)
botnet (562)
code of conduct (582)
computer addiction (581)
computer crime (556)
computer ethics (581)
computer security risk (556)
computer vision syndrome (579)
content filtering (590)
cookie (585)
copyright (582)
cracker (556)
cybercrime (556)
cyberextortionist (557)
cyberterrorist (557)
decrypt (573)
denial of service attack (562)
digital certificate (574)
digital forensics (569)
digital signature (574)
DoS attack (562)
e-mail filtering (587)
employee monitoring (590)
encryption (573)
Fair Credit Reporting Act (588)
firewall (563)
green computing (583)
hacker (556)
hardware theft (570)
hardware vandalism (570)
information privacy (584)
information theft (572)
inoculate (561)
intellectual property rights (582)
license agreement (571)
noise (575)
online security service (558)
overvoltage (575)
password (566)
personal firewall (564)
personal identification number (PIN) (568)
pharming (588)
phishing (587)
piracy (571)
power surge (575)
product activation (572)
quarantine (561)
repetitive strain injury (RSI) (579)
restore (577)
rootkit (558)
script kiddie (556)
secure site (574)
social engineering (590)
software theft (571)
spam (587)
spoofing (563)
surge protector (576)
Trojan horse (558)
trusted source (560)
unauthorized access (564)
unauthorized use (564)
undervoltage (575)
uninterruptible power supply (UPS) (576)
user name (566)
virus (558)
virus definition (560)
virus hoax (561)
virus signature (560)
Web filtering software (591)
worm (558)
zombie (562)

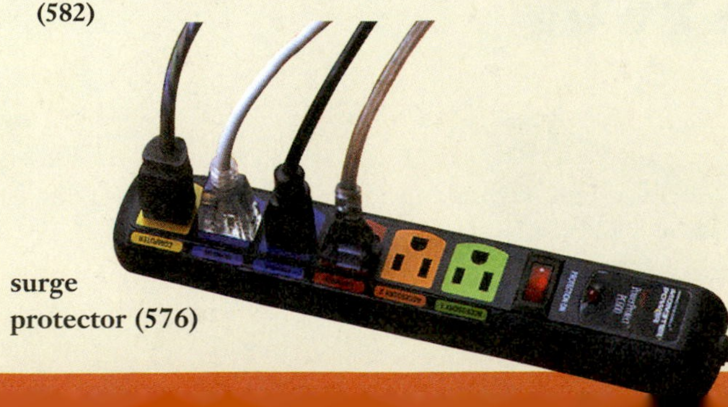

surge protector (576)

Secondary Terms

(shown in italic characters in the chapter)

1024-bit encryption (574)
128-bit encryption (574)
40-bit encryption (574)
802.11i (578)
access control (565)
access point mapping (578)
adware (588)
asymmetric key encryption (573)
authentication (565)
biometric payment (568)
blackout (575)
bot (562)
brownout (575)
Business Software Alliance (BSA) (572)
CAPTCHA (567)
carpal tunnel syndrome (CTS) (579)
CERT/CC (558)
certificate authority (CA) (574)
child (577)
ciphertext (573)
clickjacking (588)
Computer Emergency Response Team Coordination Center (558)
computer forensics (569)
crimeware (556)
CVS (579)
cyberforensics (569)
cyberwarfare (557)
cypher (573)
DDoS (distributed DoS) attack (562)
digital rights management (DRM) (582)
e-mail spoofing (563)
encryption algorithm (573)
encryption key (573)
end-user license agreement (EULA) (571)
ENERGY STAR program (583)
ergonomics (580)
fault-tolerant computer (577)
full backup (577)
grandparent (577)
hash (574)
honeypot (564)
identification (565)
intellectual property (IP) (582)
Internet Content Rating Association (ICRA) (590)
intrusion detection software (564)
IP spoofing (563)
Joule (576)
keygen (571)
macros (560)
malicious software (558)
malware (558)
network forensics (569)
offline UPS (576)
offsite (577)
online UPS (577)
parent (577)
passphrase (566)
payload (558)
phishing filter (587)
plaintext (573)
possessed object (568)
power usage effectiveness (583)
Pretty Good Privacy (PGP) (574)
private key encryption (573)
proxy server (564)
public key encryption (573)
real time location system (RTLS) (570)
Secure HTTP (S-HTTP) (575)
Secure Sockets Layer (SSL) (575)
selective backup (577)
session cookie (586)
single-user license agreement (571)
spike (575)
spim (587)
spit (587)
spyware (588)
SSID (578)
standby UPS (576)
surge suppressor (576)
symmetric key encryption (573)
system failure (575)
tendonitis (579)
three-generation backup (577)
Transport Layer Security (TLS) (575)
Underwriters Laboratories (UL) 1449 standard (576)
user ID (566)
virtual private network (VPN) (575)
war driving (578)
war flying (578)
Web bug (588)
Wi-Fi Protected Access (WPA) (578)
zombie army (562)

Checkpoint

The Checkpoint exercises test your knowledge of the chapter concepts. The page number containing the answer appears in parentheses after each exercise. The Beyond the Book exercises will help broaden your understanding of the concepts presented in this chapter.

To complete the Checkpoint exercises interactively, visit the Computer Concepts CourseMate Web site at www.cengagebrain.com and then navigate to the Chapter 11 Checkpoint resource for this book.

True/False

Mark T for True and F for False.

_____ 1. Not all breaches to computer security are planned. (556)

_____ 2. The term, cyberwarfare, describes an attack whose goal ranges from disabling a government's computer network to crippling a country. (557)

_____ 3. Many methods exist to guarantee completely a computer or network is safe from computer viruses and other malware. (560)

_____ 4. Cybercriminals install malicious bots on unprotected computers to create a zombie army. (562)

_____ 5. A honeypot is a computer that is isolated and, therefore, immune to attack. (564)

_____ 6. Biometric payment involves a customer's fingerprint being read by a fingerprint reader that is linked to a payment method such as a checking account or credit card. (568)

_____ 7. Some businesses use a real time location system (RTLS) to track and identify the location of high-risk or high-value items. (570)

_____ 8. A program called a keygen, short for key generator, creates software registration numbers and sometimes activation codes. (571)

_____ 9. With public key encryption, both the originator and the recipient use the same secret key to encrypt and decrypt the data. (573)

_____ 10. A digitial signature is a mathematical formula that generates a code from the contents of the message. (574)

_____ 11. Digital rights management (DRM) is a strategy designed to prevent illegal distribution of movies, music, and other digital content. (582)

_____ 12. Green computing involves reducing the electricity while using a computer, but the practice increases environmental waste. (583)

Multiple Choice

Select the best answer.

1. A _____ is a program that hides in a computer and allows someone from a remote location to take full control of the computer. (558)
   a. worm b. rootkit
   c. payload d. cookie

2. Malware is a term that can be used to describe _____. (558)
   a. worms b. rootkits
   c. back doors d. all of the above

3. A _____ is an assault whose purpose is to disrupt computer access to an Internet service such as the Web or e-mail. (562)
   a. denial of service attack b. zombie
   c. Trojan horse d. virus hoax

4. _____ involves the examination of computer media, programs, data and log files on computers, servers, and networks. (569)
   a. Encryption key b. E-mail filtering
   c. Digital forensics d. Trusted source

5. Physical access controls, such as locked doors and windows, usually are adequate to protect against _____. (570)
   a. software piracy b. unauthorized access
   c. hardware theft d. all of the above

6. A(n) _____ is a programmed formula that the originator of the data uses to encrypt the plaintext and the recipient of the data uses to decrypt the ciphertext. (573)
   a. botnet
   b. certificate authority
   c. encryption algorithm
   d. encryption key

7. Some organizations continually review their _____, which is a ratio that measures how much power enters the computer facility, or data center, against the amount of power required to run the computers. (583)
   a. uninterruptible power supplies
   b. public key encryption
   c. ENERGY STAR program
   d. power usage effectiveness (PUE)

8. As related to the use of computers, _____ is defined as gaining unauthorized access or obtaining confidential information by taking advantage of the trusting human nature of some victims and the naivety of others. (590)
   a. phishing b. pharming
   c. social engineering d. a virus hoax

STUDENT ASSIGNMENTS

Checkpoint

Matching Match the terms with their definitions.

_____ 1. virus (558)
_____ 2. trusted source (560)
_____ 3. quarantine (561)
_____ 4. botnet (562)
_____ 5. spoofing (563)
_____ 6. personal firewall (564)
_____ 7. passphrase (566)
_____ 8. encryption algorithm (573)
_____ 9. biometric device (568)
_____ 10. surge protector (576)

a. set of steps that can convert readable plaintext into unreadable ciphertext
b. private combination of words, often containing mixed capitalization and punctuation, associated with a user name that allows access to certain computer resources
c. protects a personal computer and its data from unauthorized intrusions
d. organization or person you believe will not send a virus infected file knowingly
e. area of the hard disk that holds an infected file until the infection can be removed
f. uses special electrical components to smooth out minor noise, provide a stable current flow, and keep an overvoltage from reaching the computer and other electronic equipment
g. group of compromised computers connected to a network such as the Internet that is being used as part of a network that attacks other networks, usually for nefarious purposes
h. translates a personal characteristic into digital code
i. technique intruders use to make their network or Internet transmission appear legitimate to a victim computer or network
j. potentially damaging computer program that affects, or infects, a computer negatively by altering the way the computer works without the user's knowledge or permission

Short Answer Write a brief answer to each of the following questions.

1. How do antivirus programs detect and identify a virus? ___________ What is a virus hoax? ___________
2. Describe the ENERGY STAR program. ___________ How should users handle obsolete computers? ___________
3. What is information privacy? ___________ List five ways to safeguard your personal information. ___________
4. What are two methods for avoiding phishing attacks? ___________ How does clickjacking work? ___________
5. Who uses content filtering and why? ___________ Describe a rating system used for content filtering. ___________

Beyond the Book Follow the book element instructions below; present your findings (brief report, presentation, discussion, or other means).

1. Ethics & Issues — Select an Ethics & Issues in this chapter (562, 568, 572, 588, 590), find a recent newspaper/magazine article that supports one point of view presented, and then evaluate the article.
2. Computer Usage @ Work — Use the Web or a recent newspaper/magazine to locate three additional unique usages of computer technology in the national and local security field (591). What makes the use of these technologies unique to the national and local security field?
3. Companies on the Cutting Edge and Technology Trailblazers — Use the Web or a recent newspaper/magazine to locate an interesting fact about McAfee, Symantec, Richard Stallman, or Gene Spafford that was not presented in the chapter (593).
4. High-Tech Talk — Locate a recent newspaper/magazine article that discusses topics related to Encryption Algorithms (592). Would you recommend the article you found? Why or why not?
5. FAQs and Web Links — Use the Web or a recent newspaper/magazine to locate three additional facts about an FAQ (559, 562, 567, 569, 577, 578, 587, 588) and Web Link (558, 562, 564, 568, 570, 572, 574, 576, 578, 582, 586, 590) that were not presented in the chapter.
6. Looking Ahead — Use the Web or a recent newspaper/magazine to discover additional uses of the technology presented in Brain Waves, Behavior Tracked to Prevent and Solve Crimes (569).
7. Innovative Computing — Use the Web or a recent newspaper/magazine to locate two additional interesting facts about RECAPTCHAs Help Digitize Newspapers, Books (567) or Customers' Behavior, Conversations Monitored (585).
8. Making Use of the Web — Visit three of the Learning sites (135) and outline the information on each Web site and the possible uses for each Web site.
9. Digital Forensics — Select a topic from the Digital Forensics feature (606) and then create a presentation about the topic using the Web or a magazine article. Discuss how the tools and techniques in the feature were used to solve a real crime.

Learn It Online

The Learn It Online exercises are interactive Web exercises designed to reinforce and expand your understanding of the chapter concepts. The descriptions below briefly summarize each exercise.

To complete the Learn It Online exercises, visit the Computer Concepts CourseMate Web site at www.cengagebrain.com, navigate to the Chapter 11 resources for this book, click the link for the exercise you want to complete, and then read the instructions..

1 At the Movies — Attack of the Mobile Viruses
Watch a movie to learn about the recent wave of viruses plaguing mobile device users and then answer questions about the movie.

2 Video and Audio: You Review It — Green Computing
Search for, choose, and write a review of a video, podcast, or vodcast that discusses green computing.

3 Student Edition Labs — Protecting Your Privacy Online and Computer Ethics
Enhance your understanding and knowledge about online privacy and computer ethics by completing the Protecting Your Privacy Online and Computer Ethics Labs.

4 Practice Test
Take a multiple choice test that checks your knowledge of the chapter concepts and review the resulting study guide.

5 Who Wants To Be a Computer Genius²?
Play the Shelly Cashman Series version of this popular game by answering questions to find out if you are a computer genius. Panic buttons are available to provide assistance during game play.

6 Wheel of Terms
Identify important key terms presented in this chapter by playing the Shelly Cashman Series version of this popular game.

7 You're Hired!
Embark on the path to a career in computers by answering questions and solving puzzles related to concepts discussed in this chapter.

8 Crossword Puzzle Challenge
Complete an interactive crossword puzzle to reinforce concepts presented in this chapter.

9 Windows Exercises
Step through the Windows 7 exercises to learn about playing audio compact discs, understanding multimedia properties, dragging and dropping Windows objects, and checking for system updates.

10 Exploring Computer Careers
Read about a career as a digital forensics examiner, search for related employment advertisements, and then answer related questions.

11 Web Apps — Dictionary.com
Learn how to use Dictionary.com to search for a dictionary entry, translate a word to other languages, and search for Web pages containing your search term.

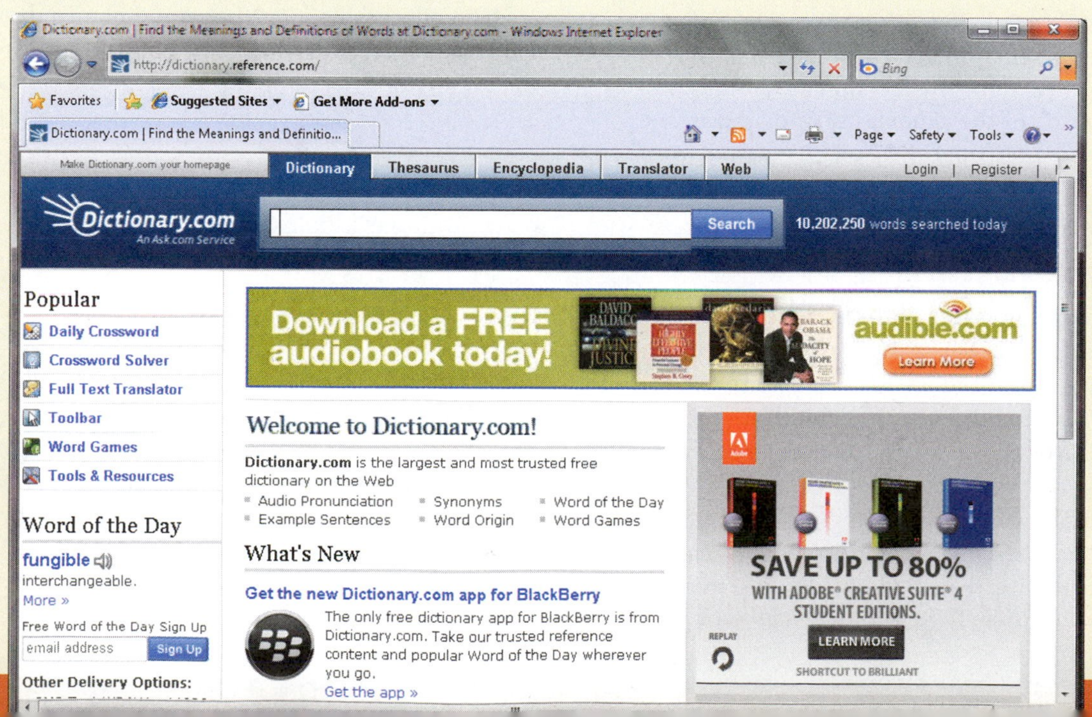

Problem Solving @ Home

The Problem Solving @ Home exercises extend your knowledge of the chapter concepts by seeking solutions to practical computer problems that you may encounter at home or school. The Collaboration exercise should be completed with a team.

In the real world, practical problems often can be solved in multiple ways. Provide one solution to each of the following problems using available resources, such as articles on the Web or in print, blogs, podcasts, videos, television, user guides, other individuals, and electronics and computer stores. You may need to use multiple resources to obtain an answer. Present your solutions in the form requested by your instructor (brief report, presentation, discussion, or other means).

1. **Infected File Detected** A message appears on your computer screen stating that your antivirus program detected an infected file on your computer and is unable to move it to quarantine. What are your next steps?
2. **Unsolicited E-Mail Attachment** You have opened an e-mail message from your best friend stating that he has attached a photo from his recent Caribbean vacation. You are unaware that your friend had taken a vacation, but you attempt to open the photo anyway. After double-clicking the attachment, the photo does not open. You immediately call your friend to ask for help, and he informs you that he did not send that e-mail message to you. What might have happened?
3. **Product Key in Use** While installing the latest version of Microsoft Office, the installation program prompts you to enter the product key. Once you finish entering the product key, you receive an error message stating that the product key already is in use. What might be causing this?
4. **Questionable Fair Use** A media company's attorney has sent you a letter stating that you are violating their rights by including a short movie clip from one of their movies in one of your videos posted on YouTube. You believe that you are within fair use guidelines by including the movie clip but also feel that you should respond to the attorney's letter. What are your next steps?
5. **Shutting Down Safely** While working on your computer, the power suddenly fails. Luckily, your computer is connected to a UPS and you are able to continue working; however, you are not certain how much time you have before the UPS battery runs out. What steps will you take to shut down your computer safely without losing data?
6. **Unauthorized Computer on Network** You are viewing the configuration for your wireless router, as well as the computers that are connected to your wireless network. In addition to the two desktop computers and one notebook computer in your house, you notice that another computer is connected to your wireless network. How could this be?
7. **Verifying Photo Validity** You are writing a research paper for your history class and have found a photo on the Web that you would like to use. You are cautious about using photos on the Web because of copyright issues and photos that have been altered digitally. How might you verify the validity of a photo on the Web?

Collaboration

8. **Minimizing Computer Threats** Because you have just started college, your parents purchased a new computer for you. You wish to protect it as much as possible from threats such as power surges and power outages, unauthorized use and vandalism, and hard disk failure. Form a team of three classmates who will research how to minimize potential threats. One team member should research ways to safeguard your computer from power surges, power outages, and other electrical variations. Another team member will research ways to safeguard your computer from unauthorized use and vandalism, and the third team member will research two backup strategies that will be used to store important backups in the event of a hard disk failure. The three team members should locate and suggest products that will help to safeguard your new computer, discuss their findings, compile them into a brief report, and then submit it to the instructor.

Problem Solving @ Work

The Problem Solving @ Work exercises extend your knowledge of the chapter concepts by seeking solutions to practical computer problems that you may encounter at work. The Collaboration exercise should be completed with a team.

In the real world, practical problems often can be solved in multiple ways. Provide one solution to each of the following problems using available resources, such as articles on the Web or in print, blogs, podcasts, videos, television, user guides, other individuals, and electronics and computer stores. You may need to use multiple resources to obtain an answer. Present your solutions in the form requested by your instructor (brief report, presentation, discussion, or other means).

1. **Unknown Computer User** When you arrive to work each day, you frequently notice that your keyboard and mouse have been moved from the location you left it in the previous day. In addition, your Web browser's history lists sites that you have not visited. You suspect that someone uses your computer while you are out of the office. What are some ways to prevent this?
2. **Forgot Decryption Password** To safeguard some of your important files from others, you decide to encrypt them. Upon attempting to decrypt the files so that you can access them, however, you are unable to remember the correct password. What are your next steps?
3. **Password Management** You must remember multiple user names and passwords to access various computer resources within your company. Each time your company introduces a new system, you must remember a new user name and password, some of which you are unable to customize. What steps will you take to manage your passwords?
4. **Problem Reinstalling Software** After recovering from a computer crash, you attempt to reinstall a program that was previously installed. When you insert the installation media, begin the installation, and type the product key, you receive an indication that you are unable to continue installing the software because you have installed it the maximum number of allowable times. What are your next steps?
5. **Surge Protector Malfunctioning** While picking up a dropped item from the floor, you notice that the lights on your surge protector are not illuminated. All the devices plugged into the surge protector appear to be functioning without issue, but you are curious as to why the lights are off. What might be wrong?
6. **Missing Security Cable Key** To protect your notebook computer from theft, you use a security cable to secure it to the desk in your cubicle. Your boss assigns you some work to take home and suggests that you take home your notebook computer. You discover, however, that you are unable to locate the key that releases the security cable from the computer. What are your next steps?

7. **Setting Up an Ergonomic Environment** After moving to a new office building, your company takes the opportunity to suggest that everyone set up an ergonomic working environment in their new office. What are some ways that you can set up an ergonomic work environment in your office?
8. **Monitored Computer Activities** You receive an e-mail message from the IT department stating that it randomly will monitor employee computers throughout the workday to ensure that they are being used for legitimate purposes. Shortly thereafter, you begin to notice that your computer slows significantly at random times once or twice per week. You suspect the performance decrease is a result of the computer monitoring. How will you address this?

Collaboration

9. **Computers in National and Local Security** National and local security agencies often use computers to protect citizens. For example, computers are used to maintain a list of individuals not cleared to board a commercial aircraft. Form a team of three people to create a list of the various ways computers help to keep us safe. One team member should research how local agencies, such as police departments, use computers to ensure security. Another team member should research ways national security agencies use computers to protect us from threats, and the last team member should research ways that private businesses use computers to guarantee security. Compile these findings into a report and submit it to your instructor.

Learn How To

The Learn How To activities step you through fundamental technology skills when using a computer. The Learn How To exercises enable you to become more proficient with these skills.

Premium Activity: To relate this Learn How To activity to your everyday life, see a visual demonstration of the activity, and complete a short assessment, visit the Computer Concepts CourseMate Web site at www.cengagebrain.com and then navigate to the Chapter 11 Learn How To resource for this book.

Learn How To 1: Back Up Files on an Offsite Internet Server

Note: The service described in this exercise allows 15 days of free access. After that time, you may be billed automatically for service unless you cancel your service in the given time frame.

Backing up files stored on your computer on another disk or computer located in a different geographical location is the ultimate safeguard for data on your computer. A good way to back up data is to use one of the services available on the Web. A leading service is found at IBackup.com. To subscribe to the IBackup service, complete the following steps:

1. Start a Web browser, type the Web address `IBackup.com` in the Address bar and then press the ENTER key.
2. When the IBackup Web page is displayed, click Signup on the top horizontal toolbar.
3. Enter your e-mail address in the E-mail Address text box and then click the Continue with Registration button to display a form (Figure 11-39).
4. Fill in the form. Select the plan you want in the Select a Storage Plan list. If you want to try the service for a short period of time before subscribing, select 5 GB 15 day Free Trial Plan.
5. To continue, you must enter credit card information. If you select the 15-day trial, your credit card will not be charged at this time, and an automatic billing at the end of 15 days will occur. After entering the required information, click the Continue button at the bottom of the page.
6. A message is displayed that confirms that you have signed up with IBackup and also provides a link for you to download the IBackup for Windows program.
7. Click the DOWNLOAD button to download the IBackup for Windows program and then follow the instructions to install the program on your computer.

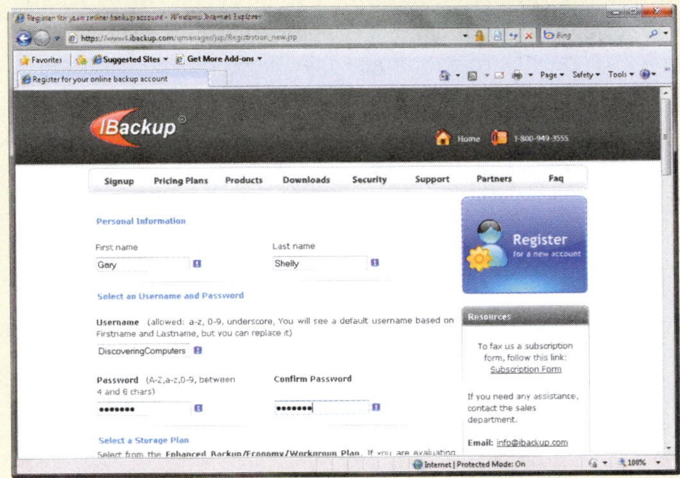

Figure 11-39

After establishing an account, you can use it for the time for which you subscribed. Complete the following steps to use the service:

1. Start the IBackup for Windows program.
2. Enter your user name and password and then click the Connect button to open a window containing your files, as well as the contents of your My IBackup folder (Figure 11-40).
3. To upload a file, locate the file in the left pane of the IBackup window and drag it to the right pane. The Backup Progress dialog box will be displayed while the file is uploading. The file will be placed in the My IBackup folder.
4. For further activities you can accomplish in this program for backing up your files, click the buttons on the top horizontal toolbar and experiment.

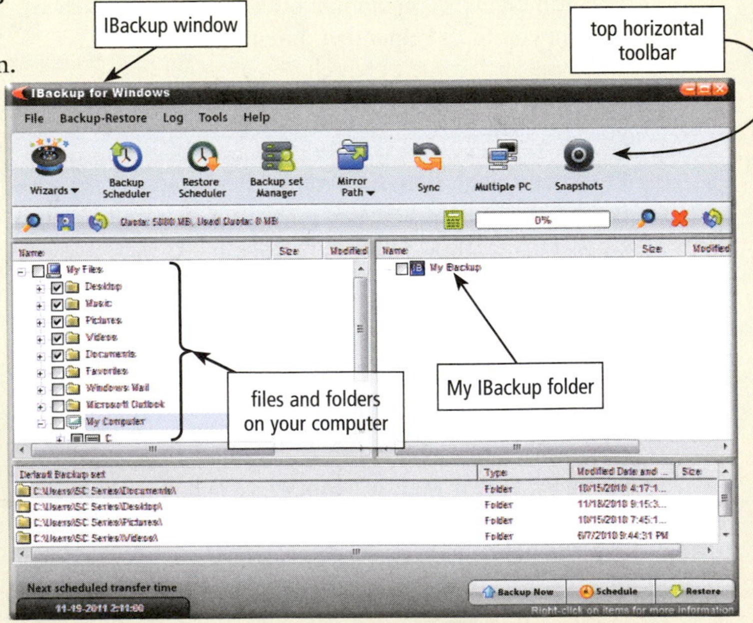

Figure 11-40

Learn How To

Exercises

1. Visit the IBackup Web site. Click View Demo and then follow the screen prompts to view all the services offered by IBackup. Which service is most appropriate for your home computer? Which service is most useful for the server that is used in the computer lab at your school? If you had critical data you needed to back up, would you use a service like this? Why or why not? Submit your answers to your instructor.
2. **Optional: Perform this exercise only for your own computer. Do not perform this exercise on a school computer.** Establish an account on IBackup.com. Upload two or more files from your computer. Download the files you uploaded back to your computer. Is this an efficient way to back up your files? Do you think the IBackup service would be useful for businesses? Submit your answers to your instructor.

Learn How To 2: Use the Windows Firewall

When you use the Internet, data is sent both from your computer to the Internet and from computers on the Internet to your computer. A firewall is a barrier that checks information coming from the Internet and either turns it away or allows it to pass through to your computer, based on your firewall settings. It also checks data being sent from your computer to the Internet to ensure your computer is not sending unsolicited messages to other computers on the Internet. A firewall can be implemented using hardware or software.

Windows contains a software firewall that starts automatically when you boot your computer. To control the firewall usage on your computer, complete the following steps:

1. Click the Start button on the Windows taskbar and then click Control Panel on the Start menu.
2. Click the System and Security link and then click Windows Firewall in the System and Security window to open the Windows Firewall window (Figure 11-41).
3. Click the Allow a program or feature through Windows Firewall link to open the Allowed Programs window (Figure 11-42). The programs and features that are checked can communicate with the Internet without your clicking a link.
4. You may want to allow programs and features that routinely communicate with the Internet, such as sports programs that display updated game scores, to have full access to your computer. To add a program to the 'Allowed programs and features' list, click the 'Allow another program' button. The Add a Program dialog box is displayed. Select a program and then click the Add button.

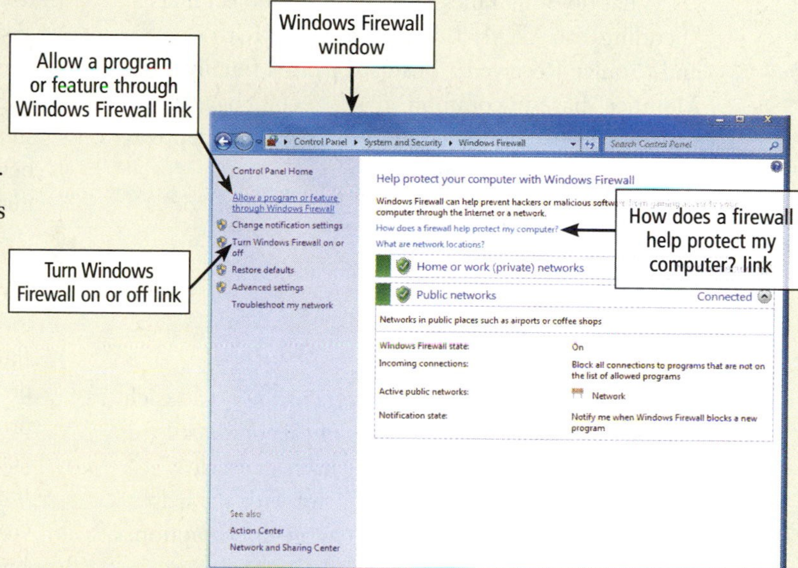

Figure 11-41

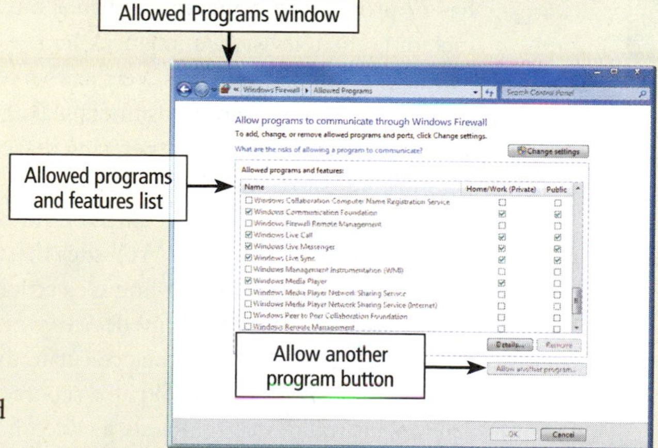

Figure 11-42

Exercise

1. Open the Windows Firewall window. Click the 'How does a firewall help protect my computer?' link. Read the information about Windows Firewall. What did you learn that you did not know? What is malicious software? What are some examples of malicious software? Submit your answers to your instructor.

STUDENT ASSIGNMENTS

Web Research

The Web Research exercises broaden your understanding of the chapter concepts by presenting questions that require you to search the Web for answers.

1 Search Sleuth

Use one of the search engines listed in Figure 2-10 in Chapter 2 on page 85 or your own favorite search engine to find the answers to the following questions. Copy and paste the Web address from the Web page where you found the answer. Some questions may have more than one answer. If required, submit your answers to your instructor. (1) Which five words are among the most commonly used passwords? (2) What do e-mail messages with the subject lines "Sending You All My Love," "Laughing Kitty," and "You've Received a Postcard from a Family Member" have in common? (3) T'ai chi, yoga, and the Alexander technique might offer some relief to computer users suffering from which injury? (4) For which purpose is a gas discharge arrestor used? (5) How many computers in the business world have antivirus software that has been disabled or never was installed properly?

2 Green Computing

The more than 1 billion computers in the world each emit an average of 1,000 pounds of carbon dioxide each year. Many home computer users can help reduce their carbon footprint with the help of devices that monitor energy consumption. Computers are not the only home devices that draw a lot of current; the average home has 27 products that always are turned on, including the television, appliances, and heating and cooling systems. Verdiem's free download, Edison, helps consumers manage their computer power usage. Smart metering devices made by Control4, Colorado vNet, and ZigBee track power usage and give automated tips on how to reduce energy costs. View online Web sites that provide information about reducing home electricity consumption. How do the monitoring devices work? How much do they cost? How do they calculate the money and energy saved per year? Write a report summarizing your findings, and include a table of links to Web sites that provide additional details.

3 Social Networking

People with unique and special talents often desire to share their passions and pastimes with others. Online social networks provide them an opportunity to share their hobbies and creations. In fact, 69 percent of online social networking members say they have a connection with special-interest Web sites. For example, members of the Sports MatchMaker (sportsmatchmaker.com) community can find people who want to play any sport or participate in any hobby at a specific date and time. Car Gurus (cargurus.com) members share their extensive automotive knowledge, and the Instructables community (instructables.com) collaborates to provide instructions for arts, crafts, food, electronics, and games. Visit these Web sites and view the members' products. Which items are popular? Which are unusual? Which photos provide details on documenting the steps necessary to complete a project? How do members share project ideas and requests for information? Summarize the information you read and viewed.

4 Blogs

More than 80,000 blogs are created daily according to Umbria Communications, a service that tracks new Internet media. Many information technology (IT) professionals maintain these blogs to tout companies' products and express personal observations. IT bloggers include Robert Scoble on video (scobleizer.com); Jeff Jaffe, Novell's chief technical officer (novell.com/ctoblog); Ed Brill on IBM (edbrill.com); and Tom Kyte on Oracle (tkyte.blogspot.com). Visit these blogs and read some of the posts. What new products are mentioned? What are the bloggers' backgrounds? What controversial topics are discussed? What personal views do the bloggers express?

5 Ethics in Action

Radio frequency identification (RFID) tags are expected to help merchants in many ways. By placing these tags on such items as prescriptions, computer peripherals, and clothing, retailers hope to reduce theft, track inventory, reduce labor costs, and keep their shelves stocked. Privacy experts, however, claim the tags can store information about consumers' shopping habits and whereabouts. Law enforcement officials, lawyers, marketers, and even thieves could use this detailed electronic data to track people at all times of the day. View Web sites that discuss using RFID tags in stores and the privacy issues that arise from their use. Write a report summarizing your findings, and include a table of links to Web sites that provide additional details.

STUDENT ASSIGNMENTS

Critical Thinking

The Critical Thinking exercises challenge your assessment and decision-making skills by presenting real-world situations associated with the chapter concepts. The Collaboration exercise should be completed with a team.

To evaluate the situations below, use personal experiences and available resources such as articles on the Web or in print, blogs, podcasts, videos, television, user guides, other individuals, and electronics and computer stores. You may need to use multiple resources to form conclusions and make recommendations.

1. Class Discussion — Unscrupulous Programmers
Your best friend, Jonathon, spends all his free time writing computer programs that interact with the Windows operating system. He recently informed you that during fall break he had written malware that randomly erases files and displays weird messages the day before Independence Day (July 3) at exactly 1:00 p.m. He plans to distribute the Trojan horse, called Happy Birthday America, via an attachment to an e-mail message. Also included with the e-mail message is a hidden program that sends the same e-mail message to all the e-mail addresses in the user's address list. The e-mail message with the attachment will be sent as spam the day after finals in May, so that it will have ample time to be distributed to millions of computers worldwide before July 3. You know that a large software company offers a hefty reward of $250,000 for turning in unscrupulous programmers. Discuss if you think it is right to inform on a friend when no profit is involved in the crime. Include in your discussion who you would notify (i.e., Jonathon's parents, the dean of students, the police, or the software company offering the reward) if you choose to turn him in.

2. Class Presentation — Ensuring Safety and Security Online
You work in an information technology department for a large enterprise. You notice that an increasing number of users are contacting the help desk complaining of slow computer performance. When a help desk representative troubleshoots the problem, he or she nearly always attributes the decreased performance to malware that is installed on the computer. Although security software is installed on each computer, users also must do their part in making sure that their computers do not become compromised. Technical support is spending too much time and money troubleshooting and cleaning these computers. As a result, they have asked you to prepare a presentation for employees that will teach them how to guard against malware and other security threats. This presentation should include information such as which Web sites are safe and unsafe, whether it is okay to download programs from the Internet and install them, and how users can protect their computers when they are away from their desks.

3. Research — Threats to Operating Systems
You work as a network analyst for a large manufacturing company that uses Windows. After the most recent virus attack, your manager asked you to analyze the feasibility of switching to a different operating system, such as Linux or UNIX. Use the Web and/or print media to research the advantages and disadvantages of switching operating systems. Create a report based on your findings to answer the following questions: Are alternative operating systems any less susceptible to viruses than Windows? Why or why not? What is Microsoft's approach to eliminating virus attacks? What types of costs are involved in changing operating systems?

Collaboration

4. Privacy Information Policy Your company has been hired by a major retailer to create a privacy information policy for the company's Web site. Your team of three classmates has been instructed to assemble a policy that not only respects an individual's privacy rights but also enables the company to collect data that can be used in targeted marketing. The company would like to collect the following information: who visits the Web site, how often they visit, which pages they view, and the amount of time they spend viewing a particular page. Using the Web and/or print media, create a policy that will include all of the preceding information. Each team member should justify a component within the policy and explain how the policy will not violate the individual's privacy rights. Include in your report examples of lawsuits brought against companies that have implemented similar policies. If any judgments were against the company, cite the specific reasons why.

Digital Forensics

FORENSICS USES SCIENCE to investigate and establish facts in criminal or civil courts. Digital forensics, the newest and fastest growing discipline in the forensics field, also can be referred to as computer forensics, network forensics, or cyberforensics. Digital forensics is the discovery, collection, analysis, and reporting of evidence found on computers and digital devices (Figure 1).

As a student in a digital forensics class, you will investigate a crime scene and observe law enforcement officials collecting evidence. After arriving at the crime scene, you expect a relatively short process that mainly involves confiscating a computer. You are surprised that the process of collecting evidence actually takes much longer than what is portrayed on the television shows you have watched.

This feature introduces students to digital forensics by presenting two real-world scenarios that involve the use of digital forensics. Throughout each scenario, students will learn the steps required to solve computer crimes by using digital forensics techniques.

Introduction to Digital Forensics

Digital forensics focuses on computers, digital devices, and networks, and requires the collection and analysis of digital evidence. Digital evidence exists on a variety of computers and digital devices, such as flash memory mobile media, external hard disks, cell phones, PDAs, copy machines, fax machines, answering machines, and GPS receivers. Depending on the type of crime, other digital devices, such as routers, portable media players, and digital cameras, also might need further examination for evidence that supports the criminal or civil case. Once the evidence is collected, law enforcement officials or digital forensics examiners will transport it to a forensics lab for investigation.

The forensic analysis of computers and digital devices specifically involves the examination of media, programs, and data and log files. Some computers and digital devices maintain *log files*, which track some or all activity on the computer or digital device. Digital forensics examiners use log files to reconstruct a perpetrator's activity with a computer or digital device, such as instant messaging (IM) conversations, Internet chat room sessions, e-mail messages, Web sites visited, files opened, and image and video files viewed. The forensic analysis of networks focuses more on

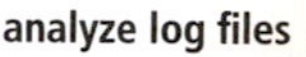


```
1) Feb 12 03:11:55 watson ipop3d[16319]: pop3
   service init from 192.168.187.35
2) Feb 12 03:11:55 watson ipop3d[16319]: Login
   user=hammer host=holmes.example.net
   [192.168.187.35] nmsgs=0/0
3) Feb 12 03:12:16 watson ipop3d[16319]: Logout
   user=hammer host=holmes.example.net
   [192.168.187.35] nmsgs=0 ndele=0
```

```
Session Start: Tue Mar 23 15:50:33 2010.
Session Ident: #Strong&40
* Now talking in #Strong&40
* Topic is 'Welcome to the BEST little channel on the net!
www.40plus.com  '
* Set by Bunni on Tue Mar 23 10:31:01
<BettyF> It sure beats the 20's we've been having, Cary
<BettyF> Hi, billy
<billy89> Hi
<abc_m> hi Cary:)
<abc_m> hi billy89
<`Cary> hey cd  how  be?
<billy89> Hi
<abc_m> not bad a bit cold but doing okay
<BettyF> How ya doing, billy?
<billy89> So... I'm just lookin' around irc...
<BettyF> and lo and behold you found us
<billy89> Doin' ok... also cold where I am... Minnesota...
Where're you?
<BettyF> Maine here
```

Figure 1 Digital forensics is the discovery, collection, analysis, and reporting of evidence found on computers, digital devices, and networks.

the activity that occurs on a network, which includes the analysis of server contents, server and router log files, network traffic, and information obtained from Internet access providers. Investigations involving digital forensics usually are thorough, and it can be difficult for a criminal to hide or permanently remove information pertaining to his or her crime once it is stored on a digital device. For this reason, digital forensics investigations can be helpful in convicting an individual of a crime.

Digital forensics is a rapidly growing field because of the increased use of computers, digital devices, and the Internet in criminal activity. As digital devices become smaller, lighter, less expensive, and easier to use, they appear at many crime scenes that police investigate. Digital forensics integrates aspects of criminal justice, computer science, and computer and network investigative techniques. In fact, many high schools and colleges realize the importance of digital forensics and offer additional courses in the field.

Cybercrimes, which are online or Internet-based illegal acts, continue to increase in both the number of incidents and the amount of money stolen, largely because cybercriminals perceive these crimes to be less risky and more lucrative than street crimes such as burglary or theft. The average bank robber, for example, nets only a few thousand dollars, and most are caught and incarcerated. Conversely, cybercrimes such as credit card theft, identity theft, and financial scams tend to net larger sums of money, and the perpetrators are more difficult to catch and convict. The problem is compounded further by the fact that access to corporate network resources makes insider jobs by employees easier.

In addition to cybercrime, investigators also use digital forensics to combat terrorism. Terrorists around the world use computers and digital devices. Thus, digital forensics analysis is an important antiterrorism tool for both criminal prosecution and intelligence gathering.

As more people and organizations store information digitally and computers are increasingly integrated into more aspects of our society, we all face increased exposure and vulnerability.

Digital Forensics Examiners

As mentioned in Chapter 11, a digital forensics examiner must have knowledge of the law, technical experience with many types of hardware and software products, superior communication skills, familiarity with corporate structures and policies, a willingness to learn and update skills, and a knack for problem solving. Digital forensics covers several overlapping areas (Figure 2).

- Law enforcement uses digital forensics as an evidence gathering and criminal investigation tool.
- Homeland security uses digital forensics for civilian and military intelligence gathering.
- Businesses and other private sector organizations use digital forensics to combat information security attacks.

Each of these areas uses the same core tools and skills in digital forensics.

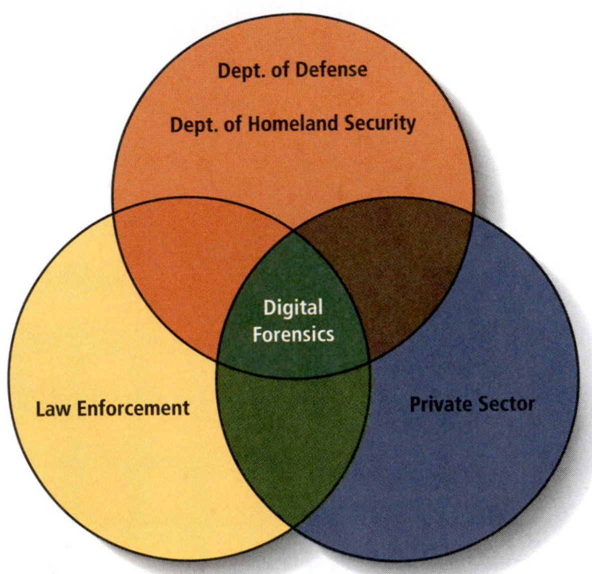

Figure 2 The domain of digital forensics is multidisciplinary, spanning the needs of the military and homeland security, law enforcement, and the private sector.

A digital forensics examiner must have knowledge of the law regardless of whether the investigation is for law enforcement or civilian purposes. Additional complexity in the law exists because computer crime statutes and users' privacy expectations vary widely from state to state and nation to nation. Because the jurisdictional boundaries of the Internet are blurred, an individual in one country can commit crimes almost anywhere in the world without leaving his or her keyboard.

Although most digital forensics examiners today engage in law enforcement investigations, the field involves more than simply obtaining evidence against a criminal. Information security professionals employ digital forensics as well. The traditional information security manager proactively protects an organization's information technology assets, such as computers and digital devices, peripherals, and storage media. Security intrusions and other events that jeopardize assets are inevitable, however. When an event compromises an asset, a digital forensics examiner often leads the incident response team to uncover how an event occurred, who was behind it, and how to prevent a recurrence. Third-party firms use digital forensics techniques for policy auditing and compliance enforcement for issues ranging from an organization's acceptable use policy (AUP) to regulations such as Sarbanes-Oxley (SOX) and the Health Insurance Portability and Accountability Act (HIPAA). (For information about these and other related laws, see Figure 11-36 on page 589.)

Digital forensics also is part of the toolkit of today's computer scientist. Many information security managers purposely place a vulnerable computer, called a *honeypot*, on their networks in the hopes that they can analyze the attacks on those computers. Carefully examining the way in which a honeypot is attacked can provide significant insight into new forms of attack, which then can be translated into new defensive tools and strategies.

A digital forensics examiner requires a working knowledge of a wide range of topics related to computers, digital devices, and networks. The most essential type of knowledge relates to how computers and digital devices store files, as well as the various file systems. The following sections illustrate some of the tasks digital forensics examiners use to search for clues in an investigation.

Digital Forensics in Action

The complexity of the digital forensics process can vary, depending on the circumstances that initially caused the investigation. The digital forensics examiner may be part of an investigative team, with the analysis of digital evidence comprising just one part of the entire investigation. The examiner looks for information pertinent to the incident or event, which a search warrant, time, and/or other circumstances may limit. The following two scenarios illustrate how digital forensics is used to collect and analyze evidence for two cybercrimes.

Scenario 1: Identity Theft

Investigators suspect that Jonathan Nash is stealing identities and then opening credit card accounts to make fraudulent purchases online. At one point, Jonathan suspected that he was being investigated for this crime and attempted to delete all incriminating files on his computer. Before Jonathan can be charged with the crime, investigators will use digital forensics to prove that he is responsible for stealing the identities and making purchases using credit cards that belong to others.

Digital forensics examiners will perform several steps, discussed in the following pages, to collect evidence that can be used to convict Jonathan of this crime.

Step 1 Gather the Materials to Analyze

The first step in the process is to gather the materials to analyze. A search warrant will guide law enforcement officials in the seizure of materials. Even with clear guidelines, law enforcement officials must consider many items for collection and examination. During this process, law enforcement personnel gather computer media, computers, mobile devices, peripherals, network hardware, and computer software.

Computer Media Media is available in a variety of forms (Figure 3). This includes hard disks, external hard disks, and optical discs. Also included are physically small, high-capacity memory devices such as USB flash drives (including versions of such devices disguised in a watch, pen, or Swiss Army knife, the last of which is shown in Figure 1 on page 607) and memory cards such as Secure Digital (SD) cards, CompactFlash cards, and xD Picture Cards.

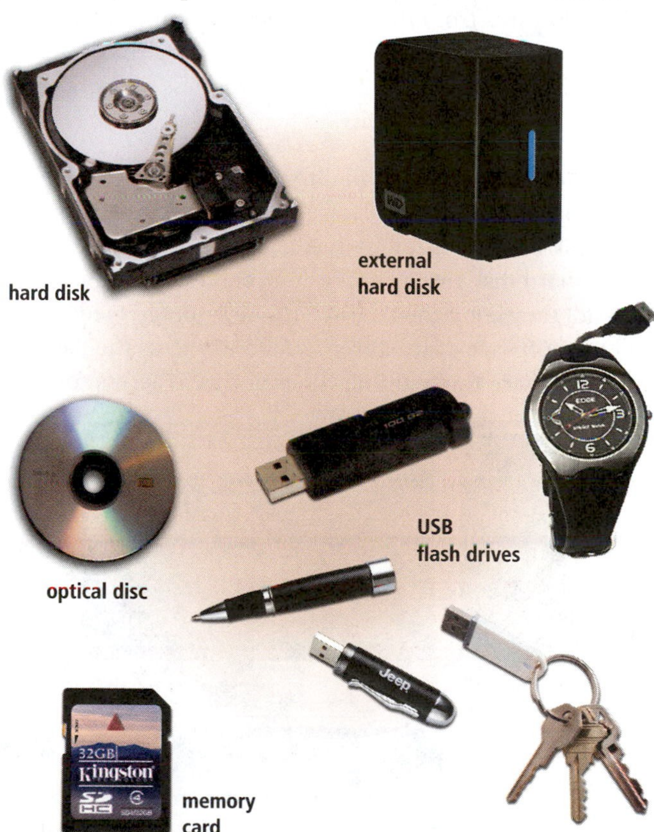

Figure 3 Digital forensics examiners analyze the data stored on various types of media.

Computers and Peripherals Every component of the computer needs to be considered for examination, and examiners generally confiscate any desktop and notebook computers; mobile devices such as smart phones, PDAs, and digital cameras; and peripherals such as keyboards and mouse devices (Figure 4). For example, examiners cannot assume that the keyboard in the forensics lab will be compatible with the computer being seized.

GPS Receivers Forensic examiners analyze an increasing number of GPS receivers each day. Examiners typically gather information such as the destinations that are programmed into the receiver, the locations where the receiver has been, and the route traveled. Some GPS receivers built into an automobile also record data about the vehicle's performance, which also can help in an investigation.

Network Hardware Homes with broadband Internet connections increasingly have networks and, therefore, multiple computers, a router, and a wireless access point. Wireless networks allow criminals to hide a networked computer easily. For example, a notebook computer or mobile device using a home's wireless network can be as far as 100 yards from the wireless access point, and thus be far outside of the immediate structure. Furthermore, the suspect may be stealing a neighbor's wireless network while engaging in criminal activity.

Computer Software Digital forensics examiners generally will not run software directly from the suspect hard disk because it might add, change, or remove data on the hard disk that is important for the investigation. Instead, they copy the data to another storage medium and use software at the forensics lab to access the data. In cases where the examiner does not have access to specialized, custom, or old software on the suspect's computer, the examiner may have to install software found at the suspect's site on a computer in the forensics lab. For this reason, examiners should seize program discs and manuals for any software with which they are unfamiliar. Any papers and books near the suspect's computer also will give the examiner a clue as to the sophistication of the user and the possible types of programs on the computer.

Scenario Specifics

In the case of Jonathan Nash, law enforcement officials obtained a search warrant to enter Jonathan's house and confiscate specific items. Officials locate an office with a computer and peripheral device that writes data on magnetic stripes. Law enforcement officials also locate various storage media, which might contain personal information or credit card information.

Step 2 Transport the Materials

Once the materials are gathered, law enforcement officials or digital forensics examiners transport them safely to a forensics lab where digital forensics examiners will examine the media for information related to the crime.

Scenario Specifics

Law enforcement officials carefully package the computer and digital devices they have obtained from Jonathan's office so that no damage will occur during transport.

Figure 4 Common digital hardware devices examined by a digital forensics examiner.

Step 3 Preserve the Media

The next step in the investigation is preserving the media. Where possible, examiners should not perform digital forensics analysis on the original media, because of the potential of accidentally changing the original evidence. Thus, the examiners typically make a copy of all media, ensuring that they do not alter the original data and information in any way and that the copy will be authenticated as identical to the original. This process is known as creating an **image**, or **imaging**.

In the extraordinary circumstances when the examiner must analyze the original media, such as a hard disk, they often use a write-protection device. A **write-protection device** prevents the examiner or the computer from inadvertently writing data and information on the media (Figure 5). Write-protection devices can cost from several hundred to several thousand dollars, depending on the types of media to which it can connect.

Figure 5 Write-protection devices prevent examiners from inadvertently altering digital evidence.

In some cases, examiners may create an image of a hard disk at the crime scene rather than transporting entire computers to the forensics lab. This is the preferable approach when the disk to be imaged is on a company's critical server and/or where seizing the computer might cause undue economic hardship to the owner. Devices such as Intelligent Computer Solutions' Road MASSter-3 fit in a small carrying case and are designed to image hard disks in the field (Figure 6).

Notebook computer hard disks represent a particular challenge for forensic analysis because many have proprietary or specialty interfaces. Additional hardware is available specifically for imaging drives for various models of Dell, Acer, HP, Lenovo, NEC, Toshiba, and other brands of notebook computers. Other specialized hardware allows for the imaging of smart phones, PDAs, and other mobile devices.

Scenario Specifics

The digital forensics examiner does not want to damage or change the original data on Jonathan's hard disk, so he creates an image of the hard disk. During the imaging process, a write-protection device ensures that nothing inadvertently is written to the original hard disk.

Step 4 Extract Evidence

The next step in the investigation requires the digital forensics examiner to extract the evidence from the media. Based on the guidelines of the investigation, the examiner determines the type of data and information on the computer that is pertinent to the case. In a case of suspected child exploitation, photos and videos are important. Chat room and e-mail logs are useful in cyberstalking cases because they might contain incriminating conversations involving the suspect. Some cybercriminals attempt to delete some or all files on their hard disk in an attempt to hide their elicit or illegal behavior. Examiners analyzing the media, however, usually are able to recover deleted files by

Figure 6 Shown here are details of the keyboard and working area of Intelligent Computer Solutions' Road MASSter-3, a portable digital forensics laboratory.

using software specially designed for this purpose (Figure 7). Examiners might encounter encrypted data on some media; if so, they must use special software to break the encryption so that they can access it.

Scenario Specifics

In this case, Jonathan attempted to delete the incriminating files but was not aware of tools that would permanently erase them. The digital forensics examiner is able to locate remnants of the files on the hard disk and is able to restore them nearly to their original form. Although the files have not been restored fully, the digital forensics examiner is able to restore enough data to retrieve potentially incriminating evidence.

Step 5 Analyze Evidence

The next step, analyzing the evidence and/or determining the root cause of the event, is the most time-consuming aspect of the process. The data and information that an examiner retrieves from the computer either can be incriminating (indicating guilt) or exculpatory (indicating innocence). Additionally, the examiner looks at the entire capacity of the medium because data and information can be hidden anywhere, including locations on the medium that appear empty. Figure 8 summarizes the common items examined during a digital forensics investigation.

(a) The display shown is from the Windows command prompt instruction dir performed on a USB flash drive. The USB flash drive contains 18 files and its volume name is TEST_USB.

(b) In an attempt to destroy evidence, the suspect deletes all the files from the USB flash drive using the Windows command del *.*.

digital forensics examiner retrieves deleted files

(c) Programs, such as WinHex (left) and EnCase (above), are used to review the file names and contents of the files deleted from the USB flash drive by the suspect.

Figure 7 The top portion of this figure shows the suspect (a) listing the files involved in criminal activity and (b) later deleting the files in an attempt to cover up the illegal activity. The lower portion of the figure shows (c) the digital forensics examiner retrieving the deleted files using special programs.

Data and Information to Examine

1. Visited Web sites
2. Downloaded files
3. Dates when files were last accessed and modified
4. Attempts to conceal, destroy, or fabricate evidence
5. Deleted or overwritten files
6. Data from RAM
7. Use of cryptography or steganography
8. File directory structure
9. Image, movie, and sound files
10. Keyword search hits
11. Contents of system files, such as the print spool, swap files, and event logs
12. Installed programs
13. E-mail messages, chat logs, instant messaging logs
14. Registry entries
15. Contents of the Recycle Bin and unallocated space
16. Antivirus, personal firewall, adware, and spyware detection software, as well as the presence of viruses, Trojan horses, rootkits, and spyware
17. Encrypted and password-protected files

Figure 8 Common items examined during a digital forensics investigation.

Digital Forensics Tools As previously mentioned, examiners use digital forensics tools to perform an analysis to ensure that no information is modified on the target media and that the examination is thorough. When a computer starts, hundreds of registry, log, and/or data files may change. Examiners never should use a suspect's disk to start a computer. Additionally, many operating systems, such as Windows, UNIX, and Linux, maintain a number of time stamps associated with every file, including the creation, last access, and last modified dates. Using ordinary utility programs to examine the contents of files usually will alter at least the last access date. Specialized analysis tools maintain the integrity of the original data so that the examiner can be sure that the results of the analysis are legally and technically valid and that nothing harms the original evidence.

A wide variety of digital forensics tools is available, each with its own use, strengths, and weaknesses. Several companies make digital forensics hardware, primarily for purposes of creating disk images. Digital Intelligence, for example, provides several forensics hardware devices, including the following:

- Forensic Recovery of Digital Evidence (FRED) is a stand-alone forensics workstation that can acquire data from all types of hard disk media, including EIDE, ATA, SATA, SAS, and SCSI hard disks (Figure 9a). This unit includes fixed hard disks for the workstation's operating system and analysis tools along with a number of bays so that forensic examiners can insert and remove other drives. For imaging situations, the examiner copies the contents of the suspect disk to a blank disk; the examiner then performs analysis on the newly copied disk.
- The Forensic Duplicator replication hardware allows the examiner to connect IDE and SATA hard disks and can replicate the contents of one disk to another (Figure 9b). The examiner also can copy the contents of one disk to a file.
- FireFly is a device that plugs directly into an EIDE, IDE, SAS, or SATA hard disk and attaches to the forensics computer via a FireWire connection (Figure 9c).

Figure 9 Three digital forensics devices.

The primary digital forensics analysis tool is software. The most widely-used specialty forensics programs today are Guidance Software's EnCase and AccessData's Forensic Toolkit, also known as FTK, which assist in gathering and analyzing data (Figure 10). No single program can perform all aspects of a digital forensics analysis. These programs provide a broad range of forensics functions (Figure 11).

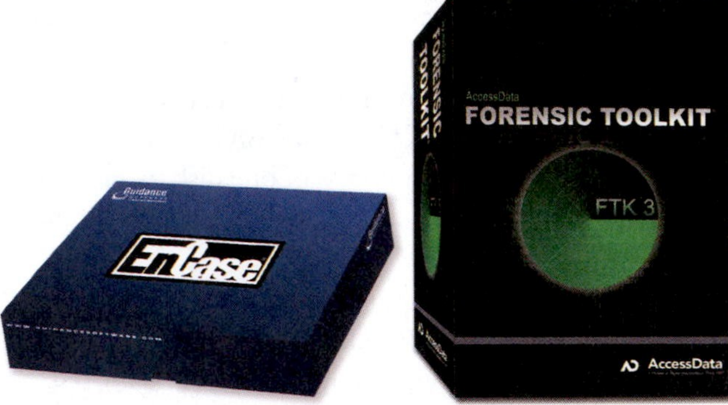

Figure 10 Popular digital forensics software.

Digital Forensics Software Tasks

1. Create disk images.
2. Recover passwords and other important information.
3. Perform file access, modification, and creation time analysis.
4. Create file catalogs.
5. View system and program logs.
6. Determine the activity of users and/or programs on a computer.
7. Recover deleted files and examine unallocated file space.
8. Obtain network information such as IP addresses and host names, network routes, and Web site information.
9. Log forensics examiner activity and aid in documentation and report writing.

Figure 11 Common tasks performed by digital forensics software.

Analyzing Mobile Devices Forensic examination increasingly requires analysis of mobile devices such as smart phones, PDAs, digital cameras, and portable media players. The amount of personal information on smart phones and PDAs, for example, includes contact lists, call history, text messages, photos and videos, e-mail messages, calendars, and documents. In some ways, analysis of mobile devices is more problematic than analysis of desktop and notebook computers, because mobile devices use a wide variety of connectors, operating environments, file structures, data formats, features, user interfaces, and operating modes. Mobile devices also can contain a variety of expansion cards including flash memory mobile media and Subscriber Identity Module (SIM) cards.

Examiners also can use mobile devices to pinpoint a person's or device's whereabouts and routes traveled. GPS is becoming more prevalent in mobile devices. Systems like OnStar use GPS technology to determine a vehicle's precise location.

Analyzing Chat Room Logs Analysis of chat room logs is another important aspect of network analysis. The log shown in Figure 1 on page 607 is a conversation between BettyF, billy89, and other members of the Internet Relay Chat (IRC) Strong&40 channel. Analysis of logs such as these can uncover evidence of cyberstalking, criminal conspiracy, harassment, or other topics of interest to the examiner.

Analyzing Browser History Logs Occasionally, it is necessary to trace a user's Web browsing path. Manual forensic analysis, which involves searching through cookies, the browser's cache, and browser history data, is difficult. Several programs are available to analyze a browser's history, although most new browsers include an incognito mode that prevents the browser from storing Web pages and addresses in the history. Some programs can locate and reconstruct file fragments from the Recycle Bin folder on the Windows desktop.

Scenario Specifics

The digital forensics examiner is attempting to locate evidence on Jonathan's hard disk that will help convict him of identity theft. In this case, the examiner has found documents and spreadsheets containing credit card numbers, saved Web pages showing receipts for items purchased, and browser history logs indicating that Jonathan regularly visited Web sites that sell stolen credit card numbers.

Step 6 Document Results

The final step in the investigation is to document the results of a digital forensics examination thoroughly, particularly when performing the examination for legal purposes. It is important to document everything, including the computer configuration and BIOS settings, the steps taken by the digital forensics examiner, and any pertinent evidence. All computer equipment, media, peripherals, or other items seized must be logged, and examiners should take photos of external and internal connections, when possible. The examiner carefully logs the handling of the evidence to demonstrate that no tampering occurred. Sample digital forensics evidence worksheets are shown in Figure 12. Figure 12a shows an evidence worksheet used when analyzing a computer. Figure 12b contains evidence worksheets used when analyzing a hard disk.

Scenario Specifics

The evidence on Jonathan Nash's hard disk and other media determine whether he is guilty of identity theft; however, the precision in collecting and analyzing the evidence is critical if it is to be admissible in a court case.

Figure 12a (computer evidence worksheet)

NIJ SPECIAL REPORT

Computer Evidence Worksheet

Case Number: ______ Exhibit Number: ______
Laboratory Number: ______ Control Number: ______

Computer Information

Manufacturer: ______ Model: ______
Serial Number: ______
Examiner Markings: ______
Computer Type: Desktop ☐ Notebook ☐ Other: ______
Computer Condition: Good ☐ Damaged ☐ (See Remarks)
Number of Hard Drives: ______ 3.5" Floppy Drive ☐ 5.25" Floppy Drive ☐
Modem ☐ Network Card ☐ Tape Drive ☐ Tape Drive Type: ______
100 MB Zip ☐ 250 MB Zip ☐ CD Reader ☐ CD Read/Write ☐
DVD ☐ Other: ______

CMOS Information Not Available ☐
Password Logon: Yes ☐ No ☐ Password = ______
Current Time: ______ AM ☐ PM ☐ Current Date: __/__/__
CMOS Time: ______ AM ☐ PM ☐ CMOS Date: __/__/__

CMOS Hard Disk #1 Settings Auto ☐
Capacity: ______ Cylinders: ______ Heads: ______ Sectors: ______
Mode: LBA ☐ Normal ☐ Auto ☐ Legacy CHS ☐

CMOS Hard Disk #2 Settings Auto ☐
Capacity: ______ Cylinders: ______ Heads: ______ Sectors: ______
Mode: LBA ☐ Normal ☐ Auto ☐ Legacy CHS ☐

Computer Evidence Worksheet

Figure 12b (hard disk evidence worksheet)

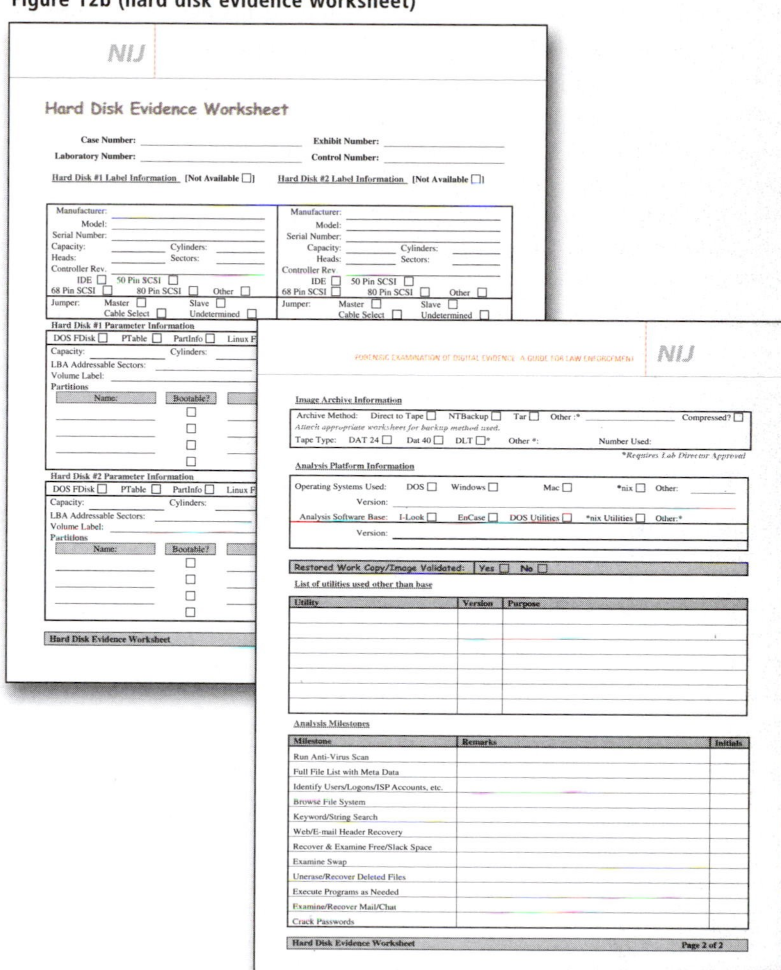

NIJ

Hard Disk Evidence Worksheet

Case Number: ______ Exhibit Number: ______
Laboratory Number: ______ Control Number: ______

Hard Disk #1 Label Information [Not Available ☐] Hard Disk #2 Label Information [Not Available ☐]

Manufacturer: ______ Model: ______ Serial Number: ______
Capacity: ______ Cylinders: ______ Heads: ______ Sectors: ______
Controller Rev. ______
IDE ☐ 50 Pin SCSI ☐ 68 Pin SCSI ☐ 80 Pin SCSI ☐ Other ☐
Jumper: Master ☐ Slave ☐ Cable Select ☐ Undetermined ☐

Hard Disk #1 Parameter Information
DOS FDisk ☐ PTable ☐ PartInfo ☐ Linux F
Capacity: ______ Cylinders: ______
LBA Addressable Sectors: ______
Volume Label: ______
Partitions
Name: | Bootable?

Hard Disk #2 Parameter Information
DOS FDisk ☐ PTable ☐ PartInfo ☐ Linux F
Capacity: ______ Cylinders: ______
LBA Addressable Sectors: ______
Volume Label: ______
Partitions
Name: | Bootable?

Hard Disk Evidence Worksheet

FORENSIC EXAMINATION OF DIGITAL EVIDENCE: A GUIDE FOR LAW ENFORCEMENT NIJ

Image Archive Information
Archive Method: Direct to Tape ☐ NTBackup ☐ Tar ☐ Other :* ______ Compressed? ☐
Attach appropriate worksheets for backup method used.
Tape Type: DAT 24 ☐ Dat 40 ☐ DLT ☐* Other *: ______ Number Used: ______
*Requires Lab Director Approval

Analysis Platform Information
Operating Systems Used: DOS ☐ Windows ☐ Mac ☐ *nix ☐ Other: ______
Version: ______
Analysis Software Base: I-Look ☐ EnCase ☐ DOS Utilities ☐ *nix Utilities ☐ Other:*
Version: ______

Restored Work Copy/Image Validated: Yes ☐ No ☐

List of utilities used other than base

Utility	Version	Purpose

Analysis Milestones

Milestone	Remarks	Initials
Run Anti-Virus Scan		
Full File List with Meta Data		
Identify Users/Logons/ISP Accounts, etc.		
Browse File System		
Keyword/String Search		
Web/E-mail Header Recovery		
Recover & Examine Free/Slack Space		
Examine Swap		
Unerase/Recover Deleted Files		
Execute Programs as Needed		
Examine/Recover Mail/Chat		
Crack Passwords		

Hard Disk Evidence Worksheet Page 2 of 2

Figure 12 Computer Evidence and Hard Disk Evidence Worksheets (from *Forensic Examination of Digital Evidence: A Guide for Law Enforcement*, National Institute of Justice).

Scenario 2: Spam Attacks

Someone is sending an unusually large number of unsolicited e-mail messages to employees of a well-known insurance company. The company's spam filter is not able to remove each message, and employees are spending too much time removing unwanted e-mail messages. As a result, employees sometimes inadvertently remove legitimate e-mail messages. The increased e-mail messages are decreasing network performance and causing the company to lose money. It is important to locate and stop those responsible for sending the unsolicited e-mail messages.

The origin of the attacks initially is unknown, because the e-mail messages appear to come from many different e-mail addresses, although the content of each message is similar. Digital forensics examiners must rely on information provided by the attacked company. The previous scenario listed six steps describing how to locate, analyze, and document the evidence. This scenario is somewhat more complex because it is not known who is responsible for the attacks. In this scenario, a digital forensics examiner might use the following techniques to locate the attacker and/or the computer network facilitating the attacks. Once the examiner finds the attacker, he or she might use the six steps in the previous scenario to link the attacker to the crime.

Analyzing Network Traffic The ability to analyze network traffic is an essential skill for a digital forensics examiner. E-mail headers are particularly important, as they provide many clues as to the origin and authenticity of e-mail messages. *E-mail headers*, which do not display in the body of the e-mail message, usually include the standard To:, From:, and Subject: lines. E-mail headers contain more information, however, than what appears at the top of an e-mail message. For example, they also can reveal the name and version of the e-mail program that created an e-mail message, the operating system used to create the e-mail message, the name and version of the mail server, internal IP addresses, and the mail server path taken by a message.

Tracking Packet Routes Examiners also must have knowledge of how the Internet works. Figure 13a shows the results from VisualRoute, listing the intermediate packet routes between a local host computer and a Web server (www.fujifilm.co.jp). VisualRoute is a utility program that lists the IP address and location of all routers with which it communicates along the path between the two computers. VisualRoute also can show a geographic map of the path (Figure 13b).

Figure 13a (route between two hosts)

Test Internet Connectivity & Trace IP Addresses

Perform connection test to www.fujifilm.co.jp Start

Connection test for www.fujifilm.co.jp completed

View: Summary | Table | Performance Graph | Analysis | Map

Hop	%loss	IP Address	Node Name	Location	ms	Graph	Network
0	0	205.234.111.204	DTG311.visualwa	*Ashburn, VA, US/*	-		Defender Technol
1	10	205.234.111.129	r03-8.iad.defende	Washington, DC,	0		Defender Technol
2	0	69.65.112.25	r01.iad.defenderh	Washington, DC,	13		Defender Technol
3	0	69.65.112.2	r02.iad.defenderh	Washington, DC,	0		Defender Technol
4	0	69.65.112.117	unknown117.112	*Ashburn, VA, US/*	17		Defender Technol
5	0	208.111.133.113	tge12-4.fr4.iad.llr	Washington, DC,	0		Limelight Network
6	0	69.28.171.213	ve5.fr3.iad.llnw.ne	Washington, DC,	0		Limelight Network
7	0	206.223.115.37	equinix-ash.he.ne	Ashburn, VA, USA	0		Equinix Inc. EQUI
8	0	72.52.92.29	10gigabitethernet	Palo Alto, CA, US/	78		Hurricane Electric
9	0	216.218.244.234	-	*Fremont, CA, US/*	193		Hurricane Electric
10	0	210.142.163.169	sto-gw2-pos2-0.g	Seto, Japan	190		Open Data Netwo
11	0	210.142.163.165	STOrk-08-giga3-1	Seto, Japan	190		Open Data Netwo
12	0	143.90.192.138	STOrw-11T2-1.nw	Seto, Japan	197		SOFTBANK TELE
13	0	219.67.158.66	66.219067158.od	*(Japan)?*	203		Open Data Netwo
14	0	211.14.3.208	ethernet2-1.core0	*(Japan)?*	176		BroadBand Towe
15	0	124.147.0.34	GigabitEthernet1-	*(Japan)?*	182		BroadBand Towe
16	0	211.14.6.33	user.FastEtherne	*(Japan)?*	176		BroadBand Towe
...	-	-	-	-	-		-
?	-	203.216.216.100	www.fujifilm.co.jp	*(Japan)?*	-		FujiFilm Software

VisualRoute Server Copyright © Visualware, Inc. | VisualRoute Home

Figure 13b (geographic map display of the route between two hosts)

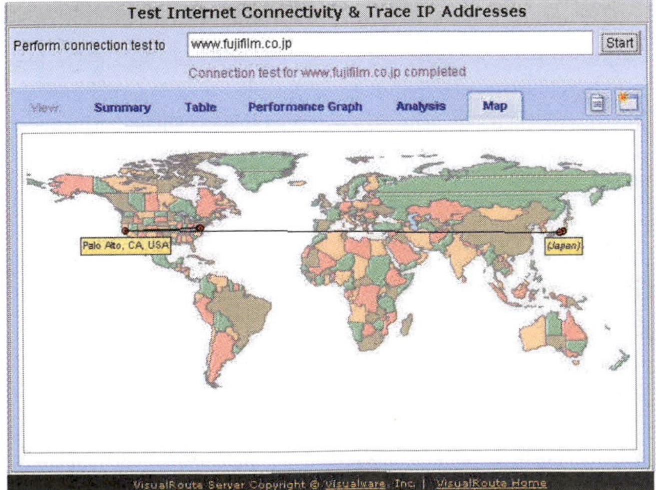

Figure 13 Tracing nodes between a local host computer and a Web server using Visualware's VisualRoute.

Analyzing Internet Access Provider Logs During a digital forensics investigation, the examiner might request logs from an Internet access provider. The Internet access provider will deliver the logs, but they will be in the raw format in which they are saved.

While the SMTP protocol forwards e-mail messages across the Internet, other protocols download e-mail messages by e-mail programs. One such protocol is the Post Office Protocol version 3 (POP3). Figure 1 on page 607 shows a set of three records from a POP3 server log showing a user logging on to check and download e-mail messages. All records show a date (February 12) and time stamp on a host named watson running the POP3 service (ipop3d) and access by a user on the host with IP address 192.168.187.35.

Analyzing a Packet Trace Packet sniffers are an important software tool in understanding network traffic. A *packet sniffer* monitors all of the traffic seen on the network port of a computer and retains a copy for later analysis. One of the most commonly used packet sniffers is tcpdump, a program for the UNIX and Linux operating systems. WinDump is the Windows version of the program.

Scenario Specifics

Digital forensics examiners were able to analyze the company's logs, as well as e-mail headers from the unwanted e-mail messages. The e-mail headers led officials to an Internet access provider in Europe. Upon requesting logs from the European Internet access provider, officials find that the IP address used to send the e-mail messages was assigned to an individual who ultimately was not aware of the crime. His computer, however, was being used as a zombie; that is, a computer controlled by an outsider without the owner's knowledge. The individual was able to help resolve the problem by locating and removing the malicious software from his computer.

Learning More about Digital Forensics

Every action a user takes on a computer or digital device leaves a trail. Deleting files really does not erase information; instead, it tells the computer that it can write new data to the space. Evidence of computer activity is stored in many places on the hard disk, some obvious and some obscure. Information about network access potentially is logged on many computers throughout the local network and global Internet. Evidence of your activities on computers and digital devices is everywhere. Using popular search engines such as Google, Yahoo!, Bing, and others, you will find links to hundreds of digital forensics sites. For a list of sources for information about digital forensics, visit the Computer Concepts CourseMate Web site at www.cengagebrain.com and then navigate to the Digital Forensics Feature resource for this book.

Notes

Chapter Twelve

Information System Development

Objectives

After completing this chapter, you will be able to:

1 Define system development and list the system development phases

2 Identify the guidelines for system development

3 Discuss the importance of project management, feasibility assessment, documentation, and data and information gathering techniques

4 Explain the activities performed in the planning phase

5 Discuss the purpose of the activities performed in the analysis phase (preliminary investigation, study current system, determine user requirements, and recommend solution)

6 Describe the various tools used in process modeling

7 Describe the various tools used in object modeling

8 Explain the activities performed in the design phase (acquire hardware and software and develop details of the system)

9 Recognize the develop programs activity is part of system development

10 Discuss the activities performed in the implementation phase (develop programs, install and test new system, train users, and convert to new system)

11 Discuss the purpose of the activities performed in the operation, support, and security phase

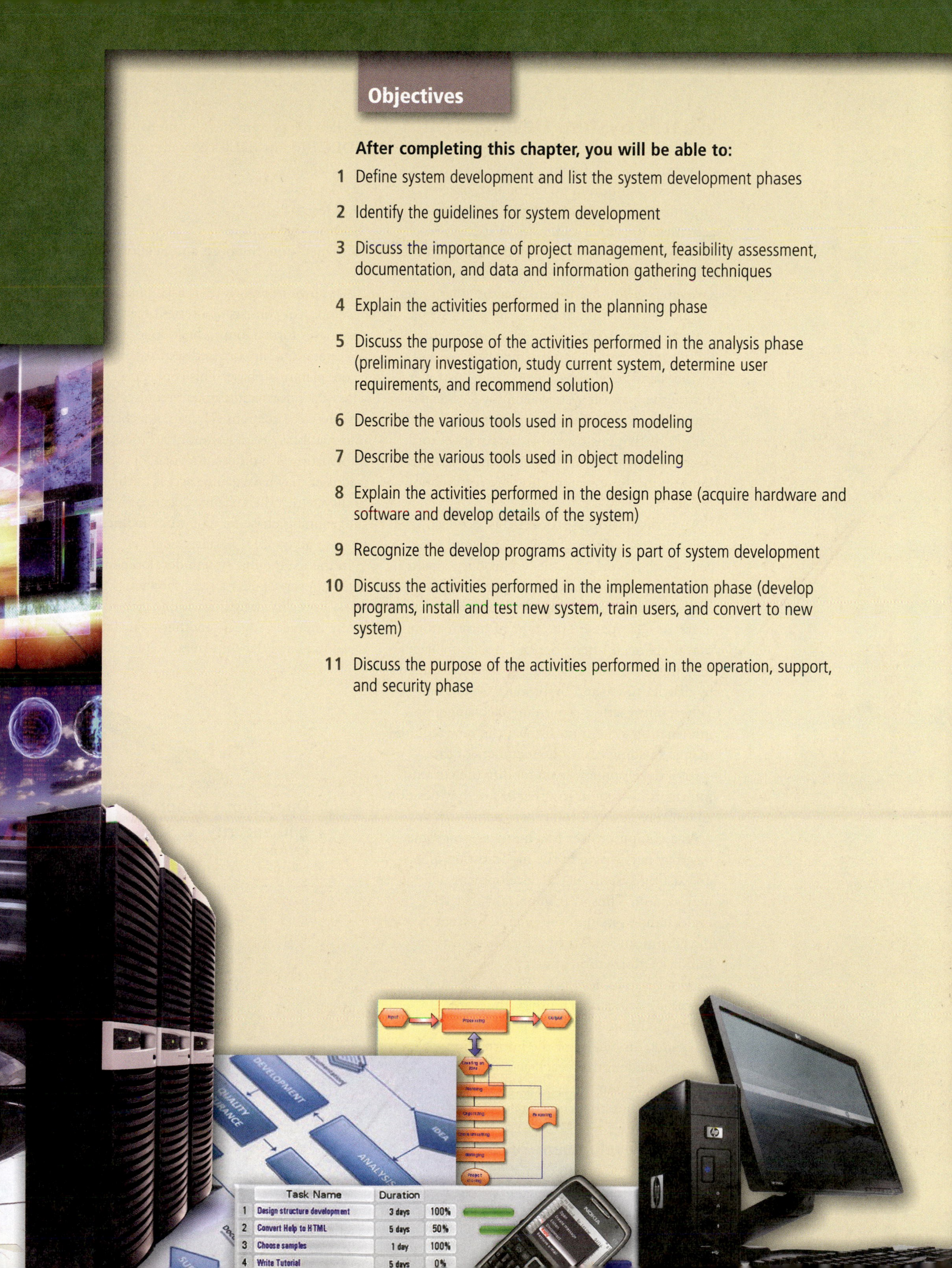

What Is System Development?

A **system** is a set of components that interact to achieve a common goal. You use, observe, and interact with many systems during daily activities. You drive a highway system to reach a destination. You use a programmable thermostat to regulate your heating and cooling systems to save energy. You use the decimal number system to calculate an amount due.

Businesses also use many types of systems. A billing system allows an organization to send invoices and receive payments from customers. Through a payroll system, employees receive paychecks. A manufacturing system produces the goods that customers order. An inventory system keeps track of the items in a warehouse. Very often, these systems also are information systems.

An **information system (IS)** is a collection of hardware, software, data, people, and procedures that work together to produce quality information. An information system supports daily, short-term, and long-range activities of users. As time passes, the type of information that users need often changes. A sales manager may want the weekly summary report grouped by district today and by product tomorrow. When information requirements change, the information system must meet the new requirements. In some cases, the members of the system development team modify the current information system. In other cases, they develop an entirely new information system.

As a computer user in a business, you someday may participate in the modification of an existing system or the development of a new system. Thus, it is important that you understand system development. **System development** is a set of activities used to build an information system.

Some system development activities may be performed concurrently. Others are performed sequentially. Depending on the type and complexity of the information system, the length of each activity varies from one system to the next. In some cases, some activities are skipped entirely.

System Development Phases

System development activities often are grouped into larger categories called **phases.** This collection of phases sometimes is called the **system development life cycle (SDLC)**. Many SDLCs contain five phases:

1. Planning
2. Analysis
3. Design
4. Implementation
5. Operation, Support, and Security

As shown in Figure 12-1, each phase of system development consists of a series of activities, and the phases form a loop. The loop forms when the operation, support, and security phase points to the planning phase. This connection occurs when the information system requires changing. A variety of situations can lead to a change in the information system. For example, users may want information in a different format, or an unauthorized user may have gained access to the information system. When change occurs or is required, the planning phase for a new or modified system begins and the SDLC starts again.

In theory, the five system development phases often appear sequentially, as shown in Figure 12-1. In reality, activities within adjacent phases often interact with one another — making system development a dynamic iterative process.

Members of the system development team follow established guidelines. They also interact with a variety of IT professionals and others during system development. In addition, they perform several ongoing activities during all five system development phases. The following sections discuss each of these items.

System Development Guidelines

System development should follow three general guidelines: group activities into phases, involve the users, and define standards.

1. Group activities or tasks into phases: Many SDLCs contain the same phases shown in Figure 12-1. Others have more or fewer phases. Regardless, all SDLCs have similar activities. For example, Figure 12-1 shows the 'Develop programs' and the 'Install and test new system' activities in the Implementation phase. Some SDLCs separate these activities in an additional phase called Construction and Testing. Other differences among SDLCs are the terminology they use, the order of their activities, and the level of detail within each phase.
2. Involve users: **Users** include anyone for whom the system is being built. Customers, employees, students, data entry clerks, accountants, sales managers, and owners all are examples of users. You, as a user, might interact with an information system at your bank, library, grocery store, fitness center, work, and school. The system development team members must remember they ultimately deliver the system to the user. If the system is to be successful, the user must be included in system development. Users are more apt to accept a new system if they contribute to its design.
3. Define standards: **Standards** are sets of rules and procedures an organization expects employees to accept and follow. Standards help people working on the same project produce consistent results. For example, one programmer might refer

System Development

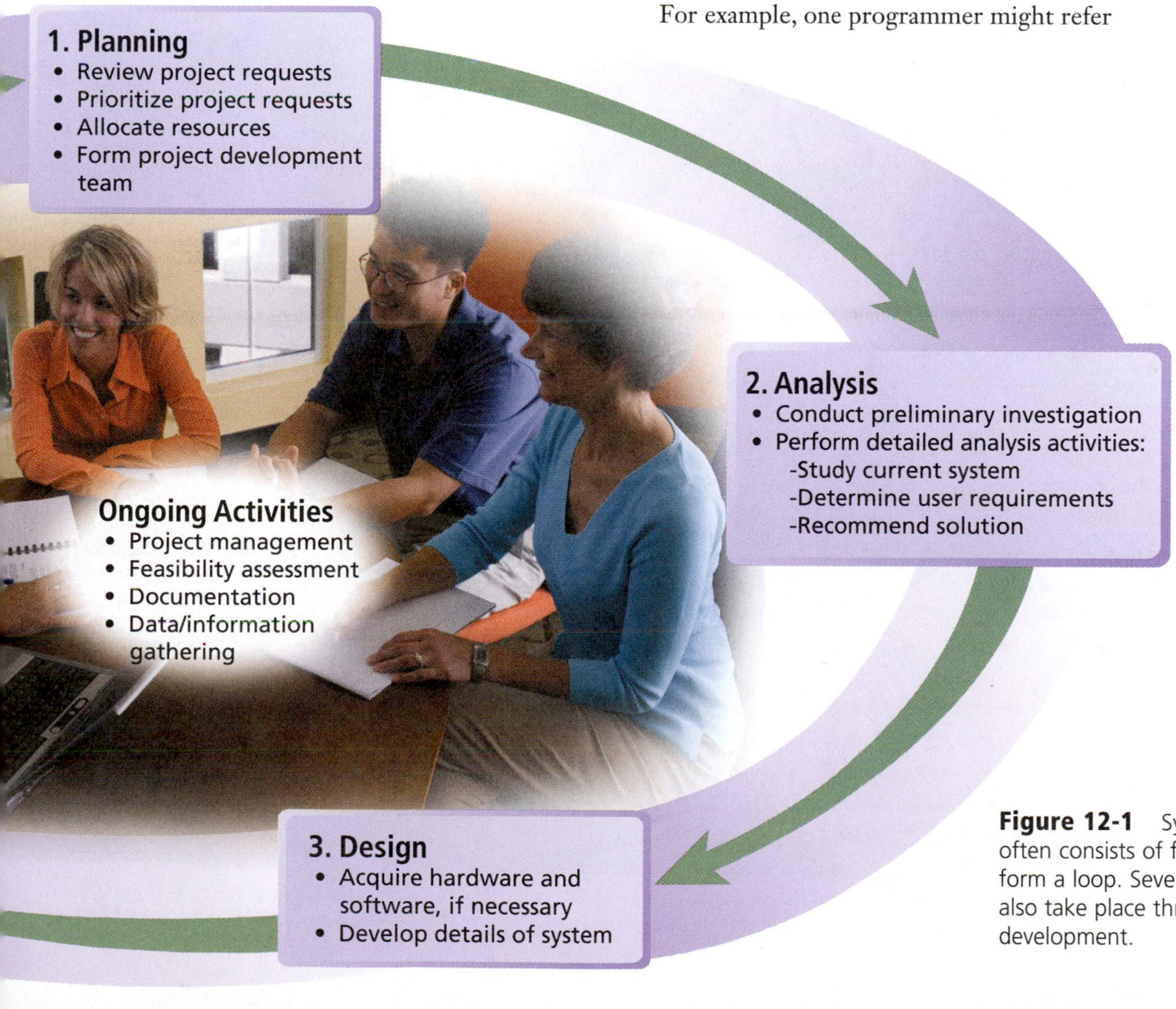

1. Planning
- Review project requests
- Prioritize project requests
- Allocate resources
- Form project development team

2. Analysis
- Conduct preliminary investigation
- Perform detailed analysis activities:
  - -Study current system
  - -Determine user requirements
  - -Recommend solution

Ongoing Activities
- Project management
- Feasibility assessment
- Documentation
- Data/information gathering

3. Design
- Acquire hardware and software, if necessary
- Develop details of system

Figure 12-1 System development often consists of five phases that form a loop. Several ongoing activities also take place throughout system development.

to a product number in a database as a product ID. Others may call it a product identification number, product code, and so on. If standards are defined, then everyone involved uses the same terms, such as product number. Standards often are implemented by using a data dictionary.

Who Participates in System Development?

System development should involve representatives from each department in which the proposed system will be used. This includes both nontechnical users and IT professionals. Although the roles and responsibilities of members of the system development team may change from organization to organization, this chapter presents general descriptions of tasks for various team members.

During system development, the systems analyst meets and works with a variety of people (Figure 12-2). A **systems analyst** is responsible for designing and developing an information system. The systems analyst is the users' primary contact person.

Depending on the size of the organization, the tasks performed by the systems analyst may vary. Smaller organizations may have one systems analyst or even one person who assumes the roles of both systems analyst and

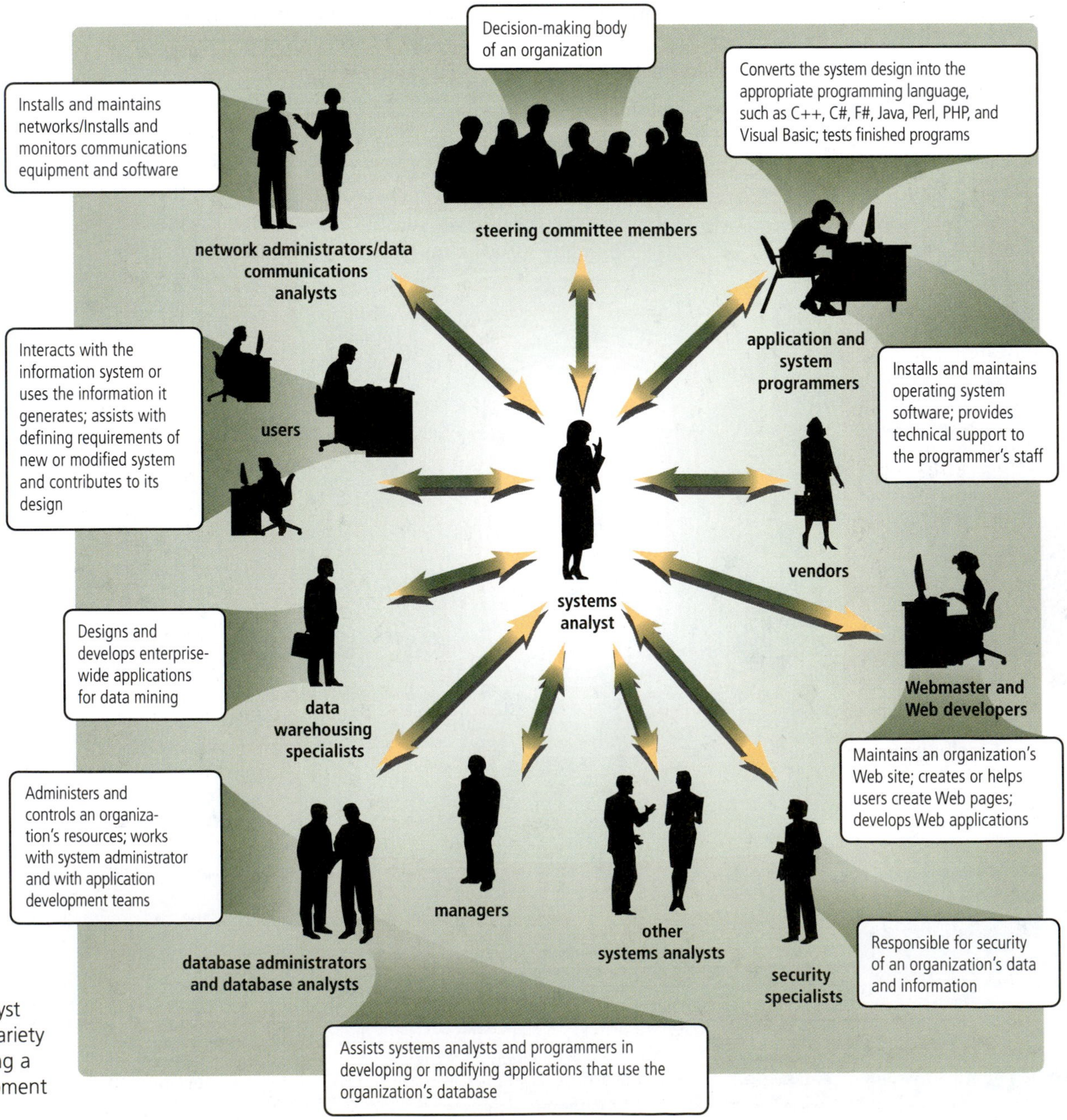

Decision-making body of an organization

steering committee members

Converts the system design into the appropriate programming language, such as C++, C#, F#, Java, Perl, PHP, and Visual Basic; tests finished programs

application and system programmers

Installs and maintains networks/Installs and monitors communications equipment and software

network administrators/data communications analysts

Installs and maintains operating system software; provides technical support to the programmer's staff

vendors

Interacts with the information system or uses the information it generates; assists with defining requirements of new or modified system and contributes to its design

users

systems analyst

Webmaster and Web developers

Maintains an organization's Web site; creates or helps users create Web pages; develops Web applications

Designs and develops enterprise-wide applications for data mining

data warehousing specialists

Administers and controls an organization's resources; works with system administrator and with application development teams

database administrators and database analysts

managers

other systems analysts

security specialists

Responsible for security of an organization's data and information

Assists systems analysts and programmers in developing or modifying applications that use the organization's database

Figure 12-2
A systems analyst meets with a variety of people during a system development project.

programmer. Larger organizations often have multiple systems analysts. Some refer to a systems analyst as a *system developer*.

The systems analysts are the liaison between the users and the IT professionals. They convert user requests into technical specifications. Thus, systems analysts must have superior technical skills. They also must be familiar with business operations, be able to solve problems, have the ability to introduce and support change, and possess excellent communications and interpersonal skills. Systems analysts prepare many reports, drawings, and diagrams. They discuss various aspects of the development project with users, management, other analysts, database analysts, database administrators, network administrators, Web developers, programmers, vendors, and the steering committee. The **steering committee** is a decision-making body in an organization.

For each system development project, an organization usually forms a **project team** to work on the project from beginning to end. The project team consists of users, the systems analyst, and other IT professionals.

Project Management

Project management is the process of planning, scheduling, and then controlling the activities during system development. The goal of project management is to deliver an acceptable system to the user in an agreed-upon time frame, while maintaining costs.

In smaller organizations or projects, one person manages the entire project. For larger projects, the project management activities often are separated between a project manager and a project leader. In this case, the *project leader* manages and controls the budget and schedule of the project, and the *project manager* controls the activities during system development. Project leaders and/or project managers are part of the project team. If the systems analyst is not the project manager, he or she works closely with the project manager.

Some organizations use extreme project management to speed development time. *Extreme project management* is a team-driven project management approach, in which a project leader is more of a participant and facilitator than a manager during the project.

To plan and schedule a project effectively, the project leader identifies the following elements:

- Goal, objectives, and expectations of the project, collectively called the *scope*
- Required activities
- Time estimates for each activity
- Cost estimates for each activity
- Order of activities
- Activities that can take place at the same time

After these items are identified, the project leader usually records them in a *project plan*. Project leaders can use **project management software** to assist them in planning, scheduling, and controlling development projects (Figure 12-3 below and on the next page).

A popular tool used to plan and schedule the time relationships among project activities is a Gantt chart (Figure 12-3a). A *Gantt chart*, developed by Henry L. Gantt, is a bar chart that

Gantt Charts

For more information, visit the Computer Concepts CourseMate Web site at www.cengagebrain.com, navigate to the Chapter 12 Web Link resource for this book, and then click Gantt Charts.

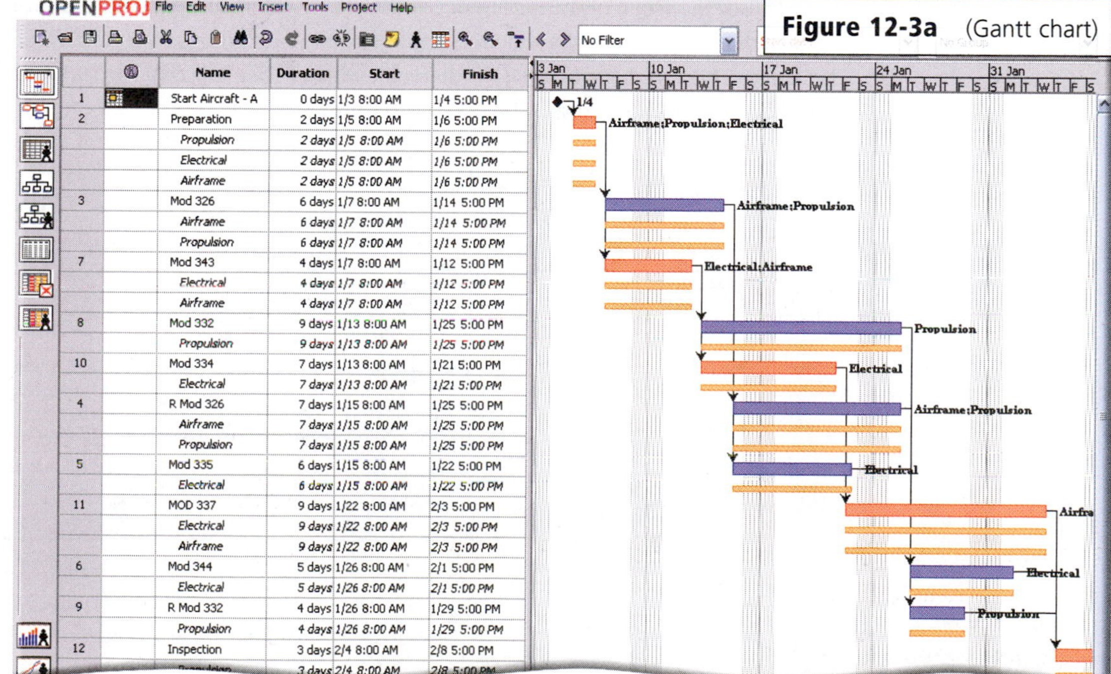

Figure 12-3a (Gantt chart)

Figure 12-3 Project management software. *(continued on next page)*

uses horizontal bars to show project phases or activities. The left side, or vertical axis, displays the list of required activities. A horizontal axis across the top or bottom of the chart represents time.

Another tool used for planning and scheduling time is called a PERT chart. Developed by the U.S. Department of Defense, a *PERT chart*, short for Program Evaluation and Review Technique chart, analyzes the time required to complete a task and identifies the minimum time required for an entire project (Figure 12-3b). PERT charts, sometimes called network diagrams, can be more complicated to create than Gantt charts, but are better suited than Gantt charts for planning and scheduling large, complex projects.

PERT Charts

For more information, visit the Computer Concepts CourseMate Web site at www.cengagebrain.com, navigate to the Chapter 12 Web Link resource for this book, and then click PERT Charts.

When the project features and deadlines have been set, the project leader monitors and controls the project. Some activities take less time than originally planned. Others take longer. The project leader may realize that an activity is taking excessive time or that scope creep has occurred. *Scope creep* occurs when one activity has led to another that was not planned originally; thus, the scope of the project now has grown.

Project leaders should use *change management*, which is the process of recognizing when a change in the project has occurred, taking actions to react to the change, and planning for opportunities because of the change. For example, the project leader may recognize the team will not be able to meet the original deadline of the project due to scope creep. Thus, the project leader may extend the deadline or may reduce the scope of the system development. If the latter occurs, the users will receive a less comprehensive system at the original deadline. In either case, the project leader revises the first project plan and presents the new plan to users for approval. It is crucial that everyone is aware of and agrees on any changes made to the project plan.

One aspect of managing projects is to ensure that everyone submits deliverables on time and according to plan. A *deliverable* is any tangible item such as a chart, diagram, report, or program file.

? FAQ 12-1

How many information system projects fail?

One study indicates that between 30 and 70 percent of information system projects fail. Approximately 25 percent of projects exceed budget restrictions, 21 percent fail to meet project requirements, and 31 percent are delivered late. These failures might occur because of changing requirements, insufficient funds, or an unreasonable schedule.

For more information, visit the Computer Concepts CourseMate Web site at www.cengagebrain.com, navigate to the Chapter 12 FAQ resource for this book, and then click Project Failures.

Feasibility Assessment

Feasibility is a measure of how suitable the development of a system will be to the organization. A project that is feasible at one point during system development might become infeasible at a later point. Thus, systems analysts frequently reevaluate feasibility during the system development project.

A systems analyst typically uses at least four tests to evaluate feasibility of a project: operational feasibility, schedule feasibility, technical feasibility, and economic feasibility.

- *Operational feasibility* measures how well the proposed information system will work. Will the users like the new system? Will they use it?

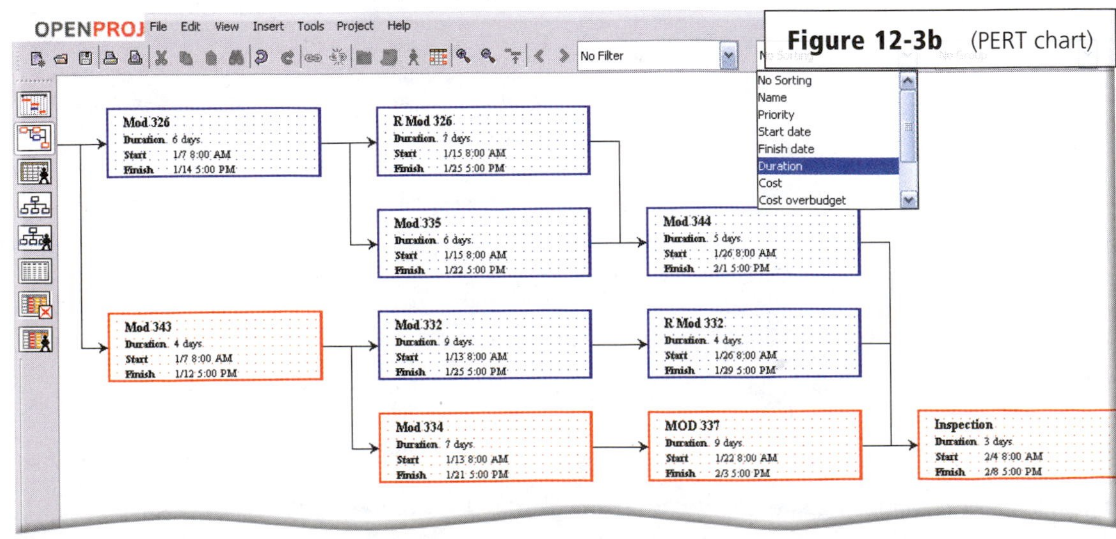

Figure 12-3b (PERT chart)

Figure 12-3 Project management software. *(continued)*

Will it meet their requirements? Will it cause any changes in their work environment? Is it secure?

- *Schedule feasibility* measures whether the established deadlines for the project are reasonable. If a deadline is not reasonable, the project leader might make a new schedule. If a deadline cannot be extended, then the scope of the project might be reduced to meet a mandatory deadline.
- *Technical feasibility* measures whether the organization has or can obtain the hardware, software, and people needed to deliver and then support the proposed information system. For most information system projects, hardware, software, and people typically are available to support an information system. The challenge is obtaining funds to pay for these resources. Economic feasibility addresses funding.
- *Economic feasibility*, also called *cost/benefit feasibility*, measures whether the lifetime benefits of the proposed information system will be greater than its lifetime costs. A systems analyst often consults the advice of a business analyst, who uses many financial techniques, such as return on investment (ROI) and payback analysis, to perform the cost/benefit analysis.

Documentation

During system development, project team members produce much documentation. **Documentation** is the collection and summarization of data and information. It includes reports, diagrams, programs, or any other deliverables generated during system development.

A *project notebook* contains all documentation for a single project. The project notebook might be a simple three-ring binder. Many organizations, however, have software that systems analysts use to create an automated project notebook.

Users and IT professionals refer to existing documentation when working with and modifying current systems. It is important that all documentation be well written, thorough, consistent, and understandable. The final information system should be reflected accurately and completely in documentation developed throughout the development project. Maintaining up-to-date documentation should be an ongoing part of system development. Too often, project team members put off documentation until the end because it is time-consuming, but these practices typically result in lower quality documentation.

Data and Information Gathering Techniques

During system development, members of the project team gather data and information. They need accurate and timely data and information for many reasons. They must keep a project on schedule, evaluate feasibility, and be sure the system meets requirements. Systems analysts and other IT professionals use several techniques to gather data and information. They review documentation, observe, survey, interview, conduct joint-application design sessions, and research.

- Review Documentation — By reviewing documentation such as an organization chart, memos, and meeting minutes, systems analysts learn about the history of a project. Documentation also provides information about the organization such as its operations, weaknesses, and strengths.
- Observe — Observing people helps systems analysts understand exactly how they perform a task. Likewise, observing a machine allows you to see how it works. Read Ethics & Issues 12-1 for a related discussion.
- Survey — To obtain data and information from a large number of people, systems analysts distribute surveys.

ETHICS & ISSUES 12-1

Do You Work Harder When Someone Is Watching?

While gathering data and information during system development, employees are involved actively in the process. They complete surveys, participate in interviews, and are observed while performing their jobs. Many researchers suggest that during observation, employees may not exhibit everyday behavior and may perform above and beyond their normal workday activities. They base this premise on the Hawthorne Effect, which is the result of a study performed in the 1920s in the Western Electric Company plant in Hawthorne, Illinois. The study discovered that productivity improved during observation, whether the conditions were made better or worse. Researchers concluded that productivity seemed to improve whenever the workers knew they were being observed.

Do you believe that you work harder when someone is watching? Why or why not? What is your opinion of the Hawthorne Effect? Do you agree with the research? Is such observation ethical, and can it have other psychological effects on employees? If productivity increases during observation, is observation a good data gathering technique in a system study? Why or why not?

Ethics & Issues

For the complete text of the Ethics & Issues boxes found in this chapter, visit the Computer Concepts CourseMate Web site at www.cengagebrain.com and then navigate to the Chapter 12 Ethics & Issues resource for this book.

- Interview — The interview is the most important data and information gathering technique for the systems analyst. It allows the systems analyst to clarify responses and probe during face-to-face feedback. To learn more about how to conduct an interview, complete the Learn How To 1 activity on pages 658 and 659.
- JAD Sessions — Instead of a single one-on-one interview, analysts often use joint-application design sessions to gather data and information. *Joint-application design (JAD)* sessions, or *focus groups*, are a series of lengthy, structured, group meetings in which users and IT professionals work together to design or develop an application (Figure 12-4).
- Research — Newspapers, computer magazines, reference books, trade shows, the Web, vendors, and consultants are excellent sources of information. These sources can provide the systems analyst with information such as the latest hardware and software products and explanations of new processes and procedures. In addition, systems analysts often collect Web site statistics such as the number of visitors, most visited Web pages, etc., and evaluate these statistics as part of their research.

Figure 12-4 During a JAD session, the systems analyst is the *moderator*, or leader, of the discussion. Another member, called the *scribe*, records facts and action items assigned during the session.

? FAQ 12-2

What types of questions are asked during an interview?

Interviewers — including systems analysts — ask two types of questions: close-ended and open-ended. Close-ended questions generally are easy to answer, such as the number of years a system has been in place. Open-ended questions, by contrast, require more explanation. For example, an open-ended question may ask the interviewee to describe three problems with the current system.

For more information, visit the Computer Concepts CourseMate Web site at www.cengagebrain.com, navigate to the Chapter 12 FAQ resource for this book, and then click Interviews.

What Initiates a System Development Project?

A user may request a new or modified information system for a variety of reasons. The most obvious reason is to correct a problem such as an incorrect calculation or a security breach. Another reason is to improve the information system. For example, if a school wants student report cards to be generated automatically from instructors' online grade books, it would have to modify the existing registration system to include this new feature. Organizations may want to improve hardware, software, or other technology to enhance an information system.

Sometimes situations outside the control of an organization require a modification to an information system. Management or some other governing body may mandate a change. For example, a school may change graduation requirements. Competition also can lead to change. After one organization provides 24-hour online customer service, others follow for fear of losing customers. Another source of change results from one organization merging with or acquiring another.

A user may request a new or modified information system verbally in a telephone conversation or written as an e-mail message (Figure 12-5a). Read Ethics & Issues 12-2 for a related discussion. In larger organizations, users write a formal request for a new or modified information system, which is called a *request for system services* or *project request* (Figure 12-5b). This document becomes the first item in the project notebook. It also triggers the first phase of the SDLC: planning.

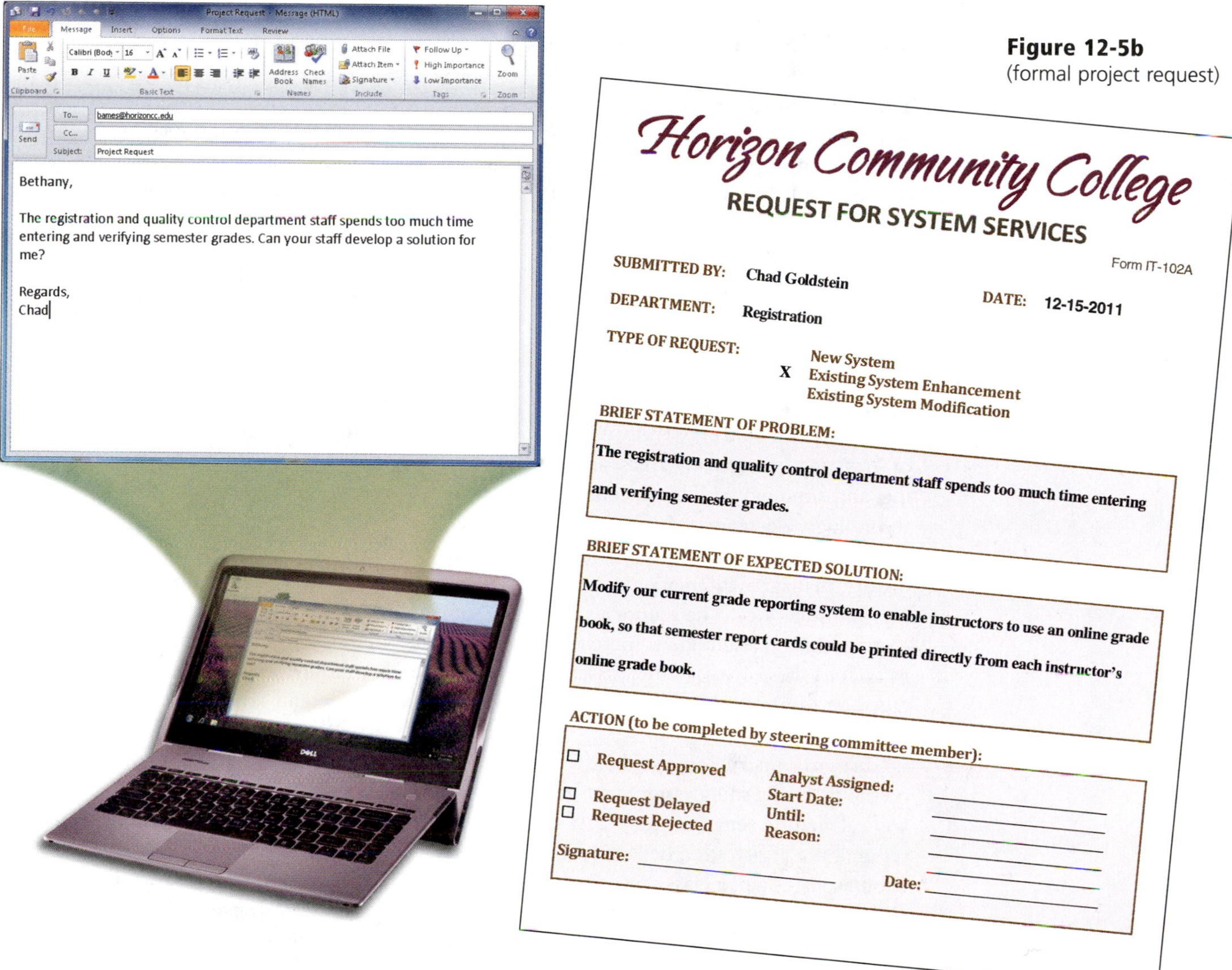

Horizon Community College

REQUEST FOR SYSTEM SERVICES

Form IT-102A

SUBMITTED BY: Chad Goldstein

DATE: 12-15-2011

DEPARTMENT: Registration

TYPE OF REQUEST:
New System
X Existing System Enhancement
Existing System Modification

BRIEF STATEMENT OF PROBLEM:

The registration and quality control department staff spends too much time entering and verifying semester grades.

BRIEF STATEMENT OF EXPECTED SOLUTION:

Modify our current grade reporting system to enable instructors to use an online grade book, so that semester report cards could be printed directly from each instructor's online grade book.

ACTION (to be completed by steering committee member):

☐ Request Approved Analyst Assigned: ______
  Start Date: ______
☐ Request Delayed Until: ______
☐ Request Rejected Reason: ______

Signature: ______ Date: ______

Figure 12-5a (informal project request)

Figure 12-5b (formal project request)

Figure 12-5 Sometimes users informally communicate a project request verbally or as an e-mail message. In larger organizations, requests often are documented on a form such as this Request for System Services.

ETHICS & ISSUES 12-2

Does E-Mail Make You Lie More?

A recent study found that people lied 50 percent more when writing business related e-mail messages than they did when writing with pen and paper. Fortunately, a second study found that the more familiarity between the e-mail sender and recipient, the level of untruths becomes less significant. Another study, though, showed that people are more likely to lie to coworkers than to strangers. Researchers offer a number of reasons for the results of the various studies. For example, one researcher found that people act in self-serving ways when typing as opposed to writing by hand. Others claim that the anonymous nature of sitting, perhaps, miles away from a faceless e-mail recipient simply makes people colder, or that the lack of facial cues, tone, and eye contact largely are to blame. For some reason, many people find it easier to protect their sense of self-worth and self-esteem when sending e-mail messages. While the effects of the studies are clear, however, researchers provide few suggestions as how to fix the problem.

Does e-mail make you lie more? Why or why not? Given the results of the studies, should readers of e-mail messages be more skeptical of e-mail content? Why? Does knowing that e-mail makes some people lie more make you reconsider how you interact with others? Why or why not? Do you find the results of some of the studies to be truthful in your own experience?

Horizon Community College — A Case Study

This chapter includes a case study to help you understand real-world system development applications. The case study appears shaded in light green immediately after the discussion of each phase in the chapter. The case is about Horizon Community College (HCC), a fictitious school.

Approximately 15,000 students are enrolled at HCC each year in its varied programs. Students can earn A.S. (Associate of Science) or A.A. (Associate of Arts) degrees in many areas: accounting, anthropology, childcare, computer technology, electronics, construction technology, forensic science, graphic design, history, management, marketing, nursing, and sociology. The school also offers certificates and adult education classes in each of these areas. Some classes are taken on campus, while others are offered online.

Currently, instructors use their own method for recording assignment grades and calculating semester grades. At semester end, the registration department distributes via e-mail a class semester grade form, which contains a list of all students in a class and an area for the instructor to record each student's final semester grade. As instructors send in their class semester grade forms, registration clerks enter each student's grade into the school's database. After grades are entered, the quality control group compares the original class semester grade forms with the entered grades to check for any errors that may have occurred during the data entry process. Then, report cards are printed and mailed to students.

With the number of enrolled students on the rise, Chad Goldstein, registrar, has noticed that it takes a considerable amount of time for the registration clerks to enter semester grades and for quality control to verify entered grades for accuracy. Lately, quality control has been finding an excessive number of data entry errors, in part due to the excessive workload on the registration clerks. For this reason, Chad would like the instructors to use an online grade book, so that report cards could be printed directly from the instructor's grade book. This change in procedure would save the registration department a great deal of time and money and eliminate data entry errors.

Chad realizes this task will require substantial school resources. He believes a systems study is necessary. He sends an e-mail message to the IT director (Figure 12-5a on the previous page). She agrees and asks him to fill out a Request for System Services form (Figure 12-5b on the previous page) and submit it to Juanita Mendez, chair of the steering committee at HCC.

Planning Phase

The **planning phase** for a project begins when the steering committee receives a project request. As mentioned earlier in this chapter, the steering committee is a decision-making body for an organization. This committee usually consists of five to nine people. It typically includes a mix of vice presidents, managers, nonmanagement users, and IT personnel.

During the planning phase, four major activities are performed: (1) review and approve the project requests; (2) prioritize the project requests; (3) allocate resources such as money, people, and equipment to approved projects; and (4) form a project development team for each approved project.

The projects that receive the highest priority are those mandated by management or some other governing body. These requests are given immediate attention. The steering committee evaluates the remaining project requests based on their value to the organization. The steering committee approves some projects and rejects others. Of the approved projects, it is likely that only a few will begin system development immediately. Others will have to wait for additional funds or resources to become available.

Planning at Horizon Community College

After receiving the project request (Figure 12-5b on page 627) from Chad, Juanita Mendez distributes it to all members of the steering committee. They will discuss the request at their next meeting. The steering committee members of HCC are Juanita Mendez, controller and chair of the steering committee; Milan Sciranka, professor; Suzy Zhao, Web developer; Donnell Carter, training specialist; Karl Schmidt, systems analyst; and Bethany Ames, IT director. Juanita also invites Chad Goldstein to the next steering committee meeting. Because he originated the project request, Chad will have the knowledge to answer questions.

During the meeting, the committee decides the project request identifies an improvement to the system, instead of a problem. They feel the nature of the improvement (to print report cards directly from instructors' online grade books) could lead to considerable savings for the school. It also will reduce data entry errors made by registration clerks.

The steering committee approves the request. Juanita points out that the school has enough funds in its budget to begin the project immediately. Thus, Bethany assembles a system development project team. She assigns Karl Schmidt, systems analyst, as the project leader. Karl and his team immediately begin the next phase: analysis.

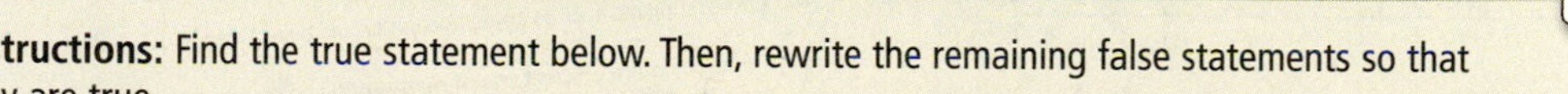

Instructions: Find the true statement below. Then, rewrite the remaining false statements so that they are true.

1. Feasibility is the process of planning, scheduling, and then controlling the activities during system development.
2. Maintaining up-to-date documentation should be an ongoing part of system development.
3. Users should not be involved throughout system development.
4. The five phases in most SDLCs are programming, analysis, design, sampling, and recording.
5. The planning phase for a project begins when the steering committee receives a Gantt chart.

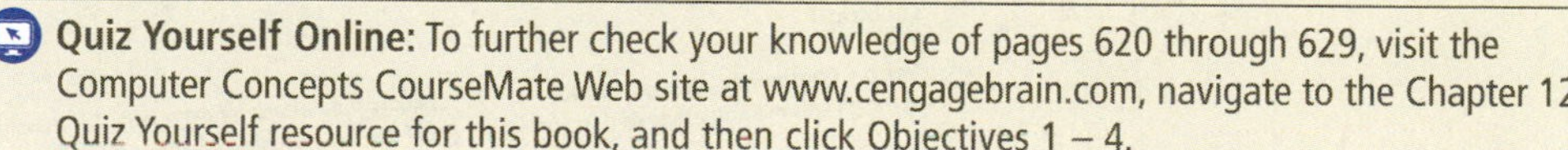

Analysis Phase

The **analysis phase** consists of two major activities: (1) conduct a preliminary investigation and (2) perform detailed analysis. The following sections discuss these activities.

The Preliminary Investigation

The main purpose of the **preliminary investigation**, sometimes called the *feasibility study*, is to determine the exact nature of the problem or improvement and decide whether it is worth pursuing. Should the organization continue to assign resources to this project? To answer this question, the systems analyst conducts a general study of the project. Then, the systems analyst

Feasibility Study

For more information, visit the Computer Concepts CourseMate Web site at www.cengagebrain.com, navigate to the Chapter 12 Web Link resource for this book, and then click Feasibility Study.

presents his or her findings in a report. Figure 12-6 shows a sample feasibility report, also sometimes known as the feasibility study.

In this phase, the systems analyst defines the problem or improvement accurately. The actual problem may be different from the one suggested in the project request. The first activity in the preliminary investigation is to interview the user who submitted the project request. Depending on the nature of the request, project team members may interview other users, too. In the case of the school, members of the team might interview the controller for data entry and quality control costs. They also might interview one or two registration clerks, quality control clerks, instructors, and students.

Horizon Community College

MEMORANDUM

To: Steering Committee
From: Karl Schmidt, Project Leader
Date: December 29, 2011
Subject: Feasibility Report of Grade Reporting System

Following is the feasibility report in response to the request for a modification to our Grade Reporting System. Your approval is necessary before the next phase of the project will begin.

Introduction

The purpose of this feasibility report is to determine whether it is beneficial for Horizon Community College to continue studying the Grade Reporting System. The registrar has indicated registration and quality control department staff spends too much time entering and verifying semester grades. This project would affect the registration department, quality control, and instructors. Students also will notice a change.

Existing System

Background

Currently, instructors use their own method for recording assignment grades and calculating semester grades. At semester end, the registration department distributes via e-mail a class semester grade form, which contains a list of all students in a class and an area for the instructor to record each student's final semester grade. As instructors send in their class semester grade forms, registration clerks enter each student's grade using the school's database. After grades are entered, the quality control group compares the original semester grade forms with the entered grades to check for any errors that may have occurred during the data entry process. Then, report cards are printed and mailed to students.

Problems

As the number of enrolled students continues to rise, the following problems have been identified with the current Grade Reporting System at Horizon Community College:

- Registration clerks and quality control spend too much time entering semester grades and verifying entered grades.
- Quality control has been finding an excessive number of data entry errors in part due to the increased workload on the registration clerks.

FEASIBILITY REPORT
Page 2

Benefits of a New or Modified System

Following is a list of benefits that could be realized if the Grade Reporting System at Horizon Community College were modified to enable instructors to use an online grade book, so that report cards could be printed directly from each instructor's grade book:

- Data entry errors of semester grades by registration clerks would be eliminated.
- Cost of supplies, such as paper and ink, would be reduced by 10 percent.
- Through a more efficient use of registration and quality control staff time, the college could achieve a 50 percent reduction in temporary clerks in the registration department.

Feasibility of a New or Modified System

Operational

A modified Grade Reporting System will require instructors enter all semester grades online. In addition to report cards being generated automatically from each instructor's grade book, students will be able to check their class progress throughout the semester.

Schedule

The established deadline for the Grade Reporting System is reasonable.

Technical

Horizon Community College already has a functional database and server. To handle the increased volume and usage of data, however, it will need to purchase a larger database server.

Economic

A detailed summary of the costs and benefits, including all assumptions, is available on our FTP server. The potential costs of the proposed solution could range from $15,000 to $20,000. The estimated savings in temporary clerks and supplies will exceed $30,000.

If you have any questions about the detailed cost/benefit summary or require further information, please contact me.

Recommendation

Based on the findings presented in this report, we recommend a continued study of the Grade Reporting System.

Figure 12-6 A feasibility report presents the results of the preliminary investigation. The report must be prepared professionally and be well organized to be effective.

In addition to interviewing, members of the project team may use other data gathering techniques, such as reviewing existing documentation. The time spent on this phase of system development is quite short when compared with the remainder of the project. Often, the preliminary investigation is completed in just a few days.

Upon completion of the preliminary investigation, the systems analyst writes the feasibility report. This report presents the team's findings to the steering committee. The feasibility report contains these major sections: introduction, existing system, benefits of a new or modified system, feasibility of a new or modified system, and the recommendation.

In some cases, the project team may recommend not to continue the project. That is, the team considers the project infeasible. If the steering committee agrees, the project ends at this point. If the project team recommends continuing and the steering committee approves this recommendation, however, then detailed analysis begins.

Preliminary Investigation at Horizon Community College

Karl Schmidt, systems analyst and project leader, meets with Chad Goldstein to discuss the project request. During the interview, Karl looks at the class semester grade forms. He asks Chad how many data entry errors that quality control identified during the last batch of report cards. Then Karl interviews the controller, Juanita Mendez, to obtain some general cost and benefit figures for the feasibility report. He also talks to several registration clerks, quality control clerks, instructors, and students. He wants to know their opinion of the current report card process.

Next, Karl prepares the feasibility report (Figure 12-6). After the project team members review it, Karl submits it to the steering committee. The report recommends proceeding to the detailed analysis phase of this project. The steering committee agrees. Karl and his team begin detailed analysis.

Detailed Analysis

Detailed analysis involves three major activities: (1) study how the current system works; (2) determine the users' wants, needs, and requirements; and (3) recommend a solution. Detailed analysis sometimes is called *logical design* because the systems analysts develop the proposed solution without regard to any specific hardware or software. That is, they make no attempt to identify the procedures that should be automated and those that should be manual.

During these activities, systems analysts use all of the data and information gathering techniques. They review documentation, observe employees and machines, distribute surveys, interview employees, conduct JAD sessions, and research. An important benefit from these activities is that they build valuable relationships among the systems analysts and users.

While studying the current system and identifying user requirements, the systems analyst collects a great deal of data and information. A major task for the systems analyst is to document these findings in a way that can be understood by everyone. Both users and IT professionals refer to this documentation.

Most systems analysts use either a process modeling or object modeling approach to analysis and design. The following pages discuss these approaches.

? FAQ 12-3

How can systems analysts build relationships with users?

Systems analysts have much more credibility with users if the analysts understand user concerns and have empathy for how the workers are feeling. If users are involved, they are more likely to accept and use the new system — called *user buy-in*. One reason systems fail is because some systems analysts create or modify systems with little or no user participation.

For more information, visit the Computer Concepts CourseMate Web site at www.cengagebrain.com, navigate to the Chapter 12 FAQ resource for this book, and then click Systems Analyst.

Process Modeling

Process modeling, sometimes called *structured analysis and design*, is an analysis and design technique that describes processes that transform inputs into outputs. Tools that a systems analyst uses for process modeling include entity-relationship diagrams, data flow diagrams, and the project dictionary. The following pages discuss these tools.

Process Modeling

For more information, visit the Computer Concepts CourseMate Web site at www.cengagebrain.com, navigate to the Chapter 12 Web Link resource for this book, and then click Process Modeling.

Entity-Relationship Diagrams An **entity-relationship diagram** (*ERD*) is a tool that graphically shows the connections among entities in a system. An *entity* is an object in the system that has data. For example, a school might have student, grades, class, room, and instructor entities.

On the ERD, entity names usually are nouns written in all capital letters. Each relationship describes a connection between two entities. In the ERD shown in Figure 12-7, a class contains one or more students, is taught by one instructor, and may or may not be held in a room. A student may or may not take classes in a given semester and, similarly, may or may not earn grades.

It is important that the systems analyst has an accurate understanding of the system. The systems analyst reviews the ERD with the user. After users approve the ERD, the systems analyst identifies data items associated with an entity. For example, the STUDENT entity might have these data items: Student ID, First Name, Last Name, Address, City, State, Postal Code, E-mail Address, Date Admitted, Major, and Photo.

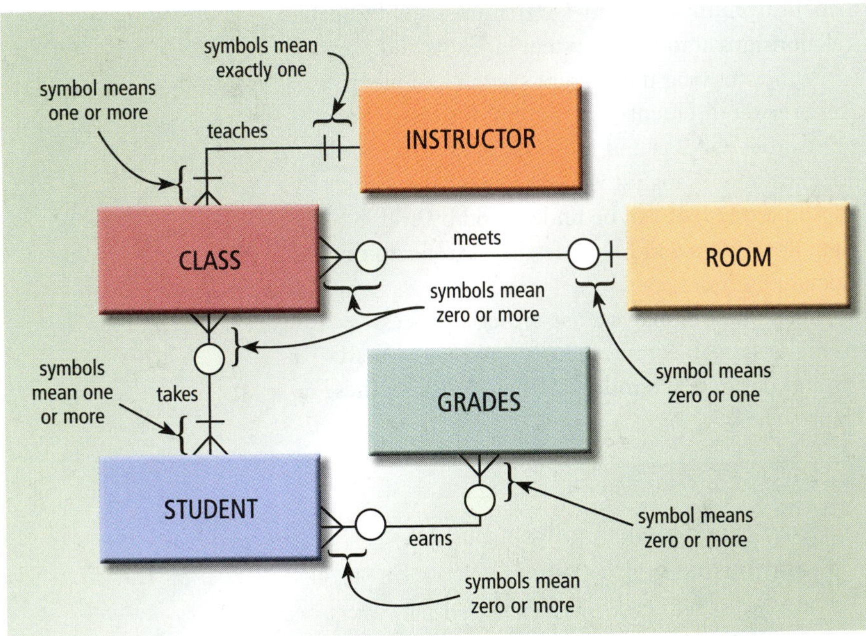

Figure 12-7 This ERD shows the relationships among entities in the Grade Reporting System at Horizon Community College.

Data Flow Diagrams A **data flow diagram** (*DFD*) is a tool that graphically shows the flow of data in a system. The key elements of a DFD are the data flows, the processes, the data stores, and the sources (Figure 12-8). A *data flow*, indicated by a line with an arrow, shows the input or output of data or information into or out from a process. A *process*, which is drawn as a circle, transforms an input data flow into an output data flow. A *data store*, shown as a rectangle with no sides, is a holding place for data and information. Examples of data stores are filing cabinets, checkbook registers, or electronic files stored on a computer. A *source*, drawn as a square, identifies an entity outside the scope of the system. Sources send data into the system or receive information from the system.

Like ERDs, systems analysts often use DFDs to review processes with users. Systems analysts prepare DFDs on a level-by-level basis. The top level DFD, known as a *context diagram*, identifies only the major process. Lower-level DFDs add detail and definition to the higher levels, similar to zooming in

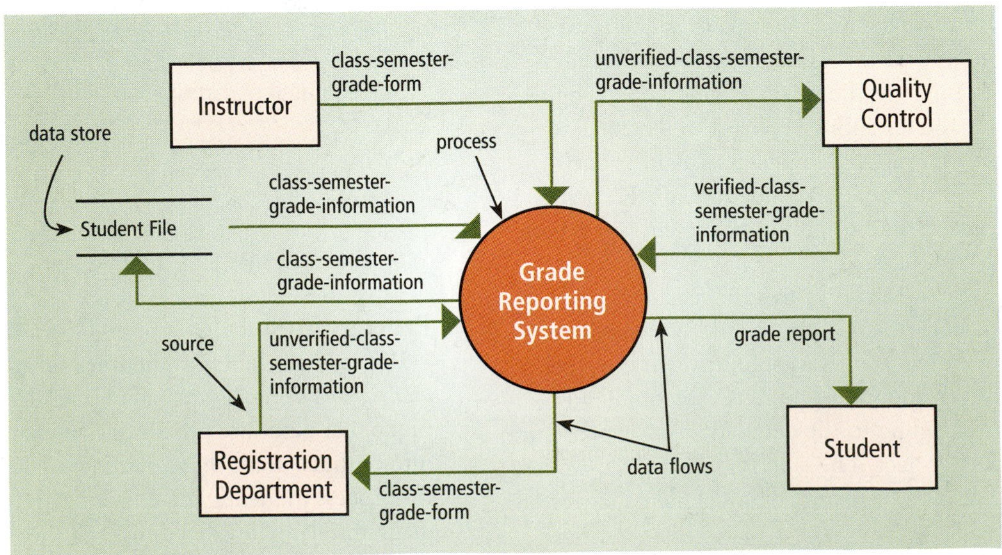

Figure 12-8 This data flow diagram, called the context diagram, has one process — the Grade Reporting System being studied at Horizon Community College. The Student File is a data store. Sources both send and receive data and information to and from the system.

on a computer screen. The lower-level DFDs contain subprocesses. For example, Figure 12-8 shows a context diagram that contains the Grade Reporting System process. This process might be split into three subprocesses: (1) gathering and organizing class semester grade forms, (2) entering and validating class semester grades, and (3) printing and distributing grade reports.

Project Dictionary The **project dictionary**, sometimes called the *repository*, contains all the documentation and deliverables of a project. The project dictionary helps everyone keep track of the huge amount of details in a system. The dictionary explains every item found on DFDs and ERDs. Each process, data store, data flow, and source on every DFD has an entry in the project dictionary. Every entity on the ERD has an entry in the project dictionary. The dictionary also contains an entry for each data item associated with the entities.

The number of entries added to the dictionary at this point can be enormous. Thus, this activity requires a lot of time.

The systems analyst uses a variety of techniques to enter these items in the project dictionary. Some of these include structured English, decision tables and decision trees, and the data dictionary.

- *Structured English* is a style of writing that describes the steps in a process. Many systems analysts use structured English to explain the details of a process. Figure 12-9 shows an example of structured English that describes the process of entering class semester grades.

Entering Class Semester Grades

For each semester class, perform the following steps:

  For each student, perform the following steps:

    Enter the grade earned.

    Verify the entered grade.

  Print the semester class entered grades.

  Create a cover sheet for quality control.

Figure 12-9 Structured English is a technique used to describe a process in the project dictionary. This structured English example describes the process of entering semester class grades. The indented text is part of a loop.

- Sometimes, a process consists of many conditions or rules. In this case, the systems analyst may use a decision table or decision tree instead of structured English. A **decision table** is a table that lists a variety of conditions and the actions that correspond to each condition. A *decision tree* also shows conditions and actions, but it shows them graphically. Figures 12-10 and 12-11 show a decision table and decision tree for the same process: determining whether a student can be enrolled in a class.

		Rules							
		1	2	3	4	5	6	7	8
Conditions	Student status (A = Active, I = Inactive)	A	A	A	A	I	I	I	I
	Prerequisites met?	Y	Y	N	N	Y	Y	N	N
	Seats available?	Y	N	Y	N	Y	N	Y	N
Actions	Student enrolled	X							
	Student not enrolled		X	X	X	X	X	X	X

Figure 12-10 This decision table describes the policy for determining whether students can be enrolled in a class at Horizon Community College. Students are enrolled if they meet all conditions in Rule #1. For example, students are enrolled if their status is active, they have met all prerequisites, and the class has seats available.

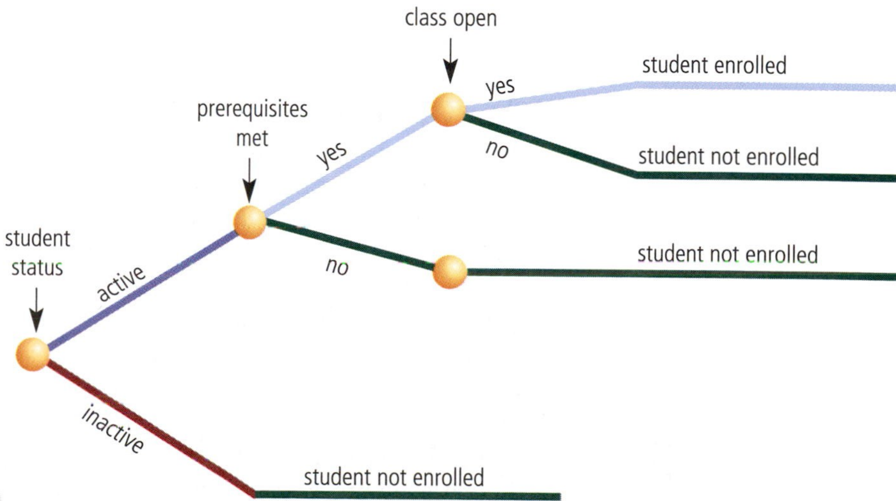

Figure 12-11 Some systems analysts prefer decision trees instead of decision tables because decision trees are graphical. The decision tree in this figure shows the same conditions as the decision table in Figure 12-10.

- Each data item has an entry in the data dictionary section of the project dictionary (Figure 12-12). The **data dictionary** stores the data item's name, description, and other details about each data item. Some DBMSs automatically generate the data dictionary. For others, the systems analyst creates the data dictionary. In later phases of system development, the systems analyst refers to and updates the data dictionary.

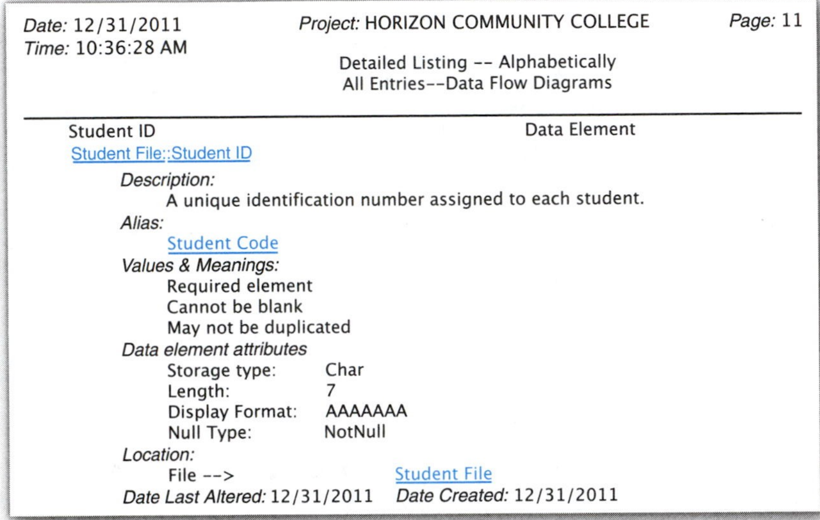

Date: 12/31/2011
Time: 10:36:28 AM
Project: HORIZON COMMUNITY COLLEGE
Page: 11

Detailed Listing -- Alphabetically
All Entries--Data Flow Diagrams

Student ID — Data Element
Student File::Student ID

Description:
A unique identification number assigned to each student.

Alias:
Student Code

Values & Meanings:
Required element
Cannot be blank
May not be duplicated

Data element attributes

Storage type:	Char
Length:	7
Display Format:	AAAAAAA
Null Type:	NotNull

Location:
File --> Student File

Date Last Altered: 12/31/2011 *Date Created:* 12/31/2011

Figure 12-12 The data dictionary records details about each of the data items that make up the data flows and entities in the system. This is a dictionary entry for the Student ID data element.

Object Modeling

Object modeling, sometimes called *object-oriented (OO) analysis and design*, combines the data with the processes that act on that data into a single unit, called an object. An **object** is an item that can contain both data and the procedures that read or manipulate that data. For example, a Student object might contain data about a student (Student ID, First Name, Last Name, Address, and so on) and instructions about how to print a student's record or the formula required to compute a student's GPA. Each data element is called an *attribute* or *property*. The procedure in the object, called an *operation* or *method*, contains activities that read or manipulate the data. For example, a school would create a new student object (method) for each new student.

Object modeling can use the same tools as those used in process modeling. Many systems analysts, however, choose to use tools defined in the UML. Although used in all types of business modeling, the **UML** (*Unified Modeling Language*) has been adopted as a standard notation for object modeling and development. The UML is a graphical tool that enables analysts to document a system. It consists of many interrelated diagrams. Each diagram conveys a view of the system.

Instead of developing their own object diagrams and steps in object-oriented system development, most organizations use an existing methodology to guide them through the system development steps. A popular methodology on the market today that uses the UML is the *Rational Unified Process* (*RUP*) by Grady Booch, Ivar Jacobsen, and James Rumbaugh.

The latest UML version includes 13 different diagrams to assist the analyst in modeling the system. Two of the more common tools are the use case diagram and class diagram. The next sections describe these two diagrams.

UML

For more information, visit the Computer Concepts CourseMate Web site at www.cengagebrain.com, navigate to the Chapter 12 Web Link resource for this book, and then click UML.

Use Case Diagram A **use case diagram** graphically shows how actors interact with the information system. An *actor* is a user or other entity such as a program. The function that the actor can perform is called the *use case*. Thus, a use case diagram shows actors and their use cases (Figure 12-13). The actor is drawn as a stick figure that connects to each use case with an arrow.

Because these diagrams are easy to understand, analysts find that the use case diagram is an ideal tool for communicating system requirements with users.

Figure 12-13 This use case diagram shows that the student needs the system for two use cases: enroll in class and earn grade.

Class Diagram A **class diagram** graphically shows classes and subclasses in a system (Figure 12-14). On a class diagram, objects are grouped into classes. Each class can have one or more lower levels called *subclasses*. Each subclass inherits the methods and attributes of the objects in its higher-level class. Every object in a class shares methods and attributes that are part of its higher-level class. This concept of lower levels inheriting methods and attributes of higher levels is called *inheritance*. In the simplified example in Figure 12-14, On Campus Class and Distance Learning Class are subclasses of the higher-level class, called Class. All classes have a Class Code, Class Section, and Instructor ID (which would be attributes in the Class object). Only on campus classes have assigned rooms and scheduled days and times, and only distance learning classes require instructor e-mail addresses and Web addresses.

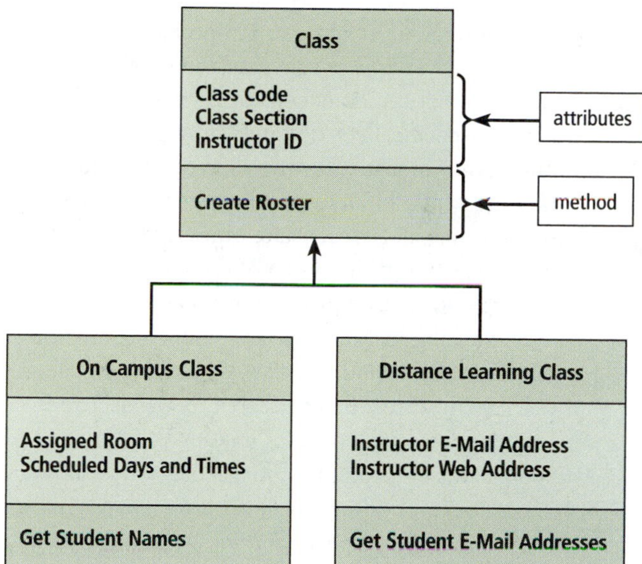

Figure 12-14 In this simplified class diagram, the Class class has two subclasses: On Campus Class and Distance Learning Class.

The System Proposal

The systems analyst has studied the current system and determined all user requirements. The next step is to communicate possible solutions for the project in a system proposal. The purpose of the *system proposal* is to assess the feasibility of each alternative solution and then recommend the most feasible solution for the project, which often involves modifying or building on the current system. The systems analyst reevaluates feasibility at this point in system development, especially economic feasibility (often in conjunction with a financial analyst). The systems analyst presents the system proposal to the steering committee. If the steering committee approves a solution, the project enters the design phase.

When the steering committee discusses the system proposal and decides which alternative to pursue, it considers whether to modify the existing system, buy packaged software from an outside source, build its own custom software, and/or outsource some or all of its IT needs to an outside firm. The final decision often is a mix of these options.

Packaged Software **Packaged software** is mass-produced, copyrighted, prewritten software available for purchase. Packaged software is available for different types of computers. Chapter 3 presented many types of application software available for personal computers. These include word processing, spreadsheet, note taking, database, document management, desktop publishing, paint/image editing, Web page authoring, personal finance, legal, tax preparation, educational/reference, e-mail, and Web browser software. Read Ethics & Issues 12-3 for a related discussion.

Vendors offer two types of packaged software: horizontal and vertical. *Horizontal market software* meets the needs of many different types of organizations. The programs discussed in Chapter 3

ETHICS & ISSUES 12-3

Do Copyrights Promote Creativity or Stifle It?

The U.S. Constitution, written more than 200 years ago, includes a clause stating that Congress must secure rights to creators of art, written material, and inventions. When Congress originally wrote the copyright law, most artists, authors, and inventors were in the upper class, and the ability to copy a work illegally was limited. Additionally, the original copyright law written in 1790 provided rights to a creator for 14 years, with a possible 14 year extension. Since then, Congress has extended rights to up to 120 years, or the lifetime of the creator plus 70 years. The digital age provides the ability for millions of people to break copyright law on a daily basis, and most people do not realize they are breaking the law. Technology to copy music, movies, art, and inventions is available to almost everyone. Opponents of current copyright law find many flaws. First, the length of copyrights lowers the incentive for creators to produce additional works because they, and their heirs, retain rights for more than 100 years. Additionally, many copyrights are held by companies, which may have an unlimited lifetime and, therefore, unlimited rights to works created by the company. They claim that copyright laws should be rewritten to encourage creativity and acknowledge the ease of copying materials.

Do copyrights promote creativity or stifle it? Why? Is the current notion of copyright outdated? Why? What are some fundamental changes to copyright law that you would suggest to lawmakers, if any? Why? How long should copyrights be in effect for a work? Why? Should corporations be treated differently by the law than individuals? Why?

Vertical Market Software

For more information, visit the Computer Concepts CourseMate Web site at www.cengagebrain.com, navigate to the Chapter 12 Web Link resource for this book, and then click Vertical Market Software.

were horizontal. If an organization has a unique way of accomplishing activities, then it also may require vertical market software. *Vertical market software* specifically is designed for a particular business or industry. Examples of organizations that use vertical market software include banks, schools, hospitals, real estate offices, libraries, and insurance companies. Each of these industries has unique information processing requirements.

Horizontal market software tends to be more widely available and less expensive than vertical market software. You can search for vertical and horizontal market software on the Web. Other sources include computer magazines, trade shows, and trade publications. A *trade publication* is a magazine written for a specific business or industry. Software for these industries often is advertised in trade publications.

Custom Software Instead of buying packaged software, some organizations write their own applications using programming languages such as C++, C#, F#, Java, JavaScript, and Visual Basic. Application software developed by the user or at the user's request is called **custom software**.

The main advantage of custom software is that it matches the organization's requirements exactly. The disadvantages usually are that it is more expensive and takes longer to design and implement than packaged software.

Outsourcing Organizations can develop custom software in-house using their own IT personnel or *outsource* its development, which means having an outside source develop it for them. Some organizations outsource just the software development aspect of their IT operation. Others outsource more or all of their IT operation.

Depending on an organization's needs, outside firms can handle as much of the IT requirements as desired. Some provide hardware and software. Others provide services such as Web design and development, Web hosting, sales, marketing, billing, customer service, and legal assistance. For example, an *Internet solutions provider* is a company that provides Web hosting services that include managing shopping carts, inventory, and credit card processing (Figure 12-15). A trend that has caused much controversy relates to organizations that outsource to firms located outside their homeland. Read Ethics & Issues 12-4 for a related discussion.

Some organizations obtain software through Web services. Recall from Chapter 9 that Web services describe standardized software that enables programmers to create applications that can communicate with other remote computers over the Internet or on an internal network. Some Web services are free; others charge a fee.

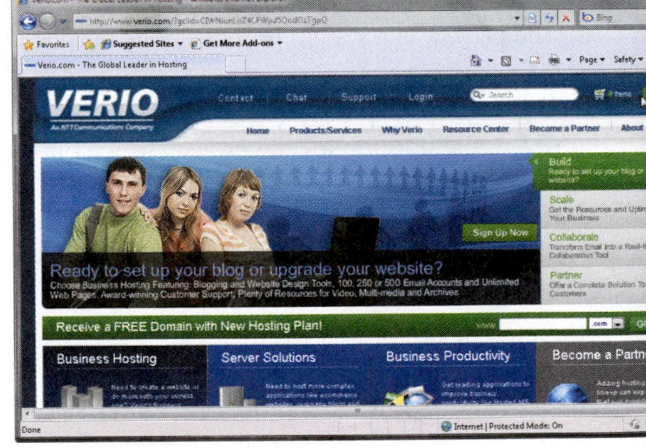

Figure 12-15 An Internet solutions provider.

FAQ 12-4

Is the level of outsourcing increasing or decreasing?

The amount of outsourcing mostly is increasing. The chart to the right shows the percentage of organizations that use outside service providers.

For more information, visit the Computer Concepts CourseMate Web site at www.cengagebrain.com, navigate to the Chapter 12 FAQ resource for this book, and then click Outsourcing.

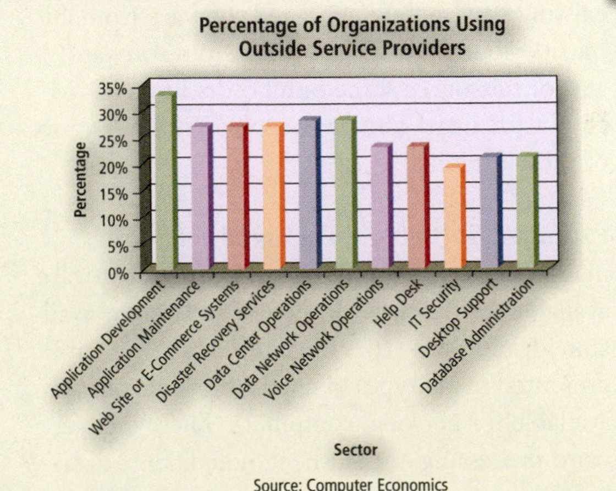

ETHICS & ISSUES 12-4

Is Outsourcing to Blame for Security Breaches?

In recent years, a common trend among organizations is the outsourcing of noncore functions. An organization's core functions include those specialties that differentiate the organization from other types of businesses or competitors. For example, one core function of a software company is the development of new programs. Noncore functions often include general business tasks. For example, the maintenance and support for an organization's computer systems may be outsourced to an outside vendor. Businesses outsource noncore functions because outside vendors often are more efficient and more cost effective than the business trying to perform the functions on its own.

Sometimes, however, when a business outsources, the outside vendors are not as careful with security and customer information as the business itself might be. One function that businesses often outsource is processing customer payments on Web sites. The business that outsources this task has spent time and effort to cultivate and then forge a relationship with its customers, and it is in the business' best interest to treat its customers well. The payment processing vendor, however, has no such bond with the customers. Often, this distance results in security breaches and stolen personal information, such as credit card numbers.

Does outsourcing lead to a lower level of security and privacy for customers? Why or why not? What can an organization do to ensure that vendors have the same level of care for customer information as the organization? Should customers hold organizations or their vendors responsible for leaks of private customer information? Why?

Detailed Analysis at Horizon Community College

Karl and his team begin performing the activities in the detailed analysis phase of the Grade Reporting System. As part of the study and requirements activities, they use several of the data and information gathering techniques available to them. They interview employees throughout the school and meet with some students. They observe instructors recording grades. Because the team is using structured analysis and design techniques, they prepare many process modeling deliverables to record their findings: an entity-relationship diagram (Figure 12-7 on page 632), a data flow diagram (Figure 12-8 on page 632), a process specification using structured English (Figure 12-9 on page 633), a process specification using a decision table (Figure 12-10 on page 633), and a data dictionary entry for a Student ID data item (Figure 12-12 on page 634). These documents all become part of the project notebook. Members of the project team refer to these documents during the remainder of the SDLC.

After two months of studying the existing system and obtaining user requirements, Karl discusses his findings with his supervisor, Bethany Ames. In addition to semester grades being printed from the online grade book, Karl recommends that students be granted access to the online grade book so that they can check their progress in a class at any given time.

Based on Karl's findings, Bethany writes a system proposal for the steering committee to review. Suzy Zhao, Web developer at Horizon Community College, developed the current Web site. Thus, Bethany recommends that Suzy's staff modify the Web site in-house. Bethany also recommends that the school invest in a larger database server to handle the additional grade book information.

The steering committee agrees with Bethany's proposal. Karl and his team begin the design phase of the project.

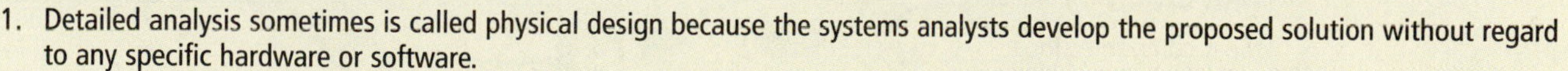

QUIZ YOURSELF 12-2

Instructions: Find the true statement below. Then, rewrite the remaining false statements so that they are true.

1. Detailed analysis sometimes is called physical design because the systems analysts develop the proposed solution without regard to any specific hardware or software.
2. Entity-relationship diagrams and data flow diagrams are tools that a systems analyst uses for object modeling.
3. Horizontal market software specifically is designed for a particular business or industry.
4. The project dictionary contains all the documentation and deliverables of a project.
5. The purpose of the preliminary investigation is to assess the feasibility of each alternative solution and then recommend the most feasible solution for the project.
6. Upon completion of the preliminary investigation, the systems analyst writes the system proposal.

Quiz Yourself Online: To further check your knowledge of pages 629 through 637, visit the Computer Concepts CourseMate Web site at www.cengagebrain.com, navigate to the Chapter 12 Quiz Yourself resource for this book, and then click Objectives 5 – 7.

Design Phase

The **design phase** consists of two major activities: (1) if necessary, acquire hardware and software and (2) develop all of the details of the new or modified information system. The systems analyst often performs these two activities at the same time instead of sequentially.

Acquiring Necessary Hardware and Software

When the steering committee approves a solution, the systems analyst begins the activity of obtaining additional hardware or software or evaluating cloud storage providers that offer the hardware or software to meet the organization's needs. The systems analyst may skip this activity if the approved solution does not require new hardware or software. If this activity is required, the selection of appropriate products or providers is crucial for the success of the information system. The activity consists of four major tasks: (1) identify technical specifications, (2) solicit vendor proposals, (3) test and evaluate vendor proposals, and (4) make a decision.

Identifying Technical Specifications

The first step in acquiring the necessary hardware and software is to identify all the hardware and software requirements of the new or modified system. To do this, systems analysts use a variety of research techniques. They talk with other systems analysts, visit vendors' stores, and search the Web. Many trade journals, newspapers, and magazines provide some or all of their printed content as e-zines. An **e-zine** (pronounced ee-zeen), or *electronic magazine*, is a publication available on the Web.

E-Zines

For more information, visit the Computer Concepts CourseMate Web site at www.cengagebrain.com, navigate to the Chapter 12 Web Link resource for this book, and then click E-Zines.

After the systems analyst defines the technical requirements, the next step is to summarize these requirements for potential vendors. The systems analyst can use three basic types of documents for this purpose: an RFQ, an RFP, or an RFI. A *request for quotation* (*RFQ*) identifies the required product(s). With an RFQ, the vendor quotes a price for the listed product(s). With a *request for proposal* (*RFP*), the vendor selects the product(s) that meets specified requirements and then quotes the price(s). Software is available that assists with the creation of a professional RFP.

Just as the depth of an information system varies, so does the length of an RFQ or RFP. Some can be as short as a couple of pages. Others consist of more than one hundred pages. Instead of an RFQ or RFP, some organizations prefer to use a request for information. A *request for information* (*RFI*) is a less formal method that uses a standard form to request information about a product or service.

Soliciting Vendor Proposals

Systems analysts send the RFQ, RFP, or RFI to potential hardware and software vendors. They have a variety of ways to locate vendors. Many publish their product catalogs on the Web. These online catalogs provide up-to-date information about and easy access to products, prices, technical specifications, and ordering information.

Another source for hardware and software products is a value-added reseller. A *value-added reseller* (*VAR*) is a company that purchases products from manufacturers and then resells these products to the public — offering additional services with the product. Examples of additional services include user support, equipment maintenance, training, installation, and warranties.

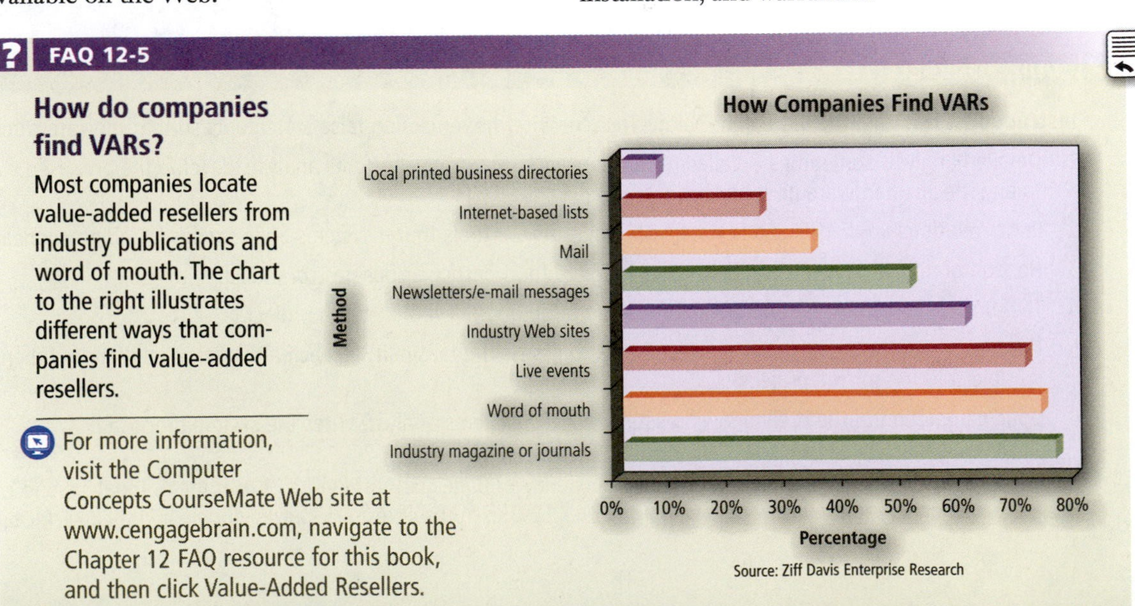

FAQ 12-5

How do companies find VARs?

Most companies locate value-added resellers from industry publications and word of mouth. The chart to the right illustrates different ways that companies find value-added resellers.

For more information, visit the Computer Concepts CourseMate Web site at www.cengagebrain.com, navigate to the Chapter 12 FAQ resource for this book, and then click Value-Added Resellers.

To be an authorized VAR, most manufacturers have requirements the VAR must meet. Various terms that identify a VAR's relationship with a manufacturer are strategic partner, business partner, authorized reseller, or solutions provider. Some VARs offer one product or service. Others provide complete systems, also known as a *turnkey solution* (Figure 12-16).

IT Consultants Instead of using vendors, some organizations hire an IT consultant or a group of IT consultants; that is, they outsource this task. An *IT consultant* is a professional who is hired based on computer expertise, including service and advice. IT consultants often specialize in configuring hardware and software for businesses of all sizes.

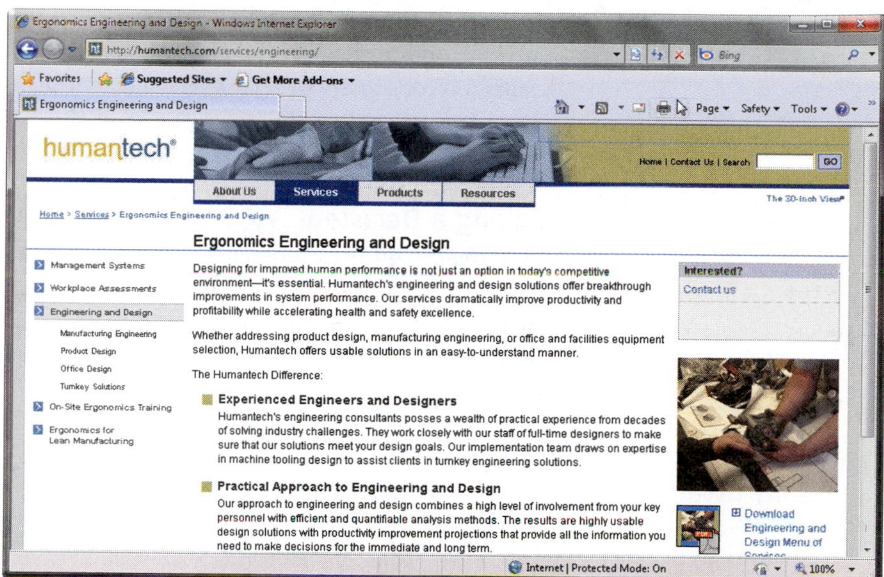

Figure 12-16 Many VARs provide turnkey solutions.

Testing and Evaluating Vendor Proposals

After sending RFQs and RFPs to potential vendors, the systems analyst will receive completed quotations and proposals. Evaluating the proposals and then selecting the best one often is a difficult task. It is important to be as objective as possible while evaluating each proposal.

Systems analysts use many techniques to test the various software products from vendors. They obtain a list of user references from the software vendors. They also talk to current users of the software to solicit their opinions. Some vendors will give a demonstration of the product(s) specified. Other vendors provide demonstration copies or trial versions, allowing the organizations to test the software themselves. Demonstration copies usually are free and have limited functionality. Trial versions are free or have minimal fees and provide full functionality for a set time (Figure 12-17). In some cases, the demonstration copies and trial versions are available to download from the Web.

Sometimes it is important to know whether the software can process a certain volume of transactions efficiently. In this case, the systems analyst conducts a benchmark test. A *benchmark test* measures the performance of hardware or software. For example, a benchmark test could measure the time it takes a payroll program to print 50 paychecks. Comparing the time it takes various accounting programs to print the same 50 paychecks is one way of measuring each program's performance. Some computer magazines

FAQ 12-6

Where do organizations find an IT consultant?

For a reliable IT consultant reference, organizations search a consultant reference guide on the Web; attend a user meeting; contact a professional organization in the industry, a hardware vendor, or a local university; look through a local newspaper; or obtain a referral.

For more information, visit the Computer Concepts CourseMate Web site at www.cengagebrain.com, navigate to the Chapter 12 FAQ resource for this book, and then click IT Consultants.

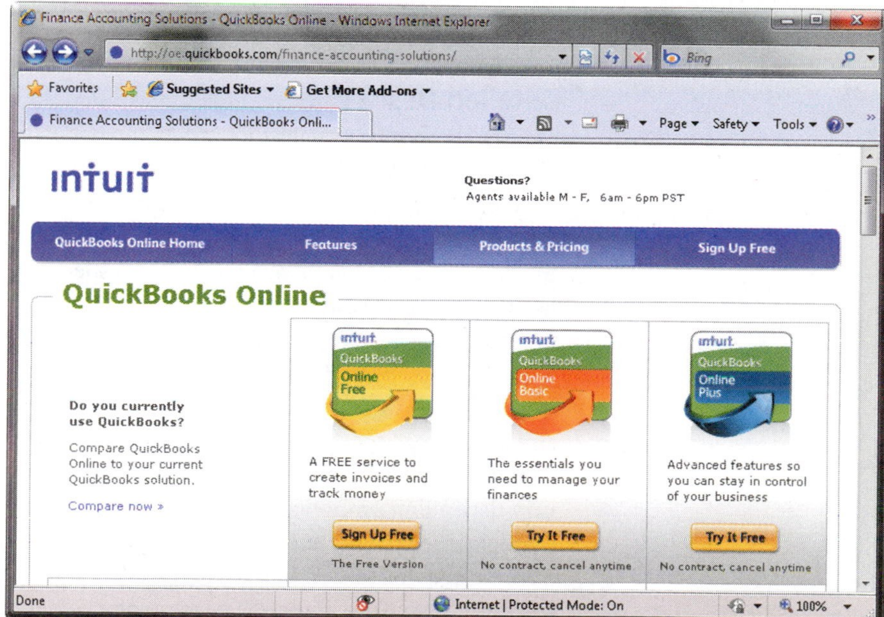

Figure 12-17 This trial version of QuickBooks can be downloaded free and expires 30 days after installation.

conduct benchmark tests while evaluating hardware and software and then publish the results for consumers to review. For a technical discussion about benchmark tests, read the High-Tech Talk article on page 648.

Making a Decision

Having rated the proposals, the systems analyst presents a recommendation to the steering committee. The recommendation could be to award a contract to a vendor or to not make any purchases at this time.

Hardware Acquisition at Horizon Community College

Karl and his team compile a requirements list for the database server. They prepare an RFP and submit it to twelve vendors: eight through the Web and four local computer stores. Ten vendors reply within the three-week deadline.

Of the ten replies, the development team selects two to evaluate. They eliminate the other eight because these vendors did not offer adequate warranties for the database server. The project team members ask for benchmark test results for each server. In addition, they contact two current users of this database server for their opinions about its performance. After evaluating these two servers, the team selects the best one.

Karl summarizes his team's findings in a report to the steering committee. The committee gives Karl authorization to award a contract to the proposed vendor. As a courtesy and to maintain good working relationships, Karl sends a letter to all twelve vendors informing them of the committee's decision.

Detailed Design

After the systems analyst identifies the data and process requirements, the next step is to develop detailed design specifications for the components in the proposed solution. A detailed design sometimes is called a *physical design* because it specifies hardware and software — the physical components required — for automated procedures. The activities to be performed include developing designs for the databases, inputs, outputs, and programs.

The length and complexity of these activities vary depending on previous decisions. For example, the systems analyst may skip many of these activities when purchasing packaged software. If an organization is developing custom software, however, these activities can be quite time-consuming.

Database Design During database design, the systems analyst builds upon the data dictionary developed during the analysis phase. The systems analyst works closely with the database analysts and database administrators to identify those data elements that currently exist within the organizations and those that are new.

With relational database systems, the systems analyst defines the structure of each table in the system, as well as relationships among the tables. The systems analyst also addresses user access privileges. That is, the systems analyst defines which data elements each user can access, when they can access the data elements, what actions they can perform on the data elements, and under what circumstances they can access the elements. The result of database design is called a *data model*. Read Looking Ahead 12-1 for a look at a future database design.

LOOKING AHEAD 12-1

Remote Solar System Objects Mapped in Database

Exploding supernovas, neutron stars, and black holes will become more than faint astronomical objects when the Large Synoptic Survey Telescope (LSST) becomes fully operable in 2016. The LSST is being constructed atop an 8,800-foot mountain in Chile.

Managing the telescope's 200,000 images of the billions of remote galaxies is a massive undertaking. A single minute of observation time generates 72 GB of data, which will be saved in a 150 PB database. Each year, 60 PB of the stored images in this world's largest nonproprietary database will be released to researchers. Each night, 30 TB of data will be sent to the United States so that astronomy buffs can view the night sky via their computers. In addition, astronomers will be able to log on to the Data Access Center at any time to view all the data collected.

Software billionaires Bill Gates and Charles Simonyi have donated $30 million for the project. Researchers are hopeful the LSST ultimately will give a graphical view of the universe's evolution from its birth to the present day.

For more information, visit the Computer Concepts CourseMate Web site at www.cengagebrain.com, navigate to the Chapter 12 Looking Ahead resource for this book, and then click LSST.

Input and Output Design During this activity, the systems analyst carefully designs every menu, screen, and report specified in the requirements. The outputs often are designed first because they can help to define the requirements for the inputs. Thus, it is very important that outputs are identified correctly and that users agree to them.

The systems analyst typically develops two types of designs for each input and output: a mockup and a layout chart. A *mockup* is a sample of the input or output that contains actual data (Figure 12-18). The systems analyst shows mockups to users for their approval. Because users will work with the inputs and outputs of the system, it is crucial to involve users during input and output design. After users approve the mockup, the systems analyst develops a layout chart for the programmer. A *layout chart* is more technical and contains programming-like notations. Many database programs provide tools for technical design (Figure 12-19).

Other issues that must be addressed during input and output design include the types of media to use (paper, video, audio); formats (graphical or narrative); and data entry validation techniques, which include making sure the entered data is correct (for example, a state code has to be one of the fifty valid two-letter state abbreviations).

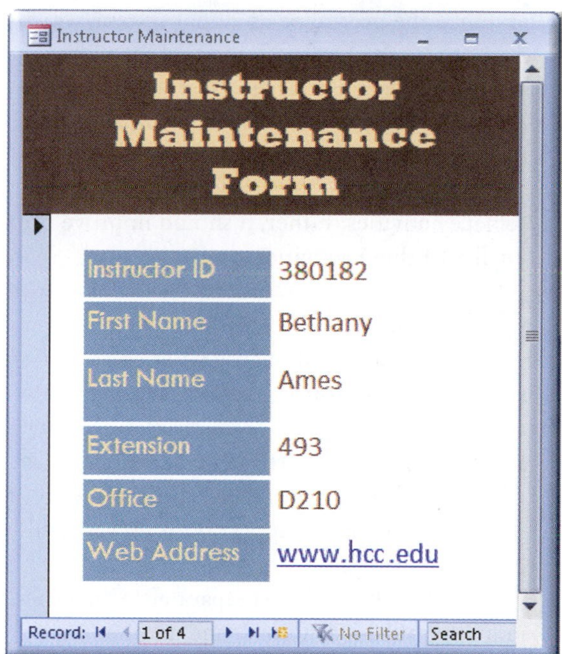

Figure 12-18 Users must give their approval on all inputs and outputs. This input screen is a mockup (containing actual sample data) for users to review.

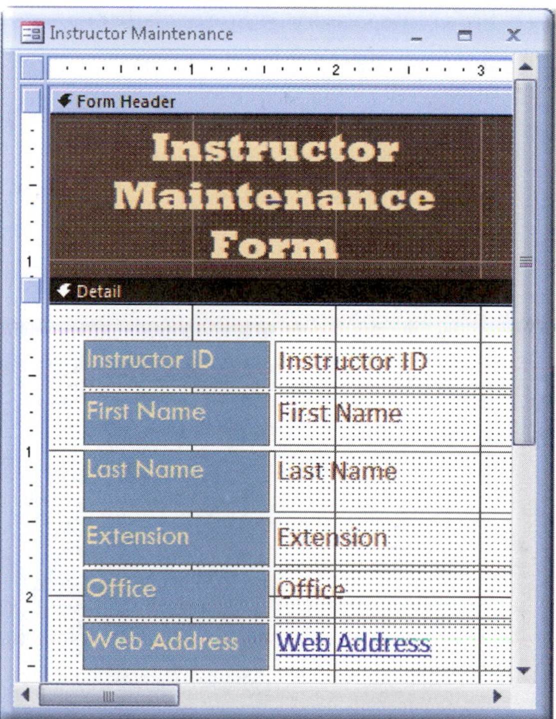

Figure 12-19 Shown here is a technical view in Access of the mockup in Figure 12-18.

Program Design During program design, the systems analyst prepares the *program specification package*, which identifies the required programs and the relationship among each program, as well as the input, output, and database specifications. Chapter 13 discusses program design at length.

Prototyping

Many systems analysts today use prototypes during detailed design. A **prototype**, sometimes called *proof of concept*, is a working model of the proposed system. The systems analyst actually builds a functional form of the solution during design. The main advantage of a prototype is users can work with the system before it is completed — to make sure it meets their needs.

The Instructor Maintenance Form shown in Figure 12-18 could be an example of a screen in a prototype of the Grade Reporting System. As soon as the users approve a prototype, systems analysts can implement a solution more quickly than without a prototype.

Some systems analysts use prototyping during the design phase. Others begin earlier in system development — during analysis or even planning.

A common problem with prototypes is they have inadequate documentation, or worse, none at all. Another drawback is that users tend to embrace the prototype as a final system, which may not be the result of an extensive analysis. Prototyping can be an effective tool if the development team and the users discipline themselves to follow all system development activities. Prototyping should not eliminate or replace activities; rather, it should improve the quality of these activities.

CASE Tools

Many systems analysts use computer software to assist during system development. *Computer-aided software engineering* (*CASE*) tools are designed to support one or more activities of system development. CASE tools typically include diagrams to support both process and object modeling.

Some CASE tools exist separately. One program might be a dictionary and another might allow you to create drawings. The most effective tools, however, are integrated (Figure 12-20).

Integrated case products, sometimes called *I-CASE* or a CASE workbench, include the following capabilities:

- Project Repository — Stores diagrams, specifications, descriptions, programs, and any other deliverable generated during system development.
- Graphics — Enables the drawing of diagrams, such as DFDs and ERDs.
- Prototyping — Creates models of the proposed system.
- Quality Assurance — Analyzes deliverables, such as graphs and the data dictionary, for accuracy.
- Code Generator — Creates actual computer programs from design specifications.
- Housekeeping — Establishes user accounts and provides backup and recovery functions.

CASE Tools
For more information, visit the Computer Concepts CourseMate Web site at www.cengagebrain.com, navigate to the Chapter 12 Web Link resource for this book, and then click CASE Tools.

Quality Review Techniques

Many people should review the detailed design specifications before they are given to the programming team. Reviewers should include users, systems analysts, managers, IT staff, and members of the system development team.

One popular review technique is an inspection. An *inspection* is a formal review of any system development deliverable. A team of four to five people examines the deliverables, such as reports, diagrams, mockups, layout charts, and dictionary entries. The purpose of an inspection is to identify errors in the item being inspected. Any identified errors are summarized in a report so that they can be addressed and corrected.

Once again, the systems analyst reevaluates feasibility to determine if it still is beneficial to proceed with the proposed solution. If the steering committee decides the project still is feasible, which usually is the case, the project enters the implementation phase.

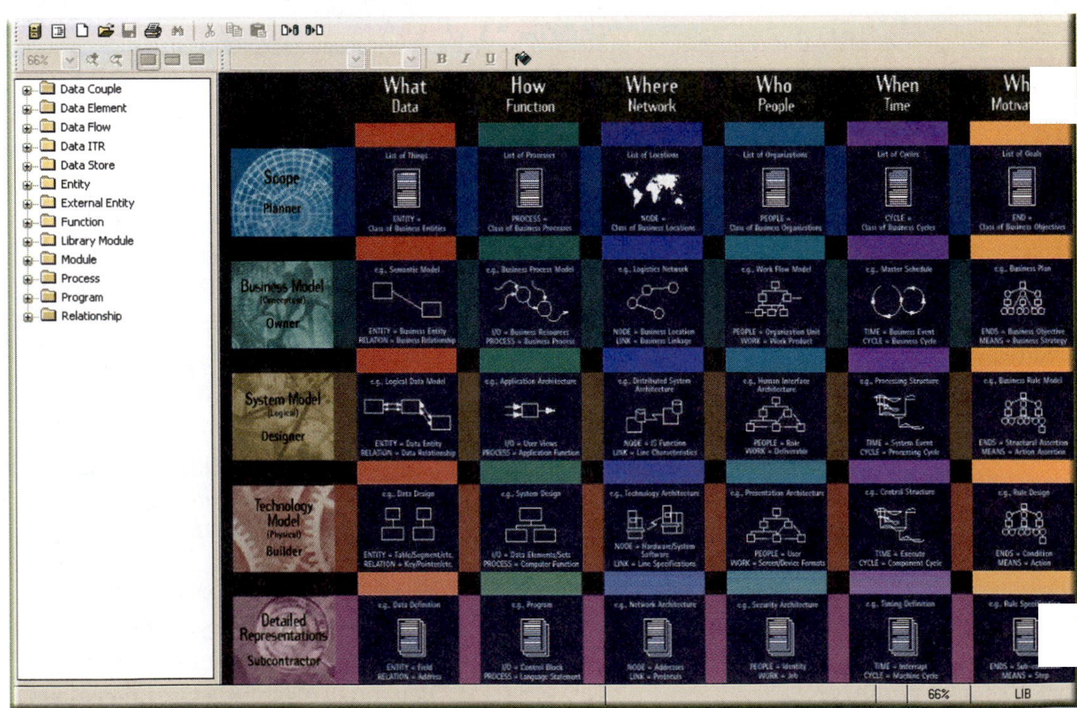

Figure 12-20
Integrated computer-aided software engineering (I-CASE) programs assist analysts in the development of an information system. Visible Analyst by Visible Systems Corporation enables analysts to create diagrams, as well as build the project dictionary.

 **FAQ 12-7**

Why do projects become infeasible late in the SDLC?

It does not happen often, but organizations cancel some projects before completion because the projects become infeasible. Projects often become infeasible either because the mission of the organization has changed and a new system is no longer needed, or because the organization finds it too costly to complete a system that meets all of their requirements.

 For more information, visit the Computer Concepts CourseMate Web site at www.cengagebrain.com, navigate to the Chapter 12 FAQ resource for this book, and then click Feasibility.

Detailed Design at Horizon Community College

As approved by the steering committee, Karl and his team begin designing the Grade Reporting System. After studying current vendor information and interviewing more users and vendors, the team designs changes to the school's database, Web site, and the associated programs. They prepare several documents including a mockup (Figure 12-18 on page 641) and a technical view in Access (Figure 12-19 on page 641).

After completing the detailed design, Karl meets with several users and IT personnel to walk through the deliverables. They locate two errors. He corrects the errors and then presents the design to the steering committee. The committee agrees with the design solution and consents to implement it.

Implementation Phase

The purpose of the **implementation phase** is to construct, or build, the new or modified system and then deliver it to the users. Members of the system development team perform four major activities in this phase: (1) develop programs, (2) install and test the new system, (3) train users, and (4) convert to the new system. Read Innovative Computing 12-1 to find out how the implementation phase was used in NASA's *Phoenix Mars Lander* Mission.

INNOVATIVE COMPUTING 12-1 

Phoenix Lander Probes Soil on Mars

Finding snow falling from Martian clouds was one of the key discoveries from NASA's *Phoenix Mars Lander* Mission. Scientists also learned that Martian soil contains calcium carbonate, which is the key component of chalk, along with salts and perhaps clay. The *Phoenix Lander's* arm dug a few inches under the surface soil and found ice.

Software engineers at Lockheed Martin wrote the programs that guided the spacecraft millions of miles in 2008 from Florida to the northern arctic plains on Mars. Engineers at the University of Arizona Lunar and Planetary Laboratory and NASA's Jet Propulsion Laboratory developed the software running the *Phoenix's* soil experiments to determine the "Red Planet's" climate, water history, soil, and chemistry. The programmers could modify *Phoenix's* schedule for the following day based on results from these experiments.

The system development team was able to prepare the *Phoenix* for launch in record time because the programmers modified software from a partially assembled lander system that had been cancelled in 2001.

For more information, visit the Computer Concepts CourseMate Web site at www.cengagebrain.com, navigate to the Chapter 12 Innovative Computing resource for this book, and then click Phoenix Mars Lander.

Develop Programs

If the organization purchases packaged software and no modifications to the software are required, the development team may skip this activity. For custom software or packaged software that requires modification, however, programs are developed or modified either by an outside firm or in-house. Programmers write or modify programs from the program specification package created during the analysis phase. Just as system development follows an organized set of activities, so does program development. These program development activities are known as the *program development life cycle*.

The program development life cycle follows these six steps: (1) analyze the requirements, (2) design the solution, (3) validate the design, (4) implement the design, (5) test the solution, and (6) document the solution. Chapter 13 explains the program development life cycle in depth. An important concept to understand is that the program development life cycle is a part of the implementation phase, which is part of the system development life cycle.

Install and Test the New System

If the organization acquires new hardware or software, someone must install and test it. The systems analysts should test individual programs. They also should be sure that all the programs work together in the system. Systems analysts do not want errors in the system after it is delivered to the users.

Systems analysts and users develop test data so that they can perform various tests. The test data should include both valid (correct) and invalid (incorrect) data. When valid test data is entered, the program should produce the correct results. Invalid test data should generate an error.

Tests performed during this step include unit tests, systems tests, integration tests, and acceptance tests. A *unit test* verifies that each individual program or object works by itself. A *systems test* verifies that all programs in an application work together properly. An *integration test* verifies that an application works with other applications. An *acceptance test* is performed by end-users and checks the new system to ensure that it works with actual data.

Train Users

According to a recent study, poor user training is one of the top ten reasons why system development projects fail. Users must be trained properly on a system's functionality. **Training** involves showing users exactly how they will use the new hardware and software in the system. Some training takes place as one-on-one sessions or classroom-style lectures (Figure 12-21). Other organizations use Web-based training, which is a self-directed, self-paced online instruction technique. Whichever method is used, it should include hands-on sessions with realistic sample data.

Figure 12-21 Organizations must ensure that users are trained properly on the new system. One training method uses hands-on classes to learn the new system.

To ensure that users are adequately trained, some organizations begin training users prior to installation of the actual system and then follow up with additional training once the actual system is installed. It is crucial that users practice on the actual system during training. Users also should receive user manuals for reference. It is the systems analyst's responsibility to create user manuals, both printed and electronic.

Convert to the New System

The final implementation activity is to change from the old system to the new system. This change can take place using one or more of the following conversion strategies: direct, parallel, phased, or pilot (Figure 12-22).

With *direct conversion*, the user stops using the old system and begins using the new system on a certain date. The advantage of this strategy is that it requires no transition costs and is a quick implementation technique. Some systems analysts call this technique an *abrupt cutover*. The disadvantage is that it is extremely risky and can disrupt operations seriously if the new system does not work correctly the first time.

Parallel conversion consists of running the old system alongside the new system for a specified time. Results from both systems are compared. If the results are the same, the organization either terminates the old system abruptly or phases it out. The advantage of this strategy is that you can fix any problems in the new system before you terminate the old system. The disadvantage is that it is costly to operate two systems at the same time.

Larger systems that have multiple sites often use a phased conversion. With a *phased conversion*, each location converts at a separate time. For example, an accounting system might convert its accounts receivable, accounts payable, general ledger, and payroll sites in separate phases. Each site can use a direct or parallel conversion.

With a *pilot conversion*, only one location in the organization uses the new system — so that it can be tested. After the pilot site approves the new system, other sites convert using one of the other conversion strategies.

At the beginning of the conversion, existing data must be made ready for the new system. Converting existing manual and computer files so that the new system can use them is known as *data conversion*.

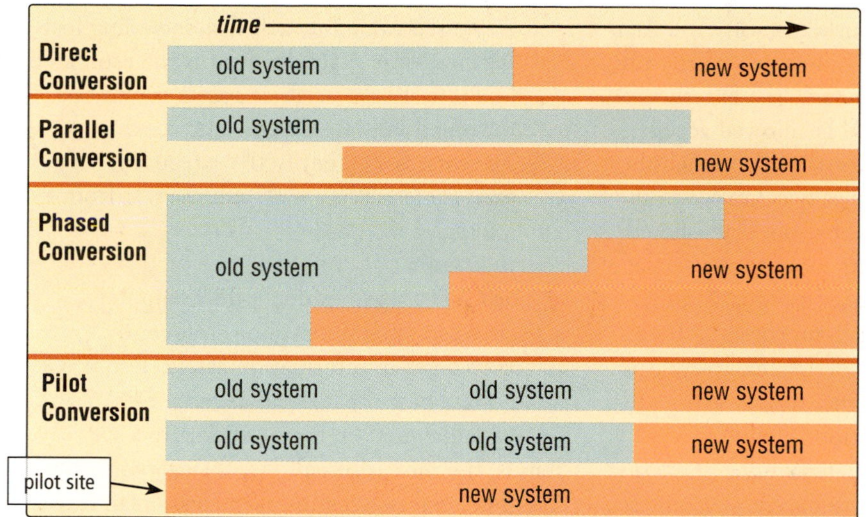

Figure 12-22 Converting from the old system to the new system usually follows one of these strategies.

Implementation at Horizon Community College

Upon receiving the program specification package, Karl forms an implementation team of Suzy Zhao, Web developer; Adam Rosen, programmer; and Stefan Davis, data modeler. The team works together to implement the Grade Reporting System.

Karl works closely with the team to answer questions about the design and to check the progress of their work. When the team completes its work, they ask Karl to test it. He does and it works great!

Karl arranges a training class for all instructors and also the employees of the registration department. During the training session, he shows them how to use the new online grade book on the school's Web site. Karl gives each attendee a printed user guide and indicates that he will e-mail them the electronic file. Karl also modifies the Web site informing students of the new online grade checking service.

Operation, Support, and Security Phase

The purpose of the **operation, support, and security phase** is to provide ongoing assistance for an information system and its users after the system is implemented. The operation, support, and security phase consists of three major activities: (1) perform maintenance activities, (2) monitor system performance, and (3) assess system security.

Information system maintenance activities include fixing errors in, as well as improving, a system's operations. To determine initial maintenance needs, the systems analyst should meet with users. The purpose of this meeting, called the *post-implementation system review*, is to discover whether the information system is performing according to the users' expectations.

Sometimes users identify errors in the system. Problems with design (logic) usually are the cause of these errors. For example, the total of a column might be incorrect. These types of errors return the analyst to the planning phase to perform *corrective maintenance*, which is the process of diagnosing and correcting errors in an information system.

Sometimes, users have enhancements or additional requirements that involve modifying or expanding an existing information system. *Adaptive maintenance* is the process of including new features or capabilities in an information system. To perform adaptive maintenance, the analyst returns to the planning phase.

During this phase, the systems analyst monitors performance of the new or modified information system. The purpose of *performance monitoring* is to determine whether the system is inefficient or unstable at any point. If it is, the systems analyst must investigate solutions to make the information system more efficient and reliable, a process called *perfective maintenance* — back to the planning phase.

Most organizations must deal with complex computer security issues. All elements of an information system — hardware, software, data, people, and procedures — must be secure from threats both inside and outside the enterprise. For example, users should be allowed access only to the data and information for which they are authorized, which typically is limited to the amount necessary to do their job. Data should be secure so that intruders cannot alter, damage, or steal data. Networks need safeguards to prevent them from being compromised. If any vulnerabilities are detected, the analyst returns to the planning phase to investigate techniques to safeguard the information system.

Organizations today often have a *chief security officer (CSO)* who is responsible for physical security of an organization's property and people and also is in charge of securing computing resources. It is critical that the CSO is included in all system development projects to ensure that all projects adequately address information security. The CSO uses many of the techniques discussed in Chapter 11 to maintain confidentiality or limited access to information, ensure integrity and reliability of systems, ensure uninterrupted availability of systems, ensure compliance with laws, and cooperate with law enforcement agencies.

Chief Security Officer

For more information, visit the Computer Concepts CourseMate Web site at www.cengagebrain.com, navigate to the Chapter 12 Web Link resource for this book, and then click Chief Security Officer.

FAQ 12-8

Are financial Web sites vulnerable?

Yes. Research indicates that vulnerabilities are common among financial Web sites. Some vulnerabilities include insecure login forms, confidential information displayed on insecure pages, and weak rules for user name and password selection. Before performing a transaction on a financial Web site, you should make sure that the Web site is secure and that the Web site has no known problems or vulnerabilities.

For more information, visit the Computer Concepts CourseMate Web site at www.cengagebrain.com, navigate to the Chapter 12 FAQ resource for this book, and then click Web Site Vulnerabilities.

Developing a Computer Security Plan

An important responsibility of the CSO is to develop a computer security plan. A **computer security plan** summarizes in writing all of the safeguards that are in place to protect an organization's information assets. A computer security plan should do the following:

1. Identify all information assets of an organization, including hardware, software, documentation, procedures, people, data, facilities, and supplies.
2. Identify all security risks that may cause an information asset loss. Rank risks from most likely to least likely to occur. Place an estimated value on each risk, including lost business. For example, what is the estimated loss if customers cannot access computers for one hour, one day, or one week?
3. For each risk, identify the safeguards that exist to detect, prevent, and recover from a loss.

The CSO should evaluate the computer security plan annually or more frequently for major changes in information assets. The CSO should recognize that some degree of risk is unavoidable; further, the more secure a system is, the more difficult it is for everyone to use. The goal of a computer security plan is to match an appropriate level of safeguards against the identified risks. Fortunately, most organizations never will experience a major information system disaster.

Organizations and individuals that need help with computer security plans can contact the *International Computer Security Association (ICSA) Labs* via the telephone or on the Web for assistance.

Operation, Support, and Security at Horizon Community College

During the post-implementation system review, Karl learns that the new Grade Reporting System is working well. Instructors find it easy to use, and students appreciate being able to check grades online. The registration department is saving time and money because they no longer have to enter or check class semester grades. Chad says his staff is working efficiently on other registration tasks, now that the Grade Reporting System has been automated. Data in the system has been accessed only by authorized users, leading him to conclude security measures work as planned.

Six months after the Grade Reporting System has been in operation, Chad would like to add the capability for students to request transcripts online. He sends an e-mail message to Karl requesting the change. Karl asks him to fill out a Request for System Services and puts him on the agenda of the next steering committee meeting. Back to the planning phase again!

 **QUIZ YOURSELF 12-3**

Instructions: Find the true statement below. Then, rewrite the remaining false statements so that they are true.

1. A computer training plan summarizes in writing all of the safeguards that are in place to protect an organization's information assets.
2. Acceptance tests measure the performance of hardware or software.
3. Activities performed during detailed design include developing designs for the databases, inputs, outputs, and programs.
4. The program development life cycle is a part of the support phase.
5. The purpose of the design phase is to provide ongoing assistance for an information system and its users after the system is implemented.
6. With a request for quotation, the vendor selects the product(s) that meets specified requirements and then quotes the price(s).
7. With parallel conversion, the user stops using the old system and begins using the new system on a certain date.

Quiz Yourself Online: To further check your knowledge of pages 638 through 646, visit the Computer Concepts CourseMate Web site at www.cengagebrain.com, navigate to the Chapter 12 Quiz Yourself resource for this book, and then click Objectives 8 – 11.

Chapter Summary

This chapter discussed the system development phases. The guidelines for system development also were presented. Activities that occur during system development, including project management, feasibility assessment, data and information gathering, and documentation, also were addressed. Throughout the chapter, a case study about Horizon Community College illustrated and reinforced activities performed during each system development phase.

Computer Usage @ Work

Textile Industry

While preparing to attend a wedding, you realize the shirt you planned to wear has a stain that will be impossible to remove before the event. You write down the size of the stained shirt, stop at a department store on your way to the wedding, purchase a new shirt of the same color and size, and quickly change shirts. As expected, the new shirt fits perfectly.

Computers assist in many aspects of the textile industry. In the past, people made fabrics and clothing articles by hand. Today, computers are speeding up and improving accuracy of the process for tasks such as designing clothing, creating patterns, and embroidering designs onto garments. Similar to how the construction and automotive industries use computer-aided design (CAD) and computer-aided manufacturing (CAM) to design and manufacture buildings and cars, the textile industry also uses CAD/CAM to design and manufacture fabrics and clothing. Recall that CAD is the use of computers and software to assist professionals with creating engineering, architectural, scientific, and other designs, and CAM uses computers and software to implement the manufacture of these designs.

CAD use begins with the design of clothing. While fashion designers often start with a vision of how they would like the finished product to appear, computers assist by showing illustrations of how certain fabrics appear on bodies of different shapes and sizes, how various designs and colors look together, and the amount of material required to manufacture the items. Once the design phase is complete and the designer makes his or her final selections, CAM helps to automate the manufacturing process and minimizes human intervention. In addition, CAM also reduces manufacturing time and decreases costs by minimizing the amount of waste generated by human error.

Computers not only assist with the design and manufacture of fabrics and clothing, but also with creating solar textiles. A solar textile is a fabric or cloth that contains a solar material that is designed to absorb sunlight and then convert the sunlight to usable energy, resulting in decreased electricity costs. Using 3-D modeling software, architects and others create designs with solar textiles, which are more flexible than traditional solar panels. In the future, you might see more solar textiles embedded in roofs and walls or being used as curtains.

The textile industry, which once relied solely on individuals to design and manufacture textiles, has made a tremendous transformation during the past decade and might play an even larger role as we continue to discover natural energy sources.

 For more information, visit the Computer Concepts CourseMate Web site at www.cengagebrain.com, navigate to the Chapter 12 Computer Usage @ Work resource for this book, and then click Textile Industry.

High-Tech Talk

Benchmarking: Testing Performance through Calculations

A benchmark is a surveyor's reference mark — a point of reference from which other measurements can be made. Benchmarking is used to evaluate various aspects of enterprises and is widely used in computer technology. Additional types of benchmarking exist, such as process benchmarking and performance benchmarking. In computer technology, a benchmark is a set of conditions used to measure the performance of hardware or software. Benchmark testing involves running a set of standard tests to compare the performance of two or more systems. Web sites and programs are available that can perform simple benchmark tests against parameters such as the speed of your computer's processor or the speed of your Internet connection. The computer industry, however, uses far more complex benchmark tests.

Suppose you are a network administrator and need to buy new servers to support your organization's e-commerce Web site. To start, you can access published benchmark results from organizations such as SPEC and TPC. Both SPEC (Standard Performance Evaluation Corporation) and TPC (Transaction Processing Performance Counsel) are nonprofit groups that define and maintain benchmarks for the computer industry. TPC, for example, tests using its TPC Benchmark W (*TPC-W*), which measures how servers perform while supporting an e-commerce Web site. Reading published benchmark test results from these groups can help you determine how one vendor's system might perform relative to another.

To understand benchmark results fully, you should understand the design and measurements (or *metrics*) used for the test. The TPC-W benchmark, for example, uses two primary metrics: WIPS and $/WIPS. *WIPS* is the number of Web Interactions Per Second that can be sustained by the *system under test*, or *SUT* (in this case, multiple servers). The *$/WIPS* is the *system cost per WIPS*, which is the total cost of the SUT divided by WIPS.

To calculate WIPS, TPC-W uses several algorithms, or formulas (Figure 12-23). One calculation is *Web Interaction Response Time* (*WIRT*), which is the time it takes to complete a Web interaction. A Web interaction might start when a user clicks a link to request a Web page and ends when the browser receives all of the data from the requested page. WIRT is calculated using the algorithm shown in Figure 12-23. Using this algorithm, if a Web interaction starts at 1:00:00 and the last byte of data is sent at 1:00:07, the WIRT is 7 seconds.

WIRT is used to calculate the number of Web interactions successfully completed during the length of the benchmark test, or *measurement interval*. During the measurement interval, the browser repeatedly cycles through requesting and then receiving a requested page, measuring the time to receive it (WIRT), and then requesting the next page. To be considered a successful Web interaction, each type of Web interaction must have a WIRT less than the TPC-specified constraint. For example, a home page Web interaction must have a WIRT of less than three seconds or it is not used when calculating WIPS.

The total number of successful Web interactions completed in a measurement interval is used to calculate WIPS. WIPS is calculated using the algorithm shown in Figure 12-23. Using this algorithm, if 14,009,400 Web interactions are completed successfully during a 30-minute test period, the WIPS rating for the system is 14,009,400/1,800 or 7,783 WIPs. The higher the WIPs rating, the more requests the Web server can handle per second.

The $/WIPS rating is determined by dividing the price of the SUT by the WIPS value (Figure 12-23). Using this algorithm, if a system rated as 7,783 WIPS costs $190,036, the $/WIPS rating is $190,036/7,783 or 24.42.

The TPC-W benchmark also measures the total number of connections a Web server can handle. Using the algorithm shown in Figure 12-23, if a Web site supports 35,000 browsers using 10 Web servers, each Web server is supporting 2 * (35,000/10), or 7,000 connections.

Data points such as WIPS, $/WIPS, and number of connections are the result of a benchmarking process. These data points provide the detailed information required to make informed purchasing decisions. For example, the WIPS and $/WIPS ratings in a benchmark report can help you better understand how the servers will perform in the real-world environment of your e-commerce Web site.

The TPC-W benchmark is just one of numerous industry benchmarks used to test different aspects of systems' performance.

Web Interaction Response Time (WIRT)

Defined by the algorithm, **WIRT** = **T2** − **T1**, where
T1 = time when the first byte of request is sent to the Web server; and
T2 = time after the last byte of a requested page is received by the browser

Web Interaction Per Second (WIPS)

Defined by the algorithm, **WI**/(**MI**), where:
WI = total number of Web interactions completed successfully; and
MI = length of the measurement interval in seconds

System Cost Per WIPS ($/WIPS)

Defined by the algorithm, **System Cost/WIPS**, where:
System Cost = entire price of the SUT, including all new hardware, software, and three-year maintenance charges; and
WIPS = Web interactions successfully completed

Total Number of Connections Supported by a Web Server

Defined by the algorithm, **2** * (**Number of Browsers/Web Servers**), where:
2 represents the 2 connections per user (one nonsecure, one secure)
Number of Browsers is the number of users browsing the Web site; and
Web Servers is the number of Web servers supporting the Web site

Figure 12-23 Some benchmark algorithms.

For more information, visit the Computer Concepts CourseMate Web site at www.cengagebrain.com, navigate to the Chapter 12 High-Tech Talk resource for this book, and then click Benchmarking.

Companies on the Cutting Edge

COMPUTER SCIENCES CORPORATION (CSC) Global IT Services Company

When the space shuttle blasted into space and docked with the International Space Station, *Computer Sciences Corporation* (*CSC*) played a major role in the mission. NASA partnered with CSC to provide support for its Center for Computational Sciences, which contains simulators and supercomputing resources for high-performance aerospace activities.

CSC's three primary lines of services are Business Solutions & Services, Global Outsourcing Services, and the North American Public Sector. Its information technology projects include managing the nation's air traffic control system, providing logistics for the U.S. Army's equipment, stopping security breaches, simplifying the U.S. Patent and Trademark Office's application process, and helping the California Department of Forestry fight wildfires.

The company has grown from a two-person operation in 1959 to an international corporation based in Falls Church, Virginia. Recently, it won the "BEST Award" from the American Society for Training and Development for its global learning and employee talent development programs.

WIKIMEDIA FOUNDATION International Movement for Free Knowledge

One of the 10 most visited Web sites in the world is Wikipedia. This online encyclopedia began in 2001, and two years later the *Wikimedia Foundation* incorporated to provide the infrastructure and support for disseminating information free of charge.

The Foundation is a nonprofit 501(c)(3) charitable corporation organized in Florida and headquartered in California. The more than 20 staff members coordinate the efforts of thousands of volunteers who provide content and serve on committees to raise funds, develop long-term plans, and oversee various projects. A network of local chapters in more than 20 countries supports the Foundation by soliciting donations, organizing events, and raising awareness of Foundation activities and the need for free Internet content.

More than 300 servers run the Wikimedia projects, and the Foundation owns this equipment along with the domain names and trademarks. The mission is to bring educational content in as many forms as possible to all areas of the world.

For more information, visit the Computer Concepts CourseMate Web site at www.cengagebrain.com and then navigate to the Chapter 12 Companies on the Cutting Edge resource for this book.

Technology Trailblazers

ED YOURDON Project Management Consultant

Much of today's structured system development life cycle is due to the methodologies *Ed Yourdon* developed more than 40 years ago. Yourdon's work in the computer industry ranges from predicting technology megatrends to recruiting and retaining employees, and much of his current research focuses on developing Web 2.0 and 3.0 strategies, products, and services.

Yourdon is considered one of the ten most influential people in the software field and was inducted into the Computer Hall of Fame. He has written 27 books; the latest, *Outsource: Competing in the Global Productivity Race* and *Death March*, provide guidance to corporate managers facing constrained resources and budgets.

Yourdon began his computer career as a programmer and then founded a consulting firm to provide advice in modern software engineering technology and project management techniques. Today, he maintains his blog, The Yourdon Report, and the Structured Analysis Wiki, and serves as a consultant in his firm, NODRUOY Inc.

TOM DEMARCO Software Development Expert

To get ahead in the corporate world, one must identify and take risks, according to *Tom DeMarco*. The software engineer is noted for his structured analysis theories, which were built on Ed Yourdon's work and led to the CASE tools used today.

In his book, *Waltzing with Bears: Managing Risk on Software Projects*, he presents the benefits of risk management and proclaims that risk brings reward, especially in the software field. He urges workers to take time to reflect upon innovation, change, and goal setting and writes about this concept in *Slack: Getting Past Burnout, Busywork, and the Myth of Total Efficiency.*

DeMarco is a fellow and senior consultant of the Cutter Consortium, an organization that helps businesses find solutions for their computer problems and supports innovative thinking and risk taking. He received the Warnier Prize and the Stevens Award for his software development contributions.

For more information, visit the Computer Concepts CourseMate Web site at www.cengagebrain.com and then navigate to the Chapter 12 Technology Trailblazers resource for this book.

STUDENT ASSIGNMENTS

Chapter Review

The Chapter Review reinforces the main concepts presented in this chapter.

To listen to an audio version of this Chapter Review, visit the Computer Concepts CourseMate Web site at www.cengagebrain.com and then navigate to the Chapter 12 Chapter Review resource for this book.

1. What Is System Development, and What Are the System Development Phases? An **information system (IS)** is hardware, software, data, people, and procedures that work together to produce quality information. **System development** is a set of activities used to build an information system. System development activities often are grouped into larger categories called phases. This collection of phases sometimes is called the **system development life cycle (SDLC)**. Many SDLCs contain five **phases**: planning; analysis; design; implementation; and operation, support, and security.

2. What Are Guidelines for System Development? System development should follow three general guidelines: (1) group activities into phases; (2) involve the **users**, which includes anyone for whom a system is being built; and (3) define **standards**, which are sets of rules and procedures an organization expects employees to accept and follow.

3. Why Are Project Management, Feasibility Assessment, Documentation, and Data and Information Gathering Techniques Important? **Project management** is the process of planning, scheduling, and then controlling the activities during system development. The goal of project management is to deliver an acceptable system to the user in an agreed-upon time frame, while maintaining costs. For larger projects, project management activities often are separated between a *project manager* and a *project leader*. Some organizations use *extreme project management*. The project leader identifies the *scope* of the project, required activities, time estimates, cost estimates, the order of activities, and activities that can take place simultaneously. The project leader records this information in a *project plan*. **Feasibility** is a measure of how suitable the development of a system will be to the organization. A **systems analyst** typically uses four tests to evaluate feasibility of a project: *operational feasibility*, which measures how well the proposed system will work; *schedule feasibility*, which measures whether established project deadlines are reasonable; *technical feasibility*, which measures whether the organization has or can obtain the hardware, software, and people to deliver and then support the system; and *economic feasibility*, also called *cost/benefit feasibility*, which measures whether the lifetime benefits of the proposed system will be greater than its lifetime costs. **Documentation** is the collection and summarization of data and information and includes reports, diagrams, programs, or other deliverables. A *project notebook* contains all documentation for a single project. To gather data and information, systems analysts and other IT professionals review documentation, observe, survey, interview, participate in *joint-application design* (*JAD*) sessions, and research.

4. What Activities Are Performed in the Planning Phase? The **planning phase** for a project begins when the decision-making body for the organization, called the **steering committee**, receives a *project request*. During the planning phase, four major activities are performed: (1) review and approve the project requests, (2) prioritize the project requests, (3) allocate resources such as money, people, and equipment to approved projects, and (4) form a project development team for each approved project.

Visit the Computer Concepts CourseMate Web site at www.cengagebrain.com, navigate to the Chapter 12 Quiz Yourself resource for this book, and then click Objectives 1 – 4.

5. What Is the Purpose of Activities Performed in the Analysis Phase? The **analysis phase** consists of two major activities: (1) conduct a **preliminary investigation**, sometimes called the *feasibility study*, to determine the exact nature of the problem or improvement and decide whether it is worth pursuing, and (2) perform detailed analysis. *Detailed analysis* involves three major activities: (1) study how the current system works; (2) determine the users' wants, needs, and requirements; and (3) recommend a solution. Detailed analysis sometimes is called *logical design*. Most systems analysts use either a process modeling or object modeling approach to analysis and design.

6. What Are Tools Used in Process Modeling? **Process modeling**, sometimes called *structured analysis and design*, is an analysis and design technique that describes processes that transform inputs into outputs. Tools

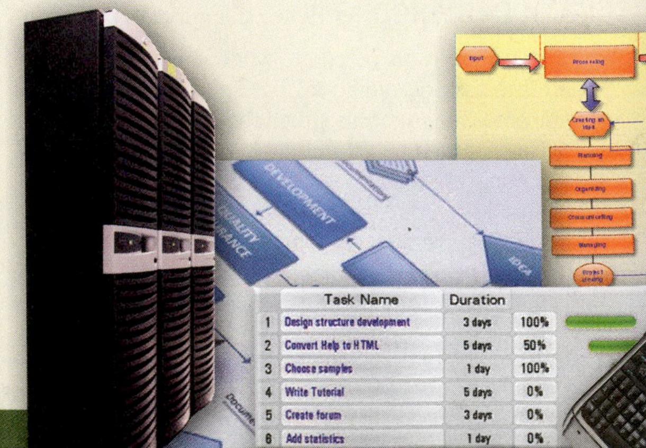

Chapter Review

used for process modeling include the following. An **entity-relationship diagram** (*ERD*) graphically shows the connections among entities in a system. An *entity* is an object in the system that has data. A **data flow diagram** (*DFD*) graphically shows the flow of data in a system. Key elements of a DFD are a *data flow*, which shows the input or output of data or information; a *process*, which transforms an input data flow into an output data flow; a *data store*, which is a holding place for data and information; and a *source*, which identifies an entity outside the scope of the system. The **project dictionary**, sometimes called the *repository*, contains all the documentation and deliverables of a project. Techniques used to enter items in the project dictionary include *structured English*, a **decision table** and/or a *decision tree*, and a **data dictionary**.

7. What Are Tools Used in Object Modeling? **Object modeling**, sometimes called *object-oriented* (*OO*) *analysis and design*, combines the data with processes that act on the data into a single unit, called an **object**. Object modeling can use the same tools as those used in process modeling, but the **UML** (*Unified Modeling Language*) has been adopted as a standard notation for object modeling and development. Two common tools in the UML are the use case diagram and the class diagram. A **use case diagram** graphically shows how actors interact with the information system. An *actor* is a user or other entity, and the *use case* is the function that the actor can perform. A **class diagram** graphically shows classes and one or more lower levels, called *subclasses*, in a system. Lower levels (subclasses) contain attributes of higher levels (classes) in a concept called *inheritance*.

Visit the Computer Concepts CourseMate Web site at www.cengagebrain.com, navigate to the Chapter 12 Quiz Yourself resource for this book, and then click Objectives 5 – 7.

8. What Activities Are Performed in the Design Phase? The **design phase** consists of two major activities: (1) if necessary, acquire hardware and software and (2) develop all of the details of the new or modified information system. Acquiring necessary hardware and software involves identifying technical specifications, soliciting vendor proposals, testing and evaluating vendor proposals, and making a decision. Detailed design includes developing designs for the databases, inputs, outputs, and programs. During detailed design, many systems analysts use a **prototype**, which is a working model of the proposed system. *Computer-aided software engineering (CASE)* products are tools designed to support one or more activities of system development.

9. Why Is Program Development Part of System Development? During the design phase, an organization can purchase **packaged software**, which is mass-produced, copyrighted, prewritten software. If suitable packaged software is not available, however, a company may opt for **custom software**, which is application software developed at the user's request to match the user's requirements exactly. Programmers write custom software from the program specification package created during the analysis phase, following an organized set of activities known as the *program development life cycle*.

10. What Activities Are Performed in the Implementation Phase? The purpose of the **implementation phase** is to construct, or build, the new or modified system and then deliver it to the users. System developers perform four major activities in this phase: (1) develop programs, (2) install and test the new system, (3) train users, and (4) convert to the new system.

11. What Activities Are Performed in the Operations, Support, and Security Phase? The purpose of the **operation, support, and security phase** is to provide ongoing assistance for an information system and its users after the system is implemented. The operations, support, and security phase consists of three major activities: (1) perform maintenance activities, (2) monitor system performance, and (3) assess system security. Organizations today often have a *chief security officer* (*CSO*) who is responsible for physical security of an organization's property and people and also is in charge of securing computing resources. The CSO develops a **computer security plan**, which summarizes in writing all safeguards that protect the organization's information assets.

Visit the Computer Concepts CourseMate Web site at www.cengagebrain.com, navigate to the Chapter 12 Quiz Yourself resource for this book, and then click Objectives 8 – 11.

Key Terms

You should know the Primary Terms and be familiar with the Secondary Terms. The list below helps focus your study.

To see an example of and a definition for each term, and to access current and additional information from the Web, visit the Computer Concepts CourseMate Web site at www.cengagebrain.com and then navigate to the Chapter 12 Key Terms resource for this book.

Primary Terms

(shown in bold-black characters in the chapter)

analysis phase (629)
class diagram (635)
computer security plan (646)
custom software (636)
data dictionary (634)
data flow diagram (632)
decision table (633)
design phase (638)
documentation (625)
entity-relationship diagram (632)
e-zine (638)
feasibility (624)
implementation phase (643)
information system (IS) (620)
object (634)
object modeling (634)
operation, support, and security phase (645)
packaged software (635)
phases (620)
planning phase (628)
preliminary investigation (629)
process modeling (631)
project dictionary (633)
project management (623)
project management software (623)
project team (623)
prototype (641)
standards (621)
steering committee (623)
system (620)
system development (620)
system development life cycle (SDLC) (620)
systems analyst (622)
training (644)
UML (634)
use case diagram (634)
users (621)

data flow diagram (632)

Secondary Terms

(shown in italic characters in the chapter)

abrupt cutover (644)
acceptance test (644)
actor (634)
adaptive maintenance (645)
attribute (634)
benchmark test (639)
change management (624)
chief security officer (CSO) (646)
computer-aided software engineering (CASE) (642)
context diagram (632)
corrective maintenance (645)
cost/benefit feasibility (625)
data conversion (644)
data flow (632)
data model (640)
data store (632)
decision tree (633)
deliverable (624)
detailed analysis (631)
DFD (632)
direct conversion (644)
economic feasibility (625)
electronic magazine (638)
entity (632)
ERD (632)
extreme project management (623)
feasibility study (629)
focus groups (626)
Gantt chart (623)
horizontal market software (635)
I-CASE (642)
inheritance (635)
inspection (642)
integration test (644)
International Computer Security Association (ICSA) Labs (646)
Internet solutions provider (636)
IT consultant (639)
joint-application design (JAD) (626)
layout chart (641)
logical design (631)
method (634)
mockup (641)
moderator (626)
object-oriented (OO) analysis and design (634)
operation (634)
operational feasibility (624)
outsource (636)
parallel conversion (644)
perfective maintenance (645)
performance monitoring (645)
PERT chart (624)
phased conversion (644)
physical design (640)
pilot conversion (644)
post-implementation system review (645)
process (632)
program development life cycle (643)
program specification package (641)
project leader (623)
project manager (623)
project notebook (625)
project plan (623)
project request (626)
proof of concept (641)
property (634)
Rational Unified Process (RUP) (634)
repository (633)
request for information (RFI) (638)
request for proposal (RFP) (638)
request for quotation (RFQ) (638)
request for system services (626)
schedule feasibility (625)
scope (623)
scope creep (624)
scribe (626)
source (632)
structured analysis and design (631)
structured English (633)
subclasses (635)
system developer (623)
system proposal (635)
systems test (644)
technical feasibility (625)
trade publication (636)
turnkey solution (639)
Unified Modeling Language (634)
unit test (644)
use case (634)
value-added reseller (VAR) (638)
vertical market software (636)

Checkpoint

The Checkpoint exercises test your knowledge of the chapter concepts. The page number containing the answer appears in parentheses after each exercise. The Beyond the Book exercises will help broaden your understanding of the concepts presented in this chapter.

To complete the Checkpoint exercises interactively, visit the Computer Concepts CourseMate Web site at www.cengagebrain.com and then navigate to the Chapter 12 Checkpoint resource for this book.

True/False Mark T for True and F for False.

_____ 1. An information system supports daily, short-term, and long-range activities of systems analysts. (620)

_____ 2. A systems analyst is responsible for designing and developing an information system. (622)

_____ 3. Operational feasibility measures whether an organization has the hardware, software, and people needed to support a proposed information system. (624)

_____ 4. Documentation should be updated only after a project is complete. (625)

_____ 5. In detailed analysis, the systems analysts develop the proposed solution with a specific hardware or software in mind. (631)

_____ 6. Structured English is a style of writing that describes the steps in a process. (633)

_____ 7. Object modeling combines the data with the processes that act on that data into a single unit, called a method. (634)

_____ 8. The only major activity of the design phase is the development of all of the details of the new or modified information system. (638)

_____ 9. Some VARs provide complete systems, known as a turnkey solution. (639)

_____ 10. During program design, the systems analyst prepares the program specification package, which identifies the required programs and the relationship among each program, as well as the input, output, and database specifications. (641)

_____ 11. With a pilot conversion, multiple locations in the organization use the new system. (644)

Multiple Choice Select the best answer.

1. _____ is a team-driven project management approach, in which a project leader is more of a participant and facilitator than a manager during the project. (623)
   a. Extreme project management
   b. The Rational Unified Process (RUP)
   c. Phased conversion
   d. Object modeling

2. A _____ analyzes the time required to complete a task and identifies the minimum time required for an entire project. (624)
   a. Gantt chart
   b. PERT chart
   c. use case diagram
   d. none of the above

3. In larger organizations, users write a formal request for a new or modified information system, which is called a _____. (626)
   a. request for proposal (RFP)
   b. joint-application design (JAD)
   c. project request
   d. data-flow design (DFD)

4. During the planning phase, the projects that receive the highest priority are those _____. (628)
   a. mandated by management or some other governing body
   b. suggested by the greatest number of users
   c. thought to be of highest value to the organization
   d. proposed by the information technology (IT) department

5. A(n) _____ lists a variety of conditions and the actions that correspond to each condition. (633)
   a. object
   b. DFD
   c. decision table
   d. ERD

6. The purpose of the _____ is to assess the feasibility of each alternative solution and then recommend the most feasible solution for the project. (635)
   a. project plan
   b. system review
   c. project request
   d. system proposal

7. _____ tools are designed to support one or more activities of system development. (642)
   a. Computer-aided software engineering (CASE)
   b. Unified Modeling Language
   c. Project management
   d. Object modeling

8. A(n) _____ test is performed by end-users and checks the new system to ensure that it works with actual data. (644)
   a. integration
   b. systems
   c. unit
   d. acceptance

STUDENT ASSIGNMENTS

Checkpoint

Matching Match the terms with their definitions.

_____ 1. system developer (623)
_____ 2. project manager (623)
_____ 3. request for system services (626)
_____ 4. process modeling (631)
_____ 5. project dictionary (633)
_____ 6. data dictionary (634)
_____ 7. object (634)
_____ 8. packaged software (635)
_____ 9. prototype (641)
_____ 10. performance monitoring (645)

a. becomes the first item in the project notebook and triggers the planning phase
b. analysis and design technique that describes processes that transform inputs into outputs
c. working model of the proposed system
d. shows how actors interact with an information system
e. controls the activities during system development
f. an item that can contain both data and the procedures that read or manipulate that data
g. stores a name, description, and other details about each data item
h. responsible for designing and developing an information system
i. contains all the documentation and deliverables of a project
j. mass-produced, copyrighted, prewritten software available for purchase
k. determines whether the system is inefficient or unstable at any point

Short Answer Write a brief answer to each of the following questions.

1. What is system development? ____________ Describe the five phases of the system development life cycle (SDLC). ____________
2. What are four types of feasibility, and what does each measure? ____________ What are six techniques used to gather data and information? ____________
3. How is UML used? ____________ How is a use case diagram different from a class diagram? ____________
4. What are the three major activities of the operation, support, and security phase? ____________ Describe each type of maintenance activity. ____________
5. What is a computer security plan? ____________ What three things should a computer security plan do? ____________

Beyond the Book Follow the book element instructions below; present your findings (brief report, presentation, discussion, or other means).

1. Ethics & Issues — Select an Ethics & Issues in this chapter (625, 627, 635, 637), find a recent newspaper/magazine article that supports one point of view presented, and then evaluate the article.
2. Computer Usage @ Work — Use the Web or a recent newspaper/magazine to locate three additional unique usages of computer technology in the textile industry (647). What makes the use of these technologies unique to the textile industry?
3. Companies on the Cutting Edge and Technology Trailblazers — Use the Web or a recent newspaper/magazine to locate an interesting fact about Computer Sciences Corporation (CSC), Wikimedia Foundation, Ed Yourdon, or Tom DeMarco that was not presented in the chapter (649).
4. High-Tech Talk — Locate a recent newspaper/magazine article that discusses topics related to Benchmarking (648). Would you recommend the article you found? Why or why not?
5. FAQs and Web Links — Use the Web or a recent newspaper/magazine to locate three additional facts about an FAQ (624, 626, 631, 636, 638, 639, 643, 646) and Web Link (623, 624, 629, 631, 634, 636, 638, 642, 646) that were not presented in the chapter.
6. Looking Ahead — Use the Web or a recent newspaper/magazine to discover additional uses of the technology presented in Remote Solar System Objects Mapped in Database (640).
7. Innovative Computing — Use the Web or a recent newspaper/magazine to locate two additional interesting facts about *Phoenix Lander* Probes Soil on Mars (643).
8. Making Use of the Web — Visit three of the Science sites (136) and outline the information on each Web site and the possible uses for each Web site.

Learn It Online

The Learn It Online exercises are interactive Web exercises designed to reinforce and expand your understanding of the chapter concepts. The descriptions below briefly summarize each exercise.

To complete the Learn It Online exercises, visit the Computer Concepts CourseMate Web site at www.cengagebrain.com, navigate to the Chapter 12 resources for this book, click the link for the exercise you want to complete, and then read the instructions.

1 At the Movies — Create a Hidden Operating System
Watch a movie to learn about keeping private files private with a hidden operating system and then answer questions about the movie.

2 Video and Audio: You Review It — Computer-Aided Software Engineering
Search for, choose, and write a review of a video, podcast, or vodcast that discusses computer-aided software engineering.

3 Student Edition Labs — Project Management and Web Design Principles
Enhance your understanding and knowledge about project management and Web design principles by completing the Project Management and Web Design Principles Labs.

4 Practice Test
Take a multiple choice test that checks your knowledge of the chapter concepts and review the resulting study guide.

5 Who Wants To Be a Computer Genius²?
Play the Shelly Cashman Series version of this popular game by answering questions to find out if you are a computer genius. Panic buttons are available to provide assistance during game play.

6 Wheel of Terms
Identify important key terms presented in this chapter by playing the Shelly Cashman Series version of this popular game.

7 You're Hired!
Embark on the path to a career in computers by answering questions and solving puzzles related to concepts discussed in this chapter.

8 Crossword Puzzle Challenge
Complete an interactive crossword puzzle to reinforce concepts presented in this chapter.

9 Windows Exercises
Step through the Windows 7 exercises to use the traffic sign tutorial and learn about Problem Reports and Solutions, creating a drawing, and capturing screen images.

10 Exploring Computer Careers
Read about a career as a systems analyst, search for related employment advertisements, and then answer related questions.

11 Web Apps — Picnik
Learn how to use Picnik to upload photos, crop photos to remove extra space, and easily e-mail photos to others.

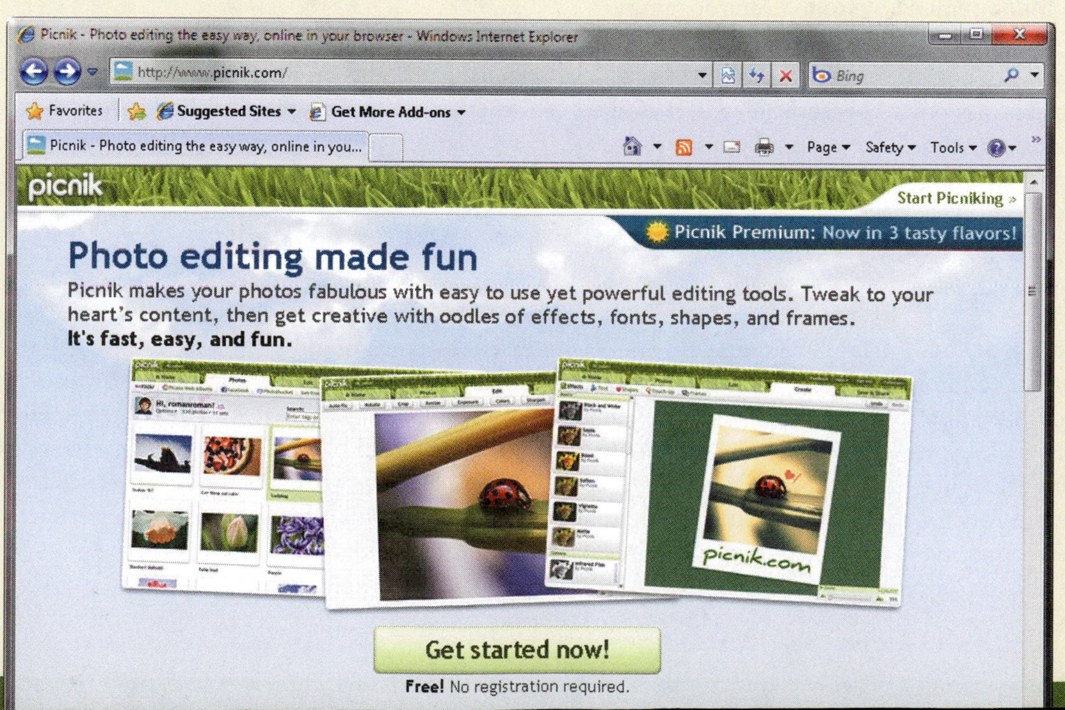

Problem Solving @ Home

The Problem Solving @ Home exercises extend your knowledge of the chapter concepts by seeking solutions to practical computer problems that you may encounter at home or school. The Collaboration exercise should be completed with a team.

In the real world, practical problems often can be solved in multiple ways. Provide one solution to each of the following problems using available resources, such as articles on the Web or in print, blogs, podcasts, videos, television, user guides, other individuals, and electronics and computer stores. You may need to use multiple resources to obtain an answer. Present your solutions in the form requested by your instructor (brief report, presentation, discussion, or other means).

1. **Trial Period Expired** During installation of a 60-day trial version of Microsoft Office, your computer displays a message stating that the trial period already has expired. What might be causing this error message to appear?
2. **Security Questions** Each time you log into your bank's Web site, it asks you to answer a series of security questions you selected when you set up your account. The Web site indicates that these security questions are used in addition to passwords to verify your identity, and asks whether you want the Web site to request the answers to those security questions the next time you log in. You do not want the Web site to ask these questions in the future, so you place a check mark in the appropriate check box. The very next day, however, the Web site asks the security questions. Why might this be happening?
3. **Direct Deposit Missing** When you check your bank account, you realize that your most recent direct deposit was not recorded. You contact the human resources manager at work, and she insists that the company paid you. What might be wrong?
4. **Learning Management System** After logging into your school's learning management system, you find that you are not able to access the videos that your instructor has posted because an error message appears stating that the page cannot be displayed. What might be wrong?
5. **Technical Support Unreachable** You are having difficulty installing a program you recently purchased. The company that created the program is located overseas, and you must make long distance calls to obtain technical support. The time difference between countries, however, makes it almost impossible to contact their technical support staff during the hours they are available. What are some other options?
6. **Web Site Vulnerability** While accessing your school's portal, you discover a vulnerability that allows you to access other students' personal information. Will you address this vulnerability with the school? If so, who will you contact, and how will you approach them?
7. **Filing Taxes Online** You are using a Web application to file your taxes for the past year. Throughout the year, you made sure that your employer withheld sufficient taxes based on your yearly income and other financial gains. After entering all your information, you are surprised to find that you still owe several thousand dollars. How might you determine whether a bug in the tax preparation Web application is returning bad data?
8. **Benchmark Results** You run a series of benchmark tests on your computer to determine whether it is running optimally. You find that your computer is performing more slowly than other computers with similar processors. What might be causing this?

Collaboration

9. **Developing a School Portal** The small private school that you attend would like to use technology to provide access to information and resources previously recorded only on paper. The school's dean asks your class to compile a list of features that students would find useful if the school creates a portal online. Form a team of three people to determine an appropriate feature set. One team member should determine what information should be made available to students, another team member should compile a list of actions, such as registering for classes, that students should be able to perform online, and the last team member should determine and justify whether it would be more cost effective to develop the portal in-house, outsource the job, or purchase an existing portal from a third-party vendor.

Problem Solving @ Work

The Problem Solving @ Work exercises extend your knowledge of the chapter concepts by seeking solutions to practical computer problems that you may encounter at work. The Collaboration exercise should be completed with a team.

In the real world, practical problems often can be solved in multiple ways. Provide one solution to each of the following problems using available resources, such as articles on the Web or in print, blogs, podcasts, videos, television, user guides, other individuals, and electronics and computer stores. You may need to use multiple resources to obtain an answer. Present your solutions in the form requested by your instructor (brief report, presentation, discussion, or other means).

1. **Upgraded Information System** Having just returned to work from a long vacation, you discover that the information system you primarily use has been upgraded to a new version. You are having difficulty learning the new version and are falling behind in your work. What are your next steps?
2. **Schedule Delay** You are working as a project manager in charge of developing a new information system. Halfway through the project, you realize that you will not meet your deadline; in fact, on your current schedule, you will deliver the system almost two months behind schedule. In addition, this delay is sure to cost your company additional money. How might you approach your manager about this?
3. **Bug in Information System** One year ago, you developed and installed an information system for a client. The client has called to inform you that she has discovered a bug in the system. The client did not purchase a technical support contract, but you want to correct your mistake. How will you respond?
4. **Information System Development** As part of a project team with six other individuals, you are developing a new information system for a financial institution. One of your teammates resigned, and your manager made you responsible for your former teammate's portion of the project. What methods can you use to determine where your teammate left off and the point from which you should continue his work?
5. **Cannot Perform Job Functions** While working with a new information system, you discover some bugs that are preventing you from performing your daily job functions. What will you do next?
6. **Replacement Information System** The information technology department within your organization has informed you that it soon will be developing a new information system that will replace an existing system. Because you have been using the existing system for quite some time, you believe you can provide valuable input concerning how the new system should be designed. What steps will you take to ensure that your feedback will be included?

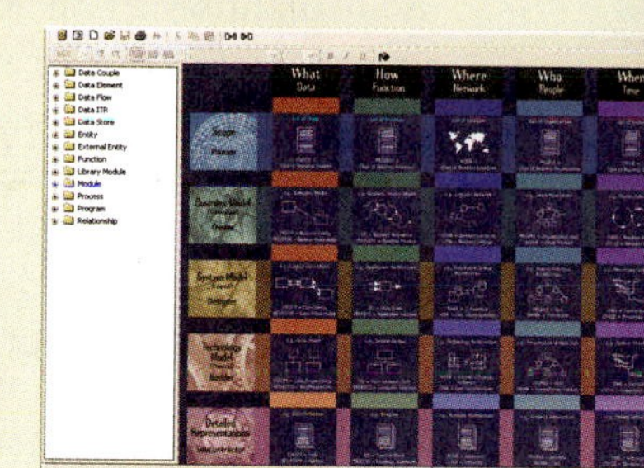

7. **Cannot Maintain Information System** As the chief information officer, you find that your organization no longer has the funds to maintain an existing information system. This means that any future bugs found in the system may not be corrected. How will you address this problem?
8. **System Upgrade Needed** Your friend informs you that his company's information system does not seem to be meeting employee expectations and might need to be modified or replaced. How will you determine where inefficiencies exist and what needs to be modified in the existing information system?

Collaboration

9. **Computers in the Textile Industry** Many businesses in the textile industry are using advancements in computer technology to aid in designing and manufacturing textiles. Department stores and companies selling clothing online also use technology to show consumers how various articles of clothing will fit or how they will match other garments. Form a team of three people to report on ways they see computers changing the textile industry. Each team member should visit local malls and Web sites and record at least three ways that computers have improved the industry. Compile the findings and then submit a brief report to your instructor.

Learn How To

The Learn How To activities step you through fundamental technology skills when using a computer. The Learn How To exercises enable you to become more proficient with these skills.

Learn How To 1: Conduct an Effective Interview

As you learned in this chapter, gathering information is a critical element in system development, because without accurate facts, it is unlikely that the finished system will perform in the desired manner. An important means of gathering information is the personal interview. Interviews are used in several stages throughout system development, and they must be thorough and comprehensive.

Prior to conducting an interview, you must determine that an interview is the best means for obtaining the information you seek. You have learned a variety of ways to obtain information, and you should use each of them appropriately. Because an interview interrupts a person's work and takes time, you must be sure the information gained in the interview justifies this interruption. Once you have determined you should conduct an interview to gather information required for system development, a variety of factors become relevant.

Goal: The most important element of a successful interview is for you to determine exactly what knowledge you hope to gain as a result of the interview. If you do not have a goal, you are unlikely to emerge from the interview with much useful information.

Do Your Homework: You should complete a variety of preparatory steps that will help ensure a successful interview. These steps include the following:

1. Gather as much information as you can from the fact-gathering processes that do not require an interview. Because an interview takes a person's time and interrupts work, you must be sure the information you are seeking is not available from other sources. Additionally, if you ask someone questions to obtain information they know is available elsewhere, you will lose credibility with them during the interview process.
2. Be sure you plan to interview the best person to obtain the information you need. To do this, you must research every person you plan to interview and understand their job, their position within the department in which they work, the knowledge they should possess relative to the information you need, the culture of their work environment, how the system being developed relates to them, and an estimate of the cooperation you can expect from them. If someone is the most knowledgeable person regarding a certain subject but is unwilling to share information other than with trusted coworkers, you likely will be better served by talking to someone else.
3. Prepare the questions you want to ask prior to setting up the interview. In this way, you can have a good estimate of the time required for the interview. While other questions will occur to you as the interview proceeds, you should have a good idea of the questions you need answered to reach your goal.
4. Prior to setting an appointment for an interview, be sure the management personnel of the people you will interview have approved. Because you will be disrupting employees' work days, you must obtain management approval before even asking for an appointment.

Make an Appointment: An appointment almost always is required. By making an appointment, you ensure the person to be interviewed will be available. Normally you should request an appointment in writing, often through the use of e-mail. In this written request, you should set a time and place for the interview, inform the interviewee what you need to know, and establish an agenda with an estimated time. You must recognize that most people do not like to be interviewed, so often you will not be seen as friendly. In addition, it might be possible that the system being developed could eliminate or change the person's job, and clearly this can establish an adversarial relationship. Your task when making an appointment, then, is to establish credibility with the interviewee and set the stage for a successful interview.

Conduct the Interview: When conducting an interview, remember that you are the "intruder." Therefore, you should be polite, prompt, and attentive in the interview. Always understand the perspective of the person being interviewed and understand his or her fears, doubts, and potential hostilities. Sometimes, the interviewee might feel he or she is in conflict with you, so by listening closely and being aware of the body language, you should be able to discern the amount of truth and the amount of hedging that is occurring. Some of the details of the interview of which you should be aware are as follows:

Learn How To

1. If possible, the interview should be conducted in a quiet environment with a minimum of interruptions.
2. The demeanor should be open and friendly, but as noted you should not expect to be welcomed with open arms.
3. Your questions should directly address the goals of the interview. Do not expect the person being interviewed to provide a tutorial. Your questions must generate answers that supply your information.
4. Your questions should be thought-provoking. Do not ask questions requiring a yes or no answer. Your questions should not lead the interviewee to an answer — rather, the questions should be open-ended and allow the person to develop the answer. As an interviewer, you never should argue with the person being interviewed, you should not suggest answers or give opinions, you should ask straightforward questions rather than compound questions, you never should assign blame for any circumstance that might come up in the interview, and you must never interrupt while the person is talking. Finally, you, as the interviewer, should not talk much. Remember, you are conducting the interview to gain information and it is the person you are interviewing who has that information. Let him or her talk.
5. Listen carefully, with both your ears and your eyes. What you hear normally is most important, but body language and other movements often convey information as well. Concentrate on the interviewee — expect that you will make much more eye contact with the person than he or she will with you. Allow silences to linger — the normal impulse in a conversation is to fill the silence quickly; in an interview, however, if you are quiet, the person being interviewed might think of additional information.
6. As you listen, concentrate on the interviewee — when points are being made, do not take notes because that will distract from what the person is saying — stay focused. When the information has been conveyed, then jot down something so that you will remember.
7. Throughout the interview, offer reinforcing comments, such as, "The way I understand what you just said is ..." Make sure when you leave the interview there are no misunderstandings between you and the person you interviewed.
8. Before you conclude the interview, be sure all your goals have been met. You likely will not have another opportunity to interview the person, so ensure you have nothing further to learn from the person.

Follow-Up: After the interview, it is recommended you send a follow-up letter or e-mail message to the person you interviewed to review the information you learned. This document should invite the interviewee to correct any errors you made in summing up your findings. In addition, for all the people you interview, keep a log of the time and place of the interview. In this way, if any questions arise regarding the interview, you will have a log.

Exercise

1. Using the techniques in this activity, conduct interviews with three students on your campus. Your interview goal is to find out about both the most successful class and the least successful class the student has completed. Why was the class successful or unsuccessful? Discuss the instructor, textbook, subject matter, and other relevant items. After the interviews, write a one-page paper summarizing your findings and identify common elements found in successful classes and in unsuccessful classes. Submit this paper to your instructor.

Web Research

The Web Research exercises broaden your understanding of the chapter concepts by presenting questions that require you to search the Web for answers.

1 Search Sleuth

Use one of the search engines listed in Figure 2-10 in Chapter 2 on page 85 or your own favorite search engine to find the answers to the following questions. Copy and paste the Web address from the Web page where you found the answer. Some questions may have more than one answer. If required, submit your answers to your instructor. (1) Who are the winners of the most recent Worldwide UML Jokes Contest? What story does the first-place winner tell in UML notation? (2) According to the *Occupational Outlook Handbook*, what education and training is recommended for a person desiring a career as a systems analyst? (3) What is the name of the document Karol Adamiecki developed in 1896? (4) How many e-zines are listed in the The Ezine Directory (ezine-dir.com), and which categories have new listings? (5) What model was created from the merger of the Objectory Process, the Booch Method, and the Object-Modeling Technique?

2 Green Computing

Corporations are touting their efforts to go green in their computing environments, but a survey of computer professionals found that less than seven percent of companies have implemented their green IT initiatives. Corporations may be choosing to practice green computing, but many times their efforts are driven by a financial goal to save electricity, not an ecological goal to reduce carbon dioxide emissions. Visit the Web sites of several companies profiled in this textbook and locate their environmentally friendly practices. Which green practices are featured? What outdated equipment has been replaced with energy-efficient machines? Is virtualization technology implemented? How are they conserving power? Write a report summarizing your findings, and include a table of links to Web sites that provide additional details.

3 Social Networking

Several Web sites provide design tools that allow you to create your own online social network and then add member profiles, discussion forums, RSS feeds, images, and surveys. A few of these Web site builders are Groupsite (groupsite.com), KickApps (kickapps.com), Nexo (nexo.com), and Ning (ning .com). Marc Andreessen, Netscape's cofounder, is Ning's chief technology officer, and the development tool he created powers more than 1.6 million social networks. Visit the online social networking development Web sites and view the page design tools provided. Compare tutorials, design templates, widgets, modules, and other layout components. What customizable tools are provided? How do these Web sites allow you to invite friends and professional contacts? How are photos and videos imported? What type of advertisements display on the free online social networks? Summarize the information you read and viewed.

4 Blogs

Creating a blog and then attracting people to read it requires a keen sense of design, marketing, and editing skills. Blogging services provide assistance in attracting visitors to a Web site and then holding their interest while they are viewing a page. Six Apart owns four blogging services: Blogs.com (blogs.com), Movable Type (movabletype.com), Vox (vox.com), and TypePad (typepad.com). Microsoft Windows Live Spaces (spaces.live.com) and Yahoo 360 (360.yahoo .com) are basic blog editors. WordPress (wordpress .com) is a blogging service with convenient editing tools. Visit these blog design Web sites and read about the features provided. Which services have blogging tools that seem easy to use? What customization tools are available? Which Web sites allow users to upload photos, videos, reader surveys, and other widgets?

5 Ethics in Action

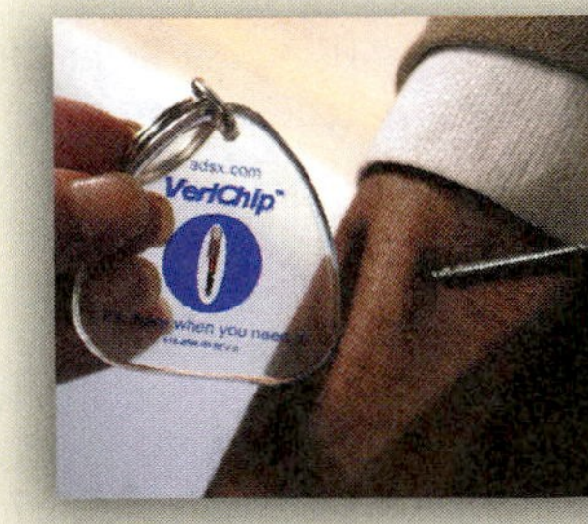

Millions of VeriChip microchips have been implanted in pets for identification purposes, but the move to humans has alarmed security experts. VeriChip's Xmark subsidiary distributes the Hugs and the Halo systems of infant protection, the RoamAlert system of wandering protection, and the MyCall emergency response system. The chips release a code when a scanner is passed over them, and this code is linked to a database that retains the person's information and can be updated. View online sites that discuss using implanted chips in humans. How can they be used to breach the confidentiality of medical records? How are they being used in nonmedical applications? Write a report summarizing your findings, and include a table of links to Web sites that provide additional details about implantable chips.

Critical Thinking

The Critical Thinking exercises challenge your assessment and decision-making skills by presenting real-world situations associated with the chapter concepts. The Collaboration exercise should be completed with a team.

To evaluate the situations below, use personal experiences and available resources such as articles on the Web or in print, blogs, podcasts, videos, television, user guides, other individuals, and electronics and computer stores. You may need to use multiple resources to form conclusions and make recommendations.

1. **Class Discussion — Offshore Outsourcing** A recent study suggests that the United States cumulatively will lose 3.4 million jobs to offshore outsourcing by the year 2015, far fewer than are lost due to new technology, domestic competition, and consumer tastes. B&L Consulting, Inc., the company you work for as a systems analyst, steadfastly has refused to use offshore outsourcing, claiming they prefer to employ homeland citizens. The company's competitors, on the other hand, have been using offshore outsourcing for some time. Of particular concern is the recent outsourcing by a competitor of the entire development of an accounting system to a firm in India. Your promotion to senior systems analyst gives you a voice on the B&L Consulting, Inc. senior management team. The major agenda item for next month's meeting is the outsourcing of the company's proposed accounts receivable system to a firm in Indonesia. Use the Web and/or other media and the material in Chapter 12 to research outsourcing and then prepare a discussion that addresses the following questions: Do you think systems can be developed entirely overseas? Why or why not? What are the major advantages and disadvantages of developing systems offshore? Is offshore outsourcing an alternative that our capitalistic economy can do without? If so, how?

2. **Class Presentation — Student Information System** You are an intern for a company that has volunteered to assist a new local community college with the development of a student information system. Your supervisor has assigned you the task of identifying the information that needs to be included in the new system. She wants you to use your school's system as the model. Analyze the data that is being recorded when students register for classes. Prepare a presentation that includes all the data that is collected and the information that is generated from that data. Include a list of suggestions for eliminating data that does not need to be recorded and adding data that currently is not recorded and information that is not generated. Include reasons why you would remove or add your suggestions.

> **Entering Class Semester Grades**
> For each semester class, perform the following steps:
> For each student, perform the following steps:
> Enter the grade earned.
> Verify the entered grade.
> Print the semester class entered grades.
> Create a cover sheet for quality control.

3. **Research — Protecting Information** For many organizations, information is their most valuable asset. Yet, information also can be the most difficult asset to protect. The primary problem is with employee information theft. Gaining ground quickly, however, is information theft by people who break into an organization's computer system via the Internet. In a test of the vulnerability of various computer systems, a Web security firm was able to make unauthorized trades at a mutual fund, access employee schedules at an airline, and change information in patient files at a health care center. Use the Web and/or print media to research how information can be protected from employees, customers, and other intruders and then prepare a report that answers the following questions: What security measures are available today? What proposals are planned for the future? Cite some examples of information theft and how the victim organization/person later was able to prevent the theft from reoccurring.

Collaboration

4. **Conversion Strategy** You are responsible for deploying a new information system at work, which will replace an old system; however, you are not certain which conversion strategy to use. It is important that your users are able to remain productive during the conversion process; furthermore, you want minimal interruption of corporate activities. Form a team of four classmates, and research the four conversion strategies (direct, parallel, phased, and pilot). Each team member should compile a list of at least two arguments for and against each conversion strategy. Then, the team members should meet to discuss their findings, decide upon the best conversion strategy to use, and then prepare a brief report describing why the conversion strategy you chose is the best one. Submit the report to your instructor.

Chapter Thirteen

Programming Languages and Program Development

Objectives

After completing this chapter, you will be able to:

1 Differentiate between machine and assembly languages

2 Identify and discuss the purpose of procedural programming languages, and describe the features of C and COBOL

3 Identify and discuss the characteristics of these object-oriented programming languages and program development tools: Java, .NET, C++, C#, F#, Visual Studio, visual programming languages, Delphi, and PowerBuilder

4 Identify the uses of these other programming languages and program development tools: 4GLs, classic programming languages, application generators, and macros

5 Describe various ways to develop Web pages, including HTML and XHTML, XML and WML, scripting languages, DHTML, Ruby on Rails, Web 2.0 development, and Web page authoring software

6 Identify the uses of popular multimedia authoring programs

7 List the six steps in the program development life cycle

8 Differentiate between structured design and object-oriented design

9 Explain the basic control structures and design tools used in designing solutions to programming problems

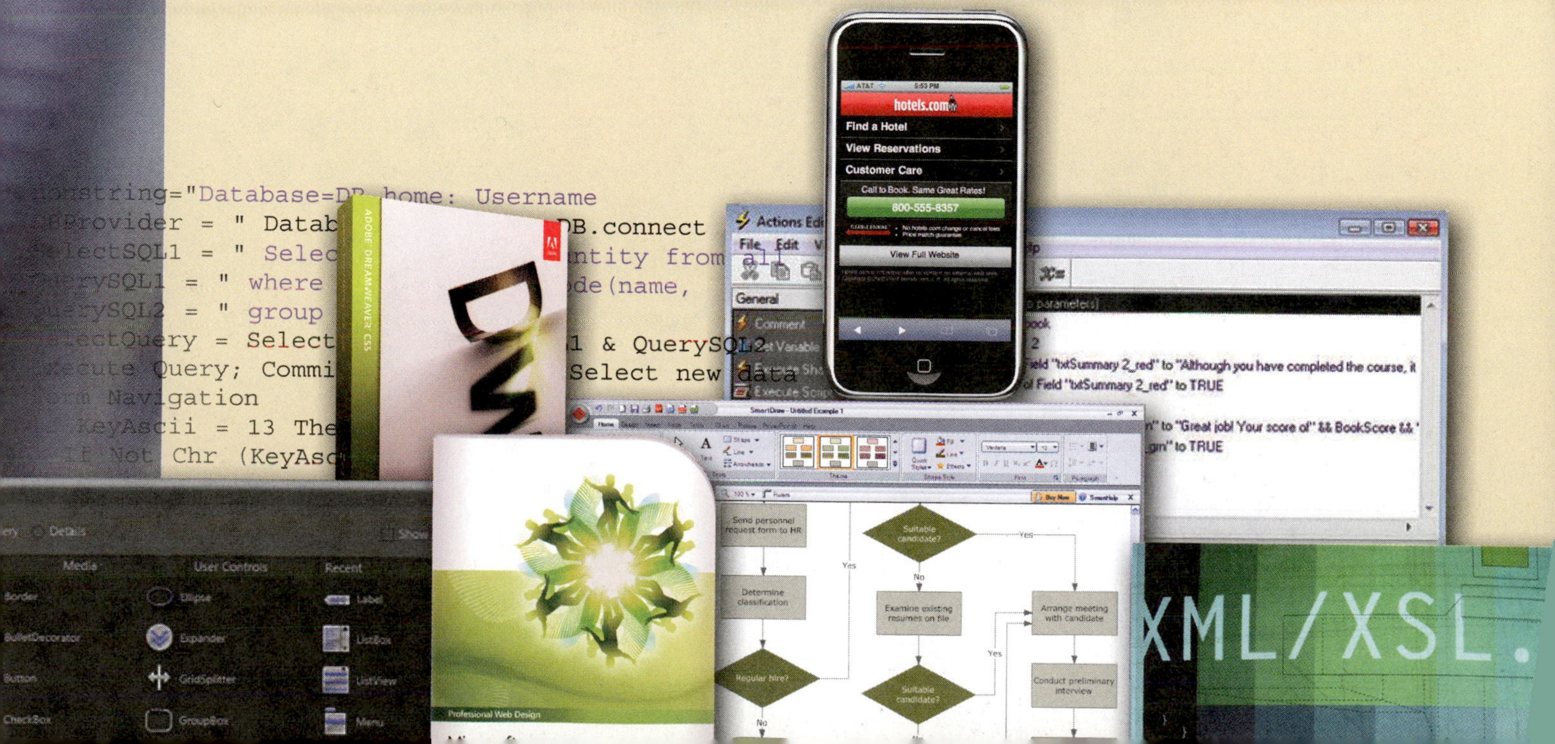

Computer Programs and Programming Languages

Although you may never write a computer program, information you request may require a programmer to create or modify a program. Thus, you should understand how programmers develop programs to meet information requirements. A **computer program** is a series of instructions that directs a computer to perform tasks. A computer **programmer**, often called a *developer*, creates and modifies computer programs.

To create a program, programmers sometimes write, or *code*, a program's instructions using a programming language. A **programming language** is a set of words, abbreviations, and symbols that enables a programmer to communicate instructions to a computer. Other times, programmers use a program development tool to create a program. A program that provides a user-friendly environment for building programs often is called a *program development tool*. Just as humans speak a variety of languages (English, Spanish, French, and so on), programmers use a variety of programming languages and tools to create programs (Figure 13-1).

Several hundred programming languages exist today. Each language has its own rules for writing the instructions. Languages often are designed for specific purposes, such as scientific applications, business solutions, or Web page development. When solving a problem or building a solution, programmers often use more than one language; that is, they integrate the languages.

Two types of languages are low-level and high-level. A *low-level language* is a programming language that is machine dependent. A *machine-dependent language* runs on only one particular type of computer. These programs are not easily portable to other types of computers. Each

Figure 13-1 Programmers must decide which programming languages and program development tools to use when they create programs.

language instruction in a low-level language usually equates to a single machine instruction, discussed further in the next section. With a *high-level language*, by contrast, each language instruction typically equates to multiple machine instructions. High-level languages often are machine independent. A *machine-independent language* can run on many different types of computers and operating systems.

The following pages discuss low-level languages, as well as several types of high-level languages.

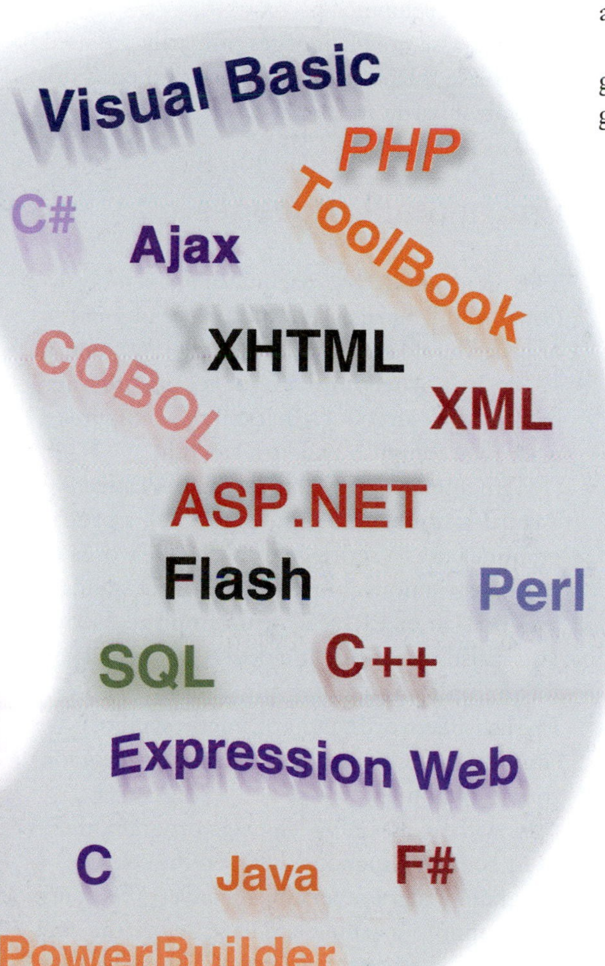

Low-Level Languages

Two types of low-level languages are machine languages and assembly languages. **Machine language**, known as the first generation of programming languages, is the only language the computer directly recognizes (Figure 13-2). Machine language instructions use a series of binary digits (1s and 0s) or a combination of numbers and letters that represents binary digits. The binary digits correspond to the on and off electrical states. As you might imagine, coding in machine language is tedious and time-consuming.

With an **assembly language**, the second generation of programming languages, a programmer writes instructions using symbolic

```
0000DE   5A50   35AA                     015AC
0000E2   47F0   2100            00102
000102   1B77
000104   5870   304E                     01050
000108   1C47
00010A   4E50   30D6                     010D8
00010E   F075   30D6    003E    010D8    0003E
000114   4F50   30D6                     010D8
000118   5050   3052                     01054
00011C   58E0   30B6                     010B8
000120   07FE
                                         00122
000122   50E0   30BA                     010BC
000126   1B55
000128   5A50   304E                     01050
00012C   5B50   3052                     01054
000130   5050   305A                     0105C
000134   58E0   30BA                     010BC
000138   07FE
```

Figure 13-2 A sample machine language program, coded using the hexadecimal number system. For information about hexadecimal, see Appendix C at the back of this book.

instruction codes (Figure 13-3). *Symbolic instruction codes* are meaningful abbreviations. With an assembly language, a programmer writes abbreviations such as A for addition, C for compare, L for load, and M for multiply.

Assembly languages also use symbolic addresses. A *symbolic address* is a meaningful name that identifies a storage location. For example, a programmer can use the name RATE to refer to the storage location that contains a pay rate.

Despite these advantages, assembly languages can be difficult to learn. In addition, programmers must convert an assembly language program into machine language before the computer can *execute*, or run, the program. That is, the computer cannot execute the assembly source program. A **source program** is the program that contains the language instructions, or code, to be converted to machine language. To convert the assembly language source program into machine language, programmers use a program called an *assembler*.

One assembly language instruction usually equates to one machine language instruction. In some cases, however, the assembly language includes macros. An assembly language *macro* generates many machine language instructions for a single assembly language instruction. Macros save the programmer time during program development.

Today, assembly languages primarily are used to increase the performance of critical tasks or to control hardware.

comments begin with an asterisk

```
*         THIS MODULE CALCULATES THE REGULAR TIME PAY
CALCSTPY  EQU     *
          ST      14,SAVERTPY
          SR      4,4
          SR      7,7
          SR      5,5
          PACK    DOUBLE,RTHRSIN
          CVB     4,DOUBLE
          PACK    DOUBLE,RATEIN
          CVB     7,DOUBLE
          ST      7,RATE
          MR      4,7
          ST      5,RTPAY
          L       14,SAVERTPY
          BR      14
*         THIS MODULE CALCULATES THE OVERTIME PAY
CALCOTPY  EQU     *
          ST      14,SAVEOTPY
TEST1     CLI     CODEIN,C'O'
          BH      TEST2
          SR      5,5
          A       5,=F'0'
          ST      5,OTPAY
          B       AROUND
TEST2     SR      4,4
          SR      7,7
          SR      5,5
          PACK    DOUBLE,OTHRSIN
          CVB     4,DOUBLE
          PACK    DOUBLE,RATEIN
          CVB     7,RATE
          MR      4,7
          MR      4,=F'1.5'
          ST      5,OTPAY
AROUND    L       14,SAVEOTPY
          BR      14
*         THIS MODULE CALCULATES THE GROSS PAY
CALCGPAY  EQU     *
          ST      14,SAVEGPAY
          SR      5,5
          A       5,RTPAY
          A       5,OTPAY
          ST      5,GRPAY
          L       14,SAVEGPAY
          BR      14
```

calculates regular time pay

evaluates overtime hours and calculates overtime pay

calculates gross pay

Figure 13-3 An excerpt from an assembly language payroll program. The code shows the computations for regular time pay, overtime pay, and gross pay and the decision to evaluate the overtime hours.

Procedural Languages

The disadvantages of machine and assembly (low-level) languages led to the development of procedural languages in the late 1950s and 1960s. In a **procedural language**, the programmer writes instructions that tell the computer what to accomplish and how to do it.

With a procedural language, often called a **third-generation language (3GL)**, a programmer uses a series of English-like words to write instructions. For example, ADD stands for addition or PRINT means to print. Many 3GLs also use arithmetic operators such as * for multiplication and + for addition. These English-like words and arithmetic symbols simplify the program development process for the programmer.

As with an assembly language program, the 3GL code (instructions) is called the source program. Programmers must convert this source program into machine language before the computer can execute the program. This translation process often is very complex, because one 3GL source program instruction translates into many machine language instructions. For 3GLs, programmers typically use either a compiler or an interpreter to perform the translation.

A *compiler* is a separate program that converts the entire source program into machine language before executing it. The machine language version that results from compiling the 3GL is called the *object code* or *object program*. The compiler stores the object code on storage media for execution later.

While it is compiling the source program into object code, the compiler checks the source program for errors. The compiler then produces a program listing that contains the source code and a list of any errors. This listing helps the programmer make necessary changes to the source code and correct errors in the program. Figure 13-4 shows the process of compiling a source program.

A compiler translates an entire program before executing it. An interpreter, by contrast, translates and executes one statement at a time. An *interpreter* reads a code statement, converts it to one or more machine language instructions, and then executes those machine language instructions. It does this all before moving to the next code statement in the program. Each time the source program runs, the interpreter translates and executes it, statement by statement. An interpreter does not produce an object program. Figure 13-5 shows the process of interpreting a program.

One advantage of an interpreter is that when it finds errors, it displays feedback immediately. The programmer can correct any errors before the interpreter translates the next line of code. The disadvantage is that interpreted programs do not run as fast as compiled programs. This is because an interpreter must translate the source program to machine language each time the program executes. Once a program is compiled, by contrast, users simply execute the object code to run the program.

Many programming languages include both an interpreter and a compiler. In this case, the programmer can use the interpreter during program development. When the program is complete and error free, the programmer can compile the program so that it runs faster when it is placed into production for users to execute.

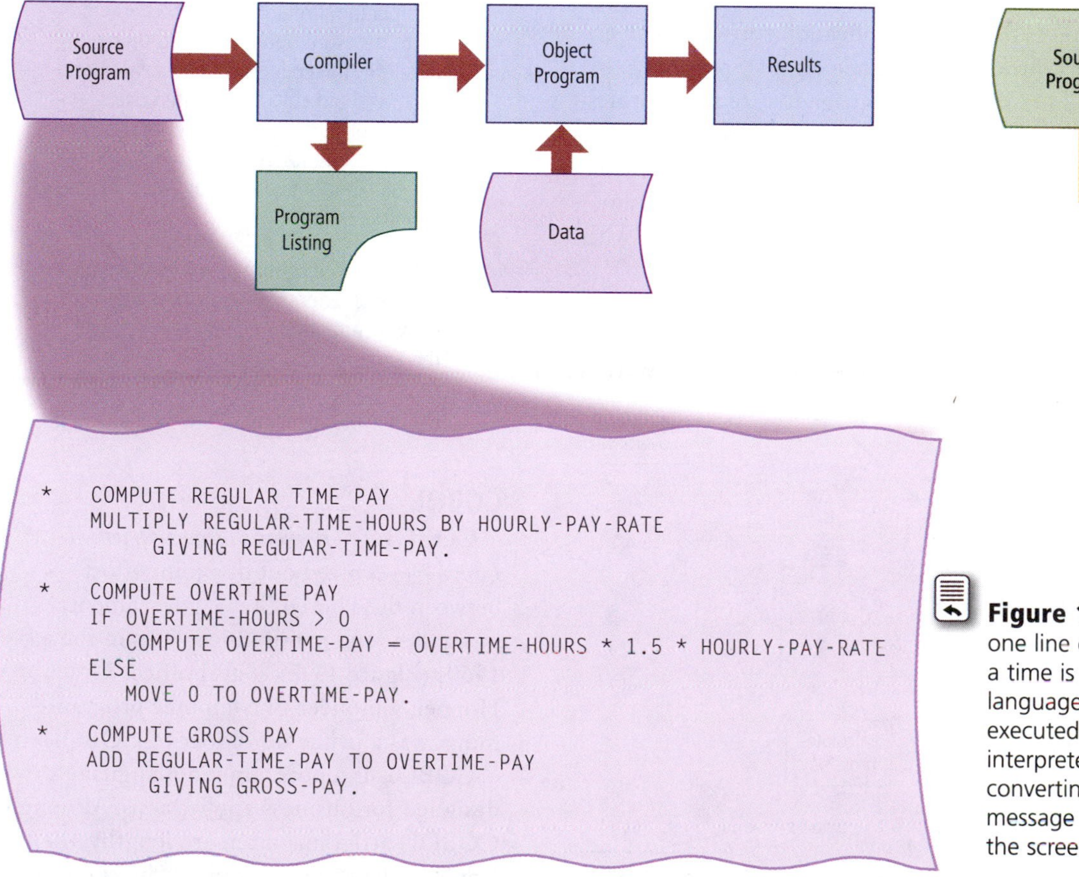

Figure 13-4 A compiler converts the source program into a machine language object program. If the compiler encounters any errors, it records them in the program-listing file, which the programmer may print when the entire compilation is complete. When a user wants to run the program, the object program is loaded into the memory of the computer and the program instructions begin executing.

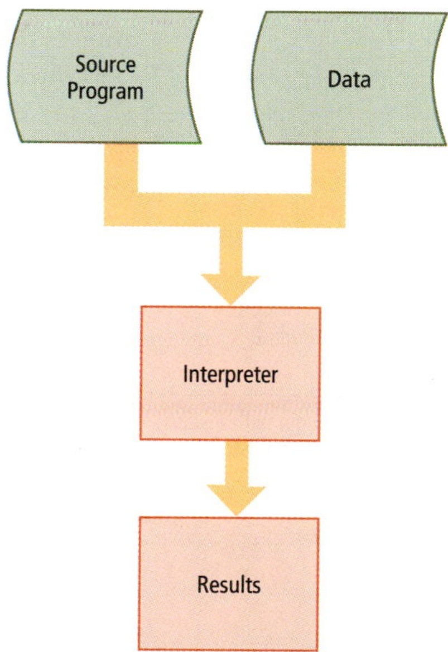

Figure 13-5 With an interpreter, one line of the source program at a time is converted into machine language and then immediately executed by the computer. If the interpreter encounters an error while converting a line of code, an error message immediately is displayed on the screen and the program stops.

Hundreds of procedural languages exist. Only a few, however, are used widely enough for the industry to recognize them as standards. These include C and COBOL. To illustrate the similarities and differences among these programming languages, the following figures show program code in these languages. The code solves a simple payroll problem — computing the gross pay for an employee.

The process used to compute gross pay can vary from one system to another. The examples on the following pages use a simple *algorithm*, or set of steps, to help you easily compare one programming language with another. Read Innovative Computing 13-1 to find out about some useful and fun online programs.

C

The **C** programming language, developed in the early 1970s by Dennis Ritchie at Bell Laboratories, originally was designed for writing system software. Today, many programs are written in C (Figure 13-6). This includes operating systems and application software such as word processing and spreadsheet programs.

C is a powerful language that requires professional programming skills. Many programmers use C for business and scientific problems. C runs on almost any type of computer with any operating system, but it is used most often with the UNIX and Linux operating systems.

C
For more information, visit the Computer Concepts CourseMate Web site at www.cengagebrain.com, navigate to the Chapter 13 Web Link resource for this book, and then click C.

comments begin with a slash followed by an asterisk

calculates regular time pay

evaluates overtime hours and calculates overtime pay

```
/* Compute Regular Time Pay                          */
rt_pay = rt_hrs * pay_rate;

/* Compute Overtime Pay                              */
if (ot_hrs > 0)
    ot_pay = ot_hrs * 1.5 * pay_rate;
else
    ot_pay = 0;

/* Compute Gross Pay                                 */
gross = rt_pay + ot_pay;

/* Print Gross Pay                                   */
printf("The gross pay is %d\n", gross);
```

calculates gross pay

prints gross pay

Figure 13-6 An excerpt from a C payroll program. The code shows the computations for regular time pay, overtime pay, and gross pay; the decision to evaluate the overtime hours; and the output of the gross pay.

INNOVATIVE COMPUTING 13-1

Online Calculators Answer Life's Questions

At practically every phase of life, people can benefit from some sort of calculator. For example, one program can help expectant parents calculate the date their child will be born and another can generate possible baby names. Once the child is born, they can use another calculator that attempts to estimate the total cost of raising the child through the teenage years.

One Web site has collected a wide variety of calculators: Your Life, Calculated. This MSN-sponsored site organizes the calculators in a variety of categories. The Career section includes a millionaire calculator to determine how much money will need to be saved each month to reach $1 million, and it also includes amortization tables and mortgage and car loan calculators.

Other tools are the tip calculator, a calculator that determines the chances of a successful personal relationship, the body mass index to measure body fat based on height and weight, the college cost calculator, and the financial aid calculator. When using online calculators, keep in mind that some are subjective in nature, and the results reflect the thoughts and/or opinions of the calculator's author.

For more information, visit the Computer Concepts CourseMate Web site at www.cengagebrain.com, navigate to the Chapter 13 Innovative Computing resource for this book, and then click Online Calculators.

COBOL

COBOL (*COmmon Business-Oriented Language*) evolved out of a joint effort between the United States government, businesses, and major universities in the early 1960s (Figure 13-7). Naval officer Grace Hopper, a pioneer in computer programming, was a prime developer of COBOL.

COBOL is a programming language designed for business applications. Although COBOL programs often are lengthy, their English-like statements make the code easy to read, write, and maintain. COBOL especially is useful for processing transactions, such as payroll and billing, on mainframe computers. COBOL programs also run on other types of computers.

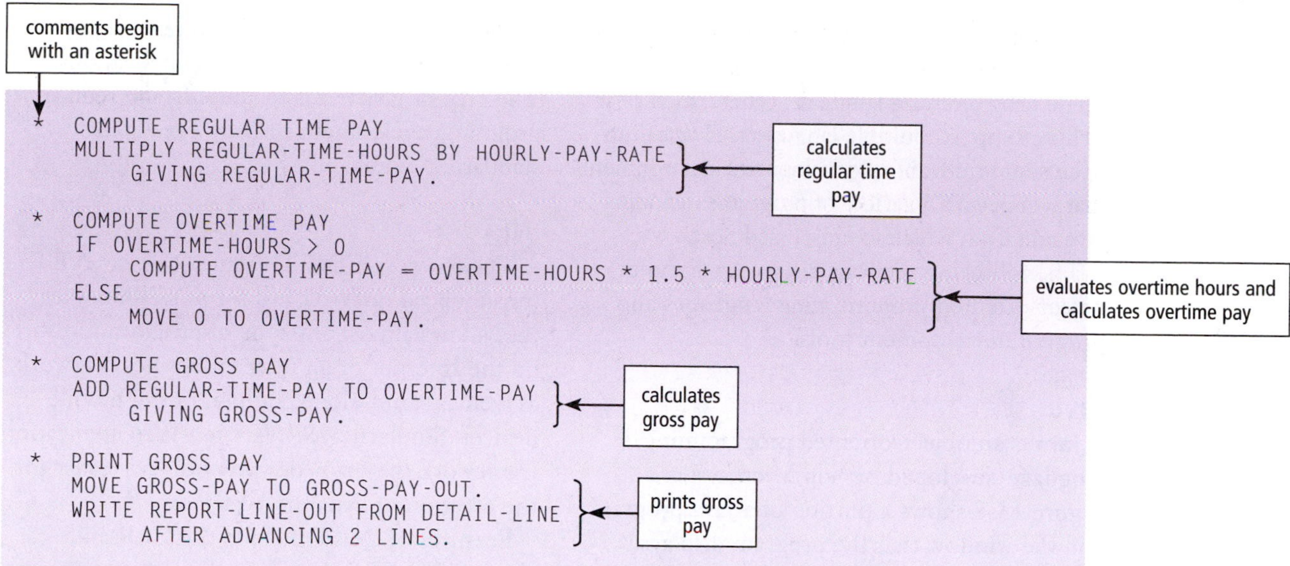

Figure 13-7 An excerpt from a COBOL payroll program. The code shows the computations for regular time pay, overtime pay, and gross pay; the decision to evaluate the overtime hours; and the output of the gross pay.

Object-Oriented Programming Languages and Program Development Tools

Computer programmers use an **object-oriented programming (OOP) language** or object-oriented program development tool to implement an object-oriented design. Recall from Chapter 12 that an *object* is an item that can contain both data and the procedures that read or manipulate that data. An object represents a real person, place, event, or transaction.

A major benefit of OOP is the ability to reuse and modify existing objects. For example, once a programmer creates an Employee object, it is available for use by any other existing or future program. Thus, programmers repeatedly reuse existing objects. For example, the payroll program and health benefits program both use the Employee object. That is, the payroll program would use it to process employee paychecks and the health benefits program would use it to process health insurance payments.

Programs developed using the object-oriented approach have several advantages. The objects can be reused in many systems, are designed for repeated use, and become stable over time. In addition, programmers create applications faster because they design programs using existing objects.

In addition to being able to work with objects, an OOP language is event driven. An *event* is an action to which the program responds. Examples of events include pressing a key on the keyboard, typing a value in a text box, moving the mouse, clicking a button, or speaking an instruction. An *event-driven program* checks for and responds to events. Some programming languages are event driven but are not complete OOP languages. Other programming languages, such as Java, C#, F#, C++, and the latest versions of Visual Basic, are complete object-oriented languages.

Object-oriented programming languages and program development tools work well in a RAD environment. **RAD** (*rapid application development*) is a method of developing software, in which a programmer writes and implements a program in segments instead of waiting until the entire program is completed. Users begin working with sections of the program as they are completed. An important concept in RAD is the use of prebuilt components. For example, programmers do not have to write code for buttons and text boxes on Windows forms because they already exist in the programming language or tools provided with the language.

Most object-oriented program development tools are IDEs. An **IDE (integrated development environment)** includes tools for building graphical user interfaces, an editor for entering program code, a compiler and/or interpreter, and a debugger (to remove errors, which is discussed later in the chapter). Some IDEs work with a single programming language; others, such as Eclipse support multiple languages. *Eclipse* is an open source, advanced development environment that works with a variety of programs including Java and C++, which are discussed next.

The following sections discuss a variety of object-oriented programming languages and program development tools.

Java

Java is an object-oriented programming language developed by Sun Microsystems. Figure 13-8 shows a portion of a Java program and the window that the program displays.

When programmers compile a Java program, the resulting object code typically is called *bytecode*, which is machine independent. Java then uses a *just-in-time (JIT) compiler* to convert the bytecode into machine-dependent code that is executed immediately. Programmers use *Java Platform, Standard Edition (Java SE)*, developed by Sun Microsystems, to create stand-alone programs for desktop computers and servers. Similarly, programmers use *Java Platform, Micro Edition (Java ME)* to create programs for smart phones and other mobile devices.

Java Platforms

For more information, visit the Computer Concepts CourseMate Web site at www.cengagebrain.com, navigate to the Chapter 13 Web Link resource for this book, and then click Java Platforms.

Java EE (Java Platform, Enterprise Edition) is a set of technologies built on Sun's Java SE that allows programmers to develop and deploy large applications for organizations, often used in Web 2.0 environments for Web applications. The goal of Java EE is to simplify and reduce program development time by developing standard, reusable objects.

.NET

The Microsoft .NET Framework, or **.NET** (pronounced dot net), is a set of technologies that allows almost any type of program to run on the Internet or an internal business network, as well as stand-alone computers and mobile devices. Similarly, *ASP.NET* is a Web application framework that provides the tools necessary for the creation of dynamic Web sites.

Features of .NET include the CLR and classes. The *CLR* (Common Language Runtime) is an environment that enables programmers to develop .NET programs using a variety of languages. A .NET-compatible language compiles the program source code into *Microsoft Intermediate Language (MSIL)*. The CLR then converts the MSIL into object code using a just-in-time compiler. The CLR supports classes so that .NET programmers can access a variety of common functions in their programs, which saves development time.

Using .NET and/or ASP.NET, programmers easily can develop Web applications, Web services, and Windows programs. Examples of languages that support .NET include C++, C#, F#, Visual Basic,

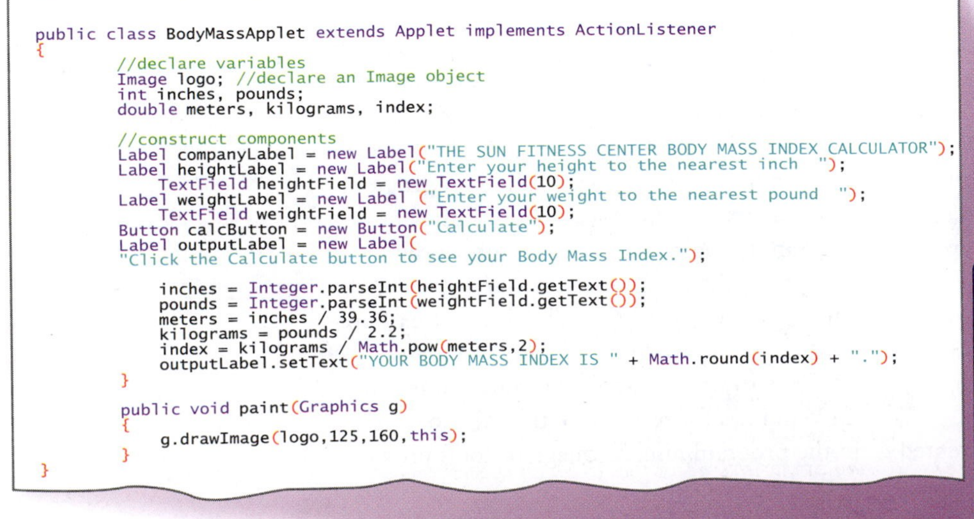

```
public class BodyMassApplet extends Applet implements ActionListener
{
        //declare variables
        Image logo; //declare an Image object
        int inches, pounds;
        double meters, kilograms, index;

        //construct components
        Label companyLabel = new Label("THE SUN FITNESS CENTER BODY MASS INDEX CALCULATOR");
        Label heightLabel = new Label("Enter your height to the nearest inch  ");
            TextField heightField = new TextField(10);
        Label weightLabel = new Label ("Enter your weight to the nearest pound  ");
            TextField weightField = new TextField(10);
        Button calcButton = new Button("Calculate");
        Label outputLabel = new Label(
        "Click the Calculate button to see your Body Mass Index.");

            inches = Integer.parseInt(heightField.getText());
            pounds = Integer.parseInt(weightField.getText());
            meters = inches / 39.36;
            kilograms = pounds / 2.2;
            index = kilograms / Math.pow(meters,2);
            outputLabel.setText("YOUR BODY MASS INDEX IS " + Math.round(index) + ".");
        }

        public void paint(Graphics g)
        {
            g.drawImage(logo,125,160,this);
        }
}
```

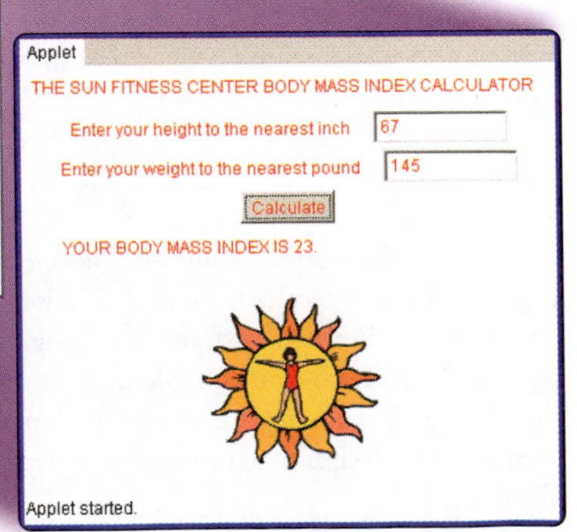

Figure 13-8
A portion of a Java program and the window the program displays.

Delphi, and PowerBuilder. The following sections discuss each of these languages.

C++

Developed in the 1980s by Bjarne Sroustrup at Bell Laboratories, **C++** (pronounced SEE-plus-plus) is an object-oriented programming language that is an extension of the C programming language. C++ includes all the elements of the C language, plus it has additional features for working with objects, classes, events, and other object-oriented concepts (Figure 13-9).

Programmers commonly use C++ to develop database and Web applications. Much application software, such as word processing and spreadsheet programs, also is written in C++. A programmer does not need C programming experience to be a successful C++ programmer.

```
// portion of a C++ program that allows users to create
// a new zip code from a string or a number and expand
// zip codes, as appropriate, to a 10-digit number

ZipC::ZipC( const unsigned long zipnum )
{
  ostringstream strInt;
  strInt << zipnum;
  code = strInt.str();
}

const string ZipC::getCode()
{
  return code;
}

void ZipC::setCode(const string newCode)
{
  code = newCode;
}

void ZipC::expand( const string suffix )
{

  if(code.length() == 5 &&          // small size?
     suffix.length() == 4)          // length ok?
  {
     code += "-";
     code.append(suffix);
  }
}
```

Figure 13-9 Sample C++ program.

C#

C# (pronounced SEE-sharp) is an object-oriented programming language based on C++ that was developed primarily by Anders Hejlsberg, Microsoft chief architect and distinguished engineer. C# has been accepted as a standard for Web applications and XML-based Web services. Recall from Chapter 9 that Web services describe standardized software that enables programmers to create applications that communicate with other remote computers over the Internet or on an internal business network.

Like Java, C# uses a JIT compiler but its resulting code is MSIL. C# applications can be built on existing C or C++ applications, saving development time for companies migrating from C or C++.

F#

F# (pronounced EFF-sharp), which is included with the latest version of Visual Studio (discussed in the next section), is a programming language that combines the benefits of an object-oriented language with the benefits of a functional language. A *functional language* is a programming language whose natural programming structure is useful in mathematical programs.

Benefits of programs written in F# include easy access to .NET libraries and performance similar to that of C# programs.

Visual Studio

Visual Studio is Microsoft's suite of program development tools that assists programmers in building programs for Windows, Windows Mobile, or operating systems that support .NET. Visual Studio includes enhanced support for building security and reliability into applications through its programming languages, RAD tools, IDE, a specialized query language called LINQ (Language Integrated Query), and other resources that reduce development time. For example, Visual Studio includes *code snippets*, which are prewritten code and templates associated with common programming tasks. *Visual Studio Tools for Office* (*VSTO*) is a set of tools integrated in Visual Studio that enables developers to create programs that work with Microsoft's Office suite, including Word, Excel, PowerPoint, Outlook, and Project. The next sections discuss the programming languages in the Visual Studio suite.

Visual Studio Tools for Office

For more information, visit the Computer Concepts CourseMate Web site at www.cengagebrain.com, navigate to the Chapter 13 Web Link resource for this book, and then click Visual Studio Tools for Office.

- **Visual Basic** is a programming language that allows programmers easily to build complex task-oriented object-based programs. Visual Basic is based on the BASIC programming language, which was developed by Microsoft Corporation in the early 1990s. This language is easy to learn and use. Thus, Visual Basic is ideal for beginning programmers.

  The first step in building a Visual Basic program often is to design the graphical user interface using Visual Basic objects (Steps 1 and 2 in Figure 13-10). Visual Basic objects include items such as buttons, text boxes, and labels. Next, the programmer writes instructions to define any actions that should occur in response to specific events (Step 3 in Figure 13-10). Finally, the programmer generates and tests the final program (Step 4 in Figure 13-10). To learn more about how to design a user interface, complete the Learn How To 1 activity on pages 708 and 709.

  An event in Visual Basic might be the result of an action that a user initiates. For example, when a user clicks a button in a Visual Basic program, the program executes the Click event. Programmers create events in Visual Basic by writing instructions (code) with its built-in programming language.

Creating a Visual Basic Program

Step 1

The developer designs the user interface, such as for the mobile device shown here. Linear Feet is a text box in which the user enters data. Pine, Oak, and Cherry are option buttons the user can click to choose the wood type. Calculate and Clear are buttons. All other objects are labels.

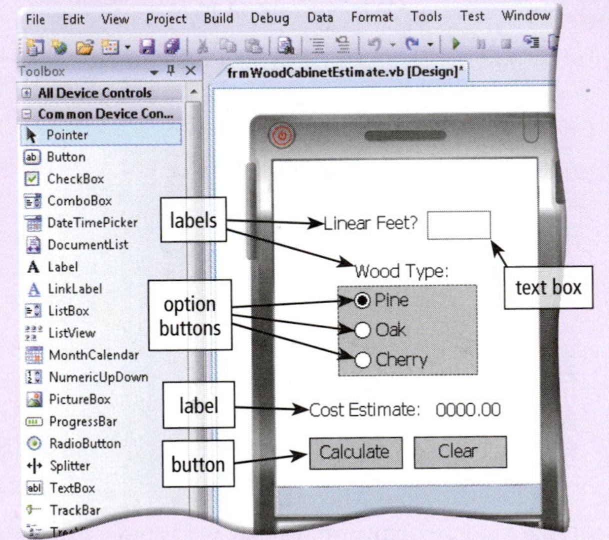

Step 2

The developer assigns properties to each object. Objects include text boxes, option buttons, buttons, labels, and the form itself.

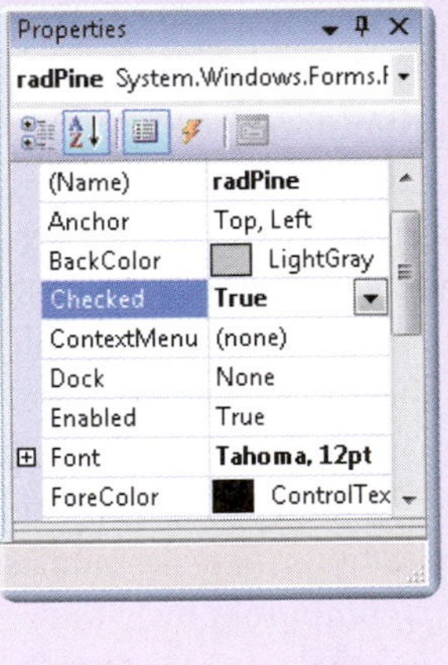

Step 3

The developer writes code to define the action of each event the user triggers.

```
Private Sub btnCalculate_Click(ByVal sender As System.Object, ByVal e As
EventArgs) Handles btnCalculate.Click
    ' The btnCalculate event handler calculates the estimated cost of
    ' cabinets based on the linear feet and the wood type.

    ' Declaration Section
    Dim decLinearFeet As Decimal
    Dim decCostPerFoot As Decimal
    Dim decCostEstimate As Decimal
    Dim decPineCost As Decimal = 100D
    Dim decOakCost As Decimal = 150D
    Dim decCherryCost As Decimal = 250D

    ' Did user enter a numeric value?
    If IsNumeric(Me.txtLinearFeet.Text) Then
        decLinearFeet = Convert.ToDecimal(Me.txtLinearFeet.Text)

        ' Is Linear Feet greater than zero
        If decLinearFeet > 0 Then
            ' Determine cost per foot of wood
            If Me.radPine.Checked Then
                decCostPerFoot = decPineCost
            ElseIf Me.radOak.Checked Then
                decCostPerFoot = decOakCost
            ElseIf Me.radCherry.Checked Then
                decCostPerFoot = decCherryCost
            End If
            ' Calculate and display the cost estimate
            decCostEstimate = decLinearFeet * decCostPerFoot
            Me.lblCostEstimate.Text = decCostEstimate.ToString("C")
        Else
```

Step 4

The developer tests the program. The Cost Estimate is displayed after the user clicks the Calculate button.

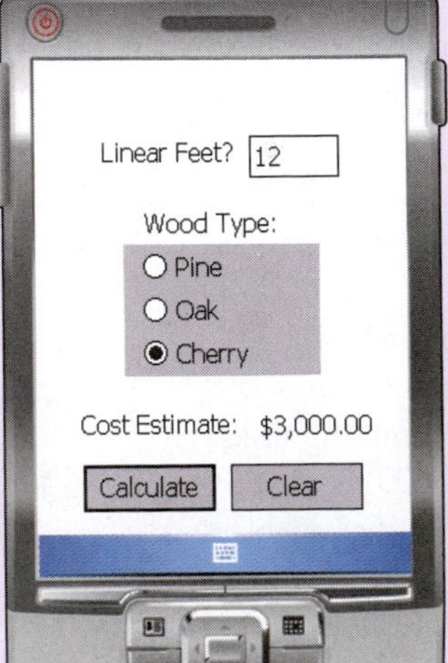

Figure 13-10 This figure shows how to create a Visual Basic program.

- **Visual C++** is a programming language based on C++. Not only is Visual C++ a powerful object-oriented programming language, it enables programmers to write Windows, Windows Mobile, and .NET applications quickly and efficiently. Features that make Visual C++ so powerful include reusable templates, direct access to machine level memory locations, an optimizing compiler, and advanced error reporting.
- **Visual C#** is a programming language that combines programming elements of C++ with an easier, rapid development environment. The purpose of Visual C# is to take the complexity out of Visual C++ and still provide an object-oriented programming language. Programmers familiar with the C/C++ programming language family often migrate to the easier-to-use Visual C#.

Visual Programming Languages

A **visual programming language** is a language that uses a visual or graphical interface for creating all source code. The graphical interface, called a *visual programming environment* (*VPE*), allows programmers to drag and drop objects to develop programs. Examples of visual programming languages include Alice, Mindscript, and Prograph.

Delphi

Borland's **Delphi** is a powerful program development tool that is ideal for building large-scale enterprise and Web applications in a RAD environment (Figure 13-11). Programmers use Delphi to develop programs quickly for Windows, Linux, and .NET platforms.

Delphi also provides visual modeling tools based on the UML. Recall from Chapter 12 that the UML (Unified Modeling Language) has been adopted as a standard notation for object modeling and development. With Delphi, programmers easily link the UML designs to the working solutions.

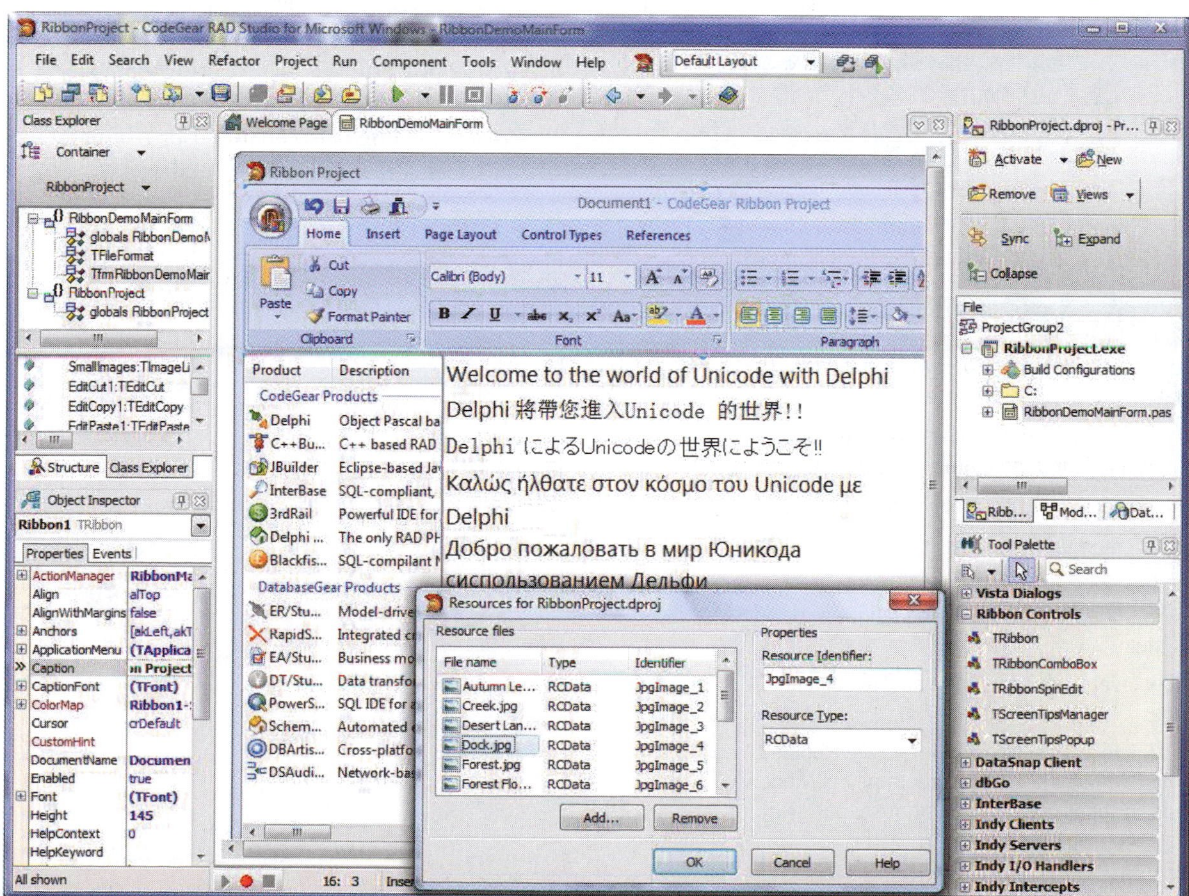

Figure 13-11 The latest version of Delphi, shown in this figure, makes Windows development tasks faster, better, and easier by supporting Microsoft's .NET Framework with both Delphi and C# languages, as well as Delphi for Windows applications in a RAD environment.

PowerBuilder

PowerBuilder, developed by Sybase, is another powerful program development RAD tool that is best suited for Web-based, .NET, and large-scale enterprise object-oriented applications. Programmers also use PowerBuilder to develop small- and medium-scale client/server applications. PowerBuilder includes a consistent interface, wizards, and many other features that enable programmers to develop applications quickly (Figure 13-12). In terms of complexity, PowerBuilder is comparable to Delphi.

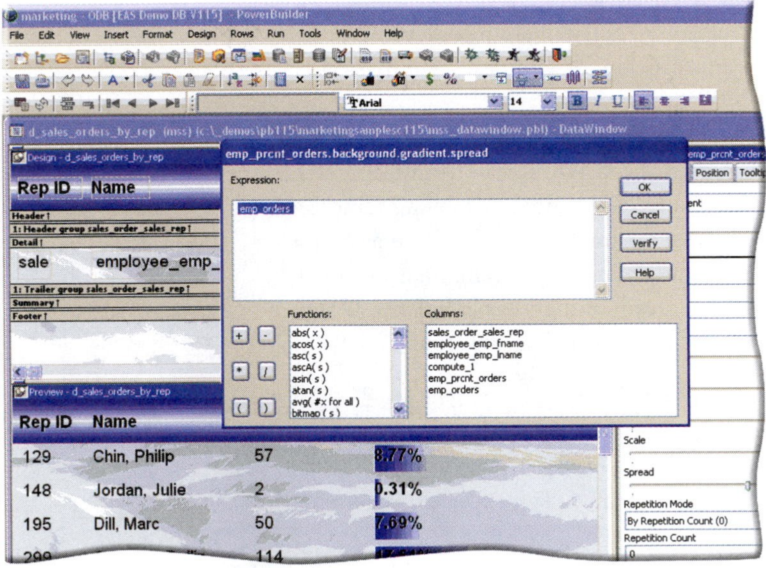

Figure 13-12 PowerBuilder is a program development RAD tool ideal for building large-scale and Web-based applications.

Other Programming Languages and Development Tools

The following sections discuss a variety of other programming languages and program development tools.

4GLs

A **4GL** (*fourth-generation language*) is a nonprocedural language that enables users and programmers to access data in a database. With a **nonprocedural language**, the programmer writes English-like instructions or interacts with a graphical environment to retrieve data from files or a database. Nonprocedural languages typically are easier to use than procedural languages. Many object-oriented program development tools use 4GLs.

One popular 4GL is SQL. As discussed in Chapter 10, **SQL** is a query language that allows users to manage, update, and retrieve data in a relational DBMS (Figure 13-13). These powerful languages allow database administrators to define a database and its structure. They also enable users to maintain and access the data in the database.

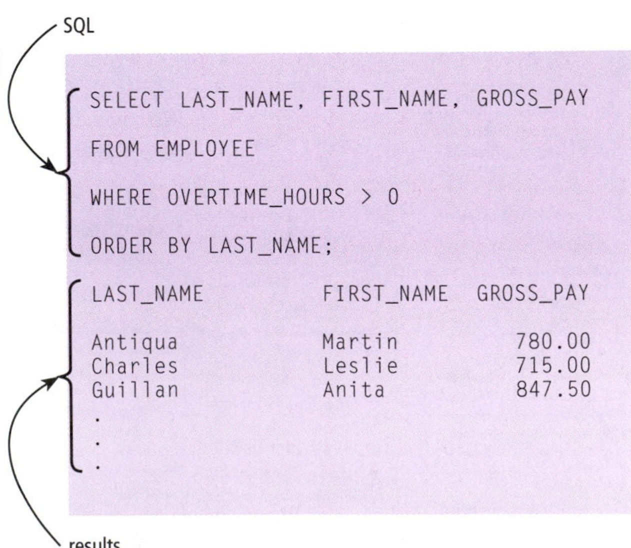

Figure 13-13 SQL is a 4GL that can be used to query database tables. This query produces an alphabetical list of those employees who receive overtime pay; that is, their overtime hours are greater than 0.

✓ QUIZ YOURSELF 13-1

Instructions: Find the true statement below. Then, rewrite the remaining false statements so that they are true.

1. An interpreter is a program that converts an entire source program into machine language before executing it.
2. C and COBOL are examples of assembly languages.
3. C# is an object-oriented programming language based on PowerBuilder.
4. Delphi is an object-oriented programming language developed by Sun Microsystems.
5. Two types of low-level languages are machine languages and source languages.
6. Visual Studio is Microsoft's suite of program development tools that assists programmers in building programs for Windows, Windows Mobile, or operating systems that support .NET.

Quiz Yourself Online: To further check your knowledge of pages 664 through 674, visit the Computer Concepts CourseMate Web site at www.cengagebrain.com, navigate to the Chapter 13 Quiz Yourself resource for this book, and then click Objectives 1 – 3.

FAQ 13-1

Why is it necessary for programmers to know SQL?

Programmers often write programs that interact with a database in some fashion. For this reason, programmers must know SQL so that their programs can communicate with the database.

For more information, visit the Computer Concepts CourseMate Web site at www.cengagebrain.com, navigate to the Chapter 13 FAQ resource for this book, and then click SQL.

Classic Programming Languages

In addition to the programming languages discussed on the previous pages, programmers sometimes use the languages listed in Figure 13-14, which were more popular in the past than today. Read Looking Ahead 13-1 for a look at the future of programming.

LOOKING AHEAD 13-1

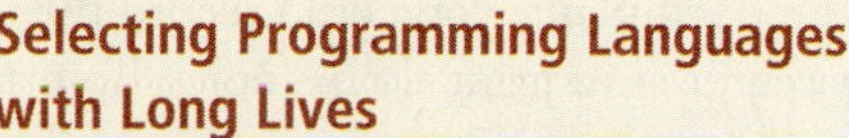

Selecting Programming Languages with Long Lives

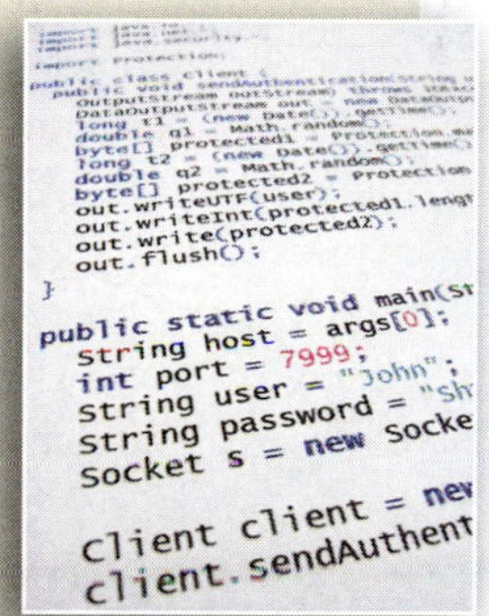

Choosing the best programming language can be a dilemma that affects programmers for years to come. If they select a language that remains popular for at least five years, chances are that employees at that time will be able to modify and enhance the code. COBOL, for example, was developed in the 1960s, and COBOL programmers still are being sought on popular employment Web sites.

Some languages that are experiencing popularity today are expected to continue growing in use. JavaScript, for example, is gaining momentum, as are Ruby on Rails and Perl. Many programs for the iPhone are written in Cocoa, and Google's App Engine uses Python, so programmers knowing these languages are in demand.

As programming evolves, some trends to watch are the blending of popular languages, the development of scripting languages for the Web and for cloud computing, the ability to insert customized code easily in a browser, and the rise of amateur programmers who will use new, graphical languages to improve their computing experience.

For more information, visit the Computer Concepts CourseMate Web site at www.cengagebrain.com, navigate to the Chapter 13 Looking Ahead resource for this book, and then click Programming Future.

Classic Programming Languages	
Ada	Derived from Pascal, developed by the U.S. Department of Defense, named after Augusta Ada Lovelace Byron, who is thought to be the first female computer programmer
ALGOL	ALGOrithmic Language, the first structured procedural language
APL	A Programming Language, a scientific language designed to manipulate tables of numbers
BASIC	Beginners All-purpose Symbolic Instruction Code, developed by John Kemeny and Thomas Kurtz as a simple, interactive problem-solving language
Forth	Similar to C, used for small computerized devices
FORTRAN	FORmula TRANslator, one of the first high-level programming languages used for scientific applications
HyperTalk	An object-oriented programming language developed by Apple to manipulate cards that can contain text, graphics, and sound
LISP	LISt Processing, a language used for artificial intelligence applications
Logo	An educational tool used to teach programming and problem solving to children
Modula-2	A successor to Pascal used for developing system software
Pascal	Developed to teach students structured programming concepts, named in honor of Blaise Pascal, a French mathematician who developed one of the earliest calculating machines
PILOT	Programmed Inquiry Learning Or Teaching, used to write computer-aided instruction programs
PL/1	Programming Language One, a business and scientific language that combines many features of FORTRAN and COBOL
Prolog	PROgramming LOGic, used for development of artificial intelligence applications
RPG	Report Program Generator, used to assist businesses with generating reports and to access/update data in databases
Smalltalk	Object-oriented programming language

Figure 13-14 Classic programming languages.

Application Generators

An **application generator** is a program that creates source code or machine code from a specification of the required functionality. When using an application generator, a programmer or user works with menu-driven tools and graphical user interfaces to define the desired specifications. Application generators most often are bundled with or are included as part of a DBMS.

An application generator typically consists of a report writer, form, and menu generator. As discussed in Chapter 10, a *report writer* allows you to design a report on the screen, retrieve data into the report design, and then display or print the report. A *form* is a window on the screen that provides areas for entering or changing data in a database. Figure 13-15 shows a sample form design and the resulting form it generates showing sample data a user may enter in the form. A *menu generator* enables you to create a menu for the application options. If you create three reports and two forms for an application, for example, the menu would contain at least six options: one for each report, one for each form, and one to exit, or quit, the application.

Macros

A **macro** is a series of statements that instructs an application how to complete a task. Macros allow users to automate routine, repetitive, or difficult tasks in application software such as word processing, spreadsheet, or database programs. That is, users can create simple programs within the software by writing macros. You usually create a macro in one of two ways: (1) record the macro or (2) write the macro.

If you want to automate a routine or repetitive task such as formatting or editing, you would record a macro. A *macro recorder* is similar to a movie camera because both record all actions until turned off. To record a macro, start the macro recorder in the software. Then, perform the steps to be part of the macro, such as clicks of the mouse or keystrokes. Once the macro is recorded, you can run it anytime you want to perform that same sequence of actions. For example, if you always print three copies of certain documents, you could record the actions required to print three copies. To print three copies, you would run the macro called PrintThreeCopies.

When you become familiar with programming techniques, you can write your own macros instead of recording them. Many programs use *Visual Basic for Applications* (*VBA*), which can work with Visual Studio Tools for Office, or a similar language as their macro

Figure 13-15a (form design)

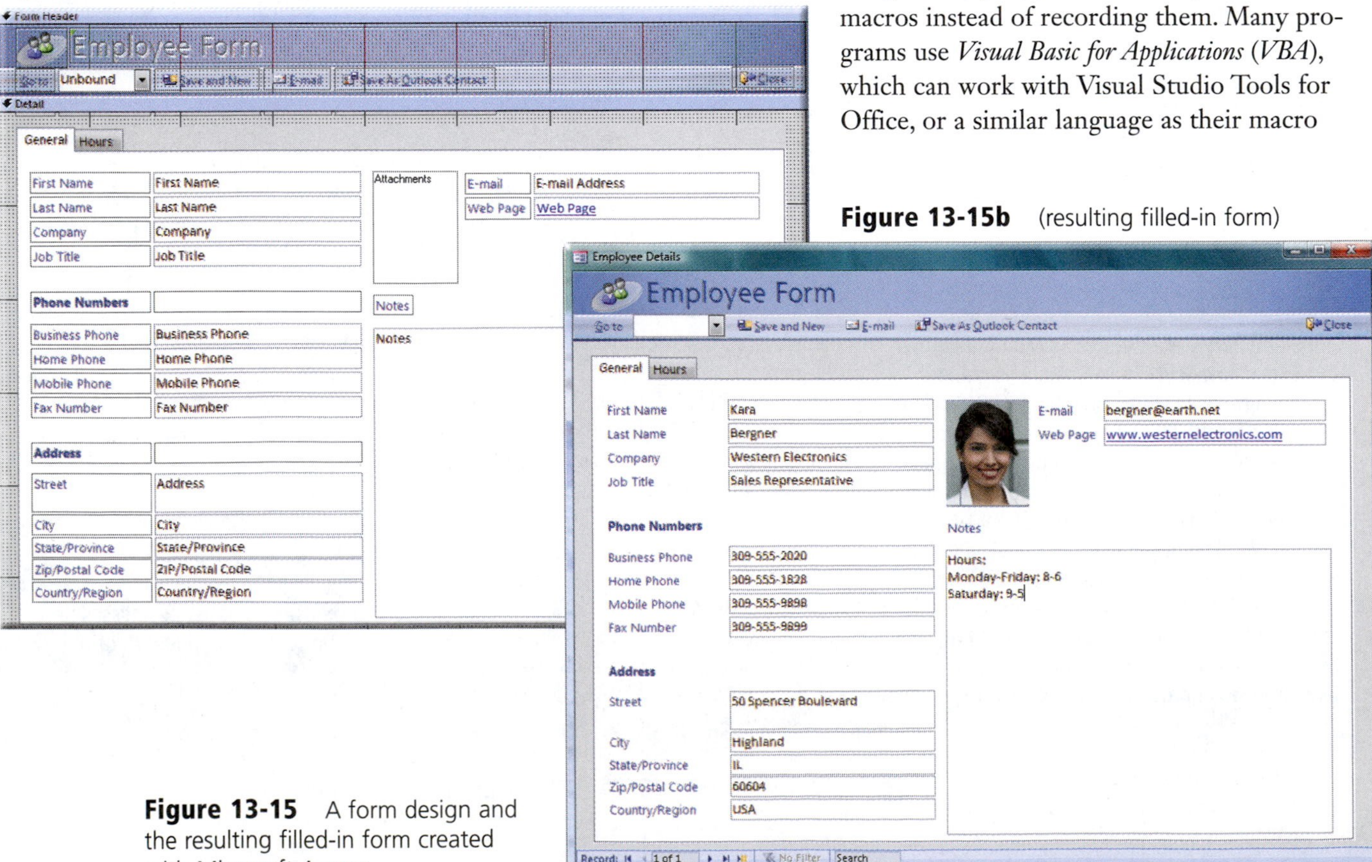

Figure 13-15b (resulting filled-in form)

Figure 13-15 A form design and the resulting filled-in form created with Microsoft Access.

programming language. The macro in Figure 13-16a shows an Excel VBA macro that automates the data entry process to determine the monthly payment, total interest, and total cost of an auto loan. Figure 13-16b shows the dialog box generated from the macro that prompts the user to enter the car model. Read Ethics & Issues 13-1 for a related discussion.

Macros

For more information, visit the Computer Concepts CourseMate Web site at www.cengagebrain.com, navigate to the Chapter 13 Web Link resource for this book, and then click Macros.

Figure 13-16a (VBA macro)

Figure 13-16b (macro dialog box in Excel window)

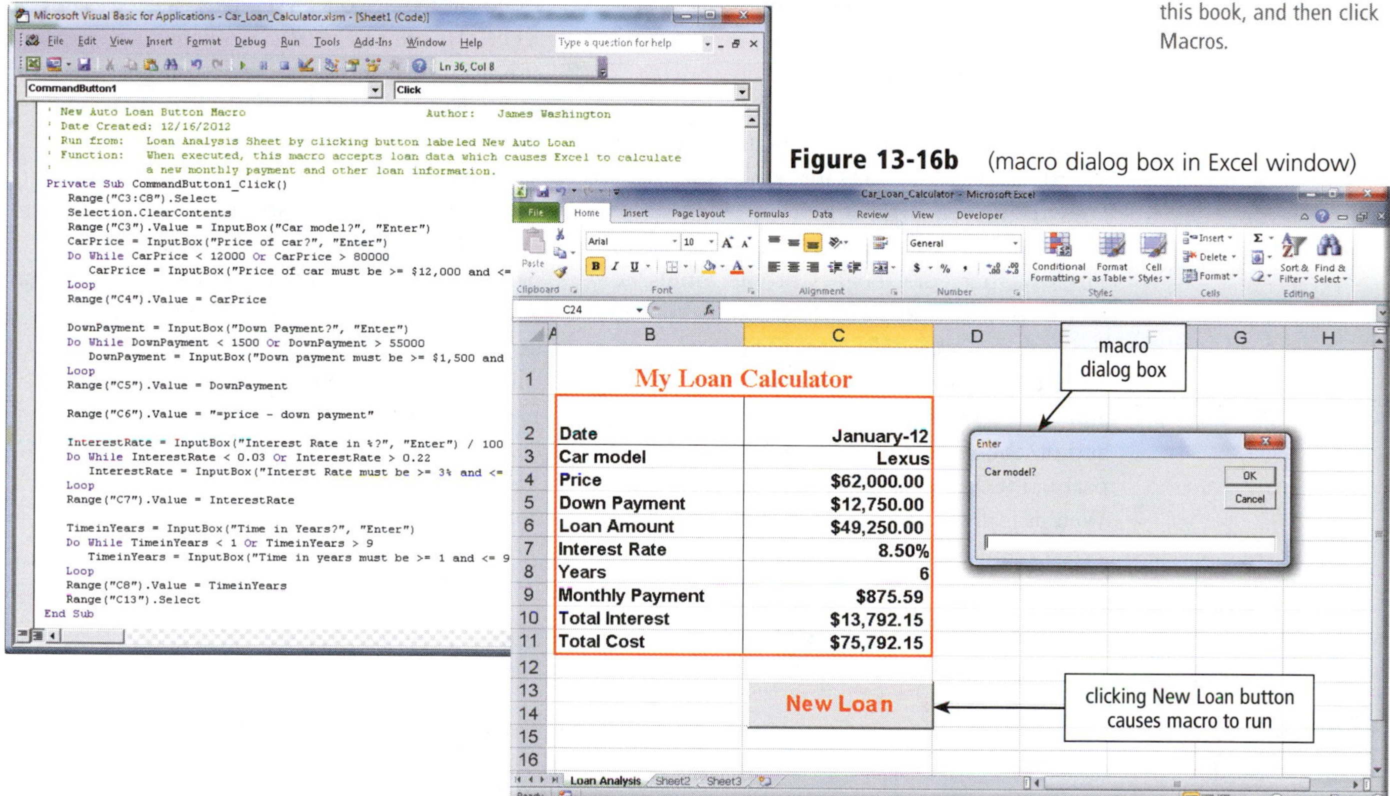

Figure 13-16 The left screen shows a VBA macro used to automate an auto loan. After a macro is written, the user clicks the New Loan button to run the macro. The right screen shows the macro guiding the user through part of the data entry process.

ETHICS & ISSUES 13-1

Who Should Be Held Accountable for Macro Security Threats?

Years ago, an individual downloaded and opened a small document that contained a virus from an Internet newsgroup. Upon opening the document, a macro was executed that sent the same document to the first 50 e-mail addresses in the person's e-mail contact list. The simple action of opening the document started a chain reaction that resulted in more than 100,000 infected computers and more than $80 million in damage. Today, such viruses, known as macro viruses, are the most common type of virus. Malware authors find that one of the easiest ways to spread viruses and worms is by distributing documents containing macro viruses. The convenience and simplicity of macros are both their greatest strengths and weaknesses. These are weaknesses because hackers find it easy to exploit technologies with such traits.

As a result of damaging macro viruses, antivirus companies and software companies have strengthened their efforts against macro viruses. Companies often prohibit employees from running macros on their computers. Both responses have made the use of macros more difficult and confusing for users, who prefer the convenience and simplicity of the earlier days. Many claim that software companies that include the capability to use macros should be responsible for making it impossible for malware authors to take advantage of security problems in the software. Software companies and others blame users who open documents from unknown sources.

Should users or software companies be held accountable for macro security threats? Why? Should a macro in a word processing document have the capability to access a person's e-mail contact list? Why or why not? How can users best be educated regarding handling documents from unknown sources?

Web Page Development

The designers of Web pages, known as *Web developers*, use a variety of techniques to create Web pages. These include some of the languages previously discussed and the languages discussed in the following sections.

HTML and XHTML

HTML (*Hypertext Markup Language*) is a special formatting language that programmers use to format documents for display on the Web. You view a Web page written with HTML in a Web browser such as Internet Explorer, Safari, Firefox, Opera, or Google Chrome. Similarly, **XHTML** (extensible HTML) is a markup language that enables Web sites to be displayed more easily on microbrowsers in smart phones and other mobile devices, as well as on desktop and notebook computers. Figure 13-17a shows part of the XHTML code used to create the Web page shown in Figure 13-17b. XHTML includes features of HTML and XML, which is discussed in the next section.

HTML and XHTML are not actually programming languages. They are, however, languages that have specific rules for defining the placement and format of text, graphics, video, and audio on a Web page. HTML and XHTML use *tags* or *elements*, which are words, abbreviations, and symbols that specify links to other documents and indicate how a Web page is displayed when viewed on the Web.

A Web page, thus, is a file that contains both text and HTML and/or XHTML tags. Examples of tags are <p> to indicate a new paragraph, <tr> to create a new row in a table, and <title> to define a document title. You can write HTML code using any text editor such as Notepad. Many programmers however, never write HTML and XHTML code because several programming languages and program development tools generate it automatically.

Figure 13-17a (portion of XHTML code)

Figure 13-17b (portion of resulting Web page)

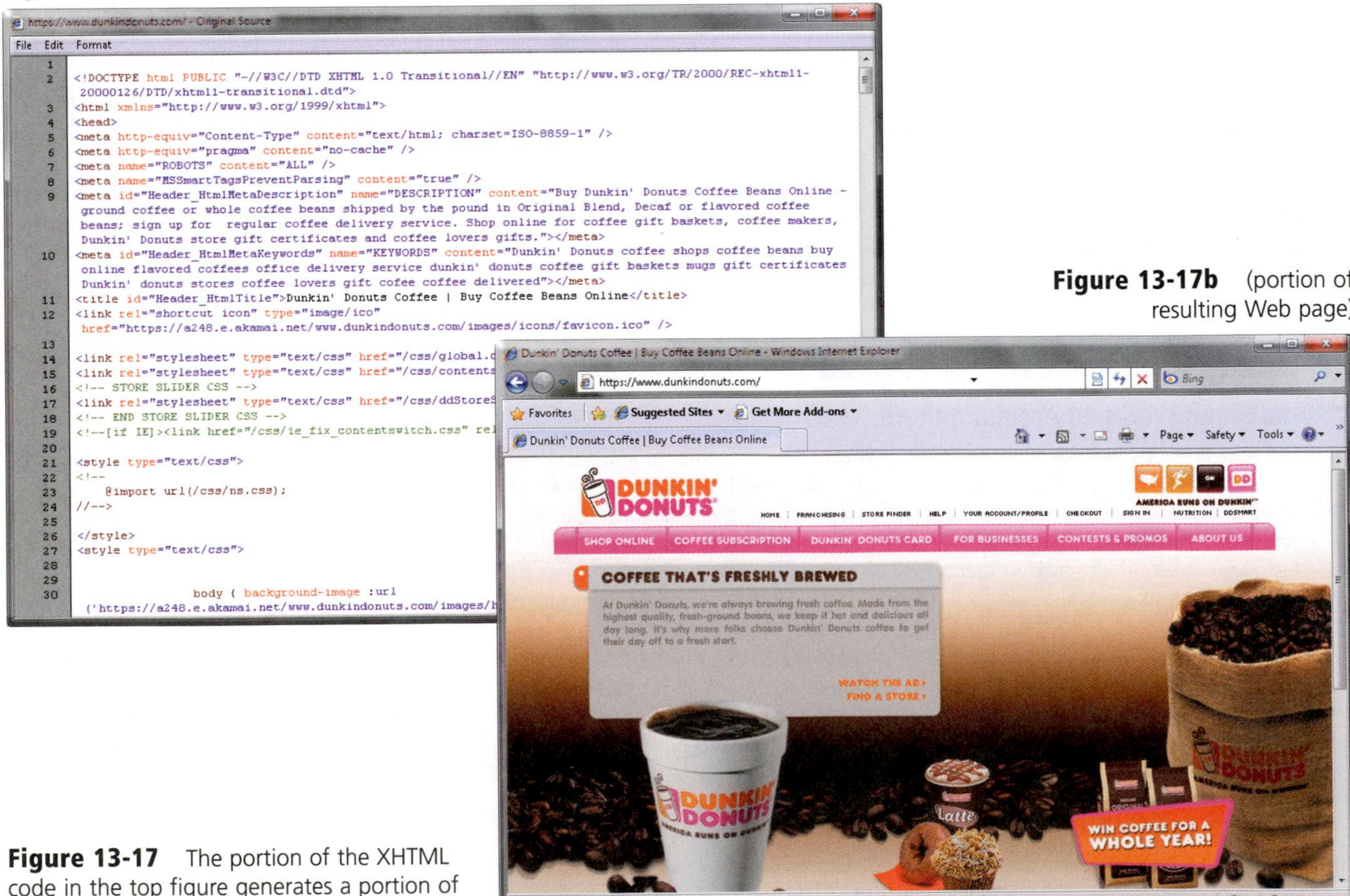

Figure 13-17 The portion of the XHTML code in the top figure generates a portion of a Web page shown in the bottom figure.

XML and WML

XML (Extensible Markup Language) is an increasingly popular format for sharing data that allows Web developers to create customized tags, as well as use predefined tags, used for developing a single Web site whose content can be formatted to display appropriately on various devices. XML separates the Web page content from its format, allowing the Web browser to display the contents of a Web page in a form appropriate for the display device. For example, a smart phone, a PDA, and a notebook computer all could display the same XML page or use different formats or sections of the XML page.

Wireless devices use a subset of XML called WML. **WML** (wireless markup language) allows Web developers to design pages specifically for microbrowsers. Many smart phones and other mobile devices use WML as their markup language.

A *style sheet* contains descriptions of a document's characteristics. (Many word processing documents use style sheets to define formats of characters and paragraphs.) XML works with *XSL* (Extensible Stylesheet Language), which is a language for creating a style sheet that describes how to present the data described in an XML document on a Web page. XML, for example, can instruct a Web browser to display data bold and centered.

An extension of XSL, called *XSLT* (Extensible Stylesheet Language Transformations), creates style sheets that describe how to transform XML documents into other types of documents. When a user requests a Web page, for example, the server uses the format described in the XSLT file to transform the XML into the appropriate format, such as WML for a smart phone microbrowser, a Web page for a notebook computer, or a label format for a mailing label program (Figure 13-18).

Two applications of XML are **RSS 2.0**, which stands for Really Simple Syndication, and **ATOM**, which are specifications that content aggregators use to distribute content to subscribers. The online publisher creates an RSS or ATOM document, called a Web feed, that is made available to Web sites for publication. News Web sites, blogs, and podcasts often use Web feeds to publish headlines and stories. Most Web browsers can read Web feeds, meaning they automatically download updated content from Web pages identified in the feed.

XML

For more information, visit the Computer Concepts CourseMate Web site at www.cengagebrain.com, navigate to the Chapter 13 Web Link resource for this book, and then click XML.

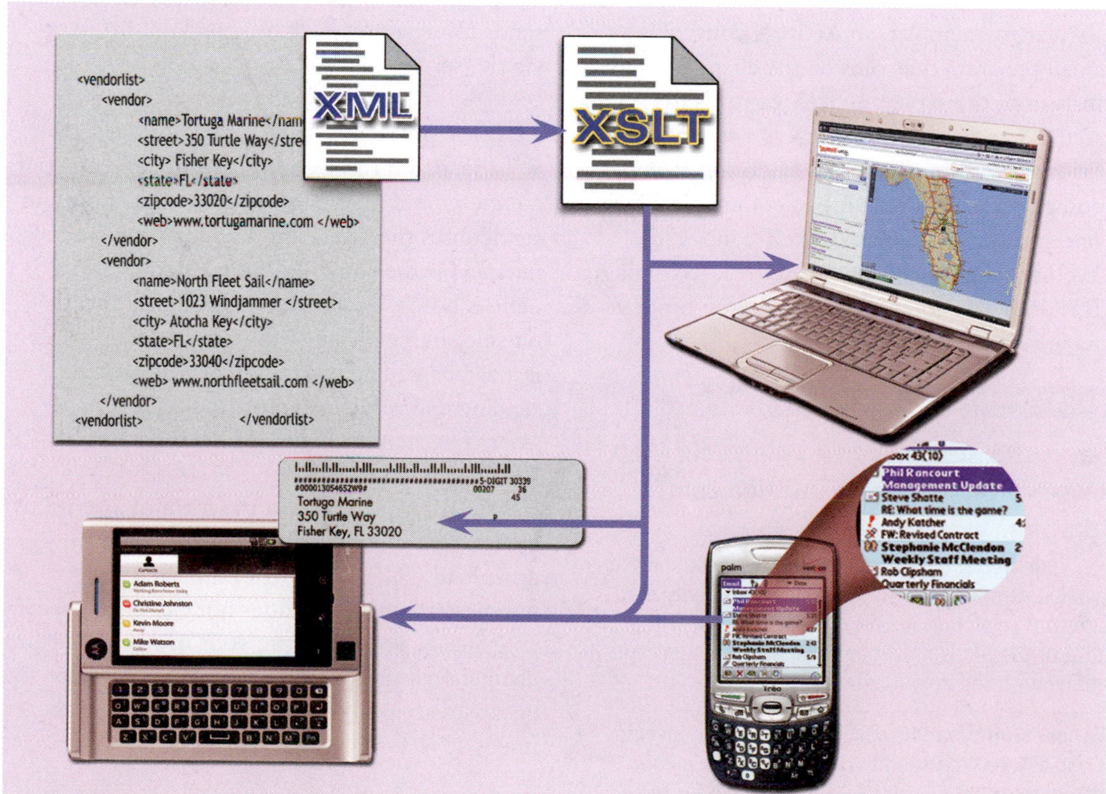

Figure 13-18 A sample XML document converted by an XSLT document for display on various devices.

Scripts, Applets, Servlets, and ActiveX Controls

Markup languages tell a browser how to display text and images, set up lists and option buttons, and establish links on a Web page. By adding dynamic content and interactive elements such as scrolling messages, animated graphics, forms, pop-up windows, and interaction, Web pages become much more interesting. To add these elements, Web developers write small programs called scripts, applets, servlets, and ActiveX controls. These programs run inside of another program. This is different from programs discussed thus far, which are executed by the operating system. In this case, the Web browser executes these short programs.

As discussed in Chapter 9, your computer is the client computer when it is connected to the Web.

- A **script** is an interpreted program that runs on the client. That is, a script runs on your computer, instead of running on a Web server.
- An **applet** also usually runs on the client inside of an interpreted program, but the applet itself is compiled. Thus, an applet usually runs faster than a script.
- Scripts and applets shift the computational work from the Web server to the client. A **servlet**, by contrast, is an applet that runs on the server.
- Similar to an applet, an **ActiveX control** is a small program that runs on the client computer, instead of the server. ActiveX controls use ActiveX technology. **ActiveX** is a set of object-oriented technologies from Microsoft that allows components on a network to communicate with one another. To run an ActiveX control, the Web browser must support ActiveX technology. If it does not, you will need a plug-in program to run ActiveX controls.

? FAQ 13-2

What is the best response when your Web browser prompts you to install a control or plug-in?

When your Web browser prompts you to install an ActiveX control or plug-in, you first should verify that the control or plug-in is from a trusted source. If the control or plug-in is not from a trusted source, do not continue with the download or installation.

For more information, visit the Computer Concepts CourseMate Web site at www.cengagebrain.com, navigate to the Chapter 13 FAQ resource for this book, and then click Web Browser Prompts.

One reason Web developers use scripts, applets, servlets, and ActiveX controls is to add special multimedia effects to Web pages. Examples include animated graphics, scrolling messages, calendars, and advertisements. Another reason to use these programs is to include interactive capabilities on Web pages. Cookies, shopping carts, games, counters, image maps, and processing forms are types of scripts, applets, servlets, and ActiveX controls that allow you to transfer information to and from a Web server.

A **counter** tracks the number of visitors to a Web site. An **image map** is a graphical image that points to one or more Web addresses. Web pages use image maps in place of, or in addition to, text links. When you click a certain part of the graphical image, the Web browser sends the coordinates of the clicked location to the Web server, which in turn locates the corresponding Web address and sends the Web page to your computer.

A **processing form**, often simply called a form, collects data from visitors to a Web site, who fill in blank fields and then click a button that sends the information. When a user clicks that button on the form, that action executes the script or applet. It transmits the data to the server, processes it, and then, if appropriate, sends information back to your Web browser via the server.

CGI Scripts

To send and receive information between your computer and a Web server, the script, applet, or servlet uses the CGI. The *CGI* (*common gateway interface*) is the communications standard that defines how a Web server communicates with outside sources. Many times, the outside source is a database. The program that manages the sending and receiving across the CGI is a *CGI script*. The steps in Figure 13-19 show how a CGI script works.

A CGI script can be in the form of a script, applet, servlet, or ActiveX control. You can download CGI scripts from the Web and purchase them. If one does not exist that meets your needs, you can write your own CGI script using a scripting language. The next section discusses scripting languages. Read Ethics & Issues 13-2 for a related discussion.

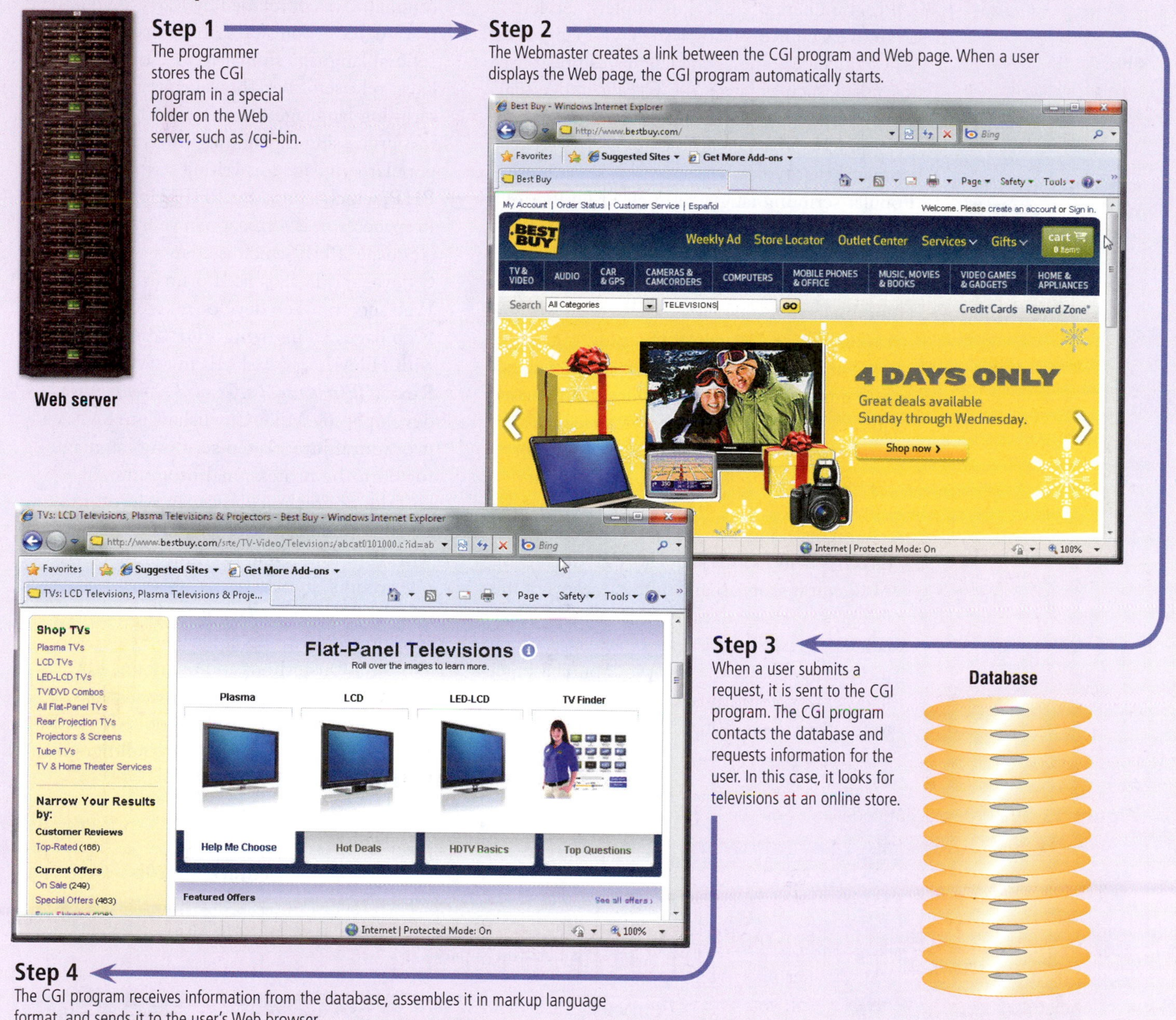

Figure 13-19 This figure shows how a CGI script works.

ETHICS & ISSUES 13-2

Should Colleges Teach Hacking?

Taking the traditional admonition "know thy enemy" literally, some colleges offer courses that teach students how to write computer viruses and other malware. One instructor teaches students how to thwart antivirus software and how to generate anonymous e-mail spam. He claims that if college students easily bypass antivirus software, then the products clearly are deficient. Proponents of such courses claim that these hacking skills enable the next generation of security experts to think like malicious hackers, thereby helping to stop the spread of malware. They liken the gained skills to physics students who learn how atomic weapons work, or biology students who learn how poisons work. Critics claim that this practice only encourages more virus authoring and hacking. Others claim that knowing how to write malware does not make someone more capable of stopping malware. Questions remain about who is responsible legally, financially, and morally if one of the students in such a course releases malicious code to the Internet or uses the knowledge acquired in the course to infect other computers purposefully.

Should colleges teach hacking? Why or why not? Should companies hire people who are trained in creating malware and computer hacking? Why or why not? What precautions should schools take if they plan to offer such courses? Who should be held responsible if a student in such a course creates destructive malware? Why?

PHP

For more information, visit the Computer Concepts CourseMate Web site at www.cengagebrain.com, navigate to the Chapter 13 Web Link resource for this book, and then click PHP.

Scripting Languages

Programmers write scripts, applets, servlets, or ActiveX controls using a variety of languages. These include some of the languages previously discussed, such as Java, C++, C#, F#, and Visual Basic. Some programmers use scripting languages. A *scripting language* is an interpreted language that typically is easy to learn and use. Popular scripting languages include JavaScript, Perl, PHP, Rexx, Tcl, and VBScript.

- **JavaScript** is an interpreted language that allows a programmer to add dynamic content and interactive elements to a Web page (Figure 13-20). These elements include alert messages, scrolling text, animations, drop-down menus, data input forms, pop-up windows, interactive quizzes, and mouse rollovers. A *mouse rollover* or *mouseover* occurs when text, a graphic, or other object changes as the user moves the mouse pointer over the object on the screen.

  Web developers insert JavaScript code directly in an HTML or XHTML document. Although it shares many of the features of the full Java language, JavaScript is a much simpler language. JavaScript is an *open language*, which means anyone can use it without purchasing a license. JavaScript thus allows the programmer to improve the appearance of Web pages without spending a large amount of money.
- **Perl** (*Practical Extraction and Report Language*) originally was developed by Larry Wall at NASA's Jet Propulsion Laboratory as a procedural language similar to C and C++. The latest release of Perl, however, is an interpreted scripting language. Because Perl has powerful text processing capabilities, it has become a popular language for writing scripts.
- **PHP**, which stands for PHP: Hypertext Preprocessor, is a free, open source scripting language. PHP, which is a language similar to C, Java, and Perl, is used primarily on Linux Web servers. Web developers create dynamic Web pages by inserting PHP scripts along with HTML or XHTML in a Web page.
- **Rexx** (*REstructured eXtended eXecutor*) was developed by Mike Cowlishaw at IBM as a procedural interpreted scripting language for both the professional programmer and the nontechnical user. In addition to all IBM operating systems, Rexx works with Windows, Mac OS, and most UNIX operating systems.
- **Tcl** (*Tool Command Language*) is an interpreted scripting language created by Dr. John Ousterhout and maintained by Sun Microsystems Laboratories. Tcl has a companion program, called Tool Kit (Tk), that allows Web developers to build graphical user interfaces.

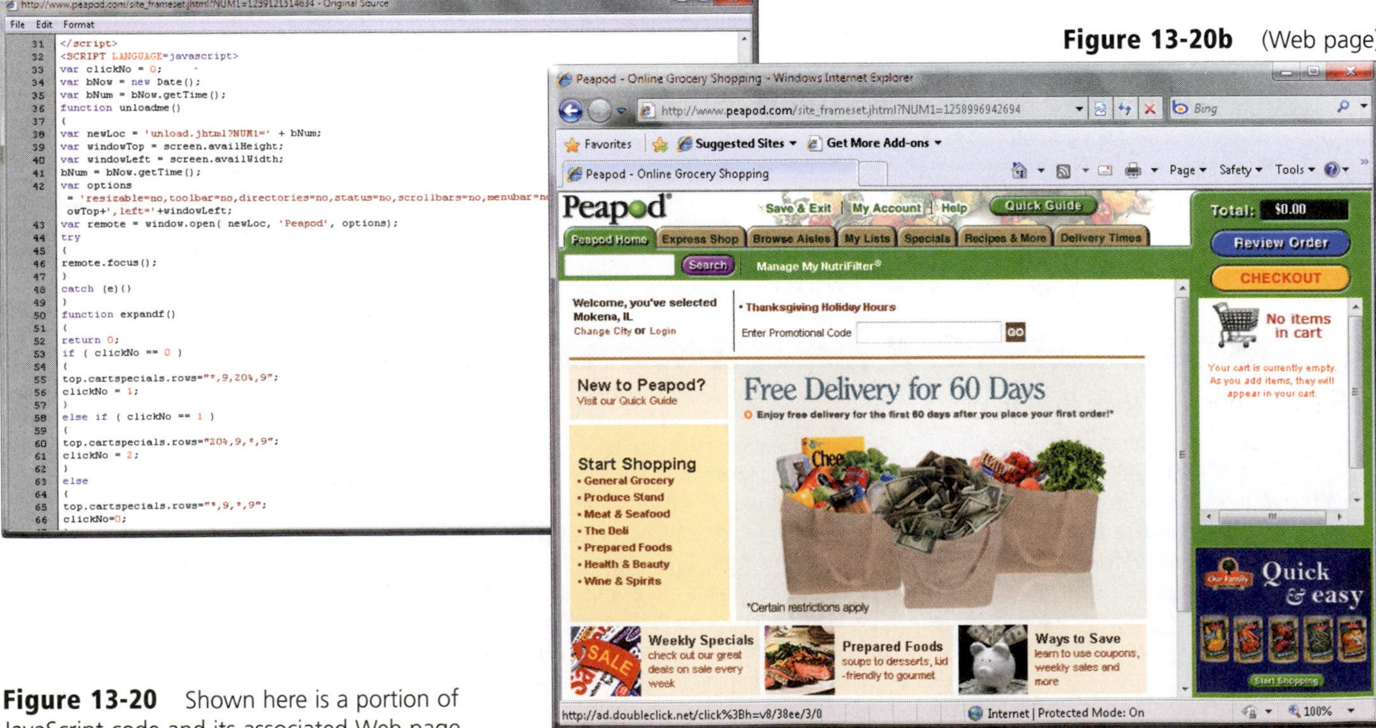

Figure 13-20 Shown here is a portion of JavaScript code and its associated Web page.

- **VBScript** (*Visual Basic, Scripting Edition*) is a subset of the Visual Basic language that allows programmers to add intelligence and interactivity to Web pages. As with JavaScript, Web developers embed VBScript code directly into an HTML or XHTML document. Programmers already familiar with Visual Basic choose VBScript as their scripting language, so that they do not have to learn a new scripting language. The latest version of Internet Explorer includes VBScript.

? FAQ 13-3

What is a "sandbox" to a developer?

A *sandbox* is an environment that allows developers to test their programs with fictitious data without adversely affecting other programs, information systems, or data. Sandboxes are used for testing purposes both by developers and users. Users often work with a sandbox to familiarize themselves with a new program or information system before they use it.

For more information, visit the Computer Concepts CourseMate Web site at www.cengagebrain.com, navigate to the Chapter 13 FAQ resource for this book, and then click Sandboxes.

Dynamic HTML

Dynamic HTML (**DHTML**) is a type of HTML that allows Web developers to include more graphical interest and interactivity in a Web page, without the Web page accessing the Web server. That is, the client's computer automatically updates and changes its own content. These Web pages display much faster than Web pages created with HTML.

Typically, Web pages created with DHTML are more animated and responsive to user interaction. Colors change, font sizes grow, objects appear and disappear as a user moves the mouse, and animations dance around the screen.

Dynamic HTML works by using the document object model, cascading style sheets, and scripting languages. The *document object model* (*DOM*) defines every item on a Web page as an object. Fonts, graphics, headlines, tables, and every other page element are objects. With DOM, Web developers can change properties, such as color or size, of any or all of these objects on the Web page.

A *cascading style sheet* (*CSS*) contains the formats for how a particular object should be displayed in a Web browser. For example, CSS specifies items such as background colors, image and link colors, fonts, and font sizes. A single DHTML document can contain multiple cascading style sheets, thus, the name cascading. As a user moves the mouse or clicks an item, a new style sheet can be applied to change the appearance of the screen.

After a Web developer has defined and formatted objects on a Web page, a scripting language such as JavaScript manipulates them. A script can move, display, hide, or change the appearance of an object as the user performs actions such as a mouse rollover.

Cascading Style Sheets

For more information, visit the Computer Concepts CourseMate Web site at www.cengagebrain.com, navigate to the Chapter 13 Web Link resource for this book, and then click Cascading Style Sheets.

Ruby on Rails

Ruby on Rails (*RoR*), also called *Rails*, is an open source framework that provides technologies for developing object-oriented, database-driven Web sites. Rails uses a free, object-oriented scripting language called *Ruby*, which is derived from a variety of languages including Ada, LISP, Perl, and Smalltalk. Rails is designed to make Web developers more productive by providing them an easy-to-use environment and eliminating time-consuming steps in the Web development process.

? FAQ 13-4

What are the popular Web programming languages?

The chart below shows the popularity of selected Web programming languages when compared to all programming languages.

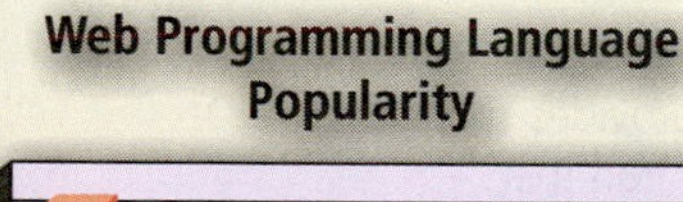

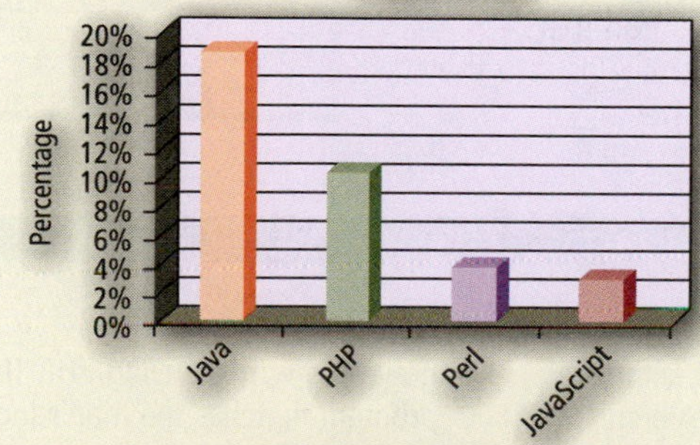

Source: TIOBE Programming Community Index

For more information, visit the Computer Concepts CourseMate Web site at www.cengagebrain.com, navigate to the Chapter 13 FAQ resource for this book, and then click Web Programming Languages.

Web 2.0 Program Development

As previously discussed, Web 2.0 refers to Web sites that provide a means for users to share personal information, allow users to modify Web site content, and have application software built into the site for visitors to use. Web 2.0 sites include social networking sites, wikis, blogs, online auctions, and Web applications such as Google Docs.

Web 2.0 sites often use RSS, previously discussed, and Ajax. **Ajax**, which stands for Asynchronous JavaScript and XML, is a method of creating interactive Web applications designed to provide immediate response to user requests. Instead of refreshing entire Web pages, Ajax works with the Web browser to update only changes to the Web page. This technique saves time because the Web application does not spend time repeatedly sending unchanged information across the network.

Ajax combines several programming tools: JavaScript or other scripting language, HTML or XHTML, XML, XSLT, and CSS. Some companies, such as Microsoft, Google, and Yahoo!, provide their Ajax toolkits at no cost. Web browsers that support Ajax include Internet Explorer, Safari, Firefox, and Opera. Examples of Web sites that use Ajax are Google Maps and Flickr.

Most Web 2.0 sites also use APIs so that Web developers can create their own Web applications. An *API* (application programming interface) is a collection of tools that programmers use to interact with an environment such as a Web site or operating system. Mapping Web sites, for example, include APIs that enable programmers to integrate maps into their Web sites (Figure 13-21).

Another use of APIs is in mashups. Recall that a mashup is a Web application that combines services from two or more sources, creating a new application. Read Innovative Computing 13-2 to find out about a Google Maps and Flickr mashup. For more information, read the Web 2.0 Program Development feature that follows this chapter.

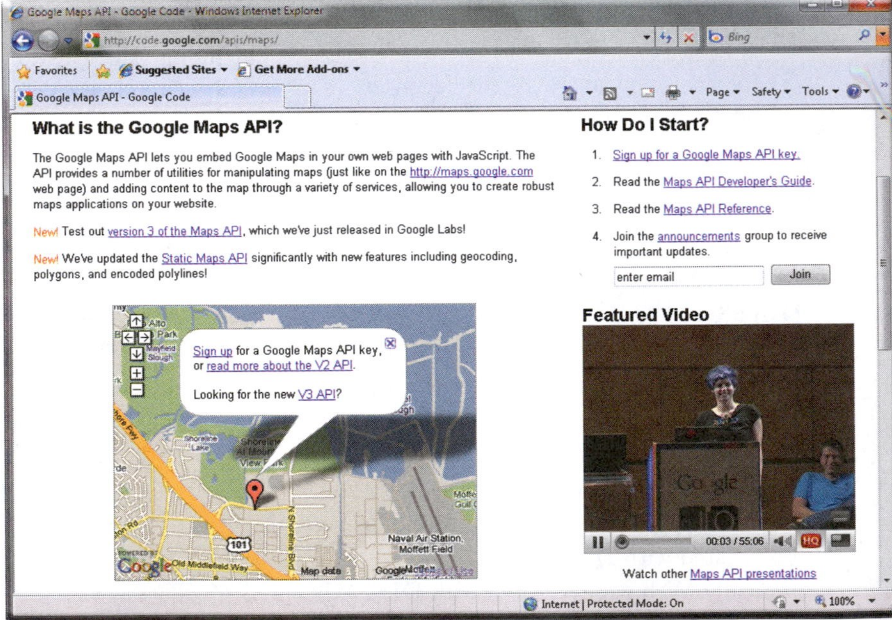

Figure 13-21 Google Maps provides tools for programmers to integrate APIs into their Web sites.

APIs

For more information, visit the Computer Concepts CourseMate Web site at www.cengagebrain.com, navigate to the Chapter 13 Web Link resource for this book, and then click APIs.

INNOVATIVE COMPUTING 13-2

View the World from Your Computer

Become a worldwide traveler without leaving home by using Earth Album, a mashup derived from Google Maps and Flickr. Simply view the world map and then click the country, region, or city of interest to display associated photos in a strip along the top of the screen. When you click one of these images, it zooms out and also displays the photographer's descriptive words, called *geotags*, that identify the photo's contents.

Early versions of Earth Album were written using Ruby on Rails, but the newest is written using PHP. The program matches the map's locations with the Flickr photos' geotags of the same location. The images change every few weeks, and the more popular images are of large cities and tourist destinations.

Besides clicking areas of the map, users can search for a specific location or click the Find Yourself link to view photos from their current geographical location. In recent years, the Earth Album Web site was recognized by both *PC Magazine* and *Time* magazine as among the best.

For more information, visit the Computer Concepts CourseMate Web site at www.cengagebrain.com, navigate to the Chapter 13 Innovative Computing resource for this book, and then click Earth Album.

Web Page Authoring Software

As Chapter 3 discussed, you do not need to learn HTML to develop a Web page. You can use **Web page authoring software** to create sophisticated Web pages that include images, video, audio, animation, and other effects.

Web page authoring software generates HTML and XHTML tags from your Web page design. With Web page authoring software, you can view or modify the HTML or XHTML associated with a Web page. Sometimes, you may add an HTML or XHTML tag that the Web page authoring software does not provide. Learning HTML and XHTML basics will enable you to fine-tune Web page formats created with authoring software.

Four popular Web page authoring programs are Dreamweaver, Expression Web, Flash, and SharePoint Designer.

- **Dreamweaver**, by Adobe Systems, is a Web page authoring program that allows Web developers to create, maintain, and manage professional Web sites. Some features of Dreamweaver include its visual environment, use of cascading style sheets, capability of manipulating code, built-in graphics editor (called Fireworks), and XML support.
- **Expression Web** is Microsoft's Web page authoring program that enables Web developers to create professional, dynamic, interactive Web sites. Expression Web requires the .NET and supports HTML, DHTML, XHTML, XML, JavaScript, and cascading style sheets. It also integrates with Visual Studio.
- **Flash**, by Adobe Systems, is a Web page authoring program that enables Web developers to combine interactive content with text, graphics, audio, and video. Features of Flash include its animation and interactive tools, professional video capabilities, easy deployment to mobile devices such as smart phones, and XML support.
- **SharePoint Designer** is a Web page authoring program that is part of the Microsoft Office and SharePoint families of products. SharePoint Designer supports ASP.NET, cascading style sheets, XHTML, and XSLT.

Multimedia Program Development

Multimedia authoring software allows programmers to combine text, graphics, animation, audio, and video in an interactive presentation. Many programmers use multimedia authoring software for computer-based training (CBT) and Web-based training (WBT). Popular Web page authoring programs typically share similar features and are capable of creating similar applications. Popular programs include ToolBook and Director.

- **ToolBook**, from SumTotal Systems, has a graphical user interface and uses an object-oriented approach, so that programmers can design multimedia applications using basic objects. These objects include buttons, fields, graphics, backgrounds, and pages.

  In ToolBook, programmers can convert a multimedia application into HTML or XHTML, so that it can be distributed over the Internet. Many businesses and colleges use ToolBook to create content for distance learning courses (Figure 13-22).
- **Director**, from Adobe Systems, is a popular multimedia authoring program with powerful features that allow programmers to create highly interactive multimedia applications.

  Director's powerful features make it well suited for developing electronic presentations, optical discs for education and entertainment, simulations, programs for kiosks, and Web applications. Web applications can include streaming audio and video, interactivity, and multiuser functionality. Users view Web applications developed in Director on the Web using the Shockwave plug-in.

Figure 13-22 A sample ToolBook application.

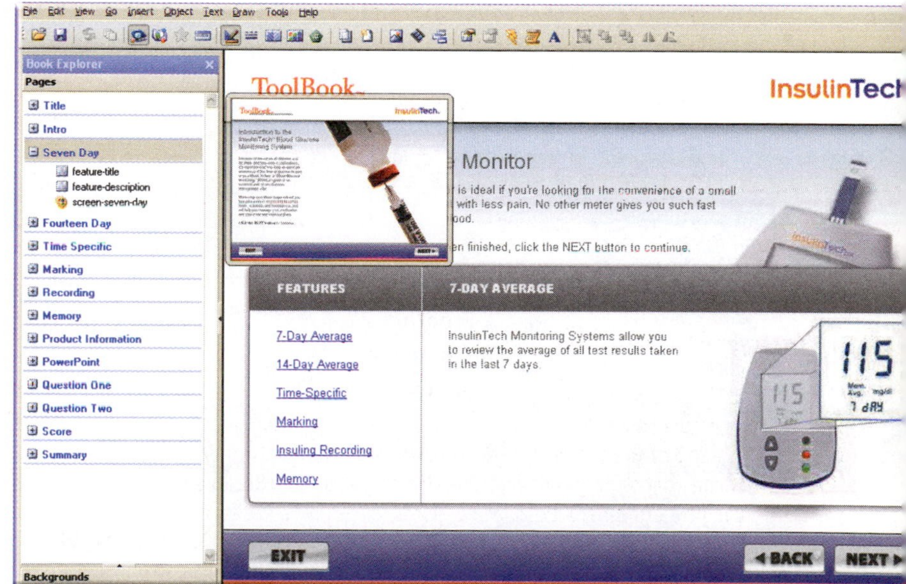

QUIZ YOURSELF 13-2

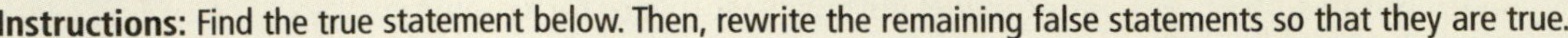

Instructions: Find the true statement below. Then, rewrite the remaining false statements so that they are true.

1. HTML and XHTML are languages that have specific rules for defining the placement and format of text, graphics, video, and audio on a Web page.
2. Interpreted HTML works by using the document object model, style sheets, and scripting languages.
3. Maps allow users to automate routine, repetitive, or difficult tasks in application software such as word processing, spreadsheet, or database programs.
4. Popular first-generation languages include JavaScript, Perl, PHP, Rexx, Tcl, and VBScript.
5. Rexx separates the Web page content from its format, allowing the Web browser to display the contents of a Web page in a form appropriate for the display device.
6. SQL is an example of a second generation language.
7. Four popular markup languages are Dreamweaver, Expression Web, Flash, and SharePoint Designer.

Quiz Yourself Online: To further check your knowledge of pages 674 through 685, visit the Computer Concepts CourseMate Web site at www.cengagebrain.com, navigate to the Chapter 13 Quiz Yourself resource for this book, and then click Objectives 4 – 6.

Program Development

Program development consists of a series of steps programmers use to build computer programs. As Chapter 12 discussed, the system development life cycle guides information technology (IT) professionals through the development of an information system. Likewise, the **program development life cycle (PDLC)** guides computer programmers through the development of a program. The program development life cycle consists of six steps (Figure 13-23):

1. Analyze Requirements
2. Design Solution
3. Validate Design
4. Implement Design
5. Test Solution
6. Document Solution

As shown in Figure 13-23, the steps in the program development life cycle form a loop. Program development is an ongoing process within system development. Each time someone identifies errors in or improvements to a program and requests program modifications, the Analyze Requirements step begins again. When programmers correct errors or add enhancements to an existing program, they are said to be **maintaining** the program. Program maintenance is an ongoing activity that occurs after a program has been delivered to users, or placed into production.

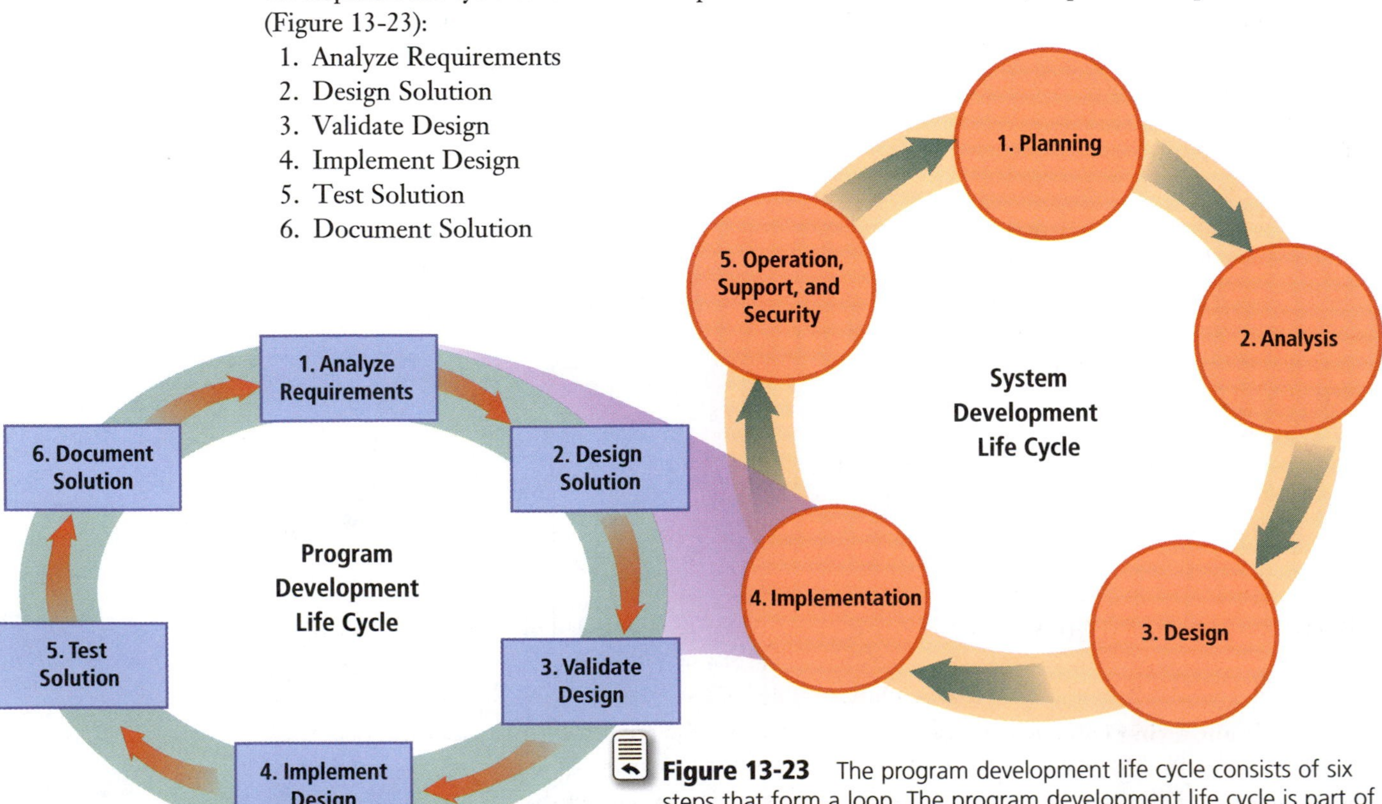

Figure 13-23 The program development life cycle consists of six steps that form a loop. The program development life cycle is part of the implementation phase of the system development life cycle.

What Initiates Program Development?

As discussed in Chapter 12, system development consists of five phases: planning; analysis; design; implementation; and operation, support, and security. During the analysis phase, the development team recommends how to handle software needs. Choices include modifying existing programs, purchasing packaged software, building custom software in-house, or outsourcing some or all of the IT activities.

If the company opts for in-house development, the design and implementation phases of system development become quite extensive. In the design phase, the systems analyst creates a detailed set of requirements for the programmers. Once the programmers receive the requirements, the implementation phase begins. At this time, the programmer analyzes the requirements of the problem to be solved. The program development life cycle thus begins at the start of the implementation phase in system development.

The scope of the requirements largely determines how many programmers work on the program development. If the scope is large, a **programming team** that consists of a group of programmers may develop the programs. If the specifications are simple, a single programmer might complete all the development tasks. Whether a single programmer or a programming team, all the programmers involved must interact with users and members of the development team throughout program development.

By following the steps in program development, programmers create programs that are correct (produce accurate information) and maintainable (easy to modify). The following sections address each of the steps in program development.

Step 1 — Analyze Requirements

The first step in program development is to analyze the requirements of the problem the program(s) should solve, so that the programmer can begin to develop an appropriate solution. In most cases, the solution requires more than one program. The Analyze Requirements step consists of three major tasks: (1) review the requirements, (2) meet with the systems analyst and users, and (3) identify input, processing, output, and data components.

First, the programmer reviews the requirements. The requirements may be in the form of deliverables such as charts, diagrams, and reports. For example, screen and report layout charts illustrate input and output requirements. Structured English, decision tables, and decision trees convey processing requirements. The data dictionary identifies the data requirements. By thoroughly reviewing these deliverables, the programmer understands the nature of the requirements.

During this step, the programmer also meets with the systems analyst and the users. This enables the programmer to understand the purpose of the requirements from the users' perspective. Recall from Chapter 12 that a guideline of system development is to involve users throughout the entire system development life cycle.

After design specifications are established, the programmer defines the input, processing, output (IPO), and data requirements for each program. Many programmers use an IPO chart to show the input, processing, and output components (Figure 13-24). An *IPO chart* identifies a program's inputs, its outputs, and the processing steps required to transform the inputs into the outputs. Programmers review the contents of the IPO chart with the systems analyst and the users. This allows programmers to be sure that they completely understand the purpose of the program.

IPO Chart

Input	Processing	Output
Regular Time Hours Worked Overtime Hours Worked Hourly Pay Rate	Read regular time hours worked, overtime hours worked, hourly pay rate. Calculate regular time pay. If employee worked overtime, calculate overtime pay. Calculate gross pay. Print gross pay.	Gross Pay

Figure 13-24 An IPO (input, process, output) chart is a tool that assists the programmer in analyzing a program.

Step 2 — Design Solution

The next step is to design the solution that will meet the users' requirements. Designing the solution involves devising a solution algorithm to satisfy the requirements. A *solution algorithm*, also called *program logic*, is a graphical or written description of the step-by-step procedures to solve the problem. Determining the logic for a program often is a programmer's most challenging task. It requires that the programmer understand programming concepts, often database concepts, as well as use creativity in problem solving.

Recall from Chapter 12 that a system can be designed using process modeling (structured analysis and design) or object modeling (object-oriented analysis and design). The approach used during system development determines the techniques a programmer uses in designing a solution. Read Ethics & Issues 13-3 for a related discussion.

Ethics & Issues

For the complete text of the Ethics & Issues boxes found in this chapter, visit the Computer Concepts CourseMate Web site at www.cengagebrain.com and then navigate to the Chapter 13 Ethics & Issues resource for this book.

ETHICS & ISSUES 13-3

Are Digital Facelifts Ethical?

While people may state that beauty is in the eye of the beholder, some researchers are claiming that beauty is just another mathematical formula to apply to a digital photo. Researchers asked people to rank a number of photos from most to least attractive. The facial proportions of those found to be most attractive, such as the distance between eyes, the shape of the jaw lines, and symmetry, were noted by the researchers. This resulted in a computer algorithm that applies these ideals to any facial photo, resulting in a digital facelift. Surprisingly, the ideals seem consistent among most cultures. Unlike photo touch-ups on magazine covers that change hair and skin color or remove wrinkles, these digital facelifts change only the proportions and location of facial features. Critics of this technology claim that beauty ideals change over time, that the software seems to make people seem more generic, and that a person's individual character is lost in the process. Furthermore, publishing such altered photos results in additional cultural pressure on people, resulting in problems ranging from low self-esteem to unnecessary surgery.

Are digital facelifts ethical? Why or why not? How might some people take advantage, for good or bad, of digital facelift technology? Should publishers of photos be required to inform their audience when such technology has been applied to a photo? Why or why not? Are digital facelifts any different from photo touch-ups done for fashion magazines? Why?

Structured Design

In **structured design**, sometimes called *top-down design*, the programmer typically begins with a general design and moves toward a more detailed design. This approach breaks down the original set of requirements into smaller, more manageable sections.

The first step in top-down design is to identify the major function of a program, sometimes called the *main routine* or *main module*. Next, the programmer decomposes (breaks down) the main routine into smaller sections, called *subroutines* or *modules*. Then, the programmer analyzes each subroutine to determine if it can be decomposed further.

Programmers use a **hierarchy chart**, also called a *structure chart*, to show program modules graphically (Figure 13-25). A hierarchy chart contains rectangles and lines. The rectangles are the modules. The main module is at the top of the chart. All other modules are placed below the main module. Modules connect by lines to indicate their relationships. In Figure 13-25, for example, the Initialization, Process, and Wrap-Up modules are subordinate to the MAIN module.

Programs developed using structured design benefit from their simplicity, reliability, readability, reusability, and maintainability. Structured design, however, does not provide a way to package the data and the program (or procedure) together. Each program has to define how it will use the data. This can result in redundant programming code that must change every time the structure of the data changes. To eliminate this problem, some IT professionals use the object-oriented approach for program development.

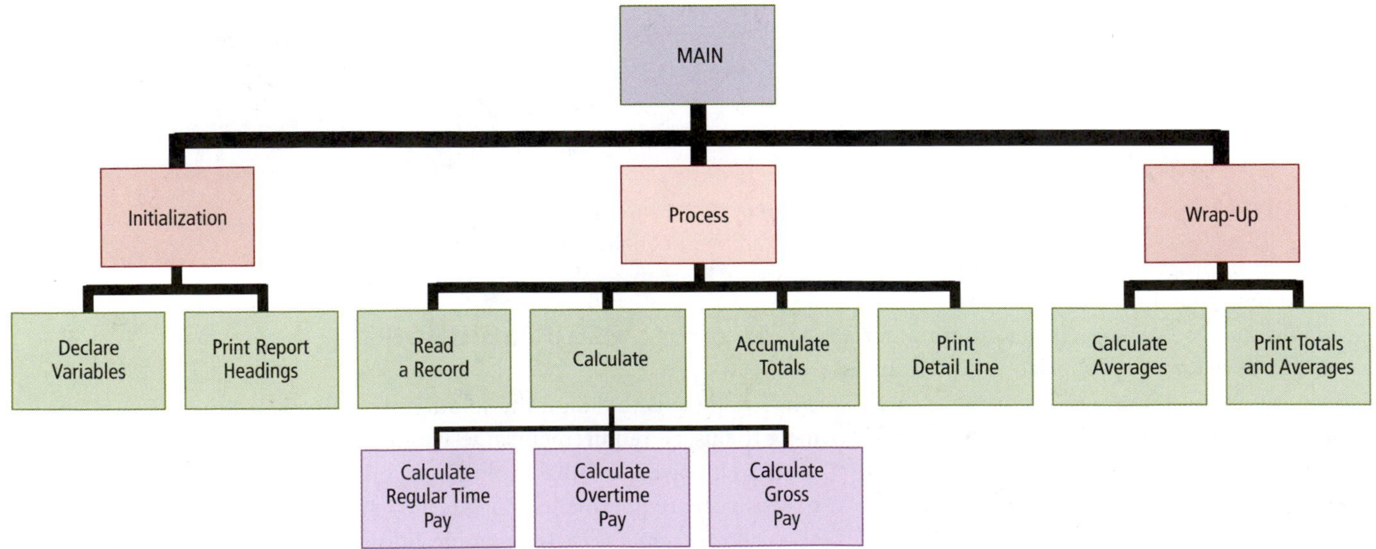

Figure 13-25 The hierarchy chart is a tool the programmer uses during structured design. On the hierarchy chart, program modules are drawn as rectangles. All modules are subordinate to the MAIN module.

Object-Oriented Design

With **object-oriented (OO) design**, the programmer packages the data and the program (or procedure) into a single unit, an object. When the structure of an object changes, any program that accesses the object automatically accesses the change.

The concept of packaging data and procedures into a single object is called *encapsulation*. That is, an object encapsulates (hides) the details of the object. Think of an object as a box, and you cannot see inside the box. The box sends and receives messages. It also contains code and data. For example, when users want to print a document, they click the Print button (the object). They probably do not know how the Print button actually communicates with the hardware to print the document. Thus, the details of the print object are encapsulated (hidden) from the user. Programmers, however, need to know how the object works, so that they can send messages to it and use it effectively.

As described in Chapter 12, objects are grouped into classes. To represent classes and their hierarchical relationships graphically, programmers use a class diagram. Figure 13-26 shows a high-level class diagram. In this diagram, a construction site needs many jobs performed, a job is completed by several workers, and each worker receives one paycheck for work performed. The 1 below the Construction Site class indicates that each Construction Site class must have at least one Job class associated with it. The 1..* above the Job class indicates that each Job class must be associated with at least one Construction Site class above it.

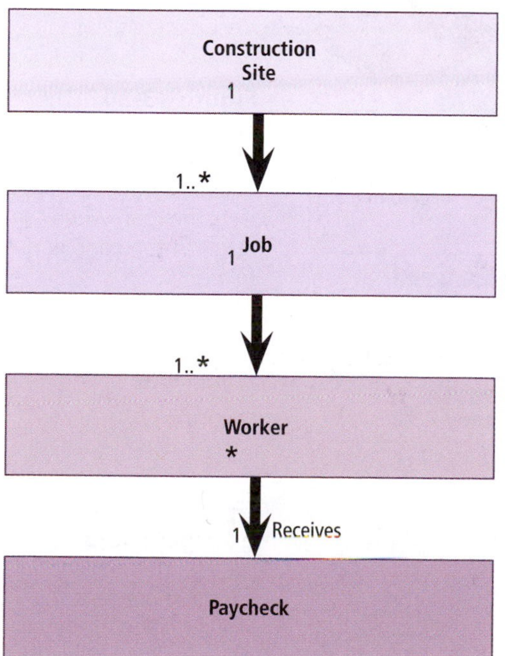

Figure 13-26 A class diagram is a hierarchical tool the programmer uses during object-oriented design.

With the high-level class diagram complete, the programmer develops a detailed class diagram that provides a visual representation of each object, its attributes, and its methods. Then, the programmer translates the methods into program instructions.

Object-Oriented Design

For more information, visit the Computer Concepts CourseMate Web site at www.cengagebrain.com, navigate to the Chapter 13 Web Link resource for this book, and then click Object-Oriented Design.

Control Structures

Whether using structured design or object-oriented design, programmers typically use control structures to describe the tasks a program is to perform. A **control structure**, also known as a *construct*, depicts the logical order of program instructions. Three basic control structures are sequence, selection, and repetition.

Sequence Control Structure

A *sequence control structure* shows one or more actions following each other in order (Figure 13-27). Actions include inputs, processes, and outputs. All actions must be executed; that is, none can be skipped. Examples of actions are reading a record, calculating averages or totals, and printing totals.

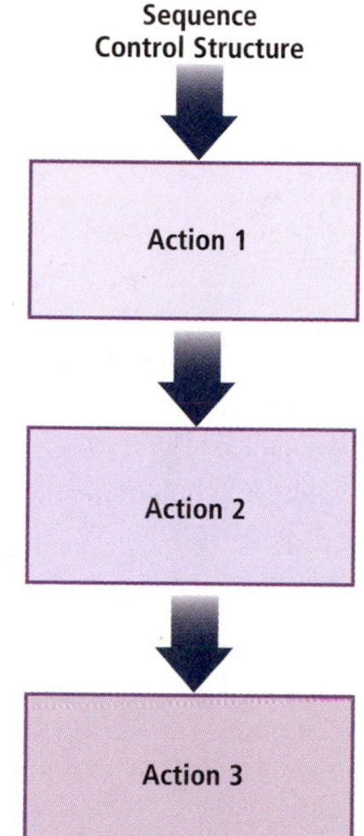

Figure 13-27 The sequence control structure shows one or more actions followed by another.

Selection Control Structure

A *selection control structure* tells the program which action to take, based on a certain condition. Two common types of selection control structures are the if-then-else and the case.

When a program evaluates the condition in an *if-then-else control structure*, it yields one of two possibilities: true or false. Figure 13-28 shows the condition as a diamond symbol. If the result of the condition is true, then the program performs one action. If the result is false, the program performs

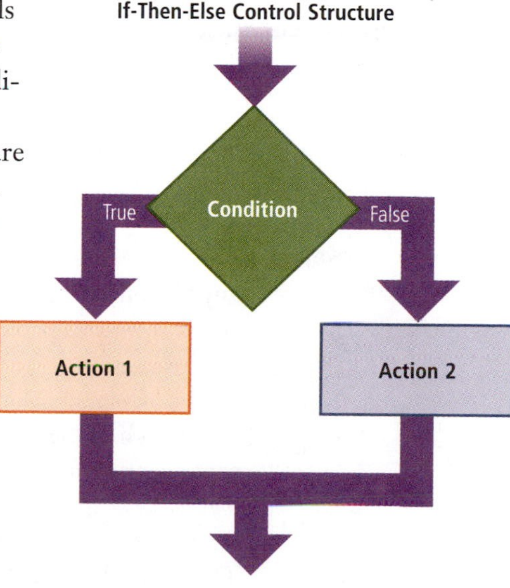

Figure 13-28 The if-then-else control structure directs the program toward one course of action or another based on the evaluation of a condition.

a different action. For example, the if-then-else control structure can determine if an employee should receive overtime pay. A possible condition might be the following: Is Hours Worked greater than 40? If the response is yes (true), then the action would calculate overtime pay. If the response is no (false), then the action would set overtime pay equal to 0.

In some cases, a program should perform no action if the result of a condition is false. This variation of the if-then-else is called the if-then control structure because the program performs an action only if the result of the condition is true.

With the *case control structure*, a condition can yield one of three or more possibilities (Figure 13-29). The size of a beverage, for example, might be one of these options: small, medium, large, or extra large. A case control structure would determine the price of the beverage based on the size purchased.

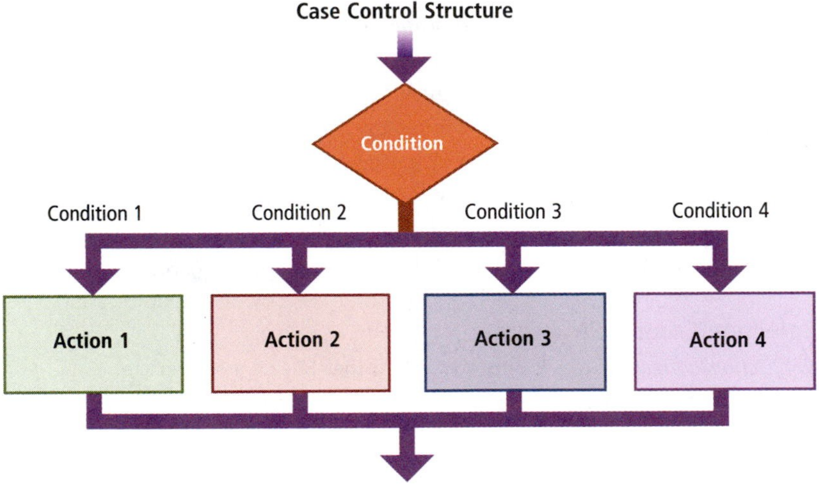

Figure 13-29 The case control structure allows for more than two alternatives when a condition is evaluated.

Repetition Control Structure The *repetition control structure* enables a program to perform one or more actions repeatedly as long as a certain condition is met. Many programmers refer to this construct as a *loop*. Two forms of the repetition control structure are the do-while and do-until.

A *do-while control structure* repeats one or more times as long as a condition is true (Figure 13-30). This control structure tests a condition at the beginning of the loop, a process called a *pretest*. If the result of the condition is true, the program executes the action(s) inside the loop. Then, the program loops back and tests the condition again. If the result of the condition still is true, the program executes the action(s) inside the loop again. This looping process continues until the condition being tested becomes false. At that time, the program stops looping and moves to another set of actions.

The do-while control structure normally is used when occurrence of an event is not quantifiable or predictable. For example, programmers frequently use the do-while control structure to process all records in a file. A payroll program using a do-while control structure loops once for each employee. This program stops looping when it processes the last employee's record.

The *do-until control structure* is similar to the do-while but has two major differences: where it tests the condition and when it stops looping. First, the do-until control structure tests the condition at the end of the loop, a process called a *posttest* (Figure 13-31). The action(s) in a do-until control structure thus always will execute at least once. The loop in a do-while control structure, by contrast, might not execute at all. That is, if the condition immediately is false, the action or actions in the do-while loop never execute. Second, a do-until control structure continues looping until the condition is true — and then stops. This is different from the do-while control structure, which continues to loop while the condition is true.

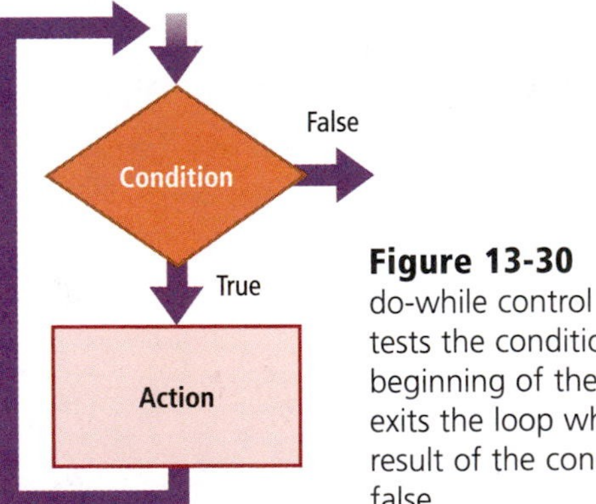

Figure 13-30 The do-while control structure tests the condition at the beginning of the loop. It exits the loop when the result of the condition is false.

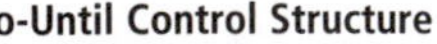

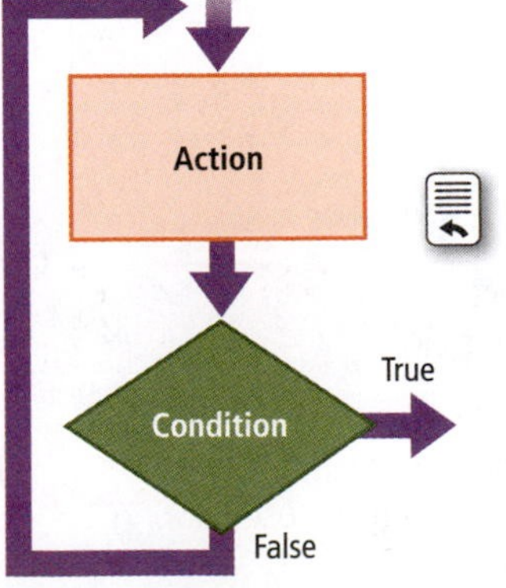

Figure 13-31 The do-until control structure tests the condition at the end of the loop. It exits the loop when the result of the condition is true.

Design Tools

To help document a solution algorithm, programmers use *design tools*. Two structured design tools are program flowcharts and pseudocode. A design tool for object-oriented design is the UML.

- A *program flowchart*, or simply **flowchart**, graphically shows the logic in a solution algorithm. The American National Standards Institute (ANSI) published a set of standards for program flowcharts in the early 1960s. These standards, still used today, specify symbols for various operations in a program's logic (Figure 13-32).

  Programmers connect most symbols on a program flowchart with solid lines. These lines show the direction of the program. Dotted lines on a flowchart connect comment symbols. A *comment symbol*, also called an *annotation symbol*, explains or clarifies logic in the solution algorithm. Figure 13-33 shows the program flowchart for three modules of the program shown in the hierarchy chart in Figure 13-25 on page 688.

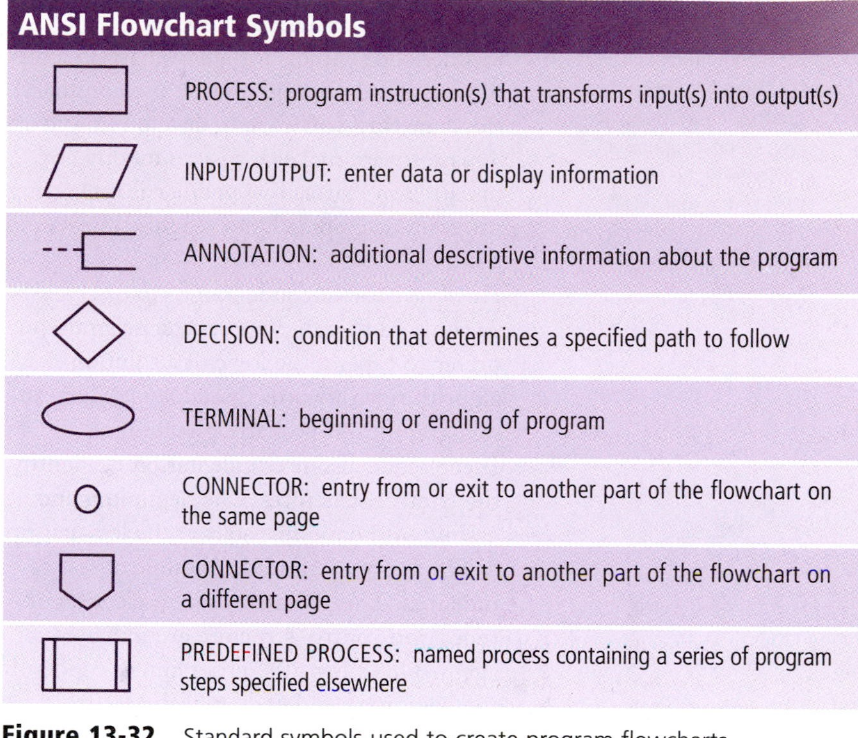

ANSI Flowchart Symbols

Symbol	Description
	PROCESS: program instruction(s) that transforms input(s) into output(s)
	INPUT/OUTPUT: enter data or display information
	ANNOTATION: additional descriptive information about the program
	DECISION: condition that determines a specified path to follow
	TERMINAL: beginning or ending of program
	CONNECTOR: entry from or exit to another part of the flowchart on the same page
	CONNECTOR: entry from or exit to another part of the flowchart on a different page
	PREDEFINED PROCESS: named process containing a series of program steps specified elsewhere

Figure 13-32 Standard symbols used to create program flowcharts.

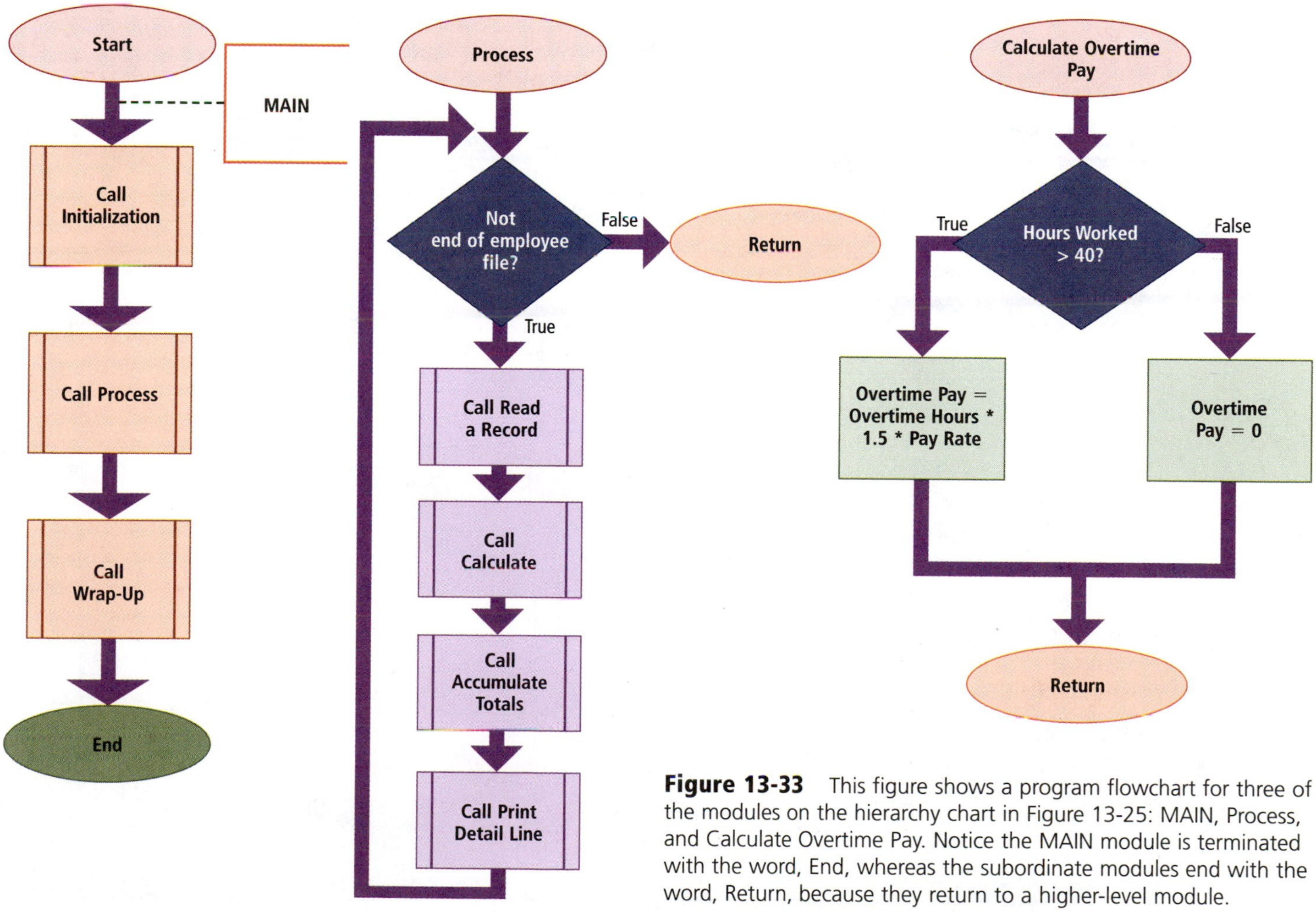

Figure 13-33 This figure shows a program flowchart for three of the modules on the hierarchy chart in Figure 13-25: MAIN, Process, and Calculate Overtime Pay. Notice the MAIN module is terminated with the word, End, whereas the subordinate modules end with the word, Return, because they return to a higher-level module.

Flowcharting Software

For more information, visit the Computer Concepts CourseMate Web site at www.cengagebrain.com, navigate to the Chapter 13 Web Link resource for this book, and then click Flowcharting Software.

In the past, programmers used a template to trace the symbols for a flowchart on a piece of paper. Today, programmers use commercial **flowcharting software** to develop flowcharts. This software makes it easy to modify and update flowcharts. Two popular flowcharting programs are SmartDraw (Figure 13-34) and Visio.

- *Pseudocode* uses a condensed form of English to convey program logic. Some programmers prefer to explain the logic of a solution algorithm with words (pseudocode), instead of a graphical flowcharting technique. Pseudocode also uses indentation to identify the control structures. The beginning and ending of the module start at the left margin.

The actions within the module are indented. The actions within a selection or repetition control structure are indented again. This allows the programmer to identify the beginning and ending of the control structure clearly. Figure 13-35 shows the pseudocode for the same three program modules as in Figure 13-33 on the previous page.

```
MAIN MODULE:

      CALL Initialization
      CALL Process
      CALL Wrap-Up

END

PROCESS MODULE:

      DO WHILE Not EOF
            CALL Read a Record
            CALL Calculate
            CALL Accumulate Totals
            CALL Print Detail Line
      ENDDO

RETURN

CALCULATE OVERTIME PAY MODULE:

      IF Hours Worked > 40 THEN
            Overtime Pay = Overtime Hours
                * 1.5 * Pay Rate
      ELSE
            Overtime Pay = 0
      ENDIF

RETURN
```

Figure 13-35 Pseudocode is another alternative method of showing program logic. This figure shows the same three modules (MAIN, Process, and Calculate Overtime Pay) as illustrated in Figure 13-33 with program flowcharts.

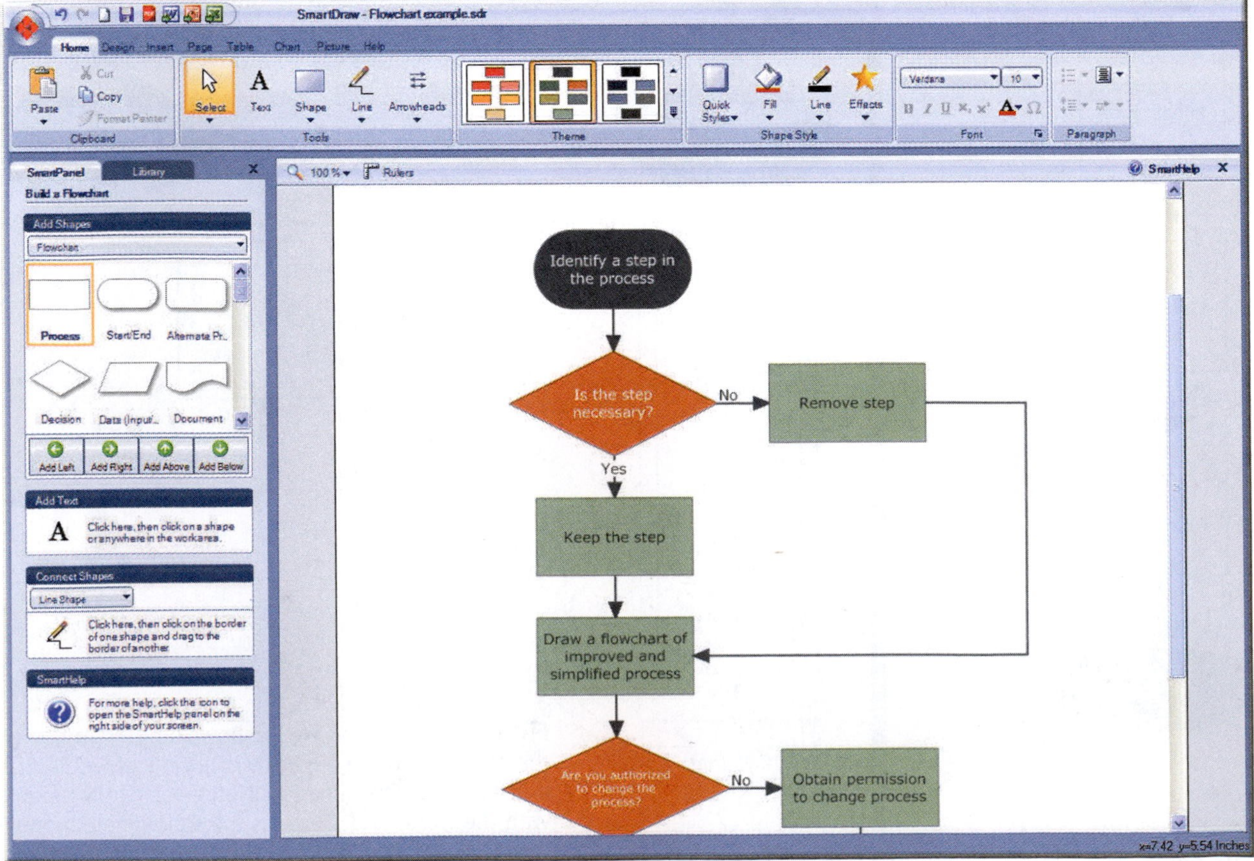

Figure 13-34 SmartDraw is a popular flowcharting program.

- As discussed in Chapter 12, the UML (Unified Modeling Language) has been adopted as a standard notation for object modeling and development. These notations are used in diagrams that present various views of the system being developed. Figure 13-36 identifies some symbols used in each of these types of diagrams.

  Two basic categories of diagrams in the UML are structural diagrams and behavioral diagrams. Examples of structural diagrams include class diagrams, component diagrams, and deployment diagrams. A class diagram shows classes and their subclasses and relationships, attributes, operations, and roles. A component diagram shows how the software components of a system interact. A deployment diagram illustrates how hardware components are connected.

  Behavioral diagrams illustrate how the processes flow among the components, classes, users, and the system being designed. Examples of behavioral diagrams include use case diagrams, activity diagrams (Figure 13-37), sequence diagrams, and state diagrams. A use case diagram shows how actors interact with the system. An activity diagram shows all the activities that occur within a use case. A sequence diagram identifies all possible paths a message takes as it moves among the actors and objects. A state diagram identifies the various changes that occur to an object over time.

Step 3 — Validate Design

Once programmers develop the solution algorithm, they should *validate*, or check, the program design for accuracy. During this step, the programmer checks the logic for accuracy and attempts to uncover logic errors. A **logic error** is a flaw in the design that causes inaccurate results. Two techniques for reviewing a solution algorithm are a desk check and an inspection.

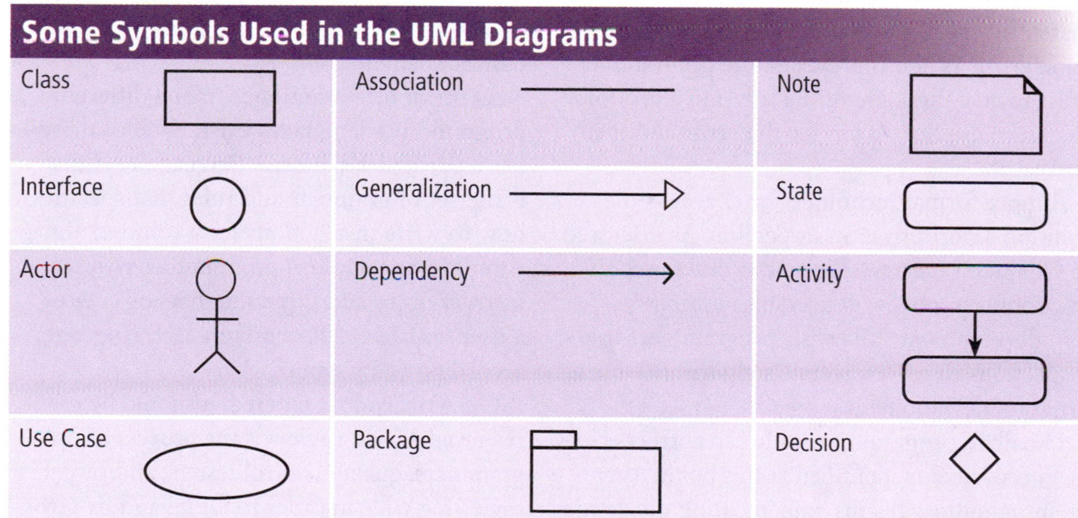

Figure 13-36 Symbols used to create diagrams in the UML.

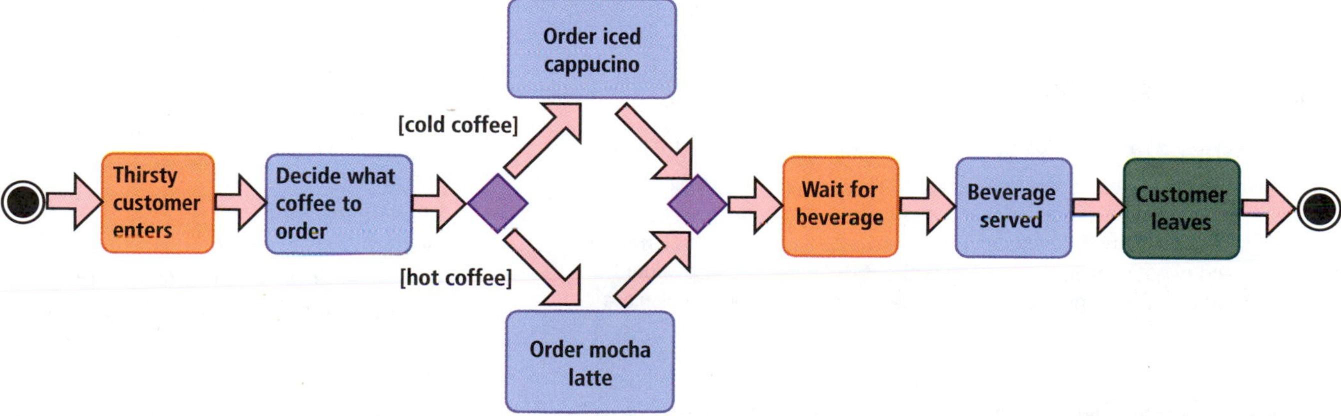

Figure 13-37 A UML activity diagram illustrating a Place Coffee Order use case.

When programmers do a *desk check*, they use test data to step through its logic. **Test data** is sample data that mimics real data the program will process once it is in production. Users should assist in the development of test data. The programmer who developed the solution algorithm usually performs the desk check, but another programmer also can perform this task. Desk checking involves five steps.

1. Develop various sets of test data (inputs).
2. Determine the expected result (output) for each set of data, without using the solution algorithm.
3. Step through the solution algorithm using one set of test data and write down the actual result obtained (output) using the solution algorithm.
4. Compare the expected result from Step 2 to the actual result from Step 3.
5. Repeat Steps 3 and 4 for each set of test data.

If the expected result and actual result do not match for any set of data, the program has a logic error. When this occurs, the programmer must review the logic of the solution algorithm to determine the reason for the error and then correct it.

A more formal technique for checking the solution algorithm is an inspection. As discussed in Chapter 12, a systems analyst often uses an inspection to review deliverables during system development. Likewise, programmers use inspections to review solution algorithms during program development.

Usually, a programmer easily can correct errors or improvements identified at this point. After the programmer begins implementing the design, errors are more difficult to fix. Thus, detecting errors and making improvements early in program development reduces the overall time and cost of program development.

? FAQ 13-5

What types of test data should be used during validation?

It is always best to test a program using alphanumeric and numeric test data. Even if a program accepts only numeric data, test with some alphanumeric data to see how it responds. Numeric test data should include both positive and negative values, with and without decimals. You also should use test data that you know is invalid to ensure that the program displays proper error messages.

For more information, visit the Computer Concepts CourseMate Web site at www.cengagebrain.com, navigate to the Chapter 13 FAQ resource for this book, and then click Test Data.

Step 4 — Implement Design

Implementation of the design includes using a program development tool that assists the programmer by generating or providing some or all code, or includes writing the code that translates the design into a computer program and, if necessary, creating the user interface. **Coding** a program involves translating the solution algorithm into a programming language (sometimes on paper) and then typing the programming language code into the computer.

You enter code using the editor provided with the programming language or any other text editor, such as Notepad, as long as the file is saved with the extension required by the programing language. If you use a standard word processing program, such as Word, you also must save the code as an ASCII file, often called plain text, instead of as a formatted word processing document. An *ASCII file* is a file that does not contain any formatting, that is, no graphics, italics, bold, underlining, styles, bullets, shading, color, etc.

As previously mentioned, many different programming languages exist. Each of these has a particular syntax. A language's **syntax** is the set of grammar and rules that specifies how to write instructions for a solution algorithm. For example, a programmer writes an instruction to add three numbers or creates a user interface differently in each language, according to its syntax.

Once the code is entered, it should be reviewed. **Code review** is the process of programmers, quality control testers, and/or peers reviewing code in order to locate and fix errors so that the final programs work correctly.

As programmers enter code into a computer, they should document the code thoroughly so that the programs can be maintained easily. Programs should include both global and internal documentation, called *comments* (Figure 13-38). *Global comments*, which usually are at the top of a program, explain the program's purpose and identify the program name, its author, and the date written. *Internal comments*, which appear throughout the body of the program, explain the purpose of the code statements within the program.

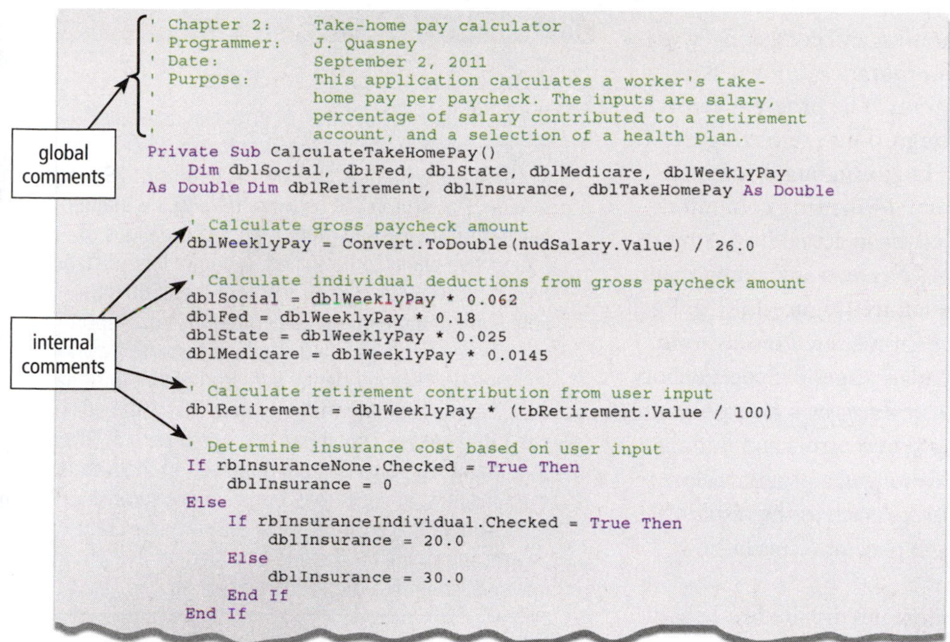


```
' Chapter 2:      Take-home pay calculator
' Programmer:     J. Quasney
' Date:           September 2, 2011
' Purpose:        This application calculates a worker's take-
'                 home pay per paycheck. The inputs are salary,
'                 percentage of salary contributed to a retirement
'                 account, and a selection of a health plan.
Private Sub CalculateTakeHomePay()
    Dim dblSocial, dblFed, dblState, dblMedicare, dblWeeklyPay
As Double Dim dblRetirement, dblInsurance, dblTakeHomePay As Double

    ' Calculate gross paycheck amount
    dblWeeklyPay = Convert.ToDouble(nudSalary.Value) / 26.0

    ' Calculate individual deductions from gross paycheck amount
    dblSocial = dblWeeklyPay * 0.062
    dblFed = dblWeeklyPay * 0.18
    dblState = dblWeeklyPay * 0.025
    dblMedicare = dblWeeklyPay * 0.0145

    ' Calculate retirement contribution from user input
    dblRetirement = dblWeeklyPay * (tbRetirement.Value / 100)

    ' Determine insurance cost based on user input
    If rbInsuranceNone.Checked = True Then
        dblInsurance = 0
    Else
        If rbInsuranceIndividual.Checked = True Then
            dblInsurance = 20.0
        Else
            dblInsurance = 30.0
        End If
    End If
```

Figure 13-38 Thorough documentation leads to maintainable programs. A program should contain global comments (at the top of the program) and internal comments (throughout the body of the program). In this Visual Basic program, the first character of the comment is an apostrophe.

Extreme Programming

As an alternative to coding in this step of program development, some companies use extreme programming to develop programs. *Extreme programming* (XP) is a strategy that proposes that programmers should immediately begin coding and testing solutions as soon as requirements are defined. The code continually is tested and refined until it works. This strategy essentially eliminates the Design Solution and Validate Design steps of traditional program development. Extreme programming also suggests that programmers work in pairs, with each communicating code to the other and generating ideas for proper solutions. Proponents of extreme programming claim it reduces the time required for program development. Extreme programming most often is used in object-oriented design.

Step 5 — Test Solution

Once a programmer codes and enters the program, the next step is to test it. Thorough testing is very important. After programmers place the program into production, many users rely on the program and its output to support their daily activities and decisions.

The goal of program testing is to ensure the program runs correctly and is error free. Errors uncovered during this step usually are one of two types: (1) syntax errors or (2) logic errors. A **syntax error** occurs when the code violates the syntax, or grammar, of the programming language. Misspelling a command, leaving out required punctuation, or typing command words, called *keywords*, out of order all will cause syntax errors. Programmers usually discover syntax errors the first time they attempt to compile or interpret the program code on the computer. When a syntax error is located, a message either is displayed on the screen immediately or is written to a log file. Either way, the programmer must review and correct all syntax errors. The procedure for testing for logic errors at this step is much like the desk checking techniques used in the Validate Design step.

Another purpose of using test data is to try to cause a **run-time error**, which is an error or event that causes the program to stop running. If the pay rate for employees cannot exceed $55.00 per hour, then the test data should use some valid pay rates, such as $25.00 and $10.50, as well as some invalid ones, such as $-32.00 and $72.50. When entering an invalid pay rate, the program should not stop running but instead should display an error message and allow the user to reenter the pay rate. If the program accepts an invalid pay rate, then it contains a logic error. If it stops running, it has a run-time error. In addition, the program should handle data exception errors such as division by zero. When users run a program, the data they enter should not cause a run-time error. They may experience a run-time error, however, if their computer does not have enough RAM or disk space to run the program.

The process of locating and correcting syntax and logic errors in a program is known as **debugging** the program. The program errors themselves are the **bugs**. Thus, removing the errors is de*bug*ging. The term bug originated when the failure of one of the first computers supposedly was traced to an actual bug. A moth lodged in the computer's electronic components was the cause of the failure (Figure 13-39). Read Ethics & Issues 13-4 for a related discussion.

Most programming languages include a debug utility. A *debug utility*, or *debugger*, assists programmers with identifying syntax errors and finding logic errors. With a debugger, a programmer examines program values (such as the result of a calculation) while the program runs in slow motion.

Some software companies distribute a beta of their software to users. A **beta** is a program that has most or all of its features and functionality implemented. Users test the beta program and send bug reports to the software company. This enables the software manufacturer to fix any errors before the software is released to the public for sale.

Beta Testers

For more information, visit the Computer Concepts CourseMate Web site at www.cengagebrain.com, navigate to the Chapter 13 Web Link resource for this book, and then click Beta Testers.

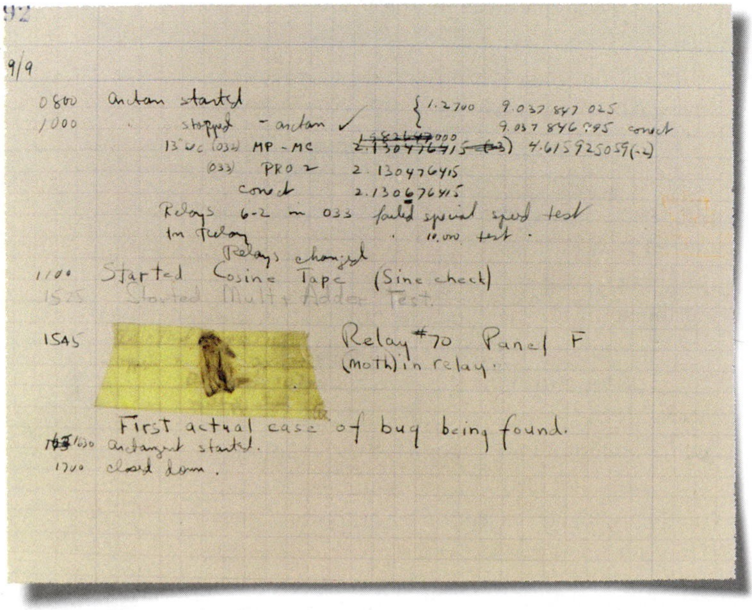

If a programmer designs a program properly during the Design Solution step, then testing in this step should not require much time. As a general rule, the more time and effort programmers spend analyzing and designing the solution algorithm, the less time they spend debugging the program.

Figure 13-39 The temporary failure of one of the first computers was traced to a dead moth (shown taped to the log book) caught in the electronic components. Some say this event is the origin of the computer term bug.

ETHICS & ISSUES 13-4

Who Is Responsible for Bugs?

The consequences of bugs, or errors, in computer programs can be staggering. A software error in a missile defense system resulted in the deaths of 29 U.S. soldiers. An error in the code controlling a Canadian nuclear facility caused more than 3,000 gallons of radioactive water to be spilled. A bug in long-distance switching software cost AT&T more than $60 million. Sometimes, employees or students who report security-related bugs are disciplined because by finding the bug, they accidently accessed secure information. Experts estimate that there are 20 to 30 bugs per 1,000 lines of code in an average program. Given that many programs contain hundreds of thousands, even millions, of code lines, bugs are not surprising. Most software licenses absolve the software creator of any responsibility for the end user getting the wrong information from a bug-riddled program.

Who should be responsible for mistakes in software? Why? If users find bugs, such as security bugs, should they be disciplined after reporting the bugs? Why? Should those who design a system or write programs for a system be legally responsible if their product results in errors or damages? Why?

Step 6 — Document Solution

In documenting the solution, the programmer performs two activities: (1) review the program code and (2) review all the documentation.

First, programmers review the program for any dead code and remove it. *Dead code* is any program instructions that a program never executes. When programmers write a program, they often write a section of code at a time. Sometimes, they decide not to use the code, but leave it in the program anyway. This dead (unused) code serves no purpose and should not exist.

Next, programmers should run the program one final time to verify it still works. After reviewing the program code, the programmer gives the program and all of its documentation to the systems analyst. The documentation includes all charts, solution algorithms, test data, and program code listings that contain global and internal comments.

The programmer should be sure all documentation is complete and accurate. This becomes especially valuable if the program requires changes in the future. Proper documentation greatly reduces the amount of time a new programmer spends learning about existing programs.

FAQ 13-6

How much documentation should a program include?

No set rule exists for the amount of documentation a program should contain, but programmers should include enough documentation to be able to understand completely the program's functionality without having to interpret each line of code.

For more information, visit the Computer Concepts CourseMate Web site at www.cengagebrain.com, navigate to the Chapter 13 FAQ resource for this book, and then click Documentation.

QUIZ YOURSELF 13-3

Instructions: Find the true statement below. Then, rewrite the remaining false statements so that they are true.

1. A language's logic is the set of grammar and rules that specifies how to write instructions for a solution algorithm.
2. An error in a program is known as a beta.
3. In structured design, the programmer typically begins with a detailed design and moves toward a more general design.
4. The concept of packaging data and procedures into a single object is called casing.
5. The program development life cycle consists of these six steps: analyze requirements, design solution, validate design, implement design, test solution, and hardcode solution.
6. Three basic control structures are sequence, selection, and pseudocode.
7. Two basic categories of diagrams in the UML are structural diagrams and behavioral diagrams.

Quiz Yourself Online: To further check your knowledge of pages 686 through 697, visit the Computer Concepts CourseMate Web site at www.cengagebrain.com, navigate to the Chapter 13 Quiz Yourself resource for this book, and then click Objectives 7 – 9.

Chapter Summary

This chapter discussed various programming languages used to create computer programs. It also presented a variety of Web development and multimedia development tools. Finally, the chapter described each step in the program development life cycle and presented the tools used to make this process efficient.

Computer Usage @ Work

Manufacturing

Manufacturing plays a crucial role in today's society. To keep up with our growing population's increasing demand for various products, organizations explore ways to streamline manufacturing processes while simultaneously minimizing costs. These organizations often find that using computers in the manufacturing process requires fewer people-hours, and products and parts are manufactured with greater accuracy and less waste.

Automakers, for example, manufacture cars on an assembly line. In the early years of car manufacturing, people were involved at all stages of the manufacturing process, and it was not uncommon to find hundreds or thousands of individuals working along the line. Although the assembly line allowed individuals to manufacture cars as quickly as they could, companies soon realized that computer-aided manufacturing (CAM) would increase output and decrease labor costs. In fact, CAM proved to be most effective when used in conjunction with computer-aided design (CAD). CAD designs an item, such as a car, to manufacture; CAM then manufactures the car according to the original design. Computers also determine the exact amount of material necessary to build the car, as well as the expected output.

Communications during the assembly process is critical. Computers automatically communicate with each other along the assembly line and provide alerts when factors arise that can interrupt the process. For example, running out of hinges that attach the door to the rest of the car's body will halt the line until someone replenishes the hinges. Computers, however, often alert individuals to low supplies before they run out and the assembly halts. Failure to detect the absence of hinges might result in the machinery that is manufacturing the car to think that it is attaching hinges when in fact it is not. This might result in damage to the door and/or the car's body further along the assembly line.

Today, computers assist with manufacturing many types of items. Although some might argue that computers perform jobs that people once held, their introduction has helped to meet our increased demand and desire for low prices.

For more information, visit the Computer Concepts CourseMate Web site at www.cengagebrain.com, navigate to the Chapter 13 Computer Usage @ Work resource for this book, and then click Manufacturing.

High-Tech Talk

Acid3 Browser Test: Verifying Standards Support

Each day, people work to develop new technologies intended to enhance a user's Web browsing experience by creating more dynamic and interactive Web pages. Simultaneously, companies such as Microsoft, Mozilla, and Google work to create new Web browser versions that include features designed to help people search and browse the Web more efficiently. In addition to providing new and exciting features with each release, new Web browsers also should support new technologies that Web developers are including in Web pages and Web applications. As presented earlier in the book, each Web browser might display a Web page with slight differences. For example, the top margin on a Web page might be twice as thick in Internet Explorer as it is in Firefox. While this might not seem significant, positioning Web page elements accurately often is necessary to display information properly, in the manner that the Web developer intends. For this reason, *The Web Standards Project* has created a series of test pages designed to inform users whether their browser supports certain Web technologies. In 1998, The Web Standards Project developed *Acid1*, the first in the series of three tests designed to test a Web browser's interpretation of the first version of basic HTML and cascading style sheets (CSS1). In 2005, The Web Standards Project introduced the *Acid2* test, which tested Web standards such as CSS positioning, CSS table formatting, and hovering effects. Throughout the past several years, new Web technologies have led companies to develop new versions of their Web browsers more frequently. The Web Standards Project released the *Acid3 Browser Test* in early 2008. During an Acid3 Browser Test, the Web browser displays a percentage counter that gradually increases. When the counter reaches 100 and displays a page similar to the one in Figure 13-40, it is an indication that the browser has passed the test.

The Acid3 Browser Test uses JavaScript to perform approximately 100 subtests. These subtests evaluate how the Web browser interprets newer Web technologies such as DOM2, ECMAScript, Media Queries, Selectors, XHTML, CSS2, CSS2.1, CSS3, and Standard Vector Graphics (SVG). To perform an Acid3 Browser Test using a Web browser, you first should ensure that the Web browser is configured with the default settings. If you have changed settings such as the default font, view, or zoom, you should return them to their original settings before performing the test. Failure to do so might result in incorrect test results. Once the browser is configured with the default settings, type `http://acid3.acidtests.org` in the Address bar and then press the ENTER key. A Web page then will be displayed with a counter beginning at zero. The counter slowly increments as the tests are performed. The counter's value increasing is indicative of the Web browser passing additional subtests. If the counter stops for more than a few seconds, does not increment smoothly, or the graphic on the screen is not arranged similarly to Figure 13-40, the Web browser has not passed the Acid3 Browser Test. If the browser does not pass the test, you first should make sure that you are using the most recent version of the Web browser and that you have downloaded and installed all updates and security patches. You also should ensure that the Web browser is performing the test with its default settings.

The Acid3 Browser Test is one of the only tests that comprehensively measures compliance with many current Web standards. If ever you must decide which Web browser to use, consider the one that passes, or comes closest to passing, the Acid3 Browser Test.

For more information, visit the Computer Concepts CourseMate Web site at www.cengagebrain.com, navigate to the Chapter 13 High-Tech Talk resource for this book, and then click Acid3 Browser Test.

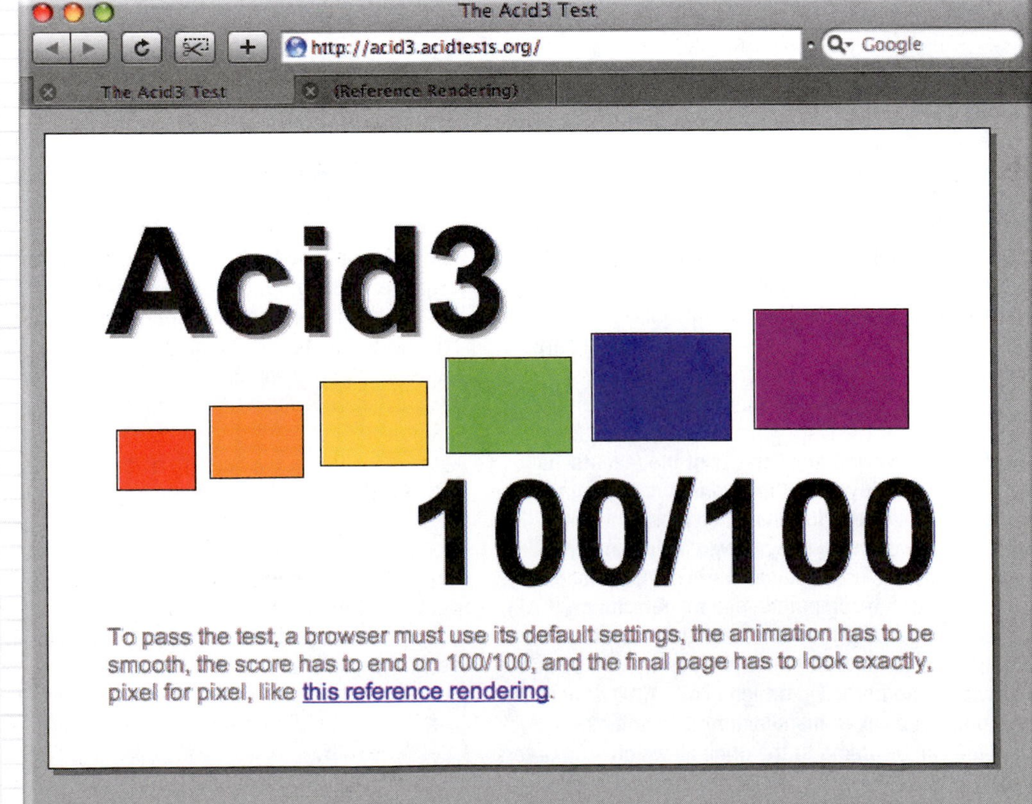

Figure 13-40 Web browsers that pass the Acid3 Browser Test display this Web page at the conclusion of the test. The version of the Safari Web browser in this figure has passed the Acid3 Browser Test.

Companies on the Cutting Edge

ELECTRONIC ARTS (EA) Entertainment Software Developer

Video gaming is one of the more popular forms of recreation among people of all ages. Game sales are increasing among all age groups, and demand for Wii products is especially high among adult gamers.

Electronic Arts (EA) is an entertainment software publishing company that develops video games for game consoles, computers, mobile devices, and the Internet. The company had thirty-one products that sold more than one million copies in a recent year, three of which sold more than five million copies: FIFA, Madden NFL, and Need for Speed Undercover.

Electronic Arts has been developing video games since 1982. From the beginning, EA has referred to its programmers as software artists who can evoke emotions from game enthusiasts. Its yearly revenues of more than $3 billion are generated from its sales of action, fantasy, sports, and strategy software for the PlayStation, Xbox, Wii, and Game Boy systems.

SUN MICROSYSTEMS Products and Services Provider

"The network is the computer" according to *Sun Microsystems'* vision. Corporation leaders believe network participation drives originality, development, and open source leadership.

Nearly every sector of society and industry uses Sun's innovative products. Its software, systems, services, and electronics help run more than five billion devices, ranging from the world's largest data centers to some of the smallest consumer electronics. The company's NASDAQ symbol is JAVA, which represents its status as being the creator and leading advocate of Java technology. Other top products are the MySQL database management system, StorageTek, and the UltraSPARC processor.

In 2010, Oracle acquired Sun Microsystems for approximately $7.4 billion. The integration of these two leading companies provides a combination of the best enterprise software with proven computer systems critical to the operation of many businesses.

For more information, visit the Computer Concepts CourseMate Web site at www.cengagebrain.com and then navigate to the Chapter 13 Companies on the Cutting Edge resource for this book.

Technology Trailblazers

ALAN KAY Computer Pioneer

The connection between music and creative thinking has been researched for years, and jazz musician and computer scientist *Alan Kay* exemplifies how people with musical talent process innovative thoughts.

Kay is president of the Viewpoints Research Institute, a nonprofit organization funded by the National Science Foundation and involved in the One Laptop per Child project. The computer scientist is credited with developing object-oriented languages and graphical user interfaces. His plans for a small, portable computer with a wireless network and storage, called the Dynabook, pioneered the concept of mobile learning in 1968; its purpose was to give children access to digital content.

He did much of his early research at the Department of Defense Advance Research Project Agency (DARPA). At Xerox's Palo Alto Research Center (PARC), he invented Smalltalk, which is the technical basis of the Apple Macintosh. He also has worked at Apple, Atari, Walt Disney Imagineering, and HP.

JAMES GOSLING Java Engineer and Architect

Songwriter and musician Neil Young has teamed with Sun Microsystems' *James Gosling* to develop a hybrid 1959 Lincoln Continental that will compete for the Automotive X prize, a contest for vehicles getting at least 100 mpg. The two Canadian-born innovators have named their car the Linc Volt, and its performance system is monitored by Java technology.

Gosling is the mastermind behind Java, and he affectionately is called the "father of Java." He was raised near Calgary, Alberta, and spent much of his free time turning spare machine parts into games. At 15, he wrote software for the University of Calgary's physics department. When he was hired at Sun, he built a multiprocessor version of UNIX, developed compilers to convert program code into machine language, and wrote a UNIX text editor.

He served as Sun's vice president and Oracle's chief technology officer until resigning in 2010. He was named an officer of the Order of Canada for demonstrating an outstanding level of talent and service to Canadians.

For more information, visit the Computer Concepts CourseMate Web site at www.cengagebrain.com and then navigate to the Chapter 13 Technology Trailblazers resource for this book.

STUDENT ASSIGNMENTS

Chapter Review

The Chapter Review reinforces the main concepts presented in this chapter.

To listen to an audio version of this Chapter Review, visit the Computer Concepts CourseMate Web site at www.cengagebrain.com and then navigate to the Chapter 13 Chapter Review resource for this book.

1. How Are Machine Languages Different from Assembly Languages? A **programming language** is a set of words, abbreviations, and symbols that enables a **programmer**, often called a *developer*, to communicate instructions to a computer. A **machine language** uses a series of binary digits, or combinations of numbers and letters that represent binary digits, and is the only language a computer directly recognizes. With an **assembly language**, a programmer writes instructions using *symbolic instruction codes*, which are meaningful abbreviations.

2. What Is the Purpose of Procedural Programming Languages, and What Are the Features of C and COBOL? In a **procedural language**, or **third-generation language** (**3GL**), a programmer writes instructions that tell a computer what to accomplish and how to do it. Programmers use English-like words to write instructions, which simplifies the program development process for the programmer. A *compiler* or an *interpreter* translates the 3GL **source program** into machine language *object code* or *object program* that a computer can execute. Standard procedural languages include C and COBOL. **C** is a powerful language that requires professional programming skills and is used for business and scientific problems. It runs on almost any type of computer or operating system. **COBOL** (*COmmon Business-Oriented Language*) is a programming language designed for business applications that uses English-like statements that are easy to read, write, and maintain.

3. What Are the Characteristics of Object-Oriented Programming Languages and Program Development Tools? Programmers use an **object-oriented programming** (**OOP**) **language** or object-oriented program development tool to implement object-oriented design. A program that provides a user-friendly environment for building programs often is called a *program development tool*. An *object* is an item that can contain both data and the procedures that read or manipulate the data. A major benefit of OOP is the ability to reuse and modify existing objects, allowing programmers to create applications faster. Often used in conjunction with OOP, **RAD** (*rapid application development*) is a method of developing software in which a programmer writes and implements a program in segments instead of waiting until the entire program is completed. OOP languages include Java, C++, and C#. **Java** uses a *just-in-time* (*JIT*) *compiler* to convert *bytecode* into machine-dependent code that is executed immediately. The Microsoft .NET framework, or **.NET**, allows almost any type of program to run on the Internet or an internal business network, as well as stand-alone computers and mobile devices. **C++** is an object-oriented extension of the C programming language. **C#** is based on C++ and has been accepted as a standard for Web applications and XML-based Web services. **F#** is a new programming language that combines the benefits of an object-oriented language with the benefits of a *functional language*. **Visual Studio** is Microsoft's suite of program development tools that assists programmers in building programs for Windows, Windows Mobile, or operating systems that support .NET. Visual Studio includes the programming languages **Visual Basic**, **Visual C++**, and **Visual C#**. A **visual programming language** uses a visual or graphical interface, called a *visual programming environment* (*VPE*), for creating all source code. Two other program development tools include **Delphi** and **PowerBuilder**.

Visit the Computer Concepts CourseMate Web site at www.cengagebrain.com, navigate to the Chapter 13 Quiz Yourself resource for this book, and then click Objectives 1 – 3.

4. What Are the Uses of Other Programming Languages and Other Program Development Tools? A **4GL** (*fourth-generation language*) is a **nonprocedural language** that enables users to access data in a database. A popular 4GL is **SQL**, a query language for relational databases. An **application generator** creates source code or machine code from a specification of the required functionality. A **macro**, which is a series of statements that instructs an application how to complete a task, allows users to automate routine, repetitive tasks.

5. What Are Web Page Program Development Techniques Such as HTML and XHTML, XML and WML, Scripting Languages, DHTML, Ruby on Rails, Web 2.0 Development, and Web Page Authoring Software? *Web developers* use a variety of techniques to create Web pages. **HTML** (*Hypertext Markup Language*) is a special formatting language that programmers use to format documents for display on the Web. **XHTML** (extensible HTML) is a markup language that includes features of HTML and XML. **XML** and **WML** are popular formats used by Web developers. A *scripting language* is an

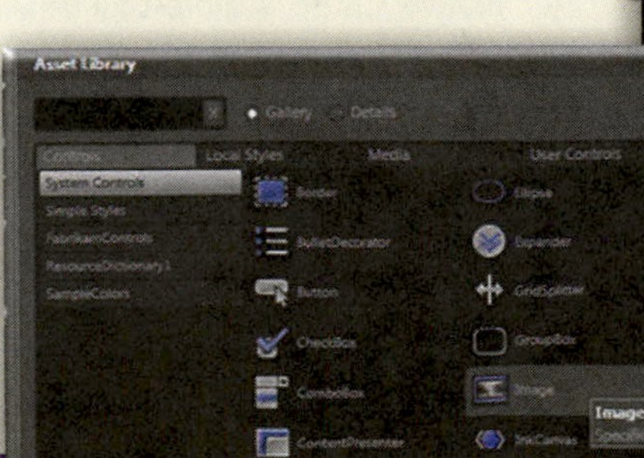

Chapter Review

interpreted language that programmers use to add dynamic content and interactive elements to Web pages. Popular scripting languages include **JavaScript**, **Perl**, **PHP**, **Rexx**, **Tcl**, and **VBScript**. **Dynamic HTML (DHTML)** is a type of HTML that allows developers to include more graphical interest and interactivity in a Web page. **Ruby on Rails** (*RoR* or *Rails*) is an open source framework that provides technologies for developing object-oriented, database-driven Web sites. Web 2.0 Web sites often use **RSS 2.0** and **Ajax**. Developers use **Web page authoring software** to create sophisticated Web pages. Four popular Web page authoring programs are **Dreamweaver**, **Expression Web**, **Flash**, and **SharePoint Designer**.

6. How Are Popular Multimedia Authoring Programs Used? **Multimedia authoring software** allows developers to combine text, graphics, animation, audio, and video into an interactive presentation. Popular authoring software includes ToolBook and Director. **ToolBook** has a graphical user interface and uses an object-oriented approach so that programmers can design multimedia applications using basic objects. **Director** has powerful features that allow programmers to create highly interactive multimedia applications.

Visit the Computer Concepts CourseMate Web site at www.cengagebrain.com, navigate to the Chapter 13 Quiz Yourself resource for this book, and then click Objectives 4 – 6.

7. What Are the Six Steps in the Program Development Life Cycle? The **program development life cycle (PDLC)** is a series of steps programmers use to build computer programs. The program development life cycle consists of six steps: (1) analyze requirements, (2) design solution, (3) validate design, (4) implement design, (5) test solution, and (6) document solution.

8. How Is Structured Design Different from Object-Oriented Design? In **structured design**, a programmer typically begins with a general design and moves toward a more detailed design. A programmer starts with the program's major function, called the *main routine* or *main module*, and breaks it down into smaller sections, called *subroutines* or *modules*. Structured design results in programs that are reliable and easy to read and maintain, but it does not provide a way to keep the data and the program together and can result in redundant programming code. With **object-oriented (OO) design**, the programmer packages the data and the program (or procedure) into a single unit, an object. Objects are grouped into classes. A detailed class diagram represents each object, its attributes (data), and its methods (procedures). The programmer translates the methods into program instructions.

9. What Are the Basic Control Structures and Design Tools Used in Designing Solutions to Programming Problems? A **control structure**, also known as a *construct*, depicts the logical order of program instructions. A *sequence control structure* shows one or more actions following each other in order. A *selection control structure* tells the program which action to take, based on a certain condition. Two types of selection control structures are the *if-then-else control structure*, which yields one of two possibilities (true or false), and the *case control structure*, which can yield one of three or more possibilities. The *repetition control structure* enables a program to perform one or more actions repeatedly as long as a certain condition is met. The two forms of the repetition control structure are: the *do-while control structure*, which tests a condition at the beginning of the loop, in a process called a *pretest*, and continues looping as long as a condition is true; and the *do-until control structure*, which tests a condition at the end of the loop, in a process called a *posttest*, and continues looping until the condition is true. Some *design tools* include a *program flowchart*, or simply **flowchart**; *pseudocode*; and the UML (Unified Modeling Language).

Visit the Computer Concepts CourseMate Web site at www.cengagebrain.com, navigate to the Chapter 13 Quiz Yourself resource for this book, and then click Objectives 7 – 9.

STUDENT ASSIGNMENTS

Key Terms

You should know the Primary Terms and be familiar with the Secondary Terms. The list below helps focus your study.

To see an example of and a definition for each term, and to access current and additional information from the Web, visit the Computer Concepts CourseMate Web site at www.cengagebrain.com and then navigate to the Chapter 13 Key Terms resource for this book.

Primary Terms

(shown in bold-black characters in the chapter)

4GL (674)
ActiveX (680)
ActiveX control (680)
Ajax (684)
applet (680)
application generator (676)
assembly language (665)
ATOM (679)
beta (696)
bugs (696)
C (668)
C# (671)
C++ (671)
COBOL (668)
code review (694)
coding (694)
computer program (664)
control structure (689)
counter (680)
debugging (696)
Delphi (673)
Director (685)
Dreamweaver (685)
dynamic HTML (DHTML) (683)
Expression Web (685)
F# (671)
Flash (685)
flowchart (691)
flowcharting software (692)
hierarchy chart (688)
HTML (678)
IDE (integrated development environment) (669)
image map (680)
implementation (694)

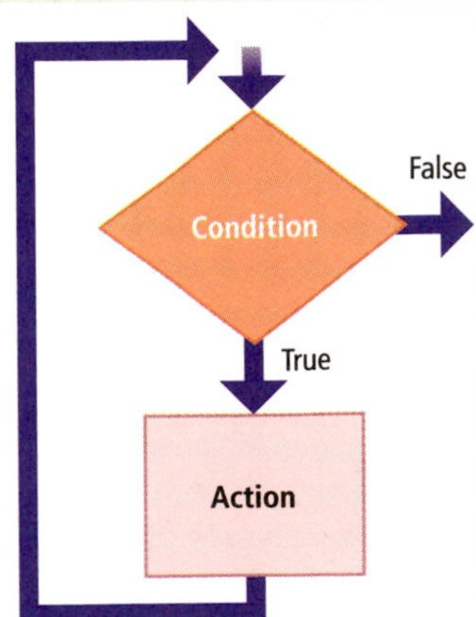

do-while control structure (690)

Java (670)
JavaScript (682)
logic error (693)
machine language (665)
macro (676)
maintaining (686)
multimedia authoring software (685)
.NET (670)
nonprocedural language (674)
object-oriented (OO) design (689)
object-oriented programming (OOP) language (669)
Perl (682)
PHP (682)
PowerBuilder (674)
procedural language (666)
processing form (680)
program development (686)
program development life cycle (PDLC) (686)
programmer (664)
programming language (664)
programming team (687)
RAD (669)
Rexx (682)
RSS 2.0 (679)
Ruby on Rails (683)
run-time error (695)
script (680)
servlet (680)
SharePoint Designer (685)
source program (666)
SQL (674)
structured design (688)
syntax (694)
syntax error (695)
Tcl (682)
test data (694)
third-generation language (3GL) (666)
ToolBook (685)
VBScript (683)
Visual Basic (672)
Visual C# (673)
Visual C++ (673)
visual programming language (673)
Visual Studio (671)
Web page authoring software (685)
WML (679)
XHTML (678)
XML (679)

Secondary Terms

(shown in italic characters in the chapter)

algorithm (668)
annotation symbol (691)
API (684)
ASCII file (694)
ASP.NET (670)
assembler (666)
bytecode (670)
cascading style sheet (CSS) (683)
case control structure (690)
CGI (common gateway interface) (680)
CGI script (680)
CLR (670)
code (664)
code snippets (671)
comment symbol (691)
comments (694)
COmmon Business-Oriented Language (668)
compiler (666)
construct (689)
dead code (696)
debug utility (696)
debugger (696)
design tools (691)
desk check (694)
developer (664)
document object model (DOM) (683)
do-until control structure (690)
do-while control structure (690)
Eclipse (670)
elements (678)
encapsulation (689)
event (669)
event-driven program (669)
execute (666)
extreme programming (XP) (695)
form (676)
fourth-generation language (674)
functional language (671)
global comments (694)
high-level language (665)
Hypertext Markup Language (678)
if-then-else control structure (689)
internal comments (694)
interpreter (667)
IPO chart (687)
Java EE (Java Platform, Enterprise Edition) (670)
Java Platform, Micro Edition (Java ME) (670)
Java Platform, Standard Edition (Java SE) (670)
just-in-time (JIT) compiler (670)
keywords (695)
loop (690)
low-level language (664)

machine-dependent language (664)
machine-independent language (665)
macro (assembly language) (666)
macro recorder (676)
main module (688)
main routine (688)
menu generator (676)
Microsoft Intermediate Language (MSIL) (670)
modules (688)
mouse rollover (682)
mouseover (682)
object (669)
object code (666)
object program (666)
open language (682)
posttest (690)
Practical Extraction and Report Language (682)
pretest (690)
program development tool (664)
program flowchart (691)
program logic (687)
pseudocode (692)
Rails (683)
rapid application development (669)
repetition control structure (690)
report writer (676)
REstructured eXtended eXecutor (682)
RoR (683)
Ruby (683)
scripting language (682)
selection control structure (689)
sequence control structure (689)
solution algorithm (687)
structure chart (688)
style sheet (679)
subroutines (688)
symbolic address (666)
symbolic instruction codes (666)
tags (678)
Tool Command Language (682)
top-down design (688)
validate (693)
Visual Basic for Applications (VBA) (676)
Visual Basic, Scripting Edition (683)
visual programming environment (VPE) (673)
Visual Studio Tools for Office (VSTO) (671)
Web developers (678)
XSL (679)
XSLT (679)

Checkpoint

The Checkpoint exercises test your knowledge of the chapter concepts. The page number containing the answer appears in parentheses after each exercise. The Beyond the Book exercises will help broaden your understanding of the concepts presented in this chapter.

To complete the Checkpoint exercises interactively, visit the Computer Concepts CourseMate Web site at www.cengagebrain.com and then navigate to the Chapter 13 Checkpoint resource for this book.

True/False Mark T for True and F for False.

_____ 1. Just as humans speak a variety of languages, programmers use a variety of programming languages and tools to create programs. (664)

_____ 2. With a procedural language, often called a third-generation language (3GL), a programmer uses a series of English-like words to write instructions. (666)

_____ 3. Programmers use Java Platform, Micro Edition (Java ME) to create programs for smart phones and other mobile devices. (670)

_____ 4. The Microsoft .NET Framework is a set of technologies that allows almost any type of program to run on the Internet or an internal business network, as well as stand-alone computers and mobile devices. (670)

_____ 5. HTML (Hypertext Markup Language) is a special formatting language that programmers use to format documents for display on the Web. (678)

_____ 6. ATOM allows Web developers to design pages specifically for microbrowsers. (679)

_____ 7. An applet usually runs slower than a script. (680)

_____ 8. Ruby on Rails is an open source framework that provides technologies for developing object-oriented, database-driven Web sites. (683)

_____ 9. Expression Web is used strictly on Linux Web servers. (685)

_____ 10. A selection control structure shows one or more actions following each other in order. (689)

Multiple Choice Select the best answer.

1. A(n) _____ reads a code statement, converts it to one or more machine language instructions, and then executes those machine language instructions. (667)
   a. compiler
   b. interpreter
   c. source program
   d. symbolic address

2. An OOP language is _____, which means an OOP language program checks for and responds to events such as pressing a key or typing a value. (669)
   a. event based
   b. interpreted
   c. event driven
   d. compiled

3. When programmers compile a(n) _____ program, the resulting object code is called bytecode, which is machine independent. (670)
   a. C
   b. assembly language
   c. Java
   d. all of the above

4. _____ is a popular fourth-generation query language that allows users to manage, update, and retrieve data in a relational DBMS. (674)
   a. SQL
   b. COBOL
   c. XML
   d. RPG

5. _____ is a subset of the Visual Basic language that allows programmers to add intelligence and interactivity to Web pages. (683)
   a. VBScript
   b. Flash
   c. Ajax
   d. SQL

6. _____ is a Web page authoring program that is part of the Microsoft Office and SharePoint families of products. (685)
   a. PHP
   b. Ajax
   c. SharePoint Designer
   d. Flash

7. _____ by Adobe Systems, is a Web page authoring program that allows Web developers to create, maintain, and manage professional Web sites. (685)
   a. Ajax
   b. Flash
   c. Expression Web
   d. Dreamweaver

8. The concept of packaging data and procedures into a single object is called _____. (689)
   a. object code
   b. encapsulation
   c. an object program
   d. a control structure

STUDENT ASSIGNMENTS

Checkpoint

Matching

Match the terms with their definitions.

_____ 1. Java (670)
_____ 2. C++ (671)
_____ 3. F# (671)
_____ 4. 4GL (674)
_____ 5. macro (676)
_____ 6. PHP (682)
_____ 7. API (684)
_____ 8. pretest (690)
_____ 9. posttest (690)
_____ 10. code review (694)

a. collection of tools that programmers use to interact with an environment such as a Web site or operating system
b. process of testing a condition at the end of a loop
c. series of statements that instructs an application how to complete a task
d. object-oriented extension of the C programming language
e. free, open source scripting language
f. process of programmers, quality control testers, and/or peers reviewing code in order to locate and fix errors so that the final programs work correctly
g. object-oriented language that uses a just-in-time compiler
h. process of testing a condition at the beginning of a loop
i. nonprocedural language that enables users and programmers to access data in a database
j. combines the benefits of an object-oriented language and a functional language

Short Answer

Write a brief answer to each of the following questions.

1. How is a compiler different from an interpreter? ____________ What is the advantage, and disadvantage, of an interpreter? ____________
2. What is a major benefit of OOP? ____________ How is RAD (rapid application development) used for developing software? ____________
3. What is included in an integrated development environment? ____________ Describe the programming languages in the Visual Studio suite. ____________
4. How is XML used? ____________ Describe two applications of XML. ____________
5. Describe two activities performed by the programmer when documenting a solution. ____________ Why is proper documentation important? ____________

Beyond the Book

Follow the book element instructions below; present your findings (brief report, presentation, discussion, or other means).

1. Ethics & Issues — Select an Ethics & Issues in this chapter (677, 681, 688, 696), find a recent newspaper/magazine article that supports one point of view presented, and then evaluate the article.
2. Computer Usage @ Work — Use the Web or a recent newspaper/magazine to locate three additional unique usages of computer technology in manufacturing (697). What makes the use of these technologies unique to manufacturing?
3. Companies on the Cutting Edge and Technology Trailblazers — Use the Web or a recent newspaper/magazine to locate an interesting fact about Electronic Arts (EA), Sun Microsystems, Alan Kay, or James Gosling that was not presented in the chapter (699).
4. High-Tech Talk — Locate a recent newspaper/magazine article that discusses topics related to Acid3 Browser Test (698). Would you recommend the article you found? Why or why not?
5. FAQs and Web Links — Use the Web or a recent newspaper/magazine to locate three additional facts about an FAQ (675, 680, 683, 694, 697) and Web Link (668, 670, 671, 677, 679, 682, 683, 684, 689, 692, 696) that were not presented in the chapter.
6. Looking Ahead — Use the Web or a recent newspaper/magazine to discover additional uses of the technology presented in Selecting Programming Languages with Long Lives (675).
7. Innovative Computing — Use the Web or a recent newspaper/magazine to locate two additional interesting facts about Online Calculators Answer Life's Questions (668) or View the World from Your Computer (684).
8. Making Use of the Web — Visit three of the Health sites (137) and outline the information on each Web site and the possible uses for each Web site.
9. Web 2.0 Program Development — Read the Web 2.0 Programming Development feature (712). Use the Web or a magazine article to research other Web 2.0 program development tools.

Learn It Online

The Learn It Online exercises are interactive Web exercises designed to reinforce and expand your understanding of the chapter concepts. The descriptions below briefly summarize each exercise.

To complete the Learn It Online exercises, visit the Computer Concepts CourseMate Web site at www.cengagebrain.com, navigate to the Chapter 13 resources for this book, click the link for the exercise you want to complete, and then read the instructions.

1 At the Movies — Electronic Arts Going Mobile
Watch a movie to learn about how Electronic Arts is tackling the mobile video game market and then answer questions about the movie.

2 Video and Audio: You Review It — Web 2.0
Search for, choose, and write a review of a video, podcast, or vodcast that discusses Web 2.0.

3 Student Edition Labs — Visual Programming and Creating Web Pages
Enhance your understanding and knowledge about visual programming and creating Web pages by completing the Visual Programming and Creating Web Pages Labs.

4 Practice Test
Take a multiple choice test that checks your knowledge of the chapter concepts and review the resulting study guide.

5 Who Wants To Be a Computer Genius²?
Play the Shelly Cashman Series version of this popular game by answering questions to find out if you are a computer genius. Panic buttons are available to provide assistance during game play.

6 Wheel of Terms
Identify important key terms presented in this chapter by playing the Shelly Cashman Series version of this popular game.

7 You're Hired!
Embark on the path to a career in computers by answering questions and solving puzzles related to concepts discussed in this chapter.

8 Crossword Puzzle Challenge
Complete an interactive crossword puzzle to reinforce concepts presented in this chapter.

9 Windows Exercises
Step through the Windows 7 exercises to learn about searching for executable files, using the Movie Box Office simulation, adjusting keyboard speed, and using the Loan Payment Calculator.

10 Exploring Computer Careers
Read about a career as a programmer, search for related employment advertisements, and then answer related questions.

11 Web Apps — Google Earth
Learn how to download and use Google Earth on your computer, fly to your neighborhood and zoom in, view satellite images of your favorite nearby businesses, and show and hide various layers.

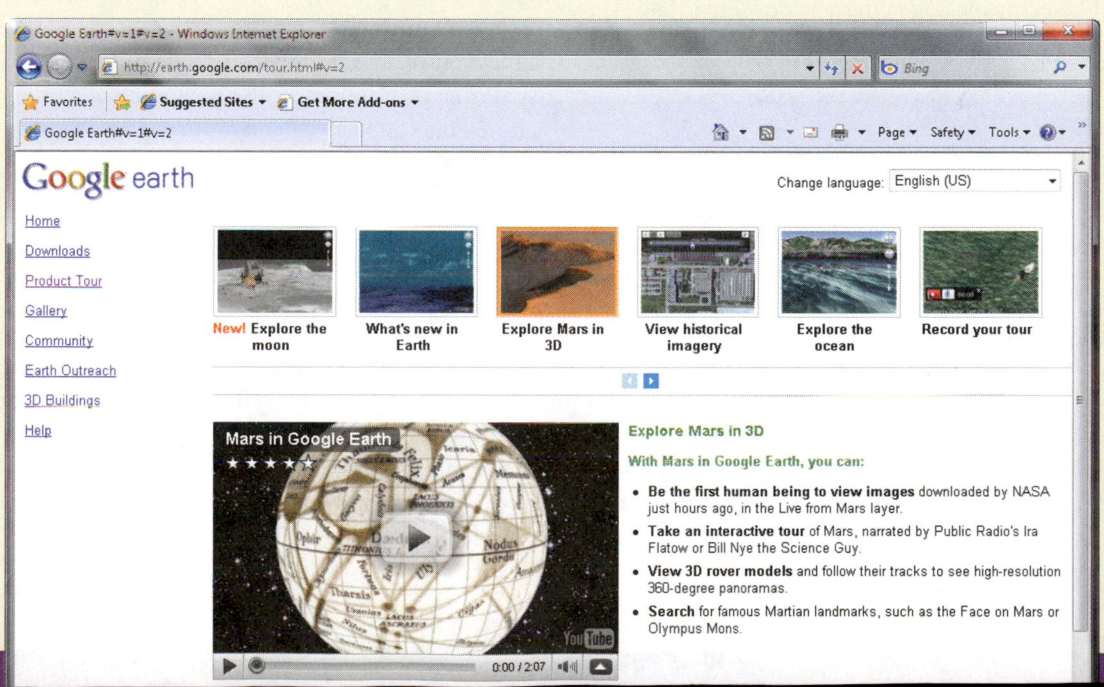

STUDENT ASSIGNMENTS

Problem Solving @ Home

The Problem Solving @ Home exercises extend your knowledge of the chapter concepts by seeking solutions to practical computer problems that you may encounter at home or school. The Collaboration exercise should be completed with a team.

In the real world, practical problems often can be solved in multiple ways. Provide one solution to each of the following problems using available resources, such as articles on the Web or in print, blogs, podcasts, videos, television, user guides, other individuals, and electronics and computer stores. You may need to use multiple resources to obtain an answer. Present your solutions in the form requested by your instructor (brief report, presentation, discussion, or other means).

1. **Incorrect Program Starts** In an attempt to open a Microsoft Word document, you double-click the document's associated icon. Instead of the document opening in Microsoft Word, however, it opens in WordPad and displays many unrecognizable characters. What might have caused this?
2. **Problem with Macro** You created a macro in one document and made it available to other documents on your computer. When you run the macro in another document, however, it does not function properly. What might be wrong?
3. **Nonfunctional Web Page** Your friend found a Web page containing classic arcade games that you played many years ago. Instead of sending you the Web address, he saved the Web page and sent it to you as an e-mail attachment. When you open the attachment on your computer, the Web page displays, but the games do not work. What might have caused this?
4. **Web Page Syntax Error** When you attempt to display a Web page, an error message appears and the Web page does not display properly on your screen. The error message cites a syntax error and asks you if you would like to debug. How will you respond?
5. **Web Browser Differences** The Internet Explorer and Firefox Web browsers both are installed on your computer, although you primarily use Internet Explorer to view Web pages. When you view your favorite Web page using Firefox instead of Internet Explorer, the Web page does not appear the same. Why does the same Web page appear differently on the two browsers?
6. **Underlined Code** While writing a program in Visual Basic, you notice that some portions of your code are underlined in red. What might be causing this?
7. **Unexplained E-Mail Message** After filling out a form on a Web page, you attempt to submit it. Upon clicking the Submit button, however, the Windows Mail program starts on your computer and displays a new, blank e-mail message that is addressed to an e-mail address you do not recognize. In addition, the e-mail message appears to have a file attached to it. What might be causing this?
8. **Requirements Not Met** While attempting to install the latest version of Windows on your computer, a message displays informing you that your computer does not meet the minimum system requirements. What are your next steps?
9. **Program Will Not Run** You have written a program to help keep track of your calorie intake. When attempting to run the program for the first time, you receive an error message indicating a syntax error. You review the program code and are unable to locate the error. What are your next steps?

Collaboration

10. **Upgrade Options** Your company has outgrown one of its existing custom software packages and needs to update the existing custom software, purchase new custom software, or purchase packaged software. You know from your computer concepts course that each option has advantages and disadvantages. Form a team of three classmates. One team member should research the advantages and disadvantages of updating the existing software, another team member should research the advantages and disadvantages of purchasing new custom software, and the last team member should research the advantages and disadvantages of purchasing new packaged software. Discuss your findings as a team, compile them into a report, and submit the report to your instructor.

Problem Solving @ Work

The Problem Solving @ Work exercises extend your knowledge of the chapter concepts by seeking solutions to practical computer problems that you may encounter at work. The Collaboration exercise should be completed with a team.

In the real world, practical problems often can be solved in multiple ways. Provide one solution to each of the following problems using available resources, such as articles on the Web or in print, blogs, podcasts, videos, television, user guides, other individuals, and electronics and computer stores. You may need to use multiple resources to obtain an answer. Present your solutions in the form requested by your instructor (brief report, presentation, discussion, or other means).

1. **Enabling and Disabling Macros** While opening a Microsoft Excel workbook, a message displays on the screen asking if you would like to enable or disable macros. You do not recall adding macros to your workbook. How will you respond?
2. **Problem Installing Custom Program** After using an application generator to create a program, you save it on a USB flash drive and give the USB flash drive to your colleague so that she can install the program on her computer. She claims, however, that the program does not work on her computer. Why might the program work on your computer, but not on her computer?
3. **Program Appears Frozen** The human resources department has just released a new program used to calculate payroll for each employee. After you enter the payroll data for each employee, you click a button to calculate everyone's pay for that pay period. After clicking the button, the program becomes unresponsive and appears frozen. What might be wrong?
4. **Database Connection Problem** You have just written a program that connects to your organization's database to retrieve customer information. When you start the program, an error message is displayed stating that there is a problem connecting to the database. What might be causing this?
5. **Unknown Language** Several years ago, a programmer who no longer is with the company wrote a program for your company using an older programming language. Your colleague has discovered a bug in the program, but nobody knows the language to be able to fix the bug. What are your options?
6. **Interface Not Intuitive** The users at work complain that the user interface in your new program is not intuitive. What might have caused this? What are your next steps?

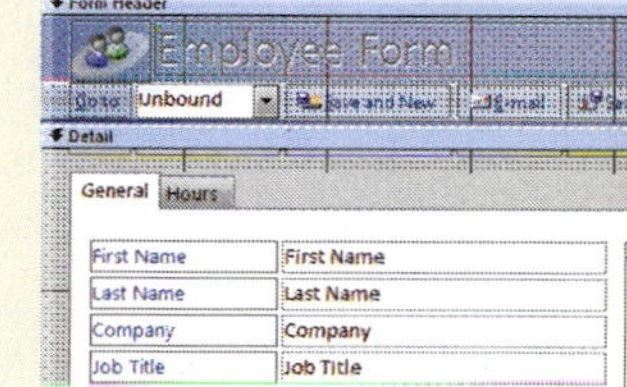

7. **Cannot Change Web Site** You are modifying your company's Web site using a text editor. When you click the Save button to save your changes, the changes are not reflected on the live Web site. What might be wrong?
8. **Old Macro** You discover that a macro you wrote using an older version of Microsoft Word does not work in the newest version of Word. What are your next steps?
9. **Control Structures** While writing a program, you must decide which control structure to use to determine whether an employee has worked overtime. Which control structure will you use, and why?

Collaboration

10. **Computers in Manufacturing** Today, computers are used in the manufacturing of nearly every type of item. Your instructor would like everyone to realize the importance of computers in today's society and requests that each person find an item and determine how computers might have been used to assist in the manufacturing process. Form a team of three people. Each team member should locate one item that he or she believes was manufactured with the help of a computer. Then, team members should research exactly how computers were used and record their findings. Finally, the three team members should compare their research to discover similarities and differences and then compile their findings into a brief report.

STUDENT ASSIGNMENTS

Learn How To

The Learn How To activities step you through fundamental technology skills when using a computer. The Learn How To exercises enable you to become more proficient with these skills.

Learn How To 1: Design and/or Evaluate a Graphical User Interface (GUI)

In most cases, when you interact with a program or a Web site, you are looking at and responding to a graphical user interface (GUI). Often, your ability to use the program or Web site effectively will depend on the design of the GUI. If it is easy to use and follow, your experience will be productive and enjoyable. Conversely, if you have to struggle to figure out how to enter data or which button to click, the GUI is defeating the purpose of the program.

Modern program designers spend 25 percent to 40 percent of their time creating and perfecting the user interface, sometimes called the presentation layer of a program. They do this because they realize the importance of user interaction with the program. If the user interface is not productive and easy to use, the user will not be satisfied with the program regardless of how well it does its work.

The user interface includes both the graphics and text shown on the screen, as well as the methods a user can use to interact with the software and cause operations to occur. Three primary means of interacting in a user interface are the keyboard, a pointing device such as a mouse, and voice input. The correct use of these tools significantly will increase the success of a user interface.

The ultimate goal of a user interface is to allow a user to interact with the interface and the underlying program in an intuitive and familiar way. If the user must stop and think how to use the interface, then the interface has failed. Therefore, if you are designing a user interface for a program, or merely evaluating a program and its user interface, you should apply a variety of guidelines to a user interface to determine its usability, including the following:

1. Using the interface should feel natural and normal. This requirement means the software developer must be aware of who the user is and the manner in which the user is accustomed to working. For example, the interface for a banking program where a teller is entering account information will be different from that of a graphic arts program that allows manipulation of graphics and photos. Both must reflect the needs of the user.
2. A graphical user interface offers a wide variety of elements (Figure 13-41), many of which can be used for similar purposes. A good user interface uses the most appropriate element for each requirement. In addition, once an element is used for a particular purpose, such as a button being used to cause a particular action, then that same element should be used for the same purpose through the program interface.
3. The elements must be arranged in the sequence in which they are used so that the user is able to move from item to item on the screen in a logical, straightforward manner. This requirement once again requires the designer to understand the needs of the user. When this rule is not followed, a confusing interface can occur (Figure 13-42). If it is followed, however, the interface is clear and easy to use (Figure 13-43).
4. The interface should be kept as simple as possible, while containing all the functionality required for the program. Generally, the simpler the interface, the more effective the interface will be.

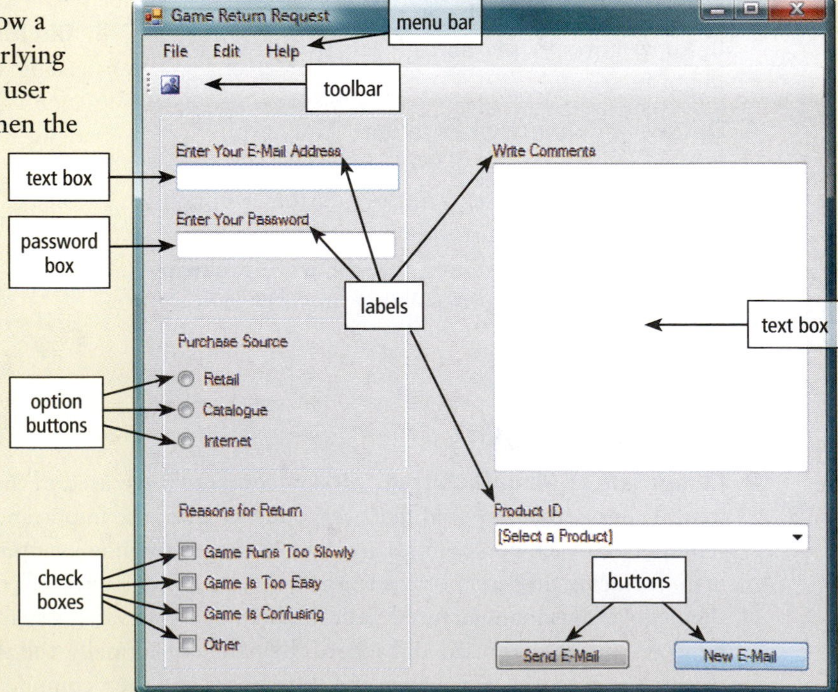

Figure 13-41

Learn How To

5. When implemented, the user interface should be intuitive, which means the user should be able to use it with little or no instruction. In fact, the user should feel that no other interface could have been designed because the one they are using is the most "natural."

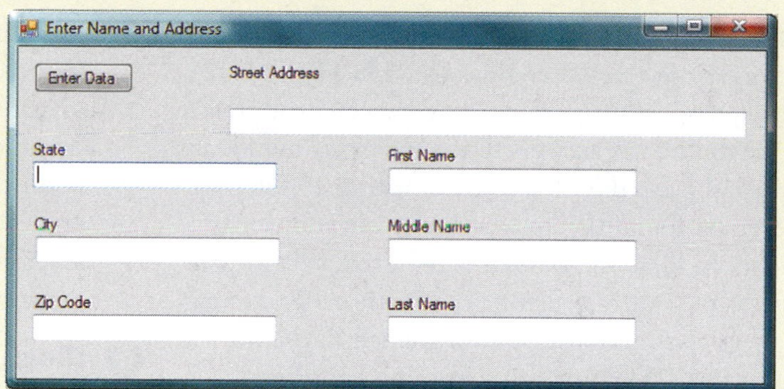

Figure 13-42

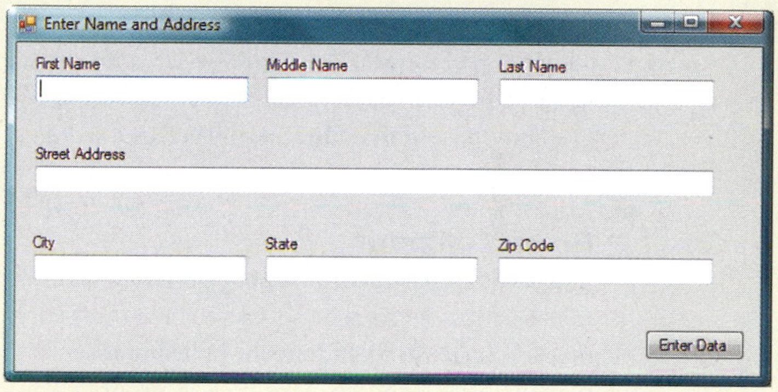

Implementing the Interface

In most cases, a graphical user interface is designed using a visual programming environment such as Visual Studio. This product allows the developer to place the GUI elements on a form, which becomes the window when the program runs. Often, the developer will produce a prototype interface, in which the elements are placed in the window but few of them are functional. This prototype allows the user to see and "feel" the interface well before the program is ready for actual implementation. Then, the users can provide feedback to the developer regarding their likes and dislikes. The developer will make adjustments, or sometimes whole new designs, to meet the needs of the users. This process can occur multiple times until the users are satisfied with the GUI design.

Figure 13-43

Evaluating Application Software

One important factor when you are a user or purchaser of software is your analysis of the user interface. As you evaluate software, it is critical to remember that the user interface is as important as the functions the software performs. If you cannot use the software effectively through the user interface, then no matter how wonderful the functions of the software might be, the software cannot be useful to you.

Exercises

1. Start three different programs from three different application software developers. For example, you could start a program from Microsoft, one from Apple, and one from Adobe. What similarities do you find in the user interface for each of these programs? What differences do you observe? Does one use color more than the others? Are different fonts used? Which do you find most effective? Why? If you had to choose one interface, which one would you choose? Why? Submit your answers to your instructor.
2. Web sites also should follow the principles of good user interface design. Visit three different sites where you can make purchases, including at least one airline site where you can make an airline reservation. Without actually buying anything (unless you want to), evaluate the procedures you had to follow in order to make the reservation or purchase. Which was the easiest to use? Which was the most difficult? Why? Did the usefulness of the user interface on the Web site influence whether you would use the Web site again? Why? Submit your answers to your instructor.
3. While both the Apple Mac OS and Windows interfaces are GUIs, they differ considerably. Conduct some common operations, such as starting and quitting a program, copying and pasting, and deleting on both a Windows computer and an Apple computer. How does using each of the interfaces differ? (Remember that the mouse is part of the user interface.) Also, start the same program, such as Microsoft Word or Adobe Photoshop, on both a Windows computer and an Apple computer. What differences between the program interfaces do you observe? Which interface do you prefer? Why? Submit your answers to your instructor.

STUDENT ASSIGNMENTS

Web Research

The Web Research exercises broaden your understanding of the chapter concepts by presenting questions that require you to search the Web for answers.

1 Search Sleuth

Use one of the search engines listed in Figure 2-10 in Chapter 2 on page 85 or your own favorite search engine to find the answers to the following questions. Copy and paste the Web address from the Web page where you found the answer. Some questions may have more than one answer. If required, submit your answers to your instructor. (1) Which programming language uses a mouse pointer shaped in the form of a turtle? (2) Which programming language did David Heinemeier Hansson create in 2003? (3) What is the purpose of a browser sniffer? (4) Which programming language was developed from a language called Oak? (5) Which topics are discussed in the first three articles listed in the News section of the W3C Web site?

2 Green Computing

The U.S. Department of Energy has determined that businesses and schools can reduce their energy consumption up to 20 percent by using asset management software. This type of program can determine energy consumption and then ensure appliances and electronic devices are operating at peak efficiency with the lowest operating costs. Visit the Web sites of several companies that have developed asset management software, including Infor (infor.com/goinggreen), Amitec Ltd. (amitec-g.com), and IBM (www-01.ibm.com/software/tivoli), and locate information about the monitoring programs. Which companies and colleges have installed this software? How does the software monitor current energy use and then measure the organization's carbon footprint? How often are the intervals set to take readings and then evaluate the data? Write a report summarizing your findings, and include a table of links to Web sites that provide additional details.

3 Social Networking

Members of online social communities face the responsibility to act civilly and follow proper etiquette rules. *The Ultimate Social Media Etiquette Handbook*, which is posted on the techipedia Web site, states the rules for managing and maintaining online social relationships. In addition, several experts offer advice, including Philipp Lenssen (antispamnews.com), Tim O'Reilly (radar.oreilly.com), and Reihan Salam (slate.com/id/2174439). Read their columns and view the techipedia Web site (techipedia.com/social-media-etiquette-handbook) to learn about the best practices to follow when participating in online social networks. How should a networker create a personalized message? How can a sender's background information be verified? When is sharing contact lists considered appropriate? Summarize the information you read and viewed.

4 Blogs

Space exploration, comets, telescopes, the International Space Station, and astrophotography are popular blogging subjects. Enthusiasts ranging from NASA astronauts (blogs.nasa.gov) to backyard astronomers (tomsastroblog.com) share their discoveries and experiences on a variety of topics. Visit these blogs along with Jonathan's Space Report (planet4589.org/jsr.html), NASA Watch (nasawatch.com), Russian Space Web (russianspaceweb.com), Space Daily (spacedaily.com), and The Write Stuff (blogs.orlandosentinel.com/news_space_thewritestuff). What are three of the more recent topics? Which images of the moon, Mars, or stars from the Hubble Space Telescope are featured? What new discoveries have been made? When is the next launch at the Kennedy Space Center? Summarize the information you read and viewed.

5 Ethics in Action

The world's largest conference for hackers, DEF CON, is held each year in Las Vegas. Attendees include experts in the fields of programming, computer security, and law enforcement. Members of Hackers for Planet Earth (HOPE), the Chaos Computer Club (CCC), and the Hacktic Network promote ethical hacking to develop software that increases freedom of expression. Visit these hackers' Web sites and read about their conferences and pursuits. Which topics do they discuss in their forums? Who are considered "true hackers"? Should some hackers be exonerated if their efforts are done with a greater purpose, such as furthering a political concern? Write a report summarizing your findings, and include a table of links to Web sites that provide additional details about hackers.

Critical Thinking

The Critical Thinking exercises challenge your assessment and decision-making skills by presenting real-world situations associated with the chapter concepts. The Collaboration exercise should be completed with a team.

To evaluate the situations below, use personal experiences and available resources such as articles on the Web or in print, blogs, podcasts, videos, television, user guides, other individuals, and electronics and computer stores. You may need to use multiple resources to form conclusions and make recommendations.

1. Class Discussion — Evaluating Macro Use As administrative assistant for the president of a local marketing company, you spend much of your time using application software, such as Word, Excel, Outlook, and Access. Your manager asked you to evaluate the use of macros to automate some of the repetitive tasks in the word processing work you do. Discuss two examples of common repetitive tasks in word processing that are not already available via buttons or commands. Include in your discussion the definition of a macro, how a macro automates a routine, what is involved in creating a macro, and how to invoke a macro.

2. Class Presentation — Evaluating Object-Oriented Programming You manage the information technology department at National Insurance, a worldwide insurance company that specializes in high-risk policies. For the past 40 years, the company has used COBOL, a procedural language, to develop new systems, such as payroll, accounts receivable, and accounts payable. Because of extensive maintenance over the years, the programs have become sluggish and difficult to maintain. Your department is about to begin a five-year major overhaul of all the current systems. Your senior advisors in the department have recommended that the company move to an object-oriented language to replace the current systems. You are not sure that this is best for the company. Use the Web and/or print media to research the advantages and disadvantages of object-oriented programming. Use your findings to create a presentation that addresses the following questions: How difficult is it for procedural language programmers and system analysts to switch to an object-oriented language? Which is easier to implement, systems implemented in a procedural language or an object-oriented language? Why? Which would you recommend for your company?

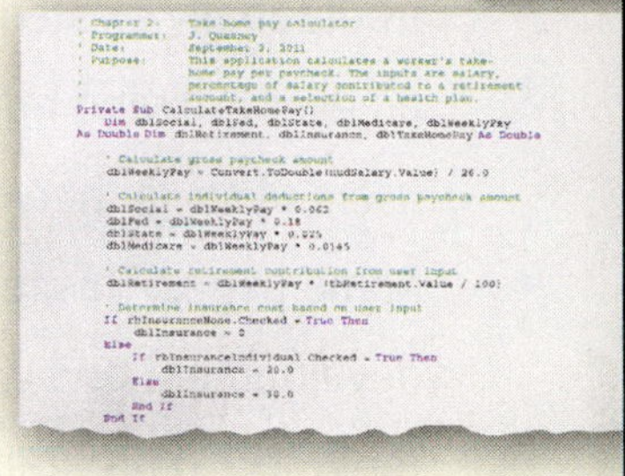

3. Research — Programming in the Future Just a decade ago, computer programs consisting of 5,000 lines of code were considered long. Today, programs can contain millions of lines of code. What will computer programming be like in the future? Some experts see such trends as continued movement toward object-oriented languages, greater participation in programming by computer users, and computers taking a more active part in programming themselves. Using the Web and/ or print media, research recent developments in programming and the impact these developments will have on the future of programming. Prepare a report on what you think programming will be like in 10 years. Be sure to address the following questions in your report: How will programming be different from what it is today? Who will be doing the programming? How will they be programming? What effect might developments in computer hardware have on programming?

Collaboration

4. Proper Interface Design Your company is moving to an electronic time card system that allows employees to electronically record their work hours. These hours then are sent to the payroll manager, who verifies the hours and processes the direct deposit. Your manager wants the interface to be intuitive so that employees easily can record their hours by the end of the pay period. Form a team of three people. One team member should identify the requirements for the interface that employees will use to record their hours. Another team member should interview at least three people and ask them how the interface best can be designed so that they can record their hours easily and accurately. The third team member should use the data from the other two team members to sketch the interface. Compile your findings and sketch into a brief report and then submit it to your instructor.

Web 2.0 Program Development

ALMOST ANY PROGRAM existing in a desktop environment can be made available as a Web application. Web 2.0 program development requires specialized tools and skills to provide Web users with programs that traditionally existed on the desktop. Web 2.0 developers always consider that their programs must be delivered to an ever-growing number of Web browsers, mobile devices, and even other Web applications (Figure 1). Everyday users of social networking Web sites may engage in Web 2.0 programming as they customize features of their home pages. This feature provides an overview of how Web 2.0 development differs from traditional program development and Web page development, and how developers take advantage of the tools and techniques used for Web 2.0 program development.

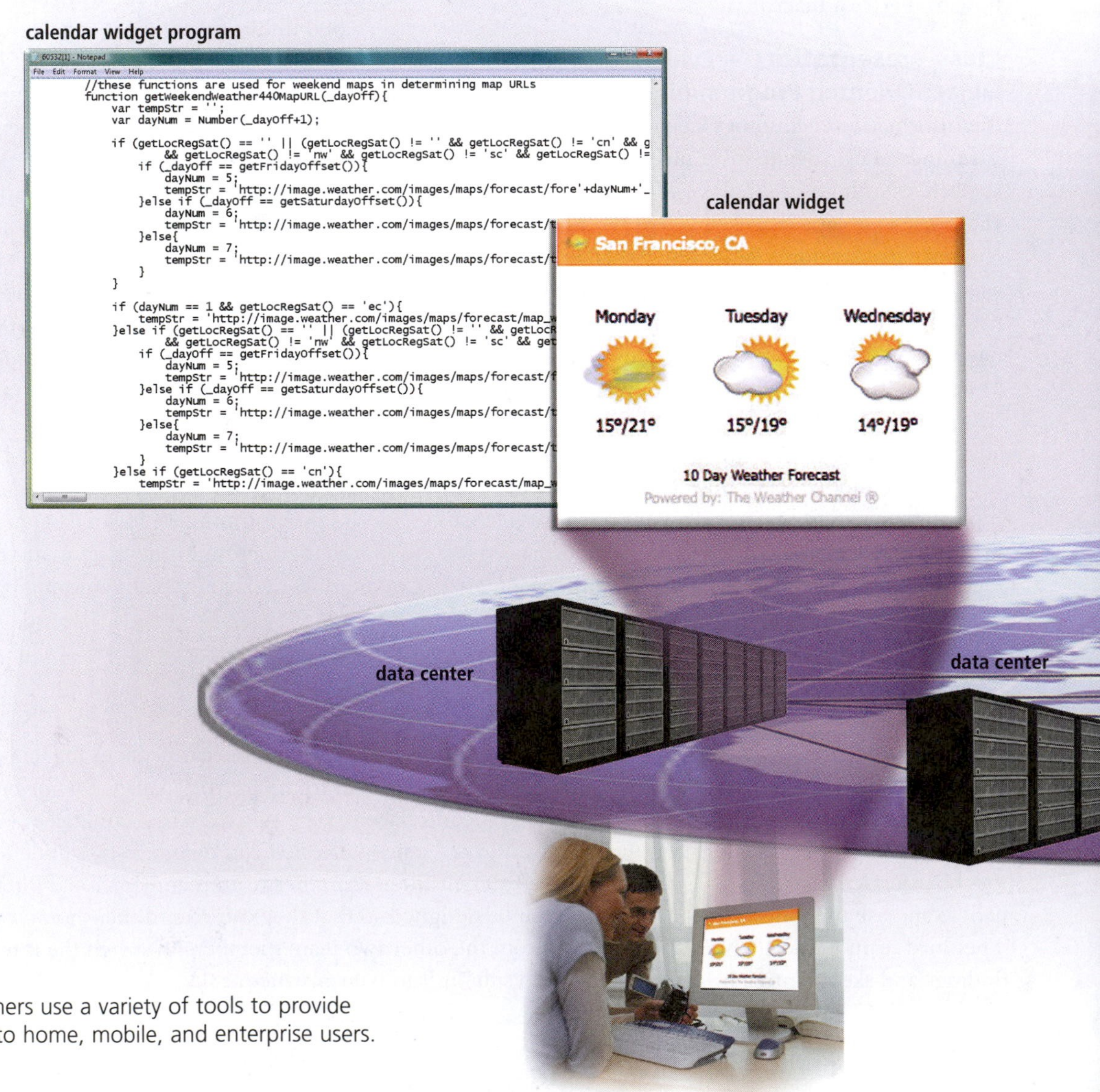

Figure 1 Programmers use a variety of tools to provide Web 2.0 applications to home, mobile, and enterprise users.

One of the main advantages of Web 2.0 program development over traditional program development is portability. That is, a Web application runs in any Web browser that supports the basic technologies of Web applications, such as HTML and JavaScript. For example, a program designed to run on a PC running a Windows operating system would require considerable reprogramming if the developer of the application decides that it also must run on Apple's Macintosh operating system. The same software designed and programmed for a Web 2.0 environment would not require reprogramming because the software would be compatible with browsers available on both operating systems. Additionally, the developer often provides the Web application for a variety of mobile devices.

Web applications typically consist of three tiers. A *tier* is a major part of a Web application, each of which can exist in separate locations or together on a network.

- First tier: This tier includes the graphical user interface, which appears in the user's Web browser. The Web browser may exist on a variety of operating systems and mobile devices.
- Second tier: The application, or logic, tier exists on the Internet or Web server. For many Web applications, this tier exists in the cloud. In this usage, the term *cloud* often refers to a large network of servers that simultaneously host a Web application.
- Third tier: The database tier stores the data necessary for the Web application. For example, in a Web application designed to function as a word processing program, the database tier stores the user's word processing documents. This tier also may be stored in the cloud.

Web applications often incorporate other Web applications. The Web application being incorporated often is called a *widget*, or sometimes a *gadget*. For example, a developer creates an interactive calendar widget that allows users of the widget to create daily to-do lists. Other Web 2.0 developers reuse the calendar widget in their own Web applications when they need to provide their users with a calendar that tracks their own to-do lists.

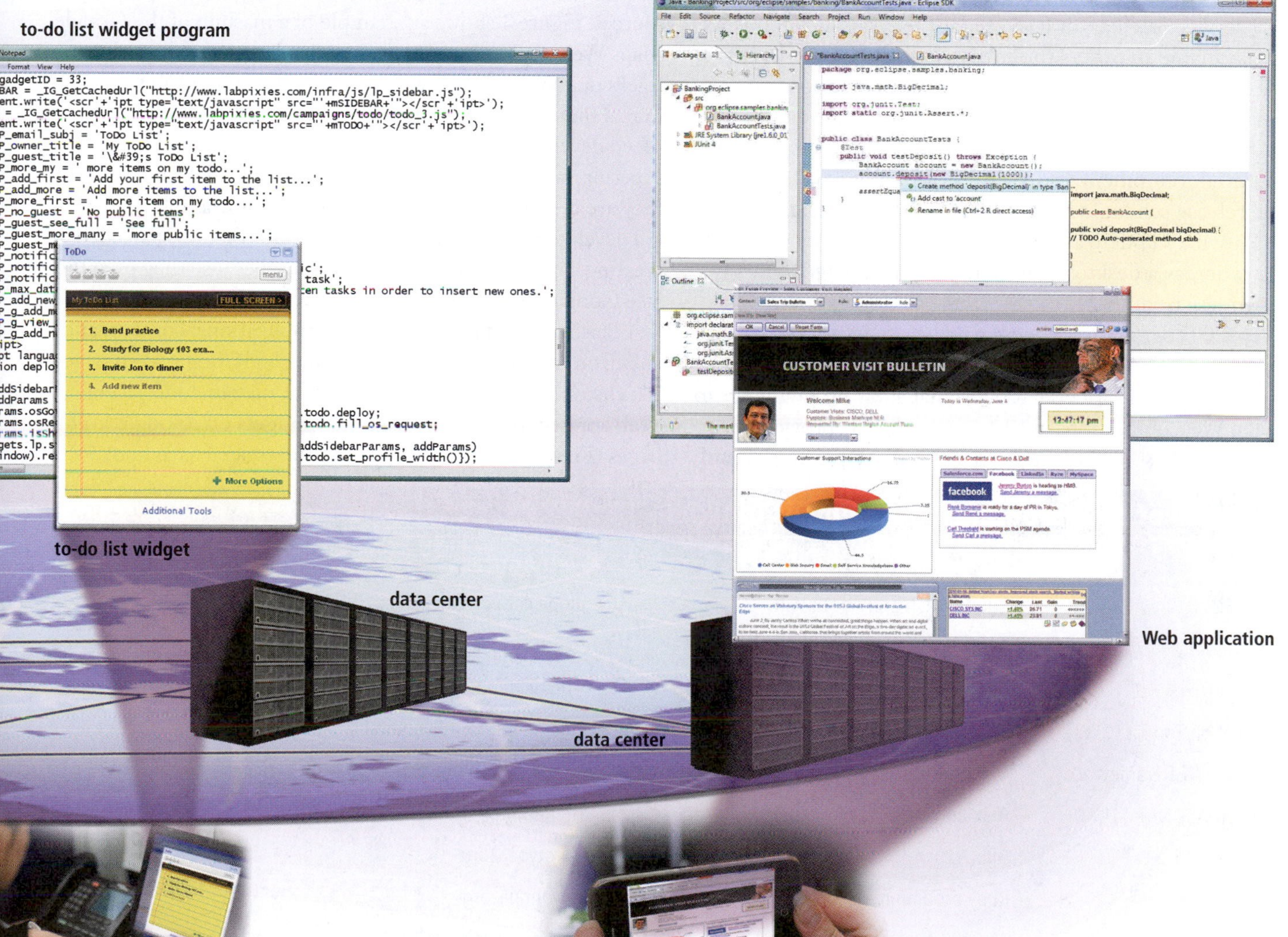

Web 2.0 Program Development Technologies

Web 2.0 program development differs from traditional Web page development mainly because it includes programming for graphical user interface elements that traditionally existed within desktop programs, such as drag-and-drop functionality and editing of Web page content. Many differences also exist between traditional desktop program development and Web 2.0 program development. Desktop programs typically are written for a single operating system, and the program code is guarded closely. Web 2.0 developers often provide the code or portions of the code for others to modify and reuse. Web 2.0 programmers design Web applications for use on multiple browsers in multiple operating systems, on mobile devices, and for syndication and mashups, which are discussed in detail in the next section. *Syndication* means that a service, such as an RSS feed, or Web application is made available to others for a fee or at no cost. For example, airlines create Web applications and syndicate them for others to incorporate the airline's flight schedules into their own Web applications. Another difference between desktop program development and Web 2.0 program development is the release schedule for new versions of the program. A company may update a Web application on a daily or weekly basis, whereas a desktop program may be updated annually or even less frequently.

Web 2.0 programmers choose whether to develop code in a text editor or to use a Web 2.0 program development toolkit. Vendors provide a variety of toolkits that allow programmers to develop Web applications quickly. Some toolkits provide programmers with sophisticated tools for code editing, testing and debugging, and deploying Web applications to Web servers. Figure 2 lists popular Web 2.0 program development toolkits. Many of the toolkits utilize Ajax (see page 684 in Chapter 13) to allow communications between the client and the Web server.

Web 2.0 Mashups and Social Networking

Web 2.0 developers often benefit from the work of other developers. One method for creating a Web application is to create a mashup. As previously described, a Web 2.0 mashup is a Web application that includes functionality, content, and data from other Web applications, content providers, and data sources. Figure 3 shows an example of a mashup of the Google Maps Web application and data from a health database that tracks ongoing public health concerns throughout the world in real time. Web 2.0 program developers create mashups to speed development time. They also create mashups to obtain superior data and services as compared to the data and services they are capable of creating themselves. For example, the Web 2.0 developers of the HealthMap mashup (Figure 3) avoided creating sophisticated mapping software because they used the free Google Maps functionality, content, and data.

A mashup often consists of Web applications, content, and data from many sources. For example, an iGoogle Web page is a customizable Web application that may include several Web applications, which are called gadgets on iGoogle Web pages (Figure 4). Other service providers such as Yahoo!

Examples of Web Program Development Toolkits

Toolkit	Technologies Used	Web Address
Adobe Flex	Adobe Flash and Adobe AIR	adobe.com/products/flex
Dojo	Ajax	dojotoolkit.org
Echo	Ajax	echo.nextapp.com/site
Google Web Toolkit (GWT)	Ajax	code.google.com/webtoolkit
Microsoft .NET Framework	Microsoft Visual Studio and .NET Framework	microsoft.com/net
Microsoft ASP.NET AJAX	Ajax and .NET Framework	asp.net/ajax
Prototype	Ajax	prototypejs.org
Ruby on Rails	Ruby programming language and Ajax	rubyonrails.org
TIBCO General Interface	Ajax	tibco.com/products/soa/composite-applications/ general-interface/default.jsp

Figure 2 Vendors provide a variety of Web 2.0 program development toolkits that help programmers speed development of Web applications.

and Microsoft Windows Live provide similar functionality. Additionally, iGoogle Web pages allow users to create additional tabs, each of which contains gadgets. A user may create a tab for news-related gadgets and another tab for game-related gadgets. You can create your own iGoogle Web page after signing up for a Google account.

Social networking sites often allow members to customize and create Web pages using Web 2.0 technologies. Third-party organizations often create widgets for use by members of social networking Web sites. Figure 5 shows a widget created by Amazon used in a Facebook member's home page, resulting in a mashup. Other examples of widgets include media players, RSS feeds (see page 92 in Chapter 2), and games. Social networking Web sites often provide toolkits to assist software developers in creating new widgets. They also often allow users to write their own programming code to customize their home pages. *User-as-developer* is a phrase that describes the notion of Web sites allowing users to add widgets/gadgets and new programming code to Web pages.

Figure 3 This HealthMap global disease alert map is a mashup of Google Maps and a database of real-time world health data.

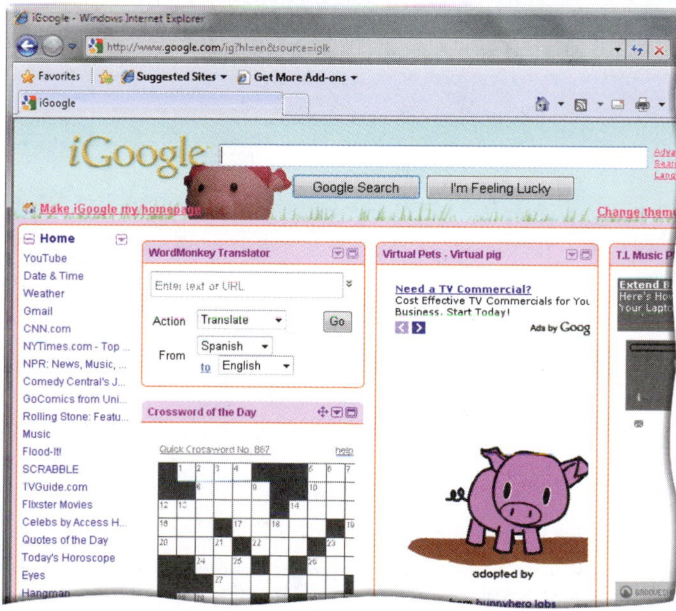

Figure 4 With iGoogle, users customize their Google home pages by choosing from thousands of gadgets.

Figure 5 Social networking Web site users increase their home pages' appeal by embedding widgets on their home pages.

Web 2.0 Program Development and the Cloud

Many organizations choose to deploy, or make available, their Web applications in a cloud computing environment, often referred to simply as the cloud. As previously defined, the term cloud can refer to a large network of servers that simultaneously host a Web 2.0 site. Distributing a Web application in the cloud means that the program developers do not require Web servers and specialists to manage the servers. The cloud provides the capability for a global presence because cloud computing environments often automatically and simultaneously distribute the Web applications to many servers throughout the world. Some cloud computing providers automatically increase available resources for a Web application when the Web application is in heavy demand. For example, if an online retailer distributes a Web application, such as an online store, in a cloud environment, and one of its products becomes a popular item, the cloud computing provider automatically increases the number of servers available to the retailer's Web application.

When working in a cloud computing environment, Web 2.0 developers must be attentive to security risks. The developer relies on the cloud computing provider to secure the Web application and, in many cases, the data needed for and generated by the Web application if the database tier also is located in the cloud. Developers also must be concerned with the reliability of a cloud computing provider. If a cloud computing provider encounters technical problems with their environment, then several thousand companies' Web applications could be at risk of becoming unavailable to users.

Using Web 2.0 Program Development Toolkits

Developers choose from a variety of toolkits and technologies when engaged in Web 2.0 program development. The following figures show how a programmer may develop two Web applications using two different tools. Figure 6 shows the development of a widget using the *Google Web Toolkit* (GWT). Figure 7 shows the development of a Web application using Microsoft's *ASP.NET AJAX* tools.

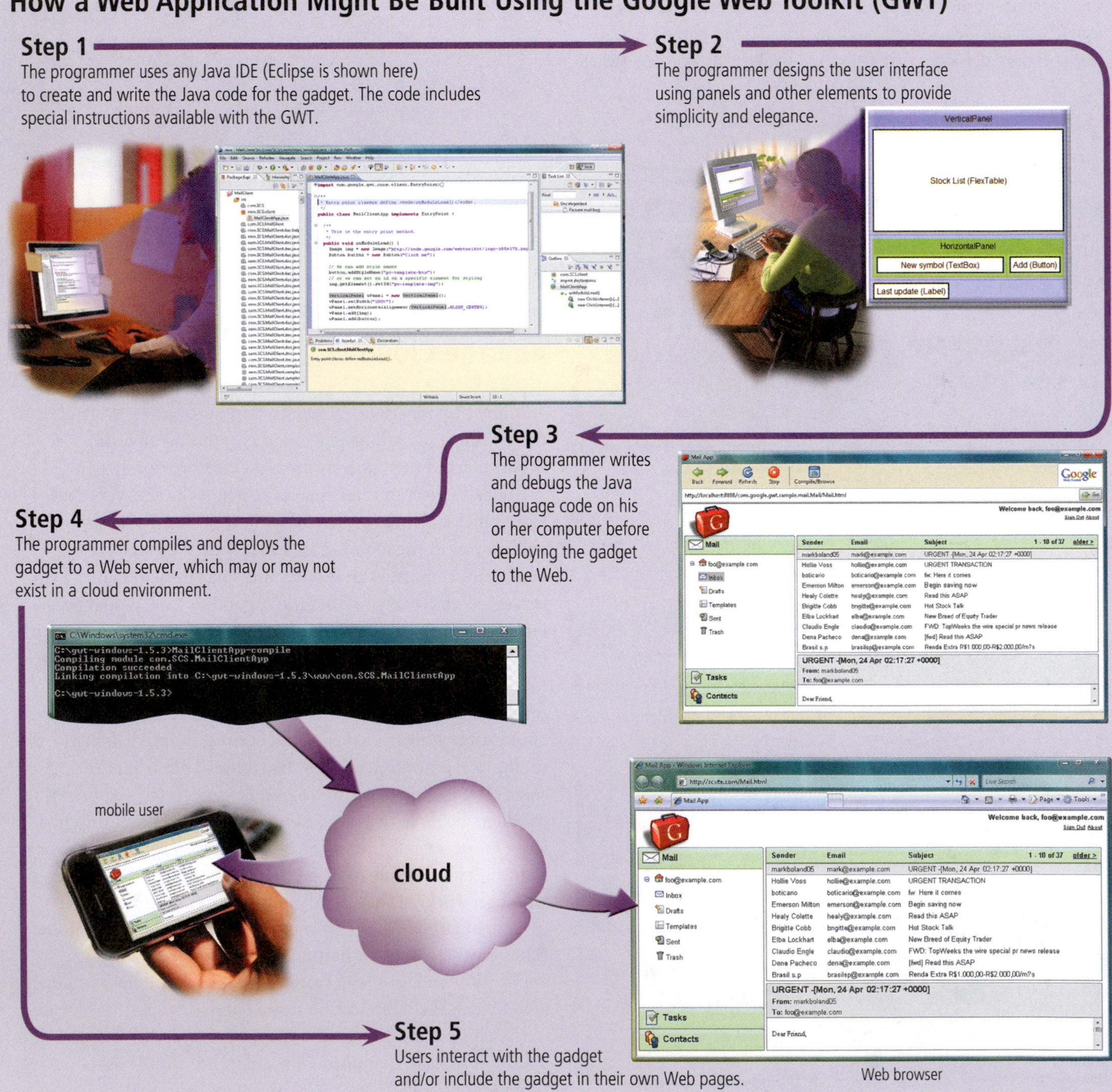

Figure 6 This figure shows how a Web application might be built using the Google Web Toolkit (GWT).

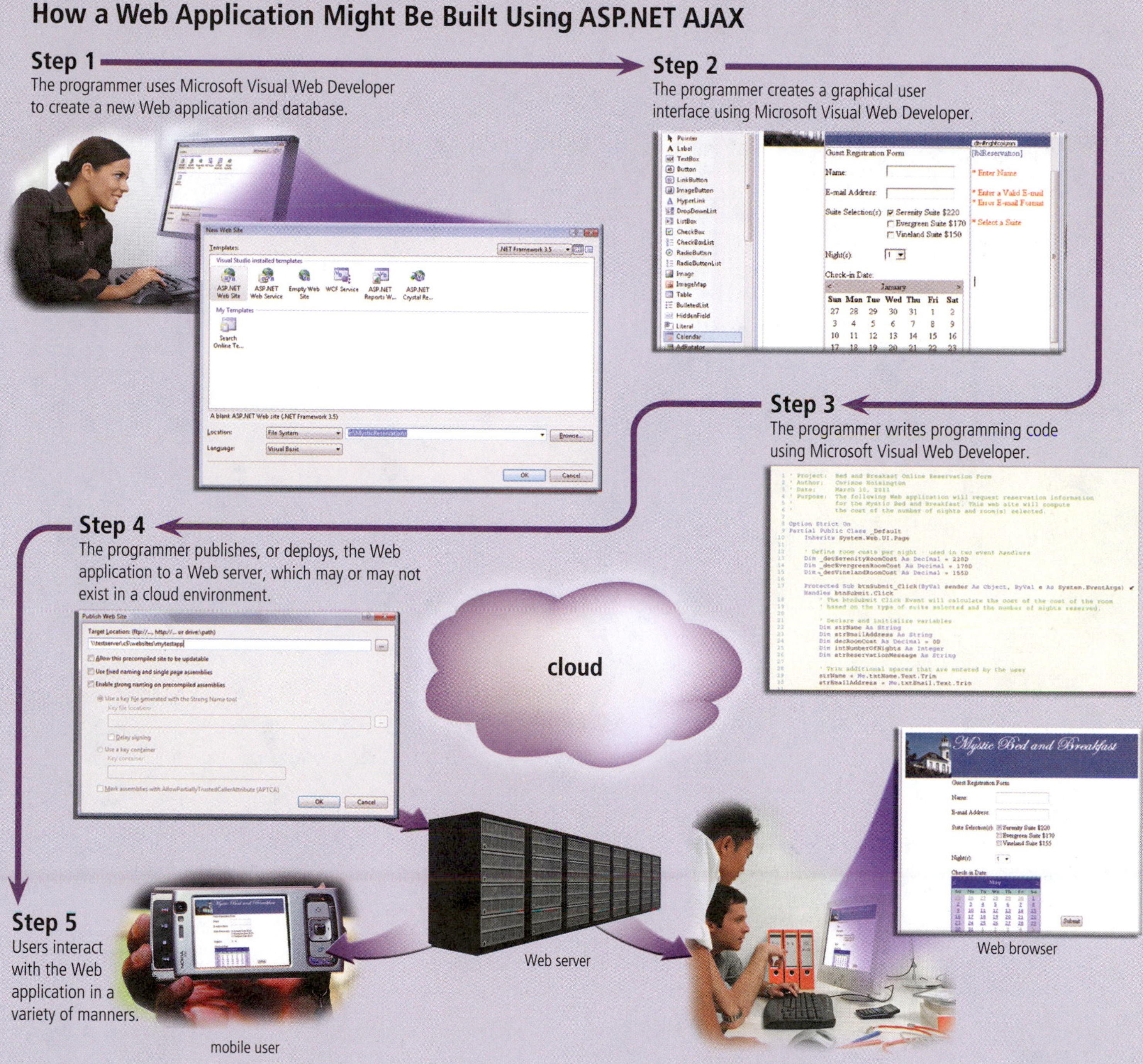

Figure 7 This figure shows how a Web application might be built using ASP.NET AJAX.

Web 2.0 Program Development: Summary

As Web applications increase in number and complexity, Web 2.0 program developers who want their Web applications to succeed make many critical decisions, including whether to use a popular toolkit or not use a toolkit at all, whether to allow others to modify and/or reuse their Web applications, whether to deploy their Web applications in the cloud, and how to manage security. With the information provided in this feature, you can begin your adventure as a Web 2.0 program developer.

Chapter Fourteen

Enterprise Computing

Objectives

After completing this chapter, you will be able to:

1. Discuss the special information requirements of an enterprise-sized corporation
2. Identify information systems and software used in the functional units of an enterprise: accounting and financial systems, human resources information systems, employee relationship management systems, computer-aided design, computer-aided engineering, computer-aided manufacturing, computer-integrated manufacturing, material requirements planning, quality control systems, marketing information systems, sales force automation, distribution systems, customer interaction management software, Web site management programs, and security software
3. Describe and list general purpose and integrated information systems used throughout an enterprise: office information systems, transaction processing systems, management information systems, decision support systems, expert systems, customer relationship management systems, enterprise resource planning systems, and content management systems
4. Describe and list types of technologies used throughout an enterprise: portals, data warehouses, communications, extranets, Web services, service-oriented architecture, document management systems, workflow, and virtual private networks
5. Describe virtualization, cloud computing, and grid computing
6. Discuss the computer hardware needs and solutions for an enterprise: RAID, network attached storage, storage area networks, enterprise storage systems, blade servers, and thin clients
7. Discuss high availability, scalability, and interoperability
8. Determine why computer backup is important and how it is accomplished
9. Discuss the steps in a disaster recovery plan

What Is Enterprise Computing?

The term, **enterprise**, commonly describes a business or venture of any size. In this chapter, the term enterprise refers to large multinational corporations, universities, hospitals, research laboratories, and government organizations. **Enterprise computing** involves the use of computers in networks, such as LANs and WANs, or a series of interconnected networks that encompass a variety of different operating systems, protocols, and network architectures.

Enterprises produce and gather enormous volumes of information about customer, supplier, and employee activity. The information flows among an assortment of entities both inside and outside of the enterprise, and users consume the information during a number of activities (Figure 14-1). Customers, suppliers, and employees interact with the enterprise in a number of ways, and computers track each interaction. Each sale of a product, purchase of a piece of equipment, or paycheck generates activity involving information systems. A *small- and medium-sized business* (*SMB*) is smaller in size than an enterprise and typically

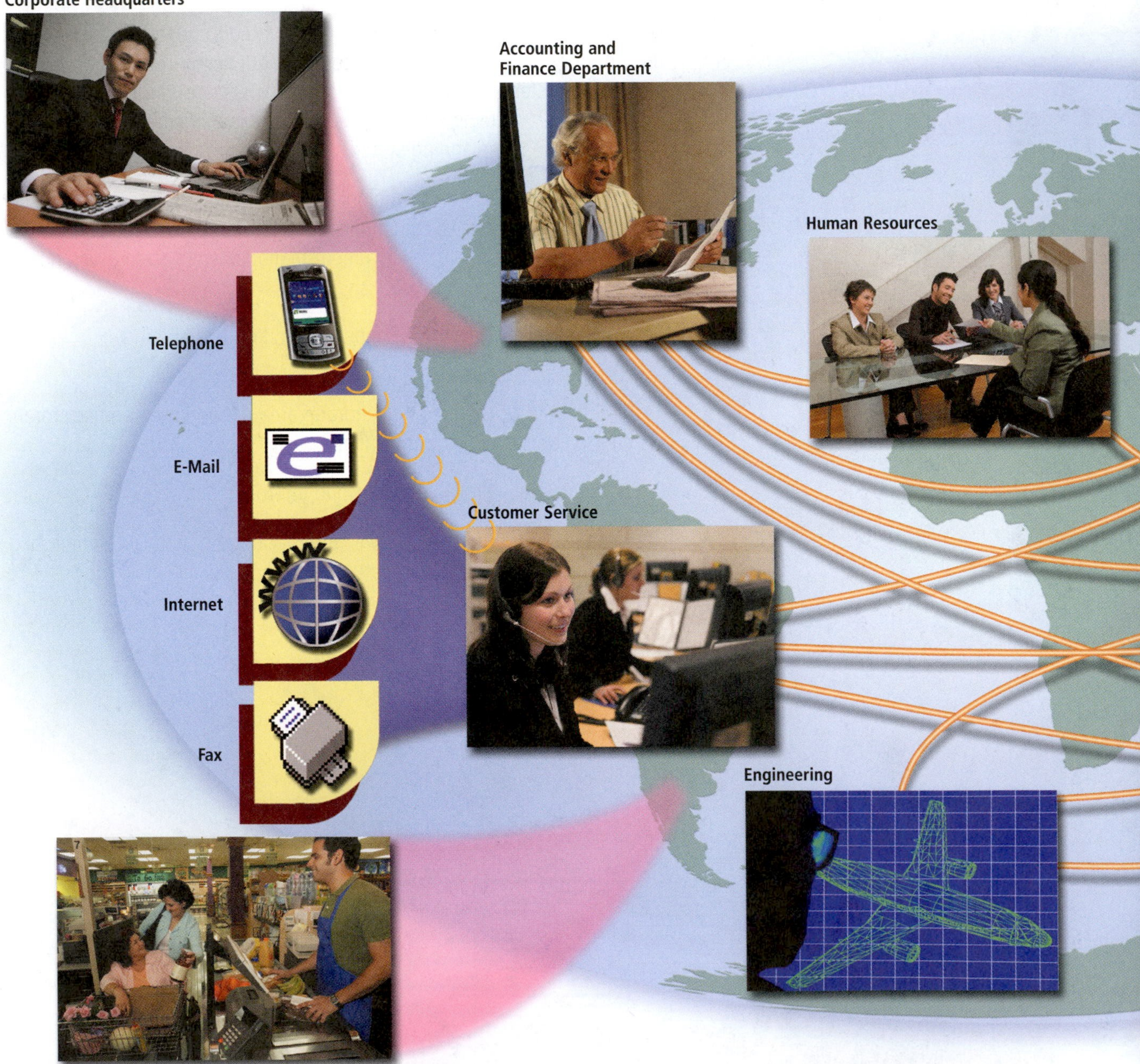

Figure 14-1 Enterprise computing involves the management of large amounts of information over an extensive geographic area and disparate groups of people.

does not have an international presence. Such entities, however, use many of the same technologies and procedures as enterprises, but on a smaller scale.

A typical enterprise consists of corporate headquarters, remote offices, international offices, and hundreds of individual operating entities, called *functional units*, including departments, centers, and divisions. Often, organizations within the enterprise may have similar responsibilities within the divisions to which they belong. For example, a large manufacturing company may organize its divisions based on the type of product that the business unit produces. Each division includes a group of engineers that designs the products. Each of the engineering groups may use similar or different information systems based on its needs or the culture of the company. Some companies allow for independence within their divisions, while others attempt to standardize systems across the enterprise.

Each type of functional unit has specialized requirements for its information systems. These units can be grouped by the functions they perform. The types of functional units within a typical manufacturing enterprise are accounting and finance, human resources, engineering,

manufacturing, marketing, sales, distribution, customer service, and information technology. These functional units are summarized later in this chapter.

Large computers connected by vast networks allow the enterprise to manage and distribute information quickly and efficiently. Procedures safeguard information when disaster strikes. Security policies ensure that people, computers, and networks access only the information they require.

When a customer visits a Web site to make a purchase, many activities occur behind the scenes at a company. A customer views an advertisement on a Web site that is created by the company's marketing department. Then the customer purchases a product at a Web site. The customer makes a credit card payment that is processed by a financial system connected to the company's bank. The company's accounting system records the payment and transaction. Next, the distribution center receives a message telling it to ship the product. The marketing department notes the advertising that was successful in generating the sale to the customer and informs the sales department that this customer may be interested in purchasing complementary products.

When the customer calls to check the status of an order, a computer routes the telephone call to the proper customer service representative who checks the status of the order in a database shared with the distribution department. Customers and employees use mobile devices to perform many of the tasks accomplished via Web sites or telephone calls. Finally, the activity generated by the purchase is detailed on management reports, and managers make decisions based on the information collected in the purchase process. For example, a manager may make a decision to order more parts for inventory because a product is selling particularly well. Companies often track customer purchases over a long period of time, whether the purchases are made over the telephone or on a Web site. Managers at the company then use this information to make a variety of decisions, such as which goods to offer in certain locations, how to best advertise goods, and which combinations of goods consumers are likely to purchase.

As just described, information is combined and analyzed by the management, and decisions are made based on the information. The divisions and departments within the enterprise use specialized hardware and software to perform their tasks. These same units may share hardware and software with each other to become more effective. Some large organizations employ enterprise-wide networks that help manage all aspects of a company and are used by many or all of the divisions and departments.

Types of Enterprises

Figure 14-1 on pages 720 and 721 shows an example of an enterprise whose main focus is in the manufacturing sector. Following is a list of examples of types of enterprises.

- Retail enterprises own a large number of stores in a wide geographical area and use their size to obtain discounts on the goods they purchase; they then seek to sell the goods at a lower price than smaller retailers.
- Manufacturing enterprises create goods on a large scale and then distribute and sell the goods to consumers or other organizations.
- Service enterprises typically do not create or sell goods, but provide services for consumers or other organizations. Examples include companies in the insurance, restaurant, and financial industries.
- Wholesale enterprises seek to purchase and then sell large quantities of goods to other organizations, usually at a lower cost than retail.
- Government enterprises include large city governments, state governments, and the departments and agencies of the federal government.
- Educational enterprises include large universities or schools that include executives, instructors, and other service personnel and whose reach extends throughout a county, a state, or the entire country.
- Transportation enterprises include airlines, regional transportation authorities, freight and passenger railroads, and trucking firms. These enterprises often include a mix of such types of transportation and have a local or an international reach.

Organizational Structure of an Enterprise

Most traditional enterprises are organized in a hierarchical manner. Figure 14-2 shows an example of an organization chart of a large manufacturing company. Managers at the first two levels at the top of the chart, including the chief executive officer (CEO), mainly concern themselves with strategic decisions and long-term planning.

The activities relating to running the business are called *supporting activities*. Supporting activities usually are separated from those activities that relate to the main mission of the company which are the *core activities*. *Operations* refer to the core activities of a business, and involve the creation, selling, and support of the products and services that the company offers. For example, in an airplane manufacturing company, a core activity may be the production of wings and cockpits, while a supporting activity may be paying vendors for the parts needed to manufacture those parts. In Figure 14-2, the chief operating officer (COO) manages the core activities. The supporting activities include financial departments and information technology (IT) departments. The chief financial officer (CFO) and the chief information officer (CIO) lead these supporting roles.

Each enterprise includes its own special needs and the organizational structure of every enterprise varies. Organizations may include all or some of the managers and departments shown in Figure 14-2. Organizations also may include additional departments or combine some of those shown.

A *decentralized* approach to information technology exists when departments and divisions maintain their own information systems. Sometimes, enterprises use outsourcing in a decentralized approach so that the company better can focus on its core skills. Some organizations maintain central computers, supported by a central information technology department, which is referred to as a *centralized* approach to information technology. Organizations decide whether to support a centralized or decentralized approach based on a number of factors, including cost, efficiency, and the interdependence of departments. A centralized approach to information systems usually reduces costs of maintenance and increases manageability. A decentralized approach allows for greater flexibility, allowing each functional unit or department to customize information systems to their particular needs. Both centralized and decentralized approaches focus on the sharing of information with other departments and divisions. Some enterprises use a combination of the approaches. For example, each of the enterprise's locations may be allowed to use their own information systems, but all locations' information systems communicate using a common data format.

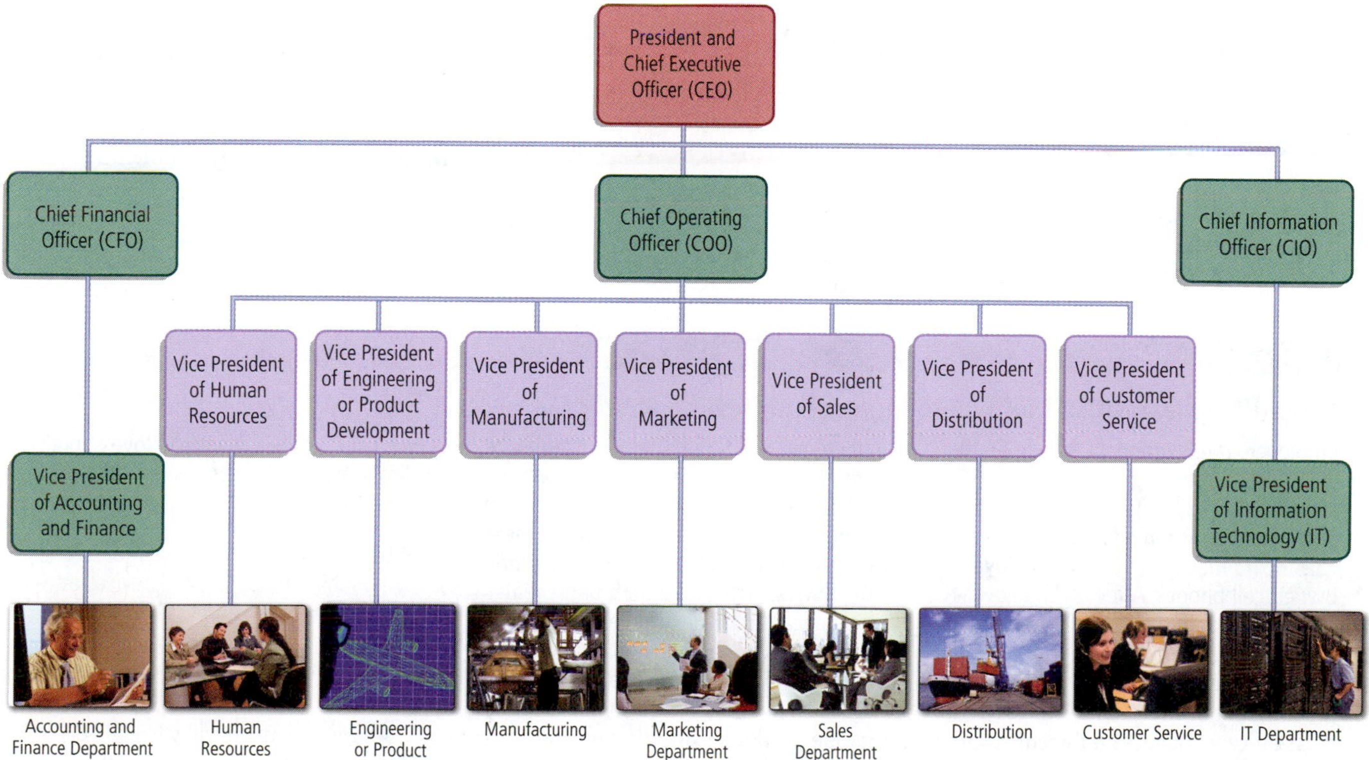

Figure 14-2 Example of an organization chart for a manufacturing enterprise illustrates the hierarchy within an enterprise.

Levels of Users in the Enterprise

In an enterprise, users typically fall into one of four categories: executive management, middle management, operational management, and nonmanagement employees (Figure 14-3). The types of information that users require often depend on their employee level in the company. Read Ethics & Issues 14-1 for a related discussion. The following paragraphs discuss the four categories of users and their information requirements.

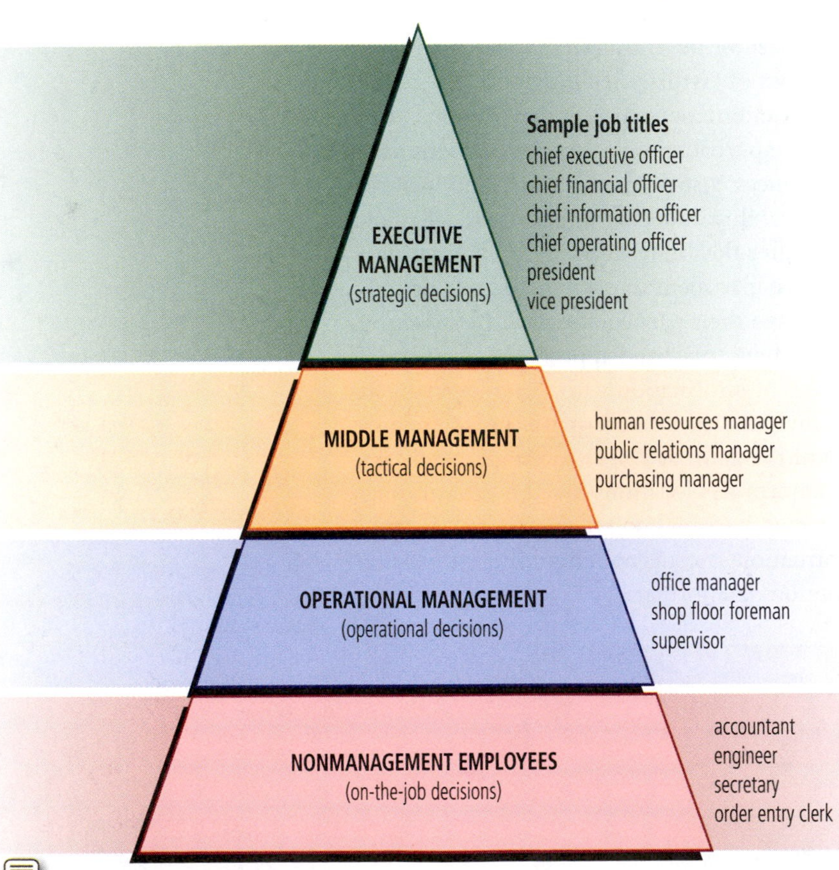

Figure 14-3 This pyramid illustrates the levels of users, sample job titles of each level of user, and the types of decisions these users make.

- **Executive management**, which includes the highest management positions in a company, focuses on the long-range direction of the company. These managers primarily are responsible for *strategic decisions* that center on the company's overall goals and objectives. Executive management oversees middle management. For example, in an airplane manufacturing company, executive management may decide when to design and build a new type of airplane.
- **Middle management** is responsible for implementing the strategic decisions of executive management. Middle managers make *tactical decisions*, which are short-range decisions that apply specific programs and plans necessary to meet the stated objectives. Middle management oversees operational management. For example, in an airplane manufacturing company, middle management may decide from which vendor to purchase parts and whether to outsource some operations.
- **Operational management** supervises the production, clerical, and other nonmanagement employees of a company. In performing their duties, operational managers make numerous operational decisions. An *operational decision* involves day-to-day activities within the company. These decisions should be consistent with and support the tactical decisions made by middle management. For example, in an airplane manufacturing company, operational management may decide the scheduling and process for building a new airplane.
- **Nonmanagement employees** include production, clerical, and other personnel. Nonmanagement employees frequently need information to perform their jobs. Today, these employees have more information available

ETHICS & ISSUES 14-1

Should Employees Use Mobile Computers and Devices at Work?

Employers rarely enforce rules prohibiting employees from listening to their portable media players while at work. Other employers do not mind personal phone calls being made at work on employee owned cell phones. A few even allow employees to plug personally owned computers into the company network. Some people argue that some or all of these practices should and could be allowed in most office workplaces if the employer uses proper security measures. They claim that because it is impossible to prevent all employees from bringing in miniature portable media players that the company should plan for all possibilities. Many companies, however, increasingly place these practices under scrutiny. They argue that the devices make data theft unpreventable because the devices can be attached to workplace computers and backups of critical company data made to the devices. Some employers now go so far as to confiscate employees' mobile computers and devices, or to terminate employment for those caught using mobile devices in the workplace. While most employers' policies disallow such devices, the rules sometimes are difficult, if not impossible, to enforce.

Should employees be allowed to use their own mobile computers and devices at work? Why or why not? Is it possible for employers to keep all personal electronics out of the office? Why? If an employer allows employees' mobile computers and devices in the office, what rules should be in effect, how should they be enforced, and what penalties should be assessed for breaking the rules?

to them than in the past. For example, in an airplane manufacturing company, a production employee may gather information regarding how to assemble a complex piece of equipment. They have access to the information necessary to make decisions that previously were made by managers — a trend called *empowering* users.

How Managers Use Information

Enterprise information is the information gathered in the ongoing operations of an enterprise-sized organization. Enterprise information begins with the day-to-day transactions that occur within a company, such as sales receipts or time cards. The company gathers and stores the information. Over time, employees collect, combine, and analyze the information. Ultimately, the role of information gathered in this way is to allow managers to make better decisions.

All employees, including managers, in a company need accurate information to perform their jobs effectively. **Managers** are responsible for coordinating and controlling an organization's resources. Resources include people, money, materials, and information. Managers coordinate these resources by performing four activities: planning, organizing, leading, and controlling.

- *Planning* involves establishing goals and objectives. It also includes deciding on the strategies and tactics needed to meet these goals and objectives.
- *Organizing* includes identifying and combining resources, such as money and people, so that the company can reach its goals and objectives. Organizing also involves determining the management structure of a company, such as the departments and reporting relationships.
- *Leading*, sometimes referred to as directing, involves communicating instructions and authorizing others to perform the necessary work.
- *Controlling* involves measuring performance and, if necessary, taking corrective action.

Figure 14-4 shows how these four management activities usually occur in an order that forms an endless cycle. During the controlling activity, managers measure actual performance against a previously established plan. Following this measurement, they may revise the plan. Revised plans may result in additional organizational and leadership activities. Managers then measure performance against the revised plan, and the cycle repeats itself. The four tasks are linked. A change in one task usually affects one or more of the other tasks.

Managers use a variety of tools and techniques to focus on information that is important to the decision-making process. These tools and techniques, including business intelligence, business process management, and business process automation, are described in the following sections.

Business Intelligence *Business intelligence (BI)* includes several types of applications and technologies for acquiring, storing, analyzing, and providing access to information to help users make more sound business decisions. BI applications include decision support systems, query and reporting, online analytical processing (OLAP), statistical analysis, and data mining. These activities are described later in this chapter.

Business Process Management *Business process management (BPM)* includes a set of activities that enterprises perform to optimize their business processes, such as accounting and finance, hiring employees, and purchasing goods and services. BPM almost always is aided by specialized software designed to assist in these activities.

Business Process Management
For more information, visit the Computer Concepts CourseMate Web site at www.cengagebrain.com, navigate to the Chapter 14 Web Link resource for this book, and then click Business Process Management.

Figure 14-4 The four management activities include planning, organizing, leading, and controlling. The activities usually are performed in a continuous sequence.

Business Process Automation *Business process automation* (*BPA*) provides easy exchange of information among business applications, reduces the need for human intervention in processes, and uses software to automate processes wherever possible. BPA offers greater efficiency and reduces risks by making processes more predictable.

Information Systems in the Enterprise

An **information system** is a set of hardware, software, data, people, and procedures that work together to produce information (Figure 14-5). A *procedure* is an instruction, or set of instructions, a user follows to accomplish an activity. For example, a company may have a procedure for its payroll system that includes a manager filling out certain forms before a new employee is added to the payroll system. An information system supports daily, short-term, and long-range activities of users in a company.

Some information systems are used exclusively by only one type of department, or functional unit, within the enterprise. General purpose information systems include categories of information systems that can be used by almost any department within the enterprise. Integrated information systems are used by multiple departments and facilitate information sharing and communication within the enterprise.

Information Systems within Functional Units

Figure 14-6 lists typical functional units, their purpose within an enterprise, and examples of programs that each might use. The sections that follow discuss the types of information systems and software used within these units. Small- and medium-sized businesses also may use some or many of these products.

Accounting and Finance Figure 14-7 illustrates the separate functions of accounting and financial systems used by accounting and finance departments. Accounting software manages everyday transactions, such as sales and payments to suppliers. Billing software helps the company reconcile purchases with customer

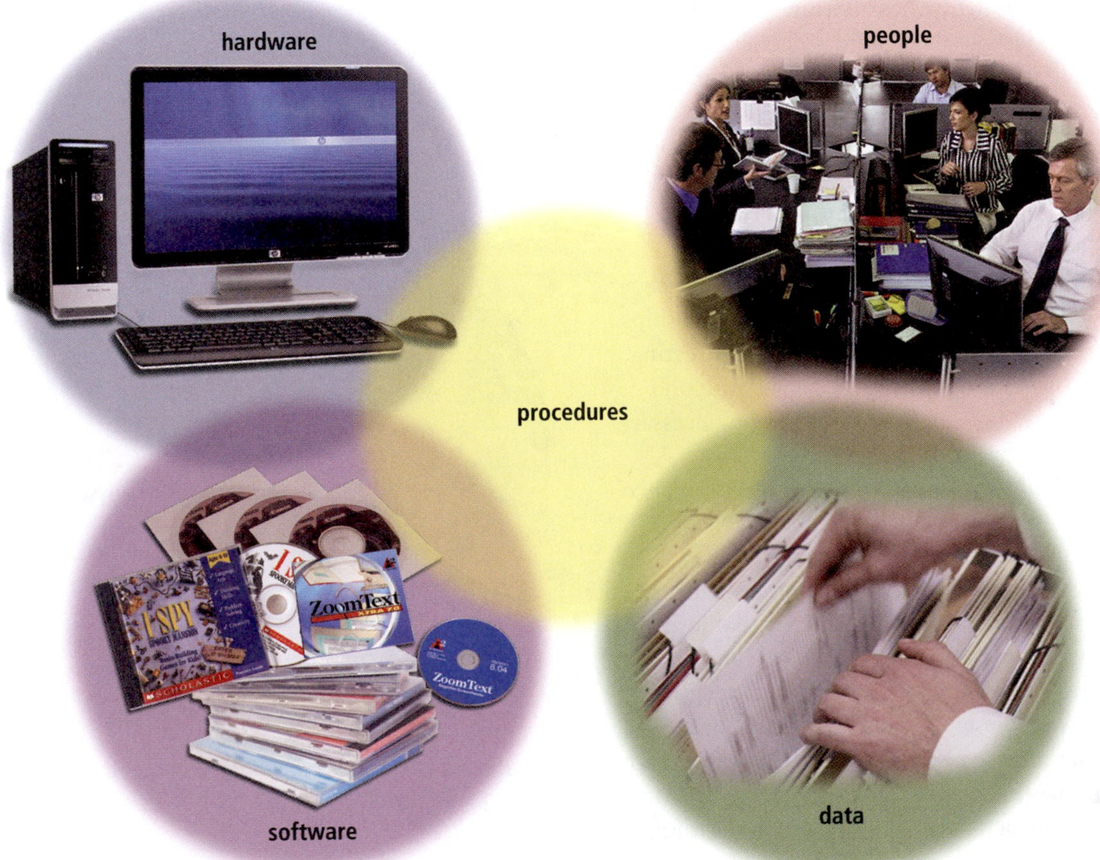

Figure 14-5
An information system typically contains five components: hardware, software, data, people, and procedures.

Functional Units within an Enterprise

Functional Unit	Description	Program Name
Accounting and Finance	Responsible for managing the business's money. Accounting department tracks every financial transaction that occurs within the company, including billing customers. Finance department manages the business's money as efficiently as possible.	Microsoft Dynamics GP Oracle Financials NetSuite
Human Resources (HR)	Responsible for recruiting and promoting employees, maintaining employee records, evaluating employees, training employees, and managing employee benefits and compensation.	Lawson Human Capital Management Oracle PeopleSoft Enterprise Human Capital Management Sage ABRA HRMS
Engineering or Product Development	Responsible for developing ideas into a product that can be used by customers. Ensures that the product can be manufactured effectively and designs the methods for manufacturing the product.	AutoCAD MicroStation ProductVision
Manufacturing	Responsible for converting raw materials into physical products.	CA-Plus MISys Manufacturing System Horizon Software MRP Plus Plexus Online
Marketing	Responsible for researching the market in which a business operates to determine the products and features that the business should develop. Determines the demographics to target with sales efforts and informs the target market about the company's products through advertising and education.	Aprimo Enterprise Oracle Marketing MarketingPilot
Sales	Responsible for selling the company's products and services.	OpenBOX Sales Force Automation Prophet SalesForce SFA
Distribution	Responsible for delivery of products to customers.	Activant Prophet 21 IBS's Advanced Inventory and Distribution Software Oracle Transportation Management
Customer Service	Responsible for maintaining a relationship with a customer both before and after a sale has been made.	SAP CRM Siebel CRM On Demand Syntellect Customer Interaction Management Suite
Information Technology (IT)	Responsible for designing, purchasing, implementing, testing, securing, and maintaining information systems for the rest of the organization. Sometimes called the information services (IS) department.	Microsoft System Center Configuration Manager VMware vCloud

Figure 14-6 An enterprise is composed of several functional units, each of which may use different programs to fulfill their needs.

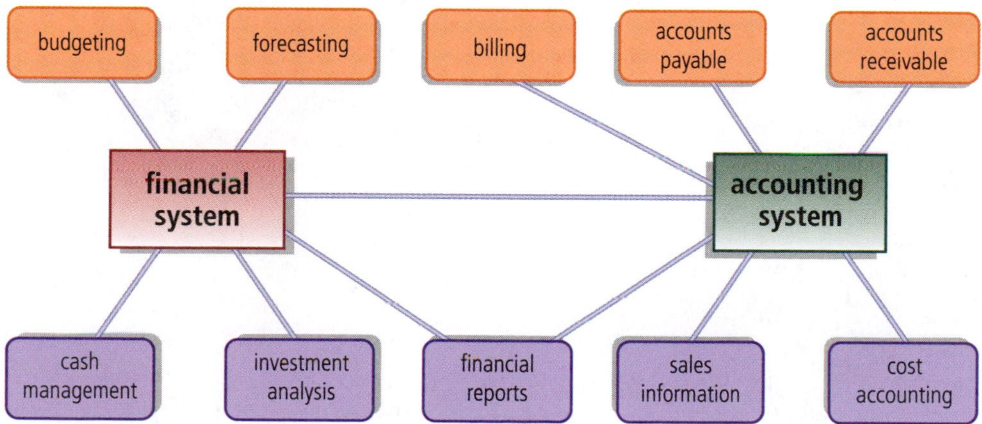

Figure 14-7 Accounting and financial systems perform different tasks but share information and produce financial reports that help management make decisions.

payments. Financial software helps managers budget, forecast, and analyze. These types of software include comprehensive and flexible reporting tools to assist managers in making decisions, provide historical documentation, and meet regulatory requirements.

Human Resources A **human resources information system (HRIS)** manages one or more human resources functions (Figure 14-8). A human resources information system and its associated software help a company such as Walmart maintain records on its more than 2 million employees. For example, when many retail employees arrive at work, they check in using an electronic clock that automatically allows managers to know who is late, early, or on time. The payroll department then can use this information when determining employee pay. An *employee relationship management (ERM) system* automates and manages much of the communications between employees and the business. For example, an employee may interact with ERM software to gather information about the employee's retirement account. Most ERM software includes a Web interface for the employees and the human resources personnel, allowing both to interact with the system when they are in the office or at home.

ERM

For more information, visit the Computer Concepts CourseMate Web site at www.cengagebrain.com, navigate to the Chapter 14 Web Link resource for this book, and then click ERM.

Engineering or Product Development Professional workers, such as engineers, require specialized software and systems to perform their tasks. **Computer-aided design (CAD)** uses a computer and special software to aid in engineering, drafting, and design (Figure 14-9). CAD offers several advantages over traditional manual drafting methods. CAD software, for example, allows engineers to view single or multiple layers of an airplane's design. The layers might include electrical systems, flight control systems, and passenger seating. Using CAD, the engineer can detect areas where the systems may interact improperly.

Computer-aided engineering (CAE) uses computers to test product designs. Using CAE, engineers can test the design of a car or bridge before it is built. These sophisticated programs simulate the effects of wind, weight, temperature, and stress on product shapes and materials.

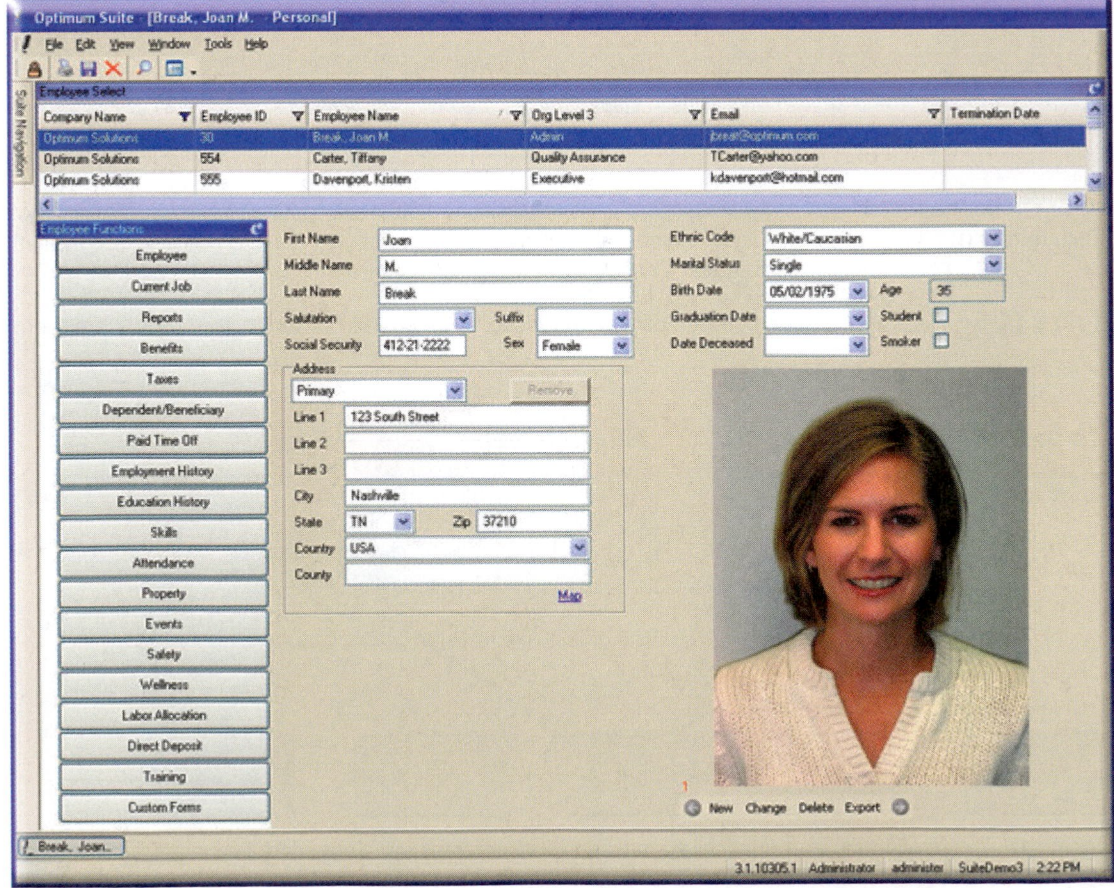

Figure 14-8 A human resources information system (HRIS) allows human resources personnel to manage employee information, such as benefits, personal information, performance evaluations, training, and vacation time.

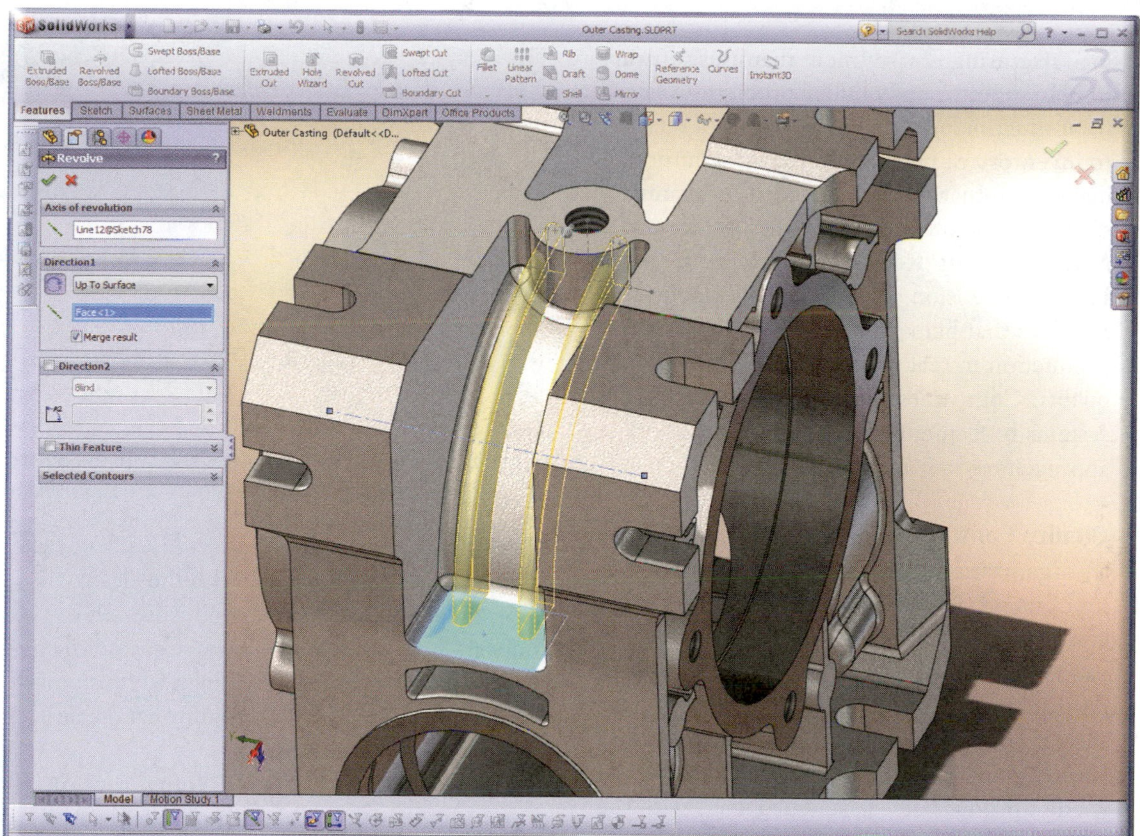

Figure 14-9 Computer-aided design (CAD) is an efficient way to develop plans for new products.

CAE also allows engineers to create a computer prototype for use in testing under a variety of conditions, such as hurricanes and earthquakes. Engineers sometimes use *3-D visualization*, which allows them to interact with a product without the need to build a prototype.

Manufacturing Manufacturing information systems not only assist in the actual assembly process, but also assist in scheduling and managing the inventory of parts and products. **Computer-aided manufacturing (CAM)** is the use of computers to control production equipment. CAM production equipment includes software-controlled drilling, lathe, welding, and milling machines.

Computer-integrated manufacturing (CIM) uses computers to integrate the many different operations of the manufacturing process, using technologies such as CAD, CAE, and CAM. Using CIM (Figure 14-10), for example, a factory can link individual processes so that production is balanced, efficient, driven by customer demand, and results in high-quality products.

Formal manufacturing methods help guide enterprises in their manufacturing processes. **Material Requirements Planning (MRP)** is an approach to information management in a

Figure 14-10 Computer-integrated manufacturing (CIM) speeds the manufacturing process and reduces product defects.

manufacturing environment that uses software to help monitor and control processes related to production. MRP focuses on issues related to inventory of parts and forecasting future demand so that materials needed for manufacturing can be on hand when they are needed. **Manufacturing Resource Planning II (MRP II)** is an extension of MRP and also includes software that helps in scheduling, tracking production in real time, and monitoring product quality. Companies use MRP and MRP II systems to facilitate an MRP or MRP II approach to their manufacturing.

MRP II

For more information, visit the Computer Concepts CourseMate Web site at www.cengagebrain.com, navigate to the Chapter 14 Web Link resource for this book, and then click MRP II.

Quality Control A *quality control system* helps an organization maintain or improve the quality of its products or services. A quality control system usually includes quality control software. *Quality control software* typically requires a great deal of continuous data gathering from the organization's ongoing processes. Using statistical analysis, the software can identify and predict product defects and problems with the company's processes. While quality control systems often are costly and disruptive to the organization, the organization typically saves more money by producing a higher quality product or service.

Marketing A *marketing information system* serves as a central repository for the tasks of the marketing functional unit. One type of marketing information system is a *market research system*, which stores and analyzes data gathered from demographics and surveys. Many companies gather information via the Web and store information about individuals' Web browsing habits and interests. For example, many companies use market research systems to analyze Web site visitors' use of the company's Web site, such as tracking the users that visit specific Web pages on a site and how long the user views the Web page. The information then is used to better market products and services to particular customers or potential customers. Figure 14-11 shows a device that tracks inventory for a marketing information system. Market research software assists in target marketing by allowing marketing personnel to query databases based on criteria such as income, gender, previous purchases, and favorite recreational activities.

Figure 14-11 Store employees use wireless devices to track inventory for a marketing information system.

Sales **Sales force automation (SFA)** software equips traveling salespeople with the electronic tools they need to be more productive. SFA software helps salespeople manage customer contacts, schedule customer meetings, log customer interactions, manage product information, and take orders from customers.

SFA software (Figure 14-12) often runs on notebook computers or other mobile devices. The notebook computer or other mobile device may connect wirelessly to the central office, allowing the salesperson to access up-to-date corporate information in real time no matter where he or she is located.

Alternatively, some SFA programs allow the salesperson to upload information to the central office at the end of the day or end of the week. The programs also allow salespeople to download updated product and pricing information.

? FAQ 14-1

When should I supply personal information to a company?

Companies gather personal information about consumers for a variety of reasons. Companies can gather information when you make a purchase, complete a survey, or enter a sweepstakes. Unless you are sure you want the company to communicate with you in some way, few reasons exist to supply personal information to a company. Ask the company why it needs the information and use your judgment. Most companies can supply you with a privacy policy upon request.

For more information, visit the Computer Concepts CourseMate Web site at www.cengagebrain.com, navigate to the Chapter 14 FAQ resource for this book, and then click Sharing Personal Information.

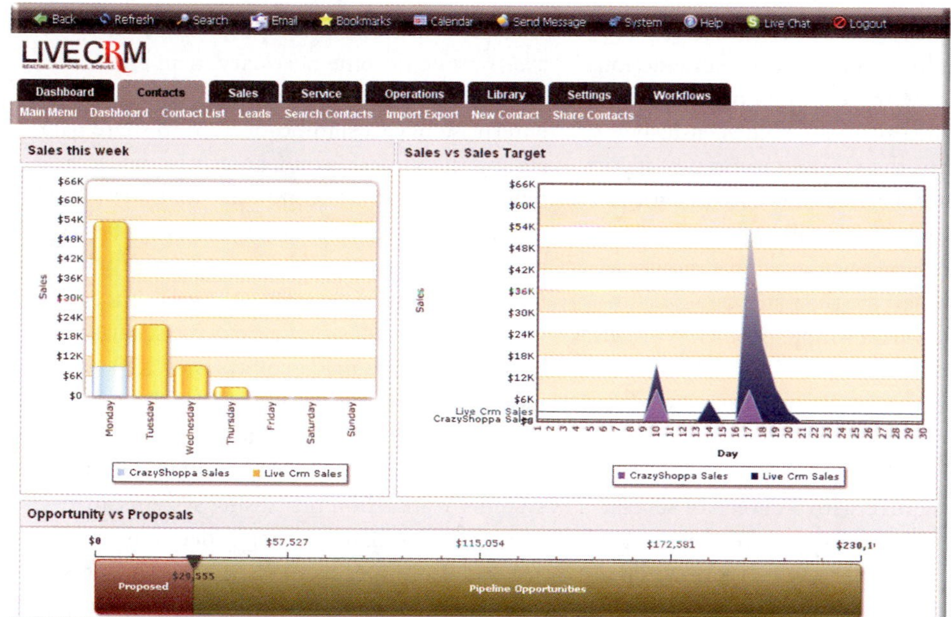

Figure 14-12 Sales force automation (SFA) software allows the sales force to manage customer and prospective customer relationships more effectively.

SFA

For more information, visit the Computer Concepts CourseMate Web site at www.cengagebrain.com, navigate to the Chapter 14 Web Link resource for this book, and then click SFA.

Distribution *Distribution systems* provide forecasting for inventory control, manage and track shipping of products, and provide information and analysis on inventory in warehouses. Some distribution systems rely on GPS and other navigation technologies to track shipping in real time. Many companies now employ RFID to track inventory and shipping. Distribution systems strive to maximize the value of each shipment made by the company while keeping costs to a minimum. Because of the complexity of the tasks of inventory management and shipping, distribution systems often integrate with quality control systems.

Customer Service **Customer interaction management (CIM)** software (Figure 14-13) manages the day-to-day interactions with customers, such as telephone calls, e-mail interactions, Web interactions, and instant

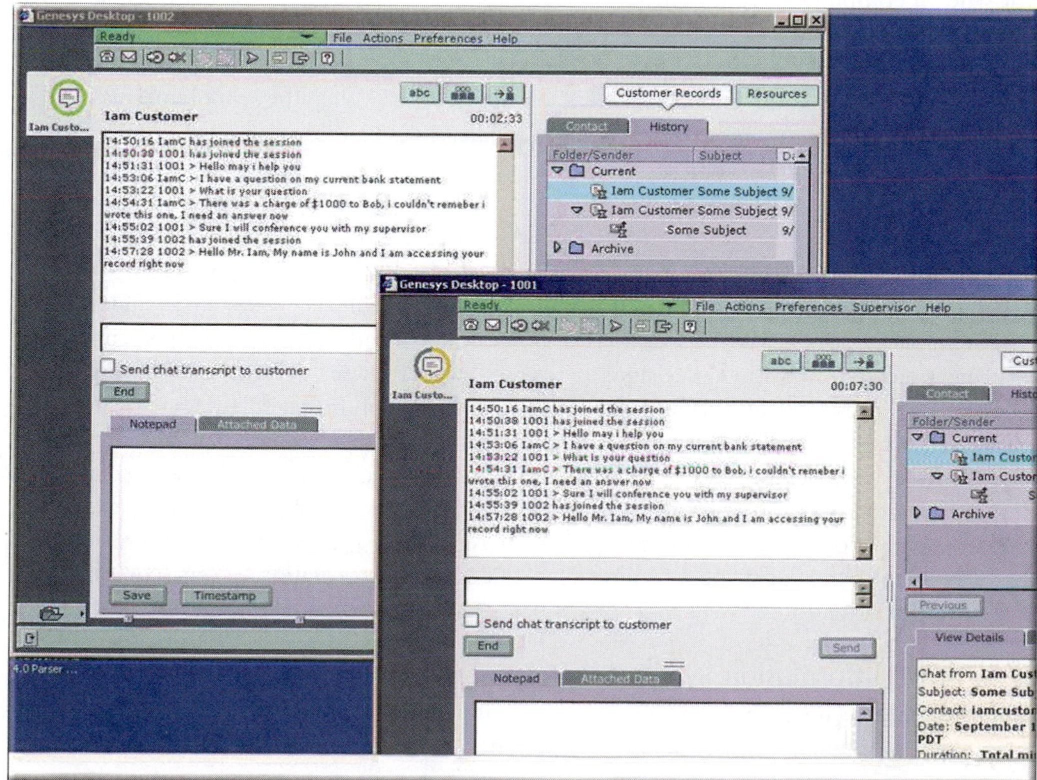

Figure 14-13 Customer interaction management (CIM) software manages and reports on daily interactions with customers, such as telephone support calls or customer support requests via e-mail.

messaging sessions. These interactions are logged so that a historical record of interactions with the customer can be viewed or analyzed at any time. A CIM program routes customer support queries to the most appropriate support person depending on the customer's situation. For example, a call from a pilot with a problem regarding an airplane during a flight requires a different level of service than an airline technician who needs to fix a simple problem with an airplane on the ground.

CIM software also assists support personnel in providing the best solutions for customers. The CIM program may provide a customer support representative with a choice of several e-mail or text messages to send to a customer in response to the problem. The representative chooses the best response and requests that the CIM software sends the e-mail or text message. Information gathered by these programs during interactions, such as reasons for the interaction and the resolution of the interaction, may be collected and made available through other information systems throughout the company.

Information Technology The information technology (IT) department makes technology decisions for the enterprise, such as a decision whether to build or buy new information systems or when a computer or information system has outlived its useful life. The overall technology strategy often is referred to as the *information architecture* of the company. Many organizations elevate the importance of information technology by including a *chief information officer* (*CIO*) executive position that reports to the CEO.

The IT department uses software to maintain hardware and software. For example, *Web site management programs* collect data designed to help organizations make informed decisions regarding their Web presence. This data might include the locations of their Web site visitors, which Web browser they use, the days and times they visit the Web site, and what keywords they entered into a search engine to locate the site. *Security software* enables the department to limit access to sensitive information.

IT Departments

For more information, visit the Computer Concepts CourseMate Web site at www.cengagebrain.com, navigate to the Chapter 14 Web Link resource for this book, and then click IT Departments.

General Purpose Information Systems

Some information systems in an enterprise cross the boundaries of functional units and are used by one or more functional units in an enterprise. These general purpose, or *enterprise-wide systems*, become necessary in an enterprise for two reasons. First, functional units within an enterprise have a significant need to share data among the units. Second, enterprise-wide systems can collect and combine data more quickly and provide executive management access to a more up-to-date and accurate view of what is happening in the organization. Advances in computing speed, storage capacity, security, and networking have made enterprise-wide systems more attractive to organizations in recent years.

General purpose information systems generally fall into one of five categories: office information systems, transaction processing systems, management information systems, decision support systems, and expert systems. The following sections present each type of these general purpose information systems.

Office Information Systems An **office information system** (**OIS**) is an information system that enables employees to perform tasks using computers and other electronic devices, instead of manually. An office information system increases employee productivity and assists with communications among employees. Some people describe an office information system as *office automation*.

Nearly every type of business or organization uses some form of office information system. For example, a school might post its class schedules on the Internet. When the school updates the schedule, students receive an e-mail notification. In a manual system, the school would photocopy the schedule and mail it to each student's house.

An office information system uses many common software products to support its activities. Typical software in such a system includes word processing, spreadsheet, database, presentation, e-mail, Web browser, Web page authoring, personal information management, and groupware. To send text, graphics, audio, and video to others, an office information system uses communications technology such as voice mail, fax, video conferencing, and electronic data interchange.

In an office information system, computers have modems, Web cams, speakers, and microphones. Employees in an office information system often use other types of hardware such as scanners, fax machines, digital cameras, smart phones, netbooks, handheld navigation devices, and other mobile devices.

Transaction Processing Systems A **transaction processing system (TPS)** is an information system that captures and processes data from day-to-day business activities. Transaction processing systems were among the first computerized systems that processed business data. Many people initially referred to the functions of these systems as *data processing*. The first transaction processing systems computerized an existing manual system. The intent of these systems was to process transactions faster, reduce clerical costs, and improve customer service.

When you make a purchase with a credit card at a store, you are interacting with a transaction processing system. A *transaction* is an individual business activity. Examples of transactions are deposits, payments, orders, and reservations. Transactions take place in real time, meaning that as soon as you make a purchase with a credit card, you can visit your credit card company's Web site and view the transaction. In an organization, clerical staff typically uses computers and special software to perform the following activities associated with a transaction processing system:

1. Recording a transaction such as an airline reservation, a customer's order, an employee's time card, or a car owner's payment.
2. Confirming an action or causing a response, such as sending an itinerary, sending a thank-you note to a customer, printing an employee's paycheck, or issuing a receipt to a car owner.
3. Maintaining data, which involves adding new data, modifying existing data, or deleting unwanted data.

Early transaction processing systems mostly used batch processing. With *batch processing*, the computer collects data over time and processes all transactions later, as a group. As computers became more powerful, system developers created online transaction processing information systems. With *online transaction processing (OLTP)*, the computer processes each transaction as it is entered. Figure 14-14 shows an example of the difference between batch processing and OLTP.

For example, when you book a flight using an airline's Web site, the airline probably uses OLTP. You use the airline's Web site to schedule your desired flights. The Web site immediately displays your itinerary and sends you a copy of your itinerary. The Web site uses OLTP to bill you online or mail an invoice to you.

Today, most transaction processing systems use OLTP. For some routine processing tasks, they also use batch processing. Many enterprise-sized organizations use batch processing to calculate paychecks and print invoices.

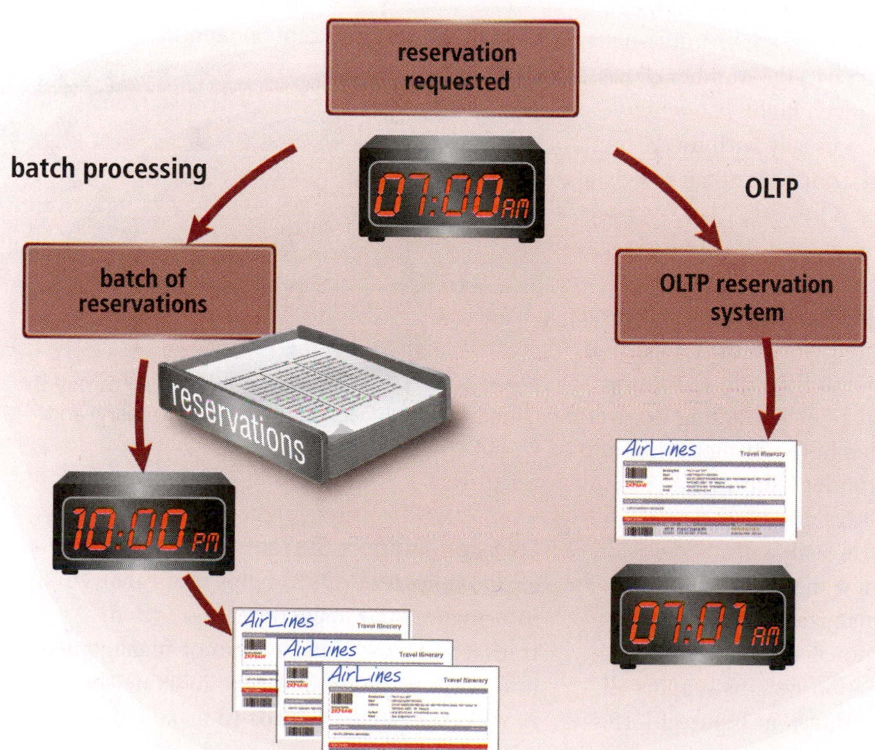

Figure 14-14 With batch processing, all airline reservations are processed together at the end of the day. With OLTP, reservations are processed immediately.

Management Information Systems A **management information system** (**MIS**) is an information system that generates accurate, timely, and organized information, so that managers and other users can make decisions, solve problems, supervise activities, and track progress. Management information systems evolved from transaction processing systems. Managers realized the computer and its software had more potential than just supporting a transaction processing system. Its capability of quickly computing and comparing data could produce meaningful information for managers.

Management information systems often are integrated with transaction processing systems. To process a sales order, the transaction processing system records the sale, updates the customer's account balance, and reduces the inventory count. Using this information, the related management information system produces reports that recap daily sales activities, summarize weekly and monthly sales activities, list customers with past due account balances, chart slow- or fast-selling products, and highlight inventory items that need reordering. A management information system focuses on creating information that managers and other users need to perform their jobs.

A management information system creates three basic types of reports: detailed, summary, and exception (Figure 14-15). A *detailed report* usually lists just transactions. For example, a Detailed Flight Report lists the number of passengers booked for a given flight. A *summary report* consolidates data usually with totals, tables, or graphs, so that managers can review it quickly and easily.

An *exception report* identifies data outside of a normal condition. These out-of-the-ordinary conditions, called the *exception criteria*, define the normal activity or status range. For example, a Premier Club Booking Exception Report notifies the airline's marketing department that some flights have not met minimum goals for booking Premier Club members.

Exception reports save managers time. Instead of searching through a detailed report, managers simply review the exception report. These reports help managers focus on situations that require immediate decisions or actions. Most information systems support all three types of reports shown in Figure 14-15.

Figure 14-15a (detailed report)

Detailed Flight Report for March 30

Flight #	Origin/ Destination	Class – Number of Passengers	Premier Club Members
1048	ORD – RSW	A – 5 B – 14 C – 89	A – 1 B – 12 C – 20
543	ORD – BMI	A – 2 B – 7 C – 15	A – 2 B – 5 C – 5
715	ORD – LAX	A – 12 B – 25 C – 123	A – 8 B – 15 C – 39
701	ORD – JFK	A – 9 B – 10 C – 7	A – 7 B – 0 C – 3

Figure 14-15b (summary report)

Summary Flight Report for March 30

Flight #	Origin/ Destination	Passengers	Premier Club Members
1048	ORD – RSW	108	33
543	ORD – BMI	24	12
715	ORD – LAX	160	62
701	ORD – JFK	26	10

Figure 14-15c (exception report)

Exception Flight Report for March 30

Flight #	Class	Origin/ Destination	Premier Club Members	Premier Club Member Goal
1048	A	ORD – RSW	1	4
701	C	ORD – JFK	3	5

Figure 14-15 Three basic types of information generated in an MIS are detailed, summary, and exception.

Decision Support Systems A **decision support system** (**DSS**) helps users analyze information and make decisions. Often, a transaction processing system or management information system does not generate the type of report a manager needs to make a decision.

A variety of decision support systems exist. Some are company specific and designed solely for managers. Others are available to everyone on the Web. Programs that analyze data, such as those in a decision support system, sometimes are called *online analytical processing* (*OLAP*) programs. Because they summarize information, these programs process many records at a time.

A decision support system uses data from internal and external sources. *Internal sources* of data might include sales orders, MRP and MRP II results, inventory records, or financial data from accounting and financial analyses. Data from *external sources* could include interest rates, population trends, costs of new housing construction, or raw material pricing.

Some decision support systems include their own query languages, statistical analyses, spreadsheets, and graphics that help users retrieve data and analyze the results. Some also allow managers to create a model of the factors affecting a decision. A product manager might need to decide on a price for a new product. A simple model for finding the best price would include factors for the expected sales volume at various price levels. The model allows the user to ask what-if questions and view the expected results.

A special type of decision support system, called an *executive information system* (*EIS*), supports the strategic information needs of executive management (Figure 14-16). An EIS presents information as charts and tables that show trends, ratios, and statistics that aid in the decision making process. Such a system typically uses external data sources such as the Dow Jones Interactive or the Internet. These external data sources provide current information about interest rates, commodity prices, and other leading economic indicators. A large number of executive managers use EIS to compile information from various departments, such as marketing, manufacturing, and finance. For example, a manager might use an EIS to analyze a company's financial trends.

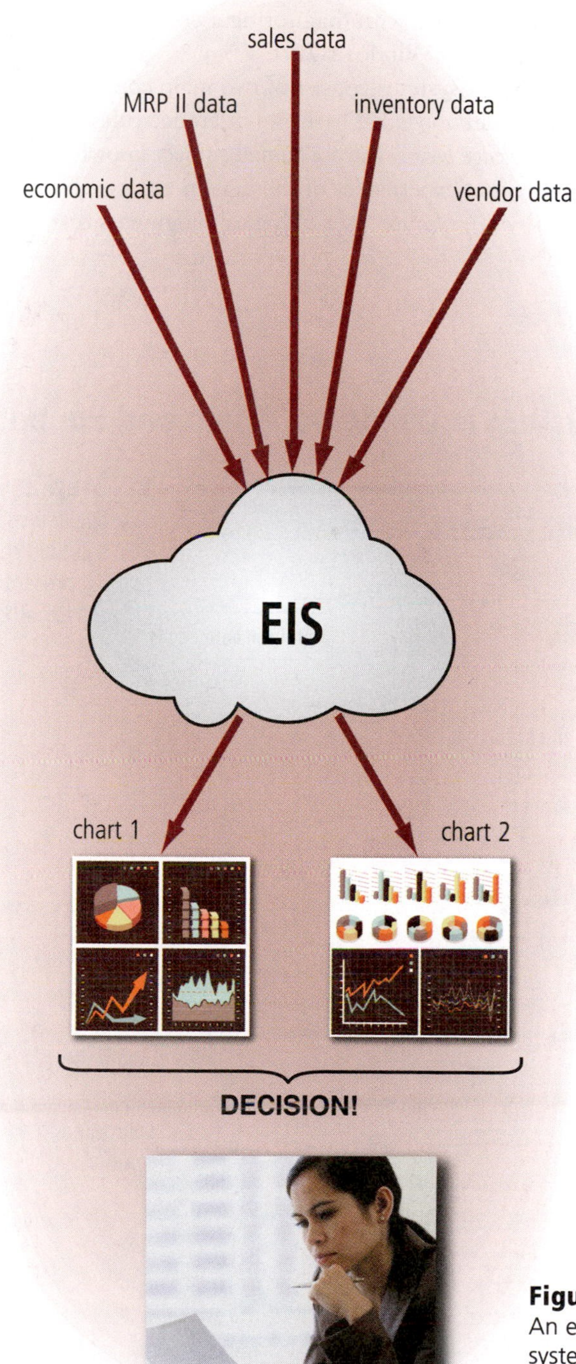

Figure 14-16
An executive information system (EIS) gathers and presents information to senior management in the form of graphics and reports used to assist in decision making.

Expert Systems An **expert system** is an information system that captures and stores the knowledge of human experts and then imitates human reasoning and decision making. Figure 14-17 shows how one expert system assists with diagnosing a computer problem in Windows 7.

Expert systems consist of two main components: a knowledge base and inference rules. A *knowledge base* is the combined subject knowledge and experiences of the human experts. The *inference rules* are a set of logical judgments that are applied to the knowledge base each time a user describes a situation to the expert system.

Expert systems help all levels of users make decisions. Nonmanagement employees use them to help with job-related decisions. Expert systems also successfully have resolved such diverse problems as diagnosing illnesses, searching for oil, and making soup.

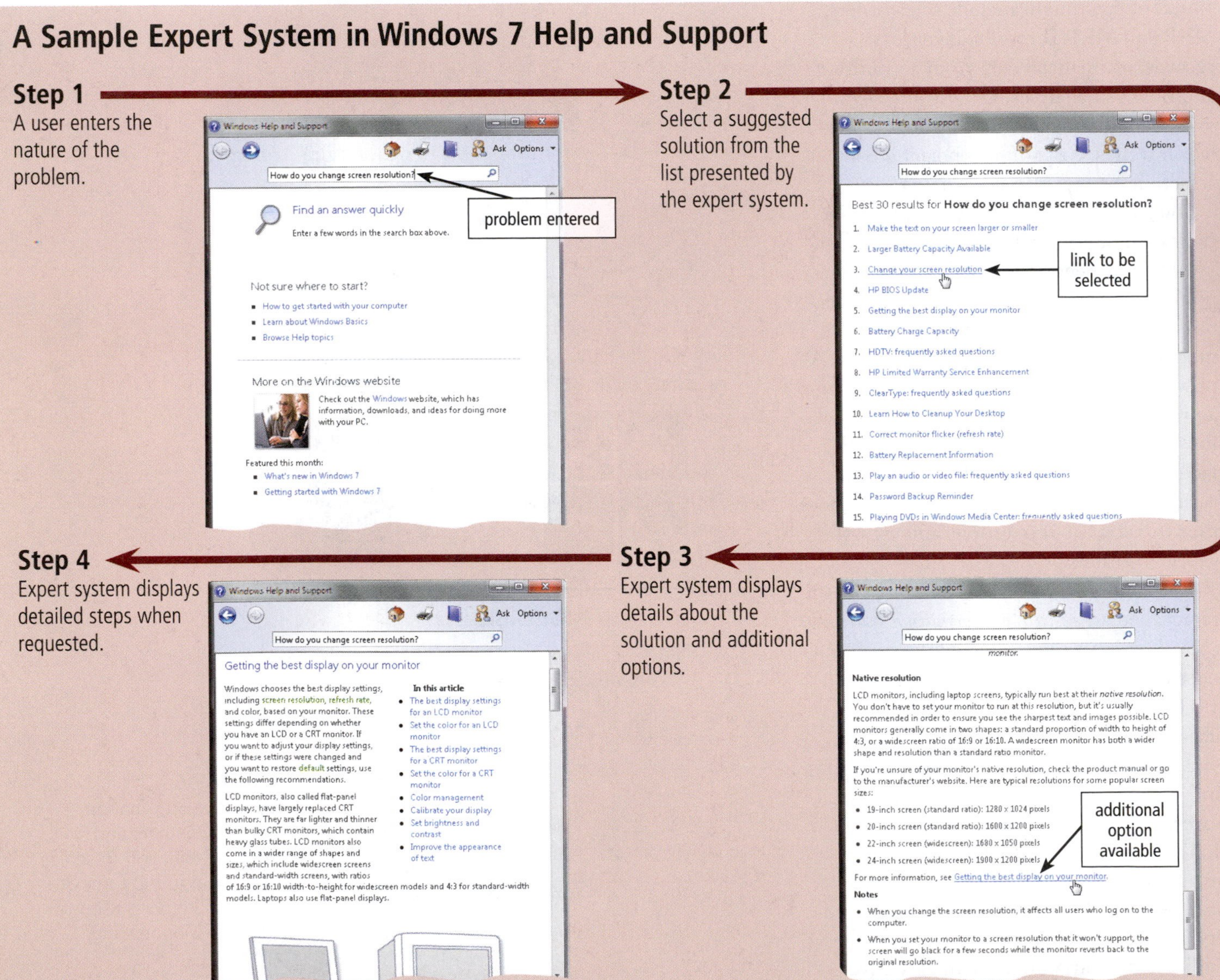

Figure 14-17 This figure shows a sample expert system in Windows 7 Help and Support.

Expert systems are one aspect of an exciting branch of computer science called artificial intelligence. **Artificial intelligence (AI)** is the application of human intelligence to computers. Artificial intelligence technology senses a person's actions and, based on logical assumptions and prior experience, takes the appropriate action to complete the task. Artificial intelligence has a variety of capabilities, including speech recognition, logical reasoning, and creative responses. New research in the field of artificial intelligence tries to mimic the way that human memory works to expedite searches for information.

Enterprises employ expert systems in a variety of roles, such as answering customer questions, training new employees, and analyzing data. Read Ethics & Issues 14-2 for a related discussion.

The knowledge and experience of a professional worker is an important asset to any business. *Knowledge workers*, such as accountants, engineers, and other professionals, include individuals whose jobs center on the collection, processing, and application of information. *Knowledge management (KM)* is the process by which an enterprise collects, archives, indexes, and retrieves its knowledge, or resources. The knowledge worker performs the tasks to develop or use the knowledge. Organizations implement *knowledge management software (KMS)* to assist in the task of knowledge management. KMS captures the expertise of knowledge workers, so that their knowledge is not lost when they leave the organization. For a more technical discussion about artificial intelligence, read the High-Tech Talk article on page 758.

Integrated Information Systems

It often is difficult to classify an information system as belonging to only one of the five general types of information systems. Much of today's application software, such as enterprise resource planning and MRP II software, supports transaction processing and creates management information system reports. Other applications provide transaction processing, management information, and decision support.

Customer Relationship Management

A **customer relationship management (CRM)** system manages information about customers, interactions with customers, past purchases, and interests. CRM mainly is used across sales, marketing, and customer service departments. CRM software tracks leads and inquiries from customers, stores a history of all correspondence and sales to a customer, and allows for tracking of outstanding issues with customers. Enterprise resource planning systems often serve as a basis for CRM.

Marketing departments use CRM software to learn about current customers and design new products based on customer experiences. The sales department uses CRM software to track the sales process from initial contact through the final purchase. The customer support organization tracks ongoing correspondence with the customer, and the CRM system may be linked to a CIM system. All of the functional units have access to each other's information, allowing for a more consistent, knowledgeable approach to managing interactions with the customer.

ETHICS & ISSUES 14-2

Can Overreliance on Artificial Intelligence and Expert Systems Be Harmful?

A woman, obviously older than 90 years of age, requested a senior discount from a ticket agent at an airport. The agent's expert system noted that a specific form of identification was needed as proof that the customer was over the age of 65. The woman did not possess the type of identification requested. Subsequently, the special fare was declined, and the woman's 70-year-old daughter wrote a scathing letter to the airline. The agent's blind trust of the expert system surely resulted in a lost customer. Artificial intelligence and expert systems often are used to aid decision making for medical situations or used in highly technical work. Users of these systems, such as physicians or engineers, often have sufficient background knowledge to question results provided by the systems. Too often, though, users are trained to rely blindly on the answers given by the system.

Some experts claim that the opposite problem often is true for such systems. A significant problem with artificial intelligence and expert systems is not overreliance, but rather a lack of trust by many users. When given the same answer to the same question by an expert system and a human, research has shown that people have a general lack of trust for the expert system as compared to another person.

Should limits be placed on where and when artificial intelligence and expert systems are used? Why or why not? Would you rely on an expert system to treat a medical problem? Why or why not? Should users be encouraged to gain more trust in artificial intelligence and expert systems? Why or why not?

Enterprise Resource Planning **Enterprise resource planning (ERP)** provides centralized, integrated software to help manage and coordinate the ongoing activities of the enterprise, including manufacturing and distribution, accounting, finance, sales, product planning, and human resources. Figure 14-18 shows how ERP fits into the operations of an enterprise. Companies such as SAP provide the fundamental framework for building these software-based systems.

The ERP system installed at each organization must be customized to match the business requirements of the enterprise. At a large organization, such a system may take four to six years to implement and cost hundreds of millions of dollars. The organization hopes to regain the investment through the advantages offered by ERP.

ERP
For more information, visit the Computer Concepts CourseMate Web site at www.cengagebrain.com, navigate to the Chapter 14 Web Link resource for this book, and then click ERP.

Advantages of ERP include complete integration of information systems across departments, better project management, and improved customer service. Project management software often is standardized across an enterprise so that different parts of the enterprise easily can integrate and collaborate on their planning and logistics. Complete integration means information is shared rapidly and management receives a more complete and timely view of the organization through the information. ERP also helps management in a company to manage better the global nature of many enterprises. The reliance on one information system, rather than up to several hundred systems, allows the IT department to focus on one type of technology and simplifies relationships with IT vendors.

Figure 14-18 Enterprise resource planning (ERP) encompasses all of the major activities throughout a business.

Content Management Systems A **content management system** (**CMS**) is an information system that is a combination of databases, software, and procedures that organizes and allows access to various forms of documents and other files, including images and multimedia content. A content management system includes information about the files and data, called *metadata*. For example, the metadata for a company's employee manual may include the author's name, revision number, a brief summary, and last revision date. The content management system also provides security controls for the content, such as who is allowed to add, view, and modify content and on which content the user is allowed to perform those operations.

Users add content to a content management system using a graphical user interface or Web page. Based on the user's actions, the content management system processes content, categorizes the content, *indexes* the content so that it later can be searched, and stores the content. Users then have access to the content stored in the system through other applications, such as an enterprise portal (Figure 14-19). Enterprise portal software gathers information from the content management system, other information sources from within the enterprise, and information external to the enterprise, such as news services.

Publishing entities, such as news services, use content management systems to keep Web sites and RSS feeds up-to-date. As news or information is published, it is categorized and updated on the appropriate sections of the Web site. For example, a sports writer may submit a story to the content management system and add metadata that indicates the story is a headline story. The content management system categorizes the story so that it is displayed as the first item with a large headline on the sports section of the Web site and RSS feeds. The content management system indexes the information in the story so that users who search the Web site based on keywords in the story will find a link to the story.

Many content management systems serve to enhance the effectiveness of groupware and collaboration software. Groupware, such as Lotus Notes from IBM, can be integrated with content management systems.

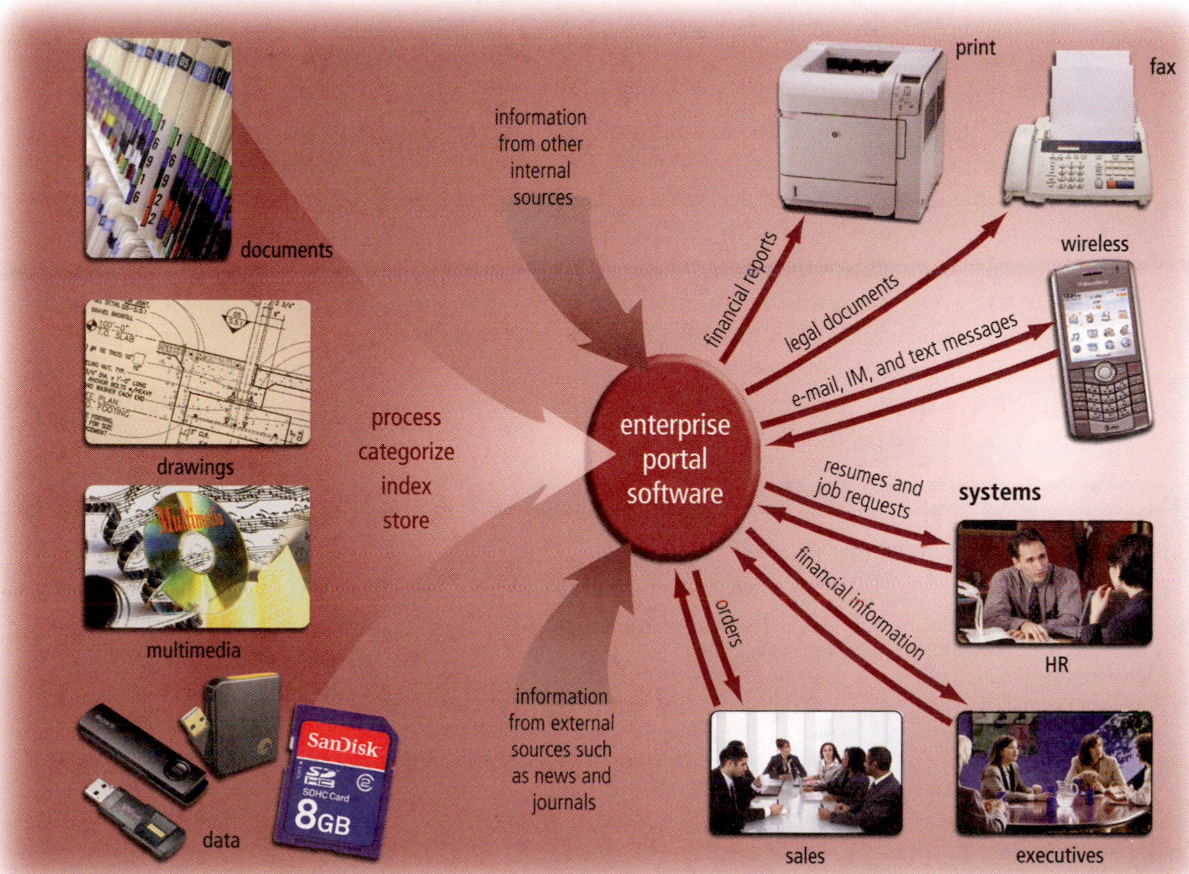

Figure 14-19 A content management system (CMS) helps a company classify and manage volumes of documents and media for future retrieval and use.

QUIZ YOURSELF 14-1

Instructions: Find the true statement below. Then, rewrite the remaining false statements so that they are true.

1. The main task of executive managers is to make short-term, tactical decisions.
2. An information system is a set of hardware, software, and people that work together to produce information.
3. A human resources information system serves as a central repository for the tasks of the marketing functional unit.
4. Customer interaction management software manages the day-to-day interactions with customers.
5. Decision support systems capture and store the knowledge of human experts and then imitate human reasoning and decision making.
6. Enterprise resource planning is a combination of databases, software, and procedures that organizes and allows access to various forms of documents and files.

Quiz Yourself Online: To further check your knowledge of pages 720 through 739, visit the Computer Concepts CourseMate Web site at www.cengagebrain.com, navigate to the Chapter 14 Quiz Yourself resource for this book, and then click Objectives 1 – 3.

Enterprise-Wide Technologies and Methodologies

Several technologies adopted by enterprises allow organizations flexibility and the ability to move swiftly in a business environment. By using standard and accepted technologies, the organization does not need to reengineer solutions to typical problems. Commonly used technologies provide the organization with a starting point to solve problems present in many large organizations.

Some of the common technologies used in enterprises include portals, data warehouses, electronic data interchange, extranets, Web services, document management systems, workflow, and virtual private networks. Most of the hardware and software that contains these technologies is located in a *data center*, which is a centralized location for managing and housing those items. Read Innovative Computing 14-1 to find out about unique data center solutions. The following sections discuss each of these technologies.

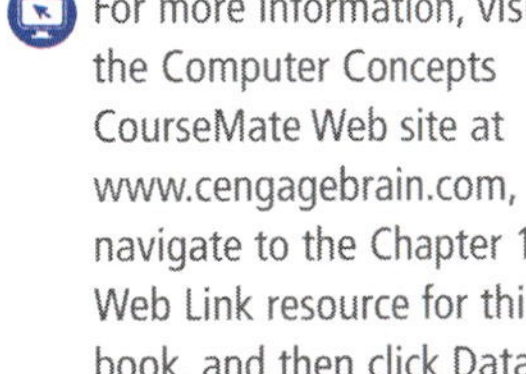

Data Centers

For more information, visit the Computer Concepts CourseMate Web site at www.cengagebrain.com, navigate to the Chapter 14 Web Link resource for this book, and then click Data Centers.

Portals

A **portal** is a collection of links, content, and services presented on a Web page and designed to guide users to information they likely are to find interesting for their particular job function. A service may include a portion of a Web page that allows the user to check package shipment status for an overnight delivery service or the ability to check airline flight schedules or flight status. Portals combine information from several business sources, both inside and outside the enterprise (Figure 14-20). A portal often includes searching capabilities or a link to a search engine, such as Google. Organizations often deploy *enterprise search* technology that allows users to perform searches across many enterprise-wide information systems and databases. Users typically can customize the portal Web site to meet their needs. The customization of users' portal pages to meet their needs is called *personalization*.

Users within a department or those working together on a project often have similar views of the portal. An executive may have access to daily

INNOVATIVE COMPUTING 14-1

Unique Data Center Storage Solutions

As data centers' sizes expand, companies are searching for groundbreaking storage solutions that do not necessarily break ground. Google, for example, is considering sea-based centers on barges docked up to seven miles offshore. Energy generated from the waves' motions could help cool and power the supercomputers running the company's search engines.

Sun Microsystems is exploring using space in abandoned coal mines. The cool groundwater would help reduce temperatures and power consumption by 50 percent, resulting in a reduction in electricity costs of at least $9 million.

Another unlikely data center location, Siberia's frozen tundra, looks promising for Microsoft's expansion plans. Currently the company is building centers adjacent to hydroelectric plants, where recycled water will cool the tens of thousands of servers. This water does not need to be drinkable, so no energy is needed to purify it at waste water treatment sites. In another energy-saving measure, Microsoft is using cool outside air instead of air conditioning systems to reduce the computers' operating temperatures.

For more information, visit the Computer Concepts CourseMate Web site at www.cengagebrain.com, navigate to the Chapter 14 Innovative Computing resource for this book, and then click Data Centers.

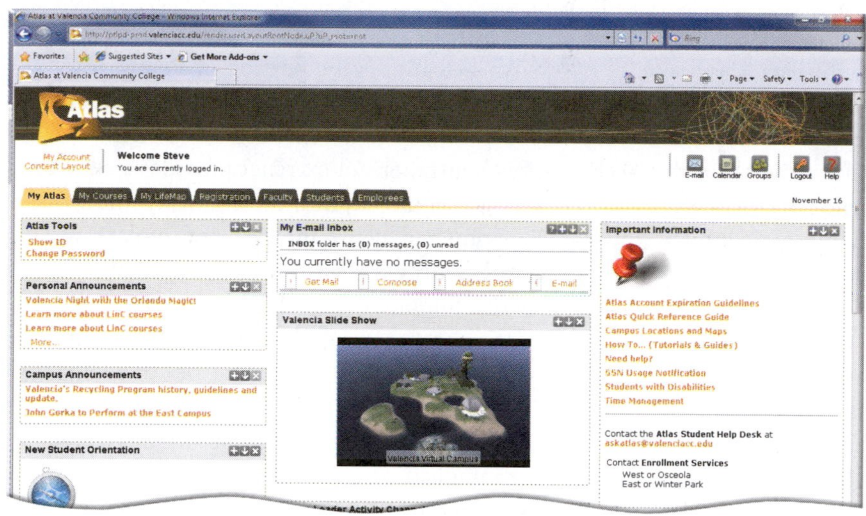

Figure 14-20 Portals allow users quick access to a multitude of information sources that they access on a regular basis.

financial summaries on the portal Web page, while a customer service representative views updates to product problems. Information from external sources included on a portal Web page can include weather, news, reference tools, and instant messaging.

Data Warehouses

A **data warehouse** is a huge database that stores and manages the data required to analyze historical and current transactions. Software, such as ERP and MRP II programs, store and access data in a data warehouse. A data warehouse may be stored in a cloud computing environment. Cloud computing is discussed later in this chapter.

Most data warehouses include one or more databases and one or more information systems storing data in the data warehouse. The data in the databases consists of transaction data required for decision making. This data may come from internal or external sources (Figure 14-21). Some data warehouses use Web farming for their external data.

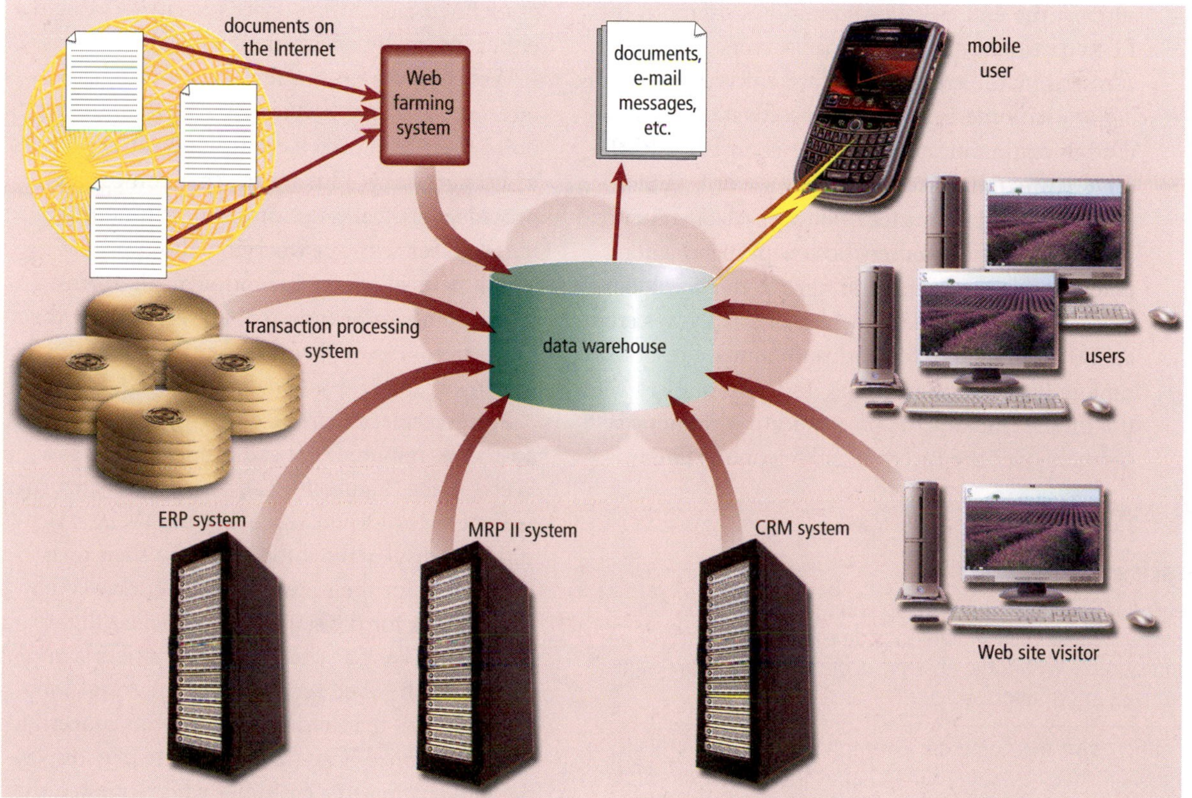

Figure 14-21 A data warehouse can receive data from a variety of sources, including company transactions, the Internet, and Web site visitor click streams.

Web farming is the process of collecting data from the Internet as a source for the data warehouse.

Another growing external source of information is a click stream. A *click stream* is a collection of every action that users make as they move through a Web site. By analyzing visitors' click streams, companies identify consumer preferences and determine which Web pages are most attractive to visitors.

Communications

The IT department, headed by the CIO, builds and maintains the electronic communications infrastructure of the enterprise. The communications infrastructure consists of hardware, software, and procedures. Examples of hardware include wired network connections, wireless network devices, routers, firewalls, servers, and a variety of long distance communications connections. Software can include e-mail, instant messaging, VoIP, and software to manage servers and end users' computers remotely. Procedures include the methods for using and managing the hardware and software. To learn about installing VoIP software on your computer, complete the Learn How To 1 activity on pages 768 and 769.

In addition to the communications software accessed by end users in the enterprise, the IT department manages the software on servers to support the end users' programs. For example, the IT department manages e-mail servers that are accessed by the end users' e-mail software programs.

For e-commerce, specialized software often is used to communicate with other computers. **EDI (electronic data interchange)** is a set of standards that controls the transfer of business data and information among computers both within and among enterprises. One of the first steps in the development of e-commerce was EDI, which originally was created to eliminate paperwork and improve response time in business interactions. Today, businesses use these standards to communicate with industry partners over the Internet and telephone lines.

? FAQ 14-2

Why do enterprises use wikis?

Enterprises are relying more heavily on wikis to create Web pages that are accessible to employees. These pages might include company information, links to information systems within the enterprise, or serve as a knowledge base for the enterprise's information systems.

For more information, visit the Computer Concepts CourseMate Web site at www.cengagebrain.com, navigate to the Chapter 14 FAQ resource for this book, and then click Enterprise Wikis.

Extranets

An **extranet** is the portion of a company's network that allows customers or suppliers of a company to access parts of an enterprise's intranet. An extranet provides a secure, physical connection to the company's network. Customers may use the extranet to place and monitor orders electronically or to make payments. Suppliers may check inventory levels of the parts they supply to the company and receive orders and payments from the company. Extranets improve efficiency by replacing the postal service, faxes, or telephone calls as the communications medium of choice. Recently, extranets have replaced or supplemented existing EDI systems.

Web Services

Web services include a relatively new set of software technologies that allows businesses to create products and B2B (business-to-business) interactions over the Internet. Web services represent an evolutionary step when compared with EDI. They send and receive requests for information from an enterprise's Web site using XML. Recall from Chapter 12 that XML is a format for sharing data that allows Web developers to create customized tags, as well as use predefined tags. Web services are made available either internally or externally.

Web services do not include traditional user interfaces, such as a Web page. Rather, users build their own interfaces to the Web services when necessary. This means that companies provide a critical piece of business functionality to a user without worrying about providing a complete solution. Two popular platforms for building and running Web services are the Sun Microsystems Java EE platform and the Microsoft .NET Framework.

For example, an airline company may provide up-to-the-minute flight status information as a Web service (Figure 14-22). Travel Web sites, such as Expedia or Orbitz, can query the Web service and then display the information on their own Web pages for their customers. The travel Web site may ask for the status of a particular flight and receive back a scheduled departure or arrival time from the Web service. How the travel Web site then uses that information is of no concern to the Web service. The travel Web site may display the information to a customer who requested the information, or it may send an e-mail notification

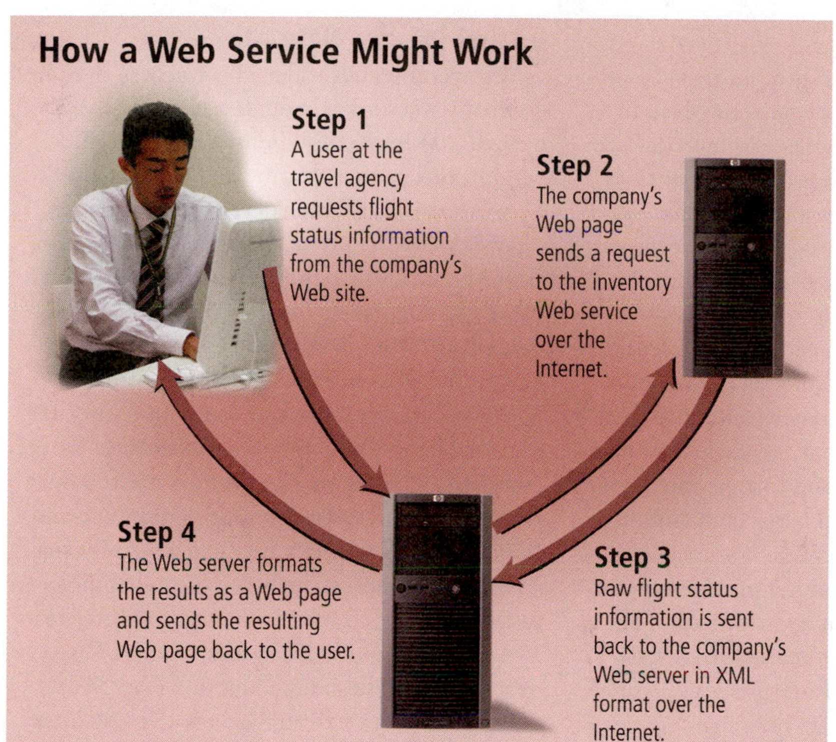

Figure 14-22 This figure shows how a Web service might work.

Web Services

For more information, visit the Computer Concepts CourseMate Web site at www.cengagebrain.com, navigate to the Chapter 14 Web Link resource for this book, and then click Web Services.

with the information to the customer. Typically, the customer or consumer of the Web service — the travel Web site in this example — must write a program to use the Web service.

Service-Oriented Architecture

Many enterprises now employ a service-oriented architecture because the company requires more communication between diverse information systems. In a *service-oriented architecture* (*SOA*), information systems provide services to other information systems in a well-defined manner over a network. For example, in a company that manufacturers airplanes, the marketing information system may provide a service in which potential airplane orders are made available to other information systems, which then can react to the potential orders.

One benefit to using an SOA is that services from multiple information systems can be combined to create new services or programs.

Document Management Systems

A **document management system (DMS)** allows for storage and management of a company's documents, such as word processing documents, presentations, and spreadsheets. A central library, or *repository*, stores all documents within a company or department. The system supports access control, security, version tracking of documents, search capabilities, and the ability for users to check in and check out documents. Users are granted access to certain parts of the repository depending on their needs. For example, one user may be responsible for creating promotional material, and therefore has the ability to create, read, and write presentations in the marketing department's repository. Salespeople need to be able only to read or copy the presentations from the repository, and therefore are granted only read privileges to the marketing department's repository.

A document management system has the benefit of tracking a document throughout its life cycle, from creation, through changes, and finally to archival. Additional information can be stored along with the document that describes the uses and history of the document. This information can include the document's creation date, the user who created the document, the project to which the document belongs, copyright information, a summary of the document, and any keywords associated with the document. This information can be used for searches within the document repository. Web application document management systems, such as Google Docs and Office Live Workspace, allow individuals and any organization to enjoy the benefits of document management systems. Google Docs provides both free and fee-based document management capabilities.

Workflow

A **workflow** is a defined process that identifies the specific set of steps involved in completing a particular project or business process. A workflow may be a written set of rules or a set of rules that exists in an information system. When an insurance company receives a claim from a customer, a workflow in the insurance company defines how the claim is validated, processed, and paid. Workflow rules trigger particular actions to be taken within the company. On an insurance claim, the first step may be to validate that the customer has a current policy and the claim form is filled out correctly. If not, the claim is rejected and the customer is notified.

A **workflow application** is a program that assists in the management and tracking of all the activities in a business process from start to finish (Figure 14-23). Enterprises use workflow applications to assist in defining complex workflows. Workflow applications also enforce the rules of the workflow once the workflow is defined and in place.

Virtual Private Network

Many companies today allow access to their company networks through a virtual private network. When a mobile user, remote office, vendor, or customer connects to a company's network using the Internet, a **virtual private network (VPN)** provides them with a secure connection to the company network server, as if they had a private line. VPNs help to ensure that transmitted data is safe from being intercepted by unauthorized people (Figure 14-24). VPNs securely extend the company's internal network beyond the physical boundaries of the company. The secure connection created over the Internet between the user's computer and the company's network is called a *VPN tunnel.* Microsoft Windows includes the capability to create VPN connections over the Internet. Programs from other vendors, such as Cisco Systems, include similar functionality. Many companies allow external access to their internal networks only via a VPN connection. Read Ethics & Issues 14-3 for a related discussion.

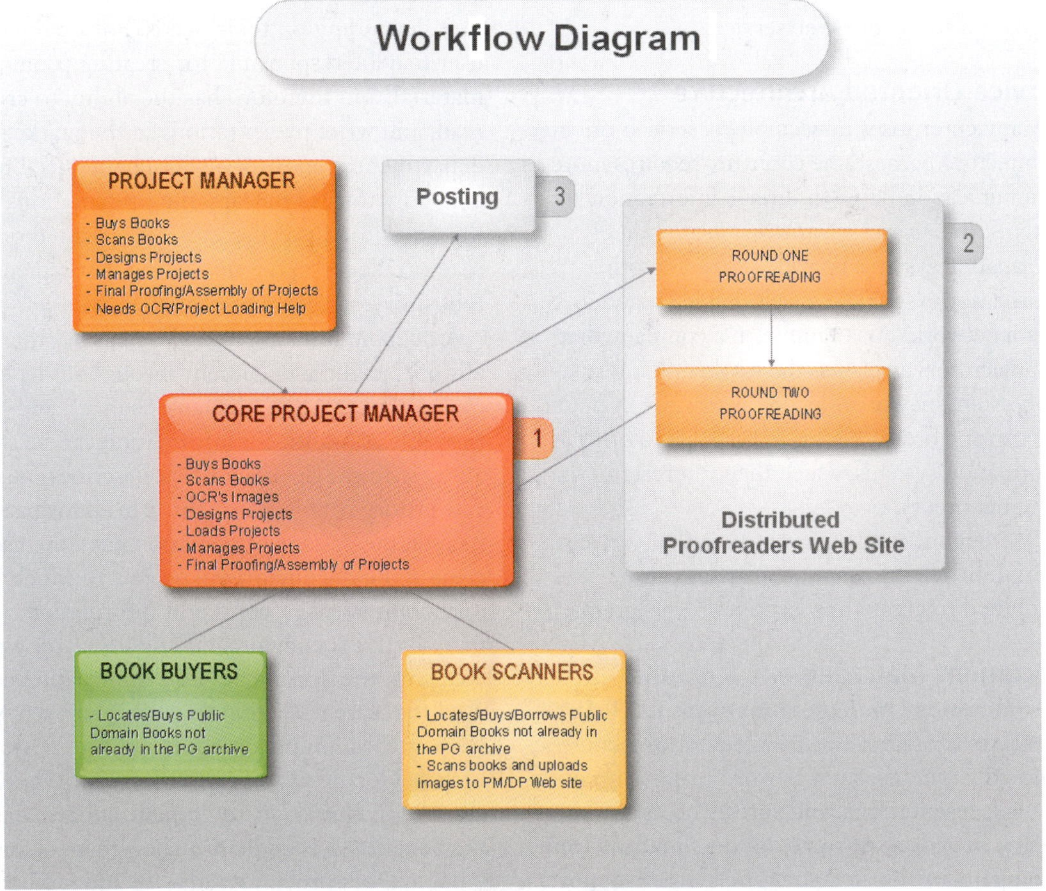

Figure 14-23 Workflow applications allow users to create visual workflows.

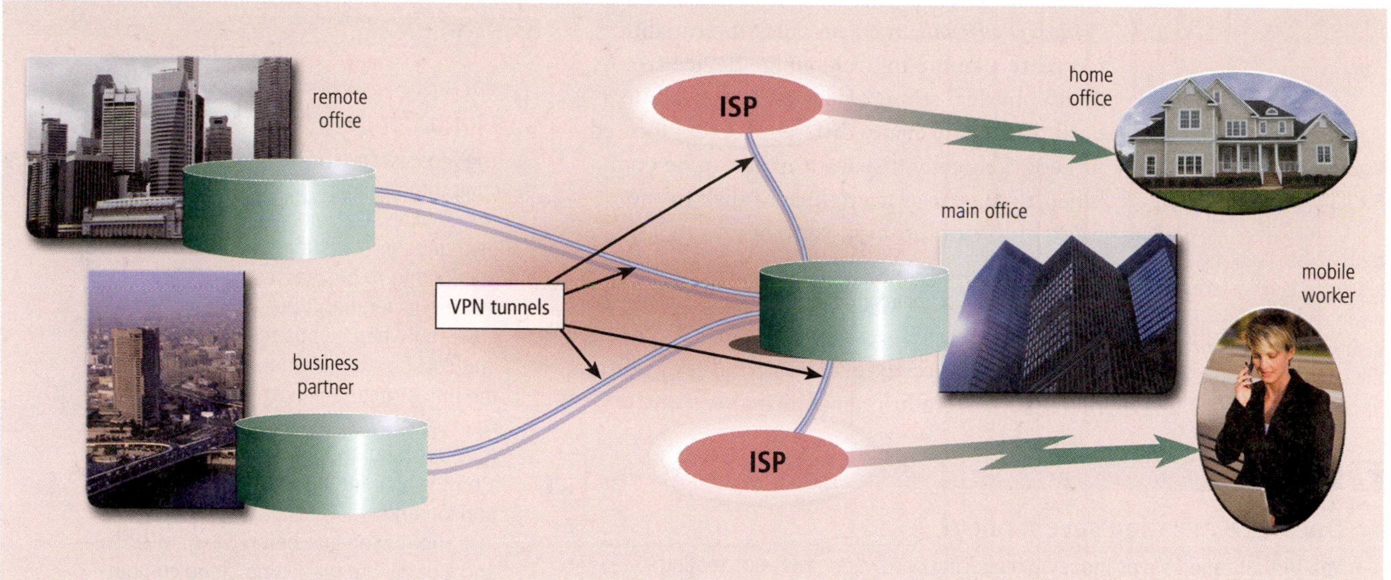

Figure 14-24 A virtual private network (VPN) allows a company to extend its internal network securely.

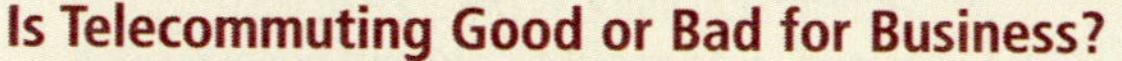
ETHICS & ISSUES 14-3

Is Telecommuting Good or Bad for Business?

Many workers dream of forever leaving the confines of their office cubicles to enjoy the pleasure of telecommuting while wearing slippers and pajamas. Proponents of telecommuting provide evidence of reduced pollution and commuting time and increased productivity due to lack of office gossip, politics, and other distractions. Managers and workers who oppose the practice claim that most people lack the self-discipline to work from home, or wherever a telecommuter may end up working. Employees more easily succumb to distractions without direct management supervision. Productivity actually may decrease because telecommuting often is not well defined. For one person, telecommuting may mean working from 8:00 a.m. to 5:00 p.m., while for another it may mean working 8 hours per day, but spreading out the work hours until 8:00 or 10:00 at night. While both work the same number of hours, coworkers find the telecommuters' staggered hours an annoyance. Many experienced workers agree that telecommuting cannot replace valuable face-to-face time with coworkers, vendors, and customers. Some workers fear telecommuting because they feel that the lack of a personal relationship with managers puts them at the top of the list for downsizing if the company experiences an economic downturn.

Is telecommuting good or bad for business? Why or why not? Are some businesses or job positions better suited for telecommuting? If so, which ones? Do some people simply lack the self-discipline to be productive while telecommuting? If so, how should managers make this determination?

Virtualization and Cloud Computing

As the cost of hardware and networking services dramatically decreases, the cost of skilled specialists to maintain complex information systems increases. These opposing trends have led to an increase in the use of virtualization and cloud computing. These technologies provide for centralized and/or outsourced management of information system infrastructure, such as servers, security, and networking. The following sections describe virtualization, cloud computing, and grid computing.

Virtualization

Due to the often dynamic nature of enterprise computing needs, IT administrators often use virtualization to adapt quickly to the change. *Virtualization* is the practice of sharing or pooling computing resources, such as servers and storage devices. *Server virtualization* provides the capability to divide a physical server logically into many virtual servers. From the end user's point of view, a virtual server behaves just like a physical server. The advantages of server virtualization are that a virtual server can be created and configured quickly, does not require a new physical server, and is easier to manage.

Storage virtualization provides the capability to create a single logical storage device from many physical storage devices. For example, hard disks from many different servers located in geographically disparate areas can be combined to appear as a single hard disk to the users of the storage. The advantages of storage virtualization are that the storage can be configured quickly, may not require the purchase of additional storage devices because the necessary capacity already may exist, and is easier to manage than traditional storage.

Virtualization

For more information, visit the Computer Concepts CourseMate Web site at www.cengagebrain.com, navigate to the Chapter 14 Web Link resource for this book, and then click Virtualization.

FAQ 14-3

Does virtualization save money?

Yes. Virtualization saves money by reducing hardware costs and creating efficiencies. Some companies also believe that because of their reduced hardware needs, they also will require fewer employees to manage their servers.

For more information, visit the Computer Concepts CourseMate Web site at www.cengagebrain.com, navigate to the Chapter 14 FAQ resource for this book, and then click Virtualization.

Cloud and Grid Computing

As the demand for computing resources increases, companies may find that using outside computing resources is more economical than building new computing capacity internally. Cloud and grid computing are two new technologies that provide flexible and massive online computing power. **Cloud computing** is an Internet service that provides computing needs to computer users. For example, an employee working during the day in California could use computing power in a Paris network system located in an office that is closed for the evening. When the company uses the computing resources, they pay a fee based on the amount of computing time and other resources that they consume, much in the way that consumers pay utility companies, such as the electric company, based on how much electricity they use. Cloud computing allows a company to diversify its network and server infrastructure. Some cloud computing services automatically add more network and server capacity to a company's Web site as demand for services of the Web site increases. The network and server capacity may be duplicated around the world so that, for example, an outage of a single server does not affect the company's operations. Read Looking Ahead 14-1 for a look at the future of cloud computing.

LOOKING AHEAD 14-1

Variable Winds Forecasted for Cloud Computing

The forecast for enterprise computing calls for partly cloudy skies. The winds of change in computing are coming to businesses in various degrees, but how and when companies and consumers will adopt the infrastructure is not clear. Most analysts agree that this revolutionary storm is brewing on the horizon and will reach just about everyone before long. Microsoft and Google are predicting cloud computing's future and are developing different business models. Microsoft is focusing on enterprise tools, while Google is working on consumer-based applications.

Small businesses should be the first widespread adopters because of cost-saving measures. Their organizational needs for occasional computing power, storage, and services make Web applications ideal. Startup companies increasingly will use pay-as-you-go assistance, such as Amazon's Web Services. Some forecasts predict that the only required hardware will be a monitor, keyboard, and mouse because all computing and storage will be performed offsite.

Large corporations, by contrast, will be slower to adopt cloud computing. Their more specific needs and concerns of security might delay their entry into this newer resource.

For more information, visit the Computer Concepts CourseMate Web site at www.cengagebrain.com, navigate to the Chapter 14 Looking Ahead resource for this book, and then click Cloud Computing.

Grid computing combines many servers and/or personal computers on a network, such as the Internet, to act as one large computer. As with cloud computing, a company may pay for the use of a grid based on the amount of processing time that it needs. Grid computing often is used in research environments, such as climate research and life science problems. For example, the SETI@home project uses a grid of millions of personal computers around the world to search radio signals for signs of extraterrestrial life.

E-Commerce

Several market sectors have taken advantage of business opportunities on the Web. The more popular market segments include retail, finance, travel, entertainment and media, and health. Figure 14-25 briefly reviews some of the more popular e-commerce market segments.

Enterprises use the Web to provide services to consumers and other businesses. Public relations, online advertising, direct mail, recruiting, credit, sales, market research, technical support, training, software consulting, and Internet access represent a few of the areas of service. Read Ethics & Issues 14-4 for additional information.

Examples of E-Commerce

Type	Purpose	Example Web Sites
E-Retail	**E-retail**, also called *e-tail,* occurs when retailers use the Web to sell their products and services.	amazon.com shopping.yahoo.com shopzilla.com
Finance	**Online banking** allows users to pay bills from their computer or mobile device, that is, transfer money electronically from their account to a payee's account such as the electric company or telephone company. With **online trading**, users invest in stocks, options, bonds, treasuries, certificates of deposit, money markets, annuities, mutual funds, and so on — without using a broker.	vanguard.com fidelity.com e-trade.com
Travel	The Web provides many travel-related services. If you need directions, you simply enter a starting point and destination, and many Web sites provide detailed directions along with a map. Users can make airline reservations and reserve a hotel or car.	orbitz.com priceline.com kayak.com
Entertainment and Media	Music, videos, news, sporting events, and 3-D multiplayer games are a growing part of the Web's future. Newsprint on the Web is not replacing the newspaper, but enhancing it and reaching different populations.	itunes.com youtube.com nytimes.com
Health	Many Web sites provide up-to-date medical, fitness, nutrition, or exercise information. Some Web sites offer the capability to listen in on health-related seminars and discussion.	webmd.com health.gov familydoctor.com drugstore.com

Figure 14-25 E-commerce allows a variety of industries to extend their relationships to their customers via the Internet.

ETHICS & ISSUES 14-4

Who Can You Trust When Making Purchases Online?

When you walk into a store, at some point in your shopping experience you almost always interact with a person directly. The online shopping experience, however, distances you from a seller who may be five hundred or five thousand miles away. For many consumers, this type of nonhuman transaction can be a source of stress and concern about the trustworthiness of the merchant. For some merchants, the distance and anonymity of the Internet provide an ideal climate for finding unknowing victims for unscrupulous activity, such as fraud. Consumer advocates and government agencies recommend many ways to avoid a bad online shopping experience. When you provide personal information, make sure that you are dealing with a secure Web site whose address begins with https:// rather than http://. Check the site's credentials, which may include seals from TRUSTe, the Better Business Bureau (BBB), or other certifying organizations. Make sure that the price you pay matches the price listed on the site and that you are not paying too much for shipping your order. When available, check reviews of the merchant offered by other consumers, but be aware that many merchants try to offer phony, positive reviews of themselves. Finally, make it a habit to rate merchants as often as possible so that others can learn from your experience.

When you shop online, how do you go about determining which online merchants are trustworthy? How do the methods that you use differ from merchants you visit when you walk into a store for the first time? Are consumer advocacy groups or the government the better choice for regulating online transactions? Why?

QUIZ YOURSELF 14-2

Instructions: Find the true statement below. Then, rewrite the remaining false statements so that they are true.

1. A portal is the portion of a company's network that allows customers or suppliers of a company to access parts of an enterprise's intranet.
2. A data warehouse is a huge database that stores and manages the data required to analyze historical and current transactions.
3. A VPN is a server that is placed on a network with the sole purpose of providing storage to users and information systems attached to the network.
4. A workflow application helps an enterprise collect, archive, index, and retrieve its resources.

Quiz Yourself Online: To further check your knowledge of pages 740 through 747, visit the Computer Concepts CourseMate Web site at www.cengagebrain.com, navigate to the Chapter 14 Quiz Yourself resource for this book, and then click Objectives 4 – 5.

Enterprise Hardware

Enterprise hardware allows large organizations to manage and store information and data using devices geared for heavy use, maximum availability, and maximum efficiency. To meet these needs, enterprise hardware often includes levels of redundancy, which means that if one piece of the hardware breaks, another part can assume its tasks. (Redundant components are discussed later in this chapter.)

Enterprises often rely on legacy systems. A *legacy system* is an information system that has existed within the organization for an extended length of time and is relied upon heavily. Enterprises often struggle with the decision to replace legacy systems with newer technology.

Enterprises use a variety of hardware types to meet their large-scale needs. The following sections discuss a variety of enterprise hardware solutions.

FAQ 14-4

How do enterprises reduce energy consumption in their data centers?

Enterprises use the power-saving practices of virtualization, high-efficiency UPSs, and power management features to reduce energy consumption in their data centers. The chart to the right shows the different techniques organizations use to save energy.

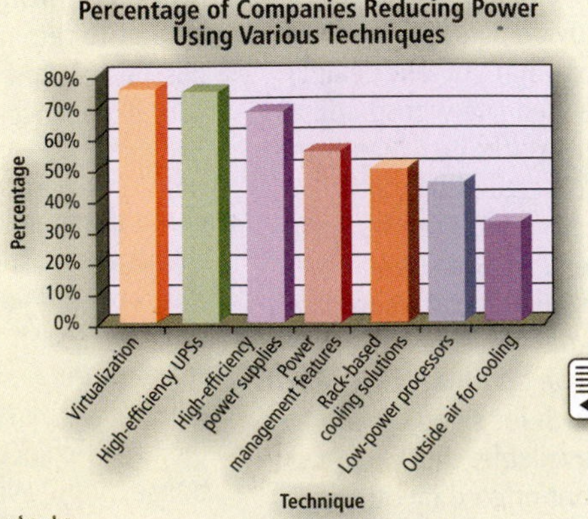

For more information, visit the Computer Concepts CourseMate Web site at www.cengagebrain.com, navigate to the Chapter 14 FAQ resource for this book, and then click Energy Reduction.

RAID

For applications that depend on reliable data access, users must have the data available when they attempt to access it. Some manufacturers provide a type of hard disk system that connects several smaller disks into a single unit that acts like a single large hard disk. As discussed in Chapter 7, a group of two or more integrated hard disks is called a **RAID (redundant array of independent disks)**. Although quite expensive for large computers, RAID is more reliable than traditional hard disks (Figure 14-26). Networks and Internet servers often use RAID.

RAID duplicates data, instructions, and information to improve data reliability. RAID implements this duplication in different ways, depending on the storage design, or level, being used. (These levels are not hierarchical. That is, higher levels are not necessarily better than lower levels.) The simplest RAID storage design is *level 1*, called *mirroring*, which writes data on two disks at the same time to duplicate the data (Figure 14-27a). A level 1 configuration enhances storage reliability because, if a disk should fail, a

Figure 14-26 A group of two or more integrated hard disks, called a RAID (redundant array of independent disks), often is used with network servers. Shown here is a rack-mounted RAID chassis including the hard disks.

duplicate of the requested item is available elsewhere within the array of disks.

Other RAID levels use a technique called *striping*, which splits data, instructions, and information across multiple disks in the array (Figure 14-27b). Striping improves disk access times, but does not offer data duplication. For this reason, some RAID levels combine both mirroring and striping. Some personal computers now include RAID storage, including striping and mirroring, to improve reliability.

Network Attached Storage and Storage Area Networks

Network attached storage (**NAS**) is a server that is placed on a network with the sole purpose of providing storage to users and information systems attached to the network (Figure 14-28a). A network attached storage server often is called a *storage appliance* because it is a piece of equipment with only one function — to provide additional storage. Administrators quickly add storage to an existing network simply by attaching a new network attached storage server to the network.

A **storage area network** (**SAN**) is a high-speed network with the sole purpose of providing storage to other servers to which it is attached (Figure 14-28b). A storage area network is a network that includes only storage devices. High-speed fiber-optic cable usually connects other networks and servers to the storage area network, so that the networks and servers have fast access to large storage capacities. A storage area network connects to networks and other servers up to seven miles away using high-speed network connections.

Both network attached storage and storage area network solutions offer easier management of storage, fast access to storage, sharing of storage, and isolation of storage from other servers. Isolation of storage from other servers lets other servers concentrate on performing a specific task, rather than consuming resources involved in the tasks related to storage. Network attached storage and storage area network systems connect to existing networks and servers in different manners, as shown in Figure 14-28. Both storage solutions include disk, tape, and optical disc types of storage.

Figure 14-27a (mirroring)

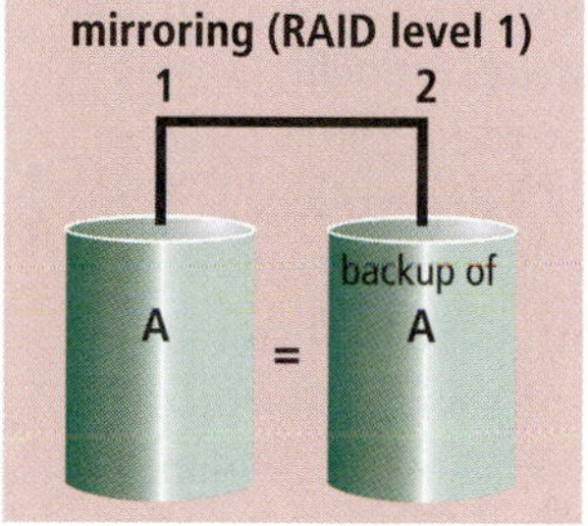

Figure 14-27b (striping)

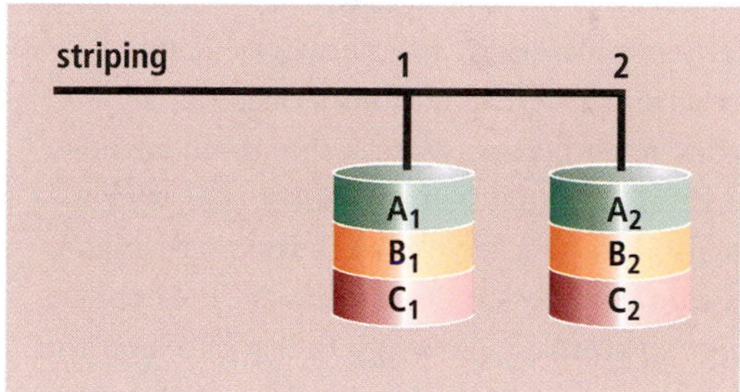

Figure 14-27 In RAID level 1, called mirroring, a backup disk exists for each disk. Other RAID levels use striping; that is, portions of each disk are placed on multiple disks.

Figure 14-28a (network attached storage on a LAN)

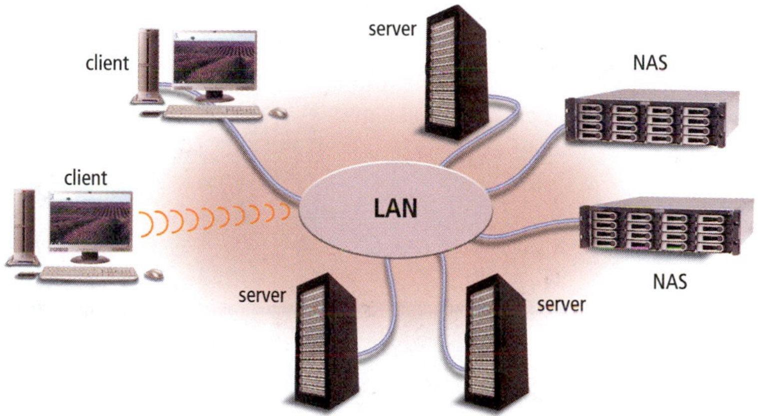

Figure 14-28b (a SAN provides centralized storage for servers and networks)

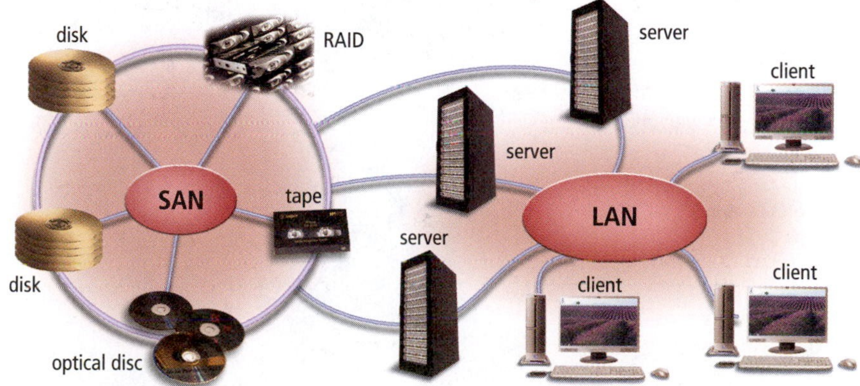

Figure 14-28 Network attached storage (NAS) and a storage area network (SAN) connect to existing servers and networks in different ways.

NAS and SAN

For more information, visit the Computer Concepts CourseMate Web site at www.cengagebrain.com, navigate to the Chapter 14 Web Link resource for this book, and then click NAS and SAN.

Enterprises sometimes choose to implement both network attached storage and storage area network solutions. A network attached storage server is better suited for adding storage to an existing network, such as a department's file server. A company typically implements a storage area network solution as central storage for an entire enterprise or a large information system, such as an enterprise resource planning system.

Enterprise Storage Systems

Many organizations use networks. Data, information, and instructions stored on the network must be easily accessible to all authorized users. The data, information, and instructions also must be secure, so that unauthorized users cannot access the network. An **enterprise storage system** is a strategy that focuses on the availability, protection, organization, and backup of storage in a company.

The goal of an enterprise storage system is to consolidate storage so that operations run as efficiently as possible. Most enterprise storage systems manage extraordinary amounts of data. For example, one large retailer manages a several-hundred TB storage system to store sales data. Read Ethics & Issues 14-5 for a related discussion.

To implement an enterprise storage system, an organization uses a combination of techniques. As shown in Figure 14-29, an enterprise storage system may use servers, RAID, a tape library, optical disc jukeboxes, Internet backup, network attached storage devices, and/or a storage area network. Enterprises often use *Fibre Channel* technology to connect to storage systems at data rates up to 4 Gbps. The following list explains these storage techniques.

- A server stores data, information, and instructions needed by users on the network.
- RAID ensures that data is not lost if one drive fails.
- A *tape library* is a high-capacity tape system that works with multiple tape cartridges for storing backups.
- An **optical disc server**, also called an *optical disc jukebox*, holds hundreds of optical discs that can contain programs and data.
- Companies using *Internet backup* store data, information, and instructions on the Web.

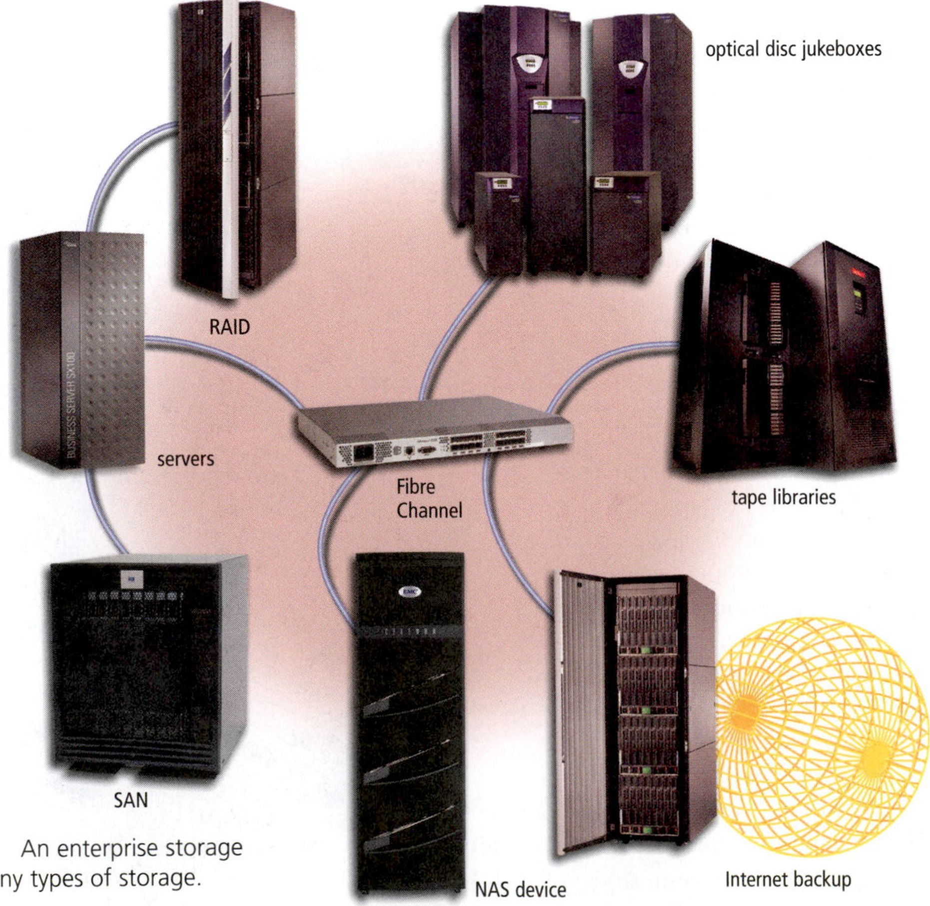

Figure 14-29 An enterprise storage system uses many types of storage.

ETHICS & ISSUES 14-5

How Much Data Should Companies Be Required to Keep?

After a string of corporate scandals, the Sarbanes-Oxley Act was signed into law in 2002, providing a myriad of financial reporting requirements and guidelines for public companies. A main focus of the law is the retention of business records. As provisions of the law slowly have come into effect, companies have been faced with massive new data storage requirements for these records. For example, all e-mail messages within a company are considered to be business records and must be retained. Deleting stored e-mail messages constitutes a destruction of evidence infraction. Penalties include 20 years in prison for any employee who alters or destroys records or documents. IT departments are faced not only with understanding this complex law, but also with ensuring accuracy of financial data, determining policies for record retention, and building storage capacity to hold all of the data. Supporters of the law cite its need due to the recent wave of corporate scandals. Opponents say that the law is overreaching and costs too much for the added benefits.

Is the Sarbanes-Oxley Act an unfair burden on companies? Why or why not? Should companies be able to engage in internal communications without the fear that those communications could be used as evidence against them later? Why or why not? Should employees or employers be held accountable if laws are violated? Why? Are such laws necessary in order to protect the public? Why or why not?

Ethics & Issues

For the complete text of the Ethics & Issues boxes found in this chapter, visit the Computer Concepts CourseMate Web site at www.cengagebrain.com and then navigate to the Chapter 14 Ethics & Issues resource for this book.

- A network attached storage device is an easy way to add additional hard disk space to the network.
- A storage area network is a high-speed network that connects storage devices.

Some organizations manage an enterprise storage system in-house. Other enterprises elect to offload all (or at least the backup) storage management to an outside organization or online Web service. This practice is known as *outsourcing*. Some vendors focus on providing enterprise storage systems to clients. A data warehouse might seek this type of outside service.

Blade Servers

A **blade server**, sometimes called an *ultradense server*, packs a complete computer server, such as a Web server or network server, on a single card, or *blade*, rather than a system unit. Each blade server includes a processor, memory, hard disk, network card, and ports on the card. The individual blades insert in a *blade server chassis* that can hold many blades. Using blade servers allows an organization to fit 16 or more blades in the physical space occupied by a typical, single server. Figure 14-30 shows a blade and a chassis that holds many blades.

Besides the savings in space offered by blade servers, blade servers require less maintenance, use less energy, generate less heat, and easily are replaced or upgraded. The use of blade servers often is undertaken as part of a company's green computing efforts. The hardware industry, however, disagrees on a standard for blade servers. A blade server made by one manufacturer often is incompatible with the blade server chassis of another manufacturer.

Blade Servers

For more information, visit the Computer Concepts CourseMate Web site at www.cengagebrain.com, navigate to the Chapter 14 Web Link resource for this book, and then click Blade Servers.

FAQ 14-5

How popular are blade servers?

One study estimates that while blade servers accounted for about 10 percent of sales in 2006, today they account for more than $5.4 billion in worldwide blade server revenue.

For more information, visit the Computer Concepts CourseMate Web site at www.cengagebrain.com, navigate to the Chapter 14 FAQ resource for this book, and then click Blade Servers.

Figure 14-30 A blade server contains several very small servers, each on its own blade within the server.

Thin Clients

A **thin client** is a small terminal-like computer that mostly relies on a server for data storage and processing. These computers are inexpensive compared to a personal computer. As shown in Figure 14-31, the system unit of a thin client usually consists of a monitor and ports. A keyboard and a mouse, or other pointing device, are attached to the system unit. A thin client typically does not contain a hard disk, and the lack of many components usually seen on a personal computer makes thin clients much easier and less expensive to maintain and repair.

The processing for a thin client usually is done on a server to which the client is attached over a network. The server may be configured in two ways — either as a virtual server on a central server or as a personal computer blade. In the first configuration, a single server is virtually divided into several personal computers. That is, one server may run 50 to more than 100 virtual servers at the same time. Each thin client shares the resources of the central server, but each individual virtual server has its own place in the memory of the central server. The second type of configuration, the *personal computer blade* (PC blade), works in much the same manner as blade servers. Individual PC blades in a blade server each act as a separate personal computer, containing a processor, memory, and hard disk.

High Availability, Scalability, and Interoperability

Enterprises measure the quality of their operations in a number of ways. Often, systems have specific requirements for availability, the capability to grow (scalability), and interoperability. One of the goals of an enterprise's hardware is to maintain a high level of availability to end users. The *availability* of hardware to users is a measure of how often it is online. Highly available hardware is accessible 24 hours a day, 365 days a year. The following sections discuss these needs in an enterprise.

High-Availability Systems

A **high-availability system** continues running and performing tasks for at least 99 percent of the time. Some users demand that high-availability systems be available for 99.9 percent or 99.99 percent of the time. *Uptime* is a measurement of availability. A system that has an uptime of 99.99 percent is nonfunctional for less than one hour per year. That one hour, called *downtime*, includes any time that the computer crashes, needs repairs, or requires installation of replacement or upgrade parts. A system with 99.9 percent availability is said to have three nines of availability, and a system with 99.99 percent availability is said to have four nines of availability.

Critical business systems demand high levels of availability. Telecommunications companies,

Figure 14-31 A thin client usually consists of a monitor, optical disc drive, keyboard, and mouse.

such as local telephone companies, rely on high-availability systems to deliver telephone service. Emergency 911 communications centers require almost 100 percent uptime for their hardware and software applications as mandated by law. Centralized accounting or financial systems must be available to gather sales and other accounting information from locations scattered around the globe.

High-availability systems often include a feature called hot-swapping. *Hot-swapping* allows components, such as a RAID hard disk or power supplies, to be replaced while the rest of the system continues to perform its tasks. A high-availability system also may include redundant components. **Redundant components**, such as redundant power supplies (Figure 14-32), allow for a functioning component to take over automatically the tasks of a similar component that fails. When a component fails, the system administrator is notified, but the computer continues to perform its tasks because a redundant component has taken its place automatically in the system.

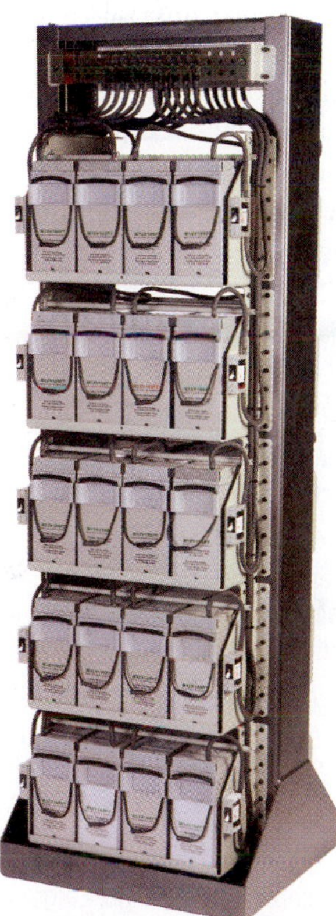

Figure 14-32 This heavy duty battery rack provides reliable backup power for enterprise hardware.

Scalability

As an enterprise grows, its information systems either must grow with it or must be replaced. **Scalability** is a measure of how well computer hardware, software, or an information system can grow to meet increasing performance demands. A system that is designed, built, or purchased when the company is small may be inadequate when the company doubles in size. When making decisions for computing solutions, managers must be careful to consider the growth plans of the company.

A company may find that its Web site is becoming overwhelmed by customers and prospective customers. If the Web site is scalable, then the Web administrator can add more Web servers to handle the additional visitors to the Web site. Similarly, an enterprise's storage needs usually grow daily, meaning that storage systems should be scalable to store the ever-growing data generated by users.

Adding more hardware often is the easiest method to grow, or scale, an information system. Because of software constraints, however, information systems may grow to a point at which adding more hardware does not achieve the return on investment required to justify the cost of the hardware. Often, at some point, a system no longer scales and must be replaced with a new system.

Interoperability

Enterprises typically build and buy a diverse set of information systems. An information system often must share information, or have **interoperability**, with other information systems within the enterprise. Information systems that more easily share information with other information systems are said to be *open*. Information systems that are more difficult to interoperate with other information systems are said to be *closed*, or *proprietary*. Recent open systems employ XML and Web services to allow a greater level of interoperability.

Enterprises own diverse hardware, software, and information systems for a variety of reasons. The enterprise may want to diversify its technology to reduce the risk of relying on just one type of technology. When a company relies on one type of technology, it risks that the technology may be limited in its ability to grow or change with the company, that the technology may become obsolete, and that the technology may become more expensive relative to competing technologies. Enterprises also grow through acquisitions of other companies, and the systems of the acquired companies must be integrated into the enterprise's existing systems.

Backup Procedures

Business and home users can perform four types of backup: full, differential, incremental, or selective. A fifth type, continuous data protection, typically is used only by large enterprises. A full backup, sometimes called an archival backup, copies all of the files in the computer. A full backup provides the best protection against data loss because it copies all program and data files. Performing a full backup can be time-consuming. Users often combine full backups with differential and incremental backups. A differential backup copies only the files that have changed since the last full backup. An incremental backup copies only the files that have changed since the last full or last incremental backup. A selective backup, sometimes called a partial backup, allows the user to choose specific files to back up, regardless of whether or not the files have changed since the last incremental backup.

With incremental backups, you have the full backup and one or more incremental backups. The first incremental backup contains changes since the last full backup. Each subsequent incremental backup contains changes only since the previous incremental backup. Figure 14-33 outlines the advantages and disadvantages of each type of backup.

Continuous data protection (CDP), or continuous backup, is a backup plan in which all data is backed up whenever a change is made. Because CDP is costly, few organizations have implemented continuous data protection, but its popularity is growing quickly as the cost for the technology falls. CDP requires little or no maintenance when compared to other backup methods. Many experts believe that CDP will replace all other types of backups in the future. Figure 14-34 illustrates an example of the hardware that might be included in a CDP system.

Backup procedures specify a regular plan of copying and storing important data and program files. Generally, users should perform a full backup at regular intervals, such as at the end of each week and at the end of the month. Between full backups, you can perform differential or incremental backups. Whatever backup procedures a company adopts, they should be stated clearly, documented in writing, and followed consistently.

Various Backup Methods

Type of Backup	Advantages	Disadvantages
Full	Fastest recovery method. All files are saved.	Longest backup time.
Differential	Fast backup method. Requires minimal storage space to back up.	Recovery is time-consuming because the last full backup plus the differential backup are needed.
Incremental	Fastest backup method. Requires minimal storage space to back up. Only most recent changes saved.	Recovery is most time-consuming because the last full backup and all incremental backups since the last full backup are needed.
Selective	Fast backup method. Provides great flexibility.	Difficult to manage individual file backups. Least manageable of all the backup methods.
Continuous	The only real-time backup. Very fast recovery of data.	Very expensive and requires a great amount of storage.

Figure 14-33 The advantages and disadvantages of various backup methods.

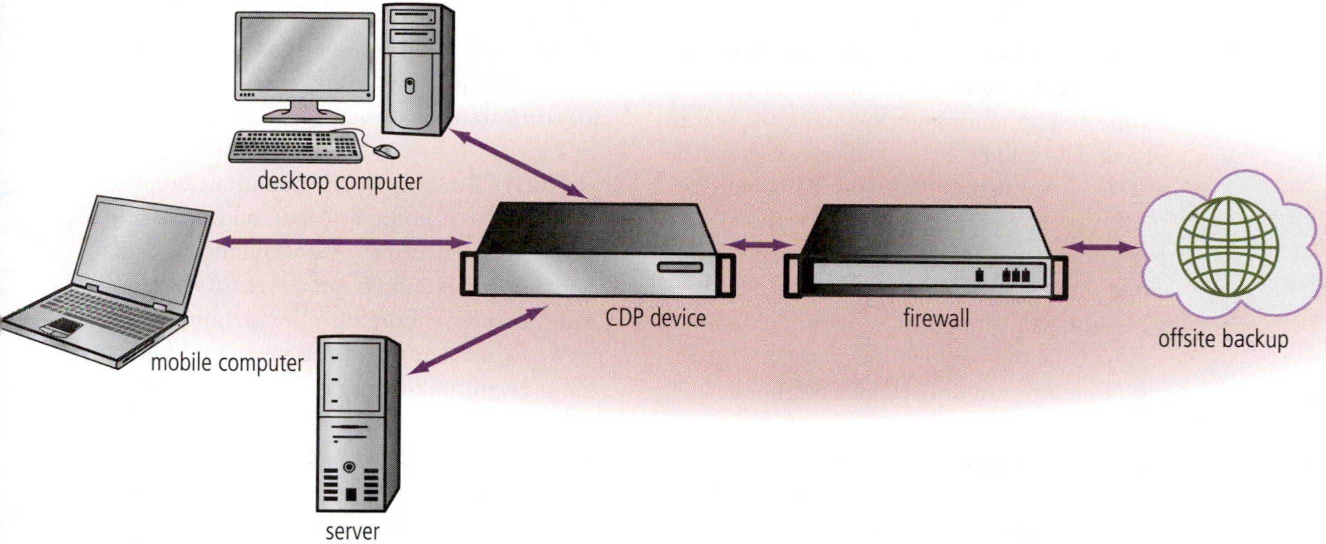

Figure 14-34 Continuous data protection (CDP) provides automatic data backup whenever data is changed in an enterprise.

FAQ 14-6

Can I use CDP at home?

Yes. The price of storage devices is decreasing, and companies that provide CDP are able to offer their services at rates much lower than what once were offered. For instance, one company allows you to back up 2 GB of data continuously for less than $60 per year.

 For more information, visit the Computer Concepts CourseMate Web site at www.cengagebrain.com, navigate to the Chapter 14 FAQ resource for this book, and then click CDP.

Disaster Recovery Plan

A **disaster recovery plan** is a written plan describing the steps a company would take to restore computer operations in the event of a disaster. Every company and each department or division within an enterprise usually has its own disaster recovery plans. A disaster recovery plan contains four major components: the emergency plan, the backup plan, the recovery plan, and the test plan.

The Emergency Plan An *emergency plan* specifies the steps to be taken immediately after a disaster strikes. The emergency plan usually is organized by type of disaster, such as fire, flood, or earthquake. Depending on the nature and extent of the disaster, the procedures that are followed in an emergency will differ. All emergency plans should contain the following information:

1. Names and telephone numbers of people and organizations to notify (e.g., management, fire department, police department)
2. Procedures to follow with the computer equipment (e.g., equipment shutdown, power shutoff, file removal)
3. Employee evacuation procedures
4. Return procedures; that is, who can reenter the facility and what actions they are to perform

The Backup Plan Once the procedures in the emergency plan have been executed, the next step is to follow the backup plan. The *backup plan* specifies how an organization uses backup files and equipment to resume information processing. The backup plan should specify the location of an alternate computer facility in the event the organization's normal location is destroyed or unusable.

When operations are so important that an organization cannot afford to lose the operations to a disaster, the organization often maintains a *hot site*, which is a separate facility that mirrors the systems and operations of the critical site. The hot site always operates concurrently with the main site, so that if either site becomes unavailable, the other site continues to meet the **organization**'s needs. The process of one system automatically taking the place of a failed system is called *failover*. A *cold site* is a site that mirrors the critical site, but does not become operational until the critical site becomes unavailable. When using a cold site, some time elapses between the disaster and when the cold site becomes functional.

The backup plan identifies these items:

1. The location of backup data, supplies, and equipment
2. The personnel responsible for gathering backup resources and transporting them to the alternate computer facility
3. A schedule indicating the order in which, and approximate time by which, each application should be up and running

For a backup plan to be successful, the organization must back up all critical resources. Also, additional people, including possibly nonemployees, must be trained in the backup and recovery procedures because organization personnel could be injured in a disaster.

The location of the alternate computer facility is important. It should be close enough to be convenient, yet not so close that a single disaster, such as an earthquake, could destroy both the main and alternate computer facilities. Some organizations preinstall all the necessary hardware, software, and communications devices at the alternate computer facility. These facilities immediately are ready in the event of a disaster. In other cases, the alternate computer facility is simply an empty facility that can accommodate the necessary computer resources, if needed. One more alternative is to enter into a *reciprocal backup relationship* with another firm, where one firm provides space and sometimes equipment to the other in case of a disaster.

Disaster Recovery Plan

For more information, visit the Computer Concepts CourseMate Web site at www.cengagebrain.com, navigate to the Chapter 14 Web Link resource for this book, and then click Disaster Recovery Plan.

The Recovery Plan The *recovery plan* specifies the actions to be taken to restore full information processing operations. As with the emergency plan, the recovery plan differs for each type of disaster. To prepare for disaster recovery, an organization should establish planning committees, with each one responsible for different forms of recovery. For example, one committee is in charge of hardware replacement. Another is responsible for software replacement.

The Test Plan To provide assurance that the disaster plan is complete, it should be tested. A disaster recovery *test plan* contains information for simulating various levels of disasters and recording an organization's ability to recover. In a simulation, all personnel follow the steps in the disaster recovery plan. Any needed recovery actions that are not specified in the plan should be added. Although simulations can be scheduled, the best test of the plan is to simulate a disaster without advance notice. Read Innovative Computing 14-2 to find an example of another type of simulation.

INNOVATIVE COMPUTING 14-2

PS3s Perform Rocket Science

Sony's PlayStation 3 has won the hearts of some gamers, but it also is finding a home in scientific labs. Astrophysicists at the University of Massachusetts networked 15 PS3s, installed Linux, and programmed the supercomputer to simulate black hole activity.

Their PS3 Gravity Grid outperforms the best desktop computers available and is powered by a Cell processor, which has six special computing engines that can perform multiple mathematical operations in a single step. The researchers claim this speed, combined with the PS3's relatively low cost, give their Gravity Grid the least expensive raw computing power per dollar of any computer available today.

The PS3s are being used for several projects. The Binary Black Hole Coalescence study estimates the properties of gravitational waves generated when two enormous black holes collide. Albert Einstein predicted these traveling ripples in his general relativity theory. Another project, called AstroPulse, searches for high-power broadband signals being sent from possible black holes, pulsars, and civilizations on distant planets.

For more information, visit the Computer Concepts CourseMate Web site at www.cengagebrain.com, navigate to the Chapter 14 Innovative Computing resource for this book, and then click PS3.

QUIZ YOURSELF 14-3

Instructions: Find the true statement below. Then, rewrite the remaining false statements so that they are true.

1. Network attached storage is a high-speed network with the sole purpose of providing storage to other servers to which it is attached.
2. Scalability refers to the ability of an information system to share information with other information systems.
3. A differential backup copies only the files that have changed since the last full or last incremental backup.
4. A full backup is the fastest backup method, requiring only minimal storage.
5. An emergency plan specifies how a company uses backup files and equipment to resume information processing.
6. The recovery plan specifies the actions to be taken to restore full information processing operations.

 **Quiz Yourself Online:** To further check your knowledge of pages 748 through 756, visit the Computer Concepts CourseMate Web site at www.cengagebrain.com, navigate to the Chapter 14 Quiz Yourself resource for this book, and then click Objectives 6 – 9.

Chapter Summary

This chapter reviewed the special computing requirements present in an enterprise-sized organization. Various types of users within an organization require different types of information systems. Large information systems become more valuable when they communicate with each other and offer users a great deal of flexibility in interacting with the information system and other users. The chapter discussed the benefits of virtualization, cloud computing, and grid computing.

Enterprises manage complex hardware, including storage area networks, RAID, and blade servers. Requirements for this enterprise hardware often include high-availability, scalability, and interoperability. The chapter also discussed the backup procedures present in a large organization.

Computer Usage @ Work

Municipal Services

You stayed up late last night and woke up late this morning. Because you take the bus to work, you hurry to get ready and arrive at the bus stop at 7:45 a.m., the exact time that the bus is scheduled to arrive. Ten minutes elapse and you are unsure whether you missed the bus or if the bus merely is running late. You call the city's transportation department to inquire about the bus, but they are unable to provide you with any information. Fortunately, the person with whom you are speaking informs you that the city currently is investing in a system that will provide exact bus arrival times at bus stops; it also will allow management to track the location of buses on their route. This technology uses a global positioning system to determine each bus's exact location and transmits that information back to a server. The server then can transmit relevant information to displays located at various bus stops throughout the city. Management also can use this information to dispatch additional buses if traffic conditions are poor, determine whether bus drivers are staying on their assigned routes, and discover whether they are obeying speed limits and other traffic laws.

After work, you arrive home to find an electrician installing a new electrical meter on your house. Your curiosity prompts you to approach the electrician to find out about the new meter, because you have had no problems with the old one. The electrician explains that in an effort to increase efficiency and save money, the power companies in the area are installing new meters that record power usage data electronically and then transmit the data wirelessly to the billing office. This new technology eliminates the need for employees to visit each house individually and reduces the possibility of human error in calculating your power consumption.

As the day ends, you watch a news story about how your city is installing sirens in strategic areas that will sound when dangerous weather approaches. These sirens either can be activated manually, or they can sound automatically when the National Weather Service issues a severe weather warning for your immediate area.

Computers have enhanced municipal services greatly during the past several years. Not only do computers provide increased opportunities for efficiency, they also provide a wealth of information to which one might not have access otherwise.

 For more information, visit the Computer Concepts CourseMate Web site at www.cengagebrain.com, navigate to the Chapter 14 Computer Usage @ Work resource for this book, and then click Municipal Services.

High-Tech Talk

Neural Networks: Learning from Experience

A *neural network* is a type of artificial intelligence system that attempts to emulate the way the human brain works. Neural networks are named after *neurons*, which are the billons of cells in the human brain that perform intelligent operations. Each neuron is like a small computer with basic capabilities. When billions of neurons are connected together, however, these cells are the intellectual capacity in the human brain, the most intelligent system known.

Neural networks are modeled on the human brain. A neural network uses an interconnected system of hundreds or thousands of specially designed circuits, also called *artificial neurons*. Like the brain's neurons, these circuits are connected together. Neural networks also are called *artificial neural networks* (*ANNs*) to differentiate the network of artificial neurons from the network of biological neurons in the human brain.

A neural network uses these circuits to create connections between inputs and outputs. The most common neural network model is the *multilayer perceptron* (*MLP*), which consists of at least three layers of circuits: a layer of input circuits, which is connected to one or more layers of hidden circuits, which are connected to a layer of output circuits (Figure 14-35). The knowledge of a neural network is housed in the hidden layers, which store the information that defines relationships between inputs and outputs.

Just as people do, neural networks learn from experience. Some neural networks are trained using a process called backpropagation, as shown in Figure 14-35. During *backpropagation*, the input data, which is the information used to make a decision, repeatedly is presented to the neural network via the input layer. The neural network then generates an output, which is the resulting decision, prediction, or response, based on the weighted connections between the inputs and outputs, as stored in the hidden layers.

The output of the neural network then is compared with the desired output, and the error is calculated based on historical or known data. This error then is fed back, or backpropagated, to the hidden layer to adjust the weights of the connection. During each repetition, the neural network learns to associate the weight of the relationship between certain inputs and outputs. It then adjusts the weights of the connections between the inputs and outputs accordingly. The hidden layers thus store a neural network's knowledge as weighted connections between inputs and outputs, which are known as *synaptic weights*. As training continues, the extent of the error decreases with each iteration, until the neural network reaches a fully trained state where it reliably produces the desired output. The neural network then is ready to produce outputs when the desired output is unknown.

Unlike humans, once trained fully, a neural network recognizes and classifies patterns in huge quantities of complex data, at high speeds that humans cannot duplicate. Uses of neural networks include a wide range of applications, such as sorting mail at the U.S. Postal Service, determining the number of jurors to call at county courthouses, and identifying police officers with a potential for misconduct. Scientists use neural networks to predict rainfall and forecast air quality. Manufacturers benefit from neural networks that allow them to test the quality of plastics and welding and determine which type of concrete to use on a highway. In health care, neural networks help predict heart attacks and cancer risk, while helping to improve treatment.

For more information, visit the Computer Concepts CourseMate Web site at www.cengagebrain.com, navigate to the Chapter 14 High-Tech Talk resource for this book, and then click Neural Networks.

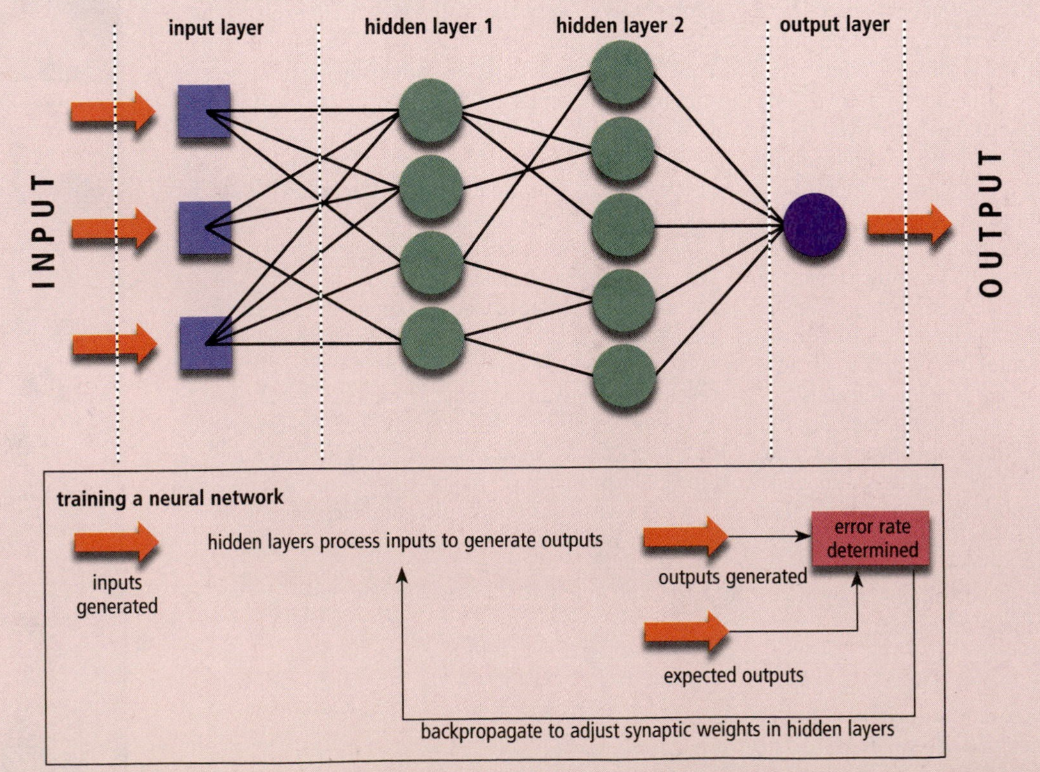

Figure 14-35 How a neural network works.

Companies on the Cutting Edge

EMC Information Management and Storage Provider

Data protection and storage are keys to running a successful business and preserving family memories. *EMC* specializes in producing innovative solutions for storing, safeguarding, and managing information so that it readily is available, searchable, and sharable.

EMC is the world leader in external storage and storage management systems. It is best known for its large-scale enterprise storage systems, and customers include financial services firms, health-care organizations, transportation companies, educational institutions, and manufacturers. Its RAID systems, networked storage systems, and storage management software are ranked at the top of the industry revenue shares.

EMC's Proven Professional certification program, aimed at validating knowledge about various IT topics, recently granted more than 45,000 certifications. EMC also has received numerous top awards for its network storage, software, and environmental practices.

IBM World's Largest Information Technology Company

Data centers consume tremendous amounts of electricity, but *IBM* is working to reduce energy consumption in these centralized locations. Its energy-efficient Active Energy Manager (AEM) tracks electricity usage and allows businesses to set a cap on total energy use for storing, networking, serving, and cooling operations.

IBM's services, consulting, and infrastructure components have helped companies develop new business ventures. Its systems supply nearly one-half of the world's supercomputing processing power, and the company is noted for its enterprise business focus in financial services, public, industrial, distribution, communications, and small- and medium-sized businesses.

The corporation was founded in 1911 when three companies merged to sell business-related gadgets, including a machine that used punched cards to catalog data. Nine years later, the company changed its name to International Business Machines (IBM). The company recently announced that more than 200 customers switched to IBM servers from Sun and HP servers.

For more information, visit the Computer Concepts CourseMate Web site at www.cengagebrain.com and then navigate to the Chapter 14 Companies on the Cutting Edge resource for this book.

Technology Trailblazers

CHAD HURLEY YouTube Cofounder and CEO

Twenty hours of video are uploaded every minute to YouTube, and much of this Web site's popularity is due to the efforts of *Chad Hurley*. He and two work colleagues at PayPal cofounded YouTube in 2005, and it grew quickly to become one of the larger Web sites. One year later they sold YouTube to Google for $1.65 billion.

Hurley says he is a user interface expert and that his interests in fine arts and business have been evident since childhood. In first grade he painted photos on plywood and attempted to sell them on his front lawn. He graduated from Indiana University of Pennsylvania with a degree in fine art, and he used his design skills in one of his first jobs after graduation to create eBay's PayPal logo.

At eBay, he envisioned the concept of adding video to the online auctions. He abandoned that idea when sellers seemed disinterested and then turned his attention to developing the YouTube concept. His goal is to allow every person worldwide to upload video content to YouTube easily and view content on any device that has a screen.

ANITA BORG Champion for Women in Technology

Women from across the globe have been inspired and encouraged to pursue a career in technology with the help of *Anita Borg*. The Anita Borg Institute for Women and Technology and the Google Anita Borg Scholarship provide programs and resources to help women develop technological innovations.

Borg died in 2003, but her accomplishments throughout her career laid the foundation for advancing women in computer science today. In 1987, she went to a technology conference that had only a few women in attendance, and shortly thereafter she formed Systers, an electronic mailing list for female engineers to exchange technology ideas. Today, the Systers list has grown to more than 3,000 members in 54 countries.

Borg's computer science research in college focused on operating systems principles, and she earned her Ph.D. degree from New York University in 1981. She then held top research positions at Nixdorf, Digital Equipment Corporation, and Xerox until her death.

For more information, visit the Computer Concepts CourseMate Web site at www.cengagebrain.com and then navigate to the Chapter 14 Technology Trailblazers resource for this book.

Chapter Review

The Chapter Review reinforces the main concepts presented in this chapter.

To listen to an audio version of this Chapter Review, visit the Computer Concepts CourseMate Web site at www.cengagebrain.com and then navigate to the Chapter 14 Chapter Review resource for this book.

1. What Are the Special Information Requirements of an Enterprise-Sized Corporation? A large organization, or **enterprise**, requires special computing solutions because of its size and geographical extent. **Enterprise computing** involves the use of computers in networks, such as LANs and WANs, or a series of interconnected networks to satisfy the information needs of an enterprise. **Executive management**, which includes the highest management positions in a company, needs information to make *strategic decisions*. **Middle management**, which is responsible for implementing the strategic decisions of executive management, needs information to make *tactical decisions*. **Operational management**, which supervises the production, clerical, and other nonmanagement employees, needs information to make an *operational decision* that involves day-to-day activities. **Nonmanagement employees** also need information to perform their jobs and make decisions. **Managers** use *business intelligence* (*BI*), *business process management* (*BPM*), and *business process automation* (*BPA*) tools to focus on information that is important to the decision-making process.

2. What Information Systems and Software Are Used in the Functional Units of an Enterprise? An **information system** is a set of hardware, software, data, people, and procedures that work together to produce information. In an enterprise, the individual *functional units* have specialized requirements for their information systems. Accounting and financial systems manage transactions and help budget, forecast, and analyze. A **human resources information system** (**HRIS**) manages human resources functions. An *employee relationship management* (*ERM*) *system* automates and manages communications between employees and the business. **Computer-aided design** (**CAD**) assists engineers in product design, and **computer-aided engineering** (**CAE**) tests product designs. **Computer-aided manufacturing** (**CAM**) controls production equipment, and **computer-integrated manufacturing** (**CIM**) integrates operations in the manufacturing process. **Material Requirements Planning** (**MRP**) uses software to help monitor and control processes related to production. A *quality control system* helps an organization maintain or improve the quality of its products or services and typically includes *quality control software*. A *marketing information system* serves as a central repository for marketing tasks. **Sales force automation** (**SFA**) software equips salespeople with the electronic tools they need. *Distribution systems* control inventory, manage and track shipping, and provide information and analysis on warehouse inventory. **Customer interaction management** (**CIM**) software manages day-to-day interactions with customers. *Web site management programs* collect data to help organizations make informed decisions regarding their Web presence. *Security software* enables the IT department to limit access to sensitive information.

3. What Information Systems Are Used throughout an Enterprise? Some general purpose information systems, called *enterprise-wide systems*, are used throughout an enterprise. An **office information system** (**OIS**) enables employees to perform tasks using computers and other electronic devices. A **transaction processing system** (**TPS**) captures and processes data from day-to-day business activities. A **management information system** (**MIS**) generates accurate, timely, and organized information, so that users can make decisions, solve problems, supervise activities, and track progress. A **decision support system** (**DSS**) helps users analyze data and make decisions. An **expert system** captures and stores the knowledge of human experts and then imitates human reasoning and decision making. **Customer relationship management** (**CRM**) systems manage information about customers. **Enterprise resource planning** (**ERP**) provides centralized, integrated software to help manage and coordinate the ongoing activities of an enterprise. A **content management system** (**CMS**) is a combination of databases, software, and procedures that organizes and allows access to various forms of documents and files.

Visit the Computer Concepts CourseMate Web site at www.cengagebrain.com, navigate to the Chapter 14 Quiz Yourself resource for this book, and then click Objectives 1 – 3.

4. What Are Types of Technologies Used throughout an Enterprise? Technologies used throughout an enterprise include the following items. A **portal** is a collection of links, content, and services presented on a Web page and designed to guide users to information related to their jobs. A **data warehouse** is a huge database that stores and manages the data required to analyze historical and current transactions. An enterprise's

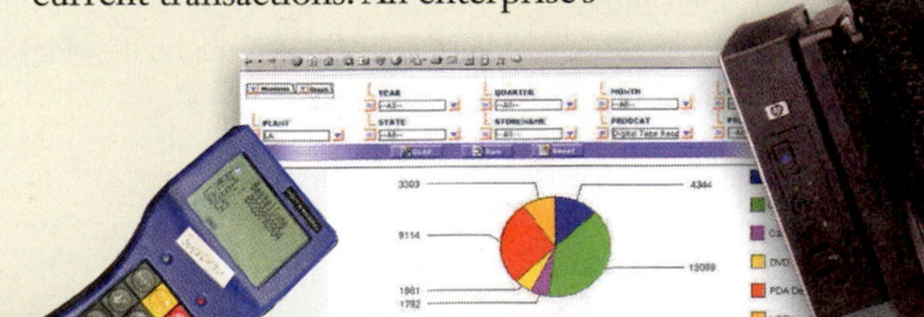

Chapter Review

communications infrastructure consists of hardware (such as wired and wireless network connections and devices, routers, firewalls, and servers), software (such as e-mail, instant messaging, VoIP, and server management), and procedures for using and managing hardware and software. An **extranet** allows customers or suppliers to access part of an enterprise's intranet. **Web services** allow businesses to create products and B2B interactions over the Internet. Many enterprises employ a *service-oriented architecture* (*SOA*) to allow better communications and services between diverse information systems. A **document management system (DMS)** allows for storage and management of a company's documents. A **workflow application** assists in the management and tracking of the activities in a business process from start to finish. A **virtual private network (VPN)** provides users with a secure connection to a company's network server.

5. What Are Virtualization, Cloud Computing, and Grid Computing? *Virtualization* is the practice of sharing or pooling computing resources, such as servers and storage devices. *Server virtualization* provides the capability to divide a physical server logically into many virtual servers; *storage virtualization* provides the capability to create a single logical storage device from many physical storage devices. **Cloud computing** is an Internet service that provides computing needs to computer users. **Grid computing**, which often is used in research environments, combines many servers and/or personal computers on a network to act as one large computer. Cloud and grid computing usually charge a fee based on usage or processing time.

Visit the Computer Concepts CourseMate Web site at www.cengagebrain.com, navigate to the Chapter 14 Quiz Yourself resource for this book, and then click Objectives 4 – 5.

6. What Are the Computer Hardware Needs and Solutions for an Enterprise? **Enterprise hardware** allows large organizations to manage and share information and data using devices geared for maximum availability and efficiency. Enterprises use a variety of hardware types to meet their large-scale needs. A **RAID (redundant array of independent disks)** is a group of integrated disks that duplicates data and information to improve data reliability. **Network attached storage (NAS)** is a server that provides storage for users and information systems attached to the network. A **storage area network (SAN)** is a high-speed network that provides storage to other servers. An **enterprise storage system** uses a combination of techniques to consolidate storage so that operations run efficiently. A **blade server**, sometimes called an *ultradense server*, packs a complete computer server on a single card, or *blade*, rather than a system unit. A **thin client** is a small, terminal-like computer that mostly relies on a server for data storage and processing.

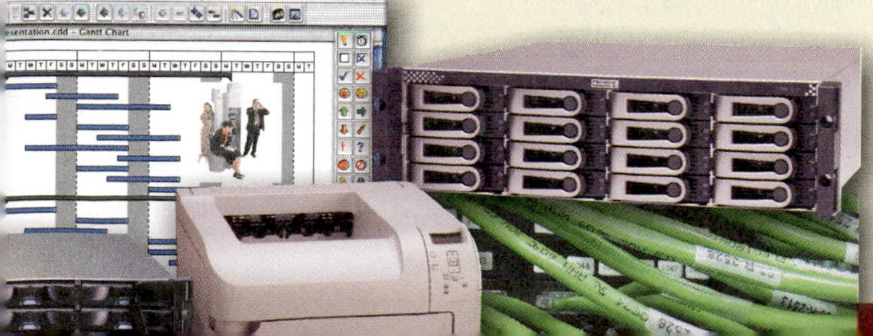

7. What Are High Availability, Scalability, and Interoperability? The *availability* of hardware to users is a measure of how often it is online. A **high-availability system** continues running and performing at least 99 percent of the time. **Scalability** is the measure of how well computer hardware, software, or an information system can grow to meet an enterprise's increasing performance demands. An information system often must share information, or have **interoperability**, with other information systems within the enterprise.

8. Why Is Computer Backup Important, and How Is It Accomplished? A backup duplicates a file or program to protect an enterprise if the original is lost or damaged. A full, or archival, backup copies all of the programs and files in a computer. A differential backup copies only files that have changed since the last full backup. An incremental backup copies only files that have changed since the last full or incremental backup. A selective, or partial, backup allows users to back up specific files. Continuous data protection (CDP), or continuous backup, is a backup plan in which data is backed up whenever a change is made. Backup procedures specify a regular plan of copying and storing data and program files.

9. What Are the Steps in a Disaster Recovery Plan? A **disaster recovery plan** describes the steps a company would take to restore computer operations in the event of a disaster. A disaster recovery plan contains four components. The *emergency plan* specifies the steps to be taken immediately after a disaster strikes. The *backup plan* stipulates how a company uses backup files and equipment to resume information processing. The *recovery plan* identifies the actions to be taken to restore full information processing operations. The *test plan* contains information for simulating disasters and recording an organization's ability to recover.

Visit the Computer Concepts CourseMate Web site at www.cengagebrain.com, navigate to the Chapter 14 Quiz Yourself resource for this book, and then click Objectives 6 – 9.

STUDENT ASSIGNMENTS

Key Terms

You should know the Primary Terms and be familiar with the Secondary Terms. The list below helps focus your study.

To see an example of and a definition for each term, and to access current and additional information from the Web, visit the Computer Concepts CourseMate Web site at www.cengagebrain.com and then navigate to the Chapter 14 Key Terms resource for this book.

Primary Terms

(shown in bold-black characters in the chapter)

artificial intelligence (AI) (737)
blade server (751)
cloud computing (746)
computer-aided design (CAD) (728)
computer-aided engineering (CAE) (728)
computer-aided manufacturing (CAM) (729)
computer-integrated manufacturing (CIM) (729)
content management system (CMS) (739)
customer interaction management (CIM) (731)
customer relationship management (CRM) (737)
data warehouse (741)
decision support system (DSS) (734)
disaster recovery plan (755)
document management system (DMS) (743)
EDI (electronic data interchange) (742)
enterprise (720)
enterprise computing (720)
enterprise hardware (748)
enterprise information (725)
enterprise resource planning (ERP) (738)
enterprise storage system (750)
e-retail (747)
executive management (724)
expert system (735)
extranet (742)
grid computing (746)
high-availability system (752)
human resources information system (HRIS) (728)
information system (726)
interoperability (753)
management information system (MIS) (734)
managers (725)
Manufacturing Resource Planning II (MRP II) (730)
Material Requirements Planning (MRP) (729)
middle management (724)
network attached storage (NAS) (749)
nonmanagement employees (724)
office information system (OIS) (732)
online banking (747)
online trading (747)
operational management (724)
optical disc server (750)
portal (740)
RAID (redundant array of independent disks) (748)
redundant components (753)
sales force automation (SFA) (730)
scalability (753)
storage area network (SAN) (749)
thin client (752)
transaction processing system (TPS) (733)
virtual private network (VPN) (744)
Web services (742)
workflow (744)
workflow application (744)

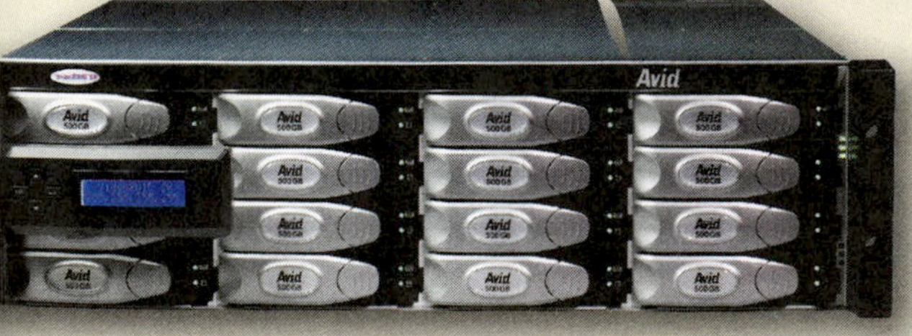

RAID (748)

Secondary Terms

(shown in italic characters in the chapter)

3-D visualization (729)
availability (752)
backup plan (755)
batch processing (733)
blade (751)
blade server chassis (751)
business intelligence (BI) (725)
business process automation (BPA) (726)
business process management (BPM) (725)
centralized (723)
chief information officer (CIO) (732)
click stream (742)
closed (753)
cold site (756)
controlling (725)
core activities (723)
data center (740)
data processing (733)
decentralized (723)
detailed report (734)
distribution systems (731)
downtime (752)
emergency plan (755)
employee relationship management (ERM) system (728)
empowering (725)
enterprise search (740)
enterprise-wide systems (732)
e-tail (747)
exception criteria (734)
exception report (734)
executive information system (EIS) (735)
external sources (735)
failover (756)
Fibre Channel (750)
functional units (721)
hot site (755)
hot-swapping (753)
indexes (739)
inference rules (736)
information architecture (732)
internal sources (735)
Internet backup (750)
knowledge base (736)
knowledge management (KM) (737)
knowledge management software (KMS) (737)
knowledge workers (737)
leading (725)
legacy system (748)
level 1 (748)
market research system (730)
marketing information system (730)
metadata (739)
mirroring (748)
office automation (732)
online analytical processing (OLAP) (735)
online transaction processing (OLTP) (733)
open (753)
operational decision (724)
operations (723)
optical disc jukebox (750)
organizing (725)
outsourcing (751)
personal computer blade (752)
personalization (740)
planning (725)
procedure (726)
proprietary (753)
quality control software (730)
quality control system (730)
reciprocal backup relationship (756)
recovery plan (756)
repository (743)
security software (732)
server virtualization (745)
service-oriented architecture (SOA) (743)
small- and medium-sized business (SMB) (720)
storage appliance (749)
storage virtualization (746)
strategic decisions (724)
striping (749)
summary report (734)
supporting activities (723)
tactical decisions (724)
tape library (750)
test plan (756)
transaction (733)
ultradense server (751)
uptime (752)
virtualization (745)
VPN tunnel (744)
Web farming (742)
Web site management programs (732)

Checkpoint

The Checkpoint exercises test your knowledge of the chapter concepts. The page number containing the answer appears in parentheses after each exercise. The Beyond the Book exercises will help broaden your understanding of the concepts presented in this chapter.

To complete the Checkpoint exercises interactively, visit the Computer Concepts CourseMate Web site at www.cengagebrain.com and then navigate to the Chapter 14 Checkpoint resource for this book.

True/False

Mark T for True and F for False.

_____ 1. The activities relating to running the business are called supporting activities. (723)

_____ 2. Business process management rarely is aided by specialized software designed to assist in these activities. (725)

_____ 3. An information system is a set of programs and procedures that work together to produce information. (726)

_____ 4. Customer relationship management software tracks leads and inquiries from customers, stores a history of all correspondence and sales to a customer, and allows for tracking of outstanding issues with customers. (737)

_____ 5. A data center is a collection of links, content, and services presented on a Web page and designed to guide users to information they likely are to find interesting for their particular job function. (740)

_____ 6. Most of the hardware and software that contains technologies, such as data warehouses, electronic data interchange, extranets, Web services, document management systems, workflow, and virtual private networks is located in a portal. (740)

_____ 7. In a service-oriented architecture (SOA), information systems provide services to other information systems in a well-defined manner over a network. (743)

_____ 8. An optical disc jukebox holds hundreds of optical discs that can contain programs and data. (750)

_____ 9. Blade servers pack a complete computer server on a single card rather than a system unit. (751)

_____ 10. Information systems that have interoperability and easily share information with other information systems are said to be open. (753)

Multiple Choice

Select the best answer.

1. _____ are smaller in size than enterprises and typically do not have an international presence. (720)
   a. Data centers
   b. Portals
   c. SMBs
   d. Web services

2. A centralized approach to information systems usually _____ manageability. (723)
   a. increases costs of maintenance and increases
   b. reduces costs of maintenance and increases
   c. reduces costs of maintenance and reduces
   d. increases costs of maintenance and reduces

3. _____ includes several types of applications and technologies for acquiring, storing, analyzing, and providing access to information to help users make more sound business decisions. (725)
   a. Business intelligence
   b. Business process management
   c. Business process automation
   d. None of the above

4. Using statistical analysis, _____ can identify and predict product defects and problems with the company's processes. (730)
   a. computer-aided engineering
   b. quality control software
   c. marketing information
   d. customer relationship management systems

5. The secure connection created between a user's computer and a company's network is called a(n) _____. (744)
   a. VPN tunnel
   b. blade server
   c. EDI portal
   d. data warehouse

6. A(n) _____ is an information system that has existed within the organization for an extended length of time and is relied upon heavily. (748)
   a. expert system
   b. high-availability system
   c. office information system
   d. legacy system

7. Enterprises often use _______ technology to connect to storage systems at data rates up to 4 Gbps. (750)
   a. Fibre Channel
   b. NAS
   c. RAID
   d. SAN

8. A(n) _____ allows a user to choose specific files to back up, regardless of whether or not the files have changed. (754)
   a. incremental backup
   b. differential backup
   c. full backup
   d. selective backup

STUDENT ASSIGNMENTS

Checkpoint

Matching

Match the terms with their definitions.

_____ 1. core activities (723)
_____ 2. quality control system (730)
_____ 3. decision support system (DSS) (734)
_____ 4. expert system (735)
_____ 5. EDI (742)
_____ 6. extranet (742)
_____ 7. workflow (744)
_____ 8. RAID (748)
_____ 9. scalability (753)
_____ 10. failover (756)

a. process that identifies the specific set of steps involved in completing a project
b. helps users analyze data and make decisions
c. process of one system automatically taking the place of a failed system
d. a set of standards that controls the transfer of business data and information among computers both within and among enterprises
e. captures and stores the knowledge of human experts and then imitates human reasoning and decision making
f. helps an organization maintain or improve the quality of its products or services
g. portion of a company's network that allows customers or suppliers of a company to access parts of an enterprise's intranet
h. business activities that relate to the main mission of a company
i. measure of how well computer hardware, software, or an information system can grow to meet increasing performance demands
j. a group of two or more integrated hard disks

Short Answer

Write a brief answer to each of the following questions.

1. What are the responsibilities of managers? ___________ What four activities do managers perform to coordinate resources? ___________
2. What is a content management system (CMS)? ___________ What type of content may be processed by a content management system? ___________
3. Describe two types of virtualization. ___________ What are cloud and grid computing, and why do companies use them? ___________
4. What are five types of e-commerce? ___________ Describe three of the five types that you listed. ___________
5. What does a backup plan contain? ___________ What factors contribute to the success of a backup plan? ___________

Beyond the Book

Follow the book element instructions below; present your findings (brief report, presentation, discussion, or other means).

1. Ethics & Issues — Select an Ethics & Issues in this chapter (724, 737, 745, 747, 751), find a recent newspaper/magazine article that supports one point of view presented, and then evaluate the article.
2. Computer Usage @ Work — Use the Web or a recent newspaper/magazine to locate three additional unique usages of computer technology in the municipal services field (757). What makes the use of these technologies unique to the municipal services field?
3. Companies on the Cutting Edge and Technology Trailblazers — Use the Web or a recent newspaper/magazine to locate an interesting fact about EMC, IBM, Chad Hurley, or Anita Borg that was not presented in the chapter (759).
4. High-Tech Talk — Locate a recent newspaper/magazine article that discusses topics related to Neural Networks (758). Would you recommend the article you found? Why or why not?
5. FAQs and Web Links — Use the Web or a recent newspaper/magazine to locate three additional facts about an FAQ (730, 742, 746, 748, 751, 755) and Web Link (725, 728, 730, 731, 732, 738, 740, 743, 746, 750, 751, 756) that were not presented in the chapter.
6. Looking Ahead — Use the Web or a recent newspaper/magazine to discover additional uses of the technology presented in Variable Winds Forecasted for Cloud Computing (746).
7. Innovative Computing — Use the Web or a recent newspaper/magazine to locate two additional interesting facts about Unique Data Center Storage Solutions (740) or PS3s Perform Rocket Science (756).
8. Making Use of the Web — Visit three of the Literature and Arts sites (139) and outline the information on each Web site and the possible uses for each Web site.
9. Enterprise Order Processing — Read the Enterprise Order Processing: A Case Study feature (772). Use the Web or a recent magazine article to research similar processes used by a real company with which you have interacted. Create a presentation about the topic.

Learn It Online

The Learn It Online exercises are interactive Web exercises designed to reinforce and expand your understanding of the chapter concepts. The descriptions below briefly summarize each exercise.

To complete the Learn It Online exercises, visit the Computer Concepts CourseMate Web site at www.cengagebrain.com, navigate to the Chapter 14 resources for this book, click the link for the exercise you want to complete, and then read the instructions.

1 At the Movies — A Tour of Lucasfilm Data Center
Watch a movie to take a tour of the Lucasfilm Data Center, the high-tech center of IT operations for a movie production company, and then answer questions about the movie.

2 Video and Audio: You Review It — Virtualization
Search for, choose, and write a review of a video, podcast, or vodcast that discusses virtualization.

3 Student Edition Labs — Project Management and Web Design Principles
Enhance your understanding and knowledge about project management and Web design principles by completing the Project Management and Web Design Principles Labs.

4 Practice Test
Take a multiple choice test that checks your knowledge of the chapter concepts and review the resulting study guide.

5 Who Wants To Be a Computer Genius^2?
Play the Shelly Cashman Series version of this popular game by answering questions to find out if you are a computer genius. Panic buttons are available to provide assistance during game play.

6 Wheel of Terms
Identify important key terms presented in this chapter by playing the Shelly Cashman Series version of this popular game.

7 You're Hired!
Embark on the path to a career in computers by answering questions and solving puzzles related to concepts discussed in this chapter.

8 Crossword Puzzle Challenge
Complete an interactive crossword puzzle to reinforce concepts presented in this chapter.

9 Windows Exercises
Step through the Windows 7 exercises to learn about changing views in Windows 7, using Windows Update, creating a desktop shortcut to the printer, and determining the brand and model of sound cards or audio devices in your computer.

10 Exploring Computer Careers
Read about a career as a CIO, search for related employment advertisements, and then answer related questions.

11 Web Apps — Microsoft Office Web Apps
Learn how to create, edit, and share documents, workbooks, presentations, and notes using Microsoft Office Web Apps.

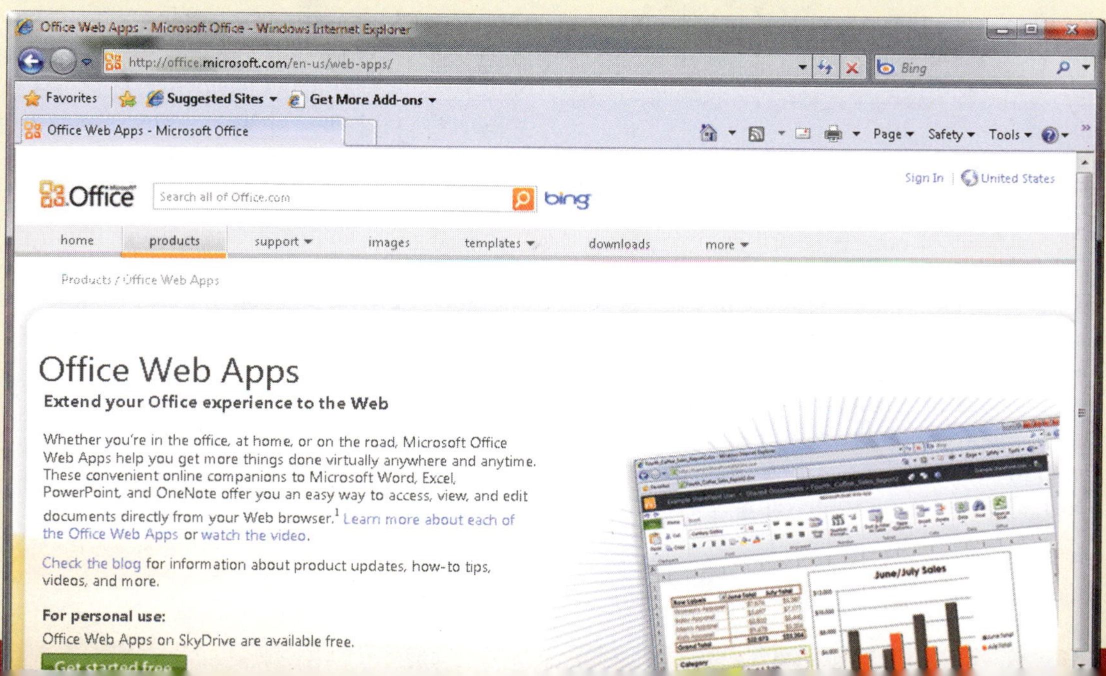

STUDENT ASSIGNMENTS

Problem Solving @ Home

The Problem Solving @ Home exercises extend your knowledge of the chapter concepts by seeking solutions to practical computer problems that you may encounter at home or school. The Collaboration exercise should be completed with a team.

In the real world, practical problems often can be solved in multiple ways. Provide one solution to each of the following problems using available resources, such as articles on the Web or in print, blogs, podcasts, videos, television, user guides, other individuals, and electronics and computer stores. You may need to use multiple resources to obtain an answer. Present your solutions in the form requested by your instructor (brief report, presentation, discussion, or other means).

1. **Online Order Status** After purchasing a new Dell computer more than a week ago, you check the status of your order on Dell's Web site. The Web site indicates that the order is pending. You have purchased Dell computers in the past and know that orders typically do not take this long. What are your next steps?
2. **Missing College Credits** Last year, you transferred to a new college and have requested that your grades be sent electronically from your previous college. It now is time for you to graduate, and you have been informed that you are missing credits for the classes that you took at your previous college. What might have happened?

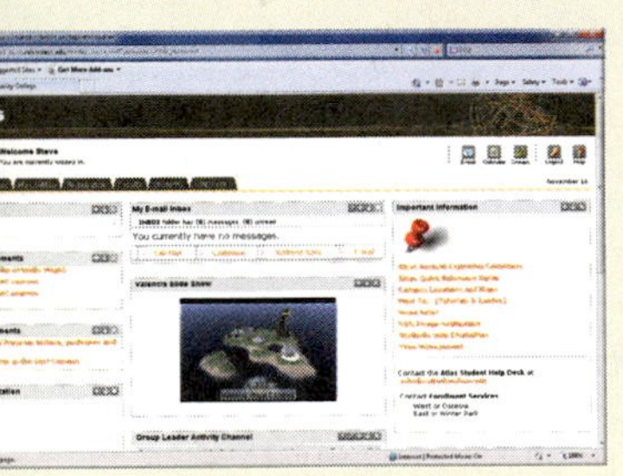

3. **Invalid Password** After typing your user name and password to log onto your school's portal, an error message displays stating that the password is incorrect. What are your next steps?
4. **Incorrect Price Displays** During the checkout process at your local supermarket, the cashier scans a can of soup, and the price on the register displays a price that is higher than the price on the shelf. What might have happened?
5. **Suspicious Account Transactions** After successfully signing up for PayPal's online payment service, you verify the balance in your checking account and notice that two suspicious transactions were conducted, each crediting your account a few pennies. Unsure of whether you now are vulnerable to identity theft, how will you proceed?
6. **Invalid Login Attempts** You regularly use online banking to check your account balance. The last time you logged on to your bank's Web site, a message displayed, indicating that there were three unsuccessful attempts to access your account earlier that day. How could this have happened?
7. **Invalid Credit Card Information** Near the conclusion of an e-commerce transaction, you enter your credit card information, and the Web site reports that your credit card information is invalid. After double-checking your credit card number, expiration date, and security code, it appears that you have entered everything properly. What are your next steps?
8. **Late Fees Assessed** Your bank recently set up an online bill payment service. You begin paying your bills online and set up each bill's payment information. One credit card company has been applying late fees to your account, although you configured the online bill payment service to pay the balances on time. What might be causing this?

Collaboration

9. **Potential Identity Theft** During a recent visit to your local supermarket, you attempt to use your debit card to pay for a purchase, but the card is declined. You return home to check the balance on your account and notice that the account contains charges that you did not authorize. It appears you are a victim of identity theft. Form a team of three classmates. One team member should research the ways that these charges might have been made. Another team member should research how to stop these charges from occurring and regain the ability to use the compromised debit card. The third team member should research ways to prevent identity theft in the future. Discuss your findings as a team, compile them into a brief report, and then submit the report to your instructor.

Problem Solving @ Work

The Problem Solving @ Work exercises extend your knowledge of the chapter concepts by seeking solutions to practical computer problems that you may encounter at work. The Collaboration exercise should be completed with a team.

In the real world, practical problems often can be solved in multiple ways. Provide one solution to each of the following problems using available resources, such as articles on the Web or in print, blogs, podcasts, videos, television, user guides, other individuals, and electronics and computer stores. You may need to use multiple resources to obtain an answer. Present your solutions in the form requested by your instructor (brief report, presentation, discussion, or other means).

1. **Negative Sales Report** You are the assistant manager of a retail store. After receiving the previous day's sales report from the store manager, you are surprised that your sales show as a negative number, when they normally are positive. How could this be?

2. **Unable to Update** Your company hosts a portal that enables you to perform tasks such as checking the information stored by the human resources department and viewing electronic paychecks. Having recently married, you access the portal to change your marital status, but the option buttons allowing you to select marital status are disabled. What might be wrong?

3. **Compromised Credit Card** An e-mail message arrives in your e-mail account stating that a Web site with which you perform a significant amount of business has been compromised. You regularly use a corporate credit card to purchase supplies from this Web site, and you are concerned that someone might have obtained your credit card information. What are your next steps?

4. **VPN Connection Troubles** A VPN connection is required to access your company's computer resources from remote locations. While working from home for the first time, you configure your computer to connect to your company's VPN, but an error message displays stating that the connection is unsuccessful. Additional attempts also produce the same error message. What might be wrong?

5. **Incorrect Pay Rate** Recently, you received a promotion that included a pay raise. You log into your company portal and verify that your rate of pay has increased. After receiving your next paycheck, however, you realize that you were paid at the previous rate of pay. Why might you not be receiving the new rate of pay?

6. **Power Outage** After a brief power outage in your workplace, you turn on your computer, log in, and attempt to access your e-mail account. When you start the e-mail program, a message displays stating that it is unable to connect to the server and cannot retrieve your e-mail messages. By visiting your favorite Web sites, you verify that the Internet connection is functioning. Why might you be unable to retrieve new e-mail messages?

7. **Missing CRM Entry** As a customer service representative for a well-known computer manufacturer, you receive a telephone call from an irritated customer who states that he has called five times about the same problem. In an effort to resolve his problem, you search for his call history using your company's CRM program. Much to your surprise, you are unable to locate any information about this customer's previous telephone calls. What might be wrong?

Collaboration

8. **Computers in Municipal Services** Municipalities are incorporating technology into most, if not all, of their services. As a student in a computer technology class, your instructor provides you with a document that lists various municipal services available in the area. Your instructor requests that teams of three people determine how computers have enhanced various services. One team member should research how computers have enhanced cable television services. Another team member should research how power and water companies benefit from computer technology, and the third team member should identify ways that municipalities can save money by using computer technology.

Learn How To

The Learn How To activities step you through fundamental technology skills when using a computer. The Learn How To exercises enable you to become more proficient with these skills.

Premium Activity: To relate this Learn How To activity to your everyday life, see a visual demonstration of the activity, and complete a short assessment, visit the Computer Concepts CourseMate Web site at www.cengagebrain.com and then navigate to the Chapter 14 Learn How To resource for this book.

Learn How To 1: Use VoIP (Voice over Internet Protocol)

Every enterprise and organization depends on reliable communications. An important means of communication is voice, or telephone, communications. In most organizations today, a telephone company is the primary vendor for providing telephone communications. In the near future, however, the Internet might be the largest provider of telephone communications.

You learned in a previous chapter about VoIP, which provides for voice communications using the Internet instead of standard telephone connections. Two advantages claimed for VoIP are improved reliability and much lower costs. Both of these advantages are attractive to businesses, and VoIP is forecasted to become the standard voice communications method within the next several years.

VoIP also is available to individual users. One primary means to use VoIP is through the service offered by Skype, a company that offers free, unlimited calls through an Internet connection. The Skype software also is free. Using Skype, you can talk to another Skype user via the Internet anywhere in the world for no cost whatsoever. If the person you call is not a Skype user, you can use Skype to call their ordinary landline or cell phone quite inexpensively. For example, to call someone on a landline telephone in the United Kingdom from anywhere in the world, the cost is approximately 2 cents per minute.

The following quote indicates the potential future of VoIP and services like Skype:

> *"I knew it was over when I downloaded Skype," Michael Powell, chairman of the Federal Communications Commission, explained. "When the inventors of KaZaA are distributing for free a little program that you can use to talk to anybody else, and the quality is fantastic, and it's free — it's over. The world will change now inevitably."*
>
> *Fortune* Magazine, February 16, 2004

To download Skype, complete the following steps:

1. Start your Internet browser, type `skype.com` in the Address bar and then press the ENTER key.
2. When the Skype home page is displayed, explore the Web site for information about using Skype. When you are ready, click the Get Skype now button.
3. When the File Download - Security Warning dialog box is displayed, click the Save button.
4. In the Save As dialog box, select the Desktop for the location of the saved file. Then, click the Save button. The Skype Setup file will download. This may take a few minutes, depending on the speed of your Internet connection, because of the large file size.
5. If the Download complete window opens, click the Close button. The SkypeSetup icon is displayed on the desktop.
6. Double-click the SkypeSetup icon on the desktop. If the User Account Control dialog box appears, click the Yes button.
7. In the Skype - Install window, select the language you would like to use, and then click the 'I agree - install' button.
8. If you do not wish to install the Google Toolbar, remove the check mark from the appropriate check box. Click the Continue installing Skype button.
9. When the installation is complete, click the Finish button.

Skype now is installed on your computer. The Skype icon should appear on your desktop. To start and use Skype, complete the following steps:

1. Drag the SkypeSetup icon on the desktop to the Recycle Bin.
2. Double-click the Skype icon on your desktop. The first time you start Skype, the Skype - Create account dialog box is displayed (Figure 14-36). In this dialog box, you enter your full name, Skype name, and password. The Skype name is the name you will use to start Skype each time, together with the password. You can use any name and password that has not already been used on Skype. Also, be sure to check the Skype End User License Agreement check box, and then click the Next button to display the next dialog box requesting your E-mail address, Country/Region, and City (Figure 14-37).
3. Enter your E-mail address, Country/Region, and City, and then click the Sign in button.
4. If your Skype name and password have not been used, Skype automatically will sign into your account and open the Skype window (Figure 14-38). If your Skype name or password already have been used by another user, you must select another Skype name or password.
5. After installing Skype, you can make calls to other Skype users anywhere in the world for no cost.
6. To learn the techniques for calling another Skype user, click Help on the menu bar, click Get Help: Answers and Support on the Help menu, and then select the subject about which you want to learn.

Learn How To

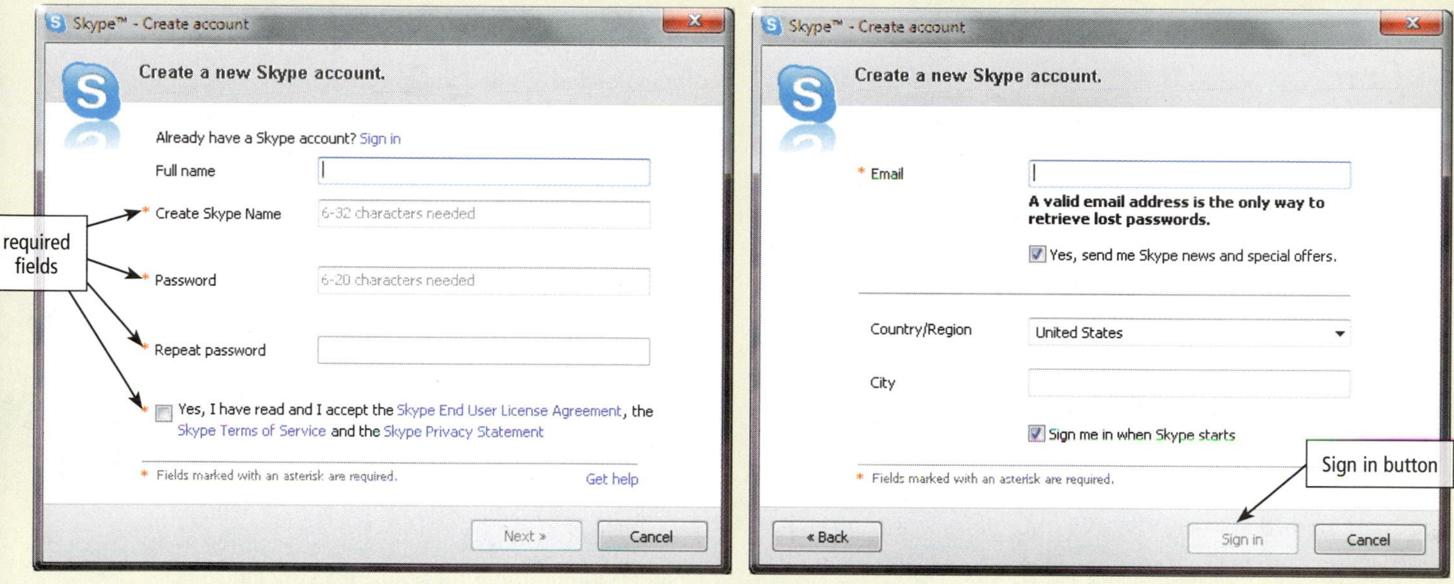

Figure 14-36

Figure 14-37

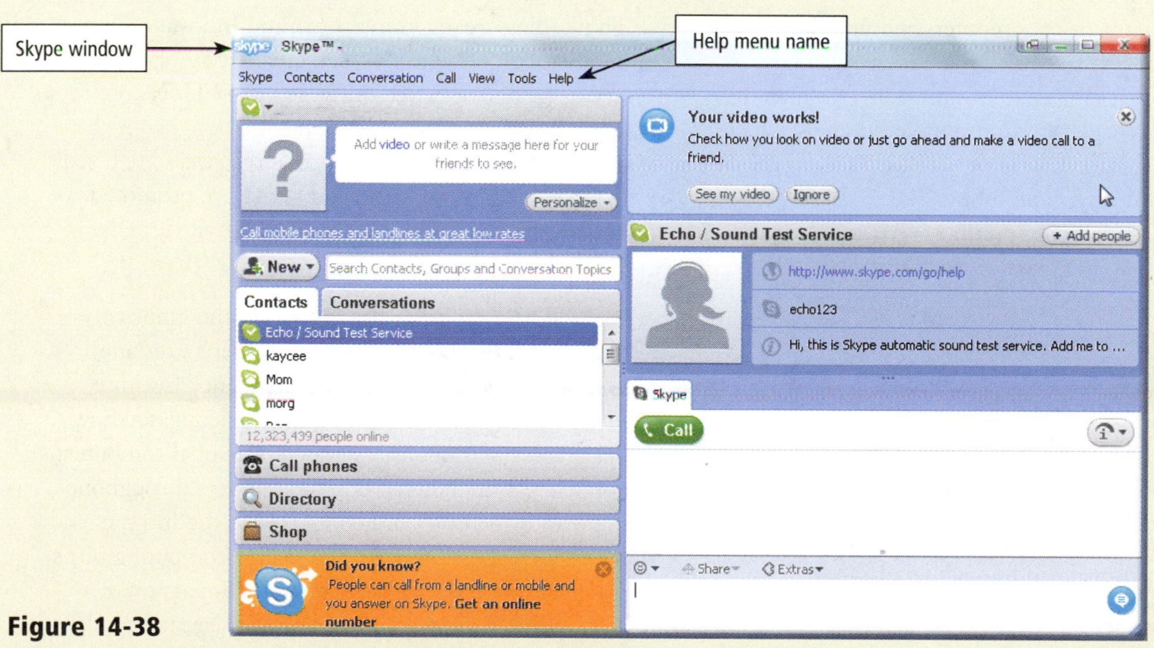

Figure 14-38

Exercises

1. Visit the Skype Web site. Examine the various screens and examples shown on the Web site. Do you think this type of service can be useful to you? Why? What are the advantages and disadvantages of using Skype? If you were calling a friend in Australia on a regular telephone, how much per minute would you have to pay? Submit your answers to your instructor.

2. **Optional: Perform this exercise only on your own computer. Do not perform this exercise on a school computer.** Establish an account on Skype. Call another member of your class who also has established a Skype account. What do you like about Skype? What do you not like? If you know someone in Europe or Asia who is a Skype user, call him or her. Do you like the fact the call is free anywhere in the world? As an option, subscribe to SkypeOut and then call someone somewhere else in the world on his or her regular telephone. Is the quality of the call good? What did you like or not like about the call? Submit your answers to your instructor.

STUDENT ASSIGNMENTS

Web Research

The Web Research exercises broaden your understanding of the chapter concepts by presenting questions that require you to search the Web for answers.

1 Search Sleuth

Use one of the search engines listed in Figure 2-10 in Chapter 2 on page 85 or your own favorite search engine to find the answers to the following questions. Copy and paste the Web address from the Web page where you found the answer. Some questions may have more than one answer. If required, submit your answers to your instructor. (1) What was the location of the latest International Supercomputing Conference? Who gave the opening keynote address, and what was the topic of this speech? (2) Where is the TSUBAME supercomputer installed? Why is it called "everybody's supercomputer"? (3) What are the primary purposes of the Virtual Private Network Consortium? (4) Which organization sponsors the Envirofacts data warehouse? (5) How many RAID levels exist?

2 Green Computing

The carbon footprint of computers running the Internet is expected to exceed that of air travel by 2020. The world's data centers emit more gas than do people living in Argentina and the Netherlands, which have a combined population of 57.2 million. As you learned in Innovative Computing 14-1 on page 740, companies are developing unique data center solutions to cope with the massive electricity demands. View online Web sites that provide information about green data centers. Which countries can profit from IBM's Liebert SiteScan? How can companies benefit by adopting the Corporate Average Data Efficiency (CADE) metric? Which countries have the world's lowest and the highest electricity rates? How are companies adopting solar power? Write a report summarizing your findings, and include a table of links to Web sites that provide additional details.

3 Social Networking

People who are at least 45 years old comprise approximately 34 percent of Internet users and quickly are becoming the largest demographic age group online. These "silver surfers" are online more than six hours per week and are making their presence known on online social networks. Monster's founder Jeff Taylor created Eons (eons.com), which is promoted as an "online gathering place for people lovin' life on the flip side of 50!" BoomerGirl Diary (boomergirl.com) and Not Over The Hill (notoverthehill.com) feature entertainment, health, financial, and travel information. Visit these Web sites and other online social networks aimed exclusively at a mature audience. Compare the content. Which groups and forums are present? What are the members' interests? Which topics are targeted toward this age group? Summarize the information you read and viewed.

4 Blogs

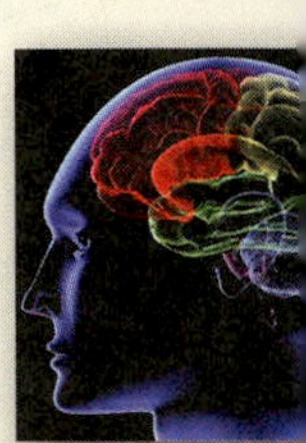

The brain's 100 billion cells work best when both halves of the brain work together. The left half, often called the judicial mind, controls logical and reasoning tasks, and the right half, referred to as the creative mind, interprets and gives meaning to stimuli. Building right-brain skills is the key to achieving professional and personal success. Many blogs contain exercises and research on developing the right brain. They include The Thinking Blog (www.thethinkingblog.com), Creative Generalist (creativegeneralist.blogspot.com), Creative Think (blog.creativethink.com), and InnovationTools (innovationtools.com). Which creativity tools and strategies are suggested on these blogs? How are enterprises incorporating creative thinking? Which mind mapping and brainstorming resources are listed? Which creativity software and books are promoted? Summarize the information you read and viewed.

5 Ethics in Action

Using grid computing, researchers at the University of Chicago, Northern Illinois University, Argonne National Laboratory, and the Max Planck Institute for Gravitational Physics in Germany simulated how black hole collisions affect gravity. Personal computers also can join millions of other computers throughout the world when they are connected to the Internet and have idle processing time. While grid computing turns inactive computer time into computational power, some critics believe some grid projects are immoral, may compromise intellectual property, and may undertake work that for-profit companies should perform. Visit Grid.org, the Open Grid Forum (ogf.org), the Globus Alliance (globus.org), and other Web sites to learn about current grid computing projects. Should for-profit companies pay grid participants for their computer time? Is data security compromised? Who sets standardization guidelines? How will companies track network resources? Write a report summarizing your findings, and include a table of links to Web sites that provide additional details.

Critical Thinking

The Critical Thinking exercises challenge your assessment and decision-making skills by presenting real-world situations associated with the chapter concepts. The Collaboration exercise should be completed with a team.

To evaluate the situations below, use personal experiences and available resources such as articles on the Web or in print, blogs, podcasts, videos, television, user guides, other individuals, and electronics and computer stores. You may need to use multiple resources to form conclusions and make recommendations.

1. Class Discussion — E-Commerce Businesses Half of all new e-commerce businesses fail within five years of their creation, and many do not last that long. While experts point to several factors, two of the most important factors to consider before embarking upon a new venture are a sound idea and financial backing. Regrettably, without the first, it often is difficult to acquire the second. Web hosting is an integral part of any e-commerce business and is an important element in any e-business plan. Select a product you believe will sell well online. Then, use Google or another search engine to research Web hosting. Discuss what you think is needed to be part of the half that succeeds. Include in your discussion the reasons you believe the product you selected will sell online and how Web hosting works.

2. Class Presentation — Artificial Intelligence Intelligent machines have intrigued humans for centuries. Today, computers and artificial intelligence (AI) capture our imagination. Categories within this topic include expert systems, neural networks, artificial life, fuzzy logic, natural language processing, and robotics. Select two of these categories to research using printed material and the Web. Evaluate the differences and similarities in your selections. Then, create a presentation to illustrate how the artificial intelligence categories you selected are used today and might be used in the future.

3. Research — Virtualization Increases in computing power allow enterprises to use virtualization to offer an increasing number of services using less hardware. Because virtualization uses less hardware, software and support costs also might decrease. As an employee in your organization's IT department, the chief information officer has asked you to research how virtualization can help create efficiencies and reduce costs. Why can virtualization reduce hardware, software, and support costs? Research an enterprise currently using virtualization. Is the experience positive? What arguments would you make to implement virtualization in your organization? Do any reasons exist why virtualization might not be a good idea? Write a report summarizing your findings, and include a table of links to Web sites that provide additional details. If required, submit your report to your instructor.

Collaboration

4. RFID Tracking A major national retail chain has grown enormously over the past several years. It has hired your team as consultants to investigate the use of radio frequency identification (RFID) as a solution to its growing inventory and supplier problems. The company wants to require that all of its suppliers use RFID on all shipments sent to the company's warehouses. The plan will require changes to every one of the company's computer systems, as well as fundamental changes in how the company does business with its stores, suppliers, and customers. Using the Web and/or print media, each team member should investigate the costs and barriers to using RFID, and contrast those with the benefits of the technology. Merge your findings into a team report that addresses the following issues: Should a large company force a specific technology on its suppliers? Why might the company opt to exclude the RFID tags from individual items? Discuss in your report how Walmart or another major retailer used RFID to solve its inventory and supplier problems. Can RFID also assist with inventory control in the store after it has been delivered by the supplier? Be sure to summarize the advantages and disadvantages of RFID.

Enterprise Order Processing: A Case Study

EVERY ENTERPRISE BUILDS its computing infrastructure in a unique manner that reflects its own specific needs. This feature presents a case study of the enterprise computing environment for a fictional company. The case study introduces the hardware, software, data, people, and procedures necessary for a computer manufacturing company to fulfill a customer's e-commerce order for a new computer. A customer order may trigger a complex chain of activities behind the scenes at the company. Figure 1 shows a timeline for the processing of a customer order. Orders must be tracked, inventory must be stocked and inventory records must be up to date, payments from customers and to vendors must be processed properly, employees must receive precise information about procedures, and management must be kept informed about the state of the company. Information systems within departments and across the company help to manage all of these activities and more.

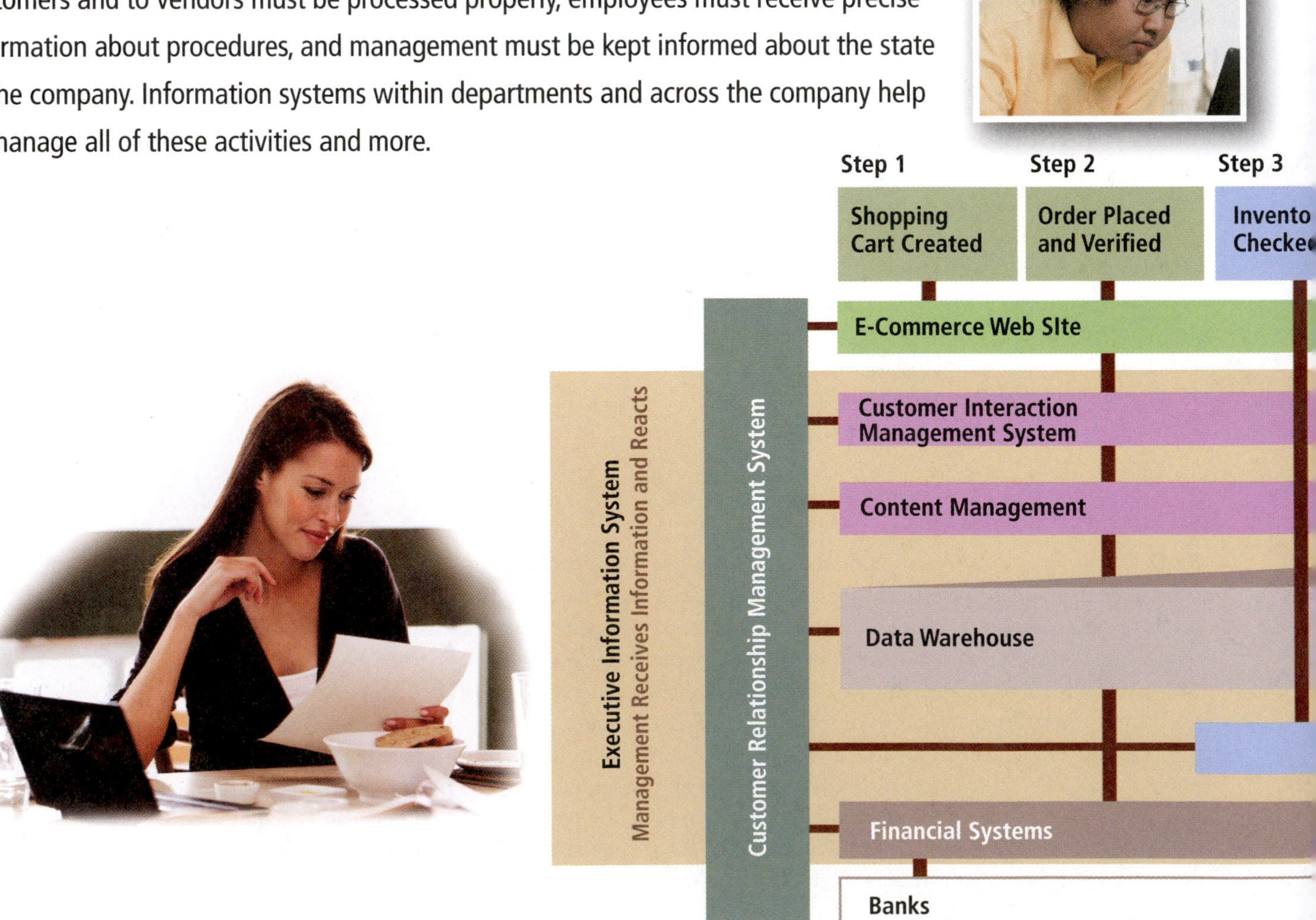

Figure 1 A typical enterprise order processing infrastructure involves several aspects of the enterprise computing environment.

Libra Computers is a large manufacturer of personal computers with 45,000 employees and 60 locations worldwide. The company accepts orders on its Web page or over the telephone. Customers select the custom components and peripherals that they would like included with their computer. Often, the company's Web site indicates which components are available and how long a particular item may take to ship to the customer, which allows customers to make informed decisions.

After a customer creates a shopping cart and places an order, the order is verified, meaning, for example, that the customer's credit card number is validated. Each customer's order is assembled after the order has been verified. The company tries not to keep the components for computers in stock in order to avoid the cost of inventory. As soon as a customer's order is verified, inventory is checked, the components are ordered from various suppliers, such as a hard disk supplier, a power supply vendor, and a WiMAX card supplier. This reduces the company's cost of holding inventory in stock and makes certain that the company does not purchase components that become obsolete or unpopular.

All components ordered from suppliers must include passive RFID tags (tiny computer chips attached to products for identification that are read via radio waves) so that Libra can track the components as they move through the manufacturing process.

During the process or after the customer receives the computer, the customer may call for assistance. Once the components for a computer are received, they are put in a bin with an RFID tag and sent on an assembly line. Workers assemble the computer, and when the computer reaches the shipping dock, the payment for the computer is processed. The computer then is shipped. Throughout the process, a customer relationship management (CRM) system tracks customer information and order history. Libra's executive information system (EIS) provides up-to-the-minute reporting of the state of many processes within the company, such as the number of orders being manufactured, delays in receiving components from suppliers, and the amount of payments and orders processed that day.

The following pages describe in more detail each of the steps in the process outlined in Figure 1.

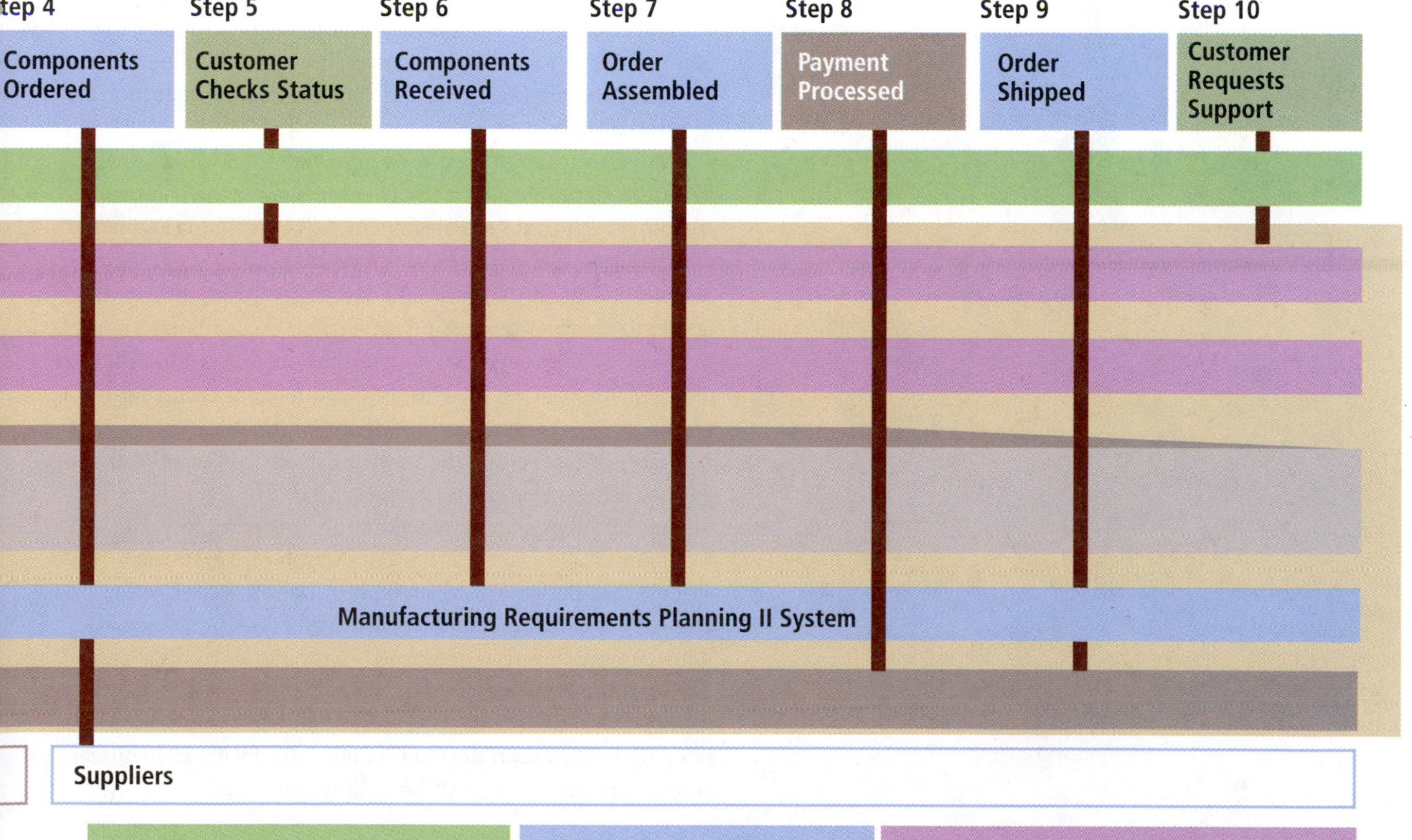

1. Shopping Cart Created

Stirling Felski needs to purchase a new computer to replace his aging and underpowered computer. After investigating computer companies and possible configurations for his new computer, he navigates to the Libra Computers' e-commerce Web site to create a shopping cart (Figure 2). The Web site is maintained on a set of approximately 1,000 high-availability blade servers. While at the Web site, Stirling investigates various processor types and components. The information about the components is kept up to date through Libra Computers' content management system (CMS). Stirling notes the availability of the components that he considers, which helps him make better decisions regarding his order.

All information systems at Libra Computers store their data in a common data warehouse. Finally, after receiving pricing information, Stirling decides to place the order.

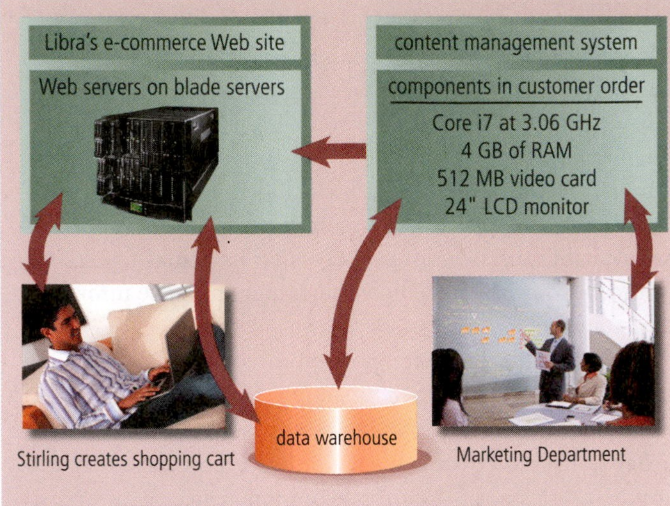

Figure 2 An e-commerce Web site often includes up-to-date information from a content management system.

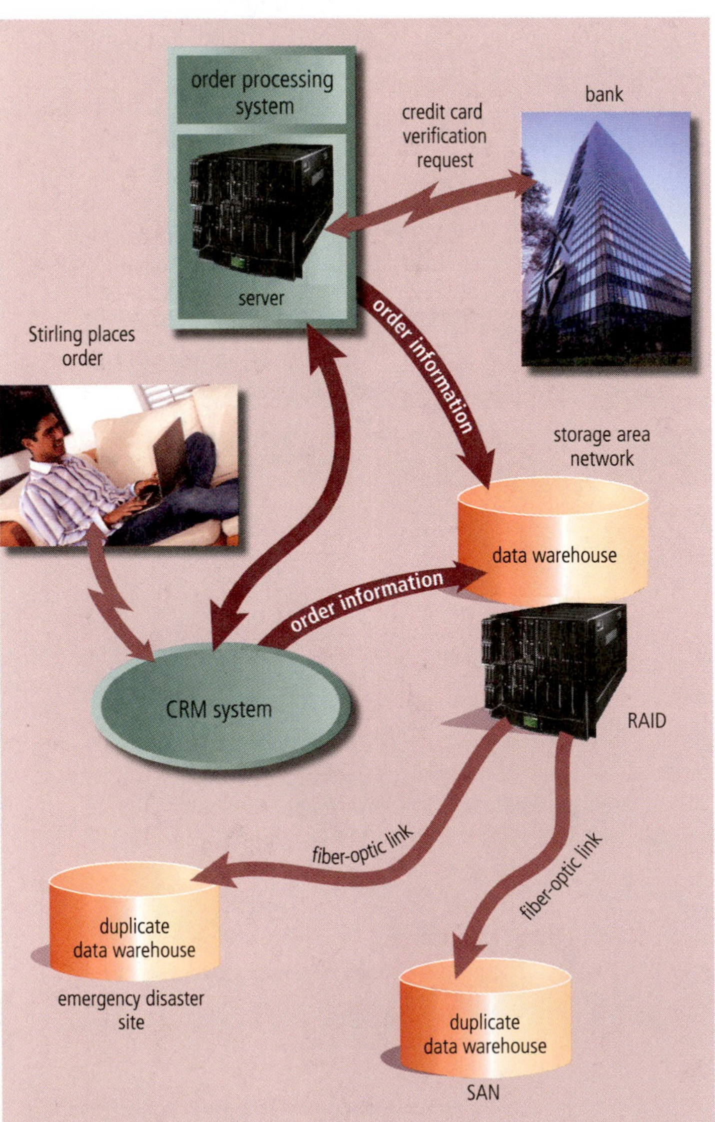

Figure 3 A customer relationship management (CRM) system helps to build trust and loyalty with customers.

2. Order Placed and Verified

Stirling places the order. Using a secure checkout Web page, he supplies his shipping information, credit card information, and contact information, such as his mailing address, e-mail address, and telephone number. He indicates that he will accept e-mail messages on his smart phone to receive status updates about the order. Data, such as Stirling's mailing address and credit card number, automatically is verified as being valid. Any access to customer information is logged in a database, and the logs frequently are audited for unauthorized or unusual access.

After submitting the required information, Stirling's order and customer information are checked against the company's customer relationship management (CRM) system (Figure 3), which determines whether he is a repeat customer or a new customer. If the order is accepted, then the order information is sent to an order processing server that uses online transaction processing to update and communicate with a number of other information systems. For example, his credit card is verified with a banking vendor. If any of the information is incorrect or inaccurate, then Stirling is notified on a Web page that the order cannot be processed. The data about Stirling and his order is stored in only one place in a data warehouse. Libra Computers' data warehouse exists on a storage area network, and every information system in the company accesses the data warehouse for its storage needs. The data warehouse is composed of thousands of disks that use RAID to help protect the data. The disks are backed up using a continuous backup procedure in which high-speed fiber-optic lines keep the data synchronized with an identical storage area network (SAN) in a different location.

3. Inventory Checked

After an order is accepted for manufacturing, the order is broken down into a list of components required from Libra Computers' suppliers (Figure 4). This processing is carried out by specialized software within the company's Manufacturing Resources Planning II (MRP II) information system. While the company does not like to keep an inventory of components in stock, some situations arise in which a component may be in inventory. If a component is found in the database of components in the inventory on hand, then the component is flagged as being necessary for the particular order. A report is sent to the stock room containing the component to instruct a worker there to set the component aside for this particular order. If the component is not found in the inventory, then an order for the component automatically is generated and sent to one of the company's suppliers.

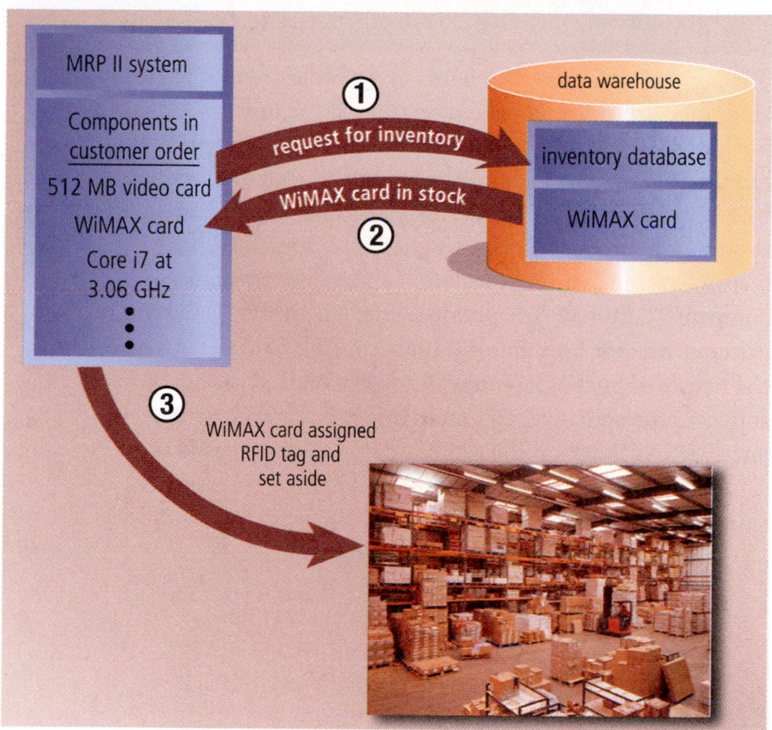

Figure 4 A Manufacturing Resources Planning II (MRP II) information system increases an enterprise's efficiency by supplying timely and accurate information.

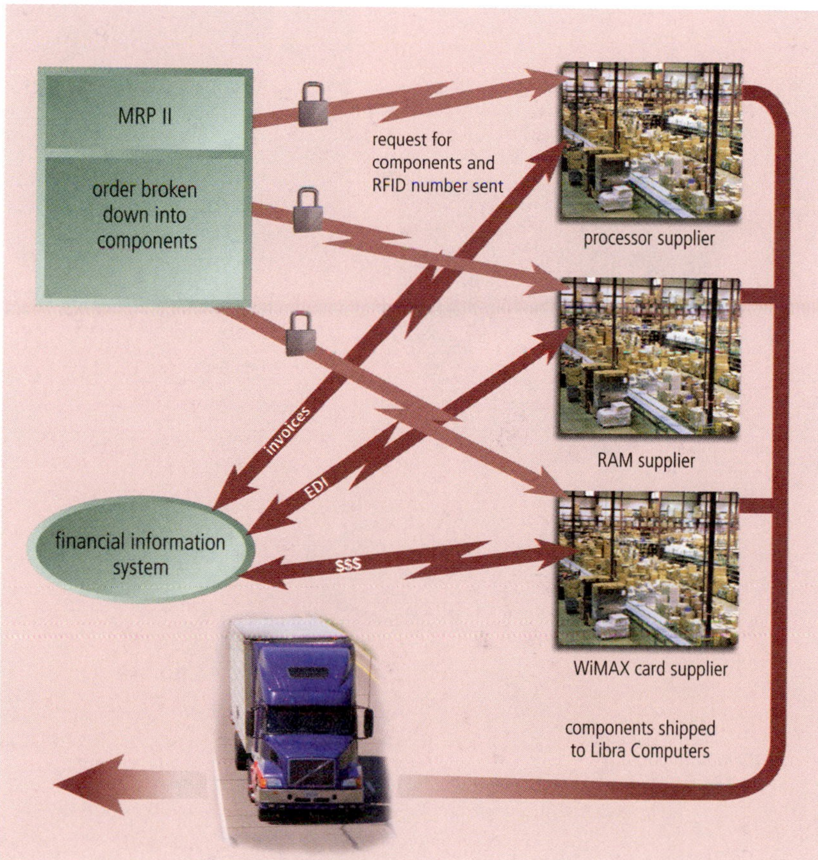

Figure 5 Just-in-time delivery, made possible with an MRP II information system, saves enterprises the cost of storing inventory of parts.

4. Components Ordered

When it is time to order components from suppliers, the MRP II system uses secure Web services on the supplier's extranet Web servers to place the orders (Figure 5). Libra Computers demands just-in-time delivery, meaning that the supplier must deliver the components to Libra exactly on the date that Libra indicates it wants the components. Libra also automatically provides an RFID number that the supplier should use on each component, and the supplier is required to affix an RFID tag to each component. Libra Computers uses the RFID tags to track the component throughout the manufacturing process. Alternatively, the company allows its suppliers to choose a number for the RFID tag and notify Libra Computers of the number. To pay its suppliers for components, Libra Computers asks that its suppliers use an electronic data interchange (EDI) system to send invoices to the company. Invoices from suppliers then are placed into the accounting system, which, using another EDI system, requests that its bank pay the supplier at the appropriate time. Payment information is recorded and reported by the company's financial information system.

5. Customer Checks Status

Stirling wants to check the status of his order to see if the computer still will ship to him on time. If the order is delayed, Stirling will have the choice to cancel the order. Rather than use the Web site to check the order, Stirling feels that he would like to talk to someone instead. All of the steps up until this point in time have been handled by automated information systems. Stirling logs into Libra's Web site and the company's customer interaction management (CIM) system prompts him for his request (Figure 6). The CIM determines the nature of Stirling's inquiry, finds a suitable customer support representative, and the CIM begins a Web conference with Stirling and the representative. When the Web conference begins, the CIM gathers customer information and order information from the customer relationship management (CRM) and Manufacturing Resources Planning II (MRP II) systems to display on the representative's computer screen. The representative easily can relay the order status to the customer.

The CIM also records the call and stores the recording and information about the Web conference in the data warehouse. The 400 support representatives at Libra use thin clients — small terminal-like computers that primarily rely on a server for data storage and processing for their work. The thin clients connect to servers, and each server can support 50 virtual servers at once. That is, fifty representatives all can share one server at a time.

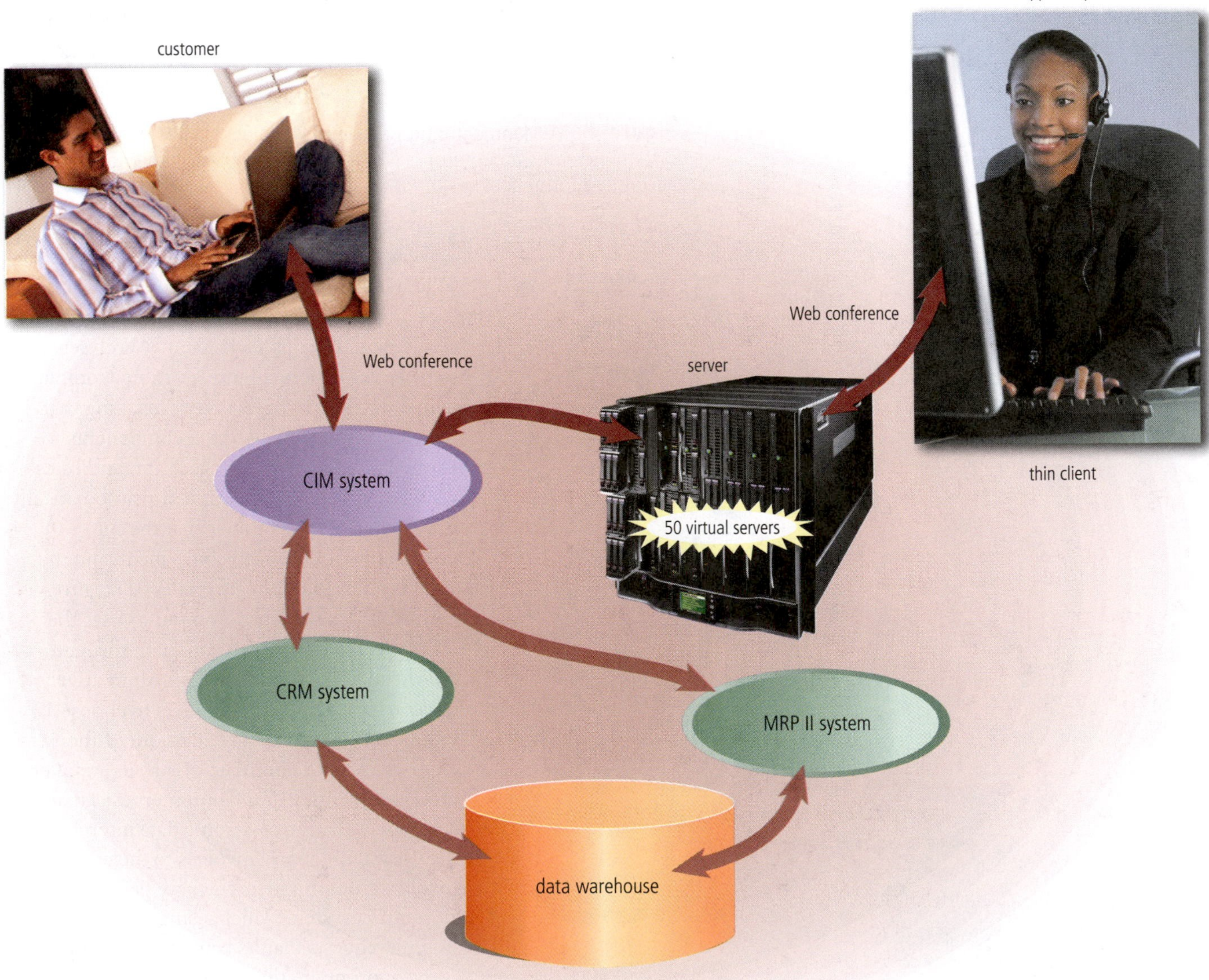

Figure 6 A customer interaction management (CIM) system allows enterprise employees consistently to engage customers.

6. Components Received

As workers at the loading docks receive components and components are acquired from inventory stocks, the components are scanned in using the RFID tags assigned to and placed on them (Figure 7). The Manufacturing Resources Planning II (MRP II) system, therefore, is able to track automatically the requests for components from various vendors. The MRP II system informs the dock workers where to store the components for future recovery when all components have been received for an order. When all the components are received, the MRP II system generates a report and assigns an RFID tag to the entire order. The workers, along with the RFID tags on the components, gather the components, place them together in a bin, tag them with the new RFID tag, and place them on a conveyor belt.

A computer-integrated manufacturing (CIM) information system then uses the order information to determine the best path along the assembly floor for the new computer. The path determined by the CIM system depends on the type of computer, the components to be installed, the urgency of the order, and the availability of workers. The CIM system uses automation to send the bin of components along the factory floor in the predetermined path.

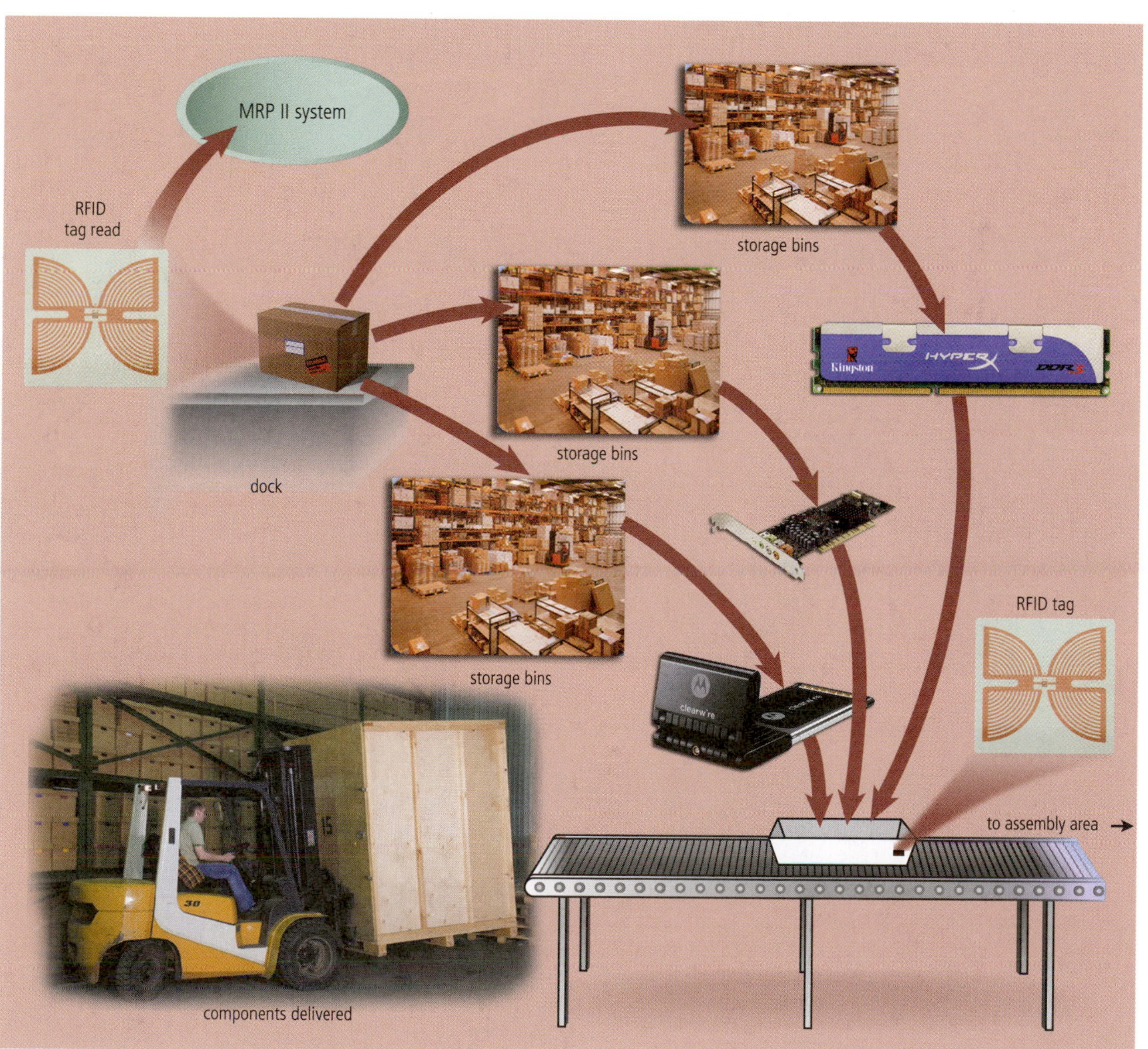

Figure 7 RFID tags provide for greater efficiency and quality because any item in an enterprise's inventory can be tracked.

7. Order Assembled

As the computer-integrated manufacturing (CIM) system guides the bin of components along the manufacturing floor, it keeps a record of what processes have been completed. When the conveyor belt brings the worker a bin, the worker uses a wireless RFID reader to verify that he or she has the correct bin and each individual component (Figure 8). The worker's thin client displays the task(s) needed to be performed by that worker. For example, the instructions may inform the workers which processor, RAM, and video card to install. If needed, more detailed instructions are maintained in a content management system. The RFID tags on each individual component are removed as they are installed in the computer. The worker can interact with the Manufacturing Resources Planning II (MRP II) system if the worker has a special request, such as informing the system that the bin contains a broken component. The MRP II system will instruct the CIM system to send the worker a replacement component. When the worker is finished with the instructed task(s), he or she informs the MRP II system and places the bin back on the conveyor belt. The CIM system takes the bin to the next worker and proceeds with this process until the computer is assembled. The last step is to take the computer to a testing environment, where the functionality of the computer is verified.

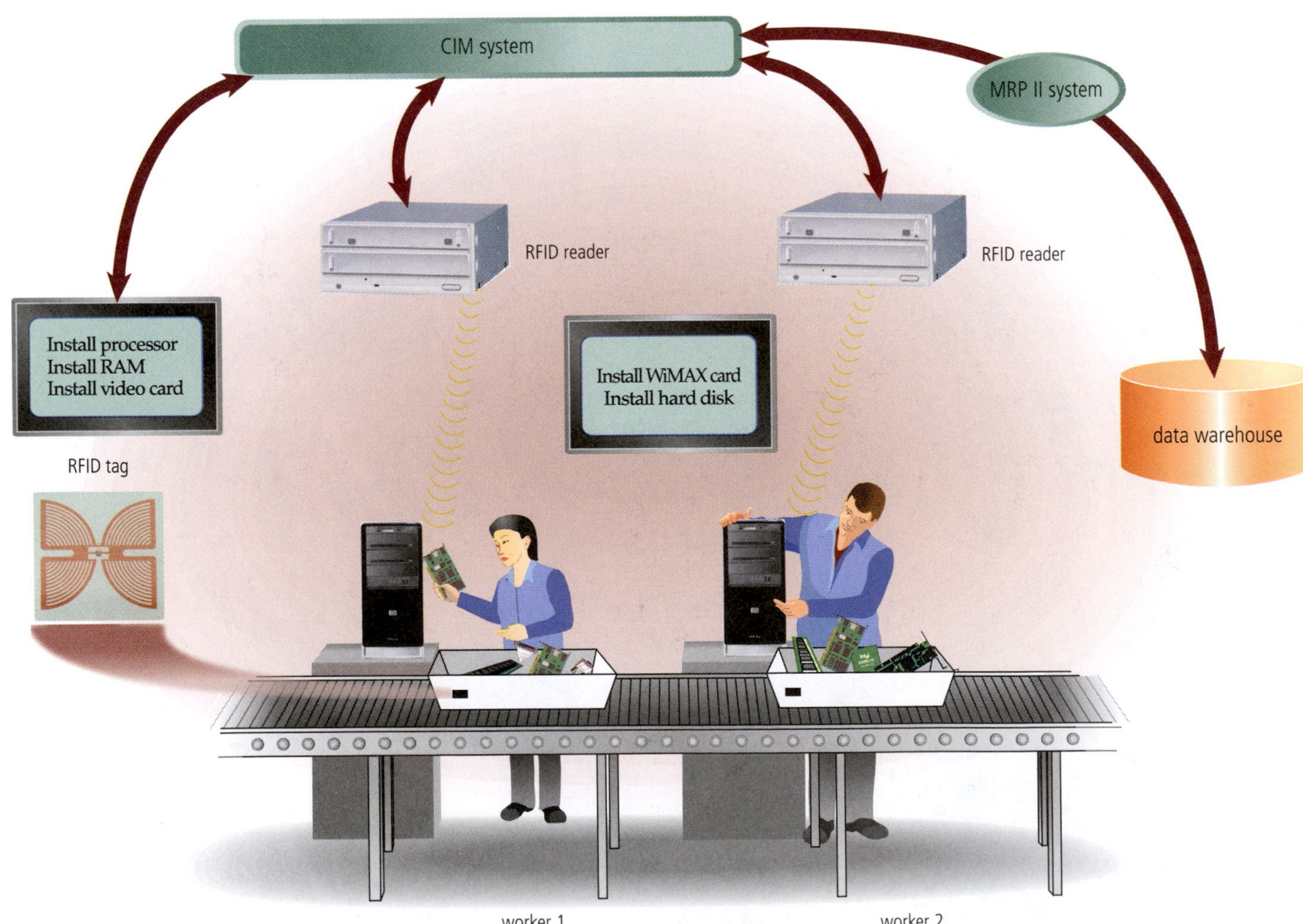

Figure 8 A CIM system, MRP II system, data warehouse, and RFID tags combine to make assembly of products efficient.

8. Payment Processed

Once Stirling's computer is assembled, tested, and ready for shipment, Libra Computers processes his payment before shipping the computer to him (Figure 9). A financial system receives notification of the request to process the payment and uses a transaction processing system to apply the charge to the customer's credit card. When the transaction processing system completes the transaction, the accounting system is updated to reflect the amount and type of transaction. The entire transaction takes less than a second. On a daily basis, Libra's bank uses electronic data interchange (EDI) to receive the money from the credit card company. Upon deposit in the bank, the bank electronically notifies Libra Computers' accounting system to inform the company of the fund transfer.

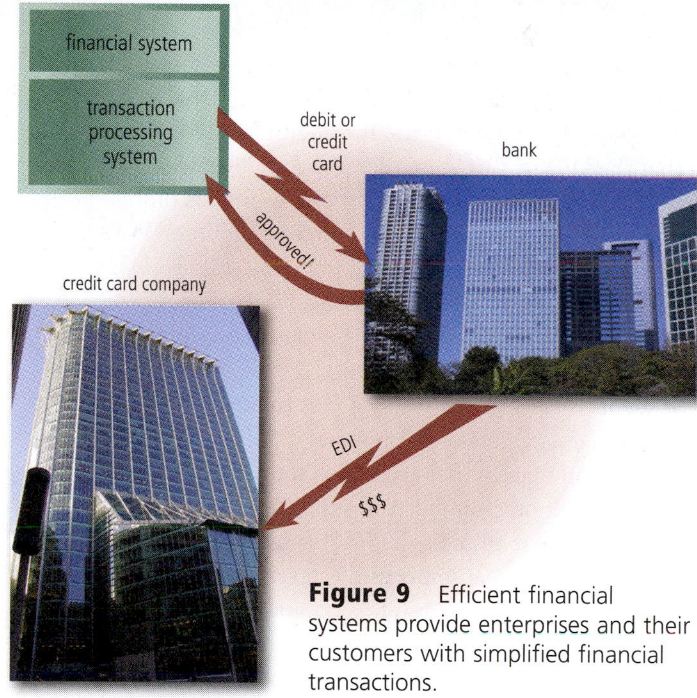

Figure 9 Efficient financial systems provide enterprises and their customers with simplified financial transactions.

9. Order Shipped

With the payment accepted, the Manufacturing Resources Planning II (MRP II) system receives its final confirmation that the order is complete (Figure 10). The MRP II system interacts with the customer relationship management (CRM) system to inform the CRM system that it should send an e-mail message to Stirling's smart phone to inform him that his order has been shipped. At the same time, the last step for the CIM is to make sure that the completed computer is sent to the shipping area. Software and hardware in the distribution system automatically read the RFID tag and determined the most cost-efficient manner in which to package the computer. The distribution system then uses artificial intelligence to determine the most cost-effective and quickest shipping method. The computer then is shipped to Stirling, and the status of the order is updated. Libra Computers uses GPS tracking and Web services at various freight and package delivery companies to track its packages automatically and any abnormalities in the shipment are reported to Libra Computers.

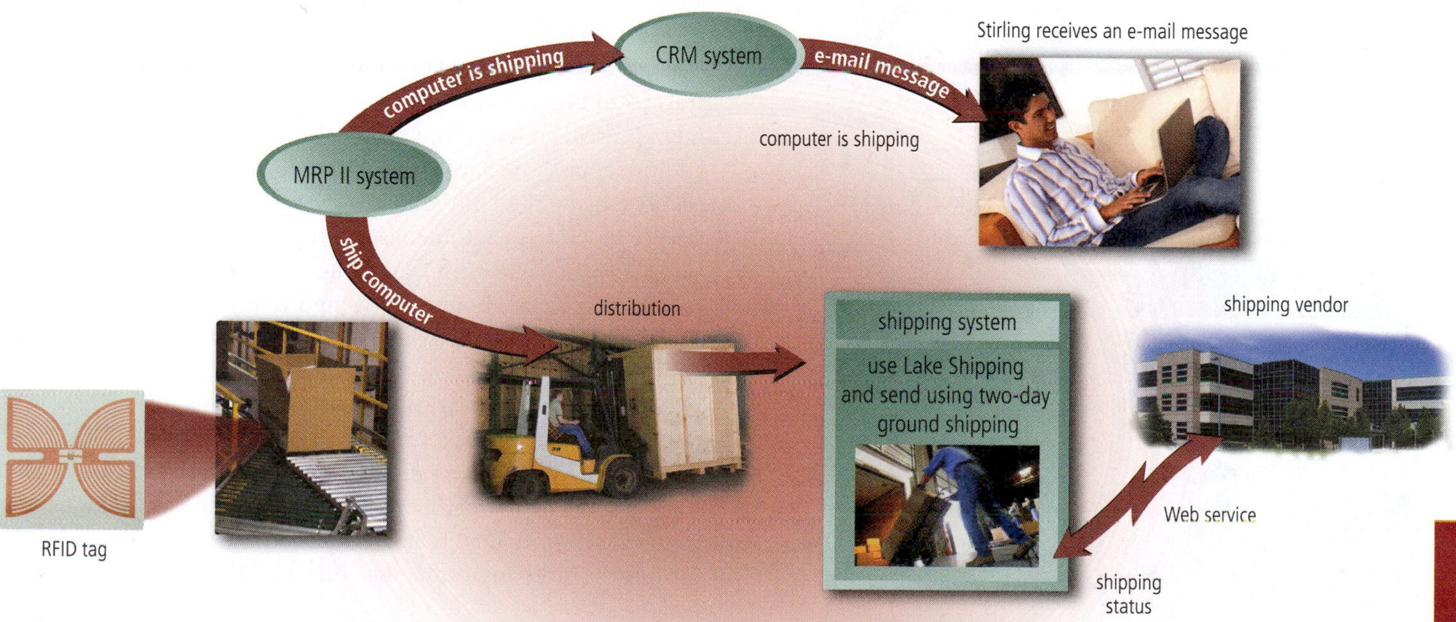

Figure 10 Multiple information systems work together to ensure a satisfying customer experience.

10. Customer Requests Support

When his new computer arrives, Stirling sets it up and attempts to use the WiMAX card on the new computer to connect to the Internet. He discovers that the WiMAX card on the new computer will not connect to the Internet as it should. Using his old computer, he navigates to the Libra Computers' Web site and clicks the technical support link (Figure 11). An expert system, loaded with documentation and information from a content management system, guides him through the diagnosis of the problem. It seems that the card simply needs to be replaced due to damage during shipping, and the customer interaction management (CIM) system supplies him with a telephone number and support reference number. When he calls, the CIM system requests his support reference number and then routes his call and customer information to a components replacement specialist. The specialist uses the Manufacturing Resources Planning II (MRP II) system to report the problem with the card and then orders a new card from the supplier using the supplier's extranet. When the part arrives at Stirling's home, the distribution system notifies the technical support personnel who call him to ask if he needs help installing the replacement.

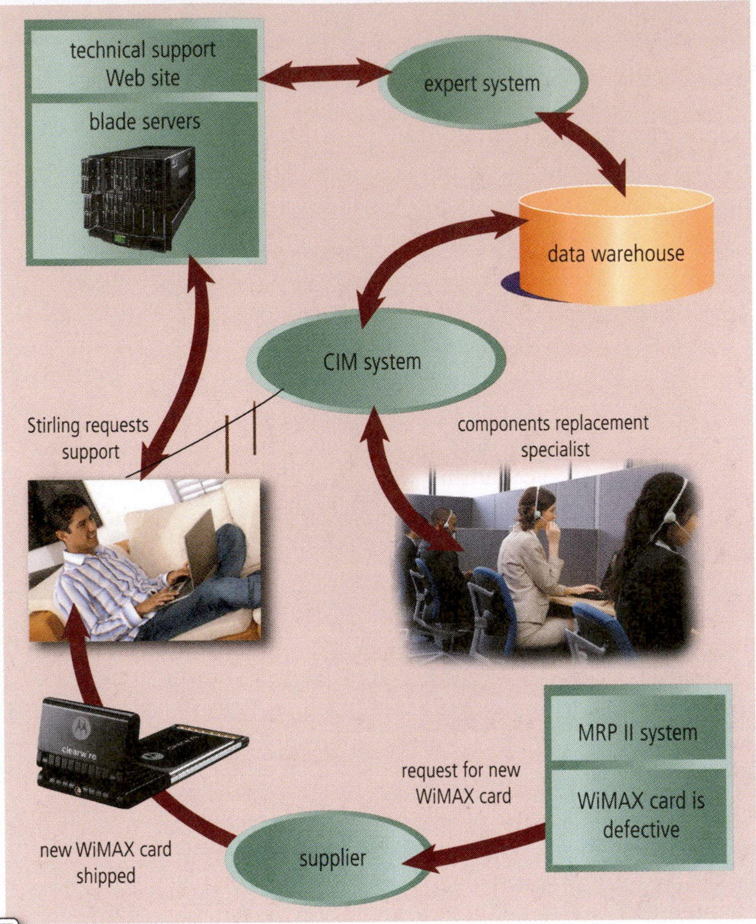

Figure 11 A request for a replacement part may involve several information systems.

Customer Relationship Management Information System Tracks Customer Experience

All of Stirling's interactions with Libra Computers are tracked in the company's customer relationship management (CRM) system (Figure 12). The CRM system performs additional tasks such as assigning Stirling a unique customer number, using the United States Postal Service updates to update his address automatically when he moves, and helps the sales team to identify when might be a good time to contact Stirling again about purchasing his next new computer. Anyone in the company who ever interacts with Stirling in the future will have access to this history. Stirling will not have to explain his past dealings with the company to the next customer support representative with whom he speaks. The CRM system stores all of its information in the data warehouse. The marketing department uses the CRM system to track customer buying habits and to target customers for future marketing campaigns based on their purchasing history.

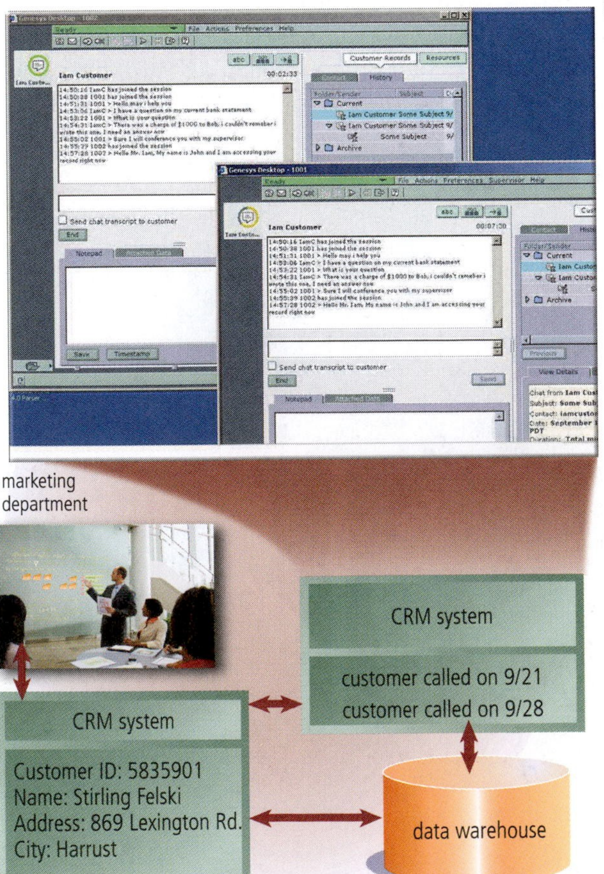

Figure 12 A CRM system provides critical information regarding the enterprise's approach to its customers.

Management Receives Information and Reacts

The executive information system (EIS) at Libra Computers is a decision support system that allows managers and executives to obtain real-time information from any information system in the company. The EIS consolidates information that is important to executives and presents a summary of information such as sales, financial, manufacturing, and service information (Figure 13). If the manager needs more detail, he or she can "zoom in" on a piece of information to see what comprises it. For example, a manager may be presented with the total number of defective components reported by customers in the last month. The manager can zoom in on that number to see a comparison of the defects from week to week within that month, and then day to day in order to look for trends. In the case of Stirling's defective WiMAX card, the chief operating officer notices a sharp increase in the number of defective cards from one particular supplier. The executive uses the Manufacturing Resources Planning II (MRP II) system to request that this supplier be excluded from future orders until the problem can be analyzed further.

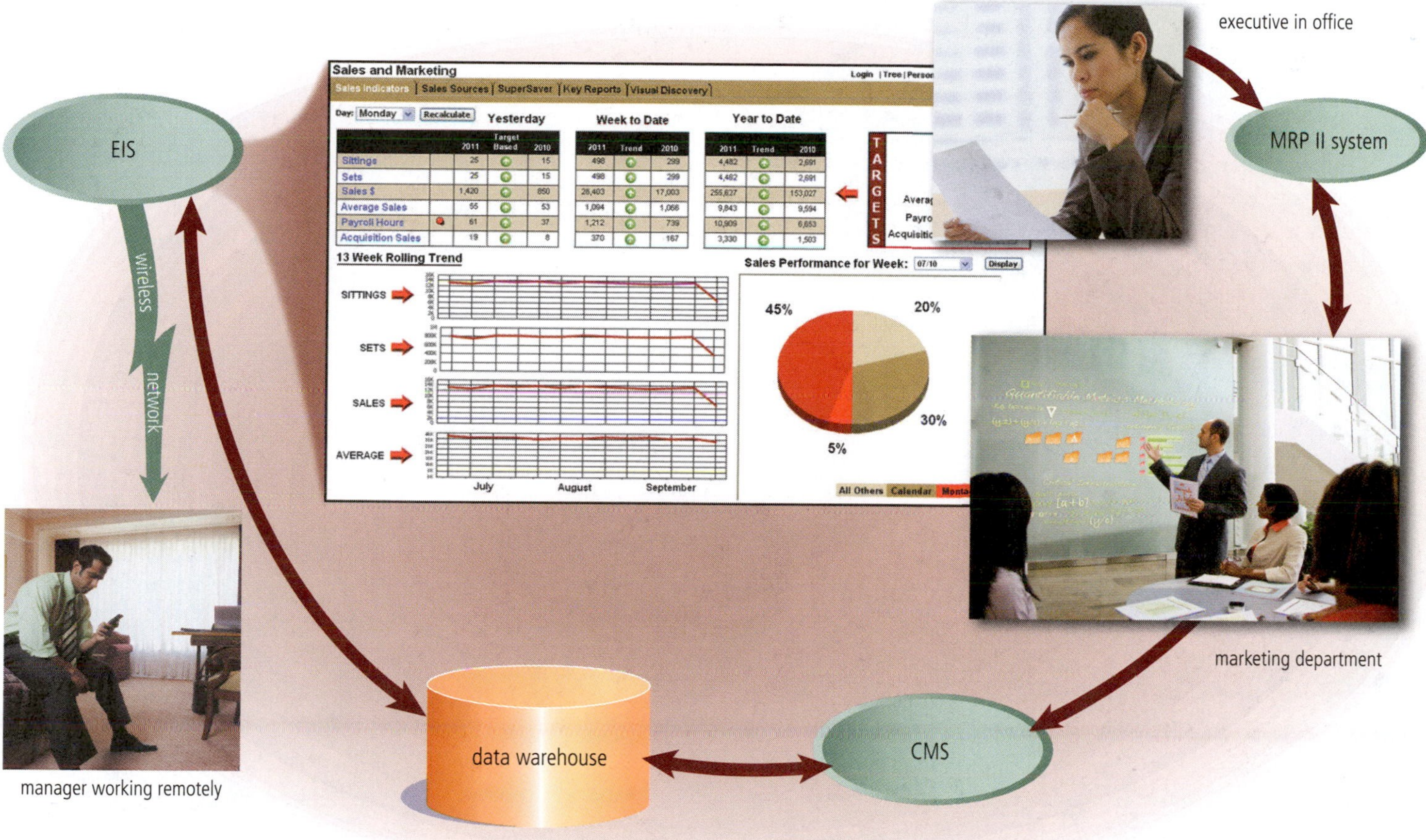

Figure 13 An executive information system (EIS) provides timely information that allows managers to make decisions quickly.

Enterprise Order Processing: *Summary*

EVERY INTERACTION that you have with an enterprise triggers a chain of events across many information systems. This case study provided an example of how hardware, software, data, people, and procedures work together to satisfy customers and meet the objectives of an enterprise.

Chapter Fifteen

Computer Careers and Certification

Objectives

After completing this chapter, you will be able to:

1. Describe career opportunities available in these segments of the computer industry: general business and government organizations and their IT departments, computer equipment field, computer software field, computer service and repair field, computer sales, computer education and training field, and IT consulting
2. Discuss functions of jobs available in an IT department
3. Distinguish between trade schools and colleges
4. Differentiate among various computer-related majors for college students
5. Identify ways to stay current with changing technology after graduation
6. List the benefits of certification for employers, employees, and vendors
7. Identify ways to prepare for certification
8. List the general areas of IT certification
9. Name some specific IT certifications in each of these certification areas: application software, operating system, programmer/developer, hardware, networking, digital forensics, security, Internet, and database system

The Computer Industry

In today's technology-rich world, a demand for computer professionals continues to grow. The U.S. Department of Labor's Bureau of Labor Statistics (BLS) reports that two of the five fastest growing occupations for individuals holding a bachelor's degree are in computer-related fields. These include data communications analysts and software engineers. Figure 15-1 identifies these and other computer-related careers available to today's college graduates. The BLS also estimates that the current IT (information technology) workforce is approximately 6.7 million people. Further, it predicts that IT will be one of the fastest growing industries for the next several years. The U.S. Department of Labor also estimates that more than 80 percent of IT employees work at organizations whose primary business is not computer related, such as banking, finance, food service, manufacturing, or transportation.

While the use of computers and the demand for computer professionals continue to grow, the number of students majoring in computer-related fields is declining. One reason is students fear homeland IT-related jobs could be outsourced (read Ethics & Issues 15-1 for a related discussion). On the other hand, administrators at colleges and universities and business executives worry that if this decline in enrollment continues, the demand for graduates majoring in computers will exceed the actual number of students graduating with computer-related degrees.

The computer industry offers many rewarding careers. These computer-related careers often require a unique combination of

Figure 15-1 The computer industry offers many rewarding careers.

hands-on skills, creative problem solving, and an understanding of the industry as a whole and your organization's specific business needs. This chapter discusses a variety of careers in the computer industry, how to prepare for these types of jobs, and available certifications.

ETHICS & ISSUES 15-1

Outsourcing Computer Jobs — A Threat to American Workers?

While the cost of skilled computer professionals has risen for companies in the United States, other countries have begun producing much less expensive skilled IT workers. To remain competitive, many companies have chosen to send computer jobs overseas, a practice known as outsourcing. Proponents say that the United States has a long history of outsourcing all types of work when the economics of the situation demands it and that the number of outsourced jobs is only two or three percent. Furthermore, with an anticipated IT worker shortage, if the government were to place restrictions on outsourcing, then American businesses could not be as competitive with their foreign counterparts.

Opponents say that outsourcing results in unemployment and decreases student interest in majoring in IT-related fields. Also, sending high-paying jobs overseas harms the economy. Outsourcing of sensitive work, such as health record maintenance or military work, could place U.S. citizens at risk. Some experts say that an increase in outsourcing is inevitable in the United States as the rest of the world becomes better educated and competitive.

Should the government limit a company's ability to outsource computer jobs to other countries? Why or why not? Should companies be criticized for outsourcing jobs? Why or why not? What are some possible alternatives to outsourcing that would help to keep a company competitive? What steps can people take in their careers to avoid becoming a victim of outsourcing? Would you pay more money for North American-based technical support? Why?

Ethics & Issues

For the complete text of the Ethics & Issues boxes found in this chapter, visit the Computer Concepts CourseMate Web site at www.cengagebrain.com and then navigate to the Chapter 15 Ethics & Issues resource for this book.

Computer salesperson
Web software developer
Desktop publisher/ compositor
IT consultant
Computer operator
Graphic designer/ illustrator
Computer security specialist/ mobile security specialist
Computer technician
Network administrator/ wireless network administrator
Database administrator
Storage administrator/analyst
Corporate trainer
Computer scientist
Technical lead
Technical writer
Chief information officer
Digital forensics examiner

Careers in the Computer Industry

With billions of dollars in annual revenue, the computer industry is one of the larger worldwide industries. This industry has created thousands of high-tech jobs, even in companies whose primary business is not computer related. Job opportunities in the computer industry generally are available in one or more of these areas:

- General business and government organizations and their IT departments
- Computer equipment field
- Computer software field
- Computer service and repair field
- Computer sales
- Computer education and training field
- IT consulting

The following pages discuss each of these areas and the career opportunities and jobs available within the areas. In the fast-paced world of technology, job titles are not standardized. Some companies are reducing their number of job titles or combining job titles into one position such as programmer/analyst.

General Business and Government Organizations and Their IT Departments

Businesses and government organizations of all sizes use computers. Without computers, very few organizations could operate in today's economy. Employees of all types, from office workers to shop foremen, use business software such as word processing to prepare basic documents. Other employees in the organization use computers for specialized activities such as the management of company finances. Read Looking Ahead 15-1 for a look at overcoming generation gaps among IT workers.

Most organizations use networks to help ensure smooth communications among employees, vendors, and customers. As discussed in Chapter 14, larger organizations use computers to answer and route telephone calls, process orders, update inventory, and manage accounts receivable, accounts payable, billing, and payroll activities. Some use computers to order raw materials automatically, control manufacturing, and ship finished goods.

Businesses and government offices use computers and the Web to provide the public with a means to access their facilities. For example, people in the United States use computers to file taxes, apply for permits and licenses, pay parking tickets, buy stamps, report crimes, apply for financial aid, and renew vehicle registrations and driver's licenses.

To manage their computers and operations, businesses and government organizations need employees to fill a variety of computer-related jobs. Most medium and large businesses and government organizations have an IT department that employs people in computer-related jobs (Figure 15-2). Employees in the **IT department** work together as a team to meet the information requirements of their organization and are responsible for keeping all the computer operations and networks running

LOOKING AHEAD 15-1

Bridging the IT Generation Gap

When younger workers are hired in the same department as older workers, the results can be frustrating or rewarding. What makes the difference is how management decides to blend the workforces.

The 80 million Generation Y workers, called millennials, who were born after 1977 bring a host of talents to the office. They generally are skilled at hands-on, experiential learning and gain skills by attempting to perform a task rather than by reading a book or attending a lecture. They multitask, prefer to work alone, accept change readily, and access information at all hours of the day.

These work habits are contrary to what older workers have experienced during their careers. To blend the cultures, managers must devise methods of fostering coexistence. The project-oriented nature of IT work appeals to the bright, creative, energetic millennials, and they perform best when given new technologies and the freedom to experiment. Enjoying new situations and challenges, they excel at mentoring less tech-savvy workers on using the innovative hardware and software and rotating among various departments to meet new people. They also thrive in an atmosphere that encourages blogging and texting, so the work environment should allow mobile social networking and communications.

For more information, visit the Computer Concepts CourseMate Web site at www.cengagebrain.com, navigate to the Chapter 15 Looking Ahead resource for this book, and then click Generation Gap.

Figure 15-2 In larger businesses and government organizations, the IT department includes professionals who set up and manage the computer equipment and software to ensure that it produces quality information for users.

smoothly. They also determine when and if the company requires new hardware or software.

An IT department provides career opportunities for people with a variety of skills and talents. Usually, these jobs are divided into six main areas. Jobs are listed in the area most often referenced, but also may fall in other areas.

1. Management — directs the planning, research, development, evaluation, and integration of technology.
2. System development and programming — analyzes, designs, develops, and implements new information technology and maintains and improves existing systems.
3. Technical services — evaluates and integrates new technologies, administers the organization's data resources, and supports the centralized computer operating system and servers.
4. Operations — operates the centralized computer equipment and administers the network, including both data and voice communications.
5. Training — teaches employees how to use components of the information system or answers specific user questions.
6. Security — develops and enforces policies that are designed to safeguard an organization's data and information from unauthorized users.

The table in Figure 15-3 on the next two pages shows some of the jobs in each of the areas of a typical IT department along with job functions, usual educational requirements (which are described later in the chapter), and national average salary ranges.

Computer Career Salaries

For more information, visit the Computer Concepts CourseMate Web site at www.cengagebrain.com, navigate to the Chapter 15 Web Link resource for this book, and then click Computer Career Salaries.

FAQ 15-1

How do computer graduates' starting salaries compare?

As shown in the chart below, computer science majors earn among the highest college graduates' starting salaries.

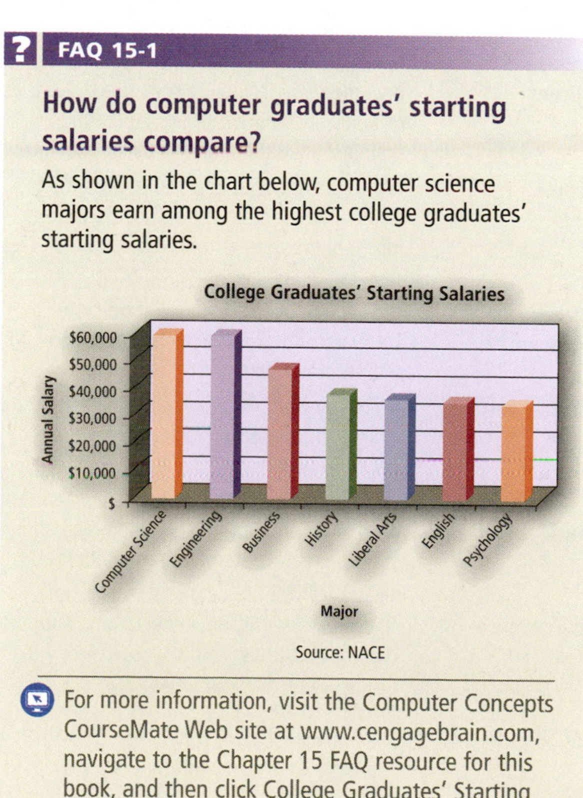

For more information, visit the Computer Concepts CourseMate Web site at www.cengagebrain.com, navigate to the Chapter 15 FAQ resource for this book, and then click College Graduates' Starting Salaries.

IT Department Jobs

Area	Job Title	Function	Usual Education Required	Annual Base Salary Range
Management	**Chief information officer (CIO)/chief technology officer (CTO)**	Directs the company's information service and communications functions	Bachelor's degree in Management Information Technology	$136,000 to $306,000
	E-commerce director	Supervises the development and execution of Internet or e-commerce systems; works with the company's marketing and customer service divisions	Bachelor's degree in Computer Information Systems or Management Information Technology	$89,000 to $190,000
	Network administrator/ wireless network administrator	Installs, configures, and maintains LANs, WANs, wireless networks, intranets, and Internet systems; identifies and resolves connectivity issues	Bachelor's degree in Computer Information Systems or Electrical Engineering Technology	$39,000 to $158,000
	Project leader/ manager	Oversees all assigned projects; allocates resources; selects teams; performs systems analysis and programming tasks; conducts performance appraisals	Bachelor's degree in Management Information Technology	$53,000 to $120,000
System development and programming	**Computer games designer/ programmer**	Designs computer games and translates the design into a computer program using an appropriate computer language	Bachelor's degree in Computer Science or Software Engineering	$49,000 to $107,000
	Computer scientist	Researches, invents, and develops innovative solutions to complex software requirements or problems	Bachelor's or master's degree in Computer Science or Engineering	$55,000 to $144,000
	Database analyst	Uses data modeling techniques and tools to analyze, tune, and specify data usage within an application area	Bachelor's degree in Computer Science or Computer Information Systems	$33,000 to $133,000
	Desktop or mobile application programmer/ developer	Converts the system design into the appropriate computer language, such as Visual Basic, Java, C#, F#, and C++	Associate's or bachelor's degree in Computer Information Systems	$42,000 to $123,000
	Software engineer	Specifies, designs, implements, tests, and documents high-quality software in a variety of fields, including robotics, operating systems, animation, and applications	Bachelor's degree in Computer Science or Software Engineering	$45,000 to $130,000
	Systems analyst	Works closely with users to analyze their requirements, designs and develops new information systems, and incorporates new technologies	Bachelor's degree in Computer Information Systems	$42,000 to $120,000
	Systems programmer	Installs and maintains operating system software and provides technical support to the programming staff	Bachelor's degree in Computer Science or Computer Information Systems	$39,000 to $122,000
	Technical lead	Guides design, development, and maintenance tasks; serves as interface between programmer/developer and management	Bachelor's degree in Computer Science	$57,000 to $131,000
	Technical writer	Works with the analyst, programmer, and user to create system documentation and user materials	Associate's or bachelor's degree in Computer Information Systems or in English	$35,000 to $94,000
	Web software developer	Analyzes, designs, implements, and supports Web applications; works with HTML, Ajax, JavaScript, and multimedia	Bachelor's degree in Computer Information Systems	$49,000 to $100,000

Figure 15-3 Some of the jobs available in each of the six main areas of a typical IT department.

IT Department Jobs *(continued)*

Area	Job Title	Function	Usual Education Required	Annual Base Salary Range
Technical services	**Computer technician**	Installs, maintains, and repairs hardware; installs, upgrades, and configures software; troubleshoots hardware problems	Associate's degree in Computer Information Systems or Electrical Engineering	$33,000 to $71,000
	Database administrator	Creates and maintains the data dictionary; monitors database performance	Bachelor's degree in Computer Information Systems or Management Information Technology	$63,000 to $107,000
	Desktop publisher/ compositor	Formats and combines text and graphics to produce publication-ready materials	Certificate or bachelor's degree in Graphic Design or Communications	$29,000 to $60,000
	Digital forensics examiner	Collects and analyzes evidence found on computers and networks	Bachelor's degree in Computer Science	$50,000 to $125,000
	Graphic designer/ illustrator	Develops visual impressions of products for advertisements and marketing materials	Certificate or bachelor's degree in Graphic Design or Communications	$35,000 to $72,000
	Quality assurance specialist	Reviews programs and documentation to ensure they meet the organization's standards	Bachelor's degree in Computer Information Systems	$45,000 to $104,000
	Storage administrator/ analyst	Installs, maintains, and upgrades storage systems; analyzes an organization's storage needs	Bachelor's degree in Computer Science or Computer Information Systems	$60,000 to $86,000
	Web designer	Develops graphical content using Photoshop, Flash, and other multimedia tools	Bachelor's degree in Computer Information Systems	$50,000 to $110,000
	Webmaster/Web administrator	Maintains an organization's Web site; creates or helps users create Web pages; oversees Web site performance	Bachelor's degree in Computer Information Systems	$46,000 to $90,000
Operations	**Computer operator**	Performs equipment-related activities such as monitoring performance, running jobs, backup, and restore	Associate's degree in Computer Information Systems	$26,000 to $59,000
	Data communications analyst/ VoIP specialist	Installs and monitors communications equipment and software; maintains Internet/WAN connections	Bachelor's degree in Computer Information Systems or Electrical Engineering Technology	$39,000 to $111,000
Training	**Computer science/ IT instructor**	Teaches students computer science and information technology skills	Master's degree in Computer Science, Computer Information Systems, Information Technology, or Computer Engineering	$34,000 to $168,000
	Corporate trainer	Teaches employees how to use software, design and develop systems, program, and perform other computer-related activities	Certificate or bachelor's degree in Computer Information Systems	$44,000 to $82,000
	Help desk specialist	Answers computer-related questions in person, on the telephone, or in a chat room	Associate's degree in Computer Information Systems	$35,000 to $56,000
Security	**Chief security officer (CSO)**	Responsible for physical security of an organization's property and people; in charge of securing computing resources	Bachelor's degree in Computer Science or Management Information Technology	$108,000 to $220,000
	Computer security specialist/mobile security specialist	Responsible for the security of data and information stored on computers and mobile devices within an organization	Bachelor's degree in Computer Information Systems or Computer Science	$47,000 to $115,000
	Network security administrator	Configures routers and firewalls; specifies Web protocols and enterprise technologies	Bachelor's degree in Computer Science or Computer Information Systems	$50,000 to $128,000
	Security administrator	Administers network security access; monitors and protects against unauthorized access	Bachelor's degree in Computer Science or Computer Information Systems	$49,000 to $118,000

? FAQ 15-2

How important is computer security?

Very important. The Computer Security Institute reports that an increasing number of software vulnerabilities are discovered each year. In one year for example, 144 large companies reported that information security attacks cost them a total of more than $41 million, according to the 13th Annual Computer Crime and Security Survey. Employees in the computer security field work to protect organizations from these vulnerabilities and breaches.

For more information, visit the Computer Concepts CourseMate Web site at www.cengagebrain.com, navigate to the Chapter 15 FAQ resource for this book, and then click Computer Security.

Computer Equipment Field

The **computer equipment field** consists of manufacturers and distributors of computers and computer-related hardware such as magnetic and optical drives, monitors, printers, and communications and networking devices. In addition to the companies that make end-user equipment, thousands of companies manufacture components used inside a computer such as chips, motherboards, cables, and power supplies.

Careers in this field are available with companies that design, manufacture, and produce computers and devices such as input, output, communications, and networking devices. Jobs include designing and fabricating computer chips, testing internal components, assembling computers and devices (Figure 15-4), and packing computers and peripherals. In addition to computer equipment-related jobs, most companies of this type include an IT department, where job opportunities may be available.

Figure 15-4 These employees assemble digital cameras.

Computer equipment manufacturers include such companies as AMD, Apple Computer, Cisco Systems, Dell, HP, IBM, Intel, Lenovo, Logitech, Lucent Technologies, Motorola, Nokia, Qualcomm, and Sun Microsystems. Many of these firms are huge organizations with thousands of employees worldwide. IBM, for example, is one of the larger computer companies with more than 398,000 employees and annual revenues of more than $103 billion.

The computer equipment industry also is well known for the many startup companies it spawns each year. These new companies take advantage of rapid changes in equipment technology, such as wireless communications, networking, multimedia, fiber optics, and recycling and green computing, to create new products and new job opportunities. Often these companies offer special incentives to influence college graduates to join their firms instead of the larger, more established companies.

? FAQ 15-3

What types of recycling programs are available for used printer ink cartridges?

Some printer ink cartridge manufacturers provide you with a bag and shipping label to return your old cartridge for recycling. If the ink cartridge manufacturer does not provide a way to recycle used cartridges, you can recycle them at various retail stores.

For more information, visit the Computer Concepts CourseMate Web site at www.cengagebrain.com, navigate to the Chapter 15 FAQ resource for this book, and then click Ink Cartridges.

Computer Software Field

The **computer software field** consists of companies that develop, manufacture, and support a wide range of software. Some software companies specialize in a particular type of software such as business software or utility programs. Other software companies, especially larger firms such as Microsoft, produce and sell many types of software.

Career opportunities in the computer software field involve designing and programming a variety of software, including operating systems and utility programs; business, graphics, multimedia, home, personal, educational, and entertainment software; network software; software development tools; and Internet and Web page authoring software.

Job titles for careers in the area of software development include project leader or project manager, desktop or mobile application programmer/developer, technical lead, software engineer, and computer scientist. Some employees develop application software such as business programs, games, simulations, Web sites, and more; others develop system software or utility programs.

A project leader or project manager analyzes software requirements, designs software solutions, and oversees the software development process. A programmer writes and tests computer programs. Programmers of Internet and Web applications often use the title, developer, instead of programmer. Technical lead personnel guide the design, development, and maintenance tasks and serve as interface between programmer/developer and management. A software engineer designs and develops software. Computer scientists draw on their theoretical educational background to research, invent, and develop innovative solutions to complex software requirements or problems. For a technical discussion about information science, read the High-Tech Talk article on page 810.

The software industry is huge, with annual sales exceeding $100 billion. Leading software companies include Adobe Systems, Apple, BMC Software, Computer Associates, IBM, Intuit, McAfee, Microsoft, Novell, Oracle, RealNetworks, Red Hat, Sybase, and Symantec. The largest software company, Microsoft, has more than 89,000 employees and annual revenues of approximately $60 billion. Read Ethics & Issues 15-2 for a related discussion.

ETHICS & ISSUES 15-2

Copying Software – A Computer Crime!

Usually, when you buy software, you legally can make one copy of the software for backup purposes. Despite the law, many people make multiple copies, either to share or to sell. Often, the sharing is done online. In a recent survey, more than 50 percent of students and 25 percent of instructors admitted that they illegally had copied, or illegally would copy, software. The Business Software Alliance, an industry trade association, believes that 35 percent of all software installed on computers worldwide is copied illegally. The illegally copied software is valued at $40 billion, and the amount is increasing annually by up to 15 percent per year. Illegally copied software costs the software industry billions of dollars a year in lost revenues, and the law allows fines up to $150,000 for each illegal copy of software. People and companies copy software illegally for a variety of reasons, insisting that software prices are too high, that software often is copied for educational or other altruistic purposes, that copied software makes people more productive, that no restrictions should be placed on the use of software after it is purchased, and that everyone copies software.

What penalty should be imposed for copying software? Why? Can you counter the reasons people give for copying software illegally? How? Would you copy software illegally, even if your boss told you to copy it? Why or why not? Should software vendors be allowed to probe your computer secretly for illegally installed software? Why or why not?

Computer Service and Repair Field

The **computer service and repair field** provides preventive maintenance, component installation, and repair services to customers. Typical job titles for workers in this field include service technician, computer repairperson, repair technician, and computer technician — all of which perform similar responsibilities.

A computer technician installs, maintains, and repairs hardware; installs, upgrades, and configures software; and troubleshoots hardware problems (Figure 15-5). A computer technician's job is challenging, designed for people who like to troubleshoot and solve problems, and possess a strong background in electronics. Computer technicians often replace a malfunctioning component, such as a hard disk, at the site of the computer equipment and then take the faulty part back for repair at an office or special repair facility. Some companies, for an additional charge, will send a computer technician to your home or place of business to perform any necessary repairs or replacements. Other companies, such as Dell and HP, offer training to an organization's employees, enabling these trained employees to function as certified technicians on the certifying company's behalf.

Many computer equipment manufacturers include diagnostic software with their computer equipment that assists computer technicians in identifying problems. Today's technology also allows computer technicians to diagnose and repair software problems from a remote

Figure 15-5 A computer technician's job requires a knowledge of electronics.

location; that is, the technician accesses the user's hard disk from a different location. Read Ethics & Issues 15-3 for a related discussion.

FAQ 15-4

How does a technician know how to diagnose a computer problem?

Most new computers include diagnostic tools that are designed to detect and report problems. Some computers also may report a problem by sounding a series of beeps through their speakers when the computer starts, or by changing the color of diagnostic lights that may be found on the computer case. Technicians can narrow down the computer problem by analyzing the pattern of beeps or diagnostic lights.

For more information, visit the Computer Concepts CourseMate Web site at www.cengagebrain.com, navigate to the Chapter 15 FAQ resource for this book, and then click Diagnostic Tools.

ETHICS & ISSUES 15-3

How Can Misuse of Information by IT Professionals Be Prevented?

In order to perform administrative and support tasks, IT workers often need to know passwords to information systems that contain confidential information. This information includes employees' salary information, confidential customer records, company trade secrets, and all of the e-mail messages circulated in an organization. One-third of IT workers admit to accessing such information secretly, and sometimes the information is leaked outside of the company. IT workers often sign agreements with organizations stating that they will not access any information that is not critical to their jobs.

Information systems at many government agencies and some organizations log all access to confidential information. Often, the logs are so large that organizations neglect to analyze the logs for unauthorized access. In some high-profile cases, organizations fired or suspended workers for such unauthorized access because log information proved unauthorized access occurred. Some people claim that licensing IT workers who have access to confidential information could help to filter out those who are more likely to snoop. At the very least, many argue that those working on information systems involving national security should go through a rigorous licensing procedure.

How can misuse of information by IT professionals be prevented? What should the consequences be for unauthorized access? Why? Would licensing and required training lessen the impact of unauthorized access? Why or why not?

Computer Sales

Computer salespeople must possess a general understanding of computers and a specific knowledge of the product they are selling. Strong people skills are important, including a keen listening ability and superior oral communications skills. Computer salespeople generally determine a buyer's needs and match these needs to the correct hardware and software. Effective computer salespeople need a thorough understanding of available products. They also must be able to discuss computers without using technical jargon.

Some salespeople work directly for computer equipment and software manufacturers such as Apple, Dell, HP, and Lenovo. Others work for resellers, including retailers that sell personal computer products, such as Best Buy, OfficeMax, Office Depot, and Staples.

The computer salesperson in a retail store often is a suitable entry-level job for students majoring in computer-related fields (Figure 15-6). Salespeople often are paid based on the amount of product they sell. More experienced corporate salespeople can be among an organization's more highly paid employees.

Figure 15-6 Computer retailers need salespeople who understand the products they sell and have solid people skills.

Computer Education and Training Field

The increased sophistication and complexity of today's computer products have opened extensive opportunities in computer-related education and training. Schools, colleges, universities, and private companies all need qualified educators. In fact, the high demand has led to a shortage of qualified instructors at the college level as instructors increasingly move to careers in private industry with the promise of higher pay.

Corporate trainers teach employees how to use software, design and develop systems, write programs, and perform other computer-related activities (Figure 15-7). Many companies use their own training departments. Corporations usually require less educational background for trainers than educational institutions require for instructors.

In a more informal setting, a help desk specialist answers hardware, software, and networking questions in person, over the telephone, or electronically via e-mail or a chat room. Educational requirements for help desk specialists are less stringent than they are for other jobs in the computer field. The help desk specialist position is an ideal entryway into the IT field.

Figure 15-7 Corporate trainers lead continuing education classes and introduce new software.

IT Consulting

Computer professionals sometimes decide to become IT consultants after gaining experience in one or more computer-related areas, such as programming, systems analysis and design, network configuration, or Web development. An **IT consultant**, typically hired based on computer expertise, provides computer services to his or her clients. Many companies hire an IT consultant to fill in for an employee on an extended leave of absence. Large enterprises often hire teams of consultants to offer advice about technology-related concerns.

IT consultants must possess strong technical skills in their specialized area and must be able to communicate effectively to clients. Qualified consultants are in high demand for tasks such as computer selection, information system design, communications, hardware and software configuration, network design and installation, and Web development. Read Ethics & Issues 15-4 for a related discussion.

ETHICS & ISSUES 15-4

Should IT Consultants Be Required to Pay for Their Mistakes?

While virtually everyone makes an occasional mistake in the workplace, some mistakes cause more damage than others. When IT consultants are paid by the hour and their mistakes lead to billing of more consulting time, some people claim that the consultants should pay the bill to fix the problem. Often, companies require IT consultants to carry liability insurance that covers a mistake such as spilling a cup of coffee on a notebook computer keyboard; however, mistakes such as deleting critical files or making unrecoverable changes to company data are not covered by insurance. Many IT consultants claim that human error is inevitable. Company employees are not held accountable financially for their mistakes; therefore, IT consultants should not be held liable for an occasional gaffe. Many companies claim that the consultants should be held to a higher standard because the consultants, in effect, have charged for making the error and then charge more for correcting it. Additionally, IT consultants who claim to be specialists should make fewer errors and, perhaps, would make fewer errors if they knew they would be held accountable.

Should IT consultants be required to pay for their mistakes? Why or why not? Is there a difference between a company employee making a costly error and a paid-by-the-hour IT consultant making an error? Why or why not? Should the decision as to who should pay for a mistake be agreed upon before a working relationship begins, or should it depend on the severity of the error? Why?

QUIZ YOURSELF 15-1

Instructions: Find the true statement below. Then, rewrite the remaining false statements so that they are true.

1. A corporate trainer installs, maintains, and repairs hardware; installs, upgrades, and configures software; and troubleshoots hardware problems.
2. A Webmaster/Web administrator is responsible for physical security of a company's property and people and is in charge of securing computing resources.
3. Career opportunities in the computer equipment field involve designing and programming a variety of software.
4. Computer sales representatives need to know how to discuss computers without using technical jargon.
5. More than 80 percent of IT employees work at organizations whose primary business is computer related.
6. Network administrators/wireless network administrators answer hardware, software, or networking questions in person, over the telephone, and/or electronically via e-mail or a chat room.

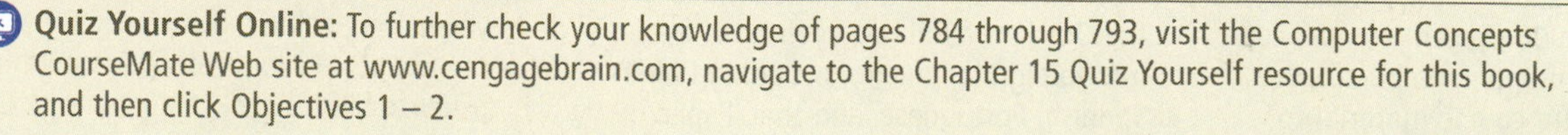

Quiz Yourself Online: To further check your knowledge of pages 784 through 793, visit the Computer Concepts CourseMate Web site at www.cengagebrain.com, navigate to the Chapter 15 Quiz Yourself resource for this book, and then click Objectives 1 – 2.

Preparing for a Career in the Computer Industry

To prepare for a career in the computer industry, you first must decide on the area in which you are interested and then become educated in that field. If you desire a formal education, several options are available, which include attending a trade school, a college that offers two-year degrees, or a college or university that offers four-year degrees. Some classes are held on campus; others are offered online. After obtaining your education, you must remain current with changes in the field. The following sections discuss various options for obtaining formal computer education and methods of remaining current after embarking on a career in the computer industry.

Attending a Trade School

A **trade school**, also called a technical school, vocational school, or career college, offers programs primarily in the areas of programming, Web design and development, graphics design, hardware maintenance, networking, personal computer support, and security. One advantage of attending a trade school is time savings. Trade schools teach specific skills instead of requiring students take a broad range of courses in the sciences and humanities. For this reason, students often complete trade school programs in a shorter time than college and university programs.

Upon completion of trade school education, students often receive a certificate. Some receive an associate's degree or higher. Many students seek full-time employment with their certificate or degree and then continue their education on a part-time basis with a two-year or four-year college. To ensure coursework will transfer, it is important that students ask their advisor if the trade school has an articulation agreement with a nearby college or university. An *articulation agreement* ensures that if you transfer to a college or university, you will receive credit for most of the courses taken at your current school.

Trade Schools

For more information, visit the Computer Concepts CourseMate Web site at www.cengagebrain.com, navigate to the Chapter 15 Web Link resource for this book, and then click Trade Schools.

As with any post-secondary school, when deciding on a trade school, you should compare curricula, laboratory facilities, instructors, and the types of jobs the school's graduates have obtained.

Entry-level jobs for students with a certificate or degree from a trade school include computer technician, desktop publisher/compositor, graphic designer/illustrator, help desk specialist, technical writer, and Web developer.

Attending a College or University

Some students attend a two-year school, called a community college or junior college. Others attend a four-year college or university. If attending a community college, students should ask their advisor if the school has an articulation agreement with a nearby college or university. As in most other industries, individuals with advanced degrees in specific fields have a better chance of success. To round out their education, many graduates augment their computer degree with a master's degree in business, education, or other field of study. Read Innovative Computing 15-1 to find out about one school that offers its course content free of charge.

At colleges and universities, three broad disciplines produce the majority of entry-level employees in the computer industry: computer information systems, computer science, and computer engineering. Another program sometimes offered is software engineering, whose definition varies depending on the school, which may combine characteristics from each of these disciplines. The characteristics of each program are summarized in Figure 15-8 and discussed in the following paragraphs.

INNOVATIVE COMPUTING 15-1

College Course Content Available Online

Whether you want to learn a new foreign language, brush up on your grammar, or study art history, you can find an online course that fits your interests. Teaching materials for thousands of colleges and universities are available free of charge on the Web.

Massachusetts Institute of Technology has one of the leading educational Web sites. More than 90 percent of its faculty and 2,600 community members have been contributing course material to the university's OpenCourseWare (OCW) project since 2001. Currently, the lecture notes, tests, and videos for more than 1,900 undergraduate- and graduate-level classes are available. No registration is required.

The more popular courses are in the areas of computer science, physics, electronics, and mathematics. Much of the OCW material has been translated into foreign languages, including Chinese, Spanish, Portuguese, and Thai. Paper copies of the course content are available to students in sub-Saharan regions without high bandwidth.

MITOPENCOURSEWARE
MASSACHUSETTS INSTITUTE OF TECHNOLOGY

For more information, visit the Computer Concepts CourseMate Web site at www.cengagebrain.com, navigate to the Chapter 15 Innovative Computing resource for this book, and then click OCW.

Computer Discipline Differences

Computer Information Systems*	Computer Science	Computer Engineering
Practical and application oriented	Theory oriented	Design oriented
Business and management oriented	Mathematics and science oriented	Mathematics and science oriented
Understand how to design and implement information systems	Understand the fundamental nature of hardware and software	Understand the fundamental nature of hardware and electronics
Certificates Degrees include A.A., A.A.S., A.S., B.A., B.S., M.S., Ph.D.	Degrees include B.S., M.S., Ph.D.	Degrees include B.S., M.S., Ph.D.

*Sometimes called Information Technology or Management Information Systems

Figure 15-8 The major differences among the computer information systems, computer science, and computer engineering disciplines.

Major in Computer Information Systems

A **computer information systems** (**CIS**), or information technology (IT), curriculum teaches students technical knowledge and skills and focuses on how to apply these skills. Types of computer courses required in a typical CIS curriculum emphasize application programming and include courses in programming, operating systems, systems analysis and design, databases, networking, and Web development. CIS curricula typically do not require majors to have a strong mathematics or physics background. In addition to academic skills, CIS majors should possess excellent people skills, a keen understanding of business operations and organizational behavior, the ability to work in teams, and solid presentation skills.

After two years of study in a CIS curriculum, students may receive an associate's degree or certificate. Entry-level jobs for students with a two-year CIS degree include desktop or mobile application programmer/developer, computer operator, computer sales representative, computer technician, graphic designer/illustrator, help desk specialist, and technical writer.

Students enrolled in four-year programs can receive a bachelor's degree with an emphasis in software development, systems analysis and design, or networking. Entry-level jobs for CIS students graduating with a bachelor's degree include desktop or mobile application programmer, computer security specialist/mobile security specialist, database analyst, e-commerce director, graphic designer/illustrator, IT consultant, network security administrator, storage administrator/analyst, systems analyst, and Web software developer.

Instead of CIS, some schools refer to this curriculum as *management information systems* (*MIS*) or *management information technology*. The main difference between a CIS curriculum and an MIS curriculum is that the ratio of business courses to computer courses is greater in an MIS curriculum.

Major in Computer Science

A **computer science** (**CS**) curriculum focuses on the theory of programming and operating systems. A computer science curriculum typically emphasizes systems programming instead of application programming. CS computer courses typically include subjects such as artificial intelligence, data communications, data and file structures, operating systems, application and systems programming, and systems analysis and design. Students also are required to take higher-level mathematics, such as calculus, and physics courses in the CS curriculum.

Entry-level jobs for graduating CS students include software engineer, storage administrator/analyst, systems programmer, digital forensics examiner, and IT consultant.

Major in Computer Engineering

A **computer engineering** (**CE**) curriculum teaches students how to design and develop the electronic components found in computers and peripheral devices. Required computer courses include application and systems programming, data and file structures, networks, and operating systems. Students also are required to take several high-level mathematics courses, at least two semesters of physics, and several electrical engineering courses in the CE curriculum.

Entry-level jobs for graduating CE students include software engineer, network security administrator, computer hardware designer, new hardware tester, and IT consultant. Computer engineers work independently or with teams of other engineers.

Computer Degrees

For more information, visit the Computer Concepts CourseMate Web site at www.cengagebrain.com, navigate to the Chapter 15 Web Link resource for this book, and then click Computer Degrees.

Searching for Computer-Related Jobs

Many companies list their job openings, internship opportunities, and career opportunities on their Web sites. They usually require initial and continuing formal education. You often can obtain a wealth of information about the firm, its employment opportunities, and its educational requirements by visiting a company's Web site (Figure 15-9). Some companies even allow job seekers to submit their resumes online. At these sites, job seekers also can post a **video resume**, which enables them to showcase their skills and abilities. To learn more about how to create a video resume, complete the Learn How To 1 activity on pages 820 and 821.

Some Web sites, such as Dice, Monster (Figure 15-10), and Yahoo! HotJobs, specialize in helping people find jobs. These job-search Web sites

Figure 15-9 Many companies' Web sites provide information about their career opportunities.

How to Use Monster to Search for a Job

Step 1
Display the Monster Web page on the screen. Type `Web software developer` in the New Search text box and then point to the Search button.

Step 2
Click the Search button to display the Job Search results page and then point to the job title for which you would like more information.

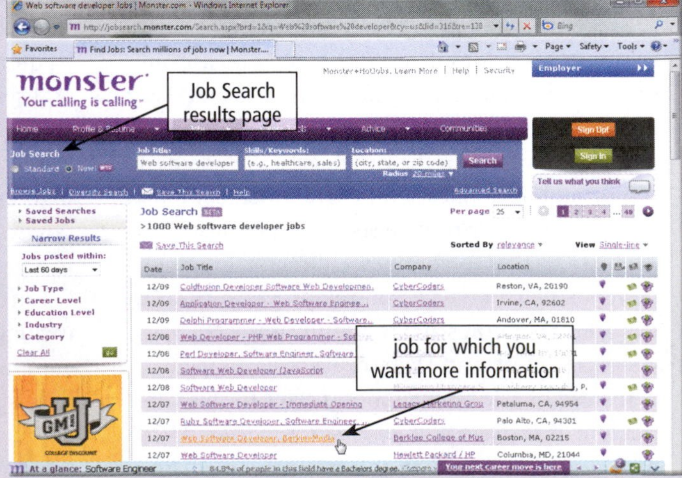

Step 3
Click the job title to display information about the available job. Read the job description. If it appeals to you, click the APPLY button and then follow the on-screen instructions.

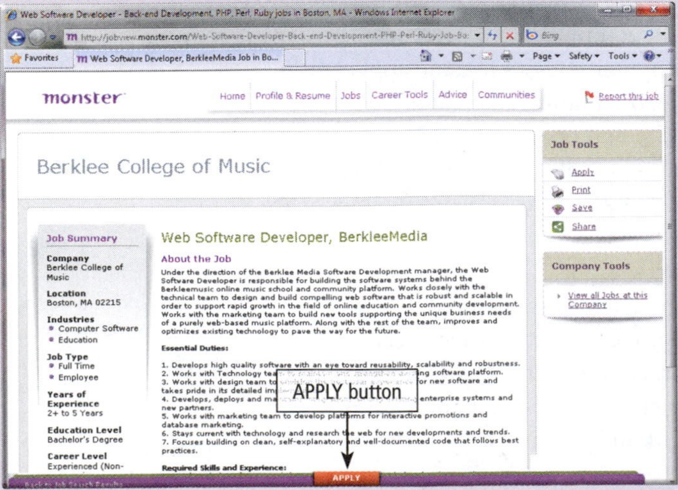

Figure 15-10 This figure shows how to use Monster to search for a job.

provide services free to job seekers — it is the employers who typically pay the fees. In addition to providing users with access to millions of job postings, these Web sites offer a variety of services, including resume writing tips, resume posting, interviewing advice, and current salary information.

? FAQ 15-5

Should I consider the 'greenness' of an organization when applying for a job?

Green organizations attempt to make everyday operational decisions that preserve natural resources and reduce waste. The desire among many to preserve the environment encourages these types of individuals to do business and/or seek employment with green organizations.

For more information, visit the Computer Concepts CourseMate Web site at www.cengagebrain.com, navigate to the Chapter 15 FAQ resource for this book, and then click Green Companies.

Planning for Career Development

Managers and educators emphasize that to remain competitive, workers in computer-related fields must keep their skills current. Someone who is an expert today finds that as technology changes, his or her career path also must change and grow. As a computer professional, you must seek methods to keep up to date on industry trends and technologies and to develop new skills. Four primary means of achieving these objectives are through professional organizations and personal networks, professional growth and continuing education activities, computer publications and Web sites, and certification.

Professional Organizations and Personal Networks

Computer professionals with common interests and a desire to extend their proficiency form computer-related professional organizations to share their knowledge. Two organizations that are influential in the computer industry are the Association for Computing Machinery and the Association of Information Technology Professionals.

The **Association for Computing Machinery (ACM)** is a scientific and educational organization dedicated to advancing knowledge and proficiency of information technology. The ACM enjoys a membership of more than 96,000 professional and student members in more than 100 countries. The focus of the ACM is computer science and computer science education. A large number of college and university computer educators are members of the ACM.

The **Association of Information Technology Professionals (AITP)** is a professional association with more than 9,000 members consisting of programmers, systems analysts, and information processing managers.

Both ACM and AITP offer the following features and benefits:

- Chapters throughout the United States, for both professionals and students
- Monthly meetings
- Workshops, seminars, and conventions
- Publications, including magazines, journals, and books that help computing professionals negotiate industry and career changes
- *Special interest groups (SIGs)* that bring together members with shared interests, needs, knowledge, and experience
- Programs to help with continuing education needs

Figure 15-11 lists several professional computer organizations. Attending professional meetings as a guest or student member provides an excellent opportunity for students to learn about the IT industry and to meet and talk with professionals in the field. Often, student chapters of professional organizations exist on college campuses. The student chapters provide students with the opportunity to develop leadership skills and to become acquainted with professionals who speak at their chapter meetings.

In addition to professional organizations, many user groups exist for a wide range of computers, operating systems, application software,

Professional Computer Organizations

For more information, visit the Computer Concepts CourseMate Web site at www.cengagebrain.com, navigate to the Chapter 15 Web Link resource for this book, and then click Professional Computer Organizations.

Professional Computer Organizations
Association for Computing Machinery (ACM)
Association for Information Systems (AIS)
Association for Women in Computing (AWC)
Association of Information Technology Professionals (AITP)
IEEE Computer Society
Independent Computer Consultants Association (ICCA)
International Systems Security Association (ISSA)
Institute of Electrical and Electronics Engineers (IEEE)
International Association for Computer Systems Security (IACSS)
National Association of Programmers (NAP)

Figure 15-11 Professional organizations help members remain current with trends in information technology.

and more. A *user group* is a collection of people with common computer equipment or software interests that meets regularly to share information. Most metropolitan areas have one or more local computer user groups that meet monthly to discuss mutual interests about computers (Figure 15-12). For anyone employed or simply interested in the computer industry, these groups can be an effective and rewarding way to learn about and continue career development.

Examples of User Groups
Apple User Groups
Association of Personal Computer User Groups (APCUG)
C/C++ Users Group (CUG)
Independent Oracle Users Group (IOUG)
Java Users Groups (JUG)
Linux Users Groups WorldWide (LUGWW)
.NET User Groups
UNIX/Linux User Groups

Figure 15-12 User groups provide computer users with a means of sharing ideas and information.

It also is wise to maintain a personal network of job-related contacts. These contacts could include current and former employers, coworkers, mentors, classmates, and instructors. Many industry professionals use their personal network to keep current with industry trends or to obtain job leads when they are seeking a change in employment.

Professional Growth and Continuing Education

Staying aware of new products and services in the computer industry is a challenging task because technology changes so rapidly. One way to stay informed is to participate in professional growth and continuing education activities such as workshops, seminars, conferences, conventions, and trade shows. These types of events provide both general and specific information about equipment, software, services, and issues affecting the computer industry.

Workshops and seminars usually last one or two days. Many companies offer training about their products in the form of books, video-based training, computer-based training (CBT), Web-based training (WBT), and instructor-led training in a classroom.

Conferences, conventions, and trade shows often last for a week. One of the larger technology trade shows in the world is the *International Consumer Electronics Show* (*CES*), which brings together more than 2,700 exhibitors and more than 110,000 attendees (Figure 15-13). At this trade show, many exhibitors demonstrate the latest developments in personal computer hardware and related peripheral devices. Read Ethics & Issues 15-5 for a related discussion.

Figure 15-13 The International Consumer Electronics Show (CES) shown here was held in Las Vegas, Nevada. More than 2,700 exhibitors displayed their newest products and services to more than 110,000 attendees.

ETHICS & ISSUES 15-5

Should Employers Be Allowed to Enforce Noncompete Agreements?

Organizations often invest a great deal of money in training IT employees and IT consultants, such as software developers, in specialized skills. IT employees and consultants often possess deep knowledge of an organization's trade secrets. To protect their investment and intellectual property, organizations often require IT employees and consultants to sign noncompete agreements. A noncompete agreement typically prevents a person from working for a competitor or working in the same specialized field for a defined period of time if the person leaves the organization. While some states prohibit noncompete agreements, court rulings continue to conflict and to be vague in determining whether noncompete agreements are legal. Organizations claim that they deserve to protect their investment in training people. Also, allowing people who possess knowledge of trade secrets to work for competitors could ruin the organization if the person shares the information. Noncompete agreements hurt IT consultants more than employees because the nature of consulting work requires consultants to move with more frequency from organization to organization than a regular employee.

Should employers be allowed to enforce noncompete agreements? Why or why not? Do noncompete agreements hurt a person's ability to compete in the job marketplace and/or enhance an organization's capability to be more competitive? Why? Should lawmakers and courts decide the legality of noncompete agreements, or should the decision be left to those who sign such agreements? Why?

Computer Publications and Web Sites

Another way to keep up to date about industry trends and technologies is to read one or more computer industry publications regularly or visit news, blogs, wikis, or technical Web sites.

Technology changes rapidly, and companies that once published their articles strictly in print have now turned to publishing only online. Magazines publishing their articles and stories online include *Computerworld*, *InfoWorld*, *PC Magazine* (Figure 15-14), and *PC World*. While some publications cover a wide range of topics, others are oriented toward a particular subject such as communications, personal computers, or a specific equipment manufacturer. Many of the more popular publications are available in public or school libraries. While some Web sites allow visitors to read their content for free, others charge a fee.

Another source for information is Web sites that discuss or share opinions, analysis, reviews, or news about technology. Popular Web sites in this category include Slashdot, The Register, AnandTech, and Tom's Hardware Guide (Figure 15-15).

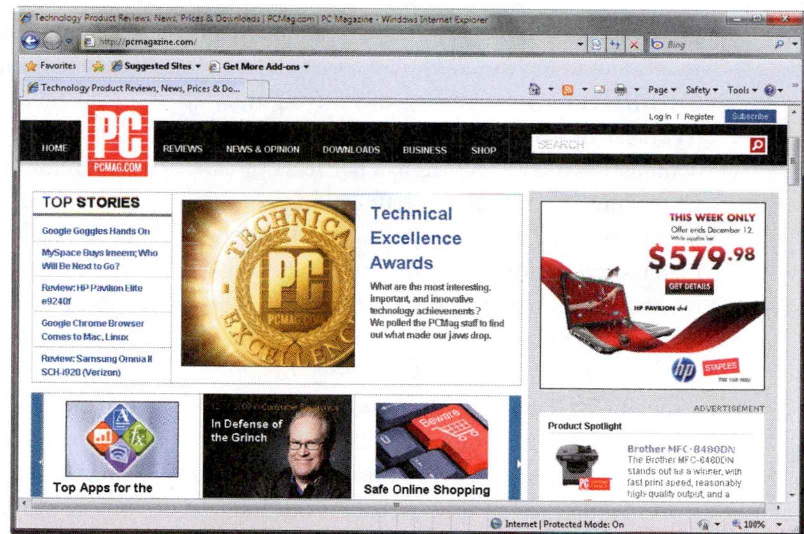

Figure 15-14 Magazines, such as the one shown here, publish their articles and stories online.

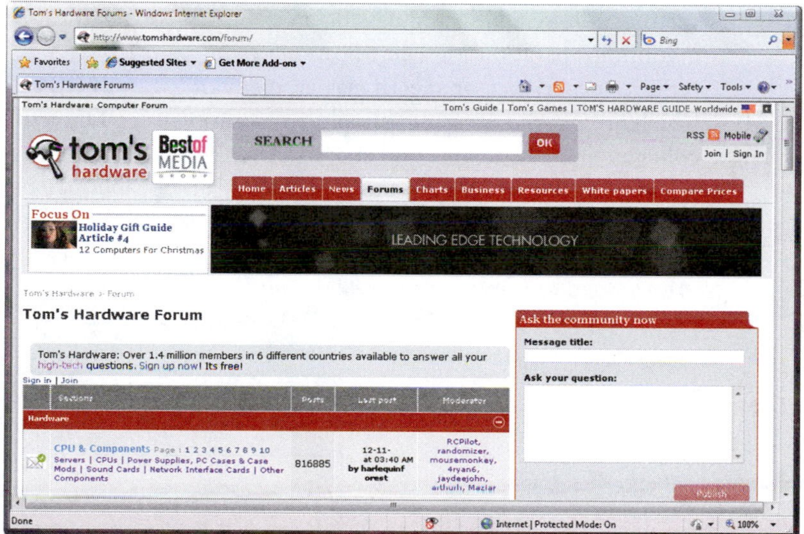

Figure 15-15 Tom's Hardware Guide, which is a popular Web site that provides news, reviews, and information about technology, also provides a forum where users can communicate with others.

✔ QUIZ YOURSELF 15-2

Instructions: Find the true statement below. Then, rewrite the remaining false statements so that they are true.

1. A transfer statement ensures that if you transfer to a college or university, you will receive credit for most of the courses taken at your current school.
2. Computer science programs focus on how to apply computing skills.
3. Job-search Web sites such as Monster provide job-search services for a fee to job seekers.
4. Students often complete trade school programs in a longer time than college and university programs.
5. Two organizations that are influential in the computer industry are the Association for Computing Machinery and the Association of Information Technology Professionals.

Quiz Yourself Online: To further check your knowledge of pages 794 through 799, visit the Computer Concepts CourseMate Web site at www.cengagebrain.com, navigate to the Chapter 15 Quiz Yourself resource for this book, and then click Objectives 3 – 5.

Certification

Certification is the process of verifying the technical knowledge of an individual who has demonstrated competence in a particular area. Companies often require certification to ensure quality and workmanship standards and to confirm their workforce remains up to date with respect to computers and technology.

Computer certification demonstrates the mastery of a skill set and knowledge base in a specific IT area. Certifications are available in many areas, including application software, operating systems, programming, hardware, networking, digital forensics, security, the Internet, and database systems. The last section of this chapter discusses specific certifications in each of these areas.

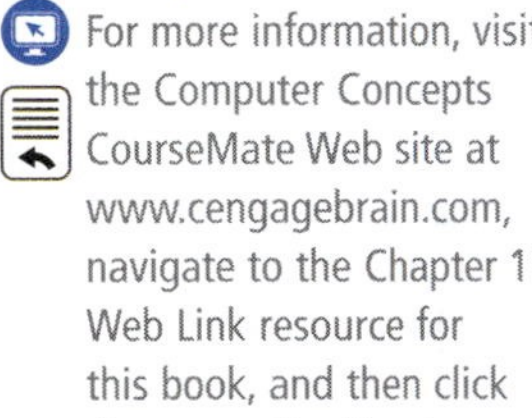

Computer Certifications

For more information, visit the Computer Concepts CourseMate Web site at www.cengagebrain.com, navigate to the Chapter 15 Web Link resource for this book, and then click Computer Certifications.

Computing professionals typically obtain a certification by taking and passing an examination. Preparation for a certification exam requires experience or special classes, many of which are offered by trade schools, community colleges, and adult education centers. After certification requirements are met, proficiency in an area is acknowledged with a certificate.

Many vendors, such as Microsoft and Cisco, offer technical certification programs for their products (Figure 15-16). These vendors, called *sponsoring organizations*, develop and administer the examinations to determine whether a person is qualified for certification. Sponsors of IT certifications include computer equipment and software vendors, independent training companies, and professional organizations.

As mentioned earlier in the chapter, some companies, such as Dell and HP, offer training and certification for their products. Other companies offer internal certifications for employees. Some of these are optional, while others are required for job retention.

Both IT professionals and users should be familiar with IT certifications. The following sections discuss certification benefits, choosing a certification, preparing for a certification, and certification examinations.

Certification Benefits

IT certification can enhance employees' careers, provide them with a better standing as industry professionals, and increase their salaries. The following paragraphs explain the benefits of certification for employees.

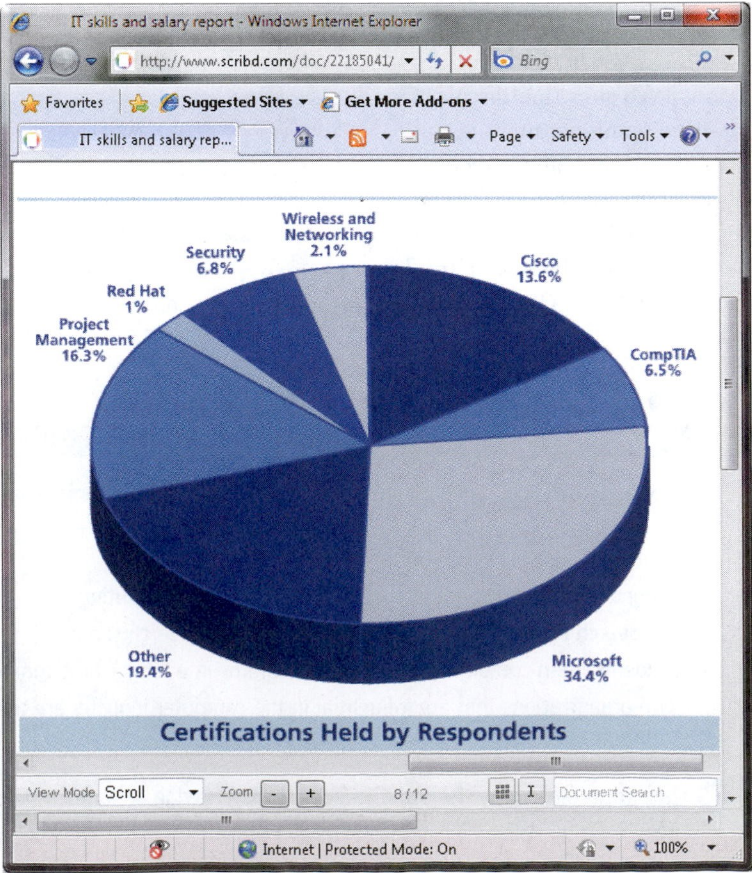

Figure 15-16 A recent report by Global Knowledge and TechRepublic shows Microsoft certifications are the most predominant.

- Career: A certification is one of the first accomplishments an employer notices on a resume. It provides a benchmark, or a means, to measure a person's skills. It can set an individual apart from other potential candidates who may be vying for a similar advancement or position.
- Professional: Certification is a personal achievement that adds credibility among peers and employers. Certification also authorizes the certificate holder to use the product's official logo or symbol on personal items, such as business cards and Web pages. As an additional bonus, some certification training can be used for college credit. Although nothing guarantees job security, certification helps give the IT professional an edge over employees without certification.
- Salary: Numerous salary surveys show that certification helps influence pay increases. Individuals with more than one area of certification can command even higher salaries. Companies often pay a bonus as an incentive for certification.

Many job listings ask for specific skills represented by certifications, and the number of companies requiring these skills is expected to grow in the future.

Vendor-sponsored certifications offer many special benefits as incentives. As shown in Figure 15-17, sponsors often provide special privileges to certified professionals, such as access to technical and product information. This may include access to secure online electronic resources, special technical support, automatic notification of updates, and access to beta products. In addition, sponsors may offer advanced training opportunities to certificate holders. Free sponsor magazine subscriptions and discounts on product-support publications and tools sometimes are available. Some sponsors even have authorized clothing lines embellished with the certification logo.

Professional organizations that offer certifications, such as the *Institute for the Certification of Computing Professionals* (*ICCP*), define standards designed to raise the competence level for the computer industry.

Certification also offers many benefits to customers, employers, and industry:

- Customer benefits of certification: Customers gain confidence in a company when IT professionals have earned a certification. Multiple certifications show that the professional can deal with many aspects of a problem, drawing from several areas of expertise. Certification implies motivation to expend extra effort, which often benefits the customer.
- Employer benefits of certification: An industry-sponsored study indicates that certified workers are more productive and knowledgeable than noncertified employees. Certified workers within the company have higher morale and job contentment, which benefits the employer.
- Industry benefits of certification: Certification is a form of industry self-regulation. It sets computer professionals' competence standards and raises the level of expertise and knowledge in the IT industry as a whole. This, in turn, enhances the reputation of the professionals in the industry.

Institute for the Certification of Computing Professionals

For more information, visit the Computer Concepts CourseMate Web site at www.cengagebrain.com, navigate to the Chapter 15 Web Link resource for this book, and then click Institute for the Certification of Computing Professionals.

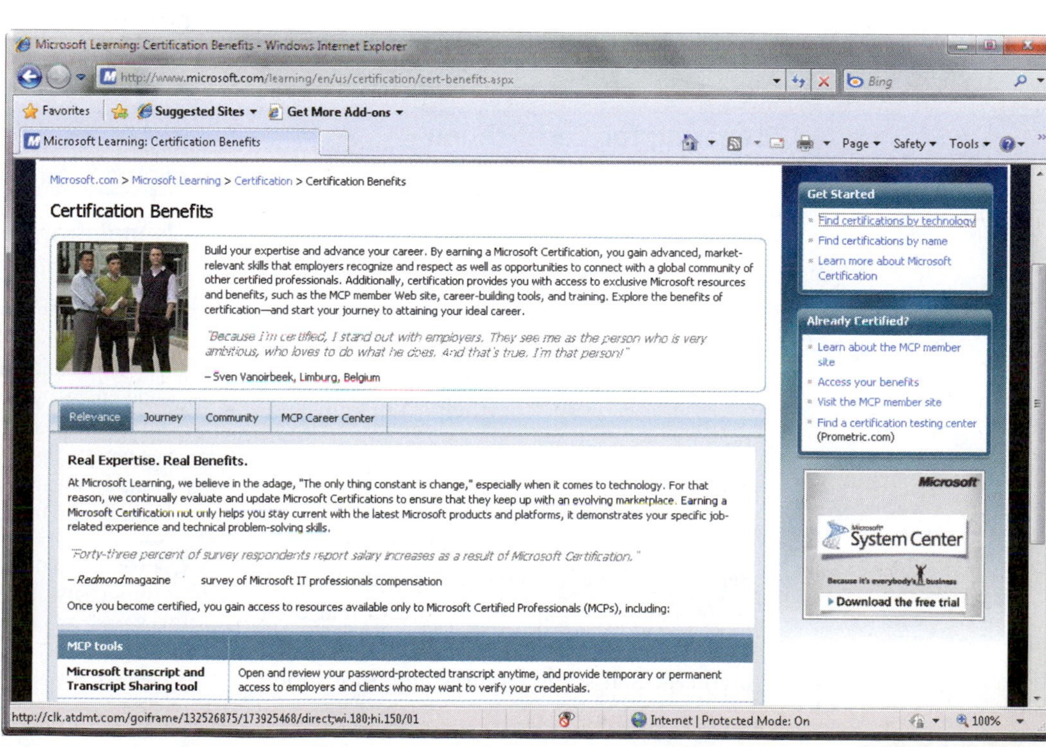

Figure 15-17 Certification sponsors often offer a variety of benefits to certificate holders.

Choosing a Certification

Certifications are not the same with respect to training and options. Selecting a certification is a personal process that requires careful thought and research. If you are considering obtaining a certification, reflect on your career goals and interests. Consider your career path during the long term. Then, assess your background knowledge and experience. Finally, research certifications to find those that best match your needs. Figure 15-18 describes factors to consider.

If you are new to the computer field, it is best to start with a general, entry-level certification. You may want to choose a certification that has immediate benefits for your current job. If you are more experienced, consider building on your existing experience with a certification that helps you reach career goals.

A certification represents a major commitment in time and money. Thoughtful research and planning can serve to guide your career to your chosen destination.

Factors to Consider when Selecting a Certification

- Consider the expenses and the time involved to obtain the certification, including how often it must be renewed
- Examine employment projections
- Look at job listings to see what certifications are sought
- Read evaluations of certifications
- Talk to people in the industry
- Think about complementary combinations of certifications to meet your goals

Figure 15-18 Factors to consider when selecting a certification.

Preparing for Certification

Most certification programs do not require academic coursework. Test results alone determine certification. Very few professionals, however, have the experience and skill set to take a certification exam without preparation. Most people prefer to follow a study program to prepare for the test. Even with experience, study serves as a review and may help to fill gaps in knowledge.

Training options are available to suit every learning style: self-study, online training classes, instructor-led training, and Web resources.

- Self-study: Flexible self-study programs help professionals prepare for certification at their own pace and supplement other training methods. Self-study requires high motivation and discipline but is the least expensive option. Hundreds of books, videotapes, and computer-based training programs on optical disc are available.
- Online training classes: Online training allows students to set their own pace in an interactive environment and combines the technological advantages of computer-based training with the connectivity of the Internet or a company's intranet. Online programs can cost about one-third the price of the traditional instructor-led programs.
- Instructor-led training: Instructor-led training is available in a variety of forms, including seminars, which typically are held for several days during a week; boot camps, which immerse students in intensive course work for up to two weeks; and academic-style classes, which span a period of several weeks or months. Some sponsors hold their own training sessions and also authorize independent training centers.
- Web resources: The certification sponsor's Web site generally contains descriptions of the available certifications, with FAQs and links to authorized training and testing centers. Many include detailed course objectives, training guides, sample test questions, chat rooms, and discussion groups. Most sell books and other training resources. Private individuals often set up Web sites to offer their own views and tips on the testing process.

Most people prefer to use a combination of these options to prepare for a certification test.

FAQ 15-6

Is mainframe specialization still a career option?

IBM reports that although mainframe sales are dropping, they still might be ideal candidates for virtualization and consolidating servers. In addition, many companies still use mainframes to support their infrastructure. In fact, one survey reports that 70 percent of the world's data exists on mainframes. For this reason, mainframe specialization still is a good career choice.

For more information, visit the Computer Concepts CourseMate Web site at www.cengagebrain.com, navigate to the Chapter 15 FAQ resource for this book, and then click Mainframes.

Certification Examinations

Authorized testing companies, such as Prometric, Pearson VUE, Brainbench (Figure 15-19), and Certiport, provide most certification exams. Many colleges also are authorized testing facilities. Certification sponsors often have a link to the testing company's Web site from their own Web page.

At the sponsor's Web site, you can use the test center locator to find a list of testing centers near you, including addresses and telephone numbers. Most testing centers allow you to pay for the test either online or by telephone with a credit card. Fees for each test range from $50 to more than $1,500, depending on the type of test. Typically, the more technical tests require higher fees. On the day of the test, you usually must present two forms of identification, one of which must be a type of photo identification.

At the testing centers, examinations are taken using computers, which process the results as you take a test. You will know immediately whether you pass the examination. Some tests are in a multiple-choice format; others are skill based.

Some tests use a technique known as *computerized adaptive testing* (*CAT*), where the tests analyze a person's responses while taking the test. The number and order of the test questions are modified to correspond to each individual's progress and demonstrated ability. Occasionally, a certification requires a hands-on lab test. The certification sponsor typically administers these tests. These examinations are much more expensive than the computerized tests. In addition, the number of testing facilities is limited.

If you do not pass an exam, you must pay the fee again to retake the test. In some cases, you can retake the test immediately; however, most people opt to review before trying to take the test again. Some training centers offer a guarantee for their program. They provide discounts, or even free sessions, for individuals who have completed their program, yet do not pass a test. Most sponsors allow candidates a set time, such as a year, in which to complete the test.

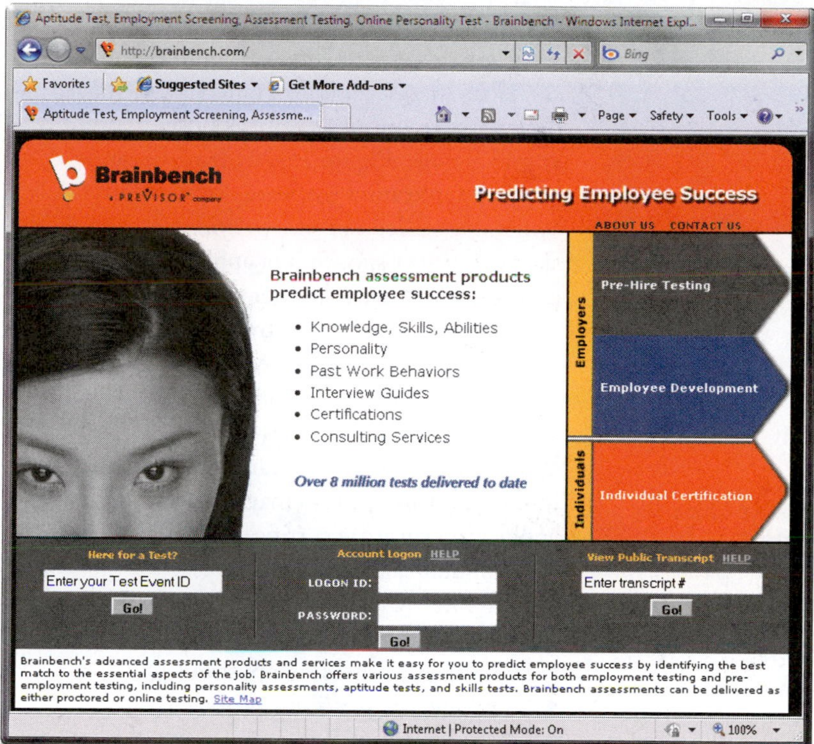

Figure 15-19 Brainbench provides assessment products designed to assess individuals' strengths and weaknesses.

A Guide to Certification

Today, more than 200 certifications are available. Some certifications have a broad focus, and others require an in-depth knowledge of a single computing aspect. Often, a sponsor establishes a series of related certifications to show levels of expertise within a single area. In addition to the certification exams that are available to the public, many companies have internal certifications available only to employees. These certifications are designed to demonstrate employees' knowledge to other employees, as well as customers.

Certifications usually are classified based on the computer industry area to which they most closely relate: application software, operating systems, programming, hardware, networking, digital forensics, security, the Internet, and database systems. Some certifications are related to more than one category. For example, a certification in networking also may indicate knowledge of hardware and operating systems.

The following pages describe the major certifications and certification sponsors in each industry area. Some certifications have components that span multiple categories. In this case, they are placed in the area for which they are known best.

Application Software Certifications

Although numerous types of application software exist, several programs have achieved national recognition for use as business and graphics tools. Figure 15-20 identifies some popular application software certifications, sometimes called *end-user certifications*, and their sponsors. Most sponsors of application software certifications have a partner training program and encourage computer-training centers to be authorized training representatives.

As with most other certifications, vendor-authorized testing facilities take registrations and administer the certification test. People in the following careers may be interested in application software certification:

- Computer sales representatives
- Computer teachers
- Corporate trainers
- Desktop publishers/compositors
- Graphic designers/illustrators
- Help desk specialists
- Office managers/workers

Microsoft Office Specialist

For more information, visit the Computer Concepts CourseMate Web site at www.cengagebrain.com, navigate to the Chapter 15 Web Link resource for this book, and then click Microsoft Office Specialist.

Application Software Certifications

Certification	Description	Sponsor
Microsoft Office Specialist (MOS) - Core	Tests a user's basic skills of Microsoft Office and other related programs	Microsoft
Microsoft Office Specialist (MOS) - Expert	Tests a user's advanced skills of Microsoft Office Word and Excel in industry applications such as budgets, publications, and collaboration	Microsoft
Microsoft Certified Desktop Support Technician (MCDST)	Tests a user's skills solving problems associated with programs that run on Windows and the operating system itself	Microsoft
Adobe Certified Associate	Tests user's expertise in a variety of Adobe software including Flash and Dreamweaver	Adobe Systems
Adobe Certified Expert (ACE)	Tests a user's expertise on Adobe software	Adobe Systems
Adobe Certified Instructor (ACI)	Demonstrates a user's ability to provide instruction on Adobe software	Adobe Systems
IBM Certified Professional for Lotus Software	Tests knowledge of Lotus programs	IBM

Figure 15-20 Application software certifications are available to anyone who works in the computer industry.

Operating System Certifications

Several options for different knowledge levels are available to those seeking operating system certifications. These certifications focus on particular skills of the user, the operator, the system administrator, and the software engineer. The table in Figure 15-21 lists a few of the certifications available in the operating systems area.

If you are interested in an occupation as an operating system administrator or software engineer, you also may benefit from certifications in networking, hardware, and the Internet. These additional certifications are linked closely to the operating system and serve to broaden expertise in that area. People in the following jobs may be interested in a certification in operating systems:

- Hardware technicians
- Help desk specialists
- Network security administrators
- IT consultants
- System administrators

Operating System Certifications

Certification	Description	Sponsor
IBM Certified Specialist	Tests knowledge of AIX operating system and network security	IBM
Microsoft Certified IT Professional (MCITP)	Tests knowledge of deploying and managing operating systems	Microsoft
Microsoft Certified Technology Specialist (MCTS)	Tests technical expertise in a specialized area including Windows and .NET environments	Microsoft
Novell Certified Linux Professional (CLP)	Tests technical expertise in installing, managing, and troubleshooting the Linux operating system	Novell
Red Hat Certified Engineer (RHCE)	Tests technical expertise of setting up and administering network services and the Linux operating system	Red Hat
Red Hat Certified Technician (RHCT)	Tests basic knowledge of setting up and managing a Linux operating system	Red Hat
Sun Certified System Administrator (SCSA)	Tests knowledge of administering the Solaris operating system	Sun

Figure 15-21 Operating system certifications test knowledge level of a specific operating system.

Programmer/Developer Certifications

Various certifications are available in the programmer/developer area. These certifications usually are supported with training programs that prepare applicants for the certification test.

If you are interested in writing application software, you also may benefit from certifications in networking and Web design. These certifications are tied closely to programming and may broaden employment opportunities.

The table shown in Figure 15-22 identifies a few of the certifications available in the programmer/developer area. People in the following jobs may be interested in a programmer/developer certification:

- Java programmers
- Mobile application developers
- Oracle database managers
- Programming consultants
- SQL programmers
- Web software developers
- XML developers

Hardware Certifications

Hardware certifications vary in scope from a narrow focus with an emphasis on the repair of a specific device to an integrated hardware solution that addresses a company's current and future computing needs. Obtaining an advanced certification in hardware implies that you have achieved a standard of competence in assessing a company's hardware needs, and you can implement solutions to help the company achieve its computing goals.

People interested in hardware certifications also may benefit from networking and operating system software certifications, which are tied closely to advanced hardware knowledge. The table in Figure 15-23 lists a few available hardware certifications. People in the following careers may be interested in hardware certification:

- Cable installation technicians
- Computer repair technicians
- Corporate trainers
- Help desk specialists
- IT consultants
- System engineers and administrators

Programmer/Developer Certifications

Certification	Description	Sponsor
Certified Software Development Associate (CSDA)	Tests basic knowledge of software development process and tools	IEEE Computer Society
Certified Software Development Professional (CSDP)	Tests advanced knowledge of software development process and tools	IEEE Computer Society
IBM Certified Solution Developer	Tests knowledge of developing XML applications with Web services	IBM
Microsoft Certified Professional Developer (MCPD)	Tests knowledge of developing Web or Windows-based applications using programs in the Visual Studio suite and the .NET Framework	Microsoft
Sun Certified Enterprise Architect (SCEA)	Tests knowledge of creating and maintaining J2EE applications	Sun
Sun Certified Java Developer (SCJD)	Tests advanced knowledge of Java programming language	Sun
Sun Certified Java Programmer (SCJP)	Tests basic knowledge of Java programming language	Sun
Sun Certified Mobile Application Developer (SCMAD)	Tests knowledge of using Java to create applications for mobile devices such as smart phones	Sun

Figure 15-22 Various certifications are available in the programmer/developer area.

Hardware Certifications

Certification	Description	Sponsor
A+	Tests entry-level knowledge of personal computer setup, configuration, maintenance, troubleshooting; basic networking skills; and system software	Computing Technology Industry Association (CompTIA)
Dell Certified Systems Expert	Tests knowledge of computer configuration and installation, troubleshooting, operating system fundamentals, and hardware replacement	Dell
IBM eServer Certified Specialist	Tests knowledge of IBM eServer line of products	IBM

Figure 15-23 Hardware certifications may test general knowledge of hardware or test knowledge of a specific type of hardware.

Networking Certifications

Network expertise is acquired through years of experience and training because so many variables exist for a total network solution. Obtaining an advanced certification in networking implies that you have achieved a standard of competence, enabling you to address the complex issues that arise when planning, installing, managing, and troubleshooting a network. Networking certification holders earn salary levels from 5 to 30 percent more than those without certification.

The table shown in Figure 15-24 identifies a few of the certifications available in the networking area. People in the following careers may be interested in network certification:

- Hardware service technicians
- Network consultants
- Network managers
- Network engineers
- System administrators

Network+

For more information, visit the Computer Concepts CourseMate Web site at www.cengagebrain.com, navigate to the Chapter 15 Web Link resource for this book, and then click Network+.

Digital Forensics Certifications

As discussed in Chapter 11, digital forensics is the discovery, collection, and analysis of evidence found on computers and networks. According to the Investigative Services Bureau, the testimonies of digital forensics certificate holders are considered highly credible during computer crimes cases.

The table shown in Figure 15-25 identifies a few of the certifications available in the digital forensics area. People in the following careers may be interested in digital forensics certification:

- Information security officers and managers
- Law enforcement officials
- Military intelligence officers
- Network administrators/wireless network administrators
- Network security administrators
- Security administrators

Networking Certifications

Certification	Description	Sponsor
Novell Certified Administrator (NCA)	Tests knowledge of Novell's networking products including NetWare, intraNetWare, and GroupWise	Novell
Novell Certified Engineer (NCE)	Tests in-depth knowledge of designing, configuring, implementing, administering, and troubleshooting the Novell network system	Novell
Cisco Certified Network Associate (CCNA)	Tests basic knowledge of installing, configuring, and operating LAN, WAN, and dial-up access services for small networks	Cisco
Cisco Certified Network Professional (CCNP)	Tests advanced knowledge of installing, configuring, and operating LANs and WANs	Cisco
Cisco Certified Internetwork Expert (CCIE)	Tests expert level knowledge in areas of internetwork communications, security, routing, and switching	Cisco
Microsoft Certified Systems Administrator (MCSA)	Tests technical expertise in one of several areas including managing and troubleshooting networks using Windows operating systems	Microsoft
Network+	Tests competency in several network areas including transmission media and topologies, protocols, and standards	Computing Technology Industry Association (CompTIA)
Sun Certified Network Administrator (SCNA)	Tests knowledge of administering Sun networks	Sun

Figure 15-24 Networking certifications usually test knowledge of a company-specific network.

Digital Forensics Certifications

Certification	Description	Sponsor
Certified Computer Examiner (CCE)	Tests core knowledge of acquisition, marking, handling, and storage of computer evidence using a particular operating system	International Society of Forensic Computer Examiners (ISFCE)
Certified Computer Forensics Examiner (CCFE)	Tests in-depth knowledge of forensic imaging, examination, collection, and reporting	Information Assurance Certification Review Board (IACRB)
Certified Electronic Evidence Collection Specialist (CEECS)	Tests basic knowledge of forensic ethics, imaging, examination, collection, and reporting	International Association of Computer Investigative Specialists (IACIS)
Certified Information Forensics Investigator (CIFI)	Tests knowledge of information forensics in areas related to auditing, incident response, law and investigation, tools and techniques, traceback, and countermeasures	International Information Systems Forensics Association (IISFA)

Figure 15-25 Digital forensics certifications usually test knowledge of the examining, collecting, and reporting of computer evidence.

Security Certifications

Security certifications measure a candidate's ability to identify and control security risks associated with any event or action that could cause a loss of or damage to computer hardware, software, data, information, or processing capability. While some security certifications focus solely on network and Internet security, others include measures to secure operating systems, application programs, and information systems, as well as the physical facility and its people.

The table shown in Figure 15-26 identifies a few of the certifications available in the security area. People in the following careers may be interested in security certification:

- Information security officers and managers
- Network administrators/wireless network administrators
- Network security specialists
- Security administrators

Internet Certifications

Internet certifications are demanding and require technical expertise in networking hardware and configuration before enrollment in an Internet certification-sponsored training program. These certifications include Web management, Web programming, and Web development certifications.

Internet-related occupations also benefit from certifications in hardware, networking, operating systems, and programming. The table shown in Figure 15-27 lists a few of the certifications available in the Internet area. People in the following careers may be interested in Internet certification:

- Internet and intranet managers
- Internet service provider staff
- Network administrators/wireless network administrators
- Webmasters
- Web software developers

Database System Certifications

Supporting a large database management system requires a professional staff. The various tasks the staff performs form a core on which the database management certifications are based. If you are interested in working with a database management system, you also may benefit from certifications in hardware, the Internet, networking, and programming.

Security Certifications

Certification	Description	Sponsor
Certified Information Systems Security Professional (CISSP)	Tests in-depth knowledge of access control methods, information systems development, cryptography, operations security, physical security, and network and Internet security	International Information Systems Security Certification Consortium (ISC)²
Security Certified Network Architect (SCNA)	Tests network security skills related to wireless security, e-mail security, digital certificates, digital signatures, and biometrics	The Security Certified Program (SCP)
Security Certified Network Professional (SCNP)	Tests skills with firewalls and defending against network intrusions	The Security Certified Program (SCP)
Security Certified Network Specialist (SCNS)	Tests basic network security skills	The Security Certified Program (SCP)
Systems Security Certified Practitioner (SSCP)	Tests basic knowledge of access controls, cryptography, data communications, and malicious code	International Information Systems Security Certification Consortium (ISC)²

Figure 15-26 Some security certifications focus on network security, while others include security for the entire enterprise.

Internet Certifications

Certification	Description	Sponsor
Certified Internet Webmaster (CIW)	Tests knowledge of Web development, security, and administration	Prosoft Learning
Certified Web Professional (CWP)	Tests advanced knowledge in areas of Web site design and development, and server administration and security	International Webmasters Association

Figure 15-27 Internet certifications are demanding and require technical expertise in networking hardware.

? FAQ 15-7

Does DBA have two meanings?

Yes; DBA stands for either database administration or database administrator. The first, database administration, is the act of managing a database. The second, database administrator, is the person who manages the database.

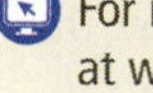 For more information, visit the Computer Concepts CourseMate Web site at www.cengagebrain.com, navigate to the Chapter 15 FAQ resource for this book, and then click DBA.

The table shown in Figure 15-28 outlines a few of the certifications available in the database area. People in the following careers may be interested in database certification:

- Database administrators
- Database analysts
- Database application developers
- Database designers

Database Certifications

Certification	Description	Sponsor
IBM Certified Solutions Expert – DB2	Tests advanced skills of administration of the DB2 database management system	IBM
IBM Certified Solutions Expert – Informix	Tests advanced skills of administration of the Informix database management system	IBM
Microsoft Certified IT Professional (MCITP)	Tests skills required to use SQL Server to design or install, manage, and maintain a database system	Microsoft
Oracle Certified Professional (OCP)	Tests knowledge of developing and deploying large-scale Oracle database management systems	Oracle
Sybase Certified Professional	Tests skills in developing and administering Sybase database management systems	Sybase

Figure 15-28 Database certifications usually test knowledge of a specific database management system.

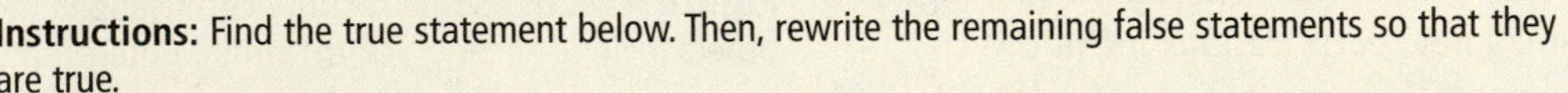

QUIZ YOURSELF 15-3

Instructions: Find the true statement below. Then, rewrite the remaining false statements so that they are true.

1. Digital forensics certifications usually test knowledge of the examining, collecting, and reporting of computer evidence.
2. If you do not pass a certification exam, you do not have to pay a fee again to retake the test.
3. Industrialization is a process of verifying the technical knowledge of an individual who has demonstrated competence in a particular area.
4. Salary surveys show that certification helps influence pay decreases.
5. The Microsoft Certified Professional Developer certification tests a user's basic (specialist) and advanced (expert) skills of Microsoft Office programs and some versions of the Windows operating system.

Quiz Yourself Online: To further check your knowledge of pages 800 through 808, visit the Computer Concepts CourseMate Web site at www.cengagebrain.com, navigate to the Chapter 15 Quiz Yourself resource for this book, and then click Objectives 6 – 9.

Chapter Summary

This chapter discussed the strong demand for computer and IT professionals and presented a variety of available computer-related careers. For additional discussion about 15 of the more popular computer careers, complete the Exploring Computer Careers exercise on the Learn It Online page in each chapter in this book. The table in Figure 15-29 lists the page number on which each career is assigned.

This chapter also focused on computer education at trade schools, computer-related majors at colleges and universities, job searches, career development planning, professional organizations, and professional growth. Information about certification preparation, examinations, and resources also was presented. Finally, specific certifications were discussed.

Learn It Online — Exploring Computer Careers Exercises

Chapter Number	Chapter Title	Job Title	Page Number
1	Introduction to Computers	Personal Computer Salesperson	47
2	The Internet and World Wide Web	Web Developer	117
3	Application Software	Help Desk Specialist	185
4	The Components of the System Unit	Computer Engineer	249
5	Input	Data Entry Clerk	295
6	Output	Graphic Designer/Illustrator	337
7	Storage	Computer Technician	389
8	Operating Systems and Utility Programs	Systems Programmer	437
9	Communications and Networks	Network Specialist	505
10	Database Management	Database Administrator	547
11	Computer Security and Safety, Ethics, and Privacy	Digital Forensics Examiner	599
12	Information System Development	Systems Analyst	655
13	Programming Languages and Program Development	Programmer	705
14	Enterprise Computing	CIO	765
15	Computer Careers and Certification	Computer Science/IT Instructor	817

Figure 15-29 Each Learn It Online page in this book contains an Exploring Computer Careers exercise. This table lists the job title and page number for each exercise.

Computer Usage @ Work

Publishing

Today, virtually any material that you read exists in electronic form. In publishing's early years, and before computers existed, authors and writers recorded content using a typewriter, which then would be duplicated and bound into a publication. When word processors were introduced, writers were able not only to type their work, but also to apply basic formatting and check their spelling. While typewriters and word processors performed their tasks adequately, they pale in comparison to the extent to which today's computers have improved the publishing process.

Computers played an essential role in this textbook's publication. Authors use word processing software to create the first draft of each chapter. This draft uses special formatting to instruct compositors how to organize and lay out the content so that it not only is attractive and readable, but has educational value. Once the first draft is complete, editors use various tools in the word processing software to make and show their changes, as well as to add comments and questions. The authors then respond to these comments and questions and make changes based upon editor feedback. The authors then send the revised electronic document to the compositor, who uses the document, along with all accompanying instructions, to create a first version of how the chapter will look once it is printed. Using desktop publishing programs, such as QuarkXPress or Adobe InDesign, the compositors perform tasks such as creating the layout, adding and formatting headings, changing fonts and font styles, adding graphical elements, and inserting page numbers. The authors, editors, and proofreaders then receive an electronic copy of the chapter, specifically a PDF file, and use document management software such as Adobe Acrobat to identify layout changes, text changes, or formatting changes that need to be made. Because multiple people review and edit each chapter, they all send their comments to an individual who then compiles all comments into one document and sends it back to the compositor for the next draft. This process continues until the authoring team requires no further changes. Once all chapters have been composed and are in their final version, the compositor then prepares and sends the files to the printer. The printer, or company hired to produce the printed textbook, then uses the files to print and bind the textbook.

Computers play an important role not only in the development of textbooks, but also in the publication of newspapers and magazines. Without computers, the publication process would be less efficient, and the final works would be more prone to errors.

For more information, visit the Computer Concepts CourseMate Web site at www.cengagebrain.com, navigate to the Chapter 15 Computer Usage @ Work resource for this book, and then click Publishing.

High-Tech Talk

Bioinformatics: Technology Collides with Biology

Informatics, also referred to as information science, refers to the gathering, processing, storing, retrieving, and organizing of information. Informatics typically combines information technology or computer science with another area of study. As we use computers to collect massive amounts of data, we also must rely on them to process the data into meaningful information. Computers continually become more powerful, requiring only seconds to process data that otherwise might require several human years to process. In fact, the informatics field is exploding in popularity.

As mentioned previously, several specializations of informatics exist, each combining computer science with another field of study. These specializations include the combination of information technology with other fields such as molecular biology (bioinformatics), biomedical sciences (biomedical informatics), chemistry (chemoinformatics), ecology (ecoinformatics), geosciences (geoinformatics), health (health informatics), neuroscience (neuroinformatics), sociology (social informatics), and veterinary medicine (veterinary informatics).

Many colleges and universities now are offering an increasing number of courses in bioinformatics. *Bioinformatics* refers to computer applications in biological sciences where biologists use computers to analyze, store, or retrieve biological information. Bioinformatics research requires extensive collaboration between biologists and computer scientists. Essentially, biologists help the computer scientists understand the research study they would like to perform, and the computer scientists design programs to collect the data, process the data, and determine the results. Throughout this entire process, the biologists work closely with the computer scientists to ensure the accuracy of the data, its processing, and the output. Computer technology has assisted in analyzing the DNA sequence, advancing the study of molecular genetics.

One of the greatest accomplishments of bioinformatics might be the *Human Genome Project*. Scientists have used computers to map the complete set of the human genome in an effort to understand more fully specific aspects of human life (Figure 15-30). At one time, scientists were unable to determine scientifically why children resembled their parents. Currently, scientists can use the genes from two individuals and predict, with great accuracy, how their children will look. While 99.9 percent of DNA is identical in all humans, computers play a critical role in determining which DNA is different and how the DNA determines human characteristics such as height and hair color. Because diseases have a genetic component, bioinformatics also will use the information from the Human Genome Project to better understand diseases plaguing humans, as well as discover ways to prevent and/or cure these diseases. Humans acquire diseases either through heredity or as a body's response to various environmental conditions. Understanding the human genome in greater detail can assist scientists in determining exactly which genes contribute to inherited diseases and possibly provide a way to prevent these genes from passing to future generations.

In addition to assisting with disease treatment and prevention, bioinformatics and knowledge of the human genome can help advance clinical medicine. An individual's genetic makeup determines both his or her physical characteristics and how his or her body might respond to certain medications and treatments. Many medications are developed that affect only a small percentage of people; thus, they never make it to pharmacy shelves. For a medication to be approved for the market, it must be effective on a wide range of individuals. Scientists can use knowledge of the similarities in the genetic characteristics of all humans to aid in developing medications that will be widely effective.

Bioinformatics, although a relatively new field, has helped us to learn much more about human life. Improvements in technology and the rate at which this field is gaining popularity might help scientists soon explain phenomenon that have mystified humans for hundreds of years.

For more information, visit the Computer Concepts CourseMate Web site at www.cengagebrain.com, navigate to the Chapter 15 High-Tech Talk resource for this book, and then click Bioinformatics.

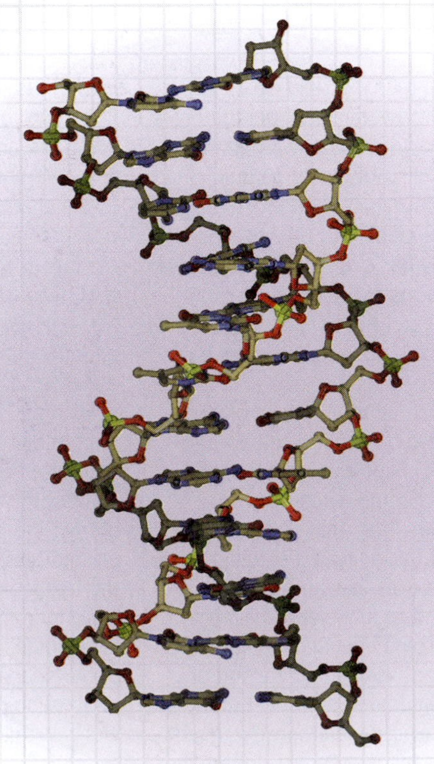

Figure 15-30 The Human Genome Project provides us with a better understanding of the genetic makeup of human beings.

Companies on the Cutting Edge

DICE Online Career Opportunities

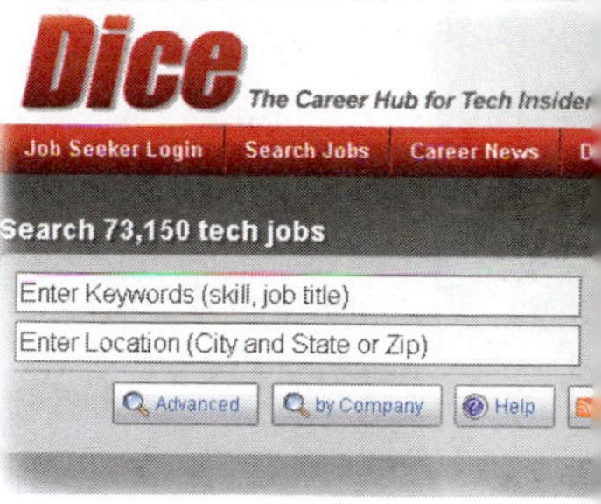

Millions of IT professionals turn to *Dice*.com each month to search for job openings, participate in discussions, and gather employment advice. This Web site is part of Dice Holdings, Inc., an Iowa-based corporation specializing in building communities of job-seeking professionals.

Dice focuses on providing services for the impending IT talent shortage. Company officials predict that demand for graduates with degrees in mathematics and science will increase dramatically as online media and services expand. Dice provides job search tools, including resume posting, job searching by both location and skill, and career news and advice listings. The DicePlay area of its Web site contains videos, games, widgets, and photos of interest to IT professionals.

Dice recently launched Dice Learning. Dice Learning provides a search engine allowing technology professionals to find information easily about technical training and certifications. Dice hopes that Dice Learning will help these professionals advance their careers.

DELL Computer Manufacturer

Every FORTUNE 100 company does business with *Dell*, making it the number one computer provider in the United States. For ten years, Dell also has been the number one computer supplier to small- and medium-sized businesses in the United States. Dell ships 140,000 computers each day, which amounts to more than a computer per second.

Founded by Michael Dell in 1984, the company prides itself on its direct approach to computer sales. Its Web site allows customers to configure and price computers and electronic components, order computers, and track their orders online. Dell also partners with Walmart, Staples, and other retail outlets to expand its distribution worldwide.

Dell is committed to practicing green computing. It is the only computer company that offers free recycling worldwide, and its global headquarters in Texas is powered by 100 percent green energy.

Dell recently confirmed that it will begin selling smart phones. The Dell Mini 3 smart phones first will be available to consumers in selected countries, including China and Brazil.

 For more information, visit the Computer Concepts CourseMate Web site at www.cengagebrain.com and then navigate to the Chapter 15 Companies on the Cutting Edge resource for this book.

Technology Trailblazers

STEVE BALLMER Microsoft CEO

Steve Ballmer's net worth of $11 billion makes him one of the world's 50 richest people. His wealth is due, in part, to his sheer enthusiasm, determination, and dedication in his role as Microsoft's CEO. This passion was evident when he once performed a crazy dance at Microsoft's 25th Anniversary employee meeting and screamed "Developers!" 14 times at a software conference.

He met Bill Gates at Harvard University and graduated in 1977 with a bachelor's degree in mathematics and economics. Ballmer was one of Microsoft's first employees; in 1980, when the company was five years old, he was appointed its first business manager. He was in charge of several divisions, including operations, sales and support, and operating systems development, until he was promoted first to president in 1998 and then to CEO in 2000.

BusinessWeek recently named him one of "The 25 Most Influential People on the Web," a fact reinforced by his invitation to give the keynote presentation at the 2009 Consumer Electronics Show in Las Vegas, Nevada.

JERRY YANG AND DAVID FILO Yahoo! Cofounders

The number of Yahoo! Games users living in the United States exceeds the entire population of Tokyo, Japan. The success of the Yahoo! Web site is due to the efforts of *Jerry Yang* and *David Filo*, who created the Yahoo! Internet navigational guide in 1994 and cofounded Yahoo! the following year.

Yang and Filo met at Stanford University, where they studied electrical engineering by day and surfed the Web at night in search of interesting Web sites. They organized their findings in a useful Yahoo! directory, *Jerry's Guide to the World Wide Web*, that they shared with schoolmates. This project grew in scope as thousands of Web sites were added each day. They hired a Stanford alumnus with expertise in artificial intelligence to create a branching hierarchy that guides users through the Web content. Yahoo! today is the most trafficked Web site.

Filo and Yang both continue to serve in their Chief Yahoo! roles. Yang, however, announced in 2008 that he would resign, but remained in his role until a replacement was found in January 2009.

 For more information, visit the Computer Concepts CourseMate Web site at www.cengagebrain.com and then navigate to the Chapter 15 Technology Trailblazers resource for this book.

STUDENT ASSIGNMENTS

Chapter Review

The Chapter Review reinforces the main concepts presented in this chapter.

To listen to an audio version of this Chapter Review, visit the Computer Concepts CourseMate Web site at www.cengagebrain.com and then navigate to the Chapter 15 Chapter Review resource for this book.

1. **What Career Opportunities Are Available in the Computer Industry?** Career opportunities in the computer industry fall into several areas. In most medium and large businesses and government offices, staff in an **IT department** is responsible for keeping all computer operations and networks running smoothly. They also determine when and if the organization requires new hardware or software. Workers in the **computer equipment field** manufacture and distribute computers and computer-related hardware. Employees in the **computer software field** develop, manufacture, and support a wide range of software. People in the **computer service and repair field** provide preventive maintenance, component installation, and repair services to customers. **Computer salespeople** determine a buyer's needs and match these needs to the correct hardware and software. Computer educators and corporate trainers teach students and employees how to use software, design and develop systems, write programs, and perform other computer-related activities. An **IT consultant** is a professional who draws upon his or her expertise in a specialized area of computers and provides computer services to clients.

2. **What Are the Functions of Jobs in an IT Department?** Jobs in an IT department fall into six main areas. Management directs the planning, research, development, evaluation, and integration of technology. System development and programming analyzes, designs, develops, and implements new information technology and maintains and improves existing systems. Technical services evaluates and integrates new technologies, administers the organization's data resources, and supports the centralized computer operating system and servers. Operations operates the centralized computer equipment and administers the network, including both data and voice communications. Training teaches employees how to use components of the information system or answers specific questions. Security develops and enforces policies designed to safeguard data and information from unauthorized users.

Visit the Computer Concepts CourseMate Web site at www.cengagebrain.com, navigate to the Chapter 15 Quiz Yourself resource for this book, and then click Objectives 1 – 2.

3. **How Are Trade Schools Different from Colleges?** A **trade school**, also called a technical school, vocational school, or career college, offers programs primarily in the areas of programming, Web design and development, graphics design, hardware maintenance, networking, personal computer support, and security. Students learn specific skills instead of taking a broad range of science and humanities courses, which can result in time savings for students.

4. **How Are the Various College Computer-Related Courses of Study Different?** Three broad disciplines in higher education produce the majority of entry-level employees in the computer industry. **Computer information systems** (**CIS**), or information technology (IT), programs teach technical knowledge and skills and focus on how to apply these skills. **Computer science** (**CS**) programs stress the theoretical side of programming and operating systems. **Computer engineering** (**CE**) programs teach students how to design and develop the electronic components found in computers and peripheral devices.

5. **How Can People Stay Current with Changing Technology?** Four primary ways to stay current with computer technology are professional organizations and personal networks, professional growth and continuing education activities, computer publications and Web sites, and certification. Professional organizations are formed by computer professionals with common interests and a desire to extend their proficiency. The **Association for Computing Machinery** (**ACM**) is a scientific and educational organization dedicated to advancing knowledge and proficiency of information technology. The **Association of Information Technology Professionals** (**AITP**) is a professional association of programmers, systems analysts, and information processing managers. Maintaining a personal network of job-related contacts can help when seeking change in employment. Professional growth and continuing education include events such as workshops, seminars, conferences, conventions, and trade shows. The *International Consumer Electronics Show* (*CES*) is one of the larger technology trade shows, bringing together thousands of vendors and more than 110,000 attendees. Computer industry publications also help to keep people informed about

Chapter Review

the latest developments in the computer industry. Another source for information is Web sites that discuss or share opinions, analysis, reviews, or news about technology. **Certification** is a process of verifying the technical knowledge of an individual who has demonstrated competence in a particular area. Computing professionals typically obtain a certification by taking and passing an examination.

Visit the Computer Concepts CourseMate Web site at www.cengagebrain.com, navigate to the Chapter 15 Quiz Yourself resource for this book, and then click Objectives 3 – 5.

6. What Are the Benefits of Certification for Employers, Employees, and Vendors? For employers, certification ensures quality workmanship standards and can help keep their workforce up to date with respect to computers and technology. For employees, certification can enhance careers, provide better standing as industry professionals, and increase salaries. For vendors, certification is a form of industry self-regulation that sets computer professionals' competence standards and raises the level of expertise and knowledge in the IT industry as a whole.

7. How Can People Prepare for Certification? Certification training options are available to suit every learning style. Self-study programs help professionals prepare for certification at their own pace and supplement other training methods. Online training classes, which are available on the Internet and on many company intranets, allow students to set their own pace in an interactive environment. Instructor-led training classes are available in a variety of forms, including seminars, boot camps, and academic-style classes. Web resources include the certification sponsor's Web site and individual Web sites. The certification sponsor's Web site can contain descriptions of certifications with FAQs and links to authorized training and testing centers. Detailed course objectives, training guides, sample test questions, chat rooms, and discussion groups often are included. Individuals also set up Web sites to offer their own views and tips on the testing process.

8. What Are the General Areas of IT Certification? Certifications usually are classified based on the computer industry area to which they most closely relate: application software, operating systems, programmer/developer, hardware, networking, digital forensics, security, the Internet, and database systems.

9. What Are Some Specific IT Certifications in Each Certification Area? Application software certifications, sometimes called *end-user certifications*, include *Microsoft Office Specialist (MOS)*, *Microsoft Certified Desktop Support Technician (MCDST)*, *Adobe Certified Associate*, *Adobe Certified Expert (ACE)*, *Adobe Certified Instructor (ACI)*, and *IBM Certified Professional for Lotus Software*. Operating system certifications include *IBM Certified Specialist*, *Microsoft Certified IT Professional (MCITP)*, *Microsoft Certified Technology Specialist (MCTS)*, *Novell Certified Linux Professional (CLP)*, *Red Hat Certified Engineer (RHCE)*, *Red Hat Certified Technician (RHCT)*, and *Sun Certified System Administrator (SCSA)*. Programmer/developer certifications include *Certified Software Development Professional (CSDP)*, *IBM Certified Solution Developer*, *Microsoft Certified Professional Developer (MCPD)*, *Sun Certified Enterprise Architect (SCEA)*, *Sun Certified Java Developer (SCJD)*, *Sun Certified Java Programmer (SCJP)*, and *Sun Certified Mobile Application Developer (SCMAD)*. Hardware certifications include *A+*, *Dell Certified Systems Expert*, and *IBM eServer Certified Specialist*. Networking certifications include *Cisco Certified Network Associate (CCNA)*, *Cisco Certified Network Professional (CCNP)*, *Cisco Certified Internetwork Expert (CCIE)*, *Microsoft Certified Systems Administrator (MCSA)*, *Network+*, *Novell Certified Administrator (CNA)*, *Novell Certified Engineer (NCE)*, and *Sun Certified Network Administrator (SCNA)*. Digital forensics certifications include *Certified Computer Examiner (CCE)*, *Certified Computer Forensics Examiner (CCFE)*, *Certified Electronic Evidence Collection Specialist (CEECS)*, and *Certified Information Forensics Investigator (CIFI)*. Security certifications include *Certified Information Systems Security Professional (CISSP)*, *Security Certified Network Architect (SCNA)*, *Security Certified Network Professional (SCNP)*, *Security Certified Network Specialist (SCNS)*, and *Systems Security Certified Practitioner (SSCP)*. Internet certifications include *Certified Internet Webmaster (CIW)* and *Certified Web Professional (CWP)*. Database certifications include *IBM Certified Solutions Expert – DB2*, *IBM Certified Solutions Expert – Informix*, *Microsoft Certified IT Professional (MCITP)*, *Oracle Certified Professional (OCP)*, and *Sybase Certified Professional*.

Visit the Computer Concepts CourseMate Web site at www.cengagebrain.com, navigate to the Chapter 15 Quiz Yourself resource for this book, and then click Objectives 6 – 9.

Key Terms

You should know the Primary Terms and be familiar with the Secondary Terms. The list below helps focus your study.

To see an example of and a definition for each term, and to access current and additional information from the Web, visit the Computer Concepts CourseMate Web site at www.cengagebrain.com and then navigate to the Chapter 15 Key Terms resource for this book.

Primary Terms

(shown in bold-black characters in the chapter)

Association for Computing Machinery (ACM) (797)
Association of Information Technology Professionals (AITP) (797)
certification (800)
chief information officer (CIO) (788)
chief security officer (CSO) (789)
chief technology officer (CTO) (788)
compositor (789)
computer engineering (CE) (795)
computer equipment field (790)
computer games designer/programmer (788)
computer information systems (CIS) (795)
computer operator (789)
computer salespeople (792)
computer science (CS) (795)
computer science/IT instructor (789)
computer scientist (788)
computer security specialist (789)
computer service and repair field (791)
computer software field (790)
computer technician (789)
corporate trainer (789)
data communications analyst (789)
database administrator (789)
database analyst (788)
desktop or mobile application programmer/developer (788)
desktop publisher (789)
digital forensics examiner (789)
e-commerce director (788)
graphic designer (789)
help desk specialist (789)
illustrator (789)
IT consultant (793)
IT department (786)
mobile security specialist (789)
network administrator (788)
network security administrator (789)
project leader/manager (788)
quality assurance specialist (789)
security administrator (789)
software engineer (788)
storage administrator/analyst (789)
systems analyst (788)
systems programmer (788)
technical lead (788)
technical writer (788)
trade school (794)
video resume (796)
VoIP specialist (789)
Web administrator (789)
Web designer (789)
Web software developer (788)
Webmaster (789)
wireless network administrator (788)

International Consumer Electronics Show (CES) (798)

Secondary Terms

(shown in italic characters in the chapter)

A+ (805)
Adobe Certified Associate (804)
Adobe Certified Expert (ACE) (804)
Adobe Certified Instructor (ACI) (804)
articulation agreement (794)
Certified Computer Examiner (CCE) (806)
Certified Computer Forensics Examiner (CCFE) (806)
Certified Electronic Evidence Collection Specialist (CEECS) (806)
Certified Information Forensics Investigator (CIFI) (806)
Certified Information Systems Security Professional (CISSP) (807)
Certified Internet Webmaster (CIW) (807)
Certified Software Development Associate (CSDA) (805)
Certified Software Development Professional (CSDP) (805)
Certified Web Professional (CWP) (807)
Cisco Certified Internetwork Expert (CCIE) (806)
Cisco Certified Network Associate (CCNA) (806)
Cisco Certified Network Professional (CCNP) (806)
computerized adaptive testing (CAT) (803)
Dell Certified Systems Expert (805)
end-user certifications (804)
IBM Certified Professional for Lotus Software (804)
IBM Certified Solution Developer (805)
IBM Certified Solutions Expert – DB2 (808)
IBM Certified Solutions Expert – Informix (808)
IBM Certified Specialist (804)
IBM eServer Certified Specialist (805)
Institute for the Certification of Computing Professionals (ICCP) (801)
International Consumer Electronics Show (CES) (798)
management information systems (MIS) (795)
management information technology (795)
Microsoft Certified Desktop Support Technician (MCDST) (804)
Microsoft Certified IT Professional (MCITP) (804, 808)
Microsoft Certified Professional Developer (MCPD) (805)
Microsoft Certified Systems Administrator (MCSA) (806)
Microsoft Certified Technology Specialist (MCTS) (804)
Microsoft Office Specialist (MOS) - Core (804)
Microsoft Office Specialist (MOS) - Expert (804)
Network+ (806)
Novell Certified Administrator (NCA) (806)
Novell Certified Engineer (NCE) (806)
Novell Certified Linux Professional (CLP) (804)
Oracle Certified Professional (OCP) (808)
Red Hat Certified Engineer (RHCE) (804)
Red Hat Certified Technician (RHCT) (804)
Security Certified Network Architect (SCNA) (807)
Security Certified Network Professional (SCNP) (807)
Security Certified Network Specialist (SCNS) (807)
special interest groups (SIGs) (797)
sponsoring organizations (800)
Sun Certified Enterprise Architect (SCEA) (805)
Sun Certified Java Developer (SCJD) (805)
Sun Certified Java Programmer (SCJP) (805)
Sun Certified Mobile Application Developer (SCMAD) (805)
Sun Certified Network Administrator (SCNA) (806)
Sun Certified System Administrator (SCSA) (804)
Sybase Certified Professional (808)
Systems Security Certified Practitioner (SSCP) (807)
user group (798)

Checkpoint

The Checkpoint exercises test your knowledge of the chapter concepts. The page number containing the answer appears in parentheses after each exercise. The Beyond the Book exercises will help broaden your understanding of the concepts presented in this chapter.

To complete the Checkpoint exercises interactively, visit the Computer Concepts CourseMate Web site at www.cengagebrain.com and then navigate to the Chapter 15 Checkpoint resource for this book.

True/False

Mark T for True and F for False.

_____ 1. A desktop or mobile application programmer/developer converts the system design into the appropriate computer language, such as Visual Basic, Java, C#, F#, and C++. (788)

_____ 2. A systems analyst specifies, designs, implements, tests, and documents high-quality software in a variety of fields, including robotics, operating systems, animation, and applications. (788)

_____ 3. A storage administrator/analyst installs, maintains, and upgrades storage systems and analyzes an organization's storage needs. (789)

_____ 4. An IT consultant typically is hired based on computer expertise and provides computer services to his or her clients. (793)

_____ 5. The main difference between a CIS curriculum and an MIS curriculum is that the ratio of business courses to computer courses is greater in a CIS curriculum. (795)

_____ 6. In general, a CS curriculum focuses on theory of programming and operating systems and typically emphasizes application programming instead of system programming. (795)

_____ 7. At some company's Web sites, job seekers can post a video resume, which enables them to showcase their skills and abilities. (796)

_____ 8. Most certification programs do not require academic coursework. (802)

_____ 9. Application software certification sometimes is called end-user certification. (804)

_____ 10. The Microsoft Certified Technology Specialist (MCTS) certification tests technical expertise in one of several areas including managing and troubleshooting networks using Windows operating systems. (804)

Multiple Choice

Select the best answer.

1. The _____ directs the company's information service and communications functions. (788)
   a. chief technology officer (CTO)
   b. project leader
   c. chief executive officer (CEO)
   d. e-commerce director

2. A _____ installs and monitors communications equipment and software and maintains Internet/WAN connections. (789)
   a. Webmaster/Web administrator
   b. help desk specialist
   c. data communications analyst/VoIP specialist
   d. network security administrator

3. A(n) _____ ensures that if a student transfers to a college or university, he or she will receive credit for most of the courses taken at the trade school level. (794)
   a. technical service
   b. user group
   c. articulation agreement
   d. tethered system

4. _____ is a business and management oriented computer discipline. (795)
   a. Computer information systems (CIS)
   b. Computer science (CS)
   c. Computer engineering (CE)
   d. All of the above

5. Both the ACM and the AITP offer _____. (797)
   a. chapters throughout the United States
   b. workshops, seminars, and conventions
   c. special interest groups (SIGs)
   d. all of the above

6. Sponsors of IT certifications include all of the following except _____. (800)
   a. independent training companies
   b. user groups and trade schools
   c. professional organizations
   d. computer equipment and software vendors

7. The _____ certification, sponsored by the IEEE Computer Society, tests basic knowledge of software development process and tools. (805)
   a. Microsoft Certified Professional Developer (MCPD)
   b. IBM Certified Solution Developer
   c. A+
   d. Certified Software Development Associate (CSDA)

8. The _____ certification tests basic knowledge of installing, configuring, and operating LAN, WAN, and dial-up access services for small networks. (806)
   a. NCA
   b. CCNA
   c. NCE
   d. Network+

STUDENT ASSIGNMENTS

Checkpoint

Matching

Match the terms with their definitions.

_____ 1. e-commerce director (788)
_____ 2. database analyst (788)
_____ 3. technical writer (788)
_____ 4. technical lead (788)
_____ 5. database administrator (789)
_____ 6. desktop publisher/compositor (789)
_____ 7. quality assurance specialist (789)
_____ 8. Webmaster/Web administrator (789)
_____ 9. corporate trainer (789)
_____ 10. chief security officer (CSO) (789)

a. teaches employees how to use software, design and develop systems, program, and perform other computer-related activities
b. formats and combines text and graphics to produce publication-ready materials
c. responsible for physical security of an organization's property and people
d. uses data modeling techniques and tools to analyze, tune, and specify data usage within an application area
e. supervises the development and execution of Internet or e-commerce systems
f. reviews programs and documentation to ensure they meet the organization's standards
g. guides design, development, and maintenance tasks
h. creates and maintains a data dictionary and monitors database performance
i. maintains an organization's Web site; creates or helps users create Web pages; oversees Web site performance
j. works with the analyst, programmer, and user to create system documentation and user materials

Short Answer

Write a brief answer to each of the following questions.

1. What is an advantage of attending a trade school? ____________ What factors should you consider when selecting a trade school? ____________
2. What are the benefits of professional growth and continuing education? ____________ What are some ways you can keep up to date about industry trends and technologies? ____________
3. How should you go about choosing a certification? ____________ Describe four options for preparing for certification. ____________
4. What is the focus of programmer/developer certification, and what other types of certification are beneficial to those interested in programmer/developer certification? ____________ Who might be interested in programmer/developer certification?
5. Describe hardware certification. ____________ Who might be interested in hardware certification? ____________

Beyond the Book

Follow the book element instructions below; present your findings (brief report, presentation, discussion, or other means).

1. Ethics & Issues — Select an Ethics & Issues in this chapter (785, 791, 792, 793, 798), find a recent newspaper/magazine article that supports one point of view presented, and then evaluate the article.
2. Computer Usage @ Work — Use the Web or a recent newspaper/magazine to locate three additional unique usages of computer technology in publishing (809). What makes the use of these technologies unique to the publishing industry?
3. Companies on the Cutting Edge and Technology Trailblazers — Use the Web or a recent newspaper/magazine to locate an interesting fact about Dice, Dell, Steve Ballmer, or Jerry Yang and David Filo that was not presented in the chapter (811).
4. High-Tech Talk — Locate a recent newspaper/magazine article that discusses topics related to Bioinformatics (810). Would you recommend the article you found? Why or why not?
5. FAQs and Web Links — Use the Web or a recent newspaper/magazine to locate three additional facts about an FAQ (787, 790, 792, 797, 802, 807) and Web Link (787, 794, 795, 797, 800, 801, 804, 806) that were not presented in the chapter.
6. Looking Ahead — Use the Web or a recent newspaper/magazine to discover additional uses of the technology presented in Bridging the IT Generation Gap (786).
7. Innovative Computing — Use the Web or a recent newspaper/magazine to locate two additional interesting facts about College Course Content Available Online (794).
8. Making Use of the Web — Visit three of the Careers sites (138) and outline the information on each Web site and the possible uses for each Web site.
9. Living Digitally — Select a topic discussed in the Living Digitally feature (824) and then present a current issue related to the topic using the Web or a magazine article.

Learn It Online

The Learn It Online exercises are interactive Web exercises designed to reinforce and expand your understanding of the chapter concepts. The descriptions below briefly summarize each exercise.

To complete the Learn It Online exercises, visit the Computer Concepts CourseMate Web site at www.cengagebrain.com, navigate to the Chapter 15 resources for this book, click the link for the exercise you want to complete, and then read the instructions.

1 At the Movies — Girls Tour the Googleplex
Watch a movie to join 70 middle-school girls as they tour the Google campus during National Engineers' week and then answer questions about the movie.

2 Video and Audio: You Review It — Computer Careers
Search for, choose, and write a review of a video, podcast, or vodcast that discusses computer careers.

3 Student Edition Labs — Careers in Technology: Getting Ahead
Enhance your understanding and knowledge about careers in technology by completing the Careers in Technology: Getting Ahead Lab.

4 Practice Test
Take a multiple choice test that checks your knowledge of the chapter concepts and review the resulting study guide.

5 Who Wants To Be a Computer Genius^{2}?
Play the Shelly Cashman Series version of this popular game by answering questions to find out if you are a computer genius. Panic buttons are available to provide assistance during game play.

6 Wheel of Terms
Identify important key terms presented in this chapter by playing the Shelly Cashman Series version of this popular game.

7 You're Hired!
Embark on the path to a career in computers by answering questions and solving puzzles related to concepts discussed in this chapter.

8 Crossword Puzzle Challenge
Complete an interactive crossword puzzle to reinforce concepts presented in this chapter.

9 Windows Exercises
Step through the Windows 7 exercises to learn about using the Character Map utility, toggle keys, and scheduling disk maintenance.

10 Exploring Computer Careers
Read about a career as a computer science/IT instructor, search for related employment advertisements, and then answer related questions.

11 Web Apps — TaxACT Online
Learn how to use TaxACT Online to sign up for a free account, download and install TaxACT on your computer, and file your federal and state taxes.

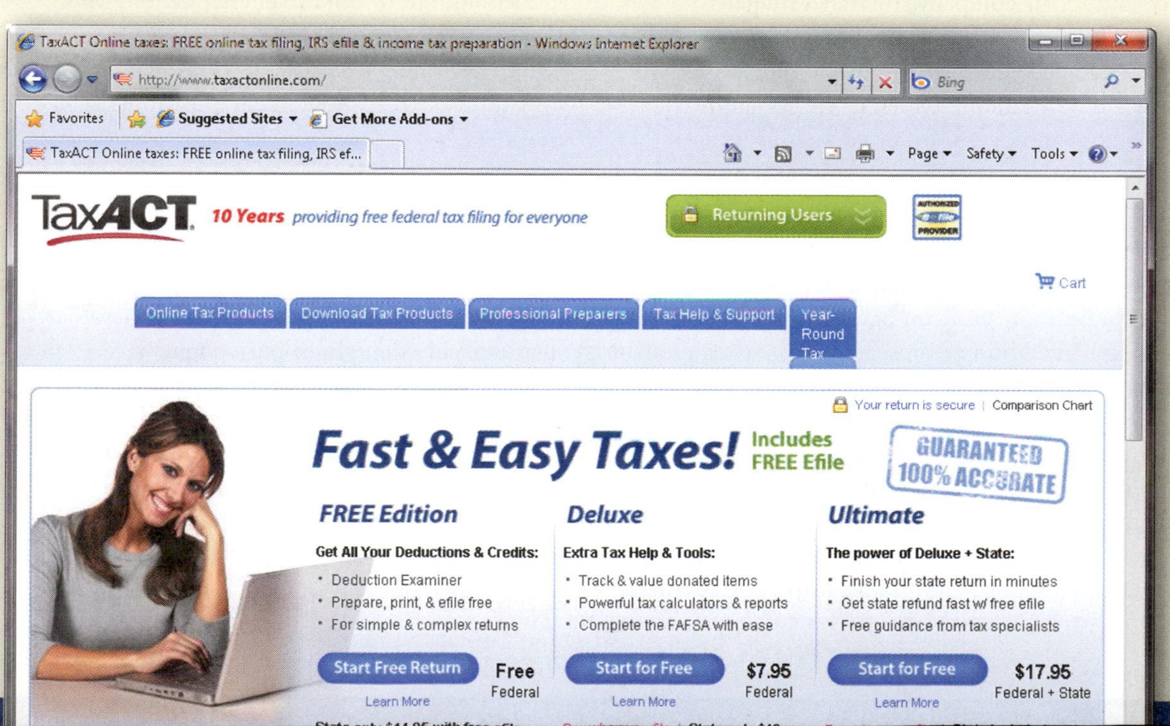

STUDENT ASSIGNMENTS

Problem Solving @ Home

The Problem Solving @ Home exercises extend your knowledge of the chapter concepts by seeking solutions to practical computer problems that you may encounter at home or school. The Collaboration exercise should be completed with a team.

In the real world, practical problems often can be solved in multiple ways. Provide one solution to each of the following problems using available resources, such as articles on the Web or in print, blogs, podcasts, videos, television, user guides, other individuals, and electronics and computer stores. You may need to use multiple resources to obtain an answer. Present your solutions in the form requested by your instructor (brief report, presentation, discussion, or other means).

1. **Differences between Job Descriptions** Your friend, who has taken some computer courses, is undecided about becoming a graphic designer/illustrator or a desktop publisher/compositor. She asks you to list two differences between the two occupations. How will you respond?
2. **Keywords for Job Search** After taking your third computer class, you realize that you would like to train people how to use computers and software. You look for a job on Monster.com and are asked to enter some keywords for your job search. What keywords will you enter to find a job that allows you to train others how to use computers and software?
3. **Online Job Search** Having decided to work in the computer equipment field, you begin your job search online. In addition to looking on job-search Web sites for available positions, where else might you find job postings?
4. **Documenting Education and Experience** You are preparing your resume to submit to a computer service and repair company. You have studied computer service and repair in various classes and want to convince your prospective employer that you are the best candidate for the job. What might convince the employer to offer you a job?
5. **Contemplating a Job Offer** After graduating from college with a degree in computer science, you send your resume to several companies. Almost immediately, you receive a job offer as a technical support representative in a midsized organization. Will you accept this job offer or wait for additional offers? Why?
6. **Selecting an Appropriate Major** You are returning to school to earn another bachelor's degree. After completing your studies, you wish to pursue a career as a network administrator. How will you respond to the question on the college's application that asks for your intended major? Why?
7. **Obtaining Additional Job Information** You are viewing a job description on Monster.com and would like more information about the position before you apply. What are two ways to find additional information about jobs posted on this Web site?
8. **Appropriate Certification** Because you hope to pursue a career as a system administrator, you would like to obtain a certification. Many certifications are available, but you want to choose the one(s) that will best prepare you for your future career. Which certification(s) will you consider?

Collaboration

9. **Learning and Demonstrating New Technology** You are preparing for a job interview for a computer technician position, and you have learned that the interviewer will ask a series of questions about new technology. In addition to researching new technologies, you also decide that you should obtain a certification that verifies your understanding of these new technologies. Finally, you should be prepared to tell your interviewer how you plan to stay current with the latest technologies. Form a team of three classmates. One team member will locate Web sites that provide information about the latest technologies. Another team member will research various certification exams and find one that will demonstrate an understanding of computer hardware, and the other team member will research ways to stay current with new technology, as it is introduced. The three team members should discuss their research, compile their findings into a report, and submit it to your instructor.

Problem Solving @ Work

The Problem Solving @ Work exercises extend your knowledge of the chapter concepts by seeking solutions to practical computer problems that you may encounter at work. The Collaboration exercise should be completed with a team.

In the real world, practical problems often can be solved in multiple ways. Provide one solution to each of the following problems using available resources, such as articles on the Web or in print, blogs, podcasts, videos, television, user guides, other individuals, and electronics and computer stores. You may need to use multiple resources to obtain an answer. Present your solutions in the form requested by your instructor (brief report, presentation, discussion, or other means).

1. **Staying Current with Technology** Having accepted a job as a computer salesperson, you now realize the importance of staying up to date with the latest technologies and products. What are three ways that you can stay current in the technology field while working full-time?
2. **Applying for Promotion** You are applying for a promotion within your organization and learn that your colleague also is applying for the same position. Although you are more qualified for the position, you learn that your colleague has falsified some information on her resume so that she appears more suitable for the promotion. What will you do?
3. **Outsourcing IT Positions** As the chief information officer for a large organization, you consider outsourcing various positions within your department to save money. What are some types of positions that easily can be outsourced? What positions might be more difficult to outsource? Why?
4. **Web Server Migration** The current Web server in your organization uses the UNIX operating system. You recently learned that your organization plans to migrate its Web site to a server that uses the Windows operating system. You are not familiar with Windows, and as the Webmaster/Web administrator, you are concerned that the migration will make your job considerably more difficult. Will you consider leaving the company? If not, what might you do to keep your job manageable?
5. **Conducting an Interview** You are preparing to conduct several interviews for candidates applying for a job as a senior systems administrator. What types of questions will you ask during the interview to determine whether they have the experience required to fulfill the job responsibilities?
6. **Budget-Cutting Measures** A rumor has been circulating in your organization that several IT positions might be eliminated in an effort to cut costs. You are not sure whether your position will be affected but want to be prepared in case your position is eliminated. How will you prepare for your possible job loss?
7. **Tough Decision** Two top candidates who applied for a job within your organization have interviewed well, and you are having difficulty selecting which candidate should be offered the job. One candidate has several certifications and only two years of job-related experience, while the other candidate has six years of experience, but no certifications. What decision will you make, and why?
8. **Training Decision** Your boss has allocated money to allow everyone in the IT department to attend training related to their job responsibilities. While researching the training available for your job as a systems administrator, you learn that you either can take a semester-long course at a local university or attend an accelerated one-week, forty-hour training course. At the end of each training session, you will be ready to become certified. Which type of training will you choose? Why?

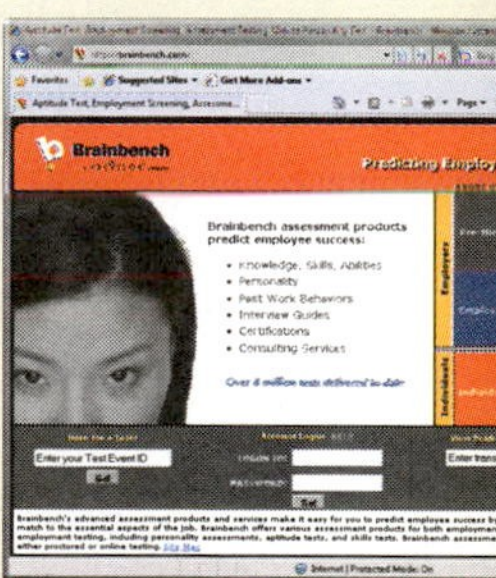

Collaboration

9. **Computers in Publishing** You have been hired to select employees for the IT department in a startup publishing company. Before you can begin hiring employees, you must familiarize yourself with the technology requirements in the publishing industry. Form a team of three people to compose a plan for creating the IT department. One team member should research the hardware requirements for people working in the publishing industry. Another team member should research the types of software used in this industry, and the third team member should compile a list of interview questions to ask each candidate.

Learn How To

The Learn How To activities step you through fundamental technology skills when using a computer. The Learn How To exercises enable you to become more proficient with these skills.

Learn How To 1: Create a Video Resume

Resumes are used to inform potential employers about your experience, education, qualifications, and other important information. When using job search services on the Web such as Monster (see Figure 15-10 on page 796), you often will submit your resume electronically.

A video resume contains a video of you speaking to your potential employer, explaining your interest in the job and why you think you are the best qualified candidate.

To create a video resume complete the following steps:

Obtain a Video Camera The first step is to obtain a video camera with which you can record your presentation. You can purchase a Web cam or a more sophisticated camera.

Record the Video When you record the video resume, you must be aware of several important elements:

1. Prepare your script: Before you start recording, write and memorize the words you will say in the video. The video should be no longer than one minute, so write your script accordingly. Remember — you are trying to impress your potential employer.
2. Set the stage: The lighting and picture in the video are critical to making a professional-appearing video. You should use adequate light so that the video is clear. Generally, you should arrange the camera for a head-and-shoulders shot.
3. Practice: You must practice your presentation in front of the camera. You can record and play back your practice recordings until you feel confident about your presentation.
4. Dress for the part: When on camera, the impression you make will be influenced by your attire and your personal grooming. You should dress as if you were doing a live interview.
5. Record the video: Your video should be no longer than one minute, but you might want to divide it into segments. For example, you could separate your statement about why you want to work for a company from your statement about your educational background. So, when you create the actual video, you may record several clips of shorter duration, and then join them together when you edit the video. To capture the video, you can use the software provided with your camera, or you can use Windows Live Movie Maker.

To use Windows Live Movie Maker, record the video on a video camera, attach the video camera to the computer, and then complete the following steps:

1. Click the Start button on the Windows taskbar, click All Programs on the Start menu, click Windows Live in the All Programs list, and then click Windows Live Movie Maker.
2. Click the Movie Maker button and then click 'Import from device' on the Movie Maker menu to begin the import process. If the Windows Live Movie Maker dialog box appears, click the OK button.
3. When the Import Photos and Videos window opens, select your video camera and then click the Import button.
4. Windows Live Movie Maker will determine how many photos and videos are on your video camera (Figure 15-31). Click the 'Import all new items now' option button.
5. Enter the name you wish to assign your video and then click the Next button.
6. Windows Live Movie Maker will import the video from your video camera (Figure 15-32). Depending on the length of your video, this process can take several minutes to complete.

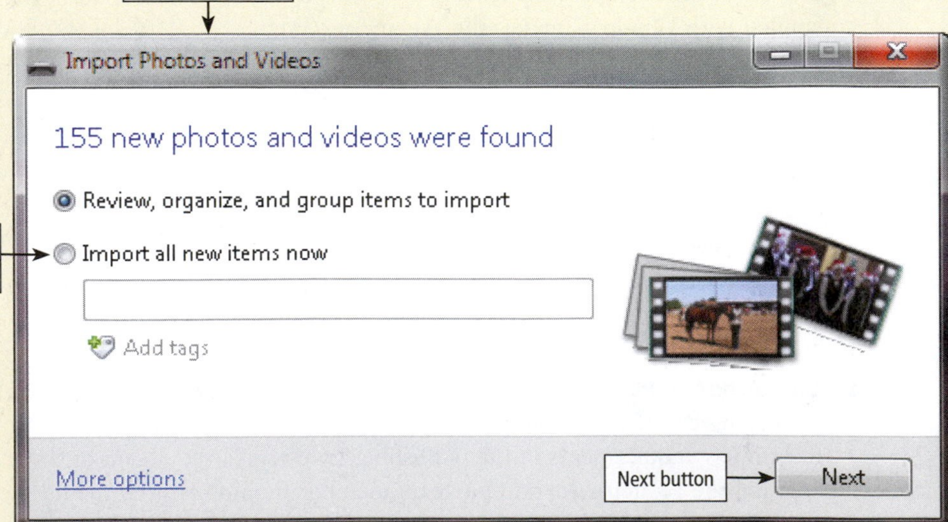

Figure 15-31

Learn How To

7. When the import process is complete, Windows Live Photo Gallery will open and display the contents from the video camera. Verify the video has imported successfully and then close Windows Live Photo Gallery.

Edit the Video After recording the video, you normally should edit it and save it in a format that can be placed in your resume. To use Windows Live Movie Maker for this process, complete the following steps:

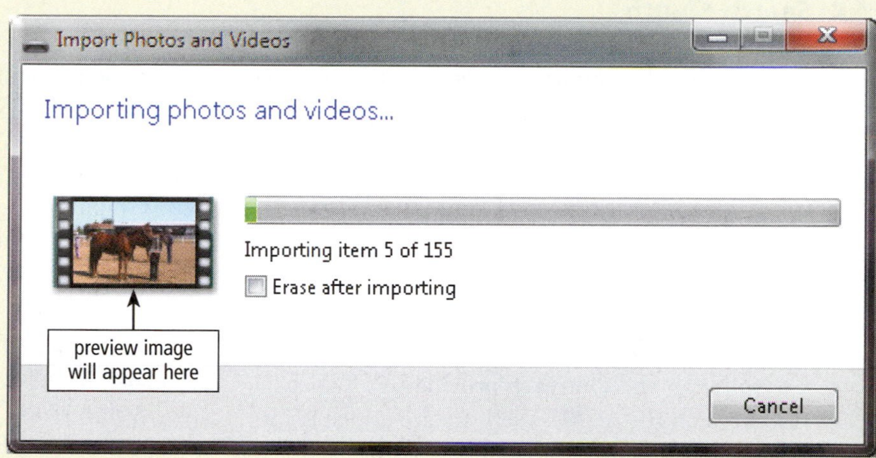

Figure 15-32

1. To create your movie, you first must import the video clips that will comprise the movie. Click the 'Add videos and photos' button on the Home tab in Windows Live Movie Maker to display the Add Videos and Photos dialog box.
2. Navigate to the location containing your imported video, select the video clip you wish to import, and then click the Open button.
3. If you have additional video clips to import, repeat the previous two steps until you have imported all video clips.
4. To learn how to edit the video resume further, click the Online help button to start Internet Explorer and display additional information about using Windows Live Movie Maker.
5. After you have completed the video, save the project by clicking the Save project command on the Movie Maker menu.
6. To save the video for inclusion in your resume, click the More button in the Sharing group on the Home tab to display a list of formats. Click the Standard-definition icon to select it and display the Save Movie dialog box. Save the movie with a name and to a location of your choice, and then click the Save button.

Import the Video into Your Resume Import the video into your resume by completing the following steps:

1. Start Microsoft Word, open the resume document, and then place the insertion point at the location where you want your video to appear.
2. Click Insert on the Ribbon and then click the Object button on the Insert tab.
3. When the Object dialog box is displayed, click the Create from File tab and then click the Browse button.
4. In the window that opens, identify where the video is stored, select the file, and then click the Open button. Click the OK button in the Object dialog box to close the dialog box and insert an icon for the video in the Word document.
5. To play the video, double-click the video icon.

Exercises

1. Write the script you would use for your video resume. Submit the script to your instructor.
2. Using Windows Live Movie Maker, create a video using the Windows Live Movie Maker sample file (C:\Users\Public\Public Videos\Sample Videos). Add transitions to make the video more interesting. Submit the video to your instructor.
3. If you have access to a video camera, use Windows Live Movie Maker to create a video resume. Place a title on the video and edit it with transitions, if appropriate. If necessary, trim the clip, ensure the clip is to your liking, and then submit the video to your instructor.

STUDENT ASSIGNMENTS

Web Research

The Web Research exercises broaden your understanding of the chapter concepts by presenting questions that require you to search the Web for answers.

1 Search Sleuth

Use one of the search engines listed in Figure 2-10 in Chapter 2 on page 85 or your own favorite search engine to find the answers to the following questions. Copy and paste the Web address from the Web page where you found the answer. Some questions may have more than one answer. If required, submit your answers to your instructor. (1) Why would a computer security specialist use software for the Metasploit Project? (2) Which services does the Buros Institute for Assessment Consultation and Outreach provide? (3) Which resources on the ACM's Web site are available for graduating students? (4) Which colleges are student chapter cohosts for the next AITP National Collegiate Conference? (5) Which Adobe product exams are available for the Adobe Certified Expert certification? (6) Which certification began in 2003 due to the efforts of John Mellon?

2 Green Computing

Each year, graphic designers, entrepreneurs, and engineers gather at the Greener Gadgets conference. Experts partner with professionals who administer Core77, a Web site with resources for graphic designers, to hold a Greener Gadgets Design Competition. Visit the Core77 Web site (core77.com) and then view the past year's winning entries. How were computers used to generate the products' designs? What technical requirements must be met, and how must the three images tell the story of the design? Then, visit the Greener Gadgets Web site (greenergadgets.com) and read the News, Blog, and Press sections. Which gadgets present green technological alternatives to the toxic chemicals, heavy metals, and low recycling rates of today's products?

3 Social Networking

Approximately 7 percent of cell phone users viewed a social network in 2009. That number is expected to triple by 2012. These 300 million users are likely to view Facebook, MySpace, Google, and Yahoo! on cell phones. Visit mobile social networking Web sites, including Peekamo (peekamo.com) and aphoot (aphoot.com). Click the links on these Web pages that provide additional information. What are the direct and indirect costs of accessing these networks? How does a user create a profile? What content is provided specifically for smart phones and other personal mobile devices? Summarize the information you read and viewed.

4 Blogs

Graphic designers develop practically every advertisement you see. These designers use computers extensively to develop their illustrations, designs, and graphics. Many graphic design blogs discuss the projects and showcase the final products. Graphic Design Basics (graphicdesignbasics.com), Web Designer Wall (webdesignerwall.com), FormFiftyFive (formfiftyfive.com), Graphic Competitions (graphiccompetitions.com), and Designers who Blog (designers-who-blog.com) are among the more popular graphic design blogs. Visit these and other design blogs and view the information presented. What advice is given for fonts and typography? Which tutorials are posted? Which Web trends are discussed? Which designs have won prizes? Summarize the information you read and viewed.

5 Ethics in Action

People studying for certification exams sometimes turn to braindump Web sites to obtain test questions that test takers recall and then post to the Web site after taking an exam. Major certification companies require test takers to sign a nondisclosure agreement. Some potential test takers, however, believe that buying these test questions makes studying efficient and effective. View online sites that contain braindumps, such as BrainDumps.com, Braindump Central (braindumpcentral.com), and TroyTec (troytec.com), and then describe the questions that are available. What is the cost of obtaining this information? What are Master Dumps? Then, view the Microsoft and Cisco Systems Web sites to read their nondisclosure agreements. What information is permitted for posting? What punishment do companies and test takers face when caught revealing exam information?

Critical Thinking

The Critical Thinking exercises challenge your assessment and decision-making skills by presenting real-world situations associated with the chapter concepts. The Collaboration exercise should be completed with a team.

To evaluate the situations below, use personal experiences and available resources such as articles on the Web or in print, blogs, podcasts, videos, television, user guides, other individuals, and electronics and computer stores. You may need to use multiple resources to form conclusions and make recommendations.

1. **Class Discussion — Illegal Activities** Your supervisor has asked your team to install software on various computers within the organization. After reviewing the terms of the license agreement, you discover that you are allowed to install the software on only one computer. You inform your supervisor that you must purchase additional licenses to install the software on multiple computers, and he applauds your effort to prevent the organization from facing a potential legal battle with the software publisher. He also asks that you educate other employees about software theft and other computer-related activities that might have legal implications. Discuss answers to the following questions: Why is it important for organizations to prevent software theft by their employees? What steps are software publishers taking to prevent software theft? What other computer-related activities in the workplace might create a legal problem for the organization?

2. **Class Presentation — Computer Animation and Programming** Some programmers consider themselves artists and they may be right — although perhaps not in the sense they had in mind. With the growing popularity of computer-animated movies, computer games, and virtual media, the call for graphic artists who also are computer programmers is expected to become a shout. The U.S. Department of Labor predicts that the demand for commercial artists with computer skills will climb nearly 40 percent by 2014. To learn about this challenging career, use the Web and/or print media to research companies that create art and movies with computers. In particular, research the animation technology internships and career opportunities with DreamWorks Animation, the company that produced *Bee Movie*, *Shrek the Third*, *Madagascar*, *Monsters vs. Aliens*, and *Kung Fu Panda*. Prepare a presentation summarizing what you think it takes to succeed in these jobs that combine artistic talent with digital skills. Include information such as locations for these jobs, salary ranges, and travel requirements.

3. **Research — Organization's Proposed Site** You are an intern working part time for the local Chamber of Commerce. Your office has just learned that a major computer chip manufacturer is considering your town for the location of their new plant. While jobs in the computer industry easily can be found throughout the United States and globally, what can you do to convince this high-tech corporation that your town is the best location? Using the Web and/or print media, research why other high-tech organizations chose their current locations. Prepare a report that explains what factors influence high-tech organizations in their choice of locations. Be certain to address tax incentives, corporate climate, employee availability, cost of living, quality of life, and other factors.

Collaboration

4. **Comparing Computer Disciplines** The computer class you are enrolled in has piqued your classmates' interest to a point where several students seriously are considering a major in one of three computer disciplines — Computer Information Systems, Computer Science, or Computer Engineering. Form a three-member team. Each team member should choose a different discipline. Using the Web, school catalogs, other media, or interviews with school counselors or advisors, each team member should determine the advantages and disadvantages of the discipline that he or she chose. Which option is more application oriented? Theory oriented? Are advanced degrees in the assigned discipline awarded at your school? As a team, merge your findings into a team report. Make sure to include in the merged report the planning and prerequisites necessary, along with which discipline offers the greatest potential for career growth and advancement.

Living Digitally

OUR DIGITAL LIVES are filled with a variety of products. We listen on portable media players to audio files we create or download. We record and view video content that matches our viewing interests. We play recorded files wherever and whenever we desire. We play games solo or with multiple friends across the globe. Our home networks link security, energy monitoring, and leisure activities throughout the house. Wherever we go in our lives, technology is a pervasive part of our daily existence.

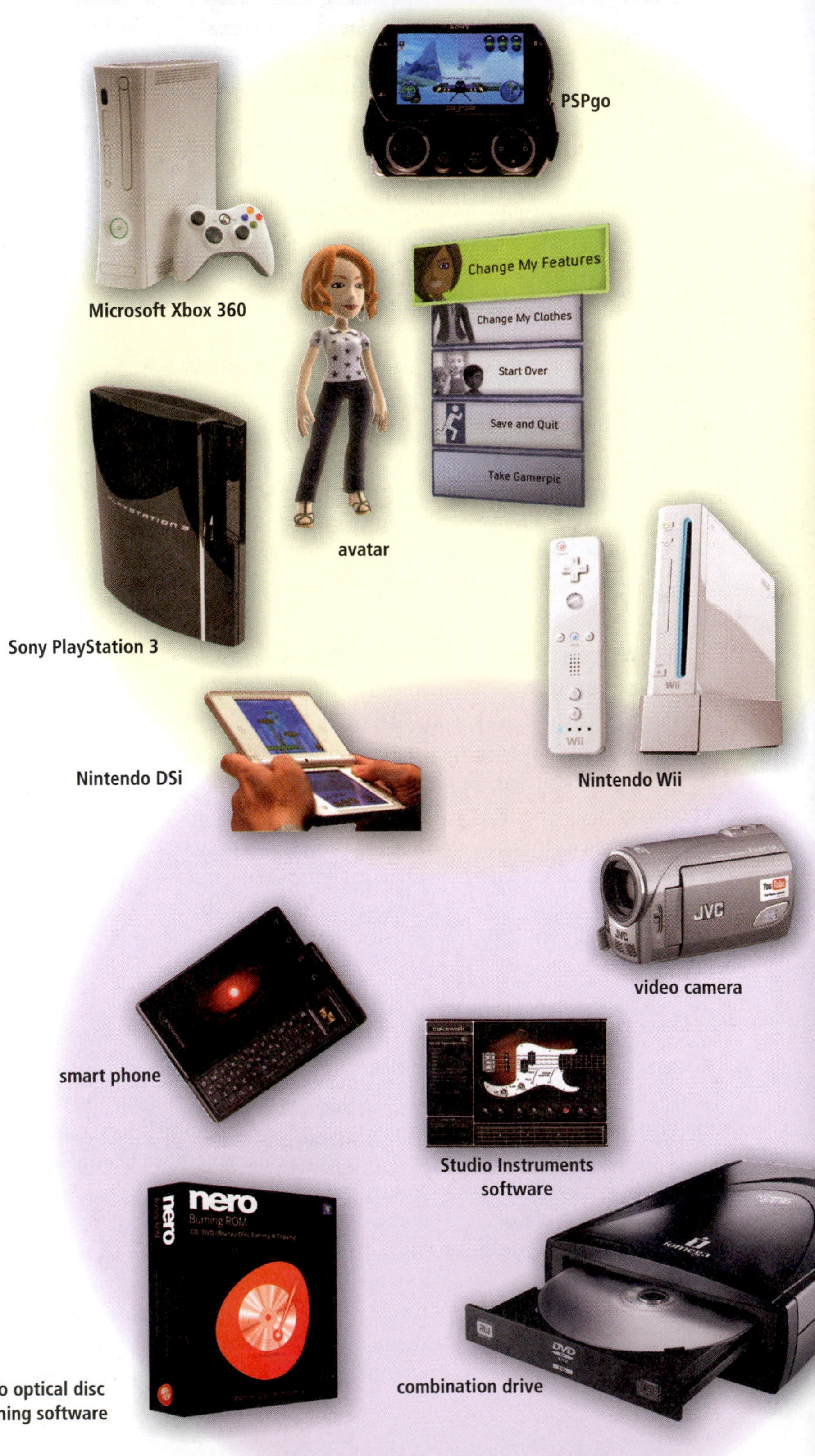

Digital products in our lives often include features that overlap in various entertainment and home automation categories.

- Audio
- Video
- Recording
- Gaming
- Digital Home

3-D video display

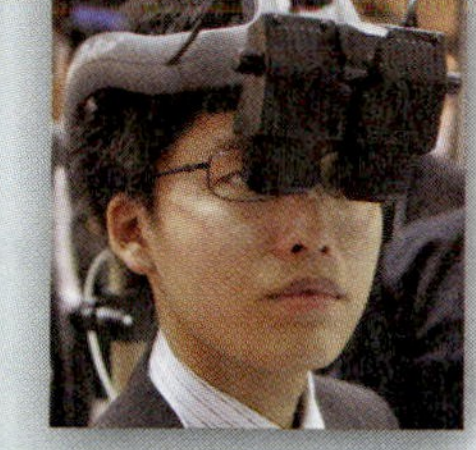
head-mounted display

flat-screen TV

Slingbox

TiVo

Rock Band

iPod/iPod touch

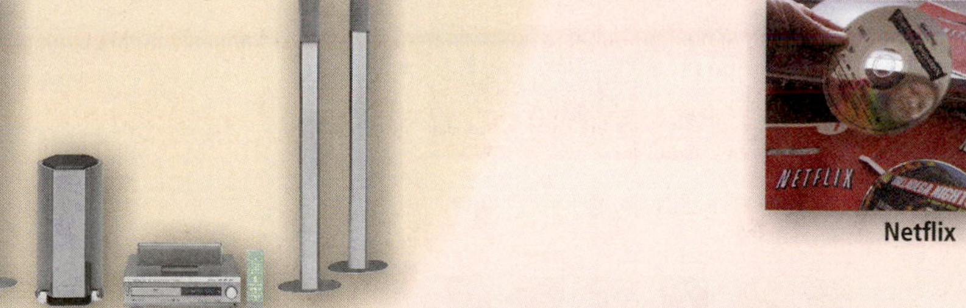

Dolby logo

speakers

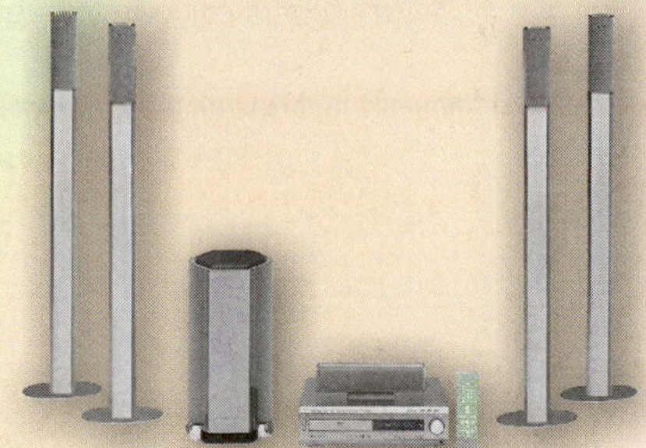
multi-room audio system

Netflix

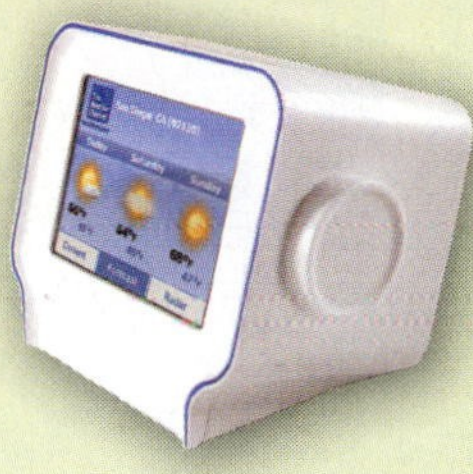
chumby

home automation dashboard

docking station

digital frames

Audio

THE MUSIC INDUSTRY is a major part of our everyday lives, and digital music sales generate more than $10 billion each year. Audio files can be played on iPods and other portable media players and mobile devices. Musicians of all skill levels can create their own music with Rock Band and Guitar Hero handheld instruments.

Figure 1 Apple has sold hundreds of millions of iPods. The iPod accessory market has grown to a billion-dollar industry, with inventors developing earbuds, cases, and docking stations.

Figure 3 Rock the night away playing set lists from some of the biggest artists and bands of all times. Customize the concert experience by selecting venues and original band members or your own personalized superstars.

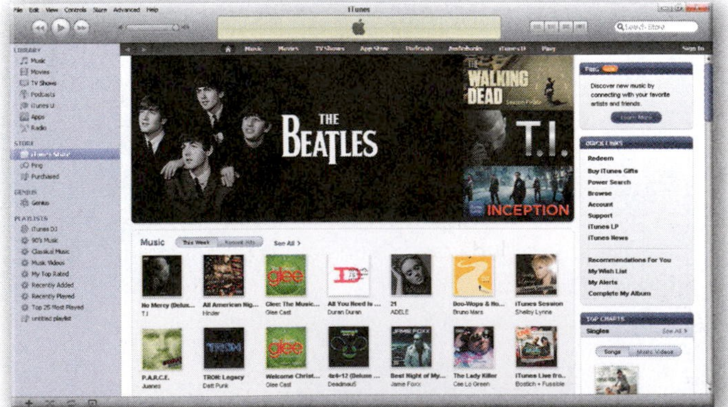

Figure 2 Music downloading services allow you to purchase individual tracks or entire albums and then download the music to a computer or portable media player. More than 500 downloading services are available; Apple iTunes and Amazon MP3 are the sales leaders.

Figure 4 Ray Dolby founded Dolby Laboratories in 1965. His company has become the world leader in defining high-quality products, including audio and surround sound in theaters, home entertainment systems, and broadcasting.

Video

WHEATHER IN A COMFY CHAIR or on the go, watching television and movies has changed dramatically. Viewers download content and then watch the programs when and where they desire on devices ranging from large flat-screen display devices to compact smart phones. Glasses and 3-D displays add a new dimension to the viewing experience.

Figure 5 A multitude of video streaming devices is infiltrating the marketplace as companies expand their services to add subscribers and bring movies and television programs to homes via a broadband Internet connection. Apple TV takes control of your home theater system by streaming HD movies, television programs, iTunes music, podcasts, and photos to display devices.

Figure 6 Experience a private video viewing with a personal head-mounted display (HMD). Video glasses can be connected to a DVD player, iPod, or game console.

Figure 7 View your favorite television programs anywhere in the world as long as you have a broadband connection and a Slingbox. This device streams video and audio from your home to any Internet-connected device.

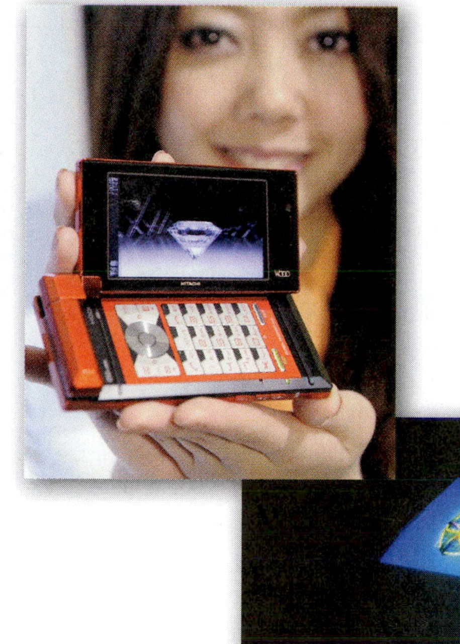

Figure 8 True 3-D video images can be seen on cell phones and video displays without special glasses or goggles. Applications include medical imaging, CAD drawings, mapping, and entertainment.

Figure 9 High-definition (HD) digital video recorders (DVRs), such as the TiVo, let you locate and record current and off-air digital broadcasts, pause and rewind live television programs, and create your own instant replays with slow motion.

Recording

WHETHER YOU ARE WORKING OUT at the gym or driving to Grandma's house for dinner, you might want to download or record your favorite audio, video, and photos to transport them from one location to another or upload them to share with friends and family. You also can record movies or television programs when you are not at home and then play them at your convenience on a home entertainment system or portable media player.

Figure 10 Use optical disc burning software to create optical discs quickly and easily with multiformat burners and rewritable drives to store your movies, photos, music, and digital data.

Figure 12 Turn your computer into a virtual bass guitar, drum set, electric piano, or string section with Cakewalk's Studio Instruments software. Then, record, edit, and mix your songs created with these virtual and real instruments and create streaming music players and playlists on your Web site.

Figure 11 Capture video using your video camera and then, with the press of a button, upload recorded clips to social networking Web sites. Each minute, more than 20 hours of video are uploaded to YouTube.

Figure 13 Capture video of friends and family, upload the clips to your computer, and use video editing software to rearrange the sequence of events, add music and titles, and record narration.

Gaming

REVENUE GENERATED BY THE VIDEO GAMING INDUSTRY quickly is approaching $100 billion. The areas experiencing the fastest growth are online and mobile gaming as new game consoles and advanced networking become mainstream.

Figure 14 The three gaming consoles — Nintendo Wii, Sony PlayStation 3, and Microsoft Xbox 360 — offer a variety of game titles.

Figure 16 In a computer role-playing game (CRPG), players interact with one another and generally attempt to accomplish a quest. Massively multiplayer online games (MMOGs) unite millions of gamers worldwide.

Figure 15 Gaming reaches all generations. The Wii game console's interactive quality appeals to players of all ages. The iPod touch's accelerometer, which detects movement and changes the display accordingly, and 3-D graphics immerse players in the action.

Figure 17 Handheld game consoles have large, high-resolution screens and incredible sound to play audio and video files and can display photos. Bluetooth and Wi-Fi technology allows networked gaming and synchronizing with other handheld units or personal computers.

Figure 18 Outdoor treasure hunters use their GPS receivers and navigational skills to create and locate hidden caches throughout the world.

Digital Home

THE AVERAGE HOUSEHOLD has 21 consumer electronics devices, and many of them are linked via home networks and broadband connections that simplify our lives and provide entertainment in innovative ways. Digital music and video are recorded and streamed to multiple devices. Meanwhile, automation systems monitor security, energy usage, and room temperatures to provide optimal conditions.

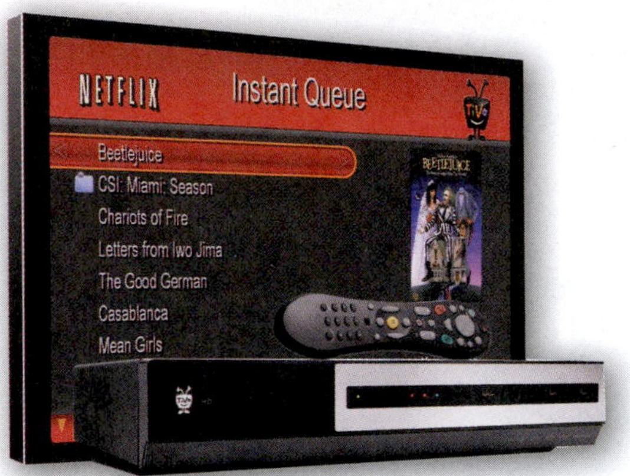

Figure 19 Set-top boxes stream movies from the Web to your televisions, computers, and mobile devices. On average, Netflix ships approximately two million DVDs each day.

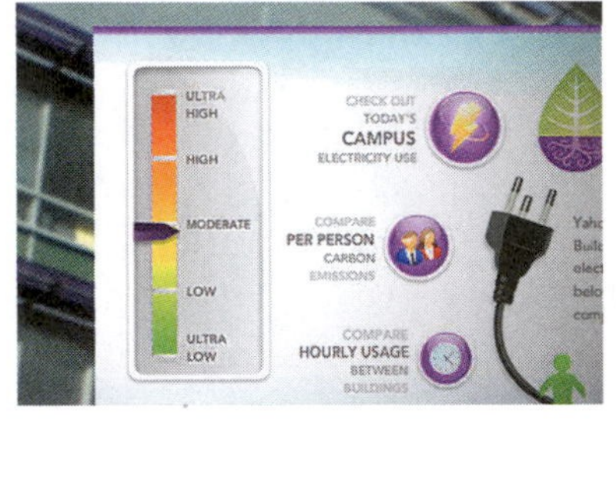

Figure 21 LED screens provide information about home electricity, gas, and water use, and they compare the rates with previous consumption.

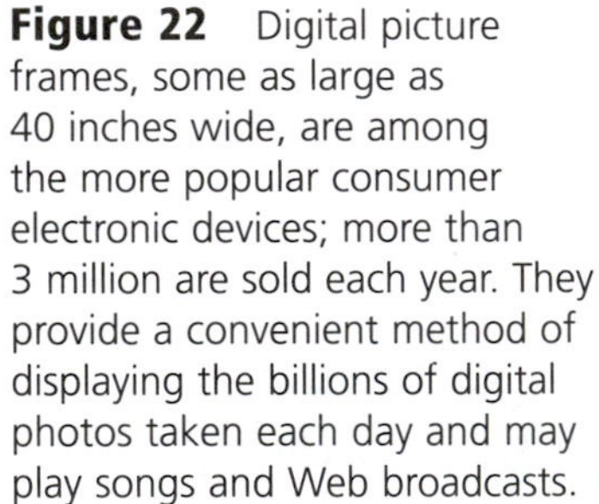

Figure 22 Digital picture frames, some as large as 40 inches wide, are among the more popular consumer electronic devices; more than 3 million are sold each year. They provide a convenient method of displaying the billions of digital photos taken each day and may play songs and Web broadcasts.

Figure 20 Program an entire home to fit your lifestyle and needs. A home automation system can set room temperatures, open and close window shades, water the grass, watch for intruders, and play music to wake you or relax you to sleep.

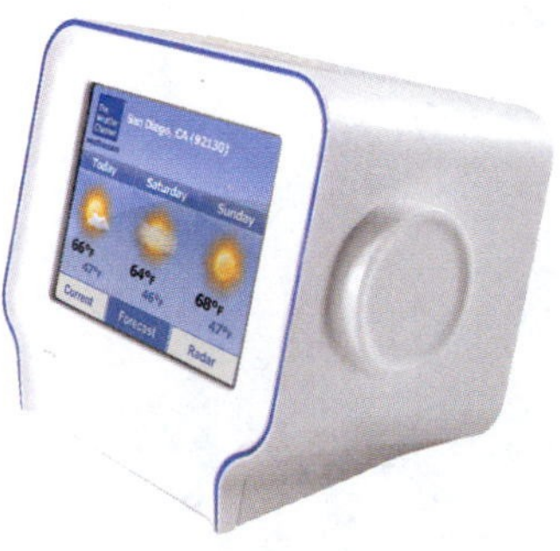

Figure 23 The wireless chumby connects to the Internet and streams news, entertainment, sports scores, video clips, interactive games, photos, and hundreds of favorite widgets.

Computer technology impacts virtually every facet of our lives. From the largest media rooms to the smallest portable media players, we can watch our favorite television programs and movies any place at any time. We can browse the Web, play games with partners on the other side of the world, listen to music we created with handheld instruments, and have fun wherever life takes us. No matter where we are, our digital lives are filled with information and entertainment.

Quiz Yourself Answers

Following are possible answers to the Quiz Yourself boxes throughout the book.

Quiz Yourself 1-1

1. A computer is ~~a motorized~~an electronic device that processes ~~output~~input into ~~input~~output.
2. A storage device records (~~reads~~writes) and/or retrieves (~~writes~~reads) items to and from storage media.
3. An ~~output~~input device is any hardware component that allows you to enter data and instructions into a computer.
4. True Statement
5. Computers have the ~~dis~~advantages of fast speeds, ~~high~~low failure rates, producing consistent results, storing ~~small~~enormous amounts of data, and communicating with others.
6. Three commonly used ~~input~~output devices are a printer, a monitor, and speakers.

Quiz Yourself 1-2

1. A ~~resource~~network is a collection of computers and devices connected together via communications devices and transmission media.
2. True Statement
3. Popular ~~system~~application software includes Web browsers, word processing software, spreadsheet software, database software, and presentation software.
4. The ~~Internet~~Web is one of the more popular services on the ~~Web~~Internet.
5. Two types of ~~application~~system software are the operating system and utility programs.

Quiz Yourself 1-3

1. A ~~desktop computer~~notebook computer (or laptop computer) is a portable, personal computer designed to fit on your lap.
2. True Statement
3. Each ~~enterprise~~home user spends time on the computer for different reasons that include personal financial management, Web access, communications, and entertainment.
4. A ~~home~~power user requires the capabilities of a workstation or other powerful computer.
5. ~~Mainframes~~Supercomputers are the fastest, most powerful computers — and the most expensive.
6. The elements of an information system are hardware, ~~e-mail~~software, data, people, and ~~the Internet~~procedures.
7. With ~~embedded computers~~online banking, users access account balances, pay bills, and copy monthly transactions from the bank's computer right into their personal computers.

Quiz Yourself 2-1

1. True Statement
2. ~~A wireless Internet service provider~~An IP address (or Internet Protocol address) is a number that uniquely identifies each computer or device connected to the Internet.
3. ~~An IP address~~A domain name, such as www.google.com, is the text version of ~~a domain name~~an IP address.
4. ~~Satellite~~Cable Internet service provides high-speed Internet access through the cable television network via a cable modem.
5. The World Wide Web Consortium (W3C) oversees research and ~~owns~~sets standards and guidelines for many areas of the Internet.

Quiz Yourself 2-2

1. True Statement
2. You cannot assume that information on the Web is correct and accurate.
3. Audio and video files are ~~downloaded~~compressed to reduce their file sizes.
4. Popular ~~portals~~players include iTunes, RealPlayer, and Windows Media Player.
5. The more widely used ~~search engines~~Web browsers for personal computers are Internet Explorer, Firefox, Opera, Safari, and Google Chrome.
6. To develop a Web page, you do not have to be a computer programmer.
7. To improve your Web searches, use ~~general~~specific nouns and put the ~~least~~most important terms first in the search text.

Quiz Yourself 2-3

1. True Statement
2. An e-mail address is a combination of a user name and ~~an e-mail program~~a domain name that identifies a user so that he or she can receive Internet e-mail.
3. ~~Business~~Consumer-to-consumer e-commerce occurs when one consumer sells directly to another, such as in an online auction.
4. FTP is an Internet standard that permits file ~~reading~~uploading and ~~writing~~downloading with other computers on the Internet.
5. ~~Spam~~Internet telephony uses the Internet (instead of the public switched telephone network) to connect a calling party to one or more called parties.
6. Netiquette is the code of ~~un~~acceptable behaviors while on the Internet.
7. VoIP enables users to ~~subscribe~~speak to other users over the Internet.

Quiz Yourself 3-1

1. True Statement
2. ~~Public-domain~~Packaged software is mass produced, copyrighted retail software that meets the needs of a wide variety of users, not just a single user or company.
3. To use ~~system~~application software, your computer must be running ~~application~~system software.
4. When a program is started, its instructions load from ~~memory~~a storage medium into ~~a storage medium~~memory.

Quiz Yourself 3-2

1. ~~Audio~~Video editing software typically includes ~~video~~audio editing capabilities.
2. ~~Enterprise computing~~Image editing software provides the capabilities of paint software and also includes the capability to modify existing images.
3. Millions of people use ~~spreadsheet~~word processing software every day to develop documents such as letters, memos, reports, mailing labels, newsletters, and Web pages.
4. Professional ~~accounting~~DTP (or desktop publishing) software is ideal for the production of high-quality color documents such as textbooks, corporate newsletters, marketing literature, product catalogs, and annual reports.
5. ~~Database~~Presentation software is application software that allows users to create visual aids for presentations to communicate ideas, messages, and other information to a group.
6. Popular ~~CAD programs~~software suites include Microsoft Office, Apple iWork, Corel WordPerfect Office, and Google Docs.
7. True Statement

Quiz Yourself 3-3

1. ~~All~~Some Web application hosts provide free access to their software.
2. ~~Computer~~Web-based training is a type of ~~Web~~computer-based training that uses Internet technology and consists of application software on the Web.
3. True Statement
4. ~~Legal~~Personal finance software is a simplified accounting program that helps home users and small office/home office users balance their checkbooks, pay bills, track investments, and evaluate financial plans.
5. ~~Personal DTP~~Photo editing software is a popular type of image editing software that allows users to edit digital photos.

Quiz Yourself 4-1

1. True Statement
2. Four basic operations in a machine cycle are: (1) ~~comparing~~ fetching, (2) decoding, (3) executing, and, if necessary, (4) ~~pipelining~~storing.
3. Processors contain a ~~motherboard~~control unit and an arithmetic logic unit (ALU).
4. The ~~central processing unit~~motherboard, sometimes called a system board, is the main circuit board of the system unit.
5. The leading processor chip manufacturers for personal computers are ~~Microsoft~~Intel and AMD.
6. The pace of the system clock, called the clock speed, is measured by the number of ticks per ~~minute~~second.
7. The system unit is a case that contains ~~mechanical~~electronic components of the computer used to process data.

Quiz Yourself 4-2

1. True Statement
2. A gigabyte (GB) equals approximately 1 ~~trillion~~billion bytes.
3. Memory cache helps speed the processes of the computer because it stores ~~seldom~~frequently used instructions and data.
4. Most computers are ~~analog~~digital, which means they recognize only two discrete states: on and off.
5. Most RAM ~~retains~~loses its contents when the power is removed from the computer.
6. Read-only memory (ROM) refers to memory chips storing ~~temporary~~permanent data and instructions.

Quiz Yourself 4-3

1. A ~~bus~~port is the point at which a peripheral attaches to or communicates with a system unit so that the peripheral can send data to or receive information from the computer.
2. An ~~AC adapter~~expansion slot is a socket on the motherboard that can hold an adapter card.
3. Built into the power supply is a ~~heater~~fan that keeps components of the system unit ~~warm~~cool.
4. ~~eSATA~~USB ports can connect up to 127 different peripherals together with a single connector.
5. The higher the bus clock speed, the ~~slower~~faster the transmission of data.
6. True Statement

Quiz Yourself 5-1

1. A keyboard is an ~~output~~input device that contains keys users press to enter data in a computer.
2. A ~~stylus~~graphics tablet is a flat, rectangular, electronic plastic board.
3. A ~~trackball~~touchpad is a small, flat, rectangular pointing device commonly found on notebook computers, including netbooks and many Tablet PCs.
4. True Statement
5. Operations you can perform with a ~~wheel~~mouse include point, click, right-click, double-click, triple-click, drag, right-drag, rotate wheel, free-spin wheel, press wheel button, tilt wheel, and press thumb button.

Quiz Yourself 5-2

1. True Statement
2. DV cameras record video as ~~analog~~digital signals.
3. Video games and computer games use a ~~Web cam~~game controller as the input device that directs movements and actions of on-screen objects.
4. Many smart phones today have a built-in camera so that users easily can ~~type text~~take pictures.
5. The ~~lower~~higher the resolution of a digital camera, the better the photo quality, but the more expensive the camera.

Quiz Yourself 5-3

1. A fingerprint reader captures curves and indentations of a ~~signature~~fingerprint.
2. After swiping a credit card through ~~an MICR~~a magstripe (or magnetic stripe card) reader, a POS terminal connects to a system that authenticates the purchase.
3. ATMs ask you to enter a password, called a ~~biometric identifier~~PIN (or personal identification number), which verifies that you are the holder of the bankcard.
4. Four types of ~~source documents~~scanners are flatbed, pen, sheet-fed, and drum.
5. Retail and grocery stores use the ~~POSTNET~~UPC (Universal Product Code) bar code.
6. RFID is a technology that uses ~~laser~~radio signals to communicate with a tag placed in an object, an animal, or a person.
7. True Statement

Quiz Yourself 6-1

1. A ~~lower~~higher resolution uses a greater number of pixels and thus provides a smoother image.
2. An output device is any type of ~~software~~hardware component that conveys information to one or more people.
3. Documents often include ~~text~~graphics to enhance their visual appeal and convey information.
4. Types of ~~pixels~~flat-panel displays include LCD monitors, LCD screens, and plasma monitors.
5. True Statement

Quiz Yourself 6-2

1. A ~~laser~~thermal printer generates images by pushing electrically heated pins against heat-sensitive paper.
2. A ~~photo~~laser printer creates images using a laser beam and powdered ink, called toner.
3. An ink-jet printer is a type of nonimpact printer that forms characters and graphics by spraying tiny drops of liquid ~~nitrogen~~ink onto a piece of paper.
4. Printed information is called ~~soft~~hard copy.
5. True Statement

Quiz Yourself 6-3

1. A digital light processing (DLP) projector uses tiny ~~lightbulbs~~mirrors to reflect light.
2. Many personal computer users attach surround sound ~~printer~~speaker systems to their computers to generate a higher-quality sound.
3. True Statement
4. Some game controllers include ~~real-time action~~force feedback, which is a technology that sends resistance to the device in response to actions of the user.

Quiz Yourself 7-1

1. Disk ~~recording~~caching consists of a memory chip(s) on a hard disk that stores frequently accessed items.
2. True Statement
3. SATA is a hard disk interface that uses ~~parallel~~serial signals to transfer data, instructions, and information.
4. ~~Storage media~~A storage device is the computer hardware that records and/or retrieves items to and from ~~a~~ storage ~~device~~media.
5. Users can move an ~~internal~~external hard disk from computer to computer as needed by connecting the disk to a USB port or FireWire port on the system unit.

Quiz Yourself 7-2

1. ~~Cloud storage~~A solid state drive (SSD) is a storage device that typically uses flash memory to store data, instructions, and information.
2. A USB flash drive is a flash memory storage device that plugs in a ~~parallel~~USB port on a computer or mobile device.
3. Flash memory cards are a type of ~~magnetic~~solid state media, which means they consist entirely of electronic components and contain no moving parts.
4. True Statement

Quiz Yourself 7-3

1. A ~~CD-RW~~CD-ROM is a type of optical disc on which users can read but not write (record) or erase.
2. A ~~DVD-RAM~~Picture CD is a single-session disc that stores digital versions of film using a jpg file format.
3. DVDs have ~~the same~~much greater storage capacities ~~as~~than CDs.
4. Optical discs are written and read by ~~mirrors~~a laser.
5. ~~Single session~~Multisession means you can write on part of the disc at one time and another part at a later time.
6. True Statement

Quiz Yourself 8-1

1. A ~~buffer~~driver is a small program that tells the operating system how to communicate with a specific device.
2. A ~~cold~~warm boot is the process of using the operating system to restart a computer.
3. A password is a ~~public~~private combination of characters associated with the user name that allows access to certain computer resources.
4. Firmware that contains the computer's startup instructions is called the ~~kernel~~BIOS.

5. The program you currently are using is in the ~~background~~foreground, and the other programs running but not in use are in the ~~foreground~~background.
6. Two types of system software are operating systems and ~~application~~utility programs.
7. True Statement

Quiz Yourself 8-2

1. ~~BlackBerry~~Palm OS devices use Palm OS as their operating system.
2. Examples of ~~embedded~~server operating systems include Windows Server 2008, UNIX, Linux, Solaris, and NetWare.
3. Windows 7 Starter uses Windows ~~Aero~~Vista Basic.
4. True Statement
5. ~~Aero Flip 3D~~Linux is a UNIX-type operating system that is open source software.

Quiz Yourself 8-3

1. A ~~pop-up blocker~~file compression utility shrinks the size of a file(s).
2. An ~~anti-spam~~antivirus program protects a computer against viruses by identifying and removing any computer viruses found in memory, on storage media, or on incoming files.
3. True Statement
4. You should ~~uninstall~~back up files and disks regularly in the event your originals are lost, damaged, or destroyed.
5. ~~Web filtering~~Disc burning software writes text, graphics, audio, and video files to a recordable or rewritable disc.
6. ~~Fragmenting~~Defragmenting a disk is the process of reorganizing it so that the files are stored in contiguous sectors.

Quiz Yourself 9-1

1. A ~~cybercafé~~hot spot is a wireless network that provides Internet connections to mobile computers and other devices.
2. A ~~Web folder~~GPS (global positioning system) is a navigation system that consists of one or more earth-based receivers that accept and analyze signals sent by satellites in order to determine the receiver's geographic location.
3. True Statement
4. ~~Receiving~~Sending devices initiate an instruction to transmit data, instructions, or information.
5. Users can send pictures and sound files, as well as short text messages, with ~~text~~picture messaging.

Quiz Yourself 9-2

1. A wireless LAN is a LAN that uses no physical wires.
2. An intranet is an internal network that uses ~~video conferencing~~Internet technologies.
3. Five types of digital ~~dial-up~~dedicated lines are ISDN lines, DSL, FTTP, T-carrier lines, and ATM.
4. In a client/server network, ~~servers~~clients on the network access resources on the ~~client~~server.
5. In a networked environment, any ~~un~~authorized computer user can access data and information stored on other computers on the network.
6. True Statement

Quiz Yourself 9-3

1. A ~~cable~~dial-up modem converts a computer's digital signals to analog signals before they are transmitted over standard telephone lines.
2. A ~~hardware firewall~~wireless access point is a communications device that allows computers and devices to transfer data wirelessly among themselves or to transfer data wirelessly to a wired network.
3. True Statement
4. ~~Analog~~Digital signals consist of individual electrical pulses that represent bits grouped together into bytes.
5. ~~Physical~~Wireless transmission media send communications signals through the air or space using radio, microwave, and infrared signals.
6. The ~~lower~~higher the bandwidth, the more data, instructions, and information the channel transmits.
7. Most wireless home networks use ~~powerline cables~~Wi-Fi.

Quiz Yourself 10-1

1. A ~~coding scheme~~check digit is a number(s) or character(s) that is appended to or inserted in a primary key value.
2. A ~~database~~field is a combination of one or more related characters or bytes and is the smallest unit of data a user accesses.
3. A ~~record~~database is a collection of data organized in a manner that allows access, retrieval, and use of that data.
4. ~~Data~~Information is processed ~~information~~data.
5. ~~Hierarchy of data~~File maintenance procedures include adding records to, modifying records in, and deleting records from a file.
6. True Statement

Quiz Yourself 10-2

1. A DBMS is ~~hardware~~software that allows you to create, access, and manage ~~an operating system~~a database.
2. A ~~query~~data dictionary contains data about files and fields in the database.
3. ~~Backup and recovery procedures~~Access privileges for data involve establishing who can enter new data, modify existing data, delete unwanted data, and view data.
4. To reduce data entry errors, well-designed forms should ~~rollback~~validate data as it is entered.
5. True Statement

Quiz Yourself 10-3

1. Data warehouses often use a process called ~~OQL~~data mining to find patterns and relationships among data.
2. ~~Object-oriented~~Relational databases store data in tables.
3. True Statement
4. Relational database users refer to a file as a table, a record as a ~~column~~row, and a field as a ~~row~~column.
5. SQL is a ~~data modeling~~query language that allows users to manage, update, and retrieve data.
6. The database ~~analyst~~administrator requires a more technical inside view of the data than does the ~~database administrator~~data analyst.

Quiz Yourself 11-1

1. A ~~back door~~denial of service (DoS) attack is an assault whose purpose is to disrupt computer access to an Internet service such as the Web or e-mail.
2. True Statement
3. A biometric device translates a personal characteristic into ~~an analog~~a digital code that is compared with a digital code stored in the computer.
4. Computer viruses, worms, Trojan horses, and rootkits are malware that acts without a user's knowledge.
5. Perpetrators of cybercrime and other intrusions fall into seven basic categories: hacker, cracker, ~~CERT/CC~~script kiddie, corporate spy, unethical employee, ~~trusted source~~cyberextortionist, and cyberterrorist.
6. ~~Shorter~~Longer passwords provide greater security than ~~longer~~shorter ones.
7. Updating an antivirus program's ~~quarantine~~signature file protects a computer against viruses written since the antivirus program was released.

Quiz Yourself 11-2

1. An end-user license agreement (EULA) ~~permits~~does not permit users to give copies to friends and colleagues, while continuing to use the software.
2. Encryption is a process of converting ~~ciphertext~~plaintext into ~~plaintext~~ciphertext to prevent unauthorized access.
3. Mobile users are ~~not~~ susceptible to hardware theft.
4. True Statement
5. Two ~~backup~~wireless security standards are Wi-Fi Protected Access and 802.11i.
6. To prevent against data loss caused by a system failure, computer users should ~~restore~~back up files regularly.

Quiz Yourself 11-3

1. A ~~code of conduct~~copyright gives authors and artists exclusive rights to duplicate, publish, and sell their materials.
2. Factors that cause ~~CVS~~tendonitis or CTS (carpal tunnel syndrome) include prolonged typing, prolonged mouse usage, or continual shifting between the mouse and the keyboard.
3. ~~Phishing~~Digital forensics is the discovery, collection, and analysis of evidence found on computers and networks.
4. True Statement
5. Users should not store obsolete computers and devices in their basement or attic.
6. You cannot assume that information on the Web is correct.

Quiz Yourself 12-1

1. ~~Feasibility~~Project management is the process of planning, scheduling, and then controlling the activities during system development.
2. True Statement
3. Users should ~~not~~ be involved throughout system development.
4. The five phases in most SDLCs are ~~programming~~planning; analysis; design; ~~sampling~~implementation; and ~~recording~~operation, support, and security.
5. The planning phase for a project begins when the steering committee receives a ~~Gantt chart~~project request.

Quiz Yourself 12-2

1. Detailed analysis sometimes is called ~~physical~~logical design because the systems analysts develop the proposed solution without regard to any specific hardware or software.
2. Entity-relationship diagrams and data flow diagrams are tools that a systems analyst uses for ~~object~~process modeling.
3. ~~Horizontal~~Vertical market software specifically is designed for a particular business or industry.
4. True Statement
5. The purpose of the ~~preliminary investigation~~system proposal is to assess the feasibility of each alternative solution and then recommend the most feasible solution for the project.
6. Upon completion of the preliminary investigation, the systems analyst writes the ~~system proposal~~feasibility report.

Quiz Yourself 12-3

1. A computer ~~training~~security plan summarizes in writing all of the safeguards that are in place to protect an organization's information assets.
2. ~~Acceptance~~Benchmark tests measure the performance of hardware or software.
3. True Statement
4. The program development life cycle is a part of the ~~support~~implementation phase.
5. The purpose of the ~~design~~operation, support, and security phase is to provide ongoing assistance for an information system and its users after the system is implemented.
6. With a request for ~~quotation~~proposal, the vendor selects the product(s) that meets specified requirements and then quotes the price(s).
7. With ~~parallel~~direct conversion, the user stops using the old system and begins using the new system on a certain date.

Quiz Yourself 13-1

1. A~~n~~ ~~interpreter~~compiler is a program that converts an entire source program into machine language before executing it.
2. C and COBOL are examples of ~~assembly~~procedural languages.
3. C# is an object-oriented programming language based on ~~PowerBuilder~~C++.
4. ~~Delphi~~Java is an object-oriented programming language developed by Sun Microsystems.
5. Two types of low-level languages are machine languages and ~~source~~assembly languages.
6. True Statement

Quiz Yourself 13-2

1. True Statement
2. ~~Interpreted~~Dynamic HTML works by using the document object model, style sheets, and scripting languages.
3. ~~Maps~~Macros allow users to automate routine, repetitive, or difficult tasks in application software such as word processing, spreadsheet, or database programs.
4. Popular ~~first generation~~scripting languages include JavaScript, Perl, PHP, Rexx, Tcl, and VBScript.
5. ~~Rexx~~XML separates the Web page content from its format, allowing the Web browser to display the contents of a Web page in a form appropriate for the display device.
6. SQL is an example of a ~~second~~fourth generation language.
7. Four popular ~~markup languages~~Web page authoring programs are Dreamweaver, Expression Web, Flash, and SharePoint Designer.

Quiz Yourself 13-3

1. A language's ~~logic~~syntax is the set of grammar and rules that specifies how to write instructions for a solution algorithm.
2. An error in a program is known as a ~~beta~~bug.
3. In structured design, the programmer typically begins with a ~~detailed~~general design and moves toward a more ~~general~~detailed design.
4. The concept of packaging data and procedures into a single object is called ~~casing~~encapsulation.
5. The program development life cycle consists of these six steps: analyze requirements, design solution, validate design, implement design, test solution, and ~~hardcode~~document solution.
6. Three basic control structures are sequence, selection, and ~~pseudocode~~repetition.
7. True Statement

Quiz Yourself 14-1

1. The main task of executive managers is to make ~~short~~long-term, ~~tactical~~strategic decisions.
2. An information system is a set of hardware, software, data, procedures, and people that work together to produce information.
3. A ~~human resources~~marketing information system serves as a central repository for the tasks of the marketing functional unit.
4. True Statement
5. ~~Decision support~~Expert systems capture and store the knowledge of human experts and then imitate human reasoning and decision making.
6. ~~Enterprise resource planning~~A content management system (CMS) is a combination of databases, software, and procedures that organizes and allows access to various forms of documents and files.

Quiz Yourself 14-2

1. ~~A portal~~An extranet is the portion of a company's network that allows customers or suppliers of a company to access parts of an enterprise's intranet.
2. True Statement
3. A VPN ~~is a server that is placed on a network with the sole purpose of providing storage to users and information systems attached to the network~~provides mobile users, remote offices, vendors, or customers a secure connection to the company network server, as if they had a private line.
4. A workflow application ~~helps an enterprise collect, archive, index, and retrieve its resources~~is a program that assists in the management and tracking of all the activities in a business process from start to finish.

Quiz Yourself 14-3

1. ~~Network attached storage~~A storage area network is a high-speed network with the sole purpose of providing storage to other servers to which it is attached.
2. ~~Scalability~~Interoperability refers to the capability of an information system to share information with other information systems.
3. A differential backup copies only the files that have changed since the last full ~~or last incremental~~ backup.
4. ~~A full~~An incremental backup is the fastest backup method, requiring only minimal storage.
5. An ~~emergency~~backup plan specifies how a company uses backup files and equipment to resume information processing.
6. True Statement

Quiz Yourself 15-1

1. A ~~corporate trainer~~computer technician installs, maintains, and repairs hardware; installs, upgrades, and configures software; and troubleshoots hardware problems.
2. A ~~Webmaster/Web administrator~~chief security officer is responsible for physical security of a company's property and people and is in charge of securing computing resources.
3. Career opportunities in the computer ~~equipment~~software field involve designing and programming a variety of software.

4. True Statement
5. More than 80 percent of IT employees work at organizations whose primary business is not computer related.
6. ~~Network administrators/wireless network administrators~~Help desk specialists answer hardware, software, or networking questions in person, over the telephone, and/or electronically via e-mail or a chat room.

Quiz Yourself 15-2

1. ~~A transfer statement~~An articulation agreement ensures that if you transfer to a college or university, you will receive credit for most of the courses taken at your current school.
2. Computer ~~science~~information systems programs focus on how to apply computing skills.
3. Job-search Web sites such as Monster provide job-search services for ~~a fee~~free to job seekers.
4. Students often complete trade school programs in a ~~longer~~shorter time than college and university programs.
5. True Statement

Quiz Yourself 15-3

1. True Statement
2. If you do not pass a certification exam, you ~~do not~~ have to pay a fee again to retake the test.
3. ~~Industrialization~~Certification is a process of verifying the technical knowledge of an individual who has demonstrated competence in a particular area.
4. Salary surveys show that certification helps influence pay ~~decreases~~increases.
5. The Microsoft Certified ~~Professional Developer~~Application Specialist certification tests a user's basic (specialist) and advanced (expert) skills of Microsoft Office programs and some versions of the Windows operating system.

Computer Acronyms

Acronym	Description	Page
0NF	zero normal form	540
1NF	first normal form	540
2NF	second normal form	540
3DES	Triple Data Encryption Standard (Triple-DES)	592
3GL	third-generation language	666
3NF	third normal form	540
4GL	fourth-generation language	674
AAC	Advanced Audio Coding	95
AC	alternating current	239
ACE	Adobe Certified Expert	804
ACI	Adobe Certified Instructor	804
ACM	Association for Computing Machinery	797
ADA	Americans with Disabilities Act	286
ADSL	asymmetric digital subscriber line	484
AES	Advanced Encryption Standard	592
AGP	Accelerated Graphics Port	238
AI	artificial intelligence	737
AIFF	Audio Interchange File Format	95
AIS	Association for Information Systems	797
AITP	Association of Information Technology Professionals	797
Ajax	Asynchronous JavaScript and XML	684
ALGOL	ALGOrithmic Language	675
ALU	arithmetic logic unit	213
AMD	Advanced Micro Devices	216, 217
ANN	artificial neural network	758
ANSI	American National Standards Institute	691
AOL	America Online	78, 89, 111
APCUG	Association of Personal Computer Users Group	798
API	application programming interface	684
APL	A Programming Language	675

Acronym	Description	Page
ARPA	Advanced Research Projects Agency	75
ARPANET	Advanced Research Projects Agency network	75
ASCII	American Standard Code for Information Interchange	221
ASF	Advanced Streaming (or Systems) Format	95
ATC	advanced transfer cache	227
ATM	Asynchronous Transfer Mode	485
ATM	automated teller machine	284
AUP	acceptable use policy	565
AWC	Association for Women in Computing	797
B2B	business-to-business	100
B2C	business-to-consumer	98
BAN	body area network	471
BASIC	Beginner's All-purpose Symbolic Instruction Code	675
BD-R	Blu-ray Disc recordable	376
BD-RE	Blu-ray Disc rewritable	376
BD-ROM	Blu-ray Disc read-only memory	375
BI	business intelligence	725
BIOS	basic input/output system	400
bit	binary digit	221, 518
BLOB	binary large object	518
BLS	Bureau of Labor Statistics	784
BMP	bit map	93
BPA	business process automation	726
BPM	business process management	725
BSA	Business Software Alliance	572
BSB	backside bus	237
btw	by the way	108
C2C	consumer-to-consumer	100
CA	certificate authority	574
CAD	computer-aided design	160, 728

Acronym	Description	Page
CAE	computer-aided engineering	728
CAI	computer-aided instruction	171
CAM	computer-aided manufacturing	38, 729
CAPTCHA	Completely Automated Public Turing test to tell Computers and Humans Apart	567
CASE	computer-aided software engineering	642
CAT	computerized adaptive testing	803
CATV	cable television	483
CBT	computer-based training	171
CCD	charge-coupled device	272
CCE	Certified Computer Examiner	806
CCFE	Certified Computer Forensics Examiner	806
CCIE	Cisco Certified Internetwork Expert	806
CCNA	Cisco Certified Network Associate	806
CCNP	Cisco Certified Network Professional	806
ccTLD	country code top-level domain	80
CD	compact disc	8, 94, 97, 375
CDMA	Code Division Multiple Access	495
CDP	continuous data protection	754
CD-R	compact disc-recordable	373
CD-ROM	compact disc read-only memory	372
CD-RW	compact disc-rewritable	373
CE	computer engineering	795
CEECS	Certified Electronic Evidence Collection Specialist	806
CEO	Chief Executive Officer	723
CERT/CC	Computer Emergency Response Team Coordination Center	558
CES	Consumer Electronics Show	798
CF	CompactFlash	364
CFO	Chief Financial Officer	723
CGI	Common Gateway Interface	537, 680
CIFI	Certified Information Forensics Investigator	806
CIM	computer-integrated manufacturing	729
CIM	customer interaction management	731
CIO	chief information officer	732, 788
CIPA	Children's Internet Protection Act	589

Acronym	Description	Page
CIS	computer information systems	795
CISSP	Certified Information Systems Security Professional	807
CIW	Certified Internet Webmaster	807
CLP	Novell Certified Linux Professional	804
CLR	Common Language Runtime	670
CMOS	complementary metal-oxide semiconductor	229
CMS	content management system	739
coax	coaxial cable	493
COBOL	COmmon Business-Oriented Language	55, 668
COO	Chief Operating Officer	723
COPPA	Children's Online Privacy Protection Act	589
CPU	central processing unit	7, 213
CRM	customer relationship management	737
CRPG	computer role-playing game	829
CRT	cathode-ray tube	313
CS	computer science	795
CSC	common short code	464
CSDA	Certified Software Development Associate	805
CSDP	Certified Software Development Professional	805
CSO	chief security officer	646, 789
CSS	cascading style sheet	683
CTO	chief technology officer	788
CTS	carpal tunnel syndrome	579
CUG	C/C++ Users Group	798
CVS	computer vision syndrome	579
CWP	Certified Web Professional	807
DA	database analyst	538
DBA	database administrator	538
DBMS	database management system	515
DC	direct current	239
DDoS attack	distributed denial of service attack	562
DDR SDRAM	double data rate synchronous dynamic random access memory	225
DES	Data Encryption Standard	592
DFD	data flow diagram	632

Acronym	Description	Page
DHCP	Dynamic Host Configuration Protocol	110
DHTML	Dynamic Hypertext Markup Language	683
DIMM	dual inline memory module	225
DL	distance learning	176
DLP projector	digital light processing projector	326
DMCA	Digital Millennium Copyright Act	589
DMS	Document Management System	743
DNS	domain name system	80
DOM	document object model	683
DoS attack	denial of service attack	562
dpi	dots per inch	273, 316
DRAM	dynamic random access memory	225
DRM	digital rights management	582
DSL	Digital Subscriber Line	76, 484
DSS	decision support system	734
DTP	desktop publishing	160
DTV	digital television	312
DV camera	digital video camera	275
DVD	digital versatile disc or digital video disc	8, 26, 64, 68, 97, 375
DVD+R	digital versatile disc or digital video disc recordable	376
DVD-R	digital versatile disc or digital video disc recordable	376
DVD+RAM	digital versatile disc or digital video disc + random access memory	376
DVD-ROM	digital versatile disc or digital video disc read-only memory	375
DVD+RW	digital versatile disc or digital video disc + rewritable	376
DVD-RW	digital versatile disc or digital video disc + rewritable	376
DVI	Digital Video Interface	310
EB	exabyte	354
e-commerce	electronic commerce	30, 32, 62, 63, 98, 100,109
ECPA	Electronic Communications Privacy Act	589
EDGE	Enhanced Data GSM Environment	495
EDI	electronic data interchange	471, 742
EEPROM	electrically erasable programmable read-only memory	228
e-filing	electronic filing	167

Acronym	Description	Page
e-form	electronic form	530
EFS	Encrypting File System	592
EFT	electronic funds transfer	471
EIDE	Enhanced Integrated Drive Electronics	361
EIS	executive information system	735
e-mail	electronic mail	12, 31, 74, 75, 77, 78, 81, 88, 89, 91, 98, 100, 101, 102, 103, 105, 108, 109, 142, 144, 150, 156, 157, 159, 173,174, 176
ENIAC	Electronic Numerical Integrator and Computer	54
ERD	entity-relationship diagram	632
e-retail	electronic retail	99, 747
ERM system	employee relationship management system	728
ERP	enterprise resource planning	738
eSATA	external Serial Advanced Technology Attachment	361
EULA	end-user license agreement	571
EVDO	Evolution Data Optimized	495
e-zine	electronic magazine	638
FAQ	frequently asked questions	14, 108
fax	facsimile	320, 321
FEK	file encryption key	592
FORTRAN	FORmula TRANslator	55, 675
FRED	Forensic Recovery of Digital Evidence	613
FSB	front side bus	237
FTP	File Transfer Protocol	107, 462, 482
FTTB	Fiber to the Building	484
FTTH	Fiber to the Home	484
FTTP	Fiber to the Premises	76
fwiw	for what it's worth	108
fyi	for your information	108
GB	gigabyte	223, 354
GBps	gigabytes per second	355
Gbps	gigabits per second	478
GHz	gigahertz	216
GIF	Graphics Interchange Format	93
GIGO	garbage in, garbage out	516
GIS	geographic information system	534

Acronym	Description	Page
GLBA	Graham-Leach-Bliley Act	589
GPRS	General Packet Radio Service	595
GPS	global positioning system	466
GPU	graphics processing unit	310
GSM	Global System for Mobile Communications	495
gTLD	generic top-level domain	80
GUI	graphical user interface	15, 402
GWT	Google Web Toolkit	714, 716
HD	high density	375
HD VMD	high-density Versatile Multilayer Disc	375
HDMI	High-Definition Media Interface	310
HDTV	high-definition television	312
HIPAA	Health Insurance Portability and Accountability Act	380
HMD	head-mounted display	308
HP	Hewlett-Packard	319, 331
HR	Human Resources	727
HRIS	Human Resources Information Systems	728
HTML	Hypertext Markup Language	678
HTPC	home theater PC	20
http	Hypertext Transfer Protocol	82, 462
IACRB	Information Assurance Certification Review Board	806
IACSS	International Association for Computer Systems Security	797
IBM	International Business Machines	55, 56, 57, 58, 67, 76, 146
ICANN	Internet Corporation for Assigned Names and Numbers	80
I-CASE	integrated computer-aided software engineering	642
ICCA	Independent Computer Consultants Association	797
ICCP	Institute for the Certification of Computing Professionals	801
ICRA	Internet Content Rating Association	591
ICSA Labs	International Computer Security Association Labs	646
IDE	integrated development environment	669
IDEA	International Data Encryption Algorithm	592

Acronym	Description	Page
IEEE	Institute of Electrical and Electronics Engineers	797
IM	instant messaging	104
IMDb	Internet Movie Database	125
imho	in my humble opinion	108
IOUG	Independent Oracle Users Group	798
IP	intellectual property	582
IP address	Internet Protocol address	79, 110
IPng	Internet Protocol Next Generation	110
IPO chart	input, processing, output chart	687
IPv6	Internet Protocol version 6	80,110
IR	infrared	494
IrDA	Infrared Data Association	235, 480
IS	information system	27, 620
ISDN	Integrated Services Digital Network	484
ISP	Internet service provider	78
ISSA	International Systems Security Association	797
IT	information technology	27
JAD session	joint-application design session	626
JIT compiler	just-in-time compiler	670
JPEG	Joint Photographic Experts Group	93
JUG	Java Users Groups	798
K	kilobyte	223
KB	kilobyte	223, 354
KBps	kilobytes per second	355
Kbps	kilobits per second	480
KM	knowledge management	737
KMS	knowledge management software	737
L1 cache	Level 1 cache	227
L2 cache	Level 2 cache	227
L3 cache	Level 3 cache	227
LAN	local area network	57, 472
LCD	liquid crystal display	308
LINQ	Language Integrated Query	671
LISP	LISt Processing	675
LUGWW	Linux Users Group WorldWide	798
M2	Memory Stick Micro	364

Acronym	Description	Page
Mac OS	Macintosh Operating System	415
Mac OS X	Macintosh Operating System X	415
MAN	metropolitan area network	473
MB	megabyte	223, 354
MBps	megabytes per second	355
MBps	megabits per second	375
MCAP	Microsoft Certified Application Professional	804
MCAS	Microsoft Certified Application Specialist	804
MCDST	Microsoft Certified Desktop Support Technician	804
MCITP	Microsoft Certified IT Professional	804, 808
m-commerce	mobile commerce	98
MCPD	Microsoft Certified Professional Developer	805
MCSA	Microsoft Certified Systems Administrator	806
MCTS	Microsoft Certified Technology Specialist	804
MFP	multifunction peripheral	320, 329, 331
MHz	megahertz	229
MIB	Medical Information Bureau	380
MICR	magnetic-ink character recognition	281
MIS	management information system	734
MLP	multilayer perception	758
MMOG	massively multiplayer online game	829
MMS	multimedia message service	464
modem	modulate/demodulate	8, 461, 485
MP	million pixels	273
MP3	Moving Pictures Experts Group Audio Layer 3 (MPEG-3)	94, 95
MPEG	Moving Pictures Experts Group	96
MRAM	magnetoresistive random access memory	225
MRP	Material Requirements Planning	729
MRP II	Manufacturing Resource Planning II	730
μs	microsecond	229
ms	millisecond	229
MSIL	Microsoft Intermediate Language	670
MSN	Microsoft Network, The	78, 81, 85, 89
MT/ST	Magnetic Tape/Selectric Typewriter	56

Acronym	Description	Page
MX	mail exchange	382
NAP	National Association of Programmers	797
NAS	network attached storage	360, 749
NCA	Novell Certified Administrator	806
NCE	Novell Certified Engineer	806
NET Act	No Electronic Theft Act	589
netiquette	Internet etiquette	108
NIC	network interface card	487
NLQ	near letter quality	322
ns	nanosecond	229
NSF	National Science Foundation	75
OCP	Oracle Certified Professional	808
OCR	optical character recognition	279
OIS	office information system	732
OLAP	online analytical processing	735
OLE	object linking and embedding	59
OLED	organic light emitting diode	308
OLTP	online transaction processing	733
OMR	optical mark recognition	279
OO	object-oriented	634, 689
OODB	object-oriented database	534
OOP language	object-oriented programming language	669
OQL	object query language	535
OS	operating system	398
OSI reference model	Open Systems Interconnection reference model	498
OSP	online service provider	78
P2P	peer-to-peer	475
PATRIOT Act	Provide Appropriate Tools Required to Intercept and Obstruct Terrorism Act	589
PB	petabyte	354
PC	personal computer	19, 20
PCI bus	Peripheral Component Interconnect bus	238
PCIe	PCI Express	238
PCL	Printer Control Language	319
PCS	Personal Communications Services	496
PDA	personal digital assistant	22
PDF	Portable Document Format	158

Acronym	Description	Page
PDL	page description language	319
PDLC	program development life cycle	686
Perl	Practical Extraction and Report Language	682
PERT	Program Evaluation and Review Technique	624
PGP	Pretty Good Privacy	574
PHP	PHP: Hypertext Preprocessor	682
PILOT	Programmed Inquiry Learning Or Teaching	675
PIM	personal information manager	156
PIN	personal identification number	284, 568
pixel	picture element	273, 278, 308
PL/I	Programming Language One	675
PNG format	Portable Network Graphics format	93
POP	Post Office Protocol	103
POP3	Post Office Protocol 3	103
POS	point of sale	284
POST	power-on self test	400
ppi	pixels per inch	273
Prolog	PROgramming LOGic	675
PROM chip	programmable read-only memory chip	228
ps	picosecond	229
PSTN	public switched telephone network	482
PUE	power usage effectiveness	583
QBE	query by example	528
QT	QuickTime	95
RA	RealAudio	95
RAD	rapid application development	669
RAID	redundant array of independent disks	360, 748
RAM	random access memory	224
RDRAM	Rambus dynamic random access memory	225
Rexx	REstructured eXtended eXecutor	682
RFI	request for information	638
RFID	radio frequency identification	280, 481
RFP	request for proposal	638
RFQ	request for quotation	638
RHCE	Red Hat Certified Engineer	804

Acronym	Description	Page
RHCT	Red Hat Certified Technician	804
RIAA	Recording Industry Association of America	64
RIMM	Rambus inline memory module	225
ROM	read-only memory	228
RoR	Ruby on Rails	683
RPG	Report Program Generator	675
rpm	revolutions per minute	358
RSI	repetitive strain injury	579
RSS 2.0	Really Simple Syndication	92, 679
RTLS	real time location system	570
RUP	Rational Unified Process	634
SAN	storage area network	749
SAS	serial-attached SCSI	235, 362
SATA	Serial Advanced Technology Attachment	361
SCEA	Sun Certified Enterprise Architect	805
SCJD	Sun Certified Java Developer	805
SCJP	Sun Certified Java Programmer	805
SCMAD	Sun Certified Mobile Application Developer	805
SCNA	Security Certified Network Architect	807
SCNA	Sun Certified Network Administrator	806
SCNP	Security Certified Network Professional	807
SCNS	Security Certified Network Specialist	807
SCSA	Sun Certified System Administrator	804
SCSI	small computer system interface	235, 362
SD	Secure Digital	364
SDHC	Secure Digital High Capacity	364
SDLC	system development life cycle	620
SDRAM	synchronous dynamic random access memory	225
SFA	sales force automation	730
S-HTTP	secure hypertext transfer protocol	575
SIGs	special interest groups	797
SIMM	single inline memory module	225
SMB	small- and medium-sized business	720
SMS	short message service	463
SMTP	simple mail transfer protocol	103

Acronym	Description	Page
SOA	service-oriented architecture	743
SOHO	small office/home office	30
SQL	Structured Query Language	534, 674
SRAM	static random access memory	225
SSCP	Systems Security Certified Practitioner	807
SSD	solid state drive	363
SSID	service set identifier	578
SSL	Secure Sockets Layer	575
SUT	system under test	648
SVG	Standard Vector Graphics	698
SVGA	Super Video Graphics Array	311
SXGA	Super Extended Graphics Array	311
TB	terabyte	223, 354
Tcl	Tool Command Language	682
TCP/IP	Transmission Control Protocol/ Internet Protocol	478
TFT display	thin-film transistor display	308
TIFF	Tagged Image File Format	93
TLD	top-level domain	80
TLS	Transport Layer Security	575
TPC-W	Transaction Processing Performance Council Workload	648
TPS	transaction processing system	733
TTL	Time To Live	382
ttfn	ta ta for now	108
tyvm	thank you very much	108
UL 1449 standard	Underwriters Laboratories 1449 standard	576
UMD	Universal Media Disc	375
UML	Unified Modeling Language	634, 692
UMPC	Ultra-Mobile PC	22
UMTS	Universal Mobile Telecommunications System	495
UNIVAC I	UNIVersal Automatic Computer	54
UPC	Universal Product Code	280
UPS	uninterruptible power supply	576
URL	Uniform Resource Locator	82
USB	universal serial bus	234, 367
user ID	user identification	410
UWB	ultra-wideband	480

Acronym	Description	Page
UXGA	Ultra Extended Graphics Array	311
VAN	value-added network	471
VAR	value-added reseller	638
VBA	Visual Basic for Applications	676
VBScript	Visual Basic, Scripting Edition	683
VoIP	Voice over Internet Protocol	100, 325
VPE	visual programming environment	673
VPN	virtual private network	575, 744
VR	virtual reality	96
VSTO	Visual Studio Tools for Office	671
W3C	World Wide Web Consortium	76
WAN	wide area network	473
WAP	Wireless Application Protocol	482
WAV	Windows waveform	95
WBT	Web-based training	181
Wi-Fi	wireless fidelity	76, 479
WiMAX	Worldwide Interoperability for Microwave Access	482
WIPS	Web Interactions Per Second	648
WIRT	Web Interaction Response Time	648
WISP	wireless Internet service provider	462
WLAN	wireless local area network	472
WMA	Windows Media Audio	95, 98
WML	wireless markup language	679
WPA	Wi-Fi Protected Access	578
WQXGA	Wide Quad Extended Graphics Array	311
WSXGA	Wide Super Extended Graphics Array	311
WUXGA	Wide Ultra Extended Graphics Array	311
WWW	World Wide Web	80
WXGA	Wide Extended Graphics Array	311
XGA	Extended Graphics Array	311
XHTML	Extensible Hypertext Markup Language	678
XML	Extensible Markup Language	468, 679
XP	extreme programming	695
XSL	Extensible Stylesheet Language	679
XSLT	Extensible Style Language Transformations	679
YB	yottabyte	354
ZB	zettabyte	354

Coding Schemes and Number Systems

Coding Schemes

As discussed in Chapter 4, a computer uses a coding scheme to represent characters. This section of the appendix presents the ASCII, EBCDIC, and Unicode coding schemes and discusses parity.

ASCII and EBCDIC

Two coding schemes that represent characters in a computer are ASCII and EBCDIC. The **American Standard Code for Information Interchange**, or ASCII (pronounced ASK-ee), coding scheme is the most widely used coding scheme to represent data. The **Extended Binary Coded Decimal Interchange Code**, or EBCDIC (pronounced EB-see-dik), coding scheme sometimes is used on mainframe computers and high-end servers. As shown in Figure C-1, the combination of bits (0s and 1s) is unique for each character in the ASCII and EBCDIC coding schemes.

When a computer uses the ASCII or EBCDIC coding scheme, it stores each represented character in one byte of memory. Other binary formats exist, however, that the computer sometimes uses to represent numeric data. For example, a computer may store, or pack, two numeric characters in one byte of memory. The computer uses these binary formats to increase storage and processing efficiency.

Unicode

The 256 characters and symbols that are represented by ASCII and EBCDIC codes are sufficient for English and western European languages but are not large enough for Asian and other languages that use different alphabets. Further compounding the problem is that many of these languages use symbols, called **ideograms**, to represent multiple words and ideas. One solution to this situation is Unicode. **Unicode** is a 16-bit coding scheme that has the capacity of representing all the world's current languages, as well as classic and historical languages, in more than 65,000 characters and symbols.

Unicode is implemented in several operating systems, including Windows, Mac OS, and Linux. Unicode-enabled programming languages and software include Java, XML, Microsoft Office, and Oracle. Some experts believe that Unicode eventually will replace all other coding schemes.

ASCII	SYMBOL	EBCDIC
00110000	0	11110000
00110001	1	11110001
00110010	2	11110010
00110011	3	11110011
00110100	4	11110100
00110101	5	11110101
00110110	6	11110110
00110111	7	11110111
00111000	8	11111000
00111001	9	11111001
01000001	A	11000001
01000010	B	11000010
01000011	C	11000011
01000100	D	11000100
01000101	E	11000101
01000110	F	11000110
01000111	G	11000111
01001000	H	11001000
01001001	I	11001001
01001010	J	11010001
01001011	K	11010010
01001100	L	11010011
01001101	M	11010100
01001110	N	11010101
01001111	O	11010110
01010000	P	11010111
01010001	Q	11011000
01010010	R	11011001
01010011	S	11100010
01010100	T	11100011
01010101	U	11100100
01010110	V	11100101
01010111	W	11100110
01011000	X	11100111
01011001	Y	11101000
01011010	Z	11101001
00100001	!	01011010
00100010	"	01111111
00100011	#	01111011
00100100	$	01011011
00100101	%	01101100
00100110	&	01010000
00101000	(	01001101
00101001	)	01011101
00101010	*	01011100
00101011	+	01001110

Figure C-1

A Unicode code for a symbol (Figure C-2) is obtained by appending the symbol's corresponding digit in the left-most column to the end of the symbol's corresponding three-digit code in the column heading. For example, the Unicode for the capital letter C is 0043. In Unicode, 30,000 codes are reserved for future use, such as ancient languages, and 6,000 codes are reserved for private use. Existing ASCII coded data is fully compatible with Unicode because the first 256 codes are the same.

Parity

Regardless of the coding scheme used to represent characters in memory, it is important that the computer store characters accurately. For each byte of memory, most computers have at least one extra bit, called a **parity bit**, that the computer uses for error checking. A parity bit can detect if one of the bits in a byte has been changed inadvertently. While such errors are extremely rare (most computers never have a parity error during their lifetime), they can occur because of voltage fluctuations, static electricity, or a memory failure.

Computers are either odd- or even-parity machines. In computers with odd parity, the total number of on bits in the byte (including the parity bit) must be an odd number (Figure C-3). In computers with even parity, the total number of on bits must be an even number. The computer checks parity each time it uses a memory location. When the computer moves data from one location to another in memory, it compares the parity bits of both the sending and receiving locations to see if they are the same. If the computer detects a difference or if the wrong number of bits is on (e.g., an odd number in a computer with even parity), an error message is displayed. Many computers use multiple parity bits that enable them to detect and correct a single-bit error and detect multiple-bit errors.

	003	004	005	006	007
0	0 0030	@ 0040	P 0050	` 0060	p 0070
1	1 0031	A 0041	Q 0051	a 0061	q 0071
2	2 0032	B 0042	R 0052	b 0062	r 0072
3	3 0033	C 0043	S 0053	c 0063	s 0073
4	4 0034	D 0044	T 0054	d 0064	t 0074
5	5 0035	E 0045	U 0055	e 0065	u 0075
6	6 0036	F 0046	V 0056	f 0066	v 0076
7	7 0037	G 0047	W 0057	g 0067	w 0077
8	8 0038	H 0048	X 0058	h 0068	x 0078
9	9 0039	I 0049	Y 0059	i 0069	y 0079
A	: 003A	J 004A	Z 005A	j 006A	z 007A
B	; 003B	K 004B	[005B	k 006B	{ 007B
C	< 003C	L 004C	\ 005C	l 006C	| 007C
D	= 003D	M 004D	] 005D	m 006D	} 007D
E	> 003E	N 004E	^ 005E	n 006E	~ 007E
F	? 003F	O 004F	_ 005F	o 006F	DEL 007F

Figure C-2

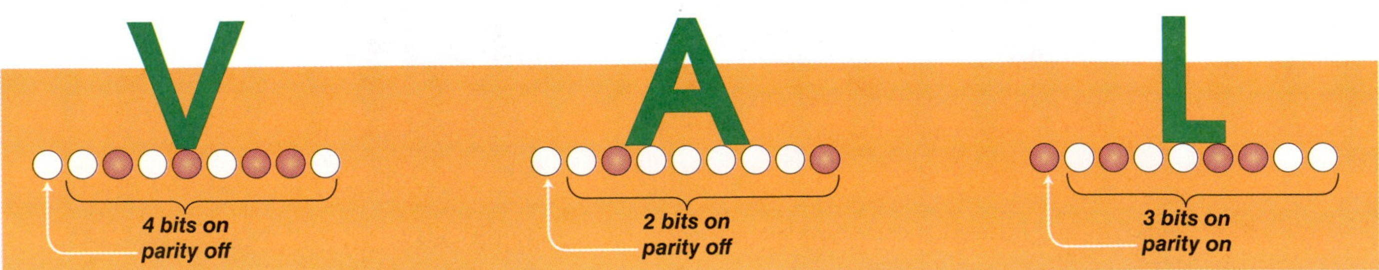

Figure C-3

Number Systems

This section of the appendix describes the number systems used with computers. Technical computer personnel require a thorough knowledge of this subject, but most users need only a general understanding of number systems and how they relate to computers.

The binary (base 2) number system is used to represent the electronic status of the bits in memory. It also is used for other purposes such as addressing the memory locations. Another number system commonly used with computers is **hexadecimal** (base 16). The computer uses the hexadecimal number system to communicate with a programmer when a problem with a program exists, because it would be difficult for the programmer to understand the 0s and 1s of binary code. Figure C-4 shows how the decimal values 0 through 15 are represented in binary and hexadecimal number systems.

DECIMAL	BINARY	HEXADECIMAL
0	0000	0
1	0001	1
2	0010	2
3	0011	3
4	0100	4
5	0101	5
6	0110	6
7	0111	7
8	1000	8
9	1001	9
10	1010	A
11	1011	B
12	1100	C
13	1101	D
14	1110	E
15	1111	F

Figure C-4

The mathematical principles that apply to the binary and hexadecimal number systems are the same as those that apply to the decimal number system. To help you better understand these principles, this section starts with the familiar decimal system, then progresses to the binary and hexadecimal number systems.

The Decimal Number System

The decimal number system is a base 10 number system (deci means ten). The base of a number system indicates how many symbols it uses. The decimal number system uses 10 symbols: 0 through 9. Each of the symbols in the number system has a value associated with it. For example, 3 represents a quantity of three and 5 represents a quantity of five.

The decimal number system also is a positional number system. This means that in a number such as 143, each position in the number has a value associated with it. When you look at the decimal number 143, the 3 is in the ones, or units, position and represents three ones (3×1); the 4 is in the tens position and represents four tens (4×10); and the 1 is in the hundreds position and represents one hundred (1×100). The number 143 is the sum of the values in each position of the number ($100 + 40 + 3 = 143$). The chart in Figure C-5 shows how you can calculate the positional values (hundreds, tens, and ones) for a number system. Starting on the right and working to the left, the base of the number system, in this case 10, is raised to consecutive powers (10^0, 10^1, 10^2). These calculations are a mathematical way of determining the place values in a number system.

When you use number systems other than decimal, the same principles apply. The base of the number system indicates the number of symbols that it uses, and each position in a number system has a value associated with it. By raising the base of the number system to consecutive powers beginning with zero, you can calculate the positional value.

power of 10	10^2	10^1	10^0
positional value	100	10	1
number	1	4	3

$$1 \quad 4 \quad 3 =$$
$$(1 \times 10^2) + (4 \times 10^1) + (3 \times 10^0) =$$
$$(1 \times 100) + (4 \times 10) + (3 \times 1) =$$
$$100 + 40 + 3 = 143$$

Figure C-5

The Binary Number System

As previously discussed, binary is a base 2 number system (bi means two), and the symbols it uses are 0 and 1. Just as each position in a decimal number has a place value associated with it, so does each position in a binary number. In binary, the place values, moving from right to left, are successive powers of two (2^0, 2^1, 2^2, 2^3 or 1, 2, 4, 8). To construct a binary number, place ones in the positions where the corresponding values add up to the quantity you want to represent and place zeros in the other positions. For example, in a four-digit binary number, the binary place values are (from right to left) 1, 2, 4, and 8. The binary number 1001 has ones in the positions for the values 1 and 8 and zeros in the positions for 2 and 4. Therefore, as shown in Figure C-6, the quantity represented by binary 1001 is 9 (8 + 0 + 0 + 1).

The Hexadecimal Number System

The hexadecimal number system uses 16 symbols to represent values (hex means six). These include the symbols 0 through 9 and A through F (Figure C-4 on the previous page). The mathematical principles previously discussed also apply to hexadecimal (Figure C-7).

The primary reasons the hexadecimal number system is used with computers are (1) it can represent binary values in a more compact and readable form, and (2) the conversion between the binary and the hexadecimal number systems is very efficient.

An eight-digit binary number (a byte) can be represented by a two-digit hexadecimal number. For example, in the ASCII code, the character M is represented as 01001101. This value can be represented in the hexadecimal number system as 4D. One way to convert this binary number (4D) to a hexadecimal number is to divide the binary number (from right to left) into groups of four digits, calculate the value of each group, and then change any two-digit values (10 through 15) to the symbols A through F that are used in the hexadecimal number system (Figure C-8).

power of 2	2^3	2^2	2^1	2^0
positional value	8	4	2	1
binary	1	0	0	1

$$1 \quad 0 \quad 0 \quad 1 =$$
$$(1 \times 2^3) + (0 \times 2^2) + (0 \times 2^1) + (1 \times 2^0) =$$
$$(1 \times 8) + (0 \times 4) + (0 \times 2) + (1 \times 1) =$$
$$8 + 0 + 0 + 1 = 9$$

Figure C-6

power of 16	16^1	16^0
positional value	16	1
hexadecimal	A	5

$$A \quad 5 =$$
$$(10 \times 16^1) + (5 \times 16^0) =$$
$$(10 \times 16) + (5 \times 1) =$$
$$160 + 5 = 165$$

Figure C-7

positional value	8421	8421
binary	0100	1101
decimal	4	13
hexadecimal	4	D

Figure C-8

Index

C

E

O

P

Q

S

T

Credits

Chapter 1: Opener © Gazimal/Getty Images; Collage: Courtesy of SanDisk Corporation; PRNewsFoto/Apple; Courtesy of Logitech; Courtesy of Apple; Courtesy of Hewlett-Packard Company; PRNewsFoto/Polaroid Corporation; © Oleksiy Maksymenko Photography/Alamy; Courtesy of Nokia; © Hugh Threlfall/Alamy; PRNewsFoto/Nintendo; 1-1© Noel Hendrickson/Getty Images; PRNewsFoto/Apple; © David L. Moore - Lifestyle/Alamy; © Jupiterimages/Comstock Images/Alamy; © curved-light/Alamy; © Brad Wilson/Getty Images; © Jupiterimages/Thinkstock/Alamy; Courtesy of Adobe Systems, Inc; Adobe product screenshot(s) reprinted with permission from Adobe Systems Incorporated; 1-3 Courtesy of Hewlett-Packard Company; Courtesy of Logitech; Courtesy of Logitech; Courtesy of Kingston Technology Corporation; Courtesy of NETGEAR; Courtesy of SanDisk Corporation; Courtesy of SanDisk Corporation; Courtesy of LaCie; Courtesy of Hewlett-Packard Company; Courtesy of Hewlett-Packard Company; Figure 1-4 Courtesy of Seagate Technology; 1-5 © Wm. Baker/GhostWorx Images/Alamy; © Jupiterimages/ Thinkstock/Alamy; 1-6 © LdF/iStockphoto; Courtesy of Acer America, Inc; Courtesy of Hewlett-Packard Company; Courtesy of Hewlett-Packard Company; 1-7 PRNewsFoto/Verizon Wireless, Achille Bigliardi; Courtesy of Dell, Inc; PRNewsFoto/VerizonWireless; Courtesy of Hewlett-Packard Company; Courtesy of Nokia; © Oleksiy Maksymenko Photography/Alamy; Courtesy of Hewlett-Packard Company; Courtesy of Microsoft Corporation; Courtesy of Hewlett-Packard Company; 1-11 © Tony Freeman/PhotoEdit; 1-12 Courtesy of Hewlett-Packard Company; Courtesy of Hewlett-Packard Company; Courtesy of Kingston Technology Corporation; Courtesy of Corel Corporation; Courtesy of Hewlett-Packard Company; 1-15 Courtesy of Dell, Inc; 1-16 Courtesy of Apple; 1-17© Dmitry Bomshtein/iStockphoto; 1-18© PSL Images/Alamy; 1-19 (top) © Oleksiy Maksymenko Photography; (bottom) Courtesy of Nokia; 1-20 © Yunus Arakon/ iStockphoto; 1-21 Courtesy of Intermec Technologies Corporation; 1-22 Courtesy of Apple; 1-23 Courtesy of Sony Electronics Inc; © eva serrabassa/iStockphoto; 1-24 © Ian Leonard/Alamy; © ST-Images/Alamy; © Graham Hebditch/Alamy; 1-25 Courtesy of Hewlett-Packard Company; 1-26 Courtesy of IBM Corporation; 1-27 Courtesy of IBM Corporation; 1-28 Courtesy of Toyota; Courtesy of Daimler Mercedes-Benz; © Jupiterimages; 1-29 © Stockbyte/Getty Images; © Heather Gail Delaney/Alamy; Courtesy of Xerox Corporation; Jose Luis Pelaez, Inc./Getty Images; Courtesy of Fujitsu Technology Solutions; 1-30 Courtesy of Intuit; © Kin Images/Getty Images; Courtesy of Apple; © Editorial Image, LLC/Alamy; 1-31 © Dwayne Newton/PhotoEdit; 1-32 © Lester Lefkowitz/Getty Images; © iStockphoto; © Myrleen Ferguson Cate/PhotoEdit; © blue jean images/Getty Images; 1-33 © Darryl Bush/San Francisco Chronicle/Corbis; 1-34 © Justin Pumfrey/Getty Images; 1-35 © Kin Images/Getty Images; © Dwayne Newton/PhotoEdit; © Myrleen Ferguson Cate/PhotoEdit; © Darryl Bush/San Francisco Chronicle/Corbis; © Justin Pumfrey/Getty Images; 1-36 © Thomas Barwick/Getty Images; 1-38 AP Photo/The Post-Tribune, Leslie Adkins; 1-39 © Pigeon Productions SA/Getty Images; 1-40a AP Photo; 1-40 Reza Estakhrian/Getty Images; 1-42 Courtesy of Garmin Ltd; Looking Ahead 1-1 iStockphoto; Innovative Computing 1-1 Courtesy of Banner Health; Innovative Computing 1-2 © Stockbyte/ Getty Images; Computer Usage @ Work © Digital Vision; HTT1-1 1-44 © Henryk Sadura/Alamy; Looking Ahead 1-1 iStockphoto; Trailblazer 1 © Justin Sullivan/Getty Images; Trailblazer 2 © Rob Kim/Landov. **Special Feature 1:** 1937 Courtesy of Iowa State University; 1937 Courtesy of Iowa State University; 1937 Courtesy of Iowa State University; 1943 Photo courtesy of The Computer History Museum; 1943 Photo courtesy of The Computer History Museum; 1945 From The Shelby White and Leon Levy Archives Center, Institute for Advanced Study, Princeton, NJ, USA/ Photo: Alan Richards; 1946 From the Collections of the University of Pennsylvania Archives; 1947 © IBM Corporate Archives; 1947 © IBM Corporate Archives; 1951 Courtesy Unisys Corporation; 1952 Courtesy of Hagley Museum and Library; 1953 © IBM Corporate Archives; 1957 © IBM Corporate Archives; 1957 © IBM Corporate Archives; 1957 Courtesy of the Department of the Navy; 1958 Courtesy of Texas Instruments; 1958 Courtesy of Texas Instruments; 1958 Courtesy of Texas Instruments; 1959 © IBM Corporate Archives; 1960 Courtesy of Hagley Museum and Library; 1964 © IBM Corporate Archives; 1964 © IBM Corporate Archives; 1964 © IBM Corporate Archives; 1965 Courtesy of Dartmouth College; 1965 Courtesy of Hewlett-Packard Company; 1969 © IBM Corporate Archives; 1970 © IBM Corporate Archives; 1971 Courtesy of Intel Corporation; 1971 Courtesy of Intel Corporation; 1975 Photo courtesy of Computer History Museum; 1975 Courtesy of Palo Alto Research Center; 1976 © Bettmann/CORBIS; 1979 Photo courtesy of Computer History Museum; 1980 © IBM Corporate Archives; 1980 © Doug Wilson/CORBIS; 1981 © IBM Corporate Archives; 1982 Courtesy of Zoom Telephonics, Inc; 1983 © PARS International; 1983 © IBM Corporate Archives; 1984 ©SSPL/The Image Works; 1984 Courtesy of Hewlett-Packard Company; 1986 © Lane V. Erickson/ Shutterstock.com; 1989 ©Photo: Fabian Bachrach. Courtesy of W3C; 1989 Courtesy of Intel Corporation; 1989 ©Wolfgang Kaehler/Corbis; 1991 ©NMPFT/SSPL/The Image Works; 1992 Courtesy of Microsoft Corporation; 1993 Courtesy of Intel Corporation; 1993 Courtesy of Microsoft Corporation; 1993 © Costa Cruise Lines/Getty Images; 1993 Courtesy of Garmin International; 1994 AP Photo/Paul Sakuma; 1994 Courtesy of Mark D. Martin; 1994 Courtesy of Netscape Communications Corporation; 1994 Courtesy of Larry Ewing and The Gimp; 1995 PRNewsFoto/eBay, Inc; 1995 Courtesy of Oracle; 1995 © Reuters/Landov; 1996 Courtesy of Microsoft Corporation; 1996 Courtesy of Palm, Inc; 1997 iStockphoto; 1997 Associated Press; 1998 Newscom; 1998 Courtesy of Google; 1998 Courtesy of Microsoft Corporation; 1998 © Brad Cherson/ Alamy; 1999 Courtesy of Intel Corporation; 1999 Courtesy of Microsoft Corporation; 1999 © CLM/Shutterstock.com; 1999 © Tan Kian Khoon/Shutterstock.com; 2000 AP Photo/PR Newswire; 2000 Courtesy of Microsoft Corporation; 2000 Courtesy of Microsoft Corporation; 2000 © B Busco/Getty Images; 2000 Courtesy of Intel Corporation; 2001 Wikimedia Foundation; 2001 Courtesy of Microsoft Corporation; 2001 Courtesy of Microsoft Corporation; 2002 © Yoshikazu Tsuno/AFP/Getty Images; 2002 Courtesy of Intel Corporation; 2003 Courtesy of ViewSonic Corporation; 2002 Courtesy of Intel Corporation; 2002 © Scott Goodwin Photography; 2002 Courtesy of Palm, Inc; 2003 © LWA- JDC/CORBIS; 2003 © Royalty-Free/CORBIS; 2003 © Jim Cummins/CORBIS; 2003 © Ed Bock/CORBIS; 2003 © Koichi Kamoshida/Getty Images; 2003 Courtesy of Microsoft Corporation; 2003 © Getty Images; 2003 © REUTERS/Mannie Garcia; 2003 Courtesy of MySpace; 2004 ISSEI KATO/Reuters/Landov; 2004 Courtesy of Facebook; 2004 Associated Press; 2004 Courtesy of Facebook; 2004 Courtesy of Sony Electronics Inc; 2004 Courtesy of SanDisk Corporation; 2004 Courtesy of Larry Ewing and The Gimp; 2004 ©Apple Computer/Handout/Reuters/Corbis; 2004 Courtesy of Palm, Inc; 2005 HANDOUT/KRT/ Newscom; 2005 Courtesy of Microsoft Corporation; 2005 © PRNewsFoto/Microsoft Corp; 2006 © Courtney Weittenbiller/iStockphoto; 2006 AP Images/ Nintendo; 2006 AP Images/Kevork Djansezian; 2006 © Reinhold Tscherwitschke; 2006 Courtesy of Intel Corporation; 2006 Courtesy of Intel Corporation; 2006 PRNewsFoto/Nintendo; 2007 © Neville Elder/Corbis; 2007 Courtesy of Intel Corporation; 2007 © Oliver Leedham/Alamy; 2007 © Suzy Bennett/Alamy; 2007 Courtesy of Apple; 2007 iStockphoto; 2007 Courtesy of Microsoft Corporation; 2007 PRNewsFoto/Sony Electronics, Inc; 2007 Courtesy of Microsoft; 2008 AP Photo/Paul Sakuma; 2008 Justin Sullivan/Getty Images; 2008 Courtesy of Dell Inc; 2008 Courtesy of Apple; 2008 AP Photo/Mark Lennihan; 2008 Courtesy of Microsoft Corporation; 2008 Courtesy of Mozilla; 2008 AP Photo/Paul Sakuma; 2008 Courtesy of Microsoft Corporation; 2008 iStockphoto; 2009 Courtesy of Coby Electronics Corporation; 2009 © Alex Segre/Alamy; 2009 Courtesy of Microsoft Corporation; 2009 Courtesy of Intel Corporation; 2009 © Arthur Turner/Alamy; 2010 Courtesy of Microsoft Corporation; 2010 Courtesy of AMD; 2010 Courtesy of Toshiba America Electronic Components, Inc; AP Photo/Paul Sakuma; 2011© iStockphoto; 2011 © PSL Images/ Alamy; 2011 PRNewsFoto/Verizon Wireless; 2011 © Joshua Kristal/Alamy; 2011 Courtesy of HTC Corporation. **Chapter 2:** Opener © Jose Luis Pelaez Inc./Getty Images; Opening Collage © ST-Images/Alamy; Courtesy of Cisco; 2-1 Courtesy of Microsoft Corporation; 2-2 PRNewsFoto/AT&T Inc; © Blend Images/Alamy; © image100/Alamy; © UpperCut Images/Alamy; © Stockbyte/Alamy; © Dann Tardif/Corbis; 2-3 Step 1 © ngirish/iStockphoto; 2-3 Step 2 © blue_Iq/iStockphoto; 2-3 Step 3 ARRIS C4® CMTS Courtesy of Arris Systems, Inc; 2-3 Step 4 © Stephen Chernin/Getty Images; 2-3 Step 6 Courtesy of Fujitsu Technology Solutions; 2-7 © ST-images/Alamy; 2-21 Courtesy of Hewlett-Packard Company; © titi matei/iStockphoto; © Glowimages/Getty Images; Courtesy of Hewlett-Packard Company; 2-25 Step 1, © Colin Young-Wolff/PhotoEdit; 2-25 Step 2, © Mark Evans/iStockphoto; 2-25 Step 3, © Andrew Lewis/ iStockphoto; 2-25 Step 4, © Alexander Hafemann/iStockphoto; 2-25 Step 5, Courtesy of Fujitsu Technology Solutions; 2-25 Step 6, © Ed Hidden/iStockphoto; 2-25 Step 7, © Oksana Perkins/ iStockphoto; 2-25 Step 8, © Bill Aron/PhotoEdit; 2-27 Step 1 Courtesy of Hewlett-Packard Company; 2-27 Step 2 Courtesy of Hewlett-Packard Company; 2-27 Step 3, Courtesy of Juniper Networks, Inc; 2-27 Step 4 Courtesy of Hewlett-Packard Company; 2-29 Step 2 Courtesy of Fujitsu Technology Solutions; 2-29 Step 3 Courtesy of Microsoft Corporation; 2-29 Step 4 Courtesy of Acer America, Inc; 2-29 Courtesy of Hewlett-Packard Company; 2-29 Step 5 Courtesy of Hewlett-Packard Company; 2-30 Courtesy of Sony Electronics Inc; Courtesy of Hewlett-Packard Company; (center) © Blend Images/Alamy; 2-31 Courtesy of Cisco; Courtesy of Siemens; © Argunova/Shutterstock.com; Courtesy of Logitech; Courtesy of Hewlett-Packard Company; Computer Usage @ Work © Picture Contact/Alamy; Trailblazer 1 © EPA/Landov; Trailblazer 2 AP Photo/Craig Ruttle; Looking Ahead 2-1 Courtesy of W3C; Innovative Computing 2-1 Courtesy of Microsoft Corporation; Innovative Computing 2-2 PRNewsFoto/Brookstone, Inc. **Special Feature 2:** © Photodisc/Alamy; © iStockphoto; © Digital Vision/Alamy; © Digital Vision/Alamy; © Alex Segre/Alamy. **Chapter 3:** Opener © Janis Christie/Getty Images; Collage © Getty Images; Courtesy of Corel Corporation; Courtesy of Microsoft Corporation; Courtesy of Microsoft Corporation; Courtesy of Microsoft Corporation; Courtesy of Nokia; Pinnacle Systems, Inc., a part of Avid Technology, Inc; Courtesy of Cakewalk Inc; Courtesy of Intuit Inc; 3-1 Courtesy of Microsoft Corporation; Courtesy of Adobe Systems Incorporated; Courtesy of Corel Corporation; 3-2 © Brooke Slezak/Getty Images; Courtesy of Hewlett-Packard Company; Courtesy of Hewlett-Packard Company; 3-14 Courtesy of Microsoft Corporation; 3-15 Courtesy of Research In Motion; PRNewsFoto/Verizon Wireless; Courtesy of Research In Motion; Courtesy of DataViz Inc; 3-16 Courtesy of Computer Systems Odessa Corporation; 3-17 Courtesy of Microsoft Corporation; 3-20 © Artiga Photo/Corbis; 3-21 Courtesy of Quark Inc; 3-22 © Picture Contact/Alamy; 3-23 Courtesy of Adobe Systems Incorporated; 3-24 Courtesy of Cakewalk Inc; 3-25 Courtesy of SumTotal Systems Inc; 3-26 Courtesy of Microsoft Corporation; 3-28 Courtesy of Intuit Inc; 3-28b © Digital Vision/Getty Images; 3-29 Courtesy of Nolo; 3-30 Courtesy of 2nd Story Software, Inc; 3-32 Courtesy of Corel Corporation; 3-33 Courtesy of Corel Corporation; 3-35 Courtesy of Encore, Inc., a Navarre Corporation Company; 3-36 Pinnacle Systems, Inc., a part of Avid Technology, Inc; 3-37 Courtesy of IMSI/Design; 3-38 Courtesy of Microsoft Corporation; 3-39 Courtesy of Encore Software, Inc. a Navarre Corporation Company; 3-40 AP Photo/Tony Giberson; 3-41a © Bernhard Classen/Alamy; 3-41b © Lon C. Dhiel/PhotoEdit; 3-41c © Fred Prouser/Reuters/Corbis; 3-46 Courtesy of Moodle; Computer Usage @ Work, © iStockphoto; Trailblazer 1 AP Photo/Steven Senne; Trailblazer 2 © Tom Wagner/Corbis; Looking Ahead 3-1 Courtesy of Microsoft Corporation; Innovative Computing 3-1 © Tetra Images/Getty Images; Innovative Computing 3-2 © Wave Royalty Free/Alamy; Web Research © Brian Stablyk/ Getty Images. **Special Feature 3:** Figure 1 Courtesy of Microsoft Corporation; Courtesy of Verizon Wireless; © Alex Slobodkin/iStockphoto; © Image Source Black/Alamy; © iStockphoto; © David Hancock/Alamy; Courtesy of Skype; © CostinT/iStockphoto; Figure 3 Courtesy of Microsoft Corporation; © Stephen Wilkes/Getty Images; Figure 5 © CAP/Getty Images; Figure 7 © Picturenet/Getty Images; Courtesy of Research In Motion; © Gary Corbett/Alamy; Courtesy of Microsoft Corporation; Figure 9 Courtesy of Jive Software; © Jeff Greenberg/Alamy; Figure 11 © David R. Fraizer/PhotoEdit; © Jochen Tack/Alamy; Courtesy of Parliant Corporation; Figure 13 Courtesy of Cisco Systems, Inc; © Alex Slobodkin/iStockphoto; Courtesy of Zoom Technologies; Figure 15 © Reggie Casagrande/Getty Images; Figure 17 Courtesy of NASA; © PhotoAlto/Alamy; Figure 18 AP Photo/Screenshot, Peter Zschunke; Figure 21 Courtesy of Microsoft Corporation; p206a © John Lund/Drew Kelly/Sam Diephuis/Getty Images; p206b © Photodisc/Alamy; p206c © MIXA/Alamy; p206 © MIXA/Getty Images; p207 © Corbis RF/ Alamy; p207 © Tetra Images/Getty Images. **Chapter 4:** Opener © E Dygas/Getty Images; Collage Courtesy of Advanced Micro Devices; © imagebroker/Alamy; © Lenscap/Alamy; Courtesy of Intel Corporation; Courtesy of Kingston Technology Corporation; Courtesy of Hewlett-Packard Company; Courtesy of Hewlett-Packard Company; © Dino Ablakovic/iStockphoto; Courtesy of Intel Corporation; Courtesy of Creative Technology Ltd; 4-1 Courtesy of Dell, Inc; Courtesy of Apple; PRNewsFoto/Apple; © Mark Ralston/AFP/Getty Images; Courtesy of Palm, Inc; Courtesy of SanDisk Corporation; Courtesy of Microsoft Corporation; 4-1 Courtesy of FUJIFILM U.S.A; Courtesy of Hewlett-Packard Company; © iStockphoto; Courtesy of Dell, Inc; 4-2 Courtesy of Creative Technology Ltd; Courtesy of Sapphire Technology; Courtesy of Intel Corporation; Courtesy of Kingston Technology Corporation; Courtesy of Hewlett-Packard Company; Courtesy of Hewlett-Packard Company; 4-3 Courtesy of Intel Corporation; 4-5 © Paul Paladin/Shutterstock.com; 4-8 Courtesy of Intel Corporation; Courtesy of Advanced Micro Devices; 4-9 © KirstyPargeter/iStockphoto; 4-10 Courtesy of Puget Custom Computers; 4-12 © iStockphoto; 4-15 Courtesy of Logitech; Courtesy of Hewlett-Packard Company; 4-16 © Wayne Eastep/Getty Images; 4-18 Courtesy of Seagate Technology LLC; Courtesy of Kingston Technology Corporation; Courtesy of ViewSonic Corporation; Courtesy of Seagate Technology LLC; Courtesy of Kingston Technology Corporation; 4-20 © Andrew Howe/iStockphoto; © Jaroslaw Wojcik/iStockphoto; 4-23 © Kim Jae-Hwan/Getty Images; Courtesy of Creative Technologies Ltd; 4-25 © WireImageStock/Masterfile; © WireImageStock/Masterfile; 4-27 © Andrew Howe/iStockphoto; 4-28 © David Kilpatrick/Alamy; © Sandeep Subba/iStockphoto; Courtesy of USB Implementers Forum; 4-29 Courtesy of Hewlett-Packard Company; 4-30 Courtesy of Hewlett-Packard Company; 4-32 © Alina Solovyova-Vincent/iStockphoto; © Ruslan Kerimov/iStockphoto; © Sascha Burkard/iStockphoto; Courtesy of Hewlett-Packard Company; © Potapova Valeriya/iStockphoto; © iStockphoto; 4-33 Courtesy of Belkin International; 4-34 Courtesy of Nokia;

Courtesy of Acer Inc; 4-35 Courtesy of Motion Computing, Inc; 4-36 Courtesy of Intel Corporation; Courtesy of Kingston Technology Corporation; 4-37 Courtesy of Hewlett-Packard Company; 4-38 © Kin Images/Getty Images; © Dwayne Newton/PhotoEdit; © Myrleen Ferguson Cate/PhotoEdit; © Darryl Bush/San Francisco Chronicle/Corbis; © Justin Pumfrey/Getty Images; 4-39 © Paul Maguire/Alamy; Courtesy of Merridrew Enterprises; © Lon C. Diehl/PhotoEdit Inc; © Gary Herrington Photography; Courtesy of Belkin International, Inc; © Felicia Martinez/PhotoEdit; Computer Usage @ Work © Gary Dineen/NBAE/Getty Images; Trailblazer 1 © Yoshikazu Tsuno/AFP/Getty Images; Trailblazer 2 © Andy Rain/Bloomberg via Getty Images; Innovative Computing 4-1 © China Photos/Getty Images; Innovative Computing 4-2 AP Photo/iRobot Corp; Looking Ahead 4-1 Felix Schmidberger; Web Research © Mikael Karlsson/Alamy **Chapter 5:** Opener © D. Hurst/Alamy; Collage Courtesy of Hewlett-Packard Company; Courtesy of Logic3 plc; Courtesy of Logic3 plc; © Hugh Threlfall/Alamy; PRNewsFoto/Metrologic Instruments, Inc; Courtesy of Wacom Technology Corporation; Courtesy of APC by Schneider Electric; Courtesy of Hewlett-Packard Company; Courtesy of Logitech; Courtesy of Logitech; Courtesy of Logitech; Courtesy of Plantronics, Inc; 5-1 © Medioimages/Getty Images; © Carmen Martínez Banús/iStockphoto; © Getty Images; © Beaconstox/Alamy; © Tetra Images/Alamy; © Keith Morris/Alamy; © Christopher Dodge/Shutterstock.com; © Denkou Images/Alamy; © BlueSoul/Shutterstock.com; © Daniel Acker/Bloomberg via Getty Images; © iStockphoto; © iStockphoto; © KAKIMAGE/Alamy; © Bonnie Kamin/PhotoEdit; © Stefan Klein/iStockphoto; © Anatoly Vartanov/iStockphoto; © Phil Degginger/Alamy; © Sandeep Subba/iStockphoto; © Natalie Jezzard/Alamy; © iStockphoto; 5-2 Courtesy of Microsoft Corporation; 5-4 © InstinctDesign/Shutterstock.com; 5-5 © Alex Segre/Alamy; PRNewsFoto/Verizon Wireless; © Alex Segre/Alamy; 5-6 Courtesy of Microsoft Corporation; 5-7 Courtesy of Gyration; 5-9 © Jupiterimages; 5-10 Adam Balatoni/iStockphoto; 5-11 © Photodisc/Getty Images; 5-12Courtesy of Dell, Inc; AP Photo/Paul Sakuma; 5-13 © Henry George Beeker/Alamy; 5-14 Courtesy of Microsoft Corporation; 5-15 © Chris Rout/Alamy; 5-16 © 2licht/Alamy; © vario images GmbH & Co.KG/Alamy; © Ronald Karpilo/Alamy; 5-17 Courtesy of Nokia; Courtesy of BoxWave Corporation; Courtesy of Nokia; 5-18 Courtesy of Verizon Wireless and plawa feinwerktechnik GmbH & Co; 5-19 Courtesy of Logitech; © Arthur Turner/Alamy; Courtesy of Logic3 plc; © ST-images/Alamy; Handout/MCT/Newscom; PRNewsFoto/SplitFish GameWare Inc; 5-20 Courtesy of Sony Electronics Inc; 5-21 © Andersen RossGetty Images; 5-22 Courtesy of Nuance; 5-23 © ICP/Alamy; 5-24 Courtesy of Corel Corporation; Courtesy of Sony Electronics Inc; 5-25 © Corbis Premium RF/Alamy; 5-26 © Steve Chenn/CORBIS; 5-27 Courtesy of Hewlett-Packard Company; Courtesy of C-Technologies/Anoto Group AB; Courtesy of Visioneer, Inc; Courtesy of AZTEK, Inc.; 5-28 Courtesy of Hewlett-Packard Company; Courtesy of Acer Inc; 5-31 © Andy Sacks/Getty Images; 5-32 © Colin Young-Wolff/Photo Edit; © Phil Degginger/Getty Images; 5-33 Courtesy of Intermec Technologies; 5-34 © Spencer Grant/Photo Edit; 5-36 Courtesy of Intermec Technologies; 5-37 Courtesy of UPEK Inc; 5-38 Courtesy of Recognition Systems, Inc; 5-39 AP Photo/Canadian Press, Adrian Wyld; © Robert F. Balazik/Shutterstock.com; 5-40 © Robin Nelson/PhotoEdit; 5-41 © Bill Aron/PhotoEdit; 5-42 AP Photo/Al Behrman; 5-43 © Kin Images/Getty Images; © Dwayne Newton/PhotoEdit; © Myrleen Ferguson Cate/PhotoEdit; © Darryl Bush/San Francisco Chronicle/Corbis; © Justin Pumfrey/Getty Images; 5-44 © STUART WALKER/Alamy; 5-46 Courtesy of NaturalPoint, Inc; Computer Usage @ Work © Chloe Johnson/Alamy; Trailblazer 1 Toshiyuki Aizawa/Bloomberg via Getty Images; Trailblazer 2 AP Photo/Michael Schmelling; Innovative Computing 5-1 Courtesy of Microsoft Corporation and Avid Technology; Innovative Computing 5-2 Courtesy of Intel Corporation; Looking Ahead 5-1 AP Photo/Georgia Tech, Gary W. Meek; Web Research © iStockphoto. **Chapter 6:** Opener © David R. Frazier Photolibrary, Inc./Alamy; Collage Courtesy of Nokia; Courtesy of Nokia; Courtesy of Logitech; PRNewsFoto/SANYO; Courtesy of Hewlett-Packard Company; Courtesy of Hewlett-Packard Company; © image100/Corbis; Courtesy of Palm, Inc; YONHAPNEWS AGENCY/Newscom; Courtesy of FUJIFILM USA; Courtesy of Palm Inc; 6-1 Image(s) reprinted with permission from ViewSonic Corporation; Courtesy of Hewlett-Packard Company; PRNewsFoto/Verizon Wireless; Courtesy of HTC and Microsoft Corporation; Courtesy of Nokia; Courtesy of Apple; Courtesy of Logitech; Courtesy of Sony Electronics Inc; Courtesy of Corel Corporation; © Getty Images; Courtesy of Corel Corporation; © Oleksiy Maksymenko/Alamy; 6-2 PRNewsFoto/Envision Peripherals Inc; 6-3 Courtesy of Hewlett-Packard Company; 6-4 Courtesy of Hewlett-Packard Company; © iStockphoto; © AFP/Getty Images; Courtesy of Nokia; Courtesy of Apple; 6-6 Courtesy of Advanced Micro Devices; 6-8 PRNewsFoto/LG Electronics, Inc; 6-9 AP Photo/Tina Fineberg; 6-10 Image(s) reprinted with permission from ViewSonic Corporation; 6-13 Courtesy of Hewlett-Packard Company; © Gari Wyn Williams/Alamy; Courtesy of Nokia; © Michael Newman/PhotoEdit; Courtesy of Canon; 6-14 Courtesy of Hewlett-Packard Company; Courtesy of Xerox Corporation; PRNewsFoto/Americas Best Value Inn; © JurgaR/iStockphoto; PRNewsFoto/Tabblo Inc; 6-16 Courtesy of Hewlett-Packard Company; 6-17 Courtesy of Hewlett-Packard Company; 6-18 Courtesy of Hewlett-Packard Company; 6-20 Courtesy of Hewlett-Packard Company; 6-21 Courtesy of Mitsubishi Digital Electronics America, Inc; Courtesy of Epson America, Inc; 6-22 Courtesy of Canon; 6-23 Courtesy of Intermec Technologies; 6-24 Courtesy of Hewlett-Packard Company; 6-25 Courtesy of Oki Data Amercas, Inc; 6-26 Courtesy of Creative Technology Ltd; 6-27 © Royalty-Free/Corbis; 6-28 © Hugh Threlfall/Alamy; Courtesy of Apple; 6-29 © Purestock/Getty Images; PRNewsFoto/SANYO; 6-30 Copyright 2001–2007 SMART Technologies Inc. All rights reserved; 6-31 Courtesy of Logic3 plc; Courtesy of Logitech; © picturesbyrob/Alamy; 6-32 © Kin Images/Getty Images; © Dwayne Newton/PhotoEdit; © Myrleen Ferguson Cate/PhotoEdit; © Darryl Bush/San Francisco Chronicle/Corbis; © Justin Pumfrey/Getty Images; 6-34 Courtesy of Enabling Technologies; © Don Farrall/Getty Images; Computer Usage @ Work Courtesy of NASA; 6-35 © Mark Evans/iStockphoto; Trailblazer 1 © Fujifotos/The Image Works; Trailblazer 2 Norm Betts/Bloomberg via Getty Images; Innovative Computing 6-1 Courtesy of EDGE Tech Corp; Looking Ahead 6-1 Photo: Greg Reekie, Courtesy of Xerox Corporation; PS@Home Courtesy of Hewlett-Packard Company. **Special Feature 6:** Opener top © SuperStock/Alamy; Opener middle © Design Pics Inc./Alamy; Opener bottom © Somos Images LLC/Alamy; Figure 1 © Balázs Öcsi/iStockphoto; Courtesy of JVC U.S.A; PRNewsFoto/VIZIO; © Blend Images/Alamy; Courtesy of Sony Electronics Inc; © Alex Slobodkin/iStockphoto; Courtesy of Microsoft Corporation; © Silvrshootr/iStockphoto; Figure 2 Courtesy of Sony Electronics Inc; © Royalty-Free/CORBIS; Courtesy of JVC U.S.A; Figure 3 Courtesy of Hewlett-Packard Company; © mbirdy/iStockphoto; Courtesy of JVC U.S.A; screenshot photo © Ben Blankenburg/iStockphoto; Figure 4 © zoomstudio/iStockphoto; Courtesy of Hewlett-Packard Company; Courtesy of Pinnacle Systems Inc; Courtesy of Pinnacle Systems Inc; © Matej Pribelsky/iStockphoto; Courtesy of Sony Electronics Inc; screenshot photo © Pete Saloutos/GettyImages; Figure 5 Courtesy of Microsoft Corporation; Figure 7 Courtesy of Pinnacle Systems Inc; Figure 8 Courtesy of Pinnacle Systems Inc; Figure 9 Courtesy of Pinnacle Systems Inc. **Chapter 7:** Opener © Asiaselects/Alamy; Collage Image copyright OnlyVectors, 2009. Used under license from Shutterstock.com © mediacolor's/Alamy; PRNewsFoto/Panasonic; PRNewsFoto/Toshiba Storage Device Division; Courtesy of Kingston Technology Corporation; Courtesy of Hewlett-Packard Company; Courtesy of Western Digital Corporation; Courtesy of Lexar Media; 7-1 © Luis Carolos Torres/iStockphoto; Courtesy of Western Digital Corporation; Courtesy of Western Digital Corporation; PRNewsFoto/EMC Corporation; Courtesy of Hewlett-Packard Company; © Bill Storage/iStockphoto; © imagebroker/Alamy; © bluliq/Shutterstock.com © vario images GmbH & Co.KG/Alamy; © MedioImages/Getty Images; © Bill Aron/PhotoEdit; © Profimedia International s.r.o./Alamy; Courtesy of SanDisk Corporation and Lexar Media; Courtesy of USB Implementers Forum Inc; © Bill Storage/iStockphoto; Courtesy of SanDisk Corporation; 7-3 © ImageState Royalty Free/Alamy; -Courtesy of Hewlett-Packard Company; Courtesy of Kingston Technology Corporation; 7-5 Courtesy of Hewlett-Packard Company; Courtesy of Seagate Technology LLC; 7-9 Courtesy of Western Digital Corporation; 7-12 Courtesy of Intel Corporation; 7-13 Courtesy of NETGEAR; 7-14 Courtesy of Western Digital Corporation; Courtesy of Iomega; 7-15 Courtesy of Hitachi Global Storage; 7-16 © Lit Liu/iStockphoto; 7-17 Courtesy of Toshiba America Electronic Components; 7-18 ©Melissa King Shutterstock.com; Courtesy of Lexar Media; © Lenscap/Alamy; Courtesy of Hewlett-Packard Company; © Niels Poulsen/Alamy; Courtesy of SanDisk Corporation; Courtesy of Kingston Technology Corporation; 7-19 Courtesy of Pretec; Courtesy of SanDisk Corporation; Courtesy of Lexar Media; 7-20 Courtesy of Delkin Devices, Inc; Courtesy of Lexar Media; 7-21 Courtesy of SanDisk Corporation; 7-22 © imagebroker/Alamy; Courtesy of USB Implementers Forum Inc; 7-25 © Jeffrey Coolidge/Getty Images; 7-29 Courtesy of Merriam-Webster Inc; Courtesy of Imation Corp; Courtesy of Caliper Corporation; 7-30 Courtesy of Microsoft Corporation; © Gary Herrington Photography; 7-31 Jay Laprete/Bloomberg via Getty Images; Courtesy of Hewlett-Packard Company; Courtesy of Shutterfly, Inc; 7-32 © 3DProfi/Shutterstock.com; Courtesy of Caliper Corporation; 7-34 © Koichi Kamoshida/Getty Images; Courtesy of Sony Computer Entertainmnet America LLC; 7-35 Courtesy of Sony Electronics Inc; 7-36 © Derek Mitchell/Alamy; 7-37 Copyright © Bill Aron/Photo Edit; 7-39 © Wes Thompson/CORBIS; 7-40 © Kin Images/Getty Images; © Dwayne Newton/PhotoEdit; © Myrleen Ferguson Cate/PhotoEdit; © Darryl Bush/San Francisco Chronicle/Corbis; © Justin Pumfrey/Getty Images; Computer Usage @ Work © Chris Rank/Bloomberg via Getty Images; Trailblazer 1 AP Photo/Kevin Sullivan; Trailblazer 2 Courtesy of IBM Research; Innovative Computing 7-1 Courtesy of Findaway World (www.playaway.com); Innovative Computing 7-2 Courtesy of MoxyCard; Looking Ahead 7-1 The Long Now Foundation; Web Research © Robert Sullivan/Getty Images. **Chapter 8:** Opener © Eric Draper/Getty Images; Collage: Courtesy of Microsoft Corporation; © Jason Brindel Commercial/Alamy; Courtesy of Research In Motion, Courtesy of Symantec Corp; PRNewsFoto/RealNetworks, Inc; 8-1 © Valeriy Kryvsha/iStockphoto; 8-1 Courtesy of Dell Inc; 8-1 Courtesy of Hewlett-Packard Company; 8-8 Step 1 Courtesy of Micron Technology, Inc; 8-8 Step 2 Courtesy of Seagate Technologies; 8-9 Courtesy of Hewlett-Packard Company; 8-9 Courtesy of Western Digital Corporation; 8-9c Courtesy of Printronix; 8-13 Courtesy of Microsoft Corporation; 8-19AP Photo/Peter Zschunke; 8-20 Courtesy of KDE e.V; 8-22 PRNewsFoto/Brother International Corporation; 8-23 Courtesy of Microsoft Corporation; 8-24 Reuters/David Becker/Landov; 8-25 © Jason Brindel Commercial/Alamy; 8-26 Courtesy of Research In Motion; 8-34 Courtesy of Axialis Software; 8-35 Courtesy of Check Point Software Technologies Ltd; 8-37 Courtesy of Symantec Corp; 8-38 Courtesy of Rhapsody International, Inc; 8-39 Courtesy of Nero AG; 8-40 Courtesy of Symantec Corp; Computer Usage @ Work © Keith Morris/Alamy; 8-41 Courtesy of Dell, Inc; Trailblazer 1 Photo © Tony Avelar/Bloomberg via Getty Images; Trailblazer 2 © Kim Kulish/CORBIS; Innovative Computing 8-1 © Ingram Publishing/Superstock Limited/Alamy; Looking Ahead 8-1 Tingrui Pan/UC Davis photo; Web Research © Jurgen Reisch/Getty Images. **Special Feature 8:** Figure 1 © Heidi Kristensen/iStockphoto; Courtesy of Dell, Inc; © Tony Tremblay/iStockphoto; Courtesy of Apple; Courtesy of FUJIFILM USA; 1 AP Photo/Paul Sakuma; Courtesy of Apple; 1 Courtesy of Dell, Inc; p445 Courtesy of Hewlett-Packard Company; Figure 2 (page 446, top to bottom) Courtesy of SanDisk Corporation; Courtesy of Avid Technology; Courtesy of Seagate Technology LLC; Courtesy of Microsoft Corporation; Courtesy of Hewlett-Packard Company; 2 Courtesy of Logitech; Courtesy of Microsoft Corporation; Courtesy of Logitech; Courtesy of US Robotics; ©Alex Slobodkin/iStockphoto; Courtesy of Microsoft Corporation; Courtesy of Sony Electronics Inc; Figure 2 (page 447, top to bottom) Courtesy of Hewlett-Packard Company; Courtesy of Hewlett-Packard Company; Courtesy of Intel Corporation; Courtesy of Kingston Technology Corporation; Courtesy of UMAX; 2 Courtesy of Creative Technology Ltd; Courtesy of Logitech; Courtesy of SanDisk Corporation; Courtesy of Belkin International Inc; Courtesy of Advanced Micro Devices, Inc; Courtesy of Logitech; © Norman Chan/iStockphoto; p450 Courtesy of Dell, Inc; Courtesy of Hewlett-Packard Company; Courtesy of Hewlett-Packard Company; Figure 5 PRNewsFoto/Mindjet LLC; Figure 6 Courtesy of Fujitsu Technology Solutions; Figure 7 © MadTatyana/Shutterstock.com; Figure 8 Courtesy of Motion Computing; p452 Courtesy of Nokia; Figure 9 Courtesy of Verizon Wireless; PRNewsFoto/Verizon Wireless; PRNewsFoto/Verizon Wireless; Courtesy of Microsoft Corporation; Figure10 Courtesy of Apple; p454 Courtesy of FUJIFILM USA; Figure 11 Courtesy of SanDisk Corporation; © Muhammad Khairul Syahir Bin Abd Haki/iStockphoto; © SasPartout/Shutterstock.com **Chapter 9:** Opener © Michael DeYoung; Collage: Courtesy of Belkin International; © David Anderson/Shutterstock.com; © Natalia Siverina/Shutterstock.com; © Hugh Threlfall/Alamy; PRNewsFoto/RealNetworks; Courtesy of Cisco; Courtesy of NETGEAR; Courtesy of Garmin Ltd; © Nicola Stratford/iStockphoto; Courtesy of Nokia; 9-1 Courtesy of IBM Corporation; © zentilia/iStockphoto; © Simon Smith/iStockphoto; Courtesy of Nokia; Courtesy of Nokia; Courtesy of Microsoft Corporation; Courtesy of Toyota U.S.A; PRNewsFoto/NAVIGON; © 2009 Jupiter Images Corporation; © 2009 Jupiter Images Corporation; © Mark Evans/iStockphoto; ©Simon Vine/Alamy; © Keith Binns/iStockphoto; © Luca di Filippo/iStockphoto; AP Photo/Koji Sasahara; © Long Ha/iStockphoto; © Alex Slobodkin/iStockphoto; 9-3 © David J. Green - Lifestyle/Alamy; © Tom Grill/Corbis; © Rob Wilkinson/Alamy; 9-4 Courtesy of NETGEAR; Courtesy of Intel Corporation; Courtesy of SMC Networks; © Justin Sullivan/Getty Images; © James Leynse/Corbis; 9-5 © Rudi Von Briel/PhotoEdit, Inc; 9-6 Courtesy of Garmin Ltd; © StockShot/Alamy; © Jasper James/Getty Images; Courtesy of Lok8u; © Fredrik Broman/Getty Images; Courtesy of Nokia; 9-7 Courtesy of Citrix Systems, Inc; 9-8 © Andersen Ross/Getty Images; Courtesy of Hewlett-Packard Company; © Javier Pierini/Getty Images; © Elena Elisseva/Shutterstock.com; 9-9 © jossnat/Shutterstock.com; © Luca di Filippo/iStockphoto; Courtesy of Symantec Corp; © Johanna Goodyear/iStockphoto; © by_nicholas/iStockphoto; 9-10 © Image Source/Imagestate; 9-11 Courtesy of Hewlett-Packard Company; © Jim Goldstein/Alamy; Courtesy of Nokia; ©Natalia Siverina/ Shutterstock.com; © terekhov igor/Shutterstock.com; Courtesy of Hewlett-Packard Company; 9-12 Courtesy of Toyota U.S.A; 9-13 Courtesy of Hewlett-Packard Company; 9-14 Courtesy of Hewlett-Packard Company; Courtesy of Fujitsu Technology Solutions; 9-15 Courtesy of Hewlett-Packard Company; Courtesy of Western Digital; Courtesy of Seagate Technology LLC; 9-16 Courtesy of Hewlett-Packard Company; Courtesy of Cisco; © jossnat/Shutterstock.com; 9-17 © Jakub Semeniuk/iStockphoto; 9-18 Courtesy of Hewlett-Packard Company; 9-19 Courtesy of Fujitsu Technology Solutions; © Yuji Mori/Getty Images; 9-21 Step 1a © James Leynse/Corbis; Step 1b © Getty Images; © Peter Titmuss/Alamy; Step 2 © James Leynse/Corbis; Step 3 Courtesy of Hewlett-Packard Company; 9-22 PRNewsFoto/Verizon Wireless; 9-23 Courtesy of Hewlett-Packard Company; 9-26 Courtesy of Motorola; 9-27© Erik S. Lesser/Landov; ©tiridifilm/iStockphotp; © image100/Alamy; Courtesy of Hewlett-Packard Company; 9-28 © cheyennezj/Shutterstock.com; Courtesy of Cisco; 9-29 Courtesy of Cisco; Courtesy of SMC Networks; 9-30 © CLEO PHOTOGRAPHY/Photo Edit; © F64/Getty Images; © Michael Newman/Photo Edit; © Bonnie Kamin/Photo Edit; ©Natalia Siverina/Shutterstock.com; 9-31 Courtesy of Cisco; Courtesy of Hewlett-Packard Company; Courtesy of Acer America Inc; Courtesy of Motorola, Inc; Courtesy of Dell, Inc; 9-32 Courtesy of Hewlett-Packard Company; Courtesy of NETGEAR; 9-33 PRNewsFoto/Verizon Wireless; Courtesy of Hewlett-Packard Company; © Natalia Siverina/Shutterstock.com; © Arkadiusz Stachowski/iStockphoto; 9-34 Courtesy of Hewlett-Packard Company; Courtesy of Motorola; Courtesy of Fujitsu Technology Solutions; Courtesy of IBM Corporation; 9-36 Courtesy of Hewlett-Packard

Company; 9-37 Courtesy of Hewlett-Packard Company;© Vladislav Ageshin/iStockphoto; 9-40 © Words and Meanings/Mark Sykes/Alamy; 9-41 © Vince Streano/CORBIS; Computer Usage @ Work © eliandric/iStockphoto; Trailblazer 1 © Kim Kulish/Corbis; Trailblazer 2 © Wolfgang Von Brauchitsch/Bloomberg News via Getty Images; Innovative Computing 9-1 AP Photo/The Charlotte Observer, Jeff Willhelm; Innovative Computing 9-2 © shapecharge/iStockphoto; Courtesy of Sling Media; Looking Ahead 9-1 "A wireless body area network of intelligent motion sensors for computer assisted physical rehabilitation" Emil Jovanov, Aleksandar Milenkovic, Chris Otto, and Piet C de Groen, J Neuroengineering Rehabil. 2005; 2: 6. Published online 2005 March 1. doi: 10.1186/1743-0003-2-6.PMCID: PMC552302 reproduced under Creative Commons License 2.0; Innovative Computing 9-2 © shapecharge/iStockphoto; Courtesy of Sling Media; Web Research © Konstantin Inozemtsev/iStockphoto. **Chapter 10:** Opener © Jack Hollingsworth/Getty Images; 10-1 Step 1 Courtesy of FujiFilm USA; © Alex Mares-Manton/Getty Images; Step 2 Courtesy of Seagate Technology LLC; Step 3 Courtesy of Hewlett-Packard Company; Steps 5 & 6 © Alex Mares-Manton/Getty Images; Courtesy of Zebra Technologies International, LLC; desktop PC Courtesy of Hewlett-Packard Company; 10-1 background © Don Smetzer/Alamy; 10-2a © Marcin Balcerzak/iStockphoto; 10-7c © zhang bo/iStockphoto; 10-9 © Davis Barber/PhotoEdit; © Davis Barber/PhotoEdit; 10-25 © Bernhard Classen/Alamy; Trailblazer 1 Courtesy of the National Academy of Engineering; Trailblazer 2 © Justin Sullivan/Getty Images; Innovative Computing 10-1 Courtesy of Challenge Online Games, Inc; Innovative Computing 10-2 David Paul Morris/Getty Images; Looking Ahead 10-1 © SMC Images/Getty Images; Computer Usage @ Work Hans Neleman/Getty Images; Web Research Courtesy of Google. **Chapter 11:** Opener © Jose Luis Pelaez Inc./Getty Images; Collage: © Peter Macdiarmid/Getty Images; © TM_Design/Alamy; Courtesy of Microsoft Corporation; Courtesy of Symantec Corp; Newscom; © Tomasz Piotrowski/Alamy; Courtesy of Tripp Lite; 11-1 Courtesy of Hewlett-Packard Company; © imagebroker/Alamy; © Mustafa Deliormanli/iStockphoto; © PhotoAlto/Alamy; © blickwinkel/Alamy; © avatra images/Alamy; © Ingvald Kaldhussæter/iStockphoto; © Jupiterimages/BrandX/Alamy; 11-3 Step 3a © Christoph Weihs/iStockphoto; 11-3 Step 3b © Ruslan Dashinsky/Shutterstock.com; 11-6 Courtesy of McAfee, Inc; 11-8 Courtesy of SonicWALL, Inc; Courtesy of Check Point Software Technologies Ltd; Courtesy of Fujitsu Technology Solutions; Courtesy of Hewlett-Packard Company; 11-14 © Paulo Whitaker/Reuters/Landov; 11-15 Courtesy of Kensington Computer Products Group; 11-21 © David Young-Wolff/PhotoEdit; 11-22 Courtesy of APC by Schneider Electric; 11-24 © Marcela Barsse/iStockphoto; © Krystian Nawrocki/iStockphoto; 11-25 Courtesy of Hewlett-Packard Company; © Daniel Laflor/iStockphoto; 11-26 © C Squared Studios/Getty Images; 11-28 ©Paramount/Courtesy Everett Collection; 11-33 Courtesy of Hewlett-Packard Company; 11-37 Courtesy of ContentWatch Inc; Innovative Computing 11-1 Courtesy of Marko V. Sakal/ www.askthecomputerwizard.com/blair/; Innovative Computing 11-2 © Andrew Olney/Getty Images; Looking Ahead 11-1 © Ann Cutting/Getty Images; Computer Usage @ Work © Ben Edwards/Getty Images; Trailblazer 1 Courtesy of Dr. Eugene Spafford/Purdue University; Trailblazer 2 REUTERS/Simon Kwong; Web Research © Trevor Fisher/iStockphoto. **Special Feature 11:** Opener AP Photo/Daniel Hulshizer; Figure 1 Courtesy of Guidance Software, Inc; Courtesy of Intelligent Computer Solutions, Inc; Photopress/Victorinox; Courtesy of EDGE Tech Corp; © Image Source Pink/Alamy; Figure 3 Courtesy of Seagate Technology LLC; Courtesy of Western Digital Corporation; Courtesy of EDGE Tech Corp; Courtesy of Kingston Technology Corporation; Courtesy of EDGE Tech Corp; © JUPITERIMAGES/Thinkstock/Alamy; Courtesy of Kingston Technology Corporation; © Art Directors & TRIP/Alamy; Figure 4 Courtesy of Hewlett-Packard Company; © CostinT/iStockphoto; © Tony Tremblay/iStockphoto; Courtesy of Hewlett-Packard Company; Courtesy of Garmin Ltd; © Jakub Semeniuk/iStockphoto; © Carsten Reisinger/Shutterstock.com; © Albo003/Shutterstock.com; Courtesy of Research In Motion; Figure 5 Courtesy of Intelligent Computer Solutions, Inc; Figure 6 Courtesy of Intelligent Computer Solutions, Inc; Figure 7 © UK Stock Images Ltd/Alamy; Courtesy of Intelligent Computer Solutions, Inc; © Jen Petreshock/Getty Images; Figure 9a,b,c Courtesy of Digital Intelligence, Inc; Figure 10 Courtesy of Guidance Software, Inc; Courtesy of AccessData Corp; Figure 13 Courtesy of Visualware, Inc. **Chapter 12:** Opener © Colin Anderson/Getty Images; Collage: © Branislav Senic/Alamy; Courtesy of Computer Systems Odessa Corporation; Courtesy of Nokia; Courtesy of Hewlett-Packard Company; © Eimantas Buzas/Shutterstock.com; 12-1 © Purestock/Getty Images; 12-3a&b Courtesy of SERENA Software, Inc. | www.serena.com; 12-4 © Digital Vision/Getty Images; 12-5 Courtesy of Dell, Inc; 12-20 Courtesy of Visible Systems Corporation; 12-21 © Ciaran Griffin/Getty Images; Computer Usage @ Work MARC ROMANELLI/Alamy; Trailblazer 1 Courtesy of Ed Yourdon; Trailblazer 2 © James Robertson/Courtesy of Tom DeMarco; Innovative Computing 12-1 Courtesy of NASA; Looking Ahead 12-1 Michael Mullen Design, LSST Corporation; Learn HowTo © Chabruken/Getty Images; WebResearch AP Photo/David Kohl. **Chapter 13:** Opener © Corbis Super RF/Alamy; Collage Courtesy of Sum Total Systems, Inc; Courtesy of Adobe Systems Incorporated; PRNewsFoto/hotels.com; © Stockbyte/Getty Images; © Ermin Gutenberger/iStockphoto; Courtesy of Microsoft Corporation; Courtesy of SmartDraw; 13-1 © JUPITERIMAGES/BananaStock; 13-11 Courtesy of Embarcadero Technologies; 13-12 Courtesy of Sybase Inc; 13-15b PhotosIndia.com/Getty Images; 13-18 (top right) Courtesy of Hewlett-Packard Company; (bottom right) PRNewsFoto/Verizon Wireless; (bottom left) PRNewsFoto/Verizon Wireless; 13-19 Courtesy of Hewlett-Packard Company; 13-22 Courtesy of SumTotal Systems, Inc; 13-34 Courtesy of SmartDraw; 13-39 Courtesy of the Naval Surface Warfare Center, Dahlgren, VA, 1988. U.S. Naval Historical Center Photograph; Computer Usage @ Work AP Photo/Abdeljalil Bounhar; Trailblazer 1 Courtesy of Viewpoints Research Institute, Inc; Trailblazer 2 © A Prabhakar Rao/The India Today Group/Getty Images; Innovative Computing 13-1 © Rafal Zdeb/iStockphoto; Looking Ahead 13-1 © Krzysztof Zmij/iStockphoto; Web Research © Carmen Martínez/iStockphoto; Critical Thinking © Ryan McVay/Getty Images. **Special Feature 13:** Figure 1 © Alex Slobodkin/iStockphoto; © Selahattin Bayram/iStockphoto; © STOCK4B-RF/Getty Images; Alpatkin Alexander/ITAR-TASS/Landov; © flashfilm/Getty Images; Figure 3 www.healthmap.org by Clark FreifeldandJohn Brownstein. Copyright © 2010; Figure 6 Step1 © Digital Vision/Getty Images; Step 2 © Jupiterimages/Thinkstock/Alamy; Step 5 © Sergio Dionisio/Getty Images; Figure 7 Step 1 © Zlatko Kostic/iStockphoto; Step 3 © Image Source Black/Alamy; Step 5 (l) © Ethan Miller/Getty Images; Step 5 (r) © Alex Slobodkin/iStockphoto **Chapter 14:** Opener © Markus Moellenberg/zefa/Corbis; Collage: © Joris van Caspel/iStockphoto; Courtesy of Hewlett-Packard Company; Courtesy of Computer Systems Odessa Corporation; Courtesy of Information Builders; PRIME NEWSWIRE; © imagebroker/Alamy; Courtesy of Promise Technology, Inc; 14-1 © Dean Sanderson/iStockphoto; © Dennis Hallinan/Alamy; © Colin Gray/Getty Images; © Jack Hollingsworth/Getty Images; © imagewerks/Getty Images; © blue jean images/Getty Images; © Dan Moore/iStockphoto; © Jon Feingersh/Getty Images; © Norman Chan/iStockphoto; © iStockphoto; © MAURICIO LIMA/AFP/Getty Images; © Lester Lefkowitz/Getty Images; © Bambu Productions/Getty Images; 14-2 © blue jean images/Getty Images; © Dean Sanderson/iStockphoto; © Dennis Hallinan/Alamy; © MAURICIO LIMA/AFP/Getty Images; © Jon Feingersh/Getty Images; © Bambu Productions/Getty Images; © iStockphoto; © Colin Gray/Getty Images; 14-5 Courtesy of Hewlett-Packard Company; © AAGAMIA/Getty Images; © Franziska Richter/iStockphoto; © David Kilpatrick/Alamy; © Bonnie Kamin/PhotoEdit; © David Young-Wolff/PhotoEdit; © shuedan/ Shutterstock.com; 14-8 Courtesy of Optimum Solutions, Inc; 14-9 Courtesy of Dassault Systèmesqa SolidWorks Corp; 14-10 AP Photo/Ted S. Warren; 14-11 © Corbis Super RF/Alamy; 14-12 LiveCRM Courtesy of Genesis Interactive (www.livecrm.co.nz); 14-13 Courtesy of Genesys Telecommunications Laboratories, Inc, an Alcatel Lucent Company; 14-16 (top) © Akkul/iStockphoto; (bottom) Tetra Images/Getty Images; 14-18 © Laurence Dutton/Getty Images; Courtesy of Computer Systems Odessa Corporation; © Ryan McVay/Getty Images; © Lisa F. Young/iStockphoto; © White Packert/Getty Images; © LWA/Getty Images; © VEER/Getty Images; © Paul Mckeown/iStockphoto;© Andy Sacks/Getty Images; © Inti St Clair/Getty Images; © Diane Diederich/iStockphoto; © blue jean images/Getty Images; © choicegraphx/iStockphoto; 14-19 Courtesy of Hewlett-Packard Company; Slobo Mitic/iStockphoto; Courtesy of Nokia; © LWA/Getty Images; © LWA/Getty Images; © Diane Diederich/iStockphoto; Courtesy of SanDisk Corporation Courtesy of Sony Electronics, Inc; Courtesy of Seagate Technology LLC; © Felix Clouzot/Getty Images; © Chad McDermott/iStockphoto; © Stefan Klein/iStockphoto; 14-21 PRNewsFoto/Verizon Wireless; Courtesy of Hewlett-Packard Company; © Vlad Kochelaevskiy/iStockphoto; 14-22 Step 1 © Studio Paggy/Getty Images; Steps 2 & 3 Courtesy of Hewlett-Packard Company; 14-23 Courtesy of Computer Systems Odessa Corporation; 14-24 © Ariel Skelley/Getty Images; © Tom Grill/Corbis; © Charles C. Place/Getty Images; © Hisham F Ibrahim/Getty Images; © image100/Corbis; 14-26 Courtesy of Avid Technology Inc; 14-28a Courtesy of Promise Technology, Inc; Courtesy of Hewlett-Packard Company; © Vlad Kochelaevskiy/iStockphoto; 14-28b Courtesy of Hewlett-Packard Company; Courtesy of Avid Technology Inc; © Vlad Kochelaevskiy/iStockphoto; 14-29 Courtesy of Alliance Storage Technologies; Courtesy of Fujitsu Technology Solutions; Courtesy of Hewlett-Packard Company; Courtesy of EMC Corporation; 14-30 Courtesy of Hewlett-Packard Company; 14-31 Courtesy of Hewlett-Packard Company; 14-32 Courtesy of Telect, Inc; Innovative Computing 14-1 © Eric Foltz/iStockphoto; Innovative Computing 14-2 Courtesy of Dr. Guarav Khanna; Looking Ahead 14-1 © Nadezda Firsova/iStockphoto; Computer Usage @ Work © Justin Kase zsixz/Alamy; Trailblazer 1Reuters/Landov; Trailblazer 2 Courtesy of Anita Borg Institute for Women and Technology-www.anitaborg.org; WebResearch © Vasiliy Yakobchuk/iStockphoto. **Special Feature 14:** Page 772 (top) © Roger Wright/Getty Images; page 772 (middle) © Keith Brofsky/Getty Images; page 772 (bottom) © Shannon Fagan/Getty Images; Figure 1 © Hugh Sitton/Getty Images; Figure 2 Courtesy of Hewlett-Packard Company; © Jon Feingersh/Getty Images; © Andres Rodriguez/Alamy; Figure 3 © Jupiterimages; Courtesy of Hewlett-Packard Company; © Andres Rodriguez/Alamy; Figure 4 © Masterfile (Royalty-Free Division) www.masterfile.com; Figure 5 © ImageState/Alamy; © David R. Frazier Photolibrary, Inc./Alamy; Figure 6 © Andres Rodriguez/Alamy © Sandy Jones/iStockphoto; Courtesy of Hewlett-Packard Company; Figure 7 Courtesy of Kingston Technology Corporation; Creative Technology Ltd; Courtesy of Intermec Technologies; 7e Carlos Cordero Pérez/La Nacion de Costa Rica/Newscom; © Anton Gvozdikov/iStockphoto; © Masterfile (Royalty-Free Division) www.masterfile.com; Figure 8 Courtesy of Intermec Technologies; Figure 9 © Jupiterimages; © Neil Cameron/Alamy; Figure 10 Courtesyof Intermec Technologies; © Image Source Black/Alamy; © Tay Jnr/Getty Images; © Tara Flake/iStockphoto; © Ed Hidden/iStockphoto; © Anton Gvozdikov/iStockphoto; Figure 11 Courtesy of Hewlett-Packard Company; © MIXA Co., Ltd./Alamy; Carlos Cordero Pérez/La Nacion de Costa Rica/Newscom; Figure 12 Courtesy of Genesys Telecommunications Laboratories, Inc, an Alcatel Lucent Company; © Jon Feingersh/Getty Images; Figure 13 © Tetra Images/Getty Images; © Jon Feingersh/Getty Images; © DreamPictures/Getty Images; Courtesy of Information Builders. **Chapter 15:** Opener © PhotoAlto/Alamy; Collage © fStop/Alamy; © JUPITERIMAGES/Thinkstock/Alamy; Courtesy of Research in Motion; PRNewsFoto/SANYO Electric Co., Ltd; Courtesy of Apple; Courtesy of Apple; Courtesy of Hewlett-Packard Company; Courtesy of Microsoft Corporation; Courtesy of Nokia; 15-1 © image100/Alamy; 15-2 © Arcaid/Alamy; 15-4 Kevin Lee/Bloomberg via Getty Images; 15-5 © Paul Thompson Images/Alamy; 15-6 Bill Greenblatt/UPI/Landov; 15-7 © Stockbyte/Alamy; 15-13 Steve Marcus/Reuters/Landov; Computer Usage @ Work © geogphotos/Alamy; 15-30 © Roberto Sanchez/iStockphoto; Trailblazer 1 © Kim Kulish/Corbis; Trailblazer 2 AP Photo/Marcio Jose Sanchez; Innovative Computing 15-1 Courtesy of MIT; Looking Ahead 15-1 © Lourens Smak/Alamy; Web Research © Asia Images Group/Getty Images. **Special Feature 15:** page 824: © Synthetic Alan King/Alamy; © Kevork Djansezian/Getty Images; Courtesy of Microsoft Corporation; AP Photo/Mark Lennihan; Tomohiro Ohsumi/Bloomberg via Getty Images; © Lightly Saled/Alamy; PRNewsFoto/JVC Company of America; PRNewsFoto/Verizon Wireless; Courtesy of Cakewalk; Courtesy of Nero AG; Courtesy of Iomega; page 825: Courtesy of Barco; © Roca/Shutterstock.com; © N_design/iStockphoto; Courtesy of Sling Media, Inc; AP Photo/Shizuo Kambayashi; AP Photo/Akira Suemori; Courtesy of Apple; PRNewsFoto/TiVo Inc; © Markos Dolopikos/Alamy; PRNewsFoto/Logitech; PRNewsFoto/Sony Electronics, Inc; AP Photo/Paul Sakuma; Courtesy of Chumby Industries; Exceptional Innovation, maker of Life | ware™; PRNewsFoto/Memorex; AP Photo/Joerg Sarbach; Figures 1 PRNewsFoto/Cambridge SoundWorks; Figure 3 (top) © Chris Polk/FilmMagic/Getty Images; Figure 3 (bottom) Courtesy of Activision Publishing, Inc; Figure 4 © Judith Collins/Alamy; Figure 5 Courtesy of Apple; Figure 6 PRNewsFoto/Myvu Corporation; Figure 7 Courtesy of Sling Media, Inc; Figure 8 (top) Yoshikazu Tsuno/AFP/Getty Images; Figure 8 (bottom) Courtesy of Physical Optics Corporation; Figure 9 PRNewsFoto/TiVo Inc; Figure 10 (left) Courtesy of LaCie; Figure 10 (right) Courtesy of Nero AG; Figure 11 (left) Courtesy of Facebook; Figure 11 (top right) © Colin Young-Wolff/PhotoEdit; Figure 11 (bottom right) PRNewsFoto/JVC Company of America; Figure 12 Courtesy of Cakewalk; Figure 13 PRNewsFoto/SANYO Fisher Company; Figure 14 (left) © Lightly Salted/Alamy; Figure 14 (middle) Courtesy of Microsoft Corporation; Figure 14 (right) John MacDougall/AFP/Getty Images; Figure 15 (top) © Juice Images/Alamy; Figure 15 (bottom) Daniel Acker/Bloomberg via Getty Images; Figure 16 AP Photo/Eckehard Schulz; Figure 17 (left) © jamalludin/Shutterstock.com; Figure 17(middle) © Kevork Djansezian/Getty Images; Figure 17 (right) © Hugh Threfall/Alamy; Figure 18 AP Photo/The Lawrence Journal-World, Scott McClurg; Figure 19 PRNewsFoto/TiVo Inc; Figure 20 (top & bottom right) Exceptional Innovation, maker of Life | ware™; Figure 20 (bottom left) Courtesy of NuVo Technologies Inc; Figure 21 Copyright © Lucid Design Group www.luciddesigngroup.com; Figure 22 Courtesy of ViewSonic Corporation Figure 23 Courtesy of Chumby Industries.